ENCYCLOPEDIA OF WOMEN AND AMERICAN POLITICS

ENCYCLOPEDIA OF WOMEN AND AMERICAN POLITICS

LYNNE E. FORD

Facts On File
An imprint of Infobase Publishing

Encyclopedia of Women and American Politics

Copyright © 2008 by Lynne E. Ford

Facts On File, Inc.
An imprint of Infobase Publishing
132 West 31st Street
New York NY 10001

Library of Congress Cataloging-in-Publication Data

Encyclopedia of women and American politics / [edited by] Lynne E. Ford.
p. cm.
Includes bibliographical references and index.
ISBN-13: 978-0-8160-5491-6 (hc : alk. paper) 1. Women in politics—United States—Encyclopedias. 2. Women legislators—United States—Encyclopedias. 3. United States—Politics and government—Encyclopedias. I. Ford, Lynne E.
HQ1236.5.U6E52 2007
973.03—dc22   2007004331

Facts On File books are available at special discounts when purchased in bulk quantities for businesses, associations, institutions, or sales promotions. Please call our Special Sales Department in New York at (212) 967-8800 or (800) 322-8755.

You can find Facts On File on the World Wide Web at http://www.factsonfile.com

Text design by Cathy Rincon and Kerry Casey

Printed in the United States of America

VB Hermitage 10 9 8 7 6 5 4 3 2 1

This book is printed on acid-free paper and contains 30% post-consumer recycled content.

CONTENTS

LIST OF ENTRIES

CONTRIBUTORS

SCOTT BEEKMAN, Ohio University

ANGELA BOSWELL, Henderson State University

JANA BRUBAKER, Northern Illinois University

LAURA M. CALKINS, Texas Tech University

PAULA F. CASEY, Independent Scholar

KYLE E. CIANI, Illinois State University

PATRICIA WALSH COATES, Cedar Crest College

MICHAEL DAVID COHEN, Harvard University

KRISTIN A. CONTOS, Southern Methodist University

SARA CROWLEY, Texas Christian University

CLAIRE CURTIS, College of Charleston

JULIE DAVIS, College of Charleston

LEANNE DUSTAN, York University

BILLIE FORD, Independent Scholar

HOLLIS FRANCE, College of Charleston

DELIA C. GILLIS, Central Missouri State University

DAVID M. GREENSPOON, McMaster University

LISA G. GUINN, Ferris State University

JEAN S. HAMM, East Tennessee State University

ROSE M. HARRIS, Nicholls State University

MARSHA HASS, College of Charleston

LYNDA HINKLE, Rutgers University–Camden

TERESA BLUE HOLDEN, Greenville College

KRISTA JENKINS, Fairleigh Dickinson University

MEGAN JONES, University of Delaware

T. ALYS JORDAN, Florida State University

CHRISTINE KNAUER, Eberhard Karls University, Tuebingen, Germany

CHANA REVELL KOTZIN, Independent Scholar

ANGELA KOUTERS, Independent Scholar

THEA LAPHAM, Independent Scholar

KATHLEEN A. LAUGHLIN, Metropolitan State University

J. CELESTE LAY, Tulane University

KIMBERLY K. LITTLE, Ohio University

JOLANTA MACEK, Franklin University

JENNIFER DAVIS McDAID, The Library of Virginia

JOHN THOMAS McGUIRE, State University of New York at Oneota

CYNTHIA MELENDY, University of Maine

CARYN E. NEUMANN, Ohio State University

ANGELA O'NEIL, Ohio Historical Society

LAURA R. PRIETO, Simmons College

MARIA ELENA RAYMOND, Independent Scholar

SHARON ROMERO, Independent Scholar

PAUL C. ROSIER, Villanova University

JENNIFER ROSS-NAZZAL, NASA Johnson Space Center, Oral History Project

SCOTT A. SHELTON, California University of Pennsylvania

HAROLD L. SMITH, University of Houston–Victoria

CANDIS STEENBERGEN, Concordia University

LAURA TUENNERMAN-KAPLAN, California University of Pennsylvania

EILEEN V. WALLIS, California State University–Fresno

HOWELL WILLIAMS, Florida State University

EDITH ZACK, Bar Ilan University, Israel

INTRODUCTION

The story of women's integration into American politics is nearly 500 years old but far from finished. There are countless examples of extraordinary women professing beliefs, adopting causes, and behaving in ways that defy the norms and expectations of their times. Victoria Woodhull, born in 1838, was married three times, the first when she was 15 years old. She started the first female brokerage house on Wall Street in 1870. She formed the Equal Rights Party and, in 1872, became its nominee for president of the United States, with abolitionist Frederick Douglass as her running mate. At the age of 19, Charlotte Woodward participated at the Seneca Falls Convention and signed the Declaration of Sentiments and Resolutions. Although she never emerged as a national leader in the movement, she remained a steadfast advocate for women's rights throughout her lifetime. She was the only Seneca Falls participant alive to see the Nineteenth Amendment ratified. U.S. senator Mary Landrieu, a Democrat from Louisiana, was elected to the state legislature at the age of 23 and was greeted by catcalls from her male colleagues. Although the first U.S. Supreme Court was seated in 1790, it was 1981 before the first woman, Justice Sandra Day O'Connor, joined the Court. Understanding why women have been willing to risk their lives, toil in obscurity, and endure the opprobrium of their peers requires that we try to appreciate the strict limits that gender has imposed on women. In the simplest terms, the history of women's engagement in American politics is the story of women's struggle to be treated as human beings—"separate and equal."

Due in large part to the success of women's rights movements, it is difficult for our modern sensibilities to comprehend what a radical change in patterns of male power and privilege developing a distinctly independent status for women requires. Any time one group makes demands that require another group to relinquish the power and privilege it currently enjoys, conflict ensues. *Patriarchy* literally means "rule of" (*arch*) "fathers" (*patri*). Patriarchy characterizes the control men have exercised over social, economic, and political power and resources, not only in the United States but throughout the world. Patriarchal systems are ancient in origin and ubiquitous. Liberal philosopher John Stuart Mill, writing in 1869, captured the pervasiveness of patriarchy's reach in this passage from *The Subjection of Women*: "Whatever gratification or pride there is in the possession of power, and whatever personal interest in its exercise, is in this case not confined to a limited class, but common to the whole male sex. . . . The clodhopper exercises, or is to exercise, his share of the power equally with the highest nobleman." Mill recognized that all men are empowered by patriarchy, regardless of their individual ability to exercise their power and privilege wisely. Likewise, all women are disempowered by patriarchy, regardless of their innate abilities for leadership and for the wise exercise of power. Patriarchy assumes that all women, by nature, are incapable of equality, and it therefore limits women's claims to natural and political rights. Patriarchal assumptions have been used to organize civil society. Until women organized to challenge the limits patriarchy imposed on their autonomy, their interests were ignored.

THE POWER OF THE SEPARATE SPHERES IDEOLOGY IN RENDERING WOMEN INVISIBLE

The long-standing and persistent belief that men and women naturally occupy separate spheres is derived from the patriarchal belief that men are meant to rule. The separate spheres ideology promotes the belief that due to women's role in reproduction, they are best suited to occupy the private sphere of home and family. Alternatively, men are designed to occupy the public sphere of work and politics. Until the mid-1800s, common law, known as *coverture,* contributed to women's lack of power in the public sphere by defining married couples as one entity entirely represented in civil society by the husband. English jurist William Blackstone wrote in 1765: "By marriage, the husband and wife are one person in law: that is, the very being or legal existence of the woman is suspended during the marriage, or at least is incorporated and consolidated into that of the husband; under whose wing, protection and *cover,* she performs every thing . . . [she] is said to be covert-baron, or under the protection and influence of her husband, her baron, or lord; and her condition upon marriage is called her *coverture."* As a practical matter, a married woman could not execute contracts independent of her husband, nor could she buy or sell property; dispose of personal assets like jewelry, clothing, and household items; control the destiny of her children; or serve as their guardian apart from her husband's consent. Coverture rendered married women civilly dead. U.S. Supreme Court justice Bradley wrote in *Bradwell v. Illinois* (1873), "It is true that many women are unmarried and not affected by any of the duties, complications, and incapacities

arising out of the married state, but these are exceptions to the general rule. The paramount destiny and mission of woman are to fulfill the noble and benign offices of wife and mother. This is the law of the Creator. And the rules of civil society must be adapted to the general constitution of things, and cannot be based upon exceptional cases." Therefore, all women were "covered" by male privilege, regardless of their marital status.

A gendered construction of citizenship for women differed from male citizenship in important ways. The same line of reasoning that denied married women property, guardianship of their children, and independent thought and action found its way into debates over suffrage and subsequent Supreme Court rulings that rendered married women both sentimental and legal dependents of their husbands. Women's role in the private sphere was, by definition, incompatible with full participation in society. The separate spheres ideology, although not originally defined in law, clearly identified the activities available for women as consistent with their primary role as childbearers and nurturers.

For working-class and lower-class women and for women of color, the separate sphere limited their access to the productive labor pool and depressed the wages paid for their work. Opportunities for work outside the home closely paralleled women's duties within the home. Immigrant women in the 1840s and 1850s, for example, worked in sex-segregated industries like textile, clothing, and shoe manufacturing. Teaching, sewing, and, later, nursing were also seen as consistent with women's domestic responsibilities, although the pay was almost negligible. Slave women in the South were at the bottom of the hierarchy in every respect. They were subject entirely to the white male patriarchal ruling class, and as such, African-American women did not enjoy any of the privileges of autonomy that accompanied the separate station enjoyed by white women in the middle and upper classes.

In the mid 19th century, white women's role within the home was raised to new heights of glorification for middle- and upper-class women. A "cult of domesticity" (also known as the "cult of true womanhood") reassured this class of woman of the importance of keeping true to their roles. The home was her exclusive domain, giving her a certain degree of autonomy. Women in this class were encouraged to work on behalf of suitable social reform causes, such as abolition, temperance, or woman and child poverty. Ironically, the interactions between women while fulfilling these rather limited public roles led them to view their own conditions in new and critical ways and eventually to organize in promotion of women's rights. Women joined the U.S. delegation to the World Anti-Slavery Convention held in London in 1840, only to be relegated to the sidelines because of their sex. As Elizabeth Cady Stanton and Lucretia Mott sat in the balcony, watching their male colleagues in the abolitionist movement debate, they planned the first meeting to talk about the "social, civil, and religious rights of women." In 1848, more than 300 people gathered for the Seneca Falls Convention and ratified the Declaration of Sentiments and Resolutions, in effect a declaration of independence from the shackles of dependence and civil invisibility.

The struggle to be "separate and equal" began in earnest following the Seneca Falls Convention. A careful look at the Declaration of Sentiments and Resolutions indicates just how large a task lay ahead (see the document in the appendix). The document mirrors the Declaration of Independence (1776) in form, word, and intent, grounding women's claims to autonomy and equality firmly within the liberal tradition of individualism. The facts submitted in support of the declaration characterize the multitude of ways sex limited women's lives. Although suffrage was one demand, most of the document was a condemnation of the limits that patriarchy and the private sphere placed on women's autonomy. The pursuit of suffrage rights led women to realize that full participation in the public

sphere would require far more than the right to vote alone. In fact, gaining the right to vote required that women change the attitudes about women's dependence and the social norms that reinforced women's dependence. By the time the Nineteenth Amendment was ratified in 1920, women had made significant progress on most of the issues raised in the Declaration of Sentiments and Resolutions. In a liberal democracy, each individual casts a vote. Women had to gain their status as "individuals" before they could gain the right to vote.

WOMEN AND POLITICAL PARTICIPATION: GOING FROM THE OUTSIDE TO THE INSIDE

Since women were largely excluded from conventional forms of politics and political participation until they won the vote in 1920, it is easy to overlook their activism and serious engagement with politics. Even though women were "outsiders" prior to suffrage, the range of activities they undertook, the tactics they employed, and the issues they cared about were political. In prerevolutionary America, women organized public demonstrations to protest the high cost of food and household goods and boycotted English tea to protest high taxes. To promote these activities, they formed organizations such as the Daughters of Liberty and the Anti-Tea Leagues. During the Revolutionary and Civil Wars, women participated both on the battlefield and in more traditional tasks consistent with their gender role, such as nursing, cooking, and sewing clothes for soldiers. Although not yet seated in power, women nonetheless lobbied those closest to them for early political recognition. Abigail Adams issued the now famous plea to her husband John Adams to ". . . remember the ladies and be more generous and favorable to them than your ancestors. . . . If particular care and attention is not paid to the ladies, we are determined to foment a rebellion, and will not hold ourselves bound by any laws in which we have no voice or representation." Her husband's response was to laugh at the very prospect. Rejected (or at best ignored) in the constitutional framework, women organized through voluntary associations and social movements. Progressive women's organizations founded in the early 20th century provided a model for the development of the welfare state in the 1930s, and women were integral in the leadership and success of the abolition, temperance, and Progressive movements.

When modern political campaigns began, women participated by performing duties "consistent with their temperament" (gender roles) by providing food, acting as hostesses and social organizers, and cleaning up afterward. Today women can be found as political actors and activists in their own right—as well as integrated into the many professions and occupations that make up the economy and the full public sphere. However, the struggle for full equality is hardly over. In 2007 women still make up a relatively small proportion of the highest positions in politics (16 percent of the U.S. Congress; 23 percent of state legislatures), business (ten women are CEOs of Fortune 500 companies; women make up 15 percent of senior executives in the nation's largest companies), and the professions (while 30 percent of all lawyers are women, women make up only 5 percent of managing partners in large firms; women make up 45 percent of the graduating class in medical school, only 14 percent of the highest-paying specialties, and 12 percent of the professor rank in medical schools). They continue to be most underrepresented in areas that have historically been defined as within the male domain or the public sphere. The wage gap, occupational segregation, the glass ceiling, and the sticky floor are all modern legacies of patriarchy and the separate spheres ideology. Individual women and women collectively through organizations continue to brazenly challenge barriers to full autonomy and political equality, and little by little, decade by decade, century by century, progress is made.

THE ORGANIZATION OF THIS VOLUME

The history of women in American politics is first and foremost the attempt to carve out a separate and distinct legal existence for women; and, secondly, the long struggle to lay claim to equal political, social, and economic rights that justly accrue to autonomous human beings. The entries in this volume profile individuals, organizations, movements, policies, laws, court decisions and the events most pertinent to women's struggle for separate and equal status in American politics. This compilation is by no means exhaustive. This volume should serve as a point of reference and as a beginning for those interested in learning more about women's roles in American politics, but it is not a replacement for a comprehensive analytical history of women's movements. To that end, you will find additional readings associated with most of the entries included here and a full bibliography of books, articles, and resource Web sites at the end of the volume. In order to really understand the complexities of women's public and private status in the 21st century, you need to know and understand the history of women's pursuit of autonomy and political identity. I encourage you to read widely and voraciously!

The entries in this volume were selected to represent the major social and political reform movements (for example, abolition, temperance, labor, and suffrage). In reading these entries, you will note that often a woman's involvement with one cause will lead her to meet activists involved in other reform efforts, and thus the many points of intersection between women's interests and causes are made evident with cross-references. Women's rights activists in a given time period share characteristics with one another, but are distinctly different from other women of their time. Entries include individual activists as well as the many associations and organizations they established or promoted (for example, Margaret Sanger and the American Birth Control League,

Alice Paul and the Congressional Union and National Women's Party). The entries have been presented alphabetically, but the cross-referencing as well as inclusion of broad conceptual entries (for example, suffrage, abortion, birth control movement) allow you to pursue a chronological read through history and the development of movements if you so choose. Because women have brought a distinctive set of demands to the policy process, several examples of major policy areas are included as well (for example, birth control, abortion, wage equity, welfare, family policy, and Social Security). Specific legislative initiatives or laws (for example, Title VII, Title IX) are linked to U.S. Supreme Court decisions that interpret their implementation (for example, *Meritor Savings Bank v. Vincent* and *Grove City v. Bell*) and to the agencies that administer the law (for example, Equal Employment Opportunity Commission). There is an entry for each First Lady who actually occupied the White House while her husband was president. Although these entries are also listed alphabetically and integrated throughout the volume, if you were to read them in the order in which each woman served as first lady, the entries also tell the story of women's proximity to political power and demonstrate the ways that denying women the opportunity to independently contribute to our nation's development limited the nation itself.

The story of women in American politics is multidimensional. Women pursuing real change are often opposed most vehemently by other women. Therefore, entries have been selected to present both sides of historical developments and contemporary controversies (for example, suffrage and anti-suffrage, feminism and anti-feminism, National Organization for Women and Independent Women's Forum, Gloria Steinem and Phyllis Schlafly). Some entries represent "firsts" for women (for example, Madeline Albright, first woman secretary of state; Jeannette Rankin, first woman elected to the House of Representatives; Seneca Falls Convention in 1848, first women's rights convention). The choice of entries is also intended to represent women's racial, ethnic, and ideological diversity. This is especially important since the women's movement can be appropriately criticized at times as being narrowly focused on the interests of middle- and upper-class women to the detriment of working and poor women, or on the interests of white women to the detriment of women of color. Those struggles within the organizations and within the movements themselves are essential to a full understanding of where we stand today. There will inevitably be oversights and omissions, and for that I apologize in advance.

We have consciously chosen *not* to include a separate entry for every woman ever to have served in the U.S. House of Representatives, the U.S. Senate, and in other public offices. However, you will find an entry for each of the 81 women in the 109th Congress. There are a number of tables included among the appendices that list all of the women to have served in various capacities (for example, U.S. House and Senate, Executive Cabinet, and first ladies) as well as empirical data on trends in the proportion of women serving in political office at the state and federal levels. There are also a number of excellent databases online (for example, the Center for American Women and Politics, www.cawp.rutgers.edu). Since one of the demands listed in the Declaration of Sentiments and Resolutions was to give women a public voice (by custom and law, women were prohibited from speaking in public before mixed audiences), examples of women's rhetoric from different points in time have also been included in the appendices.

Many people have worked to make this volume possible. Two of my colleagues in political science at the College of Charleston were instrumental in conceptualizing the volume, in creating the list of entries, and in writing many of the same: Claire Curtis and Hollis France. Current and former students have participated in the project as well, notably Jamie Lauren Huff and Angela Kouters. Owen Lancer at Facts On File has been patient and encouraging even as repeated deadlines slid by and the project was delayed by children and competing professional obligations. In the end, it is the many scholars from a wide variety of disciplines who agreed to write entries that made this volume possible. I thank them for their interest, their expertise, and their insightful entries. Finally, projects like this are not ever possible without the love and support of family, and I thank them for it.

L. E. F.

A

Abbott, Edith (1876–1957) *social worker, educator, author* Edith Abbott, born in Grand Island, Nebraska, on September 26, 1876, was the older sister of GRACE ABBOTT. Her mother, Elizabeth Griffin Abbott, was an abolitionist and women's SUFFRAGE leader. Abbott graduated from the University of Nebraska in 1901 and earned her doctoral degree in economics from the University of Chicago in 1905. The recipient of a Carnegie fellowship, she also studied at the London School of Economics and Political Science. Upon returning to the United States in 1906, she joined her sister at JANE ADDAMS'S HULL-HOUSE and worked to promote women's suffrage and the improvement of housing for the poor. She also began to advocate for new solutions to poverty. The following year, Abbott taught economics at Wellesley College, and in 1908 she became assistant director of the Research Department of the Chicago School of Civics and Philanthropy. Abbott served as dean of the School of Social Service Administration, University of Chicago, from 1924 to 1942. In 1926, she helped establish the Cook County Bureau of Public Welfare. She assisted in drafting the Social Security Act of 1935 and served as special consultant to Harry Hopkins, adviser to President Franklin D. Roosevelt. Abbott wrote extensively and published widely about the need for public welfare, the responsibility of the state in solving social problems, and in defining the field of social work. She also produced studies on women in industry and problems in the penal system. She died on July 28, 1957.

Further Reading
Barbuto, Domenica M., ed. *The American Settlement Movement: A Bibliography*. Bibliographies and Indexes in American History, no. 42. Westport, Conn.: Greenwood Press, 1999.
Costin, Lela B. *Two Sisters for Social Justice: A Biography of Grace and Edith Abbott*. Urbana: University of Illinois Press, 1983.

Abbott, Grace (1878–1939) *social worker, head of Children's Bureau* Grace Abbott was born on November 17, 1878, and raised in Grand Island, Nebraska. Her father was the state's lieutenant governor, and her mother was an abolitionist and suffragist. Grace received her bachelor's degree from Grand Island College in 1898 and taught for several years at Grand Island High School. She did graduate work in political science and in law at the University of Chicago, receiving

1

Grace Abbott, 1929 (Library of Congress)

a master's degree in 1909. The year before, greatly attracted to the pioneering social work of Jane Addams, she became a resident of Hull-House in Chicago and collaborated with Addams for over a decade.

Abbott shared Addams's interest in the cause of world peace, and she worked effectively to advance women's suffrage. She became preoccupied with the problems of immigrants very early. For more than 20 years, many Americans had been worried that the flood of immigrants—as many as a million in a single year—arriving from eastern and southern Europe constituted a severe threat to American life and institutions. These "new immigrants," as they were called, seemed dangerously "different" in language, dress, religion, and their disposition to cluster in the cities (as most people in this era were also doing). Other Americans, like Addams and Abbott, believed that it was not the immigrants who were "new," but America. Increasingly

urban, industrial and impersonal to them, the problem was how to help the newcomers find and maintain their families, get jobs, and learn to play a knowledgeable part in a democracy.

From 1908 to 1917, Abbott directed the Immigrants' Protective League in Chicago. Close personal contact with immigrants made her aware of how difficult it was for new arrivals from Poland, Italy, or Russia to find the relatives or friends they depended on; to get jobs that were not exploitative; and to avoid being abused by the political machines. A trip in 1911 to eastern Europe deepened Abbott's understanding of the needs and hopes of the immigrants. Her point of view is eloquently summarized in her *The Immigrant and the Community* (1917). To Abbott, the "new immigrants" were every bit as desirable as additions to the United States as were the older arrivals. In modern American society, they needed help; and, while the states and local philanthropic organizations such as the Immigrants' Protective League could help, the federal government had an important role to play. It was wrong, she argued, to concentrate on restricting or excluding immigration; the government should plan how to best accommodate and integrate the newcomers.

Abbott was not successful in redirecting federal policy; the Immigration Act of 1924 drastically reduced the number of new immigrants. But her writings and her work with the Immigrants' Protective League helped develop a more widespread and generous understanding of the difficulties immigrants encountered.

In 1912, Congress established the Children's Bureau in the recognition that children were entitled to special consideration in schools, in the workplace, in the courts, and even in the home. In 1916, Congress passed a law prohibiting the interstate shipment of products made by child labor. It remained for the Children's Bureau to make the law effective. Julia Lathrop, the first head of the bureau, asked her friend Abbott to head up the child labor division in 1917. Abbott proved to be an exceptionally able administrator. However, within a year the Supreme Court invalidated the 1916 law as an infringement on the rights of the states to deal with child labor as they thought best. Abbott resigned and for the rest of her life worked to secure an amendment to the Constitution outlawing child labor. To her regret, this effort, too, was frustrated by states-rights sentiments and by the concern that the amendment would jeopardize the rights of parents and churches to supervise the rearing of children.

After a brief period back in Illinois, Abbott returned to Washington in 1921 as the new head of the Children's Bureau. Probably her most important responsibility was to administer the Sheppard-Towner Maternity and Infancy Protection Act (1921), which extended federal aid to states that developed appropriate programs of maternal care. Abbott had been appalled to find that infant mortality was higher in the United States than in any country where records were kept, and she was convinced that the best way to reduce that mortality was to improve the health of the mother, before and after childbirth. The Supreme Court rejected challenges to this dramatic extension of federal government responsibilities for social welfare. Abbott, while seeing to it that more than 3,000 centers across the country met federal standards, showed herself sensitive to the special concerns of localities. Though Congress terminated the program in 1929, the act, as administered by Abbott, was a pioneering federal program of social welfare.

Abbott never lost faith that the American people would, when properly informed and led, support enlightened welfare programs. She was optimistic that the New Deal of Franklin Roosevelt and her old friend Frances Perkins would realize many of her dreams. She had the satisfaction of helping to draft the Social Security Act of 1935, which, among other things, provided federal guarantees of aid to dependent children. Ill health prompted her to resign in 1934. She became professor of public welfare at the University of Chicago, where her sister, Edith Abbott, was a dean. She lived with Edith until her death on June 19, 1939.

Further Reading

Abbott, Grace. *The Immigrant and the Community.* Englewood, N.J.: Jerome S. Ozer, 1971.
———. *The Child and the State.* Chicago: University of Chicago Press, 1938.
Chambers, Clarke A. *Seedtime of Reform: American Social Service and Social Action, 1918–1933.* Minneapolis: University of Minnesota Press, 1963.
Costin, Lela B. 1983. *Two Sisters for Social Justice: A Biography of Grace and Edith Abbott.* Urbana: University of Illinois Press, 1983.

—Cynthia Melendy

abolitionist movement, women in the

Although Quakers in Pennsylvania had opposed slavery from its inception, there was no national movement in America until William Lloyd Garrison began his crusade during the early 1830s. In December 1833, the Philadelphia Quakers, the New England Garrisonians, and the New York Reformers met with freed blacks to form the American Anti-Slavery Society. Garrison wrote the primary goals for the organization: to achieve immediate emancipation of all slaves and bring about an end to racial segregation and discrimination.

Women encountered the first of many obstacles to their participation when meeting organizers permitted them to attend but refused to allow them to speak from the floor or join the society. Immediately following this meeting, a group of black and white women organized the Philadelphia Female Anti-Slavery Society. African-American women had already begun to organize, forming one of the first abolitionist groups in 1832, the Female Anti-Slavery Society of Salem, Massachusetts. Similar groups formed throughout New England, and in 1837, when the National Female Anti-Slavery Society convened in New York, delegates from 12 states attended. Like other social-reform organizations at the time, however, the composition of most female antislavery societies followed social conventions of racial segregation. Perhaps the best-known female abolitionist was

HARRIETT TUBMAN (1820–1911), an escaped slave from Maryland who risked her life repeatedly to rescue more than 300 slaves via the Underground Railroad.

The commitment to end slavery led women to test all kinds of social constraints, including the prohibition against women speaking in public. FRANCES WRIGHT, Maria Stewart, ANGELINA GRIMKÉ, and SARAH GRIMKÉ all suffered criticism from the public, the press, and the pulpit for addressing mixed audiences of men and women in the 1830s. By the next decade, women's frustration over their limited role within the movement prompted some to take action on behalf of their own sex. At the 1840 World Anti-Slavery Convention held in London, delegates voted to seat only men, relegating the women to the galleries above. U.S. delegates LUCRETIA MOTT and ELIZABETH CADY STANTON spent hours discussing the discrimination they faced as women. In 1848, they organized the SENECA FALLS CONVENTION, the first convention for women's rights in the United States. Delegates at the Convention drafted the DECLARATION OF SENTIMENTS AND RESOLUTIONS in support of women's rights.

Further Reading

Evans, Sara. *Born for Liberty: A History of Women in America*. New York: Free Press, 1997.

Jeffrey, Julie Roy. *The Great Silent Army of Abolitionism: Ordinary Women in the Anti-Slavery Movement*. Chapel Hill: University of North Carolina Press, 1998.

abortion   A woman's right to decide whether or not to terminate her pregnancy has become one of the most controversial issues of contemporary gender politics. Pro-choice advocates argue that only a woman, often in consultation with her doctor and/or partner, can make such a difficult decision. Abortion opponents characterize the issue in moral terms, arguing that the fetus is a human life from the point of conception.

In 1821, Connecticut became the first state to enact abortion legislation, making it illegal to terminate a pregnancy after quickening (the first recognizable movement of the fetus, usually occurring in about the fourth month). In the mid-19th Century, spurred mainly by the medical community, a movement to tighten abortion regulation resulted in uniform abortion prohibition laws throughout the United States. Outside of exceptions to preserve the life of the mother, these laws stayed in place until the 1960s. Prohibiting abortion by law did not end the practice of abortions, however. Illegal abortions were frequent throughout this period, although the COMSTOCK ACT of 1873 made them harder to obtain and drove providers further underground. The Comstock Act primarily targeted "obscene literature," but it also forbade distribution of information or devices for birth control, abortion, and information on sexually transmitted diseases. By 1930, an estimated 800,000 illegal abortions were performed annually, and between 8,000 and 17,000 women died every year as a result.

Some early feminists, such as SUSAN B. ANTHONY, opposed abortion on the grounds that it endangered women's lives. These feminists believed that women's equality would only be possible when abortion was no longer necessary. They argued that prevention was more important than punishment and blamed circumstances, laws, and men for driving women to seek abortions. Later feminists advocated access to safe and effective birth control as a means of preventing abortions. The first step in this approach came in 1965 when the Supreme Court decided GRISWOLD V. CONNECTICUT. Connecticut law made it illegal for anyone, including married couples, to obtain birth control drugs and devices. The Supreme Court ruled that the ban on contraception violated the constitutional right to marital privacy. In 1972, the Court extended the right to use contraceptives to all people, regardless of their marital status (EISENSTADT V. BAIRD).

Throughout the 1960s and 1970s, states liberalized abortion laws by adding exceptions in cases of rape or incest, and for a variety of health reasons. In 1970, New York became the first state to allow abortion "on demand." Elective abortions performed by a licensed physician were completely legal for the first 24 weeks but considered to be homicide after that point. Groups such as the National Abortion Rights Action League and the Clergy Consultation Service on Abortion worked to liberalize abortion laws in other states. In 1973, in the case of ROE V. WADE, the Supreme Court struck down national and state laws regulating abortion. Under *Roe*, no state could regulate abortion during the first trimester (three months) of pregnancy. During this period, the Court found that the right to privacy "is broad enough to encompass a woman's decision whether or not to terminate her pregnancy." The Court also found two compelling state interests that could justify restrictions on abortion services. In the second trimester (fourth to sixth month), states could regulate abortion to protect maternal health. In the final trimester, when the fetus was potentially viable outside the woman's womb, states could not only regulate abortion, they could ban abortion to protect fetal life. In the years following *Roe*, the Court consistently struck down state laws that had the intent to or effect of limiting access to abortion.

The *Roe* decision marks a turning point in the politicization of abortion. To some, the decision suggested that women would no longer be forced to seek illegal abortions and that women's lives would be protected. To others, however, the decision meant that even more pregnancies would be terminated. Opponents organized and quickly mobilized as the "pro-life movement" in an attempt to make abortion illegal again. Catholic bishops were the first to organize, and they were soon joined by a variety of other constituencies united by the goal of overturning *Roe v. Wade*. More than two dozen resolutions to overturn the decision by constitutional amendment were introduced in Congress immediately following the 1973 decision. The Human Life Amendment, stating that life begins at conception and that ending it was murder, failed to

pass Congress and had little public support. Alternate pro-life strategies involved changing the composition of the Supreme Court, organizing conservative Christians into a pro-life voting block in support of Republican, anti-abortion candidates, adoption of the HYDE AMENDMENT prohibiting the use of federal funds for abortions, and state legislation requiring parental notification for minors seeking abortions. President Ronald Reagan appointed three new justices to the Court during his tenure (SANDRA DAY O'CONNER, Antonin Scalia, and Anthony Kennedy), and George H. W. Bush followed with two appointments (David Souter and Clarence Thomas). The new justices tended to be more conservative than their predecessors, and although the Court maintained the central holding in *Roe*, it allowed more restrictions and regulations, provided they did not pose an "undue burden" on a woman's ability to obtain an abortion. In 1988, the Reagan administration issued new regulations for federally funded family planning clinics, prohibiting medical personnel from discussing abortion with their clients. The GAG RULE was upheld by the Court (*RUST V. SULLIVAN*, 1991) but rescinded by President Clinton in 1993 (it was reinstated by President George W. Bush). Abortion opponents frustrated by the incremental approach to overturning *Roe* began adopting confrontational and violent tactics to prevent abortions.

Joseph Scheidler founded the Pro-Life Action League (PLAL) in 1980. PLAL dispatches sidewalk counselors to clinics to dissuade women from going through with abortions and conducts "face the truth tours" across the country by displaying huge posters of aborted fetuses. Randall Terry founded OPERATION RESCUE, a militant anti-abortion organization, in 1987. The group's aim is to prevent abortions by holding large demonstrations outside abortion clinics, destroying clinic property and equipment, blockading clinics, and physically surrounding women as they attempt to enter clinics. Although Operation Rescue promotes itself as a "peaceful civil disobedience movement," other like-minded groups at the fringes of the movement have adopted destructive tactics that include bombings, arson, assault, and the murder of abortion providers. On Christmas day in 1984, three abortion clinics were bombed. Those convicted called the bombings "a birthday gift for Jesus."

Pro-choice forces believed *Roe* signaled a victory for women's health and safety and organized primarily to protect the status quo. *WEBSTER V. REPRODUCTIVE HEALTH SERVICES* (1989) issued a direct threat to *Roe* and a new call to action for pro-choice advocates. The Missouri law in question stated that life began at conception and barred the use of public funds for abortions, prohibited abortions in public hospitals, and required viability testing after 19 weeks. In an amicus curiae brief, the solicitor general of the United States asked specifically that *Roe* be overturned. A record number of interest groups participated by submitting amicus briefs, 81 in all. The Court returned a split decision, 4-1-4. Four justices appeared willing to overturn *Roe v. Wade,* but they could not get a fifth to join them in a majority decision. Justice Sandra Day O'Connor, the first woman appointed to the Court and the only woman serving at the time, refused to join her colleagues in reversing *Roe* but did vote to uphold the Missouri restrictions in question, creating a 5-4 decision on the merits of the case. The majority of the Court held that Missouri's restrictions did not impose an "undue burden" on a woman's privacy or her access to abortion services.

In 1992, the Court again issued a divided opinion in *PLANNED PARENTHOOD OF SOUTHEASTERN PENNSYLVANIA V. CASEY.* The case involved Pennsylvania's Abortion Control Act, which included compulsory anti-abortion counseling by doctors, a 24-hour waiting period after counseling, reporting requirements by doctors and clinics, spousal notification, and parental consent that required at least one parent to accompany the minor to the clinic (or judicial approval). The Bush administration again urged the Court to use this case to overturn *Roe.* Four jus-

tices signaled that they would have overturned *Roe* entirely (Chief Justice William Rehnquist, Byron White, Scalia, and Thomas), but the decision was controlled by a three-justice plurality. O'Connor, Kennedy, and Souter specifically upheld the central holding in *Roe,* and on this point alone, they were joined by John Paul Stevens and Harry Blackmun. The majority opinion itself upheld all of the provisions in the Pennsylvania statute except spousal notification. The practical result of this decision has been to give states more latitude in adopting restrictions on abortion. Eighty-seven percent of counties in the United States have no abortion provider. Since 1995, states have enacted more than 380 anti-choice measures, and Congress has voted 166 times with anti-choice politicians winning all but 32 of those votes. Abortion is becoming less available even though it remains legal.

The divided Court in both *Webster* and *Casey* energized pro-choice advocates. Organizations such as the National Abortion Rights League (NARAL) adopted a more proactive strategy. The NATIONAL ORGANIZATION FOR WOMEN (NOW) filed a lawsuit against the Pro-Life Action League, Operation Rescue, and several individuals, including PLAL's founder Joseph Scheidler, who is named in the suit. NOW argued that trespassing, arson, the theft of fetuses, physical attacks, and threats against abortion clinics and abortion providers constituted extortion and came under the Racketeer Influenced and Corrupt Organizations (RICO) statute. NOW claimed that the actions of anti-abortion groups constituted a coordinated national conspiracy to prevent a legal activity from taking place. In *NOW v. Scheidler* (1994), the Court had to decide whether RICO was limited to enterprises with an economic motive, or whether it could be applied more broadly. The Court ruled that RICO prohibitions were not restricted to profit-making organizations, clearing the way for a federal judge to issue an injunction forbidding Scheidler and the other defendants from further violations of the RICO Act in 1999. Scheidler appealed to the Supreme Court, however, and in an 8-1 decision (Scheidler v. NOW, 2003), the Court held that abortion opponents did not commit extortion because they did not "obtain" property from the abortion supporters, thus leaving this pro-choice strategy in question.

Congress took action in 1994 to protect women's access to clinics by passing the FREEDOM OF ACCESS TO CLINIC ENTRANCES ACT (FACE). FACE prohibits the use of force, threats of force, physical obstruction, and property damage intended to interfere with people seeking or providing reproductive health services. About the same time, abortion opponents narrowed their focus to a specific procedure known as "partial birth abortion." Congress passed prohibitions on partial birth abortions in 1995 and 1997, but President Clinton vetoed both bills.

On September 28, 2000, the Food and Drug Administration (FDA) approved mifepristone, also known as RU-486, to terminate early pregnancies (defined as 49 days or less). RU-486 was developed in 1980 and has been used in Europe and China by more than 620,000 women since it came on the market in 1988. The drug is administered in pill form in doses spaced two days apart. Women are required to return to their doctor 14 days later to make sure that the pregnancy has been terminated. Mifepristone causes an abortion by blocking the action of progesterone, a hormone essential for sustaining pregnancy. The drug prevents an embryo from attaching to the uterine wall during the earliest stages of gestation. At this point in a pregnancy, an embryo is no larger than a grain of rice. This treatment regimen is effective in about 95 percent of all cases. Under the terms of FDA approval, mifepristone can be distributed by physicians who must also be able to provide surgical intervention in cases of incomplete abortion or severe bleeding (or they must have made plans in advance to have others provide such care). Side effects from RU-486 include cramping (sometimes severe) and bleeding over a period of 9–16 days. The advantages to mifepristone are that surgical complications are avoided and that it can be administered much

earlier in a pregnancy than a surgical abortion, which is generally not performed until the sixth or seventh week of pregnancy. One disadvantage is that the process may take several days rather than one visit to a clinic or hospital.

Since FDA approval in 2000, more than 360,000 women have used mifepristone to end an unintended pregnancy. However, opponents have renewed their efforts to have mifepristone removed from the market, arguing that the FDA acted hastily in its approval of the drug and ignored its safety concerns. In November 2003, two members of the House of Representatives unsuccessfully introduced the RU-486 Suspension and Review Act or "Holly's Law," named for Holly Peterson, an 18-year-old California woman who had died of a severe infection one week after taking mifespristone. The bill called for immediate suspension of the FDA's approval of RU-486 and directed the General Accounting Office to conduct a six-month independent review of the process the FDA used to declare RU-486 "safe and effective." Following the November 2004 election, the legislation was reintroduced and supporters vowed to renew their efforts to gain FDA suspension. The bill is unlikely to pass in the 110th Congress now controlled by Democrats. The FDA has already required mifepristone's label to be changed to acknowledge that there are risks associated with any abortion and that physicians prescribing the drug should instruct patients to contact them if they experience any excessive bleeding or bacterial infection.

In 2003, President George W. Bush signed the Partial Birth Abortion Ban Act. On June 1, 2004, District Court judge Phyllis Hamilton declared the act unconstitutional, saying it infringed on a woman's right to choose. At present, the ruling applies only to the nation's 900 or so Planned Parenthood clinics and their doctors, who perform about half of the 1.3 million abortions done each year in the United States. The U.S. Supreme Court heard oral arguments on two cases challenging the lower court rulings on the Partial Birth Abortion Ban of 2003: *Gonzales v. Carhart* and *Gonzales v. Planned Parenthood Federation of America.* Both cases were argued in autumn 2006 and a decision by the Court was delivered on April 18, 2007. The 5-4 ruling consolidated both cases under *Gonzales v. Carhart* and upheld the 2003 law—the first ever to ban a specific abortion procedure. *Roe v. Wade* was not overturned by this decision. Justice Anthony Kennedy wrote the majority opinion and was joined by Chief Justice John Roberts and Justices Samuel Alito, Antonin Scalia, and Clarence Thomas. Justice Ruth Bader Ginsburg was joined in dissent by Justices Stephen Bryer, David Souter, and John Paul Stevens. This was the first abortion case heard by the Court since Justice Sandra Day O'Connor's retirement and subsequent replacement by Justice Alito.

Those challenging the 2003 law raised two central concerns. First, the law does not provide a "health exception" for pregnant women facing a medical emergency—and the holding in *Planned Parenthood v. Casey* (1992) was widely believed to require a health exception. Second, a similar Nebraska law banning this abortion procedure was declared unconstitutional in 2000 (*Stenberg v. Carhart*) because it was found to impose an "undue burden" on a woman's ability to procure an abortion. The burden imposed by the Nebraska law was defined differently by various justices (Ginsburg, Stevens, and O'Connor wrote separate opinions but joined with the majority) but included the "fear of prosecution, conviction, and imprisonment" as well as the position that forcing physicians to use procedures other than what they judged to be safest, and the lack of a health exception. The decision in *Gonzales v. Carhart* (2007) does not overturn *Stenberg* but clearly signals that this new Court is prepared to relax the definition of "undue burden" it imposed.

In her dissent, Justice Ruth Bader Ginsberg, now the only woman remaining on the Court, said the federal ban and the Court's "defense of it cannot be understood as anything other than an effort to chip away at a right declared again and again by this Court—and with increasing comprehension of its centrality to women's lives." Abortion-rights advocates also expressed concern over the politicized terms used throughout Justice Kennedy's majority opinion, including *abortion doctor* to describe specialists who perform gynecological services, and *unborn child* or *baby* to describe a fetus. The term *partial birth abortion* is highly charged and, when understood broadly, refers to a number of late-term abortion procedures, including dilation and extraction and dilation and evacuation. The 2003 law and subsequent ruling in *Gonzales v. Carhart* ban only the procedure known as dilation and extraction (known also as D & X), a procedure that accounts for less than 1 (.08) percent of all abortions performed in the United States.

The public's position on the issue of abortion remains essentially constant, with a majority (somewhere around 55 percent) favoring abortion rights. However, the issue is complicated, and scholars have found that opinion varies depending on how the question is framed. Circumstances regarding the pregnancy can vary support or opposition by as much as 60 points. When a woman's health or life is in danger, support increases to 80 or 85 percent. However, when the question indicates that a woman is seeking an abortion because she has too many children, support drops to 25 percent. Overall, a majority believes that abortion is morally wrong, but a majority of the public continues to support legal abortion and to oppose an amendment to the Constitution prohibiting abortion.

The issue of abortion shapes political opinions and partisanship as well. In the 1980s, the Republicans added an anti-abortion plank to the party platform, while the Democratic Party strongly supported abortion rights. Some scholars attribute a portion of the GENDER GAP in electoral politics to this issue. Women, regardless of race, class, or religion, are more likely to support a pro-choice candidate. Pro-choice groups like EMILY'S LIST (Democratic candidates) and WISH LIST (Republican candidates) formed to advance and financially support pro-choice female candidates for public office. There is evidence to suggest that pro-choice women may have provided the winning margins for President Bill Clinton in 1992 and 1996 as well as the winning margins in many other gubernatorial and House and Senate races. President Clinton delivered on his promise to support abortion rights by overturning the gag rule, lifting the ban on fetal tissue research, ending the ban on abortions at overseas U.S. military medical facilities, and suspending the Mexico City Policy, which denied U.S. aid to international family planning organizations that provided abortion services. President George W. Bush reinstated many of these policies upon taking office in 2001.

Vermont is the only state in the nation that has not passed a statute regarding abortion since the 1973 *Roe v. Wade* decision. In every other state, legislators have introduced laws that in most cases restrict, condition, or regulate the right of a woman to seek an abortion. The majority of state actions have been invalidated by federal courts, and some have resulted in appeals to the Supreme Court. Even so, states continue to pass legislation on abortion at an astounding rate. In 2005, state legislators considered more than 500 bills aimed at limiting access to abortion in their state. Twenty-three states have adopted parental consent laws requiring at least one parent to sign a statement approving the abortion procedure; 12 other states have parental-notifications laws that require doctors to notify parents prior to performing the procedure. The Supreme Court requires all of these laws to have a "judicial bypass" remedy allowing minors to substitute the consent or notification of a judge for that of a parent. In 2006, the Court held that a New Hampshire parental-notification law must allow doctors to perform an abortion in a medical emergency without notifying a parent (*Ayotte v. Planned Parenthood of Northern New England*, 2006). Twenty-eight states require doctors to provide counseling about the risk of abortion and the availability of alternatives. Three states (Min-

nesota, Mississippi, and Texas) require doctors to warn women that abortion can increase the risk of breast cancer (a fact not supported by scientific evidence), and another seven states offer or require a sonogram before an abortion (Alabama, Arkansas, Indiana, Michigan, Oklahoma, Utah, and Wisconsin). Waiting periods prior to an abortion are common forms of regulation and are found in 24 states. Thirty-nine states require abortions to be performed by a licensed physician and a majority of states have laws that require abortions to be performed in a hospital after a certain point in the pregnancy. Forty-six states allow health care workers to refuse to participate in an abortion.

South Dakota became the latest test for the Supreme Court's willingness to overturn the core holding in *Roe v. Wade*. On March 6, 2006, South Dakota governor Mike Rounds signed a bill that would effectively ban all abortions by making it a felony for doctors to perform any abortion, except to save the life of the woman. The bill was intentionally and very carefully crafted to set up a legal challenge to *Roe v. Wade*. An immediate court challenge blocked the law's implementation, and a petition drive to overturn the law landed it on the November 7, 2006, ballot as "Referred Law 6." Voters in South Dakota were asked to affirm the law or reject it. By a margin of 56 to 44 percent, the voters rejected the law.

The battle over abortion is far from over. The core holding in *Roe v. Wade* that recognizes a woman's constitutional right to have an abortion is now viewed as so vulnerable by pro-choice advocates that some states have taken steps to ensure that abortion remains legal within the state even if *Roe* is overturned. To date these include Nebraska, Hawaii, Maryland, Maine, Washington, Connecticut, and California. In another 10 states, the state supreme court has already determined that the state constitution would protect a woman's right to abortion in the absence of *Roe* (Alaska, California, Florida, Massachusetts, Minnesota, Montana, New Jersey, New Mexico, Tennessee, and West

Virginia). Similarly, a number of states have adopted "trigger laws." Four states (Louisiana, Illinois, Kentucky, and South Dakota) have adopted provisions that will make abortion immediately illegal in the state if federal policy permits the change—in other words, if *Roe v. Wade* is overturned. Regardless of what the Supreme Court does relative to *Roe,* it seems likely that the states will remain the battleground over abortion rights.

See also BIRTH CONTROL MOVEMENT.

Further Reading

Baird, Robert, and Stuart Rosenbaum. *The Ethics of Abortion: Pro-Life v. Pro-Choice.* New York: Prometheus Books, 2001.

Blanchard, Dallas A. *The Anti-Abortion Movement and the Rise of the Religious Right: From Polite to Fiery Protest.* New York: Twayne Publishers, 1994.

Gorney, Cynthia. *Articles of Faith: A Frontline History of the Abortion Wars.* New York: Simon and Schuster, 2000.

Tribe, Lawrence. *Abortion: A Clash of Absolutes.* New York: W. W. Norton, 1992.

Weddington, Sarah. *A Question of Choice.* New York: Penguin Books, 1993.

Abzug, Bella (Bella Savitzky Abzug) (1920– 1998) *congressperson, activist*

Born on July 24, 1920, in New York City to Russian immigrants one month prior to ratification of the Nineteenth Amendment, Bella Abzug was a tireless advocate for equal rights, peace, and justice. She was also the first Jewish woman to serve in the U.S. House of Representatives, serving from 1971 to 1977.

Abzug earned her B.A. from Hunter College in 1942. Two years later, she married Martin Abzug, with whom she had two daughters. She received her law degree from Columbia University School of Law in 1947. In her legal practice, she specialized in labor and civil rights cases. She also defended people accused of subversive activities by Senator Joseph McCarthy in the 1950s and was a lawyer for the Civil Rights Congress and the American Civil Liberties Union. In 1961, she cofounded Women Strike

for Peace (WSP), in response to U.S. and Soviet nuclear testing. In 1971, she successfully ran for Congress as an anti–Vietnam War candidate. Her slogan, "This woman's place is in the House . . . the House of Representatives!" captured the novelty of her candidacy at a time when there were only 12 women in the House.

In 1971, Abzug, along with SHIRLEY CHISHOLM, BETTY FRIEDAN, and GLORIA STEINEM, founded the NATIONAL WOMEN'S POLITICAL CAUCUS (NWPC), dedicated to increasing women's participation in politics. While in Congress, she was a strong advocate of the EQUAL RIGHTS AMENDMENT, child care, women's credit rights, equal pay, welfare reform, and the public's access to information. She coauthored the Gov-

Bella Abzug, 1971 (LIBRARY OF CONGRESS)

ernment in the Sunshine Act (1976) and the Right to Privacy Act (1974). On her first day in office, she introduced a bill to withdraw troops from Vietnam by July 4, 1971; it failed. She was the sponsor of legislation in 1973 creating Women's Equality Day, and she wrote the bill that created the NATIONAL WOMEN'S CONFERENCE held in 1977. Following the conference, President Jimmy Carter appointed Abzug cochair of the National Advisory Committee for Women, but he dismissed her six months later after she criticized his economic policies as adversely affecting women. In 1977, she resigned her House seat in order to run in the Democratic primary for the all-male U.S. Senate; she lost by less than 1 percent. Although she was a candidate for mayor of New York and sought to regain her House seat in 1978 and 1986, she never again held elective office.

Abzug was active in the international women's movement, participating in the UNITED NATIONS DECADE FOR WOMEN Conferences in Mexico City (1975), Copenhagen (1980), and Nairobi (1985). Together with other women activists, Abzug cofounded the Women's Foreign Policy Council, which led to the creation of the Women's Environment and Development Organization (WEDO) in 1990. WEDO monitors governments' actions relative to international agreements involving women's rights. The United Nations honored her in 1996 with a peacekeeper's blue beret for her many contributions to peace. The UN Environment Program named her as one of the world's 25 great environmentalists.

Abzug's trademark hat began as a way for her to be taken seriously as a lawyer. As she explained, "When I was a young lawyer, I would go to people's offices and they would always say, 'Sit here. We'll wait for the lawyer.' Working women wore hats. It was the only way they would take you seriously. . . . When I got to Congress, they made a big deal of it. So I was watching did they want me to wear it or not? They didn't want me to wear it, so I did." She died on March 31, 1998, at the age of 77.

Further Reading

Abzug, Bella, and Mim Kelber. *Gender Gap: Bella Abzug's Guide to Political Power for American Women.* Boston: Houghton Mifflin, 1984.

Hyman, Paula E., and Deborah Dash Moore, eds. *Jewish Women in America: An Historical Encyclopedia.* New York: Routledge Press, 1997.

Achtenberg,   Roberta (1950–) *assistant secretary of fair housing and equal opportunity, Department of Housing and Urban Development*   Roberta Achtenberg was the first openly lesbian woman to be appointed to a high-ranking cabinet position. Born on July 20, 1950, in Los Angeles, California, she earned a B.A. in history from the University of California–Berkeley in 1972, and a J.D. from the College of Law, University of Utah, in 1975. Law provided a means for Achtenberg to pursue her passion for social justice issues. As a senior in college, she worked as an intern on welfare rights cases. While in law school, she acknowledged her sexual orientation as a lesbian and ended her marriage. Working first as a teaching fellow at Stanford Law School and later as professor of law at the New College of California School of Law (1976–81), she began to develop an interest and expertise in civil rights law as it pertains to gay and lesbian family issues. From 1982 until 1988, she worked as a staff attorney for the organization Equal Rights Advocates, Inc., directing the Lesbian Rights Project, before serving as Executive Director for the National Center for Lesbian Rights (1989–90). She pursued litigation as a strategy to win more rights and recognition for gays and lesbians in the workplace and for gay families, particularly those with children. In 1989, she won a California case recognizing the right of gay couples to adopt. Working with the National Lawyers Guild and the Anti-Sexism Committee of the San Francisco Bay area chapter, Achtenberg edited one of the first legal guides to gay rights, *Sexual Orientation and the Law* (New York: C. Boardman Company, 1985). In 1985, Achtenberg and her partner, San Francisco municipal court judge Mary C. Morgan, had a son, Benjamin.

Achtenberg's career in politics began locally in San Francisco, first as a community leader and later as an elected official when she was elected to the Board of Supervisors for the City and County of San Francisco. In an effort to focus attention on the needs of children, she and others pioneered a "children's budget," setting aside a percentage of the city's general fund to support children's services. Similarly, she supported the Beacon Initiative, a program that transforms public school buildings into community centers for parents and children. Open 14 hours a day, schools provide access to a variety of social services, computer labs, career development services, art and recreation, leadership training, and health services. She was named the Management Volunteer of the Year in 1989 by the United Way of the Bay Area and the Woman of the Year (Third Senate District) by the California State Senate in 1993. Achtenberg was unsuccessful in her bid to win a seat in the California State Assembly in 1988. She was also defeated in her campaign for mayor of San Francisco.

Achtenberg supported Bill Clinton's bid for the White House in 1992, serving as the national cochair of the Clinton-Gore campaign in 1992 and again in 1996. When she addressed convention delegates at the 1992 Democratic National Convention held in New York City, she became the first open lesbian to address either national party convention. In 1993, President Clinton appointed Roberta Achtenberg to serve as assistant secretary for fair housing and equal opportunity at the U.S. Department of Housing and Urban Development (HUD). On May 23 that year, she successfully won Senate confirmation over the vehement objections of North Carolina's Senator Jesse Helms and other conservatives; Helms referred to her as "that damned lesbian."

In winning confirmation, Achtenberg became the first openly gay person ever to hold a subcabinet position. As assistant secretary,

she served as the chief law enforcement officer for the Federal Fair Housing Act guaranteeing nondiscrimination in housing on the basis of race, ethnicity, gender, disability, or being a family with children. Working with HUD secretary Henry Cisneros, Achtenberg undertook an initiative to end the practice of "red lining," an illegal practice in which banks discriminate in giving loans for home purchases in low-income areas of town. She was a recipient of Vice President Gore's National Performance Review Golden Hammer Award for her efforts to improve the efficiency and effectiveness of the 54 HUD offices. She served as assistant secretary from 1993 to 1995, and then served as a senior advisor to Secretary Cisneros until 1997.

Achtenberg and her family returned to California in 1997. She became the senior vice president for public policy at the San Francisco Chamber of Commerce, a position she still holds. She was appointed to the California State University Board of Trustees by Governor Gray Davis in 1999, served as vice chair from 2004 to 2006, and became chair of the board in May 2006. She also serves on the Board of Directors of the Federal Home Loan Bank of San Francisco, and on the Board of Directors for San Francisco EARN, an organization dedicated to breaking the cycle of poverty by helping low-income workers invest their assets and build wealth. Achtenberg continues to work toward ending all forms of discrimination and for a number of progressive economic initiatives.

acquaintance rape (date rape)

Acquaintance rape, also referred to as date rape, has increasingly been recognized as a form of illegal sexual conduct, often as a by-product of DOMESTIC VIOLENCE. Rape is the perpetuation of an act of sexual intercourse with a person against her will and consent, either when her will is overcome by force or fear resulting from the threat of force or by drugs administered without consent; or when, because of mental deficiency, she is incapable of giving consent; or when she is below the legal age of consent. Acquaintance rape remains a controversial topic because of a lack of agreement on the definition of *consent*. Prosecution of date rape is problematic for the same reason. In 1994, Antioch College in Ohio adopted one of the first policies delineating consensual sexual behavior. The person initiating the contact must take responsibility for obtaining the other participant's verbal consent as the level of intimacy increases. Other prevention strategies today include education and awareness programs offered at most colleges and universities.

Further Reading
Warshaw, Robin. *I Never Called it Rape.* New York: HarperPerennial, 1994.
Wiehe, Vernon, and Ann Richards, eds. *Intimate Betrayal: Understanding and Responding to the Trauma of Acquaintance Rape.* Thousand Oaks, Calif.: Sage Publishers, 1995.

acquired immunodeficiency syndrome (AIDS)   The AIDS epidemic was first recognized in the United States in 1981. HIV (human immunodeficiency virus), the virus that causes AIDS, was not isolated until 1983. From 1981 through 1987, the average life expectancy for someone diagnosed with AIDS was 18 months. Early in the epidemic, few women were among those diagnosed with AIDS. Today, however, AIDS represents a growing health threat to women of all ages, but especially young women and women of color. In 2001, HIV/AIDS was the leading cause of death for African-American women ages 20–24 and 35–44. In the same year, AIDS was the sixth leading cause of death among all women between 25–34 years of age and the fourth leading cause of death among all women ages 35–44.

Women with AIDS make up an increasing proportion of the epidemic. In 1992, women accounted for an estimated 14 percent of adults and adolescents living with AIDS; by the end of 2003, this percentage had grown to 22 percent.

The rate of AIDS diagnoses of African-American women was approximately 25 times the rate for white women and four times the rate for Hispanic women in 2003. Women represent 22 percent of all people living with AIDS in the United States. Over 95 percent of AIDS cases and deaths occur outside of the United States. The majority of those living with AIDS live in Africa and Asia. Although sub-Saharan Africa makes up one-tenth of the world's population, two-thirds of the world's HIV-positive population and more than 80 percent of all AIDS deaths occur there.

The transmission of HIV can be prevented, and AIDS can be treated by antiretroviral therapy. Risk factors include sex without a condom, injection drug use, and limited access to health care. Transmission can also occur from mother to child during birth if not prevented with drug therapy. Women are particularly at risk due to inequality in relationships with men. They may be unaware of their partner's risk factors and may not insist on condom use out of a fear that their partner may abuse them or leave them. A woman is approximately twice as likely as a man to contract HIV infection during vaginal intercourse, and the presence of a sexually transmitted disease (gonorrhea or syphilis) increases the likelihood of acquiring or transmitting HIV infection.

Further Reading
ACT UP/NY Women and AIDS Book Group. *Women, AIDS, and Activism.* Boston: South End Press, 1990.

Adams, Abigail (Abigail Smith Adams)
(1744–1818) *first lady*   Abigail Adams was born Abigail Smith on November 11, 1744, in Massachusetts, raised in an influential colonial family, and received little formal schooling. Her father was a Congregationalist minister who urged her to educate herself from his extensive library; her self-education was sufficient for her to oversee the education of her own children, although she often wrote that girls could advance through the

Abigail Smith Adams (LIBRARY OF CONGRESS)

benefits of a more formal education. Abigail joined the Congregational church at age 15 and was influenced by this denomination's Arminian sect, which denied predestination and instead focused on rationality and living a moral life for the sake of the world now, not for the sake of one's soul in the afterlife. This religious background gave her the foundation for her views on women, the importance of education, and the obligation to work to improve the world here and now.

Abigail Smith met John Adams in 1759 and married him in 1764. She bore five children, one of whom died in infancy; another, John Quincy, became the sixth president.

While her husband John was away in Philadelphia for the Continental Congress and during the Revolutionary War, Abigail Adams was largely by herself in Braintree, raising her children and running the farm successfully despite many hardships. This period saw the beginning of the correspondence for which she is most famous. In a time when women's writing was not usually published, letter writing was a way to disseminate ideas without offending the sensibilities of the time. Adams wrote extensively to her husband and friends and later to her son, John Quincy, outlining her wiews on political issues of the day and relating her impressions of her own life.

In 1776, Adams wrote the letter to her husband for which she is most famous in women's rights circles: "I desire you would remember the ladies and be more generous and favorable to them than your ancestors. Do not put such unlimited power into the hands of the husbands. Remember, all men would be tyrants if they could. . . . [We] will not hold ourselves bound by any laws in which we have no voice or representation." Adams understood the demands the colonists were making on Britain and saw clearly the link between that demand for liberty and the condition of women and slaves. John Adams's response was, famously, "as to your code of laws, I cannot but laugh."

Despite her husband's bemused attitude, Abigail Adams adhered to certain ideas central to 18th-century feminist thought in the United States. She believed in the necessity of educating girls, particularly because they became the women who would raise the next generation. She emphasized the moral influence women had over men, but also believed that women must be able to fulfill their own capabilities. She advocated changing laws that were written for the benefit of men and at the expense of women (for example, laws prohibiting married women from owning property). She also abhorred slavery and considered southern slave owners to have insufficient "passion for Liberty," given their willingness to enslave others. Over the objections of her neighbors, she saw to the enrollment of a black boy in the Braintree schools in 1792, arguing that he was a free man like any other. Again in this incident, Adams recognized the necessity of education in preparing for a life of equality.

Abigail went to France and England with John from 1783 to 1788; in her letters she noted the disdain she received from many of the English nobility. During John's vice presidency (1789–97) and presidency (1797–1801), Abigail split her time between Philadelphia (then the capital) and Massachusetts. She and John moved into the White House in Washington in 1800. She took the role of first lady seriously and believed that respect for the office of the presidency would come, in part, through an adherence to formal entertaining, as she had witnessed in Europe. She was considered to have too much influence over her husband politically and was sometimes referred to as "Her Majesty." Suspicious about the influence of the French Revolution and the value of a free press, she was clear in her support for the Alien and Sedition Acts of 1798, which made it a crime to criticize John Adams's presidency.

In 1801, John and Abigail Adams retired to Braintree to live on a farm they called Peacefield. Adams continued her extensive correspondence and wrote often on the political issues of the day. She followed closely the political career of her son, John Quincy Adams. She also continued to emphasize the importance of education for girls and the role women must play in raising their children to be active participants and citizens. Adams's correspondence (which was extensive) and journals (particularly of her trips to Europe) are available through the Massachusetts Historical Society, and provide telling insight into the life of an 18th-century woman whose beliefs were ahead of her time. She died on October 28, 1818.

Further Reading

Gelles, Edith B. *Portia: The World of Abigail Adams.* New York: Routledge, 2002.

Keller, Rosemary. *Patriotism and the Female Sex: Abigail Adams and the American Revolution.* New York: Carlson Publishers, 1994.

Withey, Lynne. *Dearest Friend: The Life of Abigail Adams.* New York: Touchstone, 2001.

—Claire Curtis

Adams, Annette (Annette Grace Abbott Adams) (1877–1956) *jurist*

Born on March 12, 1877, Annette Adams was one of the first female school principals in California, one of the first two women to receive a law degree from the University of California (1912), one of the first women to be admitted to the California Bar (1912), the first woman to serve as a U.S. attorney (1918–20), the first woman appointed assistant U.S. attorney general (1920–21), the first woman to serve as an appellate court justice in California (1942–52), and the first woman named as presiding justice of the Third District Court of Appeal of California (1942). In 1950, she became the first woman to serve as judge pro tempore on the California Supreme Court, sitting for one case in honor of the court's 100-year anniversary.

Although Annette Adams had a stellar career as an attorney and judge, she had difficulty getting work as an attorney after being admitted to the bar. Law firms in San Francisco and elsewhere had a "no females" policy. Women attorneys were referred to in the early 1900s media as "Portias," unqualified women masquerading as attorneys. She understood the scrutiny she was under, remarking, "When a woman fails men say women have failed; so it is the [duty] of each woman to succeed individually that women collectively may be called successful."

Annette Adams retired from the California Court of Appeals in 1952. After a long illness, she died at her home in Sacramento on October 26, 1956.

Further Reading

Horton, Joey Dean. "'Girl' Lawyer Makes Good: The Story of Annette Abbott Adams" (1997). *Women's Legal History Biography Project,* Stanford University. Available online. URL: http://womenslegalhistory.stanford.edu/papers/aaahtml.html. Accessed on January 7, 2007.

Adams, Louisa (Louisa Catherine Johnson Adams) (1775–1852) *first lady*

Louisa Catherine Johnson was born in London on February

12, 1775, to an American merchant father (Joshua Johnson) and an English mother (Catherine Nuth Johnson). The outbreak of the American Revolution made for tense times in London, so Johnson moved his family to France. Louisa became fluent in French and developed a love for French literature and music. The family ultimately had eight daughters and one son. Louisa's parents recognized her abilities early in life and encouraged her to develop them. Louisa became an accomplished singer and harpist, but gender norms dictated that she marry rather than pursue a career in music.

In 1783, the family moved back to London, and Louisa was enrolled in a boarding school along with two of her sisters. When Joshua Johnson's business fortunes took a turn for the worse, the girls left school and were instructed at home by a governess. In 1790, President George Washington appointed Johnson the U.S. consul, and the family moved to a large house in Cooper's Row where they often entertained visiting Americans. In 1795, 28-year-old John Quincy Adams, the son of Vice President John Adams, was introduced to the Johnson family. He showed an interest in Louisa, and although both families voiced objections to the union, they were engaged in May 1796. Before the couple could be married, John Quincy Adams left for The Hague, thereby postponing their nuptials.

The year-long period of engagement was extraordinary by 18th-century standards and served as a harbinger of a difficult marriage for Louisa. Adams argued that he was not yet financially prepared for marriage, even after President Washington promoted him to the post of minister to Portugal, thereby doubling his salary. Letters from Adams to Louisa written during this year were often harsh and critical. Writing on February 7, 1797, in response to her plea to put their personal happiness ahead of his career, he said, "To serve my country at her call is not merely an ambition, but a duty. My duty to my country is in my mind the first and most imperious of all obligations; before which every interest and every feeling inconsistent with it must forever disappear." The wedding finally took place on July 26, 1797, after Louisa's father reportedly agreed to pay their passage to Lisbon. Soon after, the couple learned that the new president of the United States, John Adams, had changed his son's diplomatic post from Lisbon to Berlin.

Louisa Adams suffered several miscarriages and bouts with poor health prior to giving birth to her first son, George Washington Adams, in 1801. Three months later, the family sailed to back to the United States, where she finally met her husband's family. Of the meeting she wrote: "Do what I would there was a conviction on the part of the others that I could not *suit*." This was the first of many occasions where Louisa expressed feelings of inadequacy. Later in life she wrote an unpublished autobiography titled *The Diary of a Nobody*. She was pregnant 11 times in the first 13 years of her marriage, but only three children, all sons, survived to adulthood.

John Quincy Adams's election to the Senate in 1803 marked the start of a sustained argument over where the couple should reside. She preferred Washington (near her family) to Quincy (near his family) and refused to move north with him. He later wrote that he did not want to be apart from her, and they compromised, agreeing to spend summers in Quincy and winters in Washington. In spring 1808, Adams resigned from the Senate and announced that he would accept a teaching position at Harvard and practice law. However, in 1809 he accepted the post of minister plenipotentiary to Russia and announced that Louisa must accompany him but leave their two oldest sons behind. "To the end of time," she wrote, "life to me will be a succession of miseries only to cease with existence." An unhappy life in Russia was brightened by the birth of a daughter, Louisa Catherine Adams, in 1811, only to grow dim again upon the baby's death from dysentery at the age of 13 months.

In 1814, Adams was reassigned to London to negotiate the treaty ending the War of 1812.

Since the post was likely to be short-term, Adams went alone, leaving Louisa in Russia with their third son, Charles Francis. In December, he sent for her, asking that she meet him in Paris. In mid-February 1815, she left St. Petersburg on what would become a six-week journey through severe conditions at the height of the Napoleonic Wars. Her survival made her a heroine in her husband's eyes for a brief time.

In spring 1817, President James Monroe appointed Adams his secretary of state. Louisa dreaded the return to the explicitly political life of Washington, but the next eight years prepared her well for the duties of first lady. She sought to confront critics who labeled her "snobbish" by opening her home on Tuesday evenings. Guests found her musical abilities and her charm as a hostess very pleasing. First Lady ELIZABETH MONROE's policy of limited entertaining, combined with the death of ABIGAIL ADAMS, left Louisa Adams the center of Washington's social-political power circle until the election of 1824.

That year, Adams lost both the popular and electoral vote to General Andrew Jackson, but a crowded field left Jackson without the electoral vote margin required to win the presidency outright. The House of Representatives ultimately chose John Quincy Adams president in 1825. Louisa and John moved into the White House under a cloud, and neither ever really rallied from it. Louisa described the White House as a "dull and stately prison." In a letter to her son George she wrote: "There is something in this great unsocial house which depresses my spirits beyond expression and makes it impossible for me to feel at home. . . ." Their marriage once again deteriorated with ill effects on Louisa's health and John Quincy Adams's effectiveness as president.

Jackson defeated Adams in the election of 1828. Although Louisa looked hopefully toward a long period of retirement in the tradition of her in-laws, she was again disappointed when her husband returned to politics as a congressman. Further, two of her three sons died within

five years. John had a far more successful final career in Congress than can be said of his presidency. He joined forces with the antislavery movement and enlisted Louisa's help in cataloging antislavery petitions.

To the end, their uneasy partnership showed that although Louisa was a loyal supporter of John Quincy Adams's political career, she was not afraid to speak her own mind when the subject was politics or anything else. Although she is often described by biographers as frail and prone to physical ailments and depression, she lived what Lyman Butterfield (editor in chief of the Adams Papers) called "an extraordinarily varied and arduous life and survived a marriage of more than five decades to one of the most trying of men." In 1846, John Quincy Adams suffered a stroke but survived to celebrate their 50th wedding anniversary in 1847. He suffered a fatal stroke on the floor of the House of Representatives and died on February 23, 1848. Louisa Adams continued to live in Washington until her death on May 15, 1852. Upon her death, Congress adjourned for her funeral, a first for a first lady or for any woman.

Further Reading

Mayo, Edith P. "Louisa Adams: Ahead of Her Time." In *The Smithsonian Book of First Ladies: Their Lives, Times, and Issues,* edited by Edith P. Mayo, 39–44. New York: Henry Holt and Company, 1996.

Schneider, Dorothy, and Carl J. Schneider. *First Ladies: A Biographical Dictionary.* New York: Checkmark Books, 2001.

Shulman, Holly Cowan. "Louisa Catherine Johnson Adams." In *American First Ladies: Their Lives and Their Legacy,* 2nd ed., edited by Lewis L. Gould, 45–56. New York: Routledge, 2001.

Addams, Jane (1860–1935) *social worker, sociologist, reformer*   Born in Illinois on September 6, 1860, Jane Addams was the founder of HULL-HOUSE, a settlement house in Chicago that brought together members of all classes in education, civic reform, and political activities. She was raised in a wealthy, politically active family;

her father was a Republican state senator who provided her with an excellent education. She attended Smith College and went on to medical school; however, with the death of her father and consequent new family responsibilities, she abandoned her plan for a career in medicine, transferring her energy instead to social work and reform. While traveling in Europe, she visited Toynbee House, a settlement house in London, and decided to bring the SETTLEMENT HOUSE MOVEMENT to the United States.

As a young woman, Addams was deeply influenced by Ralph Waldo Emerson's idea of self-reliance, but as she experienced the world, she recognized the impact that social and working conditions had on people's lives and prospects. She also recognized the lack of her own

Jane Addams, 1912 (LIBRARY OF CONGRESS)

firsthand knowledge of life about the working class and recent immigrants. Thus, with the money she inherited from her father she founded Hull-House with her friend Ellen Gates Starr. Hull-House emerged out of a tradition of settlement houses where educated people would "settle" among the working class, both to offer assistance and to learn about the problems facing working-class people. Hull-House grew to be a 13-building settlement house providing day care and children's programs; English classes; citizenship classes; music, art, and theater classes; and employment and other services. Hull-House brought middle- and upper-class visitors and volunteers (some of whom, like FLORENCE KELLEY, were residents) into contact with the largely poor, working-class, immigrant neighborhood. Addams's philosophy of social reform was that the rich and poor could learn from one another and that the world could improve only through democratic reform based on understanding of each side for the other. Reformers involved with Hull-House succeeded in lobbying the Illinois state legislature to pass child labor laws and mandatory education laws. These state laws established a ground from which national legislation concerning child labor could be argued. (The first federal laws against child labor were passed in 1916, although they were later declared unconstitutional. Not until 1938, with the passage of the Fair Labor Standards Act, were minimum-age requirements effectively legislated.)

Addams was committed to the settlement house movement, workers' rights, children's rights, civil rights, and woman's SUFFRAGE. She was a member of the executive board of the National Association for the Advancement of Colored People (NAACP) and president of the National Conference of Charities and Corrections (known today as the National Conference of Social Work). She also served as vice president of the NATIONAL AMERICAN WOMAN'S SUFFRAGE ASSOCIATION (NAWSA) from 1911 to 1914. She was instrumental in the peace movement that emerged in the first part of the 20th century, establishing, with CHARLOTTE PERKINS

GILMAN, the WOMEN'S PEACE PARTY; and in 1915, with EMILY GREENE BALCH, the Women's International League for Peace and Freedom (WILPF). Addams recognized the connections between these disparate organizations, arguing that only through communal efforts among races, classes, and genders could reform occur. She argued in a 1906 lecture on "The Newer Ideals of Peace" that "[i]f we once admit the human dynamic character of progress, then it is easy to understand why the crowded city quarters become focal points of that progress." She found in her work in Chicago that the very conditions of life for immigrants there—crowded, difficult, and surrounded by people of differing ethnicities and religious backgrounds—necessitated a new way of looking at how humans got along with one another. The necessity for "kindliness" that the city demanded provided a foundation for her arguments for a peace that was not simply "not war," but rather the basis for a more progressive community. She was honored in 1910 by Yale University with the first honorary degree ever granted to a woman.

Labeled a communist sympathizer during World War I, Addams continued her work for peace as an essential first step for any further reform movements. In 1917, with support from Addams, Crystal Eastman founded the National Civil Liberties Bureau (which in 1920 became the American Civil Liberties Union [ACLU]) in order to give a constitutional foundation to people's right to speak out about peace. Despite the criticism of Addams, Herbert Hoover (then head of the U.S. Food Administration) asked her to help raise money for war-relief activities because of her popularity as a public speaker.

After the war, Addams continued with her work at Hull-House, and she pressed for continued legislation on child labor and for unemployment benefits. She further pursued her peace work by traveling worldwide to speak and network with women on the need for peaceful democratic reform. In 1931, she became the first woman to be awarded the Nobel Peace

Prize. The presentation at the Nobel awards ceremony declared: "Jane Addams combines all the best feminine qualities which will help us to develop peace on earth." This reflected the view, not held by Addams herself, that women were particularly suited to peace and reform work for their nurturing and maternal qualities.

Despite this celebration of Addams's work, she continued to push for the necessity of reform and worked to bring about practical, beneficial changes to the lives of working class and immigrant people while simultaneously arguing for a progressive change in thinking among all peoples concerning human advancement. Addams fell ill soon after receiving the Nobel Peace Prize and never fully recovered. She died on May 21, 1935.

Further Reading

Addams, Jane. *Twenty Years at Hull-House.* New York: Macmillan, 1930.
Davis, Allen F. *American Heroine: The Life and Legend of Jane Addams.* London: Oxford University Press, 1973.
Elshtain, Jean Bethke. *Jane Addams and the Dream of American Democracy: A Life.* New York: Basic Books, 2002.

—Claire Curtis

Adkins v. Children's Hospital **(261 U.S. 525)** **(1923)** In 1918, Congress passed a law establishing the the District of Columbia Minimum Wage Board. The law set the minimum wage for women and children working in the District of Columbia. For example, a weekly salary for women employed anywhere food was served was $16.50, while it was $15.50 for women working in printing and $15 for laundry workers. Congress acted to "protect the health and morals of women from degrading living conditions" by establishing a wage floor. The question for the Supreme Court was whether or not Congress had the power to set a minimum wage for women, or if this kind of wage-fixing was an unconstitutional restriction on the individual's liberty to contract (protected by the due process clause of the Fifth Amendment). This case exposed the competing strategies of women's rights advocates. ALICE PAUL and other supporters of a legal-equality approach did not favor any forms of PROTECTIVE LEGISLATION (limits on maximum work hours, minimum wage, or place of employment), while others in the movement, including JANE ADDAMS and organizations such as the League of Women Voters and the National Consumer's League, favored the laws as a means to improve women's overall welfare. This case, coming just three years after SUFFRAGE was won, characterized the major division in the post-suffrage movement for women's rights by pitting equality as promoted by the EQUAL RIGHTS AMENDMENT against the special treatment inherent in protective legislation. In declaring the law unconstitutional, Justice George Sutherland, writing for the 5-3 majority, argued "We cannot accept the doctrine that women of a mature age may be subjected to restrictions on their liberty of contract which could not lawfully be imposed in the case of men under similar circumstances." Some in Congress viewed this decision, among others, as an example of the U.S. Supreme Court overstepping its boundaries and encroaching on the legislative domain and the states' powers. By 1937, Franklin D. Roosevelt had been elected, and the Court's makeup had also changed. The ruling in *West Coast Hotel Co. v. Parrish* (1937) explicitly overturned the ruling in *Adkins* and upheld the constitutionality of minimum wage legislation for women enacted by the State of Washington. The Court's reasoning returned to the philosophy of protectionism when it accepted the state's claim that minimum wage laws for women were necessary to protect their health and ability to support themselves.

See also *MULLER V. OREGON*; PROTECTIVE LEGISLATION.

Further Reading

Baer, Judith A. *The Chains of Protection: The Judicial Response to Women's Labor Legislation.* Westport, Conn.: Greenwood Press, 1978.

The OYEZ Project. *Adkins v. Children's Hospital*, 261 U.S. 525 (1923). Available online. URL: http://www.oyez.org/cases/case?case=1901-1939/1922/1922_795. Accessed on January 5, 2007.

affirmative action Affirmative action programs are designed to remedy past discrimination based on race, ethnicity, or sex by increasing the recruitment, promotion, and job training opportunities in employment and by removing barriers to admission to educational institutions.

Affirmative action started in the mid-1960s. In a speech at Howard University in 1965, President Lyndon Johnson said, "We seek . . . not just equality as a right and a theory but equality as a fact and equality as a result." In September 1965, Johnson issued Executive Order 11246, which called upon employers who received federal contracts to "take affirmative action to ensure that applicants are employed, and that employees are treated during employment, without regard to their race, creed, color, or national origin." Under the policy, federal contractors were required to search aggressively for qualified people of color to apply for job vacancies. In 1967, Executive Order 11375 expanded the policy to include women. TITLE VII OF THE CIVIL RIGHTS ACT OF 1964 and subsequent amendments provided women with a strong legal tool to combat employment discrimination and TITLE IX OF THE EDUCATION AMENDMENTS OF 1972 provides the basis for affirmative action for women in education.

Affirmative action has become a controversial policy because of the perception of "reverse discrimination" when a preference for a candidate from an underrepresented group displaces (or is perceived to displace) someone from the majority group. A number of Supreme Court decisions have shaped affirmative action policy. In *Bakke v. University of California* (1978), the Court ruled against a medical school admissions affirmative action program that reserved 16 out of 100 seats for minority students. Even though "quotas" were declared unconstitutional, the Court also found that "race conscious" admissions policies that considered race as one of a number of factors were constitutional. The Court maintained that the inclusion of minority students would create a diverse student body, and this was beneficial to the educational environment as a whole. In 1996, however, the Court appeared to reverse its position on diversity in *Hopwood v. University of Texas,* noting that "educational diversity is not recognized as a compelling state interest." In 1997, 54 percent of the California electorate supported Proposition 209, ending affirmative action in hiring, admissions, and promotions.

In 2003, the pendulum appeared to have swung back in favor of some limited affirmative action programs due to two cases involving the University of Michigan's undergraduate admissions program (*Gratz v. Bollinger*) and its law school (*Grutter v. Bollinger*). In a 5-4 decision in *Grutter,* the Court ruled that race could be one of many factors considered when it furthers "a compelling interest in obtaining the educational benefits that flow from a diverse student body." In the *Gratz* case, the court ruled (6-3) that universities could not rely on formulaic policies that do not provide "individualized consideration" of applicants.

Women in particular have benefited from affirmative action policies designed to remove educational and occupational barriers. Between 1970 and 1995, the proportion of women physicians tripled from 7.6 percent to 24.4 percent. Between 1972 and 1996, the percentage of women awarded science and engineering degrees increased from 30 to 46 percent for bachelor's degrees and 19 to 41 percent for master's degrees. Even today, women remain underrepresented in most traditionally male dominated professions and blue-collar jobs. Wages remain unequal. In 2000, the Department of Labor reported that only 9.9 percent of all engineers, 1.2 percent of all auto mechanics, and 1.7 percent of all carpenters were women. While white men constituted 43 percent of the

2000 workforce, they hold 95 percent of senior management jobs. Only 4.1 percent of top-earnings officers in Fortune 500 companies are women. In 2003, the General Accounting Office reported that women earned 20.3 percent less than men in 2000, even when accounting for differences in occupation and time spent outside of the paid labor force. In 1983, the WAGE GAP was 19.6 percent. Affirmative action has not entirely solved the problems associated with sex discrimination.

See also GLASS CEILING.

Further Reading

Feminist Majority Foundation. Affirmative Action Information Center. "Origins of Affirmative Action for Women." Available online. URL: http://www. feminist.org/other/ccri/aafact1.html. Accessed on January 5, 2007.

Johnson, Roberta Ann. "Affirmative Action Policy in the United States: Its Impact on Women." *Policy and Politics* 18 (1990): 77–90.

AIDS See ACQUIRED IMMUNODEFICIENCY SYNDROME.

Aid to Families with Dependent Children (AFDC)

Aid to Families with Dependent Children (AFDC) was established by the Social Security Act of 1935 as a grant program to enable states to provide cash welfare payments for needy children who had been deprived of parental support or care because their father or mother was absent from the home, incapacitated, deceased, or unemployed. All 50 states, the District of Columbia, Guam, Puerto Rico, and the Virgin Islands operated an AFDC program. States defined "need," set their own benefit levels, established (within federal limitations) income and resource limits, and administered the program or supervised its administration. States were entitled to unlimited federal funds for reimbursement of benefit payments at "matching" rates that were inversely related to state per capita income. States were required to provide aid to all persons who were in classes eligible under federal law and whose income and resources were within state-set limits, thereby making public support an "entitlement" for people meeting the eligibility requirements.

In the face of mounting costs, Congress and the states were pressured to "reform" welfare programs in the 1990s. The PERSONAL RESPONSIBILITY AND WORK OPPORTUNITY RECONCILIATION ACT of 1996 (PRWORA) replaced AFDC, AFDC administration, the Job Opportunities and Basic Skills Training (JOBS) program, and the Emergency Assistance (EA) program with a cash welfare block grant called the Temporary Assistance for Needy Families (TANF) program. Key elements of TANF include a lifetime limit of five years (60 months) on the amount of time a family with an adult can receive assistance funded with federal funds, increasing work participation rate requirements which states must meet, and broad state flexibility on program design. Most significantly as a result of the 1996 legislation, welfare is no longer an entitlement program.

See also WELFARE POLICY; WELFARE RIGHTS MOVEMENT.

Further Reading
Abramovitz, Mimi. *Regulating the Lives of Women: Social Welfare Policy from Colonial Times to the Present.* Boston: South End Press, 1996.
Trattner, Walter I. *From Poor Law to Wefare State.* New York: Free Press, 1998.

Akron v. Akron Center for Reproductive Health (462 U.S. 416) (1983)

In 1978, the Akron City Council enacted an ordinance establishing 17 provisions to regulate ABORTION services. Five of the regulations were challenged: a requirement that all abortions performed after the first trimester to be done in hospitals; notification and consent by one parent 24 hours prior to an abortion performed on an unmarried minor; a provision that doctors counsel prospective patients to ensure consent, including the requirement that they state "the unborn child is a human life from the moment of conception"; a 24-hour waiting period; and the stipulation that fetal remains be disposed of in a "humane and sanitary manner." In a 6-3 decision, the U.S. Supreme Court affirmed ROE V. WADE and its commitment to protecting women's reproductive rights by invalidating the provisions of the Akron ordinance. Justice Lewis Powell, author of the majority opinion, noted that the provisions of the Akron ordinance were clearly intended to direct women away from choosing an abortion and constituted unreasonable infringements on a woman's constitutional right to obtain an abortion.

Further Reading
Goldstein, Leslie. *Contemporary Cases in Women's Rights.* Madison: University of Wisconsin Press, 1994.
The OYEZ Project. *Akron v. Akron Center For Reproductive Health,* 462 U.S. 416 (1983). Available online. URL: http://www.oyez.org/cases/case?case=1980-1989/1982/1982_81_746. Accessed on January 5, 2007.

Alan Guttmacher Institute (AGI)

The Alan Guttmacher Institute (AGI) is a nonprofit organization focused on sexual and reproductive health research, policy analysis, and public education. The Institute's mission is to protect the reproductive choices of all women and men in the United States and throughout the world.

AGI was founded in 1968 as the Center for Family Planning Program Development. Alan F. Guttmacher, an obstetrician-gynecologist and president of the PLANNED PARENTHOOD FEDERATION OF AMERICA (PPFA) for 12 years, nurtured the organization's early development. AGI is dedicated to providing reliable, balanced, nonpartisan information on sexual activity, contraception, abortion, and childbearing. The organization regularly publishes three journals: *Perspectives on Sexual and Reproductive Health, International Family Planning Perspectives,* and *The Guttmacher Report on Public Policy.* AGI maintains a Web page to disseminate information, analysis, and the results of its research at www.guttmacher.org.

Albright, Madeline (Madeline Jana Korbel Albright) (1937–) *secretary of state, United Nations ambassador, author* Madeleine Korbel Albright became the first woman in U.S. political history to occupy the cabinet position of secretary of state. President Bill Clinton, in his second term in office, nominated Albright, who was confirmed unanimously by the U.S. Senate as the 64th secretary of state. Albright was sworn into office on January 23, 1997. She brought a wealth of experience to the office of secretary of state. This experience was cultivated during her childhood and later solidified by a vibrant and prodigious academic and public service career in the foreign policy arena.

Albright was born Marie Jana Korbel in Prague, Czechoslovakia, May 15 1937; Madeline was a nickname given to her by her grandmother. She was introduced to foreign policy from an early age. Her father, Joseph Korbel, was a Czechoslovakian diplomat who represented his country in many foreign capitals. The family accompanied him to each of his diplomatic postings. As such, Secretary Albright constantly had to familiarize herself with various cultures. Her family fled Czechoslovakia when the Germans invaded during World War II, and they took up residence in London. While in London, Albright experienced firsthand the Nazis' bombing campaign. The family fled their native homeland for a second time in 1948, gaining political asylum in the United States after the communist takeover of Czechoslovakia.

After arriving in the United States and attending high school in Colorado, Albright went on to Wellesley College and earned a degree in political science in 1959. That same year, she married Joseph Medill Patterson Albright, the heir to a newspaper fortune. The marriage produced three daughters; however, the couple filed for divorce in 1983.

Combining motherhood and academics, Albright mothered twins while attending graduate school at Columbia University's School of Public Law and Government, where she earned her master's degree (1968) and Ph.D. (1976), with a concentration in Soviet politics. Immediately after graduate school, Albright's public service career began when she joined the staff of Senator Edmund Muskie, becoming his chief legislative assistant. Given both her former legislative expertise and knowledge of foreign affairs, she was invited to join President Jimmy Carter's National Security Council staff as a legislative liaison.

After Carter was defeated in 1980, Albright returned to the academic world. In 1981, she was awarded a fellowship at the Woodrow Wilson International Center for Scholars, where she conducted research and wrote a book about the role of the press in bringing about change in Poland between 1980 and 1982. In 1982, she joined the faculty at Georgetown University, teaching both graduate and undergraduate courses in international relations. She also became the director of women students enrolled in the foreign service program at the university's School of Foreign Service. She developed programs geared specifically to advancing professional opportunities for women in international relations. While at Georgetown, she was affiliated with the Georgetown University Center for Strategic and International Studies as a senior fellow in Soviet and Eastern European affairs.

Albright gained the attention of the Washington Democratic elite within the beltway as president of the Center for National Policy. The Democratic Party think tank was charged with generating discussion and study about domestic and international issues. She was the foreign policy adviser to the failed presidential candidacies of Walter Mondale and Michael Dukakis. However, her senior foreign policy advisory role in the successful run for the presidency of the Clinton campaign catapulted her to the position of U.S. ambassador to the United Nations.

In Clinton's second term as president, she was appointed secretary of state.

During her tenure as secretary of state, the highest-ranking women in the U.S. government, Albright was responsible for shaping U.S. foreign policy regarding the Balkans and ultimately U.S. and NATO military involvement in the former Yugoslavia. Many foreign leaders viewed Albright as outspoken and sometimes undiplomatic. In the United States, Albright was perceived by some as a "token," or merely as "Hillary's friend." However, both Democrats and Republicans generally embraced Albright. In 2003, three years after returning to civilian life, Albright published her memoir, *Madam Secretary.* Albright is currently the Mortara Distinguished Professor of Diplomacy at the Georgetown University Walsh School of Foreign Service in Washington, D.C. She serves as chairperson of National Democratic Institute for International Affairs and as president of the Truman Scholarship Foundation.

Further Reading

Albright, Madeleine, and Bill Woodward. *Madam Secretary: A Memoir.* New York: Miramax Books, 2003.

Crossette, Barbara. "A Political Diplomat: Madeline Korbel Albright." *New York Times,* 6 December 1996.

—Hollis France

Alcott, Louisa May (1832–1888) *author* Louisa May Alcott was born in Germantown, Pennsylvania, on November 29, 1832. She was the second daughter of Amos Bronson Alcott and Abigail "Abba" May. The family moved to Boston, Massachusetts, in 1834 and then to Concord in 1840. Louisa's father was a transcendental philosopher and educator who founded Fruitland, a utopian society. Ralph Waldo Emerson and Henry David Thoreau were close friends of the family during Alcott's childhood. Alcott published her first poem, "Sunlight," in 1852 under the pseudonym Flora Fairfield. In 1854, when she was 22 years old, she published her first book, *Flower Fables.* Over the course of her lifetime, she was the author of 270 published works, including her most famous novel, *Little Women,* published in 1868. *Little Women* was largely autobiographical, based on her own experiences growing up with three sisters. This book was significant to the development of social attitudes about women as individuals who were capable of individual actions and decisions, something that proved to be a necessary precursor to the advancement of women's political rights.

During service as a Civil War nurse in 1862, Alcott contracted typhoid fever and suffered from mercury poisoning (a side effect of the treatment) for the remainder of her life. *Hospital Sketches* (1863) was based on the letters she had written home from her Civil War post in Washington, D.C. Likewise, *Work: A Story of Experience,* chronicles the life of Christie Devon, an orphaned 20-year-old who refuses to choose between the shackles of an early marriage and further burdening her aunt and uncle. The story also explores working conditions, wages, and hardships for women in the 19th-century workplace.

In the 1870s, after living for a brief time in Europe, Alcott became active in the women's SUFFRAGE movement in Concord. She wrote articles for *The Women's Journal* and canvassed door to door trying to register women to vote. She was the first woman to register to vote in Concord's school, tax, and bond suffrage. In her final novel, *Jo's Boys,* she made arguments for women's rights and other social reforms. Alcott is quoted having said, "I can remember when anti-slavery was in just the same state that suffrage is now, and take more pride in the very small help we Alcotts could give than in all the books I ever wrote. . . ."

Louisa May Alcott died on March 6, 1888, two days after her father passed away. She is buried in Sleepy Hollow Cemetery in Concord, Massachusetts.

Further Reading

Anderson, William, and David Wade. *The World of Louisa May Alcott.* New York: HarperPerennial, 1995.

"Alice Doesn't Day" Women's Strike The "Alice Doesn't Day" women's strike was sponsored by the NATIONAL ORGANIZATION FOR WOMEN (NOW). On October 29, 1975, women were urged to refrain from all of their typical daily duties involving work, child care, and housework. The strike was intended "to demonstrate the dependence of the country on the 51 percent of the population which is female." Several historical accounts suggest that the strike was not as successful as many had hoped (*Time* magazine labeled it "a spectacular failure") and that antifeminist groups who promised to wear pink and bake cookies got more publicity than strikers. The strike took its name from the 1974 film *Alice Doesn't Live Here Anymore*, about a woman who tries to break out of a stultifying life as a housewife and pursue a career.

See also ANTIFEMINISM; FEMINISM.

alimony After divorce or separation, alimony is the money paid by one spouse to the other to meet the financial obligations of marriage. It is based on the common-law right of a wife to be supported by her husband, but in 1979 the U.S. Supreme Court removed its limitation to husbands to account for cases in which the wife is wealthier. Alimony is different from child support, which is the duty of both mother and father to contribute, based on ability to pay, to the support of minor children. In contemporary law, alimony is generally awarded only in cases where one spouse is unable to support himself or herself. Laws vary by state. Recent figures show that some 90 percent of U.S. divorces are free of alimony requirements. Alimony is called *spousal maintenance* in most states today. In cases of extended cohabitation, "palimony" sometimes may be awarded.

The introduction of "no-fault" divorce in nearly every state by the mid-1960s reduced the likelihood that alimony would be awarded to women. The consequences for women and their children have been grave. Statistics show that a man's standard of living typically rises in the first year following a divorce, while a woman's declines substantially. The equity between men and women assumed in no-fault divorce ignores the economic realities of the WAGE GAP, the discrimination women reentering the workforce are likely to face, and the child-care costs associated with a woman returning to work. Some feminists hailed no-fault divorce and the decline of alimony, while others cautioned women not to give up the protection alimony afforded before true equality was established.

See also COVERTURE; ORR V. ORR.

Further Reading
DiFonzo, J. Herbie. *Beneath the Fault Line: The Popular and Legal Culture of Divorce in Twentieth-Century America.* Richmond: University of Virginia Press, 1997.

Allen, Florence (Florence Ellinwood Allen) (1884–1966) *jurist* Born on March 23, 1884, and raised in Cleveland, Ohio, Florence Allen was a descendant of Revolutionary War hero Ethan Allen. After receiving a B.A. degree from Case Western Reserve University's College for Women (1904), she prepared for a career in music, studying in Berlin for two years, but returned to the United States when an injury prevented the development of a concert career. She worked as the music critic for the *Cleveland Plain Dealer* from 1906 to 1909 while pursuing a master's degree in political science and constitutional law (awarded in 1908). Allen then turned to law full-time, studying first at the University of Chicago and completing her law degree at New York University in 1913. She was admitted to the Ohio Bar in 1914.

Allen used the law as a tool to open doors for women. While establishing a law practice in Cleveland, she drove a horse and buggy across Ohio campaigning for woman's SUFFRAGE and the right for women to hold public office. In 1919, she was appointed prosecutor of Cuyahoga County; in 1920, she was elected a judge of the court of common pleas; and in 1922, she became the first woman elected to the Ohio Supreme Court. In March 1934, President Franklin D. Roosevelt named Allen to the U.S. Court of Appeals for the Sixth Circuit. She served on the court for 25 years, the last as chief judge. Among the many cases she heard was the constitutionality of the Tennesee Valley Authority in 1938. ELEANOR ROOSEVELT appealed to her husband to name Allen to the U.S. Supreme Court, but he declined. She was recognized as an expert on constitutional law and the law of patents. She published three books, two on the law and her memoirs, titled *To Do Justly.* Florence Ellinwood Allen died on September 12, 1966.

Further Reading

Allen, Florence. *To Do Justly.* Cleveland: Western Reserve Press, 1965.

Tuve, Jeanette. *First Lady of the Law: Florence Ellinwood Allen.* Lanham, Md.: University Press of America, 1984.

Allen, Paula Gunn (Paula Marie Francis Gunn Allen) (1939–   ) *author, literary critic*

Paula Gunn Allen, of Native American and Lebanese descent, is an acclaimed feminist poet, novelist, and literary critic. She was born in Albuquerque, New Mexico, on October 24, 1939. Allen's father, E. Lee Francis, was a Lebanese American and her mother, Ethel, was Laguna-Sioux-Scot. Her father owned the Cubero Trading Company and served as lieutenant governor of New Mexico from 1967 to 1970.

Allen's diverse background informs her writing. She particularly credits the woman-centered Pueblo culture for many of the insights evident in her poetry. Allen's early elementary education was at St. Vincent's Academy in Albuquerque and at a mission school in the town of San Fidel. She later attended the Colorado's Women's College and then the University of Oregon, she received her B.A. in English in 1966 and her M.F.A. in creative writing in 1968. She received her doctorate in American studies with a concentration in Native American

literature from the University of New Mexico in 1976. Paula Allen was twice married and twice divorced. She has three children.

Allen's writing career began with the publication of her first book, *Blind Lion Poems,* published in 1974. While completing her doctorate, she began teaching—first at DeAnza Community College and later at the University of New Mexico. She earned year-long postdoctoral fellowships to UCLA and the University of California at Berkeley. Grants from the Ford Foundation and the National Research Council facilitated her early study of the oral tradition in Native American literature. In 1978 and again in 1980, she received a National Endowment of the Arts Fellowship to study Native American women's writing. Simultaneously, she edited *Studies in American Indian Literature: Critical Essays and Course Designs* (1983), widely considered the definitive text in Native American literary criticism. Allen also had a distinguished teaching career with appointments at a number of institutions, including the College of San Mateo, San Diego State University, and San Francisco State University. She served as director of the Native American Studies program at San Francisco State. At the University of California–Berkeley, she was professor of Native American and ethnic studies. Her last academic post was professor of English, creative writing, and American Indian studies at the University of California at Los Angeles. She retired in 1999.

Allen's voice as a literary critic was primarily devoted to distinguishing Native American literature from European American interpretations. Her own writing explored the powerful roles women played in matrilineal Pueblo society. Her research documents Native American women's contribution to democracy and FEMINISM, refuting the notion that societies in which women were men's equal did not exist. She has also played a major role in championing the place of gay and lesbian Native Americans in the community. "Beloved Women: Lesbians in American Indian Cultures," an essay published in *Conditions: The Sacred Hoop: Recovering the Feminine in American Indian Traditions,* published in 1986, explored in detail the power of oral traditions found in Native American literature.

Through her poetry, Allen explores her multicultural heritage through images of spirits and shadows. In an interview, Allen said of her poetry, "My poetry has a haunted sense to it . . . a sorrow and grievingness in it that comes directly from being split, not in two but in twenty, and never being able to reconcile all the places that I am." Her most recent work is *Pocahontas: Medicine Woman, Spy, Entrepreneur, Diplomat*, published in 2003.

Further Reading
Gunn, Paula Allen. *The Woman Who Owned the Shadows*. San Francisco: Aunt Lute Books, 1983.
Purdy, John. "And Then, Twenty Years Later . . .": A Conversation with Paula Allen Gunn." *Studies in American Indian Literatures* 9 (1997): 5–16.

Allred, Gloria (Gloria Rachel Allred)
(1941–) *attorney* Gloria Allred is a feminist attorney who has tried numerous cases to advance women's rights. She was born on July 3, 1941, in Philadelphia and received her bachelor's degree from the University of Pennsylvania (1963), her master's degree from New York University (1966), and her law degree from Loyola University (1974).

Allred is known for her high public profile and her unconventional means of directing the public's attention to discrimination against women. For example, she once gave a chastity belt to a California state senator who supported a constitutional amendment to ban ABORTION. She has tried cases on SEXUAL HARASSMENT, employment discrimination, family law, and equal pay. Allred is the founder of the Women's Equal Rights Legal Defense and Education Fund, a California nonprofit organization working to advance women's rights. She is also the founding partner of the California law firm of Allred, Maroko, and Goldberg, which specializes in employment discrimination, harassment, and wrongful termination throughout California.

Alpha Suffrage Club In January 1913, IDA B. WELLS-BARNETT formed the first-ever voting rights union for black women in Illinois—the Alpha Suffrage Club. The group met weekly at the Negro Fellowship League Reading Room and Social Center (a refuge founded for blacks on the streets). The club began by parading in a demonstration on the streets of Chicago. The Alpha Suffrage Club also participated in the 1913 SUFFRAGE parade in Washington, D.C. In an attempt to appease southern legislators and some southern suffragists, organizers asked that the African-American women march in the back of the parade. Wells-Barnett tried to get the Illinois delegation to support her opposition to the segregation, but ultimately she and many other Alpha Club members simply refused to participate. On the day of the parade, Ida B. Wells-Barnett emerged from the crowd and joined the Illinois delegation, marching between two white suffragists. Wells-Barnett also founded the newspaper the *Alpha Suffrage Record* and served as its editor.

Further Reading
McMurry, Linda O. *To Keep the Waters Troubled: The Life of Ida B. Wells*. New York: Oxford University Press, 1998.

Alvarez, Aida (1949–) *cabinet member* President Clinton appointed Aida Alvarez administrator of the Small Business Administration (SBA) in 1997, making her the first Hispanic woman and the first Puerto Rican to hold a cabinet position. Under her leadership, the SBA tripled the number of loans granted to women-owned and minority-owned businesses.

Alvarez earned her bachelor's degree from Harvard University in 1971. She worked as a television and print journalist and as an investment banker, and she was appointed as the first director of the Office of Federal Housing Enterprise Oversight in 1993. In this capacity, she established regulatory oversight of Fannie Mae and Freddie Mac, the country's largest housing finance companies.

In 2000, Alvarez was elected to the Board of Overseers of Harvard University. Her role is to visit the graduate schools, departments and museums of the University to ensure that the university remains true to its charter as a place of learning. She also serves on the National Trust for Historic Preservation and the Coalition for Supportive Housing and is on the Board of Trustees of the Latino Community Foundation and the Board of Directors for PacifiCare Health Systems, Inc.

American Association of University Women (AAUW)

The mission of the American Association of University Women is to promote equity for all women and girls, lifelong education, and positive social change. The organization began in 1881 when Marion Talbot called a meeting of women graduates for the purpose of supporting one another and nurturing future generations of women in higher education. The Association of Collegiate Alumnae was formally established in 1882 and merged with the Southern Association of College Women in 1921 to form the American Association of University Women.

Today the AAUW operates as an umbrella for three distinct corporations sharing a unified mission. The AAUW Association is the membership arm of the organization. More than 100,000 members, 1,300 branches, and 600 college/university partners work in local communities to promote equity in education. The AAUW Educational Foundation provides funds to advance education and research. It is the largest funding source exclusively for graduate women. The Educational Foundation regularly funds, conducts, and disseminates research on issues concerning women, girls, and education. The AAUW Legal Advocacy Fund provides funding and support for women pursuing equity through the legal system. Primarily focused on sex discrimination in higher education, the fund helps female students, faculty, and administrators challenge discriminatory practices, including SEXUAL HARASSMENT, pay inequity, denial of ten-

ure and promotion, and inequality in women's athletics. The organization as a whole conducts conferences, leadership training, and outreach. AAUW's global network is the International Federation of University Women. The organization maintains a Web site at www.aauw.org.

See also TITLE IX.

Further Reading

Levine, Susan. *Degrees of Equality: The American Association of University Women and the Challenge of Twentieth Century Feminism.* Philadelphia: Temple University Press, 1995.

American Birth Control League (ABCL)

MARGARET SANGER founded the American Birth Control League (ABCL) on November 10, 1921, at the First American Birth Control Conference in New York City. The ABCL was dedicated to advancing public education by disseminating information to the medical community, social workers, and individual women; advocating legislative reform at the state and national level; and supporting research efforts aimed at developing safe, effective forms of birth control. In 1923, the ABCL opened the first birth control clinic in the United States. The Clinical Research Bureau (CRB) served married women and couples with contraceptive services. Most women were fitted with pessaries or diaphragms used with contraceptive jelly. The bureau's clinic kept detailed patient records, allowing the CRB to conduct research on the efficacy of various birth control devices and practices. In 1928, Sanger resigned as president of the ABCL and assumed full control of the CRB, renaming it the Birth Control Clinical Research Bureau (BCCRB). In 1939, the ABCL merged with the BCCRB, and in 1942 the organization adopted the name PLANNED PARENTHOOD FEDERATION OF AMERICA.

See also BIRTH CONTROL MOVEMENT.

Further Reading

Gordon, Linda. *Woman's Body, Woman's Right: A Social History of Birth Control in America.* New York: Grossman Publishers, 1976.

———. *The Moral Property of Women: A History of Birth Control Politics in America.* Urbana: University of Illinois Press, 2002.

American Equal Rights Association (AERA)

Founded on May 10, 1866, the American Equal Rights Association was formed to "secure Equal Rights to all American citizens, especially the right of SUFFRAGE, irrespective of race, color, or sex." The AERA lasted only three years because of philosophical divisions within its leadership. In 1867, Kansas voted down two consecutive referenda granting suffrage to blacks and women. During the Kansas campaign, ELIZABETH CADY STANTON and SUSAN B. ANTHONY alienated abolitionists and other suffragists by appealing to racist sentiments in their opposition to the Fifteenth Amendment, which granted only black males the right to vote. Stanton and Anthony argued for a Sixteenth Amendment guaranteeing woman suffrage, but many in the organization urged a more cautious and patient strategy calling for black franchise first and foremost. Stanton and Anthony split from the AERA in 1869 to form the NATIONAL WOMAN SUFFRAGE ASSOCIATION (NWSA). LUCY STONE and JULIA WARD HOWE, along with other notable abolition leaders dissolved the AERA and formed the AMERICAN WOMAN SUFFRAGE ASSOCIATION (AWSA). The NWSA and the AWSA joined forces again in 1890, forming the NATIONAL AMERICAN WOMAN SUFFRAGE ASSOCIATION (NAWSA).

See also ABOLITION.

Further Reading

Sherr, Lynn. *Failure Is Impossible: Susan B. Anthony in Her Own Words.* New York: Times Books, 1995.
———. *The Trial of Susan B. Anthony.* New York: Prometheus Books, 2003.

American Life League, Inc. (ALL)

Judie Brown founded the American Life League (ALL) in 1977. The organization's mission is stated as follows: "The mission of American Life League is to serve God by helping to build a society that respects and protects innocent human life from fertilization to natural death—without compromise, without exception, without apology." ALL takes pro-life positions on the issues of ABORTION, assisted suicide, bioethics, cloning, birth control, EUGENICS, and fetal research. The organization sponsors several initiatives: Crusade for the Defense of Our Catholic Church, Campus for Life, Rock for Life, and Stop Planned Parenthood International. The organization maintains a Web site to recruit members and disseminate information at www.aal.org.

See also RIGHT TO LIFE MOVEMENT.

American Woman Suffrage Association (AWSA)

The American Woman Suffrage Association was formed in 1869 by the New England wing of suffragists and abolitionists in reaction to ELIZABETH CADY STANTON and SUSAN B. ANTHONY's departure from the AMERICAN EQUAL RIGHTS ASSOCIATION. Stanton and Anthony believed that women were being ignored in the interest of pursuing SUFFRAGE for black males and argued on behalf of a federal amendment strategy that was perceived by some to be in direct competition with the ratification campaign for the Fifteenth Amendment. When

Members of the American Association of University Women meeting on the White House lawn with President Coolidge, 1924 (LIBRARY OF CONGRESS)

Stanton and Anthony split to form the NATIONAL WOMAN SUFFRAGE ASSOCIATION (NWSA), LUCY STONE and JULIA WARD HOWE formed the American Woman Suffrage Association. Stone and Howe accused the NWSA of diverting attention away from suffrage by their insistence on broad equality rights for women. At the urging of the AWSA, the Republican Party included a plank for woman suffrage in their platform of 1872 but failed to actively campaign on the issue of a Sixteenth Amendment for woman's suffrage. The AWSA eschewed a federal strategy in favor of a state-by-state campaign for woman suffrage. Once the Fifteenth Amendment was ratified, the major point of division between the AWSA and the NWSA was gone, but the bitterness lasted for another 20 years. The AWSA and the NWSA were joined in 1890 to form the NATIONAL AMERICAN WOMAN SUFFRAGE ASSOCIATION (NAWSA).

Further Reading

Corbin, Carole Lynn. *The Right to Vote.* New York: Franklin Watts, 1985.

Scott, Anne Firor, and Andrew MacKay Scott. *Half the People: The Fight for Woman Suffrage.* New York: J.P. Lippincott, 1975.

Ames, Jessie (Jessie Harriet Daniel Ames)

(1883–1972) *suffragist, reformer* Jessie Daniel Ames was born in Palestine, Texas, on November 2, 1883. She graduated from Southwestern University in Georgetown in 1902 and shortly thereafter met Roger Ames, whom she married in 1905. Her surgeon husband was rarely home, and then he died in 1914, leaving Ames to raise three children. To support her family, she joined her mother in running the telephone company in Georgetown.

Ames's prominent position in the community led her into social and business circles, and in 1916 she organized the Georgetown Equal Suffrage League. She went on to serve as state officer of the Texas Equal Suffrage Association. After women won the right to vote in the state's primary in 1918 and Texas ratified the Nineteenth Amendment in 1919, Ames founded the Texas LEAGUE OF WOMEN VOTERS, served as delegate-at-large to two National Democratic conventions, and served as state officer on the board of many different groups. Through these activities, she became discouraged by the failure of women's SUFFRAGE to initiate true equality and looked toward interracial cooperation to rectify the problems of society. As a field worker for the Commission on Interracial Cooperation, she began to identify lynching as a key to the oppression of both blacks and women. In 1930, Ames founded the ASSOCIATION OF SOUTHERN WOMEN FOR THE PREVENTION OF LYNCHING (ASWPL). By challenging the southern justification for lynching as a way to protect white women, the ASWPL helped to turn public opinion against lynching, decreasing the incidents of the crime so significantly that by the 1940s the organization was disbanded. Ames remained active in many causes throughout her life. She died in Austin, Texas, on February 21, 1972.

See also ANTI-LYNCHING MOVEMENT.

Further Reading

Hall, Jacquelyn Dowd. *Revolt against Chivalry: Jessie Daniel Ames and the Women's Campaign against Lynching.* New York: Columbia University Press, 1979.

The Handbook of Texas Online. "Ames, Jessie Harriet Daniel." Available online. URL: http://www.tsha. utexas.edu/handbook/online/articles/view/AA/fam6.html. Accessed on January 5, 2007.

Swartz, Jon D., and Joanna Fountain-Schroeder, eds., *Jessie Daniel Ames: An Exhibition at Southwestern University.* Georgetown, Tex.: Cody Memorial Library, Southwestern University, 1986.

—Angela Boswell

Anderson, Eugenie Moore (Helen Eugenie Moore Anderson)

(1909–1997) *ambassador, diplomat* Helen Eugenie Moore was born to Ezekiel Arrowsmith Moore, a Methodist minister, and Flora Belle Moore on May 26, 1909, in

Adair, Iowa. Although she studied at three colleges, she did not earn a degree. From 1926 to 1927, she attended Stephens College in Columbia, Missouri; from 1927 to 1928 she was enrolled at Simpson College in Indianola, Iowa, and she completed one more year at Carlton College in Northfield, Minnesota (1929–1930). In 1930, she married John Pierce Anderson, an artist and photographer. The couple had two children.

Eugenie Moore Anderson helped to create the Democratic-Farmer-Labor Party (DFL) of Minnesota in 1944. Four years later, as one of the few women among the leaders of the fledgling party, she was elected to an office in the national Democratic Party. In 1948, when the DFL split from the Democratic Party in a controversy over goals and ideology, Anderson supported Hubert H. Humphrey and the DFL. In 1949, she had the distinction of becoming the first American woman ambassador when President Harry Truman named her ambassador to Denmark. Upon her appointment, she remarked: "I know that he [Truman] intended my appointment to signify to all women that he recognizes our growing assumption of mature responsible citizenship, our work for the public good, not simply as women and mothers, but as citizens and as people." She earned the respect of the Danes by learning the language and was credited with moving Denmark from neutrality to alignment with the West.

When Truman's presidency ended, Anderson returned to the United States. In 1958, she ran for a U.S. Senate seat but lost in the primary. In 1962, President John F. Kennedy appointed her to head the U.S. delegation to Bulgaria. As minister to Bulgaria, she became the first American woman to represent the United States in a country allied with the Soviet Union. She found it difficult to operate in the communist environment and resigned in 1964. She served as U.S. representative to the United Nations from 1965 to 1967, served on the UN Trusteeship Council from 1965 to 1968, and then was appointed special assistant to the secretary of state. She died on March 31, 1997.

Anderson, Marian (1897–1993) *opera singer* Contralto Marian Anderson was born in Philadelphia, Pennsylvania, on February 27, 1897 (though she claimed a birth date of February 17, 1902). She began singing in the Union Baptist Church choir at the age of six, and community members supported her early musical training. She went on to study with tenor Giuseppe Boghetti. In 1924, she gave her first recital at New York's Town Hall. The performance was uneven and, unable to establish an active career in the United States, she went to study in London in 1925 and later to Germany. After touring extensively throughout Europe over the next 10 years, she returned to New York's Town Hall for a successful reprise in 1935. She became the nation's third highest concert box office draw.

In 1939, Anderson's agent and officials from Howard University tried to book her into Washington's Constitution Hall, owned by the DAUGHTERS OF THE AMERICAN REVOLUTION (DAR). DAR policy, however, stipulated that all contracts contain a clause saying "concert by white artists only." Consequently, First Lady ELEANOR ROOSEVELT resigned from the DAR in protest, and the U.S. Department of the Interior scheduled a concert on the steps of the Lincoln Memorial on April 9, 1939 (Easter Sunday). Over 75,000 people attended the concert, and millions more tuned in on the radio. Following the controversy, Anderson refused to ever sing in another segregated venue. In her autobiography, *My Lord, What a Morning,* she wrote: "There are many persons ready to do what is right because in their hearts they know it is right. But they hesitate, waiting for the other fellow to make the first move—and he, in turn, waits for you. The minute a person whose word means a great deal dares to take the open-hearted and courageous way, many others follow. Not everyone can be turned aside from meanness and hatred, but the great majority of Americans is heading in that direction. I have a great belief in the future of my people and my country."

In 1955, Anderson performed with the New York Metropolitan Opera Company as Ulrica, the *Gypsy* fortune-teller, in Verdi's opera *The Masked Ball*. With this appearance, she became the first African American to sing an important role at the Metropolitan Opera as a regular company member. In 1956, Anderson made a farewell tour throughout America and Europe, and in 1957 she toured 12 Asian nations on behalf of the U.S. State Department.

Anderson received a number of awards and honors over her lifetime. In 1963, she was given the Presidential Medal of Freedom by President Lyndon Johnson. She received honorary doctorates from more than two dozen universities and sang at the presidential inaugurals of Dwight Eisenhower and John F. Kennedy. Anderson retired in 1965 with a final concert in Philadelphia. She died on April 8, 1993, in Portland, Oregon.

Further Reading

Anderson, Marian. *My Lord, What a Morning*. New York: Viking Press, 1956.

Penn Library Exhibitions. "Marian Anderson: A Life in Song." Available online. URL: http://www.library.upenn.edu/exhibits/rbm/anderson/. Accessed on January 5, 2007.

Andrews, Fannie Fern Phillips (1867–1950)
peace activist Fannie Fern Phillips Andrews is well respected for her unrelenting efforts to promote the benefits of peace in both the United States and internationally through the medium of education. She was born Fannie Fern Phillips on September 25, 1867, in Margaretville, Nova Scotia, before moving to Lynne, Massachusetts, in 1876. In 1890, she married Edwin G. Andrews. She died on January 23, 1950, in Somerville, Massachusetts.

As a young woman, Fannie Fern Phillips Andrews occupied a privileged position unlike the majority of American women during the 1800s. She was afforded the opportunity to earn an education, first graduating from Salem Normal School (1884) (now Salem State College), then going on to Radcliffe College, where she earned a B.A. (1902), M.A. (1920), and Ph.D. (1923).

Andrews entered the teaching profession and experienced firsthand the problems within the school system. As a result, she set about the task of campaigning for education reform. In Boston in 1905, she formed one of the earliest school-affiliated parents' organizations, which was later followed by the Boston Home and School Association in 1907. While organizing for school reform, Andrews saw an opportunity to wed her second interest of peace activism with education reform. In 1908, she created and almost single-handedly ran the American School Peace League (ASPL), which changed its name in 1919 to the American School Citizenship League. ASPL's membership primarily attracted schoolteachers, a profession which in early American history primarily consisted of women.

During her tenure as secretary of ASPL, Andrews worked tirelessly to increase both the visibility of the organization and its membership. She was successful in getting a peace component integrated in the school curriculum. Like many of her peace movement colleagues, Andrews strongly believed that education was one of the key tools to building a peaceful world. As such, she persuaded the U.S. Bureau of Education to distribute pacifist literature and study courses to schools. On a trip to Britain in 1914, she was invited to establish the British equivalent of the ASPL. With World War I approaching, the development of international institutions to promote peace became her major concern. She became a strong supporter of President Woodrow Wilson's League of Nations plan while working as secretary of the Central Organization for Durable Peace and as a member of the League to Enforce Peace. She served with fellow WOMEN'S PEACE PARTY member JANE ADDAMS on the International Committee of International Congress of Women at The Hague and subsequently on the International Committee of Women for Permanent Peace. As the U.S. representative of the Bureau of Education, she attended the Paris Peace Conference. In both 1934 and 1936, she was appointed by President

Roosevelt to represent the United States at international conferences on education.

While Fannie Fern Andrews achieved many noted successes campaigning for peace, she was criticized by women in ASPL chapters who viewed her approach as too conservative. Her vision of how to obtain a peaceful world was referred to as "conservative internationalism." Andrews argued that war could be eradicated by applying the rule of law and drawing upon appropriate expertise. Many viewed her approach as one in which she attempted to work within the political structure by courting the expertise of power brokers in government. For some young women peace activists within the ASPL, this was disturbing given that the "experts" Andrews courted were primarily men who were perceived as "marginally invested in peace reform" and tended to be hawkish.

Andrews's scholarly works have all centered on the issues of war and peace. Her Ph.D. dissertation manuscript focused on the postwar mandate system in the Middle East under British rule. She followed up this work by conducting research in the Middle East and wrote the highly regarded two volume *The Holy Land under Mandate.*

Further Reading

Snider, Christy Jo. "Peace and Politics: Fannie Fern Andrews, Professional Politics, and the American Peace Movement, 1900–1941." *Mid-America: An Historical Review* 79 (1997): 72–95.
Zeiger, Susan. "The Schoolhouse vs. the Armory: U.S. Teachers and the Campaign against Militarism in the Schools 1914–1918." *Journal of Women's History* 15 (2003): 150–179.

—Hollis France

Anthony, Susan Bronwell (1820–1906) *suffragist, reformer* Best known for her work in women's rights, Susan B. Anthony was active in the rights of African Americans, working people, and women. She argued for education reform, labor laws, temperance laws, and abolition. Anthony was born into a prosperous Quaker family on February 15, 1820, in Adams, Massachusetts. Her father believed strongly in educating women and in everyone doing useful work. In 1839, Anthony started teaching at a Quaker school in New Rochelle, New York, but after her father went bankrupt she taught out of necessity and not simply as a religious mandate to help the world. As a young woman, she did not enjoy living away from her family but slowly accustomed herself to the responsibilities of teaching and the independence it afforded her. In 1845, her family moved to Rochester, New York, after her father's financial situation improved, and the following year Susan was appointed the headmistress of the girls' division at the Canajoharie Academy, east of Rochester. She was known in education circles for advocating coeducation through the argument that there was no innate difference between men and women. She also argued for colleges and universities to admit women and African Americans. In 1849, she returned to Rochester to take over her family's farm. While she left teaching as a profession, she continued to argue for the necessity of equal education for all.

Anthony did not attend the SENECA FALLS CONVENTION of 1848 or the women's rights convention held in Rochester a few weeks following, but her parents and younger sister did attend the Rochester convention, where an additional amendment to the DECLARATION OF SENTIMENTS AND RESOLUTIONS was added declaring equality for women "of whatever complexion." In 1851, Anthony met ELIZABETH CADY STANTON in Seneca Falls after a lecture by the abolitionist William Lloyd Garrison, and soon the two women were working together. Anthony's initial reform work was in the TEMPERANCE MOVEMENT. She started the Women's New York State Temperance Society with Stanton and LUCRETIA MOTT in 1853 because she was forbidden from speaking publicly, as a woman, in other temperance societies. She prepared a petition with over 20,000 signatures for the New York State Legislature to ban the sale of alcohol, but the petition was rejected because too many signatures were from women. It was because of the institutionalized sexism she found in her temperance work that Anthony decided to focus her attention on women's rights.

Anthony, Stanton, and Mott developed a system where Stanton would write lectures and Anthony would travel the state delivering them, returning to Seneca Falls to take care of the Stanton house and children while Stanton would work on further lectures. These lectures focused initially on temperance but in time linked temperance work to the need for changes in property laws, divorce laws, and, ultimately, to the need for women's SUFFRAGE. After Stanton made a presentation to the New York State Legislature in 1854, Anthony traveled throughout every county in New York State to maintain pressure on the legislature. One result of her success as a speaker was that the American Anti-Slavery Society asked her to become their New York agent, providing Anthony's first salaried work for the reform movement. Yet divisions between abolitionists and women's rights activists were emerging. Anthony was criticized for hiding Phoebe Harris Phelps, the abused wife of a Massachusetts state senator who had escaped to New York with one of her daughters in defiance of Massachusetts state law. Anthony could not understand why abolitionists were convinced that one could disobey the Fugitive Slave Act but not unjust laws concerning women.

After Abraham Lincoln's election as president, Anthony still worked with the abolition movement, organizing a "No Compromise with Slavery" tour of traveling speakers, who were attacked in the press and on stage. Anthony was further disappointed by women's rights activists who urged her to moderate her demands once the Civil War began, for fear that focus on suffrage during a time of war would be perceived as unpatriotic. (Suffrage activists faced the same argument at the outset of World War I.) Concerned that they might be accused of weakening the Union, some women's rights activists thought that the movement would be rewarded for silence on suffrage during the Civil War. Anthony, who was not certain that she trusted either Lincoln or the focus of the Civil War, advocated that women's rights activists maintain their pressure on the government. Once it became clear that Anthony could not act for women's rights during the War without criticism, she turned her attention to abolition. Charles Sumner, the senator from Massachusetts, had introduced an amendment freeing slaves in the North (as Lincoln's Emancipation Proclamation had only freed slaves in the states of the Confederacy); Anthony was asked by Henry Stanton to collect signatures in support of this amendment from Northern women. Anthony, Elizabeth Cady Stanton, and LUCY STONE started the NATIONAL WOMAN'S LOYAL LEAGUE, which organized thousands of volunteers who ultimately collected 400,000 signatures.

Despite their work for abolition, the women's rights movement experienced one of its most difficult issues with the postwar passage of the Fourteenth and Fifteenth Amendments. Anthony and Stanton could not support suffrage for black men prior to suffrage for women. Anthony wanted universal suffrage, and the Fourteenth and Fifteenth Amendments, by specifying that black men were to be granted the vote, established voting as a right particular to men. Anthony and Stanton then split with Lucy Stone, founding the NATIONAL WOMAN SUFFRAGE ASSOCIATION (NWSA), while Stone founded the AMERICAN WOMAN SUFFRAGE ASSOCIATION (AWSA).

While working for women's rights, Anthony continued her advocacy of other reform movements, including workers' rights. In 1868, she started a newspaper in Rochester, *The Revolution*, which proposed an eight-hour workday. Anthony also strove to attract working women to the women's rights movement by linking their lack of suffrage to issues such as disparities in pay between men and women. She advocated women forming their own trade unions, although she herself was accused of strikebreaking when she encouraged newspapers to hire women to do the typesetting to illustrate their equal ability to do the job. As with the tension between abolitionists and women's rights advocates, or temperance advocates and abolitionists, here too Anthony emphasized that wrongs against women should not take a back seat to wrongs against men.

In 1872, Anthony argued that women should register to vote under the equal-protection clause of the Fourteenth Amendment. Fifty women registered in Rochester, and 15 of those women as well as Anthony succeeded in voting in the presidential election. Arrested and tried, Anthony was not allowed to speak at her own trial (UNITED STATES V. SUSAN B. ANTHONY) after the prosecuting attorney claimed that she was not competent to testify. However, the judge (whose abuse of power swayed many who were not supporters of women's suffrage to support Anthony's right to a fair trial) asked if she had anything to say concerning her sentence. Anthony then spoke forcefully in her defense, declaring, "[Y]our denial of my citizen's right to vote is the denial of my right of consent as one of the governed, the denial of my right of representation as one of the taxed, the denial of my right to a trial by a jury of my peers as an offender against the law, the denial of my sacred rights to life, liberty, property." In 1873, Anthony was sentenced to pay court fees and a $100 fine. She refused to pay the fine, but her lawyer paid it on her behalf, thereby denying her the opportunity to appeal to the U.S. Supreme Court.

In 1876, in honor of the U.S. centennial, Stanton and MATILDA JOSLYN GAGE wrote an updated DECLARATION OF WOMEN'S RIGHTS, and Anthony and Stanton tried to gain an invitation to the reading of the Declaration of Independence in Congress. Anthony received a press pass from her brother and presented the Declaration of Rights to the vice president of the Senate. The new declaration shifted responsibility for the oppression of women from men per se to the U.S. government in particular. The year 1878 brought the first introduction of what

Anthony hoped would be the Sixteenth amendment—that the right to vote would not be denied on the basis of sex (referred to as the "Anthony Amendment")—but it never made it out of committee. Anthony presented her amendment to every Congress between 1879 and 1906.

In 1890, at the urging of ALICE STONE BLACKWELL, the rift between the NWSA and the AWSA was mended, and the two organizations merged to form the NATIONAL AMERICAN WOMAN SUFFRAGE ASSOCIATION. Anthony was elected vice president, and she later served as president from 1892 to 1900. She lobbied lawmakers every year for the passage of an amendment guaranteeing women's suffrage. Susan B. Anthony died on March 13, 1906, after giving a speech on the occasion of her 86th birthday, declaring, "failure is impossible." After the Nineteenth Amendment was successfully passed in 1920, her nephew, Daniel R. Anthony (the son of Anthony's brother who had provided her with the press pass to the 1876 centennial celebration) introduced the first EQUAL RIGHTS AMENDMENT to Congress in 1923.

Further Reading
Dubois, Ellen C. *Elizabeth Cady Stanton–Susan B. Anthony Reader: Correspondence, Writings, Speeches.* Boston: Northeastern University Press, 1992.
Sherr, Lynn. *Failure Is Impossible: Susan B. Anthony in Her Own Words.* New York: Times Books, 1995.
———. *The Trial of Susan B. Anthony.* New York: Prometheus Books, 2003.
Ward, Geoffrey. *Not For Ourselves Alone: The Story of Elizabeth Cady Stanton and Susan B. Anthony.* New York: Knopf, 2001.

—Claire Curtis

antifeminism   The antifeminist movement, whether as a counter to the women's SUFFRAGE campaign or to the EQUAL RIGHTS AMENDMENT and the "second wave" of FEMINISM, has at its foundation the belief that God created men and women to fulfill distinct roles. Gender equality therefore runs counter to nature. Antifeminists believe that men are created to occupy the public sphere of work and politics, while women are created to bear and nurture children in the private sphere of the home. Traditional family ideology calls for the wife to be subservient to her husband, leaving major decisions in his hands. Antifeminists perceive any action to change the basic power relationship between men and women as a threat. Thus, the two major waves of antifeminist activism coincide with the first and second wave of the women's rights movement.

Organized opposition to women's rights began immediately following the 1848 SENECA FALLS CONVENTION. The first women's rights campaign issued the DECLARATION OF SENTIMENTS AND RESOLUTIONS, calling for major reforms in marriage, property rights for women, educational opportunities, better working conditions, and the vote. As suffrage became the major organizing tool of those advancing women's rights, it became the major point of opposition for antifeminists. Antifeminists viewed the vote as a threat to the protections middle- and upper-class women enjoyed and argued that politics was rife with corruption, certainly no place for ladies. Women in the ANTI-SUFFRAGE MOVEMENT tended to come from Protestant, middle-class backgrounds, but the organizational leaders were often the wives of prominent politicians or businessmen in the community. Anti-suffrage forces actively campaigned against women's franchise and had the explicit support of business and industry, particularly among brewers and distillers fearful of women voters' support for the TEMPERANCE MOVEMENT. Anti-suffrage and antifeminist forces in the South feared that granting women voting rights would undermine Jim Crow laws.

The second wave of antifeminism centered on opposition to the Equal Rights Amendment (ERA). Two national organizations were formed to oppose the ERA and remain active today: the EAGLE FORUM, founded in 1972 by PHYLLIS SCHLAFLY, and CONCERNED WOMEN FOR AMERICA (CWA), founded in 1979 by BEVERLY LAHAYE. CWA developed a national network of anti-ERA

prayer chains that sought God's direct intervention weekly. STOP ERA, a Schlafly spin-off from the Eagle Forum, was dedicated specifically to the anti-ratification campaign in the states. Most of the opposition groups were organized on the principle of protecting what was perceived as traditional family values. Operating from their self-appointed positions of true defenders of women's interests, Eagle Forum and CWA leaders charged that the feminist agenda "deliberately degrades the homemaker." They warned women that ratification of the ERA would radically alter the balance of power within families and would free men from their traditional economic obligations to their families.

Both antifeminist movements claimed the separate-spheres ideology as the source of women's fulfillment as well as God's plan for human survival. Married women who worked outside the home did so for selfish, narcissistic reasons and threatened the health and safety of their children and the very stability of the family by doing so. Schlafly skillfully harkened back to the rhetoric of the anti-suffrage campaign by labeling the ERA the "extra responsibilities amendment," a claim reminiscent of the charge that voting constituted an "unfair burden" on women already laden with home and child-care responsibilities.

Antifeminist activists are also heavily represented in the antiabortion movement, insisting that legalized abortion, like the ERA, would undermine respect for women's traditional roles as homemakers and mothers. Antifeminists in this context have built alliances with conservative religious leaders who opposed abortion on moral grounds and right-wing politicians who wanted to protect traditional patriarchal family arrangements.

Further Reading

Kinnard, Cynthia D. *Antifeminism in American Thought: An Annotated Bibliography.* Boston: G. K. Hall, 1986.

Mansbridge, Jane J. *Why We Lost the ERA.* Chicago: University of Chicago Press, 1986.

anti-lynching movement *Lynch law* was a term coined during the latter part of the Revolutionary War when Virginian Charles Lynch and some of his neighbors appointed themselves justices to deal (often harshly) with the criminal element of their area. After the war, the Virginia legislature deemed Lynch's extralegal activities justifiable in the interest of restoring order "by any means necessary." During the antebellum period, victims of lynching were primarily rebellious black slaves or white abolitionists. Lynching peaked in the South between 1880 and 1900 when African-American men became the primary victims; it served as the ultimate deterrent to their newly established voting rights. Black men were also frequently accused (usually wrongfully) of raping white women. Between 1882 and 1923, more than 500 African Americans were lynched in Georgia alone.

African-American women were instrumental in anti-lynching campaigns, beginning in the 1890s with the work of IDA B. WELLS-BARNETT. After three black grocers were lynched in Memphis, Tennessee, Wells-Barnett sought to conduct a systematic investigation of lynching. In 1893, she detailed a decade of lynchings, analyzing the charges against the victim as well as the sex and race of the victim. As the owner and editor of *The Free Speech,* she used her voice to call attention to the brutality of lynching and argued in editorials that lynching was a strategy to eliminate prosperous, politically active African Americans. While she was away on a trip north, her newspaper office was destroyed, and, on the threat of lynching, she was warned not to return to Memphis. Wells-Barnett published and disseminated three major pamphlets: *Southern Horrors: Lynch Law in all its Phases* (1892), *The Red Record* (1895), and *Mob Rule in New Orleans* (1900).

The BLACK WOMEN'S CLUB MOVEMENT was active in the fight against lynching as well. Experienced activists by the 1920s, black women participated through organizations such as the Commission on Interracial Cooperation, the NATIONAL ASSOCIATION OF COLORED WOMEN, and the Anti-Lynching Crusaders. Groups raised funds for the anti-lynching campaign and lobbied on behalf of the Dyer Anti-Lynching Bill, first introduced in 1918. Mary B. Talbert served as the director of the Anti-Lynching Crusaders, founded in 1922 as an auxiliary of the National Association for the Advancement of Colored People, and orchestrated the campaign called A Million Women United to Stop Lynching. Their goal was to get a million women to donate at least one dollar to the anti-lynching cause. The group was also dedicated to recruiting white women into the movement. Some believed that white women held the key to controlling white men, while others simply argued that women, regardless of their color, were key to social-reform efforts. Efforts to integrate the anti-lynching movement were largely unsuccessful. JESSIE AMES established the most effective white women's organization, the ASSOCIATION OF SOUTHERN WOMEN FOR THE PREVENTION OF LYNCHING in 1930. Although the Dyer Bill never passed, black women activists were instrumental in calling the public's attention to the crime of lynching.

See also TERRELL, MARY CHURCH.

Further Reading
Giddings, Paula. *When and Where I Enter.* New York: William Morrow & Company, 1984.
Hall, Jacquelyn Dowd, Ann Snitow, Christine Stansell, and Sharon Thompson, eds. *The Mind That Burns in Each Body: Women, Rape and Racial Violence.* New York: Monthly Review Press, 1983.
Rosenbaum, Jon H., and Peter C. Sederberg, eds. *Vigilante Politics.* Philadelphia: University of Pennsylvania Press, 1976.

antimiscegenation statutes Lasting longer than slavery or school segregation, miscegenation laws were prevalent in the United States until 1967, when the Supreme Court declared the decision "to marry or not marry a person of another race resides with the individual and cannot be infringed by the State" (*LOVING V. VIRGINIA*).

Although some colonial leaders believed the practice of intermarriage between white settlers and Indians and blacks should be encouraged in order to create "one people," and in practice somewhere between 60,000 and 120,000 people of mixed descent lived in the colonies by the time of the American Revolution, the first law prohibiting miscegenation was adopted in Virginia in 1661. In 1664, Maryland adopted a law requiring a white woman who married a Negro slave to serve her husband's owner for the rest of her married life. Maryland banned interracial marriage due to questions of whether the offspring would be considered property or free. By the time of the Civil War, miscegenation statutes were in place in most of the South and were beginning to appear in northern states as well. Only Massachusetts repealed its statute in 1843 prior to the onset of the Civil War. Regardless, the mulatto slave population increased by 67 percent in the decade between 1850 and 1860 as a result of mixed unions and the rape of black women by white slaveholders.

Reconstruction and the federal government's focus on the promise of equality and equal protection of all citizens under the Fourteenth Amendment led to eight of the 11 former Confederate states to temporarily abandon their miscegenation laws. By the 1870s, legislators and judges reintroduced and expanded miscegenation law under a variety of claims, including one that interracial marriage was "unnatural" and contrary to God's will. State and federal judges reinterpreted the doctrine of equal-protection to mean "equal applicability." Since laws against interracial marriage affected blacks and whites "equally" and persons of both races were subject to the same penalties, there was no violation of the equal-protection provision of the Fourteenth Amendment. The U.S. Supreme Court affirmed this reasoning in 1883 in *Pace v. State of Alabama*.

At least 127 laws prohibiting interracial marriage and cohabitation were passed between 1865 and the 1950s nationwide, with 37 percent of the statutes passed outside of the South. In many states, punishment for both blacks and whites who ignored the laws could result in up to 10 years' hard labor. Western states expanded the law to include prohibitions against whites marrying American Indians, Asian Americans, Filipinos, and other groups. Arizona, for example, adopted a law against whites marrying Hindus. Enforcement of miscegenation statutes persisted well into the 1960s.

In 1948, California became the first state in which the court declared a miscegenation law unconstitutional. California Supreme Court justice Roger Traynor, arguing for a slim majority, wrote: "The right to marry is the right of individuals, not of racial groups." In 1964, the U.S. Supreme Court declared invalid a Florida law that provided stiffer penalties for cohabitation and adultery by interracial couples than same-race couples. *McLaughlin v. Florida* then served as important precedent for the 1967 case of *Loving v. Virginia* in which the Court declared all interracial marriage bans unconstitutional. Writing for the Court in a unanimous decision, Chief Justice Earl Warren said: "There can be no doubt that restricting the freedom to marry solely because of racial classifications violates the central meaning of the Equal Protection Clause." Although the Court's decision nullified existing state statutes, Alabama did not formally remove the miscegenation provision from its state constitution until 2000.

According to the U.S. Census Bureau, there were 1.2 million mixed-race marriages in 1990. By 2000, biracial marriages had increased by 65 percent. Today, one of every 15 marriages involves a biracial couple. Interracial marriages make up 6.7 percent of all marriages in the United States.

Further Reading

Bell, Derrick A. *Race, Racism, and American Law,* 2nd ed. Boston: Little, Brown, 1980.

Hodes, Martha, ed. *Sex, Love, Race: Crossing Boundaries in North American History.* New York: New York University Press, 1999.

anti-suffrage movement The anti-suffrage movement included both men and women, but the most visible and most vociferous opponents to women's SUFFRAGE were female. Many opponents argued that men and women were fundamentally different and that women were not suited for politics. Women "antis" drew large crowds when they speculated about a world where women voted: Women would ignore their families and household responsibilities, adopt masculine traits and habits, and bring chaos to the traditional family. Others argued that, once granted, the vote could not be restricted to white, well-educated women. This race-based campaign

of fear was especially effective in states with high immigrant populations and in the South. In other cases, business and industry organized against women's suffrage, fearing the social reforms women advocated, including temperance, improved working conditions, and fair wages.

Several organizations formed in opposition to women's suffrage. In 1911, state anti-suffrage associations formed the National Association Opposed to Woman Suffrage (NAOWS). At its height in the years 1911–16, the NAOWS claimed a membership of 350,000 devoted to home and national defense against women's suffrage, FEMINISM, and socialism.

Further Reading

Benjamin, Anne Myra Goodman. *A History of the Anti-suffrage Movement in the United States from 1895 to 1920: Women against Equality*. Lewiston, N.Y.: Edwin Mellen Press, 1991.

Marshall, Susan E. *Splintered Sisterhood: Gender and Class in the Campaign against Woman Suffrage*. Madison: University of Wisconsin Press, 1997.

Caricature depicting a "political boss" conducting chorus of a singing "procurer," "dive-keeper," "child labor employer," "grafter," "cadet," and "sweatshop owner," with female "Anti" at center stage, all opposed to women's suffrage (LIBRARY OF CONGRESS)

Armstrong, Anne (Anne Legendre Armstrong) (1927–) *diplomat, politician, counselor to the president* Anne Armstrong became the first woman to cochair the Republican National Convention in 1972, and the first woman to deliver a keynote address to the convention. She used her position to encourage other women, particularly feminists, to become active in the Republican Party.

Born on December 27, 1927, in New Orleans, Louisiana, Anne Legendre attended Vassar College and majored in English. She worked briefly for *Harper's Bazaar* before resigning to marry Tobin Armstrong. Armstrong's first political foray was in support of Democrat Harry Truman's 1948 presidential campaign, but she joined the Republican Party after her marriage to Tobin, a Texas Republican. She served as vice chair of the Texas Republican Party in 1966 and represented Texas on the national committee from 1968 to 1973.

Armstrong served in the Nixon administration as counselor to the president. She established the Office of Women's Programs in the White House and acted as President Nixon's expert on women's issues. She also served on the president's Domestic Council, the Council on Wage and Price Stability, and the Commission on the Organization of Government for the Conduct of Foreign Policy. Only after the evidence of Nixon's complicity in Watergate was incontrovertible did she join the chorus of calls for his resignation. In 1976, President Gerald Ford appointed her U.S. ambassador to Great Britain. She served as chair of the President's Foreign Intelligence Advisory Board from 1981 to 1990, and also chaired the Secretary of State's Advisory Panel on Overseas Security. She received the Presidential Medal of Freedom from President Ronald Reagan in 1987.

In 1997, George W. Bush (then governor of Texas) appointed Armstrong to the board of regents of Texas A&M University. She currently chairs the Executive Committee of the Board of Trustees at the Center for Strategic and International Studies. In February 2006, she came under media scrutiny after Vice President Dick Cheney shot 78-year-old Harry Whittington in the face on her 50,000-acre ranch while hunting. Her daughter, Katherine Armstrong, was the person who eventually broke the news of the incident to the local Corpus Christi newspaper.

Assault Weapons Ban   See VIOLENCE AGAINST WOMEN ACT.

Association for Women Journalists   The Association for Women Journalists serves as an advocate for women in journalism, sponsors round-table discussions concerning women and the press, promotes research on women in the press, and generally supports women journalists. The first chapter was formed in 1988 in Dallas–Fort Worth, Texas. When women employees of a local newspaper objected to a demeaning promotional campaign, they were all but ignored. The incident pointed to the need for an organization to help improve the representation of women in the media as well as increase the number of women in the industry. The organization is composed of seven chapters located in large cities throughout the United States, including Chicago and Denver.

Association of Southern Women for the Prevention of Lynching (ASWPL)   JESSIE DANIEL AMES (1883–1972), a Texas suffragist and civil rights activist, founded the whites-only Association of Southern Women for the Prevention of Lynching (ASWPL) in 1930. Active in both the LEAGUE OF WOMEN VOTERS and the Commission on Interracial Cooperation, Ames believed it was the responsibility of women's organizations to solve racial problems. Ames and the ASWPL rallied the support of thousands of women and public officials in Texas in the anti-lynching campaign. The goal of the ASWPL was to persuade sheriffs and judges to protect prisoners from lynch mobs. She recruited white Southern women to gain signatures to the following pledge: "We declare lynching an indefensible crime, destructive of all principles of government, hostile to every ideal of religion and humanity, degrading and debasing to every person involved. We pledge ourselves to create a new public opinion in the South which will not condone for any reason whatever acts of the mob or lynchers."

See also ANTI-LYNCHING MOVEMENT.

Further Reading
Wormser, Richard. "Jessie Daniel Ames." In *The Rise and Fall of Jim Crow*. Available online. URL: www.pbs.org/wnet/jimcrow/stories_people_ames.html. Accessed on June 26, 2006.

Atkinson, Ti-Grace (1938–)   *author*   Ti-Grace Atkinson was a major leader and strategist among radical feminists of the 1960s and 1970s. She was born on November 9, 1938, in Baton Rouge, Louisiana, but her affluent Republican family traveled extensively. She married at 17 (they were later divorced), and when her husband entered the military, she entered the University of Pennsylvania, earning a degree in fine arts. She became an art critic for *Art News* and cofounded the Institute of Contemporary Art in Philadelphia.

Atkinson's path to radical FEMINISM began when she read Simone de Beauvoir's *The Second Sex.* Correspondence with de Beauvoir led her to BETTY FRIEDAN and the mainstream woman's movement. She became an active participant in the NATIONAL ORGANIZATION FOR WOMEN (NOW) in 1967 as she pursued a Ph.D. in philosophy at Columbia University. Atkinson served as the president of the New York chapter of NOW and became an effective fundraiser for the national organization by trading on her Republican family connections. However, she became disillusioned with NOW's refusal to confront issues like ABORTION and the inequalities she saw in marriage, and ultimately she resigned her membership.

Atkinson declared that "the woman's movement was divided by those who want women to have the opportunity to join the oppressors, and those who want to destroy oppression itself." In 1968, she founded the Feminists, but she resigned in 1971 when she disagreed with the group's policies on speaking to the press. She gained notoriety for her positions on abortion, the myth of vaginal orgasm, lesbianism and feminism, prostitution and pornography, violence, and the treatment of older women. Her theories of radical feminism argued that male insecurity led to the creation of institutions to control women. Among these were romantic love, sexual intercourse, marriage, and religion.

Atkinson's solution to women's oppression requires a radical political redefinition of women's role that would free them to be human. She is the author of over 200 papers and a book, *Amazon Odyssey,* published in 1974. She is currently completing a doctoral degree at Columbia University and is associated with the faculty in philosophy at Tufts University.

Further Reading

DeLeon, David. *Leaders from the 1960s: A Biographical Sourcebook of American Activism.* Westport, Conn.: Greenwood Press, 1994.

Echols, Alice. *Daring to Be Bad: Radical Feminism in America, 1967–1975.* Minneapolis: University of Minnesota Press, 1989.

B

Baby M case (*In the Matter of Baby "M,"* 109 N. J. 396 [1988]) One of the first public exposures to contract pregnancy was the Baby M case, in which William and Elizabeth Stern contracted with Mary Beth Whitehead to have her artificially inseminated with William Stern's sperm. Ms. Whitehead was promised $10,000 on delivering the baby. The specific terms of the 1985 contract were drawn up to avoid "baby selling," illegal under New Jersey law. Although the baby girl, born in 1986, was initially turned over to the Sterns, Ms. Whitehead subsequently changed her mind and sought custody of the child, known in court documents as "Baby M." Whitehead argued that the bond between mother and child was more powerful than any contract.

In 1988, after a protracted court battle, the court sided with Ms. Whitehead and invalidated the SURROGACY contract on the grounds that money exchanged for the purpose of adopting a child was illegal under New Jersey law and therefore the contract was unenforceable. The outcome of this highly publicized case once again focused public attention on women's reproductive roles that conflict with social expectations. Those sympathetic to Whitehead's

claims pointed to the Sterns' wealth, two-career status, and impatience with the adoption process as evidence that they were unfit as parents, compared with Ms. Whitehead who already had children of her own, a seemingly stable marriage, and was motivated out of a desire to help infertile couples realize their dream. Ms. Stern, diagnosed with multiple sclerosis, was criticized for putting her own health interests ahead of having "their own" children.

In its 1988 ruling, the New Jersey Supreme Court overturned a lower-court ruling favoring the Sterns, invalidated the surrogacy contract, annulled Elizabeth Stern's adoption of Baby M, and restored Whitehead's parental rights. Writing for a unanimous court, Chief Justice Robert N. Wilentz said: "We do not know of, and cannot conceive of, any other case where a perfectly fit mother was expected to surrender her newly born infant, perhaps forever, and was then told she was a bad mother because she did not." The justices then dealt with the issue as a difference between the natural father and the natural mother, both of whose claims were entitled to equal weight. Custody was awarded to William Stern, and the trial court was instructed to set visitation for Mary Beth Whitehead.

Further Reading

Chesler, Phyllis. *Sacred Bond: The Legacy of Baby M.* New York: Times Books, 1988.

Baez, Joan (Joan Chandos Baez) (1941–   )

peace advocate, singer, songwriter   Joan Baez was born on January 9, 1941, in Staten Island, New York, to a father of Mexican descent and a mother of Scottish and Irish descent. Her father, Albert Vinivio Baez, was a noted physicist who set the tone for peace activism in the family by refusing to work on the Manhattan Project to build the atomic bomb. The family lived all over the United States and in several foreign countries due to his work. In 1956, Baez heard Martin Luther King, Jr., speak about nonviolence, civil rights, and social justice issues and later in the same year she bought her first guitar. In 1958, the family moved to the Boston area, where her father accepted a faculty position at the Massachusetts Institute of Technology. Baez enrolled in classes at Boston University and began singing in local coffeehouses. Her first national exposure came with the 1959 Newport Folk festival, and she recorded her first album, *Joan Baez,* on Vanguard Records.

Baez is best known for historical folk songs and for using her music to promote the causes of nonviolence, civil rights, and social justice. She performed "We Shall Overcome" at the 1963 March on Washington. She was an active opponent of the Vietnam War and withheld 60 percent of her income taxes as a protest against the war. At her concerts, she actively encouraged men to resist the draft, and she was arrested twice for her antiwar protests. In 1967, the DAUGHTERS OF THE AMERICAN REVOLUTION denied Baez permission to perform at Constitution Hall, reminiscent of their denial of the same privilege to MARIAN ANDERSON in 1939. In 1968, Baez married David Harris, a Vietnam draft protester. Harris was indicted for refusing to be inducted into the military and served 15 months in a Texas prison. Their son, Gabriel, was born in December 1969 while Harris was imprisoned.

Songs characterizing this time include "A Song for David" and "Fifteen Months." Baez and Harris were divorced in 1973, not long after his release.

A trip to Vietnam in the early 1970s exposed Baez to the atrocities committed on both sides of the conflict. She founded Humanitas International, a human rights organization, but those on the left objected to her criticism of the communist regime. Baez has also been active over the years in the gay rights movement, appearing at benefit concerts to defeat anti-gay legislation and on behalf of the National Gay and Lesbian Task Force. In 1998, she and singer Bonnie Raitt joined Julia Butterfly Hill at the top of a giant redwood tree where Hill had been camping for months to protect the tree from logging interests. Baez continues to support environmental causes, most recently with public appearances in support of the South Central Farm (a community garden in Los Angeles, California). When the United States invaded Iraq in 2003, she performed at antiwar rallies in San Francisco and traveled with Michael Moore's "Slacker Uprising Tour" to encourage young people on college campuses to vote for antiwar candidates in the 2004 election. Baez has also performed at benefit concerts to raise funds for Hurricane Katrina relief efforts in New Orleans and along the Gulf Coast. In 1987, she published her autobiography, *And a Voice to Sing With: A Memoir.*

Further Reading

Baez, Joan. *And a Voice to Sing With: A Memoir.* New York: Summit Books, 1987.

Hajdu, David. *Positively Fourth Street: The Lives and Times of Joan Baez, Bob Dylan, Mimi Baez Farina, and Richard Farina.* New York: Farrar, Straus and Giroux, 2001.

Bagley, Sarah (1806–ca. 1883)

reformer   Sarah George Bagley was born in Candia, New Hampshire, on April 19, 1806, to Nathan Bagley and Rhoda Witham Bagley. The family farmed and owned a small mill. In 1837, Sarah began work in a Lowell, Massachusetts, cotton mill. She was associated with a literary magazine called the *Lowell Offering,* and in 1840, she published her first short story, "Pleasures of Factory Life." Between 1842 and 1844, conditions in the Lowell mills deteriorated as a result of an economic depression. When Middlesex Mills implemented a requirement that workers tend two looms instead of one, 70 weavers walked off their job. About the same time, Sarah moved from Hamilton Mills to Middlesex Mills. Some scholars speculate that she got her job at the expense of striking workers. When conditions improved, mills raised wages, but only for men.

In 1844, Sarah and five other female weavers formed the Lowell Female Labor Reform Association (FLRA). The association lobbied for better working conditions in general, but focused primarily on lobbying the Massachusetts legislature for a 10-hour day in place of the 11–13 hour day that was the norm. The association published a newspaper called *The Voice of the Industry;* Sarah edited the women's column. Although the legislature twice held hearings on the issue, each time lawmakers deferred to the owners, claiming lawmakers did not have the power to determine the hours of work. Undaunted, the members of the association continued to gather signatures on petitions. By 1845, Bagley was working full-time to organize branches of the FLRA in other Massachusetts towns. She was also appointed corresponding secretary of the New England Working Men's Association and published numerous articles and pamphlets on labor conditions. In 1847, the mills reduced the workday by 30 minutes.

When a new telegraph office opened in Lowell in 1846, Sarah was hired as the nation's first female telegraph operator. In 1847, she was asked to run the magnetic telegraph office in Springfield, Massachusetts. When she arrived at the new position, she discovered that she would earn only two-thirds of the wages as the man she replaced. She vowed to continue her work on behalf of women's equality rights. After a year, she returned to Lowell and to the mills, but she continued to travel throughout New England speaking and writing about health care, working conditions, and women's rights. In 1850, she married James Durno, and the couple subsequently moved to Albany, New York, where they opened a homeopathic health care clinic specializing in the care of women and children. In the 1860s, they began to manufacture herbal medicines and moved to Brooklyn Heights, New York. James died in about 1873, and Sarah died a decade later.

Further Reading
Lunardini, Christine. *What Every American Should Know About Women's History: 200 Events that Shaped our Destiny.* Holbrook, Mass.: Adams Media Corporation, 1997.

Baker, Ella (1903–1986) *civil rights activist* Born in Norfolk, Virginia, on December 13, 1903, Ella Baker was an activist who stressed that social change comes about best when the work of ordinary people at the ground level can be multiplied, organized, and emphasized. As a girl, Ella learned early of slave life from her grandmother, who had been beaten by her master for refusing to marry the man he had chosen for her. Baker was educated at Shaw University in Raleigh, North Carolina, and urged the administration there to end what she considered a demeaning policy that banned the wearing of silk stockings. She graduated as valedictorian of her class in 1927 and moved to Harlem. There she joined the Young Negroes Cooperative League (YNCL), which worked to solidify the economic foundation of the black community through combining economic resources and sharing them cooperatively; she was appointed director of the YNCL in 1930. During the depression she also worked for the Works Progress Administration (WPA) on projects emphasizing literacy.

In 1940 she joined the National Association for the Advancement of Colored People (NAACP) and began traveling throughout the South to encourage the growth of local NAACP chapters. Baker's philosophy of organization and activism—that it must emerge from local, grassroots mobilization—conflicted with the top-down vision of then-NAACP president Walter White. This clash of organizational visions involved both Baker's sex and her insistence that strong leadership was not as important as the committed work of individuals on the ground. In 1952, she was named the first female president of the New York City chapter of the NAACP.

In 1955, Baker (with Bayard Rustin and Stanley Levison) formed the group In Friendship, which sought to provide economic assistance to activist groups, first during the Montgomery bus boycott and then to other activist groups throughout the South. Through the urging of Rustin and Levison, Baker was offered a staff position by Martin Luther King, Jr., in the newly formed Southern Christian Leadership Council (SCSL). Here Baker's theory of community activism clashed with King's practice of strong leadership. Ella Baker famously said: "Strong people do not need strong leaders."

In 1960, Baker helped form an organization that adhered more closely to her vision of activism: SNCC, the Student Non-violent Coordinating Committee. At Shaw University, she brought together students involved in sit-ins throughout the South and urged them to organize together. She mentored SNCC members, and her influence helped that group toward success as a largely decentralized organization that welcomed women and other nontraditional activists. She also advised those organizing the Mississippi Freedom Democratic Party (founded by FANNIE LOU HAMER), which sought to unseat the all-white Mississippi delegation to the 1964 Democratic National Convention.

Baker returned to New York City in 1964, and she continued her grassroots work there to end oppression of all forms. She died on December 13, 1986. Because Baker (as many women before her) believed in the importance of grassroots-level decentralized work, she is often not remembered as the force of change she was before, during, and after the civil rights movement. Baker epitomizes the work that so many women in the United States and around the world have done day by day to improve the lives of children, women, minorities, the poor, and the oppressed.

Further Reading

Grant, Joanne. *Ella Baker: Freedom Bound.* New York: Wiley, 1988.
Ransby, Barbara. *Ella Baker and the Black Freedom Movement: A Radical Democratic Vision.* Chapel Hill: University of North Carolina Press, 2003.

—Claire Curtis

Baker, Nancy Landon Kassebaum See KASSEBAUM, NANCY LANDON.

Balch, Emily Greene (1867–1961) *pacifist, Nobel Peace Prize winner* Born in Boston on January 8, 1867, Balch graduated from Bryn Mawr College for Women in 1889 as a member of the first graduating class. In 1893, she published *Public Assistance of the Poor in France* and in 1896 started teaching economics and sociology at Wellesley College. Balch was interested in issues ranging from child welfare to immigration and peace. In 1910, she wrote *Our Fellow Slavic Citizens,* which analyzed the conditions under which Slavic immigrants lived and the area from which they came.

Balch worked with JANE ADDAMS on both settlement house issues and, after 1915, peace issues. In 1915, Balch was a delegate at the International Congress of Women at The Hague, and she subsequently wrote *Women at the Hague: The International Congress of Women and Its Results* with Addams and Alice Hamilton. She helped Addams start the Women's International League for Peace and Freedom (WILPF) and served as its secretary from 1919 to 1922 and again from 1934 to 1935. During the interwar period, she also worked to facilitate the League of Nations in projects concerning disarmament and prodding the United States to commit to the League. She was terminated from Wellesley for her peace work (after she requested continuing leaves of absence). She then joined the editorial board at *The Nation*. In 1926, she worked on a commission studying conditions in Haiti and in the 1930s she began studies documenting the victims of rising Nazism.

Balch revised some of her pacifist views as a result of her investigation into the rise of Nazism, focusing on the need for international cooperation to avoid the conditions of war. In 1946, she received the Nobel Peace Prize for her work with the WILPF, to whom she gave her prize money. In 1959, Balch worked to help the WILPF mark the centenary of Jane Addams's birth. She died on January 9, 1961.

Further Reading
Randall, Mercedes M. *Improper Bostonian: The Life of Emily Greene Balch*. New York: Twayne Publishers, 1964.

—Claire Curtis

Baldwin, Tammy (1962–) *congressperson*
Tammy Baldwin was born on February 11, 1962, and raised in Madison, Wisconsin. She attended Smith College, where she earned bachelor's degrees in math and political science in 1984. She earned a law degree from the University of Wisconsin Law School in 1989. While still in law school, Tammy Baldwin won her first elective office as a member of the Dane County Board of Supervisors in 1986. In the same year, she served briefly on the Madison City Council, filling a vacancy and serving as an alderman. Baldwin served four terms as a Dane County supervisor from 1986 to 1994. While still serving as a supervisor, Baldwin launched a successful campaign for the Wisconsin State Assembly, where she served from 1993 to 1999.

In 1998, Baldwin won a seat in the U.S. House of Representatives, becoming the first woman elected to Congress from the state of Wisconsin and the first open lesbian elected

to Congress. Although many claimed Baldwin was too far left to win the congressional seat, she campaigned on issues of health care reform, including universal health care coverage, long-term care for the elderly, and public financing for day care. Students at the University of Wisconsin contributed to her victory with a record-high turnout among those living on campus. Baldwin has rewarded them by working to increase financial aid for higher education. On July 26, 2004, she spoke at the 2004 Democratic National Convention on the issue of health care. Congresswoman Baldwin serves on the House Committee on Energy and Commerce. She has been a leading advocate for health care reform, protecting Social Security and Medicare in the 109th Congress. She won reelection in 2006.

Further Reading
"Baldwin, Tammy." In *Biographical Directory of the United States Congress, 1774–present*. Available online. URL: http://bioguide.congress.gov/scripts/biodisplay.pl?index=B00123. Accessed on January 8, 2007.
Barone, Michael. *The Almanac of American Politics*. Washington, D.C.: National Journal Group, 2006.
"Representative Tammy Baldwin (WI)." Project Vote Smart. Available online. URL: http://votesmart.org/bio.php?can_id=BS021382. Accessed on January 8, 2007.

—Angela Kouters

Barceló, Gertrudis (María Gertrudis Barceló) (1800–1852) *pioneer, businesswoman*
Gertrudis Barceló was born in 1800 in the Mexican state of Sonora. As a young woman, she immigrated with her family to the Albuquerque area. She subsequently married and moved with her husband to Santa Fe in 1825, where she began a career in gambling establishments. She first operated a game of monte near a mining camp, then dealt cards at a saloon, and eventually came to own and operate her own sumptuous casino.

Commonly known as "La Tules," Barceló became a famous figure both within Santa Fe and among American readers of travel accounts. She first encountered public notoriety courtesy of Josiah Gregg's popular book, *The Commerce of the Prairies,* in 1844. Like other Anglo observers, Gregg represented Barceló as a "loose woman" whose smoking, drinking, and gambling habits typified Spanish-Mexican decadence. Mexicans and travelers, and later Anglo settlers, frequented her saloon and gambling hall, as did politicians and military officers who sometimes sought out Barceló's counsel on politics and business. She supported the United States during Mexican-American War (1846–48) and afterwards remained influential with the new American government of Santa Fe. She died in 1852, having become extremely wealthy and the owner of extensive property.

Barceló was hardly a typical woman in New Mexico. Her success in business and political influence were extraordinary, and as a result of her independence, her behavior was freer than that of her female contemporaries. She stands as an unusual example of the possibilities available to frontier Mexican women before conquest by the United States introduced the legal principle of COVERTURE to the region.

Further Reading

González, Deena. "La Tules of Image and Reality: Euro-American Attitudes and Legend Formation on a Spanish-Mexican Frontier." In *Building with Our Hands: Directions in Chicana Scholarship* edited by Beatríz M. Pesquera and Adela de la Torre, 75–90. Berkeley: University of California Press, 1993.

———. *Refusing the Favor: The Spanish-Mexican Women of Santa Fe, 1820–1880.* New York: Oxford University Press, 1999.

—Laura R. Prieto

Barton, Clara (Clarissa Harlowe Barton)

(1821–1912) *nurse, social activist, founder of the American Red Cross, health reformer*   Born Clarissa Harlowe Barton on December 25, 1821, in Oxford, Massachusetts, Clara Barton worked as a nurse during the Civil War and founded the American Red Cross afterward, believing that medical assistance in the time of war had to be provided by a neutral agency. Her family supported abolition and the education of girls, and Barton was expected to engage in charitable work. She spent two years nursing one of her brothers after a fall and started work as a teacher after the death of her mother caused her to leave school. After working for 10 years as a teacher, she returned to school for more advanced studies. After noticing the numbers of children who could not afford to pay the fees in the then common "subscription" schools, she opened the first free public school in New Jersey. The school was an enormous success, but Barton ultimately left over the unfairness of the salary discrepancy between herself and the man newly hired to run the school.

Barton then traveled to Washington, D.C., and started work in the patent office. When the Civil War began, she volunteered to gather and deliver supplies to the battlefield, assist surgeons, nurse soldiers, and do whatever could be done to relieve the suffering of the thousands who were wounded, many of whom would die due to the lack of medical supplies and attention. She was granted permission to travel to the front lines with her supplies, and she saw firsthand the impact of the war and the conditions facing injured soldiers and prisoners on both sides. Barton visited and treated Confederate prisoners and wounded in prisoner-of-war (POW) camps. She assisted where she could, and for her dedicated work, soldiers called her "the angel of the battlefield."

At the end of the war, Barton embarked on a search for missing soldiers, through appeals to those soldiers who had returned home. This led her to work on identifying and providing burial services for the thousands of soldiers who had died at the Andersonville POW camp. She traveled around the country looking for information from soldiers about those still missing and lecturing on her own experiences during the war. She also became interested in the SUF-FRAGE movement, in part as a result of the treatment that many female nurses received during the war. Her postwar poem "The Women Who Went to the Field" acknowledged the difficulty women faced because men presumed they could not do the difficult work of battlefield nursing and emphasized the very work these women had done, now forgotten. The poem argues at one point:

> Twas a hampered work, its worth largely lost;
> Twas hindrance, and pain, and effort, and cost:
> But through these came knowledge, knowledge
>   is power.
> And never again in the deadliest hour
> Of war or of peace, shall we be so beset
> To accomplish the purpose our spirits have met.

In 1869, Barton spoke at the first NATIONAL WOMAN SUFFRAGE ASSOCIATION (NWSA) convention in Washington, D.C., at the request of her friend SUSAN B. ANTHONY. Unlike Anthony, Barton advocated passage of the Fifteenth Amendment, granting the right to vote to black men but not yet women.   For health reasons, Barton left for Europe in 1869. During her travels, which coincided with the Franco-Prussian War, Barton first learned of the Treaty of Geneva (the precursor to the Geneva Conventions) and the Red Cross movement. She volunteered her services to the International Red Cross and was welcomed due to her experiences during the Civil War and her fame that had resulted from her speaking tour. She was honored by Germany with the Iron Cross and advised to bring the idea of the Red Cross to the United States. Barton returned home in 1873 to urge the United States to sign the Treaty of Geneva (which provided legal protections for prisoners of war) and to start a U.S. chapter of the Red Cross. In 1881, when the country finally opened is first American chapter, Barton was named president of the American Red Cross. She remained president until 1904, the same year she started

the National First Aid Society. Barton proposed directing the American Red Cross beyond wartime work to disaster relief, a charge for the Red Cross that she included in the U.S. charter. Under this particular charge, Barton was able to direct the services of the Red Cross to victims of earthquakes, floods, drought, and disease. The International Red Cross subsequently added an "American Amendment" to its charter, extending its own work beyond wartime services to include natural disasters as well. Barton retired from the Red Cross at age 83. She died on April 12, 1912, at Glen Echo, her home outside Washington, D.C.

Further Reading

Barton, William. *The Life of Clara Barton, Founder of the American Red Cross.* New York: AMS Press, 1969.

Clara Barton National Historic Site. Available online. URL: http://www.nps.gov/clba. Accessed on June 26, 2006.

Oates, Stephen B. *A Woman of Valor: Clara Barton and the Civil War.* New York: Maxwell MacMillan International, 1994.

Pryor, Elizabeth Brown. *Clara Barton: Professional Angel.* Philadelphia: University of Pennsylvania Press, 1987.

—Claire Curtis

Bass, Charlotta (Charlota Amanda Spears Bass) (1874–1969) *activist, politician, journalist*

Born Charlotta Amanda Spears in Sumter, South Carolina, on February 14, 1874, Charlotta Bass was a leading African-American journalist, civil rights activist, and women's rights advocate. At the age of 20, Bass moved to Providence, Rhode Island, to work for a small newspaper, the *Providence Watchman*. In 1910, she moved to Los Angeles, California, where she began selling subscriptions for the *Eagle*, a black newspaper founded by John Neimore. When Neimore died in 1912, she replaced him as the newspaper's managing editor and publisher. She renamed the newspaper the *California Eagle* and married

Joseph Blackburn Bass, the paper's new editor she had hired, in 1914. Joseph Bass remained the editor until his death in 1934.

Charlotta Bass campaigned for women's right to vote in California, and when women won state SUFFRAGE in 1911 in a popular referendum, she turned her attention to registering newly enfranchised black and white women. Through her work in the community and her voice in the newspaper, she became an advocate for the national campaign for women's suffrage as well as women's political participation in California and civil rights. In the 1940s, she became active in electoral politics, first in the Republican Party and later as a founding member of the Progressive Party. Her political work and her voice through editorials she wrote for the *California Eagle* attracted the attention of the FBI. Although she never identified herself as a Marxist, she believed that the most effective opposition to Hitler lay in the Soviet Union. She worked with trade union leaders in Los Angeles as well as Hollywood activists such as Paul Robeson. Although she was a member of national civil rights organizations, her most passionate work was reserved for local social-justice issues in Los Angeles. She supported the Sojourner Truth Club, a local organization dedicated to improving working conditions for black women, and was a founder of Sojourners for Truth and Justice. This organization called on women to march on Washington, D.C., in 1951 to demand that the federal government protect black citizens' civil rights at home even as it advocated the ideas of civil rights and liberties for citizens of other countries.

In 1948, Bass supported Henry Wallace for president. In the next election cycle, Bass ran as the Progressive Party candidate for vice president, making her the first African-American woman to be nominated for vice president. She ran for a seat in Congress on the Progressive Party ticket in 1950, but lost. On the basis of her community organizing and political activism, she was called before the California legislature's Committee on Un-American Activities. In 1951,

Bass sold the *California Eagle*, but she continued her political and social activism. In 1960, she published her memoir, *Forth Years: Memoirs from the Pages of a Newspaper*. She moved in the early 1960s to Lake Elsinore, California, where she turned her garage into a community reading room and worked to register African Americans to vote. In 1966, she suffered a stroke, dying three years later on April 12, 1969.

Beach, Amy (Amy Marcy Cheney Beach)

(1867–1944) *composer* Amy Marcy Cheney Beach, America's first leading woman composer, established a flourishing career in the United States and in Europe. She opened the door for professionalism at a time when women's creativity was perceived as "limited." Beach produced more than 300 compositions, including choral works (sacred and secular), chamber works, vocal and orchestral works, keyboard music, cantatas, and songs to the words of Shakespeare, Robert Burns, and Robert Browning.

Amy Cheney was born on September 5, 1867, into a distinguished middle-class, New England home. Her parents, Charles and Clara Cheney, recognized the touch of genius in their only daughter and gave her a thorough formal musical education. In 1885, she married Dr. Henry Harris Aubrey Beach, a physician who taught at Harvard and was also an amateur singer. Dr. Beach encouraged his wife to concentrate on composition rather than on performing music of famous composers who were all male. Disciplined as she was, Beach followed her husband's advice and concentrated on writing music full-time. Between 1885 and 1910, she produced large-scale works that were considered "masculine," such as Mass in E-flat, Symphony, op. 32, and Piano Concerto, op. 45, all of which were played by the most distinguished orchestras in Boston and in New York. Her Mass and her Symphony served as a turning point in the perception of women composers in general and the perception of her music in particular. These two works proved beyond any doubt her

Amy Marcy Cheney Beach (LIBRARY OF CONGRESS)

professional abilities, and she could compete on a level with male composers. For the suffragists of Beach's time, these works served as the ultimate response to the accusations that women artists imitated rather than created, that they lacked depth, and that they were the cause of art's downfall.

Amy herself became the "voice of the new woman artist" in both her musical writing and her discussions (written and spoken) about the status of women's art. As a romantic in her musical perception, she was taken by the idea of European nationalism and the challenge of weaving it into art and music. Influenced by the Czech composer Antonin Dvoák (1841–1904), whose Ninth Symphony, ("From the New World") swept the American musical community and its audience off its feet, she was determined to create an American national style. Her "Gaelic" Symphony, which fuses folk tunes played in their entirety as well as traditional music, is the result of her desire. Not only does she cope here professionally with the symphony, a genre

that was considered "male," but she also coins a new American Voice that consists of multitude cultures and, consequently, creates a musical web into which past, present (and future) are integrated.

Amy Beach died on December 27, 1944, in New York City.

Further Reading

Block-Fried, Adrienne. *Amy Beach: Passionate Victorian.* Oxford: Oxford University Press, 1998.
Samuel, Sadie Anne J. and Rhian. "Beach, Amy Marcy." In *The Norton/Grove Dictionary of Women Composers,* 44–50. New York: W. W. Norton.

—Edith S. Zack

***Beal v. Doe* (432 U.S. 438)** (1977)   In Pennsylvania, a group of pregnant females asked for and were denied nontherapeutic ABORTIONS. They sued the state, arguing that the Medicaid provisions required the state to fund abortions. In a 6-3 decision, the U.S. Supreme Court held that Title XIX of the Social Security Act does not require the funding of nontherapeutic abortions as a condition of participation in the Medicaid program established by that act. The Court pointed out that each state was allowed to set reasonable guidelines for medical procedures and could decide to fund only therapeutic abortions. This case was decided on the statute itself and did not reach any constitutional arguments. The Court pointed out, however, that it was not sure of the legality of the state's requirement that two additional doctors had to certify the abortion as medically necessary, because that might violate the relationship between doctor and patient.

In a very strong dissent, the minority pointed out that abortion itself is a "medically necessary" procedure, because pregnancy involves both safe births and terminations. Thus, since an abortion involves a medical procedure, it should be covered, as are other medical procedures for the needy, under Title XIX of the Social Security Act. One of the purposes of the Medicaid system was to allow the needy access to medical services that were available to other more fortunate individuals. Since those who can afford to, or have insurance coverage, are allowed nontherapeutic abortions, the needy should not be treated differently.

See also SOCIAL SECURITY AND WOMEN.

—Marsha Hass

Bean, Melissa (1962–) *congressperson* Melissa Luburi Bean was born in Chicago on January 22, 1962. Her father, a World World II Marine Raider and small-business owner, and her mother, a full-time homemaker, raised their family in Park Ridge, where Bean graduated from Maine East High School. She earned her B.A. in political science from Roosevelt University and currently lives in Barrington with her husband and two children.

In 2002, Bean ran for Congress against Phil Crane, the Republican incumbent of the eighth district seat for 33 years. She charged that Crane, once a leader of conservative forces in the House, had become a "do-nothing" congressman, and she focused attention on lobbyist-funded trips that he had taken. Bean lost, but she gained 43 percent of the vote. The eighth district had long been considered the most Republican district in the Chicago area.

In the 2004 election, the Democratic National Committee filtered funds into Bean's campaign since she had had a significant showing in the previous election cycle. On November 2, 2004, Bean defeated Crane with 52% of the vote. She is the first Democrat to represent the district since its formation in 1935 (it was numbered the 10th district from 1935 to 1949, the 13th from 1949 to 1973, the 12th from 1973 to 1993, and the Eighth since 1993).

Bean is a moderate Democrat. Her voting record has been a matter of controversy to some Democrats, particularly since she was one of only 15 Democrats to vote for passage of the Central American Free Trade Agreement (CAFTA) in July 2005. Before the final vote,

some labor unions sent a letter to House Minority Leader Nancy Pelosi warning they would not offer any support to Bean if she supported the CAFTA. Organized labor had played an important role in her 2004 victory, so without their continued support her seat remains in jeopardy for the Democrats.

Representative Bean serves on the House Financial Services Committee, including the Subcommittee on Capital Markets, Insurance and Government Sponsored Enterprises and the Subcommittee on Domestic and International Monetary Policy, Trade and Technology. She also serves on the House Committee on Small Business, where she is a member of the Subcommittee on Workforce, Empowerment, and Government Programs; and the Subcommittee on Tax, Finance, and Exports. Although Republicans had targeted her seat as vulnerable in 2006, she won reelection to a second term.

Further Reading
Barone, Michael. *The Almanac of American Politics.* Washington, D.C.: National Journal Group, 2006.
"Bean, Mellisa." In *Biographical Directory of the United States Congress, 1774–present.* Available online. URL: http://bioguide.congress.gov/scripts/biodisplay.pl?index=B001253. Accessed on January 8, 2007.
"Representative Melissa Bean (IL)." In *Project Vote Smart.* Available online. URL: http://votesmart.org/bio.php?can_id=MIL20905. Accessed on January 8, 2007.

—Angela Kouters

Berkley, Shelley (Rochelle Levine Berkley) (1951–) *congressperson* Rochelle (Shelley) Levine Berkley was born on January 20, 1951, in New York City. She completed junior high and high school in Las Vegas and became the first member of her family to attend college when she enrolled at the University of Nevada, Las Vegas (UNLV). She was elected student body president in 1971 and graduated with honors and a B.A. in political science from UNLV in 1972. She went on to earn a law degree at the University of San Diego School of Law, and in 1976 she returned to Las Vegas to begin her career.

Berkley is a former vice chair of the Nevada University and Community College System Board of Regents. She was appointed to the board in 1990 by the state governor and served two terms, completing her second term in 1998. Throughout her tenure, Berkley worked to keep higher education in Nevada affordable and accessible to all qualified students. Serving in the Nevada State Assembly from 1982 through 1984, she championed consumer protection for car buyers and mobile home owners, fought for tougher drunk-driving laws, and founded the Senior Law Project.

Berkley was first elected to the U.S. House of Representatives in 1998; her district includes much of the city of Las Vegas. During her tenure in Congress, Berkley has maintained a moderate voting record. She has focused on the interests of the gaming community and she unsuccessfully fought the plan to store nuclear waste at Yucca Mountain. She serves on the International Relations Committee, Transportation and Infrastructure Committee, and Veterans' Affairs Committee. Berkley was reelected in 2006.

Further Reading

Barone, Michael. *The Almanac of American Politics*. Washington, D.C.: National Journal Group, 2006.
"Berkley, Shelley. In *Biographical Directory of the United States Congress, 1774–present*. Available online. URL: http://bioguide.congress.gov/scripts/biodisplay.pl?index=B09231. Accessed on January 8, 2007.
"Representative Shelley Berkley." In *Project Vote Smart*. Available online. URL: http://votesmart.org/bio.php?can_id=CNV17938. Accessed on January 8, 2007.

—Angela Kouters

Berry, Mary Frances (1938–   ) *chair of the U.S. Civil Rights Commission* Mary Frances

Berry was born on February 17, 1938, in Nashville, Tennessee, to Frances Southall Berry and George Ford Berry. She attended public schools where her teachers encouraged her intellect and academic promise, graduating from high school with honors in 1956. She earned bachelors and masters degrees at Howard University, completed a Ph.D. in constitutional history at the University of Michigan, and earned her law degree from the University of Michigan Law School. She taught history at a number of Michigan institutions while she completed her law degree.

Active in antiwar protests and in the civil rights movement, Berry moved to the Washington, D.C., area in the 1970s. She served as acting director and later as director of the University of Maryland Afro-American studies program. From 1974 until 1976, she served as provost, becoming the highest-ranking African-American woman in the University of Maryland College Park administration. She also became a member of the bar in the District of Columbia. In 1976, she became chancellor of the University of Colorado at Boulder and professor of history and law.

Berry has effectively combined her commitment to racial justice with a scholarly career of teaching, research, and writing about African-American history. She is the author of numerous articles and seven books including *The Pig Farmer's Daughter and Other Tales of American Justice: Episodes of Racism and Sexism in the Courts from 1865 to the Present* (1999); *Black Resistance, White Law: A History of Constitutional Racism in America* (1971, 1994); *The Politics of Parenthood: Child Care, Women's Rights, and the Myth of the Good Mother* (1993); *Why the ERA Failed: Politics, Women's Rights, and the Amending Process of the Constitution* (1986); *Long Memory: The Black Experience in America*, with John Blassingame (1982); and *Military Necessity and Civil Rights Policy: Black Citizenship and the Constitution: 1861–1868* (1977).

In 1977, Berry took a leave from the University of Colorado to accept the first of many appointments in the federal government when President Jimmy Carter named her assistant secretary for education in the Department of Health, Education and Welfare (HEW); she served until 1980. From 1980 to 1982, she served as vice chair of the U.S. Commission on Civil Rights and served continuously as a commission member until she resigned on December 7, 2004. A staunch advocate of the commission's independence, she often battled with presidents of both parties over politicizing its oversight function. When President Ronald Reagan tried to remove Berry from the commission, she successfully sued to retain her seat, earning her the moniker "the woman the president could not fire." In 1993, President Bill Clinton named Berry chair of the Civil Rights Commission, a position she maintained until 2004. During Dr. Berry's tenure as chair, the commission issued reports on a number of significant political issues, including the use of voter registration purge lists in the 2000 Florida presidential elections, police practices in New York City, environmental justice, percentage plans and affirmative action, church burnings, and conditions on American Indian reservations.

Berry battled with the George W. Bush administration on a number of fronts. In 2001, the White House declared a vacancy on the Civil Rights Commission and nominated Peter N. Kirsanow, a conservative African-American lawyer from Cleveland, Ohio. Dr. Berry maintained that no vacancy existed on the commission since the seat in question was held by Victoria Wilson, appointed by President Clinton to fill the unexpired term of the late Judge A. Lion Higginbotham, who had died in 1998. Berry maintained that Wilson had been appointed to a full six-year term in her own right; the Bush administration disagreed, and the Justice Department filed suit in federal court. The case was ultimately resolved in the Bush administration's favor on May 10, 2002. (Appointment to the eight-member panel of the U.S. Civil Rights Commission is shared by Congress and the White House; each is responsible for four appointments, the four

congressional appointments rotating between Democrats and Republicans.)

In October 2004, the commission published a draft report on the civil rights record of the Bush Administration, citing failures in a number of areas and concluding that the administration "missed opportunities to build consensus on key civil rights issues and has instead adopted policies that divide Americans." Coming a month before the November 2004 presidential election, Republicans charged that the timing as well as the content was political rather than the result of an independent commission's analysis. Ultimately, the panel voted 6-1 to delay the release of the final report until after the election.

The final showdown between President Bush and Dr. Berry came over the end of her term. Berry claimed that her term ended at midnight on January 21, 2005; however, the Bush administration appointed Gerald A. Reynolds as the new chair in December. Berry briefly considered challenging the appointment but ultimately resigned, ending nearly 25 years of service by stating: "Given that the conclusion of my tenure is only a few weeks away, a legal challenge would be an unwise expenditure of resources. Therefore, I am resigning my position as commissioner on the United States Commission on Civil Rights effective immediately."

Berry is also known for her activist politics beyond the bounds of her formal positions. In 1984, she was one of several notable officials arrested during a sit-in at the South African embassy in opposition to U.S. support for South Africa while the country still practiced apartheid. Berry is unique for the breadth of her political skills and tactics in pursuit of racial justice, having seamlessly combined street protest with scholarship. Dr. Berry is the recipient of over 28 honorary doctoral degrees and numerous awards in recognition of her public service and scholarship. She is the recipient of the NAACP's Roy Wilkins Award, the Rosa Parks Award of the Southern Christian Leadership Conference, and the Ebony Magazine Black Achievement Award. She is one of 75 women featured in the book *I Dream a World: Portraits of Black Women Who Changed America.* Dr. Berry is the Geraldine R. Segal Professor of American Social Thought and Professor of History at the University of Pennsylvania.

Further Reading

Berry, Mary Frances. *Black Resistance/White Law: A History of Constitutional Racism in America.* New York: Penguin, 1995.

———. *Long Memory: The Black Experience in America.* New York: Oxford University Press, 1986.

———. *The Pig Farmer's Daughter and Other Tales of American Justice: Episodes of Racism and Sexism in the Courts from 1865 to the Present.* New York: Vintage Books, 2000.

Lanker, Brian. *I Dream a World: Portraits of Black Women Who Changed America.* New York: Stewart, Tabori and Chang, 1989.

Bethune, Mary McLeod (1875–1955) *educational leader*

Born at a time when the effects of slavery were still very much a reality, Mary McLeod Bethune rose from abject poverty, rigid segregation, and complete obscurity to become a leading figure in American politics. Her work as a pioneer educator, civil rights advocate, White House adviser, New Deal politician, and founder and leader of black women's organizations spanned more than three decades and traversed the 19th and 20th centuries. She was the contemporary of many better-known male political figures, including W. E. B. DuBois, Walter White, Ralph Bunche, and Booker T. Washington, yet she was the first black American and the first woman to have a statue erected in her honor in a public park in the nation's capital.

As a pioneering educator, Bethune established Bethune-Cookman College, the only historically black college or university (or HBCU, per the Higher Education Act of 1965) founded by a woman that still exists today. As a public servant and New Deal administrator, she pushed for equity in the armed forces, argued against segregation, and created opportunities for blacks and women by helping them to secure job training, trade skills, and employment in the armed forces. A leader and organizer of black women's political organizations, Bethune served two terms as the president of the NATIONAL ASSOCIATION OF COLORED WOMEN (NACW) and later established the NATIONAL COUNCIL OF NEGRO WOMEN (NCNW). Bethune was a savvy, politically astute, and conscientious "race woman" (advocate for the rights of the race) who, unlike other "race men and women" never separated gender from race. This allowed her to incorporate gender equality into a primarily race-based discourse and to develop women's leadership for the cause of racial justice at the national level—something no one else had ever done before.

Bethune was born Mary Jane McLeod to former slaves, Samuel and Patsy McInstosh McLeod, on July 10, 1875, near Mayesville, South Carolina. The 15th of 17 children, she was considered "entirely different from the rest" with "more of a missionary spirit—the spirit of doing for others." Her family owned the five acres of land and the log cabin in which she was born, providing the young Mary Jane with a sense of stability and belonging. Because her mother was "from one of the great royalties of Africa," Mary Jane adopted a great sense of pride in her African heritage; she believed strongly in Christ as the saviour and sought to live by Christian principles. Nonetheless, as a poor, uneducated, southern Negro, she could not help being influenced by the strict segregation and racial codes of the period. She spent most of her childhood chopping and picking cotton and recognized early on the stark economic and social inequalities that existed between whites and blacks. She saw "little white boys and girls going to school everyday, learning to read and write [and] living in comfortable homes with all types of opportunities for growth and service." Later in life, she recalled how she picked up one of the books of her white peers, only to be told sharply, "You can't read that—put that down." This statement became the uppermost thought and driving incentive in Mary's quest for education and quality.

At the age of 10, Mary began her formal education when the Northern Presbyterian Church sent Emma Wilson, a black missionary, to establish the Trinity Presbyterian Mission School in the Mayesville area. After excelling in her studies, Mary was selected as the recipient of a scholarship to continue her studies at Scotia Seminary (later Barber-Scotia College) in Concord, North Carolina. She graduated from Scotia Seminary in 1894 and then enrolled in the Bible Institute for Home and Foreign Missions in Chicago (later renamed the Moody Bible Institute after its founder, Dwight L. Moody). Her exposure to the head-heart-hand missionary curriculum at Scotia and the evangelistic reform gospel of Dwight Moody's Institute left Mary Jane McLeod with a fervent desire to spread the gospel of Jesus Christ and to help the poorest and most uneducated in society. As a result, after graduating from the Bible Institute in 1895, she applied to the Presbyterian Missionary Board for a missionary position in Africa, only to learn that there were no openings in Africa for a black missionary.

Mary then took her missionary zeal back to the deep South as a teacher, first at the Mayesville Institute (her alma mater) and then at the Haines Institute in Augusta, Georgia, where she honed her teaching skills under the watchful eye of the school's founder and principal, Lucy Craft Laney. Inspired by this pioneer educator's philosophy, Mary learned firsthand the significance of training and educating girls for service and leadership for racial uplift. During her one-year tenure at the Haines Institute (1896–97), she organized the Mission Sabbath School for 275 of the poorest children in the city. A year later, she moved to Kindell Institute in Sumter, South Carolina where she met and married a fellow teacher, Albertus L. Bethune. In 1899, the couple's only child, Albert McLeod Bethune, was born. Soon after Albert's birth, the Bethunes moved to Palakta, Florida, where Mary Bethune established the Palatka Presbyterian Mission School. After five years, they moved to Daytona Beach, Florida, where Mary sympa-

thized with the poverty-stricken and recently migrated black railroad workers and their families. Unable to share in her missionary zeal, Albertus Bethune separated from his family and returned to South Carolina, where he lived until his death in 1918.

Nonetheless, it was in Daytona, Florida, with "five little girls, [Bethune's son], a dollar and a half, and faith in God" that Mary McLeod Bethune opened the Daytona Normal and Industrial Institute in a four-room rented shack near an abandoned city dump. Using her skills as an organizer, administrator, and orator, Bethune raised enough funds to purchase 32 acres of swamp and dump property surrounding her rented building. By 1907, three years after the doors of the Daytona Institute opened, Faith Hall arose as the school's first permanent building. Over the next 10 years, Bethune acquired the financial support of wealthy vacationers to the city, including millionaire philanthropists James N. Gamble of Proctor & Gamble and Thomas H. White of White Sewing Machine. By

Mary McLeod Bethune, 1949 (LIBRARY OF CONGRESS)

1923, the school had an enrollment of over 300 girls with 25 faculty and staff members occupying eight buildings on 20 acres.

It was also in 1923 that Bethune affiliated the school with the Methodist Episcopal Church, merging Daytona Institute with the all-male Cookman Institute located in Jacksonville, Florida. Officially renamed Bethune-Cookman College in 1929, it achieved junior college accreditation only three years later and graduated its first four-year degree recipients in 1943. As a reflection of Mary McLeod Bethune, the head-heart-hand philosophy emphasized by Christian values undergirds and guides the school's curriculum even today. Bethune remained president of the college until 1942 but returned briefly as interim president during 1946–47.

While serving as president of Bethune-Cookman, Bethune traveled the country raising money and promoting civil rights issues. From the college's inception, Bethune had always insisted upon a racially integrated educational facility, and she always emphasized the necessity of preparing women for service and leadership. Therefore, it is not surprising that it was during her presidency of the college that she also began her meteoric rise to prominence as a leader and organizer in the Black Women's Club Movement. In 1920, she founded and served as president of the Southeastern Federation of Colored Women (SFCW). As president of this organization, Bethune opened an alternative educational facility for delinquent black girls because the state of Florida denied blacks access to its all-white facility. Bethune funded the alternative school through the SFCW and from her own personal finances until the state appropriated funds for it in the late 1920s.

In 1920, after the passage of the Nineteenth Amendment, Bethune led her faculty, staff, and other local women in a successful voter registration drive despite intimidating threats by the Ku Klux Klan. By 1924, she had become so well-known for her effective leadership that she was selected to serve as president of the NACW, which was considered the highest office a black woman could then achieve. As president of the NACW, Bethune provided the organization with its first national headquarters and a paid secretary. Nonetheless, she found the organization to be too decentralized and overburdened with local and state self-help projects. Because she believed that a centralized organization would be more effective in presenting a unified voice on public issues, she formed the NCNW in 1935, and for the first time in American history, black women became visible as political actors in national politics as they began to voice their concerns on major social issues. For example, the NCNW's 1938 Conference on Governmental Cooperation in the Approach to the Problems of Negro Women and Children, held at the White House and the Department of Interior, drew national attention to previously overlooked issues. As she had done for the NACW, Bethune established permanent headquarters for the NCNW and employed a full-time staff, and she published the *Afraamerican Women's Journal*. She served as the organization's president from its inception in 1935 until 1949. She also served as vice president of the National Association for the Advancement of Colored People (NAACP), president of the Association for the Study of Negro Life and History, president of the Commission on Interracial Cooperation of the National Urban League, and president of the National Association of Teachers in Colored Schools.

As White House adviser, Bethune maximized her personal friendship with First Lady ELEANOR ROOSEVELT to encourage the federal government to be more responsive the needs of African Americans and to bring the resources of the proliferating New Deal programs to black youth. She joined the New Deal administration in 1935 as a special adviser on minority affairs and in 1936 was named director of the Division of Negro Affairs for the National Youth Administration (NYA). She reorganized the Federal Council on Negro Affairs, which became known as the "Black Cabinet." This informal group of New Deal appointees met weekly at Bethune's house and advised President Franklin D. Roosevelt on issues relating to race. The Black Cabinet held two major national conferences, the most notable being the 1937 National Conference on the Problems of the Negro and Negro Youth. Bethune was not only the sole female member of this advisory group, she was its leader and was thought to have led the Black Cabinet with an iron fist inside a velvet glove.

During her unprecedented, highly visible involvement in national political affairs, Bethune publicly supported President Roosevelt's New Deal policies, including his 1941 executive order banning racial discrimination in the federal government and defense industries. As an NYA appointee, Bethune was, by all standards, the preeminent and most influential race leader in the nation. She served as director of the NYA's Division of Negro Affairs until the agency's termination in 1943. However, Bethune remained an important political figure. In 1945, she served as a special representative of the United States State Department at the charter United Nations Conference in San Francisco. In that same year, she assisted in the selection of black female candidates into the Women's Army Corps (WAC). In 1952, she traveled as the United States' official representative to the inauguration of Liberia's president, William Tubman. In 1953, she established the Mary McLeod Bethune Foundation to promote research, interracial activity, and the sponsorship of wider educational opportunities..

In ill health, Bethune wrote "My Last Will and Testament" for generations to come. In that document, she outlined nine principles by which she led her life: love, hope, the challenge of developing confidence in one another, a thirst for education, respect for the uses of power, faith, racial dignity, a desire to live harmoniously with one's fellow humans, and a responsibility to young people. She died of a heart attack in her home on May 18, 1955. Her "My Last Will and Testament" was published in the August 1955 edition of *Ebony* magazine.

Although considered nonconfrontational and conciliatory, Bethune was without a doubt both influential and effective in the political realm. Within the past 10 years, scholars have heralded Bethune as "the most illustrious black New Dealer and the most influential black woman in the annals of the country," "a pivotal figure in twentieth-century black women's history," "one of the most distinguished African-American leaders and the most prominent black woman of her time," "the most influential black woman in the United States through more than three decades," and "an extraordinary public figure." As historian Elaine Smith noted, "any freedom-loving country could be proud to claim [Mary McLeod Bethune] as its own."

Further Reading
Bethune, Mary McLeod. "Clarifying Our Vision with the Facts." *The Journal of Negro History* 23 (1938): 10–15.
Hanson, Joyce A. *Mary McLeod Bethune and Black Women's Political Activism.* Columbia: University of Missouri Press, 2003.
Holt, Rackham. *Mary McLeod Bethune: A Biography.* New York: Doubleday and Co., 1964.
Leftall, Delores C., and Janet L. Sims. "Mary McLeod Bethune—The Educator." *Journal of Negro Education* 45 (1976): 342–359.
Smith, Elaine M. "Mary McLeod Bethune." In *Black Women in America: An Historical Encyclopedia,* edited by Darlene Clark Hine, 94–105. Bloomington: Indiana University Press, 1994.

—Rose M. Harris

Biggert, Judy (Judith Borg Biggert) (1937–) *congressperson* Judy Biggert was born in Chicago, Illinois, on August 13, 1937. She earned a B.A. in international relations from Stanford University (1953) and a law degree from Northwestern University (1969), and practiced law prior to entering public service. Biggert began her legislative career in 1992, when she was elected to the Illinois House of Representatives to serve the newly created 81st district. She became the first member of the Illinois House in the 20th century to be named to leadership after serving only one term; she was reelected in 1994 and 1996. She was first elected to the U.S. Congress in 1988. She pledged to serve only six years in the House, but broke that pledge when she sought her fourth term in 2004.

In the 109th Congress, Biggert is a member of four committees—Education and the Workforce, Financial Services, Science, and Standards of Official Conduct—and of seven subcommittees. She serves as chair of the Science Subcommittee on Energy; vice chair of the Education Subcommittee on Workforce Protections; and vice chair of the Financial Services Subcommittee on Domestic and International Monetary Policy, Trade and Technology. She is also member of the WISH LIST, the Republican Majority for Choice, Republicans for Choice, the Republican Main Street Partnership, and Republicans for Environmental Protection. She was reelected to Congress in 2006.

Further Reading

Barone, Michael. *The Almanac of American Politics.* Washington, D.C.: National Journal Group, 2006.

Biggert, Judith Borg." In *Biographical Directory of the United States Congress, 1774–present.* Available online. URL: http://bioguide.congress.gov/scripts/biodisplay.pl?index=B001232. Accessed on January 8, 2007.

"Representative Judy Biggert (IL)." In *Project Vote Smart.* Available online. URL: http://votesmart.org/bio.php?can_id.=BS024405. Accessed on January 8, 2007.

—Angela Kouters

Bill of Rights for Women, NOW (1967)

The Bill of Rights for Women was introduced at the NATIONAL ORGANIZATION FOR WOMEN'S (NOW) 1967 national convention held in Washington, D.C. The Bill of Rights called for ratification of the EQUAL RIGHTS AMENDMENT (ERA), enforcement of antidiscrimination laws in employment, enactment of maternity leave policy, tax deductions for home and child-care expenses for working parents, support for day-care centers, equity in education, equal job training opportunities, and the right of all women to control their reproductive lives. The document was controversial from the start due to the centuries-old debate over which strategy most benefits women: protection and special treatment or equality. The document gave preference to the equality strategy, thereby angering labor activists who opposed the ERA.

See also FEMINISM.

birth control movement

In the United States, reproductive or fertility policy is not as explicitly stated as it is in some other countries (such as China's one-child policy), yet it is present nonetheless. Every nation-state depends on women to produce successive generations of new citizens, and the strength of a nation in part depends on a robust population. In most areas of U.S. constitutional law, the interests of the individual outweigh the interests of the state, unless the state can prove a "compelling state interest" that would warrant intruding on individual rights. In the area of reproduction, however, it is less clear that individual rights rein supreme, most particularly women's individual rights. The history of birth control in the United States has been characterized as a struggle between women's attempts to exercise control over their bodies, moralists and social purists who seek to control sexual behavior, and policy makers who seek to control birthrates. With the introduction of the birth control pill in 1960, the pharmaceutical industry has also played a central role in determining the kinds of birth control available to women and men.

The history of reliable contraception in the United States is a relatively short one. It has only been within the last 50 years that women have been able to access methods of contraception that are safe, reliable, and entirely within their control. Early forms of birth control relied on abstinence or male withdrawal; however, neither of these methods provided women any control over their fertility. Development and dissemination of contraceptives depend in large part on the public's attitude toward sexuality, current birthrates, and the positive or negative consequences of population growth. Prior to the Civil War, many states permitted ABORTION until "quickening" (when the fetus is felt moving), but soon after the war's conclusion, most states banned abortions. Succumbing to the pressure to increase the population and new restrictive attitudes toward sexuality that were promoted by organized religion as well as by social moralists, Congress passed the COMSTOCK ACT in 1873. This law was ostensibly designed to control pornography, but it included in its definition of pornography any information or product distributed for the prevention of conception or for causing abortion. The statute, in effect, likened contraception to obscenity and made it illegal to distribute (or import) information on contraception or contraceptive devices.

Various social sectors supported restricting contraceptives, and doctors were among them. In their eyes, contraception violated nature, bred immorality, damaged health, and violated the sanctity of motherhood. Many women, particularly those in the middle and upper classes, viewed contraception as a direct challenge to marital fidelity and their corresponding sphere of authority. Poor and uneducated women were most disadvantaged by unintended pregnancies and were especially vulnerable to public campaigns devoted to suppressing information or medical services. Middle- and upper-class women participated in an informal but extensive network of information, access to birth control devices illegally imported from Europe, and access to relatively safe (but still illegal) abortions.

Birth control advocates such as MARGARET SANGER and EMMA GOLDMAN worked most directly with poor, working-class women, many of whom were recent immigrants. In addition to stressing that giving birth to too many children or not adequately spacing pregnancies was harmful to women's health, Goldman, a socialist active in the labor movement, was also interested in limiting the influx of child labor, which drove down wages for everyone. Immigrants were the targets of a robust EUGENICS (selective breeding) movement that thrived by promoting fears of "race suicide" if white, middle-class birthrates declined and poor immigrant populations increased unchecked. These seemingly contradictory interests forged a nascent birth control movement that directly challenged the Comstock act.

By 1914, Sanger, who had been radicalized by her experiences with the political left and a year in France, began to publish a monthly called *Woman Rebel* in which she eventually promoted contraception as a woman's right: "A woman's body belongs to herself alone. It does not belong to the United States of America or any other government on the face of the earth. Enforced motherhood is the most complete denial of a woman's right to life and liberty. Women cannot be on an equal footing with men until they have full and complete control over their reproductive function." Many issues of *Woman Rebel* were confiscated by the post office under the Comstock act. While the newsletter did not include information on contraceptive techniques, it did publish letters from desperate readers begging for information. In response, Sanger published a brochure entitled *Family Limitation: A Nurse's Advice to Women.* Between 1914 and 1917, more than 160,000 copies were distributed, although Sanger fled to England during some of that time to avoid further prosecution under the obscenity laws.

In 1915, the National Birth Control League (NBCL) was formed. In 1916, Sanger opened the first birth control clinic in the United States in Brooklyn, New York. The clinic managed to stay open for 10 days before the New York state antivice agents shut it down. In those 10 days, Sanger and her sister, Ethel Byrne, were overwhelmed by women clamoring for diaphragms and information. A court decision in 1918 changed the focus of the movement by allowing physicians to disseminate "advice to a married person to cure or prevent disease"—a clear reference to venereal disease and a cover for distributing contraception to married women. Medicalizing the birth control issue allowed Sanger to solicit support and cooperation from physicians without directly challenging the Comstock act, and in 1921 she formed the AMERICAN BIRTH CONTROL LEAGUE (ABCL), which absorbed the NBCL. The VOLUNTARY PARENTHOOD LEAGUE, under the leadership of MARY WARE DENNETT, continued to push for the complete repeal of the Comstock Act and all of the state laws that had been adopted in its wake. The difference in strategies between Sanger and Dennett in pursuit of the goal for women's complete autonomy and access has been the subject of much debate among contemporary feminists.

In 1923, Sanger opened the first Birth Control Clinical Research Bureau (BCCRB) in New York City, staffed with female physicians and nurses to dispense diaphragms to "married women," as the law now permitted. Careful records on the efficacy of available forms of contraception were maintained. By 1938, the Sanger clinics (three in all) had served over 65,000 women. Not everyone in the medical establishment was supportive of physician's new role in providing birth control for married women. As late as 1935, the American Medical Association (AMA) had condemned all forms of contraception as "unsafe for women." In 1937, the AMA officially endorsed birth control as medical practice, and some medical schools began to include instruction in family planning into the curriculum. By the 1940s, the ABCL had merged with the BCCRB to form the Birth Control Federation of America, subsequently renamed the Planned Parenthood Federation of America, in recognition of contraception's transformation into a "family planning" tool.

By the 1950s and 1960s, most states had legalized birth control, but many state laws still prohibited the dissemination of information about contraception, and some states still pro-

hibited the possession of contraception. A 1965 landmark Supreme Court decision, however, eroded these laws. In GRISWOLD V. CONNECTICUT, a Planned Parenthood director was charged with violating a Connecticut state law that prohibited the distribution of contraceptives and information about them and also prohibited the possession of contraceptives. The Court found that although the U. S. Constitution does not explicitly state a right to privacy, a "zone of privacy" can be inferred from the language in the Bill of Rights. Connecticut's law violated that zone of privacy in the realm of marriage because it permitted police officers to search the bedroom of a married couple for evidence of contraception. The Court deemed this action to be overly intrusive and an unconstitutional violation of the right to marital privacy, and it threw out the Connecticut law insofar as it applied to married couples. The Court extended the right of privacy to unmarried persons with the ruling in EISENSTADT V. BAIRD (1972). The fundamental right to privacy established in the *Griswold* and *Eisenstadt* rulings was extended to cover a woman's right to abortion services in the first trimester in ROE V. WADE in 1973.

The Food and Drug Administration (FDA) approved an oral contraceptive for women ("the pill") in 1960. While condoms and diaphragms were revolutionized in the 19th century as a result of changes in rubber-manufacturing techniques, the pill represented the first new technology in contraception. The pill was followed by FDA approval of the sponge in 1983. The cervical cap was approved in 1988; and in 1990, a long-acting reversible contraceptive implant known popularly as NORPLANT and effective for up to five years was introduced (though this is no longer available in the United States). Depo-Povera, an injectable contraceptive that is effective for up to three months, had been widely used in other countries prior to its approval for use in the United States. Additionally, the FDA approved the sale of female condoms in the 1990s. The newest methods of contraceptives include the vaginal ring (sold as NuvaRing), the patch, and a safer version of the intrauterine device (IUD). All three require a prescription. Sterilization remains the most widely chosen form of contraception for women. However, approximately 3 million women at risk for unintended pregnancy are currently using no form of contraception. Availability and cost, along with side effects and safety concerns, are the most common reasons women offer for not using contraception or using it infrequently.

Pharmaceutical innovations in contraception for men have been virtually nonexistent. Reversible Inhibition of Sperm Under Guidance (RISUG) is an injectable compound that partially blocks the tubes that carry sperm, providing effective contraception for up to 10 years per dose. It is effective immediately, has few side effects, and has proven to be reversible in primate studies. This contraceptive has completed Phase I and II clinical trials in India but is years away from introduction into the U.S. market. Male hormonal contraception (a male "pill") is also in development, although there are no estimates as to when it will be available in the United States.

Although an FDA advisory committee voted 23-4 to recommend approval of over-the-counter sale of emergency contraceptives (sold as Plan B and also referred to as the "morning-after pill"), the FDA denied an application to switch Plan B to over-the-counter status in May 2004. The agency cited concerns about its use by women under the age of 16, but critics charged that the ruling and subsequent delays in additional hearings and action were motivated by conservative political agendas rather than scientific evidence. Finally, on August 24, 2006, Plan B was approved for over-the-counter sales in the United States to women over the age of 18. If taken within 72 hours of unprotected sex, it has an 89 percent efficacy rate. Although it was expected to be on pharmacy shelves by the end of November 2006, some major pharmacy chains (including Wal-Mart) have refused to stock the medication.

Birth control represents a path to autonomy and self-determination for women. For that very reason, those who wish to control women's sexuality and reproduction will continue to try and limit the availability of contraceptives. The struggle between feminists, moralists, and natalists is likely to continue for the foreseeable future.

Further Reading

McFarlane, Deborah R., and Kenneth J. Meier. *The Politics of Fertility Control: Family Planning and Abortion Policies in the American States.* New York: Chatham House Publishers, 2001.

Moskowitz, Ellen H., and Bruce Jennings, eds. *Coerced Contraception? Moral and Policy Challenges of Long-Acting Birth Control.* Washington, D.C.: Georgetown University Press, 1996.

Black, Shirley Temple (1928–   ) *actor, singer, ambassador*   Shirley Temple was born on April 23, 1928, in Santa Monica, California. Although perhaps most known for her fame as a child actress in the 1930s, Shirley Temple Black has had a long career in public service as well. She was the star of more than 40 films, most of them made during the 1930s before she had celebrated her 12th birthday. President Franklin Delano Roosevelt proclaimed: "As long as our country has Shirley Temple, we will be all right." The recipient of a special Academy Award for her performance in *Bright Eyes,* Shirley Temple became a unique symbol of American movies and a joyous tonic for a nation greatly troubled by the Great Depression.

Temple retired from acting in 1949 after marrying her second husband, Charles Black. She became active in Republican Party politics, running unsuccessfully for a seat in the U.S. House of Representatives in 1967. Richard Nixon appointed her U.S. representative to the United Nations in 1969. Five years later, President Gerald Ford appointed her to serve as ambassador to the Republic of Ghana. She later served as the first woman chief of protocol in the Ford White House. She also served as a foreign affairs

OCReff

officer with the State Department during the Reagan administration, and George H. W. Bush appointed her ambassador to Czechoslovakia in 1989. In 1988, she published her best-selling autobiography, *Child Star: An Autobiography*.

Black has served on the board of directors of The Walt Disney Company (1974–75), Del Monte, Bancal Tri-State, and Fireman's Fund Insurance. Her nonprofit board appointments have included the Institute for International Studies at Stanford University, the Council on Foreign Relations, the Council of American Ambassadors, the World Affairs Council, the United States Commission for UNESCO, the National Committee on U.S.-China Relations, the United Nations Association, and the U.S. Citizen's Space Task Force. Shirley Temple Black currently resides in Woodside, California.

Further Reading

Black, Shirley Temple. *Child Star: An Autobiography*. New York: McGraw-Hill, 1988.

Blackburn, Marsha (1952–) *congressperson*
A Mississippi native, Marsha Blackburn was born on June 6, 1952, and earned a degree from Mississippi State University in 1973. In 1974, she married Chuck Blackburn, with whom she had two children. Blackburn began her political career in 1977 as a founding member of the Williamson County Young Republicans. She served as chair of the Williamson County Republican Party from 1989 to 1991. Her elective political career began in 1992, when she won the Republican nomination for the Sixth district, which at the time included her home in Brentwood; she lost by 16 points to longtime congressman Bart Gordon. In 1995, she was appointed chair of the Tennessee Film, Entertainment and Music Commission. She gained elective office for the first time in 1998, when she won a seat in the Tennessee state senate. In the senate, she led efforts to prevent the passage of a state income tax championed by the governor.

Reapportionment moved her residence from the sixth to the seventh district, and the seat opened when incumbent congressman Ed Bryant decided to run for the Senate. Blackburn won the Republican primary by 20 points and easily won the general election in November. Her victory makes her the first Tennessee woman elected to Congress in her own right. She was unopposed for reelection in 2004 and beat Democratic challenger Bill Morrison in 2006 to retain her seat. Blackburn is very conservative, earning her the highest conservative voting rank of any woman in the House by the *National Journal*. She is described as antitax and probusiness and a strong supporter of family values. In the 109th Congress, she served on the House Energy and Commerce Committee.

Further Reading

Barone, Michael. *The Almanac of American Politics*. Washington, D.C.: National Journal Group, 2006.
"Blackburn, Marsha." In *Biographical Directory of the United States Congress, 1774–present*. Available online. URL: http://bioguide.congress.gov/scripts/biodisplay.pl?index=B001243. Accessed on January 8, 2007.
"Representative Marsha Blackburn (TN)." In *Project Vote Smart*. Available online. URL: http://votesmart.org/bio.php?can_id=CTN05798. Accessed on January 8, 2007.

—Angela Kouters

black feminism The term *black feminism* became popular in the 1970s with the inception of the black women's movement. It is an ideology that informs and guides the strategies and actions of women of color seeking to attain social equality. Black feminist thought emerged during a period of American history when various social movements, like the women's movement and the black nationalists, were all protesting gender and race inequalities. While black feminism questioned generally the lack of social equality in the wider American context, it specifically assessed the limits and constraints on black women's participation in both the white feminist movement and the larger black nationalist movement.

The two major issues black feminists were seeking to address centered around the relationship between black feminism and white mainstream FEMINISM, and the relationship between black feminism and the larger black male–dominated nationalist movement. Black women felt neglected and invisible within the larger women's movement. They attributed their lack of recognition and participation within the mainstream women's movement to the unwillingness of white women to recognize how perceptions of race contributed to social inequality. As a result, black feminists labeled the white feminist movement as racist. On the other hand, they also accused male-dominated black nationalist movements of reproducing the patriarchal system of female oppression and exploitation. Therefore, in addition to addressing and combating the racism inherent within the women's movement, black feminists were fighting the sexism rampant within the black male-dominated nationalist movement. Hence, black feminists initially set about the task of seeking an autonomous space to articulate the oppression and discrimination they faced based on their gender and race.

Gradually, as a diversity of black women's voices entered black feminist discourse, the core of black feminist thought was enlarged to reflect the multidimensional barriers to attaining social equality. Building on the combined gender and racial systems of domination that women of color confronted in their daily lives, groups such as the NATIONAL BLACK FEMINIST ORGANIZATION and the COMBAHEE RIVER COLLECTIVE introduced the realities of class and sexual oppression to the feminist space. While socialist feminist discourse was instrumental in expanding black feminist analysis of gender and racial oppression to include a system of the domination of class, lesbian feminists were equally important for their contribution to dismantling the centrality of heterosexuality within the larger feminist discourse.

Black feminist thought has been influential over the years in publicizing and raising awareness of the reality of sexual oppression within the black community. Furthermore, while achieving success challenging the white mainstream women's movement to eliminate racism, black feminists have also been instrumental in elevating and broadening the discourse of women's oppression based on race and sexism to include class and sexuality.

Further Reading

Collins, Patricia Hill. *Black Feminist Thought: Knowledge, Consciousness, and Politics of Empowerment.* Boston: Unwin Hyman, 1990.

hooks, bell. *Ain't I a Woman? Black Women and Feminism.* Boston: South End, 1981.

Smith, Barbara. *Home Girls: A Black Feminist Anthology.* New York: Kitchen Table Women of Color Press, 1983.

—Hollis France

Blackwell, Alice Stone (1857–1950) *writer, suffragist, feminist, editor* Born on September 14, 1857 in Orange, New Jersey, Alice Stone Blackwell was the daughter of LUCY STONE and Henry Brown Blackwell and the niece of ELIZABETH BLACKWELL. Raised in an activist household concerned with both abolition and women's rights, Alice Stone Blackwell graduated from Boston University in 1881 and became assistant editor at the *Woman's Journal,* the magazine of the AMERICAN WOMAN SUFFRAGE ASSOCIATION, started by her parents. She wrote a regular woman's column that highlighted a variety of suffrage activities and appeared in newspapers nationwide.

In 1890, Blackwell was instrumental in repairing the breach between the AWSA and the NATIONAL WOMAN SUFFRAGE ASSOCIATION, which merged in 1890 to become the NATIONAL AMERICAN WOMAN SUFFRAGE ASSOCIATION (NAWSA); she became the recording secretary for NAWSA, a post she held for 35 years. In 1899, at the national convention of NAWSA, Blackwell was one of the few white women to support a resolution from Lottie Wilson Jackson, a Michigan delegate, stating that black women should not have to travel only in smoking cars on trains. Jackson also referred to the harassment by white men that black women often received while traveling. White southerners denied this, and the resolution was defeated when SUSAN B. ANTHONY declared that without the vote, women could do little to change any part of American society.

While Alice Stone Blackwell worked for suffrage and women's rights her whole life, she also saw a connection between the situation of women in the United States and oppressed groups around the world. She was known for publicizing the plight of the Armenians in the early part of the 20th century. She also published editions of poetry from Armenians and Russians in order to raise awareness among Americans. She was an active member of the WOMAN'S CHRISTIAN TEMPERANCE UNION (WCTU), the National Association for the Advancement of Colored People (NAACP), and the Women's Trade Union League (WTUL). She wrote a biography of her mother Lucy Stone that was published in 1930. She died on March 15, 1950, at the age of 92.

Further Reading

Blackwell, Alice Stone. *Lucy Stone: Pioneer of Women's Rights.* Charlottesville: University Press of Virginia, 2001.

Merrill, Arlene Deahl, ed. *Growing Up in Boston's Gilded Age: The Journal of Alice Stone Blackwell, 1872–1874.* New Haven: Yale University Press, 1990.

—Claire Curtis

Blackwell, Elizabeth (1821–1910) *physician, educator, social reformer, suffragist* Born in England on February 3, 1821, Elizabeth Blackwell became the first female doctor in the United

States. Raised in an abolitionist family that moved to the United States in 1832, she decided to try to become a doctor as a way to avoid marriage and in particular to treat women and children. Blackwell was admitted to the Geneva Medical College (New York) after the admissions office decided to put her application up for a vote of the students, who, thinking that it was a joke, voted to admit her. She graduated first in her class in 1849 and went to Europe to continue her studies. In 1850, Blackwell responded to the Women's Rights Convention being held that year in Worcester, Massachusetts. The convention included a discussion of educating women in medicine, and Blackwell remarked on her approval of this. However, on the subject of women's rights, she said, "The great object of education has nothing to do with a woman's rights, or a man's rights, but with the development of the human soul and body" (quoted in her book *Pioneer Work*).

Blackwell returned to the United States in 1851 to start her own practice. She began by treating women and children in her home, but after she was joined by her sister Emily, who had also received a medical degree, she decided to open a clinic. (Marie Zakrzewska, whom Blackwell had met during her European training, also came to New York to help open the infirmary.) In 1852, Blackwell published a series of *Lectures on the Laws of Life,* focusing on the "physical education of girls." Although she never married, she adopted an orphan named Katherine Barry in 1854.

By 1857 Blackwell's clinic was incorporated as the New York Infirmary for Indigent Women and Children. She pursued two tracks at the infirmary, the treatment of the poor and the training of more women in medicine. During this time, she undertook a year-long tour of England and became the first woman to have her name on the British medical registry. She returned to the United States in 1859.

During the Civil War, Blackwell trained women as nurses, helping to start the Women's Central Association of Relief (this later became the Sanitary Commission), which provided supplies and information concerning health and hygiene to Union soldiers. Following the war, in 1868, she and her sister Emily opened a medical school for women at the New York Infirmary called the Women's Medical College. Blackwell became the chair of hygiene, and her sister Emily took the chair of obstetrics. The Women's Medical College remained in operation until Cornell University began to accept women medical students in 1899.

In 1869, Elizabeth Blackwell moved to London, where she founded the London School of Medicine for Women and helped to organize the National Health Society. In 1887, Elizabeth Blackwell was appointed professor of gynecology at the London School of Medicine for Children. She worked in London until 1907, but was forced to retire due to injuries sustained in a fall down some stairs. She died in Sussex on May 31, 1910.

Further Reading

Blackwell, Elizabeth. *Pioneer Work in Opening the Medical Profession to Women*. New York: Humanity Books, 2005.

black women's club movement   The black women's club movement refers to a myriad of multipurpose voluntary associations headed by educated, middle-class black women. The various associations emerged in response to the racialized context of American society in the late 19th century, when blacks faced discrimination and exclusion from the political, economic, and social arena of American life. In community after community across the United States, black women pooled their resources to address the needs of the most vulnerable and powerless in society: black women and children.

The major thrust of the various associations centered on welfare issues such as financing schools, orphanages, homes for the elderly, providing health care, and food for the poor (needs that were generally provided for whites by the local government). However, black women's clubs did not limit their participation to the welfare arena but also engaged in politically empowering activities such as mobilizing club members to pressure members of Congress for civil rights legislation; they prioritized voter registration work and focused on programs that stressed racial pride and improvement of the conditions for blacks.

While welfare issues made up the majority of the work done by the black women's club movement, it was work that emanated from the political sphere that raised the movement to national prominence. The catalyst for the black women's club movement was the ANTI-LYNCHING MOVEMENT initiated by IDA B. WELLS-BARNETT. Wells-Barnett exposed the use of lynching as a mechanism to discipline and terrorize the black community, and questioned the myth of rape as the reasoning used to justify it. In actuality, she challenged the status quo by daring to speak of the sexual abuse black women experienced at the hands of white men. Wells's deep concern about lynching became the "ideological direction of the organized movement of black women—a defense of black womanhood as part of a defense of the race from terror and abuse." It was her committed and resilient work against lynching that inspired prominent women from the New York and Boston area to establish the first two black women's club groups.

The long tradition of black women's organizing was officially formalized and institutionalized in 1896 with the establishment of the umbrella organization the NATIONAL ASSOCIATION OF COLORED WOMEN (NACW). Through the auspices of the NACW, black women's clubs across the county began to coordinate club efforts such as fund raising, civil rights action, and voter education.

Despite the valuable work done by the various black women's clubs around the country, the movement has been characterized in the press and by some scholars as elitist, paternalistic, perpetuating a class bias, and reinforcing patriarchal notions of womanhood. In seeking to improve the lives of working-class black women, the leadership and actions of middle-class women in the club movement reflected an attitude of their knowing what was in the best interests of poor women. This was evident within the larger discourse about refuting racist sexual ideology. While attempting to better the lives of working-class women, some middle-class black women simultaneously believed these women were immoral. In the words of many women within the top leadership of the movement, sexual permissiveness was a socioeconomic trait and not a racial characteristic. Hence, by distancing themselves, middle-class black women were asserting a moral superiority.

With the passing of civil rights legislation in the 1960s that eased the way toward social mobility among African Americans, the black middle class began moving out of once predominantly black neighborhoods. Such dispersal, along with the social capital black middle-class women took with them, contributed to the decline and prominence of the black women's club movement.

See also NEW ERA CLUB; RUFFIN, JOSEPHINE.

Further Reading

Batker, Carol. "Love Me Like I Like to Be: The Sexual Politics of Hurston's 'Their Eyes Were Watching God,' the Classic Blues and the Black Women's Club movement." *African American Review* 32 (1998): 199–213.

Lerner, Gerda. "Early Community Work of Black Club Women." *The Journal of Negro History* 59 (1974): 158–167.

—Hollis France

Black Women's Health Imperative

"I'm sick and tired of being sick and tired!" For over 20 years, those immortal words of political activist Fannie Lou Hamer have been the clarion call of the National Black Women's Health Project. Founded by women's health activist Byllye Avery as a self-help organization in 1983, the

NBWHP is the only national organization devoted solely to the health of 19 million black women and girls across the country. Now known as the Black Women's Health Imperative, the organization remains dedicated to providing African American women and girls the information they need to be advocates of their own health. The organization's mission includes community outreach, advocacy, resources and research, and education (CARE). Programs include the National Coalition for Health and Environmental Justice, the Black Church Initiative on Sexuality, and several videos designed to help mothers and daughters talk about health, changing bodies, and reproductive issues. The Black Women's Health Imperative maintains a Web site at www.blackwomenshealth.org.

Blanchfield, Florence Aby (1882–1971) *lieutenant colonel in the U.S. Army*

Florence Aby Blanchfield was the first woman to be commissioned in the regular army of the United States. Her military experiences as an army nurse include meritorious service in World War I and World War II.

Born on April 1, 1882, in West Virginia, Blanchfield graduated from Southside Hospital and Training School for Nurses in Pittsburgh, Pennsylvania, in 1906. She joined the Army Nurse Corps in 1917 and served in France. Between 1919 and 1935, she was stationed in the United States, the Philippines, and China. In 1935, she joined the U.S. Surgeon General's staff in Washington, D.C. Named superintendent of the Army Nurse Corps in 1943, she expanded the corps to nearly 57,000 nurses to meet the army's needs during World War II. She was awarded the Distinguished Service Medal in 1945.

Although Blanchfield proceeded through the ranks of first lieutenant, captain, and lieutenant colonel, nurses were denied the privileges and pay associated with commissioned officer status. Largely due to her efforts, however, the Army-Navy Nurse Act was passed in 1947, and nurses were integrated into the regular army and given equal rights, pay, and privileges associated with rank. In 1947, Blanchfield was commissioned as a lieutenant colonel in the regular army. She received the Florence Nightingale Medal of the International Red Cross in 1951. When she died on May 12, 1971, she was buried with full military honors in Arlington National Cemetery. The Colonel Florence A. Blanchfield Army Community Hospital at Fort Campbell, Kentucky, was named in her honor and dedicated in September 1982.

Blatch, Harriot Stanton (Harriot Eaton Stanton Blatch) (1856–1940) *feminist, suffragist, founder of the Women's Political Union*

Harriot Eaton Stanton was born in Seneca Falls, New York, on January 20, 1856. Harriot was the sixth of seven children (two girls and five boys) born to ELIZABETH CADY STANTON and Henry Brewster Stanton, both activist social reformers in the women's rights and abolitionist movements, respectively. Harriot and her siblings were socialized to politics early by their parents and leading social reformers of the day, including SUSAN B. ANTHONY, SOJOURNER TRUTH, William Lloyd Garrison, and Wendell Phillips. All of the Stanton children were expected to form their own opinions, to be educated on issues of the day, and to take an active role in the world.

After earning her bachelor's degree from Vassar College in 1878, Harriot joined the women's suffrage lecture circuit with her mother. The experience drained her, emotionally and physically, and she left soon after for Europe, working as a tutor to two women. Her experiences in Europe expanded her worldview, but in 1881 Elizabeth Cady Stanton summoned her daughter home to help her and Anthony complete the *History of Woman Suffrage.* Harriot contributed the chapter on the AMERICAN WOMAN SUFFRAGE ASSOCIATION, once a rival to her mother's own NATIONAL WOMAN SUFFRAGE ASSOCIATION, and an organization Stanton and Anthony were inclined to leave out of the book

Harriot Stanton Blatch, ca. 1911 (LIBRARY OF CONGRESS)

entirely. On the trip home, from Europe she met an Englishman, William Henry (Harry) Blatch, and the two were married on November 15, 1882, despite Harriot's concern that "marriage would destroy [her] usefulness." Under U.S. law at that time, the marriage cost Harriot her U.S. CITIZENSHIP, although she never declared loyalty to the British monarchy.

The couple lived primarily in England for nearly 20 years, and Harriot Stanton Blatch joined the Fabian Society and became active in the English suffrage movement. She held leadership positions in suffrage societies, the Woman's Local Government Society, and the Women's Liberal Federation. In 1894, she earned a Master of Arts degree from Vassar. Her thesis was based on a study of England's rural poor.

In 1902, Blatch returned to the United States and joined the Women's Trade Union

League (WTUL) and the National American Woman Suffrage Association (NAWSA). She is widely credited with rejuvenating the women's suffrage movement, which had fallen into the doldrums with few victories to show in over a decade. She was the founder and first president of Equality League of Self-Supporting Women (later known as the Women's Political Union). Blatch brought energy and controversy to the suffrage movement by importing the more militant tactics of the English suffragettes. She also worked diligently to expand the base of suffrage supporters beyond the elite and middle class to include working women and women from organized labor. She is credited with instituting open-air meetings, proselytizing suffrage on street corners and in parks all over New York. In 1908, she began organizing annual Suffrage Day parades that by 1912 were attracting over 20,000 marchers. Although the New York suffrage amendment was at first defeated in 1915, it ultimately passed in 1917, allowing Blatch to turn her attention to the campaign for a federal amendment.

In 1915, the Women's Political Union merged with Alice Paul's Congressional Union for Woman Suffrage (later known as the National Woman's Party). Both Blatch and Paul were veterans of the British suffrage campaign, and they collaborated to infuse the national movement with more militant tactics and direct political action, including demonstrations in front of the White House, hunger strikes, and grand parades.

After the ratification of the Nineteenth Amendment in 1920, Harriot Stanton Blatch joined the Socialist Party. She was an advocate of the Equal Rights Amendment, even though many socialists and labor advocates opposed the ERA in favor of maintaining protective legislation for women. Blatch authored several books, including *Mobilizing Woman Power* (1918); *A Woman's Point of View, Some Roads to Peace* (1920); and a book celebrating her mother's contributions to the suffrage movement titled, *Elizabeth Cady Stanton: As Revealed in Her Let-*

ters, Diary and Reminiscences (1922). She died on November 20, 1940.

Further Reading
Dubois, Ellen Carol. *Harriot Stanton Blatch and the Winning of Woman Suffrage.* New Haven: Yale University Press, 1997.

Bloomer, Amelia (Amelia Jenks Bloomer)

(1818–1894) *suffragist, editor, prohibitionist, journalist* Amelia Jenks Bloomer was born on May 27, 1818, in Homer, New York. She taught school at 17, worked as a governess, and then married Dexter C. Bloomer, a newspaper editor, in 1840, omitting the word "obey" from her vows; they settled in Seneca Falls, New York. Although she was present at the 1848 Seneca Falls Convention, Amelia Bloomer did not actively participate. In 1849, she inaugurated *The Lily,* a monthly newspaper devoted to the Temperance Movement and other women's rights issues. Although regarded as conservative by her peers in the movement, Bloomer became an outspoken advocate of freedom of dress after seeing Elizabeth Smith Miller (a cousin of Elizabeth Cady Stanton) wearing a costume of short skirts over large, Turkish-style pantaloons. This form of dress came to be known as the "Bloomer Costume." Ultimately, Bloomer and others abandoned the costume, fearing that the public ridicule it attracted would detract from other more substantive causes. In 1855, the Bloomers moved to Council Bluffs, Iowa, where Amelia Bloomer devoted herself to suffrage and other social reform causes and where she died on December 30, 1894.

Further Reading
Bloomer, Dexter C. *Life and Writings of Amelia Bloomer.* (1895) New York: Schocken Books, 1975.

Blow, Susan (Susan Elizabeth Blow) (1843–

1916) *education reformer* Born on June 7, 1843, in Carondelet, Missouri, Susan Elizabeth Blow opened the first successful public kindergarten in the United States. She joined the kindergarten movement under the inspiration of Friedrich Foebels, who argued the importance of kindergarten (meaning early childhood education from ages three to seven) in nurturing a child properly. The kindergarten movement, which started in Germany, emphasized socializing between children of similar ages, playing games to encourage social development, and the development of a sense of self. During a trip to Germany, Blow became interested in the kindergarten movement, and she studied in New York with one of Froebel's disciples. Blow argued that the role women were to play in early childhood development necessitated their own education. She opened the first public school kindergarten in 1873 in St. Louis. Within 10 years, every public school in St. Louis had a kindergarten. Blow taught in the kindergarten and trained teachers. After a long illness, she returned to kindergarten reform, but the emphasis of the kindergarten movement had shifted away from learning through play to school preparation. Blow continued to lecture on Froebel's technique and published numerous books about Froebel's teachings (*Symbolic Education, Educational Issues in Kindergarten*). She also taught at Teacher's College of Columbia University. She died on March 26, 1916, in New York City.

Further Reading

Froebel, Friedrich, Hernietta R. Eliot, and Susan Blow. *The Mottoes and Commentaries of Friedrich Froebel's Mother Play.* New York: D. Appleton and Company, 1895.

—Claire Curtis

Bly, Nellie (Elizabeth Cochrane Seaman)

(1864–1922) *journalist, businesswoman, social reformer*   Elizabeth Jane Cochrane was born on May 5, 1864, in Cochran's Mills, Pennsylvania. Her father was a prominent judge, who died without a will shortly after her birth. Her mother had no claim to the family's property, and the estate was auctioned. Biographers believe Nellie Bly's passion for women's rights stemmed from the helplessness she and her family felt after her father's death.

Cochrane's first job in journalism came when she was 19 years old. In response to a sexist editorial, she wrote an anonymous letter to the editor of the *Pittsburgh Dispatch* signed "Lonely Orphan Girl." The editor was so impressed with the letter that he ran an ad asking that the author introduce herself. When she presented herself the next day, the editor hired her, and she began to write articles under the pen name Nellie Bly. Bly's articles focused on women's rights and investigative reporting to advance social justice and reforms. In 1887, she joined the staff of Joseph Pulitzer's *New York World.* She immediately went undercover in a women's lunatic asylum, launching the "stunt age" in which women reporters risked their lives to break into the limelight of male-dominated newsrooms. When editors of the *World* suggested that they send a male reporter to beat Jule's Verne's fictional character Phileas Fogg's record for traveling around the world in 80 days, Bly threatened to do it for another newspaper if she was not given the assignment. She beat the record by more than a week, and when she returned to New York on January 25, 1890, she was greeted by parades, fireworks, and massive crowds. Bly's trip was memorialized in a board game, "Around the World with Nellie Bly," and on numerous Victorian trade cards. Her travelogue increased paper sales of the *World* substantially, but when Pulitzer denied her a bonus for her efforts, she resigned.

In 1895, Bly married Robert Livingston Seaman and retired from journalism. When Seaman died 10 years later, Bly took over his manufacturing company and instituted a number of labor reforms. Unfortunately, the company went bankrupt, and she fled to Europe just in time to return to reporting from behind the front lines during World War I. Bly returned to the United States in 1919 and reported for the *New York Evening Journal* until her death on January 27, 1922.

Further Reading

Kroeger, Brooke. *Nellie Bly: Daredevil, Reporter, Feminist.* New York: Three Rivers Press, 1995.

bona fide occupational qualification (BFOQ)

TITLE VII OF THE CIVIL RIGHTS ACT OF 1964 prohibits discrimination in employment because of race, sex, religion, or national origin. Men and women can be treated differently under the act if sex is determined to be a bona fide occupational qualification (BFOQ); in other words, an employer must prove that only one sex can perform the job. In using BFOQ as a defense in sex discrimination litigation, the employer must show "reasonable necessity" for his or her actions. It is not sufficient to demonstrate that customers prefer one sex to the other. The employer must demonstrate that hiring only men or only women is reasonably necessary to the normal operation of that particular business. For example, a sperm bank can legitimately refuse to hire women as donors, and men may be excluded from jobs as wet nurses.

In 1992, seven men argued that Hooters restaurant discriminated against them when they refused to hire males in front-of-house positions. Hooters argued that they were providing "vicarious sexual recreation" and therefore attempted to use female sexuality as a BFOQ. Since Hooters advertises itself as a family restaurant and not a sex business, Hooter's BFOQ did not hold up in court. Hooters settled with the plaintiffs for nearly $4 million dollars and agreed to create three gender-neutral positions called "Hooters Persons." The restaurant continues to hire only females as "Hooters Girls."

Further Reading

Dunlap, Mary C. *Sex Discrimination in Employment: Application of Title VII.* Santa Cruz: Community Law Reports, 1975.

Fredman, Sandra. *Women and the Law.* New York: Oxford University Press, 1997.

Bonney, Mary (Mary Lucinda Bonney)

(1816–1900) *educator, reformer*   Born in Hamilton, New York, on June 8, 1816, Bonney was a teacher, the founder of the Chestnut Street Female Seminary in Philadelphia and president and cofounder of the Indian Treaty-Keeping and Protective Association. Bonney was educated at the Troy Female Seminary and taught throughout the eastern United States before settling in Philadelphia. She was principal of the Chestnut Street Seminary for 38 years; in her last five years, the seminary was moved to Ogontz, Pennsylvania, and renamed the Ogontz School for Young Ladies.

Active in both the WOMAN'S CHRISTIAN TEMPERANCE UNION and in mission work for her church, Bonney turned her focus to American Indian issues when the possibility arose that lands previously reserved to tribes in treaties would be made available to white farmers for purchase. She started by collecting petitions to present to President Rutherford B. Hayes demanding that he uphold the treaties. Each petition drive was more successful than the earlier one, and she soon started the Indian Treaty-Keeping and Protective Association (later renamed the Women's National Indian Association) with AMELIA STONE QUINTON. In 1882, Quinton drafted the text of a proposal to allot land (usually 160 acres) in reservation to individual; the association received 100,000 signatures on the petition. Native Americans, replacing a system of land allocation to tribes as a whole. This proposal was made law in 1887 with the passage of the Dawes Act (named after Henry Dawes, the senator who presented the petition to the U.S. Senate). It was thought that this act would help protect Indian lands; in addition, Bonney and Quinton both believed that land ownership itself would lead to further assimilation of Indians into white, Christian culture.

After the passage of the Dawes Act, Bonney continued with missionary work among American Indians. She died on July 24, 1900.

—Claire Curtis

Bono, Mary (Mary Whitaker Bono) (1961–)
congresswoman Mary Whitaker Bono was born
in Cleveland, Ohio, on October 24, 1961, but
moved to southern California in 1963. She graduated from the University of Southern California
in 1984. She is the widow of congressman and
former singer Sonny Bono, who died in a skiing
accident on January 5, 1998. Mary Bono won the
Republican nomination for the special election
to succeed him, taking office on April 7, 1998.
She won a full term the following November and
has been reelected four times with no serious
opposition. Bono is one of four representatives
currently serving and elected to their seats following the deaths of their husbands.

Mary Bono is characterized as a moder-
ate-to-liberal member of Congress. She chose
not to attend the 2004 Republican National
Convention because of her objection to several
planks in the party's platform. She is a member
of the Republican Main Street Partnership, the
Republican Majority for Choice, Republicans for
Choice, the WISH LIST and CHRISTINE TODD WHIT-
MAN's Its My Party Too. In the 109th Congress,
Mary Bono served on the House Committee on
Energy and Commerce.

See also WIDOW'S TRADITION.

Further Reading

Barone, Michael. *The Almanac of American Politics*.
Washington, D.C.: National Journal Group,
2006.
"Bono, Mary." In *Biographical Directory of the United
States Congress, 1774–present*. Available online.
URL: http://bioguide.congress.gov/scripts/biodis-
play.pl?index=B001228. Accessed on January 8,
2007.
"Representative Mary Whitaker Bono (CA)." In *Project
Vote Smart*. Available online. URL: http://votesmart.
org/bio.php?can_=BCA16669. Accessed on Janu-
ary 8, 2007.

—Angela Kouters

**Bordallo, Madeleine (Medeleine Zeien
Bordallo)** (1933–) *congressional delegate*
Madeleine Bordallo, a resident of Tamuning,
Guam, was born in Minnesota on May 31,
1933. She moved to Guam at the age of 14 and
graduated from George Washington High
School in Mangilao, Guam, in 1951 and subsequently attended St. Mary's College in South
Bend, Indiana. She graduated from the College
of St. Catherine's in St. Paul, Minnesota, with a
degree in vocal music. Bordallo began her public career as a local radio and television broad-
caster in 1954. She was elected to the Guam
legislature in 1980 and reelected to four additional terms. Her late husband, Ricardo Bordallo, served as governor of Guam from 1975 to
1979, and again from 1983 to 1987. In 1990,
Ricardo Bordallo wrapped himself in the Guam
flag and shot himself to avoid a prison term for
bribery. That year, Madeleine Bordallo was a
candidate for governor, but she lost. From 1995
to 2002, she served two consecutive terms as
Guam's first woman lieutenant governor. In
2002, she was elected as a Democrat to the U.S.
House of Representatives, serving as a delegate
of Guam from January 3, 2003, to the present.
The first woman to represent the South Pacific
island in Congress, she ran unopposed in
2006.

In the 109th Congress, Bordallo is a member of the Armed Services Committee, serving
on the subcommittees on Readiness and Pro-
jection Forces. Congresswoman Bordallo also
serves as secretary of the Congressional Asian
Pacific American Caucus. She is a member of the
U.S.-Philippines Friendship Caucus, the Korean
Caucus, the Army Caucus, and the Navy/Marine
Corps Caucus, the Travel and Tourism Caucus,
and the Women's Caucus.

Further Reading

Barone, Michael. *The Almanac of American Politics*.
Washington, D.C.: National Journal Group,
2006.
"Bordallo, Madeleine." In *Biographical Directory of the
United States Congress, 1774–present*. Available
online. URL: http://bioguide.congress.gov/scripts/
biodisplay.pl?index=B001245. Accessed on January 8, 2007.

"Delegate Madeleine Z. Bordallo." In *Project Vote Smart*. Available online. URL: http://votesmart. org/bio.php?can_id=BGU01062. Accessed on January 8, 2007.

—Angela Kouters

Boxer, Barbara (Barbara Levy Boxer)

(1940–) *U.S. senator*   Barbara Boxer was born Barbara Levy in Brooklyn, New York, on November 11, 1940. She attended public schools in Brooklyn and graduated from Wingate High School in 1958. In 1962, she graduated from Brooklyn College with a degree in economics, and later that same year, she married Stewart Boxer. For the next three years, she worked as a stockbroker while her husband went to law school. Later, the couple moved to Greenbrae, Marin County, California, and had two children. During the 1970s, Boxer worked as a journalist for the *Pacific Sun* and as a congressional aide.

Barbara Boxer started her career in public life when she was elected to the Marin County Board of Supervisors in 1976. In 1980, she was chosen as the first woman to chair the Board of Supervisors; she was later reelected to a second term. In 1982, she was elected to represent the northern San Francisco Bay Area in the U.S. House of Representatives. As a representative, Boxer served on the powerful Armed Services Committee, and in 1984 she exposed the air force's purchase of a $7,622 coffeemaker. After 10 years in the House, she decided to run for a seat in the Senate, seeking to replace retiring senator Alan Cranston.

In 1992, Boxer was elected to the Senate, defeating Bruce Herschensohn, a conservative television commentator, by 5 percentage points after a last-minute revelation that Herschenson had attended a strip club. In 1998, she was reelected for a second term, beating Matt Fong, a former state treasurer, by 10 percentage points. She had thought she would retire in 2004 but then decided to recontest her seat to "fight for the right to dissent" against conservatives like Tom DeLay. After facing no Democratic oppo-

sition in the 2004 election, Boxer decisively defeated Republican candidate Bill Jones, a former California secretary of state, by a margin of 20 percent, garnering the highest number of votes in the history of direct elections for the U.S. Senate (with 6,955,728 votes) in the nation's most populous state, and the third highest vote total in the country in 2004.

Senator Boxer serves on the Senate Committees on Commerce, Foreign Relations, and Environment and Public Works, is the Democratic Chief Deputy Whip, and serves on the Democratic Policy Committee's Committee on Oversight and Investigations. A liberal Democrat, she is known for her advocacy of the environment and women's rights, as well as her stand against sexual harassment. As a congresswoman, she was a leader among House women who had sought to challenge the nomination of Clarence Thomas to the Supreme Court.

Further Reading

Barone, Michael. *The Almanac of American Politics*. Washington, D.C.: National Journal Group, 2006.

"Boxer, Barbara." In *Biographical Directory of the United States Congress, 1774–present*. Available online. URL: http://bioguidecongress.gov/scripts/biodisplay.pl?index=B000711. Accessed on January 8, 2007.

"Senator Barbar Boxer." In *Project Vote Smart*. Available online. URL: http://votesmart.org/bio.php?can_id=S0105103. Accessed on January 8, 2007.

—Angela Kouters

Bradwell, Myra (Myra Colby Bradwell)

(1831–1894) *lawyer, editor, Supreme Court plaintiff*   Myra Colby was born on February 12, 1831, in Manchester, Vermont, to Eben Colby and Abigail Willey Colby. She was educated at a girl's finishing school in Kenosha, Wisconsin, and later attended a seminary where she prepared to be a teacher. After moving to Illinois with her family, she met and married James Bradwell in 1852. Following a brief residency in

Memphis, where Myra worked as a teacher, the Bradwells returned to Illinois, where John prospered in law and politics. Although Myra began to study law informally, her formal law training began a few years later when James was accepted to the Illinois bar and she apprenticed as a lawyer in her husband's office. In 1868, she founded the *Chicago Legal News,* the most widely circulated legal newspaper in the United States for nearly two decades.

On August 2, 1869, Myra Bradwell passed the Illinois law exam; circuit judge E. S. William and state attorney Charles H. Reed signed her qualification documents. In September, she applied for the bar and included an additional document with her application addressing the issue of her sex. She quoted chapter 90, section 28 of the Illinois Revised Statues: "When any party or person is described or referred to by words importing the masculine gender, females as well as males, shall be deemed to be included." The Illinois Supreme Court, however, denied her admission to the bar, not because of her sex but because she was a married woman. Under the doctrine of COVERTURE, a married woman's person and all rights were "covered" by her husband. For this reason, Myra Bradwell was not considered an individual in her own right and therefore could not legally act on behalf of others in the practice of law.

Bradwell appealed her case but was again denied a law license, this time because of her sex. The state of Illinois claimed that since the legislature was silent on the question of women practicing law, it must not have intended for women to be included in the profession. Furthermore, the court claimed that if one woman was allowed into a civil office, then all civil offices would be filled with women. Bradwell then appealed to the U.S. Supreme Court. In *Bradwell V. Illinois* (83 U.S. 130, 1872), her attorney argued that women had the right to be admitted to the law profession, even though they did not have the right to vote. The opinion, authored by Justice Samuel Freeman Miller, sim-

ply upheld the Illinois Supreme Court's ruling. In a concurring opinion, however, Justice Joseph Philo Bradley argued that women were unfit not only for the practice of law, but for most civil occupations as well. In doing so, he articulated the prevailing social argument against women's participation in the public sphere:

Man is, or should be, woman's protector and defender. The natural and proper timidity and delicacy which belongs to the female sex evidently unfits it for many of the occupations of civil life. The constitution of the family organization, which is founded in the divine ordinance, as well as in the nature of things, indicates the domestic sphere as that which properly belongs to the domain and functions of womanhood. The harmony, not to say identity, of interest and views which belong, or should belong, to the family institution is repugnant to the idea of a woman adopting a distinct and independent career from that of her husband. So firmly fixed was this sentiment in the founders of the common law that it became a maxim of that system of jurisprudence that a woman had no legal existence separate from her husband, who was regarded as her head and representative in the social state; and, notwithstanding some recent modifications of this civil status, many of the special rules of law flowing from and dependent upon this cardinal principle still exist in full force in most States. One of these is, that a married woman is incapable, without her husband's consent, of making contracts which shall be binding on her or him. This very incapacity was one circumstance which the Supreme Court of Illinois deemed important in rendering a married woman incompetent fully to perform the duties and trusts that belong to the office of an attorney and counselor.

It is true that many women are unmarried and not affected by any of the duties, complications, and incapacities arising out of the married state, but these are exceptions to the general rule. The paramount destiny and mission of woman are to fulfil the noble and benign offices of wife and mother. This is the law of the Creator. And the rules of civil society must be adapted to the general constitution of things, and cannot be based upon exceptional cases.   Ironically, before the U.S. Supreme Court handed down its opinion in the case, the Illinois legislature passed a law stating: "No person shall be precluded or debarred from any occupation, profession, or employment (except military) on account of sex." In 1873, the same year the U.S. Supreme Court refused Bradwell's appeal, Alta M. Hulett was admitted to the Illinois bar and became the first woman attorney in Illinois. In order for Bradwell be admitted under the new state statute, she would have to reapply but refused to do so, stating, "My business had acquired such dimensions by the time the barriers to my admittance to the Bar were removed that I had no time to give to law practice and I didn't care to be admitted just for the privilege of putting 'Attorney' after my name."

Bradwell continued to work on the *Chicago Legal News* as the journal's publisher, business manager, and editor in chief. She used her paper to shape legal opinion and as a vehicle to advance women's rights. She and her husband were an influential advocacy team as well. Together, they worked to enact several laws advancing women's rights, namely the Married Women's Property Act (1872) and Equal Guardianship of Children (1873).

In 1890, the Supreme Court of Illinois granted Bradwell her license to practice law. Two years later, the U.S. Supreme Court did the same thing, with the help of the attorney general of the United States, Henry Harrison Miller. Both courts granted her license *nunc pro tunc* (now for then). Her official documents were dated 1869, the original year Bradwell applied, effectively making her the first woman lawyer in Illinois. Bradwell died of cancer on February 14, 1894.

Further Reading

Drachman, Virginia G. *Sisters in Law: Women Lawyers in Modern American History.* Cambridge, Mass.: Harvard University Press, 1998.

Friedman, Jane M. *America's First Woman Lawyer: The Biography of Myra Bradwell.* Buffalo, N.Y.: Prometheus Books, 1993.

Brant, Molly (Koñwatsi'tsiaiéñni, Mary Brant) (ca. 1736–1796) *tribal leader, philanthropist*

Molly (also known as Mary) Brant, or Koñwatsi'tsiaiéñni, was born around 1736 to Onondago and Wyandot parents in the Upper Mohawk castle, Canajohari, in New York. Through Brant's work as a diplomat and statesperson, her life served as a cultural bridge between the Iroquois and the British during the 18th century. During her childhood in the home of her stepfather, Canagaraduncka Brant, she received a European education. In 1752, Brant married Sir William Johnson, the first superintendent of the Indians of British North America, in a traditional Mohawk ceremony; the union produced at least seven children. Johnson never recognized Brant as anything except his "faithful housekeeper," but upon his death in 1774, Brant inherited all of his land and wealth.

Brant was a clan mother and head of a society of matrons who held great influence over councils of war and traditional Iroquois government. In this position, Brant held substantial economic power and controlled agricultural land use and the food supply. During the War for American Independence, Brant consistently encouraged the Iroquois Confederation to continue its support for Britain, and she is often hailed as one of the Loyalist heroes of the war. After the 1783 Treaty of Paris, Brant and her children were forced to flee to Quebec with 7,000 other Loyalist refugees. After the hostilities ended, Brant received a pension and compensation for her tremendous wartime losses. She built a house in Kingston, Ontario, where she died on April 16, 1796. She was buried in the churchyard at St. Paul's Anglican Church in Kingston.

Further Reading

Grumet, Robert Steven. *Northeastern Indian Lives, 1632–1816.* Amherst: University of Massachusetts Press, 1996.

Kenny, Maurice. *Tekonwatoni, Molly Brant, 1735–1795: Poems of War.* Fredonia, N.Y.: White Pine Press, 1992.

Purdue, Theda. *Sifters: Native American Women's Lives.* Oxford: Oxford University Press, 2001.

—Sharon Romero

Braun, Carol Moseley (Carole Elizabeth Boseley Braun) (1947–) *U.S. senator, ambassador*

Largely unknown outside of Illinois, Carol Moseley Braun became YEAR OF THE WOMAN's (1992) biggest (and most surprising) victor when she defeated two-term incumbent senator Alan Dixon in the Democratic primary and went on to win the seat in the November election, making her the first black woman in the U.S. Senate. Braun was born Carole Elizabeth Moseley on August 16, 1947, in Chicago, Illinois. Her father, Joseph, was a police officer and her mother, Edna, a medical technician. Carol Moseley earned a bachelor's degree in political science from the University of Illinois, Chicago (1969), and a law degree from the University of Chicago Law School (1972). In 1973, she married Michael Braun, and the couple had one son, Matthew, before divorcing in 1986. After being admitted to the Illinois bar in 1973, Carol worked as a prosecutor, with the office of the United States Attorney in Chicago from 1973 to 1977. In 1978, she won a seat in the Illinois House of Representatives, where she served until 1988, rising to the position of assistant majority leader. As a legislator, she was highly regarded and focused on education reform. Prior to her election to the U.S. Senate, she was elected as the recorder of deeds for Cook County, Illinois (from 1988 to 1992), the first African American elected to an executive position in the county.

Braun intended to seek reelection as recorder of deeds when on July 1, 1991, President George H. W. Bush nominated Clarence Thomas to the U.S. Supreme Court seat vacated by retiring Justice Thurgood Marshall. Braun was a public critic of the nomination, arguing that Thomas lacked the judicial record and experience to be serving on the highest court. When allegations by ANITA HILL were used to change the focus of the nomination process from intellectual caliber to allegations of SEXUAL HARASSMENT, the U.S. Senate Judiciary Committee was forced to extend the confirmation hearings. Anita Hill's testimony before the committee was televised, and millions of Americans watched the hearings. The image of an all-white, all-male Senate committee grilling a black woman, often in a condescending way, outraged millions of women, including Braun. In an interview with *Ebony* magazine, Braun said "The whole thing was an embarrassment. . . . To be honest, I couldn't bring myself to watch the hearings full time." When Illinois senator Alan Dixon cast his vote to confirm Thomas, it was understood as another of the many ways in which "men just didn't get" the seriousness of sexual harassment. Democratic leaders in Illinois began to focus on Braun as a candidate to replace Dixon in the Senate. In addition to his pro-Thomas vote, Dixon had voted with the Republican president 58 percent of the time, more so than any other northern Democrat, making him susceptible to replacement.

Although Braun received support from all corners of the state prior to announcing her candidacy, defeating an incumbent with a large campaign war chest and a 43-year career in politics was a different matter. She received endorsements from only two members of the Illinois congressional delegation, and even Senator Paul Simon, whose own 1990 reelection campaign Braun had cochaired, endorsed Dixon. Braun ran a grassroots, "outsider" campaign to capitalize on the strong anti-incumbent national sentiment. However, her campaign was beset by organizational problems and staff resignations, and she attracted little financial support (although GLORIA STEINEM helped with fundraising). A third candidate in the party primary, Alfred Hofeld, a multimillionaire personal injury lawyer, spent more than $5 million on ads depicting Dixon as an entrenched incumbent out of touch with his Illinois constituency, prompting Dixon to respond with $2 million in ads in his own defense. Braun benefited by staying out of the negative fray. Instead she traveled the state speaking about job creation, universal health care, and increasing support for education, while promising to bring much-needed diversity to the U.S. Senate. When all of the votes were counted, Braun won the primary with 38 percent of the vote to Dixon's 35 percent and Hofeld's 27 percent share.

At the 1992 Democratic Convention, six of the 16 women running for the U.S. Senate were introduced on stage before a national television audience in an attempt to highlight the fresh perspective Democrats would bring to Washington with Bill Clinton in the White House and more women in the Congress. Braun's campaign was widely touted by national FEMINIST groups, but within the state it was again beset by scandal and organizational problems. There were questions about proceeds from the sale of family-owned land relative to Braun's mother's nursing home bills and Medicaid rules. When Braun admitted to mishandling the money, her poll numbers plummeted. Her opponent, Republican Richard Williamson, tried to capitalize on the story by attacking her integrity. Ultimately, on November 3, 1992, she won by a margin of 10 percentage points, making her the first African-American woman to be elected to the U.S. Senate. Braun joined BARBARA BOXER, DIANNE FEINSTEIN and PATTI MURRAY as one of four new women in the U.S. Senate, raising the total to six (prior to the election, Senators NANCY KASSEBAUM and BARBARA MIKULSKI were the only two women in the Senate). She won an immediate spot on the Judiciary Committee, and in 1995 she won a seat on the powerful Senate Finance Committee, making her the first woman to do so for a full term.

Braun's record in the Senate is widely regarded as a positive one, although the specter of scandal never completely disappeared. She worked as a staunch advocate for equal opportunity. She focused her legislative work on educational reform, environmental clean-up (sponsoring a brownfields tax law), farm legislation, and transportation funding important to Illinois, and she served as an effective voice for the recognition of underrepresented groups by sponsoring the Sacagawea dollar coin and the authorization of the National Park Service's historic preservation of the Underground Railroad. At the same time, she visited Nigeria on vacation in 1996, a decision that was regarded as support for General Sani Abacha, authoritarian ruler of Nigeria with a terrible human rights record. There were also charges that Braun used campaign donations to cover personal expenses, including jewelry, clothing, and trips to foreign countries, as well as those related to an ensuing IRS investigation. The charges were never verified. By the end of her first term in 1998, she was politically vulnerable. She lost her reelection bid to Republican Peter Fitzgerald by a margin of 51 to 47 percent.

Following her defeat, Braun announced that she was retiring from politics. She vowed to refocus her attention on education. She worked briefly as a consultant to the U.S. Department of Education before being nominated as the ambassador to New Zealand and Somoa by the Clinton administration. She returned to the United States from New Zealand in 2001 and accepted a position as visiting distinguished professor at Morris Brown College. She later taught business law at DePaul University.

In 2003, Carol Moseley Braun established an exploratory committee in anticipation of the Democratic presidential nomination in 2004. She told *Black Enterprise* magazine that she was in the race "to ensure that the American dream finally gets extended to all Americans without regard to race, color, or gender." The NATIONAL ORGANIZATION FOR WOMEN (NOW) and the NATIONAL WOMEN'S POLITICAL CAUCUS endorsed her candidacy. On September 22, 2003, Braun formally announced her candidacy for the Democratic Party's nomination for president. She ran on the primary ballot in 20 states, at the time a record for any woman, but withdrew from the race on January 15, 2004 (four days before the Iowa caucuses) giving her support to fellow candidate Howard Dean. In honor of her candidacy, she was awarded the 2004 Ms. President Award by the Ms. President PAC and American Women

Presidents, organizations dedicated to encouraging women's candidacy for president. Braun currently heads a private law firm in Chicago, Moseley Braun LLC, and has recently launched a line of organic food products under the label *Ambassador Organics.*

Bray v. Alexandria Women's Health Clinic (506 U.S. 263) (1993)

In this case, various abortion clinics sued OPERATION RESCUE, an unincorporated association whose members oppose abortion, as well as six individuals. Among its many activities, Operation Rescue organizes antiabortion demonstrations in which participants trespass on and obstruct general access to the premises of abortion clinics. The main issue was whether there was a federal course of action when the protestors picketed, trespassed, and otherwise obstructed women going into and out of the clinics. In order for there to be a federal issue, the protected class would have to be defined as all women—in other words, that the protestors held an animus against women in general. The U.S. Supreme Court found no such animus, instead defining the animus as only the abortion itself. The Court noted that there were men and women on both sides of this issue, and therefore it was obvious that there was no animus toward women in general and thus no federally protected class. The court pointed out that were numerous state remedies for trespass and obstruction and that the clinics should look there for relief.

Further Reading

Bridgeman, Jo, and Susan Millns. *Law and Body Politics: Regulating the Female Body.* Brookfield, Vt.: Dartmouth Press, 1995.

—Marsha Hass

Breckinridge, Sophonisba (Sophonisba Preston Breckinridge) (1866–1948) *lawyer, political scientist, social reformer, suffragist*

Born in Lexington, Kentucky, on April 1, 1866, Sophonisba Breckinridge became the first woman admitted to the Kentucky bar in 1895. She graduated from Wellesley College in 1888, worked as a schoolteacher, and studied law in her father's office. Rather than practice law, she enrolled at the University of Chicago. In 1901, she became the first woman to receive a Ph.D. in political science, and just three years later, she became the first woman to graduate from the University of Chicago Law School.

From 1907 to 1921, Breckinridge lived in the HULL-HOUSE settlement. She began teaching at the Chicago School of Civics and Philanthropy, becoming a full professor by 1925. Her work in the area of social work education garnered international attention. Consistent with the philosophy of her colleague EDITH ABBOTT, Breckinridge advocated for a larger state role in public welfare. Abbott and Breckinridge cofounded the *Social Service Review* in 1927. Breckinridge was also active in politics, running unsuccessfully for Chicago alderman on the Progressive Party ticket in 1912. She was a member of the WOMEN'S PEACE PARTY, a delegate to the International Congress of Women (1915), a member of the Women's International League of Peace and Freedom, and an activist in the women's SUFFRAGE movement. Breckinridge was the author of 12 books and numerous scholarly articles on industrialization, immigration, and urbanization. Her training in law made her an effective lobbyist and policy advocate for the interests of women and children. She died on July 30, 1948, at the age of 82.

Further Reading

Abbott, Edith. "Sophonisba Preston Breckinridge Over the Years." *Social Service Review* 22 (1948): 416–423.

Fitzpatrick, Ellen. *Endless Crusade: Women Social Scientists and Progressive Reform.* New York: Oxford University Press, 1990.

Breedlove v. Suttles (302 U.S. 277) (1937)

This case involves the Georgia poll tax collected from every resident in the state. Citizens under

21 or over 60 years of age, the blind, and women who chose not to register to vote were exempt from the tax. In 1936, Nolen R. Breedlove, a 28-year-old male, applied to register to vote but refused to pay the poll tax. When the registrar denied Breedlove's application, he sued the tax collector Earl Suttles, claiming that the poll tax violated his constitutional rights under the Fourteenth and Nineteenth Amendments. Although the court agreed that the poll tax was a requisite to voting, it rejected the notion that paying or failing to pay the tax either conferred or denied a person the right to vote. In considering Breedlove's challenges to the exemptions, the court upheld each of them. Justice Pierce Butler, writing for the majority, reinforced the social stereotypes of women as dependents of their husbands: "In view of burdens necessarily borne by them [women] for the preservation of the race, the State reasonably may exempt them from poll taxes. . . . The laws of Georgia declare the husband to be the head of the family and the wife to be subject to him. . . . To subject her to the levy would be to add to his burden." Ultimately, the Twenty-fourth Amendment, ratified in 1964, prohibited poll taxes as discriminatory. Women continued to be "excused" from the responsibilities of citizenship well into the 1970s.

See also *TAYLOR V. LOUISIANA*.

Further Reading

Lindgren, J. Ralph, Nadine Taub, Beth Ann Wolfson, and Carla M. Palumbo. *The Law of Sex Discrimination,* 3rd ed. Belmont, Calif.: Thomson Wadsworth, 2005.

Brent, Margaret (ca. 1601–1671) *property owner, suffragist*   Born in England around 1601, Brent immigrated to the colony of Maryland in 1638 with two brothers and a sister. The Brents were Catholics fleeing persecution in England, and Maryland was a Catholic colony, although one with many Protestants living within it. The Brents were related to the Calverts, the ruling

family of Maryland, and each of the siblings was granted a large parcel of land. Margaret (and her sister) were allowed to own and run such property as unmarried women; neither ever married.

In 1645, controversies between Protestants and Catholics in Maryland (related to similar controversies happening in England at this time) caused many settlers to move to the colony of Virginia, and the status of Catholics in Maryland was dire. Governor Leonard Calvert escaped to Virginia, returning in 1646 with troops to help defend the colony. Calvert died in 1647, leaving the troops unpaid and Margaret Brent as the executor of his will. This also gave her power of attorney over Lord Baltimore's property (he was in London), as he was Calvert's brother and Calvert had previously had such power. As a result of this circumstance, Brent appealed to the legislature of the colony that she deserved a vote both as a property owner and as executor of the will. She was denied on both counts, but she did successfully solve the crisis concerning the unpaid troops by liquidating Calvert's assets and selling Lord Baltimore's cattle. This sale angered Lord Baltimore on his return, despite his being told that "all would have gone to ruin" if it had not been for Brent's work. The favor that Brent had been shown by the ruling authorities was lost. In 1651, Brent moved to Virginia, where she started another plantation, called Peace. She died there around 1671.

Brent's actions as a landowning, unmarried woman made her well respected in her colony for her ability to solve its most serious crisis. Her abilities were clearly recognized by Calvert, as was her success as both a plantation owner and as representative of Calvert's interests. Brent is remembered as the first woman in the colonies to seek a vote.

Further Reading

Masson, Margaret W. *Margaret Brent, c. 1601–c. 1671, Lawyer, Landholder, Entrepreneur.* Centreville, Md.: Tidewater Press, 1977.

—Claire Curtis

bridefare   As a part of the national welfare reform movement in the early 1990s, states were granted waivers from federal regulations in order to develop pilot reform programs. Wisconsin and West Virginia experimented with marriage incentives for unwed teens on welfare, termed *bridefare*. Under bridefare programs, the state added money to a family's monthly welfare benefits if the man and woman married. Proponents argue that marriage will stabilize families and reduce child poverty. Opponents worry that domestic violence will rise and maintain that marriage is only a cure for poverty when individuals are able to find stable jobs. In his first State of the Union address (2001), President George W. Bush proposed including $100 million dollars a year in the federal budget for experimental programs to encourage welfare recipients to marry.

See also WELFARE POLICY; PERSONAL RESPONSIBILITY AND WORK OPPORTUNITY RECONCILIATION ACT OF 1996.

Further Reading
Pollitt, Katha. "$hotgun Weddings." *The Nation* 4 February 2002. Available online. URL: www.thenation.com/dic/20020204/pollitt.

Brown, Corrine (1946–) *congressperson, activist*   Corrine Brown was born on November 11, 1946, in Jacksonville, Florida, and educated at Florida A&M University, where she received a bachelor's and master's degree. She was elected to the Florida House of Representatives in 1982 and served for 10 years before winning a U.S. House seat in Florida's third congressional district (1992). She generally has a liberal voting record in Congress but promotes military spending as a source of jobs for her district. In the 109th Congress, she served on the Transportation and Infrastructure Committee and Veterans Affairs Committee and also served as vice chair of the Congressional Black Caucus. She is a member of the Congressional Black Caucus and the Congressional Progressive Caucus.

Controversy has followed Brown since the start of her national political career. A few weeks after becoming a member of the House of Representatives in 1993, the Federal Elections Commission (FEC) began an investigation. Her former campaign treasurer claimed Brown had neglected to take action against an aide who had committed forgery, and Brown admitted to the FEC that her federal campaign reports contained several errors. In 1996, another investigation was opened into charges that Brown had improperly received and spent a $10,000 check from an account used by National Baptist Convention leader Henry J. Lyons for illegal activities. Brown admitted to receiving the check but denied she had used the money improperly. The ethics charges have hurt her very little at the polls. She ran unopposed for reelection in 2006 and retains her seat.

Further Reading
Barone, Michael. *The Almanac of American Politics*. Washington, D.C.: National Journal Group, 2006.
"Brown, Corrine." In *Biographical Directory of the United States Congress, 1774–present*. Available online. URL: http://bioguide.congress.gov/scripts/biodisplay.pl?index=B000911. Accessed on January 8, 2007.
"Representative Corrine Brown (FL)." In *Project Vote Smart*. Available online. URL: http://votesmart.org/bio.php?can_id=H0741103. Accessed on January 8, 2007.

—Angela Kouters

Brown-Waite, Virginia (Ginny Brown-Waite) (1943–) *congressperson*   Virginia (Ginny) Brown-Waite was born on October 5, 1943, in Albany, New York, and educated at the State University of New York at Albany. She earned a master's degree in public administration from Russell Sage College in 1984. She served as a staffer in the New York State senate, eventually rising to legislative director. She moved to Brooksville, Florida, in the late 1980s, where she still lives. After serving one term as a county commissioner in Hernando

County, Florida, she was elected to the Florida State Senate as a Republican from Hernando County. She served as Senate majority whip from 1999 to 2000 and was elected president pro tem of the state senate in 2000.

In 2002, Brown-Waite defeated the incumbent Representative Karen Thurman by a narrow margin to win the seat representing Florida's fifth congressional district. Brown-Waite was one of three Republicans who voted against a bill to give Terri Schiavo's parents the right to sue in federal court to keep her alive (Schiavo's home is located in the fifth district). She opposes "abstinence-only" approach to sex education and opposes plans to privatize Social Security. Brown-Waite opposes abortion and gun control and proudly displays her pistol on visits back home to her district. She is also known for having proposed the American Heroes Repatriation Act, a proposal to move American soldiers buried in France and Belgium back to the United States. In 2006, Brown-Waite defeated Democrat John Russell in the November general election.

Further Reading

Barone, Michael. *The Almanac of American Politics.* Washington, D.C.: National Journal Group, 2006.
"Brown-Waite, Virginia (Ginny)." In *Biographical Directory of the United States Congress, 1774–present.* Available online. URL: http://bioguide.congress. gov/scripts/biodisplay.pl?index=B001247. Accessed on January 8, 2007.
"Representative Virginia 'Ginny' Brown-Waite." In *Project Vote Smart.* Available online. URL: http://votesmart.org/bio.php?can_id=BS026279. Accessed on January 8, 2007.

—Angela Kouters

Buck, Pearl S. (Pearl Comfort Sydenstricker Buck) (1892–1973) *author* Born on June 26, 1892, Pearl Comfort Sydenstricker was the fourth child of Caroline and Absalom Sydenstricker. At the time of her birth, Pearl's parents were on leave from their work as Chinese missionaries. When Pearl was only a few months old, her par-

ents took the family back to China, where Pearl spent most of her early years.

Until she entered college in Virginia, Pearl received her education from her mother and a Chinese tutor. Shortly after graduating from Randolph-Macon Women's College, Pearl returned to China when her mother became ill. There she met and married a young agriculturist, John Lossing Buck. It was during the couple's three years in Anhwei, one of China's poorest districts, that Pearl Buck gathered much of the material for her China-based stories, including *The Good Earth.*

From 1920 to 1933, Pearl and Lossing taught at Nanking University. During these years, Pearl gave birth to a severely retarded daughter, underwent a hysterectomy, and adopted another daughter. In 1934, she moved to Pennsylvania to be near her institutionalized daughter. The following

Pearl Buck, ca. 1932 (Library of Congress)

year, she and Lossing divorced, and Pearl married publisher Richard Walsh, with whom she adopted six more children. In 1935, Pearl Buck received the Pulitzer Prize for *The Good Earth*, and in 1938 she was awarded the Nobel Prize in literature, becoming the first American woman so honored. Pearl Buck died on March 6, 1973.

In addition to her literary accomplishments, Buck's work against prejudice and for understanding and justice was significant. She served on the board of trustees for Howard University for 20 years and published numerous articles in journals of the National Association for the Advancement of Colored People and the Urban League. Buck and Walsh established the East and West Association in 1942 to further understanding between the West and Asia. The international Welcome House was founded by Buck in 1949 to coordinate adoptions for Asian and mixed-race children, the first agency to do so. In 1962, Buck created the Pearl S. Buck Foundation, which still provides support for children in their Asian homelands.

Further Reading
Conn, Peter. *Pearl S. Buck: A Cultural Biography*. London: Cambridge University Press, 1998.
Doyle, Paul A. *Pearl S. Buck*. Twayne's United States Authors Series. New York: Twayne Publishers, 1980.
Stirling, Nora. *Pearl Buck: A Woman in Conflict*. Piscataway, N.J.: New Century Publishers, 1983.

—Jean S. Hamm

Burns, Lucy (1879–1966) *suffragist*   Born in Brooklyn on July 28, 1879, Lucy Burns was raised by parents who believed in the equal education of boys and girls. She graduated from Vassar College in 1902, and after a few years teaching in New York City, she went to England to pursue graduate work. While in England, Burns became involved in the Women's Social and Political Union, was arrested, and went on hunger strike, a protest tactic she would take back to the United States.

In 1912, Burns returned and began working with ALICE PAUL to bring a more radical agenda to the NATIONAL AMERICAN WOMAN SUFFRAGE ASSOCIATION (NAWSA). She and Paul went on to form the CONGRESSIONAL UNION FOR WOMAN SUFFRAGE (later referred to as the NATIONAL WOMAN'S PARTY) when their strategy and tactics were not embraced by NAWSA. She helped plan the march for SUFFRAGE in Washington in March 1913, scheduling it to coincide with Woodrow Wilson's presidential inauguration to bring higher profile coverage to the issue of women's right to vote. The march included more than 8,000 women, all wearing white and demanding the right to vote; they were led by New York suffragist Inez Mulholland on horseback. Paul and Burns planned to hold Wilson responsible for the lack of female suffrage, a departure from the more moderate attempts by CARRIE CHAPMAN CATT to reason with the president. Burns and Paul both brought a new spirit of radical demand to the women's rights movement. Rather than ask for the vote by lobbying Congress, Burns demanded it forcefully, using tactics that upset men and many women as well.

Burns edited the suffrage journal *The Suffragist*, which exhorted women in the West who could vote to vote against the administration in office (the Democrats), arguing that whoever was in the office of the presidency would be held responsible for the failure to push for the passage of the "Anthony Amendment" (after SUSAN B. ANTONY). This method of blaming the party in power (meaning the party that held the executive office) was a tactic used successfully in Britain. However, the party structure in Britain was stronger than in the United States, and many saw the move against Wilson as tactically rash, even foolhardy. Burns began picketing the White House constantly, even after the United States entered into World War I. She did not support the war, objecting to the many young men who would die needlessly in her view. She picketed the White House with a sign that read: "We shall fight for the things which we have always held nearest our hearts—for democracy,

Lucy Burns, speaking to a crowd in Washington, D.C.
(LIBRARY OF CONGRESS)

for the right of those who submit to authority to have a voice in their own government." This was a quotation from President Wilson's own "war message" given on April 2, 1917, urging Congress to declare war on Germany, which was done four days later. Burns was subsequently arrested for picketing the White House during a time of war, but she and Paul persisted, urging the wives and daughters of prominent Wilson supporters to join in the picketing. While in prison, Burns, Paul, and other suffragists went on a hunger strike to further protest their arrest. Burns was able to refuse food for three weeks before she was force-fed. She was also beaten in prison for her refusal to eat. It was this violent action and the generally appalling treatment the suffragists received in the workhouse that helped turn the tide of public support toward the women. Burns (who served more time in prison than any other suffragist) was released from prison with Alice Paul and others, and ultimately the charges against them were dropped. Burns and Paul had used nonviolent direct action as civil rights activists would in the next generation. And, as with those activists, the violent reactions to their peaceful protests facilitated the gradual acceptance of their message.

Because of the change in public opinion, largely due to the tactics advocated by Burns

and others, Congress set January 10, 1918, as a deadline to vote on the Anthony Amendment. President Wilson indicated his support of the amendment on January 9, and on January 10 the House of Representatives finally passed the amendment that was first introduced by Susan B. Anthony in 1878. The Senate failed to pass the measure, and the House voted again in 1919 to pass the amendment. On June 4 that year, the Senate approved the amendment, and the last state to ratify (Tennessee) did so on August 26, 1920.

With the amendment passed, Burns moved back to Brooklyn, ended her political activism, and raised a niece left motherless by the death of her younger sister. She died in Brooklyn on December 22, 1966.

Further Reading

Ford, Linda G. *Iron Jawed Angels: The Suffrage Militancy of the National Woman's Party, 1912–1920.* Lanham, Md.: University Press of America, 1991.

Lunardini, Christine. *From Equal Suffrage to Equal Rights: Alice Paul and the National Women's Party, 1910–1928.* New York: New York University Press, 1986.

—Claire Curtis

Bush, Barbara (Barbara Pierce Bush)

(1925–) *first lady* Barbara Bush was born Barbara Pierce in New York City on June 8, 1925, to Marvin Pierce and Pauline Robinson Pierce; she was the third of their four children. Marvin Pierce worked for McCalls Publishing, and by 1946 he was president of the company. Primarily educated at private schools, Barbara attended Rye Country Day School before transferring to Ashley Hall, an exclusive private boarding school in Charleston, South Carolina, for her last two years of high school. As a junior, she attended a Christmas dance in Greenwich, Connecticut, and was introduced to George Herbert Walker Bush. George, a senior at the private boarding school Phillips Academy in Andover, Massachusetts, asked to see Barbara the next evening, and the couple continued to date throughout the Christmas holiday break from school.

Upon returning to school, George and Barbara continued their courtship by correspondence. As Barbara continued in school, George graduated and deferred college enrollment in order to join the U.S. Navy. By 1943, Barbara had graduated from Ashley Hall and George was commissioned as an ensign in the Navy. Before he was shipped overseas, the couple announced their engagement. George Bush was 19, Barbara was 18, and they became formally engaged in December 1943, setting their wedding date for December 19, 1944.

As Barbara entered into studies at Smith College, George began serving with a fighter squadron in the South Pacific. At Smith, Barbara was active in sports, serving as the captain of the freshman soccer team. Academics, however, took a backseat to athletics, fun, and George Bush. She dropped out of Smith at the start of her sophomore year to attend to the details of planning her wedding, but it was postponed when George Bush's plane was shot down over Chichi Jima on September 2, 1944. For a month, he was listed as missing in action, but, rescued by a U.S. submarine, he returned home safely to Greenwich on Christmas Eve 1944. The couple were married on January 6, 1945.

During the first few months of their marriage, George Bush received additional training with his squadron as the United States prepared for the final assault on Japan. Barbara joined him whenever she could, although the training took them to four different states. Following Japan's surrender on August 14, 1945, George Bush was discharged from active duty, and the couple headed to New Haven, Connecticut, so that George could enroll in Yale University. Under the GI Bill, George was eligible for a special program that allowed him to graduate in three years; he graduated Phi Beta Kappa in 1948. Rather than return to school herself, Barbara decided to work part-time at the Yale Coop and begin their family. George Walker Bush was

born in July 1946. The family moved to Odessa, Texas, where George had taken a job as an equipment clerk for Dresser Industries, a large company with oil-drilling subsidiaries. When he was promoted, the family moved to California, where he sold drilling bits for Dresser and where Pauline Robison ("Robin") Bush was born in December 1949. In 1950, the Bushes returned to Midland, Texas, and George cofounded his own oil drilling company, the Bush-Overbey Oil Development Company; in 1953, the company merged with three others to form Zapata Oil.

George and Barbara were active in the Midland community, establishing a YMCA and raising funds for the United Way and Cancer Crusade. A third child, John Ellis ("Jeb") was

President and Mrs. Bush with their dog, Millie, in Kennebunkport, Maine, 1991

born in 1953, but soon after his birth, Robin was diagnosed with acute leukemia. Although George and Barbara pursued aggressive forms of treatment at the Memorial Sloan-Kettering Cancer Institute in New York, Robin died seven months later in October 1953. The couple grieved intensely following their daughter's death. However, three more children followed: Neil Mallon in 1955, Marvin Pierce in 1956, and Dorothy Walker ("Doro") in 1959.

As George was establishing his business and beginning to think about politics and public service, Barbara tended the children and established their home. Although neighbors and friends called her a "supermom," Barbara later described the two decades of intensive child rearing as quite challenging. Between countless Little League games, illnesses and injuries, hours of homework, and handholding, she described herself as "dormant" and admitted to some jealousy of her husband traveling around the world. Her life gained some focus when Neil was diagnosed with dyslexia, and her own commitment to reading and literacy was channeled into working with him to overcome his reading problems. Although she does not credit Neil's dyslexia with her later devotion to literacy as a cause, it certainly appears to have intensified her belief that reading and literacy are keys to success in life.

In 1959, the Bushes moved to Houston, and in three years later, George Bush's political career began when local Republicans asked him to run for chair of the Republican Party of Harris County, one of the largest in counties in the country. Barbara campaigned with him in all of the nearly 200 precincts and discovered that she enjoyed campaigning. Two years later, George Bush ran for the U.S. Senate, but lost. In 1966, he won a seat in the House of Representatives, and the family moved to Washington, D.C. He won reelection in 1968 but lost another bid for the U.S. Senate in 1970, even though he had the solid backing of President Richard Nixon.

Now out of elective office, George Bush was appointed to a number of posts in the Nixon and Ford administrations, including ambassador to the United Nations (1971–73), chair of the Republican National Committee (1973–74), U.S. envoy to China (1974–75), and director of the Central Intelligence Agency (1976–77). When Jimmy Carter was elected president in 1976, George Bush's string of appointments came to an end. Barbara Bush had reportedly enjoyed most of his postings, but she did not believe he should chair the RNC due to the internal strife in the aftermath of Watergate. In addition, while both Bushes enjoyed the opportunities and freedom they had enjoyed in China, Barbara especially did not want to leave so soon when President Ford called George home to direct the struggling CIA. An "empty nester" by that point, she found herself back in Washington and profoundly depressed. Second-wave feminists were laying siege to the very ideals that had defined Barbara Bush's life—commitment to husband, children, and home. Although George urged her to seek professional help, she refused. Instead, with his support, she returned to volunteer work and developed a slide show on her year in China that she presented all over the country to raise money for charity.

In 1979, when George declared his intention to seek the presidency, Mrs. Bush and the Bush children hit the campaign trail on his behalf. Barbara Bush flew on commercial airliners, typically accompanied only by an aide, and covered every state except Alaska, speaking for her husband. She did not take policy positions independent of her husband, and although she was known for her press accessibility and candor, she carefully restricted her comments on political issues to reflect her husband's views. At this point, both Bushes were positioned squarely in the moderate camp within the Republican Party, and so her personal support for the EQUAL RIGHTS AMENDMENT and pro-choice stance were not seen as out of the mainstream. By May 1980, though George Bush had done relatively well, Ronald Reagan had the nomination locked up, and Bush withdrew from the race. But Reagan selected Bush as his running mate, and the team won the 1980 election handily over incumbent Jimmy Carter.

As the wife of the vice president, Barbara Bush announced that her national project would be literacy. In addition to entertaining thousands in the vice presidential residence, she traveled the nation promoting literacy and reading programs, though she intentionally kept a low profile relative to First Lady NANCY REAGAN. Although Barbara was personally popular, she was also the butt of jokes by late-night comedians for her white hair (purportedly a result of Robin's death) and matronly appearance. *Saturday Night Live* lampooned her as George Bush's mother. During the 1984 campaign for reelection, Barbara's candor and sharp tongue led her to characterize Democratic vice-presidential nominee GERALDINE FERRARO as a word rhyming with "rich." She later issued a public apology and telephoned Ferraro to offer her personal regrets for the comment. Reagan and Bush easily won reelection over Walter Mondale and Ferraro.

By 1988, George Bush was again ready to seek the nomination in his own right, and the Republican Party was ready to support his bid. Throughout the campaign that year, Barbara used a slide show of the Bush family and images of George Bush meeting with world leaders to define him and begin to shape her own role as first lady. She tried to carve out a fairly narrow role for herself organized around support for her husband and her family—just as she had lived her life so far. In doing so, she was implicitly promising to stay out of policy making and the day-to-day decisions of governing. She would, therefore, not be ROSALYNN CARTER. Likewise, she presented a very different kind of "family values" from those of the Reagans, and she sought to soften the hard edge of the Republican Party's attempt to co-opt "family values" as their own. Campaign ads often featured the Bushs with some of their 12 grandchildren. At the 1988 Republican National Convention, Barbara became the first wife of a candidate to address the convention

delegates, and she did so skillfully. Bush and his running mate, Dan Quayle of Indiana, easily defeated Michael Dukakis and Lloyd Bentsen in the election.

Barbara Bush entered the White House with eight years of service as the wife of the vice president and a good sense of how Washington worked from her nearly 20 years in social Washington. The Bushes revived the Carters' Inaugural Day practice of walking part of the parade route back to the White House and the long-forgotten tradition of holding a public reception. Not since Taft had citizens been invited to greet the president and first lady and tour the White House. Following the inauguration, she threw herself into the job. She maintained literacy as her primary national project, but added volunteerism to the mix. She established the Barbara Bush Foundation for Family Literacy, a private organization that solicited grants to support literacy programs. She toured the country promoting literacy, appeared on the *Oprah Winfrey Show* to promote reading, and established a popular radio program (*Mrs. Bush's Story Time*) on which she read to children. The books she read were then made available to children through the many literacy programs in the network. Like other first ladies before her, she also devoted time and attention to issues in the District of Columbia. She attracted attention to issues of homelessness, poverty, hunger, and ACQUIRED IMMUNODEFICIENCY SYNDROME (AIDS). She contributed to public awareness of AIDS and battled the prevalent stereotypes that a person could contract AIDS through casual contact with an infected person. During a visit to Grandma's House, a pediatric AIDS care facility, she posed for photographers while cuddling an AIDS-infected infant. Although she claims never to have lobbied directly for increased federal funding for AIDS research, treatment, and education programs, many suspect her public work influenced President Bush's call for dedicating more resources to these areas. When she was diagnosed with Graves' disease, a thyroid condition that leads to double vision and swelling of the eyes, she publicly disclosed all of the details of her treatment.

The first first lady to hire an African American as her press secretary, Barbara Bush brought attention to numerous civil rights issues. She is credited with influencing the appointment of Andrew Sullivan as secretary of Health and Human Services, the only African American in Bush's cabinet. She advocated tolerance and spoke out against prejudice in its many forms. In 1990, she was invited to deliver the commencement address at Wellesley College but found herself in the midst of a controversy. A group of graduating seniors objected to the choice of Mrs. Bush as a speaker because they viewed her as someone who largely defined herself and her successes through the lens of her husband's career and choices—a message that, they argued, Wellesley should not be sending to the class of 1990. The first lady treated the speech and the ensuing controversy as an opportunity to address the issue of diversity and argue that women were at a crossroads—facing the desire to have both a family and a career. She was accompanied by Raisa Gorbachev, wife of Soviet president Mikhail Gorbachev and known for challenging the staid role of former Kremlin wives. The conclusion to Barbara Bush's address diffused the controversy for most. "Who knows?" she said, "Somewhere out in this audience may even be someone who will one day follow in my footsteps, and preside over the White House as the President's spouse. I wish him well."

Barbara Bush was enormously popular as first lady, although she did very little to expand the role or position. Her clothing style, her white hair, and her size all combined to create an image of Mrs. Bush as "everybody's mother." By the end of President Bush's first term in office, his wife's approval ratings were three times higher than his. In 1992, she again addressed the Republican National Convention and sought to diffuse the growing divide between moderates and far right conservatives in the party. During the campaign, Mrs. Bush focused on presenting the differences between "George Bush's America" and "Bill Clinton's Arkansas." She liked to say that she was campaigning *for* her husband and not *against* anyone else. During the campaign, HILLARY RODHAM CLINTON tried to deflect conflict of interest criticism about her Arkansas law firm's business with the state of Arkansas by noting that her professional life preceded Bill Clinton's entry into public office: "I suppose I could have stayed home and baked cookies and had teas, but what I decided to do was to fulfill my profession which I entered before my husband was in public life." This led to the two women going head-to-head in a cookie recipe bake-off (Clinton won). The contrast between Barbara Bush and Hillary Rodham Clinton illuminated the inherent conflict in women's social and political advances over the 20th century and the historically private role of First Lady.

When George Bush lost the 1992 race, Barbara Bush took it personally. Always defensive when her husband was attacked by political foes or in the press, she took offense at the ways he had been portrayed in the 1992 campaign. However, on January 20, 1993, when the Bushes left the White House to return to private life, she was more philosophical noting, ". . . there is an ebb and flow to politics, and life will go on." Her life after the White House has many of the same foci and commitments: family, literacy, volunteerism, and charity work. She serves as AmeriCares ambassador-at-large, is a board member and raises funds for the Mayo Clinic Foundation, and supports a number of organizations. She remains very active with the Barbara Bush Family Fund Literacy programs, serving as its honorary chair and host of the annual fundraiser, "A Celebration of Reading."

When George W. Bush was elected president in 2000, Barbara Bush became only the second woman in U.S. history to be both the wife and the mother of U.S. presidents (the first was ABIGAIL ADAMS). She actively campaigned for George W. in 2000 and 2004 and for her son Jeb in his runs for governor of Florida. She remains fiercely protective of her family and has run into some problems in defending George W. Bush's actions as president, most especially the start and conduct of the war in Iraq. In a March 2003 interview on ABC's *Good Morning America,* she appeared callous when she said, "Why should we hear about body bags and deaths? Oh, I mean, it's not relevant. So why should I waste my beautiful mind on something like that?" When she toured the Houston Astrodome on September 6, 2005, in the aftermath of Hurricane Katrina, she again attracted negative press when she commented, "What I'm hearing, which is sort of scary, is that they all want to stay in Texas. Everyone is so overwhelmed by the hospitality. And so many of the people in the arena here, you know, were underprivileged anyway, so this is working very well for them."

Barbara Bush lives with her husband, George H. W. Bush, in Houston, Texas, and Kennebunkport, Maine.

Further Reading

Bush, Barbara. *Barbara Bush: A Memoir.* New York: Scribner's, 1994.
———. *Reflections: Life After the White House.* New York: Scribner's, 2004.
Gutin, Myra. "Barbara Pierce Bush." In *American First Ladies: Their Lives and Their Legacy,* 2nd ed., edited by Lewis L. Gould. New York: Routledge, 2001, 409–423.
National First Ladies Library. *Biographies: First Ladies of the United States.* Available online. URL: http://www.firstladies.org/biographies. Accessed on January 4, 2007.
Schneider, Dorothy, and Carl J. Schneider. "Barbara Pierce Bush" *First Ladies: A Biographical Dictionary.* New York: Checkmark Books, 2001, 329–338.

Bush, Laura (Laura Welch Bush) (1946–)

first lady Laura Welch was born on November 4, 1946, in Midland, Texas, the only child of Harold Welch and Jenna Hawkins Welch. Neither of her parents had graduated from college, but both stressed education and the value of learning, so books and reading were an important part of Laura's childhood. She apparently decided in the second grade that teaching was her calling. As she noted in a speech delivered at the 2000 Republican National Convention, "Growing up, I practiced teaching on my dolls. I would line them up in rows for the day's lessons." She attended public schools, including Midland's Robert E. Lee High School, where she was active with the yearbook and other extracurricular activities. On November 6, 1963, Laura and a friend were driving to a party when Laura ran a stop sign and collided with another car. The driver of the other car, fellow classmate Michael Douglas, was killed. No charges were filed in the case, and Laura's driving privileges were not affected. (Allegedly, the speed at which she was driving is illegible on the police report. Although the incident surfaced briefly early in the 2000 campaign, the press did not demonstrate as much interest in investigating the details of Laura Bush's past as they have done with HILLARY RODHAM CLINTON.)

In 1964, Laura Welch enrolled at Southern Methodist University in Dallas, where she majored in elementary education and joined the Kappa Alpha Theta sorority. She did not take much interest in the political turmoil engulfing other college campuses, and later could not recall a visit to campus by Martin Luther King, Jr. After graduating in 1968, she took a position teaching second grade at Kennedy Elementary School in Houston. When she realized that her favorite part of teaching involved reading and literacy, she enrolled in a masters program in library science at the University of Texas at Austin in 1970. When she finished the program, she worked briefly as a Houston school librarian before returning to Dallas, where she worked as a school librarian at Dawson Elementary School.

At various points in her life, Laura Welch crossed paths with future husband George W. Bush. They briefly attended the same junior high school and later lived in the same apartment complex in Houston, though they did not know one another then. They met when Laura's close friend and former roommate invited Laura to a barbecue in order to introduce her to George Bush. Although the two were quite different in personality and habits, they were immediately attracted to one another and married three months later in Midland on November 7, 1977. George was already a candidate for Congress, and although Laura professed not to care about politics, she quit her job as a school librarian and joined his campaign full-time after they were married. Bush lost the race, and the couple settled into a fairly traditional suburban existence. Laura Bush did not return to work but volunteered with the Junior League and enjoyed reading and gardening. Just as the couple began to think about adopting children, Laura discovered that she was pregnant with twin girls. After a difficult pregnancy, the twins were born by emergency Caesarean delivery on November 25, 1981. They were named Jenna Welch and Barbara Pierce for their grandmothers, Jenna Hawkins Welch and BARBARA PIERCE BUSH.

The Bushes remained in Midland throughout the early 1980s, George Bush tending his oil business in a rocky Texas economy and Laura tending to the twins. In 1986, George adopted a life of sobriety, sold his oil business, and moved the family to Washington, D.C., so that he could work on his father's presidential campaign. When George H. W. Bush was elected president in 1988, the family returned to Dallas, and George organized a group of investors to purchase the Texas Rangers baseball team. Laura volunteered at the girls' school and at a local hospital caring for babies with AIDS.

In 1992, George W. Bush began his bid to unseat ANN RICHARDS, the incumbent governor of Texas. Laura was reportedly cool to the idea, but she ultimately proved to be a valuable campaign asset and advocate for her husband, who won the election. As first lady of Texas, Laura Bush successfully lobbied for state funding of early reading, literacy, and early childhood development programs, which became the social issues on which she focused. In autumn 1997, for example, she held an early childhood development conference much like the one held by Hillary Clinton in the White House that same year. As Clinton was promoting the "Prescription for Reading" program nationally, Laura Bush was doing so simultaneously, on the state level. When her father died of Alzheimer's disease in April 1995, Laura began to raise funds and public awareness about the disease. The following year, she began an annual Texas Book Festival that successfully raised large amounts of money for the purchase of books throughout the state public library system, in addition to publicizing Texas writers and promoting the diversity of the state's intellectual and literary life. Along with political women in several other states, Laura Bush also participated in First Ladies Build, a Habitat for Humanity program in Austin.

After George Bush was reelected governor in 1998, speculation began about his interest in the White House in 2000. Again Laura was cool to the idea, particularly in light of their daughters' age and vulnerability to public scrutiny. Nonetheless, she joined the campaign in earnest in 1999.

The 2000 election was one of the closest in history, and the outcome was uncertain for many months, thereby making the transition to the White House unusual. Even more unusual was the fact that the former first lady, Hillary Rodham Clinton, had been elected to the U.S. Senate, representing New York. Laura Bush sought a less political and more traditional role than her immediate predecessor had played. However, the terrorist attacks of September 11, 2001, changed the landscape for everyone in U.S. politics. Following the American invasion of Afghanistan, Laura met with Afghan women. She discussed their repression under the Taliban as the topic of her radio address on November 17, 2001, marking the first time a first lady had delivered the weekly radio address.

Education and literacy have been Laura Bush's primary causes as First Lady. In 2001, she presided over a newly created event honoring American authors that was modeled on the Texas Book Festival. Within two years, the National Book Festival had inspired the Russian First Lady Ludmilla Putin to host an October 1, 2003, book festival in her nation that Laura Bush attended, along with several American authors. In testimony before the Senate Education Committee in 2002, Bush called for higher teacher salaries and better training for Head Start and day-care workers. She also served as a spokesperson and promoter of three programs that sought to build the ranks of the teaching profession. The New Teacher Project, the Troops to Teachers, and Transition to Teaching programs reach out to nontraditional constituencies (recent college graduates, former military personnel, and mid-career professionals) to recruit teachers. In March 2002, the first lady held a White House Conference on "Preparing Tomorrow's Teachers," bringing together university and business leaders, education advocates, teachers' unions, public policy organizations, and foundations to consider teacher preparation at colleges of education and professional development for experienced teachers. She has also hosted a number of conferences and symposia on early childhood education and literacy.

Laura Bush lobbied Congress to make the appropriations necessary to continue much of the work of Save America's Treasures. In January 2004, she announced the creation of a new Preserve America History Teacher of the Year award, again fusing the issue of education to an outside issue she has supported. In 2004, she revealed her effort with the White House Historical Association to renovate the Lincoln Bedroom and restore it to its original use as Lincoln's Victorian Cabinet Room. In addition, in a series similar to Hillary Clinton's salon evenings, Laura Bush has hosted the series "White House Salute to America's Authors," to celebrate the country's great literary works. Featured authors have included Mark Twain, Women Writers of the West, authors of the Harlem Renaissance, and three classic American sto-

rytellers: Truman Capote, Flannery O'Connor, and Eudora Welty.

Although her role has been far less policy-oriented than that of Hillary Clinton, Mrs. Bush has occasionally expressed opinions that differed from those of her husband's administration. For example, she has stated that she does not believe that ROE V. WADE should be overturned, that she believes the issue of gay marriage should initially be a matter of public decision and not judicial, and that she agreed with the president's opposition to stem cell research. When Supreme Court justice SANDRA DAY O'CONNOR announced her retirement, comments to the press made it seem that Mrs. Bush was advising the president to select a woman for the seat. How much influence she has over the president may never be known, but it is clear that she has his ear and may serve as a moderating influence over his presidential rhetoric as she has been over his behavior in the past.

In autumn 2005, Laura Bush announced that she would devote her attention to the plight of America's youth, particularly the fragile state of young boys. A White House Conference on Helping America's Youth to promote public awareness of the problems facing at-risk youth, gathered policymakers, research experts, foundations, faith-based and volunteer organizations, educators, coaches, and parents to exchange ideas and comments on programs and methods that have already proved successful. Laura Bush dedicated the National First Ladies' Library Education and Research Center on September 4, 2003. In her dedication speech, she stressed the need to better understand the role played by our nation's women—not just first ladies, but all generations of women.

Exactly what role Mrs. Bush will play as her second term as first lady comes to a close in early 2009 is unclear. She has become more willing in the second term to express her opinions and take public stands. She continues to be a strong advocate for public education, early childhood development, and libraries. To that end, she has accomplished a great deal.

Further Reading

Gould, Lewis L. "Laura Welch Bush." In *American First Ladies: Their Lives and Their Legacy,* 2nd ed., edited by Lewis L. Gould. New York: Routledge, 2001, 439–445.

Kessler, Ronald. *Laura Bush: An Intimate Portrait of the First Lady.* New York: Doubleday, 2006.

National First Ladies Library. *Biographies: First Ladies of the United States.* Available online. URL: http://www.firstladies.org/biographies. Accessed on January 4, 2007.

Schneider, Dorothy, and Carl J. Schneider, "Laura Welch Bush" *First Ladies: A Biographical Dictionary.* New York: Checkmark Books, 2001, 350–356.

Business and Professional Women/USA

See NATIONAL FEDERATION OF BUSINESS AND PROFESSIONAL WOMEN'S CLUBS.

Byrne, Jane (Jane Margaret Burke Byrne)

(1934–) *mayor of Chicago* Jane Margaret Burke was born in Chicago on May 24, 1934, to Edward and Katherine Burke. Her father was vice president of Inland Steel. Jane attended parochial schools in Chicago and spent her freshman year at St. Mary-of-the-Woods in Terre Haute, Indiana. She transferred to Barat College in Lake Forest, Illinois, where she earned a bachelor's degree in chemistry and biology (1955); shortly afterward, she married William P. Byrne, a marine aviator. However, soon after their first child was born in 1957, William Byrne died in a plane crash.

Byrne's first entrance into politics was through the John F. Kennedy campaign for president in 1960. After hearing him speak, she joined the campaign and assumed the job of secretary-treasurer in Kennedy's Chicago office. When Kennedy won, she was offered a position in Washington, D.C., but declined in order to stay in Chicago and pursue a graduate degree at the University of Illinois, Chicago Circle. Although she planned to go into teaching, a meeting with Mayor Richard Daley in 1964 changed her course. As Byrne describes in the foreword to *My Chicago,* Daley summoned her to his mayoral office and interrogated her about her support for Kennedy, arguing that she should have been working for the Daley machine if she wanted to go any place in politics. He advised her to go get active in her ward so that she could be known and seen. Then he said, "I can make you anything." When he asked her what she wanted to be in politics, she replied that she didn't even know if she wanted to be in politics. He ignored that and speculated, "Member of the House of Representatives—possible. Member of the Senate—possible, but not probable." They ended the meeting with Daley telling her to "check in once a month." He appointed her to a job in the Head Start program in 1964, and a year later she was moved to the Chicago Committee on Urban Opportunity. His patronage earned Byrne's loyalty, and Daley reciprocated by naming her to his cabinet. As commissioner of sales, weights, and measures, Jane Byrne became the first woman to serve in Mayor Daley's cabinet.

In 1972, Byrne attended the Democratic National Convention as a delegate and chaired the Democratic National Committee's Resolutions Committee in the following year. In 1975, Mayor Daley named Byrne cochair of the Cook County Democratic Central Committee. Although Jane Byrne was a Daley protégé, many Democratic leaders in Chicago distrusted her. When Richard Daley died of a heart attack in December 1976, the party removed Byrne from the Central Committee chair. The new mayor, Michael A. Bilandic, fired Byrne from her job as commissioner of sales after she accused him of not looking out for the public interest. Byrne responded by announcing her candidacy for the Democratic nomination for mayor of Chicago.

Her campaign was given little chance of victory. The charges of corruption she leveled at Bilandic never found any traction when investigated, and she lacked support from party regulars. However, snow proved to be her major asset. In 1979, it started to fall on New Year's

Eve and continued off and on through February, finally amounting to 78 inches of snow. The city was paralyzed. Bilandic announced that he had "taken charge" of snow removal and that residents should dig out and move their cars to the nearest school parking lot so the city could clear the streets. When reporters went to look at the school parking lots, they were buried in snow. Bilandic tried to assuage white suburbanites who worked in the city by directing the Chicago Transit Authority buses to bypass inner-city stops in favor of outlying areas. Angry black and Hispanic residents watched as buses passed them by. The weather broke in time for the February 27 primary; there was a record high turnout of voters, and Byrne won the Democratic primary. In the general election in April 1979, Jane Byrne became the first woman elected mayor of Chicago, Illinois, with 82 percent of the vote over Republican Wallace Johnson.

As mayor, Jane Byrne attracted national publicity and increased her popularity among Chicagoans by moving into the Cabrini Green public housing project in March 1981. This proved more than a stunt, as she succeeded in attracting attention to the deplorable conditions in public housing and helped improve city services to the area. She was also responsible for a number of economic redevelopment and major construction projects in the city, including the CTA rapid transit extension to O'Hare Airport and reconstruction of the Lake Shore Drive S-curve. However, her acerbic style and heavy-handed management style, coupled with the city's economic woes, alienated many of her early supporters. In 1983, she ran for reelection but lost in the Democratic primary to Harold Washington. She briefly attempted a write-in campaign during the general election, but suspended it when she realized she did not have popular support. Byrne sought elective office on two other occasions, losing again to Washington in the 1987 primary and losing when she ran for clerk of the Cook County Circuit Court in 1988. On November 12, 1990, Byrne announced her candidacy for the Democratic primary in the 1991 mayoral election. This time she lost to Richard Daley, Jr., son of the late mayor. She never again sought office in Cook County. In 1992, her memoir, *My Chicago,* was published by Northwestern University Press. She continues to reside in Chicago.

Further Reading
Byrne, Jane. *My Chicago.* Chicago: Northwestern University Press, 2004.

C

Cable Act (1922)   The Cable Act of 1922 stipulates that a foreign woman who marries a U.S. citizen does not automatically become a citizen but must go through the process of naturalization. As a result of this same act, a woman who is an American citizen does not lose her citizenship if she marries a foreigner unless she chooses to renounce it. The act states that "the right of a person to become a naturalized citizen shall not be denied to a person on account of sex or because she is a married person." However, the law covered only marriages to men who were eligible to become naturalized citizens (excluding men from China or Japan, among others). American-born women who married aliens were treated as naturalized citizens who could lose their citizenship if they lived abroad for two or more years.

See also CITIZENSHIP, RESTRICTIONS FOR WOMEN.

Califano v. Westcott (443 U.S. 76) (1979) This case challenged the basis on which unemployment benefits under Aid to Families with Dependent Children (AFDC) and Medicaid plans were awarded. The federal ADFC, Unemployed Father (AFDC-UF) program was administered through the states. In this case, Cindy Westcott was her family's primary wage earner before she lost her job. She qualified for AFDC unemployment benefits in every respect, except for her sex, and therefore her application was denied. She sued Joseph Califano, secretary of Health, Education, and Welfare, the agency that administered the program, on the basis that limiting benefits to fathers violated the Fifth and Fourteenth Amendments. A district court agreed when it determined that the sex-based requirements of the program were not substantially related to any important government interests, but rather were the result of outdated generalizations about female earners in two-paycheck families. The court ordered the state to provide benefits to families of unemployed mothers in the same way that they provided benefits to families of unemployed fathers. On appeal, the U.S. Supreme Court agreed with the district court and found the law and its application in violation of the equal-protection provisions of the Fifth and Fourteenth Amendments. Justice Harry Blackmun, writing for the majority, characterized the gender classification as the "baggage of sexual stereotypes."

Further Reading

Frost-Knappman, Elizabeth, and Kathryn Cullen-DuPont. *Women's Rights on Trial*. Detroit: Gale Publishing, 1997.

Sidel, Ruth. *Women and Children Last: The Plight of Poor Women in Affluent America*. New York: Viking, 1986.

Cammermeyer v. Aspin (850 F.Supp. 910)

(1994)   Colonel Margarethe Cammermeyer is the highest-ranking officer ever to be discharged from the military for her status as a homosexual. In 1989, Cammermeyer applied to the Army War College to receive additional training as chief nurse with the Washington National Guard. During a security check, Cammermeyer was asked about her sexual orientation, and she disclosed that she was a lesbian. The Washington National Guard did not take any action related to the disclosure; however, in October 1989, the U.S. Army began proceedings to withdraw federal recognition of her rank—effectively ending her military career. Over the course of the three-year investigation, Cammermeyer continued to serve effectively as chief nurse, and evaluations of her performance of duties found her to be superior. Nonetheless, in July 1991, the army withdrew federal recognition, and the Washington State National Guard was forced to discharge her.

Cammermeyer was honorably discharged on June 11, 1992, and she immediately filed suit against the U.S. Army in the U.S. District Court (Seattle, Washington), claiming that the discharge violated her Fifth Amendment rights. The court used the lowest level of scrutiny applied to discrimination cases. In order for the government to prevail, it had to show a "rational relationship" between the law and a legitimate government purpose. In this case, the court found that the government's discharge of Cammermeyer for being a lesbian did not have a rational relationship to the stated purpose of maintaining the readiness and combat effectiveness of its armed forces. In its opinion, the court

cited a number of other countries where homosexuals serve in the military without incident and also noted several studies commissioned by the government finding that homosexuals in the military did not create problems. The court also noted that Cammermeyer herself, a highly decorated, dedicated military professional, provided the best counterevidence to the government's argument. The district court ordered that Cammermeyer be reinstated to her former position, but the government appealed. Ultimately, the Ninth Circuit Court of Appeals denied these requests, and Cammermeyer returned to her position in the National Guard.

In 1994, Cammermeyer published her autobiography, *Serving in Silence*. In March 1997, she retired with full military privileges after 31 years of service in the U.S. military. After her retirement, Cammermeyer ran for Congress in the Second Congressional District in Washington State, but lost. She recently returned to law school.

Further Reading

Cammermeyer, Margarethe (with Chris Fisher). *Serving in Silence*. New York: Viking, 1994.

Cantwell, Maria

(1958–   ) *U.S. senator*   Maria Cantwell was born on October 13, 1958, in Indianapolis, Indiana. Her father served as a county commissioner, city councilman, state legislator, and chief of staff for U.S. congressman Andrew Jacobs. Her mother was an administrative assistant. Raised in Indianapolis, Cantwell earned her B.A. degree in public administration from Miami University in Ohio (1980) and moved to Seattle, Washington, in 1983 to campaign for Senator Alan Cranston in his unsuccessful bid for the 1984 Democratic presidential nomination.

In 1986, Cantwell was elected to the Washington state legislature at the age of 28. As a state representative, she helped write the Growth Management Act of 1990, which required cities to develop comprehensive growth plans, and she negotiated its passage. In 1992, she became the first Democrat elected to the U.S. House of Representatives from Washington's first congressional district in 40 years. During her first term, she supported President Bill Clinton's 1993 budget, and she lost her bid for reelection during the 1994 Republican landslide. Cantwell decided to leave politics after her defeat and became vice president of marketing at RealNetworks. She succeeded in the position and became a multimillionaire with her stock options.

In 2000, Cantwell reentered politics with a bid for a seat in the U.S. Senate. She spent over $10 million of her own money in the effort and won 37 percent to incumbent Republican senator Slade Gorton's 44 percent in the blanket primary. In the general election, Cantwell announced that she would spend whatever it took to win the seat, but she simultaneously supported McCain-Feingold campaign finance regulations and accused Gorton of being beholden to special-interest money. The outcome of the election turned on mail-in absentee ballots, requiring a recount. Cantwell's ultimate margin was 2,229 votes out of over 2.4 million votes cast. Her victory created a tie in the U.S. Senate between Democrats and Republicans, which lasted until James Jeffords (R-VT) became an Independent in May 2001. Cantwell's victory also meant that Washington's top three elected positions (governor and two U.S. senators) were all held by women.

In the Senate, Cantwell has worked on campaign finance reform and energy regulation. She served on the Senate Committee on Science, Commerce and Transportation, the Committee on Energy and Natural Resources, the Senate Finance Committee, and the Committee on Small Business and Entrepreneurship. She retained her seat in 2006, earning 57 percent of the vote.

Further Reading

Barone, Michael. *The Almanac of American Politics.* Washington, D.C.: National Journal Group, 2006.

"Cantwell, Maria E." In *Biographical Directory of the United States Congress, 1774–present.* Available online. URL: http://bioguide.congress.gov/scripts/biodisplay.pl?index=C000127. Accessed on January 8, 2007.

"Senator Maria Cantwell." In *Project Vote Smart.* Available online. URL: http://votesmart.org/bio.php?can_id=H4152103. Accessed on January 8, 2007.

—Angela Kouters

Capito, Shelley (Shelley Moore Capito)

(1953–) *congressperson* Shelley Moore Capito was born on November 26, 1953. A resident of Charleston, West Virginia, Capito is the daughter of Arch A. Moore, Jr., who twice served as that state's Governor (1969–77; 1985–89). She was educated at Duke University and at the University of Virginia and served two terms in the West Virginia House of Delegates.

When Second District congressman Bob Wise decided to run for governor in 2000, Capito won the Republican nomination largely because of her father's legacy. She was the first Republican to represent West Virginia in Congress since 1983, as well as the first woman elected to Congress from West Virginia in her own right. She has been reelected three times, including 2006.

In the House, Capito is chair of the Congressional Woman's Caucus. Like her father, her voting record has been very moderate, at least by southern Republican standards. She is a member of both the Republican Main Street Partnership (which supports stem-cell research) and the WISH LIST. In the 109th Congress, Capito served on the Rules Committee. In 2006, Capito won reelection over former West Virginia Democratic Party Chairman Mike Callaghan. She is married to Charles L. Capito, Jr., with whom she has three children.

Further Reading

Barone, Michael. *The Almanac of American Politics.* Washington, D.C.: National Journal Group, 2006.

"Capito, Shelley Moore." In *Biographical Directory of the United States Congress, 1774–present.* Available online. URL: http://bioguide.congress.gov/scripts/ biodisplay.pl?index=C001047. Accessed on January 8, 2007.

"Representative Shelley Moore Capito." In *Project Vote Smart*. Available online. URL: http://votesmart. org/bio.php?can_id=BS036142. Accessed on January 8, 2007.

—Angela Kouters

Capps, Lois (1938–) *congressperson*

Lois Capps was born in Ladysmith, Wisconsin, on January 10, 1938. She has lived in Santa Barbara, California, since 1960. She earned a bachelor's degree in nursing from Pacific Lutheran University, a master's degree in religion at Yale University, and a master's degree in education at the University of California, Santa Barbara (UCSB). Her husband, Walter Capps, was a religious studies professor at UCSB. Lois worked for nearly two decades as a nurse and health educator in the Santa Barbara public schools.

Walter Capps was elected to Congress in 1996 but died of a heart attack on October 28, 1997. Lois Capps first won the seat in a special election held on March 10, 1998, and again ran successfully in the regular November election. Her victory in 2000 made her the first Democrat to serve for more than one term in the district in over 50 years. Redistricting after the 2000 census favored the Democrats, and Capps has been reelected without serious opposition in each election, including 2006. With her background in nursing, Representative Capps has focused her legislative attention on HMO regulation and medical privacy issues. In the 109th Congress, she served on the House Budget Committee and the House Energy and Commerce Committee.

Further Reading

Barone, Michael. *The Almanac of American Politics.* Washington, D.C.: National Journal Group, 2006.

"Capps, Lois." In *Biographical Directory of the United States Congress, 1774–present.* Available online. URL:

http://bioguide.congress.gov/scripts/biodisplay. pl?index=C001036. Accessed on January 8, 2007.

"Representative Lois Capps (CA)." In *Project Vote Smart*. Available online. URL: http://votesmart. org/bio.php?can_id=CCA97919. Accessed on January 8, 2007.

—Angela Kouters

Caraway, Hattie (Hattie Ophelia Wyatt/ Caraway) (1878–1950) *U.S. senator*

Although born in Tennessee, Hattie Caraway moved to Arkansas soon after her marriage to Thaddeus Caraway in 1896. While her husband practiced law, she tended the farm, home, and children. Thaddeus Caraway was elected to the House of Representatives as a Democrat in 1912 and moved to the U.S. Senate in 1921. Upon his death in 1931, Arkansas governor Harvey Parnell appointed Hattie Caraway to complete his term. She was subsequently elected in a special election on January 12, 1932, making her the first woman ever elected to the U.S. Senate. She won two more elections before she was defeated in a crowded 1944 primary by William Fulbright. While in office, she declined to make any floor speeches, earning her the nickname "Silent Hattie." She supported prohibition and opposed anti-lynching

Hattie Wyatt Caraway, with her husband, Thaddeus Horatius Caraway, 1926 (LIBRARY OF CONGRESS)

legislation. While in the senate, Caraway set a number of firsts for women. She was the first woman to chair a Senate committee (Committee on Enrolled Bills), the first woman to preside over the Senate, and the first woman to run a senate hearing. When she left the Senate, Franklin D. Roosevelt appointed her to the Federal Employee's Compensation Commission, and later to the Employee's Compensation Appeals Board. She suffered a stroke in 1950 and died on December 21 that same year. The next woman representing Arkansas to serve in the Senate, BLANCHE LAMBERT LINCOLN, was not elected until 1998.

See also WIDOW'S TRADITION.

Further Reading

Kincade, Diane, ed. *Silent Hattie Speaks: The Personal Journal of Senator Hattie Caraway.* Westport, Conn.: Greenwood Press, 1979.

Carson, Julia (Julia May Porter Carson)

(1938–) *congressperson* Julia Carson was born Julia May Porter on July 8, 1938, in Louisville, Kentucky. She graduated from Crispus Attucks High School in Indianapolis, Indiana, and attended Martin University in Indianapolis as well as Indiana University–Purdue University. An early marriage did not last. Carson began her career as a secretary with the United Auto Workers, Local 550. Her political career began in 1965, when Indiana congressman Andrew Jacobs, Jr., hired her as a legislative assistant. In 1972, he encouraged her to run for the state legislature. In 1976, after two terms in the House, she was elected to the Indiana State Senate, where she remained for the next 14 years.

In addition to her legislative responsibilities, Carson worked as an executive for Cummins Engine Co. from 1972 to 1982 and operated her own small clothing business. In 1990, she was elected trustee for the Center Township, an agency providing assistance for the needy in central Indianapolis. In 1996, Carson made history by becoming the first woman and the first

African American the Indianapolis area (the seventh congressional district) has ever elected to Congress. She was sworn into office from her hospital bed following heart surgery. During her five terms in office, Carson has helped sponsor numerous pieces of legislation aimed at increasing funding for schools, curbing abuses in managed health care, increasing food safety, and blocking children's access to hand guns. Carson serves on the U.S. House of Representatives Financial Services Committee and the Committee on Transportation and Infrastructure. She is a member of the Congressional Black Caucus. Although in poor health, she won reelection in 2006 with 54 percent of the vote.

Further Reading

Barone, Michael. *The Almanac of American Politics.* Washington, D.C.: National Journal Group, 2006.

"Carson, Julia May." In *Biographical Directory of the United States Congress, 1774–present.* Available online. URL: http://bioguide.congress.gov/scripts/biodisplay.pl?index=C000191. Accessed on January 8, 2007.

"Representative Julia M. Carson (IN)." In *Project Vote Smart.* Available online. URL: http://votesmart.org/bio.php?can_id=BC032620. Accessed on January 8, 2007.

—Angela Kouters

Carson, Rachel (Rachel Louise Carson)

(1907–1964) *author, marine biologist, conservationist, environmentalist* Biologist and author Rachel Carson was born on May 27, 1907, in Springdale, Pennsylvania, and graduated from Pennsylvania College for Women (now Chatham College) in 1929. She intended to study English and become a writer; however, her love of nature led her to switch to biology. She earned a master's degree in zoology from Johns Hopkins University in 1932 and taught for seven summer sessions at the Johns Hopkins Summer School. Following postgraduate work at the Marine Biological Laboratory in Woods Hole,

Massachusetts, she took a position as an aquatic biologist with the Bureau of Fisheries in Washington, D.C. The first woman to take and pass the civil service exam, she had a 15-year career with the federal service as a scientist. In 1936, she became editor in chief of all publications for the U.S. Fish and Wildlife Service.

In 1941, Carson's first book, *Under the Sea Wind,* was published. She later published *The Sea Around Us* (1951) and *The Edge of the Sea* (1955) before publishing *Silent Spring* in 1962. *The Sea Around Us* won the John Burroughs Medal and the National Book Award. *Silent Spring* challenged the indiscriminate use of pesticides, earning the wrath of the powerful chemical industry, whose officials termed her an "alarmist." Dr. Robert White-Stevens, a spokesman for the industry, said, "The major claims of Miss Rachel Carson's book, *Silent Spring,* are gross distortions of the actual facts, completely unsupported by scientific, experimental evidence, and general practical experience in the field." The Monsanto Company parodied the book's title in an article titled "The Desolate Year," meant to describe the apocalyptic vision of insects ravaging the countryside and destroying the food supply.

Carson's writing style was so accessible to the general public that *Silent Spring* became a best seller in the United States and England. In the battle between the chemical industry and Rachel Carson, the public favored Carson's views. Carson said, "As a writer, my interest is divided between the presentation of facts and the interpretation of their significance, with emphasis, I think toward the latter." She wrote articles to teach children and young people about the natural world and to encourage their interest in interacting with nature responsibly. "Help Your Child to Wonder" was published in 1956 and was followed by "Our Ever-Changing Shore" in 1957.

Silent Spring represented a departure from Carson's previous work in that it was specifically designed to warn the public about the long-term effects of pesticides. She wrote, "There was once a town in the heart of America where all life

seemed to live in harmony with its surroundings. Then a strange blight crept over the area and everything began to change. There was a strange stillness. The few birds seen anywhere were moribund; they trembled violently and could not fly. It was a spring without voices. On the mornings that had once throbbed with the dawn chorus of scores of bird voices there was no sound; only silence lay over the fields and woods and marsh." The public debate it aroused prompted a study by President Kennedy's Science Advisory Committee. The report, released in 1963, essentially echoed Carson's call for judicious use of pesticides to maintain the quality of the nation's food and health and called for more research into potential health hazards. The committee chair, Dr. Jerome B. Wiesner, said the uncontrolled use of poisonous chemicals, including pesticides, was "potentially a much greater hazard than radioactive fallout." Carson testified before the Senate Committee on Commerce on behalf of the Chemical Pesticides Coordination Act (designed to require labels on pesticides informing users on how to avoid damage to fish and wildlife). At the same time, she urged the creation of a permanent Pesticide Commission at the federal level.

Rachel Carson, called the "mother of the modern environmental movement" by many, died on April 14, 1964 after a long battle with breast cancer. In commemoration of her achievements as a writer, biologist, and environmentalist, the U.S. Department of the Interior erected a plaque in her honor at the Carson Wildlife Refuge in Maine. The plaque is inscribed: "All the life of the planet is interrelated. Each species has its own ties to others. And all are related to the earth. This is the theme of *The Sea Around Us,* and the other sea books, and it is also the message of *Silent Spring.*"

Further Reading
Lear, Linda. *Rachel Carson: Witness for Nature.* New York: Owl Books, 1998.
Quaratiello, Arlene. *Rachel Carson: A Biography.* Westport, CT: Greenwood Press, 2004.

Carter, Lillian (1898–1983) *nurse, social activist*   Lillian Gordy was born on August 15, 1898, in Richland, Georgia, the fourth of nine children born to James Jackson (Jim Jack) and Mary Ida Nicholson Gordy. Lillian's father was the local postmaster. The family moved to Plains, Georgia, in 1921, and Lillian began training as a nurse at Wise Sanitarium. She completed her training in 1923 at the Grady Memorial Hospital School of Nursing in Atlanta. While in Plains, she met James Earl Carter, a local businessman, and the two were married on September 25, 1923. Lillian briefly gave up nursing when her first son, James Earl Carter, Jr., was born on October 1, 1924. The couple had three other children: Gloria (1926–90), Ruth (1929–83), and Billy (1937–88). In 1927, the Carters bought a 700-acre farm in Archery, just outside of Plains, and later added a fertilizer bagging plant, a peanut warehouse, and a general store to serve their black employees.

Miss Lillian, as she was affectionately called during her son Jimmy's presidential administration, broke the barriers of segregation in her husband's hometown of Plains, practicing nursing in the poor black area of town. She served as a nurse practitioner for the white and black community in Plains, but primarily she served the hundreds of black employees who worked in her husband's businesses. Jimmy Carter would later credit her actions with setting a "moral example" for him. In the late 1940s, the family moved back to Plains, and James Earl Carter, Sr., was elected to the State legislature. He died of pancreatic cancer in 1953, and Jimmy Carter left the navy to take over the family farm and businesses. Lillian found herself "bored" as a widow and took a job as housemother at the Kappa Alpha fraternity at Auburn University in Alabama, where she stayed until 1961. In 1964, she was the cochair of Lyndon Johnson's presidential campaign in Sumter County. Of the experience, she observed, "People hated Johnson down here because of his stand on civil rights and it got very ugly." In 1966, as her son Jimmy was making his first run for the governor's office in Georgia, Lillian applied for the Peace Corps, having been attracted by the organization's slogan, "Age is no barrier." After a psychological evaluation, she requested and was sent to India; she was then 68 years old. She worked in a family planning clinic and later with those suffering from leprosy. She returned to the United States after two years of service.

When Jimmy Carter decided to run for president, Miss Lillian was the first person he told. Lillian Carter gave thousands of speeches on behalf of her son and cared for Rosalynn and Jimmy's daughter Amy during the campaign. She wrote two books while her son was president: *Away from Home: Letters to my Family* (1978), based on letters she wrote while in India with the Peace Corps; and *Miss Lillian and Friends* (1979). In 1977, Miss Lillian became the first woman to receive the Covenant of Peace Prize, awarded by the Synagogue Council of America for her contributions to the "furtherance of international understanding and peace." In 1978, she received the Ceres Medal of the Food and Agricultural Organization, a United Nations agency, in recognition of her work to alleviate drought in West Africa.

Shortly after Jimmy Carter's presidency ended in 1981, Miss Lillian was diagnosed with breast cancer. Her youngest daughter Ruth was diagnosed with pancreatic cancer and died on September 26, 1983, at the age of 58. Only six weeks later, Miss Lillian died on October 30, 1983; she was 85 years old. She is buried next to her husband in Plains, Georgia.

Further Reading

Carter, Jimmy. *Sharing Good Times*. New York: Simon and Schuster, 2004.
———. *Christmas in Plains: Memories*. New York: Simon and Schuster, 2001.

Carter, Rosalynn (Eleanor Rosalynn Smith Carter) (1927–) *first lady*   Eleanor Rosalynn Smith was born on August 18, 1927, the first of four children born to William Edgar Smith

and Frances Allethea Smith, in Plains, Georgia. Rosalynn's father owned a garage, farmed, and drove a school bus; her mother was a college graduate. The family was centered on school and church. When Rosalynn was 13, her father died of leukemia. The family suffered financially, and her mother supported the family by sewing as well as working in the school cafeteria and in a grocery store. She later got a job in the Plains post office, working there until she was forced to retire at age 70.

Rosalynn was a good student and graduated valedictorian of her class. She attended a junior college in Americus, Georgia, commuting from Plains. In her teens, she formed a friendship with Ruth Carter, the younger sister of Jimmy Carter, who was then a student at the Naval Academy in Annapolis. In 1945, Rosalynn and Jimmy met at a picnic and began a courtship that continued even when Jimmy returned to school. Jimmy first proposed at Christmas, and Rosalynn accepted at the end of February 1946, setting aside her fears that at 18 years of age she was too young for marriage. They were married on July 7, 1946, and following a brief honeymoon in North Carolina, they began life in the navy, stationed in Norfolk, Virginia. Because Jimmy was at sea four days of every week, Rosalynn developed an independent life and managed the household. Their first son, Jack, was born in July 1947. When Jimmy Carter was selected for training in submarines in New London, Connecticut, in 1948, the family moved again. This was followed by a tour in Hawaii, where their second son, Chip, was born in 1950. The Carters spent time in San Diego, California, before returning to New London. In 1952, son Jeff was born. Jimmy Carter qualified to command submarines, and Admiral Hyman Rickover selected him to join the elite nuclear submarine program. The family moved to Schenectady, New York, to await the completion of the USS *Seawolf*.

As they waited, Jimmy's father, Earl, died, leaving the family business without a head. When the family returned to Plains, Jimmy decided that his first responsibility was to his family, the business, and the many citizens of Plains whom his father had been quietly helping over the years. Rosalynn Carter did not want to give up her independence to return to tiny Plains, but she did so in 1953. After initial setbacks, the business grew and prospered, largely because of Rosalynn's financial management skills. The Carters had always treated the people of Plains as one community—black or white. Jimmy advocated before the local school board for equal education for blacks and whites. Recognizing the limits of reform from the outside, he announced his candidacy for the state legislature in 1962. Rosalynn campaigned and made phone calls on his behalf. Ultimately, Jimmy won the election, but only after several court and party battles challenging corruption and cronyism in Quitman County. He was reelected in 1964. While he was at the statehouse, Rosalynn continued to run the family business. In 1967, after 21 years of marriage, Amy Carter was born.

The entire family participated in Jimmy Carter's 1970 campaign for governor. Usually Rosalynn traveled apart from Jimmy so that the couple could cover more territory. She gained confidence in her ability to speak directly to individuals, and she gained valuable public speaking skills as she grudgingly agreed to deliver prepared remarks to groups of citizens. During this campaign, Rosalynn discovered the cause that would characterize the central focus of her life in public service: mental illness. The more time she spent in private homes, the more frequently she discovered the severe financial and emotional hardship imposed by mental illness.

Jimmy Carter won the governorship in 1970, and the family moved to Atlanta. As the first lady of Georgia, Rosalynn made some immediate changes to the mansion, protocols, and schedule that signaled a more informal atmosphere than had characterized the Lester Maddox regime. She reduced the number of visible security guards, hung works throughout the public spaces created by Georgian artists, and opened the house to everyone living in selected congressional districts each Sunday afternoon. She promoted the theme of the "Public's House," much like she would do with the White House in 1976–80. Governor Carter established the Governor's Commission to Improve Services to the Mentally and Emotionally Handicapped and appointed Rosalynn to serve on the commission. In this capacity, she toured the state hospitals and came to realize that institutional care was not as effective as community-based care. Ultimately, the state mental health system increased community mental health centers from 23 to 134 during Carter's administration. Rosalynn also worked with the Women's Prison Committee, a subcommittee of the President's Commission on the Status of Women, and supported efforts to improve housing conditions and work programs for female inmates.

After one term as governor, Jimmy Carter was ready to explore a presidential run. Rosalynn supported the decision completely, and they again embarked as a team to build the support he would need to win the nomination. Once again, they campaigned separately in order to cover more area and reach more party faithful. This time, however, Rosalynn realized that she had to be as well versed on the issues central to the campaign as her husband was, and she prepared accordingly. When Jimmy secured the nomination at the 1976 Democratic National Convention, she said, "It was one of the most thrilling moments of my life. We had worked for it, planned for it, and knew it would come." This attitude stands in stark contrast to other candidate wives who dreaded the campaign to come and their life in the White House. During the presidential campaign, Rosalynn campaigned around the nation using a private campaign plane. She covered 42 states prior to the November election and joined Jimmy and the rest of the family to watch the returns come in.

When the Carters moved into the White House in 1977, Rosalynn was ready for the onslaught of public attention and the security measures that constrained her movements. His-

torians credit her positive evaluation as first lady to five factors: her relationship with the president, the organization of her staff, her political and communication skills, her personality, and her ability to focus her attention on specific goals. The office of the first lady was reorganized to provide more support for the public role Rosalynn adopted. A chief of staff for the first lady was created as a senior staff position with rank and salary comparable to the chief of staff for the president. Rosalynn Carter was an activist first lady from the start. Although she did not hold formal press conferences, she was accessible and popular with the press. Her direct access to the president and her open influence over Carter policy did not go without criticism, however. Unlike other first ladies before her, Rosalynn Carter did not have a network of Washington friends upon arriving in Washington. Having never been a congressional or cabinet wife, she was entirely new to the Washington social scene. The Carters attracted negative attention for their policy against serving hard liquor, even though it allowed them to entertain more people for a lower cost. She entertained more informally and preferred events where guests could bring their families. The populist theme of the campaign extended to entertaining, and it was not warmly embraced by official Washington.

Substantively, Rosalynn Carter was perhaps the most influential first lady since ELEANOR ROOSEVELT. At the president's invitation, she attended cabinet meetings, choosing to sit alongside staff members, and she was included in national security briefings. President Carter consulted her on nearly all matters of state, including the Camp David peace accords, major appointments, presidential speeches, and foreign policy. She used this influence to promote the appointment of qualified women to high administration posts, and as a result, the Carter administration appointed an unprecedented number of women. As first lady, Rosalynn traveled extensively throughout the country and abroad. Unlike previous presidential wives, however, she undertook a trip to Latin America in 1977 as a representative of the Carter administration. She visited seven countries and held substantive meetings with the heads of state in each, working to explain the Carter administration policies and to promote positive relations between the United States and Latin America. To prepare for the mission, Rosalynn studied Spanish and was briefed extensively by scholars and executive branch officials on the history of foreign policy with Latin America. More often than not, she was well received by foreign heads of state, even though some in the United States cautioned that sending a woman into a machismo Latin culture would not serve the U.S. interests well. Domestic reaction to the trip was also more positive than not. Network news broadcasts described her as a "two-way conduit of views" rather than as a spokesperson for the nation or an official negotiator. There were critics, of course, but the president's support for her mission was so firm that detractors were cautious not to be too openly critical.

President Carter wanted to appoint Rosalynn to chair the newly created President's Commission on Mental Health, but he was advised by the Justice Department that federal law prohibited him from appointing a close relative to a civilian position. Mrs. Carter was appointed honorary chair, along with Dr. Tom Bryant, the commission's formal chair. Rosalynn took a very active role, and the commission produced a list of 117 recommendations emphasizing community health care, including treatment of mental and emotional disabilities in health insurance programs, initiatives designed to lure more care workers to urban and rural care centers, and a commitment to expanding support for research on the causes and treatment of mental illness. Ultimately, the Mental Health Systems Act, based on the commission's three years of work, was passed by Congress and signed by the president in 1980, just prior to leaving office. Although some of the provisions were implemented, many more were casualties of the Reagan administration's reduction in domestic spending agenda.

Rosalynn Carter's other projects included programs and services for senior citizens and childhood immunization programs. She lobbied aggressively for the ratification of the EQUAL RIGHTS AMENDMENT (ERA), and joined BETTY FORD and LADY BIRD JOHNSON in support of the ERA at the Houston conference celebrating the International Year of the Woman in 1977. She also dedicated efforts to improving urban Washington, D.C. She responded positively to requests for her help in raising funds to support voluntarism, training programs for urban youth, and jobs seminars for the poor.

As the 1980 presidential race approached, Rosalynn campaigned hard for reelection. The Iranian hostage crisis and a slipping economy kept Jimmy Carter in Washington, so Rosalynn and other family members campaigned on his behalf. They found voters in a sour mood, and ultimately Ronald Reagan won all but six states.

Historians view Rosalynn Carter as an overwhelmingly effective first lady. She set many new precedents with her substantive changes to the office itself and with her public partnership with the president in promoting the administration's agenda. Only the second first lady to testify before Congress (Eleanor Roosevelt was the first), she represented the United States in meetings with foreign leaders and raised public awareness of mental illness, childhood disease, the needs of the elderly, and women's equality rights. As a former first lady, she remains very active in many of these same causes. The Carters have written and published together, and Rosalynn has published her memoirs (*First Lady from Plains*), as well as several books on living a healthy life and coping with mental illness in the family. She is active in several projects of the Carter Presidential Center and has accompanied former President Carter as an observer to foreign elections. Rosalynn and Jimmy Carter founded the Atlanta Project, an effort to fight urban poverty. Both are also active with Habitat for Humanity, a nonprofit organization dedicated to expanding the base of affordable housing in local communities across the nation.

In recognition of her work on behalf of the mentally ill, Rosalynn was presented with the Presidential Citation from the American Psychological Association. She has received numerous honorary degrees and citations. In 1999, the Carters received the Presidential Medal of Freedom, the nation's highest civilian honor. Rosalynn Carter continues to work on a variety of projects with her husband through the Carter Center.

Further Reading

Brinkley, Douglas. *The Unfinished Presidency: Jimmy Carter's Journey Beyond the White House.* New York: Viking, 1998.

Carter, Jimmy. *Keeping Faith.* New York: Bantam, 1982.

Carter, Rosalynn. *First Lady from Plains.* Boston: Houghton Mifflin, 1984.

National First Ladies Library. *Biographies: First Ladies of the United States.* Available online. URL: http://www.firstladies.org/biographies. Accessed on January 4, 2007.

Schneider, Dorothy, and Carl J. Schneider. *First Ladies: A Biographical Dictionary.* New York: Checkmark Books, 2001.

Catalyst Catalyst is a nonprofit research and advisory organization working to advance women in business. Felice Schwartz founded Catalyst in 1962 to aid women entering the workforce. Five college presidents (from Smith, Wellesley, Lawrence, Mills, and Sarah Lawrence) endorsed the idea and agreed to form the first board of directors. In 1969, Catalyst conducted its first survey of employers at the nation's top 1,000 companies on their attitudes toward hiring women. Since then, Catalyst has become one of the most significant repositories for information on issues related to women and work. The organization operates career centers; advises corporations on strategies to recruit, hire, and retain women and improve diversity in all aspects of business; works with corporations to recruit women for their boards of directors; and hosts a speaker's bureau. In 1987, Catalyst began to make awards to companies in recognition of innovative strategies adopted to advance women in management. The organization maintains a Web site at www.catalystwoment.org.

Catt, Carrie Chapman (Carrie Clinton Lane Chapman Catt) (1859–1947) *suffragist, feminist, peace activist* Key coordinator of the suffrage movement and skillful political strategist, Carrie Chapman Catt revitalized the NATIONAL AMERICAN WOMAN SUFFRAGE ASSOCIATION (NAWSA) and played a leading role in its successful campaign to win voting rights for women. Born Carrie Clinton Lane in Ripon, Wisconsin, on January 9, 1859, she moved to Iowa with her family when she was seven and began preparatory schooling there. In 1880, she graduated from Iowa State College at the top of her class, having worked her way through school by washing dishes, working in the school library, and teaching. After college, she worked as a law clerk, schoolteacher, and a principal in Mason City, Iowa. In 1883, at the age of 24, she became one of the first women to be appointed superintendent of schools. In February 1885, Lane married Leo Chapman, editor and publisher of the *Mason City Republican,* who died of typhoid fever the following year in San Francisco, California, after going there to seek new employment. Arriving a few days after her husband's death, the young widow decided to remain in San Francisco, where she eked out a living as the city's first female newspaper reporter.

In 1887, Chapman returned to Charles City, Iowa, and joined the Iowa Woman Suffrage Association as a professional writer, lecturer, and recording secretary. From 1890 to 1892, she served as the Iowa association's state organizer. In June 1890, Chapman married George Catt, a fellow Iowa State alumnus she had met during her stay in San Francisco who encouraged her SUFFRAGE activity. During this time, Catt also began to work nationally for NAWSA, speaking in 1890 at its Washington, D.C., convention.

Her writing and speaking engagements established her reputation as a leading suffragist. In 1892, she was asked by SUSAN B. ANTHONY to address Congress on the proposed suffrage amendment. In 1900, she succeeded Anthony as NAWSA president. From then on, her time was spent primarily in speechmaking, planning campaigns, organizing women, and gaining political experience.

In 1902, Catt helped to organize the International Woman Suffrage Alliance (IWSA), which eventually incorporated sympathetic associations in 32 nations. In 1904, she resigned her NAWSA presidency in order to care for her ailing husband. Grief-stricken over the deaths of George Catt (October 1905) and Susan B. Anthony (February 1906), Catt was encouraged by her doctor and her friends to travel abroad. As a result, she spent much of the following nine years as IWSA president promoting equal-suffrage rights worldwide.

In 1915, Catt returned home to resume the leadership of NAWSA, which had become badly divided under Dr. ANNA HOWARD SHAW. In 1916, at a NAWSA convention in Atlantic City, New Jersey, Catt unveiled her WINNING PLAN to campaign simultaneously for suffrage on both the state and federal levels, and to compromise on partial suffrage in the states resisting change. Under Catt's leadership, NAWSA won the backing of both houses of Congress, as well as state support for the amendment's ratification. In 1917, New York passed a state woman suffrage referendum, and by 1918, President Woodrow Wilson was finally converted to the cause. On August 26, 1920, the Nineteenth Amendment officially became part of the U.S. Constitution.

Stepping down from the presidency of NAWSA after this victory, Catt continued her work for equal suffrage, founding the new LEAGUE OF WOMEN VOTERS and serving as its honorary president for the rest of her life. In 1923, she published *Woman Suffrage and Politics: The Inner Story of the Suffrage Movement*. In her later years, Catt's interests broadened to include

Carrie Chapman Catt (LIBRARY OF CONGRESS)

the causes of world peace and child labor. She founded the National Committee on the Cause and Cure of War, serving as its chairperson until 1932 and honorary chair thereafter. She also actively supported the League of Nations. Honored and praised by countless institutions for her half-century of public service, she died of heart failure in New Rochelle, New York, on March 9, 1947.

Further Reading

Catt, Carrie Chapman, and Nettie Rogers Shuler. *Woman Suffrage and Politics: The Inner Story of the Suffrage Movement*. New York: C. Scribner's Sons, 1923.

James, Edward T., Janet Wilson James, and Paul S. Boyner, eds. "Catt, Carrie Chapman." In *Notable American Women 1607–1950: A Biographical*

Dictionary, Vol. I, 309–313. Cambridge, Mass.: The Belknap Press of Harvard University Press, 1971.

Van Voris, Jacqueline. *Carrie Chapman Catt: A Public Life.* New York: Feminist Press at the City University of New York, 1987.

—Paula Casey

Center for American Women and Politics (CAWP)

The Center for American Women and Politics (CAWP) was founded in 1971 and operates as a unit of the Eagleton Institute of Politics at Rutgers, the State University of New Jersey. CAWP serves as a bridge between academic research on women in politics and practitioners. CAWP's major programs include maintaining the National Information Bank on Women in Public Office; conducting national forums for women in public office with special focus on projects dedicated to increasing the numbers of Latina, African-American, and young women in office; providing training seminars for women candidates; doing educational outreach to faculty engaged in teaching women and politics courses; and conducting and disseminating research on major issues involving women in public office. The organization's Web site is an excellent resource for scholars and those interested in learning more about women and American politics: www.cawp.rutgers.edu.

Center for Women Policy Studies

The Center for Women Policy Studies was founded in 1972 as the nation's first feminist policy research organization. The center is dedicated to multiethnic and multicultural feminist research, policy analysis, and advocacy to bring women's voices into contemporary public policy debates. The center works directly with state legislators to bring about public policy favorable to women's interests and utilizes the results of research projects to help shape legislation and public policy. Issues include: women and ACQUIRED IMMUNODEFICIENCY SYNDROME (AIDS), violence against women and girls, welfare reform, access to health care, educational equity, work/family and workplace diversity policies, reproductive rights and health, and trafficking in women and girls. The organization maintains a Web site at www.centerwomenpolicy.org.

Chapman, Maria Weston (1806–1885) *abolitionist*

Maria Weston Chapman was a prominent leader in both female and mixed abolitionist societies, as well as a principal organizer of antislavery bazaars. Born on July 25, 1806, in Weymouth Massachusetts, she was sent to England for her schooling. Upon returning to America, she became principal of Ebenezer Bailey's Young Ladies' High School. In 1830, she married the businessman Henry Chapman.

Shortly after her marriage, Chapman took on a leadership role in the antislavery cause in Boston, founding the Boston Female Anti-Slavery Society in 1833 with 11 other women, including three of her four sisters (Caroline, Deborah, and Anne). Chapman's abolitionist organization had humble beginnings, but it quickly fostered a sizable membership. She also organized and managed large women-run antislavery fairs in Boston, which proved to be a lucrative source of funds for abolitionists. Chapman, however, did not restrict herself to female antislavery organizations; she took on executive positions in both the Massachusetts and American Anti-Slavery Societies. The support she showed for the radical and controversial abolitionist William Lloyd Garrison, coupled with a leadership style that was commonly perceived by her peers as authoritarian, frequently brought her into disagreements with other antislavery activists. In 1837 a group of conservative clergy published a pastoral letter condemning female abolitionists for departing from their traditional spheres. In response, Maria Chapman wrote a satirical poem, "The Times that Try Men's Souls," publishing it under the name "The Lords of Creation." "Confusion has seized us, and all things go wrong, / The women have leaped from 'their spheres.' / And instead of fixed stars, shoot as comets along, / And are setting the world by their ears! / . . . So freely they move in their chosen elipse, / The 'Lords of Creation' / do fear an eclipse."

The Philadelphia Anti-Slavery Convention of 1838 was the only time Maria Chapman spoke in public, and that was only to introduce fellow abolitionist ANGELINA GRIMKÉ. In 1840, Chapman was selected to join LYDIA MARIA CHILD and LUCRETIA MOTT on the executive committee of the American Anti-Slavery Society. She was also chosen as a Massachusetts delegate to the world antislavery convention held in London that year. She did not attend.

Three daughters and a son were born to Maria and Henry Chapman between 1831 and 1840. Their youngest daughter and Henry Chapman himself fell ill with tuberculosis and died in 1842. Six years after her husband's death, Maria Chapman traveled to Europe, where she bolstered the popularity of the American antislavery movement abroad. She enrolled her three surviving children in school: son Henry in Heidelberg and both daughters in Paris. When Henry completed his education, she returned to the United States in 1855 and continued her support for the abolitionist movement. When the Civil War broke out, all of Maria Chapman's sisters joined her in Weymouth. Upon issuance of the Emancipation Proclamation in 1863, Maria worked with William Lloyd Garrison to disband the antislavery organizations. She spent her remaining years devoted to educating former slaves.

Maria Weston Chapman broke from prescribed gender expectations through her active leadership in the antislavery cause and questioned the limitations placed on the role of women in American politics. Through her public leadership role within the ABOLITIONIST MOVEMENT and the financial skills she demonstrated through her work in antislavery fairs, she helped legitimize the role of women in political campaigns. Maria Chapman died of heart disease on July 12, 1885. She is buried in the family plot, along with all of her sisters, in Weymouth, Massachusetts.

Further Reading
Pease, Jane H., and William H. Pease. "The Boston Bluestocking: Maria Weston Chapman." In *Bound with Them in Chains: A Biographical History of the Antislavery Movement.* Westport, Conn.: Greenwood, 1972, 28–59.
Taylor, Clare. *Women of the Anti-Slavery Movement: The Weston Sisters.* New York: St. Martins, 1995.

—David M. Greenspoon

Chicago, Judy (Judith Cohen) (1939–   ) *painter, sculptor, installation artist*   Judy Chicago was born Judith Cohen in Chicago, Illinois, on July 20, 1939. Studying at the University of California, she received her B.A. degree Phi Beta Kappa in 1962 and her master's degree in 1964. She taught at the University of California–Los Angeles (UCLA) until 1969 and formally adopted the name of her home city the following year. Chicago was already a working artist, when, with Canadian-born artist Miriam Schapiro, she established an arts-based education program for women—the Feminist Studio Workshop—at California State University in 1970. The program produced the first art installation that was decidedly and unabashedly feminist in perspective: *Womanhouse* (1972). It has been cited as one of the strongest inspirations for the creation of a worldwide feminist art movement.

Chicago's woman-centered and woman-inspired art turned to history two years later, and she began work on what would become her most noted—and most controversial—project: *The Dinner Party.* Realized between 1974 and 1979 (with the assistance of hundreds of volunteers), *The Dinner Party* was a room-sized multimedia installation that stood as a symbolic representation of women in the history of Western civilization. Traveling to venues across six countries, the exhibit—a triangular table set for 39 women on a floor marked with the names of almost a thousand others—was well-attended and received critical acclaim. Both *The Dinner Party* and Chicago's role in the creation of the feminist art movement was celebrated in 1996 at the UCLA Museum, and a comprehensive catalog was released by the University of California Press to accompany it.

The Birth Project was Chicago's next large artistic undertaking. Similar to *The Dinner Party* in both breadth and scope, *The Birth Project* spoke to the art world's lack of imagery around the subject of birthing and sought to compile a collection of representations and present them in needlework form. Exhibited in over 100 venues, *The Birth Project* lasted for five years (from 1980 to 1985). Pieces from the collection have been conserved and are still on exhibit in public collections across the United States. During this period, Chicago also worked on a solo project—a series of pieces created with various types of media that deconstructed notions of men, masculinity, and power. Called *Powerplay*, the series of drawings, paintings, and sculpture critiqued the construction of gender in relationships of power in the Western world.

The year 1993 marked Chicago's next large artistic undertaking. *The Holocaust Project: From Darkness into Light* opened at the Spertus Museum in Chicago that year, and it continues to be shown in museums across the country to this day. Materializing from almost a decade of research, travel, and artistic creation, *The Holocaust Project* merged Chicago's multimedia (and collaborative) work with Donald Woodman's photography to create a visual and textual representation of the Holocaust that spoke not only about the event but also to a larger human experience.

By the time the millennium arrived, Chicago had already received three honorary doctoral degrees from Russell Sage College, New York (1992), from Smith College, Northampton, Massachusetts, and from Lehigh University in Bethlehem, Pennsylvania (2000). In 1996, she became the first living artist included in the archives of the Arthur and Elizabeth Schlesinger Library on the History of Women in America at Radcliffe College in Cambridge, Massachusetts. She was also the 1999 recipient of the UCLA Alumni Professional Achievement Award. Judy Chicago's enormous body of work, including installations like *Menstruation Bathroom* (1971), collaborative projects like *Resolutions: A Stitch in Time* (begun in 1994), university-based and developed works like *At Home* (2001), and her two autobiographies (1975's *Through the Flower: My Struggle as a Woman Artist* and 1996's *Beyond the Flower: The Autobiography of a Feminist Artist*) all illustrate a strong, fiercely feminist artist determined to use her craft for social change. Pushing the borders of traditional notions of gender and sexuality through artistic expression, Judy Chicago has garnered well-earned respect as an artist, teacher, writer, and social activist. Today Chicago is the founding artist of Through the Flower, a nonprofit feminist art organization housed at Rutgers University and dedicated to raising awareness of the feminist art movement.

—Candis Steenbergen

Child, Lydia Maria (1802–1880) *author, abolitionist, suffragist* A popular 19th-century author and reformer, Lydia Maria Child was born Lydia Francis on February 11, 1802. She added Maria as a middle name in 1822 and married abolitionist David Lee Child in 1828. Lydia Child was a prolific author, producing more than 50 books between the years 1824 and 1868, including historical fiction, novels, and domestic advice manuals. These works included the commercially successful *American Frugal Housewife* (1829), *The Mother's Book* (1831), and *Good Wives* (1832). She also authored numerous articles, poems, and short stories; edited collections of poetry and prose; and edited several periodicals, including *Juvenile Miscellany* (1826–34).

As an active abolitionist, reformer, and women's rights activist, Child was identified by fellow abolitionist William Lloyd Garrison as "the first woman in the Republic." In 1833,

Child published *An Appeal in Favor of that Class of Americans Called Africans,* a work she described as the first antislavery tract in favor of immediate emancipation. Although she is perhaps best known today as the editor of *Incidents in the Life of a Slave Girl* (1861), an autobiographical novel by former slave Harriet Jacobs, Child's peers recognized her as the author of numerous antislavery works over the course of three decades. After the Civil War, Child turned her reform impulses toward the treatment of freedmen and, later, Native Americans. Lydia Maria Child died on October 20, 1880.

Further Reading

Holland, Patricia G., Milton Meltzer, and Francine Krasno, eds. *The Collected Correspondence of Lydia Maria Child, 1817–1880.* Millwood, N.Y.: Kraus Microform, 1980.

Karcher, Carolyn. *The First Woman in the Republic: A Cultural Biography of Lydia Maria Child.* Durham, N.C.: Duke University Press, 1994.

—Laura Tuennerman-Kaplan

child care Unlike workers in other industrialized countries, wage-earning parents in the United States have never had access to adequate and affordable care for their children. When care was offered, it took the form of state assistance or charitable philanthropy rather than a benefit of employment. From the 1870s to the 1920s, day nurseries operated by benevolent organizations and reform groups—both secular and religiously affiliated—emerged as the primary child care solution in the United States. Settlement houses often provided day nurseries alongside their employment agencies to ensure greater opportunities for mothers to secure day labor. Advocates for increasing child care programs in the United States gained support from the presence of the Model Day Nursery exhibit at the World's Columbia Exhibition held in Chicago in 1893. That exposure led to the establishment of the National Federation of Day Nurseries (NFDN) in 1898, with affiliated chapters and associations forming during this period. Philanthropist Josephine Jewell (Mrs. Arthur) Dodge—who had founded two day nurseries in New York City—served as a leader in child care advocacy, and the number of day nurseries grew from about 175 at the turn of the century to 700 by 1916. Yet facilities remained segregated by race and ethnicity, and groups such as the NATIONAL ASSOCIATION OF COLORED WOMEN, Catholic Charities, and the National Council of Jewish Women devoted much attention to providing day-care resources for families turned away from "white only" centers.

During periods of economic stress, especially during the Great Depression and World War II, the federal government offered states some funding to provide child care facilities but these actions never came close to filling parental needs for child care; in fact, often funds were directed at employing adults and not in providing care for children. The Franklin D. Roosevelt administration directed Works Progress Administration monies toward emergency nursery schools to employ out-of-work teachers. In 1941, Congress passed the Lanham Act, which provided funds to build facilities, but eligibility for funding was limited to centers known as "war nurseries," which serviced federal, defense-contracted workers. Similarly private child care emerged during World War II. In 1943, the Kaiser Shipyards opened a child care center at the entrance of each of their two yards. The centers were open 24 hours a day, employed physicians and nurses to care for ill children, and provided hot meals for women to take home with them when they collected their children. The purpose of Kaiser's centers was to reduce absenteeism among employees who were mothers. After the war, the Kaiser centers closed, and the federal government withdrew all its support for child care, instructing women to quit work, go home, and take care of their children. Although there was some initial dip in the percentage of women with children in the workforce immediately following World War II, women never fully left the workforce, nor did they ever again embrace the traditional model of women relegated to the private sphere of the home. In 1947, slightly over one-fourth of all mothers with children between the ages of 6 and 17 remained in the labor force. By contrast, over 75 percent of mothers with children were in the workforce, and 64 percent with children under six years of age were working in 2000. The need for high-quality, affordable child care has only grown.

Very little federal attention was paid to child care in the postwar era. One exception was the Comprehensive Child Development Act of 1971 (CCDA). Sponsored by two Democrats, Senator Walter Mondale (Minnesota) and Representative John Brademas (Indiana), the measure called for low-income families to receive free child care and all other families to pay for care on a sliding scale. Congress passed the bill, but the veto by President Richard M. Nixon signaled its ultimate fate. The public's reaction to the government's sponsorship of "out-of-home" daycare reflected the co-optation of the issue by the ideological right. State-sponsored day care had become "Sovietized" in the minds of many Americans, and any national debate about the fundamental need for day care was muted.

In the 1990s, when it was evident that women's participation in the full-time work force not only included the majority of women and women with small children, but that women would work throughout the course of their lifetime rather than for a short time before marriage and children, the federal government began to reexamine the issue. Congress passed the Child Care and Development Act in 1990. Consistent with other "new federalism" programs of the decade, the legislature authorized funding in the form of block grants to states, which allowed each state to decide how the money would best serve its needs. On the one hand, this allowed a state to experiment with child care strategies that were tailored to its unique constituencies and needs. Alternatively, by not providing uniform standards for quality, training, and services, the Child Care and Development Act did not do anything to standardize the accessibility

or quality of child care nationally. Furthermore, 75 percent of the block-grant funding was targeted for low-income families, which perpetuated the myth that child care was a class issue. In autumn 1997, the Clinton administration convened a White House Conference on Child Care. The result was a proposal to increase tax credits for child care and improve the quality and accessibility of child care centers.

For two-paycheck families, reliable, high-quality child care is scarce and exorbitantly expensive. The failure to move child care policy beyond an adjunct to public assistance means that most parents must locate and pay for a provider entirely themselves. Nearly 50 percent rely on extended family or neighbors to care for their children. An estimated 5 million children are left unsupervised after the school day ends. For most families, child care constitutes a significant expenditure: For low- and middle-income families with children between the ages of three and five, child care represents the third greatest expense after housing and food. For families with higher incomes (annual income above $66,900), it represents the second greatest expense after housing. The price of child care can easily run between $4,000 and $10,000 annually. In 2006, two parents working full-time at the minimum wage can expect to earn a combined yearly income of $21,000. In 48 states, the cost of center-based childcare for a four-year-old is greater than tuition at a four-year public college.

Without subsidies from the government or employers, the private market delivers what people require at a price they can afford by sacrificing the quality of care. Low-cost day care results in low wages for child care workers. Low wages are directly correlated with high staff turnover (over 30 percent a year on average nationwide). Low pay for preschool teachers means that centers cannot recruit and retain the best workers, nor can teachers employed at substandard wages afford to seek additional training and education. An underclass of child care workers, often mothers themselves and most recently welfare mothers forced into the job market, completes the circle of inadequate resources for inadequate care. In the late 1990s, the starting salary for day-care teachers with a college degree was about $16,000. Nonprofessional starting salaries rarely run higher than minimum wage. Middle- and lower-income families lack sufficient resources to support high-quality day-care centers without government or employer subsidies.

Subsidies for the cost of child care are very limited. In a number of states, the income eligibility cutoffs for child care assistance are so restrictive that the working poor do not qualify. For example, a family of three in Missouri earning above $17,784 cannot qualify for child care assistance. Inadequate funds at the state level mean long waiting lists. For example, in 2005 there were over 48,800 children on the waiting list in Florida, 26,500 in Texas, and over 20,000 in Tennessee. Despite research demonstrating the importance of early learning to a child's development, public investments in education and development are more than seven times greater during school-aged years than during the early learning years. Business has not stepped in to fill the gap. A survey of over 1,000 American companies found that only 9 percent of businesses with 100 or more employees offer on-site child care, even though extant studies and statistics confirm that the benefits of on-site day care are vast: It aids in recruiting and retaining high-quality workers, particularly women; enhances productivity; heightens employee morale; and provides employers with a competitive edge in a changing labor market. Privatizing child care—arguably a public good—leaves parents to bear the bulk of early child care costs without any public accountability for adequate provision and quality of child care services. This will remain a central public policy issue for women and men with children for the foreseeable future.

Further Reading

Michel, Sonya. *Children's Interests/Mothers' Rights: The Shaping of America's Child Care Policy.* New Haven, Conn.: Yale University Press, 1999.

Rose, Elizabeth R. *A Mother's Job: The History of Day Care, 1890–1960.* New York: Oxford University Press, 1999.

Shibley, Janey Hyde, and Marilyn J. Essex, eds. *Parental Leave and Child Care: Setting a Research and Policy Agenda.* Philadelphia: Temple University Press, 1991.

Stoltzfus, Emilie. *Citizen, Mother, Worker: Debating Public Responsibility for Child Care after the Second World War.* Chapel Hill: University of North Carolina Press, 2003.

—Kyle E. Ciani

Child Support Enforcement Amendment

(1984) The Child Support Enforcement Amendment of 1984 was an amendment to the Social Security Amendments of 1974, which created a state-federal child-support enforcement program. The 1984 act gave states the authority to enact and test innovative approaches to child-support enforcement and collection as long as the modifications did not have an impact on disadvantaged children in need of support. Under the 1984 act, states were granted waivers to implement models of interstate collaboration among Child Support Enforcement (CSE) agencies and the ability to test new ways of reviewing and modifying child-support enforcement orders. In addition, the act allowed states to address and examine CSE case history with domestic violence, continued assurance, and noncustodial parental access to visitation. Waivers were granted to states to address fatherhood initiatives, job-training programs, parenting classes, interviewing and client referral, and paternity test establishment. The act also allocated funds for states to address CSE program performance and improvement. County governments are required to administer Child Support Enforcement programs that are in accordance with state rules and regulations regarding programs and staffing requirements. At the federal level, the Health and Human Services assistant secretary for children and families has full responsibility for the evaluation of Child Support Enforcement programs.

—Scott A. Shelton

chilly climate The term *chilly climate* is used to describe an unwelcoming or hostile environment women often face in educational settings and the business world, or as pioneers entering nontraditional occupations. Although many overt barriers to women's participation in public life have been eliminated, women still face challenges in trying to achieve full sociopolitical integration and equality. The "chilly climate" refers to an environment in which women and girls are treated differently from men in ways that are designed to send the signal that they are not welcome. Forms of this discrimination may include valuing male comments or behaviors over those of women in the classroom, defining criteria for promotion in ways that privilege traditional male qualities or activities over those of women, engaging in a form of stereotyping that devalues women's intelligence and undermines their self-confidence, and/or privileging gender behavior consistent with traditional role expectations and punishing inconsistent behavior. The use of "chilly climate" is now also used to describe a hostile or unwelcoming environment for racial or ethnic minorities.

See also GLASS CEILING; GLASS CEILING COMMISSION.

Further Reading

Hopkins, Nancy. "MIT and Gender Bias: Following Up on Victory." *Chronicle of Higher Education* 45, no. 40 (1999). Available online. URL: www.chronicle.com/colloquy/99/genderbias/background.htm.

Orenstein, Peggy. *Schoolgirls: Young Women, Self-esteem and the Confidence Gap.* New York: Anchor Books, 1995.

Chisholm, Shirley (Shirley Anita St. Hill Chisholm) (1924–2005) *congressperson, activist, author* Shirley Chisholm represents a number of firsts in American politics, chiefly being the first African-American woman elected to Congress and the first African-American woman to seek the presidential nomination. Born Shirley Anita St. Hill in Brooklyn, New York, on November 30, 1924, to immigrant parents from Guyana and Barbados, Chisholm was educated in both the Caribbean and the United States. After receiving a B.A. in sociology from Brooklyn College (1946), she went on to teach nursery school in New York City and also pursued and completed a master's degree in elementary education at Columbia University (1952). At Columbia, she met and married a Jamaican American, Conrad Q. Chisholm.

Shirley Chisholm, announcing her candidacy for presidential nomination, January 1972 (LIBRARY OF CONGRESS)

Renowned for her oratory, a skill honed while attending Brooklyn College, Chisholm expressed her desire to enter the public arena by saying, "Service is the rent we pay for the privilege of living on this earth." Her decision to enter public office and the causes she believed in were influenced by a number of experiences and events. During Chisholm's public tenure, she was respected for her unfailing commitment to women's rights, fighting racism, and ending poverty. Being a woman coupled with race and being elected in 1968 to Congress from a predominantly poor community (New York's twelfth district) made Chisholm keenly and directly aware of the discrimination, oppression, and exploitation these various groups faced.

Equal rights for women were near and dear to Chisholm's heart. She was one of the cofounders of the NATIONAL ORGANIZATION FOR WOMEN (NOW), a strong defender of abortion rights, and a supporter of the EQUAL RIGHTS AMENDMENT. Addressing the U.S. House of Representatives in 1969 concerning why equal rights legislation for women was necessary, Chisholm observed that "as a black person, I am no stranger to race prejudice. But the truth is that in the political world I have been far oftener discriminated against because I am a woman than because I am black." She went on to point out that if women were indeed equal, "why is it such an event whenever one [woman] happens to be elected to Congress?" After her election victory, Chisholm hired a staff of all women. This was a distinctive statement to the Washington power structure that women needed to be included in decision making, given that they made up half of the U.S. population.

Among minorities and the working class, Chisholm was celebrated for her unrelenting efforts to ensure equal education access. This was evident in her fight for improved education programs and expansion of day care for inner-city youth. Two of her most famous accomplishments in the area of education came during her tenure in the New York State Assembly (1964–67). Chisholm's concern about inner-city youth being able to attend college regardless

of income became a reality in 1966 with the implementation of SEEK (Search for Education, Elevation, and Knowledge), a program that provided college funding to disadvantaged youths. Additionally, Chisholm authored legislation that secured unemployment insurance for domestics and day-care providers.

During her career in Congress, Chisholm was a member of the Education and Labor Committee, where she campaigned for a higher minimum wage and federal funding for day-care facilities. Based on her fierce commitment to improving and providing resources to the poor and disadvantaged, Chisholm consistently vowed to defeat any bill proposed by the Nixon administration to increase defense funding.

In 1972, Chisholm made her historic declaration for the presidency of the United States. She declared herself a "candidate of the people" who was "unbought and unbossed." Despite her unsuccessful bid for the presidency, Chisholm maintained that this should not discourage women from running for office. She encouraged young women around the country to "feel themselves as capable of running for high political office as any wealthy, good-looking white male."

Upon her retirement from Congress in 1983, Chisholm remained active on the lecture circuit and joined the faculty of Mount Holyoke College from 1983 to 1987. In 1993, she was nominated by President Clinton to serve as U.S. ambassador to Jamaica. Shirley Chisholm died on January 1, 2005.

Further Reading
Chisholm, Shirley. *Unbought and Unbossed: An Autobiography.* New York: Houghton Mifflin Co., 1970.
Pollack, Jill S. *Shirley Chisholm.* New York: Franklin Watts, 1994.

—Hollis France

Christian-Christensen, Donna (1945–)

congressional delegate Donna Christian-Christensen, congressional delegate from the Virgin Islands and a member of an old St. Croix family, was born in Teaneck, New Jersey, on September 19, 1945. She attended St. Mary's College in Indiana and then went on to attend George Washington University School of Medicine, in Washington, D.C., earning her M.D. She interned at Pacific Medical Center in San Francisco, California, from 1970 to 1971 and did her residency in family medicine at Howard University Medical Center from 1973 to 1974. She became a board-certified physician in 1977 and served as medical director for the St. Croix Hospital in the Virgin Islands.

As a registered member of the Democratic Party of the Virgin Islands, Christian-Christensen has served as a Democratic national committeewoman, member of the Democratic Territorial Committee, delegate to Democratic Conventions from 1984 to present, and member of the Platform Committee of the Democratic National Committee from 1988 to the present. She was elected to the Virgin Islands Board of Education from 1984 to 1986 and was appointed as a member to the Virgin Islands Status Commission from 1988 to 1992.

Christian-Christensen was elected as a Democrat to the U.S. House of Representatives in 1997. She serves on the Committee on Resources Subcommittee on National Parks, where she is the ranking Democrat. She also serves on the Small Businesses Subcommittee on Regulatory Reform and Oversight, which oversees federal regulations on small businesses, and on Homeland Security's Subcommittees on Emergency Preparedness, Science and Technology; Management, Integration and Oversight; and Prevention of Nuclear and Biological Attack. She is a member of the Congressional Black Caucus and works on health issues within the caucus.

Further Reading

Barone, Michael. *The Almanac of American Politics.* Washington, D.C.: National Journal Group, 2006.
"Christensen, Donna Marie Christian." *Biographical Directory of the United States Congress, 1774–present.* Available online. URL: http://bioguide.congress.gov/scripts/biodisplay.pl?index=C000380. Accessed on January 8, 2007.
"Delegate Donna M. C. Christian-Christensen (VI). In *Project Vote Smart.* Available online. URL: http://votesmart.org/bio.php?can_id=BC032620. Accessed on January 8, 2007.

—Angela Kouters

Citizens' Advisory Council on the Status of Women (CACSW) (1963)

President Lyndon B. Johnson created the Citizens' Advisory Council on the Status of Women (CACSW) by executive order in 1963 to promote and seek the implementation of the recommendations of the late John F. Kennedy's PRESIDENT'S COMMISSION ON THE STATUS OF WOMEN (PCSW). The CACSW and the Interdepartmental Committee on the Status of Women (ICSW), like the PCSW, were located in and administratively supported by the WOMEN'S BUREAU, U.S. Department of Labor. The CACSW, chaired by Margaret Hickey (former national president of the Business and Professional Women's Clubs) and composed of former members of the PCSW, maintained a nascent women's rights coalition emerging through relationships among commission members and state commissions on the status of women. National conferences convened by the Women's Bureau and PCSW institutions brought committed feminist activists together in a national forum on a yearly basis. The NATIONAL ORGANIZATION FOR WOMEN was formed in 1966 during the third annual conference of state commissions on the status of women.

Further Reading

Cobble, Dorothy Sue. *The Other Women's Movement: Workplace Justice and Social Rights in Modern America.* Princeton, N.J.: Princeton University Press, 2004.
Harrison, Cynthia. *On Account of Sex: The Politics of Women's Issues, 1945–1968.* Berkeley: University of California Press, 1988.
Hartmann, Susan M. *From Margin to Mainstream: American Women and Politics Since 1960.* New York: Alfred Knopf, 1989.

—Kathleen A. Laughlin

citizenship, restrictions for women *Citizenship* most often refers to those in society with civil and political rights and standing to make claims against the state for the protection of both. SEPARATE SPHERES IDEOLOGY subsumed women's claims for civil and political rights. Single women, although subject to taxation by the state, held few rights within the state. Married women's status as *femmes coverts* (women "covered" entirely by their husbands' legal identity) meant that they were incapable of an independent relationship with the state and therefore were not considered full citizens. COVERTURE, imported to the colonies from the English legal tradition, defined the legal relationship between husband and wife. English jurist William Blackstone wrote: "By marriage, the husband and wife are one person in law: that is, the very being or legal existence of the woman is suspended during the marriage, or at least is incorporated and consolidated into that of the husband; under whose wing, protection and *cover,* she performs every thing . . . [she] is said to be covert-baron, or under the protection and influence of her husband, her baron, or lord; and her condition upon marriage is called her *coverture.*"

As a practical matter, coverture made the husband and wife one person—the husband. A married woman could not execute contracts independent of her husband, nor could she buy or sell property, dispose of personal assets like jewelry and household items, control the destiny of her children, or serve as their guardian without her husband's consent. Marital rape was inconceivable because husband and wife were one person. It was not until 1978, when New York included a spouse along with a stranger and an acquaintance in the list of perpetrators of rape, that marital rape was outlawed anywhere in the United States. Although women might have been citizens in a conceptual sense, marriage took away the privileges of citizenship in a real sense.

In 1907, Congress passed a law stating that women who married aliens lost their citizenship even if they remained in the United States. The

Supreme Court upheld the law as late as 1915, ruling in *Mackenzie v. Hare* that if a woman voluntarily married an alien, she must give up her citizenship and adopt the nationality of her husband. This law remained in effect until passage of the CABLE ACT of 1922, which stated that, "the right of a person to become a naturalized citizen shall not be denied to a person on account of sex or because she is a married woman." Even then, however, the law covered only marriages to men who were eligible to become naturalized citizens (excluding men from China or Japan, among others). American-born women who married aliens were treated as naturalized citizens who could lose their citizenship if they lived abroad for two or more years. Revisions to the Cable Act in the 1930s and subsequent legislation have made married women's citizenship completely independent of their husbands'.

Further Reading
Cott, Nancy F. *Public Vows: A History of Marriage and the Nation.* Cambridge, Mass.: Harvard University Press, 2002.
Hoff, Joan. *Law, Gender, and Injustice: A Legal History of the United States,* New York: New York University Press, 1991.

Civil Rights Act of 1964   The Civil Rights Act of 1964 provided the strongest tool to combat discrimination in employment, education, and public accommodations. First sent to Congress by President John F. Kennedy in 1963, the legislation stalled in a legislature controlled by southern Democrats. Not until Lyndon Johnson assumed the presidency following Kennedy's assassination was there real effort applied to winning its passage.

The law was primarily intended to eliminate racial discrimination, but in TITLE VII OF THE CIVIL RIGHTS ACT OF 1964, sex was included along with the other protected categories of race, color, religion, or national origin. Now singularly powerful in combating gender discrimination in employment, Title VII resulted from an amendment offered by Congressman Howard Smith, a conservative southern Democrat from Virginia. Smith was determined to undermine the prohibitions against race discrimination at the core of the act by suggesting that men and women should be treated equally in the workplace. He was sure that the inclusion of sex would derail the bill. While accounts of his precise motivations vary, the Smith amendment did, in fact, survive to become one of the most powerful federal protections against employment discrimination that extended to cover sex as well as race. The Civil Rights Act of 1964 created the EQUAL EMPLOYMENT OPPORTUNITY COMMISSION (EEOC) as the enforcement agency. The EEOC is charged with investigating allegations of employment discrimination, and since an amendment in 1972, it is empowered to bring lawsuits against employers.

The law has since been amended three times. The first change extended the authority of the EEOC and expanded coverage to include public employers and educational institutions. The second amendment, known as the PREGNANCY DISCRIMINATION ACT (1978), declared that classifications based on pregnancy and pregnancy-related disabilities fall within the meaning of "sex" under Title VII. Third, the CIVIL RIGHTS ACT OF 1991 amended Title VII to reverse the effects of several Supreme Court rulings in the late 1980s that made job discrimination suits harder to win.

Further Reading

Jasper, Margaret C. *Employment Discrimination Under Title VII.* New York: Oceana Publications Inc, 1999.

Civil Rights Act of 1991   The Civil Rights Act of 1991 was designed to reverse a number of U.S. Supreme Court decisions from the late 1980s that significantly narrowed the scope of federal antidiscrimination laws as they applied to employment. Congress passed a similar bill in 1990 (the Civil Rights Act of 1990) with biparti-

san support and a number of Republican cosponsors, but President George H. W. Bush vetoed the legislation, labeling it a "quota bill." Slight adjustments to the bill and an election year looming led President Bush to sign the 1991 act.

Congress initiated both acts in response to the Supreme Court's decisions in *Ward's Cove Packing Company, Inc v. Antonio* (1989), *Patterson v. McLean Credit Union* (1989), *Price Waterhouse v. Hopkins* (1989), and *Martin v. Wilks* (1989). These cases involved challenges to hiring decisions under TITLE VII OF THE CIVIL RIGHTS ACT OF 1964 and claims of workplace discrimination brought under Section 1981 of the Civil Rights Act of 1866. Congress believed that each of these decisions made it more difficult for women and minorities to prove discrimination and harassment in the conditions of employment and in the hiring and firing policies of private corporations. Specifically, the decision in *Ward's Cove* made it more difficult for employees to prove that the company's hiring decisions, while seemingly neutral, had an illegal disparate impact on them because they now had to identify the particular policy or practice and show that it alone had produced the unlawful effect. The employer now only had to offer, rather than prove, a business justification for practices that produced a disparate impact on minorities and women. The 1991 Act allowed employees to prove their case by showing that employment practices had resulted in a disparate impact, and the employer was once again required to prove that the practice in question was a "business necessity." To avoid the "quota" label that doomed the 1990 act, Congress added, "The mere existence of statistical imbalance in an employer's workforce on account of race, color, religion, sex, or national origin is not alone sufficient to establish a prima facie case of disparate impact violation." The *Patterson* case limited employees' ability to sue for on-the-job racial discrimination because of the Supreme Court's narrow interpretation of the relevant clause in Section 1981, "make or enforce contracts," to mean hiring or firing only. Therefore, an employee who suffered discrimination on the basis of race in promotion or other advancement decisions was not covered. Congress amended the phrase in the 1991 act to cover "the enjoyment of all employment benefits, privileges, terms and conditions of the contractual relationship." Congress also expanded the remedies available to plaintiffs under the 1964 Civil Rights Act. The 1991 Act allows for a jury trial and for actions designed to recover both compensatory and punitive damages up to a limit of $300,000.

Finally, Title II of the Civil Rights Act of 1991 created the 21-member, bipartisan Federal GLASS CEILING COMMISSION. The commission's mandate was to study the barriers to the advancement of minorities and women within corporate hierarchies (the problem known as the GLASS CEILING), to issue a report on its findings and conclusions, and to make recommendations on ways to dismantle the glass ceiling.

Clark, Septima (Septima Poinsette Clark)

(1898–1987) *civil rights leader* Septima Clark was born Septima Poinsette on May 3, 1898, in Charleston, South Carolina. Upon graduating from Avery Normal Institute in 1916, Poinsette accepted a teaching position on John's Island, chiefly because black teachers were banned from the public schools of Charleston. In 1919, she returned to Charleston to teach at Avery Normal and joined the National Association for the Advancement of Colored People (NAACP). The following year, she successfully campaigned for a state law that allowed blacks to teach in Charleston's black public schools.

In 1920, Poinsette married seaman Nerie Clark. The marriage produced two children, with only the son surviving. Nerie Clark died in 1925. After returning to John's Island for two years, Septima Clark taught in the public schools of Columbia and Charleston. She earned a B.A. in English from Benedict College in 1942 and an M.A. from Hampton Institute in 1946. In 1954, the South Carolina legislature passed a law that no city or state employee could be

affiliated with a civil rights organization. At this time, Clark was serving as Charleston NAACP membership chair. Unlike many others, she refused to renounce her membership and lost her job as well as her pension. A proponent of nonviolence, she taught citizenship education at the Highlander Folk School in Monteagle, Tennessee before moving to the Southern Christian Leadership Council (SCLC) in 1961 as director of education. She died on December 15, 1987.

Clark viewed the problem of race as more significant than the problem of sex. Although she suffered and complained about discrimination by male civil rights leaders, as the first woman elected to the Executive Board of SCLC, she never focused on the specific problems of women.

Further Reading

Brown, Cynthia Stokes, ed. *Ready from Within: Septima Clark and the Civil Rights Movement.* Navarro, Calif.: Wild Trees Press, 1986.

Clark, Septima. *Echo in My Soul.* New York: E. P. Dutton, 1962.

McFadden, Grace Jordan. "Septima P. Clark and the Struggle for Human Rights." In *Women in the Civil Rights Movement: Trailblazers and Torchbearers, 1941–1965,* edited by Vicki L. Crawford, Jacquelin Anne Rouse, and Barbara Woods, 85–97. Bloomington: Indiana University Press, 1990.

—Caryn E. Neumann

Clay, Laura (1849–1941) *suffragist* Laura Clay,

born in Madison County, Kentucky, on February 9, 1849, was the daughter of Cassius Clay, a well-known abolitionist and minister to Russia when the United States purchased Alaska. She attended the University of Michigan and graduated from Kentucky State College, now Transylvania College, in 1870. After her parents' divorce in 1878, in which her mother lost her home and all marital assets, Clay became disturbed by the lack of economic and legal rights women held in Kentucky. In 1888, she founded the Kentucky Equal Rights Association with Josephine Henry. During the 22 years Clay served as its president, the association succeeded in passing laws extending women's social and economic rights in the state.

Clay also served as the auditor of the NATIONAL AMERICAN WOMAN SUFFRAGE ASSOCIATION (NAWSA) from 1896 to 1911 and chaired its membership committee, nearly tripling the membership and establishing associations in nine southern states. However, Clay broke with NAWSA over the proposed federal constitutional amendment granting woman SUFFRAGE, arguing that each state had the right to qualify its own electors. Clay campaigned against the suffrage amendment in Nashville, Tennessee. After the Nineteenth Amendment's ratification in 1920, she continued to work for the Democratic Party and women's issues. In 1920, Clay became the first woman to receive a vote for the presidential nomination from a major party when the Democrats nominated her to honor her work in political and suffrage movements. She died on June 29, 1941.

Further Reading

Fuller, Paul E. *Laura Clay and the Woman's Rights Movement.* Lexington: The University Press of Kentucky, 1975.
Irwin, Helen D. *Women in Kentucky.* Lexington: The University Press of Kentucky, 1979.
Kentucky Department for Libraries and Archives. *Laura Clay: Early Kentucky Suffragist.* Available online. URL: http://www.kdla.ky.gov/resources/KYLauraClay.htm. Accessed on June 26, 2006.

—Julie Davis

Cleveland, Frances (Frances Clara Folsom Cleveland) (1864–1947) *first lady* Frances

Clara Folsom ("Frank" to her family) was born in Buffalo, New York, on July 21, 1864, to attorney Oscar Folsom and his wife, Emma Hamon Folsom. When Oscar Folsom died in an accident in 1875, his law partner, Grover Cleveland, became administrator of the estate. Frank was well educated as a child and enrolled in Wells College in 1832. "Uncle Cleve" kept up a lively correspondence with her while she was away at school. With her mother, she visited the White House following Cleveland's election as president in 1884. President Cleveland's sister, Rose Elizabeth Cleveland, served as his official hostess with the assistance of Harriet Lane, hostess for the previous bachelor, President James Buchanan. In August 1885, Grover Cleveland proposed to Frances, and she accepted (with her mother's approval). They were married in a small ceremony in the White House on June 2, 1886. At 21, she was the youngest first lady in history. They gave two receptions following the wedding—one for the diplomatic corps and one for the general public. Soon after they were married, they moved out of the White House to a small farmhouse just outside the city. They used the White House for work and official entertaining.

Frances Cleveland was immediately popular. The press and the public hungered for details about her, and her likeness was used on numerous product advertisements. Frances relied upon Harriet Lane for advice on entertaining and managing the affairs of the White House. She was the first presidential lady to employ a secretary to assist with her correspondence, and during Cleveland's second term, a federal clerk was assigned to assist with social planning. This marked the beginning of a staff for the first lady. Frances traveled extensively throughout the country with the president, attracting crowds of well-wishers wherever they went. In Washington, she worked with charities for the poor but refused to endorse women's SUFFRAGE. She was a strong advocate of education for women and served on the board of Wells College for more than 50 years. In a subtle change to tradition, she held Saturday afternoon receptions to enable working women to attend. She helped to found the University Women's Club and urged expansion of educational opportunities for women.

Grover Cleveland lost his bid for reelection in 1888. Upon their departure from the White House, Frances reportedly told a steward, "Now, Jerry, I want you to take good care of all the furniture and ornaments in the house, for I want to find everything just as it is now when we come back again. We are coming back just four years from today." The Clevelands moved to a house in New York and on October 3, 1891, their first child, Ruth, was born. Baby Ruth quickly became as popular as her mother, and a candy bar was named for her. In 1893, as Frances had predicted, they returned to the White House; that same year, a second daughter, Esther, was born. In her second term, she was less interested in entertaining and more dedicated to the task of raising her children. Sons Richard Folsom and Francis Grover were born in 1897 and 1903, respectively. For Grover Cleveland, his second term was marked by a significant economic depression and mouth cancer, an ailment the couple kept secret fearing more disruption to the financial markets if the news leaked out.

When the Clevelands left the White House for the second time, they bought a house in Princeton, New Jersey. Tragically, Ruth died of diphtheria in 1903. Grover Cleveland died on June 24, 1908, leaving his wife and three surviving children a sizable estate. Five years later, Frances married a Princeton archeology professor, Thomas Jex Preston, Jr. In her later years, she was active in the Women's University Club and with the National Security League during World War I. Cataract surgery restored her failing eyesight, and she enjoyed returning to the White House when invited by subsequent presidential wives. Frances Cleveland Preston died on October 29, 1947.

Further Reading

Mayo, Edith P. "Frances Cleveland." In *The Smithsonian Book of First Ladies: Their Lives, Times, and Issues,* edited by Edith P. Mayo, 131–136. New York: Henry Holt and Company, 1996.

National First Ladies Library. *Biographies: First Ladies of the United States.* Available online. URL: http://www.firstladies.org/biographies. Accessed on January 4, 2007.

Schneider, Dorothy, and Carl J. Schneider. "Frances (Frank) Folsom Cleveland." In *First Ladies: A Biographical Dictionary.* New York: Checkmark Books, 2001, 139–146.

Severn, Sue. "Frances Folsom Cleveland." In *American First Ladies,* edited by Lewis Gould, 161–169. New York: Garland, 1996.

Clinton, Hillary Rodham (Hillary Diane Rodham Clinton)
(1947–) *first lady, U.S. senator*　Hillary Diane Rodham was born in Chicago, Illinois, on October 26, 1947, to Hugh Rodham and Dorothy Howell Rodham. Hillary was the first of three children (two sons followed). Hugh Rodham ran a small textile business in Chicago. In 1950, the Rodhams moved to Park Ridge, Illinois, a conservative, Republican suburb of Chicago where Hillary attended public school. Her parents placed great value on education, and both applauded her academic achievement and encouraged her to develop career aspirations. In high school, she was active with the student council and the newspaper. Named to the National Honor Society, she graduated in the top 5 percent of her class, and was voted "most likely to succeed." Rodham was also active in her church youth group. In 1962, she and her group attended a speech by Martin Luther King, Jr., in which he urged an end to racial injustice. After the speech, Rodham was introduced to Dr. King in a moment that proved formative in developing her own voice as an activist later in life. As a high school student, her political views were consistent with the Republican community in which she lived. In 1964, she campaigned for Republican presidential nominee Barry Goldwater as a "Goldwater Girl."

In autumn 1965, Rodham enrolled at Wellesley College, where she excelled as a student and quickly became involved in campus politics and student government. At this time, her politics took on a decidedly more progressive tone. Although she interned in Washington, D.C., with Secretary of Defense Melvin Laird during the summer of 1968 and attended the Republican Party convention in Miami, supporting the nomination of Nelson

Hillary Rodham Clinton (LIBRARY OF CONGRESS)

Rockefeller, she had a change of heart before the November election. She campaigned for Senator Eugene McCarthy in the election of 1968 and took part in campus protests against the war. At Wellesley's commencement in 1969, Senator Edward Brooke (R-MA) was invited to give the address, and students encouraged the university to select a student who could articulate their views about the unrest in American society. Hillary Rodham was the chosen speaker, and although she prepared a text, she altered it during Senator Brooke's speech so that she could respond to his remarks as well as articulate her own vision of the future. "The challenge now is to practice politics as the art of making what appears to be impossible, possible," she said.

In autumn 1969, Hillary Rodham became one of 30 women in the entering class of 160 students at Yale Law School. She chose Yale over Harvard because it promoted law as an avenue for social change, a perspective consistent with her personal philosophy. As a law student, she was just as active on campus as she had been as an undergraduate at Wellesley as she prepared for a life in public service and politics. She met several future political allies, including Vernon Jordan and Peter Edelman, at a LEAGUE OF WOMEN VOTERS (LWV) conference where she was invited to speak in honor of the LWV's 50th anniversary. Peter Edelman introduced her to his wife, MARIAN WRIGHT EDELMAN, founder of the Children's Defense Fund, with whom Rodham later interned, an experience that began a lifelong commitment to improving the lives and opportunities of poor children. She also briefly worked for Senator Walter Mondale's subcommittee on migrant workers and their children. She began researching the legal aspects of how children are treated in America, a line of research and writing that would eventually be used by conservative political opponents to brand her a radical and "out of step" with mainstream American parenting philosophy. In 1972, although she was eligible for graduation, Rodham decided to apply for a children's rights program at the law school so that she could continue to study children's advocacy. She wrote an article, "Children and the Law," published in the *Harvard Educational Review,* in which she tried to establish support for "children's rights."

In 1970, Rodham met fellow law student Bill Clinton while studying in the Yale law library. She reportedly walked up to him and said, "Look, if you're going to keep staring at me, and I'm going to keep staring back, I think we should at least know each other. I'm Hillary Rodham. What's your name?" Thus began their continuing personal and political partnership. Clinton had earned his undergraduate degree from Georgetown and had held a Rhodes scholarship at Oxford before enrolling at Yale. He was very vocal about his commitment to return to his native Arkansas. When he met Rodham's parents over Christmas in 1971, they expressed some reservations over his intention to pursue politics in Arkansas. Hillary's friends, too, worried that she would "disappear" into state politics rather than pursue the national stage.

During the summer of 1972, both Clinton and Rodham campaigned for Democratic candidate George McGovern. In the process, they each began to compile a network of friends and political allies in the Democratic Party. When they graduated from Yale in spring 1973, Clinton returned to Arkansas to teach at the University of Arkansas Law School and Rodham went to work for Edelman's Children's Defense Fund in Cambridge, Massachusetts. In January 1974, she was hired as a staff attorney for the House Judiciary Committee working on the impeachment of President Richard Nixon. When Nixon resigned in August 1974, she decided to move to Arkansas, where she took a position at the University of Arkansas Law School. Bill Clinton was running for a seat in Congress, and Rodham joined the campaign writing speeches and organizing his appearances. Clinton lost the campaign, but Rodham stayed in Arkansas, and the couple were married on October 11, 1975.

After her marriage, Hillary Rodham continued to use her maiden name professionally, a decision that didn't always sit well with local constituents. Bill Clinton was elected attorney general of Arkansas in 1976, and the couple moved to Little Rock, Arkansas. In Little Rock, Rodham pursued her law career, accepting an offer from the Rose Law Firm, a large and very powerful player in Arkansas politics and policy. The next year, President Jimmy Carter appointed her to the board of directors of the Legal Services Corporation, a nonprofit organization established by Congress in 1974. In Arkansas, Rodham founded Advocates for Children and Families, an organization dedicated to expanding rights for children. In 1978, Bill Clinton was elected governor of Arkansas. The first signs of what would later be known as the "Hillary Factor" were evident even in this campaign. Opponents objected to Rodham using her own name, her involvement in politics, and the fact that she had a career. For the most part, both Bill and Hillary ignored their critics. There

were also signs that Bill Clinton was unfaithful, and evidence of his infidelities during the 1970s and 1980s dogged Clinton throughout his career in elective office. Publicly, Rodham ignored the accusations, and in 1979 she became a partner in the Rose Law firm. The couple's only child, Chelsea, was born on February 27, 1980. That same year, Clinton was defeated in his bid for reelection as governor, but he won the office back in 1982. Hillary was an important factor in his comeback. She announced that she would be known as Hillary Clinton and hired a fashion consultant to advise her on her appearance.

The Clintons approached Bill's second term as governor with zeal, dedicating much of their efforts to reforming Arkansas public education system. Governor Clinton named Hillary chair of the Education Standards Committee. She spent two years investigating the state of public education in Arkansas, traveling the state and collecting data. The committee formulated a proposal calling for smaller classes and student performance testing at regular intervals. Funding for the improvements was politically assured when the committee agreed to include basic skills tests for all of the state's teachers. Teachers rallied against the provision, some calling it racist, but nevertheless it was adopted by the legislature. Hillary Clinton earned high marks for the substance of the initiative and for her adept handling of the politics of the issue; she was named Woman of the Year by an Arkansas newspaper.

As a couple, Bill and Hillary Clinton were selected by *Esquire* for its list of baby boomers most likely to leave a positive mark on history. Talk of a Clinton run for the presidency was rampant in 1987, but Bill announced that he would not seek the Democratic nomination and cited his commitment to seven-year-old Chelsea and his family. In 1988, the *National Law Journal* named Hillary Rodham Clinton one of the hundred most influential lawyers in the United States. As 1992 loomed, the Clintons again considered a run for the White House.

At first, President George Bush seemed unbeatable, and many prominent Democrats had already announced that they would sit out the 1992 cycle as a result. Clinton, now in his fifth term as governor of Arkansas, announced his intention to seek the Democratic nomination for president on October 3, 1991. Almost immediately, questions about his marriage attracted the attention of the national media. In hopes of heading off any obsession with the issue, the Clintons met the press as a couple and attempted to answer their questions. Hillary claimed, "You've got to be willing to stay committed to someone over the long run. . . . My strong feelings about divorce and its effect on children have caused me to bite my tongue more than a few times during my own marriage and to think instead about what I could do to be a better wife and partner."

In large part due to their success as collaborators in Arkansas politics, the Clintons promised a partnership presidency. Candidate Bill Clinton promised that a vote for him would guarantee the country a "two for one" deal, implying that Hillary Clinton would play a prominent and substantive role in any Clinton White House. Presumably, this was an attractive offer in 1992, since most families, with or without children, were supported by two paychecks. However, focus groups and opinion polls demonstrated the nation's ambivalence over envisioning a new role for a modern first lady. The majority of those polled favored a more traditional image for the first lady. The contrast was heightened when, in response to a question about her career, Hillary remarked, "I've done the best I can to lead my life. I suppose I could have stayed home and baked cookies and had teas." In the resulting media frenzy, conservatives characterized her remarks as demeaning to "stay-at-home" mothers. She attempted to explain her remarks: "I had understood the question to refer to the ceremonial role of a public official's spouse, and I replied that I had chosen to pursue my law practice while my husband was governor rather than stay home as an official hostess, serving cookies and tea to guests. Now, the fact is, that I've made my

share of cookies and served hundreds of cups of tea. But I never thought that my cookie-baking or tea-serving abilities made me a good, bad, or indifferent mother, or a good or bad person. So it never occurred to me that my comment would be taken as insulting to mothers (I guess including my own!) who choose to stay home with their children full time."

Ironically, the same Hillary Clinton who had devoted a good portion of her professional career to advancing the interests of children and families was labeled "anti-family" by critics on the right. Pat Buchanan, a candidate for the Republican presidential nomination, labeled her "the enemy of everything traditional in American life." Even her attempt to shield Chelsea from the press was misconstrued. A poll found that a majority of Americans thought the Clintons were childless, and when informed about the existence of daughter Chelsea, they held Hillary Clinton responsible for their misconception. Deborah Tannen, writing in an op-ed piece in the *New York Times,* summed up the feelings of the Clinton's supporters: "By what logic could it be scary rather than comforting for a president's wife, who everyone knows will have his ear, to be unusually intelligent, knowledgeable and accomplished? And to answer: by no logic at all. The hope was to incite emotions—fear and anger—that confront women who do not conform to the old molds."

Just prior to the New Hampshire primary, a tabloid called the press together to introduce Gennifer Flowers, an Arkansas woman who claimed that she and Bill Clinton had been lovers for 12 years. In a remarkable joint appearance on the television program *60 Minutes,* the Clintons acknowledged past problems in their marriage, but neither directly confirmed or denied the allegations about Flowers. During the interview, Hillary Clinton said, "I'm not sitting here because I'm some little woman standing by my man like Tammy Wynette. I'm sitting here because I love and respect him, and I honor what he's been through and what we've been through together. And you know, if that's not enough for people, then heck, don't vote for him." Her response improved her overall standings in the polls, and Bill Clinton earned the moniker "comeback kid" when he came in second in the New Hampshire primary, going on to win the nomination and, ultimately, the presidency. For the most part, the vitriolic attacks on Hillary Clinton mounted by Republicans both covertly and then very directly at the 1992 Republican National Convention in Houston, backfired. She retained the label "polarizing figure," but most came to agree that she was as skillful a politician as her husband.

As first lady, Hillary Clinton organized a staff to manage both her social obligations and her interest in playing a more substantive policy role. She set up an office in the west wing of the White House, a first for any first lady. She hired Margaret Ann Williams as her chief of staff, the first African American to hold that position. Hillary was very influential in recommending women and minorities for cabinet positions in the Clinton-Gore administration. (President Clinton appointed the most women to cabinet or subcabinet-level positions of any president in history.) Gender issues again nearly derailed the Clintons' attempts to appoint the first woman attorney general. Zoe Baird, the first nominee, was forced to withdraw because of allegations that she failed to pay employment and payroll taxes for her children's nanny. Kimba Wood, Clinton's second choice, was also forced to withdraw under similar circumstances related to child care arrangements. These issues had never been raised with regard to previous presidential appointments and were widely regarded by feminists as attacks on women pursuing nontraditional careers and their increasing presence in politics. Bill Clinton's third and ultimately successful nominee for Attorney General, Janet Reno, was unmarried and did not have any children. Ultimately, four women were confirmed to cabinet posts, including JANET RENO (attorney general), HAZEL O'LEARY (secretary of energy), Donna Shalala (secretary of health and human services), and Carol Browner (head of the Environmental Protection Agency). Clinton also appointed MADELINE ALBRIGHT as United Nations ambassador (and as secretary of state in 1997).

Hillary Clinton's first "assignment" from the president was as head of the President's Task Force on Health Care Reform. She approached this task much like she did the issue of school reform in Arkansas, voraciously consuming research on health care reform; collecting data; and soliciting opinions from the medical community, insurance interests, and consumer rights advocates. In September 1993, she appeared before a House committee on health insurance reform, becoming only the third first lady to testify before Congress. Although she was well received, and even critics acknowledged the depth of her knowledge and understanding of the issues, health care reform was not accomplished in the Clinton presidency. Critics labeled the task force proposal a form of "socialized medicine." Still others lambasted the first lady for holding task force meetings in private. A physician's interest group sued, and as a result a D.C. circuit court ruled that the first lady was a "de facto federal employee" subject to all of the rules governing federal employees actions. The implications of this ruling have not been fully investigated. For proponents, a complicated issue had produced a complicated solution that proved difficult to market to the public or to legislators. Ultimately, the Clinton administration did not push Congress for a vote on the proposal, even though Democrats controlled both houses at the time. In 1997, however, Hillary Clinton was successful with a health care initiative for children. The Children's Health Insurance Program is a federal program that provides resources through states to insure children whose parents are unable to provide health coverage.

Following the failure of the health care reform plan, Hillary Clinton took on a less public role, but she did not stop advocating for issues and causes. She is largely responsible for the Adoption and Safe Families Act of 1997 and the Foster Care Independence bill. She played host to countless White House conferences related to children's health, education, early childhood development, school violence, reading and literacy, immunization, and preventing breast cancer and other diseases. She initiated the Save America's Treasures program, designed to match federal and private donations to restore historic items. The millenium project featured monthly lectures in the East Room on issues linking America's past to its future. She oversaw the restoration of the Blue Room and the Treaty Room and hired an American chef for the White House.

The first lady and the president did not always agree on policy. She and other liberal progressives in the Democratic Party were anxious for President Clinton to push hard for policy changes and balked when he compromised with Republicans, as he did on the issue of welfare reform. The first lady often attended staff and cabinet meetings. She traveled on behalf of the administration and promoted women's rights as human rights in Africa, Asia, South America, and central Europe. In September 1995, she led the U.S. delegation to the United Nations Fourth World Conference on Women, held in Beijing, China, where she delivered a strongly worded speech in favor of women's rights and gender equality (see the appendix of this volume for a copy of the speech). In 1996, she published *It Takes a Village,* a book examining various strategies to support children and families. That same year, Bill Clinton easily won reelection to a second term.

As first lady, Hillary Clinton was never free of controversy. For most of the Clinton administration, she and the president were under investigation. Most of the probes concerned events and activities that had preceded Bill's election to the presidency (Whitewater, commodity trades, business at the Rose law firm). None of the investigations ever resulted in indictments against the Clintons. However, in summer 1994, Paula Jones, an Arkansas state employee, accused the president of sexually

harassing her in 1991. Even as that case was winding its way through the federal courts, the Monica Lewinsky scandal broke in January 1998. Bill Clinton lied to the nation and to his family about the extent of his involvement with Lewinsky, a former White House intern. As she had in the past, Hillary stood up for him, claiming that this was more evidence of a "vast right wing conspiracy" against her husband. It was not until August 1998 that she learned from one of Bill's attorneys that he would acknowledge an affair with Lewinsky when he testified before the grand jury later that day. There were accusations of sexual misconduct leveled by other women during this time as well. On October 8, 1998, House Resolution 581, introduced by Congressman Henry J. Hyde, chair of the Judiciary Committee, was approved by the House in a 258-163 vote to authorize and direct the Judiciary Committee to investigate whether sufficient grounds existed for the impeachment of the president. On December 11 and 12, the committee approved four articles of impeachment for presentation to the full House. After debate, the House approved two of the articles alleging that the president had committed perjury in his testimony to the grand jury in the Paula Jones case and about his relationship with Monica Lewinsky and that he had obstructed justice through an effort to delay, impede, cover up, and conceal the existence of evidence related to the Jones case.

The impeachment trial in the Senate began on January 7, 1999. The Senate voted on the articles of impeachment on February 12, with a two-thirds majority, or 67 senators, required to convict. On the perjury charge, the president was found not guilty with 45 senators voting for the president's removal from office and 55 against. Ten Republicans split with their colleagues to vote for acquittal; all 45 Democrats voted to acquit. On the second charge, obstruction of justice, the vote was 50-50, with all Democrats and five Republicans voting to acquit. The president remained in office—and the first lady began to focus on her own political future.

Democrats in New York had been courting Hillary Clinton to run for the Senate seat being vacated by the retiring Patrick Moynihan. She visited Moynihan in New York and then began a "listening tour" throughout the state to learn about citizens' issues and concerns. Opponents immediately labeled her a "carpetbagger," but the Clintons had purchased property in Westchester County. Hillary Clinton formally declared her candidacy for the U.S. Senate on February 6, 2000, and began campaigning full-time. Initially her Republican opponent was Rudolph Giuliani, mayor of New York, but health problems and marital issues forced him to withdraw from the race. On election night 2000, she easily defeated Congressman Rick Lazio, winning 54 percent of the vote. When she was sworn into office, she became the first first lady to be elected to office in her own right. For 19 days, she occupied the two roles simultaneously. (Her memoir, *Living History,* was published in 2003 and has sold over 3 million copies.)

In the U.S. Senate, Hillary Rodham Clinton serves on the Health, Education, Labor, and Pensions Committee; the Environment and Public Works Committee; the Special Committee on Aging; and the Senate Armed Services Committee, the first New Yorker ever to serve on that committee. Senator Clinton also chairs the Senate Democratic Steering and Outreach Committee, responsible for communicating with the public about key issues before Congress. In November 2004, Clinton announced that she would seek a second term in the Senate in 2006; she easily won reelection. She then became an early front-runner in the 2008 run for president. To date, she has a large campaign fund to draw upon.

Hillary Clinton has an established national image that makes her candidacy in 2008 a popular and controversial topic. She is widely seen as a very polarizing figure, but with her significant financial advantage, she is also seen a serious contender for the democratic nomination for president.

Further Reading
Clinton, Hillary Rodham. *Living History.* New York: Simon and Schuster, 2003.

Gould, Lewis L. "Hillary Diane Rodham Clinton." In *American First Ladies: Their Lives and Their Legacy,* 2nd ed., edited by Lewis L. Gould. New York, 2001. pp. 425–438.

National First Ladies Library. *Biographies: First Ladies of the United States.* Available online. URL: http://www.firstladies.org/biographies. Accessed on January 4, 2007.

Schneider, Dorothy, and Carl J. Schneider. "Hillary Rodham Clinton" *First Ladies: A Biographical Dictionary.* New York: Checkmark Books, 2001. pp. 339–349.

Clinton v. Jones (520 U.S. 681) (1997)

Clinton v. Jones was a SEXUAL HARASSMENT case involving Paula Corbin Jones, an employee with the Arkansas State Industrial Commission, and former president Bill Clinton. Jones alleged that Clinton, then governor of Arkansas, called her to his hotel room, where he made sexual advances to her. Jones then left the room after Clinton asked her to keep the incident between them and referred her to another employee in the governor's office who would help her if she was ever reprimanded for leaving her job to come to his hotel room.

The Supreme Court had to decide whether this case could be tried as a case of either quid pro quo or "hostile environment" sexual harassment. On the quid pro quo case, the Court decided that while Jones may have interpreted Clinton's reference to another employee as a threat to her own job safety, that threat was not sufficiently explicit to be actionable. Further, Jones's examples of tangible job loss (concerning a reassignment that the Court found provided equivalent seniority and pay opportunities) were denied, and thus no "tangible job detriment" was found. The Court also found that the incident did not provide a sufficiently "severe and pervasive" work environment, taking the "totality of the circumstances" into account.

Thus, because there was only one incident, and because Jones only interacted twice with the governor in a work-related setting after this incident, summary judgment (essentially dismissing the case as a matter of law prior to the case coming to trial) was granted to the president. The Court argued that "defendant's actions as shown by the record do not constitute the kind of sustained and non-trivial conduct necessary for a claim of hostile work environment sexual harassment."

Further Reading

Mink, Gwendolyn. *Hostile Environment: The Political Betrayal of Sexually Harrassed Women.* Ithaca, N.Y.: Cornell University Press, 2000.

—Claire Curtis

Cohen v. Brown University (103 F. 3d 155)

(1996) *Cohen v. Brown University* was a class-action suit charging that Brown University discriminated against female student athletes by violating the provisions and regulations of TITLE IX OF THE EDUCATION AMENDMENTS OF 1972. Title IX is to education what TITLE VII OF THE CIVIL RIGHTS ACT OF 1964 is to employment by basically prohibiting discrimination in education (when federal funds are involved). Although Brown University is a private institution, it does receive various forms of federal funding. This case was fought vigorously by the university in several different courts but was ultimately decided in favor of the female plaintiffs. Brown University was found in violation of Title IX because it did not fund women's athletics in a manner proportionate to the percentage of female students enrolled at Brown. Brown argued that it had an equal number of male and female teams and that they were not in violation of Title IX. However, the court found that Brown was not offering female students an appropriate number of participation opportunities (Brown offered 479 university-funded varsity positions for men, as compared to 312 for women). The

U.S. Supreme Court upheld the First Circuit Court of Appeals decision, which marked an important milestone in Title IX.

—Marsha Hass

Collins, Susan (Susan Margaret Collins)

(1952–) *U.S. senator* Born December 7, 1952, Susan Collins was raised in Caribou, a small city in northern Maine, where both her parents have served as mayor. Her family runs a fifth-generation lumber business, founded by Collins's ancestors in 1844 and operated today by two of her brothers. In 1975, she graduated St. Lawrence University, upon which she worked for former Maine senator William S. Cohen. In 1987, she joined the cabinet of Maine governor John R. McKernan as commissioner of professional and financial regulation, a position she held for five years. She then served as New England administrator of the U.S. Small Business Administration from 1992 to 1993.

In 1994, Collins ran her first campaign for public office, becoming the first woman in Maine history to receive a major party nomination for governor after winning an eight-way Republican primary in June. She lost in the general election. In December 1994, she became the founding executive director of the Center for Family Business at Husson College in Bangor, Maine, a position she held until she resigned in 1996 to run for the Senate seat being vacated by Senator Cohen. She won both a contested Republican primary and a four-way general election later that year and won reelection in 2002 with 58 percent of the vote.

Some of Collins's legislative priorities include education and homeland security. She authored a law that provided a $250 tax deduction for teachers who spend their own money on classroom supplies. Her goal of expanding access to higher education led her to coauthor the 1998 Higher Education Act and to support increases in Pell grants and other student financial aid.

In 2005, Collins was among the Gang of 14, a group of moderate senators who came together and formed a coalition to compromise on the use of the judicial filibuster, which was a highly politically charged issue because it blocked the Republican leadership's ability to have votes on some of President Bush's most controversial judicial nominees. The Senate Republicans had threatened to implement the so-called nuclear option, involving a permanent change in Senate procedure. The Gang of 14 came together in an attempt to diffuse the volatile disagreement that threatened to shut down the U.S. Senate. Under the agreement reached by the bipartisan group, the Democrats would retain the power to filibuster a Bush judicial nominee only in an "extraordinary circumstance," and the three most conservative Bush appellate court nominees would receive a vote by the full Senate.

Collins was named one of the WHITE HOUSE PROJECT's "8 in '08," meaning that she has been identified as a credible female candidate for the presidency in 2008.

Further Reading

Barone, Michael. *The Almanac of American Politics.* Washington, D.C.: National Journal Group, 2006.

"Collins, Susan Margaret." In *Biographical Directory of the United States Congress, 1774–present.* Available online. URL: http://bioguide.congress.gov/scripts/biodisplay.pl?index=C001035. Accessed on January 8, 2007.

"Senator Susan M. Collins (ME)." In *Project Vote Smart.* Available online. URL: http://votesmart.org/bio.php?can_id=BC032786. Accessed on January 8, 2007.

—Angela Kouters

Colored Women's League

The Colored Women's League was founded in 1892 in Washington, D.C. The league represents yet another example of the BLACK WOMEN'S CLUB MOVEMENT phenomenon that emerged in the 1890s.

Leaders of the Colored Women's League, such as MARY CHURCH TERRELL, Halli Quinn Brown, and Anna Julia Cooper, were all highly educated, black middle-class women committed to two key issues in American politics at the time: civil rights for black Americans and SUFFRAGE for women. To this end, leaders of the league embarked on a campaign to promote the welfare of black families and to empower black women.

The post-emancipation era witnessed blacks migrating from the South to the North hoping to achieve better opportunities in urban centers. Washington, D.C., became one of the centers of migration of largely poor and undereducated black Americans. In response to black migration to the North, the Colored Women's League formed a service-oriented club dedicated to the overall racial enrichment of black Americans. League leaders filled the vacuum left by the local District of Columbia government in meeting the needs of the black community.

The major accomplishment of the Colored Women's League was the educational initiatives it introduced. Given the fact that the leaders of the league were educators themselves as well as advocates of educational opportunities for women, they established adult education evening classes, trained kindergarten teachers, and offered free kindergarten and nursery day care for children of working mothers. League leaders were cognizant that unless black women were offered equal access to education, black women would be unable to advance politically and economically. Equally important for league leaders was the recognition that an education, which contributed to economic mobility, would be useless unless child care needs were simultaneously addressed.

The league's training program and kindergarten were later incorporated into the Washington, D.C., public school system. By 1896, the Colored Women's League had merged with one other organization to form the NATIONAL ASSOCIATION OF COLORED WOMEN (NACW).

Further Reading

Hine, Darlene Clark. *Black Women in America: An Historical Encyclopedia.* New York: Carlson Publishing, 1993.

—Hollis France

Combahee River Collective   The Combahee River Collective was established in Boston in 1974 and lasted until 1980. Its name is a symbolic recognition of the heroic act by HARRIET TUBMAN, who in 1863 freed 750 slaves near the Combahee River in South Carolina. Combahee River Collective sought to free women of color from the shackles of racial, sexual, heterosexual, and class oppression.

The collective was formed by a small group of young African-American women after they returned from the first public meeting of the NATIONAL BLACK FEMINIST ORGANIZATION (NBFO) in New York City in 1973. Unlike the NBFO, which was searching for its feminist identity and tended to be viewed as a mainstream organization, the Combahee River Collective was very clear and forthright about its identity politics. The collective's statement unequivocally makes reference to the fact that they are feminists and lesbians whose radical politics are informed by their identity.

Whereas the mainstream white women's movement tended to shy away from the use of the word *feminist* due to the perceived public perception of "feminists as man-haters" and the nationalist male-dominated black liberation movement's portrayal of "feminists as white man-hating women," members of the Combahee River Collective embraced their multiple identities unconditionally. Adding to its feminist and lesbian identities, which informed member's antiracist, antisexist and antihomophobic politics, the Combahee River Collective also adopted a class analysis of their political organizing. Recognizing that their privileged educational backgrounds placed them in a unique position to fight the interlocking systems of oppression,

their mission statement declares: "Our development must also be tied to the contemporary economic and political position of Black people. . . . [A] handful of us have been able to gain certain tools as a result of tokenism in education and employment which potentially enable us to more effectively fight our oppression. . . [A]s we develop politically we addressed ourselves to heterosexism and economic oppression." As such, the group referred to themselves as socialist feminists who believed "that work must be organized for the collective benefit of those who do the work and create the products, and not for the profit of the bosses. . . . We need to articulate the real class situation of persons . . . for whom racial and sexual oppression are significant determinants of their working/economic lives."

The writings of such African-American authors as Toni Cade, Audre Lorde, Toni Morrison, and Alice Walker were influential in galvanizing many of the members of Combahee River Collective to fight for the liberation of women of color.

—Hollis France

comparable worth   The comparable worth doctrine, also known as pay equity, is an explicit recognition of the gendered nature of work. Although the SEPARATE SPHERES IDEOLOGY may have faded over time as *the* primary organizing principle of gender relations, its legacy is very much alive today in how women and men experience work. TITLE VII OF THE CIVIL RIGHTS ACT OF 1964 makes it illegal to restrict jobs to one sex or the other based purely on sex or stereotypical assumptions about gender-linked abilities, but gender segregation is pervasive throughout the labor force. Statistics from 2005 show that three-quarters of all women who work do so in just 20 occupations, each of which is nearly 80 percent female.

The economy is organized into "men's jobs" and "women's jobs," which is eerily consistent with the public-private sphere division of labor.

For example, 2003 Bureau of Labor statistics reported that women made up 98 percent of the nation's kindergarten and preschool teachers, 84 percent of its elementary schoolteachers, 96 percent of its secretaries and administrative assistants, and 90 percent of its health care workers. Alternatively, males made up 96 percent of the nation's firefighters, 74 percent of its physicians, 97 percent of its construction workers, and 99 percent of its auto mechanics. If all occupations enjoyed the same level of prestige and pay, gender segregation in the labor force would not disadvantage women; however, that is not the case. Rates of pay in jobs dominated by women are significantly lower. The EQUAL PAY ACT of 1963 only requires equal pay when women and men are doing substantially the same work.

Comparable worth doctrine proposes that within organizations, female-dominated jobs should be compensated comparably to male-dominated jobs that are judged similar in skills, effort, responsibility, and working conditions. For example, under comparable worth doctrine, social workers (primarily female) and probation officers (predominantly male) would be paid equally even though their job titles are different. A comparable worth study in Los Angeles County California found a $20,000 annual WAGE GAP between probation officers and social workers. In 1993, Los Angeles County negotiated a settlement with female employees for more equitable pay. Comparable worth legislation is introduced in Congress each year, but it has made little progress. More progress has been made at the state and county levels.

Further Reading

National Committee on Pay Equity. "Real Life Examples of Equivalent Jobs." Available online. URL: www.pay-equity.org/PDFs/EquivalentJobs.pdf. Accessed on June 26, 2006.

Comstock Act (1873) The Comstock Act of 1873 prohibited the selling, publication, or distribution of obscene materials, including pornography and information about contraception and ABORTION. Many states, led by New York, immediately passed their own versions of antivice laws that mirrored Comstock. Anthony Comstock of the New York Society for Suppression of Vice (NYSSV), campaigned for the law, successfully bringing hundreds of cases to court before his death in 1915. One of the best-known opponents of the Comstock Act was birth control activist MARGARET SANGER, who was jailed repeatedly for the dissemination of obscene literature and contraceptive devices. Sanger established a committee to lobby the national and state legislatures to overturn the law.

Despite Sanger's legislative focus, the first success in limiting the power of "Comstockery," as use of the law came to be known, occurred not in the legislature but in the court system. In the judicial decision *The United States v. One Package* in 1936, the courts ruled that physicians prescribing contraception to prevent disease should be exempt from persecution under the law. The law would not be completely overturned in some states until the 1973 decision of *ROE V. WADE*, the landmark decision to legalize abortion. In addition to limiting the diffusion of contraceptive information, the Comstock Act was used against pornography and to censor many well-known literary works. The works of novelists D. H. Lawrence and Theodore Dreiser were censored from public consumption under the law.

See also BIRTH CONTROL MOVEMENT.

Further Reading

Beisel, Nicola. *Imperiled Innocents: Anthony Comstock and Family Reproduction in Victorian America.* Princeton, N.J.: Princeton University Press, 1997.

Sanger, Margaret. "Comstockery in America." *International Socialist Review* (July 1915): 46–49.

—Kristen A. Contos

Concerned Women for America (CWA) Concerned Women for America (CWA) was founded by BEVERLY LAHAYE in 1979 in response to what she and her allies described as the "anti-God, anti-family" rhetoric of FEMINISM. First organized to oppose the EQUAL RIGHTS AMENDMENT, CWA is organized as prayer/action chapters around the country but maintains its national headquarters in Washington, D.C. Working to bring "biblical principles" to public policy, CWA lobbies around six core issues: traditional family structure and values, sanctity of human life, parental authority in education, pornography, religious liberty and national sovereignty. The organization maintains a Web site at www.cwfa.org.

Congressional Caucus for Women's Issues: Women's Policy, Inc.

In 1977, when only 18 women (a little more than 3 percent) sat in Congress, 15 women founded the Congresswomen's Caucus, later renamed the Congressional Caucus for Women's Issues (CCWI). Since its inception, the congresswomen's caucus has been a bipartisan organization cochaired by a Democrat and a Republican. To extend the caucus's influence, the Women's Research and Education Institute (WREI) was also founded in 1977, and it remained organizationally linked to the caucus until 1985.

The caucus had two early successes in the 95th Congress: a bill preventing employer discrimination against pregnant women and gaining attention to gender disparities in federal employment and Social Security benefits. Beyond these, women had little success convincing the overwhelmingly male Congress that women's issues were not only linked to one another but were also embedded in programs that initially seemed unrelated to "women's issues." That changed in 1978 when the caucus mobilized colleagues to extend the life of the EQUAL RIGHTS AMENDMENT. Besides the extension of the deadline for ratification, which few thought possible, CCWI members put Congress on notice that they were capable of moving legislation and setting policy priorities favorable to women's interests.

The CCWI provided two functions: to advocate for women and families and to serve as an information clearinghouse on women's issues in Congress. During the 1980s and early 1990s, CCWI introduced and sponsored several omnibus legislative packages, including the ECONOMIC EQUITY ACT (first introduced in 1983), the FAMILY AND MEDICAL LEAVE ACT (first introduced in 1985, passed in 1993), the Women's Health Equity Act (passed in 1990), and the VIOLENCE AGAINST WOMEN ACT (signed in 1994). Most of these intiatives have now been adopted into law. In addition, the caucus brought new attention to the issue of breast cancer and won approval to earmark more than $500 million for breast cancer research.

The CCWI suffered organizational difficulties during the early 1980s as founding members retired, were defeated, or passed away. Attracting new members proved difficult in the 1980s, particularly among newly elected Republican women. For a variety of reasons (unwillingness to pay membership dues, wariness of affiliation with "women's issues," or a fear of alienating the conservative Reagan administration), membership lagged, and the caucus's ability to influence the legislative agenda diminished substantially. In 1981, the CCWI took dramatic steps to extend its influence and opened its membership to men. Over time, the caucus grew from one of the smallest legislative service organizations to one of the largest. New bylaws restricted membership on its executive committee to women only but retained the bipartisan co-chair arrangement, as well as its tradition of focusing on issues that united women.

When the Republicans took over Congress after the 1994 elections, rule changes stripped legislative service organizations of their budgets, staff, and office space. As a result, the CCWI reorganized as a congressional member organization, and three former staff members established a nonprofit organization called Women's Policy, Inc. (WPI) to carry on the caucus's weekly newsletter and information services. WPI maintains a Web site at www. womenspolicy.org.

See also SOCIAL SECURITY AND WOMEN.

Congressional Union for Woman Suffrage (CUWS)

In April 1913, ALICE PAUL and LUCY BURNS formed the Congressional Union for Woman Suffrage (CUWS), whose sole objective was to lobby for the passage of a federal woman SUFFRAGE amendment. Suffragists had not focused on securing a constitutional amendment since the late 19th century. Instead, the NATIONAL AMERICAN WOMAN SUFFRAGE ASSOCIATION (NAWSA) worked to secure equal rights for women using the state-by-state approach. By 1913, nine western states and the territory of Alaska had enfranchised their women. Impatient with the NAWSA, Paul and Burns established the CUWS. Although they were dissatisfied with NAWSA's campaign methods, Paul and Burns aligned the CUWS with the NAWSA, serving as an auxiliary to the association for a brief time. By 1914, however, the CUWS's members had offended NAWSA leadership with their use of militant and partisan methods, and the two organizations went their separate ways.

Influenced by their British counterparts, the Congressional Union adopted flamboyant tactics, staging publicity stunts to garner support for the Anthony Amendment (named after SUSAN B. ANTHONY). In addition, the CUWS, like the British suffragettes, believed that the party in power (the Democrats) should be held responsible for not passing woman suffrage. The union's plan stood in direct opposition to NAWSA's nonpartisanship policy. Nevertheless, in 1914 and 1916, the CUWS sent organizers to states where women could vote in congressional elections and worked to defeat Democratic Party candidates. When this strategy failed, the CUWS began picketing the White House, turning President Woodrow Wilson's own words upon him and helping to tilt public opinion in their favor. These methods attracted the media's attention, and consequently interest in

the federal woman suffrage campaign surged. In 1917, the Congressional Union merged with the NATIONAL WOMAN'S PARTY.

Further Reading

Ford, Linda G. *Iron-Jawed Angels: The Suffrage Militancy of the National Woman's Party, 1912–1920.* Lanham, Md.: University Press of America, Inc., 1991.

Irwin, Inez Haynes. *The Story of the Woman's Party.* New York: Kraus Reprint Co. 1971.

Lunardini, Christine A. *From Equal Suffrage to Equal Rights: Alice Paul and the National Woman's Party, 1910–1928.* New York: New York University Press, 1986.

—Jennifer Ross-Nazzal

contract pregnancy See SURROGACY.

Convention on the Elimination of All Forms of Discrimination Against Women (CEDAW)

(1979) The United Nations adopted the Convention on the Elimination of all forms of Discrimination Against Women on December 18, 1979. Prior to CEDAW, there was no convention that comprehensively addressed women's rights within political, cultural, economic, social, and family life. CEDAW provides a universal definition of discrimination against women as "any distinction, exclusion or restriction made on the basis of sex which has the effect or purpose of impairing or nullifying the recognition, enjoyment or exercise by women, irrespective of their marital status, on a basis of equality of men and women, of human rights and fundamental freedoms in the political, economic, social, cultural, civil or any other field."

CEDAW requires governments to take certain actions to guarantee women's rights. Article 4 permits affirmative action measures that accelerate equality and eliminate discrimination. In one of many controversial measures, Article 5 recognizes the role of culture and tradition, calling for the elimination of sex-role stereotyping. Similarly, Article 10 makes equal access to all fields of education and the elimination of stereotyped concepts of men and women an obligation. Article 11 recognizes that the right to work is a human right and mandates the end of employment discrimination. Article 12 requires countries to take steps to eliminate discrimination in health care, including providing access to family planning. It further requires that steps be taken to ensure equality in marriage and in family relations. CEDAW attempts to redress discrimination that treats men and women differently on the basis of sex.

The United States was active in drafting CEDAW, and President Jimmy Carter signed it on July 17, 1980. It was finally voted out of the Senate Foreign Relations Committee in 1994, but the Senate has yet to ratify the treaty. As of June 2000, 165 countries have ratified CEDAW, the United States being the only developed nation that has not ratified it. For CEDAW to be ratified, it needs two-thirds, or 67, affirmative votes in the Senate. Opponents believe that U.S. law would be superseded by the provisions of the treaty. However, an analysis by the State Department in the mid-1990s determined that U.S. law is consistent with the principles of CEDAW and that CEDAW is consistent with the Constitution.

Supporters of CEDAW have been frustrated by their inability to get a hearing before the Senate Foreign Relations Committee. In October 1999, a delegation of 10 congresswomen were ordered removed from a Senate Foreign Relations Committee hearing on China after they tried to present Senator Jesse Helms with a letter signed by 100 House members in support of CEDAW ratification. On November 19, 1999, Senator BARBARA BOXER, a Democrat from California, introduced a "sense of the Senate" resolution (cosponsored by seven other female Senators) to hold hearings and act on CEDAW. The resolution called for the Senate to act by March 8, 2000, INTERNATIONAL WOMAN'S DAY, and in honor of the 20th anniversary of the treaty. No action was taken. Boxer reintroduced

the resolution on April 12, 2000. State legislatures in California, Iowa, Massachusetts, New Hampshire, New York, North Carolina, South Dakota, and Vermont have endorsed U.S. ratification of CEDAW. In addition, some large city councils have taken similar action, and many professional organizations, such as the American Bar Association, have done the same.

Likening it to an international version of the ERA, many U.S. ANTIFEMINISM organizations object primarily because the treaty attempts to eliminate the differences between men and women. CONCERNED WOMEN FOR AMERICA calls CEDAW a "back-door ERA" and warns that feminists could use CEDAW to renew the drive for a federal ERA in the United States. Conservative women's organizations also argue that CEDAW liberalizes abortion by requiring access to family planning for all women and that it destroys the traditional family structure since it urges a change in traditional roles that limit women's role in society. Others worry that provisions regarding education would amount to "gender reeducation" since the treaty requires the elimination of stereotyped concepts of men and women in all forms of education.

Even without Senate action, the U.S. government had been moving toward embracing CEDAW. The United States made ratification of CEDAW one of its public commitments in the 1995 UN Conference on Women in Beijing. Protests by nongovernmental organizations at the time raised public awareness of the Senate's failure to hold hearings. On December 10, 1998, President Clinton issued Executive Order 13107, Implementation of Human Rights Treaties, in which he established an interagency working group to implement America's obligations under UN treaties on human rights "to which the United States is now or may become a party in the future." However, as of 2005, the Bush administration has not moved CEDAW forward in the U.S. Senate. The administration asked the Foreign Relations Committee to delay consideration of the treaty in 2002 and has not acted on or spoken of it since that time.

Further Reading

United Nations Division for the Advancement of Women. *Convention on the Elimination of All Forms of Discrimination Against Women.* Available online. URL: www.un.org/womenwatch/daw/cedaw/. Accessed on January 10, 2007.

Zoelle, Diana G. *Globalizing Concern for Women's Human Rights: The Failure of the American Model.* New York: St. Martin's Press, 2000.

Convention on the Political Rights of Women (1954)

The *Convention on the Political Rights of Women* was adopted by the United Nations General Assembly on December 20, 1952, and came into force on July 7, 1954. The provisions of the treaty are in accordance with provisions of the United Nations charter and of the Universal Declaration of Human Rights, and it is the first international treaty wherein ratifying states committed to the protection of political rights of their citizens. The convention is based on the recognition that every person has the right to take part in the government of his or her country (directly or indirectly) and has the right to equal access to public service. Further, participating members in the convention sought to equalize the status of men and women. As such, the convention states that women are entitled to vote in all elections on equal terms with men without discrimination, eligible for election to all publicly elected bodies, and entitled to hold public office and exercise all public functions without any discrimination.

As women in many countries did not have full political rights by the end of World War II, the United Nations President's Commission on the Status of Women sent a survey on this topic to member states. Their replies formed the basis of this convention, which along with the Convention on Nationality of Married Women (1958) and the Conventions on the Consent and Minimum Age for Marriage (1964) represent piecemeal attempts at setting international standards of nondiscrimination against women.

In 1967, the Declaration on the Elimination of Discrimination against Women outlined non-discrimination provisions more clearly and substantively. It was approved by the General Assembly by unanimous vote.

Further Reading

Cook, Rebecca, ed. *Human Rights of Women: National and International Perspectives.* Philadelphia: University of Pennsylvania Press, 1994.

Halberstam, Malvina, and Elizabeth F. Defeis. *Women's Legal Rights: International Covenants and Alternative to ERA?* Dobbs Ferry, N.Y.: Transnational Publishers Inc, 1987.

United Nations Department of Economic and Social Affairs. *The Convention on the Political Rights of Women: History and Commentary.* New York: United Nations, 1955.

—Leanne Dustan

Coolidge, Grace (Grace Anna Goodhue Coolidge) (1879–1957) *first lady*

Grace Anna Goodhue was born on January 3, 1879, in Burlington, Vermont, the only child of Andrew and Lemira Goodhue. By all accounts, Grace enjoyed a happy childhood as an extrovert who found school easy, but she was not drawn to intellectual pursuits. She spent one year living with neighbors while her father recovered from an accident. June Yale, the oldest daughter in that household, studied and taught at the Clarke School for the Deaf in Northampton, Massachusetts, and through their relationship, Grace Goodhue developed a lifelong interest in working with the deaf.

In 1898, Goodhue enrolled at the University of Vermont. After graduation, she enrolled in the training class at the Clarke School for the Deaf and taught primary and middle school for three years. She first met Calvin Coolidge while at Clarke. Coolidge, six years her senior, had graduated from Amherst College in Massachusetts and studied law at the firm of Hammond and Field. When they met, he had already served as city solicitor, clerk of the courts, and chairman of the Republican City Committee. His first invitation to Goodhue was to attend a Republican Rally at city hall. Although her mother disapproved and her friends were perplexed by her attraction to one so sullen and silent, Grace married Coolidge on October 4, 1905, in the Goodhues' home.

The couple returned from their honeymoon to resume Calvin's campaign for the school board, an election he lost. The following year, he was elected to the Massachusetts General Court, which met in Boston. Grace remained in Northampton with their infant son, John (b. 1906). From the start, the Coolidges divided their roles. He was fully engaged in building a public life and a political career and did not believe Grace should be involved in politics. So while he gradually rose through the ranks of the Republican Party and gained election to progressively higher offices, Grace remained

Grace Coolidge, 1923 (LIBRARY OF CONGRESS)

in Northampton with their children (a second son, Calvin, was born in 1908) and effectively functioned as both mother and father. Reportedly she could throw a baseball as well as any man. She continued her work with the Clarke School and got involved with community affairs and the work of her church. In 1918, Calvin Coolidge was elected governor of Massachusetts. Even then she remained in Northampton with her sons, alienating the social elite of Boston, though she commuted to Boston on a fairly regular basis and took a room at the Adams House as her husband had done. Coolidge continued to be a controlling figure in Grace's life. For instance, he agreed to buy a car as long as she agreed never to drive it.

Riots in Boston over the summer of 1919 and Coolidge's move to enlist the militia against striking unions, including the Boston police, earned him national attention, and his name was circulated as a candidate for the Republican nomination. At the convention however, Warren G. Harding won the presidential nomination, while Coolidge was nominated as vice president. When Harding and Coolidge won the 1920 election, he grudgingly agreed to move the family to Washington. The boys were enrolled in boarding school in Pennsylvania, and Grace Coolidge looked to support her husband through limited entertaining. She served as president of the Senate Ladies Club, an organization established during World War I to facilitate the women's volunteer war efforts with the Red Cross. Grace entertained the wives of senators and other Washington officials in their suite at the Willard Hotel and also accompanied Calvin to official dinners and receptions, a first in their marriage.

As the Harding administration began to unravel, Coolidge became increasingly unhappy with his marginalization as vice president. While on a trip to visit family in Vermont in August 1923, however, he and Grace received news of Harding's death. They returned to

Washington as president and first lady; he was elected to the office in 1924.

The Coolidges were sensitive to the formality of their roles throughout Calvin's terms in office. He had always kept Grace out of his political affairs, and the White House was no different. He did not consult her about their entertaining schedule and often made appointments for her. When she asked for his schedule, he replied, "Grace, we don't give that out promiscuously." Although she was well positioned by her education and predispositions to take an active role in social causes, Calvin ruled out most of her activities. Grace did not hold press conferences or even speak to the press, although they followed her every move. She dressed fashionably, albeit conservatively, and Calvin often selected her clothing. A fan of music and the theater, she invited performers to the White House. She encouraged women's causes by inviting women's groups to the White House and met with nearly every group that requested it. She was photographed often and therefore put a public face on the public role of the first lady even though she could not be described as a social activist. In the process, she brought life to an otherwise dull and fairly passive administration. She and Calvin committed to raising $2 million for the Clarke School and met that goal just before leaving the White House in March 1929.

Life in the White House included a personal tragedy. In summer 1924, the Coolidges' son Calvin developed a blister on his foot that became infected, and he died of blood poisoning, leaving Grace and Calvin devastated. Death threats against their son John, a student at Amherst, contributed to their sense of vulnerability and increased Calvin's attempts to control his wife. For example, when invited to fly with White House guest Charles Lindbergh, Grace had to decline the offer because Calvin had forbidden her to fly. For the most part, she accepted these constraints with good humor.

During a press conference in 1927, Coolidge announced that he did not intend to seek reelection in 1928. He had neither consulted his wife in this decision, nor did he feel it necessary to tell her about it when he lunched with her later that day. She learned about it in a casual conversation with a guest later in the day. Responsibilities of the White House and the loss of their son had taken their toll on both Grace's and Calvin's health. They left the White House in better repair, having undertaken major structural renovations in 1927. In the process, Grace attempted to furnish the White House with original period pieces, but she found few in storage. Those she found, she carefully cataloged. A joint resolution from Congress authorized the White House to accept gifts of period furniture to complete the project.

The Coolidges returned to Northampton, Massachusetts, after leaving the White House. In 1929, Grace Coolidge received an honorary degree from Smith College and was named one of *Good Housekeeping*'s 12 greatest women for her role as a national symbol of home and family life. Their son John was married to Florence Trumbull, daughter of the Connecticut governor. Grace wrote articles for *American Magazine* and *Good Housekeeping*, reflecting on her years in Washington. Calvin wrote a regular column for the McClure syndicate and published his autobiography. On January 5, 1933, he died unexpectedly in their home. Following his death, Grace was appointed to the board of trustees of the Clarke School, and from 1935 until 1955, she served as its chair. She also became more adventurous in her personal life, bobbing her hair, learning to drive, flying in an airplane with Governor John Trumbull, and continuing her avid interest in baseball. When the United States entered World War II, she turned her house over to the navy. She became a "household warden," trained in blackout and air raid procedures, and worked for war-bond sales and salvage campaigns. At the war's end, she moved back into her house and continued a quiet life with family and friends. She died on July 8, 1957.

Further Reading

Miller, Kristie. "Grace Anna Goodhue Coolidge." In *American First Ladies: Their Lives and Their Legacy,* 2nd ed., edited by Lewis L. Gould. New York: Routledge, 2001, pp. 257–273.

National First Ladies Library. *Biographies: First Ladies of the United States.* Available online. URL: http://www.firstladies.org/biographies. Accessed on January 4, 2007.

Schneider, Dorothy, and Carl J. Schneider. "Grace Anna Goodhue Coolidge" *First Ladies: A Biographical Dictionary.* New York: Checkmark Books, 2001, 211–219.

covenant marriage Largely a reaction to soaring divorce rates, three states (Louisiana in 1997, Arizona in 1998, and Arkansas in 2001) have adopted covenant marriage laws making marriage a legally binding contract. A covenant marriage requires that a couple seek counseling prior to marriage and permits divorce only on strictly limited terms: adultery, sexual or physical abuse, one year of abandonment, felony conviction, and separation of at least two years. In Arizona, the legislature added two other grounds for divorce: habitual drunkenness and "behaviour that imposes intolerable indignities." Couples already married can seek a covenant marriage by undergoing counseling and submitting an affidavit stating that they both agree to the terms. Proponents argue that covenant marriage strengthens and stabilizes the family, while opponents fear that making divorce more difficult will produce more conflict and potential for domestic violence. To date only 1–2 percent of all couples opt for a covenant marriage when offered the choice.

coverture Under English and United States common law, the period of a woman's marriage was referred to as coverture. A single woman, or *femme sole,* became a *femme covert* upon her marriage. The married woman lost many rights of ownership and control over her property. Under the act of coverture, the husband became the sole owner of all personal property owned by the wife before and that acquired after the marriage. He also gained the right to control all of her real property and earnings during the marriage. Coverture left the wife with no power to enter into legal contract, to sue, or to be sued in her own name. During the 18th and 19th centuries, society believed that women were naturally timid and delicate, and thus married women needed protection. Coverture was based on this patronizing and discriminatory idea. With the growing women's rights movement during the 1840s, states began passing laws that limited the scope of coverture. In 1848, the MARRIED WOMEN'S PROPERTY ACT OF NEW YORK gained nationwide attention, and eventually coverture was abolished in all of the states.

See also CITIZENSHIP, RESTRICTIONS FOR WOMEN; INTERSPOUSAL IMMUNITY.

Further Readings

Austin, Sara, and Thomas R. Kearns. *Law in Everyday Life.* Ann Arbor: University of Michigan Press, 1993.

Cott, Nancy F. *Public Vows: A History of Marriage and the Nation.* Cambridge, Mass.: Harvard University Press, 2002.

Hoff, Joan. *Law, Gender, and Injustice: A Legal History of the United States.* New York: New York University Press, 1991.

Salmon, Marylyn. *Women and the Law of Property in Early America.* Chapel Hill: University of North Carolina Press, 1986.

—Sharon Romero

***Craig v. Boren* (429 U.S. 190)** (1976) The plaintiffs in this case brought suit against Oklahoma governor David Boren, claiming that Oklahoma's beer sales law violated their Fourteenth Amendment right to equal protection. Oklahoma forbade the sale of 3.2 percent alcohol beer to males under the age of 21 and females under age 18. The state claimed the law was based on the fact that young males who drank alcohol caused more accidents than did women who drank. Therefore, the sex distinction in the law had a rational basis. The federal district court agreed, and the case went to the U.S. Supreme Court on appeal.

For women's rights activists, this case presented another opportunity to persuade the Court that sex, like race, religion, and national origin, should be subject to "strict scrutiny." Although the Court began to apply the Fourteenth Amendment's equal protection to sex-based discrimination cases, it still recognized "real differences" between males and females and used a lesser test (rational relation) in REED V. REED (1971). Future Supreme Court justice RUTH BADER GINSBURG, working with the ACLU's Women's Rights Project, advised the plaintiff's attorney to pursue a "heightened scrutiny" test for sex in this case.

In its decision, the Court articulated a three-tiered test to be applied in cases of laws discriminating on the basis of sex: heightened, intermediate, and mid-level scrutiny. Writing for the majority, Justice William Brennan said, "[s]tatutory classifications that distinguish between males and females are subject to scrutiny under the Equal Protection Clause. . . . [C]lassifications by gender must serve important governmental objectives and must be substantially related to achievement of those objectives." No longer would "loose-fitting characterizations" or sex stereotypes be accepted as a basis for gender-based statutes. State legislatures were directed to either make their laws gender-neutral or demonstrate that where laws treated men and women differently, the differences were based in fact, not generalizations. Oklahoma's law was declared unconstitutional.

The Court still applies "heightened scrutiny" to sex-based discrimination cases and has never adopted a "strict scrutiny" test similar to the one applied in racial discrimination cases. However, Justice Ruth Bader Ginsburg clarified the very narrow circumstances under which sex classifications would be constitutional in UNITED STATES V. VIRGINIA, ET AL. (1996), but she could not get enough votes to support the adoption of strict scrutiny.

Further Reading

Frost-Knappman, Elizabeth, and Kathryn Cullen-DuPont. *Women's Rights on Trial*. Detroit: Gale Publishing, 1997.

Lindgren, J. Ralph, Nadine Taub, Beth Ann Wolfson, and Carla M. Palumbo. *The Law of Sex Discrimination*, 3rd ed. Belmont, Calif.: Thomson Wadsworth, 2005.

Crandall, Prudence (1803–1890) *abolitionist, educator*   Born on September 3, 1803, in Rhode Island and raised a Quaker, Prudence Crandall opened Connecticut's first school for girls in 1831. In 1833, the school admitted Sarah Harris, a black woman from Connecticut, and the white families all pulled their daughters out of the school. Crandall then closed the school and reopened it as a boarding and day school for black girls. Eventually she was teaching 20 girls from all over the eastern seaboard. Citizens of Canterbury, Connecticut, objected to the school, and in response the Connecticut state legislature passed the Black Law, which stated that there could be no schooling in Connecticut for blacks from other states, unless the school were to receive prior written permission from the town. The Black Law stated that by educating blacks from other states, such schools would "tend to the great increase of coloured population of the state, and thereby to the injury of the people" (quoted from Crandall's trial, Crandall against the State of Connecticut, 1834).

Crandall was arrested and jailed under the Black Law, but the school remained open despite violent objections from local citizens. She only closed the school in 1834 out of fears for her students' safety. At her trial, Crandall argued that under the U.S. Constitution, citizens of one state are to be provided the privileges of other states. The prosecution then argued that free blacks were not understood to be citizens, and thus no defense on constitutional grounds could be made. Crandall's first trial ended with a hung jury, but she was found guilty in her second trial, based on the idea that blacks were not citizens and the Black Law was thus constitutional. The Black Law was repealed in 1838.

Crandall married Calvin Philleo in 1834 and moved to a homestead in Illinois, where she continued to teach and work for women's rights. The State of Connecticut formally apologized to her in 1890. She died in Elk Falls, Kansas, on January 28 that same year.

Further Reading

Petrash, Antonia. *More Than Petticoats: Remarkable Connecticut Women.* Guilford, Conn.: Globe Pequot Press, 2003.

Strane, Susan. *A Whole Souled Woman: Prudence Crandall and the Education of Black Women.* New York: W. W. Norton, 1990.

—Claire Curtis

Cubin, Barbara (1946–) *congressperson* Barbara Cubin was born on November 30, 1946, in Salinas, California, and raised in Casper, Wyoming. She holds a bachelor's degree in chemistry from Creighton University. Cubin has worked as a chemist, a social worker, and a substitute teacher in math and chemistry, and she also managed her husband's medical practice. In addition, she was an instructor in a math apprenticeship program at Casper College.

Cubin, a Republican, began her political career in 1986, when she was elected to the Wyoming House of Representatives; she served until 1992. She spent two years (1992–94) in the Wyoming Senate before running for Congress to succeed Representative Craig Thomas, who vacated Wyoming's only House seat to make a run for the U.S. Senate. Her first race was very close by Wyoming standards (Wyoming is one of the most Republican states in the nation), with Cubin winning by only seven points. In 2006, Democrat Gary Trauner came within 947 votes of defeating her, but she retained her seat.

Cubin's voting record is strongly conservative. A staunch opponent of abortion in any form,

she has consistently voted for restrictions on abortion and against funding of family planning groups that provide abortion services, counseling, or advocacy. Cubin serves as vice chair of the House Resources Committee. She is also a member of the Energy and Commerce Committee (Telecommunications Subcommittee; Commerce, Trade and Consumer Protection Subcommittee; and Health Subcommittee). On the Resources Committee, she serves on the Energy and Mineral Resources subcommittee, as well as on the subcommittee on Water and Power. Cubin also serves as communications chair of the Western Caucus and is a deputy whip.

Further Reading

Barone, Michael. *The Almanac of American Politics.* Washington, D.C.: National Journal Group, 2006.

"Cubin, Barbara L." In *Biographical Directory of the United States Congress, 1774 –present.* Available online. URL: http://bioguide.congress.gov/scripts/biodisplay.pl?index=C000962. Accessed on January 8, 2007.

"Representative Barbara L. Cubin (WY)." In *Project Vote Smart.* Available online. URL: http://votesmart.org/bio.php?can_id=CNIP7947. Accessed on January 8, 2007. .

—Angela Kouters

cult of domesticity (cult of true womanhood)   The cult of domesticity in the United States developed by the early 19th century. Promulgated through novels, religious tracts, and advice books, the cult of domesticity imposed a highly restrictive set of gender norm expectations on women (primarily white middle-class women). A "true woman" was highly desirable. Her characteristics included being submissive, self-sacrificing, highly moral, deeply religious, and asexual. She should devote herself to her husband's comforts, her children's training, and tending the home. Women who worked outside the home, even those who did so out of pure economic necessity (African-American, immigrant women, and poor women), could not aspire to true womanhood.

The cult of domesticity's expectations for women reinforced the SEPARATE SPHERES IDEOLOGY and thus served to limit women's political participation and negate any call for equality. However, the cult of domesticity also empowered middle-class white women because it defined a realm in which they practiced limited autonomy from men. Women's moral calling led them to found or join moral reform organizations dedicated to abolition, temperance, and eradicating PROSTITUTION. Feminists, although often a part of the same social movements, opposed the restrictions placed on women by the cult of domesticity. The backlash against the cult of true womanhood led to the SENECA FALLS CONVENTION in 1848 and later shaped the second wave of the feminist movement. BETTY FRIEDAN's description of the "problem that has no name" in The FEMININE MYSTIQUE can also be viewed as a backlash against the cult of domesticity and the limits that the private sphere imposed on women.

See also ABOLITIONIST MOVEMENT, WOMEN IN; FEMINISM; TEMPERANCE MOVEMENT.

Further Reading

Ellis, Sarah Stickney. "The Women of England: Their Social Duties and Domestic Habits." In *The Past Speaks, 2nd ed.*, edited by Walter Arnstein. Lexington, Mass.: D. C. Heath, 1993.

Cunningham, Minnie Fisher (1882–1964)

suffragist Minnie Fisher was born on March 19, 1882, near New Waverly, Texas. Educated by her mother, she earned a teaching certificate when she was 16. She was introduced to politics by her father, who took her to meetings of the Texas House of Representatives. In 1901, she became one of the first Texas women to earn a pharmacy degree. The following year, she married Bill Cunningham, a lawyer and insurance executive.

When Minnie Cunningham discovered that she was being paid half the salary of her

Minnie Fisher Cunningham (LIBRARY OF CONGRESS)

nondegreed male coworkers, her resentment about the inequity led to a growing interest in politics. Active in the women's SUFFRAGE movement, she served as president of the Texas Equal Suffrage Association from 1915 to 1919 and as secretary of the NATIONAL AMERICAN WOMAN SUFFRAGE ASSOCIATION's Congressional Committee during 1918–19. She then helped organize the National LEAGUE OF WOMEN VOTERS, and as its first executive secretary lobbied for the SHEPPARD-TOWNER MATERNITY AND INFANCY PROTECTION ACT OF 1921 and the CABLE ACT OF 1922. ELEANOR ROOSEVELT invited Cunningham to be a member of the Democratic Woman's Advisory Committee that proposed women's reforms at the 1924 Democratic National Convention.

Cunningham was one of the founding members of the Woman's National Democratic

Club, and from 1925 to 1928 was its resident director. After serving as the Democratic National Committee's Women's Division's acting head in 1927, Cunningham ran unsuccessfully in Texas for a U.S. Senate seat in 1928. A member of Eleanor Roosevelt's women's network during the 1930s and early 1940s, Cunningham was so successful in converting women into New Deal supporters that the Democratic National Committee staff privately considered her the South's best female political organizer. As part of the 1940s left-FEMINISM movement, Cunningham urged equal pay for black women teachers and an end to restrictions on black voting, and she supported school desegregation in the 1950s.

Further Reading

McArthur, Judith N. *Creating the New Woman: The Rise of Southern Women's Progressive Culture in Texas, 1893–1918.* Urbana: University of Illinois Press, 1998.
McArthur, Judith N., and Harold L. Smith. *Minnie Fisher Cunningham: A Suffragist's Life in Politics.* New York: Oxford University Press, 2003.

—Harold L. Smith

Curtis, Lucile Atcherson (1895–1986) *diplomatic service officer*   Lucile Atcherson Curtis was born in Columbus, Ohio, on October 11, 1894, the only child of Fred Wayland and Charlotte Ray Atcherson. Her parents doted on her and gave her the best of everything, including an education at the prestigious Columbus School for Girls. A superlative student, she graduated from Columbus at the age of 14 and was 18 when she graduated from Smith College (1913). Though she took some business courses and engaged in work as a secretary, she found she was happiest in volunteer work.

As early as 1912, Atcherson became involved in the SUFFRAGE movement, and she became the first woman from Columbus to join the NATIONAL WOMAN'S PARTY. In 1914, she began working for the Franklin County Suffrage Society for a small salary. She also helped to organize the Ohio Suffrage Association and succeeded in persuading many black women to join what was usually considered to be a white woman's cause. These activities encouraged Atcherson to broaden her horizons, and in 1917 she volunteered for overseas duty with the American Fund for the French Wounded. Her work led to the French government awarding her the Medaille de la Reconnaissance Française in 1919.

In 1920, after women had won the right vote, Atcherson applied for the Foreign Service, which involved a grueling series of tests. She and 12 men passed, and in 1922 she was appointed to the State Department's Division of Latin American Affairs, becoming the first woman to work for the Foreign Service. Initially the Senate was reluctant to approve posting a woman overseas, but in 1923 it voted overwhelmingly to appoint her as a diplomat to Bern, Switzerland. The historic appointment was hailed by the *Christian Science Monitor* as "an expansion of women's political aspirations."

In 1926, Atcherson met George Curtis, a professor of anatomy then studying in Bern. The following year, she was transferred to Panama, a posting she was not happy about, in part due to her romance with Curtis and in part because she had been repeatedly passed over for promotion. Unknown to her, she had also become the subject of increasingly harsh ratings of her job performance; one evaluation made reference to her sex being "a handicap to useful official friendships." However, it was because of her relationship with Curtis and her unhappiness over the transfer to Panama that she resigned from the Foreign Service in autumn 1927. Atcherson and Curtis were married on January 6, 1928.

Lucile and George Curtis settled in Chicago and had two daughters, Charlotte Murray Curtis, who became the first woman on the masthead of the *New York Times,* and Mary Darling Curtis. George Curtis died in 1965; Lucile lived another 21 years, suffering periodic bouts of depression. At the age of 77, she was a delegate to the White House Conference on Aging. On May 19, 1978, she and Clifton Wharton, the first black person in the U.S. Foreign Service, were honored by the State Department for their pioneering work. Lucile Atcherson Curtis died on May 9, 1986, at the age of 91.

Further Reading

Greenwald, Marilyn S. *A Woman of Times: Journalism, Feminism, and the Life of Charlotte Curtis.* Chapter 1: "A Life in Public Service." Available online. URL: http://www.nytimes.com/books/first/g/greenwald-times.html. Accessed on March 25, 2007.

D

Dall, Caroline (Caroline Wells Healy Dall)
(1822–1912) *writer, activist* Caroline Wells
Healey was born in Boston on June 22, 1822. As
a well-educated young woman, Healey was
strongly influenced by the "Conversations" (Seminars) led by the preeminent woman intellectual
of her day, Margaret Fuller. From an early age she
devoted herself to philanthropy among the poor
and found herself attracted to abolitionism and
women's rights. After a reversal in her family's
fortunes, she worked as a boarding school teacher.
On September 24, 1844, she married Rev. Charles
Henry Appleton Dall. She supported Charles's
ministry but also wrote for *Una,* a women's rights
journal. When her husband left for India as a
missionary in 1855, Dall remained in Massachusetts with their two children and became a leader
of the woman's rights movement, lecturing, writing, and organizing conventions.

Dall's most famous work was a series of
lectures, published as *The College, the Market
and the Court* (1867), in which she argued that
women should not be limited to the domestic
sphere but be allowed to contribute economically and morally to the nation. Woman's rights
did not constitute her only interest, however.
In 1865, Dall helped found the American Social
Science Association, which investigated social
conditions for use in reform efforts. For the
remainder of her life, she focused on writing,
preaching, and teaching. She published a wide
range of works, from children's literature to a
study of Shakespeare. Dall died on December 17,
1912, in Washington, D.C.

Though her intense work for women's rights
took place during only part of her life, Dall was
an important force, intellectually and organizationally, in a key time of FEMINISM's development.
Her arguments concerning women's employment and wages, in particular, prefigured those
of the next generation of feminists, most prominently CHARLOTTE PERKINS GILMAN.

Further Reading
Conrad, Susan Phinney. *Perish the Thought: Intellectual
    Women in Romantic America, 1830–1860.* New
    York: Oxford University Press, 1976.
Leach, William. *True Love and Perfect Union: The Femi-
    nist Reform of Sex and Society.* New York: Basic
    Books Inc., 1980.

—Laura R. Prieto

date rape   See ACQUAINTANCE RAPE.

Daughters of Bilitis (DOB)   Daughters of Bilitis (DOB) was launched in San Francisco in 1955 and is remembered as the first lesbian political organization founded in the United States. Del Martin (b. 1921) and Phyllis Lyon (b. 1924), who are credited with organizing and sustaining DOB, desired to develop socialization opportunities for lesbian women as an alternative to bar culture. In September 1955, Lyon and Martin met with three other lesbian couples. After a few weeks of meeting, DOB was created to provide a safe place for socializing and dancing. DOB derived its name from French poet Pierre Louys's homoerotic poem "Songs of Bilitis."

Initially the group remained small with a commitment to socializing, but members often found themselves talking about politics, their lives, and injustices experienced as lesbians. DOB extended its work to educate the public about lesbianism and improve the status of homosexuals. Throughout the 1950s and 1960s, DOB cooperated with the Mattachine Society and One, Inc., primarily male homosexual rights organizations, in holding public events and forums. Although DOB's membership was minimal, it reached many lonely lesbians through its newsletter *The Latter* when limited copies passed from friend to friend. DOB attracted a middle-class white audience, and for much of its history, the group focused on assimilation and acceptance rather than militancy. Efforts were directed to soliciting mental health professionals researching homosexuals, targeting lawyers to help change the penal code, and providing a network of services and support for lesbians. Although the national organization had disbanded by 1972, some local chapters continued to operate.

Further Reading

D'Emilio, John. *Sexual Politics, Sexual Communities: The Making of a Homosexual Minority in the United States, 1940–1970*. Chicago: University of Chicago Press, 1983.

Martin, Del, and Phyllis Lyon. *Lesbian/Women*. San Francisco: Bantam, 1972.

—Howell Williams

Daughters of Liberty   In 1765, colonists organized protests against the Stamp Act, imposed by the British to force colonists to pay a share of the costs associated with stationing troops in the colonies. This act required the colonists to pay a tax, represented by a stamp, on newspapers, playing cards, diplomas, and legal documents. Reactions to the Stamp Act included riots and boycotts of British goods. Sons of Liberty, a secret men's society, prevented stamped papers from being unloaded from British ships. The Daughters of Liberty was formed by colonial women to promote the manufacture of homespun cloth as a substitute for imported British cloth; they raised funds for General George Washington's army and circulated protest petitions.

Further Reading

Roberts, Cokie. *Founding Mothers: The Women Who Raised Our Nation*. New York: HarperCollins, 2004.

Daughters of Temperance   The Daughters of Temperance was an early women's organization supporting abstention from the use of alcohol. SUSAN B. ANTHONY, the product of a Quaker upbringing, joined the Daughters of Temperance to draw attention to the effects of drunkenness on families and campaign for stronger liquor laws. She made her first public speech in 1848 at a Daughters of Temperance supper. When Anthony returned to Rochester in 1849, she was elected president of the Rochester branch of the Daughters of Temperance and raised money for the cause. In 1853, as a representative of the Rochester Daughters of Temperance, Anthony was refused the right to speak at the state convention of the Sons of Temperance. Outraged, she collaborated with ELIZABETH CADY STANTON to found the Women's State Temperance Society with the goal of petitioning the State legislature to pass a law limiting the sale of liquor. The state legislature rejected the petition because most of the 28,000 signatures were from women. Anthony decided then that women needed the vote so that politicians could not ignore their issues. Anthony and Stanton were later criticized by organization members for talking too much about women's rights and so resigned to work full-time on women's SUFFRAGE.

Further Reading

Epstein, Barbara Leslie. *The Politics of Domesticity: Women, Evangelism, and Temperance in Nineteenth Century America.* Middletown: Wesleyan University Press, 1981.

Daughters of the American Revolution (DAR)

The Daughters of the American Revolution (DAR) was founded in 1890 and chartered by Congress on December 2, 1896. Membership is made up of female descendants of Revolutionary War patriots. The DAR headquarters in Washington, D.C., houses one of the nation's premier genealogical libraries, a collection of preindustrial American decorative arts, Washington's largest concert hall, and an extensive collection of early American manuscripts and imprints. The DAR boasts 170,000 members in 3,000 chapters across the United States and internationally. The organization focuses primarily on community voluntarism, scholarships, and support for education. In 1939, the DAR turned down MARIAN ANDERSON's request to perform at Constitution Hall. First Lady ELEANOR ROOSEVELT resigned from the organization in protest and arranged for Anderson to sing on the steps of the Lincoln Memorial.

On January 27, 2005, the DAR cohosted a ceremony with the U.S. Postal Service releasing a commemorative stamp in honor of Marian Anderson. DAR president Presley Merritt Wagoner included the following statement in her remarks: "We deeply regret that Marian Anderson was not given the opportunity to perform her 1939 Easter concert in Constitution Hall but recognize that in the positive sense the event was a pivotal point in the struggle for racial equality. Ms. Anderson's legendary concert on the steps of

Mrs. Asmead White (fourth from left), president-general of the Daughters of the American Revolution (DAR), stands with six new vice presidents–general, elected at the April 20, 1961, session of the DAR's 70th Continental Congress in Washington, D.C. (LIBRARY OF CONGRESS)

the Lincoln Memorial will always be remembered as a milestone in the Civil Rights movement. The beauty of her voice, amplified by her courage and grace, brought attention to the eloquence of the many voices urging our nation to overcome prejudice and intolerance. It sparked change not only in America but also in the DAR."

Further Reading

Anderson, Peggy. *The Daughters: An Unconventional Look at America's Fan Club—the D.A.R.* New York: St. Martin's Press, 1974.

Davis, Angela (1944–) *political activist* Angela Yvonne Davis was born in Birmingham, Alabama, on January 26, 1944. She studied both at home and in Paris between 1961 and 1967 and received her B.A. (magna cum laude) from Brandeis in 1965. While attending graduate school at the University of California at San Diego, she studied philosophy under the acclaimed Marxist theorist Herbert Marcuse. By 1968, Davis's activism was escalating; she moved to Los Angeles and became a member of both the Communist Party and the Black Panthers shortly after the death of Martin Luther King, Jr.

The following year, Davis was offered the position of lecturer in the philosophy department at the University of California, Los Angeles (UCLA). After teaching for only one year (and despite an excellent academic record at the institution), the California Board of Regents denied her reappointment because of her affiliation with the Communist Party and her advocacy of "radical" black politics. In August 1970, Davis was linked to the much-publicized attempted escape at the Marin County courtroom in which three people were killed. After a gun legally registered to her was found on the scene, Davis was charged with conspiracy, murder, and kidnapping, becoming the third woman in history to appear on the FBI's "most wanted" list, and she promptly went into hiding. She was apprehended two months later in New York and returned to California for her hearing. The trial received international attention, sparked a worldwide campaign in support of her innocence, and lasted more than 13 weeks. After spending over 16 months behind bars, Davis was released on bail and was later acquitted of all charges by an all-white jury.

Following her release from prison and riding the momentum of the "Free Angela Davis" movement, she established the National Alliance Against Racist and Political Repression, an organization that exists to this day. Davis's writings on communism and racial oppression in the United States were published in *If They Come in the Morning: Voices of Resistance* (1971). Immediately after that book's publication, she began documenting her young but active life to date, the results of which became *Angela Davis: An Autobiography* (1974, reprinted 1988). She subsequently returned to teaching, first at San Francisco State University (1979–91) and then at the University of California–Santa Cruz. She became a noted lecturer, speaking to audiences around the globe on issues of institutionalized racism and oppression. In 1980 and again in 1984, she ran for vice president of the United States as the American Communist Party's candidate.

Davis's writing has also garnered international recognition. *Women, Race & Class*, published in 1981, became an instant staple in many university courses and continues to be widely read. A collection of her speeches, given between 1983 and 1987, was published in a volume entitled *Women, Culture, and Politics* in 1989.

Davis has remained committed to social and political activism. In 1998, she co-organized "Critical Resistance: Beyond the Prison Industrial Complex," a national conference on racism and classism in the justice system held at Berkeley. Her current research reflects the event's theme, and FEMINISM, African-American studies, popular music, cultural theory, and philosophy remain at the forefront of her academic research. She holds tenure at the University of California–Santa Cruz, in the history of consciousness program, and sits on the advisory board of the Prison Activist Resource Center, still struggling to expose and extinguish racism in American institutions.

Further Reading

Davis, Angela. *Blues Legacies and Black Feminism: Gertrude "Ma" Rainey, Bessie Smith, and Billie Holiday.* New York: Pantheon Books, 1998.

———. *The Angela Y. Davis Reader.* Malden, Mass.: Blackwell Publishers, 1998.

———. *Violence Against Women and the Ongoing Challenge to Racism.* Latham, N.Y.: Kitchen Table Women of Color Press, 1992.

———, and Chela Sandoval. *Methodology of the Oppressed.* Minneapolis: University of Minnesota Press, 2000.

————, and Joy James. *Resisting State Violence: Radicalism, Gender, and Race in U.S. Culture*. Malden, Mass.: Blackwell Publishers, 1996.

Lubiano, Wahneema, ed. *The House That Race Built*. New York: Vintage Books, 1998.

—Candis Steenbergen

Davis, Jo Ann (1950–) *congressperson* Jo Ann Davis was born in Rowan County, North Carolina, on June 29, 1959, but has lived in Virginia since she was nine years old. She attended Hampton Roads Business College. Davis worked in real estate before she was elected to the Virginia House of Delegates in 1996. She was reelected in 1998.

In 2000, first-district Congressman Herb Bateman, a 17-year incumbent, announced his retirement due to health concerns. He subsequently died on September 11, 2000. Davis ran for and won the Republican nomination to succeed him, despite Governor Jim Gilmore's endorsement of her primary opponent. She went on to win easily in November. She was the second Virginia woman and the first Virginia Republican woman elected to the House in her own right. Davis was unopposed in 2002 and 2004. In 2006, she held her seat against two challengers.

Davis is a staunch conservative and one of four Pentecostals serving in Congress. Davis believes God led her to Congress. She can be counted on to vote for tax cuts for all who pay taxes and has promoted an agenda that includes pro-life legislation and support for the traditional family. She is a deputy majority whip and chairwoman of the House Intelligence Subcommittee on Intelligence Policy. She is married to Charles E. Davis II, with whom she has two children.

Further Reading

Barone, Michael. *The Almanac of American Politics*. Washington, D.C.: National Journal Group, 2006.

"Davis, Jo Ann." In *Biographical Directory of the United States Congress, 1774–present*. Available online.

URL: http://bioguide.congress.gov/scripts/biodisplay.pl?index=D000597. Accessed on January 8, 2007.

"Representative Jo Ann S. Davis (VA)." In *Project Vote Smart*. Available online. URL: http://votesmart.org/bio.php?can_id=CS040937. Accessed on January 8, 2007.

—Angela Kouters

Davis, Susan (1944–) *congressperson* Susan Davis was born on April 13, 1944, in Cambridge, Massachusetts, but has spent most of her life in California. She graduated from the University of California at Berkeley in 1964 and earned a master's degree in social work from the University of North Carolina at Chapel Hill in 1968. She worked as a social worker in San Diego before her 1983 election to the San Diego School Board, where she served until 1992. In 1994, she was elected to the California State Assembly (1994–2000). As an assemblywoman, Davis chaired the Committee on Consumer Protection, Government Efficiency and Economic Development. She authored a state law giving women direct access to their gynecologists without getting a referral from their primary care physicians.

In 2000, Davis challenged three-term Republican incumbent Brian Bilbray in what was then the 49th district, winning with 50 percent of the vote. Her district was renumbered the 53rd district after the 2000 census and redrawn to include more of San Diego. She has won reelection in each cycle with little opposition, including in 2006. She is the first Democrat to represent the district for more than one term since its creation in 1953. Davis serves on the House Committee on Armed Services and the Committee on Education and the Workforce. Her legislative priorities include defense, education, environment, health care, and veteran's affairs. She has two sons with her husband, Steve.

Further Reading

Barone, Michael. *The Almanac of American Politics*. Washington, D.C.: National Journal Group, 2006.

"Davis, Susan A." In *Biographical Directory of the United States Congress, 1774–present.* Available online. URL: http://bioguide.congress.gov/scripts/biodisplay.pl?index=. Accessed on January 8, 2007.

"Representative Susan A. Davis (CA)." In *Project Vote Smart.* Available online. URL: http://votesmart.org/bio.php?can_id=. Accessed on January 8, 2007.

—Angela Kouters

Day, Dorothy (1897–1980) *religious leader, social activist, journalist* Born on November 8, 1897, in Brooklyn, New York, Day attended the University of Illinois for two years and then moved to New York City in 1916. She wrote articles for socialist newspapers such as the *Call* and participated in demonstrations against the United States' involvement in World War I. After the birth of her daughter in 1927, Day answered her inner spiritual yearnings by converting to Roman Catholicism. In January 1933, she met Peter Maurin, a fellow Catholic and raffish lay philosopher. Day and Maurin cofounded the *Catholic Worker* newspaper, which published its first issue on May 1, 1933. The two also established "hospitality houses," which emphasized care of the poor and disadvantaged and advocated lives of personal poverty.

Controversial after World War II because of her condemnation of the Hiroshima and Nagasaki atomic bombings and her protest of civil-defense drills in New York City, Day gradually won both respect and recognition both within and outside the American Roman Catholic church by the late 1960s. She died on November 29, 1980, in New York City's Maryhouse, her hospitality house for abused women.

Dorothy Day's contribution to women's involvement in politics stands as a substantial, if indirect, one since she considered herself an anarchist. She helped refocus American Catholic women's perceptions away from ritual and opposition to international communism to issues of social concern. The tumultuous, but still-thriving, Catholic Worker movement attests to Day's powerful witness for her church and the question of its worldly mission.

Further Reading
Forest, James H. *Love Is the Measure: A Biography of Dorothy Day.* Maryknoll, N.Y.: Orbis Press, 1994.
Miller, William D. *Dorothy Day: A Biography.* New York: Harper and Row, 1982.
Thorn, William, Phillip Runkel, and Susan Moutin, eds. *Dorothy Day and the Catholic Worker Movement: Centenary Essays.* Milwaukee: Marquette University Press, 2001.

—John Thomas McGuire

Declaration of Sentiments and Resolutions (Declaration of Rights and Sentiments) (1848) LUCRETIA MOTT and ELIZABETH CADY STANTON were the driving force behind a movement to address the plight of women in 19th-century society, which resulted in the SENECA FALLS CONVENTION in 1848. This event took place eight years after they met in London at an antislavery convention and was the first public political meeting addressing women's rights and where Stanton composed the Declaration of Sentiments and Resolutions. In July 1848, over 300 men and women met in Seneca Falls, New York, for the First Women's Rights Convention. There, the declaration was debated and refined. The public release of the Declaration of Sentiments and Resolutions triggered dialogues among many women interested in equal rights and woman SUFFRAGE. The declaration was also met with strong criticism and anger. It became one of the roots of the suffrage movement when Stanton insisted that this resolution be included: "Resolved, that it is the duty of the women of this country to secure to themselves their sacred right to the elective franchise." The document is remarkable because for the first time women publicly claimed their inalienable rights and held men responsible for a host of grievances. The dozen resolutions passed demanded equal rights for women in marriage, education, religion, and employment. The document is included among the appendices to this volume.

Further Reading

Commager, Henry Steele, ed. *Documents of American History to 1898*, vol. 1. New York: Prentice Hall, 1993.
Stanton, Elizabeth Cady, Susan B. Anthony, and Matilda Gage. *History of Woman Suffrage*, vol. 1, *1848–1861*. Salem, N.H.: Ayer Co., 1985.
Yellin, Carol Lynn, and Janann Sherman. *The Perfect 36: Tennessee Delivers Woman Suffrage*. Oak Ridge: Iris Press, 1998.

—Paula Casey

Declaration of Women's Rights (July 4, 1876)

On July 4, 1876, SUSAN B. ANTHONY delivered a speech entitled "Declaration of Rights of the Women of the United States"; it was written by MATILDA JOSLYN GAGE and ELIZABETH CADY STANTON. The address was a political statement on the status of women delivered during the celebration of the nation's centennial. The content of the declaration focused on women's status as noncitizens by highlighting women's lack of civil and political rights guaranteed to men in the Bill of Rights. The address closed with this statement:

And now, at the close of a hundred years, as the hour hand of the great clock that marks the centuries points to 1876, we declare our faith in the principles of self-government; our full equality with man in natural rights; that woman was made first for her own happiness, with the absolute right to herself—to all the opportunities and advantages life affords for her complete development; and we deny that dogma of the centuries, incorporated in the codes of nations—that woman was made for man—her best interests, in all cases, to be sacrificed to his will. We ask of our rulers, at this hour, no special favors, no special privileges, no special legislation. We ask justice, we ask equality, we ask that all the civil and political rights that belong to citizens of the United States, be guaranteed to us and our daughters forever.

Defense Advisory Committee on Women in the Services (DACOWITS)

The Department of Defense Advisory Committee on Women in the Services (DACOWITS) was established in 1951 by then Secretary of Defense George C. Marshall. The committee is composed of civilian women and men who are appointed by the secretary of defense to provide advice and recommendations on matters and policies relating to the recruitment and retention, treatment, employment, integration, and well-being of highly qualified professional women in the armed forces. DACOWITS has consistently brought hard questions to the attention of military leaders who, to their credit, have made progressive changes. Coed boot camp, gender "norming" of fitness standards, rules aimed at eliminating SEXUAL HARASSMENT, and family-friendly policies are all changes instituted as a result of DACOWITS's work. The panel also was behind President Bill Clinton's 1994 move to put women on most combat ships and aircraft. In 2002, Secretary of Defense Donald Rumsfeld let the group's charter lapse and dismissed all of its members. Under its new charter, the committee's historic focus on gender integration has been watered down by a new emphasis on recruitment and retention, as well as a new spotlight on family issues. In addition, the Pentagon now controls the agenda, raising questions about the group's autonomy and continued effectiveness.

DeGette, Diana (1957–) congressperson

Diana DeGette was born in Japan on July 29, 1957, while her father served in the armed forces. She graduated with honors from Colorado College in 1979 and earned a J.D. degree from New York University in 1982. She returned to Denver and began a law practice focusing on civil rights and employment litigation. Active in Denver politics, she was elected to the Colorado House of Representatives in 1992. She became minority whip after being reelected in 1994. She is the author of a law that guarantees Colorado women unobstructed access to abortion clinics and other medical care facilities; popularly known as the "Bubble Bill," it was unsuccessfully challenged in HILL V. COLORADO (2000).

In 1995, first-district congresswoman PATRICIA SCHROEDER announced that she was retiring after 12 terms (24 years) in the House; she endorsed DeGette in the Democratic primary. DeGette won the primary with 55 percent of the vote and then won in November 1996 with 57 percent of the vote. She has since been reelected five times against token Republican opposition.

DeGette has a liberal voting record and works on feminist causes. She also has a reputation as an effective legislative strategist. She was the primary Democratic sponsor of the bill to lift President George W. Bush's limits on stem cell research in 1995, a bill that prompted Bush's first presidential veto on July 19, 2006. In the 109th Congress, she serves on the Energy and Commerce Committee. She also serves as the cochair of the Congressional Diabetes Caucus and the pro-choice caucus. She has risen through the ranks of the Democratic leadership and now serves as a chief deputy whip. After the Democrats regained control of the House in the 2006 elections, she considered running for house majority whip but chose not to challenge South Carolina's Representative Jim Clyburn.

Further Reading

Barone, Michael. *The Almanac of American Politics.* Washington, D.C.: National Journal Group, 2006.

"DeGette, Diana." In *Biographical Directory of the United States Congress, 1774–present.* Available online. URL: http://bioguide.congress.gov/scripts/biodisplay.pl?index=D000197. Accessed on January 8, 2007.

"Representative Diana L. DeGette (CO)." In *Project Vote Smart.* Available online. URL: http://votesmart.org/bio.php?con_id=BC037052. Accessed on January 8, 2007.

—Angela Kouters

DeLauro, Rosa (1943–) *congressperson* Rosa DeLauro was born March 2, 1943, in New Haven, Connecticut, and raised in New Haven's Wooster Square, where for years her grandmother owned and operated a pastry shop. DeLauro's mother, Luisa, was the longest-serving member of the New Haven Board of Aldermen (1965–98). DeLauro is a graduate of Marymount College, where she received her B.A. with honors in 1964. She earned her master's degree in international politics from Columbia University in 1966 and studied at the London School of Economics. DeLauro worked as chief of staff to Senator Christopher Dodd for seven years and then served as director of EMILY'S LIST, the Democratic pro-choice fund-raising organization. She is married to political pollster and consultant Stanley Greenburg.

DeLauro was first elected to Congress in 1990. In 2006, she was reelected to a ninth term. She has promoted legislation to require 48-hour hospital stays following mastectomies. She continues to fight, as yet unsuccessfully, to remove abortion restrictions from federal employees' health benefits. She works actively for feminist issues in the House, including, most recently, the Paycheck Fairness Act designed to strengthen the EQUAL PAY ACT OF 1963. She sits on the House Appropriations Committee and serves as ranking member of the Agriculture Subcommittee and as a member of the Labor-Health and Human Services–Education Subcommittee. She also serves on the House Budget Committee. In 1999, she was elected assistant to the Democratic leader by her colleagues, making her the second-highest-ranking Democratic woman in the House of Representatives. She was reelected to this position in 2000. In 2002, she was appointed cochair of the House Democratic Steering Committee, a position she was reelected to in 2004. She was re-elected in 2006 with 76 percent of the vote.

Further Reading

Barone, Michael. *The Almanac of American Politics.* Washington, D.C.: National Journal Group, 2006.

"De Lauro, Rosa L." In *Biographical Directory of the United States Congress, 1774–present.* Available online. URL: http://bioguide.congress.gov/scripts/biodisplay.pl?index=D000216. Accessed on January 8, 2007.

"Representative Rosa L. DeLauro (CT)." In *Project Vote Smart.* Available online. URL: http://votesmart.org/bio.php?can_id=H673103. Accessed on January 8, 2007.

—Angela Kouters

Dennett, Mary (Mary Coffin Ware Dennett)

(1872–1947) *birth control activist* Born on April 4, 1872, Mary Ware Dennett became a national figure in the battle for the repeal of obscenity laws that restricted the dissemination of birth control information. Dennett began her political career as field secretary in the SUFFRAGE movement and soon became active in socialist causes. In 1915, her career took a turn when she became head of the National Birth Control League, the first organization to lobby against obscenity legislation under the COMSTOCK ACT. Unlike fellow birth control advocate MARGARET SANGER, Dennett took a conservative approach to lobbying for sex education and the repeal of restrictive legislation. In 1918, the VOLUNTARY PARENTHOOD LEAGUE (VPL) was established, and Dennett served as its director and the editor of the *Birth Control Herald* until a policy split caused her to resign in 1925.

After her split from the VPL, Dennett concentrated on writing publications aimed at educating the public about contraception and sex. In 1926, she published *Birth Control Laws,* which outlined the history of the Comstock Act and her legislative attempts challenging it. She was convicted on obscenity charges in 1929 for repeatedly requesting a pamphlet she had written nine years earlier entitled "The Sex Side of Life: An Explanation for Young People" to be distributed through the mail. The essay was Dennett's attempt to set straight ideas on sex and sexuality for adolescents. With the help of the

American Civil Liberties Union, her conviction was overturned in 1930, and she continued to write books, letters, and articles advocating the importance of sex education and birth control information. She remained active in the peace movement during World War II and until her death on July 25, 1947.

See also BIRTH CONTROL MOVEMENT.

Further Reading

Chen, Constance M. *The Sex Side of Life: Mary Ware Dennett's Pioneering Battle for Birth Control and Sex Education.* New York: W. W. Norton & Co., 1996.

Dennett, Mary Ware. *Birth Control Laws: Shall We Keep Them, Change Them, or Abolish Them.* New York: Da Capo Press, 1926.

Gordon, Linda. *The Moral Property of Women: A History of Birth Control Politics in America.* Chicago: University of Illinois Press, 2002.

—Patricia Walsh Coates

Detzer, Dorothy

(1893–1981) *congressional lobbyist, activist* Dorothy Detzer, heralded by the *New York Times* as "the most famous woman lobbyist," campaigned for disarmament and economic justice. Her lifelong commitment to fighting against war and military armament by all countries was shaped by her personal humanitarian travel around the world and by a family tragedy that was a direct result of war.

Detzer was born on December 1, 1893, and grew up in Fort Wayne, Indiana. After graduating from high school and traveling throughout the Far East and the Philippines, she then returned to the United States and dedicated her life to social work. She enrolled in the Chicago School of Civics and Philanthropy while serving as an officer of the Juvenile Protective Association. After World War I, she left the United States for humanitarian relief work in Austria and Russia. Strongly affected by the miseries of war she witnessed in Austria and Russia, and by the death of her twin brother after an illness due to gassing during World

War I, Detzer became convinced that relief work could not by itself eliminate warfare and she became actively involved in the pacifist movement.

In 1922, Detzer joined the U.S. section of the Women's International League for Peace and Freedom (WILPF). Serving as the WILPF's national secretary, she attempted to shape and influence U.S. foreign policy and the public's attitude about war, with particular focus on the consequences of war for women and children. Her most successful lobbying efforts included a legislative investigation into the military-industrial complex launched by Senator Gerald Nye. The Nye Committee was successful in getting the president to approve a mandatory arms embargo on the sale of arms when two or more foreign states engage in war.

Coupled with her antiwar efforts, Detzer fought for economic justice focusing on the economic inequality that African countries suffered as a result of U.S. and British business concessions. She worked relentlessly for recognition of the Soviet Union in the family of nations and for Cuba's freedom from U.S. intervention, and she argued for U.S. neutrality as WWII approached. In 1933, her economic-justice efforts resulted in her receiving the Order of African Redemption by the Liberian government.

Detzer was not without her critics. Her antiwar calls and her criticism of militarism along with her call to include the Soviet Union in the family of nations caused her to garner accusations of anti-Americanism and claims of being a communist. After marrying Ludwell Denny, a journalist, in 1954, Detzer left the Washington lobbying circle in pursuit of a career as a freelance foreign journalist. She died on January 7, 1981, in Monterey, California.

Further Reading

Schott, Linda. *Reconstructing Women's Thoughts: The Women's International League for Peace and Freedom Before World War II.* Stanford, Calif.: Stanford University Press, 1997.

—Hollis France

Dewson, Mary Williams (Mary [Molly] Williams Dewson) (1874–1962) *feminist, activist* Born on February 18, 1874, in Quincy, Massachusetts, Dewson graduated from Wellesley College in 1897. After nearly 30 years of working in organizations such as the National Consumers' League and the Consumers' League of New York, Dewson entered national politics through her close friendship with ELEANOR ROOSEVELT. In 1928, she worked in the midwestern division of Alfred E. Smith's 1928 presidential campaign. Four years later, Dewson became director of the women's division of the Democratic National Campaign Committee. After Franklin D. Roosevelt's presidential election in November 1932, Dewson and Eleanor Roosevelt wanted to strengthen women's participation in the national Democratic Party. They lobbied President Roosevelt and the new chairperson of the Democratic National Committee (DNC), James A. Farley, to create a full-time directorship of the Women's Division. They were successful, and Dewson assumed the new position in October 1933.

As leader of the DNC's Women's Division from 1933 through her retirement in June 1937, Dewson increased women's participation in Democratic politics. She created a national speakers' bureau, published a monthly magazine, lobbied for the New Deal's social legislation, and made women throughout the nation local New Deal experts through the Reporter Plan. The Women's Division played a significant part in securing President Roosevelt's reelection in 1936.

After her retirement, Dewson served on the Social Security Administration's executive board until 1938 and then resided in Castine, Maine. She died on October 21, 1962, just a few weeks before the passing of her political mentor, Eleanor Roosevelt.

Dewson's contribution to women's involvement in the United States' politics stands as a large one. For the first time in Democratic Party history, women participated extensively in organizing and strategizing for national elections.

Further Reading

McGuire, John Thomas. "From the Courts to the State Legislatures: Social Justice Feminism, Labor Legislation, and the 1920s." *Labor History* 45 (2004): 225–246.

Ware, Susan. *Partner and I.* New Haven, Conn.: Yale University Press, 1987.

—John Thomas McGuire

Dix, Dorothea (Dorothea Lynde Dix)

(1802–1887) *social reformer, mental health reformer* Dorothea Lynde Dix was born in Hampden, Maine, on April 4, 1802, the daughter of Mary and Joseph Dix. Her early life was difficult owing to her mother's mental illness and her father's alcoholism. Dix was responsible for raising her younger brothers and chafed under her wealthy grandmother's desire to see her become a lady. Her first career was as a school-teacher, after she persuaded her grandmother to allow her to open a school in their home. Dix, who suffered from tuberculosis, worked as a teacher until her late 20s, when her illness forced her to take a long rest. Upon recuperation, she began her second career after visiting a women's prison in the hope of beginning Sunday school classes. The prison's population included many mentally ill and mentally challenged women. Appalled at the conditions, Dix worked for much of the rest of her life to improve treatment of the mentally ill and the incarcerated.

Initially Dix worked with members of the Massachusetts legislature to change the laws concerning the nature of institutionalizing the mentally ill. She was convinced that mental illness could be treated and was likely to be exacerbated by the appalling conditions found in the prisons where many people were housed. She was enormously influential in changing people's views about the mentally ill, and she succeeded in changing the laws of Massachusetts and many other states. She even lobbied Congress in 1854 to pass a law establishing 5 million acres of federal land for the treatment of the mentally ill. This bill was passed but then was vetoed by President Franklin Pierce.

At the outset of the Civil War, Dix became the superintendent of female nurses for the Union forces, training women to be army nurses, collecting medical supplies, and inspecting hospital facilities. At the end of the war, she returned to her work lobbying for the treatment of mental illness as an illness. She planned a number of hospital facilities for the treatment of the mentally ill, and the first facility that she planned and built in Trenton, New Jersey, contained an apartment for her retirement. She died there on July 17, 1887.

Dorothea Lynde Dix (LIBRARY OF CONGRESS)

Further Reading

Gollaher, David. *Voices for the Mad: The Life of Dorothea Dix.* New York: Free Press, 1995.

Schlaifer, Charles, and Lucy Freeman. *Heart's Work: Civil War Heroine and Champion of the Mentally*

Ill, *Dorothea Lynde Dix.* Gettysburg, Pa.: Stan Clark Military Books, 1991.

—Claire Curtis

Doe v. Bolton (410 U.S. 179) (1973)

In 1970, Mary Doe, an indigent, filed under Georgia law for a therapeutic abortion recommended by her treating physician. Georgia law made all abortions a crime unless they comply with a three-step process: (1) that the abortion be performed in a hospital accredited by the Joint Commission on Accreditation of Hospitals (JCAH), (2) that the procedure be approved by the hospital staff abortion committee, and (3) that the performing physician's judgment be confirmed by independent examinations of the patient by two other licensed physicians. Denied permission for an abortion, Doe sued the State of Georgia. The court held that while a woman's right to an abortion was not absolute, the Georgia process had deprived Doe of her rights under the Fourteenth Amendment because none of the three requirements constituted a valid exercise of law. The court noted that the Georgia law was "new" and passed in response to ROE V. WADE (410 US 179). Approximately one-fourth of the states had passed such laws, and this was the first case to test the constitutionality of the new statutes.

Further Reading

Hull, N. E. H. *The Abortion Rights Controversy in America: A Legal Reader.* Chapel Hill: University of North Carolina Press, 2004.

Rabin, Eva R. *Abortion, Politics and the Courts: Roe v. Wade and Its Aftermath,* rev. ed. New York: Greenwood Press, 1987.

—Marsh Hass

Dole, Elizabeth (Elizabeth Hanford Dole)

(1936–   ) *U.S. senator, cabinet member, president of American Red Cross*   Elizabeth Handford was born on July 29, 1936, in Salisbury, North Carolina. After graduating with honors from Duke University in 1958, she studied at Oxford Unversity, then earned a master's degree in education at Harvard University. She received a law degree from Harvard in 1965 and took a position with the Department of Health, Education and Welfare. She served as executive director of the President's Committee on Consumer Interests under President Lyndon Johnson and as deputy director of the White House Office of Consumer Affairs under President Richard Nixon. Nixon also appointed her to the Federal Trade Commission (FTC). In 1975, she married Senator Robert J. Dole and took a leave from the FTC in order to help in her husband's vice-presidential campaign.

In 1979, Dole resigned from the FTC to campaign for her husband's presidential bid. When Bob Dole withdrew from the race, Elizabeth Dole joined the Reagan-Bush campaign. In 1980, President Reagan appointed her assistant to the president for public liaison. The first woman to be named to a post in his administration, she was subsequently appointed Secretary of Transportation in 1983, making her the first woman to serve in that position. In this role, Dole focused on automobile safety requirements, the minimum drinking age, and passive restraints in vehicles. In 1989, President George H. W. Bush appointed her secretary of labor. In this capacity, Dole initiated the GLASS CEILING Study, designed to identify barriers to management and promotion opportunities for women and minorities. More than 60 percent of Dole's senior staff at the Department of Labor was made up of women or minorities.

In 1990, Dole left her cabinet post to become director of the American Red Cross. She was the first woman to hold the top position since the organization's founder, CLARA BARTON. As president of the Red Cross, Dole reformed the disaster relief program and restored credibility to the blood collection and distribution system. In 1996, she took another leave of absence to campaign for her husband's last presidential bid, but she returned immediately following the election.

In 1999, Dole resigned from the Red Cross and announced her own candidacy for the 2000 Republican presidential nomination. Despite her popularity and a second-place showing in the polls, she withdrew from the race before the primaries even began, citing a lack of money for the campaign. Research on her failed candidacy documents gender bias in the way the national press covered her campaign. Instead of focusing on her issue positions, the media highlighted her marriage to Bob Dole, her appearance, and her personality. Dole sought public office again in 2002 when she ran for a U.S. Senate seat from North Carolina. She won the election with 54 percent of the vote, defeating Erskine Bowles, a former chief of staff to President Bill Clinton, and becoming the state's first female U.S. senator. In November 2004, Dole became chair of the National Republican Senatorial Committee, a top Republican leadership post. She is expected to seek reelection to the U.S. Senate in 2008.

Further Reading

Braden, Maria. *Women Politicians and the Media.* Lexington: University of Kentucky Press, 1996.

Dole, Elizabeth, and Bob Dole. *Unlimited Partners: Our American Story.* New York: Simon & Schuster, 1996.

domestic violence   Domestic violence is an issue that sits at the intersection of the private and public spheres. The context in which domestic violence is defined affects the remedy available. Under COVERTURE laws of marriage, men were allowed to administer "corrections" to their wives since they were legally responsible for their wives' debts and conduct. Just as parents were entrusted to discipline their children, a husband as the patriarchal head of a family was entrusted to discipline his wife. The phrase *rule of thumb* is falsely said to have arisen in this context—that is, a husband's legitimate authority to use force against his wife or children was limited to the use of a stick no larger in diameter than his thumb. One of the causes the TEMPER-ANCE MOVEMENT took up was to stop women from being physically abused by their husbands. Drunken husbands not only spent the family's wages but also often returned from a night of drinking to physically assault their wives and children. Activists urged reform of divorce laws to permit women to escape domestic violence.

In the 1970s, the battered women's movement reflected the divide among feminists. Some argued that the best way to help women end the violence in their lives was to provide them with services (e.g., shelter, police protection, legal aid, and counseling) within the conventional social service sector. Other more radical feminists believed that domestic violence stemmed from economic dependency and would not cease until the basic structural gender arrangements in society changed. They favored creating autonomous alternatives to the patriarchal family and economic structures. According to this view, addressing domestic violence must begin by moving the definition of the problem from the private sphere to the public sphere. When women's battery is defined as a family problem, public institutions are unlikely to interfere. Thus, police departments have been slow to intervene in domestic disputes until recently.

A national coalition of feminist organizations successfully lobbied Congress to pass federal legislation on domestic abuse. The VIOLENCE AGAINST WOMEN ACT OF 1994 charges the Justice Department with collecting data on domestic abuse; provides money to state and local governments to fund efforts to provide services to victims and abusers; and identifies domestic abuse as a gender-based crime, which has allowed victims to sue their batterers in federal court. In 2001, 85 percent of victimizations by intimate partners were committed against women. Roughly one-third of domestic violence victims are men, but they are far less likely to report the crime or to seek shelter. In at least one case, a California man filed a sex discrimination suit because he was denied a bed in 10 different battered women's shelters. The shelters claimed that it was not clinically appropriate to house and treat male and female victims together.

See also SEPARATE SPHERES IDEOLOGY.

Further Reading

Roberts, Albert R. *Handbook of Domestic Violence Intervention Strategies: Policies, Programs and Legal Remedies.* New York: Oxford University Press, 2002.

domicile laws Domicile laws establish an individual's rights within a defined territory (most often a state) for purposes of benefits and obligations. Since most laws regarding the family are state-based, establishing permanent residency is significant. In a holdover from the days of unity in marriage, many states follow the common law assuming that a husband's residence constitutes the primary residence of a family. In the days when men provided sole financial support for the family, giving them precedence in the choice of domicile may have made sense. As women have entered the workforce on a more equal basis, where a family sets up residence is now subject to negotiation. Yet a majority of the public still believes a husband and wife should occupy one residence, and many state laws still assume that a wife has abandoned her husband if she refuses to move with him to another city. A 1985 survey showed that 72 percent of women and 62 percent of men believed that a woman *should* quit her job and move to another city if her husband got a job there, even if she had a good job in the city where they were currently living. Only 10 percent of women and 19 percent of men said that the husband should turn down the job. The rise of commuter marriages, most often necessitated by two professional careers, has caused domicile laws to begin to change, but this is often on a case-by-case basis. Some women have found it easiest to get a court order recognizing their unique residence for the purposes of university tuition, taxation, voting, licensing, and jury duty, among others.

Further Reading

Leiter, Richard A., ed. *National Survey of State Laws.* Detroit: Thomson Gale, 2004.

Dothard v. Rawlinson (433 U.S. 321) (1977) Dianne Rawlinson applied for a position as a prison guard in Alabama. She was denied the position for failing to meet the 120 lb. weight requirement for Alabama prison guards (there was also a height requirement of 5'2"). She sued under TITLE VII OF THE CIVIL RIGHTS ACT OF 1964, alleging that she had been denied employment because of her sex in violation of federal law. The court held that the height and weight requirements, while apparently neutral, had a disparate impact on females and thus were in violation of Title VII because Alabama could provide no objective evidence that the height and weight requirements were necessary to the job. While the suit was pending, Alabama redefined the position of prison guard to include a "gender" nexus in "contact" positions. The court found that Alabama had not provided evidence to support the denial of 75 percent of positions in the prison system to women. The initial height and weight requirements as well as the gender nexus were found to be arbitrary and amounted to gender discrimination under Title VII.

Further Reading

Burstein, Paul. *Discrimination, Jobs and Politics: The Struggle for Equal Employment Opportunity in the United States since the New Deal.* Chicago: University of Chicago Press, 1985.

—Marsha Hass

Douglas, Helen Gahagan (1900–1980) *actress, politician* Born on November 25, 1900, in Boonton, New Jersey, Helen Gahagan first attracted attention as a Broadway performer. She married Melvyn Douglas in 1931, and the couple moved to California. It was here, surrounded by the misery of the Great Depression, that she became politically active, left the Republican Party she had followed by family tradition, and became active in Democratic New Deal politics. In 1939, she was appointed to the national advisory committee for the Works Progress Administration. In 1944, she won election to the House of Representatives from California's 14th district, a seat she held from 1945 to 1951. She was a staunch supporter of President Harry S. Truman's Fair Deal policies, and in 1946 Truman appointed her a delegate to the United Nations General Assembly. In 1950, Helen Gahagan Douglas ran for a Senate seat from California but was defeated by Richard M. Nixon. That campaign became infamous for its "red-baiting" and vicious politics. While never calling Douglas a communist, Nixon declared her "pink right down to her underwear." Out of public office, she spent her time as a lecturer and author. In 1963, she published *The Eleanor Roosevelt We Remember*. She died on June 28, 1980, in New York City.

Further Reading

Douglas, Helen Gahagan. *A Full Life: Helen Gahagan Douglas*. Garden City, N.Y.: Doubleday, 1982.

Drake, Thelma (1949–) *congressperson* Thelma Drake was born on November 20, 1949, in Elyria, Ohio. She attended Old Dominion University and worked as a real estate agent in Norfolk, Virginia, prior to entering politics. Drake served in the Virginia House of Delegates for nine years (first elected in 1995), the first Republican from the Norfolk area sent to the state legislature since Reconstruction. She served as chair of the Virginia Housing Commission and was a member of the Chesapeake Bay Commission.

On November 2, 2004, Drake was elected to represent Virginia's second congressional district in the U.S. House of Representatives. The second district includes all of the City of Virginia Beach, parts of the cities of Norfolk and Hampton, and Accomack and Northampton Counties on Virginia's Eastern Shore. Thelma Drake was appointed to serve on the Committee on Armed Services, the Committee on Resources and the Committee on Education and the Workforce. She faced a tight reelection in 2006, and her seat was identified as a possible pick-up for Democrats. However she retained her seat, winning by 51 to 49 percent over Democrat Phillip Kellam.

Further Reading

Barone, Michael. *The Almanac of American Politics.* Washington, D.C.: National Journal Group, 2006.

"Drake, Thelma D." In *Biographical Directory of the United States Congress, 1774–present.* Available online. URL: http://bioguide.congress.gov/scripts/biodisplay.pl?index=D000605. Accessed on January 8, 2007.

"Representative Thelma D. Drake." In *Project Vote Smart.* Available online. URL: http://votesmart.org/bio.php?can_id=BS026669. Accessed on January 8, 2007.

—Angela Kouters

Dulles, Eleanor Lansing (1895–1996) *diplomat, author* Eleanor Lansing Dulles's career as a diplomat, scholar, and member of a diplomatic dynasty contributed to key national and foreign policy decisions in American politics. She was born on June 1, 1895, in Watertown, New York, into the famous Dulles family (including her brothers John Foster and Allen Welsh) that served the American public through several generations. In 1926, she earned a Ph.D. in economics from Radcliffe College. She developed a keen interest in international economics, with a focus on Europe.

Dulles entered government service in 1936. Considered one of the key architects of President Roosevelt's new Social Security system, she was principally involved in investigating the funding of Social Security. By 1942, Dulles had moved on to the State Department, where she was able to put into practice her scholarly skills in international economics. Operating in a male-dominated policy environment, Dulles went on to achieve successes despite the discrimination and prejudices women faced during this period.

In 1945, as the United States considered the possibilities of postwar economic planning, Dulles was instrumental in contributing to the U.S. position on international financial cooperation. She represented the United States at the Bretton Woods Conference, which established the International Monetary Fund and the International Bank for Reconstruction and Development. As the U.S. representative to Austria in 1949, she lent her economic expertise to the war-torn and economically ravaged country. Her most lauded accomplishment was her enthusiastic and unrelenting efforts to restore and revitalize Germany after World War II. Often referred to as "the Mother of Berlin," she is considered to have been instrumental in crafting Germany's reconstruction.

By 1959, Dulles had expanded her regional interests beyond Europe, and she became interested in economic conditions in underdeveloped countries, traveling extensively to Africa, Latin America, and South Asia. In 1962, she resigned from the State Department and returned to academia, taking up teaching positions at Duke and Georgetown universities. She continued to write and publish on various foreign policy issues. In 1980, at the age of 85, she penned her memoirs *Chances of a Lifetime* chronicling her exceptional life. She died on October 30, 1996, at the age of 101.

Further Reading

Dulles, Eleanor Lansing. *Chances of a Lifetime: A Memoir.* Englewood Cliffs, N.J.: Prentice Hall, 1980.
Dunn, Lynne Kathleen. "Joining the Boys' Club: The Diplomatic Career of Eleanor Lansing Dulles." In *Women and American Foreign Policy: Critics, Lobbyists and Insiders,* edited by Edward Crapol. Westport, Conn.: Greenwood Press, 1987.

—Hollis France

Duniway, Abigail Scott (Abigail Jane Scott Duniway) (1834–1915) *suffragist, publisher*
Born on October 22, 1834, near Groveland, Illinois, SUFFRAGE advocate, writer, and editor Abigail Jane Scott journeyed with her family to Oregon in 1852. She worked as a schoolteacher before marrying Benjamin C. Duniway in 1853; the couple had six children. In 1862, the family lost their farm, and soon after, Benjamin was disabled in an accident. In 1871, Duniway moved her family to Portland, Oregon.

As she struggled to support her family, Duniway became convinced American women needed the vote. In Portland, she founded and edited the *New Northwest,* a newspaper devoted to suffrage that she edited until it closed in 1887. In 1895, she became editor of the *Pacific Empire.* She also wrote and published five books of fiction and poetry and one on suffrage. In 1873, Duniway organized the Oregon Equal Suffrage Association and became its president. She also became vice president of the NATIONAL WOMAN SUFFRAGE ASSOCIATION (NWSA) in 1884. Despite her hard work, suffrage campaigns failed in Oregon in 1884 and again in 1900. Although she did not participate in the losing Oregon

Abigail Scott Duniway (LIBRARY OF CONGRESS)

campaign in 1905–06, Duniway did participate in suffrage campaigns in other western states. Her work helped suffrage win in Idaho in 1896 and in Washington in 1910. She led two more unsuccessful Oregon campaigns before suffrage was finally won there in 1912. Duniway became the first women to register to vote in that state. She died on October 11, 1915. Her leadership and organizational skills had contributed to the growth of the suffrage movement in both the Pacific Northwest and nationally, and she deserves much of the credit for her region's suffrage victories.

Further Reading

Duniway, Abigail Scott. *Path Breaking: An Autobiographical History of the Equal Suffrage Movement in Pacific Coast States.* New York: Schocken Books, 1971.

Moynihan, Ruth Barnes. *Rebel For Rights: Abigail Scott Duniway.* New Haven, Conn.: Yale University Press, 1983.

—Eileen V. Wallis

Dworkin, Andrea (1946–2005) *feminist, writer*
Andrea Dworkin was born in Camden, New Jersey, on September 26, 1946. She began her degree in English at Bennington College in Vermont in 1964 with the financial support of scholarships and loans from her father. Her defiant persona and prolific life as a writer began when she was very young, and her active mind and burgeoning FEMINISM found academic life dull and misogynist. She would leave and return to school twice before receiving her degree in 1969.

Dworkin's university years involved making ends meet with a variety of part-time jobs, ranging from receptionist to waitress to sex worker, and she was an active participant in the Student Peace Union and resistance movements against the war in Vietnam. In 1965, she was arrested for protesting the war and jailed, where her brutal treatment by police and medical staff led to a grand jury investigation of the prison. After the trauma, Dworkin left school, went to

Greece, worked, and wrote poetry. In 1966, she published her first work: a small collection of poems called *Child*. Shortly thereafter, she left her abusive marriage and lived very much like a fugitive, running from place to place and hiding from the man who persistently and aggressively pursued her.

While on the run, Dworkin met Ricki Adams, a feminist and activist who helped her and broadened her mind regarding feminism. They discussed gender oppression and political and social issues, and eventually they planned the book that became *Woman Hating*. Published in 1974, *Woman Hating* tackled sex roles, pornographic images and writing, history, foot-binding practices, and mythology. It also attacked counterculture pornography of the era, particularly sex newspapers such as *Suck, Oz,* and *Screw,* papers created by "people who share our values, our concerns—people who talk of liberation." The book stirred controversy in the mainstream realm, caused conflict among Dworkin's friends and acquaintances (particularly those working within the culture), and firmly established her as a militant feminist writer and thinker as well.

During the 1980s, Dworkin met Catherine A. MacKinnon, a noted lawyer, feminist, and activist with whom she wrote *Pornography and Civil Rights: A New Day for Women's Equality* (1988) and edited *In Harm's Way: The Pornography Civil Rights Hearings* (1997). Controversial in both focus and stance, Dworkin and MacKinnon's work on pornography—grounded in the idea that it was another form of sex discrimination and should be legally recognized as such—led to their draft of an ordinance that would deem pornography a violation of women's civil rights. Although it was adopted by a couple of city councils, it was never enacted.

Dworkin's work—fiction and nonfiction—tackled sexism, equal rights issues, misogyny, pornography, battery, and the patriarchy. While the extremism of her views and the texts that emerged from them have often been anathematized by feminists, nonfeminists and antifeminists alike, her writing demanded change: from long-established power relations and structures, from the social world, from men, and from women. As GLORIA STEINEM, quoted on the dust jacket of Dworkin's novel, *Mercy* (1990), said: "In every century, there are a handful of writers who help the human race to evolve. Andrea is one of them."

Dworkin suffered from nearly incapacitating osteoarthritis during her final years, but she continued to publish articles until a month before her death on April 9, 2005. She was 58 years old.

Further Reading

Dworkin, Andrea. *Intercourse.* New York: The Free Press, 1987.
Dworkin, Andrea. *Heartbreak: The Political Memoir of a Feminist Militant.* New York: Basic Books, 2002.
Strossen, Nadine. *Defending Pornography: Free Speech, Sex, and the Fight for Women's Rights.* New York: New York University Press, 2000.

—Candis Steenbergen

Dyer, Mary (Mary Barrett Dyer) (ca. 1611–1660) *religious leader, Quaker martyr*

Born in England around 1611, Mary Barrett married William Dyer in 1633 and immigrated to Massachusetts Bay Colony around 1634. Mary and William Dyer were supporters of ANNE HUTCHINSON and her views concerning the covenant of grace. Mary Dyer first came into trouble with the colonial authorities through the birth of a stillborn child in 1637. The birth was attended by Hutchinson, who had buried the body (on the advice of John Cotton) instead of immediately turning it over to the governing council for examination. Upon discovering this, the governing authorities had the child's body exhumed, and it was described as "monstrous." The deformed stillbirth was used as a sign that Satan had influenced Dyer through Hutchinson.

Dyer and her husband were excommunicated and banished and followed Hutchinson to Rhode Island, where Dyer converted to Quakerism. Quakers believed that God was within humans in the form of an "inner light" and that God did not distinguish between men and women. In 1657, Dyer returned to Massachusetts, unaware that Quakers were being arrested upon their arrival in the colony. She managed to get a letter to her husband, who came from Rhode Island to plead for her release. She was freed on the condition that she not return to Massachusetts. However, she did return to convert people to Quakerism, and consequently she was arrested again and sentenced to death. Once more she was released into the authority of her husband upon agreement that she would not return under pain of execution. When she returned in 1660, she was hanged on June 1 that year.

Further Reading

La Plante, Eve. *American Jezebel: The Uncommon Life of Anne Hutchinson, the Woman Who Defied the Puritans.* New York: HarperCollins, 2004.
Plimpton, Ruth. *Mary Dyer: Biography of a Rebel Quaker.* Wellesley, Mass.: Branden Books, 1994.

—Claire Curtis

E

Eagle Forum Founded in 1972 by PHYLLIS SCHLAFLY, the Eagle Forum is an ultraconservative national grassroots organization of the New Right affiliated with the Republican Party. It has numerous state and city chapters, and Schlafly has been its president and most prominent spokesperson since its founding. The Eagle Forum reports a current membership of 80,000 men and women. Since the organization's opposition to the EQUAL RIGHTS AMENDMENT (ERA), however, grassroots activities have been predominantly female. The *Phyllis Schlafly Report,* the *Eagle Forum Newsletter,* and the *Education Report* are its official publications. More than the *Phyllis Schlafly Report,* the *EF Newsletter* contains news, information, and guidelines for effectively launching and organizing grassroots activities on a local level, and it calls for donations for the Eagle Trust Fund. Schlafly also communicates with her supporters via a weekly radio program heard nationwide on 40 stations. The Eagle Forum makes effective use of high-tech media, especially with their homepage www.eagleforum.org. With the Teen Eagles and the Eagle Forum Collegians, it reaches out to high school and college students to form future conservative leaders and activists. It organizes the Eagle Council, an annual meeting that trains conservative speakers.

The Eagle Forum's original project was to stop the ERA from becoming part of the Constitution. The organization supports conservative and pro-family policies at every level of government and describes itself as "the alternative to women's lib." It champions traditional family values and gender roles and opposes women's liberation, linking it to a national downfall. Among other issues, it also has been fighting federal support for day care, sex and AIDS education, reproductive rights, protections against SEXUAL HARASSMENT, gay and lesbian rights, the United Nations, immigration, and multiculturalism.

See also ANTIFEMINISM.

Further Reading

Critchlow, Donald T. *Phyllis Schlafly and Grassroots Conservatism: A Woman's Crusade.* Princeton, N.J.: Princeton University Press, 2005.

Felsenthal, Carol. *The Biography of Phyllis Schlafly: The Sweetheart of the Silent Majority.* Garden City, N.Y.: Doubleday & Company, Inc, 1981.

Hardisty, Jean. *Mobilizing Resentment: Conservative Resurgence from the John Birch Society to the Promise Keepers.* Boston: Beacon Press, 1999.

—Christine Knauer

Eddy, Mary Baker (Mary Morse Baker Glover Eddy) (1821–1910) *writer, religious leader* A writer, publisher, and advocate of Christian Science, Mary Baker Eddy was born Mary Morse Baker on July 16, 1821, in Bow, New Hampshire. She was the youngest of six children of Mark and Abigail Ambrose Baker. Because her early childhood was punctuated with chronic illness, she received both formal and informal education. In 1843, Baker married George Washington Glover, who died six months later. Widowed, in financial despair, and pregnant, she returned to her parent's home in declining health to deliver her son, George Washington Glover II, in 1844 and remained with her family until her mother's death in 1849. Two years later, her son George, now age seven, was relocated and raised by friends. In hopes of reuniting with her son, Mary married Dr. Daniel Patterson, a dentist, in 1853, but Patterson refused to allow George to reside in their New Jersey home. In 1862, Mary Patterson, continuing to struggle with chronic illness, received treatment from Phineas Quimby, a traveling mesmerist who healed patients using hypnosis. Although her health improved dramatically as a result of his treatment, she suffered a relapse and came to believe that Quimby's healing powers flowed more from the strength of his personality and training in hypnosis than from some divine principle. However, she continued to study with Quimby until his death in 1866. One month after his death, a severe fall on the ice left her bedridden again. Without Quimby to help, she turned to her Bible and read deeply about Jesus' healing work. When she found herself suddenly well, she attributed her recovery to the discovery of Christian Science. She devoted the next nine years to intensive study of the scriptures and healing activity.

In an era where women had limited access to the public sphere as leaders, this atypical woman lectured, published, and organized followers of Christian Science. Her first teaching manuscript "The Science of Man" (1869) was used in her first class in 1870. As her work continued, she divorced Daniel Patterson in 1873

Mary Baker Eddy (LIBRARY OF CONGRESS)

after a 13-year separation. In 1875, she led her first Sunday service at Good Templars Hall in Lynn, Massachusetts, and published *Science and Health,* focusing on Christian Science principles. The following year, her work advanced with the publication of *The Science of Man* and formation of the Christian Scientist Association. In 1877, she married Asa Gilbert Eddy, who supported her work in Christian Science until his death in 1882.

In 1879, Mary Baker Eddy formalized the Christian Science movement into Churches of Christ, Scientist, located in Boston, Massachusetts, and in 1881 she became the church's first ordained pastor (1881). Her organizational skills and advocacy of Christian Science became institutionalized into the Metaphysical College

(1881) and the National Christian Scientist Association (1886). Eddy's publishing career progressed with *Unity of Good* (1887), *Retrospection and Introspection* (her autobiography, 1892), *Rudimental Divine Science* (1908), *Poems* (1910), and numerous other works. She further contributed to the development of Christian Science in establishing the Christian Science Publishing society (1898). The publishing society published *Christian Science Journal* (1898), *Christian Science Sentinel* (1898), and *Christian Science Monitor* (1908). Eddy's distinguished achievements remain vibrant in the 21st century with 134 churches worldwide, her writings translated into 17 languages, and the formation of the Mary Baker Eddy Library.

Eddy contributed to the transition of America religiously, socially, and journalistically by challenging both the common Protestant understanding of healing and traditional medical healing practices and by incorporating new concepts of how the body and spirit functioned. She carved a space within the public sphere as a writer, publisher, and theologian in the 19th and early 20th century of America. She died on December 3, 1910, at the age of 89.

Further Reading

Gill, Gillian. *Mary Baker Eddy*. Reading, Mass.: Perseus Books, 1998.

Knee, Stuart E. *Christian Science in the Age of Mary Baker Eddy*. Westport, Conn.: Greenwood Press, 1994.

Parker, Gail Thain. *Mind Cures in New England: From the Civil War to World War I*. Hanover, N.H.: University Press of New England, 1973.

Peel, Robert. *Mary Baker Eddy: The Years of Authority*. New York: Holt Rinehart and Winston, 1977.

T. Alys Jordan

Edelman, Marian Wright (1939–) *lawyer, activist, children's advocate* The leading advocate for children's interests in the United States and the founder of the Children's Defense Fund, Marian Wright Edelman learned the value of service to others and the ethic of changing the world one small step at a time from her father. Marian Wright, the youngest of five children, was born on June 6, 1939, in segregated Bennettsville, South Carolina. Her father, Arthur Wright, was a Baptist preacher who placed great value on education and service to others. All five children participated in study sessions around the kitchen table every evening, whether they had assignments or not. Arthur Wright urged his children not to let anything get in the way of their education.

Marian enrolled at Spellman College in Atlanta, Georgia, in 1956. In her junior year, she studied in Geneva, Switzerland, on a Merrill scholarship and spent the following summer in the Soviet Union on a Lisle fellowship. In a *New Yorker* interview, she credits that year with giving her the confidence that she "could navigate in the world and do just about anything." At Spellman in her senior year she joined the early civil rights movement, helping to organize students to protest segregation with sit-ins in Atlanta. Volunteer work with the National Association for the Advancement of Colored People (NAACP) led her to choose to study law over graduate work in Russian and a career in the Foreign Service as she had planned upon graduation in 1960. Law would offer her a more direct means to represent impoverished African Americans and continue the struggle against segregation and discrimination, even though she claimed not to have any interest in or aptitude for law. She attended Yale Law School and earned a degree in 1963. As a law student, she worked with the Northern Student Movement (associated with the Student Nonviolent Coordinating Committee, SNCC) and traveled to Mississippi to register black voters over spring break in her senior year.

Upon graduation, she spent a year as a staff attorney for the NAACP Legal Defense and Education Fund in New York before moving to Jackson, Mississippi, to direct the fund's office there. In doing so, she became the first black female attorney to practice in Mississippi. The summer of 1964 was a dangerous one of violence and fear in Mississippi, as the Ku Klux Klan brutalized any blacks who tried to challenge segregation as the status quo. In addition to her legal work, Wright helped to establish a Head Start program for poor children in Mississippi. In 1967 she led U.S. senators Robert Kennedy and Joseph Clark on a tour to expose the abject poverty of the Mississippi Delta, where families lived without lights or running water. During this trip she met Peter Edelman, Senator Kennedy's assistant. A year later she moved to Washington, D.C., to marry Peter and move her social justice work closer to the source of political power. Together, the Edelmans have three sons.

The assassinations of Martin Luther King, Jr., and Senator Robert Kennedy roiled the social justice community. Edelman helped to organize King's Poor People's Campaign, including the mass demonstration for social and economic justice in 1968. As a result of her work with poor women, she began to expand her activism to focus on child-care legislation and encouraged Congress to take up comprehensive childhood development initiatives. In 1971, she helped to assemble a broad coalition of groups in support of the childhood development bill only to see it vetoed by President Richard Nixon. Work on children's issues appealed to her as a way to cut across issues of race and class while working for social change. In 1973, Edelman founded the Children's Defense Fund (CDF) to protect and promote the interests of all children. The CDF is dedicated to research, advocacy, and outreach and is funded entirely by private foundations in order to maintain its independence. The CDF plays a critical role in all issues affecting children, from teen pregnancy to foster care to child care, by documenting problems and developing solutions grounded in research. Edelman and the CDF have been successful in bringing attention to children's issues and increasing federal funding for education and anti-poverty programs, regardless of which political party controls government at the time. Recently the CDF's focus has been on pregnancy prevention and promoting high quality standards and full funding for child-care initiatives.

In 1992, with the election of President Bill Clinton, Edelman believed she had a strong ally in the White House. Edelman was a friend of the Clintons, and First Lady HILLARY RODHAM CLINTON had interned with the Children's Defense Fund while at Yale Law School. The CDF launched its "Leave No Child Behind" campaign in 1992, with the goal of full funding for Head Start, insurance for every child and pregnant woman, vaccinations for all children, and an expanded children's tax credit for parents. The Stand for Children march in 1996 attracted more than 200,000 people and was organized by a coalition that included the NAACP, the March of Dimes, the Salvation Army, and the National Urban League. The purpose was to protest the "neglect of children in the world's richest country" and to bring renewed visibility to issues of child poverty and need. When the Clinton administration supported welfare reform legislation that cut $54 billion in federal aid to food stamps and child and family nutrition, Edelman became one of the administration's biggest critics. The CDF developed a program to document the effects of the new welfare legislation. In 2000, Edelman was awarded the Presidential Medal of Freedom, the highest civilian honor in the United States.

The Marian Wright Edelman Institute for the Study of Children, Youth, and Families has been established at San Francisco State University. The institute houses an interdisciplinary bachelor's degree in child and adolescent development. In addition to the degree program, the mission of the institute is to promote collaboration among faculty, to create public outreach, social advocacy, and other partnerships between the institution and the community, and to foster research and scholarly work. The institute and its many programs can be accessed online (http://edelman.sfsu.edu/default.htm).

Edelman continues her work as president of the Children's Defense Fund and her full-time advocacy for the rights of all children. She is the author of several books, including *The Measure of Our Success: A Letter to My Children and Yours* (Beacon Press, 1992) and *I'm Your Child, God: Prayers for Children and Teenagers* (Hyperion Books, 2002). The Children's Defense Fund maintains a Web site. The URL is http://www.childrensdefense.org.

Further Reading

"Marian Wright Edelman," *Contemporary Black Biography.* Vol. 42. Farmington Hills, Mich.: Thomson Gale, 2004. Available online. URL: http://galenet.galegroup.com. Accessed on June 15, 2007.

Edelman, Marian Wright. *Families in Peril: An Agenda for Social Change.* Cambridge, Mass.: Harvard University Press, 1987.

Eisenhower, Mamie (Mamie Geneva Doud Eisenhower)

(1896–1979) *first lady* Mamie Geneva Doud was born on November 14, 1896, in Boone, Iowa, to John Sheldon and Elvira Mathilde Carlson Doud. Her father ran the family meatpacking business and accumulated wealth and success at an early age. Mamie was raised in privilege, tended by household servants, and not expected to do very much for herself. Like other girls of privilege of this time, Mamie's formal education beyond the eighth grade consisted of finishing school and lessons in dance, voice, and piano. She was fond of beautiful things and attentive to fashion. Mamie was taught to run a household with servants, learning from her mother, "If you don't learn how to cook, nobody will ask you to do it."

In 1903, the family moved from Iowa to Colorado in search of a better climate for her mother's health. Mamie herself experienced rheumatic fever at age seven that left lasting heart damage and negatively affected her stamina and general health for the rest of her life. She made her debut at the Douds' winter home in San Antonio, Texas, in 1915. There she met Second Lieutenant Dwight David Eisenhower. When "Ike" proposed to Mamie soon after Christmas in 1915, her father objected and tried to warn her of the hardships (most especially financial difficulties) she would face as a military wife. Nevertheless, the couple were married on July 1, 1916, and moved into Infantry Row at Fort Sam Houston.

Mamie was hardly prepared for life as an army wife, but she did not dare complain to her family. True to her father's predictions, there was not much money and no domestic help. She learned from Ike basic cooking, and for the first time she maintained her own household. She complained when Ike was away from home for long periods, but accepted his response: "Mamie, there's one thing you must understand. My country comes first and always will. You come second." She gradually adjusted to her new way of life and made a home for them as best she could.

The Eisenhowers were popular, and soon, wherever they were posted, their quarters

Mamie Doud Eisenhower (LIBRARY OF CONGRESS)

became known as "Club Eisenhower." Mamie's social graces helped Ike's career, and they were often entertained by people of rank. When the United States entered World War I, Ike was assigned training missions within the United States. Their first son, Doud Dwight, was born on September 24, 1917. Mamie gave birth at a military hospital at Fort Sam Houston while Ike was away. Caring for the child alone exhausted her dangerously, and she fell into a coma. She recovered, but her rather delicate health and a fear of early death colored her ability to deal with all sorts of situations and produced such problems as claustrophobia; fear of flying; fear of insects; a lack of physical stamina; and Ménière's disease, which disturbed her balance when standing. For the rest of the war and its immediate aftermath, Mamie joined Ike whenever it was possible, but often she endured long periods of separation. On January 2, 1921, their son died of scarlet fever. Mamie was overcome with grief, and Ike worried about a complete nervous breakdown.

In autumn 1921, Ike was sent to Panama as executive officer to the commandant, General Fox Conner. Mamie was pregnant again and worried about the environment in Panama but accompanied him there, only to find the living conditions far worse than she could have imagined. She endured but returned to San Antonio to give birth to a son they named John Sheldon Doud, in honor of her father. Two months later, she and the baby returned to Panama and stayed until 1923, when she again returned to San Antonio to restore her own health. When she rejoined Ike again, she had made her peace with the life required of her. She became close friends with Virginia Conner, who helped her become active in fund-raising efforts for the base hospital. Throughout the remainder of their military posts, Mamie dedicated herself to providing a tranquil home, serving as a ready hostess to advance Ike's career. Assignment to the general staff school at Fort Leavenworth, Kansas, assured Ike access to the highest ranks. In 1928, they were assigned to Paris, where he prepared a book on the battlefields of World War I. Mamie enjoyed the post, and their apartment attracted American diplomats and military personnel. In 1929, Ike became chief of staff to General Douglas MacArthur, and the couple returned to Washington. The Great Depression added more strain to the couple's tight family budget as the army cut salaries.

In 1935, the Eisenhowers faced another turning point as Ike wrestled with whether to stay in the army or leave in favor of more lucrative private-sector offers. Mamie confided that she did not believe he belonged in civilian life, and Ike left for the Philippines. Mamie initially stayed in Washington, but when Ike did not return, she joined him in the Philippines, only to find that he had carved out an independent life for himself. In 1939, with World War II looming, the Eisenhowers transferred back to Washington. Mamie continued to fulfill her role as an army wife, making the best of her situation. However, in 1942 Ike (now General Eisenhower) was appointed European theater commander and left for England. Mamie stayed in Washington, withstanding painful rumors of an affair between Ike and his official driver, Kay Summersby. He returned to Washington when the war ended in 1945, and they settled into their finest army accommodations to date. For three years they were comfortable and worked to readjust to married life in one another's company. Ike retired from the army in 1948 and was installed as president of Columbia University. This hiatus was short-lived, and Ike took a leave from his academic post to assume command of North Atlantic Treaty Organization (NATO) forces in 1951. Mamie accompanied him to France but never adjusted to the staid lifestyle there. After returning to the United States, the Republican Party began actively courting Ike for the presidential nomination. The couple appeared together at the party convention in Chicago, but privately Mamie dreaded the publicity his candidacy would bring. She proved an able campaigner, though, and used the knowledge she had gained from living all over the United

States to the campaign's advantage. She granted press interviews and accepted invitations to speak to women's clubs—both black and white. She proved an invaluable asset to the ticket, and the public adored her; two campaign songs were written for her. When the Eisenhower-Nixon ticket was sworn into office in 1953, moving into the White House was an easy adjustment for a woman who had already moved some 30 times in the course of her marriage.

As first lady, Mamie Eisenhower was the epitome of the nation's attempt to return to normalcy and the rise of the consumer culture. She devoted attention to her wardrobe, preferring American designs and designers. She dressed simply but elegantly and appeared on the New York Dress Institute's list of the 12 best-dressed women every year she was in the White House. The couple purchased their very first home together while in the White House—a farm in Gettysburg, Pennsylvania. Their son John, now married and with children of his own, was a frequent visitor to the White House and the farm. Mamie entertained extensively in the official residence, welcoming more heads of state than any other president's wife. She opened the White House to citizens of all walks of life, working in quiet ways for the advancement of African Americans and women. She also reinstated the White House Easter egg roll (discontinued during the war) as an integrated event and invited MARIAN ANDERSON to sing at Ike's inaugural in 1957. She did not play a role as adviser to her husband on political matters, believing that was entirely his realm. She did worry about his health, however, particularly after his heart attack in 1955. In 1960, she urged Richard Nixon not to ask Ike to campaign on his behalf, fearing a second attack would be fatal.

In 1961, the Eisenhowers left the White House for their farm in Pennsylvania, where they enjoyed family and friends. Ike Eisenhower died in 1969, and Mamie lived on for another 10 years, increasingly withdrawn from the public eye. She died of a stroke on November 1, 1979, and was buried beside her husband at the Eisen-

hower Center in Abilene, Kansas. Her legacy as first lady is largely limited to that of role model for a postwar nation. A lifetime of support for her husband's military career prepared her well for the social expectations that constrained her as first lady. She did not appear bothered by her limited influence, but rather relished her husband's success.

Further Reading

National First Ladies Library. *Biographies: First Ladies of the United States.* Available online. URL: http://www.firstladies.org/biographies. Accessed on January 4, 2007.
Schneider, Dorothy, and Carl J. Schneider. "Mamie Geneva Doud Eisenhower." *First Ladies: A Biographical Dictionary.* New York: Checkmark Books, 2001. pp. 261–270.
Young, Mark. "Mamie Geneva Doud Eisenhower." In *American First Ladies: Their Lives and Their Legacy,* 2nd ed., edited by Lewis L. Gould, pp. 311–319. New York: Routledge, 2001.

Eisenstadt v. Baird (405 U.S. 438) (1972)

Following a presentation on contraception to students at Boston University, William Baird was convicted of a felony under a Massachusetts statute after giving contraceptive foam to an attendee. The Massachusetts law required that only a registered physician or a registered pharmacist (pursuant to a valid prescription) could provide items of contraception to married people, and then only to prevent sexually transmitted disease, not contraception. Single persons could not receive any items of contraception for any purpose. The Supreme Court found the statute to violate the Fourteenth Amendment because it treated single and married persons differently without a substantial state interest in doing so.

See also BIRTH CONTROL MOVEMENT; *GRISWOLD V. CONNECTICUT.*

Further Reading

McFarlane, Deborah R., and Kenneth J. Meier. *The Politics of Fertility Control: Family Planning and*

Abortion Policies in the American States. New York: Chatham House Publishers, 2001.

—Marsha Hass

Elders, Joycelyn (Minnie Lee Jones, Minnie Joycelyn Lee) (1933–) *U.S. surgeon general, physician*

Joycelyn Elders was born Minnie Lee Jones on August 13, 1933, in Schaal, Arkansas, the first of eight children born to Haller and Curtis Jones. Her mother taught her to read, and she attended school when she could, balancing the 13-mile trip to school with the need to work with her family in the cotton fields near her home. When she earned a scholarship to Philander Smith College in Little Rock, Arkansas, her father was hesitant to let her go since the family needed her labor, but her paternal grandmother intervened. While in college, she took changed her name to Minnie Joycelyn Lee; later she simply used Joycelyn.

Lee studied biology and chemistry but did not aspire to be a doctor until she heard Edith Irby Jones, the first African American to study at the University of Arkansas School of Medicine, speak at the college. After earning her B.A. in biology in 1952, Lee joined the U.S. Army's Women's Medical Specialist Corps, and in 1956 she entered the University of Arkansas School of Medicine on the G.I. Bill. As the only black student in the medical school, she was required to eat with the cleaning staff in a separate university dining room, even though the Supreme Court decision in *Brown v. Board of Education of Topeka Kansas* (1954) had outlawed separate educational facilities.

Joycelyn Lee married Oliver Elders in 1960, the same year she earned her medical degree. She interned in pediatrics at the University of Minnesota, but returned to Little Rock for her residency. She developed a specialty in pediatric endocrinology, particularly in juvenile diabetes. Recognizing that juvenile diabetes presented a significant risk to pregnant teenagers, she began a public advocacy campaign to prevent pregnancy among her patients. Soon

Elders's activism extended beyond her immediate patients to sexually active teenagers in Arkansas. Arkansas's teen pregnancy rate was significantly higher than the national average in 1987. Dr. Elders told the *Boston Glove* that a poor teenager with a baby was "captive to a slavery the Thirteenth Amendment did not anticipate."

In 1987, Governor Bill Clinton named Dr. Joycelyn Elders director of the Arkansas Department of Health. In this new role, Elders urged more direct government action and began a public education campaign promoting contraceptive use among sexually active teens. After a visit to the state's first school-based health clinic, she helped to open 18 others in concert with an expanded sex education curriculum throughout the state. Almost immediately, she faced opposition from political conservatives and religious fundamentalists. In 1989, the Arkansas state legislature adopted a K–12 personal health and hygiene curriculum that included instruction in sex education, substance abuse prevention, self-esteem, and shared male/female sexual responsibility.

When President Bill Clinton nominated Elders for U.S. surgeon general, criticism from the right intensified. Elders did not back away from her programs or her published comments on issues ranging from television condom ads to RU 486 and abortion. Her Senate confirmation appeared stalled, but support from the American Medical Association and popular former surgeon general C. Everett Koop, in addition to her dogged determination to stand her ground, resulted in a positive vote on September 7, 1993. When she assumed her post, she became the first African American and the second female to direct the U.S. Public Health Service. Her platform included teen pregnancy; tobacco use; national health care; ACQUIRED IMMUNODEFICIENCY SYNDROME (AIDS) education, prevention, and treatment; gun control; and drug and alcohol abuse.

Elders never escaped controversy and was watched carefully by her conservative critics. In 1994, she had just finished a speech at the

United Nations marking World AIDS Day when she was asked whether she would ever consider promoting masturbation as a means of preventing teenagers from engaging in riskier sexual activity. She replied: "With regard to masturbation, I think that it is something that is part of human sexuality and a part of something that should perhaps be taught." In the ensuing furor over these comments, she was forced to resign after only 15 months in office. Had the political climate been less volatile for the president, she might have survived. However, Elders stood by her comments and never apologized. She returned to the practice of medicine but did not give up her public advocacy work. Joycelyn Elders retired from medicine in 1999, but she continues to promote the public health issues she cares most about.

Further Reading

Elders, M. Joycelyn. *Joycelyn Elders: From Sharecroppers' Daughter to Surgeon General of the United States of America.* New York: William Morrow, 1996.

Emerson, Jo Ann (1950–   ) *congressperson*
Jo Ann Emerson was born on September 16, 1950, in Bethesda, Maryland. In 1972, she graduated from Ohio Wesleyan University with a degree in political science. Prior to being elected to the U.S. House of Representatives, she served as senior vice president of public affairs for the American Insurance Association, as director of state relations for the National Restaurant Association, and as deputy communications director for the National Republican Congressional Committee. She married Bill Emerson in 1975.

Bill Emerson was first elected to Congress in 1980, but he died of cancer on June 22, 1996. Jo Ann decided to run for the House of Representatives after Bill's death, but a Missouri state law prohibited her from filing to run in the Republican primary, so she ran as an independent against Democrat Emily Firebaugh and Republican Richard Kline in the general election

and as a Republican against Firebaugh in the special election to finish the last two months of her late husband's term. She won both elections easily, and she has been reelected five times, including the 2006 election, without serious opposition. In 2002, Emerson decided not to run for the U.S. Senate against Jean Carnahan, a fellow congressional widow.

On May 24, 2005, Emerson was one of 50 Republicans to vote in favor of overturning President George W. Bush's ban on federal funding for stem cell research. She cast her yea vote the day after her mother-in-law passed away from Alzheimer's disease. In the 109th Congress, Emerson has served on the House Appropriations Committee. She is the first woman elected to Congress from the state of Missouri. Married to Ron Gladney, she has two children and six stepchildren.

Further Reading

Barone, Michael. *The Almanac of American Politics.* Washington, D.C.: National Journal Group, 2006.
"Emerson, Jo Ann." In *Biographical Directory of the United States Congress, 1774–present.* Available online. URL: http://bioguide.congress.gov/scripts/biodisplay.pl?index=E000172. Accessed on January 8, 2007.
"Representative Jo Ann Emerson (MO)." In *Project Vote Smart.* Available online. URL: http://votesmart.org/bio.php?can_id=. Accessed on January 8, 2007.

—Angela Kouters

EMILY's List (Early Money is Like Yeast)
EMILY's List has become the United States' largest grassroots political network. The group's mission is to elect pro-choice, Democratic women to federal, state, and local offices. It was founded by ELLEN R. MALCOLM in 1985, and in 1986 the organization helped elect BARBARA MIKULSKI of Maryland to the U.S. Senate. The acronym stands for "Early Money Is Like Yeast," and the group's primary function has been to

help raise money by bundling contributions from individuals to those candidates who have passed the group's selection process. Members of the group pay $100 to join and then commit to contributing at least another $100 to a minimum of two candidates per election cycle. Individuals write checks directly to the campaigns of their choice, but the money is channeled through EMILY's List. In 1992, the group spawned a similar Republican organization called the WISH LIST (Women in the Senate and the House) that funds pro-choice Republican women.

In addition to financial support, EMILY's List helps recruit and train candidates, and they mobilize Democratic women to get to the polls in support of its candidates. EMILY's List is criticized by some because they do not track many aspects of their candidates' records other than reproductive rights, and some of their candidates have voted against progressive proposals supported by a majority of Democrats. The organization maintains a Web site at www.emilyslist.org

—J. Celeste Lay

England, Lynndie (1982–) U.S. soldier

United States Army Reserve private Lynndie England, a native of Ashland, Kentucky, was one of at least six U.S. soldiers directly involved in the Abu Ghraib prison scandal in Iraq. Photographs made public in May 2004 showed PFC England posing with naked Iraqi prisoners. A cigarette dangling from her mouth, she was seen smiling in several photographs, pointing to the genitals of detainees and holding the end of a leash attached to a naked male Iraqi prisoner. The photographs shocked the public's sensibilities and led to an investigation of all forms of prisoner abuse in Iraq. While the Bush administration claimed that the soldiers had acted independently, England claimed that she was "ordered" to appear in the photographs by "persons in my higher chain of command." Her first trial ended when the military judge declared a mistrial. A military jury subsequently convicted her on six counts in connection with the prisoner abuse scandal.

Of the seven reservists from the 372nd Military Police Company who faced charges, three were women. The commander of the 800th Military Police Brigade, army reserve brigadier general Janis Karpinski, was in charge of military prisons in Iraq. The top U.S. intelligence officer in Iraq, in charge of reviewing the status of detainees before their release, was Major General Barbara Fast. Since the earliest SUFFRAGE campaigns, feminists have argued that women should be in positions of power because they would exercise it with more care and less violence than men do. Abu Ghraib presented evidence to the contrary and led feminists to rethink many of their assumptions about women's essential nature. Journalist Barbara Ehrenreich wrote: "What we have learned from Abu Ghraib, once and for all, is that a uterus is not a substitute for a conscience. This doesn't mean gender equality isn't worth fighting for for its own sake. It is. If we believe in democracy, then we believe in a woman's right to do and achieve whatever men can do and achieve, even the bad things. It's just that gender equality cannot, all alone, bring about a just and peaceful world."

On September 26, 2005, Lynndie England was convicted of one count of conspiracy, four counts of maltreating detainees, and one count of committing an indecent act. She was sentenced to three years for her crimes and given a dishonorable discharge. She is currently serving her term at the Naval Consolidated Brig Miramar in San Diego, California.

See also MILITARY SERVICE.

Further Reading

Ehrenreich, Barbara. "A Uterus is no Substitute for a Conscience: What Abu Ghraib Taught Me." *ZNet*, May 21, 2004. Available online. URL: http://www.zmag.org/content/showarticle.cfm?ItemID=5571. Accessed on June 30, 2006.

Equal Credit Opportunity Act (ECOA)

(1974) As women entered the workforce in greater numbers throughout the 1960s and 1970s, many found that despite their earnings they were being denied credit in their own name. In many cases they needed a male cosigner before they could get loans or credit cards. In 1974, the Equal Credit Opportunity Act (ECOA) became law; it banned discrimination in access to credit on the basis of sex or marital status and was later amended to include race, religion, national origin, and age. As a result of the ECOA, a creditor may not discount income because of sex or marital status, refuse to consider regular alimony and child support as income, consider the race of people in the neighborhood where one wants to buy a house, or consider whether a phone is listed in the applicant's name. The ECOA is credited, among other things, with helping women start businesses and take out mortgages in their own names. Until 1970, women's mortgage activity was not tracked; today women are a major force in the home-buying market. According to the Center for Women's Business Research, the number of women-owned businesses in the United States grew at twice the rate of all firms between 1997 and 2002. The Small Business Administration reports that women-owned businesses account for 28 percent of all privately owned businesses, and they employ 9.2 million people. Women-owned businesses contribute $2.38 trillion in revenue to the U.S. economy. This would not have been possible without the ECOA.

Further Reading

Gelb, Joyce, and Marian L. Palley. *Women and Public Policies*. Richmond: University of Virginia Press, 1996.

Equal Employment Opportunity Act (1972)

The Equal Employment Opportunity Act of 1972 was required to expand the jurisdiction and powers of the EQUAL EMPLOYMENT OPPORTUNITY COMMISSION (EEOC). The NATIONAL ORGANIZATION FOR WOMEN (NOW) formed in 1966 in part to agitate and lobby for greater enforcement of provisions of TITLE VII OF THE CIVIL RIGHTS ACT OF 1964 outlawing sex discrimination in employment and to put teeth in the EEOC. The Equal Employment Opportunity Act broadened the power of the EEOC by authorizing the commission to sue for compliance rather than relying solely on voluntary compliance. In addition, the law expanded the EEOC's jurisdiction to include small businesses, federal and state employees, and educational institutions.

Further Reading

Burstein, Paul. *Discrimination, Jobs, and Politics: The Struggle for Equal Employment Opportunity in the United States Since the New Deal*. Chicago: University of Chicago Press, 1998.

U.S. Economic Employment Commission. *EEOC History: The Law.* "Equal Employment Opportunity Act of 1972." Available online. URL: http://www.eeoc.gov/abouteeoc/35th/thelaw/eeo_1972.html. Accessed on January 4, 2007.

Equal Employment Opportunity Commission (EEOC)

The EEOC was established to enforce TITLE VII OF THE CIVIL RIGHTS ACT OF 1964 prohibitions against discrimination, including sex discrimination, in employment. The EEOC originally was only authorized to investigate and resolve individual complaints of employment discrimination, but in 1972 Congress expanded the EEOC's power to include initiating lawsuits against employers, and it extended the jurisdiction of the EEOC to federal, state, county, and municipal workplaces.

The EEOC was not very energetic in its enforcement of antidiscrimination laws related to sex. Only under the leadership of ELEANOR HOLMES NORTON did the agency develop strategies addressing entire industries or sectors of employment where sex discrimination was present. These were called "patterns and practice" lawsuits. In 1980, the EEOC issued regulations defining sexual harassment as illegal. However, with the appointment of Clarence Thomas as

EEOC chair, the rate of litigation plummeted, and the agency returned to a philosophy of resolving complaints on an individual basis. Many areas of law that were of interest to women, including SEXUAL HARASSMENT, COMPARABLE WORTH, and equal pay, became low priorities. Following ANITA HILL's widely publicized 1991 charges of sexual harassment against Clarence Thomas, complaints filed with the EEOC increased steeply.

Further Reading

U.S. Economic Employment Commission. *EEOC History.* "35 Years of Ensuring the Promise of Opportunity." Available online. URL: http://www.eeoc. gov/abouteeoc/35th/history/index.html. Accessed on January 4, 2007.

Equal Pay Act (1963)   The Equal Pay Act was passed as an amendment to the FAIR LABOR STANDARDS ACT (1938) on June 10, 1963, and became effective on June 11, 1964. The Fair Labor Standards Act prohibited classifying jobs and wages according to age or sex, provided a minimum wage for some job classifications, and required fair treatment for wage and hourly workers. When women flooded the workforce during both world wars, government took action to alleviate the fear that women in men's jobs would depress wages. Policy dictated that women holding "men's jobs" be paid "men's wages" in order to protect men's jobs and wage rates. Since attitudes about women working were still largely ambivalent, policy directed at equalizing wages based on a doctrine of equality did not surface until the Kennedy administration sent an equal-pay bill to Congress. The WOMEN'S BUREAU, led by ESTHER PETERSON, argued that fairness dictated equal pay for men and women. Initially, the Women's Bureau pursued "equal pay for comparable work" but relented under pressure from employers who argued that defining comparable work would invite excessive government intrusion. By the time Congress took action in 1963, 23 states already had equal-pay laws on the books.

The Equal Pay Act requires that when men and women perform the same (or substantially the same) job in the same place and under the same conditions, they must receive equal pay. However, seniority, merit, and measures related to the quantity and quality of the work provide a legal basis for pay differentials, as do "any other factor other than sex." Initially, the law covered only wage and hourly employees and exempted employers with fewer than 25 employees. In 1972, the law's protections were extended to workers in small firms not covered by minimum-wage laws, professionals including teachers, and state and local government employees. Enforcement moved from the Department of Labor exclusively to the EQUAL EMPLOYMENT OPPORTUNITY COMMISSION (EEOC) in 1978, but that move did not result in more stringent enforcement of the law. To date, enforcement is the result of an individual or group of workers filing a claim with the EEOC rather than aggressive action on the part of government to equalize pay. Although women earned just 58 cents for every dollar earned by a man in 1968, the prevailing 23 percent wage gap in 2005, more than 40 years after the law was passed, suggests that both the law and its enforcement have not rectified the problem of wage discrimination.

See also EQUAL PAY DAY; WAGE GAP.

Further Reading

U.S. Economic Employment Commission. EEOC History. The Law. "Equal Pay Act of 1963." Available online. URL: http://www.eeoc.gov/abouteeoc/ 35th/thelaw/epa.html. Accessed on January 4, 2007.

—Scott A. Shelton

Equal Pay Day   Each year, the National Committee on Pay Equity (NCPE) organizes the national observance of Equal Pay Day to raise awareness about unfair pay for women and people of color in the United States. In 2005, for example, Equal Pay Day was celebrated on

Tuesday, April 19. Equal Pay Day is observed to indicate how far into each successive year a woman must work to earn as much as a man earned in the previous year and symbolizes the day when women's wages catch up to men's wages from the previous week. Because women earn less on average, they must work longer for the same pay. The NCPE encourages women to wear red on Equal Pay Day to symbolize how far women and minorities are "in the red" with regard to their pay. The WAGE GAP represents how much, on average, women earn to a man's dollar. The national wage gap for all college-educated women in 2005 is $.72, but it varies by state. The District of Columbia has the lowest wage gap (women make 86 cents for every dollar a man earns) and Wyoming has the largest wage gap in the country at $.63. The National Committee on Pay Equity maintains a Web site at www.pay-equity.org.

See also EQUAL PAY ACT.

Equal Rights Amendment (ERA)   The Equal Rights Amendment (ERA) was designed to make equality of women and men a part of the U.S. Constitution. Its aim was to invalidate federal and state laws that discriminated against women on the basis of sex. In 1923, the NATIONAL WOMAN'S PARTY (NWP) under ALICE PAUL first introduced the ERA to Congress. (For many years, it was known as the Alice Paul Amendment.) For the NWP, the ERA was a natural extension to the access to political power gained through suffrage and the only way to ensure that equality was extended into the workplace, the church, education, health care, and family law. To other women, however, the ERA was a potential threat to the PROTECTIVE LEGISLATION and broad social reforms enacted to protect women in the workplace and accommodate their special burdens relative to chidlbirth and family responsibilities. Labor unions immediately opposed the ERA and remained in active opposition until 1973. Between 1923 and 1970, the amendment was submitted to Congress in

various forms in each session, but it was always rejected.

With the second wave of FEMINISM in the 1960s, there was a growing societal consensus about the need for institutionalizing women's equality. The women's movement, especially the NATIONAL ORGANIZATION FOR WOMEN (NOW) and ERAmerica, passionately pursued the ERA's adoption and ratification in the 1970s. Two additional factors made it possible for the ERA to gain congressional support at this time. First, when the CIVIL RIGHTS ACT OF 1964 was enacted, the inclusion of sex in TITLE VII OF THE CIVIL RIGHTS ACT OF 1964, forbidding discrimination in employment on the basis of sex, effectively dismantled any remaining protective legislation that discriminated *in favor* of women. Labor unions were now free to support the amendment. Perhaps most importantly, women used political pressure to focus the public's attention on Congress's failure to act as well as a rarely used parliamentary procedure to free the ERA proposal from the House Judiciary Committee where it had been held captive for decades.

In 1970, the Pittsburgh chapter of NOW staged a protest interrupting public hearings on granting the vote to 18-year-olds (ultimately ratified as the Twenty-sixth Amendment), prompting Senator Birch Bayh to promise to hold Senate hearings on the ERA. The record of those hearings detailing the various ways women experienced discrimination across all sectors of life created a compelling case in favor of the ERA. Simultaneously, Congresswomen MARTHA GRIFFITHS and Enid Green mounted a discharge petition drive to free the ERA from the House Judiciary Committee. A discharge petition is a procedural mechanism for circumventing committee inaction and bringing a resolution directly to the floor of the House of Representatives. It is a bold move and rarely successful. Of the 829 petitions filed prior to Griffith's, only 24 bills were ever successfully discharged, and of those, only 20 passed the House, of which only two were enacted into law. Yet Griffiths not only managed to persuade 218 House members to sign the discharge petition, she also got 332 of the 435 members to vote for the discharge resolution on the floor, effectively removing the ERA from the Judiciary Committee's grasp. On the Senate side, however, the resolution was amended to exempt women from the draft, effectively killing the chances for congressional passage in 1970. It was not until 1972, after more than a year of successive hearings, failed amendment attempts, and wording changes, that both houses of Congress successfully passed the bill by the constitutionally required two-thirds margin, enabling the resolution to be sent to the states.

Initially states competed over the honor of ratifying the amendment quickly. Hawaii, for example, voted to ratify the ERA on the same day that it was passed by the U.S. Senate. Within one year after Congress's approval, 30 of the required 38 states had ratified the ERA.

By 1973, however, anti-ERA groups had formed to halt its ratification on the state level. The most prominent and effective was PHYLLIS SCHLAFLY's organization called STOP ERA. The ERA's adversaries managed to raise doubts over the amendment's effects and usefulness. Opponents argued that the ERA was unfair to women and labeled it the "extra responsibilities amendment." They were successful in painting a dire image of a gender-neutral America where women were drafted into war, forced into the workplace against their will, left destitute after divorce by the elimination of alimony, and compelled to share public restrooms with men. By 1977, 35 of the 38 states required had ratified the amendment, but the tide was turning decidedly against ratification. In 1978, Congress granted an unprecedented extension to the period of time during which states could consider the amendment. However, when the period expired on June 30, 1982, not a single additional state had ratified the ERA, and several were actively working to rescind their previous positive vote.

Although the ERA has been reintroduced into each session of Congress since 1982, it has

Women protesting the Equal Rights Amendment in front of the White House, 1977 (LIBRARY OF CONGRESS)

never again been sent to the states. The failed amendment read: "Equality of rights under the law shall not be denied or abridged by the United States or any State on account of sex; The Congress shall have the power to enforce, by appropriate legislation, the provisions of this article; This amendment shall take effect two years after the date of ratification."

Recently a new legal strategy to rejuvenate the Equal Rights Amendment has emerged. The ERA would have become the Twenty-seventh Amendment to the Constitution if it had achieved ratification by 1982. Instead, the "Madison Amendment" governing congressional pay raises, which was sent to the states for ratification in 1789, became the Twenty-seventh Amendment in 1992. ERA supporters argue that acceptance of the Madison Amendment means that Congress has the power to maintain the legal viability of the ERA and the existing 35 state ratifications. If so, only three more states are needed to ratify the amendment to make the ERA a part of the U.S. Constitution. The legal rationale for the "Three-State Strategy" was developed by three law students in an article, "The Equal Rights Amendment: Why the ERA Remains Legally Viable and Properly Before the States," published in the *William & Mary Journal of Women and the Law* in 1997. The Congressional Research Service analyzed this legal argument and concluded that the acceptance of the Madison Amendment does imply that ratification of the ERA by three more states could allow Congress to declare ratification accomplished.

There have been a number of bills introduced into the U.S. House of Representatives and the U.S. Senate requiring Congress to certify the ERA if three additional states vote positively for ratification. To date, none have been passed by Congress. Ratification bills have since been introduced into six states (Florida, Illinois, Mississippi, Missouri, Oklahoma, and Virginia), and supporters seek to do the same in the remaining nine unratifying states (Alabama, Arizona, Arkansas, Georgia, Louisiana, Nevada, North Carolina, South Carolina, and Utah).

Support for constitutional equality remains high. A 2001 public opinion poll demonstrated historically high public support for the issue, but it also suggested that mobilizing public support in favor of ratification will be difficult. While 96 percent of respondents supported constitutional equality for women and men, and 88 percent want the Constitution to explicitly guarantee equality, 72 percent mistakenly believe that the Constitution already includes this provision.

Further Reading

Becker, Susan. *The Origins of the Equal Rights Amendment: American Feminism Between the Wars*. Westport, Conn.: Greenwood, 1982.

Berry, Mary Frances. *Why ERA Failed: Politics, Women's Rights and the Amending Process of the Constitution*. Bloomington: Indiana University Press, 1986.

Mansbridge, Jane. *Why We Lost the ERA*. Chicago: University of Chicago Press, 1986.

—Christine Knauer

Equal Rights Association   Founded in 1866, the Equal Rights Association fought for the political rights of blacks and of white women. Proposed by white woman suffragists SUSAN B. ANTHONY, ELIZABETH CADY STANTON, and LUCY STONE and supported by such black rights advocates as Frederick Douglass, the association lobbied state legislatures, state constitutional conventions, and white male voters in the Northeast and Midwest to alter state constitutions that discriminated against one or both groups. Most importantly, it advocated the right to vote for all adult Americans, regardless of gender or race.

The Equal Rights Association won few state battles. Democrats supported SUFFRAGE for white women, but not for blacks. Republicans favored voting rights for black men, but not for women. Finally, disagreement over two amendments to the federal Constitution split the reformers both ideologically and organizationally. The Fourteenth Amendment's (ratified 1868) identification of voting rights with "male" Americans, combined with the Fifteenth Amendment's (ratified 1870) extension of suffrage to black men but not to women, convinced white members by 1869 that white women's rights must come either instead of those for blacks or only after them. Those who rejected African Americans' rights in favor of white women's formed the NATIONAL WOMAN SUFFRAGE ASSOCIATION under the leadership of Anthony and Stanton. Those willing to defer women's rights until after black men's formed the AMERICAN WOMAN SUFFRAGE ASSOCIATION, led by Stone.

Having built on two decades of overlap between the women's and black rights movements, the Equal Rights Association revealed in its failure that postbellum America could not accommodate such broad reform. The politics of Reconstruction placed woman suffrage in opposition to black rights. From then on, these groups would struggle separately for the rights of citizens.

Further Reading

DuBois, Ellen Carol. *Feminism and Suffrage: The Emergence of an Independent Women's Movement in America, 1848–1869*. Ithaca, N.Y.: Cornell University Press, 1978.

Stanton, Elizabeth Cady, Susan B. Anthony, and Matilda Joslyn Gage, eds. *History of Woman Suffrage*, vol. 2. New York: Fowler & Wells, 1882.

—Michael David Cohen

Equity in Prescription Insurance and Contraceptive Coverage Act

The Equity in Prescription Insurance and Contraceptive Coverage Act (EPICC) was first introduced in 1997 to address insurance discrimination against women, but it has yet to pass and be signed in to law. The legislation requires private health plans to cover FDA-approved prescription contraceptives and related medical services to the same extent that they cover prescription drugs and other outpatient medical services. To date, 22 states have passed laws or promulgated regulations requiring private health plans that cover prescription drugs to include coverage for prescription contraception. Fourteen others require this of at least some insurers. Health plans routinely cover other prescription drugs, but 28% of employers still fail to provide coverage for all five FDA-approved reversible methods of contraception.

In December 2000, the EQUAL EMPLOYMENT OPPORTUNITY COMMISSION (EEOC) ruled that an employer's failure to cover prescription contraceptives in the same manner as other preventive health services constitutes sex discrimination in violation of TITLE VII OF THE CIVIL RIGHTS ACT OF 1964. In 2001, the U.S. District Court for the Western District of Washington ruled that an employer's failure to cover prescription contraceptives in its otherwise comprehensive prescription drug plan constitutes sex discrimination in violation of Title VII of the CIVIL RIGHTS ACT OF 1964, as amended by the 1978 PREGNANCY DISCRIMINATION ACT. The court found that "the law is no longer blind to the fact that only women can get pregnant, bear children, or use prescription contraception. The special or increased healthcare needs associated with a woman's unique sex-based characteristics must be met to the same extent, and the same terms, as other healthcare needs."

Further Reading

Center for Reproductive Rights. "Contraceptive Coverage for All: EPICC Act is Prescription for Women's Equality." Available online. URL: http://www.crlp.org/pub_fac_epicc.html. Accessed on January 4, 2007.

Eshoo, Anna (Anna Georges Eshoo) (1942–)

congressperson Anna Eshoo was born on December 13, 1942, in New Britain, Connecticut. She attended Canada College, where she received her associate of arts degree (1975). In 1981, Eshoo worked as chief of staff for California Assembly Speaker Leo McCarthy, and a year later she was sworn in as a member of the San Mateo County Board of Supervisors, becoming president of the board in 1986.

In 1992, Eshoo decided to run for congress and was successful in her bid. She has represented the 14th congressional district of California for seven consecutive terms. She easily won reelection to an eighth term in 2006. Appointed in January 2003 to the House Intelligence Committee, she also serves on the House Energy and Commerce Committee. She is the only member of Assyrian descent serving in Congress and is the primary sponsor of a bill to protect Assyrian Christians from religious persecution in Iraq. She has been a strong advocate for women's rights and has supported legislation on pay equity, pension reform, and reproductive choice.

Further Reading

Barone, Michael. *The Almanac of American Politics.* Washington, D.C.: National Journal Group, 2006.

"Anna Georges Eshoo." In *Biographical Directory of the United States Congress, 1774–present.* Available online. URL: http://bioguide.congress.gov/scripts/biodisplay.pl?index=E000215. Accessed on January 8, 2007.

"Representative Anna G. Eshoo (CA)." In *Project Vote Smart.* Available online. URL: http://votesmart.org/bio.php?can_id=H0284103. Accessed on January 8, 2007.

—Angela Kouters

eugenics The word *eugenics* was first used in 1883 by Sir Frances Galton, the distant cousin of Charles Darwin, to refer to the study or use of selective breeding to improve a species over time. Eugenics became entangled with claims for women's rights and access to birth conrol when white feminists, including EMMA GOLDMAN and CHARLOTTE PERKINS GILMAN, argued that only women who could control their fertility would be able to produce high-quality children. If the future of the country depended on future generations of citizens, the production of the future generations depended on women, and therefore women should enjoy the same civil and political rights as men. Ironically, this argument was turned on its head as nativists urged healthy, white, middle-class women to bear more children. The U.S. Supreme Court ruled compulsory sterilization legal in 1927, thereby empowering the government to determine which women were fit to conceive and bear children.

Eugenics was largely discredited following World War I and the later revulsion over Nazi racial extermination policies. However, a contemporary argument equates prenatal testing for physical and developmental deformities with eugenics.

See also BIRTH CONTROL MOVEMENT.

Further Reading

Cuddy, Lois A., and Claire M. Roche. *Evolution and Eugenics in American Literature and Culture, 1880–1940.* Lewisburg, Pa.: Bucknell University Press, 2003.

F

Fair Labor Standards Act (1938)

Fair Labor Standards Act (1938) The Fair Labor Standards Act of 1938, as amended, provides for minimum standards for both wages and overtime entitlement and spells out administrative procedures by which covered work time must be compensated. This was the first national minimum wage law to sustain a constitutional challenge. In addition to establishing a minimum wage of $.25 an hour, the Act also established 40 hours as the maximum number of hours in a regular workweek before overtime pay was required (typically set at time-and-a-half). The provisions of the Fair Labor Standards Act covered both men and women. The legislation also banned oppressive child labor. Congress has amended the act several times to increase the minimum wage and extend coverage to more sectors of the workforce. The current federal minimum wage rate is $5.15, but the Democratically controlled 110th Congress passed legislation on April 20, 2007, to increase the federal minimum wage to $5.85 per hour (60 days after the president signs the bill into law), then $6.55 per hour a year later, and $7.25 per hour a year after that. States can set a minimum wage rate higher than that established under the act, but they may not fall below the federal rate.

Further Reading
U.S. Department of Labor. "The Fair Labor Standards Act (FLSA)." Available online. URL: http://www.dol.gov/compliance/laws/comp-flsa.htm. Accessed on January 4, 2007.

Faludi, Susan

Faludi, Susan (1959–) *journalist, author* Susan Faludi was born on April 18, 1959, in New York City. After attending Harvard University, where she graduated summa cum laude with a B.A. degree in 1981, she became a copy clerk for the *New York Times* and a reporter for various newspapers throughout the nation. In 1990, she worked with the *Wall Street Journal* in San Francisco, and she won a Pulitzer Prize in 1991 for explanatory journalism. In the same year, *Backlash: The Undeclared War Against American Women* was published, skyrocketing her into feminist fame as she argued that the media was actively working to stereotype and distort women's images to return the culture to its prefeminist state. She received a National Book Critics Circle Award for the book in 1992.

Backlash had a profound effect on the development of THIRD-WAVE FEMINISM, as women coming out of the conservative Reagan era began to

175

reconsider their identification as women and as feminists. In March 1992, Faludi appeared with GLORIA STEINEM on the cover of *Time,* suggesting that she was the bridge to a new generation of feminists. In 1999, she released her second book, *Stiffed: The Betrayal of the American Man,* in which she argued that despite the fact that most power lies with men, most men have little power and that men are also victims of the culture and gender confusion. This book failed to have much impact and was criticized by both feminists and many of the men with whom she was sympathizing. Currently living in Los Angeles, California, Faludi continues to write for various magazines such as *The New Yorker, Esquire,* and *The Nation.*

Further Reading

Faludi, Susan. *Backlash: The Undeclared War Against American Women.* New York: Crown, 1991.
———. *Stiffed: The Betrayal of the American Man.* New York: W. Morrow & Co, 1999.

—Lynda Hinkle

Family and Medical Leave Act (FMLA)

(1993)   Implementation of the Family and Medical Leave Act (FMLA) provided the first comprehensive program in the United States to assist wage earners with dependent-care responsibilities. Signed into law by President Bill Clinton on February 5, 1993, FMLA signaled his first official act as president and took effect six months later on August 5, 1993. The act stipulates that businesses with 50 or more employees must provide any employee with dependent-care needs up to 12 weeks of unpaid leave and job retention in order to care for their relative. Employees may request time for needs as diverse as the care of newborns or adopted children and a disabled or seriously ill relative. The measure represents, however, a significantly modified version of the Parental and Disability Leave Act introduced in 1985 by Representative PATRICIA SCHROEDER, (D-CO). That measure attempted to provide universal employer coverage for Ameri-

can workers by offering them 18 weeks of job-protected leave to care for newborn, newly adopted, or seriously ill children, and allowances for a 26-week leave for cases of prolonged medical illness among employees or their dependents. Supporters renamed the bill in 1987 and compromised on the length of leaves, securing congressional support; however, President George H. W. Bush twice vetoed the measure.

Further Reading

Hyde, Janet Shibley, and Marilyn J. Essex, eds. *Parental Leave and Child Care: Setting a Research and Policy Agenda.* Philadelphia: Temple University Press, 1991.
Kaitlin, Katharine Karr. "Congressional Responses to Families in the Workplace: The Family and Medical Leave Act of 1987–1988." In *More Than Kissing Babies? Current Child and Family Policy in the United States,* edited by Francine H. Jacobs and Margery W. Davies. Westport, Conn.: Auburn House, 1993.
National Partnership for Women and Families. "Family and Medical Leave Act." Available online. URL: http://tinyurl.com/ysO7x8. Accessed on January 4, 2007.
Wisensale, Steven K. *Family Leave Policy: The Political Economy of Work and Family in America.* London: M. E. Sharpe, 2001.

—Kyle E. Ciani

family leave policy   The United States remains one of only three countries (along with Australia and Libya) without paid family leave. FAMILY AND MEDICAL LEAVE ACT (FMLA) regulations, finally signed into law by President Clinton in 1993, are limited to companies with more than 50 employees and merely guarantee that an employee's job or a similar job will be available upon their return from up to 12 weeks of unpaid leave. When Representative PATRICIA SCHROEDER of Colorado first introduced the Parental and Disability Leave Act in 1985, no one would join her in sponsoring it. After eight years and two George H. W. Bush presidential vetoes of revisions of Schroeder's legislation, the FMLA applies to barely half the workforce in the United States and has not amounted to undue interference in the private market as business once feared. Policies such as the FMLA that mandate job-guaranteed leave but do not require wage replacement are of limited value to most workers, particularly the working poor. The FMLA did, however, assert a public interest in family care, and that opened an important door.

The FMLA provides up to 12 weeks of unpaid job-protected leave to care for a newborn child or a sick family member, or to deal with one's own illness. Proposals introduced in the 106th Congress attempted to extend FMLA coverage to employers with 25 or more employees, to eliminate the hours-of-service requirement (currently an employee has to have worked for 1,250 hours in the last year to qualify for coverage), to allow employees to take FMLA leave to address domestic-violence situations, and to extend the FMLA to allow parents to attend and participate in school events, teacher-parent conferences, and field trips. Under the Clinton administration, the Department of Labor granted a waiver to states in order to allow voluntary experimentation with funding paid leave through unemployment insurance (UI). In 2002, 16 states were actively considering proposals to use the so-called baby UI regulation. Before any state could adopt and implement new legislation, the Bush administration rescinded the UI regulation. Skirting the objections to using UI funds for otherwise able-bodied workers with emergent family responsibilities, California pursued a paid-leave policy using temporary disability insurance. In September 2002, California became the first state to adopt legislation to provide up to 12 weeks of partial wage replacement to workers who take leave for approved family situations. The California Family Temporary Disability Insurance program, funded entirely by employee contributions, will provide 55 percent (up to $728 per week) of eligible workers' pay. The cost to workers is minimal—estimated to average $27 a year for most. California remains the only state to have adopted a wage replacement policy for family leave.

Results of the National Study of the Changing Workforce suggest that women's decision to work part-time in order to care for children or family limits their ability to access FMLA leave. Although 86 percent of fathers covered under the FMLA had worked the required 1,250 hours, only 73 percent of mothers met that requirement. As a result, the study estimated that only 41 percent of employed women were covered by the FMLA, compared to 49 percent of men. Even when employees are covered by the FMLA, the likelihood is that their leave must be unpaid. Two-thirds of workers who are eligible for leave opt not to take it because of financial reasons, and one in 11 who used FMLA leave was actually forced onto public assistance to make ends meet.

Americans strongly support providing paid family leave. In a Center for Policy Alternatives survey, 68 percent of women and 56 percent of men would be more likely to vote for a candidate who favors expanding the FMLA. A 2000 survey found that 80 percent of adults and 88 percent of parents with children six or younger support "paid parental leave that allows working parents of very young babies to stay home from work for their children." The same survey found that 85 percent of adults support expanding "disability or unemployment insurance to help families afford to take time off from work to care for a newborn, a newly adopted child, or a seriously ill family member." Only 14 percent of those surveyed said that they opposed such measures. Both business and government get mediocre marks from survey participants on their efforts to make changes in the workplace that would help workers meet the needs of their young children. Fifty-nine percent of those surveyed said that employers are doing a fair or poor job, whereas 63 percent said that government is doing a fair or poor job in assisting workers.

Opponents of the regulations to allow states to use unemployment insurance funds to pay for family leave argue that the practice will be too expensive and will bankrupt states' unemployment insurance funds, particularly in times of economic recession when unemployment rates are high. The Employment Policy Foundation (EPF) characterizes the policy change as "pitting the 'haves' (those with jobs) versus the 'have-nots' (the unemployed)." EPF cautions that notification and reporting requirements can limit personal freedom and privacy rights. In response to unfavorable comparisons of the current FMLA with more generous European family-leave policies, the EPF argues that the U.S. economy benefits from a free-market approach that allows workers to negotiate benefits privately with their employers.

For two-paycheck families, reliable, high-quality CHILD CARE is scarce and exorbitantly expensive. The failure to move child-care policy beyond an adjunct to public assistance means that most parents are on their own to locate and pay for a provider. Nearly 50 percent rely on extended family or neighbors to care for their children. An estimated 5 million children are left unsupervised after the school day ends. It is a patchwork system at best, and for most families it constitutes a significant expenditure. For low- and middle-income families with children between the ages of three and five, child care represents the third greatest expense after housing and food. For families with higher incomes (annual income above $66,900), it represents the second greatest expense after housing. The price of child care can easily run between $4,000 and $10,000 annually. In 48 states, the cost of center-based child care for a four-year-old is greater than tuition at a four-year public college. Subsidies for the cost of child care are very limited. In a number of states, the income eligibility cutoffs for child-care assistance are so restrictive that the working poor do not qualify. For example, a family of three in Missouri earning above $17,784 cannot qualify for child-care assistance.

Inadequate funds at the state level mean long waiting lists. There are 48,800 children on the waiting list in Florida, 26,500 in Texas, and more than 20,000 in Tennessee. Despite research demonstrating the importance of early learning to a child's development, public investments in education and development are more than seven times greater during school-aged years than during the early learning years. Business has not stepped in to fill the gap. A survey of more than 1,000 American companies found that only 9 percent of businesses with 100 or more employees offer on-site child care even though extant studies and statistics confirm that the benefits of on-site day care are vast: It aids in recruiting and retaining high-quality workers, particularly women; enhances productivity and heightens employee morale; and provides employers with a competitive edge in a changing labor market. Privatizing child care—arguably a public good—leaves parents to bear the bulk of early child-care costs without any public accountability for adequate provision and quality of child-care services.

Internationally, support for families takes a variety of forms. Whether any one country has adopted a policy relating to family support depends on a number of factors, including structural economic factors (capitalist versus socialist economy); need created by changing social and economic factors; and the activity of family advocacy groups, employers and business owners, women's organizations, and religious groups. These "policy inputs" influence the "policy output" in each country and help explain why there are differences across national boundaries. Family policy may take the form of cash benefits or assistance (health insurance, education, Social Security, or employment) to boost the family's standard of living; indirect cash transfers in the form of tax credits or deductions for dependent children, family allowances, and means-tested family benefits; employment benefits granted to workers with family responsibilities (maternity and parental leave, child-care leave); direct services to families (on-site child care, after-school programs); housing subsidies for families with children; or legislation that is consistent with the state's population policies (access to contraception, abortion services, infertility treatments, or adoption). The United States has a large number of policies at the state and federal levels that affect families, but the dominance of attitudes that support family autonomy and limited government involvement, as well as the

FAMILY LEAVE POLICIES IN THE UNITED STATES AND 10 PEER NATIONS, 2002

COUNTRY	TYPE OF LEAVE PROVIDED	PAYMENT RATE
United States	12 weeks of family leave	Unpaid
Canada	17 weeks of maternity leave 10 weeks of parental leave	15 weeks at 55% of prior earnings 55% of prior earnings
Denmark	28 weeks of maternity leave 1 year of parental leave	60% of prior earnings 90% of unemployment benefit rate
Finland	18 weeks of maternity leave 26 weeks of parental leave child-rearing leave until child is 3	70% of prior earnings 70% of prior earnings Flat rate
Norway	52 weeks of parental leave 2 years of child-rearing leave	80% of prior earnings Flat rate
Sweden	18 months of parental leave	12 months at 80% of prior earnings, 3 months flat rate, 3 months unpaid
Austria	16 weeks of maternity leave parental leave until child is 3 years old	100% of prior earnings 18 months of unemployment benefit; 6 months unpaid
France	16 weeks of maternity leave parental leave until child is 3 years old	100% of prior earnings unpaid for one child; paid at flat rate for two or more children
Germany	14 weeks maternity leave 3 years parental leave	100% of prior earnings Flat rate for 2 years, unpaid for third year
Italy	5 months maternity leave 6 months parental leave	80% of prior earnings 30% of prior earnings
United Kingdom	18 weeks maternity leave 13 weeks parental leave	90% for 6 weeks, flat for 12 weeks unpaid

Source: Waldfogel, Jane. "International Policies toward Parental Leave and Child Care. Table 1: Childbirth-Related Leave Policies in the United States and 10 Peer Nations." In *The Future of Children,* Princeton-Brookings Web site. Available online. URL: http://tinyurl.com/2uybm2. Accessed on June 30, 2006.

reinforcement of gender ideologies, has limited the coherence and reach of family policy. The issues associated with balancing work and caring for families loom large for individual families, and particularly for women within families, but receive very little positive public attention.

Although the right of a mother to leave employment after pregnancy was affirmed internationally in the United Nations' International Labour Office Maternity Protection Convention, adopted in 1952, the United States lagged far behind other nations in even meeting the bare minimum requirement of 12 weeks of maternity leave. Of the 138 UN member nations, the United States was the only country that made this leave optional. In other countries, a mandatory minimum is enforced, and in several the minimum leave is compulsory. Parental leave, entitling both mother and father to spend time with their children, is offered in 36 of 138 member nations. In 25 nations, including nine of the 14 European Union members, parental leave is paid (see the table accompanying this entry). The most generous parental- or maternity-leave policies offer high levels of compensation to offset a loss of earnings overall. In all cases, job guarantees are built into the policy so that parents are not penalized for taking time off. The barrier to paid leave in the United States is not economic but rather ideological.

Further Reading

Ford, Lynne E. *Women and Politics: The Pursuit of Equality.* Boston: Houghton Mifflin, 2006.

Glass, Jennifer L., and Sarah Beth Estes. "The Family Responsive Workplace." *Annual Review of Sociology* 23 (1997): 298–314.

National Partnership for Women and Families Web site. Available online. URL: http://www.nationalpartnership.org. Accessed on January 4, 2007.

Family Support Act of 1988   The Family Support Act of 1988, signed into law by President Ronald Reagan on October 13, 1988, was the first of several attempts to reform WELFARE POLICY (specifically AID TO FAMILIES WITH DEPENDENT CHILDREN). The intent of the legislation was to reduce long-term dependence on welfare through job training, work requirements, educational support, and more aggressive enforcement of child support by requiring states to freeze wages of delinquent parents. Under the law, one parent in a two-parent family was required to work in a private or public sector job for at least 16 hours a week as a condition of receiving benefits. Young parents were required to stay in school or return to school to complete a minimum of a high school diploma. States were mandated to provide child-care and Medicaid benefits. At the signing ceremony, President Reagan characterized the intent of the law: "The Family Support Act says to welfare parents, 'We expect of you what we expect of ourselves and our own loved ones: that you will do your share in taking responsibility for your life and for the lives of the children you bring into this world.'"

See also WELFARE RIGHTS MOVEMENT; PERSONAL RESPONSIBILITY AND WORK OPPORTUNITY RECONCILIATION ACT.

Feinstein, Dianne (1933–) *U.S. senator* Dianne Feinstein was born on June 22, 1933, and in 1955 received a B.A. in history from Stanford University, where she served as student body vice president in her final year. Feinstein's career is a history of firsts: The first woman to serve as president of the San Francisco Board of Supervisors, San Francisco's first woman mayor, the first woman to be nominated by a major party for governor of California, among the first women to be considered for selection as a vice presidential nominee for a major party, and the first woman elected to represent California in the U.S. Senate. Feinstein was elected to the Senate in 1992 to fill the remaining two years of then-Senator Pete Wilson's term when he resigned to become California's governor. In 1994, she was elected to her first full six-year term in the Senate; she was reelected easily in 2006.

Senator Feinstein serves on the Judiciary Committee, where she is the ranking member of the Terrorism, Technology and Homeland Security Subcommittee; the Appropriations Committee, where she is the ranking member of the Military Construction and Veterans Affairs Subcommittee; the Energy and Natural Resources Committee; the Select Committee on Intelligence; Homeland Security Subcommittee of Appropriations and the Rules and Administration Committee. Her legislative record is a curious mix of progressive and conservative issues. Feinstein supported the war in Iraq; she has claimed that President Bush misled her on the reasons for going to war. She was the original Democratic cosponsor of a bill to extend the USA Patriot Act. Feinstein is a firm supporter of capital punishment and of a constitutional amendment to ban the desecration of the American flag. At the same time, she has voted against the North American Free Trade Agreement (NAFTA), the Defense of Marriage Act, and school prayer, and she fought against welfare reform that she viewed as harmful to women's interests.

Feinstein is a strong supporter of ABORTION rights and gun control. In 1993, she led the fight to ban assault weapons. The ban was successfully passed as part of the Violent Crime Control and Law Enforcement Act of 1994. In 2004, when the ban was set to expire, Feinstein sponsored a 10-year extension of the ban as an amendment to the Protection of Lawful Commerce in Arms Act, but the act itself failed. The assault weapons ban has yet to be revived.

Further Reading

Barone, Michael. *The Almanac of American Politics.* Washington, D.C.: National Journal Group, 2006.

"Feinstein, Dianne." In *Biographical Directory of the United States Congress, 1774–present.* Available online. URL: http://bioguide.congress.gov/scripts/biodisplay.pl?index=F000062. Accessed on January 8, 2007.

"Senator Dianne Feinstein (CA)." In *Project Vote Smart.* Available online. URL: http://votesmart.org/bio.php?can_id=S0103103. Accessed on January 8, 2007.

—Angela Kouters

Felton, Rebecca Latimer (Rebecca Ann Latimer Felton) (1835–1930) *U.S. senator*

Rebecca Latimer Felton was the first woman to serve in the United States Senate, although only for one day (November 21–22, 1922) as a result of a special appointment upon the death of Thomas E. Watson. A successor to Watson had been elected and Congress had already adjourned, but an outcry from women forced President Warren G. Harding to convene a special session of Congress so that Felton could travel to Washington to take her seat. She was admitted after a day and a half of debate among her "colleagues" (during which she waited outside the Senate chambers) as to whether or not to admit a woman. After she entered and was sworn in, Felton, then 87 years old, delivered a speech in which she declared that she would not be the last woman they would see in Congress: "A Senator of the U.S., a woman, is still a sort of political joke with our masculine leaders in party politics. . . . But the trail has been blazed!

The road is apparently rough—maybe rocky—but the trail has been located. It is an established fact. While it is also a romantic adventure, it will ever remain an historical precedent—never to be eased."

Rebecca Ann Latimer was born near Decatur, Georgia, on June 10, 1835. In 1852, she graduated at the top of her class from Madison Female College. The commencement speaker was Dr. William H. Felton, a physician and state legislator. Latimer and Felton were married the next year, and she became his counselor and secretary, promoting his political ambitions and career by writing his speeches and editorials. Dr. Felton was elected to Congress and served three terms (1875–81). Having served as his campaign manager, Rebecca then served as his secretary during this time while also dedicating herself to progressive reforms and women's rights. She worked on behalf of woman SUFFRAGE, prohibition, and vocational educational opportunities

Rebecca Latimer Felton (LIBRARY OF CONGRESS)

for women, and against the convict leasing system. She became the South's best-known and most effective champion for women's suffrage, although her views on race were far from progressive as she described the greatest threat to white rural women in Georgia as coming from "black rapists." She condemned anyone who spoke out against the South's racial policies. During her life, Felton wrote numerous articles and editorials as well as two books, *My Memoirs of Georgia Politics* (1911) and *Country Life in Georgia in the Days of My Youth* (1919). She died on January 24, 1930.

Further Reading

Talmadge, John E. *Rebecca Latimer Felton: Nine Stormy Decades*. Athens: University of Georgia Press, 1960.

Whites, LeeAnn. "Rebecca Latimer Felton and the Wife's Farm: The Class and Racial Politics of Gender Reform." *Georgia Historical Quarterly* 76 (1992): 354–372.

Feminine Mystique, The   BETTY FRIEDAN published the most influential text of FEMINISM's "second wave," *The Feminine Mystique*, in 1963. Friedan traced her initial idea for the book to a questionnaire she had sent to 200 of her Smith College classmates on the occasion of their 15th reunion. Many women's responses described a sense of frustration and dissatisfaction even though their lives—as suburban, middle-class housewives and mothers—represented the cultural ideal for American women in the 1950s. Whereas the women themselves saw their lack of fulfillment as an individualized problem of adjustment, Friedan perceived a more systemic process at work. She traced the roots of the "problem that has no name" to the way consumer culture (especially the mass media) and Freudian psychology encouraged women to seek happiness solely through serving their families and not through self-actualization. She cited articles in women's magazines, statistics, personal accounts, and other sources as evidence for the pervasiveness of the "feminine mystique" and its pernicious effects.

Throughout the study, Friedan criticized the emotional and economic dependence of women on their husbands and the ideas that this fostered. Calling the suburban home a "comfortable concentration camp" (a resonant term in the aftermath of the Holocaust), she issued a ringing call for women to pursue higher education and careers instead of succumbing to child rearing and housewifery as their full-time occupations. Only by rejecting the sex role prescribed for them could women achieve a real sense of self-worth. Along with the civil rights movement, *The Feminine Mystique* catalyzed the women's liberation movement in the 1960s. The controversial book sold almost 3 million copies in three years and initiated a nationwide debate. Friedan consequently became a nationally recognized public figure and a leading spokesperson for feminism.

Further Reading

Bradley, Patricia. *Mass Media and the Shaping of American Feminism*. Jackson: University Press of Mississippi, 2003.

Horowitz, Daniel. *Betty Friedan and the Making of the Feminine Mystique: The American Left, The Cold War, and Modern Feminism*. Amherst: University of Massachusetts Press, 1998.

Meyerowitz, Joanne. "Beyond the Feminine Mystique: A Reassessment of Postwar Mass Culture, 1946–1958." In *Not June Cleaver: Women and Gender in Postwar America, 1845–1960*, edited by Joanne Meyerowitz, 229–262. Philadelphia: Temple University Press, 1994.

—Laura Prieto

feminism   Feminism provides the most direct challenge to the gendered world, as well as to PATRIARCHY, capitalism, and the sexist assumptions that women's differences from men render them inherently inferior. Feminism is a complex and somewhat paradoxical ideology that defies a single definition. In fact, feminists are rarely in agreement with one another over the ultimate aims of feminism or the means to achieve its goals. Although many feminists exhibit a commitment to absolute legal and practical equality, some feminists have argued for separate spheres of influence and an emphasis on difference and complementarity rather than equality. As Rebecca West wrote in 1913 in an oft-quoted passage, "I myself have never been able to find out precisely what feminism is. I only know that people call me a feminist whenever I express sentiments that differentiate me from a doormat or a prostitute."

As a word and concept, *feminism* is a relatively recent addition to the lexicon, emerging only in the 1910s to express a broader set of goals than the SUFFRAGE movement embraced. According to historian Nancy Cott, people in the 19th century talked about the "advancement of woman," the cause of woman, or woman's rights and woman SUFFRAGE. To modern ears, the use of the singular "woman" sounds awkward—both grammatically and conceptually. Nineteenth-century women's consistent usage of the singular *woman* symbolized the unity of the female sex. However, there is not one single definition of feminism, but rather a wide array of approaches to advancing women's rights. Cott identifies three characteristics that can be found in all feminist ideas: (1) a belief in equality, defined not as "sameness" but rather as opposition to ranking one sex superior or inferior to the other, or opposition to one sex's categorical control of the rights and opportunities of the other; (2) a belief that women's condition is socially constructed and historically shaped rather than preordained by God or nature; and (3) a belief that women's socially constructed position situates them on shared ground, enabling a group identity or gender consciousness sufficient to mobilize women for change.

As an ideology, feminism has spawned a number of different "brands," among them liberal feminism, radical feminism, Marxist-socialist feminism, global feminism, BLACK FEMINISM, ecofeminism, and gender feminism. Scholars dif-

fer on how to label and divide the complex terrain of feminist theory. Philosopher Rosemarie Tong distinguishes among these theories based on the locus of women's oppression in each. For example, liberal, radical, Marxist-socialist, and global feminists, as well as ecofeminists to some extent, attribute women's subordination to macro-level institutions, such as patriarchy, capitalism, or colonialism. Gender feminists, sometimes also called cultural feminists or maternal feminists, focus on the microcosm of the individual, claiming the roots of women's oppression are embedded deep within a woman's psyche. A brief critical and comparative review of each approach to feminism follows.

Liberal Feminism

This is perhaps the oldest strand of feminism, based on the same belief that promoted individual autonomy over aristocratic privilege in the French Revolution and the U.S. Revolutionary War. Liberalism stresses the importance of rational thought, autonomous action, and choice on the part of each person. Reason is what most clearly distinguishes humans from other forms of animal life. Individual autonomy empowers an individual to make choices in her or his own best interests, thereby elevating individual rights above the common good. Liberal theorists believe that the political and legal systems can be used to promote a liberal agenda for all people. Applied to feminism, early liberal feminists such as Britons Mary Wollstonecraft (author of *A VINDICATION OF THE RIGHTS OF WOMAN*), John Stuart Mill, and Harriet Taylor Mill stressed the importance of educating and enfranchising women, and of providing them with equal access to both opportunities and resources in society.

Liberal feminists tend to work *within* the existing political system and structures to eradicate all forms of sexual discrimination. Contemporary liberal feminists believe that by reforming the legal and political system to allow women equal access to opportunities and resources, men and women can achieve a state of equality. Liberal feminists target laws that distinguish between men and women because of sex. For example, the DECLARATION OF SENTIMENTS AND RESOLUTIONS, issued by women at the SENECA FALLS CONVENTION in 1848, is a liberal feminist document. It calls for the reform of laws restricting women's right to hold property, control resources, and vote. The U.S. suffrage movement and suffrage organizations, such as the NATIONAL AMERICAN WOMAN SUFFRAGE ASSOCIATION, extended women's liberal feminist claims that suffrage was an essential step in achieving political and social equality across three generations. The proposed EQUAL RIGHTS AMENDMENT and the United Nations CONVENTION ON THE ELIMINATION OF ALL FORMS OF DISCRIMINATION AGAINST WOMEN are examples of contemporary legal reforms in the liberal feminist tradition.

A variety of criticisms have been leveled against liberal feminism. Early and contemporary liberal feminists alike have concentrated almost exclusively on the public sphere. Women's unpaid labor in the home, DOMESTIC VIOLENCE, marital rape, and traditional practices that discriminate against women in many cultures are not addressed within the liberal approach because they occur in the private sphere. These issues are labeled *personal* and therefore are not subject to public scrutiny or redress in the public policy arena. Radical feminists charge that liberal feminism has been co-opted by the male establishment since its goals are to reform the existing system rather than to replace it, as radical feminists demand. Global feminists equate liberal feminists' embrace of individualism with Western values that do not fit well in other cultures where community values are favored over the individual. Additionally, individualism makes sex solidarity and the development of a unified movement difficult. Conservative critics charge that liberal feminists, by concentrating on ending legal sex discrimination in society, are out of touch with mainstream women who still value marriage, motherhood, and family—all traditionally private sphere concerns. Finally, liberal feminism has been labeled racist, classist, and heterosexist, suggesting that liberal

feminism speaks only to concerns of white, middle- and upper-class, heterosexual women and the history of the women's movement offers ample evidence that the concerns of women of color, the working poor, and lesbians have been on the periphery of the liberal feminists' agenda.

Radical Feminism

Radical feminism is difficult to define because of the many subgroups within the larger framework. However, there are some common distinguishing features. Unlike liberal feminists who believe that it is possible to produce systemic reforms that would yield women more rights (ultimately leading to equality of rights), radical feminists believe it is the "sex-gender system" itself that is the source of women's oppression. Radical feminists are interested in women's liberation from the bonds of this system and therefore have advocated a total revolution. For this reason, scholars often classify women's organizations as either "reform-minded" or "revolutionary" and link them to liberal or radical feminist theory accordingly.

Radical feminist theory spawned a variety of activist groups in the 1960s. Many, although not all, were associated with the political left. Such radical organizations as the REDSTOCKINGS, Women's International Terrorist Conspiracy from Hell (WITCH), the Feminists, and the New York Radical Feminists were among some of the largest groups formed.

Radical feminists argue that sexism, as the first form of human oppression, must take precedence over other forms of oppression and must be eradicated first. Beyond agreement on this basic issue, radical feminists differ on the best way to eliminate sexism. Radical-libertarian feminists believe that femininity, sex, and reproductive roles limit women's development. They often promote androgyny (eliminating masculine-feminine distinctions) as a way to overcome the limits of femininity and to break the socially constructed link between sex and gender. Radical-cultural feminists, on the other hand, believe that female-feminine qualities are vastly superior to male-masculine characteristics. Women should not try to be like men, but rather they should try to be like women. By this they mean a return to women's essential nature. Therefore, culturally associated feminine traits—interdependence, community, sharing, emotion, nature, peace, and life—should be celebrated over hierarchy, power, war, domination, and death. Androgyny simply clouds the female nature with undesirable male qualities. For these reasons, radical-cultural feminists are often associated with LESBIAN SEPARATISM.

Critics of radical feminism often target the stark choices women have been asked to make. Issues of separatism, lesbianism, and the promotion of reproductive technology over traditional means of conception and biological motherhood draw fire from conservative critics who charge that radical feminists are out to eradicate the family. Others criticize radical cultural feminists' belief in the essential nature of women, charging that it unnecessarily polarizes men and women.

Marxist-Socialist Feminism

In contrast to liberal theory's emphasis on the individual, Marxist-socialist feminism stresses the collective aspect of human development. Men and women, through production and reproduction, have collectively created a society that, in turn, shapes them. Capitalism and patriarchy work hand in hand, although Marxist-socialists believe that capitalism, more than sexism, is at the root of women's oppression. Women's economic dependence on men gives them little leverage in other aspects of society. However, rather than singling out women as *the* oppressed class, Marxist-socialist theories focus on the worker. Woman's situation can then only be understood in terms of her productive work and its relationship to her life. In a capitalist system, women are exploited both in the marketplace (lowest-paying and most menial jobs) and at home (no wages for their domestic labor). Marxist-socialist feminists advocate public policy that

aims to redistribute wealth and opportunity. For example, some have argued that women be paid a wage for their housework; others have concentrated their actions on issues of the workplace outside the home and the disparities in pay and position between men and women. The concept of "equal pay for equal work" does not cover women working in traditional occupations that are undervalued. Advocates of equal pay for jobs of COMPARABLE WORTH argue that wage inequities will persist as long as jobs are segregated on the basis of gender.

Critics of Marxist-socialist feminism most often point to the sizable gap between the ideal and the reality in contemporary Marxist-socialist regimes (those remaining and those recently dissolved). Women have filled the majority of low-status and low-paying occupations and, contrary to theory, are still taking primary responsibility for home and child care.

Global Feminism

In global feminism, the forces of colonialism and nationalism have conspired to divide the world into *the haves,* known as the First World, and the *have nots,* known as the Third World. Global feminists seek to expand feminist thought to include issues vital to women in the Third World. They argue that economic and political oppression are every bit as severe as sexual oppression. For global feminists, the personal and political are one. The way in which various forms of oppression interconnect and affect women has been the focus of many global feminists. Some charge that First World women are blinded by sexual oppression. As a result, they overlook their own complicity in the oppression of women caused by multinational corporations and exploitative labor practices. Others suggest that color, class, and nationality cannot be separated from sex when addressing the forms of oppression people face. Western feminists, they argue, have been too narrow in their agendas, particularly liberal feminists who were guided by legal reforms in the public sphere. Political participation is a hollow victory for those who cannot feed their families, earn a living wage, control their reproduction, and live free of violence.

Cultural practices that Western feminists and others deem exploitative or damaging to women have presented the most vexing problems for global feminists. Dowry, bride price, female circumcision, and many religious customs are examples of practices that, when taken out of a cultural context, are indefensible in any feminist theory. However, the importance and power of culture, tradition, and religion make passing judgment on these and other issues problematic. Differences among women of various cultures present many challenges to global feminists who attempt to create a feminist theory and set of practices that unite rather than divide women.

Black Feminism

One of the thorniest questions arising in black feminist thought is: Who can be a black feminist? Does authentic voice flow from one's race, one's experiences with the dual oppressions of race and gender, or one's ideas and ideologies regardless of race and gender? The core of the black feminist tradition encompasses several themes: the legacy of struggle, the experience born of multiple oppressions, and the interdependence of thought and action. Black feminists often express frustration that white women seem incapable of understanding the "multiple jeopardy" that black women face on a daily basis. Sexism cannot be separated from racism or classism or any of the other "isms" women must deal with. To pursue a single-minded gender equality strategy is to ignore profound forms of oppression and to exclude women of color from the women's movement. Black women have experienced discrimination in the women's movement and continue to press feminists to expand the definition of feminism. Alice Walker has offered the term *womanist* as an alternative to feminist, saying that "womanist is to feminist as purple is to lavender." A womanist is at heart a *humanist* pursuing political action as a means to human empower-

ment—including both men and women of all races, ethnicities, and abilities.

Critics of black feminism are most often African-American women themselves. Some critics argue that black feminists have failed to confront sexism strongly enough as it occurs within the black community. Believing that black males are under siege by the dominant white community, some black women have been reticent to press for stronger laws protecting women's interests, believing that black males would be disproportionately harmed in the process.

Ecofeminism

The term *ecofeminism* was coined by French feminist François d'Eabonne in 1974. Ecofeminism is a variant of ecological ethics and the branch of feminism that most resembles global feminism in its emphasis on "connectedness." In this case, however, feminists are interested in the connections between all living things—human and nature. Ecofeminists charge that patriarchy's hierarchical framework not only damages women but harms nature as well. "Because women have been 'naturalized' and nature has been 'feminized' it is difficult to know where the oppression of one ends and the other begins," says Rosemary Tong. Therefore, the liberation of one cannot be affected apart from the liberation of the other. A main goal of ecofeminists is to make visible the "woman-nature" connections and, where they are harmful to women or nature, to dismantle them. Ecofeminists disagree over how closely women should be associated with nature, but all agree that ending women's and nature's oppression should be a joint endeavor. In this sense, the environment is a feminist issue.

Critics of ecofeminism warn that equating women with nature harkens back to essentialist arguments that limit women's public influence. Others charge that feminists should invest their energy in understanding other women and in bridging the divide between nations and cultures before addressing nature. To ecofeminists, the interests of women and of nature are indistinguishable.

Gender Feminism

Unlike any of the theories previously described, gender feminism argues that the root of women's oppression lies somewhere at the intersection of biology, psychology, and culture. They believe that the traits culture associates with women and femininity are superior in many respects to masculine traits, and therefore both men and women should strive to develop relational webs. The issues most closely associated with gender feminism include the superiority of women's moral development, women's ways of knowing and thinking, and women's mothering abilities. Because gender feminists argue that men and women are developmentally different, they are sometimes also known as *difference feminists*. However, difference in this case works in favor of women. Among the best-known gender feminists is CAROL GILLIGAN, who challenges Lawrence Kohlberg's theory of moral development in her book *In a Different Voice* (1982). She argues that Kohlberg's widely accepted model of moral development does not account for differences between male and female moral development. While males resolve moral dilemmas using an *ethic of justice,* females use an *ethic of care.* While Gilligan did not at first argue that one was superior to the other, her work has been widely used to promote gender feminism's claim to women's moral superiority.

Maternalism, a subset of gender feminism, celebrates the power of women's reproductive capacity. Mothers in many Latin American nations, for example, have politicized motherhood in opposing dictatorships, raising sensitive political questions, and serving as visible reminders of the repression of immoral regimes. In the United States, mothers' movements are enjoying a contemporary resurgence. On Mother's Day 2000, tens of thousands of mothers marched on Washington, D.C., in the Million Mom March to protest gun violence against children and to petition the government to take action in the form of tougher gun control legislation.

Critics of gender feminism argue that associating women with caring reinforces the traditional view of women as nurturers rather than women who are autonomous and strong. Particularly in relation to electoral politics, a nurturant posture of care has proven to be a somewhat limited virtue depending on the domestic political climate in any one election. Others charge that labeling women as the only sex responsible for caring releases men from important social and familial obligations and unnecessarily polarizes men's and women's gender roles. Some also object to the nomenclature of maternal feminism, arguing that not all women are or aspire to be mothers.

See also ANTIFEMINISM; GENDER STEREOTYPES; LESBIAN SEPARATISM; SEPARATE SPHERES IDEOLOGY; THIRD-WAVE FEMINISM.

Further Reading
Chodorow, Nancy. *The Reproduction of Mothering: Psychoanalysis and the Sociology of Gender.* Berkeley: University of California Press, 1978.
Collins, Patricia Hill. *Black Feminist Thought: Knowledge, Consciousness, and the Politics of Empowerment.* Boston: Unwin Hyman, 1990.
Cott, Nancy F. *The Grounding of Modern Feminism.* New Haven, Conn.: Yale University Press, 1987.
Daly, Mary. *Gyn/Ecology: The Metaethics of Radical Feminism.* Boston: Beacon Press, 1978.
Firestone, Shulamith. *The Dialectic of Sex: The Case for Feminist Revolution.* New York: Bantam Books, 1970.
Ford, Lynne E. *Women and Politics: The Pursuit of Equality.* Boston: Houghton Mifflin, 2002.
Gilligan, Carol. *In a Different Voice: Psychological Theory and Women's Development.* Cambridge, Mass.: Harvard University Press, 1982.
Jagger, Allison M. *Feminist Politics and Human Nature.* Totowa, N.J.: Roman and Allanheld, 1983.
Morgan, Robin, ed. *Sisterhood is Global: The International Women's Movement Anthology.* Garden City, N.Y.: Anchor, 1984.
Okin, Susan Moller. *Women in Western Political Thought.* Princeton, N.J.: Princeton University Press, 1979.
Tong, Rosemarie Putnam. *Feminist Thought: A More Comprehensive Introduction.* Boulder, Colo.: Westview Press, 1998.
Whelan, Imelda. *Modern Feminist Thought: From the Second Wave to "Post Feminism."* New York: New York University Press, 1995.

Feminist Majority Foundation See SMEAL, ELEANOR.

Fenwick, Millicent (Millicent Hammond Fenwick) (1910–1992) *congressperson* At the age of 64, Millicent Hammond Fenwick was elected to the U.S. House of Representatives from New Jersey. She was highly respected among her peers and political analysts for her forthrightness, quick wit, and candor. Refusing to tow the official Republican Party line, Fenwick was often labeled as a maverick in Republican circles as she lambasted public officials who engaged in hypocrisy and abused the public's trust. America's most trusted newsman of the time, Walter Cronkite, heralded her as the "conscience of Congress."

Born Millicent Hammond on February 25, 1910, in New York City, Fenwick lived a life of privilege the first 28 years of her life. Her father was a financier and later a diplomat. Her mother, the granddaughter of the founder of Stevens Institute of Technology in New Jersey, died in the sinking of the *Lusitania* in 1915. Her father's appointment as U.S. ambassador to Spain disrupted Fenwick's formal schooling, but she educated herself, learning to speak Italian, French, and Spanish fluently. In 1929, she attended Columbia University.

Millicent Hammond married at a young age, but her separation and later divorce from Hugh Fenwick left her a single mother of two. Lacking enough money to cover expenses, she set about the task of finding a job rather than accept financial assistance from her family. Eventually she joined the staff of *Vogue* magazine as a caption writer and worked her way up to associate editor.

Fenwick acknowledged that her Republican political leanings were first conceived as she saw the power Adolf Hitler was amassing in Germany. From that point on, she grew to distrust government. However, despite her distrust of government intervention, she was still considered to be a moderate Republican. Socially liberal and

fiscally conservative, Fenwick was a passionate consumer rights and civil rights advocate who was also a committed member of the National Association for the Advancement of Colored People (NAACP). It was, in fact, her involvement in civil rights that led her into politics.

Elected to Congress in 1974, Fenwick opposed congressional pay raises and the use of political action committee (PAC) money. One year after taking office, she joined a congressional delegation to the Soviet Union, where they were confronted with the stories of Soviet dissidents about vast human rights abuses. Upon her return, Fenwick introduced legislation to establish an oversight committee for the Helsinki accords to ensure that all signatory countries upheld their commitment to protect human rights.

After her unsuccessful run for the U.S. Senate in 1982, Fenwick was appointed the first U.S. ambassador to the United Nations Food and Agricultural Organization in Rome (1983–87). Upon her retirement from public service at the age of 77, she moved back to her hometown of Bernardsville, New Jersey, where she died on September 16, 1992.

Further Reading

Fenwick, Millicent. *Speaking Up*. New York: Harper and Row, 1982.

Schapiro, Amy. *Millicent Fenwick: Her Way*. New Brunswick, N.J.: Rutgers University Press, 2003.

—Hollis France

Ferguson, Miriam (Miriam Amanda "Ma" Wallace Ferguson) (1875–1961) *first woman governor of Texas* Miriam "Ma" Ferguson was born Miriam Amanda Wallace on June 13, 1875, in Bell County, Texas. She studied at Baylor Female College for three years (1894–97), and in 1899 she married James Ferguson, with whom she had two daughters, Dorrace and Ouida. In 1915, James Ferguson campaigned for governor of Texas in 1915 and won. In 1917, however, he was impeached by the Texas legislature due to questionable loans and finances. Because of this, he could not run again for governor, and therefore Miriam launched her own gubernatorial campaign in 1924—an interesting turn of events considering her husband's support for the ANTI-SUFFRAGE MOVEMENT.

It was clear throughout her campaign that Miriam, if elected, would not serve by herself but would actively involve James in the administration and affairs of the state. She ran on an anti-Ku Klux Klan ticket and won. Her first term as governor saw a continuation of the political controversies that had plagued her husband. Many in the state chastised the Ferguson administration for alleged bribery and for giving favorable contracts to supporters. Miriam—or "Ma" Ferguson, as reporters referred to her—lost the 1926 campaign, but she recaptured the governor's office in 1932. In the throes of the Great Depression, the state was in debt, and Ferguson attempted to assuage the financial crisis with the Texas Relief Commission. Yet controversy followed her during her second term as well, and "Ma" Ferguson did not seek another term until a failed campaign run in 1940. She died on June 25, 1961, at the age of 86.

Further Readings

Nalle, Ouida Ferguson. *The Fergusons of Texas, or "Two Governors for the Price of One": A Biography of James Edward Ferguson and His Wife.* San Antonio: Naylor, 1946.
Paulissen, May Nelson, and Carl McQueary. *Miriam: The Southern Belle Who Became the First Woman Governor of Texas.* Austin: Eakin Press, 1995.

—Sara Crowley

Ferguson v. City of Charleston (532 U.S. 67)

(2001)   Concerned about the number of expectant mothers using crack cocaine and delivering babies at risk due to this drug use, the Medical University Hospital and the Charleston Solicitor's Office, in conjunction with the local police, instituted a drug-testing program for pregnant women who sought prenatal care through the emergency room of the only public hospital in Charleston. Women testing positive for cocaine were arrested. A group of patients sued, alleging unreasonable search and seizure as a result of the tests, which were warrantless and for which permission had not been sought or obtained. The U.S. Supreme Court found that the testing violated the Fourth Amendment and did, in fact, amount to an unreasonable search and seizure. The state hospital had argued that it was necessary to "scare" these drug users into abstinence and/or treatment programs and that the ends justified the testing. The Court disagreed and held that permission or warrants had to be obtained. The hospital's use of law enforcement to force patients into drug therapy and counseling triggered the protections of the Fourth Amendment.

Further Reading

Center for Reproductive Rights. *In the Courts: The Center's Cases.* "Pregnant Women's Rights: *Ferguson v. City of Charleston*: A Case Summary." Available online. URL: http://www.reproductiverights. org/crt_preg_ferguson.html. Accessed on January 4, 2007.

—Marsha Hass

Ferraro, Geraldine (Geraldine Anne Ferraro)

(1935–) *congressperson, vice-presidential nominee*   In 1984, Geraldine Ferraro became the first woman to be placed on a major national party ticket as a vice-presidential candidate when Democratic presidential nominee Walter Mondale selected her as his running mate. Although the Democratic Party's presidential bid was unsuccessful, Ferraro's groundbreaking selection actualized the possibility that a woman could be elected to the presidency the near future. Twenty years later, Ferraro's historic candidacy continues to be credited for the influx of women political candidates at both the national and local levels.

Born on August 26, 1935, to working-class immigrant parents in Newburg, New York, Ferraro taught in the New York City school system after graduating from Manhattan College in 1956. While teaching grade school, she worked her way through Fordham Law School at night. In 1960, she earned her J.D. degree and married John Zacarro. After being admitted to the bar in 1961, Ferraro established a law practice, and 13 years later she joined the Queens County district attorney's office. During her tenure at as an assistant district attorney, she earned a reputation for defending the interests of the most vulnerable in society: children, women, and the elderly. Ferraro claims that it was during her district attorney days that she transitioned from a conservative to a liberal philosophy. In 1978, she was elected to the U.S. House of Representatives from New York's ninth congressional district.

Ferraro's three terms in Congress brought many benefits for women and the elderly, including her sponsorship of the Women's Economic Equity Act (1974), which abolished pension discrimination against women, increased job training opportunities for displaced homemakers, and gave displaced homemakers equal access to opening individual retirement accounts. Serving on the Select Committee on Aging, she continuously fought against cuts in Social Security and Medicare for the elderly.

Ferraro gained the confidence of Walter Mondale while serving as chief of the Democratic Platform Committee. However, her lack of foreign policy experience and her husband's dubious financial dealings plagued her candidacy and may have contributed to the Democratic ticket's defeat in 1984 to the Republicans. Following the election, Ferraro ran unsuccessfully for the U.S. Senate. Since leaving national office, she has immersed herself in the foreign policy arena and continues to champion women's role in the political sphere. In 1993, President Bill Clinton appointed Ferraro as the U.S. head delegate to the United Nations Human Rights Commission. She serves on the board of the National Democratic Institute of International Affairs and as a member of the Council of Foreign Relations. Ferraro continues to be actively involved supporting various organizations and groups seeking to increase women's leadership roles in politics.

Further Reading

Breslin, Rosemary, and Joshua Hammer. *Gerry! A Woman Making History.* New York: Pinnacle Books, 1984.

Ferraro, Geraldine. *Ferraro, My Story.* Toronto and New York: Bantam Books, 1985.

—Hollis France

Fillmore, Abigail (Abigail Powers Fillmore)

(1798–1853) *first lady* Abigail Powers was born in Stillwater, New York, on March 17, 1798, the youngest of seven children of Lemuel and Abigail Newland Powers. When she was two, her father died, and her mother moved the family to the Finger Lakes region of New York where other relatives were settling. Young Abigail was taught to read by her mother and educated herself by reading her father's library. When she was 16, she began to work as a teacher at the New Hope Academy. She met Millard Fillmore three years later, and for a brief time, he was her student; he later became her colleague as they both taught at the academy. Abigail and Millard were engaged in 1819, but her family, who objected to her marrying beneath her social position, kept them apart for the better part of seven years. Eventually, however, they married on February 5, 1826, and settled in East Aurora, New York, where she continued teaching while he practiced law. In 1828, their first child, Millard Powers Fillmore, was born, and Millard Sr. was elected to the state legislature. Leaving Abigail, he went alone to Albany.

In 1830, the couple moved to Buffalo, where Millard opened a law practice with a friend. They established themselves in the community, working to improve public education and establishing a lending library. In 1832, Abigail bore another child, a girl they named Mary Abigail (called Abby), and Millard won a seat in the U.S. Congress. He returned to Buffalo upon completion of his two-year term, but was reelected to Congress as a Whig in 1836. This time Abigail accompanied him to Washington, but they sent the children to live with relatives in upstate New York. She attended to her duties as a congressman's wife by paying calls, keeping herself informed by reading the newspapers and editorials of the day, and attending ceremonial affairs, and she consulted frequently with her husband.

In 1842, Abigail suffered an accident that left her unable to walk or stand for long periods without pain. Although she sought treatment, she never fully recovered. Millard abandoned his congressional career and returned to practicing law. Later, 16-year-old Powers joined the firm as his clerk, while young Abby pursued on advanced study of music. In 1847, Millard was elected controller, and he returned to Albany. As his career advanced, Abigail's health deteriorated. In 1849, Millard was elected vice president with Zachary Taylor, but Abigail did not accompany him to Washington. When Taylor died suddenly in office and Millard Fillmore assumed the presidency, she moved into the White House.

Although she found it difficult, Abigail Fillmore attempted to perform her formal duties as first lady, continuing the traditions of Tuesday morning receptions, Friday evening levees, and Thursday dinners for guests. She designated her daughter Abby as official hostess when she was unable to preside. Her main contribution as first lady was to urge her husband to ask Congress for an appropriation to establish a library in the White House. She received $2,000, which she used to purchase several hundred books and renovate a second-floor parlor as a library.

Abigail Fillmore's final public appearance was at the inauguration of Franklin Pierce as her husband's successor. The day was dreadfully cold with snow in the air, and Abigail caught a cold. Although the family only planned to stay in the Willard Hotel for a few days before making the journey home, Abigail became seriously ill with pneumonia and died within a few weeks

on March 30, 1853. She was remembered in press accounts of her death as "a lady of great strength of mind."

Further Reading

National First Ladies Library. *Biographies: First Ladies of the United States.* Available online. URL: http://www.firstladies.org/biographies. Accessed on January 4, 2007.

Schneider, Dorothy, and Carl J. Schneider. "Abigail Powers Fillmore." *First Ladies: A Biographical Dictionary.* New York: Checkmark Books, 2001. pp. 83–87.

First Lady of the United States The title First Lady of the United States is not a constitutional role but rather an unofficial title given to the official White House hostess. The term was first used when DOLLEY MADISON was eulogized as "America's First Lady." Typically, the first lady is the wife of the sitting president of the United States, but not always. If a president is a widower or bachelor, a female relative or a close friend can be his first lady. Contemporary first ladies have expanded the role of official hostess to include a more public role. First ladies are often known for their dedication to a specific cause. For example, NANCY REAGAN adopted the issue of drug awareness and is known for the "Just Say No" slogan. LAURA BUSH, the current first lady, worked on the problem of literacy in her husband's first term but announced that she would focus on the health and well-being of juvenile boys in the Bush administration's second term. HILLARY RODHAM CLINTON took her political involvement further when President Bill Clinton appointed her to chair a task force on health care reform. The public did not respond well to the ambiguity between her unofficial status and official political duties.

As more professional women serve in the role of first lady, there will likely be more challenges to the role expectations. When a woman is elected president of the United States, the social role typically performed by the spouse of the president will undergo another examination.

Americans have already started to think about a "first gentleman's" role as a result of HILLARY RODHAM CLINTON's candidacy for the Democratic nomination for president in 2008.

Further Reading

Meijer, Molly, ed. *Inventing a Voice: The Rhetoric of American First Ladies of the Twentieth Century.* Lanham, Md.: Rowman & Littlefield, 2004.
The White House. *First Ladies' Gallery.* Available online. URL: http://www.whitehouse.gov/history/firstladies. Accessed on January 4, 2007.

Flynn, Elizabeth Gurley (1890–1964) *labor organizer, American Civil Liberties Union founder* Elizabeth Gurley Flynn was born in Concord, New Hampshire, on August 7, 1890; the family moved to New York in 1900. Converted to socialism by her parents, Thomas and Annie Gurley Flynn, Elizabeth Flynn delivered her first speech, "What Socialism Will Do for Women," at the age of 16. As a result of her political activities, she was expelled from public high school. In 1906, she became a member of the Industrial Workers of the World (IWW), and the next year she began organizing workers in the garment, mining, and restaurant sectors. Although often arrested, she was never convicted of any criminal activity.

Flynn was particularly concerned with women's rights and was an ardent supporter of BIRTH CONTROL and women's SUFFRAGE. She was critical of the leadership in the trade union movement for being male-dominated and ignoring the particular needs of women. She joined the Communist Party in 1936, and during World War II she campaigned for equal opportunity and pay for women as well as day-care centers for working women. In 1942, she ran for Congress and attracted over 50,000 votes in a losing effort.

In 1951, Flynn was arrested and charged with violating the Alien Registration Act. She was found guilty and served two years in the women's prison at Alderson, West Virginia. Upon her release from prison, she wrote *The Alderson Story: My Life as a Political Prisoner,* published in 1955. In 1961, she became the national chairperson of the Communist Party. She died on September 5, 1964, while making a trip to the Soviet Union. Elizabeth Gurley Flynn was given a state funeral in Red Square before her remains were flown back to the United States for burial in Chicago near several colleagues from the Communist Party.

Further Reading

Flynn, Elizabeth Gurley, and Rosalyn Fraad Baxandall. *Words on Fire: The Life and Writings of Elizabeth Gurley Flynn.* New Brunswick, N.J.: Rutgers University Press, 1987.

Fonda, Jane (Lady Jayne Seymour Fonda) (1937–) *actor, activist* Jane Fonda was born on December 21, 1937, in New York City to actor Henry Fonda and his second wife, socialite Frances Seymour Brokaw. After her mother committed suicide in 1950, Fonda was sent to New York to attend the Emma Willard School. She subsequently attended Vassar College but left after two years and moved to Paris, where she began modeling, studied acting, and became involved in radical politics. Her acting career began in 1954 when she appeared with her father in a performance of *The Country Girl*. Six years later, she joined drama teacher Lee Strausberg's Actors Studio (1958). In the 1960s she moved from stage to film and averaged nearly two movies a year. In 1971, she won her first Academy Award for Best Actress in *Klute*. She won a second Academy Award in 1978 for her role in *Coming Home,* the story of a disabled Vietnam veteran's return from war. Between 1969 and 1986, she was nominated for five Best Actress Awards by the Academy. She has appeared in more than 25 major motion pictures over the four decades of her acting career to date. During the 1980s and 1990s she released more than 20 best-selling exercise videos. Although she announced her retirement from the movies in 1991, she returned to the screen in

2005 (*Monster-in-Law*) and again in 2007 (*Georgia Rule*).

In addition to acting, Fonda is best known for her political activism beginning in the 1960s in support of the civil rights movement and in opposition to the Vietnam War. Fonda befriended major leaders of the American Left, including ANGELA DAVIS and activist Tom Hayden, whom she later married. In 1971, she helped found FTA, a troupe of antiwar actors and musicians that entertained American servicemen. She briefly returned to Paris, where she met with Vietnamese Communist negotiators at the Paris Peace Talks before traveling to Hanoi, North Vietnam, in July 1972.

While in North Vietnam, Fonda made several radio broadcasts condemning American military policy and briefly met with American prisoners of war held in Hanoi. Fonda's actions became highly controversial, particularly among American Vietnam War veterans, who nicknamed her "Hanoi Jane." She was criticized for her interactions with the Vietnamese communist leadership and for her accusations about American "war crimes" in Vietnam. Fonda's antiwar activities were investigated by Congress and the FBI, but she was never charged with criminal activity. In an appearance on *60 Minutes* (March 31, 2005), Fonda said that although she had no regrets about her antiwar activism or her trip to North Vietnam in 1972, she did regret the widely circulated photograph of her seated on an antiaircraft gun and its use as anti-American propaganda. Most recently she has been a critic of the war in Iraq and argues that it will turn people against the United States rather than end the threat of terrorism.

In addition to peace and civil rights causes, Fonda has been a longtime supporter of women's rights, even though she admits that she once feared calling herself a feminist because she mistakenly believed that all feminists were "anti-male." She has worked to end violence against women and girls through the V-Day campaign, to promote women's reproductive rights and to prevent teen pregnancy by establishing the Jane Fonda Center for Adolescent Reproductive Health at Emory University in Atlanta, Georgia (2002), and to promote women's entrance into politics.

During the 1980s, Fonda became a highly successful entrepreneur, in addition to continuing her film career. While living in Atlanta, Georgia, in the 1990s, she became an advocate for inner-city women and women's health issues, including domestic violence. Divorced from media magnate Ted Turner in 2001, she continues to produce films and speak on environmental and social justice issues. Fonda maintains homes in New Mexico and Georgia. In 2005, she published her autobiography *My Life So Far*.

Further Reading

Andersen, Christopher. *Citizen Jane: The Turbulent Life of Jane Fonda.* New York: Henry Holt, 1990.

Fonda, Jane. *My Life So Far.* New York: Random House, 2005.

Holzer, Henry Mark, and Erika Holzer. *'Aid and Comfort:' Jane Fonda in North Vietnam.* Jefferson, N.C.: McFarland, 2002.

—Laura M. Calkins

Ford, Betty (Elizabeth Ann Bloomer Ford)

(1918–) *first lady* Elizabeth Ann Bloomer was born on April 8, 1918, in Chicago, Illinois, to William Stephenson and Hortense Neahr Bloomer. Although she preferred to be called Elizabeth, she was always known as Betty. The family moved to Grand Rapids, Michigan, when Betty was two years old. Her father was a traveling salesman and her mother was from a wealthy family background. Betty began taking dance lessons when she was eight years old, and she planned for a performance career. Later she taught dance lessons and particularly enjoyed the physical liberation modern dance afforded her. When the stock market crashed in 1929, Betty added modeling to the money she earned from teaching dance. She viewed First Lady ELEANOR ROOSEVELT as a role model for women's independence.

In 1936, Betty's father died of accidental carbon monoxide poisoning. That same year, Betty finished high school and begged to go to New York for professional dance instruction. She and her mother compromised on the Bennington School of Dance at Bennington College in Vermont. There she spent two summers studying with legendary dance-choreographer Martha Graham as well as with dancers such as José Limón. During the fall and winter, she returned to Grand Rapids to teach dance and to model. She still longed to study and perform with Graham in New York, and for a brief period she did. As a member of Graham's auxiliary troupe, Betty Bloomer performed with the Graham Dancers in Carnegie Hall. Her mother persuaded her to return to Grand Rapids for one more six-month trial, after which if she was still set on a professional career in dance, she would have her mother's support.

Betty expanded her dance lessons, modeled, and worked as a fashion coordinator for Herpolsheimer's department store. She met and married Bill Warren, a furniture dealer, in 1942. As Bill changed jobs, the couple moved throughout the Midwest. Betty always found work and held on to jobs more successfully than her husband. At the point when she was ready to file for divorce, she learned that Bill had slipped into a diabetic coma while in New York and was not expected to live. He recovered enough to return to Grand Rapids, and they lived together with his parents for a time. After two years, Bill recovered fully, and Betty initiated divorce proceedings. Friends later introduced her to Gerald R. Ford, World War II veteran, Michigan football hero, and lawyer. Although she balked at beginning another relationship, she agreed to meet him to talk for a few minutes.

By the time Betty's divorce was finalized in 1947, she and Gerald Ford were dating regularly. Ford proposed in February 1948 but cautioned her that he intended to run for the U.S. House of Representatives. They set the wedding for October 15, 1948, between the September primary and the November general election. Their honeymoon was a series of rallies, football games, and speeches. Betty continued to work but helped with the campaign when she could. Gerald Ford won the election, and the couple moved to Washington, D.C.; he was reelected with little trouble in each successive election.

As a congressional wife, Betty sat in on hearings, entertained constituents, and helped out in the office on the weekends. She became active in the bipartisan Congressional Club, made up of wives of Supreme Court justices, cabinet members, and members of the House and Senate. Between 1950 and 1957, the Fords had four children: Michael (1950), John (1952), Steven (1956), and Susan (1957). Betty Ford devoted herself to raising her children, and Gerald tended to his political career. The Fords bought a house in Alexandria, Virginia, but returned to a house in Grand Rapids, Michigan, each summer.

In 1956, Gerald Ford won the post of minority leader in the U.S. House. With this elevation, Betty became more politically active, working with Republican women and traveling with her husband. The busier she became, the more troubled she was by arthritis and a pinched nerve in her neck. A dependence on pain medication and alcoholism led to a collapse in 1965. Work with a therapist helped her to regain confidence and to admit that, like other women of her times, she suffered from what BETTY FRIEDAN had labeled the "feminine mystique." She wrote: "I was beginning to feel sorry for myself. . . . He gets all the headlines and applause, but what about me? On the one hand, I loved being the 'wife of'; on the other hand, I was convinced that the more important Jerry became, the less important I became." She did not mention or deal with her addiction to painkillers and alcohol, conditions she hid even from her family.

Gerald Ford's position as minority leader and their close ties to other Republicans meant foreign trips and campaigning for presidential candidate Richard Nixon. When the Republicans failed to retake the House of Representatives in the 1972 election, Ford began planning his retirement in order to return to his law practice. However, Vice President Spiro Agnew's resignation led Nixon to pick Ford as his new vice president—the first to be selected under the terms of the Twenty-fifth Amendment. Ford easily won Senate confirmation and was sworn into office on December 6, 1973.

As the wife of the vice president, Betty Ford quickly established a reputation for candor with the press. When asked about the 1973 ROE V. WADE decision, she agreed "that it was time to bring ABORTION out of the backwoods and put it into the hospitals where it belonged." Meanwhile, the investigations into Watergate heightened, and when there was no question about Nixon's involvement in the cover-up, the House began moving toward impeachment, and the president's advisors urged him to resign. On August 8, 1974, Richard Nixon resigned the presidency, and Gerald R. Ford was sworn in as president. His ascension made him the first person in the nation's history to hold the two highest offices without being elected to either. When Ford pardoned Nixon a month later, the country was furious, and his standing in the polls plummeted by 20 points almost overnight. Many believed Ford had cut a deal with Nixon, thereby robbing the nation of learning the truth about the extent of the corruption in the Nixon administration and what the president himself had been party to. Ford argued that he acted alone, and that the pardon was the only way to put Watergate behind the nation and move forward. Both Fords later acknowledged that the pardon most likely cost the Republicans the 1976 election.

In September 1974, doctors found a suspicious lump in Betty Ford's right breast. The lump proved to be cancerous, and doctors performed a radical mastectomy. Since the cancer had spread to three nodes, she began chemotherapy as well. Betty Ford turned her personal ordeal into a call for other women to undergo checkups. One of those who heeded the call was Happy Rockefeller, wife of Vice President Nelson Rockefeller. She wound up losing both breasts to cancer.

Betty Ford used her position to advocate for other women's causes as well. She worked for ratification of the EQUAL RIGHTS AMENDMENT, promoted women's history during the nation's bicentennial celebrations, advocated the appointment of women to cabinet-level posts, and urged equality of rights in relation to social security, education, and credit. As first lady, she also promoted the arts, working closely with the National Endowment for the Arts. Her style of entertaining emphasized all things American— art, cuisine, cutlery, crystal, silver, and china. Her love of dance filled the White House with entertainers, dancers, and musicians.

Betty Ford was very active in the 1976 presidential campaign. Her popularity ratings were higher than the president's, and campaign buttons bore such slogans as, "Keep Betty in the White House" or "Betty's Husband for President." The loss to Jimmy Carter and Walter Mondale was devastating, and Betty delivered Gerald Ford's concession speech because he was hoarse with laryngitis. She left the White House in a depressed state of mind. Leaving Washington after 28 years was difficult.

Betty would later admit that she was often in a fog as first lady. The stress of two assassination attempts on President Ford, intensive campaigning, and physical pain led her to rely more heavily on prescription drugs and alcohol. Early in their California retirement, her family intervened and persuaded her to seek treatment. With courage, she publicly disclosed her addiction, hoping to help other addicts in the process. In 1982, she founded the Betty Ford Center for Drug and Alcohol Rehabilitation in Rancho Mirage, California. Her efforts were specifically targeted at women addicts. Discovering that nine out of 10 wives of addicts stay with them, but nine out of 10 husbands of addicts leave, she set up a therapeutic support system for women at the center. Although the center is now known for the many celebrities it has treated, they have to queue up on the waiting list alongside Medicaid recipients. Betty Ford heads the board that runs the center and continues to advocate for the latest developments in the treatment of addiction.

Betty Ford was the most outspoken feminist first lady since Eleanor Roosevelt, a woman she repeatedly said she admired. Her position as a wife, mother, and vocal supporter of equal rights for homemakers gave her leeway to urge women to take advantage of the feminist movement's successes. Her personal courage and candor saved lives. In 2003, Betty Ford published *Healing and Hope: Six Women from the Betty Ford Center Share Their Powerful Journeys of Addiction and Recovery.* She continues to serve as the chairman of the board of directors of the Betty Ford Center.

Further Reading

Ford, Betty. *The Times of My Life.* New York: Harper Row, 1978.

———. *A Glad Awakening.* Garden City, NY: Doubleday, 1987.

National First Ladies Library. *Biographies: First Ladies of the United States.* Available online. URL: http://www.firstladies.org/biographies. Accessed on January 4, 2007.

Schneider, Dorothy, and Carl J. Schneider. "Elizabeth Ann (Betty) Bloomer Warren Ford" *First Ladies: A Biographical Dictionary.* New York: Checkmark Books, 2001, 301–318.

Weidenfeld, Sheila Rabb. *First Lady's Lady: With the Fords at the White House.* New York: Putnam, 1979.

Foxx, Virginia (Virginia Ann Foxx) (1943–   )
congressperson Virginia Ann Foxx was born on June 29, 1943, in New York. She is a graduate of the University of North Carolina (UNC) at Chapel Hill, where she received her A.B. degree in English in 1968 and M.A.C.T. in sociology in 1972. In 1985, she earned her doctorate in education with a specialization in curriculum and teaching/higher education from the University of North Carolina at Greensboro. Foxx began her career as a secretary and research assistant at UNC-Chapel Hill. She taught at Caldwell Community College and was a sociology instructor at Appalachian State University, where she also

held several administrative positions, including assistant dean of the general college. From 1985 to 1987, Foxx served as deputy secretary for management in the North Carolina Department of Administration under Governor Jim Martin. Prior to her election to the North Carolina Senate in 1994, she served as president of Maryland Community College from 1987 to 1994.

Foxx served 10 years in the North Carolina Senate before deciding to run for Congress. She sponsored a constitutional amendment to ban same-sex marriage and a bill to deny Social Security rights to illegal aliens. In 2004, when Congressman Richard Burr of the fifth district decided to run for the U.S. Senate, Foxx was one of the first candidates to join the race; she emerged victorious from one of the most expensive and nastiest primary elections in North Carolina's history. In September 2005, she was one of 11 members of Congress to vote against the $51 billion aid package to victims of Hurricane Katrina.

Foxx is the third woman in North Carolina history to serve in the U.S. House. She has a very conservative voting record, supporting gun rights and staunchly opposing ABORTION rights. In the 109th Congress, Foxx served on the House Committee on Agriculture, the House Committee on Education and the Workforce, and the House Committee on Government Reform. She was reelected in 2006.

Further Reading

Barone, Michael. *The Almanac of American Politics.* Washington, D.C.: National Journal Group, 2006.

"Foxx, Virginia Ann." In *Biographical Directory of the United States Congress, 1774–present.* Available online. URL: http://bioguide.congress.gov/scripts/biodisplay.pl?index=F000450. Accessed on January 8, 2007.

"Representative Virginia Ann Foxx (NC)." In *Project Vote Smart.* Available online. URL: http://votesmart.org/bio.php?con_id=BS024152. Accessed on January 8, 2007.

—Angela Kouters

Freedom of Access to Clinic Entrances Act (FACE) (1994)

Congress passed the Freedom of Access to Clinic Entrances Act (FACE) in 1994 as a response to increased violence against ABORTION providers. Following the 1993 murder of Dr. David Gunn, a Pensacola, Florida, physician killed for having performed abortions within that community, as well as the 1994 murders of four other health care workers at abortion clinics throughout the United States, President Bill Clinton signed and implemented the FACE Act in an attempt to eliminate what appeared to be a growing problem that the states had failed to address on their own. FACE made it a federal crime to engage in any activity or threatened activity that utilized force and was aimed at any abortion provider, with criminal and financial penalties implemented at the federal level. The act also prohibited physical vandalism to structures that provided abortion services. While FACE restricted the protest activities of abortion opponents, it did not prohibit those protests. Anti-choice activists may still protest in whatever fashion they choose as long as that protest does not impede the daily operations of the targeted clinic.

FACE attached both civil and criminal penalties to violations of the legislation, and it allowed states some latitude in implementation, such as the establishment of buffer zones around specific clinics. Opponents of FACE characterized the legislation as a violation of the First Amendment's guarantee of freedom of speech, yet these charges were unfounded. FACE allowed for such legal forms of nonviolent protest as distributing literature to and shouting at persons entering the facilities.

See also RIGHT TO LIFE MOVEMENT.

Further Reading

Beckman, Linda J., and S. Marie Harvey, eds. *The New Civil War: The Psychology, Culture, and Politics of Abortion.* Washington, D.C.: American Psychological Association, 1998.

Feldt, Gloria, and Laura Fraser. *The War on Choice: The Right-Wing Attack on Women's Rights and How to Fight Back.* New York: Bantam Books, 2004.

Jelen, Ted G., ed. *Perspectives on the Politics of Abortion.* Westport, Conn.: Praeger, 1995.

—Kimberly K. Little

Freeman, Jo (Joreen Freeman) (1945–)

feminist scholar, teacher, author   Jo Freeman was born on August 26, 1945, in Atlanta, Georgia, and raised in Los Angeles, California. After many years working in electoral politics as a youngster, she plunged into the student social movements while an undergraduate at the University of California, Berkeley. She was a member of many groups, including the Young Democrats, SLATE, the Berkeley Free Speech Movement (FSM), and the Bay Area civil rights movement.

Upon graduating from Berkeley in 1965, Freeman joined the field staff of the Southern Christian Leadership Conference (SCLC) in Atlanta, primarily doing voter registration. She spent a year in Alabama and several months in Mississippi. She was run out of Mississippi when the *Jackson Daily News* exposed her as a professional agitator, citing her participation in the FSM. Transferred to Chicago, she soon left the SCLC to work for the West Side *TORCH,* a community newspaper where she learned journalism and photography.

Freeman's visibility increased sharply in the late 1960s when she became a feminist activist. With other Chicago women, she organized one of the first women's liberation groups in autumn 1967. This became the mother group for many of the small women's liberation groups that spread around the country. In spring 1968, Freeman started and served as editor for *Voice of the Women's Liberation Movement,* the nascent movement's first newsletter. She later helped to restart the Chicago chapter of the NATIONAL ORGANIZATION FOR WOMEN (NOW).

Freeman received her Ph.D. in political science from the University of Chicago in 1973. She became active in the NOW New York City chapter in 1974 after moving there for her first teaching job. She taught at the State University of New York for four years and spent two years in Washington, D.C., first as a Brookings fellow and then as an American Political Science Association congressional fellow. She returned to New York to get her law degree from New York University School of Law in 1982 and practiced law in New York until retiring in 2001 in order to write full-time.

Freeman is best known for her prolific writing and editing, which has attracted worldwide attention. She authored two books on women and politics, both of which won political science prizes for scholarship. She wrote a third book on her experiences at Berkeley as an undergraduate. The fifth edition of her introductory women's studies textbook is still in print and a leading book in its field. Her popular essay "The Tyranny of Structurelessness," which addresses the early women's liberation movement, was translated into many languages and found an audience among people and groups far removed from FEMINISM. Her scholarly study "On the Origins of Social Movement," is considered a classic. She has reported on feminist activities and issues of interest to women while covering the Democratic and Republican national nominating conventions every four years since 1976.

Further Reading

Freeman, Jo. *At Berkeley in the Sixties: Education of an Activist, 1961–1965.* Bloomington: Indiana University Press, 2004.

———. *A Room at a Time: How Women Entered Party Politics.* Lanham, Md.: Rowland and Littlefield, 2000.

———. *Women: A Feminist Perspective.* Mountain View, Calif.: Mayfield Publishing Co., 1995.

—Maria Elena Raymond

French, Marilyn (1929–   ) *author* Marilyn French was born in New York on November 21, 1929. After receiving her B.A. from Hofstra College, Long Island, in 1951, French married and became a suburban wife. By the early 1960s, however, she had divorced, and academic study drew her back. She resumed her education in English, first at Hofstra College (where she earned her M.A. in 1964) and then at Harvard University (receiving a Ph.D. in 1972). Her doctoral dissertation would become her first published book: *The Book as World: James Joyce's Ulysses,* published in 1976. That same year, she was appointed a fellow of Harvard in 1976. She also taught English at a number of colleges on the East Coast.

While French had become a "serious" writer during the 1950s and had already published one book of nonfiction, her most notorious and celebrated work would come a year later in the form of fiction. Her now-infamous *The Women's Room,* published in 1977, became an almost instant success. Grounded in the ideology of the still-burgeoning feminist movement but written in accessible, engaging language, *The Women's Room* describes the life of Mira, a housewife, and her journey of self-discovery, independence, and fulfillment, finding all three without a man. Mira's feminist tale was translated into more than 20 languages, became a best seller in both the United States and in Europe, and was adapted to a made-for-TV movie in 1980.

Giving up teaching for writing full-time and riding on the success of *The Women's Room,* French published her second novel, *The Bleeding Heart,* in 1980. This book takes on marriage as a problematic institution in modern America. French's selection of themes—the inequality of the sexes, the negative effects of patriarchal institutions, and hostility toward women—touched the minds and reflected the experiences of many women. These themes would permeate her works of nonfiction as well, particularly 1985's *Beyond Power: On Women, Men, and Morals,* a controversial collection of historical essays on the treatment of women by men over centuries, and *The War Against Women* (1992). *The War Against Women,* a study of the patriarchal oppression that plagues American institutions and the women who occupy them, also speaks of a male-dominated world society, one that had responded to the feminist movement with increased violence.

In 1998, a piece of French's own story was published. In *A Season in Hell,* French recounts her learning, at 61 years old, that she had cancer and that there was little hope for survival. Her story speaks of her illness, her negative experiences of treatment by physicians, and of a battle she won despite the odds.

A writer, thinker, and cancer survivor, French has published books that have affected millions of women of her generation. Her writing continues to stir discussions and be read in women's studies courses, remaining a solid part of the second-wave feminist canon. Still active as a writer, she published *In the Name of Friendship* in 2006.

Further Reading

French, Marilyn. *The Women's Room.* New York: Random House, 1977.
———. *Beyond Power: On Women, Men, and Morals.* New York: Ballentine Books, 1985.
———. *The War Against Women.* New York: Random House, 1994.
———. *In the Name of Friendship.* New York: The Feminist Press, 2006.

—Candis Steenbergen

Friedan, Betty (Bettye Naomi Goldstein)

(1921–2005) *author, feminist* Betty Friedan was born Bettye Naomi Goldstein on February 4, 1921, in Peoria, Illinois. After graduating *summa cum laude* from Smith College in 1942, she received a prestigious fellowship to begin graduate studies in psychology at Berkeley, where she studied with the renowned psychologist Erik Erikson. Although she was offered a second and more prestigious fellowship to continue her work, she turned it down because it threatened the boyfriend she was seeing at the time. She moved to New York's Greenwich Village and worked for a labor newspaper. In 1947, she married Carl Friedan, with whom she had three children. (The marriage would end in divorce in 1969.) She worked as a freelance magazine writer and labor journalist as well as homemaker in the suburbs of New York City.

As her 15th college reunion approached, Betty Friedan sent questionnaires to 200 Smith classmates asking them about their experiences since graduation. Their responses, as well as those collected from graduates of Radcliffe and other colleges, along with scores of personal interviews, led Friedan to research and write her most famous book, the FEMININE MYSTIQUE (1963), a profoundly influential study of the dissatisfaction that many middle-class suburban housewives felt. It begins: "Gradually, without seeing it clearly for quite a while, I came to realize that something is very wrong with the way American women are trying to live their lives today. I sensed it first as a question mark in my own life, as a wife and mother of three small children, half-guiltily, and therefore half-heartedly, almost in spite of myself, using my abilities and education in work that took me away from home." The book is credited with triggering the second wave of FEMINISM in the 1960s.

The Feminine Mystique made Friedan a nationally recognized figure, and she helped found the NATIONAL ORGANIZATION FOR WOMEN (NOW) in 1966, serving as NOW's president from 1966 to 1970. In 1970, she led the Women's Strike for Equality March in New York, on the 50th anniversary of women's SUFFRAGE. Carrying banners that read "Don't Cook Dinner—Starve a Rat Tonight!" or "Don't Iron While the Strike is Hot," marchers drew attention to women's unpaid household labor and continuing sex discrimination in the workplace. Focusing on individual rights and political equality for women, Friedan demanded enforcement of the provisions against sex discrimination contained in the EQUAL PAY ACT (1963) and the CIVIL RIGHTS ACT OF 1964. Friedan was a founder of two other influential women's rights organizations: the National Abortion and Reproductive Rights Action League (NARAL) in 1969 and the NATIONAL WOMEN'S POLITICAL CAUCUS in 1971. She was also the founder of The First Women's Bank and Trust Company (1973), which is no longer in business.

Although she is generally celebrated as the mother of second-wave feminism, *The Feminine*

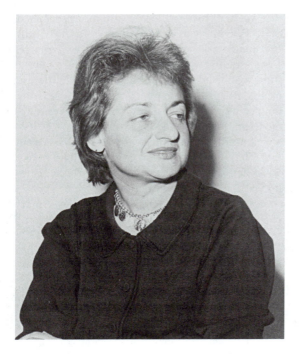

Betty Friedan, 1960 (LIBRARY OF CONGRESS)

Mystique and Friedan's activist agenda were not without critics. Many feminists criticized the book's limited representation of women. The problems of suburban domesticity were born of economic prosperity, and the book does not address the issues faced by millions of poor, working-class women. The feminist Rosemarie Tong writes: "Friedan seemed oblivious to any other perspectives than those of white, middle-class, heterosexual, educated women who found the traditional roles of wife and mother unsatisfying." African-American activist bell hooks extends that criticism even farther, particularly in defining the agenda of second-wave feminism, in noting that Friedan "did not discuss who would be called in to take care of the children and maintain the home if more women like herself were freed from their house labor and given equal access with white men to the professions. She did not speak of the needs of women without men, without children, without homes."

Indeed, Friedan split with NOW in 1970 because she believed that the organization was devoting too many resources to lesbian issues. Her 1981 book *The Second Stage* warned the women's movement against dissolving into factionalism and a preoccupation with sexual and identity politics. She believed that once the movement passed the initial phases, it should focus on working with men to remake private and public arrangements that work against full lives with children for both women and men. Friedan argued that a truly equitable marriage and family would require reorganizing many aspects of conventional middle-class life, from the greater use of flex time and job sharing, to company-sponsored day care, to new home designs to permit communal housekeeping and cooking arrangements. Some denounced her as reactionary, but almost two decades later, working women still struggle in a largely unreconstructed private sphere with little to no support from government or employers.

Friedan's later work (*The Fountain of Age*, 1993) studied the relationship between sex roles and the aging process. In her final book, *Life So Far* (2000), she accused her former husband of physically abusing her during their marriage. He repeatedly denied the accusations, claiming he was the victim of a "drive-by shooting by a reckless driver savagely aiming at the whole male gender." Through more than five decades of activism, Friedan showed the ability not only to formulate feminist theory but also to develop her thinking in response to social and cultural change. This has made her one of the most significant political and intellectual leaders in 20th-century feminism. Betty Friedan died of congestive heart failure on February 4, 2006, her 85th birthday.

Further Reading

Friedan, Betty. *Life So Far.* New York: Simon & Schuster, 2000.

Hennessee, Judith. *Betty Friedan: Her Life.* New York: Random House, 1999.

hooks, bell. *Feminist Theory: From Margin to Center.* Cambridge, Mass.: South End Press, 2000.

Horowitz, Daniel. *Betty Friedan and the Making of the Feminine Mystique: The American Left, The Cold War, and Modern Feminism.* Amherst: University of Massachusetts Press, 1998.

Tong, Rosemarie. *Feminist Thought.* Boulder, Colo.: Westview Press, 1998.

—Laura Prieto

Frontiero v. Richardson (411 U.S. 677)

(1973)   In order to increase participation in the armed services, Congress passed laws granting servicemen similar employment benefits to those offered by civilian employers. Married service personnel could apply for extra housing allowance and comprehensive medical and dental benefits for their dependents. It was assumed that the male serviceman was "head of household," and no showing had to be made of true dependency of the wife and children. Female service persons, however, had to prove that their husband and children were, in fact, dependents. Sharon Frontiero, a female lieutenant in the air force, applied for benefits for her husband, a student attending college on Veterans Administration (VA) benefits. It was determined that he was not a dependent because his VA benefits covered over 50 percent of his expenses. Frontiero sued, and the Supreme Court agreed with her that she should be treated as a "serviceman" and that gender was not an appropriate reason to discriminate in benefits.

Further Reading

Hoff, Joan. *Law, Gender, and Injustice: A Legal History of U.S. Women.* New York: New York University Press, 1991.

—Marsha Hass

G

Gage, Matilda Joslyn (1826–1898) *suffragist, activist, lecturer* This suffragist, historian of women, author, lecturer, women's rights activist and theorist, advocate for civil rights, and abolitionist was born in Cicero, New York, an eastern suburb of Syracuse, on March 24, 1826. The daughter of Dr. Hezekiah Joslyn, she was raised in an abolitionist home that was a station on the underground railroad and was taught multiple languages. She married Henry Gage, a merchant, in 1845. They had five children.

Matilda Gage made her first public speech at the third national Women's Rights Convention in Syracuse in 1852, and rapidly became a leader in the women's rights movement. Throughout her career, Gage was among the more radical leaders of the movement, and, like ELIZABETH CADY STANTON, she focused particularly on the role of social and religious institutions as well as civil concerns. Her writing focused on significant accomplishments of women in invention, in military affairs, and in history. Gage coauthored the first three volumes of *History of Woman Suffrage* with Stanton and SUSAN B. ANTHONY. She also worked with Stanton on *The Woman's Bible,* and in 1893 she published *Woman, Church and State,* her most widely known solo publication.

In 1879, Gage's newspaper, *The National Citizen and Ballot Box,* published the early sections of *A History of Woman Suffrage,* including Stanton's account of the 1848 SENECA FALLS CONVENTION. The newspaper was used prior to printing in book form in order to provide an opportunity for comment.

As the country moved toward the right in the late 1880s, carried along by a conservative religious movement that had as its goal the creation of a Christian state, Gage decided it was time to launch a full-scale attack on the "bulwark of woman's slavery"—the church. Believing that the danger to religious liberty and a secular state was immediate, Gage and Stanton began talking of the need for a feminist anti-church organization. Anthony, in the meantime, was increasingly moving toward a single-minded focus on the vote. When Anthony led her followers in merging the two existing SUFFRAGE organizations, thereby bringing in the conservative WOMAN'S CHRISTIAN TEMPERANCE UNION forces, Gage left the suffrage movement and formed the anti-Church group she had been considering, the Woman's National Liberal Union. This organization was viewed as one of the most radical in the country, and Gage's mail was intercepted by the government.

Stanton, meanwhile chose to become president of Anthony's combined NATIONAL AMERICAN WOMAN SUFFRAGE ASSOCIATION rather than join Gage's group. Anthony denounced Gage's "secession" (as she called it) from the suffrage ranks, and Gage spent her last eight years estranged from most of her movement allies and friends of the previous 40 years. Estrangement was not the only price Gage paid for her uncompromising radical vision. Anthony and Stanton became the icons of the suffrage movement, and Gage's contributions were largely overlooked. She died in Chicago on March 24, 1898, and was buried in the cemetery at Fayetteville, New York, where she had lived most of her life.

Further Reading

Gage, Matilda Joslyn. *Woman, Church and State: A Historical Account of the Status of Women through the Christian Ages.* Watertown, Mass.: Persephone, 1980.

Wagner, Sally Roesch. *A Time of Protest: Suffragists Challenge the Republic 1870–1877.* Aberdeen: Sky Carrier Press, 1996.

———. *Matilda Joslyn Gage: She Who Holds the Sky.* Aberdeen: Sky Carrier Press, 1998.

—Paula Casey

gag rule The gag rule is connected to the ABORTION debate in American politics. It is a tool employed by antiabortion forces to peel away at the *ROE V. WADE* case legalizing abortion in the United States. The gag rule has its historical precedent in the 1834 U.S. Congress in which proslavery factions in the House of Representatives effectively utilized parliamentary mechanisms to postpone or shorten discussion by abolitionist forces. In the 1980s, the antiabortion forces adopted this little-known technical parliamentary device in an attempt to silence abortion rights advocates. Antiabortion forces employed the services of their surrogates and supporters in the legislative, judicial, and executive branches to restrict abortion services by denying public funding.

Antiabortion forces began their attack on abortion rights with the HYDE AMENDMENT prohibiting the use of Medicaid to fund abortions except in a case where a women's health was at risk. This law disproportionately affected poor women and women of color who lacked financial resources to gain access to an abortion. In 1991, antiabortion forces scored another major success with the Supreme Court ruling in *RUST V. SULLIVAN* that the federal government had the right to suspend funding to clinics where abortion counseling is provided.

Many reproductive rights activists perceived the government's argument as one that imposed a "gag rule" because it restricted professional health care providers from engaging in free speech. Doctors argued that this law, which was implemented by Congress, impinged on doctor-patient relations. In 1993, the law was finally rescinded under the tenure of pro-choice Democratic president Bill Clinton. The Senate Labor and Human Resources Committee lifted the gag rule banning abortion counseling in federally funded clinics.

Antiabortion activists not satisfied with limiting the gag rule to the domestic arena began campaigning to export antiabortion ideology overseas. Beginning in 1984, the global gag rule was introduced in Mexico City by the Reagan administration and continued unchanged during the George H. W. Bush tenure. The Mexico City policy denies U.S. funding to any nongovernmental organization that engages in abortion-related activities internationally. Abortion-related activities are classified as providing counseling, lobbying, or clinical services.

Within two days of taking office in 1993, President Clinton rescinded the Mexico City policy. However, Clinton agreed to continue the provision that restricted U.S. Agency for International Development monies from going toward abortion-related services. In 1999, Clinton struck a compromise with the Republican-dominated Congress and agreed to reinstate a limited gag rule for one year. This one-year installment prohibited providers of abortion-related services from using any other funds they receive for those services, and they must certify that they are complying. A waiver was included that allowed groups who refused to certify to continue receiving some U.S. funds as long as they are not used for abortion-related services. In 2001, the pendulum swung once again in favor of the antiabortion forces. On his first full day in office, President George W. Bush reinstated the Mexico City policy.

See also RIGHT TO LIFE MOVEMENT.

Further Reading

Cohen, Susan A. "Global Gag Rule: Exporting Anti-abortion Ideology at the Expense of America Values." *The Guttmacher Report: On Public Policy* 4, no. 3 (2001): 1–3.

Gorney, Cynthia. *Articles of Faith: A Frontline History of the Abortion Wars.* New York: Simon and Schuster, 2000.

—Hollis France

Garfield, Lucretia (Lucretia Rudolph Garfield) (1832–1918) *first lady* Lucretia (Crete) Rudolph was born on April 19, 1832, in Garrettsville, Ohio, to Zebulon and Arabella Mason Rudolph. Sickly as a child, she was an avid reader. In 1850, she entered Western Reserve Eclectic Institute, and she pursued a career in teaching upon graduation.

Crete met James A. Garfield as a fellow student at the Eclectic Institute and corresponded during the years he was away at Williams College. Their courtship was happiest when restricted to letters; in person they often quarreled, and throughout their engagement James pursued other women (a practice that would continue well into their marriage). Even so, they were married on November 11, 1858. In 1859, James was elected to the Ohio Senate, but the onset of the Civil War called him into service for the Union. He was an effective military leader and rose through the ranks. The Garfields' first child, Eliza, was born on July 3, 1860. In 1862, an illness required James to return to Ohio to recuperate. The birth of their second child in

October 1863, Harry Augustus, was followed by Eliza's death from diphtheria three months later. In all, the Garfields had seven children, five of whom survived infancy.

James Garfield was elected to the U.S. House of Representatives in 1863 and quickly rose through the Republican leadership ranks. Crete did not accompany him to Washington, but in 1864 James confessed that he had fallen in love with Lucia Gilbert Calhoun. Crete forgave the affair, and James promised to stop seeing Mrs. Calhoun. Thereafter, Crete accompanied James to Washington during the congressional session. They built a house in Washington in 1870 so that the family could be together both in Washington and in Ohio. Most of Crete Garfield's attention was devoted to her children and domestic duties. Although she argued that women should content themselves with performing their domestic duties well, she resented that domesticity was an end in itself for women. An educated woman, she wrote, "To be half civilized with some aspirations for enlightenment, and obliged to spend the largest part of the time the victim of young barbarians keeps one in a perpetual ferment." Nevertheless, she did not support women's SUFFRAGE, arguing ironically that it would disturb domestic peace.

James Garfield ran for and won the presidency in 1880. Lucretia understood her husband's election as bringing "a terrible responsibility . . . to him and to me," and she undertook her duties as first lady with great dignity and a sense of purpose. She was unaccustomed to entertaining on such a grand scale, and so she sought advice from wives of her husband's cabinet officers who were more familiar with Washington's social expectations. Only three months after moving into the White House, Crete fell ill with malaria. James stayed by her side until she was well enough to move to New Jersey to fully recuperate away from the swamps of Washington. On July 2, 1881, a disappointed petitioner for a patronage job shot President Garfield. Crete returned to the White House immediately, only to watch him suffer and die of an incurable infection on September 18, 1881.

Upon her departure from the White House, Crete Garfield received $360,000 raised by public subscription, a $50,000 grant from Congress, and a $5,000 annual widow's pension. She survived her husband by some 37 years, spending most of her retirement out of the public eye with her children and grandchildren. She died of pneumonia in California on March 13, 1918.

Further Reading

National First Ladies Library. *Biographies: First Ladies of the United States.* Available online. URL: http://www.firstladies.org/biographies. Accessed on January 4, 2007.

Peskin, Allen. *Garfield.* Kent, Ohio: Kent State University Press, 1998.

Schneider, Dorothy, and Carl J. Schneider. "Lucretia Rudolph Garfield." *First Ladies: A Biographical Dictionary.* New York: Checkmark Books, 2001, 133–138.

Geduldig v. Aiello **(417 U.S. 484)** (1974) The issue in this case was whether the California Disability Insurance Fund discriminated against females due to a lack of pregnancy coverage under most circumstances. The Supreme Court found that it did not. This case preceded the GENERAL ELECTRIC COMPANY V. GILBERT (1976) case that served as the basis for Congress's passage of the PREGNANCY DISCRIMINATION ACT in 1978. This is the first important case in a group of cases asserting gender discrimination in pregnancy, disability, or benefit coverage.

—Marsha Hass

gender gap   The gender gap references any differences between men and women in a variety of settings, from television viewing habits to college attendance. In political science, it is most often referred to as the difference between men and women with regard to voting behavior— both in terms of turnout and preferences.

Although women had once voted at lower rates than their male counterparts, women now outnumber men at the polls. A partisan gender gap was first noticed in the 1980 presidential election. Men gave 53 percent of their vote to Ronald Reagan, compared to only 47 percent of women, creating a six-point gender gap. In 1996, this gap increased to 11 points when 54 percent of women voted for Bill Clinton, while only 43 percent of men did so. This gap is also present in races for lower level offices; gaps of at least four percentage points were found in 1996 in six of 11 gubernatorial contests and 28 of 34 senatorial elections. In all but one of these elections, women favored Democrats over Republicans. The gap is politically very meaningful: In eight Senate races in 1996, women handed Democrats their victory. The gender gap remained large in 2000, but even with 54 percent of women voting for Al Gore in 2000, the 11-point gap failed to materialize in a win for this Democratic candidate.

According to many pollsters and scholars, the gender gap emerges from different issue concerns on the part of women and men, and from the assumption that Democratic candidates pay more attention to "women's issues" than do Republican candidates. It often follows that women care more about "caregiving" issues, such as health care and education, while men concern themselves with taxes, the economy, and international issues.

Some scholars criticize this approach to the gender gap because it describes women as if they were one unified bloc when in reality the gender gap is driven by certain types of women. For example, when breaking down women by race in the 1996 election, although 54 percent of women supported Clinton, only 48 percent of white women supported him. Similarly, between 1992 and 1996, Clinton was able to increase his support among less-educated women at higher rates than women with college degrees. Even so, in the current political climate, college-educated women remain a substantial voting bloc for Democrats.

Further Reading

Kahn, Kim Fridkin. *The Political Consequences of Being a Woman.* New York: Columbia University Press, 1996.

Mueller, Carol. *The Politics of the Gender Gap.* Newbury Park, Calif.: Sage Publications, 1998.

Tolleson-Rinehart, Sue, and Jyl Josephson, eds. *Gender and American Politics.* Armonk, N.Y.: M.E. Sharpe, 2000.

—J. Celeste Lay

gender stereotypes Gender refers to the attributes, behaviors, personality characteristics, and expectations associated with a person's biological sex within a given culture. While sex is biologically determined, gender is socially constructed and varies by time and place. Gender stereotypes occur when one applies generic attributes, opinions, or roles to either gender without considering the individual or the context. Gender stereotypes lead to assumptions about what men and women are *supposed* to do, and they have proven detrimental to both sexes in achieving full integration into all aspects of society. Gender stereotypes are evident in the way we dress, the toys we assign as appropriate for boys and girls, the jobs that guidance counselors may point young men and women toward, media images of women and men, and the ways families operate and assign authority.

The problem with gender stereotyping arises when a person or group of people do not conform to social expectations associated with their gender. Women faced this limitation when they began to lobby for SUFFRAGE and other rights associated with the public sphere. The U.S. Supreme Court relied on gender stereotypes consistent with women's place in the private sphere in a number of cases, including MULLER V. OREGON and BRADWELL V. ILLINOIS. For the most part, the Court's opinions today require that employers, educational institutions, and others evaluate individual attributes rather than rely on social and gender stereotypes of a group. Stereotypes are notoriously inaccurate for most

members of the group. As a result of research in psychology, biology, child development, sociology, and political science (and other disciplines as well), there are many books and articles that focus on dispelling gender stereotypes and bias in children.

See also SEPARATE SPHERES IDEOLOGY.

Further Reading

Basow, Susan. *Gender Stereotypes: Traditions and Alternatives.* Monterey, Calif.: Brooks/Cole Publishing, 1986.

Crawford, Susan Hoy. *Beyond Dolls and Guns: 101 Ways to Help Children Avoid Gender Bias.* Portsmouth, N.H.: Heinemann Press, 1995.

General Electric Company v. Gilbert (429 U.S. 125) (1976) This very important case was the basis for the PREGNANCY DISCRIMINATION ACT passed by Congress in 1978. General Electric (GE) provided its employees with coverage for nonoccupational sickness and accidents. Pregnancy was specifically *not* covered. The Supreme Court found that excluding pregnancy coverage was not gender discrimination since both men and women were treated the same under the policy. The Court found that GE's plan was insurance coverage with certain risks covered, while others were not, and thus there was no gender discrimination. While the Court noted that only women could get pregnant, it was unwilling to consider exclusion of pregnancy coverage discrimination under TITLE VII OF THE CIVIL RIGHTS ACT OF 1964. Congress responded with new legislation, essentially adding pregnancy to Title VII.

Further Reading

Kirp, David L., et al. *Gender Justice.* Chicago: University of Chicago Press, 1986.

Mezey, Susan Gluck. *Elusive Equality: Women's Rights, Public Policy, and the Law.* Boulder, Colo.: Lynne Rienner, 2003.

Wisensale, Steven K. *Family Leave Policy: The Political Economy of Work and Family in America.* London: M.E. Sharpe, 2001.

—Marsha Hass

General Federation of Women's Clubs (GFWC)

The General Federation of Women's Clubs (GFWC), founded in 1890 at the apex of the woman's club movement that began shortly after the Civil War, was the first national women's voluntary association in the United States. Although the GFWC endorsed policy resolutions throughout its history, including advocacy of social reforms during the progressive era and early support for the EQUAL RIGHTS AMENDMENT, voluntary service and charitable giving in local communities has remained the group's primary mission over its long history. Consequently, the GFWC's membership was comprised of white, middle-class women who did not work outside of the home well into the 20th century. Wide-ranging national program goals related to improving the lives of women and children and the promise of local autonomy enabled the GFWC to attract millions of women into club work from the burgeoning suburbs after World War II; the GFWC claimed to represent 11 million women in the 1950s. The contemporary GFWC supports over 150,000 projects in local communities and has raised millions of dollars for local charities.

Further Reading

Blair, Karen J. *The Clubwoman as Feminist: True Womanhood Redefined, 1868–1914.* New York: Holmes and Meier Publishers, 1980.

Scott, Anne Firor. *Natural Allies: Women's Associations in U.S. History.* Urbana: University of Illinois Press, 1992.

—Kathleen Laughlin

Gilbreth, Lillian (Lillien Moller Gilbreth)

(1878–1972) *psychologist, engineer, author*   Best known as the mother of the 12 children immortalized in the novel *Cheaper by the Dozen*, Lillian Moller Gilbreth was also an innovative engineer who used the newly emerging field of time motion study to analyze the actions of workers both in factories and in the home.

Born on May 24, 1878, into an upper-middle-class family in Oakland, California, Lillian Evelyn Moller pursued a college degree at the University of California at Berkeley over her father's objections that such an education was not necessary for a woman who would simply need to know how to run a household. Moller ultimately graduated with both a B.A. and an M.A. in literature (and spoke at her own graduation, becoming the first woman to do so in the University of California system). She met her husband, Frank Gilbreth, while in Boston prior to leaving for a trip to Europe. Her marriage to Gilbreth in 1904 provided Moller with her life's work, for Frank Gilbreth was at the beginning of a lifelong fascination with efficiency, time management, and the improvement of how workers do their work.

Lillian Gilbreth earned a Ph.D. in psychology at Brown University in 1915. The Gilbreths worked together, under the auspices of their company, Gilbreth, Inc., to improve the efficiency of workers by engaging in time-motion studies where the actions of workers doing their jobs would be analyzed and then broken down into the most efficient series of motions. Lillian Gilbreth drew on her background in psychology to further study the effect time management had on workers, focusing particularly on stress and sleep deprivation.

After her husband's death in 1924, Gilbreth continued to work toward greater workplace and household efficiency. She was the first female member of the American Society of Mechanical Engineers and the first female professor at Purdue University. Gilbreth recognized that the work women did in their homes was also deserving of study and innovative technologies. She wrote two books in the 1920s focused on women: *The Homemaker and her Job* and *Living with Our Children.* Both books argued that women must acknowledge the value of the work they do in the home and that the best way to raise healthy, happy children is to create an efficient home where women are freed to consider their own happiness, as well as the happiness of children and husbands.

In her later life, Gilbreth helped General Electric design more efficient household appliances. She also worked to design kitchens that could be used by the physically challenged. She patented a number of household inventions, including the foot-pedal trashcan. During the Great Depression, after President Herbert Hoover asked her to join the Emergency Committee for Unemployment, Gilbreth started a program called Share the Work. During World War II, she consulted with munitions factories about their management practices. In 1966, she received the Hoover Medal from the American Society of Civil Engineers and was the first woman elected to the National Academy of Engineering. She was honored with multiple honorary degrees, and she worked well into her 80s. She died on January 2, 1972, in Phoenix, Arizona.

Further Reading
Lancaster, Jane. *Making Time: Lillian Moller Gilbreth, A Life Beyond Cheaper by the Dozen.* Boston: Northeastern University Press, 2004.
Gilbreth, Lillian. *As I Remember: An Autobiography of Lillian Moller Gilbreth.* Norcross, Ga.: Engineering and Management Press, 1998.

—Claire Curtis

Gilligan, Carol (1936–) *psychologist* Carol Gilligan was born on November 28, 1936, in New York City. She graduated with honors from Swarthmore College in 1958, received a master's degree in clinical psychology from Radcliffe University in 1960, and earned her doctorate in social psychology from Harvard University in 1964.

Gilligan is best known for her research on the moral development of adolescent girls. In the 1970s, she worked closely with Lawrence Kohlberg, known for his research on moral development and his stage theory of moral development, justice, and rights. Gilligan's work challenges the generalizations of Kohlberg's theory as applied to women. Kohlberg's stage theory of moral development privileges the male view of individual rights and rules over women's point of view of development in terms of its caring effect on human relationships. Gilligan developed a new psychology for women based on rethinking the meaning of self and selfishness. She asked four questions about women's voices: Who is speaking, in what body, telling what story, and in what cultural framework is the story presented? Her theory was published in 1982 in her most famous book, *In a Different Voice: Psychological Theory and Women's Development.* Her work spawned the development of "difference feminism." Gilligan asserted that women have differing moral and psychological tendencies than men. According to Gilligan, men think in terms of rules and justice, and women are more inclined to think in terms of caring and relationships.

There have been many critics of Gilligan's work, but Christine Hoff Sommers has directly challenged its content and the legitimacy, saying that Gilligan has failed to produce the data for her research. Sommers condemns the fact that Gilligan used anecdotal evidence, that researchers have not been able to duplicate her work, and that the samples used were too small. Sommers also thinks the field of gender studies needs to be put to the test of people from fields such as neuroscience or evolutionary psychology, rather than from the area of education, and feels strongly that promoting an antimale agenda hurts both males and females. The debate moved into the mainstream in a widely read exchange in *The Atlantic Monthly* in 2000.

Since 1997, Gilligan has been on the faculty at Harvard University, where she continues her research on gender, development, and education.

Further Reading
Gilligan, Carol. *In a Different Voice: Psychological Theory and Women's Development.* Cambridge, Mass.: Harvard University Press, 1982.
Sommers, Christine Hoff. *The War Against Boys: How Misguided Feminism Is Harming Our Young Men.* New York: Simon and Schuster, 2001.

Gilman, Charlotte Perkins (Charlotte Anna Perkins Stetson Gilman) (1860–1935)

feminist, political writer   Born on July 3, 1860, in Hartford, Connecticut, the grandniece of HARRIET BEECHER STOWE, Charlotte Anna Perkins was raised in poverty after her father left her mother in Charlotte's early childhood. She only received four years of formal education, yet she still attended the Rhode Island School of Design, financing her tuition by selling watercolors and prints. Though initially determined not to marry in order to fulfill her ambition for a career to help change the status of women, she wed Charles Stetson in 1884 and gave birth to her only child, Katherine, that same year. After the birth of her daughter, Gilman suffered from depression that was treated with a rest cure rather than physical or intellectual engagement. After the failure of this cure, Charlotte left her husband and moved to California in 1888; after Stetson remarried, she sent Katherine to live with him. It was her experience with the conflict between motherhood and the pursuit of a career (particularly a career that emphasized the independence of women) that influenced many of Charlotte Gilman's later writings.

Gilman's most famous works were the short story *The Yellow Wallpaper* (1890), a fictionalized account of a woman suffering through a rest cure similar to Gilman's own, and the nonfiction *Women in Economics* (1898), which argued that political and social independence for women was contingent on their ability to be financially independent. Without that financial independence, she argued, women would remain in a socially produced inferior position. Gilman met JANE ADDAMS in 1895 and lived in HULL-HOUSE for a few months. In 1900, she married her cousin, George Houghton Gilman, who was supportive of her career. In 1909, she began publishing the progressive journal *The Forerunner*. It was in this journal that Gilman's utopian work *Herland* was first published. *Herland* (1915) describes a country of only women visited by three American men. It is a society based on motherhood, egali-

Charlotte Gilman, ca. 1900 (LIBRARY OF CONGRESS)

tarianism, self-sufficiency and the pursuit of one's talents. *Herland* was followed by *With Her in Ourland* (1916), recounting the trip of one of the Herland women into Europe and the United States of the First World War years.

Gilman's major achievement was to challenge traditional notions of what it means to be a woman and to advocate that changing the conditions under which women live (subordination) would change the world for the better by liberating women. As did some other early women's rights activists, Gilman supported racist and nativist ideas. However, her overall philosophical outlook, that there were no innate differences between men and women, could be applied to all humans. She died on August 17, 1935.

Further Reading

Gilman, Charlotte Perkins. *The Living of Charlotte Perkins Gilman: An Autobiography.* Madison: University of Wisconsin Press, 1991.

Hill, Mary A. *Charlotte Perkins Gilman: The Making of a Radical Feminist, 1860–1896.* Philadelphia: Temple University Press, 1980.

Lane, Ann J. *To Herland and Beyond: The Life and Works of Charlotte Perkins Gilman.* Charlottesville: University Press of Virginia, 1997.

Rudd, Jill, and Val Gough, eds. *Charlotte Perkins Gilman: An Optimist Reformer.* Iowa City: University of Iowa Press, 1999.

—Claire Curtis

Ginsburg, Ruth Bader (1933–) *Supreme Court justice*   Joan Ruth Bader was born in Brooklyn, New York, on March 15, 1933. Her parents, Nathan Bader and Celia Amster Bader, were both children of Jewish immigrants. When Ruth was one year old, her older sister Marilyn died of meningitis. Nathan Bader worked as a furrier and clothier, at times owning his own small shop. Nathan and Celia stressed hard work and the importance of education in raising Ruth. Celia was from a family who had subscribed to the view that college was only for boys; when she graduated from high school, she worked to put her brother through Cornell University and then, as expected, married and began her family. She was, however, determined that Ruth would set high goals for herself, pursue her ambitions, and have the education and career Celia could not have herself.

Ruth Bader attended public schools in Brooklyn and received a number of awards for outstanding achievement. While she was in high school, her mother was diagnosed with cervical cancer and died the day before Ruth's graduation. In September 1950, Ruth enrolled at Cornell University. During the first semester of her freshman year, she met Martin Ginsburg, a sophomore; a year later, they announced their engagement. As they planned for a life together, they both decided to enter the field of law. While Ruth completed her senior year, Martin was enrolled at Harvard Law School. Ruth graduated summa cum laude from Cornell in 1954, first in her class and with high honors in government and distinction in all subjects. She was elected to Phi Beta Kappa and Phi Kappa Phi. Soon after her graduation, She and Martin were married.

Their plans to continue together at Harvard were interrupted when Martin was drafted into the U.S. Army. The couple spent two years in Lawton, Oklahoma, where Martin was stationed at Fort Sill. Ruth worked at the local Social Security office; when she became pregnant, she was demoted to a less prominent (and less visible) position. Jane Ginsburg was born on July 21, 1955.

In autumn 1956, Martin returned to law classes at Harvard, where Ruth also enrolled; she was one of nine women in a class of over 500 students. At the start of the year, the dean of Harvard Law School, Erwin N. Griswold, held a dinner party at his home. He invited all of the entering female students and a number of the faculty, asking each woman in turn to justify why she had taken a seat that might otherwise have gone to a qualified male applicant. The women suffered other indignities as well—for example, they were not permitted in the periodicals room at the Harvard Law Library. By the conclusion of her second year, Ruth was ranked in the top 10 students in her class and she made the law review. During this year, Martin was diagnosed with testicular cancer, but neither withdrew from law school. Ruth hand-copied the notes taken by other students in Martin's classes so that he could continue to study and graduate with his class. Upon receiving his law degree in 1958, Martin accepted a job with a prestigious New York City law firm, and as a result Ruth transferred to Columbia Law School, where she was one of 12 female students.

In 1959, Ruth Bader Ginsburg graduated from Columbia, tied for first place in her graduating class, having again made law review. She was admitted to the New York bar (1959); however, not a single law firm in New York would hire her. While her gender served as one strike against Ginsburg, the fact that there were virtually no Jewish lawyers at that time became strike two. Her determination to overcome both obstacles, however, eventually landed her a position as a law clerk for Judge Edmund L. Palmieri at the United States District Court for the Southern District of New York. After two years, she took a position with the Columbia Law School Project on International Procedure, which allowed her to study the judicial system of Sweden in 1962. While she was at the University of Lund, she became aware of the ongoing dialogue about sex roles and the debate over how best to accomplish gender equality. In 1963, she became an assistant professor at Rutgers School of Law, the second woman in the institution's history. In 1965, when she became pregnant again, she resolved to say nothing to her colleagues, fearing a similar demotion as during her first pregnancy. She gave birth to James Thomas Ginsburg on September 8, 1965, and returned to the classroom in time for the start of the fall semester. In her five years at Rutgers, Ruth Ginsburg produced four books and eight articles. Most of her work concerned the Swedish legal system or comparative law. In 1969, she was awarded an honorary doctorate of law by the University of Lund for her significant contributions to the study of Swedish law. In that same year, Ginsburg was promoted to professor and granted tenure at Rutgers.

In autumn 1968, a group of female law students approached Ginsburg and asked her to teach a seminar on women and the law. Ginsburg agreed and then confined herself to the library, where she read every article and case on the subject. She was both amazed and outraged at how little scholarship on women and the law had been written. Thus began the next phase of her career, devoted to social activism in pursuit of equality for women and men under the law. Ginsburg attributes her conversion to feminism to Simone de Beauvoir's *The Second Sex,* published in 1949. The timing of her feminist awakening coincided with major advances in women's equality under federal statute including adoption of the EQUAL PAY ACT of 1963 and TITLE VII OF THE CIVIL RIGHTS ACT OF 1964. Ginsburg took up the challenge of taking such laws and making them real for women through enforcement in the courts. By 1969, the legal status of women had become the primary focus of

Ginsburg's academic career. She helped women law students create a new journal, the *Women's Rights Law Journal,* and helped to organize one of the first academic conferences on women and the law held in 1970.

Ginsburg's career highlights include assisting the New Jersey affiliate of the American Civil Liberties Union (ACLU) in litigating sex discrimination cases. Her association with the ACLU led to her involvement in the case of REED v. REED (1971). The case involved an Idaho law that stated, "Where there are several persons equally entitled to administer the estate of a person dying intestate, males must be preferred to females." Sally Reed had applied to be the administrator of her late son's estate, but was rejected because of this law. Reed sued, arguing that the law violated the equal-protection clause of the Fourteenth Amendment and was therefore unconstitutional. The Idaho Supreme Court found the law constitutional, setting up an appeal to the U.S. Supreme Court. Ginsburg was added to the team of ACLU lawyers working on the case, and she became the principal author of the amicus curiae brief. The brief argued that under the equal-protection clause of the Fourteenth Amendment, all classifications by sex were "suspect" and should be subject to the same "strict scrutiny" that courts gave to classifications based on race. Under this reasoning, classifications based on sex could only be valid if they were found necessary to promote a "compelling state interest." Sex discrimination cases were being decided using the "rational basis" test. Under this line of reasoning, laws and practices that treat men and women differently would be upheld unless they were found to be "wholly irrational or arbitrary."

Ginsburg's ACLU brief, referred to as the "grandmother brief" because so many of its arguments were repeated in subsequent sex discrimination cases, argued that it was no longer credible to assume that women as a class were necessarily less able than men to perform any number of duties. Any automatic preference of men to women where the preference was totally unrelated to the task, she argued, was a violation of "the equal protection of the laws." On November 21, 1971, the U.S. Supreme Court ruled in favor of Sally Reed and declared the Idaho statute unconstitutional. Although the court did not aopt "strict scrutiny" as the standard in sex discrimination cases, it did announce that all statutes that classify by sex were to be "subject to scrutiny."

Even while the *Reed* decision was pending with the Court, the ACLU organized a permanent project dedicated to women's rights. The ACLU Women's Rights Project was founded in 1972, and Ruth Bader Ginsburg and Barbara Feigen-Fasuteau were selected as codirectors. The goal of the organization was to establish precedent on the basis of carefully chosen litigation in order to end discrimination on the basis of sex and eradicate sex stereotypes that limited women's opportunities. Key to Ginsburg's strategy was the concept of gender equality as including both men and women. Nearly two out of every three cases the Women's Rights Project pursued had a male as a plaintiff.

In 1972, Ginsburg became the first female full professor at Columbia University School of Law and the first woman ever to receive tenure. She divided her time between academia and the Women's Rights Project. Her first appearance before the U.S. Supreme Court was in the case of *FRONTIERO V. RICHARDSON* (1973). The case offered an opportunity to challenge classifications by sex in federal law. Sharon Frontiero was a married lieutenant in the air force. When she applied for increased benefits to cover her husband, she was refused. Under federal law, wives were automatically defined as a dependent, while husbands of active-duty females were required to prove that over half his support came from her earnings. Ginsburg argued that the different treatment of men and women in the military arbitrarily and unreasonably discriminated against them and therefore violated the due-process clause of the Fifth Amendment. Ginsburg again appealed to the justices to apply "strict scrutiny" where

classifications were based on sex. Although the Court ruled in favor of Frontiero, only four justices joined in the majority opinion, declaring that "classifications by sex, like classification based on race, alienage, and national origin, are inherently suspect and must therefore be subjected to close judicial scrutiny," meaning that the standard was not adopted as precedent. In all, Ginsburg argued six cases before the Supreme Court between 1972 and 1978, and lost only one (*Kahn v. Shevin,* 1974). In *CRAIG V. BOREN* (1976) the Court finally adopted Ginsburg's language of "heightened scrutiny" in reviewing gender-based classifications in the law.

In 1980, President Jimmy Carter appointed Ginsburg to the U.S. Court of Appeals for the District of Columbia Circuit. Martin Ginsburg moved to Washington, D.C., and became a professor at Georgetown University Law Center. The resignation of Justice Byron White in 1993 created an opening on the U.S. Supreme Court. In appointing Ruth Bader Ginsburg to fill the seat, President Bill Clinton referred to her as the "Thurgood Marshall of gender equality law." The Senate voted 97-3 to confirm Ginsburg, and she took the oath of office on August 10, 1993. On the bench, she is a persistent questioner during oral argument and prolific in the number of opinions she writes. She is the author of the 1996 majority opinion admitting women to the Virginia Military Institute (*UNITED STATES V. VIRGINIA,* 1996). Relying on many of the very cases she had won as a litigator, Justice Ginsburg declared, "A government policy that treats the sexes differently must have an exceedingly persuasive justification. . . . Women seeking and fit for a VMI quality education cannot be offered anything less under the Commonwealth's obligation to afford them genuinely equal protection." On October 5, 2002, Ruth Bader Ginsburg was inducted into the National Women's Hall of Fame in Seneca Falls, New York.

Further Reading

Bayer, Linda. *Ruth Bader Ginsburg*. Philadelphia: Chelsea House Publishers, 2000.

Campbell, Amy Leigh. *Raising the Bar: Ruth Bader Ginsburg and the ACLU Women's Rights Project.* Philadelphia: Xlibris Corporation, 2004.

—Thea Lapham

Glaspie, April (April Catherine Glaspie)

(1942–) *American diplomat* April Glaspie made her mark in the U.S. diplomatic core as a veteran of 25 years in the foreign service and the first American woman appointed ambassador to an Arab country. She gained notoriety as U.S. ambassador to Iraq during the events leading up to the Gulf War and later on as senior advisor to the United Nations mission to Somalia in 1993.

Born in Vancouver, Canada, on April 26, 1942, and educated in the United States in California and later at John Hopkins University in Maryland, Glaspie joined the U.S. State Department in 1966. The State Department culture at the beginning of her career dictated that the upper-level jobs, such as ambassadorial postings, were limited to men. Despite this barrier to women's advancement, Glaspie worked diligently to compile an outstanding dossier while serving at the Middle East desk. Her first field service was a posting to Cairo, where her expertise of the Middle East region came to the attention of visiting Secretary of State Henry Kissinger. She was subsequently promoted to the position of deputy chief of mission to Syria. While posted in Damascus, she was instrumental in getting the Syrian government to aid in freeing American hostages from a highjacked TWA plane. She was later called "a genuine heroine" by Secretary of State George Shultz and awarded a top political reporting officer citation.

In 1989, Glaspie was appointed U.S. ambassador to Iraq, becoming the first female U.S. ambassador to the Arab world. Her historic appointment was soon tainted by Iraq's invasion of Kuwait in 1990. Iraq produced a transcript of a conversation between Iraqi president Saddam Hussein and Ambassador Glaspie in which, on behalf of the U.S. government, she allegedly sanctioned Iraq's actions by leading the president to believe that the United States would do nothing to intervene if he invaded Kuwait. This became a major embarrassment for the United States, and officials distanced themselves from Glaspie, claiming that her version of U.S. policy on Iraq's invasion of Kuwait was incorrect.

Glaspie was next assigned to the UN Mission in New York and later to South Africa as consul-general in Cape Town. She held the post until her retirement from the State Department in 2002. Glaspie now lives as a private citizen and has consistently refused to comment on her actions in Iraq.

Further Reading
Blumenthal, Sydney. "April's Bluff: The Secrets of Ms. Glaspie's Cable," *New Republic* 5 August 1991, 8–11.
Cockburn, Alexander. "Women in the News." *Nation* 18 October 1993, 415.

—Hollis France

glass ceiling   The glass ceiling has been defined as an invisible, artificial barrier that determines the level to which a woman or other member of a demographic minority can rise in an organization. The first reference in print to the "glass ceiling" has been attributed to a 1984 quote from *Working Woman* editor Gay Bryant: "Women have reached a certain point—I call it the glass ceiling. They're in the top of middle management and they're stopping and getting stuck." The organized women's movement and academicians moved quickly to document examples of the glass ceiling as an explanation for why there were so few women in the highest political offices, in top corporate jobs, and in the professions. In 1991, the GLASS CEILING COMMISSION was created by the CIVIL RIGHTS ACT OF 1991. The secretary of labor was charged with studying the problem and preparing recommendations for combating the limitations imposed by the glass ceiling.

Further Reading

Kelly, Rita Mae. *The Gendered Economy: Work, Careers, and Success.* Newbury Park, Calif.: Sage Publications, 1991.

Lindgren, J. Ralph, and Nadine Taub. *The Law of Sex Discrimination.* St. Paul, Minn.: West Publishing, 1993.

Glass Ceiling Commission   Created by the CIVIL RIGHTS ACT OF 1991, the Glass Ceiling Commission was charged with studying the problem known as the GLASS CEILING, the invisible barrier to the advancement and other minorities. Secretary of Labor Robert Reich convened and chaired the 21-member body appointed by the president and congressional leadership. The commission worked to identify glass-ceiling barriers and identify practices and policies that promote employment advancement opportunities for women and minorities.

In November 1995, the commission issued its final report, "A Solid Investment: Making Full Use of the Nation's Human Capitol." The report begins: "The glass ceiling is a reality in corporate America. Glass ceiling barriers continue to deny untold numbers of qualified people the opportunity to compete for and hold executive level positions in the private sector." For example, 97 percent of managers of *Fortune* 1000 Industrial and *Fortune* 500 companies are white, and 95–97 percent are male; African-American men with professional degrees earn 21 percent less than their white counterparts holding the same degrees in the same job categories. Commission recommendations focused on business and government, calling on CEOs to make a visible commitment to workforce diversity throughout their organizations and government agencies to lead by example through a careful examination of their practices for promoting qualified minorities and women to senior management and decision-making positions. A summary of the specific recommendations can be found in the commission's final report, A Solid Investment: Making Full Use of the Nation's Human Capital (1995).

Further Reading

Falk, Erica. *The Glass Ceiling Persists.* Philadelphia: The Annenberg Public Policy Center of the University of Pennsylvania, 2004.

U.S. Glass Ceiling Commission. *A Solid Investment: Making Full Use of the Nation's Human Capital* (Final Report of the Commission). Washington, D.C.: U.S. Government Printing Office, 1995. Available online. URL: http://digitalcommons.ilr.cornell.edu/key_workplace/120/. Accessed June 26, 2007.

Goldman, Emma (1869–1940) *anarchist author, lecturer, feminist, birth control advocate* Best known as an extreme activist who was deported from the United States, Emma Goldman considered anarchism a natural vehicle for women's rights, particularly rights to birth control, workplace equality, and sexual freedom. She argued that "every love relation should by its very nature remain an absolutely private affair. Neither, the State, the Church, morality, or people should meddle with it" (from "Jealousy: Causes and a Possible Cure," 1912).

Born in Russia on June 27, 1869, Goldman immigrated to the United States when she was 15, settling with two of her sisters in Rochester, New York, in 1885. She began work in a garment factory and married, thus attaining U.S. citizenship, in 1886—also the year of the Haymarket affair. In that incident in Chicago, seven anarchists were sentenced to death after a bomb was thrown at a group of police officers during a protest concerning strikebreakers at a nearby factory. The men were sentenced for justifying the use of violence in bringing about revolutionary change, although it is clear, in retrospect, that none of the men charged had thrown the bomb. This event helped to awaken Goldman's radical conscience and instigated her shift toward political activism. In 1889, she abandoned her husband and moved to New York City, where she began work with an anarchist newspaper (*Freiheit*) and found work at another factory. She became involved with a variety of trade union activists, including Alexander Berkman, her lover and lifelong friend who was later convicted of trying to kill Henry Frick of Carnegie Steel (because of the company's labor practices and its response to the Homestead strike). Goldman and Berkman were convinced that the right kind of violence would help to awaken the minds of workers and compel them to revolution. Goldman believed that violence could be justified to bring about change. She lectured extensively after Berkman's arrest and was jailed herself in 1893 for her claim in public lectures that workers could steal bread if they needed it. During this time, she also studied nursing and considered studying to be a doctor, but she rejected this idea when it became clear that her political activities would not be viewed positively.

In 1901, Goldman was arrested again because Leon Czolgosz, who assassinated President William McKinley, claimed he had been influenced by Goldman's speeches. She was acquitted and continued her lecturing, branching out by the early 1900s to the topics of free speech, sexual freedom, and birth control (the 1873 COMSTOCK ACT had made the presentation of all contraceptive information illegal). In 1906, Goldman started a new anarchist magazine, *Mother Earth,* which pursued a variety of topics: free speech, birth control, women's rights, worker's rights, objections to the draft, and education reform. Jailed again in 1916 for passing on information about birth control, Goldman entered her most famous period of activism with the start of World War I and the subsequent success of the Russian Revolution. She was arrested and imprisoned in 1917 because of her antidraft activism, and after her release from jail she was deported to the USSR. She left the Soviet Union in 1921, publishing an account of her dissatisfaction with the Bolshevik Revolution in *My Disillusionment with Russia.*

In 1921, she settled in Britain and continued lecturing. Fearing deportation, she married Welsh miner James Colton in order to gain British citizenship. Goldman was not allowed to visit the United States until 1934, when she was granted a visa for a lecture tour. She traveled to Spain in 1936 in support of the revolution there, although she was once again disillusioned by the anarchists' willingness to side with communists. After the Spanish Civil War, she moved to Toronto. She died on May 14, 1940, and was buried in Chicago, near the site of the Haymarket affair, although she had not lived in the United States since her deportation in 1919.

Further Reading

Falk, Candace. *Love, Anarchy and Emma Goldman.* New Brunswick, N.J.: Rutgers University Press, 1990.

Goldman, Emma. *Living My Life.* New York: AMS Press, 1970.

———, and Alix Kates Shulman, ed. *Red Emma Speaks: An Emma Goldman Reader.* New York: Schocken Books, 1982.

—Claire Curtis

Emma Goldman, 1910 (LIBRARY OF CONGRESS)

Gonzales v. Carhart (550 U.S.___) (2007)

See ABORTION.

Granger, Kay (1943–   ) *congressperson* Kay Granger was born on January 18, 1943, in Greenville, Texas, and earned a B.S. degree from Texas Wesleyan University in 1965. She was elected to the Fort Worth city council in 1989 and she was elected mayor of Fort Worth in 1991.

After the retirement of Congressman Pete Geren in 1996, both the Democratic and Republican parties worked to recruit Granger. Eventually, after declaring that she was a Republican, she won the seat by a narrow margin. In the 106th Congress, she was given a seat on the Appropriations Committee, and in the 107th, she added the Budget Committee to her duties. She was reelected in 1998 by a surprisingly safe margin given that the district is former Democratic House Speaker Jim Wright's old district. She has not had a serious challenge to her seat yet, and she ran unopposed in 2002.

Granger is a member of the Republican Main Street Partnership (which supports stem cell research), the Republican Majority for Choice, Republicans for Choice, and the WISH LIST (all support ROE V. WADE). She has generally supported legislation favoring women's interests, including backing the Food Drug Administration's approval of the RU-486 abortion pill. In 2003, she proposed a national gynecological cancer detection program. In January 2005, she toured Iraq. With ELLEN TAUSCHER, Granger conducted a training session for women candidates. She was reelected in 2006 and will serve as the vice chair of the House Republican Conference in the 110th Congress.

Further Reading

Barone, Michael. *The Almanac of American Politics.* Washington, D.C.: National Journal Group, 2006.

"Granger, Kay." In *Biographical Directory of the United States Congress, 1774–present.* Available online. URL: http://bioguide.congress.gov/scripts/biodisplay.pl?index=G000377. Accessed on January 8, 2007.

"Representative Kay Granger (TX)." In *Project Vote Smart.* Available online. URL: http://votesmart.org/bio.php?can_id=BC032299. Accessed on January 8, 2007.

—Angela Kouters

Grant, Julia (Julia Dent Grant) (1826–1902) *first lady* Julia Dent was born on January 26, 1826, at White Haven Plantation, near St. Louis, Missouri, into a wealthy slaveholding family. Her father, Frederick Dent, was a farmer and her mother, Ellen Bray Dent, the daughter of Methodist missionaries. Julia was the fifth of eight children and the first daughter. She was largely educated at home or in a log cabin school nearby. She preferred the outdoors to study.

In 1844, the Dents invited soldiers stationed near their home to visit. Ulysses S. Grant, a former West Point classmate of Julia's brother, was among them. He visited her frequently, and they enjoyed riding, fishing, and social occasions with her family. Although Julia's mother supported the relationship, her father opposed Grant's antislavery position and his opposition to the Mexican War. Grant's parents, ardent abolitionists, objected to his marriage into a slaveholding family. Ulysses proposed, but the marriage was postponed for three years while he fought in the Mexican War. The couple were married on August 22, 1848. Their honeymoon was a boat trip down the Mississippi and a trip to Ohio to meet his parents. From there, she accompanied him to his post at Sackett's Harbor, establishing the pattern that characterized the rest of their marriage. The birth of their first child, Frederick Dent, sent her back to St. Louis while he continued in a series of army postings. His desire to rejoin his family led him to resign his commission in 1854. As a civilian, he took up farming on 60 acres that Julia's father had given her as a wedding gift. Daughter Ellen (Nellie) was born on the farm in 1855. By all accounts, the Grants had an exceptionally happy family life. A national economic depression and illness forced Ulysses Grant to sell the

Julia Dent Grant, ca. 1870 (LIBRARY OF CONGRESS)

farm and look for less physical work. In 1858, a second son, Jesse Root, was born.

The onset of the Civil War in April 1861 split the Dent and Grant families as Julia and Ulysses were solidly pro-Union. In August 1861, he was commissioned a brigadier general in the U.S. Army; she remained behind as he moved from post to post. In November 1861, Julia made her first of many battlefield visits with the children. She believed that the family's presence gave morale to Ulysses and the other soldiers and did no harm to the children. She urged her husband on and offered advice, which historians argue he most often ignored. Julia became nearly as recognizable a public figure as General Grant himself. Following the fall of Vicksburg, she and the children joined him once more. When a horse injured him, she was there to tend to his convalescence, and she briefly moved to Washington when Ulysses was named supreme

commander of the Union forces. Following the war, he was named general in chief, a largely ceremonial position created especially for him. The Grants enjoyed support from President Andrew Johnson, and Julia Grant opened their home for receptions and dinner parties.

Ulysses S. Grant was elected president in 1868 and inaugurated on March 4, 1869. Julia looked forward to her life as first lady and found the public and press alike receptive to her overtures. She entertained regularly and quite elaborately in the White House, and unlike nearly all of her predecessors, she enjoyed her life as first lady. She hoped for a third term in office, although Ulysses did not. Without her knowledge, he mailed a letter to the Republican Convention announcing his decision not to run. The Grants welcomed Rutherford and Lucy Hayes to the White House with a state dinner and an informal luncheon on inaugural day.

The Grants traveled around the world after leaving the White House and settled in New York two years later. To earn money following a financial disaster, Grant worked on his memoirs, completing them just before he succumbed to throat cancer on July 23, 1885. Julia wrote her own memoirs, making her the first first lady to do so, although they were never published. As a widow, she lived in New York and Washington, traveling often to see her children and grandchildren. She died on December 14, 1902.

Further Reading

National First Ladies Library. *Biographies: First Ladies of the United States.* Available online. URL: http://www.firstladies.org/biographies. Accessed on January 4, 2007.

Porter, Horace. *Campaigning with Grant* New York: Bison, 2000.

Schneider, Dorothy, and Carl J. Schneider. "Julia Dent Grant" *First Ladies: A Biographical Dictionary.* New York: Checkmark Books, 2001, 112–123.

Grasso, Ella (Ella Rosa Giovanna Oliva Tambussi Grasso) (1919–1981) *politician* Born on May 10, 1919, in Windsor Locks, Connecticut,

Ella Rosa Giovanna Oliva Tambussi graduated from Mount Holyoke College with honors in 1940 and received an M.A. there in 1942. In 1942, she married Thomas A. Grasso, with whom she had two children. During World War II, she served as assistant director of research for the Connecticut office of the War Manpower Commission and became active in local Democratic politics. In 1952, she was elected to the Connecticut state legislature and served two terms. Between 1956 and 1958, she served on the Democratic National Committee. In 1958, she was elected to the first of three terms as Connecticut's secretary of state. In 1970 and again in 1972, she was elected to the U.S. Congress. In order to be accessible to her Connecticut constituents, Grasso installed a 24-hour toll-free "Ella-Phone" remarking, "It's my way of bringing government closer to the people and the people closer to government."

In 1974, Grasso was elected governor of Connecticut, making her not only the first female governor of Connecticut but also the first woman to hold a state governorship having been elected in her own right (previous women governors had been wives of former governors). She was reelected by a large majority and began a second four-year term, but resigned on New Year's Eve in 1980 because of illness. She died on February 5, 1981.

Although holding the distinction as the first woman elected governor, Grasso did little to advance feminist causes. She opposed legalized ABORTION and did not actively support affirmative action. Although she personally supported the EQUAL RIGHTS AMENDMENT, she did not campaign for it. Throughout her public life, she was known for her plain style and commitment to using government to serve people.

Further Reading

Bysiewicz, Susan. *Ella: A Biography of Ella Grasso.* Old Saybrook, Conn.: Peregrine Press, 1984.

Griffiths, Martha Wright (1912–2003) *congressperson*   Martha Wright was born on January 29, 1912, in Pierce City, Missouri. While at

the University of Missouri, she met and married Hicks W. Griffiths. They attended the University of Michigan Law School and in 1940 were the first married couple to graduate in the same year. They practiced law in Detroit, Michigan, as Griffiths and Griffiths.

Martha Griffiths won her 1948 Democratic bid to the Michigan House of Representatives. She subsequently failed in an attempt to gain a U.S. congressional seat in 1952, but Governor G. Mennen Williams appointed her as the first woman judge to the Detroit Recorder's Court. She served until 1954, when she was elected to the U.S. House of Representatives as the first Democratic woman from Michigan. In Congress, she was a member of the Joint Economic Committee of Congress, chair of the House Subcom-

Martha Griffiths, in Washington, D.C., 1970 (LIBRARY OF CONGRESS)

mittee on Fiscal Policy, and the first woman on the powerful Ways and Means Committee. One of Griffiths's most important contributions was her fight to include the word *sex* in TITLE VII OF THE CIVIL RIGHTS ACT OF 1964. She is also known for spurring the congressional vote on the EQUAL RIGHTS AMENDMENT (ERA). Griffiths mounted a discharge petition drive to free the ERA from the House Judiciary Committee, chaired by the very powerful Emanuel Celler. A discharge petition is a procedural mechanism for circumventing committee inaction and bringing a resolution directly to the floor of the House of Representatives. It is a bold move and rarely successful. Of the 829 petitions filed prior to Griffith's, only 24 bills were ever successfully discharged, and of those, only 20 passed the House. Of those 20, only two were enacted into law. Not only did Griffiths manage to convince 218 House members to sign the discharge petition, but she also got 332 of the 435 members to vote for the discharge resolution on the floor, effectively removing the ERA from the Judiciary Committee's grasp. The House and Senate approved the amendment, but eventually the ERA fell three states short of the 38 needed for ratification.

Griffiths left Congress in 1974 and subsequently served on several corporate boards. In 1984, she became the first woman lieutenant governor of Michigan and thus was the first woman to serve in all three state government branches (legislative, judicial, executive). On April 22, 2003, Martha Wright Griffiths died of pneumonia in Armada, Michigan.

Further Reading

Brett Harley, Rachel, and Betty McDowell. *Michigan Women: Firsts and Founders,* vol. II. Lansing: Michigan Women's Studies Association, 1995.

Commission on the Bicentenary by the Office of the Historian, U.S. House of Representatives. "Martha Wright Griffiths." In *Women in Congress, 1917–1990.* Washington, D.C.: GPO, 1991, 358–63.

George, Emily. *Martha W. Griffiths.* Washington, D.C.: University Press of America, 1982.

—Jolanta Macek

Grimké, Angelina (Angelina Emily Grimké Weld)

(1805–1879) *abolitionist, activist*   Born on February 20, 1805, in Charleston, South Carolina, and raised, by her sister, SARAH GRIMKÉ, Angelina Grimké's life was deeply impacted by her abhorrence of slavery and her sister's conversion to Quakerism. Growing up in a family of slave owners, Angelina witnessed firsthand the degradations of slavery. At a young age, she witnessed the whipping of a female slave her age, and from that point she sought to challenge her father's view about slavery. Left behind after Sarah moved to Philadelphia in 1829, Angelina converted to Quakerism and moved to Philadelphia to be with her sister. In 1835, she sent a letter to William Lloyd Garrison's abolitionist newspaper *the Liberator* concerning her knowledge of the reality of slavery and her stance against it ("it is my deep, solemn, deliberate conviction, that this is a cause worth dying for"). As she was the daughter of a slave owner and a southerner, Grimké's letter had great impact. Angelina and Sarah were asked by the members of the ABOLITIONIST MOVEMENT to deliver a series of public lectures on the horrors of slavery. The sisters began to publish antislavery pamphlets (*An Appeal to the Christian Women of the South, An Epistle to the Clergy of the Southern States,* and *An Address to Free Colored Americans*); however, they were criticized by the Quaker community, both for their stance on the need for immediate abolition (Quakers at this time were arguing for a gradual route to emancipation) and for the public nature of their demand. As Quakers (not simply as women), they were not supposed to publicly present their views.

Angelina left the Quakers to become active in the abolitionist movement, but as a woman who wanted to link the wrongness of slavery to the wrongness of women's subordination, she was criticized by the abolitionist community. Furthermore, Angelina and Sarah's speaking tour attracted criticism from many quarters because they were female.

In 1838, Angelina appeared before the Massachusetts State Legislature with antislavery petitions signed by 20,000 women. In the same year, she married abolitionist and social reformer Theodore Weld, with whom she worked to publish *American Slavery As It Is*, a collection of firsthand accounts of slavery. Angelina bore three children, and in the early 1850s Weld started a utopian community, Raritan Bay Union, which included a boarding school where the children of ELIZABETH CADY STANTON were educated. Grimké's public life largely ended with the birth of her children (although she and Weld did find and help raise and educate their nephew born of a Grimké brother and one of his slaves). She died on October 26, 1879.

Further Reading

Browne, Stephen H. *Angelina Grimké: Rhetoric, Identity and the Radical Imagination.* East Lansing: Michigan State University Press, 2000.

Lerner, Gerda. *Grimké Sisters from South Carolina: Pioneers for Women's Rights and Abolition* Oxford: Oxford University Press, 1998.

—Claire Curtis

Grimké, Sarah Moore (1792–1873) *abolitionist*

Sarah Grimké was born on November 26, 1792, and raised in Charleston, South Carolina, in a family of wealthy slave owners. After the death of her mother, Sarah took over the duties of raising her younger sister, ANGELINA GRIMKÉ. At an early age, Sarah recognized the wrongness of slavery, and on a trip to Philadelphia with her father, she first encountered the Quakers. She was then in her 20s, and after her return to Charleston she decided to move to Philadelphia and convert. Angelina and Sarah both started writing antislavery pamphlets (*An Appeal to the Christian Women of the South, An Epistle to the Clergy of the Southern States* and *An Address to Free Colored Americans*) and were asked to deliver a series of public lectures. Both sisters were criticized for speaking out publicly—something women of the time did not do—and they saw the parallel between their work on abolition and the issue of women's rights. Sarah also wrote *Letters on the Equality of the Sexes*, arguing that reference to biblical arguments concerning female inferiority merely reflected the patriarchal society in which the Bible was written: "I ask no favors for my sex. . . . All I ask our brethren is, that they will take their feet from off our necks, and permit us to stand upright on that ground which God designed for to occupy."

Both sisters were criticized virulently for associating abolition with what was termed "the woman question." Abolitionists accused them of diluting the essential focus on slavery, and the mainstream press and many churches demonized them as unmarried, unnatural women who were engaged in un-Christian work by violating the strictures that a woman stay at home. Despite these criticisms, both sisters continued speaking out on both issues, arguing in essence that the issue at hand was the Constitution, and whether one was a woman or a slave, the Constitution protected the rights of all. Sarah moved to the Raritan Bay Union in Raritan Bay, New Jersey, with her sister and her sister's husband, Theodore Weld, and helped raise Angelina's children and a nephew from Charleston. The Union established a progressive boarding school that promoted co-education. Sarah and Angelina worked as teachers. Sarah died on December 23, 1873.

See also ABOLITIONIST MOVEMENT.

Further Reading

Lerner, Gerda. *Grimké Sisters from South Carolina: Pioneers for Women's Rights and Abolition* Oxford: Oxford University Press, 1998.

———. *The Feminist Thought of Sarah Grimké* Oxford: Oxford University Press, 1998.

—Claire Curtis

Griswold v. Connecticut (381 U.S. 479) (1965)

Two Connecticut criminal laws were challenged in this landmark case. The first prohibited the use of contraceptives by married couples and the second made "assisting or abetting" the use of contraceptives illegal. After examining a female patient, a doctor made a recommendation for appropriate contraception. This physician worked for the Connecticut chapter of the PLANNED PARENTHOOD FEDERATION OF AMERICA. Both the physician and the head of the chapter were found guilty and fined, and this lawsuit followed. In a heated opinion, the Supreme Court found that there was a right to privacy in the marital relationship and that contraceptives and contraceptive information should be available under the First Amendment. One cannot make informed decisions without information, and thus the dissemination of that information is protected.

See also BIRTH CONTROL MOVEMENT.

Further Reading

Moskowitz, Ellen H., and Bruce Jennings, eds. *Coerced Contraception? Moral and Policy Challenges of Long-acting Birth Control.* Washington, D.C.: Georgetown University Press, 1996.

McFarlane, Deborah R., and Kenneth J. Meier. *The Politics of Fertility Control: Family Planning and Abortion Policies in the American States.* New York: Chatham House Publishers, 2001.

The OYEZ Project. "*Griswold v. Connecticut,* 381 U.S. 479 (1965)." Available online. URL: http://www.oyez.org/cases/case?case=1960–1969/1964/1964_496. Accessed on January 5, 2007.

—Marsha Hass

Grove City College v. Bell (465 U.S. 555)

(1984)　Grove City College is a private institution that refused to accept federal financial aid so that it would not be subject to federal legislation and control. However, students accepted Basic Educational Opportunity Grants. The Department of Education sent Grove City a federal form to certify that there was no discrimination in its programs. Grove City refused to sign the certification, saying none of its programs received federal funds and therefore it was not subject to the nondiscrimination requirements under TITLE IX OF THE EDUCATION AMENDMENTS OF 1972. This case significantly, albeit briefly, undermined the effectiveness of Title IX as an antidiscrimination tool. In this decision, the Supreme Court removed the applicability of Title IX in athletics programs by stating that only those programs or activities that receive direct federal financial assistance are under the umbrella of Title IX. Since most athletics programs do not directly receive federal money, they would be free of the requirement that they provide gender equity in university athletics. Congress overturned the action in 1988 with passage of the Civil Rights Restoration Act (over the veto of President Ronald Regan). The law mandates that all educational institutions that receive any type of federal financial assistance, whether direct or indirect, be bound by Title IX legislation.

Further Reading

The OYEZ Project. "*Grove City College v. Bell,* 465 U.S. 555 (1984)." Available online. URL: http://www.oyez.org/cases/case?case=1980–1989/1983/1983_82_792. Accessed on January 05, 2007.

—Marsha Hass

Guerrilla Girls　The Guerrilla Girls are a group of anonymous women who use pseudonyms (names of women artists), gorilla costumes, and vibrant pop art to reinvent FEMINISM in the arts. Beginning in 1985, the Guerrilla Girls began working to subvert the patriarchal systems evident in visual art, lobbying to see women and people of color included in what is viewed and taught as "great art," and exhibited in more venues. The group formed as a response to a Museum of Modern Art exhibition called "An International Survey of Painting and Sculpture," which included only 13 women out of the 169 artists represented. Using political posters and stickers strategically placed in havens for traditional art (such as behind the scenes at Sundance and throughout famous museums) and protests staged in gorilla masks, the Guerrilla Girls have created media events that raise awareness for women artists. They have also published a number of books such as *Bitches, Bimbos and Ballbreakers: The Guerrilla Girls' Illustrated Guide to Female Stereotypes; The Guerrilla Girls' Bedside Companion to the History of Western Art;* and *Confessions of the Guerrilla Girls,* and their posters have appeared on billboards and in magazines such as the *Nation.* They tour college campuses and attend conferences to lobby for their agenda, which includes such wide-ranging issues as the war on terror, representation of women at film awards ceremonies, representation of women and people of color within the visual art world, ABORTION, ACQUAINTANCE RAPE, and stereotypes. Many of the projects, posters, and stickers that the Guerrilla Girls have developed since their inception can be seen on their Web site at www.guerrillagirls.com.

Further Reading

Guerrilla Girls. *Bitches, Bimbos and Ballbreakers: The Guerrilla Girls' Illustrated Guide to Female Stereotypes.* New York: Penguin Books, 2003.
———. *The Guerrilla Girls Bedside Companion to the History of Western Art.* New York: Penguin Books, 1998.

—Lynda L. Hinkle

Guinier, Lani (Carol Lani Guinier) (1950–)

legal scholar, professor   Born on April 19, 1950, to a Jamaican father and a Jewish mother, Lani Guinier grew up in a working-class neighborhood in Queens, New York. Her father served as chair of the Afro-American Studies department at Harvard University. Guinier attended public schools before receiving her bachelor's degree from Radcliffe College in 1971. She attended Yale Law School, graduated with her J.D. in 1974, and immediately thereafter clerked for Damon J. Keith, the chief judge of the U.S. District Court in the Eastern District of Michigan. In 1977, Guinier took a position with the Civil Rights Division of the U.S. Department of Justice. From 1981 to 1988, she served as assistant counsel for the Legal Defense and Educational Fund of the National Association for the Advancement of

Colored People (NAACP). In 1988, she was appointed associate professor at the University of Pennsylvania Law School. As a legal scholar, Guinier researched and wrote extensively about ways to expand minority rights (particularly minority voting rights) within a democracy governed by the majority. James Madison's essays warning against the dangers to democracy when any majority tyrannizes a minority guide much of this work. In 1998, she moved to Harvard University, where she became the first black woman tenured professor.

On April 29, 1993, President Bill Clinton nominated Professor Guinier for head of the Justice Department's Civil Rights Division. Immediately, conservative opponents seized upon her scholarly writing to characterize Guinier as "the quota queen," a reference to a number of reform proposals included in her scholarship to change the "winner-take-all" electoral system in the United States. Most Americans did not get a chance to really learn about Guinier's ideas because President Clinton withdrew her nomination before Senate hearings could even get started. Guinier used a 1994 book to articulate her ideas and to comment on the political controversy surrounding her nomination. In *The Tyranny of the Majority,* she spoke of a "censorship imposed against me [that] points to a denial of serious public debate or discussion about racial fairness and justice in a true democracy." Although Guinier's ideas about fairness in a democracy often use race as an example, her theoretical framework and reform proposals are designed to assure any numerical minority group a fair chance at representation.

Professor Guinier's achievements have been recognized with numerous awards, including the Champion of Democracy Award from the National Women's Political Caucus; the Margaret Brent Women Lawyers of Achievement Award from the American Bar Association (ABA) Commission on Women in the Profession; the Rosa Parks Award from the American Association of Affirmative Action; the Sacks-Freund Award for Teaching Excellence from Harvard Law School;

and the Harvey Levin Teaching Award, given to her by her students at the University of Pennsylvania Law School. Professor Guinier continues to write and disseminate her ideas through publications and two collaborative online projects: www.minerscanary.org and www.racetalks.org. Both projects are designed to facilitate productive public discussion about race.

Further Reading

Guinier, Lani. *Lift Every Voice: Turning a Civil Rights Setback into a New Vision of Social Justice.* New York: Simon and Schuster, 1998.

———. *Tyranny of the Majority.* New York: The Free Press, 1994.

H

Hamer, Fannie Lou (1917–1977) *civil rights leader* The woman known as being "sick and tired of being sick and tired," was born Fannie Lou Townsend, on October 6, 1917, Montgomery County, Mississippi. She was the youngest of 20 children in a family of sharecroppers on a cotton plantation. Her grandparents had been slaves. Because of her fieldwork, she never received more than six years of formal education. In 1942, she married Perry Hamer, a sharecropper on a neighboring farm. The couple adopted two children.

Fannie Lou Hamer's civil rights work started in 1962 when she attended her first meeting of the Student Nonviolent Coordinating Committee (SNCC) in Ruleville, Mississippi. At that meeting, she learned for the first time that African Americans had a constitutional right to vote. When SNCC leaders asked for a volunteer to go to the courthouse to register to vote, Hamer agreed to lead a group of 17 people to register. At the courthouse, the group was arrested and severely beaten by police. Once released, she was fired and thrown off of the farm where she had worked as a timekeeper for 18 years. She said later, "I guess if I'd had any sense, I'd have been scared—but what was the point of being scared? The only thing they could do to

me was to kill me, and it seemed like they'd been trying to do that a little bit at a time ever since I could remember." Later that same year, she took a bus to Indianola, Mississippi, to try again to register. Along the way, she led those assembled in spiritual hymns (for example, "Go Tell It on the Mountain" and "This Little Light of Mine") to bolster their courage and resolve. Ultimately, she did register to vote, but was harassed by police and received repeated death threats by the Ku Klux Klan. Later in 1963, she became a field organizer for SNCC and traveled extensively around the country speaking and registering people to vote. She participated in "Freedom Summer" in 1964 and was elected vice chair of the newly founded the Mississippi Freedom Democratic Party (MFDP). The MFDP was organized to challenge Mississippi's all-white delegation to the Democratic National Convention. Hamer, along with others from the MFDP, was invited to testify before the Democratic Party's Credential's Committee. There she gave an impassioned speech about her own voter registration ordeal and equated the Democratic Party's willingness to seat the MFDP with freedom in America itself. Several television networks aired the speech on that evening's newscast, and the Credentials Committee was deluged with thousands of calls and telegrams urging them to recognize the MFDP. President Lyndon Johnson, an incumbent due to the assassination of John F. Kennedy, had the most to lose if the convention fractured, and he sent several operatives to try and negotiate with the MFDP. A compromise was brokered that gave the MFDP two seats in return for other critical concessions. Although the deal was endorsed by Martin Luther King, Jr., and the Southern Christian Leadership Conference, Hamer objected, accusing Senator Hubert Humphrey (who was then campaigning for the vice presidential nomination) of selling out 400 black people's lives for a job, "Now if you lose this job of Vice-President because you do what is right, because you help the MFDP, everything will be all right. God will take care of you. But if you take [the nomination] this way, why, you will never be able to do any good for civil rights, for poor people, for peace, or any of those things you talk about. Senator Humphrey, I'm going to pray to Jesus for you." Hamer was blocked from participating in any other negotiations and ultimately the deal fell through entirely. Two delegates from MFDP were given speaking privileges rather than full rights as delegates. However, after the convention in 1968, the party adopted a requirement that the states' delegation representation be proportional to the state's population in terms of race and one-half female. Hamer was a member of the Mississippi delegation at this convention.

Hamer's activism extended beyond voting rights to include opposition to the Vietnam War and work on behalf of Head Start, farm cooperatives, and Martin Luther King, Jr.'s Poor People's Campaign. She worked with the NATIONAL COUNCIL OF NEGRO WOMEN (NCNW) to improve life for poor minorities in Mississippi and in the 1970s, helped to convene the NATIONAL WOMEN'S POLITICAL CAUCUS in the state. Fannie Lou Hamer died of breast cancer on March 14, 1977, at the age of 59. She is buried in her hometown of Ruleville, Mississippi. By risking her own life, she helped to win full citizenship for countless other African Americans through voting rights and educational initiatives.

Harding, Florence (Florence Mabel Kling Dewolfe Harding) (1860–1924) *first lady*

Florence Mabel Kling was born in Marion, Ohio, on August 15, 1860, to Amos and Louisa Kling. Her wealthy father was a strict disciplinarian and did not hesitate to whip Florence when she displeased him. However, he saw to it that she was educated and learned about business and finance from his own experiences. Florence became increasingly rebellious as she matured. In 1880, she eloped with Henry DeWolfe and soon gave birth to a son, Marshall. Two years later, her husband abandoned her with the baby, and she returned to Marion. Her father, however, refused to take her back into his home, so she supported herself by giving piano lessons. Ultimately, her parents offered to adopt her son and raise him, but they did not offer to give her shelter as well. In 1886, she was divorced from DeWolfe. Florence continued to show interest in her son, and throughout her life, she kept a room available for him. (Marshall died young, leaving a wife and two children, and Florence looked after them from a distance as well.)

Sometime during the late 1880s, Florence met Warren G. Harding, and they were married on July 8, 1891. Harding was publisher of the *Marion Star* at the time, and marriage to Florence launched a business and political partnership. She believed that he held great potential: He was handsome, a good public speaker, and attracted followers (particularly women) wherever he went. Her demands on him, historians report, forced him to seek refuge at the Kellogg Battle Creek Sanitarium in Michigan. While he was away, the circulation manager at the paper resigned. Florence Harding went into the office to help out and ended up taking over business operations. Rather than continue to sell the *Star* from the office, she employed newspaper boys to deliver it. In the 14 years she worked for the paper, she modernized the presses, subscribed

Florence Kling Harding, ca. 1920 (LIBRARY OF
CONGRESS)

to a wire service, made sure customer accounts
were current, and hired a woman reporter—
reportedly the first in Ohio.

In 1899, Warren Harding announced as a
candidate for the state senate. Florence Harding became his campaign manager and courted
the press to his advantage. He won the seat,
and Florence accompanied him to Columbus.
A popular and successful senator, Harding was
elected as lieutenant governor before winning a
seat in the U.S. Senate in 1914. While Florence
was hospitalized for a kidney-related illness,
Harding reportedly began a long-term affair
with her best friend, Carrie Phillips. When
Florence discovered the infidelity, she briefly
considered divorce but realized that she would

lose the business and political relationships that
she had worked so hard to develop and so maintained the marriage, even though she was both
hurt and angered by his betrayal. Nonetheless,
she stayed by his side and continued to work to
advance his political fortunes.

As a senator's wife, Florence Harding
attended Senate debates on SUFFRAGE, a cause
she vigorously supported. By all accounts, she
was the first avowedly feminist first lady, one
who believed in equality for women and advocated it in her words and deeds. She encouraged
her husband to use his political positions to
advance women's causes as well. She participated actively in the Ladies of the Senate Club,
worked with the Red Cross, and adopted the
cause of wounded American soldiers as her own,
referring to them as "her boys." Although she
did not fit well in the Washington social circle,
she developed a strong friendship with the mining heiress and socialite Evalyn Walsh McLean.
One of Florence Harding's great causes included
the health and safety of animals. She gave generously to the Animal Rescue League and the Society for the Prevention of Cruelty to Animals.

When Warren Harding was mentioned for a
run for the presidency, Florence consulted with
astrologer Marcia Champrey, who reportedly
predicted that Harding would win but die in
office. Florence spoke publicly against Warren's
nomination, fearing that he would succumb to
the job at the expense of his health. Ultimately
she was convinced to support his bid for office,
and on November 2, 1920, she became the first
woman to vote for her husband for president.

As first lady, Florence continued to work
on behalf of women's rights and expanded public participation. She hosted the first women's
tennis tournament on the White House lawn,
was the first to hold press conferences for
women reporters, and was a strong advocate of
organizations like the Girl Scouts because she
believed girls should be as active and physically
fit as boys. She accepted honorary membership
in the NATIONAL WOMAN'S PARTY, although she
maintained she was a firm Republican partisan.

Mrs. Harding also brought popular culture to the White House by welcoming jazz, musical theater, and moving pictures. She reinstated the public's access to the White House, which had been closed by EDITH WILSON, and welcomed tourists back onto the grounds and into the first-floor rooms. Before her husband's inauguration, she donned a helmet and goggles and took a ride in a "hydro aeroplane"—making her the first first lady to fly.

For all of her political acumen, Florence Harding did not have good insights into personal motives or sense when corruption was brewing. She recommended a number of appointments to the president that ultimately embroiled his administration in scandal as officials were charged with profiteering, secret oil lease deals, and bootlegging. Warren Harding proved to be more formidable as a candidate than as a governing president. As word of the scandals began to leak out, he embarked on a cross-country train journey labeled "The Voyage of Understanding." The president's health deteriorated during the journey, forcing Florence to deliver remarks on his behalf.

Warren Harding died on August 2, 1923, in the Palace Hotel in San Francisco. Florence accompanied her husband's body back to the White House, where the president lay in state, and then went on to Marion, Ohio, where the burial took place. She moved from the White House to Evalyn McLean's home, but took up a more permanent residence at the Willard Hotel. In the final year of her life, she attempted to gather up as many of her husband's letters and papers as she could find. She destroyed most, leaving little to tarnish his reputation (or hers). Although Congress did not grant her the usual presidential widow's pension, she lived comfortably on the proceeds of her husband's estate and drew an annual salary as a contributing editor to the *Marion Star*.

Florence Harding died on November 21, 1924, and is buried beside her husband in Marion. Her legacy is one of activism and independence of mind in an era that did not discredit her for either. She was the first presidential wife to vote and encouraged other women to do likewise.

Further Reading

Gutin, Myra G. *The President's Partner: The First Lady in the Twentieth Century.* New York: Greenwood Press, 1989.
National First Ladies Library. *Biographies: First Ladies of the United States.* Available online. URL: http://www.firstladies.org/biographies. Accessed on January 4, 2007.
Sferrazza, Anthony Carl. *Florence Harding: The First Lady, the Jazz Age, and the Death of America's Most Scandalous President.* New York: Morrow, 1998.

Harman, Jane (1945–   ) *congressperson* Jane Harman was born Jane Lakes in New York City on June 28, 1945, and grew up in Los Angeles, where she attended public school. She earned her B.A. degree from Smith College in 1966 and her J.D. from Harvard School of Law in 1969. Harman worked as an attorney, served as special counsel to the Department of Defense, and was deputy secretary to the cabinet in the Carter White House. Harman began her career on Capitol Hill as chief counsel and staff director for the Senate Judiciary Subcommittee on Constitutional Rights. She is currently a member of the Council of Foreign Relations, the Aspen Institute, and the University of California–Los Angeles (UCLA) School of Public Affairs Advisory Board.

Harman first ran for Congress in 1992, won her seat, and served from 1993 to 1999. She left Congress to run for governor of California in 1998 but was defeated in the Democratic primary by then Lieutenant Governor Gray Davis. While out of office, she served as a regent's professor at UCLA, teaching public policy and international relations. She won back her House seat in 2000 and has been easily reelected in each subsequent election, including 2006. She is a member of the Blue Dog Coalition, a group of conservative congressional Democrats composed mostly of southerners, making her a rarity. She is also the ranking member of the House Permanent Select Committee on Intelligence.

Harman was rumored to be on 2004 Democratic presidential nominee John Kerry's "short list" for vice president, but Kerry selected North Carolina Senator John Edwards instead.

In 2006, although the Democrats regained control of the House and Harmon might have been in line for chair of the Intelligence Committee, House Speaker NANCY PELOSI passed her over in favor of Texas representative Silvestre Reyes. Harmon and Pelosi have been described as political rivals, but more likely the choice was because of an October 2006 Justice Department probe launched to investigate whether Harmon had enlisted wealthy donors and the American Israel Public Affairs Committee to lobby then House Minority Leader Pelosi to retain Harmon on the Intelligence Committee. Harmon has denied the charges, but since the Democrats can attribute some of their 2006 electoral success to the ethical lapses of Republican incumbents in the 109th Congress, even the allegation was enough to remove Harmon from consideration.

Further Reading

Barone, Michael. *The Almanac of American Politics.* Washington, D.C.: National Journal Group, 2006.

"Harman, Jane F." In *Biographical Directory of the United States Congress, 1774–present.* Available online. URL: http://bioguide.congress.gov/scripts/biodisplay.pl?index=H000213. Accessed on January 8, 2007.

"Representative Jane Herman (CA)." In *Project Vote Smart.* Available online. URL: http://votesmart.org/bio.php?can_id=BC032299. Accessed on January 8, 2007.

—Angela Kouters

Harriman, Pamela (Pamela Beryl Digby Churchill Harriman) (1920–1997) *ambassador, political fundraiser*

Pamela Harriman's life story, beginning in her homeland of England, prepared her for a successful career as a socialite, fundraiser, and ambassador. Born Pamela Beryl Digby on March 20, 1920, in Hampshire, England, she was a member of an aristocratic family. Her father was the 11th baron Digby, and her mother was the daughter of a baron. From the early age of 19, Pamela began eschewing the lingering Victorian notions of womanhood that limited a woman's goals to marriage. On October 4, 1939, she married Randolph Churchill, and as Winston Churchill's daughter-in-law, she played an essential role in entertaining many of the world's top leaders. As her marriage to Randolph soured, however, she began romantic liaisons with some of the world's most powerful men, many of whom were also married. The couple finally divorced, and Pamela subsequently had the marriage annulled.

Pamela Churchill had numerous romantic liaisons and another marriage and divorce before marrying one of her longtime paramours, Averell Harriman, on September 27, 1971. Harriman, former governor of New York, lifelong Democrat, and millionaire, died in 1986, leaving his wife Pamela $75 million. Pamela Harriman used her wealth and accumulated political connections to continue her husband's passion to elect Democratic Party candidates.

Key Democratic Party leaders like President Bill Clinton credit Harriman with the rebirth of the Democrats in the 1990s. She began a political action committee (PamPAC) and established her house in Georgetown as the epicenter for Democratic Party strategy sessions. She also engineered the successful campaigns of key black Democrats and aided Clinton's presidential victory in 1992. As a sign of gratitude, the Clinton Administration awarded her the ambassadorship to France. The French embraced Harriman with open arms, welcoming her fluent French skills and her efforts to soothe tension in Franco-American over issues such as NATO expansion, the Middle East, and trade. Harriman died on February 5, 1997, while still serving as U.S. ambassador to France.

Further Reading

Smith Sally B. *The Life of Pamela Churchill Harriman: Reflected Glory.* New York: Simon & Schuster Inc., 1996.

—Hollis France

Harris, Katherine (1957–) *congressperson*
Katherine Harris was born on April 5, 1957, in
Key West, Florida. She received her bachelor's
degree from Agnes Scott College and earned an
executive master's degree from the Kennedy
School of Government in 1997. Before entering
politics, Katherine Harris was vice president of
a commercial real estate firm and a marketing
executive at IBM.

Harris entered politics in 1994 by winning
election to the Florida Senate. As Florida's secretary of state (1999–2002), she presided over
the 2000 presidential election controversy, even
though she had served as candidate George W.
Bush's campaign cochair for Florida since October 1999. Prior to the election, the secretary of
state's office hired a private firm to purge the
voter registration rolls of felons. Thousands of
individuals, many of them African-American
voters, were incorrectly removed from the voter
lists and therefore ineligible to vote in 2000. It
was Harris who certified that Republican candidate George W. Bush had defeated Al Gore in
the popular vote of Florida (based on a series of
vote counts, some original and some recounts)
and thus certified the Republican slate of electors. Her ruling was challenged and overturned
on appeal by the Florida Supreme Court, but
this was reversed by U.S. Supreme Court, which
awarded the presidency to Bush in a 5-4 decision (*Bush v. Gore*, 2000).

In 2002, Harris ran for the congressional
district vacated by retiring Republican representative Dan Miller and won the seat by a 10-point
margin; she was reelected in 2004 by a comfortable margin. Harris considered running for the
seat of retiring Senator Bob Graham in 2004 but
was reportedly urged not do so by staff at the
Bush White House who were promoting Secretary of Housing and Urban Development Mel
Martinez to run. (Martinez narrowly defeated
challenger Betty Castor.)

On June 7, 2005, Harris announced her
intention to run for the Republican nomination
to challenge incumbent Democrat senator Bill
Nelson in the 2006 election. Although the state

Republican Party did not endorse her candidacy,
and Florida governor Jeb Bush and White House
strategist Karl Rove refused to endorse her
candidacy, Harris persisted. Her campaign was
plagued by ethics investigations related to allegedly illegal campaign contributions given by
Mitchell Wade, a defense contractor. Wade pled
guilty to laundering over $32,000 in campaign
contributions through his employees in order to
evade the contribution limits. Harris trailed in
the polls throughout the 2006 Senate race and
was soundly defeated in November.

Further Reading
Barone, Michael. *The Almanac of American Politics.*
Washington, D.C.: National Journal Group, 2006.
"Harris, Katherine." In *Biographical Directory of the
United States Congress, 1774–present.* Available
online. URL: http://bioguide.congress.gov/scripts/
biodisplay.pl?index=H0001035. Accessed on Jan-
uary 8, 2007.

—Angela Kouters

Harris, Patricia (Patricia Roberts Harris)
(1924–1985) *secretary of health, education, and
welfare* Described by former president Jimmy
Carter as "a cabinet officer extraordinaire" who
was "strong, competent, tough, [and] obsessed
with concern for the poor, the bereft, the inarticulate, the elderly, the homeless, the weak, and
the student," Patricia Roberts Harris proved
many times over to be an able governmental
administrator, an astute attorney, and a shrewd
policy maker. Emerging from a humble background, Harris achieved several historical firsts
as an African-American woman: the first
appointed as an ambassador, the first to hold a
deanship of an American law school, the first to
serve as a delegate to the United Nations, the
first to hold an appointment in a president's
cabinet, and the first to hold a second presidential cabinet appointment.

Harris was born on May 31, 1924, in Matoon,
Illinois, to Bert Fitzgerald, a pullman car waiter,
and Hildren Brodie Roberts, an actuarial clerk

for an insurance company; she was raised by her mother. Harris's passion for those considered "marginal" can be partially explained by her early exposure to racism. She attended Howard University, where she graduated summa cum laude with an A.B. degree in political science and economics in 1945. While at Howard, Harris became involved in the burgeoning civil rights movement by leading a group of students to stage sit-ins and demonstrations at segregated restaurants and department stores. After leaving Howard, Harris enrolled at the University of Chicago, earning a master's degree in industrial relations.

In 1949, Harris returned to Washington, D.C., to further her graduate studies at American University, during which time she worked as assistant director of the American Council on Human Rights. From 1953 to 1959, she served as executive director of the second oldest national black sorority, Delta Sigma Theta. Harris organized the first national business office for the sorority and, as one of its lobbyists, was responsible for the organization's national lobbying campaign that culminated in the passage of the CIVIL RIGHTS ACT OF 1964 and the Voting Rights Act 1965. In 1955, Harris met and married attorney William Beasley Harris, who encouraged her to pursue a legal career. She entered George Washington University's law school in 1957 and graduated at the top of her class three years later. After graduation, she worked briefly in the Criminal Division of the U.S. Department of Justice and later as a faculty member of Howard University's law school. Harris's advocacy work on behalf of blacks, women, and the poor intensified as she began serving as cochair of the National Women's Committee for Civil Rights—an appointment made by President John F. Kennedy in 1963.

Beginning an impressive list of firsts, in 1965 Harris was named U.S. ambassador to Luxembourg and became the first African-American woman named an American envoy. In 1966, she became the first African-American woman to serve as a delegate to the United Nations. After completing her diplomat duties, Harris returned to Howard University as the dean of the law school—another first for an African American woman—but resigned within 30 days after unresolved tensions between protesting law students and the university's president. She later joined a prestigious D.C. law firm and simultaneously held several board appointments, including service on the board of directors of the National Association for the Advancement of Colored People (NAACP) Legal Defense Fund, the American Civil Liberties Union, the national YWCA, the Twentieth Century Fund, and Chase Manhattan.

In 1971, Harris was appointed chair of the Democratic Party's Credentials Committee for its 1972 convention and was charged with the responsibility of enforcing newly adopted rules designed to encourage greater participation from the young, minorities, and women. In 1977, President Jimmy Carter appointed her secretary of housing and urban development (HUD), making Harris the first African-American woman to hold a cabinet-level position. During her tenure as secretary of HUD, Harris instituted several new policy initiatives that were designed to fulfill the promises made to the poor under President Lyndon Johnson's Great Society program. Specifically, she was able to increase subsidized housing for the poor and provide millions of dollars for renovating and upgrading neighborhoods that were scheduled for "slum clearance." She also instituted the Urban Development Action Grant program as an incentive for bringing economically stable businesses to urban areas. Harris addressed housing discrimination by establishing regulations with the Federal Mortgage Association that would allow millions of low-income families to obtain first-time mortgages.

In 1979, Patricia Roberts Harris was appointed to the largest cabinet post, secretary of the Department of Health Education and Welfare (HEW), becoming the first African-American woman appointed to two cabinet-level positions. As secretary of HEW, she was able to protect many of the social programs that were targeted for budget cuts. In addition, it was during Harris's tenure that HEW became more attentive to women's colleges and the concerns of women students. She assigned a special assistant to serve as a liaison with women's colleges, and through her work with those colleges she became instrumental in pushing for the passage of funding for women's sports under TITLE IX OF THE EDUCATION AMENDMENTS OF 1972. HEW was renamed the Department of Health and Human Services (HHS) in 1980 when Congress established a separate Department of Education. Because of this reorganization, Harris was the first to serve as secretary of HHS. To her credit, she was noted for restoring order and direction to two disorganized and demoralized federal agencies. She served as secretary of HEW until Carter's loss to Ronald Reagan in the 1980 presidential election.

In 1982, Harris made an unsuccessful bid for the mayorship of Washington, D.C. Despite a long career of advocating for blacks, the poor, and women, Harris was characterized as an aloof, middle-class black whose real concern was achievement, not social change. As a result, she lost to incumbent Marion Barry after a bitter campaign. In 1983, Harris returned to George Washington University law school as a full-time law professor. She held this position until her death from cancer on March 23, 1985.

Further Reading

Bigelow, Carlisle Barbara. "Patricia Roberts Harris" *Contemporary Black Biography: Profiles from the International Black Community,* vol. 2. Detroit: Gale Research, 1992. Available online. URL: http://galenet.galegroup.com

Carter, Jimmy President. "Eulogy for Patricia Roberts Harris." *Howard Law Journal* 29 (1985): 415–416.

Harris, Patricia Roberts. "The Undeveloped Resource." In *Rebels in Law: Voices in History of Black Women Lawyers,* edited by Jay Clay Smith, Jr. Ann Arbor: University of Michigan Press, 1998, 186–189.

—Rose M. Harris

Harrison, Anna Symmes (Anna Tuthill Symmes Harrison) (1775–1864) *first lady*

Anna Tuthill Symmes was born to John Cleves and Anna Tuthill Symmes on July 25, 1775, in Sussex County, New Jersey; her mother died the following year. Her father, an officer in the Continental Army, determined that he could not raise her himself, and so she was raised by her maternal grandparents on Long Island. She received an excellent education and is the first first lady to be formally educated. When she was 14, she rejoined her father on his land near Cincinnati. In 1795, at the age of 20, she met and married William Henry Harrison, an officer in the American Revolutionary War; together they had 10 children.

William Henry Harrison rose to the rank of general and achieved fame after defeating Chief Tecumseh at the Battle of Tippecanoe in 1811. At the time, he was serving as the governor of the Indiana Territory. In 1814, the Harrisons' oldest

Anna Tuthill Symmes Harrison (LIBRARY OF CONGRESS)

child was married, and their last child was born. Harrison was elected to Congress in 1816 and departed for Washington leaving, Anna and the children behind. He returned to the territories with his election to the Ohio state legislature in 1819, but left again for Washington in 1824 after being elected to the U.S. Senate from Ohio. Harrison first campaigned for the presidency during the election of 1836, but a crowded field left him little chance for victory. In 1840, Harrison was the sole candidate for the Whig party on a ticket with a southern Democrat, John Tyler. Harrison was a popular military hero, and his campaign emphasized his log-cabin roots.

Anna Harrison was 65 years old when William Henry Harrison won the presidency. In relatively poor health and despondent over the deaths of several of their children over the previous decade, she did not immediately accompany her husband to Washington for the inaugural. Instead, she designated her daughter-in-law, Jane Irwin Harrison, to serve as hostess until she arrived. However, she never assumed her official duties as first lady since President Harrison died within a month of taking office, the victim of pneumonia contracted on the day of his inaugural. In 1855, Anna moved in with her only surviving son, John Scott Harrison (father to future president Benjamin Harrison), in North Bend, Ohio, where she lived until her death on February 25, 1864.

Although she never actually assumed the duties of first lady, Anna Harrison nevertheless achieved many firsts among those holding the position. She was the first to be formally educated as a child, the oldest woman to become first lady, and the first to become widowed while her husband was in office. As a result, she was the first former first lady to receive a pension and the first to be the grandmother of a future president, Benjamin Harrison (1889–93).

Further Reading

National First Ladies Library. *Biographies: First Ladies of the United States.* Available online. URL: http://www.firstladies.org/biographies. Accessed on January 4, 2007.

Shulman, Holly Cowan. "Anna Tuthill Symmes Harrison." In *American First Ladies: Their Lives and Their Legacy,* 2d edition, edited by Lewis L. Gould, 57–64. New York: Routledge, 2001.

Harrison, Caroline (Caroline Lavinia Scott Harrison) (1832–1892) *first lady*

Caroline (Carrie) Lavinia Scott was born on October 1, 1832, in Oxford, Ohio. She was the third of five children born to Miami University professor John Witherspoon Scott and Mary Potts Neal Scott. The family valued education highly, and Carrie loved literature and the arts. She attended the Oxford Female Institute in 1852, an institution founded by her father, and studied music, English literature, drama, art, and painting. She took over for a piano teacher who fell ill midsemester and continued teaching at Oxford after she graduated in 1853.

Carrie Scott met Benjamin Harrison, one of her father's students and the grandson of President William Henry Harrison, while she was in college. Following his graduation in 1852, he moved to Cincinnati to study law but returned to marry Caroline on October 20, 1853. They began their married life on the Harrison family farm in North Bend, Ohio. In early 1854, Benjamin was admitted to the bar, and they moved to Indianapolis, where he set up a practice. Times were lean until he was asked to join a practice with William Wallace, a candidate for the Marian County clerkship who needed help in the office while he campaigned. The partnership prospered, and the Harrisons moved to a larger house and hired help for Caroline, her physical condition somewhat weakened by two births (Russell Benjamin, b. 1854; Mary Scott, b. 1858). Caroline devoted increasing attention to her activities with First Presbyterian Church, where she taught Bible study and directed the choir, and to charitable causes such as the Indianapolis Orphan's Asylum. In 1860, she was appointed to the board of managers, a seat she held until her death.

As Benjamin Harrison's law practice flourished, he turned his attention to politics. In quick succession, he was elected city attorney in 1857, secretary of the Republican State Central Committee the following year, and reporter of the state supreme court in 1860. The onset of the Civil War brought changes to both Harrisons. Benjamin became a colonel in the Indiana regiment of the Union army in the summer of 1862, while Caroline supported the war effort through the Ladies Patriotic Association and the Ladies Sanitary Commission. On at least two occasions, she and the children visited Benjamin's encampment in Tennessee and Kentucky. On an extended furlough and visit with family in Pennsylvania in 1864, all four of the Harrison family fell ill with scarlet fever. They recovered, but Caroline took the children back to Indianapolis, and Benjamin rejoined his troops. He returned to Indianapolis to a hero's welcome in June 1865, but Caroline worried that his reputation would lead to progressively higher political office and lengthier separations. Harrison promised to turn his attentions to his law practice and his family, and he did so. Within five years, he was one of the most prominent attorneys in the state. They built a larger house, and Caroline Harrison supervised its design and construction. She entertained, founded a literary circle for intellectual stimulation, took art classes, and continued her painting.

In 1872, when Benjamin expressed interest in seeking the Indiana state governorship, Caroline supported his decision. Although he lost the nomination, he was tapped as the Republican nominee in 1876, ultimately losing in the general election. By this time, Caroline had made her peace with Benjamin's extended absences during campaigns and had grown to enjoy her own public role as the "candidate's wife." On a vacation in 1877, the couple called upon President and Mrs. Rutherford B. Hayes, and two years later, the Hayes enjoyed the Harrisons' hospitality on a visit to Indiana. Benjamin Harrison later stumped for James Garfield and earned a cabinet post, but declined in favor of the U.S. Senate seat he had won in 1880. Caroline and daughter Mary (now 22) moved to Washington and took up residence in a boarding house. Her position as a senator's wife gave Caroline access to Washington society, even though she did not entertain much herself due to her health. Benjamin Harrison lost his bid for reelection to Democratic-engineered gerrymandering, but he emerged two years later as a contender for the Republican presidential nomination. Presidential election strategies of this era were characterized as "front-porch" campaigns, as the candidate and his wife received guests and potential voters at their home rather than stumping around the country. Thousands of people trooped through their Indianapolis home.

Benjamin Harrison's election as president in 1888 focused press and public attention on Caroline. Although she had been entertaining within political circles for some time, she was unprepared for the volume of requests and visitors that followed them to Washington and relied on her daughter Mary and her daughter-in-law to assist as hostesses in the White House. She ended the custom of handshaking in her reception lines and brought dancing and drink back to the White House. Substantively, she divided her attentions beyond the White House to Washington charities such as the Garfield Hospital and the Washington City Orphan Asylum. She undertook a campaign to renovate and enlarge the White House with an overtly political strategy, lobbying for support by inviting congressmen and journalists to inspect the White House and soliciting the help of former first ladies in making the case. Architect Fred Owen drew three plans—one for an entirely new building, one for changes to the present structure, and one that called for two new wings to be added with a botanical conservatory connecting the two. Unsuccessful in getting Congress to agree with her choice of the third set of plans, Caroline was forced to undertake more modest restorations to the existing building. She focused on ridding the building of rats, modernizing the kitchen facilities, installing bathrooms, and, most controversially, adding electric lights. In addition, she created an inventory of the contents of the White House, detailing the history of each piece of furniture and art. She restored as much of the White House china as she could find and started the extensive collection of china of former first ladies that still exists today.

On matters social and political, Caroline Harrison was more active with regard to women's interests than any of her predecessors. She worked to expand educational opportunities for women, including raising funds for a medical school at Johns Hopkins University on the condition that it admit women. She helped to found the DAUGHTERS OF THE AMERICAN REVOLUTION (DAR) in 1890 and served as its first president-general. In this capacity, she gave a number of public lectures urging people to remember the essential role that women had played in the founding of the nation. The DAR promoted citizenship education and worked to perpetuate the memory of the American Revolution.

During much of her stay in the White House, Caroline suffered from a variety of illnesses, many respiratory in nature. In spring 1892, she was diagnosed with tuberculosis. Although she briefly recovered at a retreat in the Adirondack Mountains, she suffered a setback in September and asked to be returned to the White House. She died on October 25, 1892. It was an election year, and out of respect for the president's lady, neither Benjamin Harrison nor Grover Cleveland actively campaigned for the presidency. Two weeks following her death, Harrison lost his bid for reelection.

Although not an activist in the women's movement, Caroline Harrison nonetheless was willing to lend her name and her position to various causes in the advance of women's education and recognition of their role in building the nation. This has given her an enduring legacy.

Further Reading

Mayo, Edith P. "Caroline Harrison." In *The Smithsonian Book of First Ladies: Their Lives, Times, and Issues.* New York: Henry Holt and Company, 1996.
Means, Marianne. *The Women in the White House.* New York: Random House, 1963.
National First Ladies Library. *Biographies: First Ladies of the United States.* Available online. URL: http://www.firstladies.org/biographies. Accessed on January 4, 2007.
Schneider, Dorothy, and Carl J. Schneider. "Caroline (Carrie) Lavinia Scott Harrison" *First Ladies: A Biographical Dictionary.* New York: Checkmark Books, 2001, 147–154.

Harris v. Forklift Systems, Inc. (510 US 17)

(1993)   In 1986, Teresa Harris sued her former employer, Forklift Systems, Inc., under TITLE VII OF THE CIVIL RIGHTS ACT OF 1964 for an abusive and hostile environment that she alleged was created by the company president, Charles Hardy. She charged that Hardy often insulted her because of her gender and made her the target of unwanted sexual innuendos. For example, Hardy had told Harris on several occasions, in the presence of other employees, "You're a woman, what do you know" and "We need a man as the rental manager." Hardy occasionally asked Harris and other female employees to get coins from his front pants pocket, and he threw objects on the ground in front of Harris and other women and asked them to pick the objects up. Harris claimed that Hardy's sexually harassing conduct caused her to suffer psychological distress, with symptoms similar to post-traumatic stress disorder. When Harris threatened to resign, Hardy said he "was only kidding" and apologized. However, when the behavior continued, Harris left the company and filed suit with the EQUAL EMPLOYMENT OPPORTUNITY COMMISION. The company maintained that while Hardy's actions were boorish, Ms. Harris had not suffered any material damages and therefore did not have cause to sue under Title VII.

The issue was whether the actions were sufficiently severe and pervasive to constitute an impermissible hostile environment under Title VII. The district court, while agreeing that Hardy was vulgar, that Harris had been the subject of a continuing pattern of sex-based harassment, that Harris had been offended by the conduct, and that the conduct would have offended a "reasonable manager," nonetheless concluded that Harris had not suffered a serious psychological injury and therefore Hardy's conduct did not create a hostile work environment. The case was dismissed. Upon appeal, the Sixth Circuit Court affirmed the district finding. However, the U.S. Supreme Court, in a unanimous decision, ruled that while conduct that is merely offensive does not violate Title VII, the law does provide protection long before the impermissible conduct leads to severe psychological distress. In other words, the protections afforded by Title VII begin *before* the harassment leads to a psychological break. Therefore, a plaintiff alleging SEXUAL HARASSMENT need not demonstrate any psychological harm. The conduct must be shown to create an objectively hostile environment, one that a "reasonable person" would find hostile or abusive. The Court did not go so far as to adopt the "reasonable woman" or "reasonable victim" standard promoted by some feminists.

Further Reading

Gregory, Raymond F. *Unwelcome and Unlawful: Sexual Harassment in the American Workplace.* Ithaca, N.Y.: Cornell University Press, 2004.

MacKinnon, Catherine. *Sexual Harassment of Working Women.* New Haven, Conn.: Yale University Press, 1979.

—Marsha Hass

Harris v. McRae, (448 U.S. 297) (1980)

In 1976, Congress passed the HYDE AMENDMENT, which prohibited using federal Medicaid funds to pay for abortion except to save a woman's life. Cora McRae, a pregnant Medicaid recipient who wished to terminate her pregnancy, challenged the amendment and took action against PATRICIA ROBERTS HARRIS, secretary of health and human services. McRae, on behalf of other indigent women similarly situated and several hospitals providing abortion services, sued on the grounds that the Hyde Amendment violated the right to

privacy, the due-process clause of the Fifth Amendment, and the religion clauses of the First Amendment. Medicaid is a cost-sharing program involving the states and the federal government. After Congress refused to pay the federal share, the question evolved into whether the state could do the same.

In a 5-4 ruling, the U.S. Supreme Court held that the Hyde Amendment was constitutional and that states participating in the Medicaid program were not obligated to fund medically necessary abortions under Title XIX of the Social Security Act. The Court found that a woman's freedom of choice did not carry with it "a constitutional entitlement to the financial resources to avail herself of the full range of protected choices." The Court further ruled that because the equal-protection clause was not a source of substantive rights and because poverty did not qualify as a "suspect classification," the Hyde Amendment did not violate the Fifth Amendment. Finally, the Court held that the coincidence of the funding restrictions of the statute with tenets of the Roman Catholic Church did not constitute an establishment of religion. Feminists decried the decision as one that created two classes of women: those entitled to rights under the Constitution because they could afford to pay for them and those who were not entitled to the freedom of choice because they were not using their own monies.

—Marsha Hass

Hart, Melissa (1962–) *congressperson*

Melissa Hart was born on April 4, 1962, in North Hills, Pennsylvania, and graduated from North Allegheny High School and Washington Jefferson College. After earning her J.D. from the University of Pittsburgh School of Law (1987), she practiced law for a major Pittsburgh law firm. Hart is the first Republican woman to represent Pennsylvania at the federal level. Prior to her election to the U.S. House of Representatives in 2000, she served in the Pennsylvania State

Senate (1991–2000), where she chaired the Finance Committee.

Widely viewed as an upcoming star within the new class of Republicans, Hart had a conservative voting record in Congress, particularly on reproductive rights issues. She was a sponsor of the Unborn Victims of Violence Act and the original sponsor of the Born-Alive Infants Protection Act. In 2005, Hart won an appointment on the House Ways and Means Committee. She also played an active role in the race for House majority leader following the resignation of Congressman Tom Delay. As a top whip for Rep. John Boehner (R-OH), she worked to secure votes for him in the race in his successful bid for the position in February 2006. Hart has also played a leadership role within the Republican National Party. In 2004, she was appointed cochair of the Platform Committee for the Republican National Convention. With U.S. senator Bill Frist, she helped to craft the Republican Party platform.

In 2006, Hart was challenged by Democrat Jason Altmire, a 38-year-old health care professional. Hart's seat was considered "safe" going into the election, but as the election neared, her poll numbers sagged and her challenger's popularity surged. Altmire defeated Hart for the seat, by a margin of 52 to 48 percent. Hart has recently been mentioned as a candidate for the U.S. Senate when Senator Arlen Specter retires.

Further Reading

Barone, Michael. *The Almanac of American Politics.* Washington, D.C.: National Journal Group, 2006.
"Hart, Melissa A." In *Biographical Directory of the United States Congress, 1774–present.* Available online. URL: http://bioguide.congress.gov/scripts/biodisplay.pl?index=H001033. Accessed on January 8, 2007.

—Angela Kouters

Hartford Accident and Indemnity Co. v. Insurance Commissioner of the Commonwealth of PA (482 A.2d 542) (1984)

This is an important case because it challenged the notion that gender could be the basis for insurance premiums in the automobile casualty realm. The challenge was brought initially by a 26-year-old male who objected to being charged $148 more than a similarly situated female based on actuarial data that showed men had more accidents than females. The Supreme Court pointed out that using gender as the main criterion for setting rates was unjust discrimination and had nothing to do with actual risk of any particular driver. The Court observed that how often and how far a car was driven could be much more predictive than the driver's gender. While insurance companies are allowed to set rates based on risks, those rates may not unjustly discriminate. This case was the beginning of a series of cases challenging gender-based rates and payouts.

Further Reading

Hoff, Joan. *Law, Gender, and Injustice: A Legal History of the United States.* New York: New York University Press, 1991.

—Marsha Hass

Hayes, Lucy (Lucy Ware Webb Hayes)

(1831–1889) *first lady*   Lucy Ware Webb was born on August 28, 1831, in Chillicothe, Ohio, to Dr. James Webb and Maria Cook Webb; she was the only daughter of three children born to the couple. The family was prosperous, and both parents were strong temperance advocates. In 1833, James Webb died of cholera. In 1844, the family moved to Delaware, Ohio, where Lucy attended prep school and sat in on college classes at Ohio Wesleyan University, even though women were not officially permitted to enroll. She graduated from Cincinnati Wesleyan Female College in 1850. She met Rutherford B. Hayes shortly before her graduation, and they were married on December 3, 1852. The couple remained close to both their families and lived with various family members until moving into their own home in 1854. The Rutherfords had seven children, five surviving to adulthood.

Lucy Hayes's temperance background and her college degree both suggest that she might have become active in the movement for women's rights, but she did not play that role. Her sister-in-law, Fanny Platt, encouraged her to become active in public affairs and took her to a lecture by LUCY STONE. (Platt died in childbirth two years later.) Lucy's interest in politics was stimulated by the antislavery principles of the Republican Party, and she encouraged her husband to enter politics, but the Civil War delayed this. Rutherford joined the Ohio Volunteer Infantry and was wounded in active duty several times over the course of the war. In 1863, he was posted to West Virginia, and the family followed. Lucy mothered the officers and enlisted men, mending their clothing and writing for those with limited educations. In 1864, Colonel Hayes's Ohio supporters nominated him for Congress; although he did not campaign, he was elected in October 1864. Hayes left the army a brigadier general and took his seat in Congress in 1865. Lucy did not accompany him to Washington but visited as often as she could. In 1867, she encouraged him to run for the governorship of Ohio. Lucy was actively involved in her husband's career and in reform movements. She actively worked to raise money to found a home for soldier's orphans and supported her husband's efforts at prison reform but declined to speak publicly in favor of temperance or women's SUFFRAGE. Activists and social reformers saw her as the embodiment of the "new woman." Despite having a college degree, however, she refused to advocate for women in higher education and the professions.

After Rutherford served two terms as governor and conducted an unsuccessful Senate campaign, he and Lucy returned to Ohio. A third term as governor in 1875 put him in line for the Republican nomination for president in 1876. A crowded field left the outcome of the election in doubt for months before Congress declared Hayes the president. Lucy and Rutherford learned the news as they were making their way to Washington.

Lucy Webb Hayes, 1877 (LIBRARY OF CONGRESS)

Lucy Hayes took up her position as first lady at a time when gender roles were in flux. Suffragists and women's rights advocates looked expectantly to the White House for support in their efforts to expand opportunities for women in all spheres of life. Despite Lucy's obvious interest in politics and strong principled convictions, she did not use her position to advance the cause of women. Instead, she took up the traditional duties associated with the president's lady.

As had been their custom since marriage, Rutherford and Lucy Hayes forbade alcohol to be served in their home. Although Rutherford made the decision, Lucy was labeled "Lemonade Lucy" as a result. Card playing and dancing were also banned at the White House. Lucy enlisted a number of female relatives to assist her in entertaining, but the presidential couple ended the practice of large evening receptions open to the general public that had taken their toll on the White House, replacing these occasions with opportunities for the public to tour the White House and meet with the president. Lucy gave women's luncheons and began the tradition of hosting receptions for the diplomatic corps. During the Hayes tenure, indoor plumbing was installed in the White House, along with the first telephone. Lucy and Rutherford Hayes also initiated the annual Easter egg roll, a tradition that continues today.

Upon Rutherford's retirement, he and Lucy returned to Ohio, where she continued to serve as president of the Methodist Episcopal Women's Home Missionary Society. She refused to endorse woman suffrage and worked against liberalizing immigration policies. Eight years after leaving the White House, Lucy Hayes suffered a pair of strokes and died on June 25, 1889. Her husband died three years later.

Further Reading

Mayo, Edith P. "Lucy Hayes." In *The Smithsonian Book of First Ladies: Their Lives, Times, and Issues*, edited by Edith P. Mayo, 117–121. New York: Henry Holt and Company, 1996.

National First Ladies Library. *Biographies: First Ladies of the United States*. Available online. URL: http://www.firstladies.org/biographies. Accessed on January 4, 2007.

Schneider, Dorothy and Carl J. Schneider. "Lucy Ware Webb Hayes" *First Ladies: A Biographical Dictionary*. New York: Checkmark Books, 2001, 124–132.

Height, Dorothy Irene (1912–) activist, president of the National Council of Negro Women

Dorothy Height is best known for her work in the civil rights movement. She was born on March 24, 1912, in Richmond, Virginia, and later quickly established herself as a dedicated student. Her oratory skills earned her a scholarship to New York University, where she earned a degree in education and a master's degree in educational psychology. She did further postgraduate work at Columbia University and the New York School of Social Work. She is the recipient of nineteen honorary doctorates from colleges and universities.

While working as a caseworker for the welfare department in New York in 1937, Dr. Height joined the NATIONAL COUNCIL OF NEGRO WOMEN (NCNW). That same year, she began work with the Harlem YWCA and quickly advanced to a position with the national YWCA, where she was active in developing its leadership training and interracial and ecumenical education programs. During the YWCA's 1946 convention, Height coordinated the introduction of a policy to integrate its facilities nationwide, and she was elected national interracial education secretary of the organization. In 1965, the YWCA named Dr. Height the first director of its new Center for Racial Justice, and five years later, the YWCA National Convention adopted the One Imperative: "To thrust our collective power towards the elimination of racism, wherever it exists by any means necessary."

Height served as the president of NCNW for over 40 years, from 1957 to 1998. Working closely with Martin Luther King, Jr., Roy Wilkins, Whitney Young, A. Philip Randolph, and others. Height participated in virtually all of the major civil and human rights events throughout the 1950s and 1960s. She has received numerous awards in recognition of her tireless efforts. In 1989, President Ronald Reagan presented her with the Citizens Medal Award for distinguished service to the country; in 1994, President Clinton presented her with the Presidential Medal of Freedom; and in 2004, she was awarded the Congressional Gold Medal. In honoring Dorothy Height, Senator Hillary Clinton said: "So today we honor a hero. A hero of the civil rights movement, a hero of the women's movement, a hero on behalf of African Americans and particularly the black family reunion movement, a woman who embodies everything that makes our nation great. We do this today in some small measure to thank you for a life of service and dedication and to recognize that we are all richer and better because Dr. Dorothy Height passed our way."

Further Reading

Height, Dorothy. *Open Wide the Freedom Gates: A Memoir.* New York: Public Affairs Press, 2003.

Herseth Sandlin, Stephanie (1970–) *congressperson*

Stephanie Herseth was born on December 30, 1970, and raised on her family's farm near Houghton, South Dakota. There is a legacy of public service in her family: Her paternal grandfather, Ralph Herseth, was governor; her paternal grandmother, Lorna Herseth, was South Dakota's secretary of state; and her father, Lars Herseth, served for 20 years in the state legislature and ran for governor in 1986.

Herseth received her undergraduate, graduate, and law degrees from Georgetown University. She ran for South Dakota's lone U.S. House of Representatives seat in the 2002 election but lost to Bill Janklow. In early 2004, Janklow resigned his seat after he was convicted of manslaughter in a traffic-accident case, triggering a special election. Herseth was selected as the Democratic nominee, and she beat GOP candidate Larry Diedrich with 51 percent of the vote in the election held on June 1, 2004. The regular election in November was a rematch, and Herseth was elected to a full term with 53.4 percent of the vote. Herseth is the first woman in South Dakota state history to win a full term in Congress.

Herseth is widely regarded as a moderate in Congress and walks a fine line between the positions adopted by the national Democratic Party and the more conservative makeup of her constituency in South Dakota. She is a member of the Blue Dog Coalition and has the support of the National Rifle Association. She supports ABORTION rights, research into renewable energy sources, and farm supports. In the 109th Congress, she served on the House Committee on Agriculture, the House Committee on Veterans Affairs, and the Committee on Resources. She was reelected in 2006. In March 2007, she married Max Sandlin, a former congressman from Texas, and took the name Herseth Sandlin.

Further Reading

Barone, Michael. *The Almanac of American Politics.* Washington, D.C.: National Journal Group, 2006.

"Herseth Sandlin, Stephanie." In *Biographical Directory of the United States Congress, 1774–present.* Available online. URL: http://bioguide.congress.gov/scripts/biodisplay.pl?index=H001037. Accessed on January 8, 2007.

"Representative Stephanie Herseth." In *Project Vote Smart.* Available online. URL: http://votesmart.org/bio.php?can_id=MSD24249. Accessed on January 8, 2007.

—Angela Kouters

Hill, Anita Faye (1956–) *lawyer*

Anita Hill was born in rural Oklahoma on July 30, 1956. She graduated with honors from the University of Oklahoma and received her law degree from Yale University School of Law, one of 16 African Americans in a class of 160. She worked on the staff of the EQUAL EMPLOYMENT OPPORTUNITY COMMISSION (EEOC) in Washington, D.C. (1981–83), before joining the law faculty of Oral Roberts University and, later, the University of Oklahoma.

On October 6, 1991, Anita Hill's life was dramatically and irrevocably changed when her charges of SEXUAL HARASSMENT against her former EEOC supervisor, Clarence Thomas, were made public on the eve of his confirmation as a Supreme Court justice. On that date, NINA TOTENBERG of National Public Radio alleged that the committee had suppressed allegations of sexual harassment against Thomas brought by Hill. On October 8, Democratic congresswomen marched from the House to the Senate to demand an investigation. The Senate relented, and new hearings were called with Anita Hill as the primary witness. Her testimony before the Senate Judiciary Committee was televised, giving many voters, particularly female voters, their first glimpse of the all-male, all-white committee. Interest in the hearings was incredibly intense. Senator Paul Simon reported receiving nearly 20,000 letters on the subject, compared to fewer than 16,000 on the Gulf War. Millions watched the televised hearings, which had a larger audience than the football games that were on at the same time. Women were outraged at what many perceived as unfair and condescending treatment of Hill. Tee shirts proclaiming "I Believe Anita Hill," "He did it," and "She Lied" sprang up across the country. A full episode of a prime-time sitcom, *Designing Women,* was dedicated to the controversy. After the show's airing, CBS received more than 1,500 phone calls—the largest number in the network's history in response to a single show; most were positive. Clarence Thomas was ultimately confirmed by the narrowest margin in U.S. Senate history.

The issue of sexual harassment in the workplace was moved from the private to the public sphere because of Anita Hill's allegations and willingness to speak out. Today Hill is a professor of social policy, law, and women's studies at Brandeis University at the Heller School for Social Policy and Management.

Further Reading

Hill, Anita Faye, and Emma Coleman Jordan, eds. *Race, Gender, and Power in America: The Legacy of the Hill-Thomas hearings.* New York: Oxford University Press, 1995.

Smitherman, Geneva, ed. *African American Women Speak Out on Anita Hill–Clarence Thomas.* Detroit: Wayne State University Press, 1995.

Hills, Carla Anderson (1934–   ) *secretary of housing and urban development, trade representative, lawyer*   Carla Anderson was born on January 3, 1934, in Los Angeles, California. She received her bachelor's degree from Stanford University in 1955 and her law degree from Yale University Law School in 1958. That same year, she married Roderick M. Hills, with whom she has four children.

Carla Anderson Hills entered politics in 1959 as an assistant U.S. attorney. After a period in private practice, she was appointed assistant attorney general in the Civil Division of the U.S. Department of Justice. In 1974, President Gerald Ford appointed Hills secretary of housing and urban development. She served in the cabinet until 1977, when she again returned to private law practice. She served as chair of the Urban Institute from 1983 until 1988. In 1989, President George H. W. Bush appointed her to be the U.S. trade representative. In this capacity, she was the president's chief advisor in international trade policy and was instrumental in acting for the United States in the drafting of the North American Free Trade Agreement.

Since leaving government in 1993, Hills has established a consulting firm (Hills & Company, International Consultants) that advises companies on global trade and investment issues in emerging markets. She has served as president of the National Association of Women Lawyers, as vice chairman of the Council of Foreign Relations, and as a trustee with the Forum for International Policy. She is on the board of directors of AOL Time Warner, Chevron Texaco, Lucent Technologies, and American International Group, Inc. In 2000, Hills was awarded the Aztec Eagle, the highest honor given by the Mexican government to a noncitizen of that country.

Hill v. Colorado (530 U.S. 703) (2000)   In 1993, Colorado passed a law intended to regulate protesters outside of health clinics. One part of the law requires that anyone within a zone of 100 feet of a medical facility's entrance needs to obtain permission of the passersby before approaching them within eight feet to pass out literature, educate them, or counsel them in any way. Leila Hill, Audrey Himmelmann, and Everitt W. Simpson, Jr., were protesters and sidewalk counselors at a clinic that performed ABORTIONS in Colorado. They filed suit against the state, challenging the law as a violation of their First Amendment right to free speech.

This case presented the U.S. Supreme Court with the opportunity to revisit the issue of free speech and restrictions applied to protestors at health care facilities. In a previous case (*Schenck v. Pro-Choice Network of Western New York,* 1997), the Court had distinguished between fixed buffer zones and "floating bubbles." Fixed zones were found to be constitutional because it was necessary to allow people to enter and exit freely. The question in this case was whether the eight-foot provision within the 100-foot zone constituted a "floating" or "fixed" area. The Court reviewed the First Amendment rights of both sides. In a 6-3 decision, the Court found the statute constitutional because it was narrowly drawn and balanced the rights of the protestors with those of the unwilling listeners. The Court found that, rather than speech, the statute was a restriction on "place." The court noted the disagreement over whether the statute was "content related" and held that it was not because it applied to all facilities and all kinds of protestors. Furthermore, the buffer zone does not cut off communication entirely between protestors and passersby, but leaves open "alternative communication channels."

Further Reading

Hull, N.E.H. *The Abortion Rights Controversy in America: A Legal Reader.* Chapel Hill: University of North Carolina Press, 2004.

The OYEZ Project. "*Hill v. Colorado,* 530 U.S. 703 (2000)." Available online. URL: http://www.oyez.org/cases/case?case=1990–1999/1999/1999_98_1856. Accessed on January 9, 2007.

—Marsha Hass

Hishon v. King & Spalding (467 U.S. 69)

(1984) Under TITLE VII OF THE CIVIL RIGHTS ACT OF 1964, it is unlawful to discriminate in employment on the basis of sex. This case involves Elizabeth Anderson Hishon, an attorney with King & Spalding in Atlanta Georgia. Recruited directly out of Columbia Law School,

Hishon agreed to join the firm only after being assured that she would be considered for partnership in the firm "on a fair and equal basis" after five or six years of service in which her evaluations were satisfactory. After five years of more than satisfactory evaluations, she was twice rejected for promotion to partnership and was terminated. She sued, arguing that she was the victim of sex discrimination.

The district court dismissed the case, arguing that Title VII did not cover partnership decisions. When the Court of Appeals agreed, Hishon appealed to the U.S. Supreme Court in order to determine if Title VII provisions applied to partnership decisions. The Supreme Court ruled unanimously that Title VII protection did extend to the law firm's partnership decisions. Chief Justice Warren Burger, writing for the majority, stated that "the contractual relationship of employment triggers the provision of Title VII governing 'terms, conditions, or privileges of employment.'" He went on to say that verbal agreements triggered Title VII protections just as a formal contract would, and therefore if King & Spalding had promised that Hishon would be considered for partnership, then the firm must do so without discrimination on the basis of sex. The Court sent the case back to the lower courts for trial. Instead, Hishon settled with King & Spalding for an undisclosed sum. By that time, she was a partner with another firm.

This case, as well as PRICE WATERHOUSE V. HOPKINS (1989), raises the issue of the GLASS CEILING and demonstrates the difficulty in establishing clear sex discrimination in cases where intangible qualities are a factor in determining promotion decisions. In Ann Hopkins's case, the Supreme Court found that sex stereotyping had played a role in her partnership denial. The Hishon case never made it that far.

Further Reading

Frost-Knappman, Elizabeth, and Kathryn Cullen-DuPont. *Women's Rights on Trial.* Detroit: Gale Publishing, 1997.

Hobby, Oveta Culp (1905–1995) *secretary of health, education, and welfare* Oveta Culp Hobby, first secretary of the Department of Health, Education and Welfare, first commanding officer of the Women's Army Corps, and chairman of the board of the *Houston Post,* was born in Killeen, Texas, on January 19, 1905. She attended Baylor Female College and worked as a cub reporter on the Austin *Statesman.* Hobby served as the legislative parliamentarian for the Texas House of Representatives (1925–31, 1939–41) and studied at the University of Texas Law School. On February 23, 1931, she married former Texas governor William P. Hobby, when she was 26 and Hobby was 53. The couple had two children, each born on her birthday. Hobby authored a handbook on parliamentary law and helped her husband run the *Houston Post,* reviewing books, editing copy, and writing editorials. Her colleagues took note of her organizational skills, tenacity, and political savvy, and nicknamed the young editor "Miss Spark-Plug."

Oveta Hobby, ca. 1953 (Library of Congress)

In 1941, Hobby went to Washington, D.C. to take charge first of the Women's Interest Section of the War Department Bureau of Public Relations then the Women's Army Corps (1942–45). Hobby commanded more than 200,000 women at more than 200 posts in every theater of wartime operations and successfully fought for legislative action giving WACs the rights and privileges of soldiers.

In 1953, President Dwight D. Eisenhower named Hobby as chair of the Federal Security Agency. Later that year, the post was elevated to a cabinet position and renamed the Department of Health, Education, and Welfare. Hobby became its first secretary (the only woman in Eisenhower's cabinet) and during her tenure announced the development of the Salk vaccine. She resigned in 1955 and resumed her career with the *Post.* She died on August 16, 1995.

Further Reading

Handbook of Texas Online. "Hobby, Oveta Culp." Available online. URL: http://www.tsha.utexas.edu/handbook/online/articles/HH/fho86.html. Accessed on January 9, 2007.

—Jennifer Davis McDaid

Hodgson v. Minnesota (497 U.S. 417) (1990) This case involved a challenge to a Minnesota statute that set up requirements for an abortion by a minor under the age of 18. The statute required a 48-hour waiting period after the notification of both parents. The district court found that this requirement served no useful purpose and made the section over-broad and, as such, unconstitutional. As to the other section providing a judicial bypass of the 48-hour notification requirement, the Appeals Court found that section constitutional, saving the entire statute. Since the section required a thoughtful decision, an expedited court hearing before a judge, and the help of an attorney, the U.S. Supreme Court determined that Minnesota had overcome the defective section requiring 48-hour notice to both parents. The decision of the Court of Appeals was upheld. Both the majority and dissenting opinions show a divided Court and concern about abortions by minors.

Further Reading

Hull, N. E. H. *The Abortion Rights Controversy in America: A Legal Reader.* Chapel Hill: University of North Carolina Press, 2004.
The OYEZ Project. "*Hodgson v. Minnesota,* 497 U.S. 417 (1990)." Available online. URL: http://www.oyez.org/cases/case?case=1980–1989/1989/1989_88_1125. Accessed on January 09, 2007.

—Marsha Hass

Hoey, Jane (Jane Margueretta Hoey) (1892–1968) *social worker, government official*

A social worker, welfare administrator, and government official, Jane Margueretta Hoey was also a pioneer for women as director of the Bureau of Public Assistance and, later, the Bureau of Family Services of the Social Security Administration. Born in 1892, she received a B.A. from Trinity College, Washington, D.C., in 1914 and earned a master's degree in political science from Columbia University and a diploma from the New York School of Philosophy, both in 1916. Her career began in local government in 1916 when she was appointed assistant secretary of the Board of Child Welfare of New York City. Her superior was Harry Hopkins. By 1935, Hopkins and other close associates had gone to Washington to work in President Franklin Roosevelt's New Deal administration. In 1934, the president created the Committee on Economic Security, whose members included Hopkins and FRANCES PERKINS. Hoey joined the Committee on Child Welfare, and after the enactment of the Social Security Act in 1935, she became director of the Bureau of Public Assistance within the Social Security Administration. She held this position until she was dismissed when Dwight D. Eisenhower and the Republicans took control of the executive branch in 1953. After leaving the bureau, she became director of social research for the National Tuberculosis Association. In 1967, a year before her death, the Columbia School of Social Work established the Jane M. Hoey Chair in Social Policy.

Further Reading

Social Security Online History. "Jane Hoey." Available online. URL: http://www.ssa.gov/history/janehoey.html. Accessed on January 9, 2007.

Hoffman, Anna Rosenberg   See ROSENBERG, ANNA.

Holm, Jeanne (Jeanne Marjorie Holm) (1921–) *major general in the U.S. Air Force*

Jeanne Holm served the United States with honor, becoming the first woman in American military history to be promoted to the rank of major general. During her career, Holm believed that as one of America's major institutions for protecting its core values and security, the U.S. military needed to change its practice of excluding women from combat.

Holm was born in Portland, Oregon, in 1921. In 1942, during the height of America's involvement in World War II, Holm enlisted in the army. Her military career parallels efforts by the U.S. military to promote gender integration. Advances in technology and communications during World War II led to the need for more support personnel for combat troops and led the military to open up some positions to women. Women served primarily in voluntary positions and were housed in separate military service units for women. Holm's initial enlistment in the army was in the Women's Army Auxiliary Corps (WAAC). She demonstrated her leadership skills early and, following officer candidate school, received a commission as a third officer, or WAAC second lieutenant.

After serving in numerous command positions in the army, Holm took advantage of the Women's Armed Services Integration Act signed by President Truman in 1948 to make the transition to the air force. As director of women in the

Air Force (1965–1973) she worked to strengthen and expand job opportunities and assignments for women in the military. She consistently questioned the traditional roles of women in the military being limited to ministering to the wounded or administrative positions, and she called upon the military to eliminate the artificial line between "combat" and "noncombatant" positions. Holm posed the question: "Is it right to expect military men to face the risks inherent in the military profession, while attempting to protect or shield the women who take the same oath and draw the same pay, get the same training and wear the same uniform?"

In 1973, she was promoted to Major General and named Director of the Air Force Personnel Council and Assistant Secretary for Manpower. She served as Special Assistant to the President for women from 1976 until 1977 when she returned to the Pentagon as undersecretary of the Air Force.

See also WOMEN'S ARMY CORPS.

Further Reading

Holm, Jeanne. *Women in the Military: An Unfinished Revolution.* New York: Random House, 1992.

—Hollis France

hooks, bell (Gloria Jean Watkins) (1952–)
author, scholar   bell hooks is a leading public intellectual who provides provocative critiques of American politics and culture. hooks's scholarship contributes to the national conversation on diversity in American politics. She provokes and encourages critical thinking about the interconnectedness of race, class, gender, and sexuality in contributing to a more diverse America.

Born Gloria Jean Watkins on September 25, 1952, in Kentucky, hooks changed her name to pay homage to both her mother and maternal grandmother. She adopted the lower-case spelling of her name to draw attention to her message rather than to her as the author. Growing up in a patriarchal, working-class, black southern household, hooks became acutely aware

at an early age of the convergence of class and race. She received her B.A. from Stanford University in 1973, her M.A. in 1976 from the University of Wisconsin, and her Ph.D. in 1983 from the University of California–Santa Cruz. hooks's scholarship invites readers to explore how access to resources in a capitalist society affects various groups based on both race and gender. Her book *Feminist Theory: From Margin to Center* (1984) examines what it means to be a feminist and what it takes to end sexism and sexist oppression. hooks eschews the notion that only women can be feminists. She believes that it is necessary for both men and women to be feminists in order to end sexist oppression. Currently hooks is making an effort to reach out to younger working-class populations. She writes articles for popular magazines that have a younger African-American audience. Topics addressed by hooks include hip hop, the images of black women, the O. J. Simpson case, and images of black masculinity.

hooks has been a professor of African and Afro-American studies and English at Yale University, an associate professor of Women's Studies and American Literature at Oberlin College, and a distinguished lecturer of English Literature at the City College of New York.

See also BLACK FEMINISM; FEMINISM.

Further Reading

hooks, bell. *Ain't I a Woman: Black Feminism.* Boston: South End Press, 1981.

—Hollis France

Hooley, Darlene (1939–) *congressperson*
Darlene Hooley was born on April 4, 1939, on the family farm in Williston, North Dakota. Her family moved to Salem, Oregon, when she was eight. After graduating from high school in Salem, Hooley went on to receive a B.S. degree from Oregon State University and subsequently became a reading, music, and physical education teacher. She served on the Park District Board before her election to the West Linn City

Council (1976–80). This was followed by her election to the Oregon State Legislature (1980–86) and to the Clackamas County Board of Commissioners (1986–96).

First elected to the U.S. House of Representatives in 1996, Hooley was selected president of the class of freshman House members in 1997. She serves on the House Committee on Science, the Financial Services Committee, and the House Committee on Veterans' Affairs. She also serves as a senior whip for the Democrats. She tends to have a moderate, liberal-leaning voting record. A supporter of Oregon's assisted suicide law, she has championed consumer credit rights and opposed the use of military force in Iraq. Hooley has been consistently reelected, including in 2006.

Further Reading

Barone, Michael. *The Almanac of American Politics.* Washington, D.C.: National Journal Group, 2006.

"Hooley, Darlene." In *Biographical Directory of the United States Congress, 1774–present.* Available online. URL: http://bioguide.congress.gov/scripts/biodisplay.pl?index=H000762. Accessed on January 8, 2007.

"Representative Darlene Hooley (OR)." In *Project Vote Smart.* Available online. URL: http://votesmart.org/bio.php?can_id=BC033437. Accessed on January 8, 2007.

—Angela Kouters

Hoover, Lou (Lou Henry Hoover) (1874–1944) *first lady*

Lou Henry was born on March 29, 1874, to Florence Weed and Charles Delano Henry, in Waterloo, Iowa; her father had wanted a boy and so had named her Lou. Her mother was trained as a teacher, and her father worked in banking. In 1884, the family moved to Whittier, California, and Lou joined her father in his love of outdoor activities. They enjoyed camping, hiking, riding horses, and studying rocks and flowers together. As she matured, he included her in his banking business and taught

her how to keep the books, while her mother taught her cooking and sewing. After graduating from high school, Lou studied to be a teacher, earning her certificate at 19. She worked for a time as a cashier in her father's bank and then as a substitute teacher in the Monterey schools until a lecture by Stanford University geology professor, John Casper Branner, changed her life. In the fall of 1894, she enrolled at Stanford, majoring in geology (the first woman to do so). She studied Latin and participated actively in sports on campus. In the geology lab, Dr. Banner introduced Lou to one of his most promising senior students, Herbert Hoover. The two were instantly compatible, and although Hoover graduated in 1895, they maintained their courtship through letters as he established his career in mining. Lou graduated in 1898, becoming the first woman to earn a degree in geology. She searched in vain for employment in the field of geology, but nobody would hire a woman.

Herbert had been offered a position in Australia that resulted in his appointment as head of all mining operations in China. The position came with a significant increase in pay, and he wired Lou a marriage proposal, which she accepted by return cablegram. The couple were married as soon as Herbert returned to the United States, on February 10, 1899, and they immediately set off for China. During their passage, Lou studied the Chinese language, and she and Herbert immersed themselves in the study of Chinese history and culture. They settled in Tientsin, and Lou set up their household, but the outbreak of the Boxer Rebellion, a violent reaction to foreign intervention in the Chinese economy, led to a siege on Americans and other foreigners living in Tientsin. Lou armed herself with a revolver, took her turn on watch, and rolled bandages and cared for the injured in a makeshift hospital.

In late 1900, the Hoovers left China for London. Herbert's work required him to travel around the world, and Lou most often accompanied him; because of her training in geology, she served as his unpaid assistant. Together

Lou Henry Hoover, ca. 1930 (LIBRARY OF CONGRESS)

they studied mining law and cataloged the mining laws of the world. The birth of their son, Herbert Clark Hoover, in 1903 did not slow Lou and Herbert's collaboration. With a nurse willing to travel, the baby accompanied them, and by the time he was one year old, he had circled the globe twice. When Allen Henry Hoover was born in 1907, he was added seamlessly to the family's travels, always with London as their home base.

In 1908, Herbert established his own mining consulting firm, through which he earned a considerable income. The couple collaborated on a translation of a 16th-century mining text, *De Re Metallica,* which had been lost to the mining industry. For five years, Lou and Herbert worked on the project together: She researched the language translation while he replicated the lab experiments to verify the correct interpretation of the text. They published the translation in 1912 at their own expense, and in 1914 the Mining and Metallurgical Society of America bestowed a gold medal upon the Hoovers for this major scientific accomplishment.

The couple had decided to educate their sons in the United States and made plans to return to California and build a house near the Stanford campus. The onset of the war meant that only Lou and the two boys took up residence in California. At the outbreak of World War I, when Herbert Hoover was tapped to oversee U.S. relief efforts in Belgium and northern France, Lou Hoover left her sons in California and returned to Europe to help. She served as the president of the American Women's War Relief Fund, and assisted Americans stranded in Europe in securing passage to America. Within three weeks, more than 40,000 U.S. citizens were sent home. Initially the Hoovers were able to serve as brokers with the Germans in arranging economic development and relief efforts in Belgium. Once the United States became a combatant, Lou focused her efforts on raising money in the United States for overseas relief efforts. She embarked on a speaking tour, raising hundreds of thousands of dollars for the cause. President Woodrow Wilson appointed Herbert Hoover as director of the Food Administration in the United States. The family took up residence in Washington and developed incentives for Americans' to conserve scarce food items by adopting meatless and wheatless meals—a campaign known as "Hooverizing." Lou Hoover opened her home to the *Ladies Home Journal* to assure a skeptical public that they, too, were conserving. As the size of the federal government expanded as a result of the war, Lou Hoover took an interest in the influx of young single women drawn to Washington's jobs. She helped establish the Food Administration Women's Club, providing housing, good nutrition, and opportunities for recreation to women; she rented a large house for the club. At war's end, Lou devoted the same care and attention to returning injured veterans, making sure they had medical care during their passage home, through a program called Canteen Escort Service.

In 1921, President Warren G. Harding appointed Herbert Hoover secretary of commerce, lengthening their stay in Washington. As a cabinet wife, Lou Hoover conspired with other wives to end the practice of leaving calling cards and hosting teas in favor of more substantive activities. She encouraged young women to combine motherhood with a career and urged girls and teenagers to educate themselves for a career. Her work with the Girl Scouts stemmed from her belief in the importance of outdoor activities for girls. From 1922 to 1925, Lou Hoover served as the national president of the Girl Scouts, embarking on a fund-raising initiative to support expanded programming and leadership training for girls. In 1922, she helped found the National Amateur Athletic Federation and was selected as its only female vice president. Within that organization, she founded the Women's Division to advance the ideals of sports for the sake of play rather than competition.

In 1928, when Herbert Hoover won the Republican nomination for president, Lou campaigned by his side but remained largely silent about political issues featured in the campaign. Upon her husband's inauguration in March 1929, Lou Hoover entered the White House as one of the most accomplished first ladies to hold the position. As first lady, she became the first to deliver regular radio broadcasts, to be identified with civil rights issues, and to undertake the development of specific programs to combat poverty associated with the Great Depression. Her entertaining was somewhat constrained by the economy, but the Hoovers regularly spent their own money to cover the costs. She sparked a controversy when, in hosting the traditional tea for congressional wives, she included Jessie DePriest, wife of Oscar DePriest, the first African American elected to Congress since Reconstruction. Several southern state legislatures publicly berated Mrs. Hoover for this action, but President Hoover signaled support for his wife by inviting the presidents of Hampton Institute and Tuskegee Institute to the White House. In another break with precedent, Lou included pregnant women in the White House receiving line and encouraged gender-neutral hiring policies for civil service appointments.

A spirit of voluntarism and generous philanthropy characterized much of Lou Hoover's life, and this continued while she was in the White House. The volume of requests for assistance exceeded her ability to reply, so she employed a staff and granted nearly every request. At her death, her private papers revealed hundreds of uncashed checks sent as repayment for "loans" to people she never knew. Working with several organizations, she encouraged economic relief efforts to take the form of war relief. She mobilized the girls active in Girl Scouts in the relief efforts at the local level, steadfastly believing that voluntarism could solve the nation's economic woes, even as the nation had begun to blame her husband for its misery. The election of 1932 confirmed that attribution of blame, and Franklin Delano Roosevelt was swept into office.

For the Hoovers, life after the White House continued to center on voluntarism, this time using their Palo Alto home on the Stanford University campus as their base. Lou and Herbert enjoyed time with their family and treated their grandchildren to the same outdoor adventures they had experienced as children. She continued her association with the Girl Scouts and was elected president of the National Girl Scouts Council. When World War II broke out, the Hoovers moved to New York and devoted themselves to war relief efforts. Lou helped Herbert to establish Dutch and Norwegian relief committees and worked with the Salvation Army to clothe European war refugees. While in New York, she died of a heart attack on January 7, 1944. She was buried in Palo Alto, but her body was moved to West Branch, Iowa, following Herbert Hoover's death and burial in 1964. Their house in Palo Alto was deeded to Stanford University and now functions as the president's residence.

Lou Hoover was a feminist to her core. She was educated in a nontraditional field only to face discrimination when she tried to find a job. Her marriage to Herbert Hoover offered her an opportunity to work in mining and geology in spite of her sex. She was a devoted partner who maintained independent positions and pursuits. Her dedication to advancing the status of women was unmatched by any previous first lady and set the tone for her successor, ELEANOR ROOSEVELT.

Further Reading

Allen, Anne Beiser. *An Independent Woman: The Life of Lou Henry Hoover.* Westport, Conn.: Greenwood, 2000.

National First Ladies Library. *Biographies: First Ladies of the United States.* Available online. URL: http://www.firstladies.org/biographies. Accessed on January 4, 2007.

Schneider, Dorothy, and Carl J. Schneider. "Lou Henry Hoover" *First Ladies: A Biographical Dictionary.* New York: Checkmark Books, 2001, 220–229.

Howe, Julia Ward (1819–1910) *author, suffragist* Julia Ward Howe, now best known as author of "The Battle Hymn of the Republic," was famous in her lifetime as a poet, essayist, lecturer, reformer, and biographer. She worked to end slavery, helped to initiate the women's movement in many states, and organized for international peace.

Born on May 27, 1819, in New York City, Julia Ward was the third of six children of Julia Rush Cutler and Samuel Ward. While in Boston, she visited the New England Institute for the Blind (later the Perkins Institute) where met Dr. Samuel Gridley Howe, who became her husband in 1843. She published poetry in two anthologies in 1848 and a play and a volume of poems in 1857. During the Civil War, both Julia and her husband worked with the Sanitary Commission in Washington. Hearing the popular song "John Brown's Body," she wrote the words to "The Battle Hymn of the Republic," later published by *The Atlantic* in February 1862.

A believer in woman SUFFRAGE, Howe was a founder of the New England Woman's Club and served as the president of the New England Woman Suffrage Association (1868–77 and 1893–1910). She also led the formation of the AMERICAN WOMAN SUFFRAGE ASSOCIATION when its members separated from the National Association, and she presided over the Massachusetts Suffrage Association from 1870 to 1878 and 1891 to 1893. In 1872, she initiated a Mothers' Peace Day observance on the second Sunday in June, which later became the popular Mother's Day holiday now celebrated in May. She was the first woman elected to the American Academy of Arts and Letters in 1908. After she died on October 17, 1910, services were held in Boston at the Church of the Disciple and at Symphony Hall, where there were overflowing crowds.

Further Reading

Clifford, Deborah. *Mine Eyes Have Seen the Glory: A Biography of Julia Ward Howe.* Boston: Little, Brown, 1979.

Julia Ward Howe, ca. 1908 (LIBRARY OF CONGRESS)

Grant, Mary Hetherington. *Private Woman, Public Person: An Account of the Life of Julia Ward Howe from 1819–1868*. Brooklyn: Carlson Publishing, 1994.

Howe, Julia Ward, and Carrie Chapman Catt. *Reminiscences, 1819–1899*. Boston and New York: Houghton Mifflin, 1899.

—Cynthia Melendy

Hoyt v. Florida (368 U.S. 57) (1961)

The issue in this case involved a Florida statute that allowed women to opt out of jury service. This was accomplished by exempting all women unless they registered and asked to serve on juries. The state rationale was that women should be allowed to decide for themselves if their lifestyles and family responsibilities made jury service possible. Men, of course, were not given this choice and were all subject to jury duty unless granted an exemption. Mrs. Hoyt challenged the statute on the two grounds that she was entitled to a jury of her peers and, because she had been accused of murdering her husband, that women would be more understanding. The Supreme Court rejected both challenges, noting first that women could serve if they so wished, and thus Florida had not denied women the right to participate. As to the second issue, that a jury containing women might be more amenable to her defense, the Court pointed out that this was not required by the Constitution. The state could not impermissibly exclude classes of jurors but had only to offer a pool of jurors from which a particular jury might be empanelled. The Court pointed out that this statute was part of an enlightened viewpoint addressing the issue of women's rights. This decision would ultimately be overturned by TAYLOR V. LOUISIANA in 1975.

Further Reading

The OYEZ Project. "Hoyt v. Florida, 368 U.S. 57 (1961)." Available online. URL: http://www.oyez.org/cases/case?case=1960–1969/1961/1961_31. Accessed on January 9, 2007.

—Marsha Hass

Huerta, Dolores (Dolores Clara Fernandez Huerta) (1930–) *cofounder of United Farm Workers, labor organizer, social activist*

Dolores Clara Fernandez was born on April 10, 1930, in Dawson, New Mexico. Her father, Juan Fernandez, was a migrant farmworker, a coal miner, and union activist. In 1938, he was elected to the New Mexico state legislature. Her parents were divorced when Dolores was three, and she grew up with her mother, Alicia Chavez, in Stockton, California. Her mother supported the family by working as a cook, though later she purchased two hotels and a restaurant business. Dolores and her four siblings were often cared for by their grandfather, Herculano Chavez, a disabled miner. As a girl, Dolores and her siblings learned the importance of community activism from their mother. Dolores was active in her community through her Girl Scout troop, a diverse collection of African-American, Chinese, Filipino, Latina, and Anglo girls, at a time when segregation and racism were prevalent. Dolores graduated from Stockton High School and married Ralph Heal. They had two daughters, but divorced within a few years. Dolores earned a teaching certificate at Stockton Community College in 1955 but only taught for one year, believing she could do more for the children of migrant farmers as an activist than she could as a teacher. She married Ventura Huerta, and together the couple had five children before divorcing. Dolores later entered a long-term relationship with Richard Chavez, brother of activist Cesar Chavez. Huerta is the mother of 11 children.

Dolores Huerta began work as an activist with the Community Service Organization (CSO), cofounding the Sacramento chapter in 1955. In 1960, she co-founded the Agricultural Workers Association. In each case, the organization was dedicated to improving the lives of Chicano workers by offering language classes, assistance in obtaining citizenship, advocating for old-age pensions for noncitizens, and the right to take licensing tests in Spanish. During this time she met Cesar Chavez, then the executive director of the CSO. In 1962, she and Chavez founded the National Farm Workers Association, which later became the United Farm Workers (UFW) of America. Their first major action was a grape picker's strike and nationwide boycott in order to win a labor contract for the farmworkers. Huerta negotiated on behalf of the workers a three-year collective bargaining agreement with the UFW. Her pickets, strikes, and boycotts resulted in her being arrested more than 20 times. In 1974, she helped to found the Coalition of Labor Union women (CLUW) in recognition of the extra challenges women workers, particularly women working in the fields, often face. Huerta-led boycotts of lettuce, grapes, and Gallo wine were instrumental in pressuring state lawmakers to adopt the California Agricultural Labor Relations act of 1975, the first law to grant farmworkers the right to collectively organize and bargain for better wages and working conditions.

Huerta has lobbied on behalf of numerous laws in support of farmworkers and migrant rights, including the Immigration Act of 1985, which extended some rights to guest workers who lacked citizenship yet worked and paid taxes in the United States. In 1988, she was severely injured in a police beating she received while protesting in San Francisco against then Vice President George H. W. Bush. In a settlement, the City of San Francisco paid her a reported $825,000 in damages. Huerta is the recipient of numerous awards in recognition for her lifetime of dedication to labor and worker's rights. She is the recipient of more than six honorary doctorates, including one from Princeton University in 2006. Five California elementary schools and one high school are named in her honor. She has been awarded the Woman of Courage award from the NATIONAL ORGANIZATION FOR WOMEN (NOW) and the American Civil Liberties Union Bill of Rights Award. In 1993, she was inducted into the National Women's Hall of Fame.

Dolores Huerta continues to work on behalf of farmworker's rights and women's rights as the president of the Dolores Huerta Foundation. She is an officer in the United Farm Workers, the Coalition for Labor Union Women, and the California AFL-CIO. She serves as a board member for the FEMINIST MAJORITY. In 2002, Huerta was awarded the Puffin Foundation/Nation Institute Award for Creative Citizenship. The grant of $100,000 allowed her to establish the Dolores Huerta Foundation's Organizing Institute. The foundation focuses on community organizing and leadership training in low-income communities and with underrepresented populations.

Further Reading
Ferriss, Susan, Ricardo Sandoval, and Diana Hembree, eds. *The Fight in the Fields: Cesar Chavez and the Farmworkers Movement.* New York: Harcourt Brace, 1997.

Hull-House   Hull-House, founded in 1889 in Chicago by JANE ADDAMS and Ellen Gates Starr, was the first midwestern social settlement. Housed in a rundown mansion in the middle of Chicago's slums, it was designed to bring various segments of society together by crossing boundaries of class and ethnicity. Addams's and Starr's simply stated mission was to be "good neighbors." The United States was rapidly diversifying in the mid- to late 1800s as it began absorbing a large influx of European immigrants attracted to the opportunities offered by industrialization. One of the chief aims of Hull-House was to ameliorate the accompanying dehumanizing conditions, such as overcrowding and sweatshop labor. In addition, Addams and Starr wanted to create an environment where college-educated women could engage in legitimate work as an alternative to the traditional roles of wives and mothers. Hull-House thus became a gathering place not only for immigrants but also for thinkers and activists of every political stripe.

Addams and other women residents inserted themselves into the political sphere by fighting for woman's SUFFRAGE and sponsoring legislation to limit the hours of working women, recognize labor unions, abolish child labor, establish juvenile courts, make school attendance compulsory, and ensure safe working conditions in factories. The Progressive Party adopted many of these reforms as part of its platform in 1912. The residents also helped to influence and administer the programs of the New Deal. Hull-House closed in 1963, but its work continues at several community centers.

See also SETTLEMENT HOUSE MOVEMENT.

Further Reading

Brown, Victoria Bissell, ed. *Twenty Years at Hull-House: With Autobiographical Notes.* Boston: Bedford/St. Martin's, 1999.

Bryan, Mary Lynn McCree, and Allen Freeman Davis, eds. *100 Years at Hull-House.* Bloomington: Indiana University Press, 1990.

—Jana Brubaker

Hutchinson, Anne (Anne Marbury Hutchinson) (1591–1643) *religious leader*

Born in England in July 1591, Anne Marbury was 21 when she married William Hutchinson, a cloth merchant and Puritan. The couple immigrated to Massachusetts Bay Colony in 1634, one year after John Cotton, their minister. After they arrived in Massachusetts Bay, they were admitted to membership in Cotton's Boston church (despite a brief dispute that Anne had with one of the religious elders on her ship during her passage). Anne Hutchinson began to work in the colony as a midwife and also began to offer spiritual support to women in childbirth. This turned into a biweekly series of expositions on the sermons given by the ministers of the Boston church. The popularity of Hutchinson's expositions grew, and soon her audience included men as well as women.

Hutchinson's teachings concerned the distinction between the covenant of grace and the covenant of works. A covenant of works argues that one's saved status can be judged by one's works, or good deeds; these works are an outward manifestation of an inward state. A covenant of grace, on the other hand, argues that emphasis on works denies the singular nature of God's grace. Hutchinson believed fervently in the covenant of grace, and she issued criticisms of ministers who did not adhere to her understanding of that grace. Hutchinson, and those who agreed with her, were termed *antinomians,* since denying a doctrine that espoused the necessity of good works would be to claim that we need not obey any laws of the state (*antinomian* means "against the law").

Hutchinson was publicly criticized for her meetings, and after she persisted in maintaining them she was brought in front of the General Court and charged with disturbing the peace of the colony. She was banished after being declared "a woman not fit for our society." She and her husband went with their children to Rhode Island, where they founded the town of Pocasset and established the colony's first civil government. After William died in 1642, Anne took a number of her children to the Dutch colony in New York. There, in August 1643, she and five of her children were killed in an Indian raid, but she left behind a legacy for future generations of American women. Her influence, both on the government of the Massachusetts Bay Colony itself and on certain individuals, such as MARY DYER, was as a woman willing to speak against authority in defense of what she believed to be right.

Further Reading

Battis, Emery J. *Saints and Sectaries: Anne Hutchinson and the Antinomian Controversy in Massachusetts Bay Colony.* Chapel Hill: University of North Carolina Press, 1962.

Hall, David D., ed. *The Antinomian Controversy 1636–1638: A Documentary History.* Durham, N.C.: Duke University Press, 1990.

LaPlante, Eve. *American Jezebel: The Uncommon Life of Anne Hutchinson, the Woman Who Defied the Puritans.* New York: HarperCollins, 2004.

—Claire Curtis

Hutchison, Kay Bailey (Kathryn Ann Bailey Hutchison)

(1943–) *U.S. senator* Kathryn Ann (Kay) Bailey was born in Galveston, Texas, on July 22, 1943. She graduated from the University of Texas in 1962 and received her law degree from the University of Texas in 1967. Following her graduation from law school, she was the legal and political correspondent for a local TV station.

In 1972, Bailey was elected to the Texas State House of Representatives marking the first time a Republican woman had done so in the history of the state. She remained a member of the Texas State House of Representatives until 1976, when she was nominated to become the vice chairman of the National Transportation Safety Board, a post she held until 1978. In 1978, Kay Bailey married Ray Hutchison, a lawyer, and moved to Dallas, where she was named senior vice president and general counsel of Republic Bank Corp. She later cofounded Fidelity National Bank of Dallas and owned McCraw Candies, Inc., a manufacturing company with national distribution.

Kay Bailey Hutchison was a candidate for the U.S. House of Representative in 1982 but was defeated. She temporarily left politics and became a bank executive and businesswoman until 1991, when she was elected Texas state treasurer. This marked the first time a Republican woman had ever been elected to a statewide office in Texas.

In 1993, Hutchison was elected as the first woman to represent Texas in the U.S. Senate in a special election to fill the seat vacated when Lloyd Bentsen became secretary of the treasury in the Bill Clinton administration. Seven years later, more than 4 million Texans reelected her to a second full term—at the time the largest number of votes ever garnered in the state. In 2001, she was elected vice chairman of the Senate Republican Conference, becoming one of the top five leaders of Senate Republicans and the only woman. She has been reelected to that post three times. Having been reelected in 2006, she was selected as the chair of the Republican Policy Committee. In the Senate, she serves on the Committee on Appropriations, the Committee on Commerce, Science and Technology, the Committee on Rules and Administration, and the Committee on Veteran's Affairs.

In February 2006, the WHITE HOUSE PROJECT named Senator Hutchison one of "8 in '08," signaling that she is a credible female candidate for the presidency in 2008. Hutchison has published two books since she was elected to the U.S. Senate. The first was written with colleagues in 2000 and is titled *Nine and Counting: the Women of the Senate*. The most recent book, *The Spirited Women who Shaped Our Country,* was published in 2004.

Further Reading

Barone, Michael. *The Almanac of American Politics*. Washington, D.C.: National Journal Group, 2006.

"Hutchison, Kathryn Ann Bailey (Kay)." In *Biographical Directory of the United States Congress, 1774–present*. Available online. URL: http://bioguide. congress.gov/scripts/biodisplay.pl?index= H001016. Accessed on January 8, 2007.

"Senator Kay Bailey Hutchison (TX)." In *Project Vote Smart*. Available online. URL: http://votesmart. org/bio.php?can_id=S0852103. Accessed on January 8, 2007.

—Angela Kouters

Hyde Amendment

Named after Representative Henry J. Hyde, a Republican from Illinois, the Hyde Amendment prohibits the federal government from paying for the cost of ABORTIONS covered under state Medicaid plans. The original language of the amendment attached to the Appropriations Act of 1977 stated: "None of the funds contained in this Act shall be used to perform abortions except where the life of the mother would be endangered if the fetus were carried to term." Congress has since passed revisions that allow for funding in cases of rape or incest, but these provisions vary by year.

Federal and state restrictions on public funding for abortions make it extremely difficult—often impossible—for Medicaid recipients to exercise their constitutional right to safe and legal abortion. In practice, these women do not have the same rights as other American women who can finance an abortion out-of-pocket or through private insurance coverage. Nor do Medicaid-eligible women have the same rights as men who depend on publicly funded health care, since in no case are covered medical services that men need restricted by the federal Medicaid program's standard for reimbursement as it does for abortions. Claims that the Hyde Amendment violates the equal-protection clause of the Fifth Amendment's due-process clause as well as the free-exercise clause of the First Amendment, denying women the right to choose abortion as established by ROE V. WADE (1973), were brought before the U.S. Supreme Court in 1980. The Court upheld the constitutionality of the Hyde Amendment in HARRIS V. MCRAE (1980), holding that the states have a right to encourage childbirth and cannot be compelled to fund abortions once federal funds are withheld. At this time, 17 states allocate funds to maintain abortion coverage for Medicaid recipients, while 33 states do not fund abortions at all.

A 1984 study conducted by researchers from The ALAN GUTTMACHER INSTITUTE showed that 44 percent of women on Medicaid who obtained abortions that year paid for them with money earmarked for living expenses, such as food, rent, and utilities. Some women are forced to carry unwanted pregnancies to term. Studies have shown that 18–33 percent of Medicaid-eligible women who want abortions but live in states that do not provide funding have been compelled to give birth. Civil liberties advocacy organizations such as the American Civil Liberties Union (ACLU) have established projects intended to defeat the Hyde Amendment.

Further Reading

Levy, Dana, Charles Tien, and Rachelle Aved. "Do Differences Matter? Women Members of Congress and the Hyde Amendment." *Women and Politics* 23 (2001): 105.

I

Immigrants' Protective League (IPL) The Immigrants' Protective League (IPL) existed as a voluntary association headed by white, educated, middle-class women. The IPL set about the task of targeting the concerns and issues of newly arriving immigrants, specifically immigrant women. The agenda of the IPL served the purpose of the larger reform movement in the United States during the 19th century that sought to address the social ills confronting the urban working class. At the end of the 19th century, the United States witnessed a large influx of eastern and southern European immigrants. Many of these immigrants settled in large urban centers and were immediately confronted with poverty, discrimination, and an unfamiliar cultural landscape. To help alleviate many of the problems faced by immigrants, the IPL was launched in Chicago in 1908 by such noted figures as JANE ADDAMS and GRACE ABBOTT.

Immigrant women seeking the IPL's services underwent an "Americanization" process by assimilating American values, ideas, and beliefs. Embodied in this process were underlining themes of patriarchal notions of womanhood, nationalism, and sexuality. Instrumental to the IPL's program of Americanization was a wom-

an's relationship to nation building through her reproductive role. The immigrant woman was seen as a transmission agent who would pass on the lessons she herself learned in language, civics, and housekeeping classes.

In 1967, the IPL merged with Travelers Aid, an organization founded in 1888 to assist young and solitary newcomers to the city of Chicago. Despite the merger, they continued working as two separate organizations until 1980, when they incorporated as Travelers and Immigrant Aid (TIA), with a mission "to serve the poor and vulnerable." In 1995, TIA was absorbed into Heartland Alliance.

Further Reading
Ewen, Elizabeth. *Immigrant Women in the Land of Dollars: Life and Culture of the Lower East Side, 1890–1925.* New York: Monthly Review Press, 1995.
Lissak, Rivka Shpak. *Pluralism and Progressives: Hull House and the New Immigrants, 1890–1919.* Chicago: University of Chicago Press, 1989.

—Hollis France

Independent Women's Forum (IWF) The Independent Women's Forum (IWF) is a conservative, nonprofit, nonpartisan, antifeminist organization based in Washington, D.C. Founded in 1992, the organization claims: "The Independent Women's Forum was established to combat the women-as-victim, pro-big-government ideology of radical FEMINISM. We seek to restore, strengthen, and extend that which promotes women's wellbeing by advancing the principles of self-reliance, political freedom, economic liberty, and personal responsibility." IWF offers an alternative ideological approach to engaging women in politics. The organization supports a legal department, programming on college campuses, and specific issue-related projects—many aimed at quality of life issues for women surrounding work-family pressures. The organization maintains a Web site at: www.iwf.org.

See also ANTIFEMINISM.

International Ladies' Garment Workers' Union (ILGWU)

Founded in 1900 as an organization dominated by Jewish and Italian immigrants, the International Ladies' Garment Workers Union (ILGWU) was one of the most important and progressive unions in the United States. In 1909, 20,000 New York shirtwaist makers, mostly women, launched a 14-week strike called "The Uprising," followed several months later by a strike of 60,000 cloak makers. In the negotiations that followed, the ILGWU was recognized by the industry and won higher wages as well as important new benefits for its members, such as health examinations. In 1911, 146 workers, most of them young women, were killed in the TRIANGLE SHIRTWAIST COMPANY FIRE, leading to a public call for laws to protect workers. The union's membership rose and fell with the vagaries of the economy and pressures on wages created by international trade. In 1995, the ILGWU combined forces with the Amalgamated Clothing and Textile Workers' Union to form UNITE (Union of Needletrades, Industrial and Textile Employees). In 2004, UNITE merged with HERE (Hotel Employees and Restaurant Employees International Union) to form

UNITE HERE, a union representing more than 450,000 members, as well as more than 400,000 retirees.

Further Reading

Bernstein, Irving. *Turbulent Years, A History of the American Worker 1933–1941.* Boston: Houghton Mifflin, 1979.
Dubinsky, David and A. H. Raskin. *David Dubinsky: A Life With Labor.* New York: Simon & Schuster, 1977.

International Women's Day (IWD)

International Women's Day (IWD; celebrated each year on March 8) is an occasion marked by women's groups around the world. This date is also commemorated at the United Nations and is designated in many countries as a national holiday. Women, who are often divided by national boundaries and by ethnic, linguistic, cultural, economic, and political differences, are encouraged to come together to celebrate International Women's Day and reflect on nine decades of struggle for equality, justice, peace, and development.

The first International Women's Day was on February 28, 1909, the last Sunday of the month. The origins of IWD are found in women's struggle for the vote as well as social and economic rights. Demonstrations coinciding with socialist labor struggles, the peace movement, and international gender solidarity formed the early basis for IWD. International Women's Day continued to be commemorated in the West into the 1920s but faded for several decades until it was revived by the growth of FEMINISM in the 1960s and 1970s. During International Women's Year in 1975, the United Nations began the tradition of celebrating IWD on March 8. The growing international women's movement, which has been strengthened by four global UN women's conferences, has helped make the commemoration a rallying point for coordinated efforts to demand women's rights and participation in the political and economic process. Increasingly, IWD is a time to reflect on progress made, to call for change.

The theme for International Women's Day in 2006 was the role of women in decision-making. Although progress in meeting the goal of full participation has been slow, there have been milestones. In January 2006, for example, the proportion of women in national parliaments reached a new global high (16.4% in both houses combined). There are now 11 women heads of state or government in countries on every continent. Chile, Spain, and Sweden have gender parity in government.

See also UNITED NATIONS DECADE FOR WOMEN.

Further Reading

United Nations. *International Women's Day.* Available online. URL: http://www.un.org/events/women/iwd/2006/history.html. Accessed on January 9, 2007.

interspousal immunity   Interspousal immunity has its common-law origins in COVERTURE, the rule that husband and wife were one person upon marriage. This meant that as a matter of substantive law, a tort committed by one spouse against the other could not be a source of liability. Second, as a matter of procedure, neither spouse could sue the other during the marriage because one cannot sue oneself. In criminal matters, one spouse could not be compelled to testify against the other since doing so would constitute a form of self-incrimination prohibited by the Fifth Amendment. Women were defenseless as victims of domestic violence, particularly in cases of marital rape. As women gained legal independence beginning in the late 1840s and the theory of unity dissolved, most states abolished immunity between husband and wife in negligence actions. The principle of interspousal immunity has been dismantled by the states (largely through specific court actions). Pressure on the courts to reform this archaic legal principle came from activists working against domestic violence.

See also MARRIED WOMEN'S PROPERTY ACT (1848).

Further Reading

Hoff, Joan. *Law, Gender, and Injustice: A Legal History of the United States,* New York: New York University Press, 1991.

Ireland, Patricia (1945–   ) *women's rights leader*   Born on October 19, 1945, in Oak Park, Illinois, Patricia Ireland began her work life in 1967 as a flight attendant for Pan American Airlines before earning a law degree from the University of Miami in 1975. While working as a corporate attorney, Ireland engaged in activism centered on a number of political issues, particularly those that concerned international women's rights and human rights causes.

Ireland was active in the NATIONAL ORGANIZATION FOR WOMEN (NOW) programs even before she was selected as executive vice president and treasurer in 1987. She subsequently served as the organization's president for 10 years (1991–2001). During her tenure, NOW focused its programming and outreach on protecting and expanding reproductive rights, electing more women to state and national political offices, and developing alliances with other civil and human rights organizations. In the area of ABORTION rights, Ireland helped to initiate the lawsuit *NOW v. Scheidler.* In 1992, the "Elect Women for a Change" campaign provided trained volunteers and organizational support to feminist candidates for Congress. Ireland developed closer organizational ties and issue affinities with welfare and poor women's rights activists; national civil rights leaders; and lesbian, gay, bisexual, and transgender rights groups. Ireland was the prime architect of NOW's Global Feminist Program. During her tenure at NOW, Ireland represented the organization and women's interests at six international conferences around the world.

In May 2003, Ireland was named to head the YWCA of the United States, but in October that same year, the organization announced Ireland's termination. Colleagues at NOW argued that Ireland had been forced out due to pressure orchestrated by conservative groups such as the Traditional Values Coalition. Conservatives objected to her abortion rights positions and her publicly acknowledged lesbian relationship.

See also FEMINISM.

Further Reading
Ireland, Patricia. *What Women Want.* New York: Dutton Books, 1996.
Wingfield, Brian. "Y.W.C.A. Chief Dismissed 6 Months After Being Hired," *New York Times* 20 October 2003.

iron-jawed angels   The term *iron-jawed angels* refers to the suffragists who were jailed for trespassing during their White House sidewalk protests. Once unjustly imprisoned, the women refused to eat and were force-fed through clenched jaws.

ALICE PAUL organized and coordinated the actions of hundreds of women to call on President Woodrow Wilson to pressure Congress to consider and pass a federal SUFFRAGE amendment (known by then as the SUSAN B. ANTHONY Amendment). On January 10, 1917, the first "Silent Sentinels" appeared in front of the White House. These were women who stood motionless holding banners that read, "Mr. President, What Will You Do for Woman Suffrage?" and "How Long Must Women Wait for Liberty?" These suffragists were the first picketers ever to appear before the White House.

At first the pickets attracted sympathy from the public, and donations poured in from women nationwide. However, in 1917, while other suffragists debated how to respond to the country's war on Germany, Alice Paul's NATIONAL WOMAN'S PARTY (NWP) stepped up efforts to call attention to women's disenfranchisement. Ignoring the war, NWP picketers carried signs reading: "Kaiser Wilson, have you forgotten your sympathy with the poor Germans because they were not self-governed? Twenty million American women are not self-governed. Take the beam out of your eye." As the rhetoric heated up, police began arresting picketers, some of whom were physically attacked by daily crowds of onlookers. Each time police arrested a marcher or a woman was felled by attack, another woman was there to take her place. States sent delegations to the picket lines, and those who could not picket sent donations to support those marching in their place. When jailed, women refused to pay their fines and remained in jail. In an attempt to scare off new picketers, prison terms of up to 60 days were imposed. The women engaged in several hunger strikes to protest their unjust incarceration. Prison officials responded by force-feeding them through the nose, a dangerous and terribly painful practice. Public reaction was swift and overwhelmingly sympathetic to the suffragists, prompting early releases. Women released from prison capitalized on the public's sympathy by campaigning for suffrage in their prison garb.

In February 2004, HBO Films premiered *Iron Jawed Angels* starring Hillary Swank as Alice Paul, Frances O'Connor as LUCY BURNS, Julia Ormond as INEZ MILHOLLAND, and Anjelica Huston as CARRIE CHAPMAN CATT. The film won praise from reviewers and feminists alike and helped millions of men and women "discover" the suffrage cause and its leaders and heroines.

Further Reading
Kraditor, Aileen. *The Ideas of the Woman Suffrage Movement: 1890–1920.* New York: Norton, 1981.
Stevens, Doris. *Jailed for Freedom: American Women Win the Vote.* Troutdale, Oreg.: NewSage Press, 1995.

J

Jackson-Lee, Sheila (1950–) *congressperson, judge, activist*   Sheila Jackson-Lee was born on January 12, 1954, in Queens, New York, and earned a bachelor's degree in political science from Yale University (1972) and a law degree from the University of Virginia Law School (1975). Jackson-Lee moved to Houston after her husband, Dr. Elwyn C. Lee, took a job at the University of Houston. Her husband is the vice chancellor of the University of Houston System and vice president for student affairs at the University of Houston.

Jackson-Lee made two unsuccessful bids for local judgeships before becoming a municipal judge (1987–90). In 1989, she was elected to an at-large seat on the Houston City Council; she served until 1994. As a council member, Jackson-Lee was an advocate for gun safety and supported an ordinance that punished parents who did not keep their guns away from children. She also worked for expanded summer hours at city parks and recreation centers as a way to combat gang violence.

Jackson-Lee was first elected to Congress in 1994. She sits on the House Committee on the Judiciary, the Committee on Science, and the Committee on Homeland Security. She is the ranking Democrat on the Subcommittee on Immigration, Border Security, and Claims. Sheila Jackson-Lee is the first vice chair of the Congressional Black Caucus. She was reelected in 2006.

Further Reading

Barone, Michael. *The Almanac of American Politics.* Washington, D.C.: National Journal Group, 2006.

"Jackson-Lee, Sheila." In *Biographical Directory of the United States Congress, 1774–present.* Available online. URL: http://bioguide.congress.gov/scripts/biodisplay.pl?index=J000032. Accessed on January 8, 2007.

"Representative Sheila Jackson-Lee (TX)." In *Project Vote Smart.* Available online. URL: http://votesmart.org/bio.php?can_id=. Accessed on January 8, 2007.

—Angela Kouters

Johnson, Eddie Bernice (1935–) *congressperson*   Eddie Bernice Johnson was born on December 3, 1935, in Waco, Texas, educated in nursing at St. Mary's College, University of Notre Dame, and became a psychiatric nurse and psychotherapist. She received her B.S. degree from

258

Texas Christian University in 1967 and her master's in public administration from Southern Methodist University in 1976.

Johnson was the first African-American woman ever to win elected public office in Dallas. In 1972, she began her career in public service when she was elected to the Texas House of Representatives. She chaired the Labor Committee, becoming the first woman in Texas history to lead a major Texas House committee, and subsequently was an administrator for the U.S. Department of Health, Education and Welfare from 1977 to 1981. Johnson was elected to the Texas State Senate in 1986. As a state senator, she was on the redistricting committee, where she was instrumental in shaping the district she represents. She was subsequently elected to the U.S. House of Representatives in 1992.

As the chair of the Congressional Black Caucus (2000–01), Johnson was a leading voice in opposition to the Authorization for Use of Military Force Against Iraq Resolution of 2002. She sits on the House Transportation and Infrastructure Committee and serves as the ranking Democratic member of the Subcommittee on Water Resources and Environment. Johnson has sponsored legislation designed to reauthorize federal welfare programs with stronger antidiscrimination provisions, remedy environmental injustice, and reform the tax code and the payroll tax. She was reelected in 2006 with 80 percent of the vote.

Further Reading

Barone, Michael. *The Almanac of American Politics.* Washington, D.C.: National Journal Group, 2006.

"Johnson, Eddie Bernice." In *Biographical Directory of the United States Congress, 1774–present.* Available online. URL: http://bioguide.congress.gov/scripts/biodisplay.pl?index=J000126. Accessed on January 8, 2007.

"Representative Eddie Bernice Johnson (TX)." In *Project Vote Smart.* Available online. URL: http://votesmart.org/bio.php?can_id=H3985103. Accessed on January 8, 2007.

—Angela Kouters

Johnson, Eliza (Elizabeth [Eliza] McCardle Johnson)

(1810–1876) *first lady* Elizabeth McCardle was born on October 4, 1810, in Greeneville, Tennessee, the only child of John and Sara Phillips McCardle. Her father, a shoemaker by trade, died in 1826, leaving Eliza and her mother to support themselves by sewing quilts. Home-schooled by her mother, she was a voracious reader and may have received some formal education at Rhea Academy.

Andrew Johnson was serving as a tailor's apprentice in North Carolina, but fled to Tennessee on foot to avoid completing his apprenticeship. He set up a tailor's shop in Greeneville, and a year after the two met, Eliza and Andrew were married on May 17, 1827. As he established his tailoring business, she reportedly taught him to write and read. He was anxious to improve himself, and she read to him as he worked, encouraged him to join the debating society to learn public speaking, and supported his quest for his first political position as local alderman.

Between 1828 and 1852, Eliza Johnson had five children; all survived to adulthood. Andrew Johnson was first elected to the state legislature in 1835 and to the U.S. House of Representatives in 1842. She did not join him in Washington, nor did she move to Nashville upon his election as governor of Tennessee in 1853. In 1857, Johnson was elected to the U.S. Senate, and Eliza joined him briefly in Washington 1861, but she returned to Greeneville as the Civil War began. Tuberculosis weakened Eliza Johnson's health, and alcoholism in her two oldest sons distracted her attention. Andrew Johnson's public position against secession had resulted in threats against his life and endangered the family. President Lincoln appointed Johnson military governor of Tennessee, making him responsible for the territory held by Union forces. The Johnsons' Greeneville home was confiscated by Confederate forces; his papers were scattered and his assets frozen. Eliza Johnson was ordered to leave the area, but she requested and received a reprieve until her health improved enough to allow her to travel. She made her way to Nashville accompanied by family, but they were regarded as the enemy and harassed by Confederate forces such that they had difficulty finding accommodations.

On March 4, 1865, Andrew Johnson was rewarded by his loyalty to the Union and sworn in as Abraham Lincoln's vice president. The assassination of President Lincoln a month later elevated Johnson to the presidency. Eliza Johnson had no desire to serve as First Lady. Perhaps because of the difficulties suffered by Mary Todd Lincoln at the hands of the public and press, but more likely because of her own private nature and fragile health, she shunned any public role as first lady and appointed her daughter, Martha Johnson Patterson, to serve in her place. Like other wives before her, she created a private space for herself on the second floor of the White House and occupied herself with her family rather than the affairs of the country.

Johnson's presidency was beset with problems. Although Republicans controlled the Congress, they doubted Johnson's allegiance to the Union based on his decisions to pardon Confederates and move toward Reconstruction. The standoff between the executive and legislative branches over issues related to civil rights of freed slaves and reconstruction of southern states led to an effort to impeach President Johnson and remove him from office. Johnson retained office by a single Senate vote and completed his term. In March 1869, the family turned the White House over to Julia and Ulysses S. Grant and returned to Greeneville. Andrew Johnson ultimately returned to politics, being elected to the U.S. Senate in 1875. However, while visiting his wife and daughter in Tennessee, he suffered a stroke and died on July 31, 1875. Eliza was too infirm to attend his funeral. She died six months later on January 15, 1876.

Further Reading

Anthony, Carl Sferrazza. *First Ladies: The Saga of the President's Wives and Their Power, 1789–1961.* New York: William Morrow, 1990.

Bendict, Michael Les. *The Impeachment and Trial of Andrew Johnson.* New York: Norton, 1999.

National First Ladies Library. *Biographies: First Ladies of the United States.* Available online. URL: http://www.firstladies.org/biographies. Accessed on January 4, 2007.

Schneider, Dorothy, and Carl J. Schneider. "Eliza McCardle Johnson." *First Ladies: A Biographical Dictionary.* New York: Checkmark Books, 2001, 107–111.

Trefousse, Hans Louis. *Andrew Johnson: A Biography.* New York: Norton, 1997.

Johnson, Lady Bird (Claudia Alta Taylor Johnson) (1912–2007) *first lady*

Claudia Alta Taylor was born on December 22, 1912, in Karnack, Texas, to Thomas Jefferson ("TJ") Taylor and Minne Lee Patillo Taylor. Claudia was the Taylors' third child and only daughter. Legend has it that she acquired her nickname Lady Bird as a child when an African-American cook compared her beauty to that of an East Texas beetle, the ladybird. Lady Bird's mother was from an influential family and felt trapped by the isolation of Texas. She read constantly to her daughter and traveled to Chicago to attend the opera. When Lady Bird was five, her mother, pregnant again at age 44, fell down a flight of stairs and died from the complications of a miscarriage. Her father called in her mother's Aunt Effie Patillo to help raise his daughter. From that point, Lady Bird spent the academic year in Texas and summers with her mother's family in Alabama.

Although her love of reading made school easy for her, Lady Bird was shy. When the one-room school in Karnack closed, she was educated by a tutor and then attended high school in Marshall, Texas. High school was painful since no one had helped her transition from a tomboy to a young woman. She graduated third in her class at 15 years old, too young to enroll in college, so she spent the next two years at St. Mary's Episcopal School for Girls. In 1930, Lady Bird enrolled at the University of

Texas at Austin and flourished. She majored in history, wrote articles for the *Daily Texan,* and served as publicity manager for the University of Texas Sports Association, a group of female athletes. She earned a B.A. degree in 1933, but stayed an extra year to complete a major in journalism.

By 1934, Lady Bird was ready to embark on a career, but the Great Depression limited her options. Around this time, she was introduced to Lyndon Baines Johnson, an aide for a Texas congressman in Washington. Johnson proposed on their first date, but Lady Bird declined. They began a correspondence, however, and Johnson returned to Texas to meet with her father. Her father approved of the couple, but still Lady Bird refused his proposal. Finally she agreed to travel with Johnson to visit friends in Austin, and on the way Johnson persuaded her to marry him—a marriage he arranged immediately by calling upon friends to obtain a marriage license on short notice. After a brief honeymoon in Mexico, the couple returned to Washington. For a month, they lived in the basement of the Dodge Hotel before taking a one-bedroom apartment.

Lady Bird found Lyndon to be demanding, short-tempered, and consumed by politics. She didn't complain but instead applied her energies to learning how to be a congressional wife from other wives and learning about her husband from her mother-in-law. In 1935, they returned to Texas when Lyndon was appointed director of the Texas National Youth Administration (NYA), a Great Depression program that created meaningful work opportunities for young people. In Texas, the Johnsons decided together that the works projects would focus on beautifying the roadways and building roadside parks. In 1937, Lyndon decided to seek a seat in Congress. Lady Bird worked diligently on his election, contributing $10,000 from her mother's estate to finance the successful campaign. Lyndon's next attempt was for a Senate seat in 1941, but the popular Texas governor Pappy O'Daniel defeated him.

Lady Bird Johnson, ca. 1962 (LIBRARY OF CONGRESS)

When the country entered World War II, Lyndon Johnson left his congressional office to Lady Bird to run and went on active duty with the Navy Reserves. By all accounts, Lady Bird ran the office efficiently and was sensitive to the needs of Texas constituents under duress due to rationing and other war efficiency measures. Johnson returned home in 1942 when President Roosevelt urged all elected members of Congress to resume their domestic political duties. The couple had two children in the mid-1940s: Lynda Bird (b. 1944) and Lucy Baines (b. 1947). (Both daughters would later be married in the White House.)

In 1943, the Johnsons purchased radio station KTBC in Lady Bird's name with $17,000 from her mother's estate. While Lady Bird tended to the daily management and rebuilding efforts in Texas, Lyndon used his influence with the Federal Communication Commission to expand transmission strength and win permission to broadcast 24 hours a day. By the mid-1950s, the station was a powerful political tool and a financial success.

In 1948, Lyndon attempted another run at the Senate with Lady Bird by his side. This time, Lyndon won by a suspect 87-vote margin in the primary and took the November election by a wide margin. In Washington, he quickly mastered the politics of the Senate, emerging as the youngest minority leader in history; in 1954, the same year he was reelected to the Senate, he became majority leader. Lady Bird supported his climb by hosting dinner parties at all hours and welcoming visitors on a moment's notice. After a heart attack in 1955, Lyndon took a brief rest at the LBJ Ranch before resuming his political climb. Lady Bird helped him lose weight and eliminate a lifetime smoking habit. When he returned to Washington, he had his eye on the presidency. Although he did not win the nomination in 1956, it was clear to Lady Bird that more would be expected of her, and she enrolled in a public speaking class through the Capital Speakers Club to lessen her fears of appearing in public.

When John F. Kennedy asked Johnson to join the ticket in 1960 as a way to heal the rift in the Democratic Party, Lady Bird encouraged her husband to accept even though she knew he did not relish playing second fiddle to Kennedy. During the 1960 campaign, Lady Bird proved to be a real asset campaigning in the South, making several whistle-stop tours through the region. As wife of the vice president, she often filled in for First Lady JACQUELINE KENNEDY, who did not like the ceremonial duties associated with the role. Lady Bird traveled extensively with Lyndon as he made several foreign tours on the president's behalf. The Johnsons were with the Kennedys on November 22, 1963, when the president was assassinated, and Lady Bird watched as her husband was sworn into office on Air Force One.

As first lady, Mrs. Johnson made a number of important contributions. She developed a staff that went well beyond a social secretary, hired a staff director and press secretary, and brought professional staff from the Department of the Interior to oversee the continuing restoration of the White House begun under the Kennedy administration. Lady Bird kept a formal diary of her activities and later published a portion of her entries as A White House Diary (1970). She enjoyed a positive relationship with the press, although she did not hold formal press conferences. During the campaign for the presidency in 1964, she again helped the ticket in the South by campaigning from the "Lady Bird Special." Once assured that they would occupy the White House for the next four years, Lady Bird turned to identifying the causes she most favored. Although her efforts were many and varied, the two causes to which she devoted the most energy included Head Start and a national beautification campaign. Working directly with Sargent Shriver, head of the Office of Economic Opportunity, she visited Head Start classrooms and lobbied Congress for funding to continue the program. Her efforts dedicated to beautification of the natural environment, however, proved to be her lasting legacy.

Working with the president and various advisors, Lady Bird first turned her attention to the city of Washington itself. She worked directly with Walter Washington, head of the national Capitol Housing Agency, on identifying projects for local neighborhoods. In summer 1965, youth and local residents were enlisted in a clean-up campaign. The first lady called on a network of friends to donate the money needed to support the local efforts and employ youth in the process. During the summer of 1966, 250 African-American young people were employed to clean up playgrounds and beautify neighborhoods. Lady Bird's later efforts included the area surrounding the Capitol and incorporated urban planners and architects. Her collaboration with Walter Washington helped him become the first African-American mayor of Washington, D.C.

Lady Bird Johnson's efforts nationally involved her directly in policy formation and passage of the Highway Beautification Act of

1965. This legislation sought to limit billboard advertising along America's roadways, but it encountered stiff opposition from industry. Lady Bird directly lobbied members of Congress and participated in strategy sessions to get the legislation passed. Critics denounced the law as the "president's wife's bill," but for his part, Lyndon made no secret of his promise to her to pass the bill if at all possible. In the end, it was passed and signed into law on October 22, 1965. A subsequent bill passed in 1968 severely weakened the anti-billboard provisions, but by that time Johnson's term was ending, and the Vietnam War had sapped much of the power from his presidency.

The emerging women's and civil rights movements placed even greater pressures on the White House. Lady Bird encouraged Congress to take up legislation to help women balance the competing demands of work and family. She was horrified at the violence perpetrated against African Americans protesting discrimination. As a southerner who had been raised with blacks, she was somewhat confused by the new fury expressed over their oppression. Johnson's Great Society efforts were dwarfed by the incredible poverty in inner cities and the despair it induced. War protesters heckled her at public appearances. She was therefore not disappointed when the president announced that he "would neither seek nor accept the nomination of his party" for reelection in 1968. When they left the White House for Texas in early 1969, she continued to pursue her interests and found much in life to satisfy her. Lyndon, on the other hand, was not well-suited to private life, and he experienced a rapid decline. He died on January 22, 1973.

Following her husband's death, Lady Bird carried on her work in conservation and gave the LBJ Ranch to the National Park Service (although retaining a lifetime interest). In 1982, she donated 60 acres in East Texas for the National Wildflower Research Center, which she founded with actress Helen Hayes. She continued to advocate for conservation and for planting native plants and wildflowers along the nation's highways. When her son-in-law, Charles Robb, sought elective office in Virginia, she campaigned on his behalf while continuing to run the family businesses. In 1982, she announced that she was retiring from public life.

Lady Bird Johnson continued to live at the LBJ Ranch in Stonewall, Texas, spending her final years at her home in Austin. Her legacy as first lady grows from, but dramatically expands on, the political work accomplished by ELEANOR ROOSEVELT. Lady Bird was a policy maker and an influential lobbyist on matters that interested her, and she effectively used her role to accomplish improvements in environmental legislation and support for Head Start programs. She died on July 11, 2007, and was buried next to her husband in the family cemetery in Stonewall, Texas.

Further Reading

Gould, Lewis L. *Lady Bird Johnson and the Environment.* Lawrence: University Press of Kansas, 1999.

Johnson, Lady Bird. *A White House Diary.* New York: Holt, Rinehart, and Winston, 1970.

National First Ladies Library. *Biographies: First Ladies of the United States.* Available online. URL: http://www.firstladies.org/biographies. Accessed on January 4, 2007.

Schneider, Dorothy, and Carl J. Schneider. "Claudia Alta Taylor (Lady Bird) Johnson." *First Ladies: A Biographical Dictionary.* New York: Checkmark Books, 2001, 280–291.

Johnson, Nancy (Nancy Lee Johnson)

(1935–) *congressperson*   Nancy Elizabeth Lee was born on January 5, 1935, in Chicago, Illinois. She earned a bachelor's degree from Radcliffe College (1957) and attended the University of London's Courtauld Institute (1957–58). She married Dr. Theodore Johnson, with whom she has three daughters. Nancy Lee Johnson was active in community affairs as a volunteer before entering electoral politics. She was elected to the Connecticut State Senate in 1976 and served for three consecutive terms before being elected to the U.S. House of Representatives in 1982, representing first the sixth district and then the fifth district of Connecticut (following the elimination of the 6th district).

Nancy Johnson is a member of various moderate/liberal Republican groups such as the WISH LIST, the Republican Main Street Partnership, and Republicans for Choice. In the 109th Congress, Johnson was a senior member of the House Ways and Means Committee and the first woman to chair one of its subcommittees. She also served on the Joint Committee on Taxation. Johnson lost her seat in November 2006 to challenger Chris Murphy. A prominent issue in the campaign was Johnson's support for the Iraq War and her support for the invasion in 2003. Although she vastly outspent Murphy, she lost the election by over 12 points. After she left Congress, she became a resident fellow at Harvard University's Institute of Politics.

Further Reading

Barone, Michael. *The Almanac of American Politics.* Washington, D.C.: National Journal Group, 2006.
Johnson, Nancy Lee. *Biographical Directory of the United States Congress, 1774–present.* Available online. URL: http://bioguide.congress.gov/scripts/biodisplay.pl?index=J000163. Accessed on January 8, 2007.

—Angela Kouters

Johnson v. Calvert (5 Cal. 4th 84; 851 P.2d 776) (1993)

This case involved an unsuccessful claim of parental rights by a gestational surrogate in California. By contract, Anna Johnson was implanted with an embryo created by the egg and sperm of a husband and wife, Crispina and Mark Calvert. Johnson ultimately gave birth to a child and sued to claim her parental rights. The California Supreme Court ruled that a gestational surrogate does not have the rights of a biological mother. A woman who, by agreement, has a zygote implanted in her and carries the fetus to term "provides a necessary and important service" but has no rights or status as "birth mother." The court refused to consider arguments challenging the constitutionality of SURROGACY itself, based on the contention that it is a form of involuntary servitude, tends to degrade women, and is rife with race and class exploitation issues.

Further Reading

Robertson, John A. *Children of Choice: Freedom and New Reproductive Technologies.* Princeton, N.J.: Princeton University Press, 1996.
Saetnan, Ann Rudinow, Nelly Oudshoorn, and Marta Kirejvzyk. *Bodies of Technology: Women's Involvement With Reproductive Medicine.* Columbus: Ohio State University, 2000.

Jones, Mary Harris ("Mother" Jones) (1837–1930) *labor activist*

The woman who became known as "Mother" Jones for her intense involvement in the labor movement, was born Mary Harris in Cork, Ireland, on August 1, 1837 (although she claimed a birthdate of May 1, 1830). Her father, a tenant farmer in Ireland, immigrated to the United States and sent for his family in 1838. Mary was the first in her family to graduate from high school. She enrolled in a teacher's college and found work as a teacher in Toronto, Canada, and Monroe, Michigan. She left teaching when she moved to Chicago in 1859 and instead opened a dressmaking shop. In 1861, she moved to Memphis, Tennessee, and resumed work as a teacher. There she met George E. Jones, a member of the Iron Molder's Union. They were married in 1861, and Mary gave birth to four children in six years. Tragically, George and her four children died in a yellow fever epidemic in 1867, leading Mary to dress in black for the rest of her life.

Jones returned to Chicago that year and resumed her work as a seamstress until the Great Chicago Fire in 1871 claimed her shop. In search of community and a sense of belonging after so much personal tragedy, she joined the Knights of Labor, a progressive reform organization dedicated to organizing all workers regardless of their race, sex, or trade. The Knights advocated an eight-hour workday and better living conditions. In 1894, Mary Jones began to work as an organizer for the United Mine Workers and traveled extensively throughout Colorado, Arizona, Michigan, Minnesota, West Virginia, and Pennsylvania. She was involved in strikes and had a knack for attracting the attention of the media with the power of her speeches, public protests, and symbolic gestures. For example, in 1903, she organized a march of more than 100 child mill workers to President Theodore Roosevelt's residence in New York. She worked undercover in mills in the South to expose abusive child labor practices. In 1913, she was present for the Colorado Coal Strike and the Ludlow Massacre where 20 women and children living in a miner's tent colony were killed by the Colorado militia. Jones

testified before Congress and lobbied President Wilson to bring an end to the violence and establish grievance committees for the mines.

Although Mary Jones urged women to participate actively through labor organizations in promoting their own welfare and their families' interests, she did not support woman's SUFFRAGE. The reasons for her opposition are not entirely clear. It may have stemmed from her general distrust of government and politicians. More likely, however, it had to do with class interests. She saw the world as divided into those who created wealth and those who owned it, with all other distinctions, such as race and gender, insignificant. She wrote in 1925, "The plutocrats have organized their women. They keep them busy with suffrage and prohibition and charity."

A self-described "hell raiser" she was often at odds with the establishment, particularly with the law. Approaching her eighties, she continued to participate in strike actions with street car, garment, and steel workers. She was jailed during a mine strike in West Virginia in 1913, but an outpouring of support led to her release. She wrote an autobiography, published in 1925 by the Charles Kerr Company. A few months before she died, she was captured speaking on film by the Movietone News. Mary Jones died on November, 30, 1930, and was buried at Mount Olive Hill, a miner's cemetery in Mount Olive, Illinois. Miners later erected a granite monument at her gravesite in her honor. There are numerous tributes to her life and work, including a progressive magazine named for her (*Mother Jones*, available at www.motherjones.com). In 1992, she was inducted into the U.S. Department of Labor's Hall of Fame, located in Washington, D.C.

Further Reading

Gorn, Elliott J. *Mother Jones: The Most Dangerous Woman in America.* New York: Hill and Wang, 2001.

Jones, Mary Harris. *The Autobiography of Mother Jones.* Chicago: Charles Kerr Company, 1925.

—Caryn E. Neumann

Mary Harris Jones ("Mother" Jones), ca. 1902. (LIBRARY OF CONGRESS)

Jones, Stephanie Tubbs (1949–) *congressperson* Stephanie Tubbs was born in Cleveland, Ohio, on September 10, 1949. She received her undergraduate degree in social work from Case Western Reserve University in 1971 and earned a law degree from Case Western Reserve University School of Law in 1974. In 1976, she married Mervyn L. Jones, Sr. Her career in public service began in 1981 when she won election to a municipal judgeship for Cleveland. She subsequently served on the Court of Common Pleas of Cuyahoga Country from 1983 to 1991. In 1991, she became the first African-American and female Cuyahoga County prosecutor.

In 1998, Jones was elected to the U.S. House of Representatives for Ohio's 11th district, succeeding Congressman Louis Stokes. She has been active with the National Democratic Party, serving as a cochair of the Democratic National Committee and, in 2004, as chair of the platform committee at the Democratic National Convention. Her legislative agenda includes advocacy for wealth development, equitable access to health care and quality education, and legal restriction on predatory lending. On January 6, 2005, she joined Senator BARBARA BOXER in objecting to the certification of the 2004 U.S. presidential election results for Ohio because of a number of irregularities at the polls.

Jones was the sponsor of the "Count Every Vote" Act of 2005. As the first African-American woman to serve on the Ways and Means Committee, she has worked against any efforts to privatize Social Security. Although she was encouraged by Democratic leaders to run for Ohio governor in 2002, she declined. She was reelected to Congress in 2006 with 83 percent of the vote and now chairs the House Committee on Standards of Official Conduct (known also as the Ethics Committee).

Further Reading
Barone, Michael. *The Almanac of American Politics.* Washington, D.C.: National Journal Group, 2006.
"Jones, Stephanie Tubbs." In *Biographical Directory of the United States Congress, 1774–present.* Available online. URL: http://bioguide.congress.gov/scripts/biodisplay/pl?index=J000284. Accessed on January 8, 2007.
"Representative Stephanie Tubbs Jones (OH)." In *Project Vote Smart.* Available online. URL: http://votesmart.org/bio.php?can_id=C0H45325. Accessed on January 8, 2007.

—Angela Kouters

Jordan, Barbara Charline (1936–1996) *congressperson, activist* Barbara Charline Jordan was born to Arlyne and Reverend Benjamin Jordan on February 21, 1936, in Houston, Texas, and attended Houston's segregated public schools. She graduated magna cum laude from Texas Southern University, where she won honors for her debate talents. When she enrolled in law school at Boston University, she was the only woman in her class of 128. She received her law degree in 1959 and returned to Houston to establish her practice.

Elected to the Texas Senate in 1966 after two unsuccessful runs for a seat in the Texas House of Representatives in 1962 and 1964, Jordan became the first black woman elected to that position in U.S. history, as well as the first black person since 1883. During her second term (1968), Jordan was elected president pro tem of the Senate. In the tradition of the Texas Senate, she served a day as governor of Texas, becoming the first black female governor in the United States. She was the primary sponsor of Texas's first minimum-wage law, written broadly to cover farmworkers and others not included in the federal minimum-wage statute.

In 1972, elected as the representative of a newly created congressional district, Jordan became the first black Texan in the U.S. Congress. Her intellect and forceful personality propelled her to powerful positions as a member of the House Judiciary Committee, the House Committee on Government Operations, and the Steering and Policy Committee of the Democratic Caucus. The general public got their first close look at Jordan when, in 1974, she made of a future run for the White House. However, she retired after three terms in Congress due to the onset of multiple sclerosis.

After leaving Congress, Jordan turned to education and was a professor for 16 years, teaching at the Lyndon B. Johnson School of Public Affairs at the University of Texas at Austin. She was the recipient of 25 honorary doctorate degrees from colleges and universities, including Tuskegee Institute, Princeton, and Harvard. She continued to serve on special political commissions and spoke at political gatherings and symposiums. Sixteen years after delivering her first keynote address at the Democratic National Convention, she again was invited to give the keynote address at the 1992 convention. In 1994, she was awarded the Presidential Medal of Freedom, the highest civilian award in the United States.

Barbara Jordan's talent for speech and debate, fostered in high school and continued during four years on the debate team of Texas State University, helped take her to record heights in her life. Through her words and actions, she became a renowned champion of equal opportunity and equal legal rights for everyone. When she spoke, people listened and reacted. The sound of her voice commanded attention, the tone garnered respect. Jordan died at the age of 59 on January 18, 1996, in Austin, Texas, from viral pneumonia as a complication of leukemia.

Barbara Jordan, giving the keynote address at the Democratic National Convention, July 12, 1976 (LIBRARY OF CONGRESS)

the opening statement during the televised impeachment hearings of President Richard M. Nixon. (See the appendices of this volume for the text of this speech.) So began one of many statements that are now routinely quoted in textbooks, collections of historical speeches, all in acknowledgment of Jordan's extraordinary ability to make words connect with ordinary people. When she made a riveting speech at the 1976 Democratic National Convention, there began political speculation about the possibility

Further Reading

Jordan, Barbara, and Shelby Hearon. *Barbara Jordan—A Self-Portrait.* New York: Doubleday & Co., 1979.

Safire, William, ed. *Lend Me Your Ears: Great Speeches in History.* New York: W.W. Norton & Co., 1997.

—Maria Elena Raymond

K

Kaptur, Marcia (Marcia [Marcy] Carolyn Kaptur) (1946–) *congressperson* Marcia Kaptur was born on June 17, 1946, in Toledo, Ohio, and graduated from St. Ursula Academy in Toledo in 1964. She received a B.A. degree from the University of Wisconsin in 1968 and an M.A. from the University of Michigan in 1974. She attended the University of Manchester in the United Kingdom in 1974 and did postgraduate study in urban planning at the Massachusetts Institute of Technology in 1981. Kaptur served on the Toledo-Lucas County Planning Commission from 1969 to 1975 and was director of planning for the National Center for Urban Ethnic Affairs from 1975 to 1977. From 1977 to 1979, she served in the Carter administration as a domestic policy advisor.

Kaptur was first elected to the U.S. House of Representatives in 1982. She serves on the House Committee on Appropriations and has pushed for more portraits and statues of women throughout the U.S. Capitol. Kaptur represented Ohio as a delegate to the 2000 and 2004 Democratic National Conventions. When one of her constituents, Roger Durbin, suggested the creation of a World War II memorial in Washington, D.C., Kaptur spearheaded the project, and the memorial opened in 2004. In 2006, she received over 70 percent of the vote and won reelection to her 13th consecutive term in office. Kaptur is now the senior woman in the House of Representatives.

Further Reading

Barone, Michael. *The Almanac of American Politics.* Washington, D.C.: National Journal Group, 2006.

"Kaptur, Marcia Carolyn (Marcy)." In *Biographical Directory of the United States Congress, 1774–present.* Available online. URL: http://bioguide.congress.gov/scripts/biodisplay.pl?index=K000009. Accessed on January 8, 2007.

"Representative Marcy Kaptur." In *Project Vote Smart.* Available online. URL: http://votesmart.org/bio.php?can_id=. Accessed on January 8, 2007.

—Angela Kouters

Kassebaum, Nancy Landon (Nancy Landon Kassebaum Baker) (1932–) *U.S. senator* Nancy Landon Kassebaum (now Baker) is a Republican who represented the state of Kansas in the U.S. Senate from 1978 to 1997. Born on July 29, 1932, in Topeka, Kansas, she is the daughter of Alfred M. Landon (1887–1987), who was governor of Kansas from 1932 to 1937 as well as the 1936 Republican presidential nominee. Nancy Landon graduated from the University of Kansas in 1954 with a B.S. in political science and earned her M.A. in diplomatic history from the University of Michigan in 1956. In June 1955, she married businessman Philip Kassebaum (they divorced in 1975).

While raising four children on a farm in Maize, Kansas, Nancy Kassebaum was involved with the local school board, the Kansas Governmental Ethics Committee, and the Kansas Committee for the Humanities. In 1975, she joined Senator James Pearson's staff in Washington, D.C. Upon his retirement in 1978, she decided to run for his seat and defeated eight other Republicans in the primary. The only woman in the Senate at the time of her election and the first to serve in that body on her own merits rather than succeeding a deceased husband, she was reelected in 1984 and 1990. In 1996, she did not seek reelection.

When the Republicans secured a Senate majority after the 1980 election, Kassebaum became a member of the Foreign Relations Committee, where she focused on African issues. Kassebaum was known for her moderate views and willingness to oppose the Reagan administration when she supported sanctions on South Africa to abolish apartheid. She earned a reputation for building coalitions and for pragmatic positions on policy. She supported the EQUAL RIGHTS AMENDMENT and the Strategic Arms Limitation Treaty. Kassebaum was an early proponent of term limits, supported ABORTION rights and gun control, and was the first woman to chair a major U.S. Senate committee, the Labor and Human Resources Committee in 1995. She is noted for her efforts to improve education, child care, and health care; promote fiscal responsibility; and overhaul foreign aid programs.

Since 1996, Kassebaum has been married to former senator Howard Baker, Jr. (R-TN), who served as chief of staff (1987–89) under President Ronald Reagan and was appointed by President George W. Bush as ambassador to Japan, serving in that post from 2001 to 2005. In 1996–97, Nancy Kassebaum Baker served as the first Mary Louise Smith chair in woman and politics at Iowa State University.

Further Reading

Kassebaum, Nancy Landon. "To Form a More Perfect Union." *Presidential Studies Quarterly* 18 (1988): 241–249.

Marshall-White, Eleanor. *Women, Catalysts for Change: Interpretive Biographies of Shirley St. Hill Chisholm, Sandra Day O'Connor, and Nancy Landon Kassebaum.* New York: Vantage Press, 1991.

—Paula Casey

Kelley, Florence (1859–1932) *social reformer, labor activist*   Born in Philadelphia on September 12, 1859, Florence Kelley was the daughter of U.S. congressman William D. Kelley (1814–90), who showed her the conditions under which poor and immigrant children worked and lived. Kelley graduated from Cornell University in 1882 and Northwestern University law school in 1894. In, 1884, she married Lazare Wishniewski, a Polish doctor with whom she had three children. After studying in Europe and publishing a translation of Friedrich Engels's *The Conditions of the Working Class in England,* Kelley divorced her husband and, moved to Chicago in 1891. There she moved into JANE ADDAMS'S HULL-HOUSE and began work documenting the living and working conditions of those within one square mile of the settlement house. This experience resulted in a constant use of facts and data to uphold all of her calls for economic and social reform.

In 1893, Kelley was appointed the first female factory inspector in Illinois. In this role, she worked to document the effects of long hours on all workers, paying particular attention to women and children. In 1898, she testified at the NATIONAL AMERICAN WOMAN SUFFRAGE ASSOCIATION convention on "Working Women's Need of the Ballot," arguing that any worker who is disenfranchised is largely unable to work for changes in industry, and that when women lack the vote, they are necessarily subordinated in comparison with their fellow male workers. "By impairing [a woman's] standing in the community the general rating of her value as a human being, and consequently as a worker, is lowered."

Kelley worked to establish child labor laws, and in 1899 (after moving to New York), she helped start the National Consumer's League (NCL), which worked to establish a minimum wage and a limited workday. The NCL also started a "white label" initiative, which resulted in the display of an NCL white label on all products from companies with progressive labor practices (no child labor and following workday regulations). In 1905, Kelley started the Inter-Collegiate Socialist Society with Upton Sinclair and Jack London. She traveled extensively throughout the United States to speak to students on college campuses and was criticized in the *Congressional Record* for her influence among young people.

With the help of the lawyer (and future Supreme Court justice) Louis Brandeis, Kelley sought to challenge the argument that limited working hours were unconstitutional. To do this, she gathered data in support of the claim that extended working hours were harmful to the health of women and children. This case, MULLER V. OREGON (1908), established that laws limiting women to a 10-hour workday were constitutional. Kelly also fought for the establishment of a U.S. Children's Bureau. In 1909, she helped found the National Association for the Advancement of Colored People (NAACP), and in 1921 she was instrumental in the passage of the SHEPPARD-TOWNER MATERNITY AND INFANCY PROTECTION ACT. Florence Kelly died in Philadelphia on February 17, 1932.

Further Reading

Sklar, Kathyrn K. *Florence Kelley and the Nation's Work: The Rise of Woman's Political Culture.* New Haven, Conn.: Yale University Press, 1997.

———. *Notes of Sixty Years: The Autobiography of Florence Kelley.* Chicago: Charles H. Kerr, 1986.

—Claire Curtis

Kelly, Sue (Susan Weisenbarger Kelly)

(1936–) *congressperson* Susan Weisenbarger was born on September 26, 1936, in Lima, Ohio, where she attended public schools and graduated from Lima Central High School. She attended Denison University in Granville, Ohio, earning a B.A. degree in 1958, and then earned her master's degree from Sarah Lawrence College in 1985. Kelly started her career as a biomedical researcher in Boston, Massachusetts, for the New England Institute for Medical Research. After marrying Edward Kelly and moving to New York State, she owned businesses renovating buildings and selling flowers while raising four children.

In 1994, Sue Kelly decided to run for Congress. She won her seat in a crowded field and was subsequently reelected to five consecutive terms. In January 2001, Rep. Kelly was appointed as chair of the House Financial Services Oversight and Investigations Subcommittee. In this role, she was an active proponent for corporate reform and increased federal oversight of corporate affairs. Kelly held the first congressional hearings on the Enron and Global Crossing bankruptcies as well as on the WorldCom accounting fraud. Following these hearings, she was an author of the Sarbanes-Oxley corporate reform bill, which has helped ensure corporate responsibility and restore investor confidence.

Kelly initially voted against the Partial Birth Abortion Ban bill in 1996 but changed her vote in 2003. In 1998, she called on feminists to explain why they were not outraged by President Bill Clinton's personal behavior. She voted in favor of two of the four impeachment indictments against President Clinton. For a brief time, HILLARY RODHAM CLINTON's residence in Chappaqua, New York, was in Kelly's 19th district (it is now in the 18th district). She called the first lady a "carpetbagger" who did not understand New York's issues.

Kelly served as chair of the House Page Board from 1998 until 2001. When the scandal involving Congressman Mark Foley's inappropriate emails to teenage House pages broke in October 2006, questions were raised as to whether Kelly knew about Foley's behavior during that time. She refused to participate in a LEAGUE OF WOMEN VOTERS debate in her district (she was represented by an empty chair on stage) and refused to appear on the popular television program *The Colbert Report*. Instead, Stephen Colbert interviewed her Democratic opponent, John Hall. In the November 2006 election, Kelly lost her seat to Hall by a margin of 51-49.

Further Reading

Barone, Michael. *The Almanac of American Politics.* Washington, D.C.: National Journal Group, 2006.

"Kelly, Sue W." In *Biographical Directory of the United States Congress, 1774–present.* Available online. URL: http://bioguide.congress.gov/. Accessed on January 8, 2007.

—Angela Kouters

Kennedy, Jacqueline Bouvier (Jacqueline Lee Bouvier Kennedy Onassis, Jackie Kennedy)

(1929–1994) *first lady* Jacqueline Lee Bouvier was born on July 28, 1929, in Southampton, New York, to stockbroker John and Janet Lee Bouvier. Jacqueline and her younger sister, Caroline Lee, grew up in a family plagued by debt, alcoholism, and the separation of their parents. Following a divorce in 1936, the girls lived with their mother and her second husband, Hugh Auchincloss. Jacqueline was educated in private schools, including Miss Porter's School in Farmington, Connecticut. She received instruction in social dance, ballet, horseback riding, and music. Her own interests were in poetry and short stories, and some of her earliest work appeared in the local paper.

Jacqueline, also known as Jackie, enrolled at Vassar in 1947 and spent her junior year studying at the Sorbonne in Paris. She returned to complete her senior year at George Washington University, graduating in 1951. That year, she entered a nationwide *Vogue* Prix de Paris contest. The prize was a scholarship to the Sorbonne and a year divided between Paris and New York. The contest required applicants to design an entire issue of the magazine, and Jacqueline emerged as the winner among 12 finalists. Her mother and stepfather persuaded her to refuse the prize in favor of a summer in Europe and a full-time job as an inquiring photographer with the *Washington Times Herald*. Her daily column involved posing a question and running the response with a picture. She interviewed average citizens and high-profile politicians.

Jackie Bouvier met John Fitzgerald Kennedy in May 1952, as he was completing a third

Jacqueline Lee Bouvier Kennedy, 1961 (JFK LIBRARY)

term in the House of Representatives. He was elected to the Senate from Massachusetts later that year. The couple married on September 12, 1953, in a large society wedding in Newport, Rhode Island, and lived with family for much of their early marriage. Jackie had an uneasy relationship with the Kennedy clan, but Joseph Kennedy saw her as an asset to his son's chances for the presidency. With Jack Kennedy serving in the U.S. Senate, the couple rented a row house in Georgetown, where Jacqueline entertained and studied to be a Washington hostess. She supported her husband's career by tending to his wardrobe and attending Senate debates when he spoke. She did not care for women's groups but joined the Senate wives in Red Cross work and in fund-raising for the arts.

In 1956, two disappointments coincided. Jack failed in his bid to be the Democratic nominee for vice president, and Jacqueline gave birth to a stillborn daughter. In 1957, however, she gave birth to a healthy daughter, Caroline. Jackie joined Jack in his campaign for reelection to the U.S. Senate, using her language skills and social graces to attract voters. In 1959, she again campaigned actively with him as he sought the Democratic nomination for president. She granted television interviews and wrote a newspaper column titled "Campaign Wife." Toward the end of the campaign, she withdrew from most public campaigning due to her advancing pregnancy. However, she continued to be photographed and brought style to maternity fashion, rescuing the condition of pregnancy from isolation women often experienced. As Jack Kennedy's election appeared more certain, the Kennedy family hired Letitia Baldridge to serve as Jacqueline's assistant and to shape her image as first lady. Kennedy was elected on November 4, 1960, and son John Kennedy, Jr., was born prematurely by Caesarean section on November 21.

Upon Jack's election, Jacqueline Kennedy announced that she would devote her time to restoring the White House to its original splendor. She secured an extra appropriation from Congress to renovate the family quarters to accommodate a young family and appealed to the public for additional funds for the restoration effort, producing a television tour of the restored mansion. She also created a White House guidebook that sold millions of copies and is still updated in every administration, and she succeeded in acquiring museum status for the White House along with a permanent curator. Thanks to her efforts, White House property may only be removed to the Smithsonian Institute, ending a longstanding practice among past presidents of distributing contents of the White House as mementos to friends and supporters. After the restoration of the White House was complete, Jackie extended her reach to the Blair House, Lafayette Square, and the Victorian homes that surrounded the White House. She consulted urban planning experts in how best to revitalize Pennsylvania Avenue and extended her interest in historic preservation to treasures around the world.

Jacqueline Kennedy worked to protect the privacy of her children and to guarantee as much normalcy in daily life as possible. Security concerns dictated that Caroline be educated in the White House, but Jacqueline invited other children to join the school there. She maintained a distant and difficult relationship with the press, even though she herself had worked as a journalist. The public hungered for details about the urbane Kennedy couple and their photogenic children, but Jackie insisted that some aspects of their life were off-limits. Her experience, however, had also taught her the value of a well-placed quote or article, and so she allowed Press Secretary Pierre Salinger to coordinate public relations efforts and made overtures to the press by including a small press pool at White House dinners.

As first lady, Jackie Kennedy was extraordinarily popular throughout the United States and abroad. Enthusiastic crowds led President Kennedy to introduce himself to Parisians as "the man who accompanied Jacqueline Kennedy to Paris." Travel to Venezuela and Columbia offered the chance for her to speak Spanish to gathered crowds. At home, she introduced a number of innovations in executive entertaining. She brought renowned entertainers into the White House to perform for guests, adopted round tables to encourage conversation at formal dinner parties, and abolished the formal receiving line in favor of a small cocktail gathering before dinner. She raised money for the arts and cultural community in Washington and throughout the nation.

The death of the Kennedys' infant son Patrick, born on August 7, 1963, brought a state of mourning to the White House. Jacqueline departed for a tour of the Greek Isles and when she returned she agreed to accompany Jack to Dallas, Texas. On November 22, 1963, as they rode together in an open motorcade through the streets of Dallas, John F. Kennedy was shot and killed. Jacqueline Kennedy stood next to Vice President Lyndon Johnson as he was sworn in as president on Air Force One and stayed with her husband's body as it was flown back to Washington. In the days that followed the assassination, she worried about where she and her children would go upon leaving the White House and participated actively in planning a funeral that would befit Kennedy's legacy. Following the funeral, she and her children moved to a house in Washington owned by Averell Harriman. They lived there until 1964, when they moved to New York City.

Jacqueline Kennedy devoted herself to raising her children and promulgating the legacy of her husband's presidency as a promise cut short. The Camelot myth provided a way to raise funds in support of the Kennedy Library in order to continue the work and promote the ideals of John F. Kennedy. She supported Jack's brother Robert's candidacy for the Senate from New York but recoiled when he was assassinated in 1968: "I hate this country. I despise America and I don't want my children to live here any more. If they're killing Kennedys, my kids are number-one targets."

In October 1968, Jacqueline married wealthy Greek shipping magnate Aristotle Onassis. The Onassis children disliked her, and the Kennedy camp disapproved. The relationship required her to be away from her own children in school in New York. After Onassis died in 1975, she returned to New York City and took an editorial job with Viking Press and, later, Doubleday, producing a number of best-selling books. She continued to promote the arts and raise money for preservation efforts. Her daughter Caroline graduated from law school, married Edwin Schlossberg, an exhibit designer, and together they had three children. John F. Kennedy, Jr., ultimately passed the bar in New York on his third attempt but gravitated toward publishing interests.

In January 1994, Jacqueline was diagnosed with non-Hodgkin's lymphoma; she died at home on May 19 that year. John and Caroline defined the themes of her life as "her love of words, her emphasis on family, and her desire for adventure." She is buried in Arlington National Cemetery near John F. Kennedy and their two children who died in infancy. Her son, John F. Kennedy, Jr., was killed in a plane crash on July 16, 1999.

Further Reading

Baldridge, Letitia. *Of Diamonds and Diplomats*. Boston: Houghton Mifflin, 1968.

Bradford, Sarah. *America's Queen: the Life of Jacqueline Kennedy Onassis*. New York: Viking, 2000.

Caroli, Betty Boyd. "Jacqueline Lee Bouvier Kennedy Onassis." In *American First Ladies: Their Lives and Their Legacy*, 2nd ed., edited by Lewis L. Gould. New York: Routledge, 2001, 321–334.

National First Ladies Library. *Biographies: First Ladies of the United States*. Available online. URL: http://www.firstladies.org/biographies. Accessed on January 4, 2007.

Schneider, Dorothy, and Carl J. Schneider. "Jacqueline Lee (Jackie) Bouvier Kennedy." *First Ladies: A Biographical Dictionary*. New York: Checkmark Books, 2001, 271–279.

Kilpatrick, Carolyn Cheeks (1945–   ) *congressperson*   Born on June 25, 1945, in Detroit, Carolyn Jean Cheeks graduated from the Detroit

High School of Commerce, attended Ferris State University from 1968 to 1970, and received a B.S. degree from Western Michigan University in 1972. After earning an M.S. from the University of Michigan in 1977, she worked as a teacher and was a member of the Michigan State House of Representatives (1979–96). She is currently a member of the Detroit Substance Abuse Advisory Council. A marriage to Bernard Kilpatrick ended in divorce.

In 1996, Kilpatrick defeated incumbent U.S. representative Barbara-Rose Collins in the Democratic primary. She was subsequently elected to the 105th Congress and in every election since, including November 2006. Kilpatrick serves on the House Committee on Appropriations. In December 2006, Kilpatrick was unanimously selected as chair of the Congressional Black Caucus for the 110th Congress. She is the mother of Kwame Kilpatrick, who was elected to fill his mother's seat in the Michigan State House and was subsequently elected mayor of Detroit in 2001.

Further Reading

Barone, Michael. *The Almanac of American Politics.* Washington, D.C.: National Journal Group, 2006.

"Kilpatrick, Carolyn Cheeks." In *Biographical Directory of the United States Congress, 1774–present.* Available online. URL: http://bioguide.congress.gov/scripts/biodisplay.pl?index= K000180. Accessed on January 8, 2007.

"Representative Carolyn Cheeks Kilpatrick (MI)." In *Project Vote Smart.* Available online. URL: http://votesmart.org/bio.php?can_id=BC036076. Accessed on January 8, 2007.

—Angela Kouters

King, Coretta Scott (1927–2006) *civil rights activist*

Born in Marion, Alabama, on April 27, 1927, Coretta Scott spent her childhood on a farm owned by her parents, Obie Leonard and Bernice McMurray Scott. As a young child, Coretta walked five miles every day to attend a

Coretta Scott King, at the Democratic National Convention in New York, 1976 (LIBRARY OF CONGRESS)

one-room schoolhouse. The only high school was nine miles away, too far to walk, so her mother hired a bus and drove all of the African-American children in the area to Lincoln High School, a private black institution with an integrated faculty. After graduation, Coretta attended Antioch College in Ohio, where she received her B.A. in music and elementary education in 1949. Her older sister, Edythe, had been the first full-time black student to live on campus.

Coretta Scott joined the Antioch chapters of the National Association for the Advancement of Colored People (NAACP) as well as the Young Progressives, attending the Progressive Party convention in 1948 as a student delegate. In 1951, she enrolled at Boston's New England Conservatory of Music and subsequently met Martin Luther King, Jr., a doctoral candidate at Boston University School of Theology. They married on June 18, 1953. Coretta shocked Martin's father, the Reverend Martin Luther King, Sr., who presided over the wedding, by demanding that the promise to obey her husband be removed from the ceremony.

The Kings had four children: Yolanda Denise (1955), Martin Luther III (1957), Dexter Scott (1961), and Bernice Albertine (1963). Although supportive of Martin's work, Coretta focused on raising children and teaching music.

She accompanied Martin to major civil rights events and raised funds for the Southern Christian Leadership Conference (SCLC) by performing at "freedom concerts." In 1962, Coretta King served as a Women's Strike for Peace delegate to the 17-nation Disarmament Conference in Geneva, Switzerland. She struggled to find a balance between her desire to be active in the movement and the desire (and expectation) that she stay at home and raise her four children. "Martin was a very strong person, and in many ways had very traditional ideas about women," she said in a 1982 interview with the *New York Times Magazine*. "He'd say, 'I have no choice, I have to do this, but you haven't been called.' And I said, 'Can't you understand? You know I have an urge to serve just like you have.'"

Martin Luther King, Jr., was assassinated on April 4, 1968. Following his death, Coretta King committed herself to the civil rights movement and worked to promote his message of nonviolent resistance. Just four days after her husband's death, she led a march of 50,000 people through the streets of Memphis, and later that year she took his place in the Poor People's March to Washington. Although she used his words in an effort to keep his spirit alive in the movement, she gradually inserted her own decidedly feminist voice. When she spoke at the Lincoln Memorial on June 19, 1968, she called upon women to "unite and form a solid block of woman power to fight the three great evils of racism, poverty, and war." She also served on the board of directors of the NATIONAL ORGANIZATION FOR WOMEN.

In 1969, Coretta Scott King published her autobiography, *My Life with Martin Luther King, Jr.* While her activities within the movement continued, she focused most of her energy toward building the Martin Luther King, Jr., Center for Nonviolent Social Change in Atlanta, Georgia. The center's responsibilities include an exhibition hall, King's boyhood home, a library containing King's papers, and a museum. Coretta Scott King was instrumental in the adoption of a national holiday in honor of her husband and in encouraging communities to honor Martin Luther King, Jr., with a day devoted to service. The first holiday in honor of King was celebrated on January 20, 1986.

Loretta Scott King remained active in civil rights and women's rights and continued to be the driving force behind the expansion of the King Center. She died on January 30, 2006, in Mexico, where she was seeking nontraditional treatment for advanced ovarian cancer. She was the first woman and the first African American to lie in state in the Georgia Capitol, where more than 40,000 people filed past her body. More than 115,000 waited in line to pay their respects at a wake held at the historic Ebenezer Baptist Church, where Martin Luther King, Jr., and his father had both preached. The funeral was held at New Birth Missionary Baptist Church, where Bernice, the youngest of the King's four children, is pastor. The six-hour service featured remarks from President George W. Bush and three former presidents (Carter, Bush, and Clinton) as well as countless politicians and leaders in the civil rights movement past and present. Many who spoke challenged mourners to carry on the Kings' legacy. In November 2006, the bodies of Coretta Scott King and Martin Luther King, Jr., were laid to rest in a new mausoleum at the King Center.

Further Reading
Carson, Clayborne. "King, Coretta Scott" *Black Women in America, A Historical Encyclopedia,* edited by Darlene Clark Hine, 205–206. New York: Carlson Publishing Inc., 1993.
King, Coretta Scott. *My Life With Martin Luther King, Jr.* New York: Henry Holt & Co., 1969.

Kirkpatrick, Jeane J. (Jeane Duane Jordan Kirkpatrick) (1926–2006) *United Nations ambassador* Jeane Duane Jordan was born on November 19, 1926, in Duncan, Oklahoma, the daughter of Welcher F. and Leona Jordan. Her father was an oil wildcatter. She attended Stephens College in Missouri for two years and then moved to New York, where she earned a bachelor's degree from Barnard College (1948) and a master's degree from Columbia University (1950). After working as a research analyst with the Office of Intelligence Research at the U.S. State Department, she studied at the Institute de Science Politique in Paris from 1952 to 1953. In 1955, she married Evron M. Kirkpatrick, also a political scientist. She worked intermittently for the U.S. Department of Defense. In 1968, she earned a doctorate in political science at Columbia University and was appointed assistant professor at Georgetown University. She was promoted to full professor in 1973.

Dr. Kirkpatrick was the first woman appointed to serve as permanent representative of the United States to the United Nations and as a member of Ronald Reagan's cabinet and National Security Council. She served as a member of the president's Foreign Intelligence Advisory Board (1985–90) and the Defense Policy Review Board (1985–93), and she also chaired the Secretary of Defense Commission on Fail Safe and Risk Reduction of the Nuclear Command and Control System (1992). Kirkpatrick headed the U.S. delegation to the Human Rights Commission in 2003. She received numerous awards and recognitions, including the Medal of Freedom in 1985 and the Department of Defense Distinguished Public Service Medal in 1992. In 1993, she cofounded Empower America, a conservative public policy organization. She was the author of several books and monographs, including *The Withering Away of the Totalitarian State* (1992), and was the Leavey professor of government at Georgetown University as well as a senior fellow at the American Enterprise Institute, a conservative think tank in Washington, D.C. Dr. Jeane Kirkpatrick died at her home in Bethesda, Maryland, on December 7, 2006. She was 80 years old.

Further Reading

Harrison, Pat. *Jeane Kirkpatrick.* New York: Chelsea House, 1991.

Kreps, Juanita (Juanita Morris Kreps)

(1921–   ) *economist, secretary of commerce, director of the New York Stock Exchange*   Juanita Morris was born in Lynch, Kentucky, on January 11, 1921. She received a B.A. from Berea College (1942), an M.A. in economics from Duke University (1944), and a doctorate in economics from Duke (1948). She married Clifton H. Kreps, a fellow economist, in 1944. Kreps taught economics at Denison College in Ohio as well as at other institutions, returning to Duke in 1955. There she served as the last dean of the Woman's College and facilitated the merger of the women's and men's programs. In 1972, she was the first woman to be appointed a James B. Duke professor, the university's highest academic honor. The next year, she was named Duke's first female vice president.

Kreps served as the first woman director of the New York Stock Exchange. In 1977, she became the first woman to serve as U.S. secretary of commerce, having been appointed by President Jimmy Carter. She served as secretary from January 23, 1977, to October 31, 1979. Kreps is the author of numerous scholarly articles and books, including *Sex in the Marketplace: American Women at Work* (1971).

Further Reading

Grossman, Mark. *Encyclopedia of the United States Cabinet,* 3 vols. Santa Barbara, Calif.: ABC-CLIO, 2000, 183–189.

—Hollis France

Kunin, Madeleine May (1936–   ) *governor of Vermont*

Born on September 28, 1933, in Zurich, Switzerland, Madeleine May Kunin immigrated to the United States with her family in 1940. She earned a bachelor's degree from the University of Massachusetts in 1956, a master's degree from Columbia University in 1957, and a second master's degree from the University of Vermont in 1967. She married Dr. Arthur Kunin, with whom she had four children. Taking note that there were no women on the Burlington Board of

Aldermen, Kunin announced herself as a candidate in 1972; she lost that election by 16 votes. The next fall, she won a seat in the Vermont House of Representatives and served three terms. In 1978, she was elected lieutenant governor.

After an unsuccessful run for governor in 1982, Kunin was elected Vermont's first woman governor in 1984. She won reelection twice, making her the first woman in the country to win three terms in office. Kunin's focus in the legislature and as governor included environmental issues, education, and poverty. As governor, she was praised for her fiscal responsibility and for education reform. She made a point to hire women in her administration.

In 1992, Kunin served as a member of President Bill Clinton's transition team and was rewarded with appointment as deputy secretary of education in 1993. In this position, she established the Office of Educational Technology, chaired the National Science and Technology Council's Committee and headed efforts to simplify the national student loan system. Within the Clinton administration, she also served on the President's Council on Sustainable Development and the board of the National Environmental Education and Training Foundation. Kunin was a member of the President's Interagency Council on Women and took part in the U.S. delegation to the World Conferences on Women in Copenhagen and Beijing. Knopf published her political memoir, *Living a Political Life,* in 1994. Today Kunin has dual appointments at the University of Vermont in Burlington and St. Michael's College in Colchester, in the departments of political science, as a distinguished visiting professor. She divorced Arthur Kunin in 1995 and married John Hennessey in 2006.

L

Ladies Association of Philadelphia The Ladies Association of Philadelphia was founded in 1780 as a way to raise money and supplies for General George Washington's army and aid the patriots' efforts in the Revolutionary War. Esther De Berdt Reed was the first president. Through a door-to-door campaign that marked the first example of direct canvassing, the women raised well over $300,000 to support the war effort. The Ladies Association stipulated, however, that the money was to be used to provide "an extraordinary bounty" instead of the things the soldiers should "receive from Congress or the states." George Washington took exception to the women's intention and tried to negotiate directly with several of the women's husbands in order to direct the use of the funds himself. Ultimately, at least part of the money was used to purchase linen, which the ladies then sewed into shirts for the troops. When Esther Reed died suddenly of dysentery, Sarah Franklin Bache (daughter of Benjamin Franklin) took over leadership of the group. So that the soldiers knew whom to thank for their bounty, Bache directed each woman to sew her name into the collar of each shirt.

Further Reading

Roberts, Cokie. *Founding Mothers: The Women Who Raised our Nation.* New York: HarperCollins, 2004.

LaHaye, Beverly (1929–) *religious activist* Beverly LaHaye was born Beverly Jean Ratcliffe on April 30, 1929. While attending Bob Jones University in the late 1940s, she married Tim LaHaye at the age of 18. The shy mother of four followed her husband as he pastored different Baptist churches. The LaHayes eventually landed in San Diego, where Beverly began to participate with her husband in public speaking events. In 1971, the couple joined the Family Life Seminars to tour the country and educate Christians about family life. Six years later, Beverly LaHaye saw a Barbara Walters television interview with feminist BETTY FRIEDAN. LaHaye asserts that she resented the fact that Friedan claimed to speak for all American women. In response to the interview, LaHaye organized a female prayer group to discuss the women's movement, specifically the EQUAL RIGHTS AMENDMENT (to which she objected). Her organizing efforts grew, and in 1979 she founded Concerned Women for America (CWA).

CWA claims to be the nation's largest public policy women's organization with the goal to protect and promote biblical values in all levels of government. CWA's pro-family agenda opposes homosexuality, abortion, and UN conferences on the rights of women and children. Agendas are driven at the local level by Prayer Action Chapters that telephone and write legislators while also praying for them. In addition to chairing CWA, LaHaye broadcasts *Beverly LaHaye Live,* a daily radio show that encourages men and women to lead the fight in culture wars by taking political action. LaHaye's numerous books, television appearances, and advocacies instruct women to be submissive wives, mothers and leaders within a context of family life.

See also antifeminism.

Further Reading

Brown, Ruth Murray. *For a "Christian America": The History of the Religious Right.* Amherst, N.Y.: Prometheus Books, 2002.

Kinnard, Cynthia D. *Antifeminism in American Thought: An Annotated Bibliography.* Boston: G.K. Hall, 1986.

Mansbridge, Jane J. *Why We Lost the ERA.* Chicago: University of Chicago Press, 1986.

—Howell Williams

Landrieu, Mary (Mary Loretta Landrieu)

(1955–) *U.S. senator* Mary Landrieu was born on November 23, 1955, in Arlington, Virginia, and grew up in an old New Orleans political family. The eldest of nine children born to Moon Landrieu, mayor of New Orleans during the 1970s, she attended Ursuline Academy and then went on to earn B.A. in sociology from Louisiana State University (1977).

In 1979, at the age of 23, Landrieu became the youngest woman ever elected to the Louisiana state legislature. She once noted that she was "greeted with whistles the first time she

addressed the chamber and [her colleagues] once put rubber snakes in her desk." In the state legislature, she focused on protecting victims of domestic abuse and strengthening child-support laws. After eight years as a state representative, Landrieu was elected state treasurer on a platform of reform and fiscal responsibility. As treasurer, she opened up the state contract system, which had long been criticized for cronyism, and she was a critic of Governor Edwin Edwards's attempt to legalize gambling.

Landrieu decided to run for governor in 1995. She lost in her first defeat by only 8,983 votes. Almost immediately, she began campaigning for the Senate seat being vacated by Bennett Johnson. In one of the closest elections in Louisiana history, Landrieu won (1996).

During her tenure in the Senate, Landrieu has compiled a moderate to conservative voting record. She supports elimination of the estate tax and better fiscal management of resources. In 2004, she was one of only six Democrats to vote against renewing the ban on assault weapons. In 2005, she was among the "Gang of 14" who forged a compromise to avoid a showdown over the issue of Senate filibusters on judicial nominations. She voted to support the appointment of John Roberts as chief justice of the U.S. Supreme Court, but against the nomination of Samuel Alito as justice. In the wake of the devastation of Hurricane Katrina, Senator Landrieu has become a national spokeswoman for victims of the hurricane and the rebuilding of New Orleans. She attracted some criticism early for her seemingly detached understanding of the scale of devastation along the Gulf Coast. She was quoted as praising the Bush administration for its handling of the situation early in the disaster, but has since become a harsh critic of the federal response.

In the Senate, Landrieu serves on the Committee on Appropriations, Committee on Natural Resources, the Committee on Homeland Security and Governmental Affairs, and on the Committee on Small Business and Entrepreneurship. Reelected in 2002, when her margin of victory was largely dependent on Orleans Parish, she will face election again in 2008.

Further Reading

Barone, Michael. *The Almanac of American Politics*. Washington, D.C.: National Journal Group, 2006.

"Landrieu, Mary L." In *Biographical Directory of the United States Congress, 1774–present*. Available online. URL: http://bioguide.congress.gov/scripts/biodisplay.pl?index=L000550. Accessed on January 8, 2007.

"Senator Mary L. Landrieu (LA)." In *Project Vote Smart*. Available online. URL: http://votesmart.org/bio.php?can_id=BC037760. Accessed on January 8, 2007.

—Angela Kouters

League of Women Voters (LWV) (National League of Women Voters)

The National League of Women Voters (NLWV) was established in 1920 following successful ratification of the Nineteenth Amendment granting women the right to vote. Women associated with the NATIONAL AMERICAN WOMAN SUFFRAGE ASSOCIATION (NAWSA) under CARRIE CHAPMAN CATT's leadership had been persuaded to act as nonpartisans in the battle for SUFFRAGE, and many remained active in the organization in its new nonpartisan incarnation as the NLWV. Rather than directly entering electoral politics, the NLWV dedicated its efforts to educating newly enfranchised women, studying national legislation and social policy, and participating in local civic matters. Catt's earlier admonition against allegiance to any one party held, and the league separated itself from partisan politics entirely, even refusing to endorse specific candidates or to promote women from within its own ranks as candidates. "Naturally, this course has failed to please extremists of either brand," said the league's first president, Maud Wood Park, in 1924. "The partisan radicals call the League conservative, the thorough-going reactionaries are sure that it is radical or worse."

Today the League of Women Voters (LWV, the name adopted in 1946) continues in a strictly nonpartisan fashion. The LWV's work is based on the philosophy that citizens who have well-researched and unbiased information will make wise decisions. The league helps citizens ensure that their voices are heard at the local, state, and national levels and through coalition-building around shared issues. As it has from its founding, the LWV adopts an annual national platform of issues through a process of consensus building. Delegates from state-based affiliates convene in even-numbered years to select issues for the league's attention. The first issues the LWV adopted included support for collective bargaining, child labor laws, minimum wage, a joint federal-state employment service, compulsory education, and equal opportunity for women in government industry. One of its early legislative successes was passage of the SHEPPARD-TOWNER MATERNITY AND INFANCY PROTECTION ACT (1921), a bill that provided federal aid for maternal and child care programs. More recently, the LWV was instrumental in winning passage of the National Voter Registration Act (1993) as a means of registering more Americans to vote, simplifying procedures in the states and reshaping government's role in the registration process. Contemporary issues include campaign finance reform, gun control legislation, and health care reform. The League of Women Voters maintains a Web site at www.lwv.org.

Further Reading

Fowler, Robert Booth. *Carrie Catt: Feminist Politician*. Boston: Northeastern University Press, 1986.

Stuhler, Barbara. *For the Public Record: A Documentary History of the League of Women Voters*. Westport, Conn.: Greenwood Press, 2000.

Lease, Mary Elizabeth (Mary Ellen Elizabeth Clyens Lease)

(1853–1933) *populist reformer* Activist, writer, and member of the Populist Party, Mary Elizabeth Clyens was born in Ridgeway, Pennsylvania, on September 11, 1853. After moving to Kansas to work as a teacher, she met and married Charles L. Lease in 1873. The couple lost their farm in the Panic of 1873, and in 1874 they moved to Denison, Texas, where four of their five children were born and Mary studied law.

In 1883, the Lease family moved back to Kansas, where Mary pursued her interest in the SUFFRAGE and labor movements. Following her admission to the Kansas bar in 1885, Lease entered politics, running in 1888 for a local office on the Union Labor party ticket. She lost the election and soon switched to the Populist ticket. Populism sought to organize farmers in order to pursue economic and social change, including the popular election of senators, government control of railroads, woman suffrage, free silver, and prohibition. A gifted and powerful public speaker, Lease gave more than 160 speeches for the Populist cause during the campaigns of 1890 alone. Newspapers mocked Lease with the nicknames "Yellin' Mary Ellen" and "Mary Yellin' Lease."

Lease fought the fusion of the Populist and Democratic parties in the election of 1896 but did reluctantly stump for fusion candidate William Jennings Bryan. Following the Populists' 1896 defeat, Lease moved to New York City, where she worked as a writer and lecturer. She divorced her husband in 1902. Lease faded from political life after 1918 but is today remembered as one of the most influential figures in American populism. Mary Elizabeth Lease died in Callicoon, New York, on October 29, 1933.

Further Reading

Lease, Mary Elizabeth. *The Problem of Civilization Solved.* Chicago: Laird & Lee, 1895.

McNall, Scott G. *The Road to Rebellion: Class Formation and Kansas Populism, 1865–1900.* Chicago: University of Chicago Press, 1988.

Stiller, Richard. *Queen of Populists: The Story of Mary Elizabeth Lease.* New York: Crowell, 1970.

—Eileen V. Wallis

Ledbetter v. Goodyear Tire and Rubber Co. (550 U.S. ___) (2007)

Lilly Ledbetter, the lone female supervisor at a tire plant in Gadsden, Alabama, filed suit alleging that her pay was substantially less than that of the male supervisors employed in the same plant owing to illegal sex discrimination and, therefore, constituted a violation of Title VII of the Civil Rights Act of 1964. Ledbetter argued that as a result of poor performance evaluations because of her sex, her pay raises over time did not keep pace with those of her male counterparts such that upon her retirement in 1998, her salary was substantially lower. Goodyear disputed her characterization of the performance evaluations as a form of sex discrimination but maintained that Ledbetter's suit was time barred. Title VII requires that an individual wishing to bring suit must do so within 180 days after the alleged unlawful employment practice occurred. Ledbetter argued that she was discriminated against over the course of her entire 19-year career with Goodyear and that each subsequent paycheck was a separate act of discrimination.

The Supreme Court's 5-4 majority decision (May 29, 2007), written by Justice Samuel Alito (joined by Chief Justice Roberts and Justices Scalia, Kennedy, and Thomas), held that the effects of past discrimination do not restart the clock for filing claims with the EEOC and that Ledbetter's suit was therefore not timely because she could not demonstrate specific acts of discrimination within the proscribed time period. Justice Alito wrote that "current effects alone can't breathe life into prior, uncharged discrimination. We apply the statute as written, and this means that any unlawful employment practice, including those involving compensation, must be presented within the period described by the statute." Ledbetter argued that discrimination in pay is different from other types of employment discrimination and thus should be governed by a different rule. However, Alito responded that "because a pay-setting decision is a discrete act that occurs at a particular point in time, these arguments must be rejected."

Justice RUTH BADER GINSBURG (joined by Justices Stevens, Souter, and Breyer) countered in dissent that "pay disputes often occur, as they did in Ledbetter's case, in small increments; only over time is there strong cause to suspect that discrimination is at work." She further claimed that women may be reluctant to file suits in federal court over small amounts, particularly when they are trying to succeed in a "male-dominated workplace, in a job filled only by men before she was hired, understandably may be anxious to avoid making waves." For the second time in the 2006 term, Ginsburg read aloud her dissent from the bench, a significant statement for a justice and a rare occurrence. The first instance came with her dissent in GONZALES V. CARHART, when the majority upheld the 2003 Partial Birth Abortion Ban Act. Ginsburg is the only female justice on the Supreme Court since Alito replaced Justice SANDRA DAY O'CONNOR in January 2006. Since O'Connor's departure and the resulting conservative shift in the Court, Ginsburg has been far sharper in her criticism that the majority is undermining hard-fought gains in women's rights, many won by Ginsburg herself while a practicing attorney for the ACLU's Women's Rights Project.

Women's rights organizations joined Ginsburg in characterizing this opinion as a major setback for women and for civil rights, while business groups such as the U.S. Chamber of Commerce called it a "fair decision" that "eliminates a potential wind-fall against employers by employees trying to dredge up stale pay claims."

Lee, Barbara

Lee, Barbara (1946–) *congressperson* Barbara Lee was born on July 16, 1946, in El Paso, Texas. She was educated at Mills College and earned an M.S.W. from the University of California–Berkeley in 1975. Lee was a staff member for Representative Ron Dellums from 1976 to 1986 and a member of the California State Assembly (1990–96) and the California State Senate (1996–98) before entering the U.S. House of Representatives in a special election to fill the seat of retiring congressman Ron Dellums. She was elected in 1998.

Lee is the most senior Democratic woman on the House International Relations Committee, where she serves on the Africa and the Western Hemisphere Subcommittees. She also serves on the House Financial Services Committee, where she sits on the Housing and Domestic and International Monetary Policy Subcommittees. She is the cochair of the Congressional Progressive Caucus, whip for the Congressional Black Caucus (CBC), and a aenior Democratic whip. She also serves as chair of the CBC Task Force on Global HIV/AIDS and is cochair of the CBC Haiti Task Force.

In 2001, Congresswoman Lee cast the only vote against the U.S. invasion of Afghanistan. The daughter of a retired lieutenant colonel in the U.S. Army, Lee said on the House floor: "I am convinced that military action will not prevent further acts of international terrorism against the United Sates. There must be some who say, 'Let's step back for a moment and think through the implications of our actions today—let's more fully understand the consequences.'" The price for Lee's vote of conscience was 24-hour police protection in the face of numerous death threats. In her office, the phone lines shut down under the weight of thousands of phone calls from all over the country—many irate, some of them threatening. She responded: "Some people are calling me un-American and all that. I know that I'm unified with our country. . . . I know that my actions are as American as anyone else's. I'm trying to preserve the people's right to have some kind of oversight and some say in the cycle of violence that could occur if we go into war without an end in sight. The Congress has a responsibility to provide the checks and balances and to exercise some oversight. I don't believe we should disenfranchise the people of America in the war-making decision-making process." Congresswoman Lee was reelected to office in 2006.

Further Reading

Barone, Michael. *The Almanac of American Politics.* Washington, D.C.: National Journal Group, 2006.

"Lee, Barbara." In *Biographical Directory of the United States Congress, 1774–present.* Available online. URL: http://bioguide.congress.gov/scripts/biodisplay.pl?index=. Accessed on January 8, 2007.

"Representative Barbara J. Lee (CA)." In *Project Vote Smart.* Available online. URL: http://votesmart.org/bio.php?can_id=BS026786. Accessed on January 8, 2007.

—Angela Kouters

Lemons v. City and County of Denver (620 F.2d 228, 229 [10th Cir.]) (1980)

This case was an early attempt to use the concept of COM-PARABLE WORTH to challenge pay inequities in the field of nursing under TITLE VII OF THE CIVIL RIGHTS ACT OF 1964. The suit was based on the proposition that nurses were underpaid in city positions and in the community in comparison with other, different jobs which they asserted were of equal worth to the employer. The claim was made on the basis of disparate impact analysis, an approach that the courts viewed with some skepticism in the 1980s. The U.S. District Court ruled that Title VII was not meant to be applied to entire fields of employment (nursing in this case) and noted that the idea of comparable worth applied in this sense was "pregnant with the possibility of disrupting the entire economic system of the United States." In order to demonstrate wage discrimination in a comparable-worth claim under the EQUAL PAY ACT or Title VII, the court held that the act in question must be a specific discretionary practice (for example, the use of hiring tests or the configuration of fringe benefits) rather than a wide-ranging, economically constrained policy such as paying market wages. The U.S. Supreme Court denied certiorari.

Further Reading

Burstein, Paul. *Discrimination, Jobs, and Politics: The Struggle for Equal Employment Opportunity in the United States Since the New Deal.* Chicago: University of Chicago Press, 1998.

Lenroot, Katherine (Katherine Frederica Lenroot) (1891–1982) *activist*

Katherine Lenroot was born on March 8, 1891, in Superior, Wisconsin, to Clara Pamela Clough and Irvine Luther Lenroot, an influential Republican senator who served the state in a number of elected positions. Katharine Lenroot is best known for her long association with the U.S. Department of Labor's Children's Bureau, joining the Bureau in 1915 as a special investigator and retiring in 1951 as its third chief. Her commitment to public service likely grew from her father's example and her connections to prominent scholars at the University of Wisconsin. There she studied social science with Richard Ely and John Commons, graduating in 1912 with a B.A. in economics. Upon graduation, Lenroot took a position with the Industrial Commission of Wisconsin, where she conducted cost-of-living surveys to assess the effectiveness of the state's new minimum-wage law. A project of the Children's Bureau Social Service Division, Lenroot's involvement kept her in touch with her lifelong friend, Emma O. Lundberg, a fellow Wisconsin graduate and director of the surveys. In January 1915, she moved to Washington, D.C., to join Lundberg and the Children's Bureau as one of 26 special agents employed in its social service division. For a brief period from 1921 to 1922, Lenroot directed the bureau's editorial division, but when GRACE ABBOTT became the Bureau's second chief in 1921, she appointed Lenroot as her assistant chief. In 1934, Lenroot succeeded Abbott to become the third chief of the Children's Bureau, retiring from that position in 1951. Her policy development work on both the Social Security Act (passed in 1935) and the FAIR LABOR STANDARDS ACT (passed in 1938) centered on maternal and infancy health concerns as well as establishing expanded services for disabled, neglected, and dependent children.

Lenroot served as president of the National Conference of Social Work in 1935, executive secretary of the White House Conference on Children in Democracy in 1940, and secretary of the United Nations' Temporary Social Commission in 1946. Tulane University bestowed an honorary law degree upon Lenroot in 1948. Always speaking for the children, her speech to the graduating class noted: "We are prodigal in our dreams for children but often miserly in our deeds."

Further Reading

Gordon, Linda. *Pitied But Not Entitled: Single Mothers and the History of Welfare.* New York: Free Press, 1994.

Lindenmeyer, Kriste. *"A Right to Childhood": The U.S. Children's Bureau and Child Welfare, 1912–46.* Urbana: University of Illinois Press, 1997.

Muncy, Robyn. *Creating A Female Dominion in American Reform, 1890–1935.* New York: Oxford University Press, 1991.

Ware, Susan. *Beyond Suffrage: Women in the New Deal.* Cambridge, Mass.: Harvard University Press, 1981.

—Kyle E. Ciani

lesbian separatism In the early 1970s, after encountering misogynistic attitudes and practices in the gay liberation movement and anti-lesbian discrimination in the women's liberation movement, some lesbian feminists opted for a strategy of separation. In seeking to minimize their contacts with men, lesbian separatists created women-only communes and houses, political groups, and businesses, as well as women-only events such as music concerts and poetry readings. Lesbian separatists subscribed to a radical feminist philosophy that views gender differences in terms of essentialism. Unlike the liberal feminists of the mainstream women's movement, who argued that gender was a social construction, lesbian separatists contended that the differences between men and women are rooted in nature. Thus, women naturally possessed a female energy characterized by its warmth, nurturing, and pacifist qualities. Men, on the other hand, were aggressive, competitive, and destructive. Because men could not, or would not, ever change their ways, lesbian separatists believe that it was necessary for women to exclude them from their lives.

See also FEMINISM.

Further Reading

Seidman, Steven. *The Social Construction of Sexuality.* New York: Norton, 2003.

Liliuokalani (1838–1917) *queen of Hawaii* Queen Liliuokalani was the last reigning monarch of Hawaii. First settled by Polynesian voyagers sometime in the 8th century, Hawaii saw a massive influx of American settlers during the 19th century, most coming to exploit the islands' burgeoning sugar industry. In 1887, under pressure from U.S. investors and American sugar planters, King Kalakaua (Liliuokalani's brother) agreed to a new constitution that stripped him of much of his power. However, in 1891, Liliuokalani ascended to the throne and refused to recognize the constitution of 1887, replacing it instead with a constitution that restored the monarchy's traditional authority. Two years later, a revolutionary "committee of safety," organized by Sanford B. Dole, a Hawaiian-born American, staged a coup against Queen Liliuokalani with the support of U.S. minister John Stevens and a division of U.S. Marines. On February 1, 1893, Stevens recognized Dole's new government on his own authority and proclaimed Hawaii a U.S. protectorate. Dole submitted a treaty of annexation to the U.S. Senate, but Democrats largely opposed it, especially after it was revealed that most Hawaiians did not want annexation. President Grover Cleveland sent a new U.S. minister to Hawaii to restore Queen Liliuokalani to the throne under the 1887 constitution, but Dole refused to step aside and instead proclaimed the independent Republic of Hawaii, which was organized into a U.S. territory in 1900.

In 1895, Liliuokalani was arrested and forced to reside in Iolani Palace after weapons were found in the gardens of her home. In 1896, she was released and returned to her home at Washington Place, where she lived for the next two decades and composed many Hawaiian songs, including the popular "Aloha Oe." Liliuokalani died on November 11, 1917.

Further Reading
Allen, Helena G. *The Betrayal of Liliuokalani: The Last Queen of Hawaii 1838–1917.* Honolulu: Mutual Publishing, 1991.

Lincoln, Blanche (Blanche Lambert Lincoln)
(1960–) *U.S. senator* Blanche Lincoln was born on September 30, 1960, in Helena, Arkansas, attended Arkansas public schools, graduated from Randolph-Macon Woman's College in 1982. She worked as staff assistant to Congressman Bill Alexander after graduation and served in his office until 1984. In 1992, Lincoln challenged her former boss in the Democratic primary, won, and took his seat in the House, where she served until 1997. She did not seek reelection in 1996 because she was pregnant with twin boys, but she returned to politics in 1998 with a bid for the U.S. Senate seat being vacated by incumbent Democrat Dale Bumpers. She won and became the youngest woman ever elected to the United States Senate, as well as the second woman ever to represent Arkansas in that body.

In the Senate, Lincoln serves on the Finance Committee; the Special Committee on Aging; and the Agriculture, Nutrition, and Forestry committee. She also chairs the Forestry, Conservation, and Rural Revitalization subcommittee, and in the past, she has served on the Select Committee on Ethics. She is a member of the Rural Health Caucus, the Senate Social Security Task Force, and the New Democrat Coalition. Lincoln is also a founding member of the Senate Centrist Coalition, a bipartisan group of senators who advocate governing from the center.

Lincoln is often discussed as a presidential contender for the Democratic Party. She is a coauthor of *Nine and Counting: The Women in the Senate,* published in 2000. Senator Lincoln won reelection in 2004 and will run again in 2010.

Further Reading
Barone, Michael. *The Almanac of American Politics.* Washington, D.C.: National Journal Group, 2006.
"Lincoln, Blanche Lambert." In *Biographical Directory of the United States Congress, 1774–present.* Available online. URL: http://bioguide.congress.gov/scripts/biodisplay.pl?index=L000035. Accessed on January 8, 2007.
"Senator Blanche L. Lincoln (AR)." In *Project Vote Smart.* Available online. URL: http://votesmart.org/bio.php?can_id=H0131103. Accessed on January 8, 2007.

—Angela Kouters

Lincoln, Mary Todd (Mary Ann Todd Lincoln)
(1818–1882) *first lady* Mary Ann Todd was born in Lexington, Kentucky, on December 13, 1818, the fourth of seven children born to businessman Robert Smith Todd and Elizabeth Parker Todd. Her early childhood was happy and relatively privileged, but that changed upon her mother's death when she was six. Her father remarried, but an increasingly large second family distracted her stepmother. Mary Todd was well educated and excelled at school. As she matured, she developed a sharp tongue and a habit of mimicking people. As a young woman, she expressed her opinions "rather than asking questions and listening raptly to men's answers."

In 1836, Mary traveled to Springfield, Illinois, to live with a married sister. There, in 1839, she met Abraham Lincoln, an attorney. Although their differences were great in many ways, they fell in love and planned to be married. She had brushed off other suitors, including Stephen Douglas, whom she reportedly told, "I can't consent to be your wife. I shall become Mrs. President, or I am the victim of false prophets, but it will not be as Mrs. Douglas." Neither Mary nor Abraham was in any hurry to marry.

She feared losing her civil and legal rights when she married, and he worried whether he could make her happy and about his ability to support her. An argument at a party in 1841 broke off their engagement and plunged Lincoln into a severe depression. Mary, too, had regrets and wanted to resume the relationship. In 1842, Lincoln's depression lifted and the couple were married almost immediately.

Lincoln practiced law (often riding circuit for a month at a time), and he and Mary resided in a boarding house in Springfield. On August 1, 1843, she gave birth to the first of four sons (Robert Todd). With money from Mary's father, the Lincolns built a house where three more sons were born (Edward, William, and Thomas). After one term in the Illinois state legislature, Abraham Lincoln was elected to the U.S. Congress in 1846. Mary and their two sons moved to Washington with him, but they moved back to Springfield after one term.

In 1850, Edward died of tuberculosis. Mary Lincoln suffered from migraine headaches and frequent episodes of aberrant behavior. Even so, she never faltered in her support for her husband's political career. She prodded him to run for successively higher offices and worked to bolster his fragile self-confidence. The Republican Party nominated Lincoln as a candidate for the U.S. Senate in 1858. Although he was little known and lost the race, the debates with his opponent, Stephen A. Douglas, attracted widespread favorable attention. In 1860, the Republican National Committee came to Springfield to notify Lincoln of his nomination for the presidency. Mary campaigned for him actively, writing letters to clarify his positions, speaking with reporters who came to Springfield, and making "speeches" (the *New York Times* characterization of her explicitly political conversations) on his behalf. She was thrilled when he came home calling, "Mary, Mary, *we* were elected."

Mary and the children made the train trip from Springfield to Washington alone. Fearing assassination attempts, the newly elected president entered the city separately and without fanfare. Mary enjoyed the attention of the crowds along the route. She did not exhibit a very complex understanding of the impending Civil War or what it would mean for Lincoln's presidency or her time as first lady. Although the war broke out soon after the inaugural, Mary Todd Lincoln made her first priority seeking and receiving an allowance from Congress to refurbish the White House. She made several trips to New York and Philadelphia to select furnishings and other decor, quickly exhausting the four-year allowance in under a year. The ensuing scandal embarrassed the president, and he threatened to cover the expenses from his own salary. Chastened but not deterred, Mary sold White House furniture and reduced the staff to cut expenses. Measures of economy did not extend to her clothing, however. She employed seamstress Elizabeth Keckley to design her gowns, favoring elaborate styles, bright colors, and striking patterns. In these pursuits, Mary did not earn the admiration of the press or public that she sought. As a hostess, however, Mary Lincoln was well regarded in Washington. She entertained enthusiastically, regularly hosting gatherings of as many as 4,000 guests. Mary viewed entertaining as a sign of Union stability and as a way to raise the morale of union troops.

Mary's extravagance in dress and design was not the only point of criticism during her time as first lady. As a native of Kentucky, her allegiance to the Union was questioned, especially as most of her family supported the Confederacy. Her southern accent and public mourning over the death of her brother-in-law, a soldier in the Confederate forces, even led some to raise charges of treason. But Mary was an ardent abolitionist who encouraged her husband's antislavery disposition and actions. She considered the Emancipation Proclamation of 1863 a personal victory as she had lobbied the president vigorously. Meanwhile, southerners viewed her as a traitor. To counter these accusations, Mary extended her official activities as first lady to review troops, comfort the wounded in local hospitals, and raise funds in support of the Union effort.

In February 1862, William and Tad fell seriously ill, most likely from typhoid contracted through contaminated drinking water. Tad eventually recovered, but William died. Her grief was inconsolable, drawing even more criticism for her "indulgence." William's death increased her aberrant behavior. She refused to leave her room, avoided spending time with Tad, and sought out spiritualists whom she believed could reunite her with her favorite son. Although Abraham Lincoln campaigned for a second term, he believed it would bring more misery. Both he and Mary had forebodings of his death as the second term began. On April 14, 1865, as the couple sat holding hands in the balcony of Ford Theater, assassin John Wilkes Booth bullet's ended any hope Mary might have held for happiness. She blamed herself for the president's death and took to her bed for more than a month. She did not vacate the White House for the new administration until May 23, in part because she felt she had nowhere to go. Finally she departed for a series of Chicago hotels, burdened by her grief, hysteria, and considerable debt.

The remainder of Mary Lincoln's life was a series of tragedies and personal indignities. Crushing debt accumulated during her years in the White House dwarfed the income from Abraham Lincoln's estate and led Mary to embark on a series of money-raising schemes. She enlisted the help of Elizabeth Keckley to sell her clothing (referred to as "Mrs. Lincoln's Secondhand Clothing Sale"), petitioned friends for money, and lobbied Congress for a pension in the amount of her husband's salary had he served a second term. Although she was successful in raising funds, they were not sufficient to cover her debts or to purchase a home for herself and her sons. Her bizarre behavior during this time ended most of her friendships and strained her relationship with Robert, her oldest son. Intermittently, Mary sought refuge from creditors and medical relief of her ailments in

Europe. When Congress awarded her an annual widow's pension of $3,000 in 1871, she returned to the United States with Tad. On July 15, 1871, Tad died suddenly, and Mary was again plunged into depression and more bizarre behavior.

In 1875, Robert Lincoln swore out a warrant against his mother, charging her with lunacy. With an incompetent defense attorney selected by her son, she was forced to defend her sanity before an all-male jury and a series of medical witnesses paid by Robert to certify that she was insane. Her eccentricities and independence worked against her by 19th-century standards of womanhood. The jury verdict was insanity, and she was committed against her will to an asylum in Batavia, Illinois. She lost all of her property and the balance of her inheritance to Robert. Robert's motivations are impossible to discern. Mary's behavior and profligate spending were no doubt an embarrassment, but there is little evidence that she was a danger to herself or to society.

Within four months, Mary managed to free herself with the help of MYRA BRADWELL (the first woman lawyer in the United States). Released to the care of her sister, Elizabeth Edwards, she sued Robert for return of her property, and on June 15, 1876, another court found her mentally competent. Mary demanded that Robert return every gift she had ever given him and all of the property he had gained as a result of her institutionalization. Robert, now President Garfield's secretary of war and politically influential in his own right, began to spread rumors about his mother's hysteria. Once again she fled to Europe, only to return when blindness left her unable to care for herself. She spent the last year of her life in a New York medical hotel, urging Congress to raise her annual pension to that awarded Lucretia Garfield ($5,000). Although Congress agreed, it was Robert who was the beneficiary. Mary Todd Lincoln died intestate on July 16, 1882, and Robert inherited $84,000.

Mary Todd Lincoln's political ambition and independence of thought and action made her an easy target since she refused to be wholly governed by the gender expectations of her times. In other respects, her ego and lack of self-control led her to view entering the White House as a personal triumph to be enjoyed irrespective of the Civil War gripping the nation. Social conventions stifled her personal ambition, forcing her to work through her husband. In doing so, she no doubt played an essential role in fostering the political career of one of the nation's most important public figures. Her obvious affection for her husband led her to support him through the darkest days of the Civil War, in many cases rising above her own limitations and infirmities to do so.

Further Reading

Baker, Jean H. *Mary Todd Lincoln: A Biography.* New York, Norton, 1987.

National First Ladies Library. *Biographies: First Ladies of the United States.* Available online. URL: http://www.firstladies.org/biographies. Accessed on January 4, 2007.

Schneider, Dorothy, and Carl J. Schneider. "Mary Ann Todd Lincoln" *First Ladies: A Biographical Dictionary.* New York: Checkmark Books, 2001, pp. 95–106.

Shulman, Holly Cowan. "Mary Ann Todd Lincoln." In *American First Ladies: Their Lives and Their Legacy,* 2nd ed., edited by Lewis L. Gould. New York: Routledge, 2001, pp. 113–129.

Lockwood, Belva (Belva Ann Bennett McNall Lockwood) (1830–1917) *lawyer, women's rights advocate*

Born on October 24, 1830, in Royalton, New York, to Lewis Johnson and Hannah Green Bennett, Belva Ann Bennett began teaching at the age of 15. In 1848, she married Uriah H. McNall, with whom she had a daughter before he died in 1853. To support herself, Belva returned to teaching and also attended Genesee College, from which she graduated in 1857. After a period of teaching in New York, she moved to Washington, D.C., where she set up her own school. In March 1868, she married Ezekiel Lockwood, who eventually took over running her school to allow her to attend law school. In 1871, she finally won admission to National University Law School after being rejected by Georgetown University, Howard University, and what is now George Washington University.

In 1873, following her graduation from National University Law School, Belva Lockwood was admitted to the bar of the District of Columbia and opened a small law office out of her home. After being twice denied admission to the Supreme Court bar on account of her gender, Lockwood successfully lobbied Congress to strike down that barrier in 1879. The following year, she became the first woman to argue before the Court. In her most important case, *United States* v. *Cherokee Nation* (1906), she won long-overdue payment promised to the Cherokee people in numerous land treaties.

A champion of women's political and economic rights, Lockwood was a local leader of the NATIONAL WOMAN SUFFRAGE ASSOCIATION and was later an officer in the NATIONAL AMERICAN WOMAN SUFFRAGE ASSOCIATION. She delivered lectures across the country and was involved in the International Council of Women. In 1884 and 1888, the Equal Rights Party nominated her for president of the United States on a platform of "equal and exact justice to every class of our citizens, without distinction of color, sex, or nationality." Lockwood traveled throughout Europe on behalf of the pacifist movement in the years leading up to World War I. In 1912, she was selected as attorney general of the American Woman's Republic, a suffrage organization and theoretically independent nation governed from its capital in St. Louis by a female president, cabinet, and congress. She died in Washington, D.C., on May 19, 1917.

Lockwood's most important legacy lies in the legal opportunities she helped open for women, especially the right to argue before the nation's highest court. Her many efforts on behalf of the rights of women and racial minorities and against war, however, highlight the diversity of causes for which activist women fought in the Gilded Age and Progressive Era, and which a few feminists managed to combine in one career.

Further Reading

Norgren, Jill. "Before It Was Merely Difficult: Belva Lockwood's Life in Law and Politics." *Journal of Supreme Court History* 23 (1999): 16–42.

Winner, Julia Hull. *Belva A. Lockwood.* Lockport, N.Y.: Niagara County Historical Society, 1969.

—Michael David Cohen

Lofgren, Zoe (1947–) *congressperson* Originally named Sue, Zoe Lofgren was born on December 21, 1947, in San Mateo, California. She attended Gunn High School in Palo Alto, earned her B.A. at Stanford University (1970), and a J.D. from Santa Clara University (1975). She was a staff assistant to Congressman Don Edwards and worked on the impeachment of President Richard Nixon. After two years as partner at a law practice in San Jose, she was elected first to a community college board and then to the Santa Clara County Board of Supervisors, where she served for 13 years.

In 1994, Don Edwards decided to retire after 32 years in Congress. Lofgren won the Democratic nomination against the predictions of many and went on to win overwhelmingly in the general election. She is currently the chair of the 33-member California Democratic Congressional Delegation. She serves on the Judiciary Committee and as a ranking member of a subcommittee of the Homeland Security Committee. She rarely faces opposition and has won each reelection easily, including in 2006. She is married to John Marshall Collins, with whom she has two children.

Further Reading

Barone, Michael. *The Almanac of American Politics.* Washington, D.C.: National Journal Group, 2006.

"Lofgren, Zoe." In *Biographical Directory of the United States Congress, 1774–present.* Available online.

URL: http://bioguide.congress.gov/scripts/bio display.pl?index=L000397. Accessed on January 8, 2007.

"Representative Zoe Lofgren (CA)." In *Project Vote Smart.* Available online. URL: http://votesmart.org/bio.php?can_id=CNIP5803. Accessed on January 8, 2007.

—Angela Kouters

***Loving v. Virginia* (388 U.S. 1)** (1967)   Richard and Mildred Loving were married in 1958 in Washington, D.C., because their home state of Virginia still upheld the antimiscegenation law which stated that interracial marriages were illegal. After their wedding, they returned to Caroline County, Virginia, to live together. In 1959, they were prosecuted and convicted of violating the state's antimiscegenation law. They were each sentenced one year in jail, but the judge promised them that the sentence would be suspended if they agreed to leave the state and not return for 25 years. Forced to move, they returned to Washington and, in 1963, initiated a suit challenging the constitutionality of the antimiscegenation law. In March 1966, the Virginia Supreme Court of Appeals upheld the law, but in June 1967, the U.S. Supreme Court unanimously ruled it unconstitutional.

In a unanimous decision, the Court held that distinctions drawn according to race were generally "odious to a free people" and were subject to "the most rigid scrutiny" under the equal-protection clause of the Fourteenth Amendment. The Virginia law, the Court found, had no legitimate purpose "independent of invidious racial discrimination." The Court rejected the state's argument that the statute was legitimate because it applied equally to both blacks and whites and found that racial classifications were not subject to a "rational purpose" test under the Fourteenth Amendment. Thus, in 1967, the 16 states which still had ANTIMISCEGENATION STATUTES laws on their books were forced to erase them.

Further Reading

The OYEZ Project. "Loving v. Virginia," 388 U.S. 1 (1967). Available online. URL: http://www.oyez.org/cases/case?case=1960-1969/1966/1966_395. Accessed on January 10, 2007.

Low, Juliette (Juliette "Daisy" Magill Kinzie Gordon Low)

(1860–1927) *activist, founder of the Girl Scouts* Juliette Gordon Low is known for founding the Girl Guides, subsequently the Girl Scouts of the USA, one of the first programs aimed directly at developing self-reliance in girls. Born Juliette Magill Kinzie Gordon on October 31, 1860, in Savannah, Georgia, she was known as Daisy from an early age. In her teens, Daisy attended boarding school in Virginia and a French school in New York City. She traveled extensively and developed a lifetime interest in the arts.

In 1886, Daisy Gordon married William Mackay Low, and the couple moved to England. As every Girl Scout knows, Juliette Low suffered from profound hearing loss—a result of chronic ear infections as a child and a punctured eardrum suffered on her wedding day when a grain of rice lodged in her ear. Historians speculate that Low's disability led to her interest in including girls with disabilities in Girl Scouts. In 1911, six years after her husband's death, she met Sir Robert Baden-Powell, founder of the Boy Scouts and Girl Guides. She quickly returned to the United States and dedicated her energy to establishing an American version of the Girl Guides. On March 12, 1912, Low gathered 18 girls in Savannah, Georgia, and formed the first troop. A year later, the incipient organization was renamed Girl Scouts of the United States, and it was incorporated in 1915.

In developing the Girl Scout movement in the United States, Low brought girls of all backgrounds into the outdoors, giving them the opportunity to develop self-reliance and resourcefulness. She encouraged girls to prepare not only for traditional homemaking but also for possible future roles as professional women in the arts, sciences, and business and for active citizenship outside the home. Girl Scouts welcomed disabled girls at a time when they were excluded from many other activities. In 1947, the organization was renamed Girl Scouts of the United States of America, and it was chartered by Congress in 1950. Today Girl Scouts of the USA has a membership of nearly 4 million girls and adults, and more than 50 million women in the United States are Girl Scout alumnae.

Juliette Low died of breast cancer on January 17, 1927, and was buried in her Girl Scout uniform in Savannah. After her death, she was recognized in many ways for her contributions to girls' development. In 1948, President Harry S. Truman authorized a stamp in her honor, one of the first to honor a woman. On October 28, 1979, Juliette Low was inducted into the National Women's Hall of Fame in Seneca Falls, New York. In 1983, President Reagan signed a bill naming a new federal building in Savannah in honor of Low, only the second federal building to be named after a woman. Her birthplace

Juliette Low (LIBRARY OF CONGRESS)

in Savannah is now known as the Juliette Gordon Low Girl Scout National Center.

Further Reading

Brown, Fern. *Daisy and the Girl Scouts: The Story of Juliette Gordon.* New York: Whitman, 1996.
Girl Scouts of the USA. Girl Scout History. Available online. URL: http://www.girlscouts.org/who_we_are/history. Accessed on January 4, 2007.

Lowell, Josephine Shaw (1843–1905) *activist, philanthropist* Josephine Shaw Lowell was a philanthropist and reformer who led the charity organization movement in New York. She was born on December 16, 1843, in Roxbury, Massachusetts. The Civil War took the lives of both her brother, Robert Gould Shaw, commander of the 54th Massachusetts regiment, and her husband, Charles Russell Lowell, who died less than a year after they wed in 1863. Their daughter Carlotta was born weeks later and became her mother's companion for life. The young widow subsequently made the problem of poverty her life's work. She began by inspecting conditions at prisons, poorhouses, and other charitable institutions in New York. Her reports advocated a more professional, depoliticized approach to state welfare. Lowell helped found such institutions as the Charity Organization Society of the City of New York in 1881 and the state's first reformatory for women, in addition to the Consumer's League of New York. Increasingly drawn into politics, the groups she joined, formed, and led successfully challenged the Tammany political machine during the 1894 mayoral election in New York City. Lowell later joined the Anti-Imperialist League to oppose the annexation of the Philippines. Illness encroached on her activism, however, and she died in New York City on October 12, 1905.

Josephine Shaw Lowell believed there was a need for both private and public institutions, in that the government should reserve public relief for the truly helpless and deserving while private charity would cover the rest. She sought to replace sentimentality with social science and fought for greater social responsibility and accountability in the government. While an antebellum moral zeal characterized her reform work, Lowell's career marks a turning point in the 20th-century transition to professionalism.

Further Reading

Lowell, Josephine Shaw. *Public Relief and Private Charity.* New York: G. P. Putnam's Sons, 1884.
Stewart, William Rhinelander. *The Philanthropic Work of Josephine Shaw Lowell.* New York: The Macmillan Co., 1911.
Waugh, Joan. *Unsentimental Reformer: The Life of Josephine Shaw Lowell.* Cambridge, Mass.: Harvard University Press, 1997.

—Laura R. Prieto

Lowey, Nita (1937–) *congressperson* Nita Lowey was born on July 5, 1937, in New York City and graduated from Mount Holyoke College with a bachelor's degree in marketing in 1959. From 1975 to 1985, she served as the deputy director of the Division of Economic Opportunity, and from 1985 until 1988, she was the assistant secretary of state for New York. Lowey was first elected to the House of Representatives in 1988. In 2001, she was chosen as the first female chair of the Democratic Congressional Campaign Caucus. She is currently a member of the House Homeland Security Committee and the House Appropriations Committee and is also the ranking member of the Foreign Operations Appropriations Subcommittee.

Lowey has consistently been a strong supporter of public broadcasting, and she appeared at a congressional hearing with Sesame Street characters Bert and Ernie in support of funding for the Corporation for Public Broadcasting. She has not faced much political opposition in her elections and strongly considered running for the Senate in 2000, but stepped aside when Hillary Rodham Clinton announced her candidacy. Lowey is a strong supporter of Abortion and reproductive rights and has cochaired the CONGRESSIONAL CAUCUS FOR WOMEN'S ISSUES. Lowey was reelected to her seat in 2006.

Further Reading

Barone, Michael. *The Almanac of American Politics.* Washington, D.C.: National Journal Group, 2006.

"Lowey, Nita M." In *Biographical Directory of the United States Congress, 1774–present.* Available online. URL: http://bioguide.congress.gov/scripts/biodisplay.pl?index=L000480. Accessed on January 8, 2007.

"Representative Nita M. Lowey (NY)." In *Project Vote Smart.* Available online. URL: http://votesmart.org/bio.php?can_id=H2742103. Accessed on January 8, 2007.

—Angela Kouters

Luce, Clare Boothe (Ann Clare Boothe Brokaw Luce) (1903–1987) *congressperson, writer, diplomat*

Clare Boothe Luce had success in life as an editor, a playwright, politician, journalist, and diplomat. She was born Ann Clare Boothe in New York City, to William Franklin and Ann Snyder Boothe, who separated when Clare was 8 years old. Although initially inclined to pursue a life in the theatre, Boothe developed an interest in SUFFRAGE after meeting a New York suffragist while on a European tour with her parents; she was then in her early 20s. In 1930, after a brief and violent marriage to George Tuttle Brokaw that produced one daughter (Ann Clare Brokaw), she joined the staff of *Vogue* magazine. In 1931, she became associate editor of *Vanity Fair* and served until 1934. In 1935, Clare Boothe married Henry Luce, founder and publisher of *Time* magazine and *Fortune*. In the latter half of that decade, she wrote a number of plays that opened to fairly cool reviews on Broadway.

During World War II, Henry and Clare Luce traveled extensively, reporting on the war and conditions in Germany, China, Africa, India, and Burma for *Life* magazine. In 1942, Clare traded on this international experience and

Clare Boothe Luce, 1932 (LIBRARY OF CONGRESS)

sought a seat in the U.S. House of Representatives from Connecticut. Campaigning as an anti-Roosevelt conservative, she won the seat and began a political career characterized by her fervent anticommunist rhetoric and calls for isolationism. After serving two terms in the House, she returned to writing as solace for the loss of her only child, Ann, to an automobile accident in 1944. She converted to Catholicism and wrote a series of articles describing her conversion.

In 1952, Luce campaigned for Eisenhower and was rewarded with an appointment as ambassador of Italy; illness forced her to resign in 1956. When Eisenhower tried to appoint her ambassador to Brazil in 1959, the nomination met with opposition among some Democrats. Luce never assumed her position, being forced to withdraw over some ill-chosen remarks about her Senate opponents. She remained active in Republican Party politics at the national level, supporting archconservative Barry Goldwater for president in 1964.

In 1967, Henry Luce died and Clare retired from the public eye. In the last years of her life, she returned to Washington, D.C., when Ronald Reagan appointed her to the President's Foreign Intelligence Advisory Board. In 1983, she was honored with the Presidential Medal of Freedom. She died of a brain tumor on October 9, 1987.

Further Reading

Morris, Sylvia. *Rage for Fame: The Ascent of Clare Booth Luce.* New York: Random House, 1997.

Lyon, Mary (1797–1849) *educator*   Mary Lyon was born on a farm in Buckland, Massachusetts, on February 28, 1797. She attended the village school from age four until 13. With no formal training, but with a reputation as a good student, Lyon accepted her first teaching job at the age of 17. Despite economic hardships, she furthered her education by attending lectures and sitting in on classes, and through practical experience, she developed a philosophy for teaching and learned to run a school.

In 1834, Lyon turned her attention to founding an institution of advanced learning for females. After tireless fund-raising, travel, building, and organizing, Mary Lyon opened Mount Holyoke Female Seminary in South Hadley, Massachusetts in November 1837. Lyon's school was distinctive in providing tough entrance exams, a curriculum equivalent to men's colleges (science and math classes were required), affordable tuition, and an institution free of denominational control or a wealthy founder's influence. She expanded traditional Victorian expectations for women as maternal moral exemplars and religious educators by asserting that female public education should build well-rounded, disciplined, and strong-minded citizens to mold the future and transform society. Lyon's education system exemplified the Christian principles of domestic labor, benevolence, and cooperation, all of which she assumed necessary for women to contribute to the public good.

Lyon's seminary was a great success, and attendance grew over the years. Twelve years after its founding, Lyon died, on March 5, 1849; she was buried on the school grounds. Her legacy was enormous. Lyon linked women with public life through women's higher education. Mount Holyoke graduates taught and founded schools from Georgia to Japan. The school received its collegiate charter in 1888, when it became Mount Holyoke Seminary and College. In 1893, Mary Lyon's seminary assumed its present name of Mount Holyoke College. One of its most famous graduates was Secretary of Labor FRANCES PERKINS.

Further Reading

Gilchrist, Beth Bradford. *The Life of Mary Lyon.* Boston: Houghton Mifflin, 1910.

Lansing, Marion, ed. *Mary Lyon through Her Letters.* Boston: Books, 1937.

Porterfield, Amanda. *Mary Lyon and the Mount Holyoke Missionaries.* New York: Oxford University Press, 1997.

—Howell Williams

M

MacKinnon, Catharine Alice (1946–) *attorney, feminist scholar* Catherine Alice MacKinnon was born in Minneapolis, Minnesota, on October 7, 1946. She studied at Smith College, receiving her B.A. in Government in 1969, and went on to study law, earning a J.D. from Yale in 1977. A social activist and feminist during her graduate school days, MacKinnon became interested in gender inequality in the workplace, particularly with regards to SEXUAL HARASSMENT and women's rights. While still a law student, she expanded a paper into book form and published *Sexual Harassment of Working Women: A Case of Sex Discrimination* (1979), her first book. A landmark study, MacKinnon's argument was simple: Workplace sexual harassment was a violation of women's civil rights. In 1986, her argument materialized in the Supreme Court's decision in Mentor Savings Bank v. Vinson ruling that sexual harassment was indeed sex discrimination, effectively proving MacKinnon right.

While working toward a Ph.D. in political science from Yale University Graduate School (which she received in 1987), MacKinnon actively engaged in public discussions of social and legal rights and issues; practiced law; and taught at a number of prestigious American law schools, including the University of Chicago, Harvard, Stanford, and Yale. By the time she received a tenured position at the University of Michigan's law school, she had joined forces with ANDREA DWORKIN, a noted feminist writer, to take on issues of pornography and the exploitation of women. Together they wrote *Pornography and Civil Rights: A New Day for Women's Equality* (1988) and edited *In Harm's Way: The Pornography Civil Rights Hearings* (1997). Controversial in both focus and stance, MacKinnon and Dworkin's work on pornography—grounded in the idea that it was another form of sex discrimination and should be legally recognized as such—led to their draft of an ordinance that would deem pornography a violation of women's civil rights. Although it was adopted by a couple of city councils, it was never enacted.

MacKinnon's other books, *Feminism Unmodified* (1987), *Toward a Feminist Theory of the State* (1989), and *Only Words* (1993), further articulated her arguments against sexual harassment, the patriarchal structure of the law, and pornography. While inciting heated debates among feminists and nonfeminists alike, MacKinnon's ideas played a significant role in the transformation of American educational institutions by bringing feminist theory and ideology into the curriculum of legal studies. Not surprisingly, her work also permeated other women's issues, including rape, ABORTION, and women's rights both at home and abroad. A lawyer, professor, writer, activist, and public speaker, MacKinnon has earned her reputation as an aggressive and provocative theorist and feminist iconoclast. In 2005, she was elected a fellow of the American Academy of Arts and Sciences. She is the Elizabeth A. Long professor of law at the University of Michigan.

See also FEMINISM.

Further Reading

MacKinnon, Catherine A. *Sexual Harassment of Working Women: A Case of Sex Discrimination.* New Haven, Conn.: Yale University Press, 1979.
———, and Andrea Dworkin. *Pornography and Civil Rights: A New Day for Women's Equality.* Minneapolis: Organizing Against Pornography, 1988.
———, and Andrea Dworkin, eds. *In Harm's Way: The Pornography Civil Rights Hearings.* Cambridge, Mass.: Harvard University Press, 1997.

—Candis Steenbergen

Madison, Dolley (Dorothea Dandridge Payne Todd Madison) (1768–1849) *first lady* Dolley Madison was born Dorothea Dandridge Payne, the eldest of nine children, on May 20, 1768. Her Quaker parents, John and Mary Coles Payne, settled their family in Virginia. The family lived as pacifists during the Revolutionary War, forbidden by the Quaker religion to participate in any form of combat. Upon the conclusion of the war in 1783, John Payne emancipated his slaves and sold his plantation. In search of a stable Quaker community and a new start in business, the family moved to Philadelphia, where John Payne established himself as a merchant in laundry starch. In 1789, Payne's business failed and the Quaker community disowned him because he could not pay his business debts; he died a recluse in 1792. Immediately following her husband's death,

Mary Payne supported the family by opening a boarding house for the leaders of the new nation. Dolley loved the sophistication and style of Philadelphia and did not want to return to Virginia. After turning down several proposals for marriage, she accepted a proposal from Quaker John Todd, Jr., a lawyer. They were married on January 7, 1790.

John Todd was successful in his law practice, and the couple were financially secure and able to purchase many luxuries. The couple had two sons: John Payne Todd (b. 1790) and William Temple Todd (b. 1792). In autumn 1793, a devastating epidemic of yellow fever struck Philadelphia, claiming 5,000 lives within a few weeks. Dolley Todd took her sons to a resort outside the city, but John Todd stayed in the city to care for his afflicted parents. Within one week, Dolley Todd lost her infant son William, her husband, and her in-laws to the plague. At age 25, she was a widow with a young son. She returned to Philadelphia and resettled with the help of a large circle of friends and the close-knit Quaker community. The custom of the day anticipated the quick remarriage of young widows.

In May 1794, Aaron Burr, a boarder with her mother and a close family confidant, introduced Dolley to his friend, James Madison. Madison was 43 years old and had never married. He was well known for his role in framing the U.S. Constitution and the Bill of Rights, as well as for his work as an elected representative from Virginia and a leader of the Republican Party. Dolley wrote to her friend Eliza Collins: "In the course of this day I give my Hand to the Man who of all others I most admire." On September 15, 1794, the couple were married at Harewood, her sister Lucy Washington's estate. The Quakers disowned Dolley for marrying outside the faith, thus freeing Dolley to enjoy the fashions, theater, music, and books that she had been denied previously. She took easily to managing the affairs of the Madisons' two households: a three-story brick home in Philadelphia and the Montpelier estate in Virginia. The Madisons entertained constantly and opened their home to politicians of all factions.

When John Adams assumed the presidency in 1797, the Madisons left Washington in favor of Montpelier. However, Thomas Jefferson's election in 1801 returned them to Washington when James Madison was appointed secretary of state. Both Jefferson and his vice president, Aaron Burr, were widowers, and so when Jefferson entertained he often asked Dolley or her sister Anna to serve as hostess. This began Dolley Madison's nearly 16-year role as America's first lady. Jefferson eschewed the formality introduced by MARTHA WASHINGTON and ABIGAIL ADAMS in favor of small, highly informal gatherings. Although she actively followed politics, even visiting the congressional gallery and the Supreme Court, Dolley expressed no political opinions of her own. She carefully avoided any appearance of influencing what she called the "public business."

On March 4, 1809, James Madison became the nation's fourth president, and Dolley officially assumed the role of first lady. She is widely recognized for her accomplishments as a hostess and for decorating the White House, thus providing a public social space for the executive branch. In both aspects, she was conscious of defining new rules of etiquette appropriate to a new republic. With her husband's approval and a small allowance from Congress, she and architect Benjamin Henry Latrobe decorated the presidential mansion during the first two years of the administration. Thomas Jefferson had furnished the White House with personal furnishings from his home, Monticello. When Jefferson retired, he took everything with him, leaving the Madisons to inhabit a large and virtually unfurnished executive mansion. In past administrations, the president's home was also a public arena and therefore the president himself often made decisions regarding decoration and furnishing. Madison turned the enterprise over to Dolley completely. Working with Latrobe, Dolley carefully skirted the conflicting pressures of a populist Republican constituency and the Federalist preference for formality and elegance befitting the power of the office. Biographer Holly Shulman described her accomplishment: "She molded a presidential palace just fine enough for Federalist ideas, just sophisticated enough for the new nation's international image, and yet simple enough to soothe Republican fears."

This victory was to be short-lived. On August 24, 1814, the British invaded Washington and burned the White House to a shell. In the month preceding the attack, while the president was away inspecting the army, Dolley packed up trunks of cabinet papers, silver, the crimson curtains from the Oval Room, a few books, and, most famously, the Gilbert Stuart portrait of George Washington. Even as late as the afternoon of August 23, Dolley stayed in Washington awaiting the return of the president. Finally she fled the city, stopping at a series of homes along the way. By August 28, she and James Madison had returned to Washington, only to find it devastated and smoldering. She wrote a friend: "Everything belonging to the publick, our own valuable stores of every description, and a part of my clothers had burned. I confess that I was so unfeminine as to be free from fear, and willing to remain in the *Castle*. If I could have had a cannon through every window, but alas! those who should have placed them there, fled before me, and my whole heart mourned for my country!" In the aftermath of the siege, Dolley helped a group of women establish an orphanage in Washington and resumed public entertaining in the Octagon House. She and James never returned to the White House.

In March 1817, James Madison retired from office, and James Monroe was inaugurated. At the end of Madison's second term, the entire District of Columbia honored the president and his wife with a series of farewell parties. James lived for another 20 years and never once returned to Washington. Streams of guests, however, came to visit them at Montpelier. Entertaining such large numbers of guests took money, and the Madison's assets steadily dwindled due to economic hardships for Virginia planters and sizable gambling debts incurred by Dolley's only son, Payne Todd. James Madison spent a good portion of his final years organizing his papers both as a public service and in the hope that their sale might provide for his wife.

James Madison died on June 28, 1836. In 1837, Congress bought part of his papers for $30,000, including his meticulous accounts of the debates at the Constitutional Convention of 1787. In October 1837, Dolley Madison returned to Washington, hoping that residence there might speed the publication of the remainder of her husband's papers. She resumed her active social life, even on a restricted income, while her son continued to drain her assets as administrator of Montpelier in her absence. Eventually she was forced to sell the estate, retaining only "the family burial place, some of the furniture, and some few of the black people." James Madison's body servant Paul Jennings, who stayed on with her even in her impoverished widowhood, was eventually sold to Daniel Webster, who agreed to let him earn his freedom. Jennings later wrote about taking Dolley Madison groceries and giving her money from his own pocket.

In 1844, the House of Representatives unanimously passed a resolution "that a committee be appointed on the part of this house to wait on Mrs. Madison, and to assure her that, whenever it shall be her pleasure to visit the House, she be requested to take a seat within the Hall." In 1847, Dolley sold the remainder of her husband's papers to Congress for $25,000. Her son's reputation led Congress to issue $5,000 immediately to pay off her loans and to invest the other $20,000 in a trust from which she would receive the income. Her will divided the trust fund equally between her son Payne and sister Anna but left all of her material possessions (including her slaves) to Payne. Dolley Madison died on July 12, 1849, and was buried in Congressional Cemetary. In 1858, her nephew Richard Cutts, had her body transferred to the family burial ground at Montpelier.

As the leading lady of Washington before and after her formal period as first lady, Dolley Madison served with grace and distinction. She helped the nation develop a distinctively American style in the presidential mansion that lives on today.

Further Reading

National First Ladies Library. *Biographies: First Ladies of the United States*. Available online. URL: http://www.firstladies.org/biographies. Accessed on January 4, 2007.

Schneider, Dorothy, and Carl J. Schneider. "Dolley Payne Todd Madison." *First Ladies: A Biographical Dictionary*. New York: Checkmark Books, 2001, pp. 23–34.

Shulman, Holly Cowan. "Dolley Payne Todd Madison." In *American First Ladies: Their Lives and Their Legacy*, 2nd ed., edited by Lewis L. Gould. New York: Routledge, 2001, pp. 21–36.

Malcolm, Ellen R. (1947–   ) *political activist*
Ellen R. Malcolm is founder and president of EMILY'S LIST. She was born in Montclair, New Jersey, in 1947. Her father, William Reighley, was cofounder of International Business Machines Corporation (IBM) and a Republican. Malcolm changed her political orientation while in college and became an active Democrat. While a student at Hollins College in 1968, she campaigned for Senator Eugene McCarthy and worked for Common Cause throughout the early 1970s. She served as press secretary for the NATIONAL WOMEN'S POLITICAL CAUCUS (NWPC) and as press secretary for ESTHER PETERSON, then President Jimmy Carter's special assistant for consumer affairs. Frustrated by the lack of support for women candidates and the low numbers of women in political office, Malcolm organized a group of friends and established EMILY's List in 1985. The acronym EMILY stands for "early money is like yeast" (it makes the dough rise).

As a political action committee (PAC), EMILY's List raises money for Democratic, pro-choice women candidates. Members of EMILY's

List pay $100 to join and then commit to contributing at least another $100 to a minimum of two candidates per election cycle. Instead of writing the check to EMILY's List, members write checks directly to the campaigns of their chosen candidates identified on the list. The checks are mailed to EMILY's List and then "bundled" and send directly to the candidate. In this way, the organization is able to facilitate the donation of larger sums of money than current Federal Election Commission regulations would allow a PAC to contribute. According to the organization's Web site, EMILY's List has helped send 11 pro-choice Democratic women to the U.S. Senate and 60 to the U.S. House of Representatives, and it has helped elect eight governors since its founding. EMILY's List is now the largest PAC, with over 73,000 members.

The recipient of numerous awards and honors, Malcolm was named one of America's most influential women in 1998 by *Vanity Fair* magazine and, in 1999, one of the 100 Most Important Women in America by *Ladies' Home Journal*. In 1992, Malcolm was among *Glamour* magazine's Women of the Year.

Further Reading

EMILY's List Web site. Available online. URL: http://www.emilyslist.org/. Accessed on January 10, 2007.

Maloney, Carolyn (Carolyn Bosher Maloney)

(1948–) *congressperson* Carolyn Maloney was born on February 19, 1948, in Greensboro, North Carolina, and graduated from Greensboro College in 1970. She relocated to New York City and worked as an administrator with the New York City Board of Education and as teacher in the city schools. From 1977 until 1982, she worked on the staff for the New York Legislature. She was elected to the New York City Council in 1982 and served as a council member for 10 years.

In 1992, Maloney was elected to the U.S. House of Representatives, upsetting 14-year Republican incumbent Bill Green. Despite being heavily outspent, she rode Bill Clinton's coattails into office. She is the first woman ever to represent the district and has been reelected in each cycle with no significant Republican opposition, including the November 2006 election. Maloney serves on the Committee on Financial Services, the Committee on Government Reform and Oversight, and the Joint Economic Committee, and she is the chair of the Democratic Task Force on the Homeland Security Department. In December 2006, Maloney was named vice chairwoman of the Joint Economic Committee for the 110th Congress.

Further Reading

Barone, Michael. *The Almanac of American Politics.* Washington, D.C.: National Journal Group, 2006.
"Maloney, Carolyn Bosher." In *Biographical Directory of the United States Congress, 1774–present.* Available online. URL: http://bioguide.congress.gov/scripts/biodisplay.pl?index=H000087. Accessed on January 8, 2007.
Project Vote Smart. Available online. URL: http://votesmart.org/bio.php?can_id=H2681103. Accessed on January 8, 2007.

—Angela Kouters

Mankiller, Wilma (Wilma Pearl Mankiller)

(1945–) *principal chief of the Cherokee Nation* As a result of Wilma Mankiller's election as principal chief of the Cherokee Nation, she became the first woman in modern history to lead a major Native American tribe. Born in Tahlequah, Oklahoma, on November 18, 1945, she studied sociology and worked as a social worker in California in the 1960s. In the mid-1970s, she returned to Oklahoma to reclaim her ancestral property, Mankiller Flats. In 1977, she took a position in economic development with the Cherokee Nation. In 1983, she was asked by principal chief Ross Swimmer to run as his deputy chief. When he resigned in 1985 to become head of the Bureau of Indian Affairs, Mankiller assumed the duties of the chief. She won the post in her own right in 1987 and was reelected in 1991 with 82 percent of the vote. "Prior to my election," says Mankiller, "young Cherokee girls would never have thought that they might grow up and become chief."

Mankiller's administration brought renewed attention to the tribe as she focused on the high unemployment rate and low educational attainment of her people. She worked to improve community health care and emphasized the necessity of retaining Cherokee traditions by founding the Institute for Cherokee Literacy. After being diagnosed with cancer, she did not seek reelection in 1995. She was inducted into the National Women's Hall of Fame in 1993, and in 1998 President Clinton awarded her the Presidential Metal of Freedom. She is the recipient of 18 honorary degrees and she serves as a trustee of the Ford Foundation.

Further Reading
Mankiller, Wilma P., with Michael Wallis. *Mankiller: A Chief and Her People.* New York: St. Martin's Press, 1993.

Mansell v. Mansell (490 U.S. 581) (1989)
The parties in this case were divorced in 1979. The divorce decree incorporated a separation agreement that divided the husband's veteran's disability pay. The issue of the state court's authority to divide such pay was never raised in the divorce case, and the divorce decree became final. Several years later, the husband filed a collateral attack on the divorce decree, arguing for the first time that the court lacked authority to divide his disability pay. There were two issues presented. First, could the judgment be reopened since the issue was not raised in the original agreement; and second, could the state rule that federal disability pay be divided. Ultimately, the U.S. Supreme Court ruled on the merits that federal law supercedes state law, and therefore the benefit could not be divided. The Uniform Service Former Spouse Protection

Act (USFSPA) was passed in 1983 to govern in these situations.

Further Reading
Justia.com U.S. Supreme Court Center. "*Mansell v. Mansell,* 490 U.S. 581 (1989)." Available online. URL: http://supreme.justia.com/us/490/581/case.html. Accessed on January 10, 2007.

Mansfield, Arabella (Belle Aurelia Babb Mansfield) (1846–1911) *attorney*
The nation's first woman lawyer, Arabella Mansfield was born Belle Aurelia Babb on May 23, 1846, at Sperry Station in Des Moines County, Iowa. After graduating from Iowa Wesleyan College in 1866, she taught political science, English, and history at Simpson College in Indianola, Iowa, until her marriage in 1868 to John M. Mansfield, a professor at Iowa Wesleyan. She joined the Iowa Wesleyan faculty in that year as a teacher of English and history. Mansfield studied law with her husband, and together they applied for admission to the Iowa bar in 1869. Sympathetic examiners certified Arabella Mansfield as the first female lawyer in the country. Although she joined the National League of Lawyers in 1893, she never practiced law but instead returned to academia, where she remained until her death on August 2, 1911, in Aurora, Illinois.

March for Women's Lives (1992, 2004)
The NATIONAL ORGANIZATION FOR WOMEN (NOW) has organized a number of public demonstrations to raise awareness about issues affecting women and most especially threats to ABORTION rights. NOW began organizing the marches in the mid-1980s, but the March for Women's Lives in 1992 and 2004 were collaborative efforts with other organizers to draw attention to antiabortion law cases pending before the Supreme Court. NOW's estimate for the 1992 March in Washington, D.C., was 750,000 supporters. Organizers also hoped to mobilize pro-choice voters in anticipation of the 1992 presidential election.

The 2004 March for Women's Lives was organized by seven sponsors: the Feminist Majority, NOW, NARAL Pro-Choice America, the PLANNED PARENTHOOD FEDERATION OF AMERICA, the Black Women's Health Imperative, the National Latina Institute for Reproductive Health, and the American Civil Liberties Union. Organizers estimated that 1.15 million women and men participated in the April 25, 2004, march. The demonstration was in protest of the Bush administration's actions limiting women's rights, particularly in the area of reproductive choice.

Upon taking office in 2001, President Bush issued an executive memorandum reinstating the global GAG RULE on international family-planning assistance. Bush timed his action to coincide with the 28th anniversary of the *ROE v. WADE* decision. Under the global gag rule, foreign family-planning agencies may not receive U.S. assistance if they provide abortion services, including counseling on abortion or referrals to other clinics, or lobby to make or keep abortion legal in their own country. On November 5, 2003, Bush signed the Partial-Birth Abortion Ban Act into law. This federal law is the first to ban a specific kind of abortion procedure known as dilation and extraction.

Organizers of the 2004 march believed that by calling attention to the Bush administration's actions, particularly the strong measures undertaken to criminalize abortion and restrict access to information and women's health services, they could motivate women to channel their anger through electoral politics in November and vote Bush out of office. They also hoped that the march would energize young women to fight to protect rights won by previous generations of feminists. Senator HILLARY RODHAM CLINTON told the crowd, "All the people are here today not only to march on behalf of women's lives but to take that energy into the election in November."

Although the 2004 march organizers labeled the event an overwhelming success, and the sheer size of the turnout sent a powerful message about women's political potential, it is impossible to tell whether the event served as an effective mobilizing tool for women in the November election. President Bush easily won a second term in office, and although more women voted than in 2000, the GENDER GAP was smaller, and more women voted for the Republican incumbent than they had in 2000. Some scholars attribute this shift among women to the influence of national security issues and the ongoing threat of terrorism, but more research on the connections between women's experience with demonstrations and their political campaign activities and vote choice is necessary before any judgments can be reached.

Further Reading

Ford, Lynne E. *Women and Politics: The Pursuit of Equality.* Boston: Houghton Mifflin, 2006.

National Organization for Women. "March for Women's Lives." Available online. URL: http://march.now.org/. Accessed on January 10, 2007.

Married Women's Property Act of New York (1848)   Before this law was passed, COVERTURE dictated that a woman could not hold property in her own name. A married woman could not make contracts, keep or control her own wages or any rents, transfer property, sell property, or bring any lawsuit. Between 1839 and 1895, this tradition was gradually reversed by a series of married women's property acts, passed in varying forms by every state in the Union. In some states, the acts were limited in scope, shaped primarily to serve the interests of fathers wishing to protect their estates from improvident sons-in-law and husbands seeking to sequester their own property from seizure for debts. The United States' first Married Women's Property Act, passed in Mississippi in 1839, guaranteed the right of married women to receive income from their property and protected it against being seized for their husbands' debts, but the law left husbands in sole charge of buying, selling, or managing the property. In other states where women's rights activists took a leading role in the campaigns, more ambitious property reform laws were passed. The New York State law passed in 1848 served as a model for similar acts passed between 1848 and 1895 across the country. By the mid-1870s, almost all the states in the North had passed a Married Women's Property Act, and by the end of the century, the southern states had as well. Although the scope of these laws varied widely from state to state, taken together they represented a major advance in women's rights and in establishing women's autonomy. The New York Statute was significant due to its scope. It included women's right to maintain control over property held upon marriage as well as property (including wages and inheritance) acquired during marriage.

Further Reading

Cott, Nancy F. *Public Vows: A History of Marriage and the Nation.* Cambridge, Mass.: Harvard University Press, 2002.
Salmon, Marylyn. *Women and the Law of Property in Early America.* Chapel Hill: University of North Carolina Press, 1986.
Shammas, Carol. "Reassessing Married Women's Property Acts." *Journal of Women's History* 6 (1994): 9–30.

Matalin, Mary (Mary Joe Matalin) (1953–)

political strategist, consultant Mary Joe Matalin was born in Chicago, Illinois, on September 19, 1953, and received a B.A. in political science in 1978. In 1981, she moved to Washington, D.C., to work at the Republican National Committee. She enrolled in Hofstra University Law School two years later but dropped out after a year. She has held a number of political jobs, including serving as political director for President George H. W. Bush's reelection campaign in 1992. During this campaign, Matalin's relationship with James Carville, who held a similar post in Bill Clinton's organization, received much attention in the press. After the election, they married and wrote a book about politics and their relation-

ship, *All's Fair: Love, War and Running for President,* published in 1994 by Random House. Matlin works as a political commentator on radio and television. She was named senior adviser to Vice President Richard Cheney in 2001 and continued in that role until 2003. In 2004, she published the book *Letters to My Daughters.*

Matsui, Doris (Doris Okada Matsui)

(1944–) *congressperson* Doris Okada was born on September 25, 1944, in an internment camp at Poston, Arizona, and grew up in Dinuba, in California's Central Valley. She earned a bachelor's degree in psychology from the University of California–Berkeley, where she met her husband, Bob Matsui. Doris Matsui was active in California politics and was an early supporter of Arkansas governor Bill Clinton's presidential campaign. When Clinton won, Matsui served on his transition team. Following the inauguration, she was appointed deputy special assistant to the president and deputy director of public liaison, working under Alexis Herman. One of her duties was to work with the Asian-American community. On December 28, 1996, the lead story on the front page of the *New York Times* reported that Doris Matsui had been active in John Huang's Asian-Pacific American Working Group to raise campaign donations from Asian Americans, which would have been illegal because of her White House position. Although Matsui was friends with Huang, the administration denied she played any role in fund-raising, and the *New York Times* admitted it had made a mistake three years after the initial story.

Matsui served in the White House from 1993 to 1998. President Clinton appointed her to the board of the Woodrow Wilson International Center for Scholars in September 2000. Matsui also served on the boards of KVIE-TV and People for the American Way. After leaving government, Matsui was director of government relations for the law firm Colleen, Shannon, Scott, stepping down in 2005 to take her seat in Congress. Following the death of her husband, 26-year incumbent Bob Matsui from complications of myelodysplastic syndrome on January 1, 2005, Doris Matsui was elected as his replacement in a special election on March 8, 2005. The Matsuis had not disclosed Bob's terminal illness to the public during his campaign for reelection. In the House, Doris Matsui, who was reelected in 2006, serves on the Rules Committee.

Further Reading

Barone, Michael. *The Almanac of American Politics.* Washington, D.C.: National Journal Group, 2006.

"Matsui, Doris Okada." In *Biographical Directory of the United States Congress, 1774–present.* Available online. URL: http://bioguide.congress.gov/scripts/biodisplay.pl?index=M001163. Accessed on January 8, 2007.

"Representative Doris K. Matsui (CA)." In *Project Vote Smart.* Available online. URL: http://votesmart.org/bio.php?can_id=MCA05731. Accessed on January 8, 2007.

—Angela Kouters

McCarthy, Carolyn (1944–) *congressperson*

Carolyn McCarthy was born on January 5, 1944, in Brooklyn, New York. She earned her LPN from Glen Cove Nursing School in 1964 and worked as a nurse in a suburb of New York City. On December 7, 1993, her husband Dennis was killed and her son Kevin was injured on a Long Island Rail Road commuter train when a gunman, Colin Ferguson, randomly opened fire on passengers. McCarthy responded to the tragedy by launching a campaign against gun violence that eventually led her to run for Congress in 1996. She defeated Republican incumbent Dan Frisa, who had a long record of votes against gun-control legislation. She has been reelected in each subsequent election, including the 2006 contest.

In the House, Congresswoman McCarthy serves on the Committee on Education and Workforce and the Committee on Financial Services. She is also one of the most vocal supporters in the House for reinstating a federal ban on semiautomatic firearms, commonly referred to as the "assault weapons ban." In addition to her efforts to reduce gun violence, McCarthy is active on issues relating to education and public health.

Further Reading

Barone, Michael. *The Almanac of American Politics.* Washington, D.C.: National Journal Group, 2006.

"McCarthy, Carolyn." In *Biographical Directory of the United States Congress, 1774–present.* Available online. URL: http://bioguide.congress.gov/scripts/biodisplay.pl?index=M000309. Accessed on January 8, 2007.

"Representative Carolyn McCarthy (NY)." In *Project Vote Smart.* Available online. URL: http://votesmart.org/bio.php?can_id=BC38252. Accessed on January 8, 2007.

—Angela Kouters

McCollum, Betty (1954–) *congressperson*

Betty McCollum was born on July 12, 1954, in South St. Paul, Minnesota. When her daughter was injured on a slide in a city park and the city council refused to take action to rectify what McCollum considered a dangerous situation, her friends urged her to run for city council herself. She won a seat in 1986 and served for three terms. McCollum served from 1993 to 2000 in the Minnesota House of Representatives and was elected assistant leader three times by her Democratic-Farmer-Labor (DFL) Party colleagues.

When incumbent Minnesota congressman Bruce Vento decided not to seek reelection in 2000 to the U.S. House due to illness, McCollum won the DFL nomination to succeed him. She was endorsed and supported by EMILY's LIST. McCollum has been reelected three times, including in 2006, without any serious opposition. In 2004, she called for Secretary of Education Rod Paige to resign after he referred to the

National Education Association (NEA) as "a terrorist organization." In the House, Representative McCollum serves on the Committee on Education and the Workforce and the Committee on International Relations.

Further Reading

Barone, Michael. *The Almanac of American Politics.* Washington, D.C.: National Journal Group, 2006.

"McCollum, Betty." In *Biographical Directory of the United States Congress, 1774–present.* Available online. URL: http://bioguide.congress.gov/scripts/biodisplay.pl?index=. Accessed on January 8, 2007.

"Representative Betty McCollum (MN)." In *Project Vote Smart.* Available online. URL: http://votesmart.org/bio.php?can_id=BS021756. Accessed on January 8, 2007.

—Angela Kouters

McGee, Anita (Anita Newcomb McGee)

(1864–1940) *activist* Anita Newcomb was born on November 4, 1864, in Washington, D.C. In 1888, she married scientist William John McGee, with whom she had three children. In 1892, she received her M.D. from Columbian University (now George Washington University). She subsequently undertook postgraduate studies in gynecology at Johns Hopkins University but stopped practicing medicine in 1896 to take on a series of leadership positions in organizations including the DAUGHTERS OF THE AMERICAN REVOLUTION (DAR).

As chair of the DAR Hospital Corps when the United States declared war on Spain (1898), McGee persuaded Surgeon General George M. Sternberg to let her committee screen nursing applicants for the U.S. Army. She was so successful that Sternberg subsequently established a Nurse Corps Division and appointed McGee acting assistant surgeon general in August 1898. McGee subsequently worked to recognize and formalize the contract nurses' contributions to the war. She helped to form the Society of Spanish-American War Nurses and lobbied extensively to establish a permanent U.S. Army Nurse Corps, finally succeeding through passage of the Army Reorganization Act of 1901. McGee later joined Spanish-American War veterans in nursing Japanese troops during the Russo-Japanese War (1904–5). Japan gave her an officer's rank and awarded her the Imperial Order of the Sacred Crown in recognition of her service.

After these events, McGee led a more private life. She died in Washington, D.C., on October 5, 1940, and was buried in Arlington National Cemetery with full military honors. Savvy at navigating political and military bureaucracy and committed to equality for women, McGee used the wartime need for nurses to gain women permanent entry into the U.S. armed forces.

Anita McGee, ca. 1940 (LIBRARY OF CONGRESS)

Further Reading

Graf, Mercedes. "Women Physicians in the Spanish-American War." *Army History* 28 (2002): 5–15, 28.

Oblensky, Florence. "Anita Newcomb McGee, M.D. (4 Nov. 1864–5 Oct. 1940)." *Military Medicine* 133 (1968): 397–400.

Sarnecky, Mary. *A History of the United States Army Nurse Corps.* Philadelphia: University of Pennsylvania Press, 1999.

—Laura R. Prieto

McGrory, Mary (1918–2004) *reporter*   Mary McGrory was born on August 22, 1918, in Boston, Massachusetts, to Mary Catherine and Edward Patrick McGrory. She graduated from the Girl's Latin School in Boston and began work as a book reviewer with the *Boston Herald.* In 1947, she began her career as a journalist with the *Washington Star,* remaining with the paper until it folded in 1981. She first attracted critical acclaim with her relentless coverage of the Josephy McCarthy hearings on communism in 1954. As one of the first of the few women columnists, she earned a loyal following with her tribute to John F. Kennedy following his 1963 assassination: "He brought gaiety, glamour and grace to the American political scene in a measure never known before. That lightsome tread, that debonair touch, that shock of chestnut hair, that beguiling grin, that shattering understatement—these are what we shall remember."

McGrory's coverage of the Watergate scandal earned her the number 20 spot on the "enemies list" that Charles Colson drafted for Richard Nixon. President George H. W. Bush also complained about McGrory's columns in his private journal, noting: "She has destroyed me over and over again." She was known for her tenacity in getting to the heart of a story. She won a Pulitzer Prize in commentary in 1974, the year Nixon resigned. She continued to work and write well into her 80s. In March 2003 she fell ill, suffering a stroke. She died in April 2004 at the age of 85.

Further Reading

Corn, David. "The Death of Mary McGrory." *Nation,* 23 April 2004. Available online. URL: www.thenation.com/biogs.capitolgames?pid=1398. Accessed on June 15, 2007.

Toner, Robin. "Mary McGrory, 85, Longtime Columnist, Dies." *New York Times,* 23 April 2004.

McKinley, Ida (Ida Saxton McKinley)
(1847–1907) *first lady*   Ida Saxton was born in Canton, Ohio, on June 8, 1847, to banker James Ashbury Saxton and Katherine DeWalt Saxton. Ida was well educated, completing her schooling at Brooke Hall Seminary in Media, Pennsylvania. Upon graduation, she embarked on an extensive tour of Europe with a group of other young women accompanied by a Canton schoolteacher as chaperone. Ida took full advantage of the experience, often diverting from the group to explore on her own. When she returned, her father offered her a position in his bank. It was not considered "proper" for women of her social position to work, but Ida was comfortable with finances and accepted the opportunity. She advanced quickly from clerk to cashier, but this early experience never led her to advocate for women's rights related to business or nontraditional occupations.

Ida Saxton probably met William McKinley at a church picnic or at the window of the bank, but the two shared an instant mutual attraction. He was a Civil War veteran and had recently been elected county prosecuting attorney. They were married on January 25, 1871, and throughout their marriage she called him "Major." Their first child, Katherine, was born on Christmas day 1871. In 1873, Ida survived a difficult labor only to see her daughter Ida die soon after birth. In that same year, her mother passed away, and Ida's episodes with migraines, convulsions, and seizures that had afflicted her throughout young adulthood increased in severity. Her will and strength of independence waned, and she became a semi-invalid. In 1875, her daughter Katherine also died, devastating Ida.

William McKinley was devoted to his wife. Even as a member of the House of Representatives, he tended to her needs and assured her that he was constantly nearby with a series of signals and notes throughout the day. Despite the seizures (undoubtledly the result of epilepsy), Ida appeared in public when she was well enough to stand. Doctors were helpless to prevent the seizures, and the family decided it best to simply ignore them whenever possible to allow Ida to function with some semblance of dignity. Guests were urged to do the same.

Ida encouraged her husband's political aspirations, avidly following the news from her confinement so that they could talk together about events of the day. She traveled with him when her health permitted. First elected to the House of Representatives in 1876, William McKinley was defeated in 1890 but elected governor of Ohio the following year. The McKinleys typically lived in hotels in Washington and Columbus in order to limit Ida's household responsibilities. This allowed her to engage in social and charitable activities as her health permitted. They entertained despite her ailments.

William McKinley's campaign for the presidency in 1896 included a Women's McKinley Club in Canton, Ohio. Buttons and other memorabilia featured a picture of Ida McKinley and represented the first time that women were actively courted. McKinley's opponents tried to gain politically from his wife's public absence by accusing her of being a spy, a Roman Catholic, and a lunatic. The Republicans countered with a biographical pamphlet on Ida McKinley's life. William was elected, and she attended the inaugural on March 4, 1897, as well as the ball that evening. To accommodate her frailness and his habit of directly assisting her, she sat in a chair directly beside him at meals and in receiving lines. Jennie Hobart, wife of the vice president, assisted with the formal hostess duties and tended to Ida's personal needs when called upon.

William McKinley won reelection in 1900 with Theodore Roosevelt as his running mate. Ida's health worsened at the start of the second

Ida Saxton McKinley, ca. 1900 (LIBRARY OF CONGRESS)

term, but in 1901 she was well enough to accompany her husband on a cross-country tour. During this trip, an infection in her finger spread to her heart, nearly killing her. As she recuperated with friends in Buffalo, anarchist Leon F. Czolgosz shot William McKinley as he toured the Pan-American Exposition on September 5, 1901. McKinley urged his friends to be careful in how they told Ida of the shooting. He died nine days later with Ida by his side. She accompanied the body back to Washington and attended all of the funeral ceremonies without assistance. Historians report that she never again suffered another seizure following McKinley's death. She returned to Canton and lived for another six years beyond her husband, dying from a stroke on May 26, 1907.

Further Reading
Mayo, Edith P. "Ida McKinley." In *The Smithsonian Book of First Ladies: Their Lives, Times, and Issues,*

edited by Edith P. Mayo, 142–146. New York: Henry Holt and Company, 1996.

National First Ladies Library. *Biographies: First Ladies of the United States.* Available online. URL: http://www.firstladies.org/biographies. Accessed on January 4, 2007.

Schneider, Dorothy, and Carl J. Schneider. "Ida Saxton McKinley" *First Ladies: A Biographical Dictionary.* New York: Checkmark Books, 2001, 155–161.

McKinney, Cynthia (1955–   ) *congressperson*   Cynthia McKinney was born on March 17, 1955, in Atlanta, Georgia. She earned a bachelor's degree in international relations from the University of Southern California (1978) and attended the Fletcher School of Law and Diplomacy; she is currently working on a Ph.D. at the University of California, Berkeley. McKinney's political career began in 1986 when her father, state representative Billy McKinney, submitted her name as a write-in candidate for a Georgia State House district even though she was living in Jamaica at the time. She won 40 percent of the vote. In 1988, she actually ran for the seat and won, making the McKinneys the first father and daughter to simultaneously serve in a state house. In 1991, her remarks from the floor in opposition to the bombing of Iraq during the Persian Gulf War resulted in many of her legislative colleagues walking out in protest.

In 1992, McKinney was elected as the first congresswoman from Georgia's newly drawn 11th district, a majority-minority district that stretched from Atlanta to Savannah. She was the first African-American woman to represent Georgia in the House. In 1995, the 11th district was declared unconstitutional by the U.S. Supreme Court in a case testing racial gerrymandering. Her district was renumbered and redrawn to take in almost all of DeKalb County. The new district included more white voters, but it was no less Democratic, and McKinney was easily reelected from this district in 1996, 1998, and 2000.

In 2002, McKinney was defeated in the Democratic primary by DeKalb County judge Denise Majette. Although McKinney protested the result in court, claiming that Republicans in the district had participated in the Democratic primary specifically to vote against McKinney, Georgia has an open primary system allowing voters to lawfully participate in whichever primary election they choose. A major issue in the 2002 campaign was McKinney's allegation that the Bush administration knew in advance about the 9/11 terrorist attacks but failed to prevent them. In 2004, Majette did not seek reelection, deciding instead to campaign for the U.S. Senate. McKinney won the Democratic primary and regained her seat, but the Democratic leadership declined to reinstate her seniority.

In the 109th Congress, McKinney served on the House Committee on Armed Services and the House Committee on the Budget. She was a dogged advocate for victims of Hurricane Katrina, at one point suggesting that if employees of a nursing home were charged with negligent homicide in the deaths of their patients in the rising flood waters, Homeland Security secretary Michael Chertoff should be similarly charged. On November 18, 2005, Congresswoman McKinney was one of only three members to vote yea on a resolution calling for the immediate withdrawal of U.S. forces from Iraq.

Cynthia McKinney lost in the August 2006 Democratic primary to Hank Johnson. On December 6, 2006, just prior to departing from the House of Representatives, she introduced legislation to impeach President George W. Bush for his failure to uphold his oath to defend the U.S. Constitution. The legislation failed.

Further Reading

Barone, Michael. *The Almanac of American Politics.* Washington, D.C.: National Journal Group, 2006.

"McKinney, Cynthia Ann." In *Biographical Directory of the United States Congress, 1774–present.* Available online. URL: http://bioguide.congress.gov/scripts/biodisplay.pl?index=M000523. Accessed on January 8, 2007.

—Angela Kouters

McMorris Rodgers, Cathy (1969–) *congressperson* Cathy McMorris was born on May 22, 1969, in Salem, Oregon, a descendant of pioneers of the Oregon Trail. She earned her B.A. in pre-law from Pensacola Christian College and an executive MBA from the University of Washington. She began her career in public service by running for the Washington State House of Representatives in 1993 and served until 2004. During her time in the state legislature, she served as the House Republican leader from 2003 to 2004, the first female to serve as minority leader. McMorris focused on improving the economy, creating jobs, and reforming government. She chaired the House Commerce and Labor Committee, the Joint Legislative Audit and Review Committee, and the State Government Committee.

McMorris was elected to Congress in 2004 at the age of 35 when George Nethercutt vacated the seat in order to run for the U.S. Senate. She is pro-life, has established a fairly conservative voting record, and was a close ally of former Speaker Tim Delay. In the 109th Congress, she served on the Committee on Armed Services, the Committee on Education and the Workforce, and the Committee on Resources. She was chosen for the Republic Steering Committee and has served as an assistant whip. She married Brian Rodgers in August 2006 and won reelection in November later that year.

Further Reading

Barone, Michael. *The Almanac of American Politics.* Washington, D.C.: National Journal Group, 2006.

"McMorris Rodgers, Cathy." In *Biographical Directory of the United States Congress, 1774–present.* Available online. URL: http://bioguide.congress.gov/scripts/biodisplay.pl?index=M001159. Accessed on January 8, 2007.

"Representative Cathy McMorris (WA)." In *Project Vote Smart.* Available online. URL: http://votesmart.org/bio.php?can_id=. Accessed on January 8, 2007.

—Angela Kouters

Mead, Margaret (1901–1978) *anthropologist* Margaret Mead did more than just study anthropology, she lived it—from wearing the native dress of the people she observed to learning their language and customs. Her gender and self-taught methods of fieldwork allowed Mead to gain access to the carefully guarded secrets and stories of many of the world's indigenous people: from the Manu'a of Samoa to the Omaha Indians of Nebraska and the Arapesh of New Guinea.

Born in Philadelphia on December 16, 1901, Mead earned her master's and Ph.D. degrees from Columbia University, but she earned her reputation as the world's most innovative and significant anthropologist in far corners of the world. Like many great women throughout history, Mead refused to live life as a spectator. Instead, she boldly went where few anthropologists, particularly women, had previously trod. Her adventurous nature also led her to become an outspoken supporter of progressive education, civil rights, economic development, sex, religion, and moral issues.

On December 8, 1939, Mary Catherine Bateson, Mead's only child, was born. Catherine's father, Mead's third husband, was anthropologist Gregory Bateson. While that marriage would subsequently end, as had the previous two, Mead adamantly refused to describe her adventures in matrimony as failures. They had simply come to an end. Instead of bemoaning their demise, the eternal optimist chose to share what she had learned along the way with other women.

From 1961 until her death, Mead wrote a monthly column for *Redbook Magazine* that offered women common-sense advice on family, social and moral issues. The prolific and well-respected writer's books include *Growing up in New Guinea* (1930), *The Changing Culture of an Indian Tribe* (1932), *Sex and Temperament in Three Primitive Societies* (1935), and *Twentieth Century Faith: Hope and Survival* (1973).

Further Reading

Mead, Margaret. *Coming of Age in Samoa.* New York: Perennial Classics, 2001.

Rice, Edward. *Margaret Mead: A Portrait*. New York: Harper & Row Publishers, 1979.

—Thea Lapham

Meritor Savings Bank v. Vinson (477 US 57) (1986)

The first Supreme Court decision on SEXUAL HARASSMENT, *Meritor Savings Bank v. Vinson* found first that both quid pro quo (this for that) sexual harassment (where sexual favors were requested in exchange for either job advancement or nondismissal) and hostile-environment sexual harassment were actionable as forms of sex discrimination. *Meritor* stressed that sexual harassment concerns unwelcome behavior and that sexual relations that were voluntary could still be seen as unwelcome. The case, which dated from 1974, involved a bank teller who had agreed to sexual relations with her boss out of a fear that she would lose her job if she did not agree. Earlier the courts had declared that because she had voluntarily had sex with Vinson, and because she was terminated for excessive sick leave, sexual harassment had not occurred. The Supreme Court's decision was important because it emphasized, first, that if the sexual advances were unwelcome then the fact that the sexual relations may have been voluntary did not matter. Second, the Court shifted the impact of sexual harassment away from merely tangible economic loss to the possibility of an adverse psychological impact. Third, the Court provided the lens of hostile environment sexual harassment to a case that had failed as a quid pro quo. Finally, the Court declared that to determine whether behavior is unwelcome the plaintiff's behavior and possible "sexually provocative speech or dress" is relevant.

Further Reading

The OYEZ Project. "*Meritor Savings Bank v. Vinson*, 477 U.S. 57 (1986)." Available online. URL: http://www.oyez.org/cases/case?case=1980-1989/ 1985/1985_84_1979. Accessed on January 10, 2007.

—Claire Curtis

Mikulski, Barbara (Barbara Ann Mikulski)

(1936–) *U.S. senator* Born on July 20, 1936, the great-granddaughter of Polish immigrants who owned a local bakery, Mikulski is the oldest of three daughters. She was raised in east Baltimore, where her parents, William and Christine Kutz Mikulski, ran a neighborhood grocery store. She received her B.A. degree from Mount St. Agnes College in Baltimore in 1958 and her M.S.W. degree from the University of Maryland School of Social Work in 1965. Mikulski began her political career by organizing neighbors to stop construction of a 16-lane highway through the historic Fells Point area of Baltimore. As a result, Barbara Mikulski became known as "the street fighter who beat the highway." In 1971, she won a seat on the Baltimore City Council. In 1976, she ran for and won a seat in the U.S. House of Representatives, serving for five terms before she was elected to a U.S. Senate seat in 1986.

Senator Mikulski was the first Democratic woman to hold a Senate seat not previously held by her husband, the first Democratic woman to serve in both houses of Congress, and the first woman to win a statewide election in Maryland. She is unofficially known as the "dean of the Senate women" because of her extraordinary and successful efforts that led to the election of six additional Democratic women in the Senate. In 1994, Senator Mikulski was unanimously elected as secretary of the Democratic Conference. She was the first woman to be elected to a Democratic leadership position in the Senate.

In the Senate, Mikulski serves on the Committee on Appropriations, the Committee on Health, Education, Labor and Pensions, and the Select Committee on Intelligence. She faces reelection in 2010.

Further Reading

Barone, Michael. *The Almanac of American Politics*. Washington, D.C.: National Journal Group, 2006.
"Mikulski, Barbara Ann." In *Biographical Directory of the United States Congress, 1774–present*. Available

online. URL: http://bioguide.congress.gov/scripts/biodisplay.pl?index=M000702. Accessed on January 8, 2007.

"Senator Barbara A. Mikulski (MD)." In *Project Vote Smart*. Available online. URL: http://votesmart.org/bio.php?can_id=S0401103. Accessed on January 8, 2007.

—Angela Kouters

Milholland, Inez (Inez Milholland Boissevain) (1886–1916) *suffragist, labor lawyer, public speaker*

Inez Milholland literally gave her life for the SUFFRAGE cause, collapsing in the midst of a speech in 1916. She is most famously recalled for her role in the NATIONAL AMERICAN WOMAN SUFFRAGE ASSOCIATION parade held on the eve of President Woodrow Wilson's inauguration in 1913. Milholland led the parade on a white charger, clad in white and gold, holding a banner that read "Forward Into Light."

Born on August 6, 1886, in Brooklyn, New York, Milholland attended grammar school in New York, high school in London, and the Willard School in Berlin before enrolling at Vassar College in 1905. When her efforts to bring two national speakers on women's suffrage to the campus met with resistance, she moved the event to an adjacent cemetery. She was denied admission to several all-male law schools (Oxford, Cambridge, Harvard, and Columbia) and so enrolled at the New York University School of Law. As a law student, she was active in a number of progressive causes, including women's suffrage, the Women's Trade Union League, the National Child Labor Committee, the National Association for the Advancement of Colored People and England's Fabian Society. In addition, she did legal work in Children's Court and as a probation worker. In 1913, she married Eugen Jan Boissevain, a Dutch businessman, while in London.

When efforts to lobby Woodrow Wilson to support a federal amendment granting women the vote failed, Milholland set off by rail on a lecture tour, hoping to convince those in the Western territories to adopt the suffrage cause and reject Wilson in the upcoming 1916 election. Milholland suffered from pernicious anemia, and the strain of travel and her heavy lecture schedule proved too much for her. She collapsed midway through a stump speech in Los Angeles California. Although her sister gave blood for two transfusions, Milholland died 10 weeks after her collapse. Her last public words were: "Mr. President, how long must women wait for liberty?"

Further Reading

Lumsden, Linda J., and William J. Jackson. *Inez: The Life and Times of Inez Milholland.* Bloomington: Indiana University Press, 2004.

Inez Milholland at the National American Woman Suffrage Association parade in Washington, D.C., on March 3, 1913 (LIBRARY OF CONGRESS)

military service   Perhaps more than any other issue, the issue of women serving in the military exposes the lingering disagreements over their appropriate role in society. For those who believe that men and women are naturally disposed to occupy different spheres in life, the military is the clearest example of a role that only men should play. The physical demands of military service exclude many citizens from active duty but are particularly challenging for the majority of women. On the other hand, as the military has become an all-volunteer force in the United States, more women have joined and served with distinction. Since women play an ever more visible role in politics and are increasingly considered qualified for the office of president and commander in chief, the military is likely to see more gender integration over time, not less.

Although women's visible service in the military, particularly among active-duty personnel in combat zones, is a contemporary phenomenon, women have served throughout America's history in unofficial support roles—as nurses and doctors in field hospitals; as spies; or as soldiers disguised as men during the Revolutionary War, the Civil War, and the Spanish-American War. It was not until 1901 and the formation of the Army Nurse Corps (and 1908 with the formation of the Navy Nurse Corps) that women's roles were made visible.

During World War I, women joined the military as enlisted personnel with the navy and marines. More than 33,000 women served in that war, and more than 400 nurses died in the line of duty. Women were permitted to enlist in a limited capacity primarily because personnel were in such short supply. Administrative tasks went unfulfilled as male soldiers were redeployed to the front lines of battle. Although the service branches requested that more women be recruited to fill desk jobs and support roles during World War I, the Pentagon refused. World War II and the pressing need for support changed that attitude somewhat. Women's branches were developed in all services: the WOMEN'S ARMY CORPS (WAC), the Navy Women's Reserve (WAVES), the Marine Corps Women's Reserve, and the WOMEN'S AIRFORCE SERVICE PILOTS (WASPS). During World War II, more than 400,000 women served at home and abroad in primarily noncombat roles.

The Women's Armed Services Integration Act of 1948 transformed the auxiliary nature of women's service to permanent status in the military. During the Korean conflict, more than 50,000 women served and more than 7,000

women were deployed to Vietnam, most as nurses. A statue memorial to women's service in Vietnam stands near the entrance to the Vietnam War Memorial in Washington, D.C.

As of 2007, women make up 15 percent of active-duty personnel in the U.S. military; an unprecedented 350,000 women are currently serving. Prior to 1967, there was a 2 percent cap limiting women's service in the military. By 2000, the proportion of enlisted women had risen to 14.7 percent. The air force has the highest proportion of women on active duty (19.3 percent), and the Marine Corps has the lowest (6.1 percent). The army reports 15.5 percent women and the navy 13.6 percent women among enlisted personnel. The Office of the Assistant Secretary of Defense identifies four factors that affect the proportion of enlisted female members: (1) Women tend to have a lower inclination to enlist than men do. (2) Combat exclusions restrict the positions in which women may serve. (3) The military personnel system is "closed," meaning that growth comes from the bottom up and from within, so the proportion of women depends primarily on the proportion of women recruited. (4) Finally, women leave the services at a higher rate than men. The increase in the proportion of women in the military has resulted in changes in nearly all aspects of military life: training programs and physical fitness regimens, assignments, living arrangements, and medical services. New policies had to be created to address pregnancy, single parents in the military, child care during peacetime and deployment, and dual-service marriages.

In 1994, Congress repealed the "risk rule" barring women from all combat situations and allowed each branch of the service to determine which positions would he open to women. Secretary of Defense Les Aspin advised, "Women should be excluded from assignment to units below brigade level whose primary mission is to engage in direct combat on the ground." *Combat* was defined as "engaging an enemy on the ground with individual or crew-served weapons, while being exposed to hostile fire and to a high probability of direct physical contact with the hostile force's personnel." As a result, thousands of previously restricted positions became open to women: 91 percent of positions in the army, 96 percent in the navy, 93 percent in the Marine Corps, and 99 percent in the air force. Although women are still prohibited from certain assignments in each branch of the service, most experts think it is only a matter of time until there is full gender integration. Department of Defense evidence suggests that mixed crews perform as well as or better than all male units, and a RAND Research Brief from 1997 reported that the integration of women has not adversely affected military readiness. Using interviews, surveys, and focus groups, the researchers probed issues of unit cohesiveness, readiness, and morale. While gender played some role in unit cohesiveness, this typically occurred only in units where conflict was already a problem. The presence of women was also cited as raising the level of professional standards. Morale was affected by gender in two areas: SEXUAL HARASSMENT and a perception of double standards related to physical standards.

Female recruits tend to have more education and better test scores than men. As technology continues to advance, women will gain more opportunities. "U.S. military superiority is in our intelligence and technology. People who remain skeptical of having women fight for their country act like we're still attacking with fixed bayonets," says Linda DePaw of the Minerva Center (a military think tank). Although pregnancy rates, sexual harassment, and sexual assault remain problems, the public's reaction to women in combat and female casualties has proved milder than predicted. According to Carolyn Becraft, a deputy assistant secretary of defense under President Bill Clinton, "It's been a non-issue."

The first Gulf War (Desert Storm, 1991) marked the largest deployment of women to a combat zone in U.S. history. More than 40,000 women served in the Gulf, comprising 7 percent of the deployed force. Their roles included flying helicopters on reconnaissance and search-and-rescue missions, driving convoys, staffing Patriot missile placements, piloting planes, and guarding prisoners of war (POWs), among others. Thirteen women were killed in the line of duty, and two were taken as POWs. Deployment of women in the current war in Iraq is even larger, although there is no official count. As of May 2005, more than 155,000 women have served or are currently serving "in theater," meaning in Iraq and the countries involved in the operation known as Enduring Freedom, which includes Afghanistan. According to the Pentagon, this number includes 16,000 single mothers. The deployment has also stretched the limits of the law on women in combat roles. According to retired air force brigadier general Wilma L. Vaught, "You've got more women carrying weapons with the possibility that they'll use them to fight or defend themselves. That's one of the big differences between this war and others. Women haven't done this type of war before." Blurred lines between front-line positions and combat support have resulted in higher female casualties, including the capture of army soldiers Jessica Lynch and Shoshana Johnson, both ambushed in a supply convoy in 2003. As of August 2007, 88 military women have been killed in Iraq (out of more than 4,060 deaths).

Events related to Operation Enduring Freedom have stimulated the public debate over women's roles in military combat. As CBS News reported in October 2004, "The unexpected realities of the war in Iraq are forcing the Pentagon to reexamine its longstanding ban on women in combat in a guerrilla war fought mainly in cities and without front lines." As part of the Pentagon's effort to reorganize the army into a more combat-ready force, mixed-gender supply companies will be attached directly to combat units.

Those opposed to women in the military, particularly in positions likely to face hostilities, often ground their opposition in the essential natures of men and women. Allan Carlson of the Family Research Council, a conservative Washington think tank, says, "Having mothers on or near the front lines violates the most basic human instincts." PHYLLIS SCHLAFLY of the EAGLE FORUM has written: "The men in our government and in the U.S. military lack the courage to stand up to feminists and repudiate their assault on family and motherhood." Conservative commentator Linda Chavez has noted: "No matter how much we modernists pretend otherwise, women are different from men, and their roles are not interchangeable. Females are not just smaller versions of males; they are also, on average, far less aggressive and more nurturing, qualities that suit them to be good mothers but not warriors."

Both advocates and opponents of an increased role for women in the modem military were confronted with the stark gender dissonance created by pictures of women among the men involved in the Abu Ghraib prison scandal. In April 2004, graphic photographs of naked male prisoners in sexualized poses, hooded prisoners connected to electrodes, and male prisoners piled naked in a jumbled human pyramid were made public. Among the U.S. military immortalized in the photographs was a smiling Private LYNNDIE ENGLAND. Specialist Sabrina Harman was pictured smiling and giving a thumbs-up sign from behind a pile of hooded, naked Iraqi prisoners. Of the seven reservists from the 372nd Military Police Company who ultimately faced criminal charges for their actions, three were women. The commander of the 800th Military Police Brigade, the unit in charge of military prisons in Iraq, was army reserve brigadier general Janis Karpinski. The notion that women were too delicate to face the horrors of war was certainly dashed, but so too was the claim that women in uniform would behave differently than men.

Military women have, for the most part, resisted any focus on their gender. Congress

may well be forced to confront gender in any future debates over military conscription. When President Jimmy Carter reactivated the draft registration process, Congress did not act on his recommendation and amend the act to include females. In ROSTKER V. GOLDBERG (1981), the U.S. Supreme Court ruled that Congress's decision to exempt women from registration "was not the 'accidental by-product' of a traditional way of thinking about females" and did not violate the due-process clause of the Fifth Amendment. The Court reasoned that because of the combat restrictions on females at the time, men and women were not "similarly situated" for the purposes of draft registration. With restrictions relaxed and women's strong performance in the 1991 Gulf War and the 2003 war in Iraq, it is hard to see how the Court could use the same reasoning in upholding women's exclusion today.

Further Reading

Sisk, Richard. "Gender Ban Ripped: Congress's Only Woman Vet Rips House Panel's Curbs on Troops." *New York Daily News* 21 May 2005.
Chavez, Linda. "Women in Combat Will Take Toll on Our Culture." Townhall. com, 30 April 2003. Available online. URL: http://tinyurl.com/2vtysp. Accessed on January 10, 2007.
Herbert, Melissa. *Camouflage Isn't Only for Combat; Gender, Sexuality, and Women in the Military.* New York: New York University Press, 1998.

Millender-McDonald, Juanita (1938–2007) *congressperson* Juanita Millender-McDonald was born on September 7, 1938, in Birmingham, Alabama. She earned a B.A. in business administration from the University of Redlands (1981), a master's in public administration from the University of Southern California (1988), a master's in education administration from California State University–Los Angeles, and a Ph.D. in public administration from the University of Southern California. She was a teacher, a member of the Carson, California, city council (1990–92), and a member of the California State Assembly (1992–96) before entering the U.S. House of Representatives in 1996. Millender-McDonald first won her seat in the House in a special election and easily won reelection in each subsequent cycle. She was returned to the House in 2006.

The congresswoman was the ranking Democrat on the House Committee on House Administration. She also served on the House Committee on Small Business and the Committee on Transportation and Infrastructure. She was considered a front-runner for the job of secretary of transportation had John Kerry been elected president in 2004. Millender-McDonald has cochaired the Caucus on Women's Issues, where she focused on Social Security reform. She led the opposition to the Unborn Victims of Violence Act (the bill would make it a crime to harm a fetus in an attack on a pregnant woman). She spoke out against genocide in Cambodia, Darfur, and other regions of the world where human rights are in danger or ignored, and worked with former Secretary of State MADELINE ALBRIGHT and Ambassador John Miller on human trafficking and women's rights issues globally. She was also a member of the Congressional Black Caucus. Millender-McDonald died of cancer on April 22, 2007. A special election on August 21, 2007, resulted in the election of Laura Richardson, former state assemblywoman.

Further Reading

Barone, Michael. *The Almanac of American Politics.* Washington, D.C.: National Journal Group, 2006.

"Millender, McDonald, Juanita." In *Biographical Directory of the United States Congress, 1774–present.* Available online. URL: http://bioguide.congress. gov/scripts/biodisplay.pl?index=M000714. Accessed on January 8, 2007.

"Representative Juanita Millender-McDonald (CA)." In *Project Vote Smart.* Available online. URL: http://votesmart.org/bio.php?can_id=BC030264. Accessed on January 8, 2007.

—Angela Kouters

Miller, Candice (1954–) *congressperson*

Candice Miller was born on May 7, 1954, in Detroit, Michigan, graduated from Lakeshore High School in St. Clair Shores, and attended both Macomb County Community College in Warren and Northwood Institute for Business Management. She served as a trustee on the Harrison Township Board (1979–80), as Harrison Township supervisor (1980–92), as treasurer of Macomb County (1992–94), and as the secretary of state of Michigan (1995–2003). She was also the chair of the Bush-Cheney campaign in Michigan in 2004.

In 2002, Miller was elected as a Republican to the U.S. House of Representatives in the seat previously held by Democrat whip David Bonior. During the 108th Congress, she was admonished by the House Ethics Committee for improperly attempting to influence the vote of fellow Michigan congressman Nick Smith on the floor of the U.S. House. In the 109th Congress, Miller served on the House Committee on Armed Services, the Committee on Government Reform, and the Committee on House Administration. She won reelection in 2006. '

Further Reading

Barone, Michael. *The Almanac of American Politics.* Washington, D.C.: National Journal Group, 2006.

"Miller, Candice S." In *Biographical Directory of the United States Congress, 1774–present.* Available online. URL: http://bioguide.congress.gov/scripts/ biodisplay.pl?index=. Accessed on January 8, 2007.

"Representative Candice S. Miller (MI)." In *Project Vote Smart.* Available online. URL: http://votesmart.org/bio.php?can_id=BMI53653. Accessed on January 8, 2007.

—Angela Kouters

Millett, Kate (Katherine Murray Millett) (1934–) *feminist writer, activist*

Katherine Murray Millett was born on September 14, 1934, in St. Paul, Minnesota. Studying first at University of Minnesota (where she graduated with first-class honors in 1956), she went on to earn a master's degree (again with first-class honors) at St. Hilda's College, Oxford University, in 1958. After teaching in the United States for a few years, she moved to Japan to teach English and study sculpting. While overseas, she met Fumio Yahima, a sculptor whom she married two years after returning to America in 1963. She began teaching in Barnard College's department of English a year later and became active in feminist politics and the civil rights movement.

In 1966, Millett became a committee member of the NATIONAL ORGANIZATION FOR WOMEN (NOW). She also returned to studying, completing a Ph.D. (with distinction) at Columbia University in 1970. Her dissertation, an interdisciplinary work that combined religion, sociology, psychology, and anthropology with literary theory and analysis, also combined academic research with grassroots activist practice and defined the objectives and potential strategies of the feminist movement. Published the year she was awarded her doctorate, *Sexual Politics* was an overnight success, catapulting Millett into the public sphere with national prominence in the feminist movement. Attacking PATRIARCHY as the root cause of women's oppression in society and proposing changes in personal and sexual attitudes, *Sexual Politics* helped rally the still-burgeoning women's rights movement and was as controversial as it was popular.

Millett soon felt the costs of being a celebrity—and a feminist. Just a year after the release of her first book, she made a film about women called *Three Lives*, and by 1973 had published another book, *The Prostitution Papers* (1973). When her third book, *Flying,* was published in 1974, the aftermath of her best seller was revealed. An autobiographical work, *Flying* outlines the distress that followed the success of *Sexual Politics* as well as the ordeals she suffered for her radical feminist views and, particularly, her coming out as a lesbian. Another autobiographical work followed, and *Sita* (describing a

hopeless love affair with another woman) was published in 1977.

Millett remained actively involved in feminist politics and activism throughout the 1970s, and she participated in demonstrations supporting the enactment of the EQUAL RIGHTS AMENDMENT (ERA) to the Constitution. At the end of the decade, she published another work of nonfiction, *The Basement: Meditation on a Human Sacrifice* (1979), a harrowing tale of the abuse, torture, and subsequent murder of a young woman orchestrated by her supposed guardian. That same year, Millett left American soil again, this time to Iran to join and support a campaign for women's rights after the revolution there. She was expelled by the then-new Islamic regime shortly thereafter. Her account of that experience and her take on the political oppression in the country under Ayatollah Khomeini was documented in *Going to Iran,* published in 1981.

While writing, traveling, and teaching, Millett continued her work as a sculptor and showed her pieces in one-woman shows in New York, Los Angeles, and internationally. She also exhibited in the Women's Building in Los Angeles in 1977 and was one of the founders of the Women's Art Colony. Despite Millett's seemingly endless energy, she fell under increased distress and mental strain, and *The Loony Bin Trip* (1990) documents her personal experience of a breakdown, hospitalization, and recovery and her story of being a psychiatric patient.

Millett now stands as a recognized name of FEMINISM's past, and her book, *Sexual Politics,* continues to be read as a seminal work in the women's liberation movements in North America and overseas.

Further Reading
Millet, Kate. *A.D.: A Memoir.* New York: Norton, 1995.
———. *Going to Iran.* New York: Coward, McCann & Geoghegan, 1982.
———. *The Loony Bin Trip.* Champaign: University of Illinois Press, 1990.

———. *The Politics of Cruelty.* New York: Norton, 1994.

———. *The Prostitution Papers.* New York: Avon, 1973.

———. *Sita.* New York: Simon & Schuster, 1992.

—Candis Steenbergen

Mink, Patsy (Patsy Takemoto Mink) (1927–2002) *congressperson*

Patsy Mink, the first Asian-American woman elected to Congress, was born Patsy Takemoto on December 6, 1927, in Paia, Maui, Hawaii, the second of two children. Of Japanese descent, her father, Suematsu Takemoto, was a land surveyor, and her mother, Mitama Tateyama, was a homemaker. Patsy and her brother Eugene grew up in segregated Hawaii, where whites and Asians lived separately. When the Japanese bombed Pearl Harbor on December 7, 1941, life changed for the Minks, although not as dramatically as for many Americans of Japanese descent living on the mainland. Because of the size of the population living on the Hawaiian Islands, Japanese Americans there were not interned during World War II. However, Mink's father was interrogated; school was limited to four days per week (with the fifth dedicated to war duty); and the Japanese-language school Patsy had attended after her classes in public school was closed. Mink aspired to be a doctor and excelled in school. In 1943, she was elected president of the student body at Maui High School, the first female to hold the office. She graduated valedictorian in 1944 and entered the University of Hawaii in Honolulu to prepare for medical school. In 1946, she transferred to Wilson College in Pennsylvania but found no pre-med program and, after a semester, transferred again to the University of Nebraska, Lincoln. She was assigned to the "International House," where all students of color resided. She wrote a letter to the editor protesting the segregation policy. She left Nebraska after only a few months because of a medical condition that required surgery. She completed her degrees in zoology and chemistry at the University of Hawaii in 1948. Although Mink wanted to attend medical school and applied to several institutions, she was not accepted, in part, she believed, because of her race and gender. Instead, Mink enrolled in law school at the University of Chicago in 1948. There she met John Mink, a geology graduate student, and the two were married on January 27, 1951. Patsy completed her law degree in the same year.

Finding a job in law proved difficult. In addition to race and gender, Mink was hampered by her status as a married woman. When she gave birth to their daughter, Gwendolyn Rachel Matsu Mink, in 1952, a fourth impediment to employment in law was added. She found work at the University of Chicago Law library, but with no prospects for work as a lawyer in sight, the family returned to Hawaii in 1952. She passed the Hawaii bar that same year, making her the first Japanese-American woman to do so, and opened her own practice. She first ran for office in 1956 and won a seat in the Hawaii Territorial House. In 1958, she won election to the Hawaii Territorial Senate and was named chairperson of the Education Committee. When Hawaii was admitted to statehood in 1959, the Territorial Houses were dissolved. Mink sought the Hawaiian seat in the U.S. House of Representatives but lost to Daniel Inouye. She continued her work in the Democratic Party and won a seat in the state senate in 1962. Her legislative focus was again on education, but she began to work explicitly on behalf of women's rights as well by supporting an equal pay law.

In 1964, she was elected to the U.S. House of Representatives, making her the first Asian-American woman elected to Congress (and one of only 12 women in the body). Serving from 1964 to 1976, Mink worked on promoting federal aid to education, women's rights, civil rights, and poverty issues. In 1972, Mink briefly ran for president, appearing only on the ballot of the Oregon Democratic primary before she withdrew. Like other women before her, Mink did not think that she would win the nomination, but she wanted to highlight issues important to women and demonstrate that the idea of a woman president was serious. In Congress, she was a strong feminist voice for abortion rights, support for day care, equal pay, civil rights, federal aid to families, and environmental protection. In 1973, she urged the impeachment of Richard M. Nixon and promoted hearings on the Watergate scandal. She was a primary proponent of TITLE IX of the EDUCATIONAL AMENDMENTS of 1974, opening academic and athletic opportunities to women.

In the election of 1976, Mink ran for a U.S. Senate seat but lost. When she left Congress, she worked briefly in the Carter administration as assistant secretary of state for oceans and international environmental affairs (1977–78), but returned to her law practice in Hawaii after one year. In 1983, she was elected to the city council of Honolulu (1983–87), but lost in the next two elections (for governor in 1986 and for mayor of Honolulu in 1988). She returned to Congress as the result of a special election in 1990 to fill the vacated seat of Representative Daniel Akaka. She was again a strong voice for women's rights, objecting to the nomination of Clarence Thomas for the U.S. Supreme Court. By 1996, she was the senior Democratic woman serving in the House. In June 2002, she was honored as a NOW Woman of Vision at the commemoration of the 30th anniversary of Title IX. Most recently, she was publicly skeptical of the government's response to the September 11, 2001, terrorist attacks. She raised concerns about the potential loss of civil liberties and the creation of the new Department of Homeland Security. She served continuously until her death at the age of 74 on September 28, 2002, of viral pneumonia brought on by a case of chicken pox. A few days before her funeral, Congress changed the name of Title IX to the Patsy Mink Act. She was elected once more, posthumously, in November 2002.

Minor, Virginia (Virginia Louisa Minor)
(1824–1894) *suffragist* Virginia Louisa Minor

was an advocate for women's SUFFRAGE in Missouri following the Civil War. Born in Virginia, on March 27, 1824, she married attorney (and distant cousin) Francis Minor in 1843, and they moved to St. Louis in 1845. Their only son died at the age of 14. In March 1867, Minor petitioned the Missouri State Legislature, arguing that citizens taxed by the government were entitled to vote. In May that year, she became the first president of the Woman Suffrage Association of Missouri (WSA). She resigned her post in 1871 when WSA affiliated itself with the AMERICAN WOMAN SUFFRAGE ASSOCIATION rather than the NATIONAL WOMAN SUFFRAGE ASSOCIATION, which argued the Fourteenth Amendment guaranteed all people citizenship and thus the vote. In 1890, Minor was elected president of the reunited St. Louis branch of the NATIONAL AMERICAN WOMAN SUFFRAGE ASSOCIATION. She resigned that post in 1892 and died in St. Louis on August 14, in 1894.

Minor is best known for her lawsuit against the St. Louis registrar for denying her the right to register to vote in 1872. Because married women could not sue in court, she and her husband filed the lawsuit jointly. She argued that the registrar denied her constitutional right based on the Thirteenth and Fourteenth Amendments, because by denying her the vote as a citizen, it placed her in a position of "involuntary servitude." The case was dismissed based on explicit reference to "male citizens" in the Missouri Constitution. Minor's appeal went to the U.S. Supreme Court in March 1875 (*MINOR V. HAPPERSETT*). The Court rejected her claim based on citizenship rights, arguing that individual states may exclude women from voting because voting was not necessarily a right of citizenship.

Further Reading
Corbett, Katharine T. *In Her Place: A Guide to St. Louis Women's History.* St. Louis: Missouri Historical Society Press, 1999.
Wheeler, Marjorie Spruill. *One Woman, One Vote: Rediscovering the Woman Suffrage Movement.* Troutdale, Oreg.: NewSage Press, 1995.

—Lisa G. Guinn

Minor v. Happersett (88 U.S. 162) (1875)

In this case, the U.S. Supreme Court ruled that the state of Missouri had been within its constitutional rights in denying VIRGINIA MINOR, a woman, the right to vote. Feminist VICTORIA WOODHULL had urged women to attempt to vote, arguing that the Fourteenth Amendment forbade the states to limit citizens' rights. This "new departure" was adopted by the NATIONAL WOMAN SUFFRAGE ASSOCIATION (NWSA), and SUSAN B. ANTHONY organized more than 70 suffragists nationwide (Minor among them) to vote in the 1872 elections. Anthony herself voted in Rochester, New York, and was subsequently arrested and jailed. At her trial, she gave an impassioned speech on the injustices of excluding women from political participation. Her case could not be appealed to the Supreme Court due to the fact that (over her objections) her lawyer had paid her fine rather than see her spend time in jail.

Virginia Minor had been denied entrance to the Missouri polls by the registrar, Reese Happersett, on the ground that the state constitution limited voting to males. With her husband (because married women could not bring legal action on their own), she sued the registrar, arguing that her rights of citizenship had been unlawfully denied. When the case reached the Supreme Court, however, the justices declared that voting was not among the privileges guaranteed to all citizens and was therefore not protected by the Fourteenth Amendment. While the Court acknowledged that women were citizens, it ruled that the Fifteenth Amendment only stated conditions that the states could not use to deny the vote, thereby leaving them free to erect other restrictions on the franchise. This decision convinced the NWSA that woman SUFFRAGE could be won only by constitutional amendment.

Further Reading

FindLaw for Legal Professionals. "U.S. Supreme Court: *Minor v. Happersett,* 88 U.S. 162 (1874)." Available online. URL: http://tinyurl.com/2sctmn. Accessed on January 10, 2007.

Linder, Douglas O. "The Trial of Susan B. Anthony, 1873." In *Famous American Trials.* Available online. URL: http://tinyurl.com/4S6nb. Accessed on January 10, 2007.

Mississippi University for Women v. Hogan (458 U.S. 718) (1982)

Joe Hogan wanted to get a degree in nursing and applied to Mississippi University for Women, a state-funded all-women's college. He was denied admission and told that as a male he could attend classes but would not receive any official credits. Hogan argued that this practice violated his equal-protection rights. The university, on the other hand, argued that its all-female policy was designed to compensate for the past discrimination against women and that it was essential to the learning environment for women.

In determining whether equal-protection rights were violated by a policy favoring one sex over the other, the U.S. Supreme Court applied the standard requiring the policy to further an important and legitimate objective of the state. In addition, the Court had to find that the practice actually met the objective. In this case, the Court ruled that the objective was illegitimate because it was solely based on sex as a criterion. The justices further ruled that the admission policy did not serve to compensate women for past discrimination because the nursing profession has always been regarded as a female profession. Finally, since Mississippi University allowed Hogan to attend college without earning credit, the claim that it wanted to create a single-sex learning environment for women was also void.

Further Reading

The OYEZ Project. "*Miss. Univ. for Women v. Hogan,* 458 U.S. 718 (1982)." Available online. URL: http://www.oyez.org/cases/case?case=1980–1989/1981/1981_81_406. Accessed on January 10, 2007.

Mitchell, Maria (1818–1889) *astronomer*

Maria Mitchell was born on August 1, 1818, in the whaling port of Nantucket, Massachusetts. Her

Quaker parents encouraged her educational pursuits. Mitchell's neighbors' reliance on celestial navigation for their livelihoods influenced her early interest in astronomy, as did the avid example of her father, a teacher. She served as the librarian of the Nantucket Atheneum for 20 years while also assisting her father in his stellar observations. In 1847, while helping with his work for the U.S. Coast Survey, she discovered a new comet, thereafter referred to as "Miss Mitchell's Comet." Worldwide celebrity ensued, including election to prestigious scientific societies. In 1865, Mitchell accepted an invitation to take charge of the observatory at the newly founded Vassar College. There she continued her research, often inviting students to work with her. She became known not only as a pioneering astronomer but also as one of Vassar's greatest teachers and mentors. Mitchell retired from Vassar in 1888 and died in Lynn, Massachusetts, on June 28, 1889.

Mitchell is remembered primarily for her scientific achievements, which were particularly remarkable for a woman of her day. She was the first woman elected to the American Academy of Arts and Sciences and to the American Philosophical Society. Both within and outside of scientific circles, however, she used her public influence to urge that women's accomplishments be recognized and rewarded fairly. Feminist concerns of this kind characterized the Association for the Advancement of Women (1873), of which she was a founder and early president.

Further Reading

Kendall, Phebe Mitchell, ed. *Maria Mitchell: Life, Letters, and Journals*. Boston: Lee and Shepard, 1986.

Rossiter, Margaret. *Women Scientists in America: Struggles and Strategies to 1940*. Baltimore: Johns Hopkins University Press, 1982.

Wright, Helen. *Sweeper in the Sky: The Life of Maria Mitchell, First Woman Astronomer in America*. New York: Macmillan Co., 1949.

—Laura R. Prieto

Mitchell, Martha (Martha Elizabeth Beall Mitchell) (1918–1976) *Watergate whistle-blower*

Born Martha Elizabeth Beall on September 2, 1918, in Pine Bluff, Arkansas, Martha Mitchell is best known for her late-night phone calls to Washington journalists to report President Richard Nixon's "dirty tricks" during the early days of the Watergate scandal. When the *Washington Post* reported that her husband, Attorney General John N. Mitchell, had authorized $250,000 to pay for bail and to hush up the Watergate burglars, Martha claimed that the White House was using John as a scapegoat to protect Richard Nixon. John Mitchell reportedly went so far as to lock Martha in a closet to keep her from phoning the press. White House tapes reveal a campaign to discredit Martha with leaked information about her alleged drinking problem. The Mitchells ultimately divorced, and when John Mitchell was sentenced for his Watergate crimes in February 1975, he said, "It could have been worse. They could have sentenced me to spend the rest of my life with Martha Mitchell." Martha Mitchell died of myeloma on May 31, 1976, at the age of 57.

Further Reading

Bernstein, Carl and Bob Woodward. *All the President's Men*. New York: Warner Books, 1974.

Thomas, Helen. *Front Row at the White House: My Life and Times*. New York: Scribner, 2000.

Mofford, Rose (Rose Perica Mofford) (1922–) *governor of Arizona*

Rose Mofford served as the first woman governor of Arizona following the impeachment of Governor Evan Mecham. Born Rose Perica in Globe, Arizona, on June 10, 1922, her first job in government was at the age of 17, as secretary to the state treasurer. She was married to "Lefty" Mofford in 1957. In 1977, she was appointed Arizona secretary of state by Governor Wesley Bolin, and she was reelected to that position in 1978, 1982, and 1986. Following Evan Mecham's impeachment in 1987, she took over as acting governor on February 2, 1988, and was sworn in as governor on April 4 after Mecham was convicted and removed from office. Mofford proved a calming influence in Arizona state politics, providing stability and removing controversial appointments. Though favored to win, she did not run for election in 1990. Mofford served most recently as an Arizona elector for Democratic candidate John Kerry in the 2004 U.S. presidential race.

Further Reading

Myers, John L., ed. *The Arizona Governors: 1912–1990.* Phoenix: Heritage Publishers, 1989.

Monroe, Elizabeth (Elizabeth Kortright Monroe) (1786–1830) *first lady* Born on November 27, 1728, in New York City, Elizabeth Kortright was the second of five children born to Laurence and Hannah Kortright. Her father was a wealthy Tory merchant who remained in the United States after the American Revolution. Elizabeth grew up in New York City and made her debut into the city's exclusive mercantile society. In 1785, she met James Monroe, then a Virginia delegate to the Confederation Congress. They were married on February 16, 1786, and lived with her father in New York until the congressional session ended. The Monroes then returned to Fredricksburg, Virginia where James somewhat reluctantly took up the practice of law to support the family; Eliza Monroe was born in 1786. In 1789, James Monroe bought Albemarle farm near Jefferson's Monticello. The Monroes spent summers there and winters near the Court of Appeals in Richmond or the U.S. Senate in Philadelphia following his election as a senator in 1790. In 1794, Monroe was appointed U.S. minister to France, where they quickly adopted French customs and language, enrolling Eliza in a French school. During this two-year term, Elizabeth performed one notable public deed with her visit to Madame de Lafayette, scheduled for execution following the French Revolution. The publicity surrounding her visit resulted in Madame Lafayette's release.

In 1797, the Monroes returned to Charlottsville, Virginia, where James worked closely with Thomas Jefferson and James Madison in building the Republican Party. In 1799, he was elected governor of Virginia. In May that same year, Elizabeth gave birth to a son who died of whooping cough 16 months later. A third child, Maria Hester, was born in 1803. After three terms as governor, James Monroe accepted President Jefferson's appointment as envoy to France to negotiate the Louisiana Purchase. He engaged in a number of diplomatic assignments in Paris and London from 1803 to 1807 before returning the family to their estate in Virginia. Their daughter Eliza married George Hay, a prominent Virginia politician, in 1808. In 1810, James Monroe was elected to the Virginia Assembly, but he left before his term expired to accept an appointment as secretary of state under James Madison. Elizabeth's arrival in Washington did not go smoothly as, among other things, she retained the French custom of returning but not initiating calls and visits.

In 1816, James Monroe was elected as the fifth president of the United States. Although the Monroes had been residents of Washington for several years, biographers describe them as strangers to social Washington. In sharp contrast to DOLLEY MADISON's gregarious social personality and active calling calendar, Elizabeth Monroe did not accept private invitations and entertained infrequently. Elizabeth called upon her daughter Eliza to help her with social commitments, only to find that Eliza's French socialization and manners also alienated Washington society. Never certain of her formal status when she acted in her mother's place, she often appeared dictatorial. The rift eventually led James Monroe to call a special cabinet meeting in 1817 to consider the protocol of receiving diplomats in Washington.

Ultimately, Elizabeth Monroe's choices in shaping her public role may have had as much to do with health problems as with precedent setting. Paying calls was exhausting, and Elizabeth suffered from a number of maladies, including rheumatism and headaches, occasional seizures, and several serious fevers. While foreign visitors approved of her reserved formality, it stood in stark contrast to her immediate predecessor, Dolley Madison, and did not sit well with most Americans.

Elizabeth Monroe's health deteriorated considerably during her husband's second term. When John Quincy Adams became president in 1825, the Monroes were unable to vacate the White House for several weeks until Elizabeth was well enough to travel. In June 1825, the first couple retired to Oak Hill, a plantation in Loudon County, Virginia. On September 23, 1830, Elizabeth Monroe died. James Monroe lived with his daughter, Maria Hester Gouverneur, in New York until his death on July 4, 1831. Almost no historical record regarding Elizabeth and James Monroe remains due to a family tradition of burning all personal correspondence.

Further Reading

Fix, Julie K. "Elizabeth Kortright Monroe." In *American First Ladies: Their Lives and Their Legacy,* 2nd ed., edited by Lewis L. Gould. New York: Routledge, 1996.

Schneider, Dorothy, and Carl J. Schneider. "Elizabeth Kartright Monroe." *First Ladies: A Biographical Dictionary.* New York: Checkmark Books, 2001, 35–41.

Moore, Gwen (Gwendolynne Sophia Moore)

(1951–   ) *congressperson* Gwen Moore was born on April 18, 1951, in Racine, Wisconsin, to a father who was a factory worker and a mother who was a public schoolteacher. Moore attended Marquette University as an expectant mother, receiving welfare benefits to support herself and her daughter. She graduated with a B.A. degree in political science and in 2000 received a certificate for senior executives in state and local government from Harvard University. Prior to elective office, Moore worked as a housing officer with the Wisconsin Housing and Economic Development Authority and as a planning analyst with the Wisconsin Department of Employment. She also served as a development specialist for the City of Milwaukee, Wisconsin, as a representative to the Wisconsin State Assembly (1989–91), and in the Wisconsin State Senate (1996–2004).

Moore was elected to the U.S. House of Representatives in 2004, earning 70 percent of the vote and defeating Republican Gerald Boyle in the general election. The first African American and the second woman to represent Wisconsin in Congress, she has introduced legislation to provide economic incentives and tax cuts to small businesses to promote job creation. She has also supported an amendment to the Truth in Lending Act to prevent so-called predatory lending. Moore supports amending the U.S. Constitution to provide for uniform national election standards and to end gender discrimination under the law. In the 109th Congress, she served on the Committee on Financial Services and the House Committee on Small Business. She is a member of the Congressional Black Caucus and the Working Group on Welfare Reform. She was reelected to the House in 2006.

Further Reading

Barone, Michael. *The Almanac of American Politics.* Washington, D.C.: National Journal Group, 2006.

"Moore, Gwendolynne S." In *Biographical Directory of the United States Congress, 1774–present.* Available online. URL: http://bioguide.congress.gov/scripts/biodisplay.pl?index=M001160. Accessed on January 8, 2007.

"Representative Gwendolynne S. Gwen" Moore (WI). In *Project Vote Smart.* Available online. URL: http://votesmart.org/bio.php?can_id=BS021367. Accessed on January 8, 2007.

—Angela Kouters

motherhood bind

The term *motherhood bind* has gained prominence in the contemporary political lexicon as more women with children seek progressively higher levels of public office. Women face a series of questions about their fitness for public service and about their ability to hold public office, regardless of whether they are mothers or not. Journalist and communication scholar Deborah Tannen described the motherhood bind in a 1992 *New York Times* opinion column: "If you're not a Mother, you're a Failed Woman. If you are a Mother, you can't have enough attention to pay to serious work. If you are paying attention to serious work, you must be a Bad Mother." Childless women candidates (or professional women in general) often face questions about their "life choices"—that is, they must explain why they do not have children. Female elected officials with children are peppered with questions about how they will handle the duties of their office and maintain their responsibilities to their children and home. For example, PATRICIA SCHROEDER, former Democratic congresswoman from Colorado, had a two-year-old daughter when she was first elected in 1972. She spent the first few days in office fielding queries from constituents, colleagues, and reporters about how she was going to "do it."

Almost 30 years later, Jane Swift became governor of Massachusetts when Paul Cellucci resigned from office to serve as ambassador to Canada in 2001. Upon taking office, she became the nation's youngest governor at age 36, and she was pregnant with twins. Even feminists challenged her ability to govern as a pregnant woman and mother of another young daughter. Wendy Kaminer, in an article for *The American Prospect,* wrote: "Today it's difficult to suggest that bearing children may even temporarily disqualify a woman from high office, or any extremely demanding and stressful full-time job. It's hard to ask the question 'Is Jane Swift fit to serve?' without calling up more than 100 years of crippling stereotypes about the emotional, moral, and physical attributes of normal women. Still, it's a question that ought to be asked. . . . Why would you want to become governor and give birth to twins more or less simultaneously, anyway? I realize that Swift

didn't plan this odd confluence of events, but she could easily have anticipated it. . . . If she intended to assume the office of governor when Cellucci moved on, Swift could have postponed her pregnancy."

Is it reasonable to expect women to postpone or forgo having children in order to pursue public office? If the PIPELINE THESIS is correct, the proportion of women holding public office will never reach parity if young women do not enter politics early and seek progressively higher levels of responsibility and office.

Further Reading
Kaminer Wendy. "Mama's Delicate Condition." *American Prospect* 12, no. 7 (April 23, 2001): Available online. URL: www.prospect.org/V12/7/kaminer-w.html.
Tannen, Deborah. "The Real Hillary Factor." *New York Times,* 12 October 1992, op-ed sec., A19.

Mott, Lucretia Coffin (1793–1880) *suffragist, abolitionist* Lucretia Mott was an advocate of equality between women and men, whites and blacks. She was simultaneously an abolitionist and a suffragist who did not want to favor one activity over the other, seeing both as essential work for creating a truly free society. She was born Lucretia Coffin on January 3, 1793, into a Quaker family and grew up among abolitionists on Nantucket, Massachusetts. In the Quaker tradition, she was educated alongside her brothers and was sent to a Quaker girls' boarding school in New York when she was 13. There she met James Mott, her future husband, whom she married in 1811; they had six children, five of whom survived to adulthood.

Active in the Quaker community, Lucretia Mott moved to Philadelphia and became a minister in 1821. In 1833, she founded the PHILADELPHIA FEMALE ANTI-SLAVERY SOCIETY as women were not admitted to traditional abolitionist groups. She traveled throughout Pennsylvania speaking out against slavery, and she and her husband James Mott provided shelter in their home for runaway slaves. She was chosen as a delegate to the World Conference against Slavery in 1840, but upon her arrival in London, she was refused a seat there because she was a woman. The debate over the inclusion of women in the conference infuriated the female delegates. Refused the opportunity to argue on their own behalf, men like Wendell Phillips had to point out the irony of refusing women (who had been duly chosen as representatives) in a conference devoted to the abolition of slavery. Many men who were against the women's participation used the argument that their inclusion would offend their hosts; yet this appeal for respect of customary beliefs was often the very argument used by Southern slave owners to support slavery.

It was at the World Conference against Slavery that Mott first met ELIZABETH CADY STANTON, who came to the convention with her husband on her honeymoon. After they were rejected as delegates, Mott and Stanton vowed to work together for the rights of women. Mott, like Stanton, was deeply influenced by Mary Wollstonecraft's VINDICATION OF THE RIGHTS OF WOMEN, which argued that women had been continually degraded throughout history and taught to think of themselves as the weaker sex. Wollstonecraft's work argued that the power of reason is available to men and women alike, and thus women, like men, must be educated in a way that best enhances that reason.

Mott and Stanton met again in upstate New York in 1848 when they worked together to organize the SENECA FALLS CONVENTION for women's rights. Mott and Stanton together wrote the DECLARATION OF SENTIMENTS AND RESOLUTIONS, and Mott opened and closed the 1848 convention. Two years later, she organized another conference, in Rochester, New York, and also in 1850 met LUCY STONE for the first time at the first NATIONAL WOMAN'S RIGHTS CONVENTION in Worcester, Massachusetts. That same year, Mott published her *Discourse on Women,* in which she drew on Wollstonecraft to argue for the equality of woman: "Of what rights is she deprived? What

privileges are withheld from her? I answer, she asks nothing as a favor, but as a right, she wants to be acknowledged as a moral responsible being. She is seeking not to be governed by laws, in the making of which she has no voice. She is deprived of almost every right in civil society, and is a cypher in the nation, except in the right of presenting a petition."

In 1852, Mott was elected president of the Woman's Rights Convention, and she attended every meeting until they were disbanded during the Civil War. It was as president of this organization that Mott presided over the "Mob Convention" of 1853 at the World's Fair in New York City. The crowd had been agitated with multiple days of newspaper accounts ridiculing both the idea of women's rights and the public display of women as speakers on their own behalf. Speakers (including SOJOURNER TRUTH) were greeted with howls of rage, catcalls, and thrown items. Mott refused to call in the police (who were contacted at one point and never came) in order to stay true to her pacifist principles. As would be seen 100 years later in the civil rights movement, the contrast between the Quaker simplicity of Mott and the brutishness of the mobs who opposed her won many supporters to her cause.

As a Quaker, Mott advocated pacifism and did not support the Civil War, although she remained staunchly against slavery and did hope that it would end as a result of the war. She distinguished between pacifism and "passivism," remarking that John Brown could be admired as a moral hero (for his passionate abolitionist stance that ended in the failed attack on Harper's Ferry to instigate a slave uprising). "Quakerism, as I understand it, does not mean quietism," Mott remarked in a speech given at the Philadelphia Anti-Slavery Society. In 1866, she joined Elizabeth Cady Stanton again to found the AMERICAN EQUAL RIGHTS ASSOCIATION (AERA); she was elected its first president. The association sent a letter to Congress in 1868 requesting that the word *male* not be used in the Fourteenth Amendment to define voters.

AERA, whose membership was diverse by race and by sex, recognized that limiting the extension of SUFFRAGE only to black men would ultimately hurt the attainment of equal rights not simply by women but by any other group. In 1870, Mott tried to mend the rift between the NATIONAL WOMAN SUFFRAGE ASSOCIATION and the AMERICAN WOMAN SUFFRAGE ASSOCIATION over the question of suffrage for black men. While she understood the tensions between asking for votes for black men without demanding an extension of suffrage to women, Mott also saw the value of reformers working together to bring about change. She advocated universal suffrage, and when the EQUAL RIGHTS AMENDMENT was first introduced in 1923, it was referred to as the Lucretia Mott amendment (later to become the ALICE PAUL Amendment).

The Motts were instrumental in the founding of Swarthmore College, which was coeducational and open to students of all races from its inception. In 1867, became involved with the Free Religious Association, a group of Quaker activists who emphasized an individual's own struggle to come to terms with the divine. In 1870, she became president of the Pennsylvania Peace Society, urging President Ulysses S. Grant to work for the abolition of slavery in Cuba. Her last public address was in 1878 in Rochester, New York, at the 30th anniversary of the Seneca Falls Convention. Lucretia Mott died on November 11, 1880.

Further Reading

Cromwell, Otelia. *Lucretia Mott.* Cambridge, Mass.: Harvard University Press, 1958.

Hare, Lloyd C. M. *The Greatest American Woman, Lucretia Mott.* New York: Negro Universities Press, 1937.

Palmer, Beverly Wilson, ed. *Selected Letters of Lucretia Mott.* Urbana: University of Illinois Press, 2002.

—Claire Curtis

Ms. magazine

Founded by feminist GLORIA STEINEM, the magazine called *Ms.* made its first debut as 30-page insert in the December 1971 issue of *New York Magazine.* Its straightforward name reflected the feminist movement's rejection of the courtesy titles "Miss" and "Mrs." that linked a woman's identity to her marital status.

Supporters praised the first monthly issue of *Ms.* published in July 1972 for its empowering articles and liberating style. Its detractors, meanwhile, viewed the publication as evil incarnate. Instead of recipes and fashion advice, *Ms.* focused on topics that mainstream publications usually avoided. From ABORTION to the EQUAL RIGHTS AMENDMENT and DOMESTIC VIOLENCE, Steinem and *Ms.* took a front-line position. By the end of its first year, the magazine had established the Ms. Foundation for Education and Communication, a nonprofit organization to raise funds benefiting women's causes in the areas of employment, reproductive health, violence against women, and issues affecting young women.

Katherine Graham, owner of the *Washington Post,* was the first person to make a major investment in the fledgling publication: $20,000. As the 1970s came to a close, however, advertising dollars became increasingly harder to come by—due largely to the constant scrutiny and attack the magazine was under because of its "radical views." From 1978 to 1987, *Ms.* was published as a nonprofit magazine through the Ms. Foundation. On December 31, 2001, the Feminist Majority Foundation assumed ownership of *Ms.,* which continues to reflect the vision of its founder.

Further Reading

Farrell, Amy Erdman. *Yours in Sisterhood: Ms. Magazine and the Promise of Popular Feminism (Gender and American Culture).* Chapel Hill: University of North Carolina Press, 1998.

Thom, Mary. *Inside Ms.: 25 Years of the Magazine and the Feminist Movement.* New York: Owl Publishing, 1998.

—Thea Lapham

Muller v. Oregon (208 U.S. 412) (1908)

Social reform was central to the Progressive Era (1890s–1920s). Beginning in the states, reformers worked to adopt a variety of statutes, including factory safety laws, workmen's compensation, minimum wages, and maximum hours. Conservatives were able to block a number of these on the basis that private property was sacrosanct and that legislatures should not be able to tell people how to use their property. The courts also sustained the "liberty to contract," claiming that employers and employees should be able to negotiate the terms of employment without state interference. The courts did acknowledge that the state had an inherent police power, by which it could interfere with property and labor contracts in order to protect the health and safety of citizens.

In *Lochner v. New York* (1905) a bare majority of the Supreme Court ruled that a 10-hour day workday law was unconstitutional because there was no demonstrated relation between the law and the workers' health or safety. The Court conceded, however, that such measures might be permissible if it could be shown that the law did in fact serve to protect health or safety.

When the state of Oregon established a 10-hour workday for women only in laundries and factories, business owners attacked it on the grounds that, like the New York law at issue in *Lochner,* it bore no relation to the women's health or safety. Future Supreme Court justice Louis Brandeis defended the state's law in *Muller v. Oregon*. In what has come to be known as the "Brandeis Brief," he covered the traditional legal precedents in just two pages and then filled over 100 pages with sociological, economic, and physiological data on the effect of long working hours on the health of women. Justice David J. Brewer's opinion for the majority, upholding the Oregon law, argued that women were in fact different from men and that these differences made the connection between the law and worker health and safety clear. Relying on GENDER STEREOTYPES, Brewer said:

That woman's physical structure and the performance of maternal functions place her at a disadvantage in the struggle for subsistence is obvious. This is especially true when the burdens of motherhood are upon her. Even when they are not, by abundant testimony of the medical fraternity continuance for a long time on her feet at work, repeating this from day to day, tends to injurious effects upon the body, and, as healthy mothers are essential to vigorous offspring, the physical well-being of woman becomes an object of public interest and care in order to preserve the strength and vigor of the race.

Still again, history discloses the fact that woman has always been dependent upon man. He established his control at the outset by superior physical strength, and this control in various forms, with diminishing intensity, has continued to the present. As minors, though not to the same extent, she has been looked upon in the courts as needing especial care that her rights may be preserved. Education was long denied her, and while now the doors of the schoolroom are opened and her opportunities for acquiring knowledge are great, yet even with that and the consequent increase of capacity for business affairs it is still true that in the struggle for subsistence she is not an equal competitor with her brother. Though limitations upon personal and contractual rights may be removed by legislation, there is that in her disposition and habits of life which will operate against a full assertion of those rights. She will still be where some legislation to protect her seems necessary to secure a real equality of right. Doubtless there are individual exceptions, and there are many respects in which she has an advantage over him; but looking at it from the viewpoint of the effort to maintain an independent position in life, she is not upon an equality. Differentiated by these matters from the other sex, she is properly placed in a class by herself, and legislation designed for her protection may be sustained, even when like legislation is not necessary for men, and could not be sustained.

It was not until the 1970s, in a series of cases, that the U.S. Supreme Court declared policy based on gender stereotypes unconstitutional.

Further Reading

Cott, Nancy F. *No Small Courage: A History of Women in the United States.* New York: Oxford Press, 2000.

Kerber, Linda K., and Jane Sherron De Hart. *Women's America: Refocusing the Past.* New York: Oxford University Press, 2004.

Murkowski, Lisa (1957–   ) *U.S. senator* The first Alaskan-born senator to serve the state and the 33rd female to serve in the U.S. Senate, Lisa Murkowski was born in Ketchikan, Alaska, on May 22, 1957. She attended public school in Fairbanks, graduated from Georgetown University with a degree in economics in 1980, and earned her law degree from the Willamette College of Law in 1985. Murkowski worked as a district attorney in Anchorage for two years and then in private practice with a commercial law firm for eight years prior to her work as a sole practitioner. She has resided in Anchorage for more than 25 years.

Lisa Murkowski was elected to three terms in the Alaska State House of Representatives, beginning in 1998. She won subsequent reelections in 2000 and 2002, and her State House colleagues selected her as house majority leader for the 2003–04 term. During her time in the State House, Murkowski served on the Alaska Commission on Post Secondary Education and chaired the labor and commerce committees as well as the military and veterans affairs committee. She was also a member of the National Council of State Legislatures, the Council of State Governments Executive Committee, and the National Order of Women Legislators.

Murkowski, a Republican, was appointed to the U.S. Senate on December 20, 2002, to fill the vacancy caused by the resignation of her father, Frank H. Murkowski. She was subsequently elected to the U.S. Senate in 2004 for the term ending January 3, 2011. A member of the Senate Energy and Natural Resources Committee, Senator Murkowski chairs its subcommittee on water and power and serves on its subcommit-

tees on energy, and public lands and forests. Murkowski also is a member of the Senate Environment and Public Works Committee, serving on the subcommittees of transportation and infrastructure, and a member of the Fisheries, Wildlife, and Water Committee. In addition, she serves on the Veterans Affairs Committee and the Indian Affairs Committee. Senator Murkowski assumed leadership roles quickly in the 108th session, being selected to serve as a deputy whip, assisting the majority whip on voting strategy and other leadership functions. She was also selected as chair of the class of new senators elected in 2002.

Further Reading

Barone, Michael. *The Almanac of American Politics.* Washington, D.C.: National Journal Group, 2006.

"Murkowski, Lisa." In *Biographical Directory of the United States Congress, 1774–present.* Available online. URL: http://bioguide.congress.gov/scripts/biodisplay.pl?index=M001153. Accessed on January 8, 2007.

"Senator Lisa A. Murkowski (AK)." In *Project Vote Smart.* Available online. URL: http://votesmart.org/bio.php?can_id=CAK67328. Accessed on January 8, 2007.

—Angela Kouters

Murray, Judith Sargent (Judith Sargent Stevens Murray) (1751–1820) *feminist writer* Judith Sargent was born on May 5, 1751, in Gloucester, Massachusetts into a family increasingly influenced by Universalism, a new strand of Protestantism emerging from England. Universalism (which has today merged with Unitarians to create the Unitarian Universalists) declares the universal salvation of souls, in direct contrast with the predestinarianism of the Puritans. This universalism extended itself, for Sargent, to the equality of the sexes. She was taught to read and write but was not formally educated beyond this. However, her family had a large library and she read extensively before her first marriage to John Stevens, a sea captain, in 1769. That marriage lasted 18 years until Stevens's death. She then married John Murray (1788), a Universalist minister whom she had first met in 1774. They had a daughter, Julia Maria, born in 1791.

An extensive letter-writer, Judith Sargent Murray began to publish essays and poems after her husband went into debt following the Revolutionary War. Her first published essay, "Desultory Thoughts upon the Utility of Encouraging a Degree of Complacency in the Female Bosom," published under the pseudonym Constantia in 1784, argued that girls should be addressed "from the early dawn of reason . . . as a rational being." She stressed the education of girls both for their own sakes and also as beings who would grow up to raise and educate their own children. This began Murray's lifelong public advocacy of education for girls and her argument that if women are treated as incapable, then they will become incapable; but if they are acknowledged as equally capable (and educated to that capability), then they will act accordingly.

Judith Sargent Murray published many essays and poems in the *Massachusetts Magazine,* including "On the Equality of the Sexes": "Is the needle and kitchen sufficient to employ the operations of a soul thus organized [as creative and lively]? I should conceive not!" She also published two recurring series, *The Gleaner,* later published as a book, and *The Repository,* in addition to a biography of her husband published a year after his death in 1815. She wrote numerous plays that were produced in Boston and was an influential woman in the 18th and early 19th centuries at a time when few voices of women were heard. Judith Sargent Murray died on June 9, 1820, in Natchez, Mississippi.

Further Reading
Kornfeld, Eve. *Creating an American Culture, 1775–1800.* Boston: Bedford/St. Martins, 2001.
Schloesser, Pauline. *Fair Sex: White Women and Racial Patriarchy in the Early American Republic.* New York: New York University Press, 1992.

Skemp, Sheila L. *Judith Sargent Murray: A Brief History with Documents,* vol. I. Boston: Bedford/St. Martins, 1998.

—Claire Curtis

Murray, Patty (Patricia Lynn Johns Murray)

(1950–) *U.S. senator*   Patty Murray was born on October 11, 1950, in Bothell, Washington, one of seven children. A graduate of Washington State University (1972), she was a preschool teacher for several years, taught at Shoreline Community College, and married Rob Murray, with whom she has two children. In 1986, while Murray was working as a citizen-lobbyist for education and environmental issues, a state politician told her she could not make a difference because she was only a "mom in tennis shoes." Nonetheless, Murray led a grassroots coalition of 13,000 parents to save a local preschool program from budget cuts and went on to serve on the local school board. In 1988, she was elected to the Washington State Senate (1988–92); in 1990, she was elected to serve as Democratic whip.

In 1992, Murray ran for the U.S. Senate becoming the first woman to represent Washington State. In 1998 and 2004, she was reelected by a wide margin, and she is currently Washington's senior senator. Murray serves as the highest-ranking Democrat and former chair of the Senate Transportation Appropriations Subcommittee. She convened Senate hearings on port security and cargo security and authored a pilot project to improve security at the nation's three largest ports. Murray helped write and pass the historic VIOLENCE AGAINST WOMEN ACT of 1994 and was a key proponent of its reauthorization in 2002. She is also first woman to serve on the Senate Veterans Affairs Committee. She has been honored for her work by the Vietnam Veterans of America, American Ex-POWs, the Veterans of Foreign Wars, the Paralyzed Veterans of America, and the Washington State Department of Veterans Affairs. She has been linked to indicted former lobbyist Jack Abramoff through campaign contributions from out-of-state Indian tribes. She has not returned the money and maintains that she has done nothing illegal. In December 2006, she was elected secretary of the Senate Democratic Conference.

Further Reading

Barone, Michael. *The Almanac of American Politics.* Washington, D.C.: National Journal Group, 2006.
"Murray, Patty." In *Biographical Directory of the United States Congress, 1774–present.* Available online. URL: http://bioguide.congress.gov/scripts/bio display.pl?index=M001111. Accessed on January 8, 2007.
"Senator Patty Murray (WA)." In *Project Vote Smart.* Available online. URL: http://votesmart.org/bio. php?can_id=S0943103. Accessed on January 8, 2007.

—Angela Kouters

Musgrave, Marilyn (1949–   ) *congressperson* Marilyn Musgrave was born on January 27, 1949, in Greeley, Colorado. She earned a bachelors degree in social studies from Colorado State University in 1972. Prior to elective office, she worked as a teacher and in business. Her career in elective office began in 1991 when she served one term on the school board of Fort Morgan. She has served in the Colorado House of Representatives (1993–97) and in the Colorado Senate (1997–2002). As a state legislator, she devoted her attention to small business and agricultural issues, particularly authoring bills to exempt farm-equipment dealers from sales tax. She is known for her support of the right to keep and bear arms and as a social conservative. As a state legislator, Musgrave voted to deny marriage rights and parental rights for gays and lesbians and sponsored a bill to prevent same-sex partners from seeing their partners' children in the hospital during an emergency. Musgrave also cast the only vote against legislation to give battered spouses paid leave from work.

In 2002, when incumbent congressman Bob Schaffer retired, Musgrave won the Republican

nomination to succeed him and went on to win the general election. In 2003, Musgrave was the lead sponsor of the Federal Marriage Amendment banning same-sex marriage. In the 109th Congress, she served on the House Committee on Agriculture, the Committee on Education and the Workforce, and the Committee on Small Business. A close ally to former Speaker Tom Delay, she has been accused of a number of ethical violations. In 2005 and again in 2006, the group Citizens for Responsibility and Ethics in Washington put Musgrave on their list of most corrupt members of Congress. Musgrave won reelection in 2006.

Further Reading

Barone, Michael. *The Almanac of American Politics.* Washington, D.C.: National Journal Group, 2006.
"Musgrave, Marilyn N." In *Biographical Directory of the United States Congress, 1774–present.* Available online. URL: http://bioguide.congress.gov/scripts/biodisplay.pl?index=M001152. Accessed on January 8, 2007.
"Representative Marilyn N. Musgrave (C0)." In *Project Vote Smart.* Available online. URL: http://votesmart. org/bio.php?can_id=BS020598. Accessed on January 8, 2007.

—Angela Kouters

Myers, Dee Dee (Margaret Jane Myers) (1961–   ) *White House press secretary* Dee Dee Myers is the first woman and the youngest person ever to serve as White House press secretary. Born Margaret Jane Myers in Philadelphia on September 1, 1961, she graduated from Santa Clara University in 1983. Before joining Bill Clinton's campaign for president in 1991, Myers worked on a variety of local, state, and national campaigns. She served as press secretary for Dianne Feinstein in her 1990 bid for governor of California and worked on the presidential campaigns of Governor Michael S. Dukakis and Vice President Walter F. Mondale. She also worked on the staffs of Los Angeles mayor Tom Bradley and California state senator Art Torres. Myers served as White House press secretary for most of the first two years of Bill Clinton's administration (January 20, 1993, to December 22, 1994). She was the first woman to serve as press secretary, in addition to being the second youngest ever. Her first months on the job were overshadowed by Clinton advisor George Stephanopoulos, who conducted the daily press briefings, but Myers finally took over after Stephanopoulos, criticized for poor public relations skills, was moved to a new position. Myers is generally considered to have been a successful press secretary. Since leaving the White House, Myers has worked as a political analyst, commentator, and writer. She is a contributing editor to *Vanity Fair* magazine and had been a consultant to the NBC television drama *The West Wing*. Myers is married to Todd S. Purdum, a correspondent for the *New York Times*; they live in Los Angeles with their two children.

Myrick, Sue (Susan Wilkins Myrick)

(1941–) *congressperson* Sue Myrick was born in Tiffin, Ohio, on August 1, 1941. She attended public school and graduated from Port Clinton High School in Port Clinton, Ohio. She then attended Heidelberg College from 1959 to 1960. Myrick is the former president and chief executive officer of Myrick Advertising and Public Relations and Myrick Enterprises. Before entering Congress, she served on the Charlotte, North Carolina, City Council and was a two-term mayor of the city of Charlotte, the first female mayor in Charlotte's history.

Myrick, a Republican, was first elected to Congress in 1994. She is currently in her seventh term representing North Carolina's ninth district, which covers portions of Union, Mecklenburg, and Gaston counties. One of only 69 women currently serving in the U.S. House of Representatives, Myrick has steadily risen in seniority and leadership. In January 2003, she was appointed deputy majority whip of the 108th Congress by Majority Whip Roy Blunt. Myrick serves on the Energy and Commerce Committee, which is the oldest legislative committee in the U.S. House of Representatives. She is also member of the subcommittees on health; environment and hazardous materials; and commerce, trade and consumer protection. She also serves on the Speaker of the House's Task Force for a Drug-Free America.

Myrick is a breast cancer survivor and cochairs the House Cancer Caucus. She sponsored a law to provide Medicaid coverage for low-income women for mammograms and pap smears. She also cosponsored a bill with NITA LOWEY to require the National Institutes of Health to investigate the connection between the environment and cancer.

Further Reading

Barone, Michael. *The Almanac of American Politics.* Washington, D.C.: National Journal Group, 2006.

"Myrick, Sue." In *Biographical Directory of the United States Congress, 1774–present.* Available online. URL: http://bioguide.congress.gov/scripts/biodisplay.pl?index=M001134. Accessed on January 8, 2007.

"Representative Sue W. Myrick (NC)." In *Project Vote Smart.* Available online. URL: http://votesmart.org/bio.php?can_id=CNIP0698. Accessed on January 8, 2007.

—Angela Kouters

N

Nannygate   Zoe Baird, a highly accomplished attorney, was nominated by President Bill Clinton in 1993 to serve as the nation's first female attorney general. During her Senate confirmation hearings, evidence was introduced that she had employed illegal immigrants to care for her children and failed to report and pay taxes for these workers. Baird was forced to withdraw her candidacy. Her successor, Kimba Wood, also a distinguished attorney, faced heightened scrutiny and was also forced to withdraw her candidacy after disclosure that she too had employed undocumented child-care workers. The incident became known as "Nannygate" and galvanized women's groups to lobby for more attention to the issue of CHILD CARE. Women also pointed out that no male appointee had been subject to the same line of questioning about domestic help. Clinton's third choice was single and childless JANET RENO, who served for two terms as the nation's first female attorney general.

Napolitano, Grace (Grace Flores Napolitano) (1936–) *congressperson*   Grace Napolitano was born on December 4, 1936, and raised in Brownsville, Texas. After high school, she married and moved with her husband, Frank Napolitano, to California, where they raised five children, and where she worked as a secretary at the Ford Motor Company for 22 years. Napolitano began her political career as a member of the Norwalk City Council, winning her first election in 1986 by only 28 votes. Four years later she won reelection by the largest vote margin recorded in city history. In 1989, Napolitano was selected by the council to serve as mayor. She subsequently served in the California Assembly (1993–98), where she focused on international trade, environmental protection, transportation, and immigration. She was instrumental in the creation of a new committee on international trade and served as chair of the Women's Caucus and vice chair of the Latino caucus.

Due to term limits, Napolitano left the California Assembly in 1998, at which time she ran for and won a seat in the U.S. House of Representatives. In the 109th Congress, she served on the House Committee on International Relations and the Committee on Resources. In 2005, Napolitano was elected chair of the Hispanic Caucus. She won re-election in 2006.

Further Reading

Barone, Michael. *The Almanac of American Politics.* Washington, D.C.: National Journal Group, 2006.

"Napolitano, Grace F." In *Biographical Directory of the United States Congress, 1774–present.* Available online. URL: http://bioguide.congress.gov/scripts/biodisplay.pl?index=N000179. Accessed on January 8, 2007.

"Representative Grace Flores Napolitano (CA)." In *Project Vote Smart.* Available online. URL: http://votesmart.org/bio.php?can_id=BS026886. Accessed on January 8, 2007.

—Angela Kouters

National American Woman Suffrage Association (NAWSA)

The National American Woman Suffrage Association (NAWSA), founded in 1890, united two suffragist organizations that had pursued opposing policies in the years after the Civil War. The NATIONAL WOMAN SUFFRAGE ASSOCIATION (NWSA), founded by ELIZABETH CADY STANTON and SUSAN B. ANTHONY in 1869, had supported a federal constitutional amendment that would grant women the vote, whereas the AMERICAN WOMAN SUFFRAGE ASSOCIATION (AWSA), organized the same year by LUCY STONE, JULIA WARD HOWE, and others, sought action through the state legislatures. The two policies represented more than differing tactics. The NWSA's insistence on immediate federal action brought the women's movement into direct competition with the campaign for black male SUFFRAGE. The AWSA recommended that women should not seek federal action until the campaign for black suffrage had been won. But after this goal was achieved with the ratification of the Fifteenth Amendment in 1870, it became clear that the Republican Party would not take up the fight for woman suffrage as the AWSA had hoped.

Residual bitterness between the two woman suffrage groups kept them apart for another 20 years, but the primary division over the Fifteenth Amendment no longer applied, and the two groups united in the NAWSA in 1890.

Under Anthony and Stanton, the NWSA had expressed an assertive FEMINISM, advocating a broad range of rights for women. With the blending into NAWSA, the women's movement became both more focused and more conservative, seeking only the vote and often justifying it in terms of women's "purifying" influence rather than equality with men. CARRIE CHAPMAN CATT, a former NAWSA president, returned and gave new life to the suffrage movement, aggressively organizing state campaigns that reached beyond NAWSA's traditional middle-class base to include immigrant and working-class women.

The suffrage movement was getting broader support from national reform groups, and in Washington, the CONGRESSIONAL UNION FOR WOMAN SUFFRAGE led by Alice Paul was bringing the militant tactics of British suffragists to a campaign for a federal amendment. Although the Congressional Union's abrasiveness offended the NAWSA leadership, it also spurred them to action. Catt herself cultivated President Woodrow Wilson, ultimately winning his support. On June 4, 1919, with 26 state legislatures petitioning Congress on behalf of woman suffrage, the Nineteenth Amendment passed by a large majority and went to the states for ratification. NAWSA disbanded, but many of its leaders were active in the founding of the National LEAGUE OF WOMEN VOTERS in the same year.

Further Reading

Catt, Carrie Chapman, and Nettie Rogers Shuler. *Woman Suffrage and Politics: The Inner Story of the Suffrage Movement.* New York: C. Scribner's Sons, 1923.

Evans, Sara M. *Born for Liberty.* New York: The Free Press, 1989.

—Paula Casey

National Association of Colored Women (NACW)

The National Association of Colored Women (NACW) formed in 1896 at a Boston meeting of national leaders of the BLACK WOMEN'S

CLUB MOVEMENT, a powerful network of organizations devoted to eliminating racial inequality by expanding economic, social, and political opportunities for African-American women and men. The NACW merged the NATIONAL FEDERATION OF AFRO-AMERICAN WOMEN and the COLORED WOMEN'S LEAGUE, a group headed by the woman who would soon take the helm as the first president of the NACW, MARY CHURCH TERRELL.

Faced with segregated financial institutions, medical facilities, fraternal organizations, and an omission from any form of organized labor, African Americans sought their own remedies to social welfare and economic inequality within their communities. The NACW network of African-American women's clubs facilitated member involvement in such social-reform measures as the establishment of community hospitals and of shelters for young women that catered to an African-American clientele. The NACW established these institutions not only as a means to assist their communities but also as a way to provide black women with increased educational opportunities. By providing African-American women with the tools necessary for improving their economic status, NACW members hoped to circumvent the risks for sexual exploitation and abuse associated with work as a live-in domestic worker, the largest employment category for black women living in the late 19th century. Committed to eliminating the racial double standard that held white women to a higher sexual morality than their black counterparts, the NACW believed that these stereotypes endangered African Americans, both women and men. False allegations of the rape of white women were given as the primary justification for the lynching of African-American men during this period, and the growing problem of lynching soon became the primary focus of the NACW as it moved into the 20th century.

See also ANTI-LYNCHING MOVEMENT.

Further Reading

Davis, Angela Y. *Women, Race, and Class.* New York: Vintage Books, 1983.
Giddings, Paula. *When and Where I Enter: The Impact of Black Women on Race and Sex in America.* New York: Bantam Books, 1984.
Guy-Sheftall, Beverly, ed. *Words of Fire: An Anthology of African-American Feminist Thought.* New York: The New Press, 1995.

—Kimberly K. Little

National Association of Women Business Owners (NAWBO)

The National Association of Women Business Owners (NAWBO) was founded in 1975 by a group of 12 women business owners in the Washington, D.C., area. Today it includes chapters in almost every U.S. metropolitan area. Membership is open to sole proprietors, partners, and corporate owners with day-to-day management responsibility. Active members who live in a chapter area automatically join both their local chapter and the national organization. There is also an at-large chapter for the women business owners outside the chapter areas. The organization is dedicated to improving the conditions under which women entrepreneurs operate. The organization offers members the opportunity to network, build alliances, and participate in professional development programming. NAWBO offers a public policy presence in Washington, D.C., and an international network of contacts through its affiliation with Les Femmes Chefs d'Entreprises Mondiales (World Association of Women Entrepreneurs) in 35 countries. The organization maintains a Web site at www.nawbo.org.

National Birth Control League

See VOLUNTARY PARENTHOOD LEAGUE.

National Black Feminist Organization (NBFO)

The National Black Feminist Organization (NBFO) was founded in 1973 in New York City; its first elected chairman was Margaret Sloan, then editor of *Ms.* MAGAZINE. The organization was made up of primarily black middle-class professional women. NBFO started as an organization seeking an independent identity for the black woman. Black women often felt invisible within the larger women's movement dominated by white women and ignored by the black liberation movement occupied primarily by black men. By creating the NBFO, black women were articulating that they would no longer allow any group or organization to define their actions, concerns, and needs.

The NBFO's purpose was twofold: (1) to address racism prevalent in the white women's liberation movement, and (2) to combat sexism embedded in the black men's liberation movement. Simultaneously addressing and combating racism and sexism, two interlocking systems of oppression, was viewed as the key to empowering and giving voice to the needs of black women. Unlike their white female counterparts in the larger woman's movement and their male counterparts in the black liberation movements, black women faced double discrimination based on their race and gender. As such, they needed a separate space, not only to discuss and address issues and concerns that directly affected them based on their dual oppression, but also to assess and establish strategies to connect their struggles to the larger political system.

The NBFO spawned chapters in major cities across the United States. In the Chicago chapter, a monthly newsletter was created along with consciousness-raising groups and workshops addressing specific issues such as reproductive rights, sterilization abuse, equal access to ABORTION, health care, CHILD CARE, police brutality, labor organizing, and antiracist organizing. While some chapters, such as the Chicago branch, were successful in creating a sense of unity and consistency, other chapters, such as the founding New York City branch, were less successful. Members of the New York chapter were constantly at odds as to what actions should be taken on specific issues. Michele Wallace, a founding member and author of "On the National Black Feminist Organization," suggests that the organization was doomed

because the membership was so diverse, including members from the Socialist Workers Party, radical lesbians, and nonfeminists. Wallace notes: "It is possible that NBFO was not meant to happen when it did. Most of the prime movers in the organization were representing some other organization and whatever commitment they might have had to black women's issues took a back seat. Women who had initiative and spirit usually attended one meeting, were turned off by the hopelessness of getting anything accomplished, and never returned again. Each meeting brought new faces . . . so NBFO has become an organization of people who actually seem to enjoy long, pointless meetings and endless squabbling."

The national structure of the NBFO was dissolved in 1977. However, independent chapters, such as the COMBAHEE RIVER COLLECTIVE, continued to operate at the local and regional level. Despite its demise, the NBFO remains one of the important black women's organizations to begin the discourse on BLACK FEMINISM in the United States.

Further Reading

Gordon, Vivian V. *Black Women, Feminism, and Black Liberation: Which Way?* Chicago: Third World Press, 1985.

Sarachild, Kathie, ed. *Feminist Revolution.* New York: Random House, 1981.

Wallace, Michell. "On the National Black Feminist Organization." In *Feminist Revolution.* New York: Random House, 1978, 174–175.

—Hollis France

National Black Women's Health Project (NBWHP)   See BLACK WOMEN'S HEALTH IMPERATIVE.

National Council of Negro Women (NCNW)   The National Council of Negro Women (NCNW) was founded by MARY MCLEOD BETHUNE on December 5, 1935, in New York

City at the 137th Street branch of the YWCA. The NCNW is considered to be the first African-American "organization of organizations." Bethune served as president from 1935 to 1949. During World War II, the NCNW sponsored a number of patriotic activities, including "We Serve America," encouraging local councils to "Buy Bonds and Be Free." Under the leadership of Dorothy Boulding Ferebee from 1949 to 1953, the NCNW focused on supporting United Nations initiatives on human rights as well as attempts to end segregation and discrimination faced by African Americans in the United States. Under the presidency of Vivian Carter Mason (1953–57), the NCNW worked primarily with the National Association for the Advancement of Colored People and other organizations to implement the landmark 1954 *Brown v. Board of Education* decision. From 1957 to 1997, DOROTHY HEIGHT, a Bethune protégé, led the organization. One of Height's greatest achievements was securing a tax-exempt status for the organization in 1966, increasing the organization's financial stability. Cheryl R. Cooper, a former AARP executive, assumed the presidency in 1997.

The NCNW has consultive status with the United Nations and provides important outreach to more than 4 million women in the United States and Africa. Some of its domestic and international projects include the Black Family Reunion Celebration; the Excellence in Teaching Award Program; local leadership development for women and girls in South Africa; the Court Network Project; the Homebuyer's Assistance Program; and a youth exchange program in the United States, South Africa, and Kenya. The NCNW has 38 nationally affiliated organizations and 254 community based-sections. The organization maintains a Web site at www.ncnw.org.

Further Reading

Giddings, Paula. *When and Where I Enter: The Impact of Black Women on Race and Sex in America.* New York: Amistad, 1996.

Papers of the National Council of Negro Women (1935–1978) can be found at the Bethune Museum and Archives National Historic Site in Washington, D.C.

—Delia C. Gillis

National Federation of Afro-American Women (NFAAW)

Founded in 1895 by JOSEPHINE RUFFIN, the National Federation of Afro-American Women (NFAAW) was the first national organization for African-American women arising out of the BLACK WOMEN'S CLUB MOVEMENT. Margaret Washington, wife of Booker T. Washington, served as the first president. In 1896, the organization merged with the COLORED WOMEN'S LEAGUE to form the NATIONAL ASSOCIATION OF COLORED WOMEN (NACW). The NACW adopted the motto "Lifting as We Climb" with the intention of demonstrating to "an ignorant and suspicious world that our aims and interests are identical with those of all good aspiring women." Founders at the merger included HARRIET TUBMAN, IDA BELL WELLS-BARNETT, and MARY CHURCH TERRELL. Mary Church Terrell was selected as the organization's first president. The NACW focused on job training, pay equity, and child care. In addition, the organization worked to advance civil rights by opposing segregation in transportation and working visibly in the ANTI-LYNCHING MOVEMENT. The organization was an early supporter of the woman's suffrage movement and publicly endorsed the federal amendment in 1912. The National Association of Colored Women's Clubs is the oldest secular African American organization in existence today and maintains a national headquarters in Washington, D.C.

National Federation of Business and Professional Women's Clubs (Business and Professional Women/USA) (BPW/USA)

The National Federation of Business and Professional Women's Clubs (BPW), known today as Business and Professional Women/USA (BPW/USA), is an advocacy group for working women. Unwavering in its commitment to equal opportunity from it founding in 1919 to the present, the BPW opposed state and federal legislation to prohibit hiring married women for public service positions during the Great Depression in the 1930s, included support for the EQUAL RIGHTS AMENDMENT in its legislative platform beginning in 1937, and proposed a federal "equal pay for equal work" act to ensure fair wages for women entering the workforce during World War II. Increased resources from an unprecedented growth in membership during the late 1940s and throughout the 1950s enabled the BPW to relocate its national headquarters to Washington, D.C., from New York City, a move that represented a commitment to political action in the postwar years, and to establish a nonprofit research and educational foundation.

In the 1960s, the BPW led efforts to pass historic federal antidiscrimination legislation, the ground-breaking EQUAL PAY ACT of 1963, and contributed to the rise of the modern women's movement as a participant in the deliberations of John F. Kennedy's PRESIDENT'S COMMISSION ON THE STATUS OF WOMEN. It also served as the primary organizer of state commissions on the status of women. In 1992, the BPW abandoned its longstanding commitment to nonpartisanship when it formed a political action committee (PAC) that endorsed Bill Clinton and Al Gore for president and vice president. Since the early 1990s, BPW/PAC has funded voter registration initiatives and has endorsed and supported candidates for national elective office. BPW/USA maintains a Web site at www.bpwusa.org.

See also FEMINISM.

Further Reading

Hartmann, Susan M. *From Margin to Mainstream: American Women and Politics Since 1960.* New York: Alfred Knopf, 1989.

—Kathleen Laughlin

National League of Women Voters See LEAGUE OF WOMEN VOTERS.

National Organization for Women (NOW)

The National Organization for Women was founded in 1966 to "take action to bring equality for all women." It is the largest feminist organization in the United States, with more than 500,000 contributing members and approximately 550 chapters organized within all 50 states and the District of Columbia.

The organization emerged out of the frustration women felt with the EQUAL EMPLOYMENT OPPORTUNITY COMMISSION's lack of attention to sex discrimination in employment. Although sex was included in TITLE VII OF THE CIVIL RIGHTS ACT OF 1964, the EEOC considered racial discrimination to be a more important priority and developed a policy of ignoring women's complaints. Because of this, Representative MARTHA GRIFFITHS took to the floor of the house prior to the Third Annual Conference of the Commissions on the Status of Women (held in Washington, D.C., June 28–30, 1966) with a speech criticizing the EEOC and its willful refusal to enforce the law.

From this experience, it became clear that women needed an advocacy organization of their own that would be as powerful as the NAACP was in pressing for rights for African Americans, and the National Organization for Women (NOW) was born. Twenty-eight women contributed $5 each and formed an organization that would focus on women's civil rights. On October 29–30, 1966, more than 300 people met in convention in Washington to give shape to the organization and elect the leadership. BETTY FRIEDAN, author of *The FEMININE MYSTIQUE,* was chosen as the first president. The organization's agenda included better education, employment, and political opportunities for women. It also sought equal pay for equal work. In the liberal climate of the 1960s, NOW grew rapidly. It pioneered the use of "Ms." as a salutation and helped make two-career families more acceptable in middle-class society. In the 1970s, NOW focused on preserving a woman's right to ABORTION established by ROE V. WADE (1973) and was a leading force in the ultimately unsuccessful effort to ratify the EQUAL RIGHTS AMENDMENT.

NOW continues to be a force in contemporary politics in the 21st century. As a measure of its success, the organization is often a favorite target of anti-feminist and conservative political groups. NOW and its activists engage in use of both traditional and nontraditional means to push for social change, doing extensive electoral and lobbying work and bringing lawsuits (see NOW v. Scheidler, for example). NOW also organizes mass marches and rallies and orchestrates immediate constituent pressure on the federal legislature or president through the use of email and the Internet. NOW was a partner in the organization of the MARCH FOR WOMEN'S LIVES, held in April 2004 on the Mall in Washington, D.C. The march attracted more than 500,000 women from multiple generations and demographic groups to give voice and express support for women's reproductive rights in the face of recent setbacks. The organization maintains a Web site at www.now.org.

See also ANTIFEMINISM; FEMINISM; YARD, MOLLY.

Further Reading

Barakso, Maryann. *Governing NOW: Grassroots Activism in the National Organization for Women.* Ithaca, N.Y.: Cornell University Press, 2004.

Rosen, Ruth. *The World Split Open: How the Modern Women's Movement Changed America.* New York: Viking, 2000.

National Organization of Black Elected Legislative Women (NOBEL/Women)   The National Organization of Black Elected Legislative Women (NOBEL/Women) is a nonprofit, nonpartisan organization primarily composed of current and former African-American women legislators. Founded in 1985 as a national organization to increase the number of African-American women serving at every level of

government, the organization sponsors forums and educational programs, and advocates on policies affecting the lives of all women. NOBEL/Women has worked actively to increase the representation of black women on corporate boards, commissions, and executive offices. The organization works to ensure the enforcement of responsible programs and policies that meet the legal, social, political, economic, educational, and health needs of women. This is largely accomplished by keeping government agencies accountable for implementing equitable laws and regulations that prohibit discrimination against women and promote participation in the public and private sector.

NOBEL/Women collaborated with the CENTER FOR AMERICAN WOMEN AND POLITICS (CAWP) to create the Leadership Institute, a vehicle to recruit, train, and prepare black women for elective office. The inaugural class of 2002 included 16 women from 12 states.

Further Reading

The National Organization of Black Elected Legislative Women (NOBEL/Women). Available online. URL: http://www.nobelwomen.org/Organization.htm. Accessed on January 11, 2007.

National Woman's Loyal League (NWLL) (Women's National Loyal League)   SUSAN B. ANTHONY and ELIZABETH CADY STANTON established the National Woman's Loyal League (also known as the Women's National Loyal League) in May 1863. In an attempt to bring an end to the Civil War with the adoption of a constitutional amendment abolishing slavery, the women organized a massive petition drive. The NWLL claimed more than 5,000 members, many of whom had suspended their campaign for SUFFRAGE during the war. In February 1864, the women presented Congress with over 100,000 signatures in support of the Thirteenth Amendment. The league submitted another 300,000 signatures in the following year. The organization disbanded when the Thirteenth

Amendment was ratified by the states on December 18, 1865.

See also ABOLITIONIST MOVEMENT, WOMEN IN THE.

Further Reading

Venet, Wendy Hamand. *Neither Ballots nor Bullets: Women Abolitionists and the Civil War.* Charlottesville: University Press of Virginia, 1991.

National Woman's Party (NWP)   In 1913, suffragists ALICE PAUL and LUCY BURNS organized the CONGRESSIONAL UNION FOR WOMAN SUFFRAGE as part of the NATIONAL AMERICAN WOMAN SUFFRAGE ASSOCIATION's (NAWSA) goal to lobby Congress for a national amendment granting women's SUFFRAGE. When NAWSA's efforts proved ineffective, Paul and Burns formed the National Woman's Party (NWP) to fight more aggressively for an immediate national amendment. NWP began by encouraging women voters in western states to boycott Democratic candidates based on President Woodrow Wilson's refusal to support women's suffrage. The tactics then moved to public displays, such as parades and picket lines, to draw attention to the issue. NWP continued to fight for women's suffrage until the passage of the Nineteenth Amendment in 1920. It then began a crusade for an EQUAL RIGHTS AMENDMENT (ERA) that would eliminate any discrimination against women. Although passed by Congress in 1972 and finally sent to the states, the ERA fell short of ratification by three states. NWP continues its fight against discrimination today.

NWP was one of the first groups to use nonviolent, unconventional tactics in its protest for women's suffrage. NWP leaders learned militant protest through participation in the British Women's Social and Political Union. NWP embraced "militancy" as defined by defying and resisting authority in defense of minority rights. From 1917 through 1919, members picketed the Democratic White House. These wartime demonstrations were deemed unpatriotic, resulting in hundreds of women being arrested and imprisoned. They protested their arrests by staging hunger strikes, which led to force-feedings, abuse, and psychological testing. Their request to be treated as "political prisoners" was repeatedly denied, and word of their treatment resulted in public outrage. NWP is credited with influencing the passage of the Nineteenth Amendment based on its direct-action campaign.

Further Reading

Cott, Nancy. "Feminist Politics in the 1920s: The National Woman's Party." *Journal of American History* 71 (1984): 43–68.

Ford, Linda. "Alice Paul and the Politics of Nonviolent Protest." In *Votes for Women: The Struggle for Suffrage Revisited*, edited by Jean H. Baker, 174–188. New York: Oxford University Press, 2002.

—Lisa G. Guinn

National Woman's Rights Convention (1850)   Two years after the SENECA FALLS CONVENTION, the first National Women's Rights Convention was held in Worcester, Massachusetts, in 1850. More than 1,000 women and men attended the event organized by LUCY STONE, Abby Kelley Foster, and Paulina Wright Davis. A "Call to the Convention" went out under the signatures of 89 individuals, including LUCRETIA MOTT and abolitionist William Lloyd Garrison. Those in attendance debated and ultimately passed resolutions supporting equal rights for women in the areas of education, marriage, and social reforms. Annual conventions were held in the decade that followed, with the exception of 1857.

Further Reading

Ken, Andrea. *Lucy Stone: Speaking Out for Equality.* New Brunswick, N.J.: Rutgers University Press, 1992.

National Woman Suffrage Association (NWSA)   In May 1869, SUSAN B. ANTHONY, ELIZABETH CADY STANTON, and other women exasperated at the collapse of the recent EQUAL RIGHTS ASSOCIATION convention in New York City, founded the National Woman Suffrage Association (NWSA). The convention split when former abolitionists, such as Frederick Douglass, accused Anthony and Stanton of racism because they had campaigned for George Francis Train, a Democratic candidate for governor of Kansas who opposed votes for blacks but favored woman SUFFRAGE. Many women delegates also felt that demands for woman suffrage should be put aside until blacks received the right to vote. Stanton and Anthony strongly wanted the Equal Rights Association to concentrate its efforts on women's issues and formed the NWSA for that purpose.

The NWSA dealt with many issues of interest to women besides suffrage, such as the unionization of women workers. In 1872, the association supported VICTORIA WOODHULL, the first woman candidate for president of the United States. In contrast, the AMERICAN WOMAN SUFFRAGE ASSOCIATION limited its efforts to securing the right to vote and tied itself closely to the Republican Party. After the 1872 election, the political differences between the two associations began to fade, but the acrimony was so great that it was not until 1890 that they finally merged (becoming the NATIONAL AMERICAN WOMAN SUFFRAGE ASSOCIATION). Despite factionalism and changes in the political climate that both delayed the progress of the suffrage movement and undermined radical reconstruction, the NWSA set a precedent for women interested in organizing independently of male-dominated politics.

Further Reading

Evans, Sara M. *Born for Liberty.* New York: The Free Press, 1989.

Stanton, Elizabeth Cady, Susan B. Anthony, and Matilda Gage. *History of Woman Suffrage, 1848–1861,* vol. 1. Reprint ed. Salem, N.H.: Ayer Co., 1985.

—Paula Casey

National Women's Conference (1977)

Chaired by Representative BELLA ABZUG (D-NY), the National Women's Conference was held on November 18–21, 1977, in Houston, Texas. It provided an opportunity to evaluate and make recommendations on the role of women in this country through a discussion of specific issues and ideas.

The conference was organized after a 1975 United Nations conference in Mexico City celebrating the International Year of the Woman, which was later extended to the UNITED NATIONS DECADE FOR WOMEN. In the United States, early in 1975, President Gerald R. Ford established a 35-member National Commission on the Observance of International Women's Year to make recommendations to promote equality between men and women. Congressional action came at the same time with Public Law 94–167, which was introduced by U.S. congresswomen BELLA ABZUG and PATSY MINK and called for the commission to organize and convene a national women's conference in 1977, supported by $5 million in federal funds. The law stipulated that prior to the national conference, meetings were to be held in all states and territories to elect delegates and to consider recommendations pertaining to women's issues that would be discussed at the national meeting. These state conventions, which drew some 130,000 participants nationwide, were held from February through July 1977. To represent the bridge between this conference and the SENECA FALLS CONVENTION of 1848, more than 3,000 relay runners carried a torch, lit in Seneca Falls in September 1977, to Houston. Texas congresswoman and Houston native BARBARA JORDAN delivered the keynote address. The conference received complete coverage on public television.

Delegates at the conference addressed 26 major topics, including the EQUAL RIGHTS AMENDMENT (ERA), ABORTION, lesbian rights, CHILD CARE, minority women, homemakers, battered women, education, rape, health, and a cabinet-level women's department. As expected, the most heated debates arose over the issues of abortion and lesbian rights. The ERA was three states short of ratification in 1977, and although the debate over the resolution was heated, delegates finally approved a call for its ratification. The only plank that did not receive action was a proposal for a federal women's department. Near the end of the conference, nonfeminist delegates walked out in protest over their lack of voice in the meeting proceedings.

The Conference's National Plan of Action was submitted to the president and Congress in March 1978, and a month later Jimmy Carter established the National Advisory Committee for Women. While progress on the national agenda established by the Houston conference has been episodic and remains incomplete, the National Women's Conference represents the last time there has been a national dialogue on women's rights endorsed by the federal government.

See also FEMINISM; INTERNATIONAL WOMEN'S DAY.

Further Reading

Handbook of Texas Online. "National Women's Conference, 1977." Available online. URL: http://www.tsha.utexas.edu/handbook/online/articles/NN/pwngq.html. Accessed on January 11, 2007.

National Women's Political Caucus (NWPC)

The National Women's Political Caucus (NWPC) was founded in 1971 to identify, recruit, train, endorse, and support women seeking office. In part fueled by frustration over the Congress's failure to act on the EQUAL RIGHTS AMENDMENT, founders BELLA ABZUG, GLORIA STEINEM, SHIRLEY CHISHOLM, and BETTY FRIEDAN called an organizing meeting in Washington, D.C. More than 300 women from 26 states attended, and the NWPC was founded. Today there are NWPC affiliates in 38 states.

The nonpartisan organization is dedicated to increasing the number of women serving in public office. To this end, the NWPC trains women in how to run successful campaigns and raise funds. The caucus leadership alternates between a Republican and a Democrat every two years. In 1975, the NWPC created the Candidate's Support Committee, a political action committee dedicated to funding female candidates exclusively. Since 1976, the NWPC has expanded its focus to include increasing the number of women in appointed positions. Through the Coalition for Women's Appointments, the caucus reviews the qualifications of hundreds of women and submits selected names and credentials to each new presidential administration for consideration. The National Women's Political Caucus also claims credit for advancing the idea of a woman for vice president in 1984, when GERALDINE FERRARO was named as the Democratic vice-presidential nominee. The NWPC has played an active role in advancing women's representation in cabinet-level positions as well as Congress. The organization maintains a Web site at www.nwpc.org, where a current list of candidate and policy endorsements can he found.

Nestor, Agnes (1880–1948) *suffragist, labor activist*

Born in Grand Rapids, Michigan on June 24, 1880, Agnes Nestor rose to prominence during a strike at the glove factory where she worked. When she was 18, she helped lead her fellow workers to demand an end to "machine rent" (a process whereby workers had to pay for the energy used to run their machines), for an end to the practice of charging workers for the needles that they used, and for a union shop. The women succeeded, and Nestor helped form the International Glove Workers Union. She held leadership positions within the union until her death; served on the board and was president of the Chicago Women's Trade Union League (WTUL); and served on the executive board of the national WTUL, an organization also supported by JANE ADDAMS and ELEANOR ROOSEVELT, which worked to persuade women to join labor organizations. Nestor also lobbied for legislation in support of a shorter workday, child labor laws,

Agnes Nestor (LIBRARY OF CONGRESS)

and women's SUFFRAGE. She was successful in changing Illinois law to achieve a 10-hour work day (a compromise from the eight-hour day she had sought, which was not achieved until the 1937). Agnes Nestor died in Chicago on December 28, 1948.

Further Reading

Jacoby, Robin Miller. *The British and American Women's Trade Union Leagues, 1890–1925: A Case Study of Feminism and Class.* New York: Carlson Publishers, 1994.

Nestor, Agnes. *Woman's Labor Leader: An Autobiography of Agnes Nestor.* Washington: Zenger Publishing Co., 1975.

—Claire Curtis

New Era Club (Women's Era Club)   The Woman's Era Club, also known as the New Era Club, began in Boston in 1893 under the leadership of its president, JOSEPHINE RUFFIN. The Woman's Era Club was composed predominantly of African American women, but it was open to all women. The club initially articulated a mission to help all who were subjugated "not the Negro alone but the Chinese, the Hawaiian, the Russian Jew, the oppressed everywhere." However, almost immediately, their attention became focused on building a national network of black women's clubs. The New Era Club's two most notable achievements were its publication of *Woman's Era*, a monthly journal that circulated nationally among black club women from 1894 to 1897, and the First Conference of Colored Women that the club hosted in Boston in 1895. This conference and publicity that the BLACK WOMEN'S CLUB MOVEMENT received through *Woman's Era* led to the formation of the NATIONAL ASSOCIATION OF COLORED WOMEN (NACW) in 1896.

Boston women vied without success for Ruffin to become the leader of the NACW. Ruffin's vision for the organization differed from that of MARY CHURCH TERRELL, who gained ascendancy in the national organization. As a result of their disagreements, the New Era Club withdrew from the NACW in April 1900. That same year, Ruffin was refused a seat as a delegate of the New Era Club at the national conference of the General Federation of Women's Clubs despite New Era's earlier admittance into that organization. This enforcement of a color line created a controversy that was unresolved until 1902. Then the organization left the decision on qualifications for state and, therefore, national federation membership up to members at the state level. The Woman's Era club disbanded shortly thereafter.

Further Reading

McHenry, Elizabeth. *Forgotten Readers: Recovering the Lost History of African-American Literary Societies.* Durham, N.C.: Duke University Press, 2004.

Streitmatter, Rodger. *Raising Her Voice: African American Women Journalists Who Changed History.* Lexington: University Press of Kentucky, 1994.

White, Deborah Gray. *Too Heavy A Load: Black Women in Defense of Themselves, 1894–1994.* New York: W.W. Norton, 1999.

—Teresa Blue Holden

New York v. Sanger (118 N.E. 637) (1918)

MARGARET SANGER was working as a home nurse in New York City when a woman in her care died of a self-induced ABORTION. Sanger left nursing to promote birth control education full-time. In direct violation of the COMSTOCK ACT of 1873, she launched a monthly magazine, *The Woman Rebel,* giving women information on birth control and on female sexuality. Because Sanger used the words *birth control,* language specifically identified in the Comstock Act as "obscene," and promised to provide information on birth control, the U.S. Post Office refused to distribute *The Woman Rebel* through the mail. Sanger was arrested in August 1914 but fled to Europe the day before her trial was scheduled to begin. When she returned the next year, the prosecutor dropped the charges.

In 1916, Sanger and her sister, Ethel Byrne, opened the first birth control clinic in Brooklyn, New York. Within 10 days, police raided the clinic, and Sanger and her sister were arrested and charged with creating a public nuisance. Ethel Byrne was sentenced to 32 days in the workhouse for distributing obscene birth control information; she began a hunger strike and was force-fed. Sanger pled her sister's case with Governor Charles Whitman and eventually won a pardon, but only in exchange for reluctantly agreeing not to reopen the clinic. Sanger herself was found guilty at a trial before the Court of Special Sessions in Brooklyn, New York, in January 1917. She was sentenced to a month in a workhouse but served her time at the penitentiary for women in Queens, New York.

Following her release, Sanger filed an appeal with the Court of Appeals of the State of New York, arguing the Comstock Act violated the federal and state constitutions by denying women information necessary to preserve their health and safety. The court ruled that the Comstock Act was within the police powers of the state. However, the act specifically exempted doctors from giving information to a married person to cure or prevent a disease. Sanger therefore opened a series of birth control clinics staffed by doctors (the precursor to PLANNED PARENTHOOD FEDERATION OF AMERICA).

Birth control was considered "obscene" material under Comstock until a 1936 court case, but it was not until the 1965 case of GRISWOLD V. CONNECTICUT that married couples were permitted to lawfully use contraceptives, and not until 1972 (EISENSTADT V. BAIRD) was birth control made legal for all persons, married or unmarried.

See also BIRTH CONTROL MOVEMENT.

Further Reading

Chesler, Ellen. *Woman of Valor: Margaret Sanger and the Birth Control Movement in America.* New York: Anchor Books, 1993.

Frost-Knappman, Elizabeth, and Kathryn Cullen-DuPont. *Women's Rights on Trial.* Detroit: Gale Publishing, 1997.

Nineteenth Amendment   See SUFFRAGE.

Nixon, Pat (Thelma Catherine Ryan Nixon)

(1912–1993) *first lady*   Thelma Catherine Ryan was born on March 16, 1912, in Ely, Nevada, to copper miner William Ryan and Kate Halberstadt Bender Ryan. She was their third child and only daughter. Her Irish father nicknamed her "Pat" in honor of St. Patrick's Day, the day after her birth, although she was known as Thelma throughout most of her childhood.

Life in the Ryan household was difficult. In 1914, the family moved to California, and everyone worked in the fields harvesting fruits and vegetables. The house had no running water or electricity. Her father was violent when he had been drinking, and his temper led Thelma to learn to suppress her own emotions and avoid confrontation. When she was 14, her mother died of cancer, and three years later her father died of black lung disease. Pat aspired to be more than a farm worker, and so applied herself to school; a good student, she graduated at the top of her high school class. Throughout the Great Depression, she scrambled for money and worked at numerous jobs. She enrolled in Fullerton Junior College and paid her tuition by working as a cleaning woman and a clerk at a local bank.

In 1931, Pat took a leave from school to drive an elderly couple across the country to New York. Instead of returning immediately, she stayed for two years working as a stenographer and as an X-ray technician following a class on radiology. She returned to Los Angeles to finish her education, again supporting herself with a range of jobs, including dental assistant, telephone operator, retail clerk, and actress in the movies. In 1937, she graduated with honors from the University of Southern California. She took a job teaching typing and shorthand at a high school in Whittier, California. She met attorney Richard Milhous (Dick) Nixon in 1938 when both were auditioning with the Whittier Community Players. They were married in a simple Quaker ceremony on June 21, 1940.

The couple set up house near his law office and she continued to teach. After the Japanese attack on Pearl Harbor in December 1942, the couple moved to Washington, and both Pat and Dick worked for the Office of Price Administration (OPA). In June 1942, in a clash with his Quaker upbringing, he resigned to join the Navy. Pat joined other wives in following their military husbands from base to base, and each time she found employment wherever they were posted. When Dick was sent overseas, she returned to work for the OPA in Washington and then in San Francisco.

In 1945, Republican Party leaders in California invited Dick to run for a House seat in the 1946 election. Pat supported his decision to accept, although she made it clear that she would not make public speeches on his behalf. Instead she served as a one-woman office staff, appearing at his side only on rare occasions. After he was elected, she took up the challenge of making a home in Washington and performing the duties expected of a congressman's wife. During this time, their two daughters were born—Patricia (called Tricia) in 1946 and Julie in 1948. As Nixon's electoral career advanced with each election cycle, Pat Nixon supported his campaigns behind the scenes and increasingly appeared by his side throughout the campaigns for Senate in 1950, the vice presidency in 1952 and 1956, and the presidency in 1960. Her interest in people and her personal warmth is said to have humanized Richard Nixon, who as a political figure often drew negative reactions. Pat Nixon proved to be an expert campaigner, although she said that politics produced the "most vicious people in the world." However, when ethical questions emerged about Nixon's use of a secret fund collected by wealthy donors, she urged him to confront his critics. In a speech that saved his candidacy, he said that his wife did not have a fur coat but instead wore "a good Republican cloth coat." He denied improperly accepting gifts but refused to return Checkers, a little dog that had been given to his young daughters.

As wife to the vice president, Pat Nixon relied upon her experience as a Senate wife in fulfilling her duties. She was a regular stand-in for Mamie Eisenhower, presided over the Ladies of the Senate Red Cross organization, and entertained frequently. She traveled with Dick on numerous foreign trips, and as she did so, she consciously broke many barriers to women. For example, in Japan she gave the first press conference ever held for women reporters. On a 1959 trip to Moscow, when she took note that no other women were attending the first banquet, she questioned Premier Nikita Khrushchev, and thereafter Mrs. Khrushchev attended. When Richard Nixon announced his candidacy for the presidency in 1960, the campaign created a separate persona for Pat Nixon to appeal to voters. She was featured in campaign slogans and on buttons, bumper stickers, and posters that read "Pat for First Lady."

When Dick narrowly lost the election, the family returned to a more private life in California—at least until 1962, when he ran for governor of California against Pat's advice and lost. In 1963, they moved to New York City, where she worked part-time in Dick's law office. When her husband was nominated for the presidency in 1968 and won the office, Pat took up the role of first lady with energy. Like many first ladies before her, she set about refurbishing the public rooms in the White House. During the time the Nixons occupied the White House, the percentage of genuine antiques used to furnish the mansion more than doubled. She also significantly enhanced the White House art collection. Pat Nixon worked to make the White House accessible to the public by installing recorded histories of the mansion for people to listen to as they waited in the public tour line. She instituted evening tours for working people and tours for the blind, and she had the White House lit at night. She was diligent in her correspondence with Americans who wrote to her. In 1971, the Nixons' daughter Tricia was married to Edward Cox in a White House rose garden ceremony.

Pat Nixon traveled extensively as first lady, visiting 29 countries, including China in 1972. When she traveled with the president, his advisers considered her a positive diplomatic asset. She traveled throughout the United States as well, promoting voluntarism and the power of individual attention to social problems. When she announced a national recruitment program, she explained, "Our success as a nation depends upon our willingness to give generously of our self for the welfare and enrichment of the life of others." Pat used the White House to honor community groups and outstanding individual volunteers. She was an advocate for the Domes-

tic Services Volunteer Act of 1970, although she did not personally lobby legislators.

Pat was tactful but honest in expressing her own political views. She was first lady during one of the most active periods of the feminist movement's second wave. She urged Richard Nixon to appoint a woman to the U.S. Supreme Court and urged the Republican Party to endorse the EQUAL RIGHTS AMENDMENT at their 1972 convention. She wore pants (even though her husband disapproved) and modeled them in a national publication. Following the decision in ROE V. WADE in 1973, the first lady publicly disclosed her support for ABORTION rights. She encouraged women to seek public office and spoke out about the need for more women representatives in Congress.

The escalation of the Watergate scandal and the persistent pressure from anti-Vietnam war and pro-civil rights protesters colored Richard Nixon's second term in office and ultimately cut it short when he resigned the presidency on August 8, 1974. As the scandal unfolded and public scrutiny increased, Pat Nixon withdrew from public life. She continued to attend official functions but was otherwise rarely seen in public. As a disgraced Nixon departed from the White House to return to California, Pat was by his side. She later said that the saddest day of her life was September 8, 1974, the day that President Gerald Ford pardoned her husband. Richard Nixon's acceptance of the pardon implied his guilt, and she continued to believe that there was a conspiracy larger than the president at the heart of Watergate.

In July 1976, Pat Nixon suffered a stroke that resulted in a temporary loss of speech and paralysis on her left side. With physical therapy, she recovered. In the 1980s, the Nixons moved to New York City and then to Saddle River, New Jersey. Pat Nixon's health continued to deteriorate, and she died on June 22, 1993; her husband followed her a year later, on April 20, 1994. They are buried on the grounds of the Richard Nixon Birthplace and Library in Yorba Linda, California.

Further Reading

Eisenhower, Julie Nixon. *Pat Nixon: The Untold Story.* New York: Simon and Schuster, 1986.

National First Ladies Library. *Biographies: First Ladies of the United States.* Available online. URL: http://www.firstladies.org/biographies. Accessed on January 4, 2007.

Schneider, Dorothy, and Carl J. Schneider. *First Ladies: A Biographical Dictionary.* New York: Checkmark Books, 2001.

Small, Melvin. *The Presidency of Richard Nixon.* Lawrence: University Press of Kansas, 1999.

Noonan, Peggy (Margaret Ellen Noonan)

(1950–) *speechwriter, columnist, author* Peggy Noonan is best known for her artful political phrasing during the Reagan and Bush presidencies. Born Margaret Ellen Noonan on September 7, 1950, in Brooklyn, New York, she graduated with honors from Fairleigh Dickinson University, where she was editor of the school newspaper. From 1975 to 1978, she wrote and broadcast the editorials and public affairs documentaries for an all-news radio station in Boston, Massachusetts. In 1978, she moved to New York and taught journalism at New York University before taking a job as a writer and producer for the CBS Radio Network, writing Dan Rather's daily radio commentary until 1984.

In 1984, Noonan became a special assistant to President Ronald Reagan, for whom she wrote speeches until 1986. She was also chief speechwriter to Vice President George H. W. Bush during his first presidential campaign penning such memorable phrases as "a thousand points of light" and a "kinder, gentler nation." She is said to have convinced George Bush to issue his now infamous call, "Read my lips, no new taxes."

In 1989, Noonan left Washington for New York, where she has completed several books, including *What I Saw in the Revolution: A Political Life in the Reagan Era,* published by Random House in 1990. Her latest book is a collection of her *Wall Street Journal* columns titled *A Heart, a Cross, and a Flag* (2003). Today Peggy Noonan works as a contributing editor for the *Wall Street Journal, Time* magazine, and *Good Housekeeping.*

Norplant

Norplant is a long-acting birth control method that will last for up to about five years. The Norplant sticks are surgically inserted into a woman's arm. Six small little sticks containing a hormone called progestin, similar to progesterone, is slowly released into the blood stream to prevent pregnancies. Within the first one and a half years, a high dose of progestin is released. After that, the level drops down to what a birth-control pill might contain for the remaining time. After the five-year period, Norplant must be removed. Because this method requires surgery for the insertion and removal, the total cost for this method of birth control can cost between $400 and $1,000 (over five years).

Norplant was approved for use in the United States in 1991 and offered women one of the first long-acting but reversible forms of contraception. However, many feel that it has also been a vehicle for infringing on the reproductive autonomy of women. Almost immediately after the Food and Drug Administration (FDA) approved Norplant, judges and legislators attempted to mandate its use by certain individual women or groups of women. Because it works automatically, is easily monitored, and cannot be removed without medical assistance, Norplant can be used more readily than other contraceptives to control women's reproduction; therefore some state legislatures considered bills that would have offered financial incentives to women on welfare to induce them to use Norplant. Kansas, Louisiana, and Tennessee all considered legislation either providing Norplant to welfare mothers free of charge or offering a one-time grant to cover the cost of insertion along with a small annual stipend (ranging from $50 to $100 a year) for each year a woman used Norplant.

Other legislation would have required women receiving public assistance either to use Norplant or lose their benefits. Some bills would have forced women convicted of child abuse or drug use during pregnancy to have Norplant implanted (Kansas, Louisiana, Ohio, South Carolina, and Tennessee all considered such legislation). In Kansas, a bill was introduced in 1991 that would have set out a new condition of probation for women convicted of narcotics possession. The law, never passed, would have mandated implantation of Norplant for any woman able to become pregnant who had been convicted of possession of narcotics. Civil liberties advocates objected immediately, and none of the invasive legislation was ever passed. Examples of coercive contraception ordered by the judicial system include a 1991 case in which, as a condition of probation, a judge in Austin, Texas, ordered the implantation of Norplant in a woman who had pleaded guilty to child abuse. Similarly, in California, a judge ordered that Norplant be inserted in a 27-year-old mother of four convicted of child abuse and that it remain there for three years beyond her term of court-supervised probation. Medical authorities objected to these court-ordered insertions because they expressly ignored contraindications to the drug.

Norplant is no longer available to women in the United States as of 2000. The FDA recalled a specific batch of Norplant manufactured in October 1999 because it believed that the capsules in that batch were not releasing enough hormones to effectively prevent pregnancy. The manufacturer removed Norplant from the U.S. market while they investigated the problem. The contraceptive has not been available since, and there is no information about when it might be available again.

See also BIRTH CONTROL MOVEMENT.

Further Reading

Boston Women's Health Collective. *Our Bodies Ourselves: A New Edition for a New Era.* New York: Simon and Schuster, 2005.

Northup, Anne (Anne Meagher Northup)

(1948–) *congressperson* Anne Northup was born on January 22, 1948, in Louisville, Kentucky, and was educated at Sacred Heart Academy and Saint Mary's College. She worked for the Ford Motor Company, as a math and economics teacher, and for the Kentucky Truck plant prior to election to public office. She and her husband, Woody Northup, have six children. In 1987, Anne Northup was elected to the Kentucky House of Representatives, where she served until 1996. She was elected to the U.S. House of Representatives in 1996.

Northup has close ties to President George W. Bush. In 1996, Bush campaigned on her behalf in her first race for the U.S. House. In 1999, Northup was one of eight members of Bush's presidential exploratory committee. During her tenure in Congress, she voted with the president 95 percent of the time despite a heavily Democratic constituency. Northup served on the House Committee on Appropriations, giving her some ability to deliver projects to her district. She was the recipient of 2004 campaign funds from former House Speaker Tom Delay's political action committee but refused to return the money when encouraged to do so. Although Northup was reelected in 2004 with 60 percent of the vote, she was defeated in 2006 by Democrat John Yarmuth. Her defeat was attributed to the combination of a Democratic-leaning district and her support for an unpopular president.

Further Reading

Barone, Michael. *The Almanac of American Politics.* Washington, D.C.: National Journal Group, 2006.

"Anne Meagher Northup." In *Biographical Directory of the United States Congress, 1774–present.* Available online. URL: http://bioguide.congress.gov/scripts/biodisplay.pl?index=N000143. Accessed on January 8, 2007.

—Angela Kouters

Norton, Eleanor Holmes (1937–) *congressional delegate* A native of Washington, D.C.,

Eleanor Holmes earned a B.A. from Antioch College (1960) and both an M.A. in American Studies (1963) and a law degree (1964) from Yale University. While clerking for a federal judge in Philadelphia, she met Edward Norton, and the couple married in 1965. For five years, Eleanor Holmes Norton worked on freedom-of-speech cases for the American Civil Liberties Union (ACLU) in New York. In 1970, she became the first woman to head the New York City Commission on Human Rights. In 1977, President Jimmy Carter appointed Norton chair of the EQUAL EMPLOYMENT OPPORTUNITY COMMISSION (EEOC). During her tenure, the agency became more proactive in litigating "patterns and practice" sex discrimination suits.

In 1990, while a tenured professor at Georgetown University Law Center, Norton was elected to represent the District of Columbia as a nonvoting delegate to the U.S. House of Representatives. Unlike a full representative, the delegate from the District of Columbia is not permitted a legislative vote. Also, she may speak only on behalf of the District and vote only in committee, not on the House floor. The District of Columbia, which has no Senate member at all, shares its limited form of congressional representation with Puerto Rico and three other U.S. territories. Unlike those territories or any other place in the United States, citizens are subject to all federal laws, including taxation, despite not being represented in Congress. In 1993, Norton successfully lobbied for the right to vote on the House floor as a representative of the District of Columbia, but in 1995 her vote was again denied. Eleanor Holmes Norton is an energetic advocate for women, African Americans, and residents of the District of Columbia.

Further Reading

Barone, Michael. *The Almanac of American Politics*. Washington, D.C.: National Journal Group, 2006.

"Norton, Eleanor Holmes." In *Biographical Directory of the United States Congress, 1774–present*. Available online. URL: http://bioguide.congress.gov/scripts/biodisplay.pl?index=N000147. Accessed on January 8, 2007.

"Delegate Eleanor Holmes Norton (DC)." In *Project Vote Smart*. Available online. URL: http://votesmart.org/bio.php?can_id=BC038592. Accessed on January 8, 2007.

O

Oberlin College Oberlin College is located in Oberlin, Ohio. Established in 1833, it was the first coeducational institution in the United States. The first 15 women admitted were limited to "ladies' courses," and they were also required to perform domestic tasks to support the school and the male student population. Over time, both requirements were phased out. Within four years, women and men took the same curriculum. In 1841, the first three women graduated, becoming the first three women in the U.S. to earn bachelor's degrees. Oberlin College also admitted students of color. In 1862, Oberlin student Mary Jane Patterson became the first African-American woman to graduate from college in the United States. Advanced education made possible women's entrance into politics and the public sphere more generally. One of Oberlin's best-known alumna was suffragist LUCY STONE, who graduated in 1847. Another was civil rights activist MARY CHURCH TERRELL, an 1884 graduate. The college's Web site is at www.oberlin.edu.

Oberlin College, class of 1898 (LIBRARY OF CONGRESS)

O'Connor, Sandra Day (1930–) *Supreme Court justice* Sandra Day was born in El Paso, Texas, on March 26, 1930, to Arizona rancher Harry A. Day and Ada Mae Wilkey Day. She grew up on the Lazy B Ranch located in southeastern Arizona. The Great Depression strained the family's ability to thrive, but by the late 1930s, the ranch was again stable. Sandra's sister Ann was born in 1938 and her brother Alan in 1939. From the age of five, Sandra lived with her maternal grandmother during the months that school was in session in order to attend the Radford School, a private academy for girls. She graduated from high school at the age of 15 and enrolled at Stanford University, graduating magna cum laude with a degree in economics in 1950. While still a senior at Stanford, she began to study law, and immediately following the completion of her undergraduate work, she enrolled in Stanford Law School. She served on the Stanford Law Review and was elected to the Order of the Coif, a legal honor society. In 1952, she married John Jay O'Connor, a fellow law student at Stanford.

Graduating third in her class at Stanford University Law School should have been enough to propel Sandra Day O'Connor into a top-level position at any law firm—but it was not. Like many women in 1952, her gender outweighed her academic achievements when it came to hiring. The only law-related job she was offered was that of a legal secretary. Deciding to pass on secretarial work, O'Connor became a deputy county attorney in San Mateo, California. In 1953, she followed her husband to Germany, where he served with the U.S. Army Judge Advocate General Corps and she worked as a civilian lawyer for the quartermaster. They returned to the United States in 1957 and settled in Maricopa County, Arizona, not too far from the Lazy B Ranch.

In 1958, Sandra gave birth to the first of three sons and opened a private practice with one partner. From 1960 to 1965, she did not practice law or hold paid employment but instead volunteered, worked in politics, served on the local zoning commission, and became active with the Republican Party in Maricopa County. She served as the county precinct officer from 1960 to 1965 and as district chair from 1962 until 1965. In 1965, she was employed as an assistant state attorney general. In 1969, the future Supreme Court justice was appointed to the Arizona State Senate to fill a vacancy left by another female senator. O'Connor subsequently won her own races for the state senate in 1970 and 1972, becoming the first woman majority leader in the state senate's history in 1972. In 1974, she was elected judge of the Maricopa County Superior Court, where she served until 1979, the year she was appointed to the Arizona Court of Appeals.

Sandra Day O'Connor, ca. 1982 (LIBRARY OF CONGRESS)

On August 19, 1981, President Ronald Reagan fulfilled a campaign promise to appoint a woman to the U.S. Supreme Court, nominating O'Connor to the seat vacated by Justice Potter Stewart. The Senate confirmed her nomination by a vote of 99-0, and she took the oath of office on September 25, 1981, becoming the 102nd justice of the United States Supreme Court and the first woman to be seated on the Court. Justice O'Connor has been described as a restrained jurist and a cautious interpreter of the constitution. On a variety of issues, she carefully sought a middle path. O'Connor was the swing vote (the fifth vote in a 5-4 decision) on numerous issues brought before the Supreme Court. Although she raised questions about the constitutional basis for the 1973 *ROE V. WADE* abortion decision, she consistently declined to provide the vote necessary to overturn the controversial decision. In 2003, she cast the fifth and deciding vote—in addition to writing the court's opinion—upholding the right of the University of Michigan Law School to use race as a factor in admissions as long as each application was processed individually (*Grutter v. Bollinger,* 1993). In *Bush v. Gore* (2000), she voted with the 5-4 majority to end the recount effort in Florida, effectively giving George W. Bush the presidential election victory.

After nearly 24 years of service on the Court, O'Connor announced her intention to retire on July 1, 2005, effective upon the confirmation of her successor. In her letter to President George W. Bush, she indicated that she wanted to spend more time with her husband, who was suffering from the early stages of Alzheimer's disease. On July 19, 2005, President Bush introduced John G. Roberts as O'Connor's successor. However, when Chief Justice William Rehnquist died on September 3, 2005, Bush withdrew Roberts's nomination for justice and renominated him for chief justice of the United States (he was confirmed in September 29, 2005). Meanwhile, Justice O'Connor faced the prospect of starting a new term with the Court when it reconvened in October. On October 3, 2005, President Bush nominated White House Counsel Harriet Miers to the seat. The reaction to the nomination was swift and almost entirely negative, based on her lack of previous experience as a judge and her close personal ties to Bush. Because her past legal experience was as a corporate attorney, there was no public record on which to judge her views on issues likely to come before the Court. Conservatives announced their intention to fight the nomination. Although the Senate Judiciary Committee scheduled hearings to begin on November 7, 2005, President Bush withdrew Miers' nomination at her request on October 27, 2005. Bush then nominated Samuel Alito on October 31, 2005. He was confirmed by the Senate on January 31, 2006, and O'Connor could finally step down.

Since her retirement from the Court, Sandra Day O'Conner has been appointed to a number of important posts. In October 2005, the College of William and Mary named her its new chancellor. The chancellor is largely a symbolic post, serving as adviser to the college president and as an advocate for the college. O'Connor was appointed to the board of the Rockefeller Foundation in June 2006. In March 2006, she was appointed to the bipartisan Iraq Study Group, also known as the Baker-Hamilton Commission, the only woman among the 10 members. The panel was charged with assessing the situation in Iraq after the 2003 U.S. invasion and making policy recommendations. The panel's report was presented to the president and released to the public on December 6, 2006.

See also AFFIRMATIVE ACTION.

Further Reading
O'Connor, Sandra Day. *The Majesty of the Law: Reflections of a Supreme Court Justice.* New York: Random House, 2004.
———, and H. Alan Day. *Lazy B: Growing Up on a Cattle Ranch in the American Southwest.* Random House, 2002.

—Thea Lapham

O'Day, Caroline (Caroline Love Goodwin O'Day) (1875–1943) *congressperson*

Born on June 22, 1875, in Perry, Georgia, Caroline Love Goodwin attended Cooper Union after high school and went to Europe to study art. She eventually settled in New York City, where she married an independently wealthy oilman, Daniel T. O'Day, in 1901. When he died in 1916, Caroline O'Day's social and political interests fully emerged and she committed herself to issues of social welfare and women's suffrage. She joined the Consumers' League of New York and served on the city's board of social welfare. In 1923, O'Day became chairperson of the Women's Division of the New York State Democratic Party. For the next five years, she collaborated with social activists ELEANOR ROOSEVELT, Marion Dickerman, and Nancy Cook in advancing progressive reform causes.

After working in the 1928 and 1932 presidential elections, O'Day ran for New York's at-large congressional seat in 1934. She won with the personal support of Eleanor and President Franklin D. Roosevelt. Successfully reelected in the late 1930s and early 1940s, O'Day was a key supporter of New Deal measures and became involved in immigration issues, particularly over the controversial entry of European refugees to the United States. In 1942, illness forced O'Day to retire from politics, and she died on January 5, 1943.

Caroline O'Day made significant contributions to women's politics in the 1920s and 1930s. As the leader of New York's Democratic women, she helped build a formidable political organization. O'Day then became an important congressperson at a time when few women ran for national political office.

Further Reading

McGuire, John Thomas. "Making the Democratic Party a Partner: Eleanor Roosevelt, the WJLC, and the Women's Division of the New York State Democratic Party, 1921–1927." *Hudson Valley Regional Review* 18 (2001): 29–47.

Swain, Martha H. "Caroline O'Day." In *American National Biography,* vol. 16, edited by John A. Garraty and Mark C. Carnes. New York: Oxford University Press, 1999.

—John Thomas McGuire

Ohio v. Akron Center for Reproductive Health (497 U.S. 502) (1990)

In this case, the U.S. Supreme Court upheld an Ohio law requiring physicians to notify or obtain written permission from one parent within 24 hours prior to performing an ABORTION on an unmarried or unemancipated minor. The requirement could be waived if the minor and an adult sibling or relative certified that the minor feared physical, sexual, or severe emotional abuse from one or the other parent upon notification. The statute provides for a judicial bypass option whereby the minor could seek a court order from a judge in lieu of parental notification. Although the Court of Appeals ruled that the law violated the Fourteenth Amendment, the U.S. Supreme Court, citing the existence of the judicial bypass, disagreed and ruled the statute constitutional.

Further Reading

The OYEZ Project. "*Ohio v. Akron Center for Reproductive Health,* 497 U.S. 502 (1990)." Available online. URL:http://www.oyez.org/cases/case?case=1980–1989/1989/1989_88_805. Accessed on January 11, 2007.

O'Leary, Hazel (Hazel Rollins Reid O'Leary)

(1937–) *secretary of energy* Hazel O'Leary was born on May 17, 1937, in Newport News, Virginia. She earned a bachelor's degree from Fisk University in 1959 and a law degree from Rutgers University in 1966. Thereafter, she worked as a prosecutor in New Jersey and was named a partner in the accounting firm Cooper and Lybrand. Her first national government appointment came during Gerald Ford's administration when she was appointed to serve as director of the Office of Consumer Affairs for the Federal Energy Administration. During the Carter administration, O'Leary served as deputy director and then director of the Economic Regulatory Administration.

After several years in the private sector as counsel for Northern State Power while the Republicans were in power, O'Leary returned to Washington as secretary of energy under President Bill Clinton in 1993. She left the administration at the end of its first term, under investigation for allegations that she had met with Chinese officials in return for a $25,000 "donation" to a charity she favored, Africare. During her tenure in the Clinton administration, she was accused of overspending on overseas travel. In 1996, she was forced to apologize to Congress when her spending exceeded the amount authorized for travel, and she resigned in January 1997.

O'Leary returned to the consulting firm, O'Leary and Associates, established with her husband, John F. O'Leary, in 1981. As a consultant, she engaged issues of national security, science and technology, energy policy, and sustainable development on behalf of her clients. From 2001 to 2002, she served as president and chief operating officer at Blaylock and Partners, an African-American investment banking firm in New York. Since 2004, she has served as president of Fisk University, her undergraduate alma mater, in Nashville, Tennessee.

Operation Rescue Operation Rescue is an anti-abortion group known for its use of confrontational civil disobedience in opposing ABORTION. Evangelical Christian Randall Terry started the group in 1986 in order to galvanize large crowds to blockade the entrances to women's clinics. The group is also known for its "sidewalk counseling," an effort to persuade a woman not to enter the clinic or to convince a pregnant woman not to seek an abortion. Demonstrators often appear at clinics with poster-sized photographs of aborted fetuses. Members of the group have also been known to detain doctors and prevent them from entering health facilities.

After Randall Terry left the organization in 1995 to become a radio talk-show host, Flip Benham, a Protestant minister, took over as head of Operation Rescue. Benham has expanded the range of issues his members protest to include pornography and same-sex partner benefits offered by corporations like Disney. In part, this change in tactic is due to court decisions and recent legislation that limit the group's direct action. In 1994, Congress passed the FREEDOM OF ACCESS TO CLINIC ENTRANCES ACT, which prohibits blocking access to abortion clinics. Operation Rescue refuses to acknowledge the law, and as a consequence, thousands of its members have been arrested. Although the group denies any participation in clinic violence or the murder of abortion providers, membership declines when violence increases. In 2000,

Benham formed a new group, Operation Save America, in order to continue clinic demonstrations unhampered by the costs associated with Operation Rescue's court-imposed restrictions and heavy fines.

See also RIGHT TO LIFE MOVEMENT.

Further Reading
Risen, James, and Judy L. Thomas. *Wrath of Angels: The American Abortion War.* New York: Basic Books, 1998.

opt-out revolution Journalist Lisa Belkin set off a firestorm with "The Opt-Out Revolution," an article published in the *New York Times Magazine* (October 26, 2003). Based on interviews with eight fellow Princeton alumni, Belkin asked, "Why don't women run the world?" and answered, "Maybe it's because they don't want to." In support of her claim, she offered a number of interview quotes and anecdotal experiences of women educated at elite institutions who left high-profile professional jobs to be full-time mothers and caregivers. Belkin's article generated an overwhelming response from feminists who argued that by "opting out," women of privilege were ignoring the need to fight for the institutional and structural changes still needed to make the workplace hospitable for women *and men* with family responsibilities. Belkin did not include any reactions from the eight featured women's spouses.

Studies demonstrate that both men and women resent working longer hours at a job with increasingly fewer benefits and less job security than ever before. A 2000 Harris poll reported that more than four-fifths of men in their 20s and 30s said that a work schedule that allowed for family time was more important to them than a high-paying job. In a 2004 article in the *New York Times Magazine,* "Look Who's Parenting," Ann Hulbert contrasts the parenting values of the baby-boom generation with the post-boomer Generation X. According to data collected by Reach Advisors, half of the

Gen-X fathers devoted three to six hours a day to domesticity and complained of too little time with their kids. Restructuring the workplace in favor of a balanced life and greater long-term economic security requires men and women to act as agents of change.

What Belkin describes as a steady social trend is, in reality, barely a trickle. Workforce participation of married women with children under age six declined from 63.7 percent in 1998 to 62.5 percent in 2001. Fifty-two percent of women with infants remain in the workforce (down from 58.7 in 1998). There have been other demographic changes that bear watching, though. About 18 percent of women ages 40–44 today have never had a child, compared with 10 percent of women in 1976. Women in this age group have, on average, 1.9 children, down considerably from the 1976 average of 3.1 children. According to the most recent Census Bureau report (2003), 44 percent of all women of child-bearing age (defined by the USCB as 15–44) are childless. Seventy-one percent of women without children participate in the labor force.

Further Reading

Belkin, Lisa. "The Opt Out Revolution." *New York Times Magazine,* 26 October 2003.

Berry, Mary Frances. *The Politics of Parenthood: Childcare, Women's Rights, and the Myth of the Good Mother.* New York: Penguin Books, 1993.

Hirshman, Linda. "Homeward Bound." *American Prospect,* 20 December 2005.

Orenstein, Peggy (1961–) *author* Peggy Orenstein is an award-winning author on issues affecting girls and women. Born in Minneapolis, Minnesota, on November 22, 1961, she earned a B.A. degree from Oberlin College in 1983. She subsequently worked in New York as an editor for *Esquire, Manhattan, Inc.,* and *7 Days;* and in San Francisco as managing editor of *Mother Jones.* In 1995, Orenstein ignited a national dialogue about girls and self-esteem with her book, *School Girls: Young Women, Self-Esteem, and the*

Confidence Gap. This work was a follow-up to a 1990 AMERICAN ASSOCIATION OF UNIVERSITY WOMEN study that found girls enter adolescence confident and optimistic, only to emerge as adults full of self-doubts and limited expectations for their futures. Orenstein's work is based on interviews with middle-school-age girls in two communities in California and exposes classroom bias, the lack of role models, and negative peer pressure as factors worthy of community and national attention.

In much the same way, Orenstein generated intense dialogue about the choices and career/family trade-offs facing women in their 30s and 40s with the publication of *Flux: Women on Sex, Love, Work, Kids and Life in a Half-Changed World* in 2001. In this work, she argues that the advances of the women's movement allow women to grow up with a sense of expanded possibilities, only to be confronted with the realities of a world in which women still experience discrimination in pay, struggle with child care options, and see little relief on the horizon. Orenstein interviewed hundreds of women to understand the personal and professional aspects of their lives and the nature of their choices. There is an autobiographical quality to this work since she is writing about her own peer group. Orenstein is a contributing writer to the *New York Times Magazine, Glamour, Mother Jones, Salon,* and the *New Yorker.* She serves on numerous boards and as an advisor to HBO documentaries.

Further Reading

Orenstein, Peggy. *School Girls: Young Women, Self-Esteem, and the Confidence Gap.* New York: Anchor Books, 1995.

Orr v. Orr (440 U.S. 268) (1979) In this case, the Supreme Court ruled that an Alabama statute requiring males, but not females, to pay ALIMONY was unconstitutional under the Fourteenth Amendment. Many states had similar laws, and these were changed to be gender neutral. Prior to this case, alimony awards were nearly always granted to the woman in a divorce based on the assumption that she was her husband's dependent. As a result of the women's movement and more women in the paid labor force, the courts began to view alimony in terms of need and ability to pay, making the sex of the payor or payee less relevant. While gender-neutral alimony laws appear to be a step toward equality for women, the realities imposed by a sex-segregated economy, the WAGE GAP, and lingering assumptions about women's traditional role in caring for children and family mean that women suffer disproportionate economic hardship relative to ex-spouses following a divorce.

Further Reading

DiFonzo, J. Herbie. *Beneath the Fault Line: The Popular and Legal Culture of Divorce in Twentieth-Century America.* Richmond: University of Virginia Press, 1997.

Ovington, Mary White (1865–1951) *suffragist, socialist, unitarian, journalist, cofounder of the NAACP* Mary White Ovington was born on April 11, 1865, in Brooklyn, New York, into a family that supported women's SUFFRAGE and had been deeply involved in the ABOLITIONIST MOVEMENT. Ovington attended Radcliffe College, though she was forced to withdraw in 1893 for financial reasons. After working as a registrar for a few years, she helped to found what came to be known as the Greenpoint Settlement in Brooklyn. She was head social worker at Greenpoint for eight years and then turned her attention to issues of race. In order to decide what needed to be done, Ovington embarked on a study concerning the social and economic conditions of African Americans in New York City. In 1911, she published *Half a Man: The Status of the Negro in New York.* During her research and writing of this book, Ovington met extensively with others interested in the intersection between issues of race, class, and gender. In 1909, she was the instigator for (and member of) the group that met and founded the National Association for the Advancement of Colored People (NAACP, with JANE ADDAMS and MARY CHURCH TERRELL). She was made secretary of the NAACP in 1910 and held various positions on the organization's board until she retired due to ill health in 1947.

Ovington was vice president of Brooklyn's National Consumer League (founded by FLORENCE KELLEY) and a member of the left-leaning Social Reform Club, but she was also a critic of socialist organizations for not doing enough to promote the cause of women and of blacks; she likewise criticized women's groups for not doing enough for women of color. She founded the Lincoln Settlement in Brooklyn and helped a variety of organizations raise money for their social reform work. She died on July 15, 1951, in Newton Highlands, Massachusetts.

Further Reading

Ovington, Mary White, with Ralph E. Luker, ed. *Black and White Sat Down Together: Reminiscences of an NAACP Founder.* New York: Feminist Press, 1995.

Wedin, Carolyn. *Inheritors of the Spirit: Mary White Ovington and the Founding of the NAACP.* Hoboken, N.J.: John Wiley and Sons, 1997.

—Claire Curtis

P

Packard, Sophia (1824–1891) *educator* Sophia Packard was born in New Salem, Massachusetts, on January 3, 1824. She was educated at the Female Seminary of Charlestown, Massachusetts, and after teaching for several years, she became a preceptor and teacher at the New Salem Academy in 1855. After holding a number of teaching jobs in the northeast, Packard toured the South in 1880 and decided to open a school for African-American women and girls in Georgia. She persuaded the Woman's American Baptist Home Mission Society to provide support and moved to Atlanta in 1881 with her long-time companion, Harriet E. Giles. Enrollment at the Atlanta Baptist Female Seminary increased rapidly, and early in 1883 the school moved from a church basement to a new facility. John D. Rockefeller paid the balance due on the note in 1884, and the school was named Spelman Seminary in honor of Rockefeller's wife and her parents. At Packard's death on June 21, 1891, Spelman Seminary had 464 students and a faculty of 34. The seminary became Spelman College in 1929 and, along with Morehouse College, became affiliated with Atlanta University.

Palmer, Alice Freeman (1855–1902) *educator* Alice Elvira Freeman was born on February 21, 1855, in Colesville, New York. She graduated from the University of Michigan in 1876, just six years after the institution began to accept female students. She later undertook graduate study in history there. In 1878, newly founded Wellesley College courted her to join its faculty, appointing her first as head of the history department, then as vice president and acting president, and finally, in 1882, as president of the college. Freeman's highly successful administration ended after six years when she resigned to marry Harvard professor George Herbert Palmer. She remained professionally active, however, as president of the Association of Collegiate Alumnae (later renamed the AMERICAN ASSOCIATION OF UNIVERSITY WOMEN [AAUW]) from 1885 to 1886, and as the first dean of women at the nascent University of Chicago, 1892–95. She also led the campaign to improve the normal school system in Massachusetts in the 1890s and contributed to the creation of Radcliffe College. She died on December 6, 1902.

In raising admissions standards at Wellesley, creating a network of academies to prepare young women for college, working to make the University of Chicago more hospitable for women students, and leading organizations like AAUW, Palmer increased both the range and the quality of educational opportunities for women in the United States. Her professional and political influence secured a place for American women in higher education. She was also an important role model who deftly combined traditional expectations like marriage with a vibrant career.

Further Reading

Bordin, Ruth. *Alice Freeman Palmer: The Evolution of a New Woman.* Ann Arbor: University of Michigan Press, 1993.
Palmer, George Herbert. *The Life of Alice Freeman Palmer.* Boston: Houghton Mifflin, 1908.

—Laura Prieto

Parks, Rosa (Rosa Louise McCauley Parks)

(1913–2005) *civil rights leader* Rosa Louise McCauley was born on February 4, 1913, in Tuskegee, Alabama. As a child, she attended the Montgomery Industrial School for Girls and then Booker T. Washington High School. She was a student at Alabama State College for a short while and married Raymond Parks, a barber, in 1932. Working as both a seamstress and a housekeeper, Rosa Parks became involved in the civil rights movement at a young age and joined the Montgomery branch of the National Association for the Advancement of Colored People (NAACP), an organization committed to social justice, in 1943. She sat as the branch's secretary until 1956.

On December 1, 1955, Parks did something that would lead to her international renown. She refused to relinquish her seat on a bus to a white passenger. According to Montgomery's racial segregation ordinances, the front seats on buses were allotted to white riders only, and African Americans were forbidden to take them. Should all of the front seats fill, black passengers (although they paid the same fare) were

required to relinquish their seats. Drivers were instructed to uphold the law and have all those who disobeyed removed, arrested, and fined. Parks's refusal to yield her seat led to her arrest and a $10 fine.

Word of Parks's defiance spread quickly, and officials of the NAACP, Montgomery church leaders, and the young Reverend Martin Luther King, Jr., believed that her action was a powerful impetus for a city-wide boycott of the city's transit system. African-American passengers—totaling almost 70 percent of all bus riders—were asked to stop using the buses until the segregation policy was revoked. The boycott was an overwhelming success, lasting more than 380 days. It ended on December 20, 1956, when the U.S. Supreme Court declared Montgomery's segregated seating unconstitutional. Parks became known as the mother of the Civil Rights movement because of her role as the primary impetus of the campaign.

The boycott cost Parks her job, and she moved to Detroit, Michigan, shortly thereafter. Working as a fundraiser for the NAACP, she was asked to manage congressman and civil rights activist John Conyers's office in 1965. She worked for Conyers for the next 25 years, until her retirement in 1988. In 1987, she cofounded the Rosa and Raymond Parks Institute for Self Development, an organization dedicated to motivating African-American youth toward progressive social change. "There are very few people who can say their actions and conduct changed the face of the nation," said Mr. Conyers, "and Rosa Parks is one of those individuals."

Parks's actions and activism were first recognized in 1970 when she was awarded the Spingarn Medal. Since that time, she has received the Martin Luther King, Jr., Nonviolent Peace Prize (1980), the ELEANOR ROOSEVELT Women of Courage Award (1984), and the International Freedom Conductor Award from the National Underground Railroad Freedom Center (1998). In addition, the Southern Christian Leadership Council established an annual Rosa Parks Freedom Award in her honor. She was inducted into the National Women's Hall of Fame in 1993 and received the Congressional Gold Medal, the United States' highest civilian honor, in 1999. Parks's autobiography, *Rosa Parks: My Story,* was published in 1992.

Rosa Parks died on October 24, 2005, at her home in Detroit, Michigan. She was 92 years old.

Further Reading

Gray, Fred. *Bus Ride to Justice: Changing the System by the System: The Life and Works of Fred D. Gray.* Montgomery: NewSouth Books, 1999.

Parks, Rosa, with Gregory J. Reed. *Quiet Strength: The Faith, the Hope, and the Heart of a Woman Who Changed a Nation.* Grand Rapids, Mich.: Zondervan, 1995.

Siegel, Beatrice. *The Year They Walked: Rosa Parks and the Montgomery Bus Boycott.* New York: Four Winds Press, 1992.

—Candis Steenbergen

Parrish, Anne (1760–1800) *educator* Born in Philadelphia, Pennsylvania, on October 17, 1760, Anne Parrish grew up in a Quaker home where charitable works were greatly valued. In 1795, Parrish established the first charitable organization for women, the House of Industry, to supply employment to poor women in Philadelphia. The following year, she founded a school for needy girls that provided instruction in regular school subjects as well as supplementary training in domestic skills. Later named the Aimwell School, the institution lasted until 1923. Parrish died in Philadelphia on December 26, 1800.

Further Reading

Haviland, Margaret Morris. "Beyond Women's Sphere: Young Quaker Women and the Veil of Charity in Philadelphia, 1790–1810." *William and Mary Quarterly* 51, no. 3 (July 1994): 419–446.

patriarchy *Patriarchy* literally means rule of (*arch*) fathers (*patri*). More generally, patriarchy characterizes the pervasive control men exercise over social, economic, and political power and resources; this is true not only in the United States but throughout the world. Historian Gerda Lerner defines the central features of patriarchal tradition:

> Patriarchy . . . means the manifestation and institutionalization of male dominance over women and children in the family and the extension of male dominance over women in society in general. It implies that men hold power in all the important institutions of society and that women are deprived of access to such power. It does *not* imply that women are totally powerless or totally deprived of rights, influence, and resources.

Liberal political theorist John Stuart Mill, writing in *The Subjection of Women* (1869), recognized that all men were empowered by patriarchy, regardless of their individual ability to exercise their power and privilege wisely:

> Whatever gratification or pride there is in the possession of power, and whatever personal interest in its exercise, is in this case not confined to a limited class, but common to the whole male sex. Instead of being, to most of its supporters, a thing desirable chiefly in the abstract, or, like the political ends usually contended for by factions, of little private importance to any but the leaders; it comes home to the person and hearth of every male head of a family, and everyone who looks forward to being so. The clodhopper exercises, or is to exercise, his share of the power equally with the highest nobleman.

FEMINISM as an ideology and women's movements as political action directly challenge the privileged position of men and demand that women be viewed as individuals rather than simply derivatives of their relationships to men. The longstanding and persistent belief that men and women naturally occupy separate spheres strengthens the power of patriarchy. The SEPARATE SPHERES IDEOLOGY promotes the belief that due to women's role in reproduction, they are best suited to occupy the private sphere of home and family. Alternatively, men are designed to occupy the public sphere of work and politics. Since power and resources in post-agrarian society derive from the public space rather than private space, controlling access to the public sphere substantially favors men. Until the mid-1800s, the common law known as COVERTURE contributed to women's lack of power in the public sphere by defining married couples as one entity represented in civil society by the husband. Therefore women could not vote, control property, or work for wages since they were indivisible from their husbands.

Controversies over patriarchal control are far from over today. Laws limiting women's reproductive freedom and autonomy are rooted in a patriarchal desire to control lineage. The use of *patronymics* (father's names) was important in establishing property rights. The practice of a woman adopting her husband's surname is a patriarchal holdover from coverture law, but even in 2000, only 9 percent of all women kept their birth surnames upon marriage. In some states, notably Kentucky and Alabama, married women are required by law to use their husband's surname on state documents like a driver's license or state tax returns. The U.S. Supreme Court upheld this sex-based requirement as recently as 1971 (*Forbush v. Wallace*). Religious traditions, cultural norms, and secular laws are powerful forces in preserving patriarchy.

Further Reading

Lerner, Gerda. *The Creation of Patriarchy.* Oxford: Oxford University Press, 1987, p. 239.

Paul, Alice (Alice Stokes Paul) (1885–1977)

suffragist leader   Alice Paul was one of the leading figures in the fight for woman suffrage and women's equality. Born on January 11, 1885, in Moorestown, New Jersey, and raised as a Quaker, she graduated from Swarthmore College in 1905 and subsequently worked at the New York College Settlement while attending the New York School of Social Work. In 1906, she left for England to work in the settlement house movement there for three years. Paul studied at university in England and returned to get her Ph.D. from the University of Pennsylvania (1912). She was chair of a major committee (congressional) of the National American Woman Suffrage Association (NAWSA) within a year, in her mid-20s, but a year later, in 1913, she and others withdrew from NAWSA to form the Congressional Union for Woman Suffrage. This organization evolved into the National Woman's Party in 1917, and Paul's leadership was key to this organization's founding and future.

In England in 1909, Paul had taken part in more radical protests for woman suffrage with

Alice Paul, ca. 1920 (LIBRARY OF CONGRESS)

the founder of the British suffrage movement, Emmeline Pankhurst, and her daughters, Sylvia and Christabel, participating in hunger strikes. Paul, who understood the importance of street theater in communicating a political position, brought back this sense of militancy, and in the United States she organized protests and rallies that led to her imprisonment three times. Her emphasis on a federal constitutional amendment for suffrage was at odds with the NAWSA position, which was to work state-by-state as well as at the federal level. Despite the often strong acrimony between the two groups, their tactics actually complemented each other: NAWSA's taking more deliberate action to win suffrage in elections meant that more politicians at the federal level had a stake in keeping women voters happy, and the NWP's militant stands kept the issue in the newspapers and at the forefront of the political world.

After the 1920 victory for the Nineteenth Amendment, Paul became involved in the struggle to introduce and pass an EQUAL RIGHTS AMENDMENT (ERA), which acquired her name. (The amendment was finally passed in Congress in 1970 and sent to the states to ratify; however, the number of states necessary never ratified within the specified time limit and the amendment failed). Paul was also active in the peace movement, stating at the outbreak of World War II that if women had helped to end World War I, the second war would not have been necessary. Paul died on July 9, 1977, in Moorestown, New Jersey, while the heated battle for the ERA was still raging.

The Alice Paul Institute (API), a not-for-profit 501(c)3 corporation based in Mount Laurel, New Jersey, was founded in 1984 by a group of dedicated volunteers to commemorate the centennial of Alice Paul's 1885 birth and to further her legacy. API has preserved the legacy of Paul and her fellow suffragists and launched the physical restoration of Paul's birthplace and family home, which was purchased in 1990. The restoration of the house began in spring 2001, and most of the project was completed during summer 2002. The Alice Paul Institute maintains a Web site at www.alicepaul.org.

Further Reading

Butler, Amy E. *Two Paths to Equality: Alice Paul and Ethel M. Smith in the ERA Debate, 1921–1929.* Albany, N.Y.: State University of New York Press, 2002.

Lunardini, Christine A. *From Equal Suffrage to Equal Rights: Alice Paul and the National Woman's Party, 1910–1928.* New York: New York University Press, 1986.

Stevens, Doris. *Jailed for Freedom*, edited by Carol O'Hare. Troutdale, Oreg.: NewSage Press, 1995.

—Paula Casey

pay equity   See COMPARABLE WORTH.

Pelosi, Nancy (Nancy Patricia D'Alesandro Pelosi) (1940–) *Speaker of the House of Representatives*

Nancy Pelosi was born Nancy Patricia D'Alesandro on March 26, 1940, in Baltimore, Maryland, to Italian-American parents. She became involved in politics at an early age as her father, Thomas D'Alesandro, Jr., was a U.S. congressman from Maryland and had also been mayor of Baltimore. Nancy D'Alesandro attended Trinity College in Washington, D.C. (graduated 1962), where she met her future husband, Paul Pelosi. When the couple married, they moved to his hometown of San Francisco; they had five children.

Pelosi became involved in Democratic politics as her children grew older, working her way up to becoming party chair for Northern California and joining forces with one of the leaders of California Democratic Party politics, fifth district congressman Phillip Burton. Pelosi was first elected to the U.S. House of Representatives on June 2, 1987, in a special election. She was elected to a full term in 1988 and has been successfully reelected in every contest since—including November 2006, when she won over 80 percent of the vote.

Pelosi is a very effective fundraiser, netting nearly $8 million for Democratic candidates in the 2002 midterm cycle. She has served on the House Committee on Appropriations and the Committee on Intelligence. She was the ranking Democrat on the Intelligence Committee for two years. In 2001, she was elected to the position of House minority whip, serving as second in command to Minority Leader Dick Gephardt of Missouri. She campaigned for candidates in 30 states and in 90 Congressional districts, earning support for future leadership positions. In 2002, after Gephardt resigned as minority leader to seek the Democratic nomination in the 2004 presidential election, Pelosi was elected Minority Leader. At the time, it was the highest leadership position ever held by a woman.

Following the Democratic victories in 2006, Nancy Pelosi was elected Speaker of the House, becoming the first woman to hold the position.

Further Reading
Barone, Michael. *The Almanac of American Politics.* Washington, D.C.: National Journal Group, 2006.

"Pelosi, Nancy." In *Biographical Directory of the United States Congress, 1774–present.* Available online. URL: http://bioguide.congress.gov/scripts/biodisplay.pl?index=P000197. Accessed on January 8, 2007.

"Representative Nancy Pelosi (CA)." In *Project Vote Smart.* Available online. URL: http://votesmart.org/bio.php?can_id=H022103. Accessed on January 8, 2007.

—Angela Kouters

Perkins, Frances (Fannie Coralee Perkins)
(1880–1965) *secretary of labor* Fannie Coralie Perkins was born on April 10, 1880, in Boston; she legally changed her name to Frances as an adult. Perkins graduated from Mount Holyoke College in 1902 and took a teaching position in Lake Forest, Illinois. While there, her interest in social service, begun at Mount Holyoke, contin-

ued to develop, and she spent much of her time working at HULL-HOUSE. She moved to New York in 1909 to study the living conditions of industrial workers and was quickly appointed to the Committee on Safety of the City of New York. In 1913, she married Paul Caldwell Wilson, with whom she had a daughter. Unusual for her time, she retained her maiden name.

When Franklin Roosevelt became governor of New York in 1928, he made Perkins industrial commissioner for the state; upon his election as president (1932), he appointed her secretary of labor. In 1945, she resigned from the cabinet, became a member of the Civil Service Commission, and worked in that agency until 1953. Perkins joined the faculty of Cornell University's School of Industrial and Labor Relations in 1957 and was still teaching at her death on May 14, 1965.

Perkins was one of Roosevelt's most trusted lieutenants and a key force in pushing FDR to protect the rights of American workers. One of the more liberal members of the FDR administration, she helped shape the policies that developed the Social Security Act, the FAIR LABOR STANDARDS ACT, the National Labor Relations Act, and the Civilian Conservation Corps. She also utilized her position as secretary of labor to guarantee that employers abided by collective bargaining laws and was perceived by labor unions as a staunch ally in the administration.

As the first woman appointed to a cabinet-level position, Perkins is a central figure in the fight for political equality, but she is also an important individual in American labor history. She was secretary of labor for slightly more than 12 years (the longest tenure ever in that position), the Department of Labor headquarters were named after her in 1980, and she was inducted into the Labor Hall of Fame in 1988.

Further Reading
Martin, George Whitney. *Madam Secretary, Frances Perkins.* Boston: Houghton Mifflin, 1976.

Pasachoff, Naomi. *Frances Perkins: Champion of the New Deal.* New York: Oxford University Press, 1991.

—Scott Beekman

Personal Responsibility and Work Opportunity Reconciliation Act (1996)

Signed into law on August 22, 1996, the Personal Responsibility and Work Opportunity Reconciliation Act (PRWORA) effectively repealed the 60-year-old federal guarantee of cash assistance to families with children (Aid to Families with Dependent Children), replacing it with block-grant funding to states for temporary assistance for poor families (Temporary Assistance for Needy Families) for up to two years, with a five-year lifetime limit. Under the new law, recipients must work after two years on assistance (with some exceptions), and the legislation establishes benchmarks for states. For example, 25 percent of all families in each state were required to be engaged in work activities or to have left the rolls after the first year, increasing to 50 percent by 2002. In addition, adults must find work or begin performing community service work (state option), and the law mandates a minimum of 30 work hours per week for parents with children over age six. States will be rewarded with financial bonuses if they reduce caseloads and penalized for not meeting other requirements.

Additional CHILD CARE services funding was approved, although states were left to create the systems for providing care within the parameters of the funds provided. As a result, child care has been scarce, and the waiting list for federally subsidized child care slots is very long in most states. Child support enforcement requirements were expanded, and proof of paternity must be produced. States may choose to deny aid to families when additional children are born. States are given full responsibility for planning and administering most assistance programs under the new law and must submit new welfare plans to the federal government in order to receive block-grant funding.

The PRWORA produced a great deal of controversy when introduced. Advocates for women and children predicted that 2.5 million people would be pushed deeper into poverty. The NATIONAL ORGANIZATION FOR WOMEN and the Children's Defense Fund lobbied against the bill's passage. Women in Congress, particularly African-American women, spoke out against what they viewed as racist and sexist assumptions motivating the new legislation. The results of the PRWORA have been somewhat difficult to measure, but by most estimates the number of individuals and families receiving public assistance has fallen since 1996. Critics attribute the early results to a robust economy and point to the increasing numbers of families working multiple jobs while still unable to rise above the federal poverty standard.

See also WELFARE POLICY; WELFARE RIGHTS MOVEMENT.

Further Reading
Ehrenreich, Barbara. *Nickel and Dimed: On (Not) Getting by in America.* New York: Owl Books, 2002.
Seccombe, Karen. *"So You Think I Drive a Cadillac?": Welfare Recipients' Perspectives on the System and Reform.* Boston: Allyn and Bacon, 1998.
Shipler, David K. *The Working Poor: Invisible in America.* New York: Knopf, 2004.

Peterson, Esther (Esther Eggertsen Peterson) (1906–1997) *consumer advocate, woman's advocate*

Born on December 9, 1906, Esther Eggertsen grew up in a Mormon family in conservative Provo, Utah, where her father was the local school superintendent. She earned a bachelor's degree from Brigham Young University in 1927 and a master's degree from Columbia University Teachers College in 1930. Her husband, Oliver Peterson—with whom she had four children—was active in the Farmer-Labor and Socialist Parties and introduced her to labor issues and leaders within the labor movement of the 1930s. Consequently, Esther Peterson became very interested in the rights of working people.

From about 1932 to 1937, Peterson taught at the Winsor School for Girls in Boston. At night she volunteered to teach classes at the Boston YWCA for domestic workers and those in the garment trades. Each summer, she worked as recreation director for the Bryn Mawr Summer School for Women Workers in Industry, where women learned techniques of speaking and organizing, as well as science, literature, history, art, and dance. Peterson became the assistant director of the Department of Cultural Activities of the Amalgamated Clothing Workers of America (ACWA) in 1938. After World War II began, she codirected the ACWA Committee on War Activities. She also organized other nonunion workers, trying especially to integrate newly hired African-American women into the union.

In 1944, Esther Peterson began her career in lobbying as the union's first legislative representative and worked to raise the minimum wage. In 1958, she became a lobbyist for the Industrial Union Department of the AFL-CIO. Three years later, President John F. Kennedy appointed her assistant secretary of labor and director of the Women's Bureau. In this capacity, she led the campaign for the EQUAL PAY ACT of 1963 and served as the director of the first PRESIDENT'S COMMISSION ON THE STATUS OF WOMEN. From 1964 to 1967 Peterson served as President Lyndon Johnson's special assistant on consumer affairs. In 1977, she headed President Jimmy Carter's consumer affairs department, a post she held until 1981. Her consumer advocacy resulted in new federal laws requiring the labeling of foods with their nutritional value, the pricing of food products per unit and the use of open dating—labeling with a date by which perishable products such as milk must be sold.

Peterson was awarded the Presidential Medal of Freedom in 1981. In 1993, she served as a Clinton appointee on the U.S. delegation to the United Nations. She died on December 20, 1997, at the age of 91.

Further Reading

Peterson, Esther, with Winifred Conkling. *Restless: The Memoirs of Labor and Consumer Activist Esther Peterson.* Washington, D.C.: Caring Publishing, 1997.

Philadelphia Female Anti-Slavery Society

James and LUCRETIA MOTT were founding members of the Pennsylvania Anti-Slavery Society, one of the oldest in the nation, founded in 1833. In the same year, Lucretia Mott, Mary Ann McClintock, and Harriet Forten Purvis helped found the Philadelphia Female Anti-Slavery Society. Like other women's social-reform movements, the purpose of the Philadelphia Female Anti-Slavery Society was to raise funds to support the movement's speakers (nearly all male). The ABOLITIONIST MOVEMENT spawned many debates among the activists about the proper role for women. Ultimately, it was women's very exclusion from the proceedings of the World Slavery Conference held in London that prompted Mott and ELIZABETH CADY STANTON to issue a call for a meeting to consider the rights of women. The SENECA FALLS CONVENTION in 1848 included many of the male and female reformers active in the abolitionist movement.

Further Reading

Yee, Shirley J. *Black Women Abolitionists: A Study in Activism 1828–60.* Knoxville: University of Tennessee Press, 1992.

Yellin, Jean Fagan. *Women and Sisters: The Anti-Slavery Feminists in American Culture.* New Haven, Conn.: Yale University Press, 1989.

Phillips v. Martin Marietta Corp. (400 U.S. 542) (1971)

This case is one of the first to apply the sex discrimination provisions of TITLE VII OF THE CIVIL RIGHTS ACT OF 1964 to employment decisions. An employer may not, in the absence of a business necessity, refuse to hire women with school-aged children. Ida Phillips applied for a job with Martin Marietta but was informed that the company did not hire women with preschool-aged children; there was no such policy regarding employment of men with preschool-aged children. Phillips sued under Title VII, arguing that she had been denied employment on the basis of her sex. The district court found no bias against women and cited the prevalence of women applicants and employees at Martin as evidence. The U.S. Supreme Court ruled unanimously, however, that applicants cannot be subject to different hiring standards on the basis of sex.

Further Reading

The OYEZ Project. "*Phillips v. Martin Marietta Corp.,* 400 U.S. 542 (1971)." Available online. URL: http://www.oyez.org/cases/case?case=1970–1979/1970/1970_73. Accessed on January 11, 2007.

Phyllis Schlafly Report

After losing the race for the presidency of the National Federation of Republican Women and withdrawing from establishment politics, PHYLLIS SCHLAFLY needed a new way to communicate with her conservative followers and gain new supporters. In 1967, therefore, she founded the *Phyllis Schlafly Report,* a monthly political newsletter that has been published ever since. Though Schlafly has not written all articles herself, the newsletter contains her conservative ideas, her ideology, and her opinions on current events. Initially, she focused primarily on foreign policy, national defense, military issues, and anticommunism. When she turned against the EQUAL RIGHTS AMENDMENT (ERA), the newsletter was an established and effective way of communicating her views, becoming the mouthpiece of STOP ERA and the EAGLE FORUM. With her anti-ERA campaign, a report was published in a double issue, one focusing on ERA and one on its pre-ERA topics. Schlafly informed her readers on her reasons for opposing the ERA and FEMINISM. The report provided anti-ERA activists with arguments and strategies to effectively rally against the ERA. It contained information and handouts to lobby state legislators and appeals for donations.

With the campaign against the amendment, subscription rates for the *Phyllis Schlafly Report* went up from 3,000 in 1967 to 35,000 in 1980. However, the actual number of readers was much higher, as Schlafly asked her subscribers to copy the reports and circulate them in their community. Schlafly and her followers distributed her newsletter to state legislatures. Many state legislators turned to the *Phyllis Schlafly Report* to inform themselves about the alleged effects of the ERA and eventually voted against it. The newsletter continues to be a platform for her antifeminist and conservative convictions.

See also ANTIFEMINISM.

Further Reading

Felsenthal, Carol. *The Biography of Phyllis Schlafly: The Sweetheart of the Silent Majority.* Garden City, N.Y.: Doubleday & Company, 1981.

—Christine Knauer

Pierce, Jane (Jane Means Appleton Pierce)

(1806–1863) *first lady* Jane Means Appleton was born in Hampton, New Hampshire, on March 12, 1806, the third of six children. Her father, Jesse Appleton, was a respected Congregationalist minister, and her mother, Elizabeth Means Appleton, came from a wealthy family. In 1807, Jesse Appleton became president of Bowdoin College in Brunswick, Maine. The children were raised on the Bowdoin campus among the families of professors in strict Calvinist tradition. Jane's father instilled a deep fear of sin in his daughter that would shape her reactions to events later in life. After he died of tuberculosis in 1819, Elizabeth Appleton moved the family back to Amherst, New Hampshire. Jane may have contracted tuberculosis herself, as she was frail and often in ill health. She was a good student, however, with an interest in literature.

When Jane Appleton was 20, she met Franklin Pierce, a graduate of Bowdoin, who was planning to study law as a means of entering politics. Although she was retiring and he gregarious, they began an eight-year courtship. Her family objected to nearly everything about Pierce, most especially his affiliation with the Democratic Party. Nevertheless, the couple married on November 19, 1834, and immediately departed for Washington so that Franklin could take his seat in the Congress as a representative for New Hampshire. He was subsequently elected to the U.S. Senate (1837–42).

Life in Washington appealed to Franklin as much as it appalled his wife. She disdained the atmosphere of political deal-making and the after-hours drinking involved. After eight unhappy years, she convinced him to give up politics and return to his law practice in Concord, New Hampshire. The birth of her sons Frank Robert (b. 1839) and Benjamin (b. 1841) after several miscarriages and stillbirths gave her even more reason to urge their return to a more healthful and stable existence. Although they did as she wished and returned to Concord in 1842, they were devastated by the death of their first son from typhus in 1843.

With the outbreak of the Mexican War (1846–48), Franklin felt the call of duty and accepted a commission as brigadier general. Before he left, he arranged for live-in help for his ailing wife and remaining son, Benny. Jane concentrated all of her energies on her son, raising him in the strict evangelical traditions in which she herself had been raised. When Franklin returned from the Mexican War, his law practice prospered, and Jane's health began to improve. But this hiatus from politics proved short-lived; when she heard that Franklin had been nominated as the Democratic candidate for president, she fainted. She began praying for him to lose and offered him no support in his active campaign for the job.

When Franklin Pierce won the presidency in 1852, Jane resigned herself to life in the White House, comforted by the thought that at least she would have Benny with her. However, on January 6, 1853, on a train ride back from Boston, the train derailed and tumbled over an embankment. Neither parent was hurt, but Benny was killed. Jane believed that God must have caused Benny's death as punishment for his parent's sins—especially the political ambitions of his father. This charge devastated Franklin. Jane did not attend the inauguration and only moved into the White House at the urging of her family. Her husband hired a New Hampshire couple with experience in managing an inn to manage the daily affairs of the White House, and Jane's aunt, Abby Kent Means, served as the official hostess.

The Pierce administration was a politically troubled one, but Jane offered no aid or solace to her husband. She sank into a deep depression, often behaving oddly, such as spending hours in the White House sitting room scribbling notes to her dead son. The president went out in Washington alone, escaping the despondency of the White House to visit the theater or galleries. Varina Davis, second wife of Jefferson Davis, gradually persuaded Jane to participate in more public events. In 1855, she attended the New Year's reception, and in 1856 the Pierces held a round of official dinners.

When they left the White House in 1857, Franklin Pierce took Jane abroad, hoping that a change in scenery would improve her health and mental state. They returned to Concord and planned to build a house. Supporters urged Franklin to consider another campaign for the White House in 1860, but he declined as Jane's health worsened. She died on December 2, 1863, and was buried in Concord beside her children.

Further Reading

Mayo, Edith P. "Jane Pierce." In *The Smithsonian Book of First Ladies: Their Lives, Times, and Issues.* New York: Henry Holt and Company, 1996, 81–83.

National First Ladies Library. *Biographies: First Ladies of the United States.* Available online. URL: http://www.firstladies.org/biographies. Accessed on January 4, 2007.

Pinchot, Cornelia Bryce (Cornelia Elizabeth Bryce Pinchot) (1881–1960) *political activist*

Cornelia Elizabeth Bryce was born in Newport, Rhode Island, to Lloyd Stevens and

Edith Cooper Bryce. Lloyd Bryce was a congressman, political advisor to Theodore Roosevelt, and United States minister to the Netherlands. Edith Cooper Bryce was the granddaughter of iron mogul Peter Cooper. Cornelia's upbringing in Rhode Island and New York provided her with a elite education, exposure to the political arena, and the company of well-placed individuals in society. She was an accomplished traveler, amateur political activist, and sportswoman by the time she met and married Gifford Pinchot in 1914, at the age of 33; he was 49.

Cornelia spent her honeymoon helping her husband campaign for a seat in the U.S. Senate from Pennsylvania, which he lost. Her political interest was not solely on behalf of her husband; before she married Gifford, Cornelia had taken part in picket lines, marches, protests, and joined organizations on behalf of workers' interests, female SUFFRAGE, child labor, and other Progressive causes. Pinchot herself ran for a seat in Congress three times from the state of Pennsylvania on the Republican ticket; she failed all three times, in 1928, 1932, and 1936. After Gifford's death in 1946, she continued her political activism, serving as the U.S. representative at the International Women's Conference (1945), as president of the Americans United for World Organization, and on the board of the Americans for Democratic Action. She lived in Washington, D.C., in her later years, entertaining political and social figures until her death at the age of 79. Her papers are housed in the Library of Congress.

Further Reading

Furlow, John W., Jr. "Cornelia Bryce Pinchot: Feminism in the Post-Suffrage Era." *Pennsylvania History* 43 (1976): 329–346.
Voda, Mary Beth Kennedy. "The Lady in Red: Cornelia Bryce Pinchot: Feminist for Social Justice." *Pennsylvania Heritage* 23 (1997): 22–31.

—Megan Jones

pink-collar ghetto   The term *pink collar ghetto* was reportedly first introduced by Louise Kapp Howe in her book *Pink Collar Workers: Inside the World of Women's Work* (1977). Howe's work examined the experiences of women working in traditionally "female" occupations such as secretary, beautician, and waitress. Her central claim was that the "equal pay" theory on which the EQUAL PAY ACT of 1963 was based would never alleviate the WAGE GAP for women working in the "pink-collar ghetto" because the wages, salaries, and prestige of these occupations were systematically marginalized. Since the majority of working women (certainly in 1977, but still today) hold jobs in employment sectors consistent with private-sphere gender roles, the Equal Pay Act promised little relief. The law requires that employers provide equal pay for equal or substantially equal work rather than for comparable work. Three-quarters of all women who work do so in just 20 occupations, each of which is nearly 80 percent female. Bureau of Labor statistics for 2003 reported that women made up 98 percent of nation's kindergarten and preschool teachers, 84 percent of its elementary school teachers, 96 percent of secretaries and administrative assistants, and 90 percent of registered nurses. Likewise, men constitute 96 percent of the nation's firefighters, 74 percent of its physicians, 97 percent of its construction workers, and 99 percent of its auto mechanics. The median income for all full-time male workers in 2001 was $29,101, compared with $16,614 for all full-time female workers.

As long as occupations are segregated by gender, the Equal Pay Act will not erase pay differentials. Many feminists advocate a COMPARABLE WORTH strategy that would pay equivalent rates based on equivalent work, even when the job title was not identical. Comparable-worth legislation would ensure that women who work as prison matrons would be paid the same as men who work as prison guards. A Fair Pay Act, designed to provide equal pay for comparable work, has been introduced into Congress repeatedly but has made little headway toward passage as of the 109th Congress.

Further Reading

Blum, Linda M. *Between Feminism and Labor: The Significance of the Comparable Worth Movement.* Berkeley: University of California Press, 1991.

Howe, Louise Kapp. *Pink Collar Workers: Inside the World of Women's Work.* New York: G. P. Putnam's Sons, 1977.

pipeline thesis   The term *pipeline thesis* refers to the theory that women will only advance to higher political office as well as to positions of responsibility in science, academia, and the professions once more women flood the "pipeline" into such jobs. This theory suggests that there is a logical progression of advancement and that once women comprise sufficient numbers of qualified candidates, they will be promoted and/or elected in proportionate numbers. Proponents of this theory therefore believe that it is only a matter of time until women achieve parity. However, given that women have been in public life and the workforce in significant numbers since the mid-1970s without making equally significant advances in the proportion of political posts or in the highest echelons in industry, critics suggest that sex discrimination clogs the pipeline and that direct action through legal intervention or policy is the only way to ensure that women are advanced. Even when men and women are similarly educated and working in the same profession, women are likely to be at the bottom of the wage and prestige scales. For example, women constitute 30 percent of all lawyers in the United States, yet they make up only 15 percent of the partners in the 250 largest law firms and only 5 percent of managing partners in large firms. Women represent 15 percent of the senior executives in *Fortune 500* companies (up from 8 percent in 1995) and earn roughly two-thirds the salaries of their male counterparts.

With regard to electing more women to office, the pipeline refers to the characteristics of electable candidates. These characteristics may depend in part on the level of office in question (national, state, or local). The higher the office, the more experience, education, and professional prestige are required. Candidates for the U.S. Senate are drawn from a select pool of individuals, many of whom come from corporate boardrooms, the ranks of senior management, prestigious law firms, or the U.S. House of Representatives. Women have only recently broken into this select group, and their numbers are still very small. In 2004, there were two women CEOs of *Fortune* 500 companies, and women held roughly 10 percent of senior management positions in the nation's largest companies, constituted only 13 percent of the partners of large law firms, held 14.9 percent of the seats in the U.S. House, and made up only 18.2 percent of full professors at doctoral-granting institutions nationwide. For many, this suggests that the reason for women's lack of representation in politics rests with their small numbers in the pipeline to elected office. In other words, there are simply not enough qualified female candidates. Advocates for more women in office are advised to be patient. As more women enter the public sphere overall, there will be more female candidates and therefore more women elected officials.

Critics of the pipeline thesis point to different factors in the relatively small number of women seeking and winning elected office. While women's numbers have been growing at the local and state legislative levels, the average age when first elected to office remains significantly higher for women than for men. Women often wait to seek office until their children are grown, which limits their ability to climb the ladder to progressively higher positions. In a study released in 1991, only 15 percent of women officeholders were 40 years old or younger, compared to 28 percent of men. Men in office were twice as likely as women to have pre-teenage children at home. While fatherhood is seen as compatible with a professional career and political office, motherhood is seen as a full-time job. Women with small children face tough questioning as candidates about how they expect to handle both jobs. Men, however, are rarely asked whether their political responsibilities will take them away from their children.

In a study conducted in the spring of 2000 for the WHITE HOUSE PROJECT Education Fund, researchers interviewed young women and men to learn more about the pipeline of the future. The study found that young people, particularly women, are extraordinarily dedicated to their communities and to solving problems within their communities. Although they hold negative attitudes about politics and politicians in general, more than four in 10 young adults would consider running for office themselves. Young women are more inclined to get involved in politics if they believe they will be able to accomplish their goals and address issues they care about through political involvement. Young women who have held leadership positions in their school or community and who have been encouraged to seek office are far more likely than other women to express a desire to seek political office. Encouragement has twice the power of any other factor in predicting whether a young woman will consider running for office. Presumably then, young women could be cultivated to fill the pipeline and seek elective office.

However, significant new research in the area of women candidates challenges both the eligibility pool and the pipeline theses in explaining why so few women seek office in each election cycle. Research by Richard Fox and Jennifer Lawless suggests that these theories may rest on a fundamentally flawed assumption: that women will respond to political opportunities in the same ways that men traditionally have. As the authors point out, little attention has been paid to the process by which gender affects men's and women's emergence as candidates for public office. They found that women overall are less likely than their male colleagues to consider running for office, undertake the steps necessary to declare a candidacy, or actually run for public office.

So what explains women's lack of ambition for political office? Fox and Lawless investigated a number of factors related to traditional gender socialization, political culture, family responsibilities, and self-perceived qualifications. They did not find any empirical support for the traditional barriers to women's entry into politics; women's ambition is not depressed by political culture, family structure, or primary caretaking responsibilities, nor by ideological motivations. Rather, women's self-perceptions of their qualifications for office and the degree to which they receive encouragement to run from a political or nonpolitical source are central to predicting whether women will seek political office. When women perceive themselves as "very qualified" for holding an elected position, they are significantly more likely to consider running.

For women, the impact of self-perceived qualifications on the decision to seek office is nearly double that for men. Fox and Lawless concluded that although women who run for office are just as likely as men to emerge as winners, the winnowing process in candidate emergence yields a smaller number of female candidates. The pool of candidates who actually run, therefore, looks very different from the eligibility pool of potential candidates. Women are significantly less likely than men to receive political encouragement to run and to assess themselves as qualified to run for office, but at the same time they are more likely to rely on their own assessment when considering whether to enter the political arena. Therefore, relying on the inevitable advance of women in the professions, as the pipeline thesis suggests, is necessary but may not be sufficient to produce more women candidates or elected officials.

See also GLASS CEILING; SEPARATE SPHERES IDEOLOGY.

Further Reading

Fox, Richard L., and Jennifer L. Lawless. "Entering the Arena? Gender and the Decision to Run for Office." *American Journal of Political Science* 48, no. 2 (April 2004): 264–280.

The Whitehouse Project. "Pipeline Research." Available online. URL: http://www.thewhitehouseproject.org/research/pipeline_research.html. Accessed on January 11, 2007.

Wilson, Marie. *Closing the Leadership Gap: Why Women Can and Must Help Run the World.* New York: Viking Press, 2004.

Pittsburgh Press v. Pittsburgh Commission on Human Relations (413 U.S. 376) (1973)

This case challenged the prevailing practice of segregating by sex help-wanted ads placed in newspapers. Although TITLE VII OF THE CIVIL RIGHTS ACT of 1964 prohibited employment discrimination on the basis of sex, the EQUAL EMPLOYMENT OPPORTUNITY COMMISSION (EEOC) refused to enforce the law and end this practice as it pertained to sex discrimination even though it had provided guidelines to end similar segregation of classified ads on the basis of race, religion, and national origin (the other protected classes under Title IV). In 1967, under pressure from the NATIONAL ORGANIZATION FOR WOMEN (NOW), the EEOC agreed to hold hearings on the issue. As a result, the agency changed its guidelines in 1968.

Individual newspapers were slow to comply. NOW dedicated its efforts to drawing public attention to those news organizations that refused to follow EEOC guidelines and integrate their classified job listings. The *Pittsburgh Press* altered its headings from "Male Help Wanted" and "Female Help Wanted" to "Jobs—Male Interest" and "Jobs—Female Interest." The Pittsburgh Commission on Human Relations ordered the newspaper to stop the practice of separate columns, but it refused. Ultimately the case ended up at the U.S. Supreme Court, where the *Pittsburgh Press* argued it required protection from interference under First Amendment rights of speech and press. Therefore the Court had to sort through competing rights. The justices did so on the basis of distinguishing between speech and commercial speech. Since the job ads were a part of the paper's commercial enterprise, they were not subject to the same level of protection as the editorial or news content would be. This decision effectively ended the practice of male and female help-wanted ads—a mere nine-years after Title VII made discrimination on the basis of sex illegal in employment.

Further Reading

Frost-Knappman, Elizabeth, and Kathryn Cullen-DuPont. *Women's Rights on Trial.* Detroit: Gale Publishing, 1997.

The OYEZ Project. "*Pittsburgh Press Co. v. Human Rel. Comm'n,* 413 U.S. 376 (1973)." Available online. URL:http://www.oyez.org/cases/case?case=1970–1979/1972/1972_72_419. Accessed on January 11, 2007.

Planned Parenthood Federation of America (PPFA)

Planned Parenthood Federation of America (PPFA) is the oldest family-planning organization in the United States. PPFA has its roots in the early BIRTH CONTROL MOVEMENT led by MARGARET SANGER. In 1921, Sanger founded the first family-planning organization, the AMERICAN BIRTH CONTROL LEAGUE (ABCL), offering an ambitious program of education, legislative reform, and research on contraceptive techniques. Sanger envisioned an organization that would consolidate birth control activism, family-planning services, and clinic access. In 1939, the ABCL merged with the Birth Control Clinical Research Bureau to form the Birth Control Federation of America, and in 1942 the organization voted to change its name to Planned Parenthood Federation of America, Inc.

PPFA has adopted a variety of political and social goals. Its early mission was to make contraception more accessible to free women from unplanned pregnancies. By the 1960s, PPFA's support of the birth control pill made contraceptive access possible to millions of women worldwide. PPFA has remained legally active at both the state and federal level, supporting such cases as *GRISWOLD V. CONNECTICUT,* which struck down state laws prohibiting contraceptive use by married couples, and ROE V. WADE, which legalized ABORTION. More recently, Planned Parenthood has been at the forefront in the effort to overturn a federal ban on third-trimester abortions, and the federation helped to organize two of the largest marches in Washington, D.C., history for abortion rights. Currently, nearly 21,000 volunteers and staff provide reproductive health care and education to almost 5 million people each year. The Planned Parenthood Action Fund remains politically active through lobbying, voter education, and electoral work. Globally, Planned Parenthood serves the international community through its involvement in Planned Parenthood Global Partners and as a member of the International Planned Parenthood Federation.

Further Reading

Kennedy, David M. *Birth Control in America: The Career of Margaret Sanger.* New Haven, Conn.: Yale University Press, 2001.

McCann, Carole. *Birth Control Politics in the United States, 1916–1945.* New York: Cornell University Press, 1994.

—Patricia Walsh Coates

Planned Parenthood of Southeastern Pennsylvania v. Casey (505 U.S. 833) (1992)

In the late 1980s, Pennsylvania amended its ABORTION laws to require informed consent and a 24-hour waiting period for women seeking abortions. Minors would need parental consent, and married women would need spousal consent in order to have an abortion in the state. Several abortion clinics and abortion-rights groups challenged these provisions. In a 5-4 decision, the Supreme Court reaffirmed the basic right of abortion under ROE V. WADE but also upheld most of the Pennsylvania provisions. The justices overturned the strict trimester formula of *Roe,* claiming that medical advances had made the formula obsolete. They imposed a new standard to determine the validity of laws designed to restrict abortions, holding that state abortion regulations cannot have the purpose or effect of imposing an "undue burden" on women seeking abortions. The Court defined an *undue burden* as a "substantial obstacle in the path of a woman seeking an abortion before the fetus attains viability." According to the justices, only the provision requiring spousal consent would fail the undue-burden test, and it was therefore stricken. The opinion for the Court was unique in that it was crafted and authored by three justices. Neither side of the abortion debate was satisfied with the ruling.

Further Reading

Casper, Gerhard. *Landmark Abortion Cases: Planned Parenthood v. Casey.* Bethesda, Md.: University Publications of America, 1993.

Friedman, Leon. *The Supreme Court Confronts Abortion: The Briefs, Argument, and Decision in Planned Parenthood v. Casey.* New York: Farrar, Straus and Giroux, 1993.

Sanger, Alexander. *Beyond Choice: Reproductive Freedom in the 21st Century.* New York: Public Affairs, 2004.

—J. Celeste Lay

Pocahontas (ca. 1595–1617) *peacemaker* Pocahontas, daughter of Powhatan, the leader of a powerful Indian confederacy in Virginia, served as her father's emissary to the settlers in the English colony of Jamestown. Pocahontas left no written record of her life or her impressions about the colonists, so researchers rely largely on English sources to tell her story. In what is probably an apocryphal story, John Smith claimed that when he was captured by Powhatan's brother in 1607, Pocahontas stepped forward to protect his life by offering her own. Beginning in 1608, she made frequent trips to the settlement, delivering messages from Powhatan and arranging for the exchange of corn, fish, and other supplies.

Relations between Powhatan and the Jamestown colonists disintegrated after John Smith returned to England in 1609. The following year, Pocahontas married an Indian named Kocoum. In 1613, she was taken hostage by Samuel Argall, who hoped to use her to gain bargaining power with the Indians. As a captive, Pocahontas began religious instruction, met widowed tobacco planter John Rolfe, and married him on April 5, 1614. Afterward, the colonists enjoyed a temporarily peaceful relationship with the Indians that lasted until Powhatan's death. Pocahontas gave birth to a son, Thomas Rolfe, in 1615. The Virginia Company recognized Pocahontas's contributions to the colony that same year and provided her and her son with an annual stipend.

In 1616, Pocahontas, her husband and son, and several Indian men and women sailed for England to encourage support of the Virginia Company and the colony. There Pocahontas was presented to James I and Queen Anne. She died on March 21, 1617, just as the Rolfes were preparing to board a ship bound home for Virginia, and was buried in a churchyard in Gravesend, England.

Further Reading

Barbour, Philip. *Pocahontas and Her World.* Boston: Houghton Mifflin Company, 1970.

Rountree, Helen. *Pocahontas's People: The Powhatan Indians of Virginia through Four Centuries.* Norman: University of Oklahoma Press, 1990.

———. "Pocahontas—the Hostage Who Became Famous." In *Sifters: Native American Women's Lives,* edited by Theda Perdue, 14–28. Oxford: Oxford University Press, 2001.

Woodward, Grace Steele. *Pocahontas.* Norman: University of Oklahoma Press, 1969.

—Jennifer Davis McDaid

Polk, Sarah Childress (1803–1891) *first lady*
Sarah Childress was born near Murfreesboro, Tennessee, to Joel and Elizabeth Whitsett Childress on September 4, 1803; she was the third of six children. The family was prosperous, religiously principled, and politically connected.

Sarah's parents believed in educating all of their children equally. After completing the primary grades, Sarah and her sister Susan were tutored at home after hours by the principal of Bradley Academy, where her brothers attended school. She was an avid reader and enjoyed reading the newspapers and engaging in conversation about the political issues of the day. General Andrew Jackson was a frequent visitor. In 1817, the sisters enrolled in Monrovian Female Academy in Salem, North Carolina, touted as the best girl's school in the South. Though their enrollment was cut short by their father's death, Sarah's educational foundation allowed her to approach the role of first lady as a political partner to the president.

Sarah met James Polk, a schoolmate of her brothers, at a reception for the Tennessee governor. Polk was a lawyer, politician, and clerk of the Tennessee court. He courted Sarah for four years before she reportedly accepted his proposal on the condition that he win a seat in the state legislature. They were married on January 1, 1824, and in 1825, James Polk was elected to the U.S. House of Representatives. Sarah stayed in Tennessee during his first year in Washington, while he lived in a boarding house with other congressmen. The Polks never had children, probably because an operation in his youth had left him sterile. Without children to tend, Sarah was free to follow politics and advocate for her husband's career on a full-time basis. In 1826, she joined him in Washington and they "messed" in a boarding house with congressmen from other states. She enjoyed the political life in Washington and frequently attended the House of Representatives when James Polk spoke. She often agreed with her husband's positions, but when her opinions dissented from his, she felt free to share her views openly. Her piety required that they attend the Presbyterian Church each Sunday, refrain from dancing and the theater, and not conduct business of any kind on Sundays. When Polk's loyalty to President Andrew Jackson won him support to become Speaker of the House, Sarah served as his personal adviser and correspondence secretary. Later she would draft and revise his speeches.

James Polk was nominated as the Democrat's presidential candidate in 1844 and narrowly defeated Henry Clay. Sarah Polk eagerly moved into the White House in March that year and at once instituted her ban against dancing, much to the dismay of the social elite in Washington. "To dance in these rooms would be undignified," she reportedly said. Sarah enjoyed entertaining, though, and gave elegant dinner parties in the White House. She talked easily with men and women alike and was popular throughout political circles. Although she did not publicly participate in governing the country, when officials came to call on the president, she was always present. She read several newspapers each day and marked articles she thought he should read. She also tended his health carefully and tried to prevent him from over-exertion. James rarely traveled outside the White House because of his health, but Sarah circulated throughout Washington and returned to him to share what she had learned. She did not take up the cause of women's rights, even though the SUFFRAGE movement was beginning and married women were advocating for greater control of their wealth and property. She is reported to have preferred men's company to that of women, and she had few close women companions.

Upon his election, James Polk had promised to serve only one term. He and Sarah therefore left Washington in 1849, intending to put politics behind them and enjoy a long retirement in Tennessee. They took a four-week tour of the South on their return to Nashville, but this exacted a toll on James Polk's health. He died on June 15, 1849, just three months after leaving the presidency. Sarah Polk outlived him by more than 40 years.

As a widow, Sarah Polk lived quietly in the house they had planned together in Nashville, Tennessee. Although heavily involved in politics

Sarah Childress Polk, 1846 (LIBRARY OF CONGRESS)

through her husband, the second half of her life was unremarkable. Tennessee politicians and visiting dignitaries frequently called upon her, and she received them all at her home. During the Civil War, she declared herself neutral and received both Confederate and Union officers. She died at her home on August 14, 1891, at the age of 87.

Further Reading

Mayo, Edith P. "Sarah Polk." In *The Smithsonian Book of First Ladies: Their Lives, Times, and Issues.* New York: Henry Holt and Company, 1996, 68–73.

Means, Marianne. *The Women in the White House.* New York: Random House, 1963.

National First Ladies Library. *Biographies: First Ladies of the United States.* Available online. URL: http://www.firstladies.org/biographies. Accessed on January 4, 2007.

Pregnancy Discrimination Act (1978)

Passed in response to the Supreme Court's decision in GEDULDIG V. AIELLO, which found that pregnancy discrimination was not illegal sex discrimination under the Fourteenth Amendment, the Pregnancy Discrimination Act law amended TITLE VII OF THE CIVIL RIGHTS ACT OF 1964 to explicitly prohibit discrimination on the basis of pregnancy, childbirth, or related medical conditions. In this sense, discrimination due to pregnancy is treated as unlawful sex-based discrimination. As a result, employers could not question potential hires about their plans to have children, and employers had to treat pregnancy just like any other temporary disability, meaning they had to provide extend benefits equally. For example, if the employer allowed workers sick time or disability for other medical conditions, they had to do so for pregnancy and recovery from childbirth as well.

Proponents of the law argued that pregnancy was a major force in limiting women's full equality in the workplace because it offered employers a way to refuse to hire women or fire women once they became pregnant. Opponents such as the Chamber of Commerce of the United States and the National Association of Manufacturers argued that the law would be too expensive for businesses and that women would abuse the benefits promised by the legislation. They argued that pregnancy, unlike other temporary disabilities, was a voluntary condition. Similar arguments were made more than two decades later in opposition to the FAMILY AND MEDICAL LEAVE ACT (1993) allowing employees to take unpaid leave to care for a new baby, an adopted infant, or a sick family member.

Further Reading

Mezey, Susan Gluck. *Elusive Equality: Women's Rights, Public Policy, and the Law.* Boulder, Colo.: Lynne Rienner, 2003.

President's Commission on the Status of Women (PCSW)   President John F. Kennedy

signed Executive Order 10980 establishing the President's Commission on the Status of Women (PCSW) on December 14, 1961. The commission was Kennedy's response to criticism from female activists in the Democratic Party for failing to appointment women to cabinet-level posts and other high-ranking positions. A 20-member panel appointed by the president from recommendations by ESTHER PETERSON, the director of the Women's Bureau, U.S. Department of Labor, included leaders of national women's organizations and labor union representatives. At the request of Peterson, who wanted the commission to be politically and administratively effective, the president also appointed cabinet secretaries from the Departments of Labor; Health, Education and Welfare; Commerce; and Agriculture, as well as the attorney general and the head of the Civil Service Commission. Former first lady ELEANOR ROOSEVELT served as chair until her death in 1962.

Seven committees—civil and political rights, education, federal employment, home and community, private employment, protective labor legislation, and social insurance—chaired by PCSW members but composed of additional consultants from the fields of education, health, and business and from the ranks of women's organizations carried out President Kennedy's mandate to make recommendations that would remove barriers to women's full participation in public life. The PCSW formalized alliances among women's organizations that until that time had managed only tenuous and tentative coalitions because of differences over support of the EQUAL RIGHTS AMENDMENT. Committee investigations and subsequent recommendations published in the commission's final report in 1965, *American Women*, publicized persistent inequality and held out the promise of collective action for women's rights.

Further Reading

Harrison, Cynthia. *On Account of Sex: The Politics of Women's Issues, 1945–1968.* Berkeley: University of California Press, 1988.

Hartmann, Susan M. *From Margin to Mainstream: American Women and Politics since 1960.* New York: Alfred Knopf, 1989.

Laughlin, Kathleen A. *Women's Work and Public Policy: A History of the Women's Bureau, U.S. Department of Labor, 1945–1970.* Boston: Northeastern University Press, 2000.

—Kathleen A. Laughlin

Price Waterhouse v. Hopkins (490 U.S. 228) (1989) Ann Hopkins was a senior manager with Price Waterhouse, an accounting firm. She was proposed for partnership in 1982, but her candidacy was deferred for a year. When the partners in her office refused to repropose her for partnership, she sued under TITLE VII OF THE CIVIL RIGHTS ACT OF 1964, charging that the firm had discriminated against her on the basis of sex in its partnership decisions. As evidence, she recounted a number of remarks by the partners that described her in stereotypical gender terms.

This case was one of the first to deal with subtle forms of sex discrimination in a professional setting. The District Court ruled in Hopkins's favor, finding Price Waterhouse had engaged in discrimination based on sex stereotyping. The U.S. Supreme Court ruled that biased comments were not sufficient proof of discriminatory motive, but the justices returned the case to the district court for trial to determine whether Price Waterhouse would have made the same decision based on factors other than sex. An employer who has allowed a discriminatory motive to play a part in an employment decision must prove by clear and convincing evidence that it would have made the same decision in the absence of discrimination. Price Waterhouse did not meet this burden.

See also GENDER STEREOTYPES.

Further Reading
The OYEZ Project. "*Price Waterhouse v. Hopkins,* 490 U.S. 228 (1989)." Available online. URL: http://www.oyez.org/cases/case?case=1980–1989/1988/1988_87_1167. Accessed on January 11, 2007.

prostitution Prostitution is the buying and selling of sexual services in exchange for money, goods, or other forms of compensation. Prostitution is illegal in the United States (with the exception of a few counties in Nevada) and in most countries around the world. Even so, there are more forms of prostitution available today than there have been at any other time in history. The modern commercial sex industry includes street prostitution, massage brothels, escort services, outcall services, strip clubs, lap dancing, phone sex, adult and child pornography, video and Internet pornography, and prostitution tourism. Increasingly, prostitution involves young girls and boys as clients attempt to avoid the dangers of HIV/AIDS and other sexually transmitted diseases prevalent among older sex worker populations. International trafficking in young girls and boys has attracted new attention, particularly in light of thousands of vulnerable child orphans following the tsunami in 2004. The international community is currently considering the proposed United Nations Convention Against Sexual Exploitation.

Perspectives on prostitution differ, with some arguing that prostitution is a legitimate choice for women and that individual freedom requires that the state permit women to engage in unfettered economic exchange. Others view prostitution as another form of economic subjugation of women, a result of the commodification of women's bodies. Others point to patterns of development and regulation as evidence that prostitution can only be understood within the context of PATRIARCHY. ANDREA DWORKIN, for example, writes: "Male dominance means that the society creates a pool of prostitutes by any means necessary so that men have what men need to stay on top, to feel big, literally, metaphorically, in every way." Prostitution tends to develop during historical periods when women are most excluded from public life. Women in the 18th and 19th centuries who were not confined by either slave labor or domestic labor in the home were assumed to be prostitutes, even though in reality they had few alternative means of survival. A similar pattern is visible in under-developed countries today, where there are few opportunities for economic survival for women who labor in the informal domestic sector.

Further Reading

Dworkin, Andrea. "Prostitution and Male Supremacy." In *Life and Death: Unapologetic Writings on the Continuing War against Women*. New York: Free Press, 1977.

Guy, Donna J. "Stigma, Pleasures, and Dutiful Daughters." *Journal of Women's History* 10 (1998): 181–191.

protective legislation   The Progressive movement was begun by a loose coalition of reformers emerging in the late 19th century, lasting from the 1890s to the 1920s. Progressives tended to be white, educated, middle-class men and women who believed society needed to respond to the changes wrought by industrialization, urbanization, and immigration. While their individual interests varied, all Progressives believed in the power of government to solve social problems. This interest in reform led many Progressives, particularly women, to carve out careers in education, public policy, and new fields such as public health and social work. Although women did not yet have the right to vote, they nonetheless shaped public policy by acting through such volunteer organizations as the Young Women's Christian Association, the National Consumer's League, professional associations, and trade unions.

One of the changes Progressives sought was protective legislation for workers. Historian Alice Kessler-Harris has identified two types of protective legislation: regulatory and restrictive or prohibitive. Regulatory protective legislation tried to mandate maximum hours, minimum wages, and safe working conditions. Restrictive or prohibitive legislation tried to keep women and children out of some jobs altogether on the grounds that those jobs were morally and/or physically dangerous. Progressive legislation that addressed all workers often ran into fierce resistance from the capitals and from the courts. Because of this, some reformers chose restrictive over regulatory legislation, stressing that women and children were particularly vulnerable and therefore entitled to special legal protection.

The length of the workday was one of the first Progressive targets: between 1909 and 1917, 19 states passed laws restricting how many hours per day a woman might work. Progressive reform groups also sought minimum or "living" wage regulations for women. In reality, protective legislation guaranteed that men and women were treated differently in the workplace, and most often the different treatment was based on GENDER STEREOTYPES of women's physical stamina and social stereotypes about women's proper place in society.

Wisconsin was the first state to adopt a protective law in 1867, and several states followed. Most laws limited women's hours of employment in manufacturing. Practically speaking, limiting the women's workday to 8 or 8.5 hours also limited their earning potential. Since female employees were subject to more regulation, employers were often reluctant to hire women. Oregon's statutes were challenged before the U.S. Supreme Court in MULLER V. OREGON (1908). In upholding the law, the Court ignored the precedent set in *Lochner v. New York* (1905), where a bare majority of the Court ruled that a 10-hour day workday law was unconstitutional because there was no demonstrated relation between the law and the workers' health or safety. The *Lochner* decision conceded, however, that such measures might be permissible if it could be shown that the law did in fact serve to protect health or safety. When the state of Oregon established a 10-hour workday for women only in laundries and factories, business owners attacked it on the grounds that, like the New York law at issue in *Lochner,* it bore no relation to the women's health or safety. Louis D. Brandeis defended the law for Oregon. In what has come to be known as the "Brandeis Brief," he covered the traditional legal precedents in just two pages, and then filled over 100 pages with sociological, economic and physiological data on the effect of long working hours on the health of women. Justice Brewer's opinion for the majority argued that women were in fact different from men and that these differences made the connection between the law and worker health and safety clear.

Women's rights advocates differed over whether protective legislation advanced women's status in society or hindered them in the labor force. The split resulted in organized labor's opposition to the EQUAL RIGHTS AMENDMENT (ERA) when it was first introduced in 1923. The passage of TITLE VII OF THE CIVIL RIGHTS ACT OF 1964, prohibiting discrimination in employment practices "because of sex," essentially ended the debate over protective legislation as a strategy for advancing women's rights. Labor interests then joined others in support of the ERA.

Further Reading

Kessler-Harris, Alice. *Out to Work: A History of Wage-Earning Women in the United States.* New York: Oxford University Press, 1982.

Leher, Susan. *Origins of Protective Labor Legislation for Women, 1905–1925. SUNY Series on Women and Work.* Albany: State University of New York Press, 1987.

Muncy, Robyn. *Creating a Female Dominion in American Reform, 1890–1935.* New York: Oxford University Press, 1991.

—Eileen V. Wallis

Pryce, Deborah (1951–) *congressperson*
Born on July 29, 1951, in Warren, Ohio, Deborah Pryce earned a bachelor's degree from Ohio State University in 1973 and a law degree from Capital University (Columbus, Ohio) in 1979. She entered private practice and served as an administrative law judge, as first assistant city prosecutor, as a senior assistant city attorney, and finally as an assistant city manager before being elected judge on the Franklin County Municipal Court.

Pryce was first elected to the U.S. House of Representatives in 1992. She was subsequently elected by her colleagues to serve as chair of the House Republican Conference, making her the fourth-highest ranking member and the highest-ranking Republican woman ever in the House of Representatives. Pryce is considered a moderate legislator. She has been a strong supporter of tax cuts and voted to give President George W. Bush authority to invade Iraq in 2003. As the war has gone badly, she has become a more vocal critic. She is pro-choice and a member of Republicans for Choice and the WISH LIST.

In the 109th Congress, Pryce served on the House Committee on Financial Services after 10 years on the House Rules Committee. The Committee on Financial Services has jurisdiction over the Federal Reserve, U.S. monetary policy, financial services technology issues, currency and coinage, and economic growth. Pryce is the fourth-ranking Republican on the committee and also serves as chair of the Domestic and International Monetary Policy Subcommittee. In 2006, she narrowly won reelection, defeating challenger Mary Jo Kilroy by 1,062 votes after a mandatory recount. At issue in the campaign was her vote on the war, her connection to disgraced congressman Mark Foley and the ensuing scandal, and her participation in organizing a fundraiser for Congressman Bob Ney (since indicted and convicted).

Further Reading

Barone, Michael. *The Almanac of American Politics.* Washington, D.C.: National Journal Group, 2006.

"Pryce, Deborah D." In *Biographical Directory of the United States Congress, 1774–present.* Available online. URL: http://bioguide.congress.gov/scripts/biodisplay.pl?index=P000555. Accessed on January 8, 2007.

"Representative Deborah D. Pryce (OH)." *Project Vote Smart.* Available online. URL: http://votesmart.org/bio.php?can_id=H3161103. Accessed on January 8, 2007.

—Angela Kouters

Q

Quinton, Amelia Stone (1833–1926) *social advocate, activist for Native American rights* Born into a Baptist family in Jamestown, New York on July 31, 1833, Amelia Stone Quinton started the Indian Treaty-Keeping and Protective Association (later renamed the Women's National Indian Association) with MARY BONNEY. Quinton was a teacher and a volunteer in the prison system when she joined the WOMAN'S CHRISTIAN TEMPERANCE UNION (WCTU) in 1874. She worked as a state organizer for the WCTU until her marriage to the Reverend Richard L. Quinton in 1877. The next year, she moved to Philadelphia and renewed her friendship with Mary Bonney. Through Bonney's concern over American Indian lands being made available to white settlers, Quinton and Bonney together started a petition drive to protest the breaking of treaties. They formed the Indian Treaty-Keeping and Protective Association to help publicize the situation with tribal lands and to organize a broader petition-gathering system.

In 1882, Quinton presented a petition with 100,000 signatures to Senator Henry Dawes of Massachusetts. The petition proposed a system of allocation of lands to individuals within tribes in order to both strengthen American Indians' legal right to land and to assimilate the Indians into white culture through land ownership and farming. Quinton's proposal also included provisions for educational and missionary work on tribal lands. Quinton traveled west and spoke extensively both to white women concerning the situation of Native Americans and to Indian women on reservations. During this time, she attracted many new members to her organization, which had branches in 28 states by 1886. In 1887, the Dawes Act was made law, granting individuals allotted portions of land and granting citizenship. Quinton then turned her attention to educational and missionary work among American Indians. She became president of the Women's National Indian Association in 1887 and served for 18 years, during which time the organization admitted men as members and was again renamed, becoming the National Indian Association. She died on June 23, 1926.

—Claire Curtis

R

Rankin, Jeannette (1880–1973) *congressperson* Born in Montana on July 11, 1880, Jeannette Rankin ran for Congress in 1916 and in winning became the first female elected to the House of Representatives. She was a pivotal figure who was active in the struggle for women's rights and in the peace movement her entire life.

Rankin was educated at both the University of Montana and the University of Washington. She worked initially as a teacher and subsequently moved to New York City to study social work. While in school, she joined the NATIONAL AMERICAN WOMAN SUFFRAGE ASSOCIATION (NAWSA) and worked as their legislative secretary. In 1913, she marched in the Woman Suffrage Parade in Washington prior to Woodrow Wilson's presidential inauguration. She decided to return to Montana later in 1913 to work for SUFFRAGE there. A year later, the Montana legislature approved the vote for women in that state, a victory that made Rankin famous in suffrage circles and contributed to her decision to run for Congress in 1916. She ran on a platform advocating women's suffrage, legislation to protect children, and pacifism. Rankin's election to the House of Representatives was due in large part to her own tireless campaigning and

also a concurrent prohibition ballot measure that energized many of Montana's women voters. Upon her victory, Rankin became the first woman to be elected to national political office. She was hailed by suffragists as their heroine and possible savior. After her win, an article in the *New York Times* (November 12, 1916) quoted Rankin as saying, "I am going to Washington to represent the women and children of the West, to work for an eight-hour work day for women and for laws providing that women shall receive the same wages as men for the same amount of work."

One of Rankin's first votes as a congresswoman was her vote against war with Germany in 1917. She subsequently introduced a bill (which failed) guaranteeing women who married foreigners that they could retain their U.S. citizenship, and she intervened to help women on the job deal with long work hours and dangerous and degrading work environments due to SEXUAL HARASSMENT. She attempted to mediate a mining strike in Montana, although she was seen not as a neutral party but as a union supporter. This support for Industrial Workers of the World may have done more than her pacifism to guarantee her defeat in her bid for a

U.S. Senate seat in 1918. However, it is as a pacifist that Rankin became best known politically. Her vote against war with Germany followed the platform of Alice Paul's NATIONAL WOMAN'S PARTY and rejected CARRIE CHAPMAN CATT's argument within NAWSA that women looked weak when they advocated for peace. Rankin's election to Congress had initially united the suffrage groups, but they fell apart over the issue of war.

In 1917, Rankin introduced the SUSAN B. ANTHONY amendment granting women the right to vote. The vote in the House of Representatives achieved enough yes votes (274 yes and 136 no votes) for a two-thirds majority, but the amendment failed in the Senate, and it did not pass both houses until 1919. While in Congress, Rankin also introduced a "maternity bill" providing federal funding for prenatal and infancy care. In 1921, this ultimately passed as the SHEPPARD-TOWNER MATERNITY AND INFANCY PROTECTION PROTECTION ACT. After running unsuccessfully for a Senate seat in 1918, Rankin left Congress in 1919 and as an independent began work for the Women's International League for Peace and Freedom. She subsequently moved to a farm in Georgia and started the Georgia Peace Society. During the 1920s, she campaigned for child labor laws, citizenship reform, and women's and children's rights.

In 1940, Rankin ran for Congress again on another pacifist platform, and again she won. Hers was the only vote registered against declaring war with Japan after Pearl Harbor; she said, "As a woman I can't go to war, and I refuse to send anyone else." This vote was singularly unpopular, although she was hailed for standing fast to her convictions. At the end of her two-year term, she chose not to run for Congress again and returned to Montana to care for her elderly mother. Upon her mother's death, her brother granted her the financial wherewithal to travel freely. She started a women's cooperative in Georgia in the early 1960s and traveled to India multiple times to study Gandhi's philosophy of nonviolence. At age 88, Rankin protested against the war in Vietnam, leading a march of 5,000 women (the "Jeanette Rankin Brigade") on Washington in 1968; she was joined by CORETTA SCOTT KING. While in Washington, she presented an antiwar petition to congressional leaders. In her last years, she worked to abolish the electoral college and advocated at-large congressional elections to replace single-member district representation. She considered a third run for Congress, but poor heath intervened.

Jeannette Rankin's life bridges the span of the women's movement of the 20th century, from the fight for suffrage in the early quarter of the century to the rise of second-wave feminism in the 1960s. Rankin will always be remembered as the first woman in Congress, and nothing can overshadow that remarkable "first." She

Jeannette Rankin, ca. 1916 (LIBRARY OF CONGRESS)

died in Carmel, California, on May 18, 1973, at the age of 92.

Further Reading

Josephson, Hannah. *Jeanette Rankin, First Lady in Congress.* Indianapolis: Bobbs-Merrill, 1974.

Lopach, James, and Jean A. Luckowski. *Jeanette Rankin: A Political Woman.* Boulder: University Press of Colorado, 2005.

Smith, Norma. *Jeanette Rankin: America's Conscience.* Helena: Montana Historical Society Press, 2002.

—Claire Curtis

Ray, Charlotte (1850–1911) *attorney* Born on January 13, 1850, in New York City, Charlotte E. Ray was the first black female attorney in the United States. Her father, Reverend Charles Bennett Ray, was a Congregationalist minister and prominent abolitionist. Ray was educated at the Institute for the Education of Colored Youth, graduating in 1869. Accepted at the Howard University School of Law, she taught at Howard's normal and preparatory school while attending law school in the evenings. She graduated from Howard in 1872 and was admitted to the bar of Washington, D.C. that same year (the D.C. bar had only recently removed the term *male* to describe those qualified for admission). Ray opened her own practice in Washington but had to close it for lack of business (likely due to the prejudice of possible clients). She moved to New York and became a teacher, attending conventions of the NATIONAL AMERICAN WOMAN SUFFRAGE ASSOCIATION and joining the NATIONAL ASSOCIATION OF COLORED WOMEN. Little is known about Ray after this point. She died on January 19, 1911.

—Claire Curtis

Ray, Dixy Lee (Marguerite Ray) (1914–1994) *scientist, governor of Washington State* Marguerite Ray was born in Tacoma, Washington, on September 3, 1914; in 1930, she changed her name legally to Dixy Lee Ray. She was attracted to the sciences from a young age and studied at Mills College in California, graduating as valedictorian of her class in 1937. She proceeded to graduate study in marine biology at Stanford University, where she earned a Ph.D. in 1945. In 1947, Ray entered the faculty of the zoology department at the University of Washington in Seattle, remaining there until 1972. During that period, she also served as director of Seattle's Pacific Science Center, which had been organized as part of the 1962 World's Fair in Seattle.

Ray was an active proponent of science education, especially for girls. She supported the expansion of nuclear power production in the United States, although she was also a critic of the American nuclear industry. In 1973, she was appointed by President Richard Nixon to the U.S. Atomic Energy Commission (AEC), becoming its first female commissioner. After six months, the president appointed her chair of the AEC. In that job, she emphasized public awareness of nuclear safety issues and defended the AEC's lengthy power plant licensing procedures.

Ray was chair of the AEC until it was disbanded in January 1975. She then served briefly as assistant secretary of state for environmental and scientific affairs.

Believing that scientists should take a more active role in politics, she ran in the Democratic gubernatorial primary in 1976. She narrowly defeated Seattle mayor Wes Uhlman to win the Democratic primary and won the general election over King County executive John Spellman with 54 percent of the vote. The very qualities that made her a compelling "outsider" as a candidate rendered her a controversial, one-term governor. She campaigned to reduce bureaucracy and as governor acted by reducing state welfare benefits. She angered environmentalists by her support for nuclear power plants and pro-development stances. In 1980, although she ran for reelection, she was defeated in the Democratic primary and retired to her farm on

Fox Island, Washington. Even in political retirement, she continued to write and speak out on the need for sound scientific knowledge to guide policy decisions. Dr. Ray died in Washington on January 2, 1994.

Further Reading:

Guzzo, Louis. *Is It True What They Say about Dixy? A Biography of Dixy Lee Ray.* Mercer Island, Wash.: Writing Works, 1980.

Ray, Dixy Lee. *The Nation's Energy Future.* Washington D.C.: Atomic Energy Commission, 1973.

———. *Trashing the Planet: How Science Can Help Us Deal with Acid Rain, Depletion of the Ozone, and Nuclear Waste (Among Other Things).* New York: HarperPerennial, 1992.

———. *Environmental Overkill: Whatever Happened to Common Sense?* New York: HarperPerennial, 1994.

—Laura M. Caulkins

Reagan, Nancy (Anne Frances Robbins Davis Reagan) (1921–) *first lady*

Anne Frances Robbins was born on July 6, 1921, in New York City, to Kenneth and Edith Luckett Robbins. Her mother, who called her daughter Nancy, was a stage actress, and her father sold used cars. Soon after Nancy's birth, the couple separated; they legally divorced in 1928. To enable her mother to continue to work, Nancy was sent to live with her aunt, Virginia Galbraith, in Bethesda, Maryland. In 1929, when Edith married neurosurgeon Dr. Loyal Davis, Nancy rejoined her mother and the family settled in Chicago, Illinois.

Dr. Davis was a very conservative Republican, and his views are said to have shaped Nancy's own politics. When Nancy was 14, Dr. David adopted her, and she took his name. Educated at Girls' Latin School in Chicago, Nancy was active in student government, played field hockey, and won the lead in the senior class production of *First Lady*. As a student at Smith College, she continued to study acting as a drama major. Upon graduation in 1943, she returned to Chicago, where she worked as a retail clerk at Marshall Field's department store and as a nurse's aid. She pursued her interest in acting, aided by her mother's network of contacts and friends, and performed in summer stock theater as well as with a touring company. In 1949, a screen test arranged by Spencer Tracy resulted in a beginner's contract with Metro Goldwyn Mayer. She appeared in several films, 11 in all between 1949 and 1958, and typically in a supporting role. In her penultimate movie, *Hellcats of the Navy* (1957), she played opposite Ronald Reagan.

In 1950, Nancy Davis met Ronald Reagan, who was then president of the Screen Actors Guild. The story goes that she discovered her name on a list of communist sympathizers in late 1949 and contacted Reagan to investigate the matter and to help her clear her name. (It turned out that there was another actress by the same name in Hollywood at the time). Some biographers dispute such noble motives in requesting the meeting and attribute the dinner to Nancy's desire to meet the newly eligible Ronald Reagan, whose marriage to actress Jane Wyman had just ended in a difficult divorce. The two apparently dated sporadically over the next two years, but they were eventually married on March 4, 1952, with actor William Holden and his wife as their only guests. Their first child, Patricia Anne, was born on October 22, 1952, and a son, Ronald, Jr., was born on May 20, 1958. Reagan had two children from his marriage to Wyman: Maureen, born in 1941, and Michael, adopted as an infant in 1946.

While Nancy Reagan tended to the children, Ronald moved from films to a position as the official spokesperson for General Electric, hosting a weekly television series called *General Electric Theater* and traveling on behalf of the corporation. During this time, he developed as a public speaker and as an ideological conservative. In 1962, when he lost his position with General Electric, he earned a living delivering public speeches. As a liberal Democrat in 1960, Reagan had spoken on behalf of Richard Nixon, and in 1962 he officially changed political parties and became a Republican. Politics consumed more of his time throughout the early 1960s, and he made his political debut in 1964 with a televised speech on behalf of conservative presidential candidate Barry Goldwater. Soon after, he announced that he would challenge two-term incumbent California governor Pat Brown. The Brown forces didn't take the former actor and a political novice very seriously until it was too late. Ronald Reagan won the 1966 election by a wide margin.

Nancy Reagan's eight years as first lady of California were rocky. She stirred controversy almost immediately when she referred to the historic governor's mansion in Sacramento as a "firetrap" unfit for their son, and the family rented a house in the Sacramento suburbs that friends had purchased for their use. Nancy quickly established a reputation as an over-protective wife, tending carefully and attentively to the governor's schedule and health. When she thought he was overbooked and growing tired, she called his staff and had items dropped from his schedule. Nancy's relationship with the public and the press could only be described as "strained." At very same time that second-wave FEMINISM was ascending, Nancy Reagan appeared to be retreating into a 1950s gendered lifestyle with few public causes and little expressed interest in public policy issues. Reporters wrote about the "gaze," a term coined for the way Nancy sat in rapt attention when her husband was speaking. Gradually, however, she found a set of causes she could call her own: the Foster Grandparents Program and the welfare of former prisoners of war returning from Vietnam. Nonetheless, the press continued to criticize Nancy Reagan for her interest in fashion, her penchant for expensive designer clothing "borrowed" but not returned, and her elite circle of friends. A 1968 *Saturday Evening Post* profile by essayist Joan Didion described California's first lady as "full of phoniness and playacting, insincere and overly dramatic."

Nancy Reagan, ca. 1981 (LIBRARY OF CONGRESS)

In 1976, Ronald Reagan unsuccessfully challenged President Gerald Ford for the Republican presidential nomination. Nancy was very involved in the campaign, giving speeches and press conferences on his behalf. She also monitored her husband's schedule and weighed in with recommendations for staffing changes when she felt his interests were not being served. This active involvement increased in his 1980 campaign for the presidential nomination and ultimately for the presidency. Publicly, Nancy confined herself to the role of Ronnie's companion at rallies, dinners, receptions, and speeches. However, insiders attested to the integral role she played in hiring the campaign staff and shaping Reagan's public image. As in the 1976 campaign, Nancy sought to offer herself as a contrast in style and substance to the incumbent first lady. She thought BETTY FORD too outspoken on public issues, particularly those related to women's rights and the EQUAL RIGHTS

AMENDMENT, and criticized ROSALYNN CARTER'S more direct participation in government and her influence over the policy agenda. By contrast, Nancy claimed to be merely a sounding board for her husband.

In November 1980, Reagan won a decisive victory over Jimmy Carter. The transition between the two presidencies was not an easy one. The Carters' low-key and cost-conscious White House did not suit Nancy Reagan's expectations. The inauguration proved to be one of the most expensive in history, estimated to cost nearly $16 million, most of it paid for with private donations. Washington society welcomed the Reagans and the return to high elegance they brought with them. Nancy Reagan quickly attracted negative attention from the press over her penchant for expensive ball gowns (again "borrowed, but not returned") and the renovations to the White House she planned to undertake. The redecoration effort was largely limited to the private residence, rather than the public areas of the mansion, and came with an estimated price tag of $800,000. Similarly, Mrs. Reagan moved to replace the White House china with a new set costing $200,000. These efforts would not have attracted nearly so much attention had the country not been gripped by a major economic recession. By the end of her husband's first year in office, Mrs. Reagan's public approval ratings showed that barely a quarter of the American public approved of the way she was handling the role of first lady. To be fair, there was certainly much ambivalence over what kind of first lady the public wanted since they were nearly equally critical of Rosalynn Carter's performance.

To reverse the torrent of negative press, the first lady's staff developed a three-pronged approach to rehabilitate her public image. First, they advised her to tone down her connections to elite society and drew the public's focus away from her designer dresses and lavish parties; second, Mrs. Reagan appeared on stage at the 1982 annual Gridiron Dinner dressed in ragged clothing and singing a parody of "Secondhand Rose"; and finally, she adopted a cause and dedicated herself to the "Just Say No" antidrug campaign. By nearly all accounts, these efforts paid off in terms of more favorable press coverage and in the public's perception of the first lady.

Mrs. Reagan faced a number of personal tragedies while in the White House. Perhaps the most frightening was the 1981 failed assassination attempt on her husband's life. Although the public was led to believe the bullet just glanced the president, medical records made public later showed that he had been shot in the chest with a .22 caliber handgun and nearly bled to death. Surgery to remove the bullet resulted in complications and an infection, thereby slowing his overall recovery. Insiders report that she doggedly protected the president's health and public image during the slow recovery. In 1985, she was again faced with a health crisis when the president underwent cancer surgery. In 1987, Nancy Reagan herself was diagnosed with breast cancer. Her choice of a mastectomy set off a firestorm of criticism. Some doctors argued that in making such a radical choice when a lumpectomy combined with radiation therapy was predicted to be equally effective may have deterred some women from treatment. Reagan countered that medical treatment was a personal choice, one that every woman must make for herself. Finally, both of her parents died during the eight years she lived in the White House.

The Reagans' relationship with their children was also the subject of extensive press coverage. Although they remained close to Maureen, the president's daughter from his first marriage, the relationship with Michael was nearly nonexistent. Daughter Patti chose to use Davis as her professional name in order to distance herself from her parents' conservative politics. In 1986, Patti published a autobiographical novel titled, *Homefront,* whose main characters sacrificed their family to political ambition. Ron, Jr., although remaining close to his parents, dropped out of Yale to join the Joffrey Ballet and pursue his lifelong dream of becoming a professional dancer. A political liberal like his sister, his lifestyle and career choices led to rampant speculation about his sexuality. Both Ronald and Nancy Reagan were criticized for promoting family values while doing little to tend to the value of their own family.

Although the Reagan presidency is widely regarded by historians as one that restored grandeur to the executive office and brought optimism back to America, the administration was plagued by scandal during its final years. The Iran-contra scandal and its subsequent investigation, White House chief of staff Donald Regan's firing and subsequent tell-all book, *For the Record* (1988), and the discovery that Nancy Reagan regularly consulted with a West Coast astrologer named Joan Quigley consumed the press's attention in the final years of the second term. Mrs. Reagan was accused of determining the president's schedule; including the date and time of significant events such as the Washington arms control summit between Reagan and Soviet leader Mikhail Gorbachev in 1987 and the Reykjavik summit in 1986. In her 1989 memoir *My Turn*, Mrs. Reagan asserted that she merely consulted with Quigley to determine good days and bad days for the president to travel out of town.

The Reagans left Washington in January 1989 after two full terms in office and returned to their ranch in California. Nancy Reagan worked on her memoirs and continued her antidrug efforts. In a handwritten letter to the nation, published in national newspapers on November 5, 1994, Ronald Reagan announced that he had been diagnosed with Alzheimer's disease. The president concluded the letter with his trademark optimism: "I now begin the journey that will lead me into the sunset of my life. I know that for America there will always be a bright dawn ahead. Thank you, my friends. May God always bless you." As the president's health failed, Nancy Reagan became his full-time caretaker and, as she had been throughout their life together, the fierce protector of his public image. As his disease progressed, she and other members of the immediate family joined the Alzheimer's Association in raising funds for research and in calling on the government to promote (rather than prohibit) embryonic stem cell research in the hope of finding a cure. President Reagan died on June 5, 2004, in Bel Air, Los Angeles, California, at the age of 93.

First Lady Nancy Reagan's legacy is a work in progress. Although she herself eschewed a direct policy role in her husband's administration, historians continue to uncover a far more active engagement in public affairs than previously known. In many respects, her tenure as first lady reflects the ambiguity of the position in a modern world. Her predecessors faced similar challenges in carving out a publicly acceptable role in a position that emerged more than two centuries ago.

Further Reading
National First Ladies Library. *Biographies: First Ladies of the United States.* Available online. URL: http://www.firstladies.org/biographies. Accessed on January 4, 2007.
Reagan, Nancy, with William Novak. *My Turn: The Memoirs of Nancy Reagan.* New York: Random House, 1989.
Reeves, Richard. *President Reagan: The Triumph of Imagination.* New York: Simon and Schuster, 2006.
Regan, Donald T. *For the Record: From Wall Street to Washington.* New York: Harcourt, 1988.
Schneider, Dorothy, and Carl J. Schneider. "Anne Francis (Nancy) Robbins David Reagan" *First Ladies: A Biographical Dictionary.* New York: Checkmark Books, 2001, 319–328.

Redstockings (Redstockings of the Women's Liberation Movement)

The name *Redstockings* combines "bluestockings," a dismissive term for educated and independent women in the 18th and 19th centuries, with "red" for social revolution. Early in 1969, after the breakup of New York Radical Women, Ellen Willis and Shulamith Firestone formed Redstockings, a group mainly active in New York City and, later, in Gainesville, Florida. Firestone soon left to form New York Radical Feminists, and a group called Redstockings West formed in San Francisco in 1970, though their activities were separate from the New York group. The East Coast Redstockings split up in 1970, but the group reformed under new leadership in 1973 and has been active ever since.

According to the Redstockings Web site (www.afn.org/~redstock/), they are a "nonprofit educational and scientific organization for the furtherance of the women's rights movement and the organized efforts of women to better their situation." From the early 1970s, the group has been influential in focusing attention on women's rights through phrases like "sisterhood is powerful" and for politicizing such things as housework, consciousness raising, and beauty pageants. Its brand of radical FEMINISM was often at odds with others in the women's rights movement, from the NATIONAL ORGANIZATION FOR WOMEN to advocates of LESBIAN SEPARATISM. Today Redstockings considers itself more of a think tank. In 1989, the group began Archives for Action, a project whose aim is "to make the formative and radical 1960s experience of the movement more widely available for the taking stock needed for new understanding and improved strategies." The group's original 1969 manifesto can be read online at http://tinyurl.com/ypeqe4.

Reed v. Reed (404 U.S. 71) (1971)   This case advanced the general cause of women's rights significantly when the U.S. Supreme Court applied the equal-protection clause of the Fourteenth Amendment for the first time in a case involving sex discrimination. Sex became a category of discrimination subject to "special" scrutiny by the U.S. Supreme Court. Idaho probate law included the following clause used in determining who should administer the estate of a person dying without a will: "Of several persons claiming and equally entitled to administer, males must be preferred to females, relatives of whole to those of half blood."

Sally and Cecil Reed both petitioned for appointment as administrator of their son Rich-

ard's estate after he committed suicide. The Idaho Probate Court ordered that Cecil Reed be appointed administrator in accordance with state code. Sally Reed appealed the court's order, arguing that Idaho's law violated her constitutional rights under the equal-protection clause of the Fourteenth Amendment. The District Court agreed and voided the two sections of the law that relied on sex and ordered that the decision be based on relative merit. However, upon appeal, the Idaho Supreme Court reinstated the Probate Court's decision (in favor of Cecil), ruling that the legislature had "evidently concluded that in general men are better qualified to act as an administrator than women."

Sally Reed appealed to the U.S. Supreme Court, and future justice RUTH BADER GINSBURG joined in her representation. Reed's team argued that women's rights were protected under the equal-protection guarantees of the Fourteenth Amendment. This time, the U.S. Supreme Court agreed. In a unanimous decision, the Court held that any classification based on sex must be "reasonable, not arbitrary" and that the distinctions made between classes of people must be based on criteria related to the objective of the statute. This case marked the first of several instances where the Court reversed its previous trend of accepting stereotypes of men and women as the basis for differential treatment. Following the *Reed* decision, lawmakers could no longer be sure that laws based on stereotypical assumptions about men and women would withstand judicial scrutiny.

See also FRONTIERO V. RICHARDSON.

Further Reading
Lindgren, J. Ralph, Nadine Taub, Beth Ann Wolfson, and Carla M. Palumbo. *The Law of Sex Discrimination*, 3rd ed. Belmont, Calif.: Thomson Wadsworth, 2005.

Reno, Janet (1938–) *attorney general*   Janet Reno was the first woman attorney general of the United States of America. Nominated by President Bill Clinton on February 11, 1993, Reno was selected as a nominee for attorney general following the unsuccessful nominations of Zoe Baird and Kimba Wood. Both of these nominees ultimately withdrew over tax issues associated with their CHILD CARE arrangements, a situation the press dubbed NANNYGATE. Reno served two complete terms in the Clinton administration, becoming the second-longest-serving attorney general in U.S. history (after William Wirt).

Reno was born on July 21, 1938, in Miami, Florida. Her father, Henry Reno, came to the United States from Denmark and worked as a police reporter for the *Miami Herald*. Jane Wood, Reno's mother, raised her children and then became an investigative reporter for the *Miami News*. In 1960, Reno earned a B.S. from Cornell University where she majored in chemistry. That same year, she became one of only 16 women in a class of more than 500 students at Harvard Law School. She received her LL.B. in 1963, but like many women lawyers of her era, she had difficulty getting a job because of her sex.

In 1971, Reno was named staff director of the Judiciary Committee of the Florida House of Representatives. In this position, she worked to revise the Florida court system. She worked for the Dade County State's Attorney's Office from 1973 until 1976, when she entered private practice. In 1978, Reno was appointed state attorney general for Dade County. She was elected to the office in November 1978 and was returned to office by the voters four more times. She focused on reforming the juvenile justice system, pursued delinquent fathers for child support payments, and established the Miami Drug Court.

In March 1993, one month after her confirmation as U.S. attorney general, Reno took responsibility for the fatal February 28 showdown at the Branch Davidian Compound in Waco, Texas, which led to a 51-day siege. In doing so, she become a target for both the right and the left. She was also criticized for her decision in the matter concerning Elián González, a young boy who became embroiled in a custody dispute between his father in Cuba and relatives in Miami. (He was returned to his father in June 2000.) Throughout her tenure, Reno emphasized using the law and its enforcement to improve society. To that end, she enforced environmental regulations and civil rights laws, cracked down on school violence, advocated victim's rights, and vigorously prosecuted white-collar crime.

In 2002, after leaving office, Reno announced as a candidate for the Democratic nomination for governor of Florida. She traveled the state in a red pick-up truck meeting voters but ultimately lost the nomination. Today Reno tours the country giving speeches on topics relating to the criminal justice system and remains a staunch advocate for the safety and interests of adolescents and children.

reproductive rights See ABORTION; BIRTH CONTROL MOVEMENT.

reproductive technology Reproductive technology refers to the variety of ways that technology is used or may one day be used in reproduction. Some examples currently in use include artificial insemination, embryo transfer, in vitro fertilization, hormone treatments, and embryo testing. Anticipated technologies include cloning and genetic engineering. Contraception is viewed as a reproductive technology as it controls fertility. The most widely used reproduction aid is artificial insemination (AI). AI can include use of a partner's sperm or use of donor sperm. Both mechanically introduce a high concentration of sperm into the vagina. Embryo transfer takes a fertilized egg from one woman's body and transfers it to another woman who carries it to gestation. In vitro fertilization is a procedure where the sperm and the egg are combined in a petri dish and then implanted into a woman's body. Hormone treatments to stimulate fertility in men and women, usually through pills or shots, may be used as a precursor to these intrusive technologies. Embryonic testing allows doctors and parents to learn information such as the child's sex or genetic diseases before birth. Like many reproductive technologies, embryonic testing has provoked controversy as some fear this will lead to increased termination of pregnancy. The ethical implications of human cloning or genetically engineering children continue to divide the science community and the general public.

Further Reading

Alpern, Kenneth D., ed. *The Ethics of Reproductive Technology.* New York and Oxford: Oxford University Press, 1992.

Saetnan, Ann Rudinow, Nelly Oudshoorn, and Marta Kirejvzyk. *Bodies of Technology: Women's Involvement With Reproductive Medicine.* Columbus: Ohio State University, 2000.

—Kristen A. Contos

Rice, Condoleezza (1954–) *National Security Advisor, secretary of state*

Condoleezza Rice represents many firsts in American politics. She became the first woman and African American to serve as National Security Advisor and the first African-American woman to hold the top diplomatic post of secretary of state.

Rice was born on November 14, 1954, at the height of the civil rights movement, in Birmingham, Alabama, to middle-class African-American parents. Growing up in the segregated South, Rice learned from an early age the importance of family and education as "armors against prejudice." Both of her parents were educators who developed a strong appreciation for classical music. This was reflected in them naming their only child after a musical notation, *con dolcezza,* meaning to play "with sweetness." Rice herself cultivated this love for classical music and is today an accomplished pianist.

Entering college at the early age of 15 and graduating by age 19 with a political science degree from the University of Denver, Rice went on to earn her master's (1975) and Ph.D. in political science (1981) from Notre Dame and the University of Denver, respectively. While in graduate school at the University of Denver, Rice was a student of MADELINE ALBRIGHT's father, Josef Korbel, a socialist democrat and former diplomat. Under Korbel's stewardship, she studied Soviet diplomacy and politics. It was during this period that she developed a fascination for international relations and Soviet politics in particular.

After graduate school, Rice joined the faculty of Stanford University and quickly carved out a niche as an arms control and disarmament specialist. Based on her expertise in these areas and as a Soviet specialist, Rice gained the attention of the foreign policy community in Washington, D.C. She worked closely with the Joint Chiefs of Staff as part of the Council on Foreign Relations and in 1989 became director of the Soviet and Eastern European Affairs section of the National Security Council. Soon the George H. W. Bush administration made her a special assistant to the president for national security affairs. During this time, Rice was instrumental in shaping the administration's Eastern European and Soviet policy.

By the time George W. Bush decided to run in the 2000 presidential election, he had begun to surround himself with many of his father's previous advisors, and Dr. Rice became his foreign policy advisor. Upon winning the election, Bush named Condoleezza Rice as his National Security Advisor. Rice's appointment was welcomed across party lines for its historic precedent. However, the Bush administration's policy toward Iraq and the events leading up to the 2003 U.S. invasion of Iraq (particularly September 11, 2001, and relations with the United Nations) marked the end of Rice's honeymoon period of bipartisan praise and support. She soon became the lightning rod for those opposed to the Bush foreign policy of preemption. Seen as one of the major architects of Bush's foreign policy, Rice came under heavy fire during the bipartisan 9/11 Commission hearings, portrayed by the left as incompetent for her failure to take seriously warnings of potential attacks on U.S. soil.

The assassination of Rice's character was highly politicized and racialized. Editorial cartoons by liberals, depicting Rice as an "ebonics-speaking, big-lipped, black mammy who just loves her 'massa'" enraged conservatives and black women's groups. Conservatives and black women's organizations repeatedly called on the democratic leadership, "civil rights leadership, and feminist organizations" to denounce the racist and sexist portrayals of Dr. Rice. While the condemnation by conservatives was viewed by many as a political opportunity to lambaste the left, the support for Rice from black women's organizations was surprising to the mainstream media. On one hand, African-American women have perceived Bush's policies as racists and antifamily, while on the other they are consciously aware of the fact that the Bush administration, unlike previous administrations, has appointed a number of African Americans to key decision-making positions. Furthermore, for African-American women, the racist depictions of Rice represent the struggles and obstacles all women of color face in a predominantly white male–controlled society.

The confirmation of Condoleezza Rice as secretary of state on January 26, 2005, by a vote of 85-13, was a cause for celebration for many within the conservative camp. However, Rice attracted the most negative votes against any nomination for secretary of state since 1825, which signaled the desire of liberals and many from within the international community to hold her accountable for the administration's failures in Iraq and in the war on terrorism writ large. As secretary of state, Rice has articulated a broad vision for U.S. foreign policy characterized by "transformational diplomacy." She believes that promoting democratic reform and basic rights, particularly in the Middle East, is the best defense against another terrorist attack. She has also undertaken a reform and restructuring initiative within the U.S. Department of State in support of transformational diplomacy. Diplomats have been redeployed to "hot spots" around the world, including India, China, Nigeria, Indonesia, and Lebanon. Diplomats are also required to serve in hardship locations and become fluent in two foreign languages, such as Chinese or Arabic. She has urged the administration to pursue regional approaches to problems that stretch across borders (such as terrorism, drug trafficking, and disease) and to partner with countries to assist in building internal mechanisms that promote self-governance and stability.

Rice's attention as secretary of state has been focused primarily on the Middle East. She has said that the Iraq War "set out to help the people of the Middle East transform their societies," and when the Iraqi people turned out to vote in large numbers in 2005 to elect a constitutional government, she declared the initiative a success, comparing it to post–World War II reconstruction efforts. She has resisted characterizing the Iraq war as a "civil war" (although admitting that the term "accurately describes key elements of the Iraqi conflict, including the hardening of ethno-sectarian identities") and went to Congress to encourage members to support the president's recommendation for a "troop surge" in February 2007. The Iraq War, more unpopular than ever in 2007, continued to shadow any accomplishments Secretary Rice may have had in other areas; however, Rice has reinvigorated her position with diplomatic activism, by promoting Israel's withdrawal from the Gaza Strip to ease the Palestinian conflict, encouraging six-party talks to get North Korea to stop its pursuit of nuclear weapons, and trying to stop Sudan's genocide. Most recently, Rice has stepped up efforts to get Iran to suspend its uranium enrichment program.

Although once widely touted as a formidable candidate for the presidency in 2008, those aspirations have faded as the War in Iraq continues and the current president's approval ratings fall to 30 percent. *Time* magazine has named Rice one of the world's 100 most influential people four times (she is only one of two African Americans to have achieved this status), and she was ranked as the most powerful woman by *Forbes* magazine in 2004.

Further Reading

Felix, Antonia. *Condi: The Condoleeza Rice Story.* New York: New Market Press, 2005.
Rice, Condoleezza, with Philip Zelikow. *Germany Unified and Europe Transformed: A Study in Statecraft.* Boston: Harvard University Press, 1995.

—Hollis France

Richards, Ann (Dorothy Ann Willis Richards) (1933–2006) *governor of Texas*

Dorothy Ann Willis was born on September 1, 1933, in Lakeview, Texas, the only child of Robert Cecil and Mildred Warren Willis. She grew up in Waco, Texas, and attended Baylor University on a debate scholarship. She married David Richards in 1953 and graduated in 1954. The couple then moved to Austin, where Ann earned a teaching certificate and taught junior high history and social studies. She and her husband had two daughters and two sons.

Richards was active in local politics, campaigning on behalf of women's rights and gay rights and progressive politicians. In 1976, she won her first elective office by defeating a three-term incumbent for a seat on the Travis County Commissioner Court. The court's first female commissioner, she served for six years. During this period, she drank heavily and sought treatment for alcohol abuse; in addition, her marriage ended in divorce. She was elected state treasurer in 1982 and again in 1986, this time without opposition. In 1988, she attracted national attention with her keynote address to the Democratic National Convention. Throughout the speech, she chastised Republican George H. W. Bush with the line: "Poor George, he can't help it. . . . He was born with a silver foot in his mouth."

When the incumbent Texas governor decided not to run in 1990, Ann Richards won the Democratic nomination over former governor Mark White. The campaign against Republican Clayton Williams was extraordinarily nasty. Williams, a successful businessman with a personal fortune, spent a considerable sum on the race and began to attract the attention of an increasingly conservative electorate; he was leading in the polls by 20 points until he made a number of political gaffes. At a public debate, Williams refused to shake Richards's hand, and just a few weeks later he publicly likened rape to a rainstorm, "as long as it's inevitable, you might as well lie back and enjoy it." Richards narrowly won the race with 49 percent of the vote.

Between January 15, 1991, and January 17, 1995, Ann Richards served as the governor of Texas. She was a popular governor, known for her sharp tongue and quick Texas wit. Richards tackled a slumping economy with a program of economic revitalization that yielded growth when the rest of the nation's economy was shrinking. Part of her strategy was to reform the regulatory institutions in the state, facilitating more competition for business and industry. She also reformed the Texas prison system, attempted to reform the way school districts were funded and operated, and introduced a state lottery. She appointed women and other minorities to over half of the positions available, and she was a strong feminist voice for progressive reforms in the interest of minority rights.

In 1994, Richards lost her reelection bid to Republican George W. Bush, winning 46 percent of the vote to Bush's 53 percent. Although she never again held public office, Richards worked as a political consultant and continued to campaign for progressive candidates in Texas and throughout the nation. She served on a number of corporate boards; was a senior adviser at the Washington law firm of Verner, Liipfert, Bernhard, McPherson and Hand; and worked for Public Strategies Inc., an Austin-based public relations and marketing firm. Richards was diagnosed with esophageal cancer in March 2006, and died at her home in Austin on September 13, 2006. She was 73 years old.

Further Reading

Morris, Celia. *Storming the Statehouse: Running for Governor with Ann Richards and Diane Feinstein.* New York: Scribner, 1992.

Tolleson-Rinehart, Sue, and Jeanie R. Stanley. *Claytie and the Lady: Ann Richards, Gender, and Politics in Texas.* Austin: University of Texas Press, 1994.

Richards, Ellen Swallow (1842–1911) *chemist, ecofeminist, educator* Ellen Henrietta Swallow was born on December 3, 1842, in Dunstable, Massachusetts, the daughter of parents who placed strong importance on education. She attended Vassar College, where she initially pursued astronomy but later switched to chemistry, earning her B.A. degree in 1870. She was the first woman to earn a degree in chemistry. After failing to find work as an industrial chemist, she enrolled at the Massachusetts Institute of Technology (MIT)—the first female student in MIT's history. Three years later, she was awarded a B.A. degree from MIT and an M.A. from Vassar for her thesis on the chemical analysis of iron ore. She received a Ph.D. from MIT in 1886.

In 1875, Ellen Swallow married Robert Richards, chair of MIT's mine engineering department. She worked as an unpaid professor for MIT—its first female professor—in programs especially created for women. From 1884 until her death, she was an instructor for the Lawrence Equipment Station, devoted to sanitary chemistry.

In 1881, Ellen Richards helped start the Association of Collegiate Alumnae, which would become the AMERICAN ASSOCIATION OF UNIVERSITY WOMEN. Richards was interested in both increasing girls' knowledge of science and in improving the domestic life in cities by focusing on achieving healthier homes. She used her house in Jamaica Plain, near Boston, as a model for sanitary living, emphasizing increased air flow, the removal of lead pipes, the directing of sewage lines away from water supplies and using plants to increase oxygen. As a result of Richard's work, Massachusetts became the first state in the country to establish water-quality standards as well as the first modern sewage treatment plant. Richards also initiated the study of home economics focusing on the most efficient way to perform household tasks. She believed in applying scientific principles to domestic situations, and her work in this area led to the creation of the field of home economics. In this way she could be considered the country's first ecofeminist. Ellen Richards died on March 30, 1911.

Further Reading

Levine, Susan. *Degrees of Equality: The American Association of University Women and the Challenge of Twentieth Century Feminism.* Philadelphia: Temple University Press, 1995.

—Claire Curtis

right to life movement The origin of the modern right to life, or pro-life, movement can be found in the 1973 U.S. Supreme Court decision on ROE V. WADE. Antiabortion activists organized quickly to begin working to overturn the decision on different fronts, lobbying Congress to enact legislation that would circumscribe *Roe*'s influence. There is no single organization dominating the movement, although the National Right to Life Committee based in Washington, D.C., maintains a high profile on a number of issues, including right to die or assisted suicide statutes, euthanasia, and human cloning. Most organizations affiliated with the movement are religiously based, many with fundamentalist Christian roots.

The movement has attracted negative public attention over the level of violence directed at ABORTION providers and women's health clinics in recent years. The 1998 shooting death of Dr. Barnett Slepian; the 1998 bombing of the New Woman, All Women Health Care Clinic in Birmingham, Alabama; the gassing of clinics in Florida; and the rash of anthrax threats against clinics across the nation following the September 11, 2001, terrorist attacks diminished public support. However, pro-life advocates have experienced a number of legislative successes under the George W. Bush administration and a Republican-controlled Congress. The Partial-Birth Abortion Ban Act, signed by President Bush in 2003, is the first federal ban on an abortion method enacted since the Supreme Court legalized abortion in 1973. The Hyde-Weldon Conscience Protection Amendment, signed in January 2005, prohibits any federal, state, or local government agency or program from discriminating against any individual or institutional health care provider because the provider does not provide, pay for, provide coverage for, or refer for abortions. In addition, President Bush reinstated the global GAG RULE upon taking office in 2001, effectively rendering U.S. foreign aid policy pro-life in character.

See also SUSAN B. ANTHONY LIST.

Further Reading

Feldt, Gloria. *The War on Choice: The Right Wing Attack on Women's Rights and How to Fight Back.* New York: Bantam Books, 2004.

Wagner, Teresa R., ed. *Back to the Drawing Board: The Future of the Pro-Life Movement.* South Bend, Ind.: St. Augustine's Press, 2003.

Roe v. Wade (410 U.S. 113) (1973)

This landmark case originated in Texas in March 1970. SARAH WEDDINGTON, an Austin attorney, brought the case on behalf of Norma McCorvey, an unmarried pregnant woman ("Jane Roe" was an alias used to protect her identity at the time). The intent of the case was to challenge the Texas abortion statute that made having or attempting to perform an ABORTION a crime, except for the purpose of saving the life of the mother. The suit claimed that the law was unconstitutional, vague, and violated the rights guaranteed to pregnant women by the First, Fourth, Fifth, Ninth, and Fourteenth Amendments.

Justice Harry Blackmun wrote the opinion for the 7-2 majority (William Rehnquist and Byron White dissented). Having already carved out a right to privacy in certain personal decisions in GRISWOLD V. CONNECTICUT (1965), Blackmun based his decision on the current state of medical knowledge and attempted to balance the privacy interests of the individual woman with the state's legitimate interest in "preserving and protecting the health of the pregnant woman . . . and that it has still another important and legitimate interest in protecting the potentiality of human life." To do so, he created an architecture wherein a full-term pregnancy is divided into trimesters (of about 3 months each). The Court ruled that a state cannot restrict a woman's right to an abortion during the first trimester; a state can regulate the abortion procedure during the second trimester "in ways that are reasonably related to maternal health"; and in the third trimester, demarcating the viability of the fetus, a state can choose to restrict or even to proscribe abortion as it sees fit.

This case has generated endless controversy among legal scholars, abortion and antiabortion rights activists, and those in the medical profession. Although the central holding in the case affirming a woman's right to an abortion in the first trimester still stands, access to abortion has been significantly curtailed by state restrictions and regulations. Federal action has restricted funding for abortion for women without private funds (for example, the HYDE AMENDMENT and *HARRIS V. MCRAE,* 1980), imposed a GAG RULE on clinics receiving federal funding (see *RUST V. SULLIVAN,* 1991), and banned late-term abortions (so-called partial birth abortions) in a law passed by Congress and signed by President George W. Bush in 2003. The federal ban was immediately challenged in court, and on June 1, 2004, District Court judge Phyllis Hamilton declared the act unconstitutional, saying it infringed on a woman's constitutionally protected right to choose. The ruling initially applied only to PLANNED PARENTHOOD FEDERATION OF AMERICA clinics and their doctors. The U.S. Supreme Court heard oral arguments on two cases challenging the lower court rulings on the Partial-Birth Abortion Ban Act of 2003: *Gonzales v. Carhart* and *Gonzales v. Planned Parenthood Federation of America*. Both cases were argued in autumn 2006, and a decision declaring the ban constitutional was delivered in the spring of 2007.

In 1992, the Supreme Court decision in PLANNED PARENTHOOD OF SOUTHEASTERN PENNSYLVANIA V. CASEY upheld *Roe* and restated that women have a constitutionally protected right to seek an abortion before fetal viability; however, the decision allowed states to restrict abortion access as long as the restrictions do not impose an "undue burden" on women. When Nebraska passed a law banning late-term or partial-birth abortions, the Court found that it violated the "undue burden" test and ruled it unconstitutional (STENBERG V. CARHART, 2000). The Nebraska statute failed to provide an exception protecting the health of the woman, and the Court determined that the definition of the procedures banned was so broad and vague that it could be interpreted to unduly limit procedures used in earlier stages of pregnancy, thus creating an undue burden. This decision effectively invalidated 29 similar state bans.

The Court also granted states more leeway in regulating the conditions under which abortions could occur. State legislatures intent on limiting abortion have adopted a wide variety of regulations, including parental consent and notification laws, mandatory waiting periods, a requirement for counseling prior to the abortion procedure, hospital and physician requirements limiting who can perform abortions and where abortions can be performed, limits on private insurance coverage for abortions, and, most recently, targeted regulation of abortion providers. By 2006, 34 states had passed laws that subjected abortion providers to reporting and licensing regulations and abortion facilities to building code regulations that are not applied in other medical instances. In 2006, another 12 states considered adopting similar laws.

Abortion has become so controversial that many doctors refuse to perform abortions and medical schools have all but stopped training new doctors in the procedure. The ALAN GUTTMACHER INSTITUTE found that in 2000, 87 percent of U.S. counties did not have a single abortion provider. One-third of American women lived in these counties, which meant they would have to travel outside their county to obtain an abortion. Of women obtaining abortions in 2000, 25 percent traveled at least 50 miles, and 8 percent traveled more than 100 miles. In South Dakota, for example, a woman may have to travel as far as 400 miles to the one abortion clinic in the state. The single doctor in South Dakota who performs abortions travels to the state from Minnesota.

South Dakota became the latest test for the Supreme Court's possible willingness to overturn the core holding in *Roe v. Wade*. On March 6, 2006, South Dakota governor Mike Rounds signed a bill that would effectively ban all abortions by making it a felony for doctors to perform any abortion, except to save the life of the woman. The bill was intentionally and very carefully crafted to set up a legal challenge to *Roe v. Wade*. An immediate court challenge blocked the law's implementation, and a petition drive to overturn the law landed it on the November 7, 2006, ballot as "Referred Law 6." Voters in South Dakota were asked to affirm the law or reject it. By a margin of 56 to 44 percent, the voters rejected the law.

The battle over abortion is far from over. The core holding in *Roe v. Wade* that recognizes a woman's constitutional right to have an abortion is now viewed as so vulnerable by pro-choice advocates that some states have taken steps to ensure that abortion remains legal within the state even if *Roe* is overturned. To date, these include Nebraska, Hawaii, Maryland, Maine, Washington, Connecticut, and California. In another 10 states, the state supreme court has already determined that the state constitution would protect a woman's right to abortion in the absence of *Roe* (Alaska, California, Florida, Massachusetts, Minnesota, Montana, New Jersey, New Mexico, Tennessee and West Virginia). Vermont is the only state in the United States that has not passed at least one law regarding abortion since the *Roe v. Wade* decision in 1973.

Further Reading

Baird, Robert, and Stuart Rosenbaum. *The Ethics of Abortion: Pro-Life v. Pro-Choice.* New York: Prometheus Books, 2001.

Gorney, Cynthia. *Articles of Faith: A Frontline History of the Abortion Wars.* New York: Simon and Schuster, 2000.

Tribe, Lawrence. *Abortion: A Clash of Absolutes.* New York: W.W. Norton, 1992.

Weddington, Sarah. *A Question of Choice.* New York: Penguin Books, 1993.

Roosevelt, Edith (Edith Kermit Carow Roosevelt) (1861–1948) *first lady*

Edith Kermit Carow was born on August 6, 1861, in Norwich, Connecticut, to Charles and Gertrude Elizabeth Tyler Carow. Her father's bouts with alcoholism and her mother's retreat into hypochondria robbed Edith of a happy childhood in her own home. However, the Carows and Roosevelts were neighbors, and Edith joined the four Roosevelt children in instruction in their home. Edith and Theodore Roosevelt knew one another and were friends throughout their childhood, while Edith considered Theodore's sister Corinne her best friend. When she was 10, Edith enrolled in the Comstock School, where she focused on music, literature, and French. As she matured, she maintained close contact with the Roosevelt family, including Theodore. Reportedly he proposed to her on several occasions between 1877 and 1878, but she argued that they were too young for marriage. In 1878, Theodore Roosevelt met Alice Lee and fell in love. They were married in October 1880. The following year, she gave a party for the couple in celebration of Theodore's first election to the New York Assembly.

Three years later, Alice died giving birth to a daughter, also named Alice. After Edith and Theodore accidentally met at his sister's house in 1885, they renewed their relationship, and they married in London on December 2, 1886. Edith and Theodore were well suited for one another: She was his intellectual equal and shared his political ambitions. When the couple returned from their honeymoon, Edith was pregnant. She insisted that little Alice come live with them, and they moved to Sagamore Hill, the house that Theodore built for his first wife in Oyster Bay, Long Island. On September 13, 1887, Edith gave birth to a son Theodore. He was followed by Kermit (b. 1889), Ethel (b. 1891), Archibald (b. 1894), and Quentin (b. 1897).

In 1889, President Benjamin Harrison appointed Theodore Roosevelt as civil service commissioner. Roosevelt subsequently served as police commissioner of New York and assistant secretary of the navy, and he shipped off to fight with the "Rough Riders" in the Spanish-American War before running for governor of New York in 1898. Upon his election as governor, the family moved to Albany, and Edith renovated the Governor's Mansion to accommodate their family. Although she implored Theodore not to seek the vice presidency, his status as a war hero led him to be drafted at the Republican convention. In September 1901, only six months after William McKinley's inauguration, he was assassinated, elevating Theodore Roosevelt to the presidency at the age of 42.

Edith accepted her role as the president's lady with some trepidation, fearing the assassination of her husband. However, she adjusted to life in the White House, and the children proved to be the source of endless press stories, amusing the nation with their animals and their antics. Edith was an experienced entertainer. The Roosevelts persuaded Congress to appropriate $500,000 for a new wing of offices on the west side of the building, leaving the entire second floor as the family's residence. The family moved to Sagamore Hill for six months as the building and renovations were completed. Edith saw to every detail. The plumbing, lighting, and heating systems were all upgraded, and in an effort to control Theodore Roosevelt's weight, she had a tennis court installed on the grounds. She added to the collection of White House china and put the collection gathered by CAROLINE HARRISON on display. She also gathered portraits of each of the former first ladies and lined the walls of a ground-floor corridor where the china was also on display.

Edith Roosevelt played a more substantive role as a diplomat and political ambassador during her husband's second term in office. She served as a conduit to the president from a trusted British ambassador during the Russo-Japanese War crisis (1904–05) and toured the country with him whenever possible. In 1905, they sailed together to inspect the construction of the Panama Canal. When Theodore Roosevelt won the Nobel Peace Prize for his mediation in the Russo-Japanese War, he and Edith agreed to use the prize money to establish the Industrial Peace Committee.

Edith Kermit Carow Roosevelt (LIBRARY OF CONGRESS)

The Roosevelts left the White House in 1908, honoring his promise to serve only one elected term as president. However, they both regretted the decision not to seek the nomination. In order to occupy her husband during his first years out of power, Edith arranged for a safari. She too found that she missed life in the White House and so traveled to Europe with her children. In March 1910, she met Theodore in Khartoum, and together they headed to Europe, where welcoming crowds awaited them at every stop. Teddy Roosevelt longed to return to the White House, but his attempts to regain prominence in the Republican Party ended with a nasty split and the election of Woodrow Wilson as president. In the process, Theodore was nearly killed by an assassin's bullet in 1912. All four Roosevelt sons enlisted in the military when the United States entered World War I, and Roosevelt longed to lead a regiment in France, but Wilson refused his request. Instead, Teddy traveled the country, recruiting for the military. On July 14, 1918, he and Edith learned that their son Quentin had been killed in the war. Her health failing and her spirits low, Edith wrote to her son Kermit: "My life is over, and I am tired of my old body anyway, and I should be glad to get rid of it."

Theodore Roosevelt entered the hospital in November 1918 and died on January 6, 1919, shortly after spending Christmas at Sagamore Hill. Edith remained active in politics, campaigning for Republicans in the 1920 election. She urged women to vote in the presidential election, exercising the franchise that was won with the ratification of the Nineteenth Amendment. She also continued to travel, write, and give generously to charities. In 1932, the Democrats nominated Franklin Delano Roosevelt, Theodore's fifth cousin (and nephew through his marriage to ELEANOR ROOSEVELT), as candidate for president. Alarmed that so many Americans believed the Democrat was her son, Edith campaigned for his opponent, Republican Herbert Hoover. On September 30, 1948, Edith Roosevelt died at her home in Oyster Bay, New York. She was 87 years old.

Further Reading

National First Ladies Library. *Biographies: First Ladies of the United States.* Available online. URL: http://www.firstladies.org/biographies. Accessed on January 4, 2007.

Schneider, Dorothy, and Carl J. Schneider. "Edith Kermit Carow Roosevelt" *First Ladies: A Biographical Dictionary.* New York: Checkmark Books, 2001, 162–171.

Roosevelt, Eleanor (Anna Eleanor Roosevelt) (1884–1962) *first lady*

Anna Eleanor Roosevelt was born in New York City on October 11, 1884, the first of three children of Anna Hall and Elliott Roosevelt. Neither of her parents worked; her mother was a wealthy socialite, and her father, brother to Theodore Roosevelt, was a charming alcoholic. When their mother died in 1892, the children went to live with their grandmother. Elliott Roosevelt died just two years later, when Eleanor was 10 years old. She was devastated by the loss of her father, who had given her the affection her grandmother had cruelly withheld, but found solace and support for developing an independent mind at Allenwood, a progressive boarding school in London; she was a student there from 1899 to 1902, excelling at languages, literature, and sports.

Eleanor returned to New York in 1902 to make her debut as required by her family's position in New York. She cared little for the social world of entertaining and turned her attention instead to her immediate family. She looked after her brother, settling him at Groton School, took classes in sociology and political economy, and worked at a settlement house, developing a reputation as a woman of substance. Her Aunt Anna Roosevelt Cowles (Theodore's sister) introduced her to politics during her uncle's presidency. In 1903, she met Franklin Delano Roosevelt, a distant cousin, and they were married in 1905 despite his mother's best efforts to prevent the union. After their marriage, she dedicated herself to her family and cared for her mother-in-law. She was not nearly as social as

Franklin and subject to periods of depression and self-doubt. Within 11 years, Eleanor bore six children; one son died in infancy.

Franklin Roosevelt served in the New York State Senate from 1910 to 1913. In 1913, Woodrow Wilson appointed him secretary of the navy, and the Roosevelts moved to Washington, D.C. Eleanor thrived in Washington, where her intellect and her linguistic skills made her stand out at diplomatic dinners. The Roosevelts entertained regularly but particularly enjoyed the once-a-month gathering of "The Club," a group of friends and political allies who gathered to debate the issues of the day. The country's entry into World War I in 1917, however, changed everyone's lives. Eleanor went from hours spent calling upon other wives to activities in support of the war effort. During this time, she learned to drive, raised funds for rehabilitation of wounded troops, and organized the Navy Red Cross.

In 1918, Eleanor discovered clear evidence of Franklin's affair with her own social secretary, Lucy Mercer. She offered Franklin an immediate divorce, which he wisely declined given the importance of Eleanor's support in building his political career and his mother's threat to cut him off financially. Franklin Roosevelt's closest political advisor, Louis Howe, advised him that without Eleanor's public-spirited outreach efforts, the public would only see his rather selfish pursuit of private pleasures.

While the marriage was never the same, the partnership continued. Eleanor resolved to build an independent life for herself, connected but not dependent on Franklin's interests or choices. To that end, she set about challenging many of the prevailing norms. She denounced the Red Scare tactics of U.S. attorney general A. Mitchell Palmer as unwarranted intrusions on fundamental civil liberties. She actively participated in organizations identified by Palmer as suspect and worked against those who supported his efforts, including the DAUGHTERS OF THE AMERICAN REVOLUTION, which had moved from a progressive to conservative organization. She developed a network of new friends and allies, mostly women who were also active in the same progressive causes. She became an active leader in the LEAGUE OF WOMEN VOTERS (LWV), the Women's Trade Union League, and the National Consumer's League.

In 1920, Franklin won the Democratic vice-presidential nomination. Although Eleanor's interests lay primarily outside the boundaries of elected office, she nonetheless agreed to campaign with Franklin. Louis Howe shrewdly included her in the major decisions of the campaign, and she developed a complementary but independent political voice while campaigning throughout the country. When the Republican Warren G. Harding won the presidency, the Roosevelts returned to Hyde Park, New York, where Franklin practiced law. Eleanor resumed her own political activities, spending Monday through Thursday in New York City and the weekend in Hyde Park with her family. This approach spared her the burden of constant entertaining at the expense of her more substantive causes. She became the chair of the LWV's Women's Joint Legislative Committee and honed her legislative strategy skills—researching and tracking legislation of interest to women, reporting monthly on the status of bills, and suggesting strategies for promoting the passage of bills of particular interest. During this time, she worked closely with CARRIE CHAPMAN CATT, journalist and publicist Esther Lape, and attorney Elizabeth Read. Her circle soon included influential social feminists Nancy Cook and Marion Dickerman.

When Franklin was stricken with poliomyelitis in the summer of 1921, Eleanor devoted herself to tending his physical and emotional needs. She also worked to keep his interest in politics and public service alive in the face of his mother's belief that his condition required him to retire from the public eye. Eleanor kept the Roosevelt name alive in Democratic circles during Franklin's recovery. Working with Cook, Dickerman, and future New York congresswoman CAROLINE O'DAY, Eleanor traveled throughout

Eleanor Roosevelt, ca. 1933 (LIBRARY OF CONGRESS)

New York encouraging women to form Democratic women's clubs. This exposure led to her selection as Democratic Women's Committee vice president and treasurer, a position she used to write extensively for the *Women's Democratic News* and various magazines. She also lectured and delivered radio addresses, activities that added to her financial independence. In 1925, with Franklin's blessing, she built a home for herself, Nancy Cook, and Marion Dickerman at Val-Kil, near Hyde Park and on Franklin Roosevelt property. In addition to operating the *Women's Democratic News*, they built the Val-Kil furniture factory and ran it with Eleanor's sons' participation. The majority of her work during this period was in support of women's direct participation in government and politics. She noted, "The whole point in women's SUFFRAGE is that the Government needs the point of view of all its citizens and the women have a point of view which is of value to the Government."

Eleanor encouraged women to learn to play the game of politics, just as men had done so successfully. Under her leadership, women gained equal representation within the New York Democratic Party. When Franklin reentered politics in his own gubernatorial race, Eleanor actively campaigned for him within the Democratic Party, effectively winning him the nomination. His election in 1928 posed some constraints on her overt political activities, but she did not accept the exclusively social role of the governor's wife. She continued to teach and organize, but with a slightly lower public profile. She spent three days each week in New York City, but returned to Albany to entertain for the weekend. During this time, she worked with the Junior League to protect women's right to work in a worsening economy when many argued that women took jobs from men who needed to feed their families. She publicly supported workers rights, was arrested on more than one picket line, and urged her husband to adopt more liberal positions. In many respects, she became Franklin's legs during his governorship. She toured and inspected state hospitals, prisons, and public works projects, reporting back to him with her observations. He taught her to be an astute observer of conditions and a careful judge of people.

The prospect of Franklin's election to the presidency in 1932 did not entirely please Eleanor, who believed that she would be consigned to a life of social teas and perpetual reception lines. Nonetheless, she campaigned on his behalf whenever asked to do so and worked diligently on grassroots organization within the Democratic Party and within the women's division particularly. She traveled extensively in this capacity, paying special attention to constituencies that the Democrats needed to win but were traditionally overlooked. When the election was decided in Roosevelt's favor, she said, "For him, of course, I'm glad—sincerely. I could not have wanted it any other way. After all, I'm a Democrat, too. Now I shall have to work out my own salvation. I'm afraid it may be a little

difficult. I know what Washington is like. I've lived there."

Although Eleanor enjoyed a good relationship with the political press, stories began to appear equating her professionalism with commercialism unbecoming to the president's lady. At Franklin's request, she resigned her positions with the Democratic National Committee, the Todhunter School, the League of Women Voters, and the Non-Partisan Legislative Committee, as well as the Women's Trade Union League. She announced that she would no longer be able to take part in commercial radio broadcasts and that she would refrain from discussing politics in her magazine articles. It pained Eleanor to disassociate herself from the causes that energized her. Confiding in Lorena Hickok, one of the only female reporters to cover the 1932 election, she said, "If I wanted to be selfish, I could wish that he had not been elected." She made numerous offers to Franklin to work within the administration—sorting mail, serving as his listening post or as his assistant in some capacity, but each was rebuffed. Undaunted, she turned to the press corps and announced that she would hold weekly meetings with female reporters. She hoped that the reporters would use their columns on her to inform the public about White House activities and to promote understanding about the ways in which politics and government functioned. She was particularly interested in reaching out to American women in this regard and so agreed to write a monthly column for *Women's Home Companion* titled "I Want You to Write to Me." She asked readers to write to her with questions or concerns, labeling her column a clearinghouse or discussion room for issues associated with the adjustments to new conditions in the world. Within a year, 300,000 people had written to her.

Eleanor transformed her social role at the White House into an ambassadorial role, greeting citizens at the door herself. She took an active role in her husband's administration whether he welcomed it or not, transforming the Lincoln Bedroom into her own study and installing a telephone. She pressed Franklin to name women to positions of power in the administration, leading to the historic appointment of FRANCES PERKINS to head the Department of Labor. She also pressed the case for social reform and an expanded role for the federal government relative to the poor, African Americans, children, and the unemployed. For critics of the New Deal, her public profile and direct involvement in recovery efforts served as a lightening rod. Eleanor paid appropriate deference to programs developed by the Roosevelt administration, but when her own research found them wanting, she did not hesitate to argue that they could be improved. When she found women's needs overlooked in federal programs, she advocated for women's divisions and then recommended the appointment of specific women to head these agencies. Her network of social reformers proved invaluable to the administration. She planned and chaired the White House Conference on the Emergency Needs of Women and turned her attention to issues of unemployed youth, helping make the case for establishing the National Youth Administration in 1935. She lobbied on behalf of artists, resulting in the creation of a Public Works Arts Project, ultimately folded into three Works Progress Administration programs: the Federal Writer's Project, the Federal Theater Project, and the Federal Art Project.

Eleanor's most vociferous efforts were in support of African Americans and ending racial prejudice. She promoted the interests of miners in West Virginia, lobbied for anti-lynching legislation, hosted cabinet wives on walking tours of Washington slums, and joined local chapters of the National Association for the Advancement of Colored People (NAACP) and the National Urban League. Her work on behalf of civil rights sharply expanded in her second term as first lady. She spoke out against poll taxes, against discriminatory practices of white landowners, and in favor of equal pay for black and white workers. She brought African Americans into the White House as her guest. Together with MARY MCLEOD BETHUNE, she convened the National Conference of Negro Women at the White House. When confronted with segregation laws in Alabama while attending the Southern Conference on Human Welfare, the first lady insisted that her chair be placed squarely between the white and African-American groups. In 1939, she resigned from the DAUGHTERS OF THE AMERICAN REVOLUTION when the organization refused to allow black contralto MARIAN ANDERSON to perform in Constitution Hall; Eleanor arranged for the concert to be held on the steps of the Lincoln Memorial instead. Her belief that civil rights was the ultimate test for American democracy intensified throughout the 1940s. In 1940, she published *The Moral Basis of Democracy* in which she urged the nation to face up to the disconnect in ideals and reality presented by racial discrimination. When World War II broke out, she equated racism in the United States with the horrors of fascism abroad, earning her the enmity of many.

The war presented Eleanor with opportunities to travel on behalf of the president. She toured factories and urged industry to hire women in jobs previously held by men. She urged the administration to create day nurseries and family restaurants to support women in the workforce. In 1942, she visited American troops (black and white) in England in camps, hospitals, and Red Cross clubs. In every case, she spoke to soldiers as individuals, asking what they needed and whom she could contact on their behalf. She wrote letters to families and placed phone calls upon her return to the United States. In August 1943, Franklin sent Eleanor to tour the South Pacific. She reported on the conditions and on the terrible toll the war was taking on the troops. These reports helped to shape the G.I. Bill designed to aid returning veterans in getting an education and buying a home.

Although Eleanor worried about her husband's failing health, she did not curtail her schedule or her commitments. Eldest daughter Anna tended to her father in Eleanor's absence—even seeing to it that he and Lucy Mercer Rutherford resumed their relationship.

Eleanor accompanied Franklin to San Diego in 1944 to accept the Democratic nomination for a fourth term, but it was Anna, not Eleanor, who accompanied FDR to Yalta and was with him when he died on April 12, 1945, in Warm Springs, Georgia. Although stung by the disclosure that Lucy Mercer was with her husband at the moment of his death, Eleanor accompanied the president's body back to Washington, D.C., and arranged for his funeral. She welcomed the Trumans to the White House and arranged for the Roosevelts' possessions, accumulated over 12 years, to be boxed and shipped to Hyde Park.

No longer bound by the many constraints imposed by the role of president's wife, Eleanor faced a freer but uncertain future. Democratic Party leaders urged her to consider public office—a seat in the U.S. Senate or a run for the governorship of New York. She declined, privately worrying to friends that her political anchor and her point of political leverage died with Franklin. She returned to Val-Kil but kept in close contact with President Truman, continuing to advocate in favor of civil rights, fair employment practices, and world peace. Truman responded by nominating her as the United States' delegate to the United Nations. In this capacity, Eleanor employed her considerable talents of persuasion and her broad political experience to shape and gain adoption of the Universal Declaration of Human Rights in 1948. During her seven years of service to the United Nations, she continued to participate in other causes as well. She pressed the Democratic Party to stay true to liberal principles, particularly as they applied to the area of civil rights. She ignored death threats as she traveled on behalf of the NAACP, exposing the violence associated with forced segregation. She was one of the first to publicly condemn Joseph McCarthy and the work of the House Un-American Activities Committee from its inception. Although disappointed by Truman, she nonetheless supported his reelection in 1948. In 1952 and 1956, she was an ardent supporter of Adlai Stevenson, even in defeat.

As the election of 1960 approached, Eleanor Roosevelt agreed to meet with John F. Kennedy. Although she did not believe he was a true liberal and feared that his tepid support of civil rights would not advance reforms, she agreed to endorse his candidacy. Upon his election, Kennedy appointed her to chair the PRESIDENT'S COMMISSION ON THE STATUS OF WOMEN. During her final two years of life, she was more dedicated than ever to advancing civil rights for African Americans. In 1962, she sponsored hearings investigating law-enforcement officials' acts against the Freedom Riders and protesters in Montgomery, Alabama.

Eleanor Roosevelt died of a rare form of tuberculosis on November 7, 1962. At a memorial service, Adlai Stevenson said: "She would rather light candles than curse the darkness, and her glow warmed the world." Roosevelt's legacy as first lady is one of personal courage and political activism on behalf of the nation's dispossessed. It is generally agreed that no other first lady in the history of the United States has touched so many lives and translated personal commitment to ideals into government action. She established a precedent for an independence that few first ladies since have adopted. She was unique in her ability to withstand the criticism of the press and the public, while actively pursuing the things that mattered most to her. The public was never entirely comfortable with her independence, but Eleanor Roosevelt's strength of character and fundamental commitment to social change allowed her to persevere.

Further Reading

Black, Allida M. "Anna Eleanor Roosevelt." In *American First Ladies: Their Lives and Their Legacy,* 2nd ed., edited by Lewis L. Gould, 285–302. New York: Routledge, 2001.

Cook, Blanche Wiesen. *Eleanor Roosevelt: Volume One, 1884–1933.* New York: Viking, 1992.

Goodwin, Doris Kearns. *No Ordinary Time: Franklin and Eleanor Roosevelt: The Home Front in World War II.* New York: Simon & Schuster, 1994.

National First Ladies Library. *Biographies: First Ladies of the United States.* Available online. URL: http://www.firstladies.org/biographies. Accessed January on 4, 2007.

Schneider, Dorothy, and Carl J. Schneider. "Anna Eleanor Roosevelt" *First Ladies: A Biographical Dictionary.* New York: Checkmark Books, 2001, 230–249.

Rosenberg, Anna (Anna M. Rosenberg Hoffman, Anna Lederer Rosenberg Hoffman)

(1902–1983) *political adviser*   Anna Rosenberg was born Anna Maria Lederer, the daughter of a prominent Jewish family in Budapest, Hungary, on June 19, 1902. Her father, Albert Lederer, ran a successful furniture factory, and her mother, Charlotte Lederer, wrote and illustrated children's books. In 1912, the family immigrated to the United States after Albert Lederer lost his business; they settled in the Bronx borough of New York City. In 1919, Anna Lederer became a naturalized American citizen and married Julius Rosenberg.

Rosenberg was appointed to the Manpower Consulting Committee of the Army and Navy Munitions Board and the War Manpower Commission in the early 1940s. In July 1944, President Roosevelt sent her to Europe to make manpower observations about the American military. For her service to the defense community and to Presidents Roosevelt and Truman, Rosenberg became the first woman awarded the Medal of Freedom in 1945 and received the United States Medal for Merit in 1947. She was appointed assistant secretary of defense in 1951, marking the first time a woman had achieve that level of government appointment in an area related to military affairs.

In 1962, Anna Rosenberg divorced her husband and married Paul G. Hoffman, the first administrator of the Marshall Plan and a top United Nations official. Anna Rosenberg Hoffman died on May 9, 1983, at the age of 81.

Further Reading

Brody, Seymour. *Jewish Heroes & Heroines of America: 150 True Stories of American Jewish Heroism.* Hollywood, Fla.: Lifetime Books, 1996.

Rosenfeld v. Southern Pacific Company (444 F. 2d 1219 [9th Cir.])

(1971)   This case arose when Leah Rosenfeld was denied the job of agent-telegrapher because company policy at Southern Pacific Company excluded women from these jobs. Southern Pacific maintained that the jobs were unsuitable for women and that California law restricted maximum work hours and imposed lifting restrictions for female employees. The company argued that in this case sex was a BONA FIDE OCCUPATIONAL QUALIFICATION. The federal district court disagreed and ruled that TITLE VII OF THE CIVIL RIGHTS ACT OF 1964 did not allow employers to make assumptions about physical characteristics and abilities of groups taken as a whole as the basis for employment decisions. Title VII prohibits using assumptions about women as a group as the basis for hiring or excluding women.

Further Reading

Hesse-Biber, Sharlene, and Gregg Lee Carter. *Working Women in America: Split Dreams* New York: Oxford University Press, 2000.

Rosie the Riveter

Rosie the Riveter was a media propaganda creation devised to encourage women to fill in for men while they were fighting World War II. During the war, so many men were sent off to combat and so much new production was needed to support the war effort that there was a gross shortage of manpower to staff factories and manufacturing plants. As a result, a print, film, and radio campaign encouraged women to leave their homes and take over jobs previously held by men for the duration of the war. "Rosie the Riveter" was the name given to the woman depicted on many of the propaganda posters. In the most famous one, she is wearing a red and white bandana to cover her hair, and she has rolled back the sleeve of her blue coverall to expose a flexed bicep. The caption above her head reads, "We Can Do It!" in bold letters.

Women responded, and they operated heavy construction machinery, worked in lumber and steel mills, unloaded freight, built dirigibles, made munitions, and much more. Although many discovered that they enjoyed the autonomy these relatively high paying jobs provided them, as men began to return home from the war, the government instituted another propaganda campaign urging women to "return to normalcy." Many did return to their prior domestic roles, but the experience demonstrated that women could hold jobs previously thought appropriate only for men. This represented the beginning of women's entrance into the full-time workforce on a permanent basis—a change that was not complete until the 1970s and 1980s.

Further Reading

Gluck, Sherna Berger. *Rosie the Riveter Revisited: Women, the War, and Social Change.* Boston: Twayne, 1987.
Goldin, Claudia. *Understanding the Gender Gap: An Economic History of American Women.* New York: Oxford, 1990.

Ros-Lehtinen, Ileana (1952–) *congressperson* Ileana Ros was born in Havana, Cuba, on July 15, 1952, but left Cuba as a child and was raised in a South Florida community. She attended public schools in Miami-Dade, Florida, and earned an A.A. degree from Miami-Dade Community College (1972), a B.A. in higher education from Florida International University (1975), and a master's in educational leadership from Florida International University (1987). In December 2004, she received her doctorate in higher education from the University of Miami. She founded a private elementary school, Eastern Academy, and served as its chief administrator. From 1983 to 1986, Ros was a Republican member of the Florida House of Representatives. She won election to the state senate and served there from 1986 to 1989. While serving in the Florida legislature, she met and married

Dexter Lehtinen, who was then also a representative and later went on to become the U.S. attorney for the Southern District of Florida.

In 1989, after the death of Congressman Claude Pepper, Ileana Ros-Lehtinen won the special election to replace him, making her the first Hispanic woman and the first Cuban American elected to the U.S. Congress. In the 109th Congress, she served on the House Committee on Government Reform and the Committee on International Relations. There is a sizable gay community in Key West, part of her district. Ros-Lehtinen has sponsored a number of gay rights bills, including a hate crimes bill, an antidiscrimination bill to protect gay federal employees, and a bill to allow homosexuals to serve openly in the military. The congresswoman was reelected in 2006.

Further Reading

Barone, Michael. *The Almanac of American Politics.* Washington, D.C.: National Journal Group, 2006.
"Ros-Lehtinen, Ileana." In *Biographical Directory of the United States Congress, 1774–present.* Available online. URL: http://bioguide.congress.gov/scripts/biodisplay.pl?index=C000435. Accessed on January 8, 2007.
"Representative Ileana Ros-Lehtinen (FL)." In *Project Vote Smart.* Available online. URL: http://votesmart.org/bio.php?can_id=H0851103. Accessed on January 8, 2007.

—Angela Kouters

Ross, Nellie Tayloe (Nellie Davis Tayloe) (1876–1977) *first female governor, director of U.S. Mint* Born on November 29, 1876, near St. Joseph, Missouri, Nellie Davis Tayloe was educated in public and private schools in Nebraska. She taught school for a few years in Omaha before moving to Cheyenne in 1902, following her marriage to William Bradford Ross. William Ross began a law practice in Wyoming and eventually became active in politics. In 1922, he was elected as Wyoming's governor. When he died in office in 1924, the secretary of state, as acting governor, called for a special election. The Democratic Party nominated Nellie Tayloe Ross to complete her husband's term. She initially declined but ultimately accepted the nomination, deciding that she was the best qualified to understand her husband's goals and work to realize them. Ross won the election by a wide margin and became the first woman governor in the United States when she was inaugurated 16 days before MIRIAM FERGUSON of Texas. She served from January 5, 1925, to January 3, 1927, losing a bid for reelection.

Following her defeat, Ross was appointed as a vice chairman of the Democratic National Committee in 1928, directing the party's women's division. She campaigned extensively for Franklin D. Roosevelt in 1932. Following his inauguration in 1933, Roosevelt appointed her as Director

of the United States Mint, a position she held until 1953. She died in 1977 at the age of 101.

Further Reading

Scharff, Virginia. "Feminism, Femininity, and Power: Nellie Tayloe Ross and the Woman Politician's Dilemma." *Frontiers* 15, no. 3 (1995): 87.

Rostker v. Goldberg (453 U.S. 57) (1981)

By a 6-3 vote, the U.S. Supreme Court ruled that the Military Service Act was constitutional and that the war powers clause in the U.S. Constitution gave Congress the power to register men and not women. The U.S. solicitor general argued that sex discrimination in the draft did serve an important government interest—that of creating a pool of registered men in the event Congress needed to reinstate the draft. Since Congress specifically excluded women from combat (not MILITARY SERVICE itself), women's exclusion was based on their combat prohibition and not their sex. The Court agreed.

The backdrop to this case is critical to understanding the nuance and the underlying politics of the decision. President Jimmy Carter reactivated the military's draft registration in 1980 in response to the Soviet Union's invasion of Afghanistan. He requested that women register as well as men, prompting a huge public outcry. Congress refused to require women to register, forcing Carter to order male-only registration to begin. Opponents of the EQUAL RIGHTS AMENDMENT (ERA) used this debate as an opportunity to argue that women would not only be required to register with the military if the ERA were ratified, but they would be sent into combat as well. Although there was no evidence that the ERA would require Congress to change the combat exclusions for women, STOP ERA forces were successful in galvanizing state legislators. The Court issued its ruling in this case on June 25, 1981. The ERA expired, unratified, on June 30, 1982.

In 1994, Congress repealed the "risk rule" barring women from all combat positions and

Nellie T. Ross (LIBRARY OF CONGRESS)

allowed each branch of the service to determine which positions would be open to women. Today over 90 percent of all positions across the four branches of the military are open to women. Therefore, the basis on which the Supreme Court decided this opinion no longer exists. Congress has so far been unwilling to entertain amendments to the Military Service Act to require women to register for the draft.

Further Reading

Frost-Knappman, Elizabeth, and Kathryn Cullen-DuPont. *Women's Rights on Trial*. Detroit: Gale Publishing, 1997.
The OYEZ Project. "*Rostker v. Goldberg,* 453 U.S. 57 (1981)." Available online. URL: http://www.oyez.org/cases/case?case=1980–1989/1980/1980_80_251. Accessed on January 11, 2007.

Roybal-Allard, Lucille (1941–) *congressperson* Lucille Roybal-Allard was born on June 12, 1941, and raised in Boyle Heights, California. A 1965 graduate of California State University at Los Angeles, she is the eldest daughter of Lucille Beserra Roybal and retired congressman Edward R. Roybal, a 30-year incumbent. In 1992, Roybal-Allard, a Democrat, became the first Mexican-American woman elected to Congress. Prior to her election to the House, she represented the 56th assembly district of California for six years (1987–92).

Roybal-Allard is a member of the House Committee on Appropriations and the Committee on Standards of Official Conduct (known as the Ethics Committee). She is the first Latina in U.S. history to be appointed to the appropriations committee. The congresswoman also serves on the Subcommittee on Homeland Security and the Subcommittee on Labor, Health and Human Services, and Education. These two subcommittees oversee funding of the Department of Homeland Security, U.S. Citizenship and Immigration Services, Coast Guard, U.S. Customs Service, Department of Labor, Department of Health and Human Services, and Department

of Education. Roybal-Allard was reelected in 2006. She is married to Edward T. Allard III, with whom she has two children.

Further Reading

Barone, Michael. *The Almanac of American Politics.* Washington, D.C.: National Journal Group, 2006.
"Representative Lucille Roybal-Allard (CA)." In *Project Vote Smart.* Available online. URL: http://votesmart.org/bio.php?can_id=H0515103. Accessed on January 8, 2007.
"Roybal-Allard, Lucille." In *Biographical Directory of the United States Congress, 1774–present.* Available online. URL: http://bioguide.congress.gov/scripts/biodisplay.pl?index=R000486. Accessed on January 8, 2007.

—Angela Kouters

Ruffin, Josephine (Josephine St. Pierre Ruffin) (1842–1924) *suffragist, civil rights activist, publisher* Josephine St. Pierre Ruffin was a Boston suffragist, African-American community leader, publisher, and civil rights activist during the last three decades of the 19th century. Born in Boston on August 31, 1842, she was the daughter of a white English mother and a black father from Martinique. She married George Lewis Ruffin—the first African American to graduate from Harvard Law School—in 1857. Josephine Ruffin's rise to prominence paralleled her husband's success as a prominent black Boston politician. She was active in predominantly white Boston women's clubs that promoted greater social and political empowerment for women. These included the New England Woman's Club, the Massachusetts Woman Suffrage Association, the Massachusetts School Suffrage Association, and the Women's Educational and Industrial Union. Through these organizations, Ruffin worked alongside LUCY STONE, JULIA WARD HOWE, and Ednah Cheney to win school SUFFRAGE for Boston women in 1879.

Ruffin's prominence in the national black community was extensive. In 1879, she led a drive to provide relief for black refugees in Kansas, and in 1893 she helped to form the predominantly black Woman's Era Club (also known as the NEW ERA CLUB), which sponsored the nationally circulated *Woman's Era* newspaper, of which Ruffin was both publisher and editor. Her editorials in *Woman's Era* encouraged readers to take actions that included civil disobedience in response to unjust Jim Crow laws. In 1900, the GENERAL FEDERATION OF WOMEN'S CLUBS refused her a seat at their national conference in Milwaukee because she was African American. This controversy created a rift between northeastern and southern club women that was finally resolved when the GFWC decided to allow states to individually determine the membership restrictions for their states.

Ruffin died in Boston on March 13, 1924, of nephritis. Extant editions of *Woman's Era* journal are available at Boston Public Library.

See also BLACK WOMEN'S CLUB MOVEMENT.

Further Reading

Brown, Hallie Quinn. *Homespun Heroines*. Xenia, Ohio: Aldine Publishing Co., 1926.

Howe, Julia Ward, and Mary Livermore, eds. *Representative Women of New England*. Reprint Services Corp, 1905.

—Teresa Blue Holden

Rust v. Sullivan (500 U.S. 173) (1991)

The national government provides funds for family-planning services (Title X of the Public Health Service Act of 1944). The Department of Health and Human Services issued regulations limiting the ability of Title X fund recipients to engage in ABORTION-related activities. Title X funds were to be used only to support preventive family-planning services. The question before the U.S. Supreme Court concerned whether these restrictions raised First and Fifth Amendment constitutional issues. The Court ruled that the regulations were a reasonable interpretation of the law, although not an exclusive interpretation. The Court further stated that although the law as applied limited forms of information, First Amendment issues were not germane since the information could be obtained elsewhere. Fifth Amendment due-process rights were not violated because the woman's ability to have an abortion was not precluded.

Further Reading

The OYEZ Project. "*Rust v. Sullivan*, 500 U.S. 173 (1991)." Available online. URL: http://www.oyez.org/cases/case?case=1990–1999/1990/1990_89_1391. Accessed on January 11, 2007.

S

Sacagawea (Sacajawea, Sakakawea) (ca. 1789–1812) *Native American interpreter for the Lewis and Clark expedition* Sacagawea (alternate spellings Sacajawea or Sakakawea) was born sometime between 1786 and 1789 on the west side of the Rocky Mountains; she grew up among her people, the Lemhi band of the Shoshoni, or Snake, Indians. At about age 14, she was captured in a raid by the Hidatsa. In 1804, she became a member of the Lewis and Clark expedition when the explorers hired as interpreter for her owner or husband, a French-Canadian fur trader named Toussaint Charbonneau. Her linguistic and culinary skills proved invaluable to the expedition. Less directly, the presence of Sacagawea and her infant son, Jean Baptiste Charbonneau (born on February 11, 1805), signaled the Corps of Discovery's peaceful intentions to the native peoples they encountered. She served as a guide for William Clark during one part of the expedition's return in 1806, after which she lived in St. Louis for a time. Sacagawea probably died at Fort Manuel in the Dakotas on December 12, 1812. Some claim, however, that she left Charbonneau around that time to live among the Comanche, who knew her as Porivo (Chief), and later still returned to the Shoshone, among whom she died in 1884.

Sacagawea is important politically, not only for her contributions to an unprecedented and highly successful scientific expedition, but also for her symbolic value. In the early years of the 20th century, suffragists (especially in the West) celebrated her as a quintessentially American icon of female achievement. She later functioned as a symbol of westward expansion and the progress of civilization. In honor of her role in the nation's past, the U.S. Mint chose to portray Sacagawea, carrying her baby on her back, on the golden dollar coin in 2000. Her myth and the mysteries that remain about her life have captured the imaginations of generations of novelists, playwrights, and artists.

Further Reading

Kessler, Donna J. *The Making of Sacagawea: A Euro-American Legend.* Tuscaloosa: University of Alabama Press, 1996.

Nelson, W. Dale. *Interpreters with Lewis and Clark: The Story of Sacagawea and Toussaint Charbonneau.* Denton: University of North Texas Press, 2003.

Slaughter, Thomas P. *Exploring Lewis and Clark: Reflections on Men and Wilderness.* New York: Alfred A. Knopf, 2003.

—Laura Prieto

Sage, Margaret (Margaret Olivia Slocum Sage) (1828–1918) *philanthropist* Born in Syracuse, New York, on September 8, 1828, and educated at the Troy Female Seminary, Olivia Slocum graduated in 1847 from the Troy Female Seminary, the school founded by EMMA WILLARD. After graduation, she worked off and on as a teacher. In 1869, she married Russell Sage, who left her $63 million upon his death in 1906. At that point, she became one of the country's premier philanthropists. Believing that women were morally superior to men, she founded the Russell Sage Foundation (in 1907), which was to be dedicated to the "improvement of social and living conditions in the United States" (according to the letter setting out the terms of her initial gift of $10 million to the foundation). This was the largest philanthropic gift ever made in the United States at the time.

The Russell Sage Foundation worked to improve the lives of the elderly and the poor and to focus attention on the growing field of social work. The foundation still exists today, focusing on advances in social science methodology in order to facilitate progress in social policies. Sage herself continued in her philanthropy, giving money to the Emma Willard School (formerly the Troy Female Seminary) and Rensselaer Polytechnic Institute. In 1916, she founded Russell Sage College, dedicated to vocational training for women. She died on November 4, 1918, having given approximately $75 million to help fund education, medical research, nature conservancy, and other individual organizations. Sage's view that only the moral superiority of women would lead to societal progress was not unusual for her time, and many women of her class saw their duty to help others through a lens of female moral superiority.

Further Reading
McCarthy, Kathleen. *Women, Philanthropy and Civil Society.* Indianapolis: Indiana University Press, 1991.

Shaw, Sondra C., and Martha Taylor. *Reinventing Fundraising: Realizing the Potential of Women's Fundraising.* San Francisco: Jossey-Bass Publishers, 1995.

—Claire Curtis

same-sex marriage One of the most recent civil rights issues involving gender is that of same-sex or gay marriage. Currently, in all but one state (Massachusetts), marriage is legal only between one man and one woman. As several states began to consider the issue of gay marriage, and couples in Hawaii sued the state for the right to marry, the U.S. Congress acted to contain any changes in state policy to only the immediate state. The federal Defense of Marriage Act (DOMA), passed by Congress and signed into law by President Bill Clinton in 1996, denies federal recognition to gay marriage and gives each state the right to refuse to recognize marriage licenses issued in other states to same-sex couples. Although the constitutionality of DOMA has yet to be formally tested before the U.S. Supreme Court, conservatives moved to head off any possibility that gay marriage might be defined as a sanctioned union and proposed the Federal Marriage Amendment, which defines marriage as a union between one man and one woman. To date, President George W. Bush has endorsed the amendment and urged Congress to take action, but no official vote has been called in either the House or the Senate.

If the U.S. Supreme Court acts to rule DOMA unconstitutional, the Federal Marriage Amendment would be the only recourse for same-sex marriage opponents. In the 2004 presidential elections, some analysts claimed that state-level Defense of Marriage Acts or constitutional bans on gay marriage on the ballot encouraged high turnout among conservative voters at a level that advantaged George W. Bush. Currently, 37 states ban same-sex marriage with DOMAs, three states have amended their constitutions to ban gay marriage, four states have laws that specifically prohibit same-sex marriage, and five states have no explicit laws. Only Massachusetts law permits same-sex couples to obtain a marriage license from the state. Vermont recognizes civil unions, and California has a domestic partnership law that extends certain state benefits to unmarried life partners.

Proponents of gay marriage argue that the right to marry is a basic human right that cannot be withheld from a class of people. In 1967, the Supreme Court appeared to recognize the right to marry by striking down ANTIMISCEGENATION STATUTES that forbade blacks and whites from marrying. In a 2003 case, *Lawrence v. Texas,* the Court ruled that privacy rights extend to same-sex couples in the same way that GRISWOLD V. CONNECTICUT extended privacy rights to heterosexual married couples in 1965. In the Texas case, Justice SANDRA DAY O'CONNOR agreed with the majority holding, noting: "A law branding one class of persons as criminal solely based on the state's moral disapproval of that class and the conduct associated with that class runs contrary to the values of the Constitution and the Equal Protection Clause, under any standard of review."

Several other nations are actively considering the issue of same-sex marriage, including Ireland, Spain, and Switzerland. In 2001, Holland moved to recognize marriage between homosexual couples, and Belgium did likewise the next year. Ontario province in Canada recognized same-sex marriages in 2003, and seven other provinces followed suit in 2004.

Further Reading

Chauncey, George. *Why Marriage? The History Shaping Today's Debate of Gay Equality.* New York: Basic Books, 2004.

Rauch, Jonathan. *Gay Marriage: Why It Is Good for Gays, Good for Straights, and Good for America.* New York: Times Books, 2004.

Sánchez, Linda (1969–) *congressperson*

Linda Sánchez was born on January 26, 1969, in Orange, California. She earned her B.A. in Spanish at the University of California–Berkeley (1991) and her J.D. from the University of California–Los Angeles (1995). In 1998, she joined the International Brotherhood of Electrical Workers (IBEW) and was elected executive secretary/treasurer of the Orange County Central Labor Council. Prior to entering public service, she was an attorney specializing in labor law. She is the younger sister of 47th district congresswoman LORETTA SANCHEZ, making them the only sisters ever to serve in Congress.

Following the 2000 Census, California's 39th district was reconfigured making it attractive for her to seek the House seat in 2002. Sánchez finished first in a six-person primary for the Democratic Party and went on to win the general election against Republican Tim Escobar by a 55–41 margin. She served on three committees in the 109th Congress: the House Committee on the Judiciary, the Committee on Government Reform, and the Committee on Small Business. In 2005, Sánchez was appointed assistant minority whip. She is a member of the Congressional Hispanic Caucus and is a founder and cochair of the Congressional Labor and Working Families Caucus. Following Hurricane Katrina, President Bush moved to suspend the Davis-Bacon Act (1934), a law that requires government contractors to pay market wages. Sánchez led the fight to overturn the president's decision, and eventually the action was rescinded. She was reelected in 2006.

Further Reading

Barone, Michael. *The Almanac of American Politics.* Washington, D.C.: National Journal Group, 2006.

"Representative Linda T. Sánchez (CA)." In *Project Vote Smart.* Available online. URL: http://votesmart.org/bio.php?can_id=MCA91748. Accessed on January 8, 2007.

"Sánchez, Loretta T." In *Biographical Directory of the United States Congress, 1774–present.* Available online. URL: http://bioguide.congress.gov/scripts/

biodisplay.pl?index=S001156. Accessed on January 8, 2007.

—Angela Kouters

Sanchez, Loretta (1960–) *congressperson*
Loretta Sanchez was born on January 20, 1960, in Lynwood, California. She received her undergraduate degree from Chapman University in Orange (1982), earned an MBA from American University in Washington, D.C. (1984), and worked as a financial analyst until entering the House of Representatives. In 1994, she ran unsuccessfully for the Anaheim City Council as a registered Republican. After changing parties, she sought her first election to the House in 1996 against controversial longtime Republican incumbent, Bob Dornan. The 1990 Census had increased the Hispanic population in the 46th district. Sanchez won the election by 984 votes, largely on the strength of support from Hispanics and blue-collar workers. She became the first Latina to represent an Orange County–based district. Dornan contested the election, alleging that some registered voters were not U.S. citizens, but he was unsuccessful. Sanchez handily defeated Dornan in a 1998 rematch and has not faced any serious opposition since then. Her district was renumbered the 47th district after the 2000 census.

In November 2002, Sanchez's younger sister, LINDA SANCHEZ, was elected from the new 39th district. They are the first pair of sisters to serve simultaneously in the U.S. Congress. In the 109th Congress, Loretta Sanchez served on the House Committee on Armed Services, the Committee on Homeland Security, and the Joint Economic Committee. She has been working to update the sexual assault crimes provision in the Uniform Code of Military Justice to bring it into compliance with federal sexual assault crime law. Sanchez won reelection in 2006.

Further Reading
Barone, Michael. *The Almanac of American Politics.* Washington, D.C.: National Journal Group, 2006.

"Representative Loretta L. Sanchez (CA)." In *Project Vote Smart.* Available online. URL: http://votesmart.org/bio.php?can_id=BC030419. Accessed on January 8, 2007.
"Sanchez, Loretta." In *Biographical Directory of the United States Congress, 1774–present.* Available online. URL: http://bioguide.congress.gov/scripts/biodisplay.pl?index=S000030. Accessed on January 8, 2007.

—Angela Kouters

Sanger, Margaret (Margaret Louise Higgins Sanger) (1879–1966) *birth control activist*
Margaret Sanger advocated for the legalization of birth control, opened the first birth control clinic in the United States in 1916, and founded the AMERICAN BIRTH CONTROL LEAGUE, which became the PLANNED PARENTHOOD FEDERATION OF AMERICA, in 1942. Born Margaret Louise Higgins, on September 14, 1879, in Corning, New York, she was the sixth of 11 children born to Michael and Anne Higgins, Irish-Catholic immigrants. Margaret was deeply affected by her mother's death from tuberculosis at the age of 50 and was convinced that Anne Higgins's frequent pregnancies played a role in weakening her health.

Margaret Higgins attended Claverack College and Hudson River Institute and began a nursing program at White Plains Hospital in 1900. In 1902, she married architect William Sanger, with whom she had three children. Margaret turned to nursing to support her family while William focused on painting. Her work in the impoverished area of Manhattan's Lower East Side strengthened Sanger's view that birth control could release women from the clutches of poverty.

In 1912 Sanger began publishing a column titled "What Every Girl Should Know" in the *New York Call* and distributing a pamphlet on *Family Limitation.* The following year, she separated from William Sanger. In 1914, she began *The Woman Rebel,* a radical feminist journal that

Margaret Sanger, 1922 (LIBRARY OF CONGRESS)

advocated for birth control. She was accused of obscenity under the COMSTOCK ACT but left for Britain before she could be tried. She returned less than a year later, and public outcry against her prosecution was so strong that the charges were dropped.

Sanger opened the first birth control clinic in the United States in the Brownsville neighborhood of Brooklyn, New York, in 1916, only to have it closed by police after nine days. In 1921, she founded the American Birth Control League, the forerunner of The Planned Parenthood Federation. A legal loophole allowed her to open a clinic, the Birth Control Clinical Research Bureau, to distribute family planning advice and contraceptives in 1923.

Sanger's association with the EUGENICS movement, which sought to use genetics to screen for desirable mental and physical traits, remains controversial. While she did work with prominent eugenicists who supported the birth control movement, her writing suggests she differed with eugenicists over the use of family planning to limit reproduction of races or nationalities.

In 1952, Sanger continued her work by founding the International Planned Parenthood Federation to address family planning in Asia and the Third World. She served as president of the group until 1959. During the 1960s, she advocated for acceptance of the birth control pill. Sanger died on September 6, 1966, a few months after the Supreme Court ruling in *GRISWOLD V. CONNECTICUT* legalized the use of birth control by married couples in the privacy of their own homes.

See also BIRTH CONTROL MOVEMENT.

Further Reading

Chesler, Ellen. *Woman of Valor: Margaret Sanger and the Birth Control Movement in America.* New York: Simon & Schuster, 1992.

Forster, Margaret. *Significant Sisters: The Grassroots of American Feminism 1839–1939.* New York: Knopf, 1985.

Kennedy, David M. *Birth Control in America: The Career of Margaret Sanger.* New Haven, Conn.: Yale University Press, 2001.

Sanger, Margaret. *Margaret Sanger: An Autobiography.* New York: Cooper Square Press, 1999.

—Angela O'Neil

Schakowsky, Jan (Janice D. Schakowsky)

(1944–) *congressperson* Jan Schakowsky was born on May 22, 1944, in Chicago and graduated from the University of Illinois in 1965. A longtime consumer rights advocate, she was responsible for a 1969 law requiring the printing of freshness dates on groceries. She was program director of Illinois Public Action, the state's largest public interest group (1976–85), and executive director of the Illinois State Council of Senior Citizens (1985–90). In 1990, she won election to the Illinois House of Representatives, serving there for four terms.

In 1998, when Sidney Yates announced that he would not seek reelection to the U.S. House of Representatives seat he had held for 49 years, Schakowsky announced her candidacy for the Democratic primary. She won in November that year with 75 percent of the vote, a margin she has maintained in every election since her first. In the House, Schakowsky serves on the Committee on Energy and Commerce, where she is a ranking member of the Subcommittee on Commerce, Trade, and Consumer Protection. She also serves on the Subcommittee on Environment and Hazardous Materials and Subcommittee on Oversight and Investigations. Schakowsky has been known for her support of women's issues while in Congress and is a close friend of Speaker of the House NANCY PELOSI.

In 2005, Schakowsky's lobbyist husband, Richard Creamer, plead guilty to failure to pay income taxes and bank fraud. Sentenced to five months in prison and 11 months of house arrest, he was released from the Federal Correction Institute in Terre Haute, Indiana, on November 3, 2006. Schakowsky was not connected with the charges and was reelected in 2006.

Further Reading

Barone, Michael. *The Almanac of American Politics.* Washington, D.C.: National Journal Group, 2006.

"Representative Janice D. 'Jan' Schakowsky (IL)." In *Project Vote Smart.* Available online. URL: http://votesmart.org/bio.php?can_id=BS024498. Accessed on January 8, 2007.

"Schakowsky, Janice D." In *Biographical Directory of the United States Congress, 1774–present.* Available online. URL: http://bioguide.congress.gov/scripts/biodisplay.pl?index=S001145. Accessed on January 8, 2007.

—Angela Kouters

Schlafly, Phyllis (Phyllis McAlpine Stewart Schlafly) (1924–) *political activist, author*

Phyllis Schlafly is an ultraconservative Republican best known for her opposition to the EQUAL RIGHTS AMENDMENT (ERA) and her ANTIFEMINISM. Born Phyllis McAlpine Stewart on August 15, 1924, in St. Louis, Missouri, Schlafly grew up in a devout Catholic family traditional in its faith and in its views of the family. A Phi Beta Kappa graduate of Washington University in St. Louis (1944), she received a master's degree in government from Radcliffe in 1945 and a J.D. from Washington University Law School in 1978. In the late 1940s, she became active in the right wing of the Republican Party. After having worked in various businesses and as a Republican campaign manager, she married Fred Schlafly in 1949, claiming that it gave her the opportunity to pursue her destined career as housewife and mother. Their marriage produced six children. Nevertheless, Schlafly never gave up her political career; she ran for Congress (unsuccessfully) in 1952 and 1970 and was actively involved in the GOP. In 1967, she founded the political newsletter the *PHYLLIS SCHLAFLY REPORT*. An ardent anticommunist, her political focus lay on national defense and military issues rather than on "women's issues."

Initially, Schalfly did not want to join the fight against the ERA. However, after reading about it, she launched an uncompromising campaign against the amendment and its supporters. With the founding of STOP ERA and the EAGLE FORUM in 1972, she became the ERA's leading opponent and organized an antifeminist countermovement that eventually helped to defeat the amendment. She argued primarily that the amendment would hurt women and families and lead to a unisex society destined for demise. Schlafly's opposition to the ERA and her antifeminism in general are intrinsically linked to her concept of national identity and national security. Since the fight against the ERA, she has continued to be an outspoken advocate of conservative issues, including positions taken on gender equality, ABORTION, and gay and lesbian rights.

Further Reading

Felsenthal, Carol. *The Biography of Phyllis Schlafly: The Sweetheart of the Silent Majority.* Garden City, N.Y.: Doubleday & Company, Inc., 1981.

Klatch, Rebecca. *Women of the New Right.* Philadelphia: Temple University Press, 1987.

Melich, Tanya. *The Republican War Against Women: An Insider's Report From Behind the Scenes.* New York: Bantam Books, 1998.

—Christine Knauer

Schmidt, Jean (Jeannette Marie Hoffman Schmidt) (1951–) *congressperson*

Jeannette (Jean) Marie Hoffmann was born in Cincinnati, Ohio, on November 29, 1951, to Augustus and Jeannette Hoffmann and earned a bachelor's degree in political science from the University of Cincinnati (1974). She worked in her father's bank, the Midwestern Savings Association, as a branch manager from 1971 to 1978 and was a fitness instructor from 1984 to 1986, when she began a four-year career as a teacher. She is married to Peter Schmidt, a stockbroker, with whom she has a daughter.

Schmidt was elected as a Miami Township trustee in 1989, finishing first of three candidates for two seats and winning 4,362 votes. In 2000, she ran for the Ohio House of Representatives seat being vacated by Sam Bateman, who was prevented by term limits from running again. In the Ohio House, she served on the Finance and Appropriations Committee; Human Services and Aging Committee; Banking, Pensions and Securities Committee; and Public Utilities Committee. In 2002, she was elected to the 125th General Assembly without opposition in both the primary and general elections.

In 2005, when Ohio congressman Rob Portman was nominated to be the U.S. Trade Representative, Schmidt decided to run in the special election to replace him. Schmidt won by a narrow margin making her the second Republican woman elected to Congress from Ohio in her own right (the first was DEBORAH PRYCE) and the first woman to represent southwestern Ohio in Congress. Two months into her term, Schmidt generated a firestorm with remarks that were understood to call Congressman John Murtha, a highly decorated Marine Corps veteran and a Democrat from Pennsylvania, a "coward" for his questioning of the Iraq war in debate on the House floor. In her remarks, she conveyed a message, allegedly from Ohio State House member Colonel Danny Bupb, asking her to send Murtha a message, "that cowards cut and run, Marines never do." After several minutes of bedlam, she asked for and received permission to withdraw her remarks, and she apologized to Congressman Murtha. Both Cincinnati newspapers condemned her remarks in editorials. Nevertheless, Congresswoman Schmidt won reelection to the House in 2006.

Further Reading

Barone, Michael. *The Almanac of American Politics.* Washington, D.C.: National Journal Group, 2006.

"Representative Jean Schmidt (OH)." In *Project Vote Smart.* Available online. URL: http://votesmart.org/bio.php?can_id=. Accessed on January 8, 2007.

"Schmidt, Jean." In *Biographical Directory of the United States Congress, 1774–present.* Available online. URL: http://bioguide.congress.gov/scripts/biodisplay.pl?index=S001164. Accessed on January 8, 2007.

—Angela Kouters

Schroeder, Patricia (Pat Schroeder, Patricia Nell Scott Schroeder) (1940–) *congressperson*

Patricia Scott Schroeder, a former Democratic congresswoman in the U.S. House of Representatives, was born on July 30, 1940, in Portland, Oregon. As a child, she was encouraged by her parents, Lee Combs and Bernice Lemoin Scott, to articulate her opinions—a trait that aided Schroeder in her future political career. Pat Scott graduated with a bachelor's degree from the University of Minnesota in 1961 and with a degree from Harvard Law School in

1964. While at Harvard, she met James Schroeder, whom she married in 1962.

In 1972, Pat Schroeder ran against incumbent Colorado Republican James D. McKewitt for a seat in the U.S. House of Representatives and won. Some politicians and constituents criticized her for being actively involved in politics while at the same time rearing two children (son Scott was six and daughter Jaime was two when Schroeder won her first campaign). She disregarded such complaints and successfully defended her seat in the House in 11 consecutive campaigns. During Schroeder's 24-year tenure in the House of Representatives, she championed many political issues pertaining to women and children, including ABORTION rights and pension sharing for ex-wives of federal workers. She also penned the FAMILY AND MEDICAL LEAVE ACT of 1993, a measure granting men and women a period of secure leave from work upon birth of a child. Schroeder co-founded the CONGRESSIONAL CAUCUS FOR WOMEN'S ISSUES in 1977 and served as its co-chair for 10 years. She chaired the Select Committee on Children, Youth and Families. In 1987, she contemplated a run for the presidency but dropped out in the early stages of the race. Pat Schroeder retired from active politics in 1996; since 1997, she has been president and chief executive officer of the Association of American Publishers.

Further Reading

Lowy, Joan A. *Pat Schroeder: A Woman of the House.* Albuquerque: University of New Mexico Press, 2003.

Schroeder, Patricia S. *24 Years of House Work . . . And the Place is Still a Mess: My Life in Politics.* Kansas City: Andrews McNeel Publishing, 1998.

—Sara Crowley

Schwartz, Allyson (1948–) *congressperson*
Born in New York City on October 3, 1948, Allyson Schwartz received a B.A. degree from Simmons College (1970) and a master's degree

from Bryn Mawr College (1972). She is married to cardiologist David Schwartz, with whom she has two sons. From 1975 to 1988, Allyson Schwartz was the executive director of the Elizabeth Blackwell Center, a women's health care center in Philadelphia, Pennsylvania. She served as deputy commissioner of the Philadelphia Department of Human Services (1988–90). In 1990, she was elected to the Pennsylvania State Senate, where she served 12 years (1990–2004). In 2004, Schwartz successfully ran for an open U.S. House seat, defeating Republican Melissa Brown by a margin of 56 to 41 percent. EMILY's LIST was her largest contributor, and the Democratic Congressional Campaign Committee also assisted in her election as a part of their "red to blue" coordinated campaign. Schwartz herself also proved to be an excellent fundraiser. In the 109th Congress, she served on the Committee on the Budget and Committee on Transportation and Infrastructure. She won reelection in 2006.

Further Reading

Barone, Michael. *The Almanac of American Politics.* Washington, D.C.: National Journal Group, 2006.

"Representative Allyson Y. Schwartz (PA)." In *Project Vote Smart.* Available online. URL: http://votesmart. org/bio.php?can_id=BS023316. Accessed on January 8, 2007.

"Schwartz, Allyson Y." In *Biographical Directory of the United States Congress, 1774–present.* Available online. URL: http://bioguide.congress.gov/scripts/ biodisplay.pl?index=S001162. Accessed on January 8, 2007.

—Angela Kouters

Seneca Falls Convention (1848) The Seneca Falls Convention, held in Seneca Falls, New York, on July 19–20, 1848, was organized by ELIZABETH CADY STANTON and LUCRETIA MOTT as the first public political meeting in the United States dealing with women's rights. As Quakers who were active in the ABOLITIONIST MOVEMENT, their concern for women's rights was heightened when Mott, as a woman, was denied a seat at an international antislavery meeting in London in 1840. Stanton and Mott, working with Martha Wright (Mott's sister), Mary Ann McClintock, and Jane Hunt, sent out a call for a women's conference to be held at the Wesleyan Chapel in Seneca Falls. The meeting attracted 240 people, including 40 men (among them Frederick Douglass, the ex-slave abolitionist). Daunted by the size of the gathering and because no woman had ever previously run a meeting like this, the organizers persuaded Mott's husband, James, to chair the meeting.

One result of the convention was the issuance of the DECLARATION OF SENTIMENTS AND RESOLUTIONS (modeled after the Declaration of Independence), enumerating the ways in which men had oppressed American women and relegated them to an inferior status. The resolutions, which accompanied the declaration of sentiments, were unanimously approved, except for Stanton's insistence on demanding the vote for women. Some participants felt this demand was too extreme; others believed women should avoid being drawn into politics. The SUFFRAGE plank did pass, but by a narrow majority. Regardless of the men's participation, the resolutions approved at the meeting explicitly blamed men for the injustices women were suffering and made clear that women must rely on themselves to achieve their emancipation.

Further Reading

Stanton, Elizabeth Cady, Susan B. Anthony, and Matilda Gage. *History of Woman Suffrage, 1848–1861,* vol. 1. Salem, N.H.: Ayer Co., 1985.

Women's Rights National Historical Park. *All Men and Women Are Created Equal—The Story of Women's Rights.* Available online. URL: www.nps.gov/wori/index.htm. Accessed on June 15, 2005.

Yellin, Carol Lynn, and Sherman, Janann. *The Perfect 36: Tennessee Delivers Woman Suffrage,* edited by Ilene Jones-Cornwell. Memphis, Tenn.: Iris Press, 1998.

—Paula Casey

separate spheres ideology (public-private split)   The separate spheres ideology was a 19th-century doctrine that there are two domains of life: the public and the domestic. Traditionally, the male would be in charge of the public domain while the female would be in charge of the domestic domain. Men were rational, instrumental, independent, competitive, and aggressive; women were emotional, maternal, domestic, and dependent. England's 19th-century emerging bourgeoisie, idealized and popularized by the sentimental novel, advice books, and medical and religious writings, emphasized the concept of a society structured around distinct, supposedly "natural," God-ordained male and female spheres. Early American culture prescribed specific tasks and subordinate status to women. Women managed the domestic sphere of rearing the children and working on the family farm, with duties such as cooking, cleaning, spinning, weaving, gardening, raising poultry, tending cattle, and trading in the local market. Under English common law, a married woman was "covered" by her husband. The name for her legal status was *femme covert,* which meant that she had virtually no rights at all. Western political theories, especially republicanism and liberalism, encouraged the concept, pronouncing the political sphere, civic virtue, and citizenship to be exclusively male preserves, and excluding women from political activity of any sort.

The concept of separate spheres was also central to common-law doctrines, which, until reforms in the mid- and late 19th century, severely restricted married women's legal rights and independence. The distinction between the public sphere of men and the private sphere of women receded during the Revolutionary War as women increasingly participated in public events.

See also COVERTURE; MILITARY SERVICE.

Further Reading

Cott, Nancy. *The Bonds of Womanhood: "Woman's Sphere" in New England, 1780–1835.* New Haven, Conn.: Yale University Press, 1977.

Welter, Barbara. "The Cult of True Womanhood: 1820–1860." *American Quarterly* 18 (1966): 154–171.

Yellin, Carol Lynn, and Sherman, Janann. *The Perfect 36: Tennessee Delivers Woman Suffrage,* edited by Ilene Jones-Cornwell. Memphis, Tenn.: Iris Press, 1998.

—Paula Casey

Seton, Elizabeth Ann (Elizabeth Ann Bayley Seton) (1774–1821) *religious educator, saint*

Elizabeth Ann Bayley was born on August 28, 1774, in New York City and was raised by her physician father and stepmother after her own mother's death in 1777. In 1794, she married William Magee Seton and prepared for a life of wealth, although she was devoted to charitable works (she started a society for the assistance of widows with small children in 1797). However, her family suffered in the yellow fever epidemic in New York, and William Seton went into debt. In order to help her husband's recovery, Elizabeth Seton sold off her silver and paid for passage on a voyage to Italy, but William Seton died in Pisa in December 1803.

While she was in Italy, Seton immersed herself in Catholic ritual and doctrine, and upon her return to New York, she decided to convert to Catholicism. Her decision to convert meant that what help her husband's family would have given to her and to her children was withheld. New York City was not an easy place to be for a Catholic convert, and the school that she helped to start in New York after returning to the United States was closed out of fears that it was seeking to proselytize Protestants to convert as well. Seton was then invited by Catholic authorities in Baltimore to come there and to start a school.

In 1809, Seton founded the Sisters of Charity, the first new community of religious women established in the United States. The Sisters devoted their community to education, the care of orphans, the poor and African Americans in Baltimore. In 1810, St. Joseph's Academy and Free School, the first free Catholic school for girls in the United States, was opened. St. Joseph's Academy started the movement for parochial education in the United States at a time when education was only available to those who could afford schooling. By the time Seton died on January 4, 1821, there were 12 Sisters of Charity communities throughout the United States and Canada running orphanages and schools.

In 1975, Elizabeth Seton was canonized, the first person born in the United States to be so honored.

Further Reading
Celeste, Marie. *Intimate Friendships of Elizabeth Ann Bayley Seton: First Native-Born American Saint, 1774–1821.* Lanham, Md.: University Press of America, 2000.

Feeney, Leonard. *Mother Seton: Saint Elizabeth of New York (1774–1821).* Cambridge, Mass.: Ravengate Press, 1975.

Seton, Elizabeth Bayley. *Collected Writings, 1793–1809.* New York: New City Press, 2000.

—Claire Curtis

settlement house movement

The settlement house movement originated in England in the early 19th century as a religious response to industrial poverty. The movement spread to the United States in the late 19th century and lasted through the Great Depression. Settlement houses were usually residential buildings that were converted into a type of community center in poor, urban neighborhoods. The volunteers were mostly middle- and upper-class women who sought to improve the lives of the poor, especially new European immigrants, by providing services that were not, at that time, provided by the government. The volunteers lived in the settlement house and sought to acquaint their neighbors with uniquely American culture, in addition to learning about the immigrants' culture. Services provided by settlement houses included but were not limited to clubs for youth, educational classes and lectures, social gatherings, arts programs, health clinics, and programs to improve sanitation and hygiene.

Two of the most famous settlement houses in the United States were HULL-HOUSE in Chicago, founded in 1889 by JANE ADDAMS; and the Henry Street Settlement in New York City, founded by Lillian Wald. Armed with firsthand knowledge about terrible housing, exploitation in the workplace, lack of occupational safety, inadequate education opportunities, and woeful health care, female reformers launched campaigns to address these urban problems, leading historians to label settlement houses "spearheads for reform." In this regard, the settlement house movement and the SUFFRAGE movement were intertwined and provided women with invaluable training in public speaking and lobbying. Likewise, settlement houses were often used as laboratories for university researchers seeking to try new programs and offer training in the new field of social work. From 1907 to 1921, SOPHONISBA BRECKINRIDGE lived in Hull-House while she taught at the Chicago School of Civics and Philanthropy.

Settlement houses are sometimes criticized today because they reflected the racism of that era by segregating whites and blacks. The Phyllis Wheatley House was founded in 1924 to provide services to African Americans living in Minneapolis, Minnesota. This house had four departments, each run by a black woman: education, recreation, music, and dramatics. Black settlement houses had a slightly different focus than those serving a primarily immigrant population. Instead of "Americanization," these residential community centers served as a hotel for African Americans visiting Minneapolis since other accommodations were closed to them. Similarly, black students studying at area universities could live in the Phyllis Wheatley House. Upon the rise of the civil rights movement, the settlement house became an important community meeting place. Currently there are about 800 settlement houses, or community centers, in the United States.

Further Reading

Barbuto, Domenica. *American Settlement Houses and Progressive Social Reform*. Phoenix: Oryx Press, 1999.

Carson, Mina. *Settlement Folk: Social Thought and the American Settlement Movement, 1885–1930*. Chicago: University of Chicago Press, 1990.

Friedman, Michael, and Brett Friedman. *Settlement Houses: Improving the Social Welfare of America's Immigrants*. New York: Rosen Pub. Group, 2004.

Lasch-Quinn, Elisabeth. *Black Neighbors: Race and the Limits Reform in the American Settlement House Movement, 1890–1945*. Chapel Hill: University of North Carolina Press, 1993.

—J. Celeste Lay

Seven Sisters Colleges   The "Seven Sisters" refers to a group of prestigious women's colleges organized in 1927 to promote private women's colleges and improve women's education. The oldest of the institutions, Mount Holyoke College (in South Hadley, Massachusetts), was founded by MARY LYON in 1837 as Mount Holyoke Female Seminary. It achieved collegiate status in 1888 and acquired its present name in 1893. Vassar College (in Poughkeepsie, New York) was founded in 1861. Wellesley College (in Wellesley, Massachusetts) was founded in 1870 by lawyer and philanthropist Henry Fowle Durant and his wife Pauline. Smith College (in Northampton, Massachusetts) was founded in 1871 by a bequest of heiress Sophia Smith. Radcliffe College (in Cambridge, Massachusetts) was founded by Harvard faculty as the Harvard Annex in 1871. Bryn Mawr College (in Bryn Mawr, Pennsylvania) was founded in 1889. It was the first women's college to grant graduate degrees, including the first doctorate in social work (1912). Barnard College (in the borough of Manhattan, New York City) was founded in 1889.

The colleges did not all remain purely single sex. Barnard was incorporated into Columbia University in 1900 although it retained its independent government. Bryn Mawr began accepting male graduate students in 1961. Vassar became coeducational in 1969 after declining an offer to merge with Yale. Radcliffe College gradually became part of Harvard University, beginning with shared responsibility over female undergraduates in 1963. In 1999, Radcliffe College was dissolved; it subsequently became the Radcliffe Institute for Advanced Study, part of Harvard University.

The Seven Sisters colleges have collectively produced many women leaders in the fields of government, law, education, business, arts and sciences, including MADELINE ALBRIGHT, BETTY FRIEDAN, and FRANCES PERKINS.

Further Reading

Horowitz, Helen Lefkowitz. *Alma Mater: Design and Experience in the Women's Colleges from Their Nineteenth-Century Beginnings to the 1930s.* New York: Knopf, 1984.

Solomon, Barbara Miller. *In the Company of Educated Women: A History of Women and Higher Education in America.* New Haven, Conn.: Yale University Press, 1986.

—Laura Prieto

sexual harassment   The history of sexual harassment in the United States can be divided into three periods: the period prior to the successful recognition of sexual harassment as a form of sex discrimination; the second period, during which the two standard forms of such harassment (quid pro quo and hostile environment) were established; and the third period of expansion, where same-sex sexual harassment was established. Sexual harassment was famously theorized by CATHERINE MACKINNON in her book *Sexual Harassment of Working Women* (1979) as a mode of men's social control over women in the workplace. MacKinnon's understanding of sexual harassment takes for granted that sexual advances or sexual conduct in the workplace references the sexual control of men over women; legal theorists in the 1990s have shifted the focus of sexual harassment away from a paradigm of male sexual control to a paradigm of sex stereotyping as itself a form of sex discrimination. Sexual harassment passed into the everyday understanding of Americans with the Supreme Court nomination hearings of Clarence Thomas and the accusations of sexual harassment set forward by ANITA HILL, his employee at the EQUAL EMPLOYMENT OPPORTUNITY COMMISSION (EEOC) in the 1980s.

After the passage of the CIVIL RIGHTS ACT OF 1964, discrimination on the basis of sex was outlawed. Prior to the passage of that act, women had no recourse for the pervasive problem of men demanding sexual favors at work. Historically, this had been a particular problem for female slaves, domestics, and any women whose class position kept them from being able to demand recourse from their male employers. Upper-class women who worked might be able to appeal to their own fathers or brothers (married women in the upper classes did not normally work outside the home) for restitution. But there was no legal remedy to protect women.

Sexual harassment is defined by the EEOC as "unwelcome sexual advances, requests for sexual favors and other verbal or physical conduct of a sexual nature . . . [creating] an intimidating, hostile or offensive work environment." There are two commonly understood forms of sexual harassment: *quid pro quo,* where promotion or demotion are tied to the performance of sexual favors, and hostile environment, where the ethos of a working environment is considered sufficiently "severe and pervasive" to negatively impact the conditions of someone's work. Sexual harassment was initially argued as a form of sex discrimination in the early 1970s. A series of cases (*Corne v. Bausch and Lomb, Tomkins v. Public Service Electric and Gas, Miller v. Bank of America*) failed to see the link between demanding sexual favors from female workers and sex discrimination on the argument that such behavior was the matter of a "personal proclivity," not part of a company policy, and that the "natural sex phenomenon" between men and women would result in far too many cases to hear.

Finally, in *Williams v. Saxbe* (1976) a lower court in Washington, D.C., declared that sexual harassment was understood as a form of sex discrimination. The court argued that male supervisors making sexual advances on female subordinates and attaching those sexual favors to job advancement or dismissal put an undue burden on female employees that was not extended to male employees (thus passing the "but for" test—"but for" a woman's sex she would not have been treated in this way). This first form of sexual harassment is understood as *quid pro quo,* harassment that takes the form of demanding *this for that*: sexual favors for job advancement (or dismissal).

Hostile environment harassment first emerged in two cases in the early 1980s: *Bundy v. Jackson* (1981) and *Henson v. City of Dundee* (1982). Here the conditions of the working environment, because of language used by coworkers, denial of job advancement, and refusal of management to remedy the working conditions, were identified as hostile or intimidating. The creation of this environment, as with the requests for sexual favors, placed an arbitrary and discriminatory condition on women's work. In 1986, the Supreme Court decided in MERITOR SAVINGS BANK V. VINSON that both forms of sexual harassment were actionable as sex discrimination. Further, they found that one need only prove that the behavior was "unwelcome." A distinction was made between *voluntary conduct* and *welcome conduct,* and the Court stated that even if sexual interaction was voluntary, that may not mean that it was welcome.

The third stage in the developing understanding of sexual harassment came in 1998 when, in *Oncale v. Sundowner,* the Supreme Court declared that sexual harassment need not be limited to opposite-sex interactions but that people of the same sex could also harass one another if such harassment stemmed from sexual desire, disparate treatment of one group of workers versus another, or a "general hostil-

ity to members of that sex." This extension of sexual harassment to same-sex scenarios has provided an innovative legal remedy for discrimination on the basis of sexual orientation (see *Rene v. MGM Grand Hotel* [2002]). In 2005, 12,679 sexual harassment charges were filed with the EEOC.

Further Reading

Gregory, Raymond F. *Unwelcome and Unlawful: Sexual Harassment in the American Workplace.* Ithaca, N.Y.: Cornell University Press, 2004.
LeMonchek, Linda, and James P. Sterba. *Sexual Harassment: Issues and Answers.* Oxford: Oxford University Press, 2001.
MacKinnon, Catherine. *Sexual Harassment of Working Women.* New Haven, Conn.: Yale University Press, 1979.

—Claire Curtis

Shaw, Anna Howard (1847–1919) *civil rights leader, minister*   Anna Howard Shaw was born in Newcastle-on-Tyne, England, on February 14, 1847, and at the age of four immigrated to the United States with her family. She grew up in Lawrence, Massachusetts, and later in rural Michigan, where life was very hard as the family struggled to hold on to their land claim. Anna Shaw's ambition to become a preacher led her to seek formal education. Taking responsibility for her own financial support, she attended Albion College for three years and then the Boston University Theological School, from which she graduated in 1878. A gifted and experienced orator by this time, Shaw was ordained as a Methodist minister. She also obtained a medical degree from Boston University Medical School in 1886, although she never practiced medicine.

Shaw then turned entirely to lecturing for her livelihood. She argued that autonomy, not motherhood, should be seen as the epitome of womanhood. Under the urging of SUSAN B. ANTHONY, Shaw embraced women's SUFFRAGE as her life's work. She served as the vice president of the NATIONAL AMERICAN WOMAN SUFFRAGE

ASSOCIATION (NAWSA) from 1894 to 1904 and then as president of the organization until 1915. Her tenure saw remarkable successes: Eight new states passed woman suffrage, and NAWSA membership rose from 17,000 to 200,000. Yet Shaw was regarded as a poor administrator, largely because she did not work cooperatively with men, whose votes were necessary to enact suffrage. In April 1917, Shaw was named chair of the Woman's Committee of the National Council of Defense. In this position, her persistence and moral courage proved effective in winning greater responsibility and fairer treatment for the Woman's Committee.

In the wake of World War I, Shaw became the first American woman awarded the Distinguished Service Medal. She died on July 2, 1919. Anna Howard Shaw was a strong, unrelenting voice for suffrage and sexual equality during the crucial final decades of women's struggle for the vote.

Further Reading

McGovern, James R. "Anna Howard Shaw: New Approaches to Feminism." *Journal of Social History* 3 (1969): 135–153.

O'Neill, William L. *Everyone Was Brave: The Rise and Fall of Feminism in America.* Chicago: Quadrangle, 1969.

Shaw, Anna Howard, with Elizabeth Jordan. *The Story of a Pioneer.* New York: Harper & Brothers, 1915.

—Laura Prieto

Dr. Anna Howard Shaw (LIBRARY OF CONGRESS)

Sheppard-Towner Maternity and Infancy Protection Act (1921)

This legislation represents the first federally funded measure in support of improving maternal and infancy care, as well as the first action taken in support of women's rights after female SUFFRAGE was secured in the United States. By funding educational programs at the state level, the Sheppard-Towner Act infused federal responsibility into improving the nation's dismal record on maternal and infant mortality.

Whereas Senator Morris Sheppard (D-TX) and Congressman Horace Towner (R-IA) bear naming rights to the act, the true crafters of the measure included a tightly organized group of female reformers devoted to improving child welfare, especially officials with the Children's Bureau. Initially introduced to Congress in 1918 by Representative JEANNETTE RANKIN (R-MT) and Senator Joseph Robinson (D-AR), concerns arose from the act's provision to offer medical care at home or in a hospital as well as an annual $4 million federal allocation. The bill that eventually passed three years later deleted all references to provision of direct patient care, opting instead for a purely educational direction. Moreover, funding was reduced to only $1.48 million for fiscal year 1921–22 and $1.24 million for the next five years. Sheppard and Towner sponsored the revised legislation, submitting it to the 66th

Congress in autumn 1920. It passed the Senate but failed in the House of Representatives in December and resurfaced in a special session of the 67th Congress in April 1921. In August, that group passed the act by a wide margin—63-7 in the Senate and 279-39 in the House—and President Warren G. Harding signed the bill into law on November 23, 1921.

Most states used their allocations from the Sheppard-Towner Act to hold health conferences; provide home visits by visiting nurses; encourage birth registration; distribute literature such as the Children's Bureau pamphlets *Infant Care* and *Prenatal Care*; and teach mothers about nutrition, hygiene, and proper CHILD CARE. Yet the act was widely contested by groups concerned with the United States adopting any form of socialized medicine. Concerns from the medical profession and politicians fearing future drift toward socialized care caused Congress to pull all funding in 1929, thereby eliminating the state programs put in place with Sheppard-Towner funds.

Further Reading

Gordon, Linda. *Pitied but Not Entitled: Single Mothers and the History of Welfare.* New York: Free Press, 1994.

Ladd-Taylor, Molly. *Mother-Work: Women, Child Welfare, and the State, 1890–1930.* Urbana: University of Illinois, 1994.

Lindenmeyer, Kriste. *"A Right to Childhood": The U.S. Children's Bureau and Child Welfare, 1912–46.* Urbana: University of Illinois Press, 1997.

Muncy, Robyn. *Creating A Female Dominion in American Reform, 1890–1935.* New York: Oxford University Press, 1991.

Schackel, Sandra. *Social Housekeepers: Women Shaping Public Policy in New Mexico, 1920–1940.* Albuquerque: University of New Mexico Press, 1992.

—Kyle E. Ciani

single-sex education   Private education in the United States was almost always divided by gender, but public schools have been largely coeducational since they were first started. Women have fought both for women's own education (for example MARY LYON started Mount Holyoke College for women) and more recently for the shift toward coeducation in America's elite private colleges. TITLE IX OF THE EDUCATION AMENDMENTS OF 1972 declared that schools receiving federal funding could not discriminate on the basis of sex. As an indirect result of Title IX and financial pressure from declining enrollments, the historically male private colleges (for example, Williams, Amherst, Bowdoin) became coeducational. This was seen as a victory for the women's rights movement. In the 1990s, the fight for coeducation shifted to the Southern public military schools: Virginia Military Institute (VMI) and The Citadel. These schools, which not only received federal funding but were in fact public schools, both became coeducational as a result of the ruling by the Supreme Court in UNITED STATES V. VIRGINIA ET AL. (1996) that VMI could not remain an all-male institution by instituting a comparable military program at Mary Baldwin College (an all-female school). After this ruling, The Citadel also went coeducational.

In May 2002, the federal government, under the No Child Left Behind Act, relaxed its guidelines concerning the separation of sexes. As a policy of educational innovation, single-sex classrooms are now allowed. Simultaneous to this shift has been a reopening of the debate among feminists concerning the value of single-sex education. While all-male education was seen as a mechanism to ensure male access to education, employment, and power, a movement to encourage single-sex classrooms within public elementary and secondary schools is growing. The AMERICAN ASSOCIATION OF UNIVERSITY WOMEN (AAUW) released a report in 1998 entitled *Separated By Sex: A Critical Look at Single Sex Education for Girls,* which did not find that single-sex education, when controlled for socioeconomic background and school selectivity, was necessarily better than coeducation. However, the AAUW does consider that there may be a need in certain coeducational schools to explore the possibility of single-sex classrooms with the goal of enhancing the overall academic experience for boys and girls. In the 2004–05 academic year, there were 34 public single-sex schools and a further 122 public schools that provided single-sex classrooms.

The advantages that advocates of single-sex education seek concern both the differences in learning styles and brain development in boys and girls and the social advantage to schooling where the opposite sex is not present. Some studies have shown that students subscribe to fewer sex stereotypes when educated in single-sex classrooms. On the other side of the debate is the argument that the world is coeducational in nature and that boys and girls must learn to interact with one another; furthermore, single-sex education has been used in the past to limit opportunities for women.

Further Reading

Datnow, Amanda, and Lea Hubbard, eds. *Gender in Policy and Practice: Perspectives on Single Sex and Co-Educational Schooling.* New York: Routledge, 2002.

Sax, Leonard. *Why Gender Matters: What Parents and Teachers Need to Know about the Emerging Science of Sex Differences.* New York: Doubleday Press, 2005.

Stabiner, Karen. *All Girls: Single Sex and Why it Matters.* New York: Riverhead Books, 2002.

—Claire Curtis

Slaughter, Louise (Louise McIntosh Slaughter) (1929–   ) *congressperson* Louise McIntosh was born on August 14, 1929, in Lynch, Kentucky. She earned a bachelor's degree in microbiology (1951) and a master's degree in public health (1953), both from the University of Kentucky. While working in market research for a chemical company, she met Bob Slaughter in San Antonio, Texas; they married, moved to Fairport, New York, and had three daughters. As her children grew, Louise Slaughter became increasingly involved with political and local community issues. She worked for Mario Cuomo as a regional coordinator in Rochester when he was New York's lieutenant governor. In 1982, local Democrats approached Slaughter and asked her to run for the state assembly. She was not expected to win but pulled off a major upset. Women's health issues and environmental legislation were her priorities in the state legislature.

After four years in the state assembly, Slaughter sought the Democratic nomination in New York's 30th congressional district and was elected in 1986. She won a 10th term in 2004 with a record 72 percent of the vote and was reelected in 2006. Slaughter serves on the Democratic Steering and Policy Committee. She is the Democratic chair of the Congressional Arts Caucus and the Bipartisan Congressional Pro-Choice Caucus. She is cochair of the Future of American Media Caucus and is former cochair of the CONGRESSIONAL CAUCUS FOR WOMEN'S ISSUES. After Martin Frost, the ranking member on the House Rules Committee, was defeated for reelection, Slaughter was appointed to the position, becoming the first female member of Congress to serve in this post. Slaughter coauthored the VIOLENCE AGAINST WOMEN ACT in 1994. In March 2004, she organized a public hearing on the issue of sexual assault in the military.

Further Reading

Barone, Michael. *The Almanac of American Politics.* Washington, D.C.: National Journal Group, 2006.

"Representative Louise McIntosh Slaughter (NY)." In *Project Vote Smart.* Available online. URL: http://votesmart.org/bio.php?can_id=H2852103. Accessed on January 8, 2007.

"Slaughter, Louise McIntosh." In *Biographical Directory of the United States Congress, 1774–present.* Available online. URL: http://bioguide.congress.gov/scripts/biodisplay.pl?index=S000480. Accessed on January 8, 2007.

—Angela Kouters

Smeal, Eleanor (1939–) *feminist, women's rights advocate*   Founder and president of the Feminist Majority Foundation, Eleanor Smeal was born in Ashtabula, Ohio, on July 30, 1939, but grew up in Erie, Pennsylvania. She graduated from Duke University with honors in 1961 and earned a master's degree in political science from the University of Florida in 1963.

Throughout the beginning of the second wave of FEMINISM in the 1960s and into the 1970s, Eleanor Smeal was a primary architect of the women's movement in pursuit of equality. She served as president of the NATIONAL ORGANIZATION FOR WOMEN from 1977 to 1982 and again from 1985 to 1987. Smeal has worked on a wide range of issues, such as ending the practice of newspaper want ads separated by sex, the integration of sexes in the Little League, and lobbying for countless major pieces of legislation to end sex discrimination (EQUAL PAY ACT of 1963, PREGNANCY DISCRIMINATION ACT of 1978, EQUAL CREDIT OPPORTUNITY ACT of 1974, VIOLENCE AGAINST WOMEN ACT of 1994, and FREEDOM OF ACCESS TO CLINIC ENTRANCES ACT of 1994, to name a few). In a move to call attention to the impact of the federal budget on women, she and her colleagues at the Feminist Majority Foundation (founded in 1987) developed a "feminist budget." She has also been active in working to elect more women to public office at the federal and state levels.

Smeal is the author of *How and Why Women Will Elect the Next President* (1984), which predicted that women's votes would be decisive in presidential politics just as the gender gap was beginning to emerge and be named. In many ways, Smeal is the public face of liberal feminism, although not nearly as controversial or as widely recognized as GLORIA STEINEM or BETTY FRIEDAN. The *World Almanac* for 1983 chose her as the fourth most influential woman in the United States; in 1979, she was named as one of *Time* magazine's "50 Faces for America's Future"; and she was featured as one of the six most influential Washington lobbyists in *U.S. News and World Report*. In 2002, she was featured as one of "21 Leaders for the 21st Century" by Women's E-news. Readers specifically pointed to her work in raising awareness about women in Afghanistan; access to safe and legal abortion services in the United States, including FDA approval of mifepristone (RU-486); and working to empower women in electoral politics. In December 2001, Smeal arranged for the Feminist Majority Foundation to become sole publisher of *Ms.* MAGAZINE. She continues to work actively for women's issues.

Further Reading

Carroll, Susan J. *Women and American Politics: New Questions, New Directions.* Oxford: Oxford University Press, 2003.

Feminist Majority Foundation Web site. Available online. URL: http://www.feminist.org. Accessed on January 15, 2007.

Inglehart, Ronald, and Pippa Norris. *Rising Tide: Gender Equality and Cultural Change around the World.* Cambridge: Cambridge University Press, 2003.

Smedley, Agnes (1892–1950) *journalist, women's rights advocate*   Agnes Smedley was born in Osgood, Missouri, on February 23, 1892. She became involved in student politics in San Diego, and after joining the Socialist Party of America in 1916, she was expelled from San Diego College. She then moved to New York City, where she became interested in the feminist movement and in the movement for Indian independence from Britain. She was arrested on espionage charges in 1918, and prominent radicals, including MARGARET SANGER, lobbied for her release.

Smedley moved to Berlin, Germany, in 1920, and her articles criticizing resurgent German nationalism were published in America's left-wing press. In 1928, she went to China, where she reported for British newspapers on China's civil wars. She became one of the few Americans to establish personal ties to the leaders of China's Communist Party, including Mao Zedong and Zhou Enlai. During this period, she also developed relationships with other journalists in the Far East, including Richard Sorge, a German spy who was active in Shanghai and Japan.

Smedley returned to the United States during World War II and became an active critic of racism and poverty, especially in the American South. After the war, she was placed under surveillance by the FBI, which suspected her of being a member of the U.S. Communist Party. She moved to a writer's colony in upstate New York, but in 1947, was accused of spying for the Soviet Union during the 1930s. The charges were not proved, and Smedley died in self-imposed exile in England on May 6, 1950.

Further Reading

MacKinnon, Janice R., and Stephen R. MacKinnon. *Agnes Smedley: The Life and Times of an American Radical.* Berkeley: University of California Press, 1988.

Smedley, Agnes. *China Fights Back: An American Woman With the Eighth Route Army.* London: V. Gollancz, 1938.

———. *Daughter of Earth: A Novel.* New York: The Feminist Press, 1987.

—Laura Caulkins

Smith, Margaret Chase (1897–1995) *U.S. senator*

Margaret Madeline Chase was born to Carrie Murray and George Emery Chase in rural Skowhegan, Maine, on December 14, 1897. After graduating from high school, she attended Colby College and then spent a few years working at a newspaper and received basic training in political leadership as a member of the NATIONAL FEDERATION OF BUSINESS AND PROFESSIONAL WOMEN'S CLUBS. In 1930, she married Clyde H. Smith, a Maine politician 21 years her senior who taught her the intricacies and practical machinery of government. Clyde Smith died on April 8, 1940, and on June 4, Margaret Chase Smith won election to the 76th Congress to fill the vacancy caused by his death. After serving five terms in the House, she entered the Senate in 1949. A moderate Republican with a long record of distaste for arrogance, Smith gave the first major speech against Senator Joseph McCarthy on June 1, 1950; she called it her Declaration of Conscience. Although she never wrote much legislation, Smith served on the Senate's most prestigious committees, Armed Services and Appropriations as well as Aeronautical and Space Sciences.

In 1964, Smith became the first woman to seek a major party's nomination for the presidency. In 1972, hurt by her defense of President Richard Nixon's Vietnam policies, she lost a reelection bid. Smith died on May 29, 1995, in Skowhegan, Maine, following a stroke.

Margaret Chase Smith was the first woman to earn a seat in both the U.S. House of Representatives and the U.S. Senate. Her sensitivity to gender discrimination, heightened through

Margaret Chase Smith, 1943 (LIBRARY OF CONGRESS)

many years in the workplace, led her to pursue a series of measures to equalize opportunities for women. She became the first congresswoman to publicly endorse the EQUAL RIGHTS AMENDMENT and had her greatest success with the Women's Armed Service Integration Act of 1948, which allowed women to pursue military careers as permanent, regular members of the armed forces.

Further Reading

Schmidt, Patricia L. *Margaret Chase Smith: Beyond Convention.* Orono: University of Maine Press, 1996.

Sherman, Janann. *No Place for a Woman: A Life of Senator Margaret Chase Smith.* New Brunswick, N.J.: Rutgers University Press, 2000.

—Caryn E. Neumann

Smith, Mary Louise (Mary Louise Epperson Smith) (1914–1997) *political organizer, women's rights activist* Mary Louise Epperson was born on October 6, 1914, in Eddyville, Iowa, and earned a bachelor's degree in social work from the State University of Iowa, now the University of Iowa, in 1935. In 1934, she married Elmer M. Smith. She worked briefly as a case worker for the Iowa Employment Relief Administration before leaving paid employment to raise her three children. After moving to Eagle Grove, Iowa, she became active in community and civic activities and with the Republican Party. She joined the Republican Women's Club and served as precinct committeewoman and county vice chair. In 1961, she was appointed to the Executive Committee of the Iowa Council of Republican Women. Three years later, Smith won election as the Republican National committeewoman from Iowa and served as a delegate from Iowa to the party's national conventions. In 1969, she became a member of the Republican National Committee's Executive Committee.

In 1974, President Gerald Ford named Mary Louise Smith to chair the Republican National Committee (RNC), making her the first woman to organize and call to order a national presidential nominating convention of a major U.S. political party. She served as national chairman of the Republican Party from 1974 to 1977. In the wake of the Watergate scandal, this was a particularly difficult time for organized Republicans. Smith advocated broad inclusivity to increase party membership and was an active supporter of the EQUAL RIGHTS AMENDMENT (ERA) and ABORTION rights for women. A cofounder of the Iowa Women's Political Caucus, she was named to the Iowa Women's Hall of Fame in 1977.

Although Mary Louise Smith remained active in Republican politics throughout the 1980s, she was alarmed when the 1980 Republican platform rescinded support for the ERA. In 1984, she resigned from the RNC and joined the Republican Mainstream Committee, a group of moderate partisans dedicated to reestablishing the party's pro-choice and pro-ERA positions and elevating the centrality of civil rights within the party. President George H. W. Bush appointed Smith to the board of directors of the National Peace Institute in 1990. She dedicated her work in the 1990s to the pro-choice cause, serving as a founder of the National Republican Coalition for Choice and a member of the steering committee for Pro-Choice America. She was the cofounder of the Louise Noun–Mary Louise Smith Women's Archives housed at the University of Iowa Libraries, opening in 1992. In 1995, Iowa State University and the College of Liberal Arts and Sciences established the Mary Louise Smith Chair in Women and Politics. The chair is host to nationally renowned political leaders, scholars, and activists each year. The woman holding the Mary Louise Smith Chair serves as a leader, mentor, and role model for young women interested in politics. Smith died of lung cancer on August 22, 1997.

Snowe, Olympia (Olympia Jean Bouchles Snow) (1947–) *U.S. senator* Olympia Jean Bouchles was born on February 21, 1947, in

Augusta, Maine, the daughter of immigrants from Greece. When both her parents died before she was 10, her aunt and uncle, who worked in a textile mill, raised her. Snowe graduated from St. Basil's Academy in Garrison, New York, in 1962 and completed her secondary education at Edward Little High School in Auburn, Maine. She graduated with a degree in political science from the University of Maine at Orono in 1969. Shortly after her graduation, she married Peter Snowe, a Republican State Legislator.

In 1973, Peter Snowe was killed in a car accident, and Olympia Snowe was appointed to his seat. She was reelected in 1974 and then was elected to the Maine Senate in 1976. In the senate, she chaired the Joint Standing Committee on Health and Institutional Services, where she gained particular recognition for her work on health care issues.

In 1978, Snowe was elected to serve in the U.S. House of Representatives and became the youngest Republican woman ever elected to the House. While serving as a representative, she married John McKernan, then the governor of Maine, in 1989; she thus served concurrently as both a U.S. representative and as first lady of Maine from 1989 to 1995. She was reelected to her House seat seven times before deciding to run for the U.S. Senate in 1994 following the retirement of Senator George Mitchell. She won, and in 2001, Senator Snowe became the first Republican woman ever to secure a full-term seat on the Senate Finance Committee, as well as only the third woman in history to join the panel. The Finance Committee is considered one of the most powerful in Congress.

In 2005, Snowe was among the Gang of 14, a group of moderate senators who brokered a compromise on the use of the judicial filibuster against judicial nominees. The WHITE HOUSE PROJECT has named Snowe one of "8 in '08," indicating that she is a credible female candidate for the presidency in 2008. Snowe lists among her top legislative priorities several areas of interest to women: contraceptive coverage, prescription drug coverage, and CHILD CARE funding. Senator Snowe was reelected in 2006 with 74 percent of the vote.

Further Reading

Barone, Michael. *The Almanac of American Politics.* Washington, D.C.: National Journal Group, 2006.

"Senator Olympia J. Snowe." In *Project Vote Smart.* Available online. URL: http://votesmart.org/bio.php?can_id=H1630103. Accessed on January 8, 2007.

"Snow, Olympia Jean." In *Biographical Directory of the United States Congress, 1774–present.* Available online. URL: http://bioguide.congress.gov/scripts/biodisplay.pl?index=S000663. Accessed on January 8, 2007.

—Angela Kouters

Social Security and women The current Social Security system was established under the Social Security Act in 1935. Numerous changes have been made since its inception, but the basic philosophy has remained intact. The Social Security system is an example of a gender-neutral law because it does not treat men and women differently in the law itself, though men and women experience the system in varied ways as a result of differences in employment and wage patterns. Social Security is particularly important for women because women are less likely than men to have a private pension. Women also live an average of seven years longer than men, and because of pay inequities and time spent away from work to raise their children, they have lower lifetime earnings than men. In 2000, women made up 60 percent of Social Security beneficiaries. Half of women age 65 and older would be poor if not for Social Security benefits, and for the 25 percent of elderly women who live alone, Social Security is their only source of income. Without Social Security, the poverty rate for women over 65 would have been 52.9 percent in 1995.

Although some adjustments to the laws have been made to recognize women's increased participation in the labor force, the Social Security system is premised on 1930s traditional gender roles in families, which characterizes a tiny fraction of modern families. Social Security was intended to be a supplement to private pension plans and savings accumulated over the course of a lifetime, but only about half of men and a quarter of retired women earn additional income from private pensions.

Under the current Social Security system, workers are eligible to retire with full benefits at age 65 and to receive partial benefits at age 62. However, for workers born after 1937, eligibility for retirement with full benefits is age 67. Social Security benefits are based on the 35 years of highest taxable earnings of at least $520 each quarter of the year. The benefit formula is a progressive calculation, and the five lowest-earning years (including years with zero earnings) in an individual's working life are dropped. A married person is eligible for the larger of either 100 percent of his or her own retired-worker benefit or 50 percent of his or her spouse's retired-worker benefit. A woman whose benefit, based on her own work record, is less than or equal to the spousal benefit she could claim is said to be "dually entitled" and does not gain additional benefit from having worked. A man is similarly entitled to benefits from his wife's accounts, but in reality nearly all who use the spouse's benefit are women. This may change if more men opt to help raise children by either reducing the number of hours they work or by leaving the paid labor force entirely for a period of time.

Several reform proposals are being actively considered in Congress. The most common type of reform, and one President George W. Bush promised to push toward adoption in his second term, includes some aspect of privatization of the current system by diverting some or all of the current payroll tax dollars to an individually held private investment account. This, however, has not been acted upon in Congress. The plans differ in how much would be diverted (all or only a percentage) and in what type of private account the money would be invested. Some people would like to see individual reform initiatives that will

invest primarily or solely in equities (stocks), whereas others would prefer a more conservative investment strategy in bonds or in some split between the two that could change over the course of one's lifetime, becoming more conservative as retirement nears. Some plans call for collective investment of the trust fund assets or the collective investment of only some of the assets to try to increase the size of the trust fund itself. The Task Force on Women and Social Security, a joint project of the National Council of Women's Organizations and the Institute for Women's Policy Research, has made several proposals that would strengthen Social Security for women. Among its many recommendations is the provision of a "family service credit," which could include an earnings credit and a provision for a number of "drop-out years" in calculating benefits.

Further Reading
Berkowitz, Edward D. *America's Welfare State: From Roosevelt to Reagan.* Baltimore: Johns Hopkins University Press, 1991.
Patterson, James T. *America's Struggle against Poverty in the Twentieth Century.* Cambridge, Mass.: Harvard University Press, 2000.

Solis, Hilda (1957–) *congressperson* Hilda Solis was born on October 20, 1957, in Los Angeles, California. She earned a bachelor's degree from California State Polytechnic University, Pomona (1979), and a master's in public administration from the University of Southern California (1981). She has served in the White House Office of Hispanic Affairs, as an analyst with the Office of Management and Budget, and as a member of the California State Assembly (1992–94) and the California State Senate (1994–2000). In 2000, she received the John F. Kennedy Profile in Courage Award, the first woman and the first Latina recipient.

In 2000, Solis won election to Congress by beating an 18-year incumbent, Matthew Martinez, in the Democratic primary. There was not a Republican in the race, but Solis beat challengers from the Libertarian, Green, and Peace and Freedom parties to win with 79 percent of vote in the general election. Solis serves on the House Committee on Energy and Commerce and the Subcommittee on Energy and Air Quality, and she is the ranking member on the Subcommittee on Environment and Hazardous Materials. She has been working to reduce teen pregnancies in the Hispanic community with community-based intervention programs. Although she is Catholic, she is pro-choice with regard to ABORTION. Along with other pro-choice Catholic Democrats, she signed a letter to Cardinal Theodore McCarrick of Washington, D.C., urging him reconsider refusing communion to pro-choice legislators. Solis was reelected in 2006.

Further Reading

Barone, Michael. *The Almanac of American Politics.* Washington, D.C.: National Journal Group, 2006.

"Representative Hilda L. Solis (CA)." In *Project Vote Smart.* Available online. URL: http://votesmart. org/bio.php?can_id=BS021498. Accessed on January 8, 2007.

"Solis, Hilda." In *Biographical Directory of the United States Congress, 1774–present.* Available online. URL: http://bioguide.congress.gov/scripts/biodisplay.pl?index=S001153. Accessed on January 8, 2007.

—Angela Kouters

Solomon, Hannah (Hannah Greenebaum Solomon) (1858–1942) *social welfare activist*

A lifelong social welfare activist, Hannah Greenebaum was born in Chicago on January 14, 1858, the fourth of 10 children of Sarah and Michael Greenebaum, both German-Jewish immigrants. She married Henry Solomon in 1879 and had three children. Hannah Solomon's commitment to social activism found expression beyond her own community in the newly founded Chicago Woman's Club (CWC), to which she and her sister were elected as the first Jewish members in 1877. Her involvement in the

CWC demonstrated the value of networking and cooperation with religious, secular and government organizations for the general good of all, a lesson she took throughout her work during the Progressive era. Solomon's own religious identity as a Jewish woman, however, led her to create, in 1893, the first national Jewish women's service and education organization: the National Council of Jewish Women (NCJW). This organization encouraged Jewish women to engage in social work, informed by the principles of Judaism. Cooperating with JANE ADDAMS of HULL-HOUSE, Solomon brought legal and work training services to Russian-Jewish immigrants through the NCJW.

Addressing the needs of immigrants exposed Solomon to the general conditions of the underprivileged, and her contributions to Chicago were wide-ranging, including rebuilding Park Ridge (Industrial) School for Girls and investigating the city's sanitation system. During World War I, she led women's civilian war efforts as chairperson of the City Ward Leaders committee. A proponent of women's rights, Solomon served as treasurer to the National Council of Women and was an interpreter for her close friend SUSAN B. ANTHONY at the International Council of Women meeting in Berlin in 1904. Solomon's belief that a woman's sphere was "the whole wide world" opened the way for Jewish women to contribute directly to their own communities and beyond. She died in Chicago on December 7, 1942, at the age of 84.

Further Reading

Rogow, Faith. *Gone to Another Meeting: The National Council of Jewish Women, 1893–1993.* Tuscaloosa: University of Alabama Press, 1993.

Solomon, Hannah. *Fabric of My Life.* New York: Bloch Publishing Company, 1946.

—Chana Revell Kotzin

Southern Women's League for the Rejection of the Susan B. Anthony Amendment

The first ANTI-SUFFRAGE organization was formed

in Massachusetts in 1868 but was not formalized and named until 1895, when it became known as the Massachusetts Association Opposed to the Further Extension of Suffrage to women (MAOFEWS). Between 1869 and 1910, the movement gathered members and money as anti-suffrage organizations formed in many other states and dedicated their efforts to defeating state referenda. In 1911, the state organizations joined together to form the National Association Opposed to Woman Suffrage (NAOWS). Southern states were slow to form anti-suffrage organizations, however, believing that custom and tradition would do more to defeat woman suffrage than any organization ever could. Alternatively, southern women may have concluded that the national suffragist forces presented little threat because they rarely ventured into the reluctant southern states. In a contrary example, Virginia suffragists formed an organization in 1912. While they claimed a membership list of more than 2,000 two years later, according to Elna Green, they rarely met and they "held no public meetings, and . . . consistently avoided newspaper debates and controversies." By far, the most active state association affiliated with NAOWS was formed in Alabama and claimed more than 1,600 members in 1916. Its motto, "Home Rule, State's Rights, and White Supremacy," reflected the primary arguments against women's suffrage in the South.

When Congress passed the Susan B. Anthony Amendment and sent it to the states for ratification on June 4, 1919, the southern strategy changed. The Alabama state association reorganized as the Southern Women's Anti-Ratification League and began to lobby members of the state legislature through letters, petitions read by male supporters. and sympathetic press coverage. After the amendment was defeated, Alabama anti-suffragists decided to maintain their organization to combat other changes if, in fact, the Nineteenth Amendment was ratified. They changed their name to the Southern Women's League for the Rejection of the Susan B. Anthony Amendment (commonly known as

the Southern Rejection League) and announced plans to cooperate with existing anti-suffrage associations and to lead the fight in states without formal anti-suffrage organizations, making it a southern regional organization.

Although it never fully achieved the status of a regional organization nor developed the leadership structure outside of Alabama that would have sustained it for any length of time, it did frame the argument against suffrage so prevalent in the South in its "Declaration of Principles" concerning the primacy of state's rights, white supremacy, and chivalry. The Southern Rejection League produced leaflets, broadsides, and editorials bearing their stamp. These were widely distributed throughout the southern states and often relied on scare tactics linking suffrage with socialism, communism, atheism, and anarchy. The anti-suffrage battle in the southern states warned women not to be gullible and think that the vote would benefit them. Instead, it would be a burden on them that would interfere with their duties at home. Marriage and family could even be jeopardized—a husband and wife could be torn asunder if they disagreed politically, and politically involved women might decide to have fewer children. Ultimately, according to this line of reasoning, the supremacy of the Anglo-Saxon race could even be threatened. By granting the vote to women, the argument went, the South could find itself on a slippery slope that might eventually result in black domination. The Southern Rejection League maintained its organization and continued working through the summer of 1920, but once the federal amendment was ratified, it lost focus and disbanded.

Further Reading

Green, Elna C. *Southern Strategies: Southern Women and the Woman Suffrage Question.* Chapel Hill: University of North Carolina Press, 1997, 106.

McRae, Elizabeth Gillespie. "Caretakers of Southern Civilization: Georgia Women and the Anti-Suffrage Campaign, 1914–1920." *Georgia Historical Quarterly* 82 (1998): 801–828.

Yellin, Carol Lynn, and Sherman, Janann. *The Perfect 36: Tennessee Delivers Woman Suffrage*, edited by Ilene Jones-Cornwell. Memphis, Tenn.: Iris Press, 1998.

—Paula Casey

Stabenow, Debbie (Deborah Ann Stabenow) (1950–) *U.S. senator*

Debborah Ann Stabenow was born on April 29, 1950, and grew up in the small town of Clare, Michigan. She attended Michigan State University, where she received her bachelor's degree in 1972 and master's in social work in 1975. Before running for public office, she worked with youth in the public schools. She was first elected to the Ingham County Board of Commissioners in 1974, while she was still in graduate school, and was the youngest person and first woman to chair the board. In 1979, she was elected to the Michigan House of Representatives, where she served until 1991. While in the state house, she became the first woman to preside over the chamber. She served in the state senate from 1991 to 1994.

In 1994, Stabenow ran for governor of Michigan but lost in the Democratic primary to Howard Wolpe. He then asked her to join his ticket as lieutenant governor in the general election, which they lost. In 1996, she won a seat in the U.S. House of Representatives and served two terms representing Michigan's 8th congressional district. Stabenow was an advocate for gun control, ABORTION rights, and tax cuts for small businesses while in the House.

In 2000, Stabenow won election to the U.S. Senate, making her only the second person from Michigan to have served in both houses of the Michigan State Legislature and in both houses of the United States Congress. She is a member of the Senate Committee on Budget, the Committee on Banking, Housing and Urban Affairs, the Committee on Agriculture, Nutrition and Forestry, and the Special Committee on Aging. Stabenow became the third-ranking Democrat in the U.S. Senate on November 16, 2004, when she was elected by her colleagues to be secretary of the Democratic Caucus. As caucus secretary, she assists Senate minority leader Harry Reid in setting the Democrats' agenda and priorities. Following the 2006 elections, the Democrats regained the majority in the Senate, and Stabenow was reelected with 57 percent of the vote. She currently chairs the Democratic Steering Committee in the 110th Congress.

Further Reading
Barone, Michael. *The Almanac of American Politics*. Washington, D.C.: National Journal Group, 2006.
"Senator Debbie Ann Stabenow (MI)." In *Project Vote Smart*. Available online. URL: http://votesmart.org/bio.php?can_id=BC035954. Accessed on January 8, 2007.
"Stabenow, Deborah Ann." In *Biographical Directory of the United States Congress, 1774–present*. Available online. URL: http://bioguide.congress.gov/scripts/biodisplay.pl?index=S000770. Accessed on January 8, 2007.

—Angela Kouters

Stanton, Elizabeth Cady (1815–1902) *social rights activist, women's rights advocate*

Born in Johnstown, New York, on November 12, 1815, Elizabeth Cady was raised in a strict Presbyterian household. In her later life, she used the death of her older brother, when she was 11, as an explanatory catalyst for her drive to improve the situation of women. Upon her brother's death, Elizabeth Cady Stanton recounts that her father said, "Oh my daughter I wish that you were a boy!" to which she replied, "I will try to be all my brother was." Cady excelled in school, and through the influence of her brother-in-law, Edward Bayard, she was sent to the Troy Female Seminary, run by EMMA WILLARD. After her graduation, she met her husband, Henry Brewster Stanton, at the house of Gerrit Smith, her cousin and a wealthy abolitionist. Against her father's wishes, she married Stanton in 1840, and the couple went immediately to London for the

Elizabeth Cady Stanton (LIBRARY OF CONGRESS)

World Anti-Slavery Convention. While Elizabeth Cady Stanton was not at the convention as a delegate, those women who were, including LUCRETIA MOTT, were not allowed to sit with men and participate. It was from Mott that Stanton was urged to read Mary Wollstonecraft's, *A VINDICATION OF THE RIGHTS OF WOMAN* in addition to works by FRANCES WRIGHT, SARAH GRIMKÉ, and ANGELINA GRIMKÉ. Mott and Stanton decided to hold a convention to promote the rights of women.

In 1845, the Stantons moved to Boston, and Elizabeth gave birth to her first three (of seven) children. (Her offspring would include feminist and suffragist HARRIOT STANTON BLATCH.) In Boston, Stanton encountered many of the abolitionists and transcendentalists about whom she had read, but her husband's law practice was not successful, and in 1847 they moved to Seneca Falls, New York. It was there in 1848 that Stanton was invited to tea at a friend's house, where Lucretia Mott was visiting. After a discussion about their dissatisfaction concerning the status of women, they decided to hold a public meeting. An ad appeared on July 11 in the *Seneca County Courier* inviting people to "a woman's rights convention . . . to discuss the social, civil and religious condition and rights of Woman." Stanton and her friends then wrote the Declaration of Sentiments, based on the Declaration of Independence. The result of the successful SENECA FALLS CONVENTION was publication of the DECLARATION OF SENTIMENTS AND RESOLUTIONS. The document was adopted both at Seneca Falls and at a convention in Rochester, New York, two weeks later. Stanton insisted that a resolution demanding SUFFRAGE be included. Many, including Mott, were concerned that such a demand would marginalize supporters. But Stanton won the argument (with help from Frederick Douglass), and she began her fight for women's suffrage.

Stanton met SUSAN B. ANTHONY in 1851 after a lecture given by William Lloyd Garrison in Seneca Falls. They began to work together, with Anthony traveling around the country giving speeches written by Stanton. (Anthony would go to Seneca Falls and help Stanton take care of the children while Stanton wrote the speeches she would deliver.) In 1854, Stanton appeared before the New York State Legislature with a 6,000 signature petition arguing for enhanced property rights and 4,000 signatures for women's suffrage: "We are persons; native, free born citizens; property holders, tax payers; yet we are denied the exercise of our right to the elective franchise." Stanton's father sharply criticized the address and told her that if she appeared publicly again espousing such ideas, he would disown her.

Stanton was subsequently elected president, at Anthony's urging, of the newly formed Women's State Temperance society. Stanton and Anthony both connected the work of the TEMPERANCE MOVEMENT to suffrage, urging women to recognize that if, as men claimed, a woman's vote was held in proxy by her husband, then temper-

427 Stanton, Elizabeth Cady

ance candidates would not win. If this was the case, then women should have their own vote to elect their chosen candidates. The society also worked to change divorce laws so that drunkenness would be seen (as adultery already was) as grounds for divorce. The society under Stanton and Anthony's tutelage was short-lived as more conservative women, concerned that the issue of temperance was taking a back seat to suffrage and women's rights, allowed men to hold office and vote. With these male members, the platform that included suffrage was defeated and Stanton and Anthony both left the society.

Stanton's father died in 1859, the same year as John Brown's failed slave uprising in Harper's Ferry, which led to the confinement of Stanton's cousin, Gerrit Smith. She spoke again before the New York legislature in 1860, noting the comparison between the condition of the slave and the condition of woman. The legislature passed a bill allowing for all women to hold property, to keep their earnings if married, to sue and to hold custody of their children. After this first legislative success of the women's movement, other states soon followed.

During the Civil War, Stanton and Anthony worked for emancipation, but after the war an argument arose among women's rights activists concerning the Fourteenth and Fifteenth Amendments to the Constitution, granting suffrage to men, regardless of race. In 1869, this split resulted in the founding of two organizations advocating women's rights: the NATIONAL WOMAN SUFFRAGE ASSOCIATION (NWSA), founded by Cady Stanton and Anthony, and the AMERICAN WOMAN SUFFRAGE ASSOCIATION, founded by LUCY STONE. Stanton served as president of the NWSA from 1860 to 1890. The NWSA turned its immediate attention to the fight over women's inclusion in the Fifteenth Amendment and divorced itself entirely from the Republican Party and the "Negro Suffrage" question, whereas the AWSA continued to support the Fifteenth Amendment as written, vowing to support a Sixteenth Amendment dedicated to woman suffrage. Of the two organizations, the NWSA was more

revolutionary because at first it refused to admit men, attacked the institution of marriage, and published essays on "free love" in its journal, *The Revolution.* Stanton, in particular, targeted the church as a primary source of sexism in society, which led her to reject the Bible. The AWSA maintained a working relationship with abolitionists of both sexes, and its membership reflected a more conservative, middle- and upper-class slice of society. AWSA's publication, the *Woman's Journal,* supported the institutions of family, church, and marriage. By 1890, old animosities between the NWSA and AWSA had faded sufficiently for a merger to take place. The new organization, the NATIONAL AMERICAN WOMAN SUFFRAGE ASSOCIATION (NAWSA), elected Elizabeth Cady Stanton president and Anthony vice president. Stanton resigned in 1892, delivering the speech "The Solitude of Self," which argued that women, like men, must be fully equipped with the tools to lead an independent life as women, for with women and with men "each soul lives alone forever." Stanton went on to write many important books, documents, and speeches of the women's rights movement. In 1881, the first volume of *The History of Woman Suffrage,* a substantial work containing the full history, documents, and letters of the woman's suffrage movement, was published. While Stanton, in addition to Anthony and Gage, wrote the first three volumes, the work was eventually completed in 1922 by Ida Harper.

In 1895, Stanton published *The Woman's Bible,* a feminist analysis of the Bible. She died on October 26, 1902, in New York City. Her role in the women's movement of the 19th century had often been overshadowed by Anthony.

Further Reading

Dubois, Ellen C. ed. *Elizabeth Cady Stanton–Susan B. Anthony Reader: Correspondence, Writings, Speeches.* Boston: Northeastern University Press, 1992.

Griffith, Elisabeth. *In Her Own Right: The Life of Elizabeth Cady Stanton.* Oxford: Oxford University Press, 1985.

Stanton, Elizabeth Cady, Susan B. Anthony, and Matilda
    Joslyn Gage, eds. *History of Woman Suffrage.* 3
    vols. Rochester, N.Y.: Charles Mann, 1881.
Ward, Geoffrey. *Not for Ourselves Alone: The Story of
    Elizabeth Cady Stanton and Susan B. Anthony.* New
    York: Knopf, 2001.

—Claire Curtis

Stanton v. Stanton (421 U.S. 7) (1975) This
case challenged a Utah statute setting the age of
majority at 18 for females and 21 for males.
Although it involved court-ordered child support payments, the real issue for women was the
reasoning behind Utah's distinction between
males and females. Thelma Stanton challenged
the Utah law as a violation of the equal-protection clause of the Fourteenth Amendment. Her
husband, James Stanton, countered that the law
had a rational basis and should therefore be
upheld. In ruling in favor of James, the Utah
Supreme Court articulated the rationale behind
the sex distinction in the law, noting that "generally it is the man's primary responsibility to
provide a home and its essentials and it is a salu-
tary thing for him to get a good education and/or
training before he undertakes those responsibilities." The court noted that girls tended to
mature before boys and also tended to marry
earlier. On this basis, the Utah court ended
child-support payments to the Stantons' daughter at age 18, but continued support payments
for their son until age 21.

On appeal, the U.S. Supreme Court overturned the decision. Justice Harry Blackmun,
writing for the majority, stated: "No longer is
the female destined solely for the home and the
rearing of the family, and only the male for the
marketplace and world of ideas. . . . Women's
activities and responsibilities are increasing
and expanding. Coeducation is a fact, not a rarity. The presence of women in business, in the
professions, in government, and indeed, in all
walks of life where education is desirable, if not
always a necessary antecedent is apparent and

a proper subject of judicial notice." By the time
this decision was issued, TITLE IX OF THE EDUCA-
TION AMENDMENTS OF 1972 had already ended
sex-based admission, enrollment, and quota
systems hampering educational equity.

Further Reading
Lindgren, J. Ralph, Nadine Taub, Beth Ann Wolfson,
    and Carla M. Palumbo. *The Law of Sex Discrimi-
    nation,* 3rd ed. Belmont, Calif.: Thomson Wad-
    sworth, 2005.

state status of women commissions State
commissions on the status of women gave the
modern women's movement immediate and
ongoing political authority in the mid- to late
1960s by mobilizing civically engaged volunteers
and professionals to formulate policies on wom-
en's issues. Leaders of national women's organizations and labor union activists participating in
the deliberations of John F. Kennedy's PRESIDENT'S
COMMISSION ON THE STATUS OF WOMEN (PCSW)—
formed by executive order in 1961 and charged
to recommend ways to eliminate legal and customary barriers to women's full participation in
civic life—founded state-wide alliances led by
the NATIONAL FEDERATION OF BUSINESS AND PRO-
FESSIONAL WOMEN'S CLUBS to establish similar
commissions in the states. There were active
commissions in all 50 states by 1967, and all but
nine of these were established by gubernatorial
executive order modeled closely on Kennedy's
Executive Order Establishing a President's Commission. Consequently, governors' commissions
were required to submit reports on women's status in the areas of education, political and civic
status, and home and community at the end of a
mandatory authorization period, usually from
one to two years.

Commission investigations and public hearings drew public attention to sex discrimination, and subsequent recommendations gave
women's organizations with disparate programs
a unified agenda for social change. Recommendations often included establishment of a

permanent commission on the status of women. Many governors reestablished commissions in the 1970s as a response to the social revolution of the 1960s. Commissions often served as the location for organizing and sustaining coalitions to ratify the EQUAL RIGHTS AMENDMENT in the 1970s and 1980s. Sixteen states have active commissions that serve as clearinghouses for information on the status of women.

Further Reading

Laughlin, Kathleen A. *Women's Work and Public Policy: A History of the Women's Bureau, U.S. Department of Labor, 1945—1970.* Boston: Northeastern University Press, 2000.

—Kathleen A. Laughlin

Steinem, Gloria (1934–   ) *feminist, journalist, women's rights advocate, founder and original publisher of Ms. Magazine*   The founder of MS. MAGAZINE, the NATIONAL WOMEN'S POLITICAL CAUCUS, and the Women's Action Alliance, Gloria Marie Steinem was born in Toledo, Ohio, on March 25, 1934. Steinem experienced an erratic early education due to her father's absence and her mother's mental illness; her parents eventually divorced. Overcoming these early difficulties, in 1952 Steinem was accepted to and enrolled in Smith College, where she began her interest in women's issues and politics, including campaigning for Adlai Stevenson. After graduation in 1956, Steinem traveled to India for two years. She returned home with a book manuscript and the hope that she would be hired as a journalist. Turned down by magazines and publishing houses, she became a freelance writer instead. She achieved some notoriety after her exposé of her undercover experience as a Playboy bunny was published in *Esquire* in 1963. However, Steinem was still not taken seriously in the world of journalism, and she was not able to write the kind of political pieces that her undergraduate degree in government had prepared her to do.

By 1968, that had changed. Steinem covered George McGovern's presidential campaign, and this work led to her being hired as an editor for *New York* magazine. Now given the chance to pursue what interested her, she wrote about the United Farm Workers strike in California, the assassination of Martin Luther King, Jr., and how women, as a group, experienced oppression. In 1970, she published the article "After Black Power, Women's Liberation," which won the Penney Missouri Journalism award. Steinem saw herself as bridging the gaps between privileged white women, working-class women, and women of color, recognizing that a FEMINISM that does not bridge that gap is not a feminism that will really be able to end oppression.

In the early 1970s, Steinem marched for passage of the EQUAL RIGHTS AMENDMENT, worker's

Gloria Steinem, 1972 (LIBRARY OF CONGRESS)

rights, and ABORTION rights. She added her voice to the multitudes of women who admitted to having had illegal abortions, and she urged legislative and judicial officials to make abortion legal. She began a lecture series with Dorothy Pitman Hughes, a black activist who had started a community day-care movement in New York. Together, in 1971, Hughes and Steinem formed the Women's Action Alliance (WAA), which provided information on how to combat sex discrimination in the workplace and how to effect social change in women's own communities. The WAA funded many activities that sought to introduce girls and women to nontraditional fields of study and employment, but it was dissolved in 1997 due to lack of funds.

It was also in 1971 that Steinem, with BETTY FRIEDAN, BELLA ABZUG, and SHIRLEY CHISHOLM, started the National Women's Political Caucus to help identify, fund, and publicize women running for political office. Later that year, Steinem produced a onetime insert to *New York* magazine, with articles that argued for the need to legalize abortion and to challenge the sexual stereotypes present in the English language. This insert was the first edition of what would become the feminist journal *Ms.* The following year Steinem also founded the Ms. Foundation in 1972 to fund women's causes, again illustrating her desire to not simply write about a better world but to try and help produce that world. She urged the Democratic National Convention of 1972 to focus more particularly on women's issues, specifically reproductive rights. Women were largely ignored at the 1972 convention, and Steinem's critical stance toward the possibility that electoral politics could change the country from above emerged in part from these experiences. *McCall's* magazine named her Woman of the Year in 1972.

Steinem was now on track for the work that she has continued to this day. She is an activist for women's rights, worker's rights, and social justice as well as a writer who seeks to reach all kinds of women concerning the issues of most concern to them. In the 1980s and 1990s, she published four books: *Outrageous Acts and Everyday Rebellions* (1983), *Marilyn: Norma Jean* (about Marilyn Monroe as a female icon; 1986), *Revolution from Within: A Book of Self-Esteem* (1992), and *Moving beyond Words* (1994). Steinem edited *Ms* for 15 years and then worked to revamp and restart the magazine after it lost readership (during which time it was sold to a group of Australian feminists and then sold again to a publishing conglomerate) in the late 1980s. The magazine subsequently reemerged without advertisements and now exists as a feminist journal that does not need to rely on advertising, particularly the kind typically found in women's magazines. Since 2001, *Ms.* has been published by the Feminist Majority Foundation.

The Ms. Foundation founded the popular TAKE OUR DAUGHTERS TO WORK DAY in 1993 and pursues a number of initiatives encouraging female-owned businesses, promoting equal pay for equal work, establishing battered women's shelters, and building ties among women across a variety of ethnic, racial, and class-based lines. Gloria Steinem is on the advisory council for the international women's rights organization Equality Now, the advisory board for the feminist activist community, feminist.com, and the board of directors of choice USA, and she is a signatory to the Not In Our Name Project protesting, in part, the war in Iraq and treatment of prisoners by the U.S. military. She was inducted into the National Women's Rights Hall of Fame in 1993.

Steinem continues to work to end the oppression of women around the world and the oppression of all peoples by a system marked by patriarchy and capitalism. Her focus has always been on political change at the grassroots level; in 1982, she said, ". . . we may disagree on analyses in the long run: I don't think feminism *can* just be imitative or integrationist. By definition, it must transform. But in the short run, there are goals we agree on. And it's in the short run that we must act." (*Outrageous Acts,* 1983)

See also NATIONAL ORGANIZATION FOR WOMEN.

Further Reading

Bradley, Patricia. *Mass Media and the Shaping of American Feminism, 1963–1975.* Jackson: University Press of Mississippi, 2003.

Heilbrun, Carolyn. *The Education of a Woman: The Life of Gloria Steinem.* New York: Bantam Doubleday Dell, 1995.

Steinem, Gloria. *Outrageous Acts and Everyday Rebellions,* by Gloria Steinem. New York: Holt Rhinehart, 1983.

———. *Moving Beyond Words: Age, Rage, Money, Power, Sex, Muscles: Breaking the Boundaries of Gender.* New York: Simon and Schuster, 1994.

Stenberg v. Carhart (530 U.S. 913) (2000)

Stenberg v. *Carhart* dealt with the issue of a state's ability to prohibit all late-term ABORTIONS (known as partial-birth abortions by opponents). This case was closely decided by the U.S. Supreme Court in a 5-4 decision and turned on the question of a woman's health. Justice Stephen Breyer, writing for the majority, said that "a risk to a woman's health is the same whether it happens to arise from regulating a particular method of abortion, or from barring abortion entirely." This decision supports a doctor's determination of what is in the best interests of the woman's health over the state's outright ban of certain abortion procedures.

On November 5, 2003, President Bush signed a law banning partial-birth abortions. The Partial-Birth Abortion Ban Act of 2003 makes it illegal for doctors to take overt action to abort a late-term fetus—one in its second or third trimester. The bill makes no exemption for a woman whose health is at risk by carrying the pregnancy to term, nor does it take into account ailments or deformities the child may suffer in life. The language in the federal legislation is very similar to Nebraska's late-term abortion law already declared unconstitutional by the U.S. Supreme Court in *Stenberg* v. *Carhart* (2000). Three federal judges in three different locations have issued injunctions citing the undue burden the law places on a woman's right to make her own medical decision about abortion without interference from the government.

Further Reading

The OYEZ Project. "*Stenberg v. Carhart,* 530 U.S. 914 (2000)." Available online. URL: http://www.oyez.org/cases/case?case=1990–1999/1999/1999_99_830. Accessed on January 11, 2007.

Stone, Lucy (1818–1893) *suffragist*

One of the most famous orators for abolitionism and women's rights, Lucy Stone was born on August 13, 1818, near West Brookfield, Massachusetts. In defiance of her father, who disapproved of education for women, Stone paid for her own tuition at OBERLIN COLLEGE, where she graduated in 1847 (one of the first women from Massachusetts to earn a college degree). She was asked to write a graduation address, but because she would not have been able to deliver it herself, women being forbidden to publicly address an audience of men and women, she refused to write it. After graduation, she began a lifelong commitment to speaking out about slavery and women's rights.

As an orator, Stone became famous. In a time when women were not supposed to speak to mixed audiences, Stone earned a living and became famous for her speeches. While on the lecture circuit for the Massachusetts Anti-Slavery Society, she received appeals from many women (ELIZABETH CADY STANTON and LUCRETIA MOTT among them) to start lecturing on women's rights. In 1849, she finished her contracted work with the Anti-Slavery Society and turned her attention to lecturing on the "woman question." She addressed the issue of women's rights in upstate New York during a movement to make the People's College coeducational. In 1850, she helped to organize the first Massachusetts women's rights convention, held in Worcester. In the same year, she addressed the Massachusetts state legislature concerning a civil rights amendment for women.

Stone met Henry Blackwell (brother to ELIZABETH BLACKWELL) after he witnessed this

Lucy Stone (LIBRARY OF CONGRESS)

address, and the two eventually married in 1855 in a ceremony that stressed egalitarianism. Stone kept her maiden name, starting a movement of "Lucy Stoners," women who retained their own names after marriage. In 1857, her only daughter, ALICE STONE BLACKWELL, was born, and Stone cut back on her lecturing in order to take care of Alice. Henry Blackwell experienced financial difficulties in this period, and the couple moved often, ultimately settling in Chicago, where Stone resumed some of her lecturing to urge the Illinois State Legislature to take up the issue of women's SUFFRAGE and married women's property rights. Stone and Blackwell worked in Kansas to halt the expansion of slavery into new Western territories. Their antislavery work was hampered by racism, but many Kansas residents were willing to support women's suffrage.

After the Civil War, Stone worked with SUSAN B. ANTHONY to bring abolitionists together with women's rights activists in order to guarantee the vote to black men and women together. With the passage of the Fourteenth and Fifteenth Amendments, which failed to grant the vote to women, the two split over the tactics of how to achieve the vote for women. Stone was offended by the racism inherent in some of the calls by suffragists to oppose passage of the Fifteenth Amendment. One argument used against the inclusion of the word *male* in the second section of the amendment was that women should not be ruled over by "ignorant men." This veiled reference to freed male slaves was of concern to Stone and others. The conflict boiled over at the AMERICAN EQUAL RIGHTS ASSOCIATION meeting in May 1870. Stone, a delegate from Massachusetts, urged a continuation of the combined effort to work for civil rights and women's rights. Stanton formed the NATIONAL WOMAN SUFFRAGE ASSOCIATION (NWSA) after the convention in order to fight against passage of the Fifteenth Amendment. Stone helped form the AMERICAN WOMAN SUFFRAGE ASSOCIATION (AWSA) in response to Stanton's NWSA. The AWSA argued that votes for women would be best achieved using a state-by-state approach. Stone sought to grant more power to the voices of women who were not from the well-connected groups that she felt were over-represented in earlier suffrage organizations. The AWSA also reached out to southern women, gaining delegates from Confederate states. Stone's daughter would mend this rift with the merger of the two organizations in 1890 as the NATIONAL AMERICAN WOMAN SUFFRAGE ASSOCIATION.

In 1870, Stone and Blackwell started the women's rights magazine *Woman's Journal,* in which they advocated for married women's property laws, divorce reforms, equal rights. It was through the *Woman's Journal*—which stayed in circulation for 60 years—that Stone's goal of outreach to women across the United States was achieved. By publishing the works of popular writers, such as HARRIET BEECHER STOWE, Stone's journal reached and was read by a wide audience. The *Woman's Journal* also followed state-by-state attempts to gain suffrage. The territories of Wyoming and Utah granted suffrage in 1869. Referenda held in Colorado, Michigan, Nebraska, and Kansas all failed, but in 1883 the vote was granted to women in the territory of Washington (although the Supreme Court took away that vote in 1887). Stone's tactics appeared to work, at least in the West, but no eastern state managed to successfully grant suffrage.

Stone gave her last lecture in 1893 at the World's Fair in Chicago, declaring, "I think, with never-ending gratitude, that young women of today do not and can never know at what price their right to free speech and to speak at all in public has been earned. . . . Now all we need is to continue to speak the truth fearlessly, and we shall add to our number those who will turn the scale to the side of equal and full justice in all things." She died of cancer on October 18, 1893.

See also ABOLITIONIST MOVEMENT, WOMEN IN THE.

Further Reading

Blackwell, Alice Stone. *Lucy Stone, Pioneer of Woman's Rights.* Charlottesville: University Press of Virginia, 2001.

Kerr, Andrea Moore. *Lucy Stone, Speaking Out for Equality.* New Brunswick, N.J.: Rutgers University Press, 1994.

Million, Joelle. *Woman's Voice, Woman's Place: Lucy Stone and the Birth of the Woman's Rights.* Westport, Conn.: Praeger Press, 2003.

—Claire Curtis

STOP ERA

STOP ERA   In October 1972, PHYLLIS SCHLAFLY founded STOP ERA in order to halt the ratification of the EQUAL RIGHTS AMENDMENT (ERA). As an acronym, the name of her organization stands for *Stop Taking Our Privileges with this Extra Responsibility Amendment.*

With her background in politics and her experience in grassroots activism, Schlafly could rely on an extensive conservative network to organize the anti-ERA movement. As the national chairperson, she was its official spokesperson and primary leader. With Schlafly behind it, STOP ERA was present on the national level, and with her loyal supporters, it was active on the local level as well. The *PHYLLIS SCHLAFLY REPORT,* the *EAGLE FORUM NEWSLETTER,* and Schlafly's book *The Power of the Positive Woman* (1977) all delivered arguments and guidelines for the views and grassroots activities of her supporters. STOP ERA organized workshops and state conferences and developed state chapters.

Right-wing organizations, churches, and religious (especially fundamentalist) networks were the recruiting field for STOP ERA. The movement brought together members of all denominations and right-wing groups and was most successful in the South and the Midwest. Its members were mainly women. Schlafly effectively involved women in politics who had previously not been politically active. The antifeminists of STOP ERA were more likely to be middle-class, white housewives, somewhat older than their feminist counterparts. They joined the movement principally out of fear of losing their femininity and female rights with the passage of the ERA. The STOP ERA activists protested against the ERA most effectively on the local level. They organized demonstrations; picketed their legislators; distributed leaflets, buttons, and pamphlets; and raised doubts over the usefulness of the ERA for women and the nation in general. In 1980, the STOP ERA women succeeded in compelling the Republican convention to remove the ERA from its agenda. Though the ERA failed to achieve ratification, attempts to revive it have meant that STOP ERA continues to this day.

See also ANTIFEMINISM.

Further Reading

Brady, David W., and Kent L. Tedin. "Ladies in Pink: Religion and Political Ideology in the Anti-ERA Movement." *Social Science Quarterly* 54 (1976): 564–575.

De Hart, Jane Sherron. "Gender on the Right: Meaning Behind the Existential Scream." *Gender & History* 3 (1991): 246–267.

———, and Donald G. Mathews. *Sex, Gender, and the Politics of the ERA: A State and the Nation.* New York: Oxford University Press, 1990.

Solomon, Martha. "The Positive Woman's Journey: A Mythical Analysis of the Rhetoric of Stop-ERA." *Quarterly Journal of Speech* 65 (1979): 262–274.

—Christine Knauer

Stowe, Harriet Beecher (1811–1896) *writer, abolitionist*

Harriet Beecher was born in Litchfield, Connecticut, on June 14, 1811. Her father, Lyman Beecher, was a Congregationalist minister committed to abolition, and her brother, Henry Ward Beecher, became a well-known minister and abolitionist. Her brother Charles and sister Catherine also became prominent activists. In 1832, Harriet moved to Cincinnati with her family, and there she met and married Calvin Stowe, in 1836; they had seven children. She worked as a teacher and began to write books and primers for children. Cincinnati, across the river from the slave state Kentucky, was also where Harriet Beecher Stowe learned firsthand about slavery.

In 1850, the Stowe family moved to Brunswick, Maine, when Calvin Stowe became a professor at Bowdoin College. The passage of the Fugitive Slave Act in that same year galvanized many northerners in the ABOLITIONIST MOVEMENT for now the North was legally implicated in slavery in a new way. This development influenced Harriet Beecher Stowe's decision to write about slavery. In Brunswick, she started writing her most famous work, *Uncle Tom's Cabin.* Initially serialized in the abolitionist newspaper *The National Era,* it was published in book form in 1852. *Uncle Tom's Cabin* outlines the evils of slavery through a variety of characters, primarily focusing on Tom, a slave who is sold to relieve his master's debts at the outset of the novel. Tom's life and ultimate death at the hands of the cruel plantation overseer Simon Legree both educated northerners to the realities of slavery and established Tom as the upright, Christian slave who did not deserve his fate.

The book was an immediate best seller and was translated into 60 different languages. While Stowe has been criticized in the 20th century for portraying slavery as an evil institution without laying any blame on the perpetrators of that institution, *Uncle Tom's Cabin* did succeed in raising public awareness about slavery, especially among northerners. President Lincoln is reported to have said to Stowe, "So you're the little women who wrote the book that started this Great War." Stowe subsequently traveled and lectured on slavery, writing a nonfiction book, *A Key to Uncle Tom's Cabin* (1853) that provided documentation for the story she had told in the novel. She wrote many other novels before her death on July 1, 1896, but she is best remembered for *Uncle Tom's Cabin* and the

Harriet Beecher Stowe, ca. 1880 (LIBRARY OF CONGRESS)

impact it had on shifting northern sentiment concerning slavery.

Further Reading

Boydston, Jeanne, Mary Keeley, and Anne Margolis. *The Limits of Sisterhood: The Beecher Sisters on Women's Rights and Woman's Sphere.* Chapel Hill: University of North Carolina Press, 1988.

Johnston, Johanna. *Harriet and the Runaway Book: The Story of Harriet Beecher Stowe and Uncle Tom's Cabin.* New York: Harper and Row, 1977.

Weinstein, Cindy, ed. *The Cambridge Companion to Harriet Beecher Stowe.* Cambridge: Cambridge University Press, 2004.

—Claire Curtis

suffrage   The history of the right to vote in the United States reveals the expansion of enfranchisement in our democracy. In colonial America, property and race qualifications limited the right to vote, whereas suffrage today is open to all citizens at the age of 18. The colonists regarded suffrage as a privilege; Americans today consider it a right. But this interpretation obscures long periods in which various groups—women, blacks, and paupers—were disenfranchised. Women were excluded because of a presumed incapacity for sound reasoning. Only in New Jersey were they enfranchised: The New Jersey Constitution of 1776 granted the vote to all inhabitants "worth" 50 pounds who had resided in a voting place for one year. In subsequent years, election officials interpreted the provision literally and permitted propertied women to vote. New Jersey, however, was the exception, though the revolutionary struggle had significantly expanded the electorate as all states ended religious restrictions on voting. At war's end, the eligible electorate numbered from 60 to 90 percent of free males, with most states edging close to the high end of that range.

In 1848, ELIZABETH CADY STANTON and LUCRETIA MOTT issued a call for participation in a meeting organized to talk about the "social, civil, and religious rights of women." More than 300 people participated in the two-day SENECA FALLS CONVENTION and ratified the DECLARATION OF SENTIMENTS AND RESOLUTIONS, as drafted by Stanton. The Declaration of Sentiments began: "We hold these truths to be self-evident: that all men and women are created equal" and then listed 18 injuries "on the part of man toward woman," including exclusion from the franchise, COVERTURE in marriage, denial of property rights, blocking access to higher education, and undermining "confidence in her own powers . . . and willing to lead a dependent and abject life." The list was a curious mix of political and personal grievances against men. All of the resolutions passed unanimously at the convention with the exception of suffrage, which passed by a narrow margin.

Of all of the Declaration's demands, the franchise was the most radical and controversial among the conference participants, as well as among women throughout the country. Even Mott counseled Stanton against including suffrage in the Declaration's resolutions, saying, "Thou will make us ridiculous. We must go slowly." The reticence among Seneca conventioneers to embrace woman suffrage immediately was a bellwether of the long struggle ahead. Within months of the Seneca Falls meeting, women's rights conventions were held in other cities, beginning in Rochester, New York. SUSAN B. ANTHONY, a tireless crusader for suffrage later in the movement, was slow to join at first. She heard about the Rochester meeting from her mother and sister, but she was already immersed in the abolition and temperance movements and felt those causes more consistent with her Quaker beliefs. In 1851, when men in Akron, Ohio, directly challenged women's ability even to hold such conventions, let alone demand civil and political rights, a former slave named SOJOURNER TRUTH responded forthrightly from the floor with her now-famous "Ain't I a Woman?" speech (see appendix of this volume).

Since the domestic role of women was primary, few people argued the merits of female enfranchisement. Although suffrage had always been regulated by state constitutions, statutes,

Suffragettes Audre Osborne and Mrs. James Stevens, ca. 1917 (LIBRARY OF CONGRESS)

and local ordinances, woman suffragists after the Civil War hoped for national enfranchisement alongside newly freed black men. In 1863, Stanton and Anthony organized the NATIONAL WOMAN'S LOYAL LEAGUE in the North to promote the emancipation of all slaves through constitutional amendment. The amendment proposed universal suffrage and was intended to include freed slaves and women. Many abolitionists objected to women's inclusion in the suffrage clause, fearing that it would cause the amendment to fail. The Republican Party argued that an attempt to enfranchise women would jeopardize efforts to enfranchise black men in the South, a move the party saw as essential to strengthening Republican control in the Southern states.

The AMERICAN EQUAL RIGHTS ASSOCIATION (AERA) was formed in 1866 to further advance the cause of universal suffrage, and many active in the organization believed that suffrage was already implied in the language of citizenship. Several prominent African-American reformers held leadership positions in the AERA, including Harriet Purvis, Sarah Redmond, and Sojourner Truth. Black men and women active in the movement clearly linked women's rights with the vote and focused their efforts on universal suffrage and universal reforms. However,

the AERA was embroiled in a struggle between those whose first priority was black male suffrage and those who were dedicated first to woman suffrage. The tension found a target in the Fourteenth Amendment. If the Fourteenth Amendment was ratified as proposed, the word *male* would appear in the U.S. Constitution for the first time, thereby establishing two categories of citizens: male and female. Suffragists disagreed among themselves as to how they ought to react to the language of the proposed amendment. Anthony and Stanton believed that it should be defeated unless it included women, while others, such as LUCY STONE, argued that it was "the Negroes' hour, and that the women must wait for their rights."

White female suffragists left the AERA, blaming male abolitionists for sacrificing women in the name of expediency. The disunity resulted in the dissolution of the AERA and the formation of two rival organizations for women's rights in 1869: first, the NATIONAL WOMAN SUFFRAGE ASSOCIATION (NWSA), led by Stanton and Anthony, and later, the AMERICAN WOMAN SUFFRAGE ASSOCIATION (AWSA), led by LUCY STONE and Henry Ward Beecher. The NWSA turned its immediate attention to the fight over women's inclusion in the Fifteenth Amendment and divorced itself entirely from the Republican Party and the "Negro suffrage" question, whereas the AWSA continued to support the Fifteenth Amendment as written, vowing to advocate for a Sixteenth Amendment dedicated to woman suffrage. The disagreement with abolitionists and the divide among suffragists is significant because it signals an end to women's quest for universal suffrage and a start to the often ugly nativist and racist rhetoric and action that characterized some claims to the woman's vote. Black male suffrage became national in 1870 when the Fifteenth Amendment prohibited states from discriminating against potential voters because of race or previous condition of servitude—but not sex.

The division of suffragists between the NWSA and the AWSA created a loss of focus, and the WOMAN'S CHRISTIAN TEMPERANCE UNION (WCTU) filled the void, taking up the cause of suffrage. FRANCES WILLARD, WCTU president from 1879 to 1897, linked suffrage to the TEMPERANCE MOVEMENT by arguing that only women could be counted on to cast the votes necessary to prohibit the sale and consumption of alcohol. Alcohol abuse was a leading cause of domestic violence, abandonment, and poverty for women and children. The WCTU was larger than any women's suffrage organization and contributed vast resources to the cause during Willard's presidency. As a result, the western territory of Wyoming granted women the vote in 1869, and state legislatures in other regions (except for the South) considered woman suffrage legislation.

From 1869 to 1874, NWSA members urged female activists to adopt a more revolutionary strategy. Missouri suffragists VIRGINIA MINOR and her husband Francis took the lead in developing a reinterpretation of the Fourteenth Amendment and applying its definition of citizenship to enfranchise women. VICTORIA WOODHULL took the same argument to the 1871 NWSA convention in the District of Columbia. Calling the strategy a "new departure," she urged delegates to adopt the tactic in their own communities. In the November election of 1872, several women attempted to vote. Sojourner Truth went to the polls in Battle Creek, Michigan, and attempted to vote, but she was turned away. Susan B. Anthony and a small group of women voted in Rochester, New York. Anthony was arrested several weeks later and charged with "illegal voting." Rather than pay her fine and win her release, Anthony instead applied for a writ of habeas corpus, in an effort to get her case before the Supreme Court.

Although Anthony's case did not reach the Court, Virginia Minor had been arrested for voting in Missouri, and her case was eventually heard by the Supreme Court. Minor argued that in denying her the vote, the state of Missouri had denied her rights under the Fourteenth Amendment guarantee to the privileges and immunities of citizenship. The right to vote, she claimed, was a privilege of citizenship. The Court rejected her claim in MINOR V. HAPPERSETT (1875). While admitting that women may be citizens, the justices stated that not all citizens were voters. The Court based its opinion on the fact that the federal Constitution does not explicitly grant women the right to vote (". . . if it had been intended to make all citizens of the United States voters, the framers of the Constitution would not have left it to implication") and the fact that no new state added to the Union after ratification had granted suffrage to women. Without constitutional instruction, the states could decide for themselves who had the privilege of voting. The ruling in Minor led suffragists to the inevitable conclusion that a legal strategy would not advance their cause, and therefore they were left with only two choices: a federal amendment or constitutional amendments in each state.

By 1890, old animosities between the NWSA and AWSA had faded sufficiently for a merger to take place, and the NATIONAL AMERICAN WOMAN SUFFRAGE ASSOCIATION (NAWSA) was formed. The merger did not immediately inject new enthusiasm or success into the movement. In fact, suffrage leaders referred to this period as "the doldrums." After Utah and Idaho enfranchised women in 1896, no other state gave women the vote until 1910, when the state of Washington acted. Women formed literary and social organizations as well, eventually leading to the women's club movement. During the same period, African-American women organized into clubs, initiating the BLACK WOMEN'S CLUB MOVEMENT. Most of the early black women's clubs (1880s–1895) were not affiliated with national organizations and formed to deal with local issues facing women of color. In 1896, the largest national black women's clubs merged to form the NATIONAL ASSOCIATION OF COLORED WOMEN (NACW), with MARY CHURCH TERRELL at the helm as president. The rise of the NACW coincided with the disenfranchisement of black males in the South, and therefore issues on its agenda included "Jim Crow" laws and lynchings, as well as women's suffrage. Organization of southern white women came last and required the NAWSA to adopt a questionable "states' rights" policy on organizational structure, allowing segregated organizations to flourish in the South. These efforts to exclude African-American women did not go unchallenged. By the end of the century, the founding leaders of the suffrage movement—Stanton, Stone, and Anthony—were aging and dying. CARRIE CHAPMAN CATT briefly replaced Stanton as president of the NAWSA in 1900, before ANNA HOWARD SHAW assumed the role in 1904. Shaw represented the "intergenerational" leaders of the suffrage movement and provided a bridge between the pioneers and the younger new leadership, including ALICE PAUL and LUCY BURNS. Shaw concentrated the NAWSA's efforts on state referendums and on lobbying state legislatures, forgoing a federal amendment for a time.

HARRIOT STANTON BLATCH (Elizabeth Cady Stanton's daughter), Alice Paul, and Lucy Burns traveled to England to participate in a new method of campaigning for women's suffrage pioneered by Emmeline Pankhurst. On their return, Paul and Burns lobbied the NAWSA to return to a federal amendment strategy. Rather than begging for their rights, they intended to demand them. Although the NAWSA formed a congressional committee in 1912, support for a federal strategy was so meager that the committee was given an annual budget of just $10. In 1913, the congressional committee planned to hold a massive parade in Washington, D.C., designed to coincide with Woodrow Wilson's presidential inauguration. The March 3 parade was intended to put both Congress and President Wilson on notice that women would not wait any longer for action on the suffrage question. On the day of the parade, some 8,000 marchers, including 26 floats, 10 bands, and five squadrons of cavalry with six chariots, participated. More than half a million people watched as the parade headed down Pennsylvania Avenue toward the White House. Trouble started when spectators began insulting participants

and pushing the crowd into the parade line. As police stood idle, the situation deteriorated into a near riot. In all, 175 calls for ambulances were sent out, and more than 200 people were treated at local hospitals. The publicity generated by the parade horrified the NAWSA leaders but thrilled Paul, Blatch, and Stone.

In 1914, Paul broke with NAWSA and established the CONGRESSIONAL UNION FOR WOMAN SUFFRAGE as an independent organization dedicated to fighting for a federal amendment. Paul focused her attention on Woodrow Wilson. She organized pickets in front of the White House and called on Wilson to pressure Congress to consider and pass the federal amendment (known by then as the Susan B. Anthony Amendment). On January 10, 1917, the first "Silent Sentinels" appeared. These were women who stood motionless holding banners that read, "Mr. President, What Will You Do for Woman Suffrage?" and "How Long Must Women Wait for Liberty?" These suffragist picketers were the first pickets ever to appear before the White House. The Congressional Union became the NATIONAL WOMAN'S PARTY (NWP) in 1917 and stepped up efforts to call attention to women's disenfranchisement with more picketing. Police began arresting picketers. When jailed, women refused to pay their fines and remained in jail. In an attempt to scare off new picketers, prison terms of up to 60 days were imposed. The women engaged in hunger strikes to protest their unjust incarceration. Prison officials responded by force-feeding them through clenched jaws or through the nose, a dangerous and terribly painful practice. Public reaction was swift and overwhelmingly sympathetic to these IRON-JAWED ANGELS, prompting early releases. Women released from prison capitalized on the public's sympathy by campaigning for suffrage in their prison garb.

Meanwhile, Carrie Chapman Catt had taken over the leadership of NAWSA. Under Catt's leadership, NAWSA pursued a state-based strategy for a federal amendment labeled the "Winning Plan." Under Catt's plan, each state would be accorded the resources and attention in proportion to its chances of passing a state constitutional amendment. Members would also lobby Congress to pass the Anthony Amendment. As women won suffrage rights in increasing numbers of states, pressure mounted on Congress to pass the Nineteenth Amendment and send it to the states for ratification. In 1919, by a one-vote margin in each house, the Nineteenth Amendment was passed by Congress and sent to the states. The battle for ratification lasted for 15 months. On August 26, 1920, by a one-vote margin in Tennessee, the 36th and final state to ratify, the Anthony Amendment was added to the Constitution.

Further Reading

Flexner, Eleanor, and Ellen Fitzpatrick. *Century of Struggle: The Women's Rights Movement in the United States.* Cambridge, Mass.: Belknap Press, 1996.
Graham, Sara Hunter. *Woman Suffrage and the New Democracy.* New Haven, Conn.: Yale University Press, 1996.

—Paula Casey

surrogacy (contract pregnancy)   Surrogacy is an arrangement by which one woman agrees to bear a child for another woman. Commercial surrogacy began in the United States in the 1970s. Typically the surrogate mother is artificially inseminated and agrees to carry the fetus to term and then deliver the baby to third-party parents. The surrogate relinquishes her parental rights, and the parent or parents receiving the baby initiate a legal adoption of the child. Usually there is a contract involved (which may or may not be enforceable) that outlines all parties' intentions and financial obligations.

The question of whether surrogacy in general is moral or legal was brought to center stage when the highly publicized BABY M CASE went to court in New Jersey in 1987. Mary Beth Whitehead, the surrogate mother, gave birth to a girl, whom she named Sara Elizabeth Whitehead, but refused to give the child to William Stern (the biological father) and his wife Elizabeth. The first court ruling in 1987 granted custody of Melissa (as the Sterns had named her) to the Sterns on the grounds that the contract was binding, but this ruling was overturned by the New Jersey Supreme Court on February 2, 1988, and the case was remanded to family court. Ultimately, William Stern was granted custody, but Mary Beth Whitehead maintained visitation rights.

The law on surrogate arrangements varies by state. In very few states can surrogacy arrangements be enforced as a binding contract, and no money can be exchanged beyond the intended parents' willingness to cover expenses. Critics charge that this forces women into indentured servant–like arrangements in exchange for their reproductive labor. Feminists are divided on the issue of surrogacy: Some argue that a woman must have complete control and autonomy over her body, while others are more persuaded by the likelihood of exploitation, particularly of poor women.

See also REPRODUCTIVE TECHNOLOGY.

Susan B. Anthony List   The Susan B. Anthony List is a membership organization with an associated political action committee (PAC) dedicated to supporting pro-life candidates for public office. The membership's ultimate goal is to end abortion in the United States, and their strategy involves electing sufficient numbers of pro-life officials and mobilizing pro-life women to be active in politics. Thus, SUSAN B. ANTHONY's name is invoked because of her tireless dedication to involving women in politics and political life, as well as her position against ABORTION. Anthony argued that abortion destroyed children and women and amounted to a false choice for women as long as they did not control their own bodies or their own destinies. The organization maintains a Web site at www.sba-list.org.

See also RIGHT TO LIFE MOVEMENT.

T

Taft, Helen (Helen Herron Taft, Nellie Taft) (1861–1943) *first lady* Helen (Nellie) Herron was born in Cincinnati, Ohio, on June 2, 1861, to Harriet Collins and John Williamson Herron. Her father, an attorney, was well connected in Republican circles, being a classmate of Benjamin Harrison and a law partner with Rutherford B. Hayes. Nellie was well-educated, attending the Miss Nourse School in Cincinnati from 1866 to 1879 and taking some classes at the University of Cincinnati. Nellie excelled in school, particularly in music. Her parents believed in expanded opportunities for women and raised her to demand more of herself than commonly expected of women. Nellie herself appears to have been ambivalent; though she worked in her father's law office and studied the law, she also enjoyed the pleasures of social world occupied by women of her means. She taught school between 1881 and 1883 and briefly considered opening her own school. At 16, her family visited the White House, which is said to have instilled dreams in Nellie of returning as first lady. While she may have comfortably pursued a career by this point in history, dreaming of the presidency for herself was practically impossible, leaving her to pursue her ambitions through marriage.

Before their courtship, Nellie Herron and William Howard Taft had been acquainted through their families' long friendship. They are said to have noticed one another in 1883 at a salon organized to discuss ideas and politics. He proposed to her on May 1, 1885, but she delayed her acceptance and insisted that their engagement remain a secret. She reportedly felt little physical attraction to Taft but believed him to be sufficiently ambitious and likely to succeed. They were married on June 19, 1886, and settled into a house overlooking the Ohio River. William Howard Taft was appointed as a judge of the superior court of Ohio. He enjoyed the work, but Nellie feared it would not give him the exposure required to seek the presidency. His ultimate career goal appears to have been the U.S. Supreme Court, while she had the presidency in mind for him. In 1890, President Benjamin Harrison appointed Taft solicitor general of the United States. The Tafts enjoyed the social life of Washington, and Nellie was disappointed when they returned to Ohio with an appointment to the Federal Circuit Court. Riding circuit required Taft to be gone for long periods and Nellie filled her time caring for their children (Robert, b. 1889; Helen, b. 1891;

and Charles, b. 1897) and pursuing civic causes. She became the executive director of the Cincinnati Orchestra.

In 1900, President William McKinley asked Taft to head a commission to establish a civilian government in the Philippine Islands. Nellie viewed this as an opportunity for advancement, and she pressed her husband to accept the post. Both William and Nellie were successful in the Philippines—he in building political consensus and improving civil and social services and she in bridging the cultural divide and eroding the color line that existed under military rule. She opened their house to everyone, she and her children studied Spanish, and she frequented the Luneta, a sort of town square that combined music with social interaction. In July 1901, William Howard Taft was installed as the first American governor-general of the Philippines. The family moved into the Malacanan Palace, the traditional home of the island's ruler. Nellie continued to entertain, throwing lavish outdoor parties, and maintained weekly receptions to which she welcomed everyone regardless of race or class. Although she enjoyed her role, she found it exhausting and tried to escape to China for a much-needed rest. Her trip was cut short by William's illness and hospitalization. Doctors recommended that Taft recuperate away from the islands and the family returned to Washington, only to return in 1902 for what amounted to a brief stay.

In October 1902, President Theodore Roosevelt offered Taft a seat on the U.S. Supreme Court, but he declined, preferring to finish his work in the Philippines. Within six months, however, he and Nellie returned to Washington, and Taft became Roosevelt's secretary of war. Nellie's role as wife of a cabinet secretary hardly compared to the glory she had experienced as "queen" of the Philippines, and she renewed her quest to win the presidency for her husband.

In 1908, because Roosevelt had signaled that he would serve only one elected term, Nellie now expected him to throw his endorsement behind William for the Republican nomination. She was furious at his delay and made several trips to see the president to press her husband's case. Roosevelt viewed this as decidedly "unwomanly" but nonetheless respected her political insights and signaled his support. Having been offered a coveted position on the U.S. Supreme Court yet again, Taft was a reluctant campaigner. Once the nomination was his, Nellie campaigned vigorously on his behalf, attracting yet another rebuke from Roosevelt. On November 3, 1908, Taft was elected president, and Nellie Taft had achieved her ambition.

As first lady, Nellie broke with tradition on the day of the inaugural by accompanying her husband in his carriage on the ride from the Capitol swearing-in ceremony to the White House. To her, this signaled the character of the political partnership that had brought them both to the White House. Once installed as first lady, she continued her participation in the business of governing by attending public and private

Helen Harron Taft, 1909 (LIBRARY OF CONGRESS)

meetings with the president and was said to sit outside cabinet meetings. "I do not believe in a woman meddling in politics or in asserting herself along those lines," she said, "but I think any woman can discuss with her husband topics of national interest and, in many instances, she might give her opinion of questions with which, through study and contact, she has become familiar." She is best remembered for her role in establishing West Potomac Park as a meeting place along the Potomac River. She renamed the road leading to the park Potomac Drive and installed a bandstand where the Marine Band would play every Wednesday and Saturday evening. She modeled this on the Luneta park she had enjoyed so much in the Philippines.

William Taft was less enamored of the presidency. He thought it an "awful agony" yet sought the Republican nomination in 1912 in a fight so protracted and bitter that Theodore Roosevelt split from the Republicans to form the Bull Moose Party. The divide among Republicans resulted in the election of Democrat Woodrow Wilson, a fate so obvious to Nellie that she started packing to leave the White House before the election had even taken place. Life after the White House was rewarding for William, however. He taught at Yale University until President Warren Harding appointed him chief justice of the Supreme Court in 1921. Nellie Taft enjoyed their return to Washington society. Her children were successful as adults: Robert became a prominent U.S. senator from Ohio, Charles was a successful lawyer, and Helen enjoyed a distinguished career in academia, earning a Ph.D. from Yale and a law degree from George Washington University.

William Howard Taft died in 1930. Nellie lived on in Washington for another 13 years, dying on May 22, 1943. She was the first first lady to be buried in Arlington Cemetery (joined now by JACQUELINE KENNEDY).

Further Reading:

Cordery, Stacy A. "Hellen (Nellie) Herron Taft." In *American First Ladies: Their Lives and Their Legacy,* 2nd ed., edited by Lewis L. Gould. New York: Routledge, 2001, 213–225.

National First Ladies Library. *Biographies: First Ladies of the United States.* Available online. URL: http://www.firstladies.org/biographies. Accessed on January 4, 2007.

Schneider, Dorothy, and Carl J. Schneider. "Helen (Nellie) Herron Taft." *First Ladies: A Biographical Dictionary.* New York: Checkmark Books, 2001, 172–181.

Tailhook scandal In September 1991, naval aviators belonging to the Tailhook Association, an organization supporting sea-based aviation, held their annual convention in Las Vegas. The revelry became assaultive, alleged Lt. Paula Coughlin, as male aviators "formed a gauntlet down a narrow hallway and tore at her clothes, grabbed at her breasts, and seized her buttocks with such force she was hoisted airborne." Other women reported that they were thrown to the ground, had their clothes torn off, and were molested by drunken airmen. In all, 119 navy and 21 Marine Corps officers were referred by Pentagon investigators for possible disciplinary actions. None of these cases ever went to trial, however, and nearly half were dropped for lack of evidence. Twenty-eight junior officers were eventually disciplined for "indecent exposure" and "conduct unbecoming an officer." None of the aviators were charged with sexual assault, and Coughlin's charges against a specific marine captain for sexual molestation were dropped for lack of evidence. The investigation and disciplinary hearings stretched on for more than three years, culminating in the resignation of Secretary of the Navy Lawrence Garrett III and the early retirement of Admiral Frank Kelso, the navy's top officer, who was found to have witnessed several incidents but failed to intervene. Women following the progress of the investigation were introduced to the dark side of military culture. Outraged that sexual assault charges were dismissed as "high-jinks" and dismayed to learn that the "gauntlet" had been a fixture at

Cannon, received a wireless telegram from an unidentified source "J.O.," ordering him to avoid all political interviews. Sherman found himself in the uncomfortable position of maintaining silence concerning his knowledge of whether or not Roosevelt had made a personal appeal for campaign funds.

Sherman's congressional career came to an end in 1908 when he was selected, somewhat to the chagrin of the party's Roosevelt wing, as Taft's running mate. While there are few who questioned Sherman's party loyalty or his organizational skills, some wondered whether or not he was suitable for the responsibilities of the office. Three assassinations of presidents in forty-three years, one as recently as 1901, might well have prompted caution concerning the qualifications of the second man on the ticket. Furthermore, because of Sherman's close affiliation with the standpatters, the progressive wing of the Republican Party would have preferred Jonathan Dolliver of Iowa, or at least Dolliver's Iowa colleague, Albert B. Cummins. Albert J. Beveridge of Indiana and Charles Evans Hughes of New York (who himself harbored presidential aspirations) were other possibilities. None of these men was interested, and Roosevelt and Taft, although not enthusiastic, acquiesced in the selection of "Sunny Jim."

The New York delegation strongly supported Sherman throughout the Chicago Republican convention. Sherman's main qualifications were his parliamentary skills. Also, he was well liked in the Senate, had been an effective Congressional Campaign Committee chairman, came from a doubtful state, and of course was acceptable to the party's conservative wing. His candidacy also received a boost when House Speaker Joe Cannon made an unprecedented appearance before the convention and gave a rousing speech in support of Sherman's nomination.

Some Progressives like W.R. Nelson, editor of the *Kansas City Star*, protested that the second post on the ticket should go to someone who could strengthen the cause against Bryan,

"not to please reactionaries." One concern of progressives was Sherman's general hostility to labor, exemplified by his support of injunctions in labor disputes, which progressives wished to see modified. Samuel Gompers, president of the American Federation of Labor, referred to Sherman's place on the Republican ticket as a "slap in the face." However, the Taft-Sherman Republican ticket swept easily to victory, defeating William Jennings Bryan, the perennial Democrat standard bearer, by more than a million votes.

Sherman, who wanted a job that was seemingly scorned by more-renowned men, was at least a competent vice president during a period that saw growing divisions within Republican Party ranks. Sherman, it was generally conceded, presided over the Senate with "skill and affability." In 1909, he became the first vice president to be include on the inaugural medal, an honor repeated only by Richard Nixon in 1957 and Spiro Agnew in 1973. Despite declining health and reports that he might retire from politics, Sherman was renominated in 1912—becoming only the seventh vice president in U.S. history to achieve this distinction. No Republican vice president had been renominated since the party's beginning in 1856. The *New York Times* in an editorial on December 23, 1911, stated that in spite of rumors, Sherman's retirement was unlikely; "his alert mind and persuasive speech will be actively employed for the good of his party, the country and Mr. Sherman."

Ideologically, Sherman remained a conservative throughout his life, a fact that his selection as Taft's running mate on a relatively progressive platform in 1908 could not change. He was a man of limited horizons and belonged, as an November 9, 1912, editorial in *Outlook* put it, to the type of men "who conserve the material interests rather than advance the spiritual interests of the nation." However, his executive ability, geniality, parliamentary skill, and devotion to the country's business interests contributed to his consistent reelection and gradual emergence as a party stalwart. During the heyday of Progressivism, he would be included among the ranks of the standpatters who resisted reform championed by the progressives. "Sunny Jim," insisted author William Manners, "during a long twenty years in the House had not backed a single thing of value." Henry Pringle in his biography of President Taft referred to him as a "conservative political hack."

Certainly, this assessment is true if one examines Sherman's views on the tariff, railroad reform, conservation, and antitrust legislation, all important issues to the Progressives. The battle over the Payne-Aldrich tariff bill perhaps best illustrates Sherman's standpattism. It appeared in 1908 that Taft (with Sherman as his running mate) adhered to the Progressive demand for lower rates. Taft, however, vacillated and accepted the Payne-Aldrich bill, which failed to meet the Progressives' demands and threatened by 1910 to split party ranks. Sherman, who had always favored protection, found the legislation to his liking. He even advised Taft to warn Republicans that "any person who tries to defeat the party wishes must necessarily be considered hostile."

The controversial Payne-Aldrich tariff bill, he felt, signified that the party had "fulfilled every campaign pledge." He not only supported the bill, to the chagrin of Progressives like Dolliver of Iowa and even Theodore Roosevelt, but dared venture into the Middle West, where antagonism toward the legislation was strongest. This effort was sharply resented by those midwestern Republican insurgent congressmen who valiantly fought to ward off Old Guard party dominance. Sherman even dared ascribe the return of prosperity and the increase in wages to the tariff—arguing that its provisions did not go far enough. Some insurgents went so far as to advocate reading Sherman out of the party.

Nor does Sherman seem to have shared the Progressive desire to protect the nation's natural resources. As vice president during the Ballinger-Pinchot controversy, Sherman sided with the Old Guard. Ballinger was the secretary of the interior who aroused the suspicions of Louis Glavis, government agent, and Gifford Pinchot, head of the Forest Service, by transferring rich Alaska coal deposits to the Guggenheim-Morgan interests. The charges of corruption against Ballinger led to demands by the Progressives that a special investigative committee be appointed. This meant that Sherman, as vice president, appointed the committee, which Progressives like Dolliver of Iowa correctly predicted would consist mostly of standpatters.

However, Sherman was somewhat more flexible in other matters. He supported labor's demands for an eight-hour day and a child-labor law for the District of Columbia. As a congressman, he favored safety legislation for railroad employees and a limited measure of federal control over industrial and transportation corporations. Sherman was a member of the House committee that worked out a compromise with the Senate in the passage of the Hepburn Act in 1906, a bill that mildly strengthened the regulatory powers of the Interstate Commerce Commission. He was among those who sponsored legislation along the lines of the Pure Food and Drug Act, contributing as early as 1902 a measure that prevented the false branding of food and dairy products from the state or territory in which they were made. However, in congressional hearings on Pure Food and Drug legislation itself in 1906, Sherman remarked that the legislation was designed to "protect not the pocketbook so much as it is the stomachs of the American people," and he opposed compulsory labels that stipulated the weight of cans and bottles. Dr. Harvey W. Wiley, Department of Agriculture chief chemist and a crusader for reform, referred to Sherman as "short weight Jim" and reminded everyone that the New York congressman was a canner.

Sherman was particularly interested in the nation's Indian policy and headed the Committee on Indian Affairs for twelve years prior to his vice-presidential nomination in 1908. He was quite proud of the fact that he was a descendent of early nineteenth-century historian of

Indians Henry Schoolcraft. The Riverside, California, Indian school was named in Sherman's honor, and he received the Indian name of Wau-be-ka-chuck (Four Eyes). He also collected numerous Indian artifacts. While Sherman's work as chairman of the Committee on Indian Affairs appears to have won high praise from Congress and may have played a role in his obtaining the vice-presidential nomination in 1908 when the "Indian States" supported him, it does not stand up under close scrutiny. Sherman's goal, as Committee on Indian Affairs chairman and as vice president, was to advance the policy of severalty stemming from the Dawes Act of 1887—that is, to break up the traditional tribal arrangement and encourage the Indians to become individual farmers—a misguided policy that was eventually deemed disastrous to the well-being of the tribes, who were separated from much of their land.

The vice president's lack of sensitivity was revealed in a speech before 400 prominent men and women at a conference held in 1911 at Lake Mohonk, New York, where he stated that the government had fulfilled all of its treaty obligations with the Indians. Chief Choctaw Victor Locke, finding this assertion ridiculous wrote: "If the Commission of which he was chairman took that view we have the explanation of many evils of the past fifteen years." Between 1883 and 1912, Lake Mohonk was an annual conference instituted by a member of the Indian Commission, Alfred Smiley and supported by such well-known humanitarians as Henry Dawes (Dawes Act author and Senate Committee on Indian Affairs chairman) and the Indian Rights Association. Sherman shared their goal of lifting the Indian to a "higher plane of civilization" and believed the day would come when the Native American would be self-supporting. He often attended Lake Mohonk Conferences, and feeling that great progress was being made in solving the Indian problem through education, he supported federal appropriations for education for Native American children. Furthermore, his colleagues in Congress credited him with endeavoring to reduce fraud in the government management of Indian Affairs.

Sherman, during the U.S. acquisition of a global empire in the 1890s, advocated government support in the completion of an interoceanic Nicaraguan Canal as early as 1896. Furthermore, he fathered the first bill advocating laying a cable to the Philippine Islands, and he also advocated strengthening both the army and the navy in order to give it a two-ocean capability. Sherman also stressed the importance of an improved revenue-cutter service and was among those congressmen who launched an investigation of hazing at the Military and Naval academies. Sherman considered hazing nonsense and brutal and believed that the American people were opposed to it.

There were a few hints of political scandal during Sherman's twenty-six years in national politics. One ugly tale surfaced in the presidential election of 1908, when it was rumored that he had diverted congressional campaign funds in order to secure reelection to Congress and that he had invented dummy corporations to exploit tribal oil lands in Oklahoma. Supposedly, Sherman had secured for a relative a position paying ten dollars a day for inspecting clothing for Indians. He ignored the charges, which were not pressed by the Democrats, as he triumphed in his last campaign. The charges were of little consequence and did not impede Sherman's nomination as Taft's running mate in 1908. However, Sherman's culpability in Indian policy cropped up again in 1910 while he was vice president. Oklahoma lawyer and lobbyist J.F. McMurray was seeking congressional approval for contracts he had solicited pertaining to the sale of Choctaw and Chickasaw land rights in coal and tar. McMurray and his accomplices, who represented the tribal nations, were to receive exorbitant fees of up to $3 million for their efforts. Senator Thomas P. Gore of Oklahoma, who attacked the contracts, was offered a bribe of between $25,000 and $50,000 for dropping his opposition, but he instead reported the incident, thereby setting forth an investigation during which, along with several other senators, a "higher up" was alleged to be involved. The "higher up" turned out to be Vice President Sherman, who stoutly denied the accusations, and even Gore acknowledged that there was no evidence to implicate him. However, Sherman's critics pointed out that as a congressman he had been Committee on Indian Affairs chairman, making it likely that he had knowledge of the McMurray contracts.

One of Sherman's main interests throughout his life was the law. His familiarity with the legislative process was enhanced by his considerable parliamentary skills—Sherman's peers regarded him as one of the best presiding officers in American history. While chairing a session at the fourteenth annual meeting of the American Academy of Political and Social Sciences in Philadelphia in 1910, Sherman delivered an address explaining the mechanism of legislation by which a bill made its way through Congress. He also equated American greatness with the Founding Fathers' constitutional wisdom and their national respect for the law. The vice president, in a not unusual surge of early twentieth-century patriotism, argued that the progress of the United States was "tied with respect for law." He expanded his address by pointing out that the United States occupied only 5 percent of the world's area, with just 7 percent of the population, while "commercially and financially we about equal one-half of all the rest of mankind."

As the Taft-Roosevelt conflict intensified, Sherman sided with President Taft and would be in position for the unique distinction of receiving the vice-presidential nomination on the Republican ticket for the second time. President Taft, elected as a Progressive in 1908, soon found himself in difficulty with the more liberal wing of the party. The president's support of conservation and tariff reform seemed weak and angered Progressive forces who sought to maintain control of the party organization. Taft's once cordial relationship with Roosevelt cooled. This conflict escalated prior to the 1910 midterm elections. Vice President Sherman traveled from Washington, D.C., to Milwaukee and criticized the Progressives for "arraying class against class and interest against interest."

Several weeks later, the struggle between Sherman and Roosevelt forces in New York intensified when the predominantly Old Guard Republican Committee, without consulting Roosevelt, nominated Sherman for temporary chair of the state convention. However, during the Republican convention at Saratoga, the Old Guard forces were thwarted and Roosevelt was elected. Roosevelt was alarmed over the decline of liberal Republicanism in the state and hoped to rally support for progressive candidate Henry L. Stimson as governor. President Taft played an ambiguous role during the contest (at first appearing to support Sherman and then denying it). This served to further the divisions within the Republican Party prior to the campaign of 1912, which would pit two Republican candidates (Roosevelt on the Progressive ticket and Taft) against an articulate and progressive Democrat, Woodrow Wilson. Sherman, never a strong Roosevelt supporter, said that Roosevelt's defeat in the election was essential "both for the life of our party and the continuation of all government."

Sherman, reluctant to accept renomination because of his declining health, would not live to see the outcome of the election, in which all Republican forces went down to defeat as Woodrow Wilson became the first Democrat to win the White House since Grover Cleveland. The vice president had actually been in ill health for nearly four years, suffering from Bright's Disease. His health worsened while on vacation in August 1912, and he was rushed back to Utica, where he slowly improved. While Sherman had the best medical advice available, he did not always follow that advice. His health was dealt a final, fatal blow when, contrary to his physician's insistence that he speak only five minutes to a visiting delegation that was to notify officially him of his renomination, he insisted upon speaking for thirty minutes. "You may know all about medicine," he told his physician, "but you don't know about politics."

The effort was too much and the vice president never recovered, dying on October 30, 1912. Throughout late summer there had been rumors of his impending resignation from the ticket, but there was no pressure from the Taft forces to bring this about.

Overall, Sherman's vice-presidential years were uneventful. He was an efficient spokesman for the GOPs conservative wing, he was generally supportive of the president in the struggles over conservation (Ballinger-Pinchot) and the tariff (Payne-Aldrich) and in trying in 1912 to thwart Theodore Roosevelt's renewed presidential aspirations. But he was not at the center of decision making. Furthermore, no one in the party considered Sherman as a possible future aspirant for the presidency, nor does he appear to have harbored such ambitions. Although Sherman had been in ill health for some time, his death at age fifty-seven shocked both the nation and the Republican Party.

The vice president's untimely death did not help Taft forces in the 1912 election because he could not be replaced at that late date. While Sherman's premature demise did not cause Taft's defeat, the lack of a second candidate on the ticket did create some confusion as Taft came in third in the popular balloting. Sherman was the seventh vice president to die in office and the first candidate in either major party to die between nomination and the date set for election. Although James Schoolcraft Sherman hardly qualified for a place among the nation's great men, and although his congressional and vice-presidential achievements were no more than average, he was well liked and respected by both major political parties.

The vice president's body lay in state in the rotunda of the Utica Courthouse, where as many as 5,000 mourners filed by the casket, with 25,000 others outside in the streets. Even the Army–Holy Cross football game at West Point was canceled due to the vice president's death. The funeral was held on November 4 in the First Presbyterian Church of Hamilton College. The vice president was buried in Forest Hill Cemetery in Utica. President William Howard Taft summed up the nation's feelings when he said: "Those who knew him loved him; those who knew the services he rendered to his country respected him."

REFERENCES

There is no full biography of Sherman, but short articles appear in some standard biographical compilations, such as *The Dictionary of American Biography*. Material on his life and career comes from publications such as *The Congressional Record* and *The New York Times*. Specific articles: "Career in Congress," *Independent*, May 28, 1908, 1188–1189; "James S. Sherman," *Independent*, June 24, 1908, 1424–1426; "Republican Candidates," *Outlook*, June 27, 1908, 410–412; "Sunny Jim Sherman," *Current Literature*, 45 (August 1908), 151–155; William E. Weed, "James S. Sherman, Republican Candidate for Vice-President," *Review of Review*, 38 (August 1908), 167–171; "Vice President Sherman and the Tariff," *Independent*, May 5, 1910, 993–994; "Portrait," *Literary Digest*, November 9, 1912, 827; "The Death of Vice-President Sherman," *Outlook*, November 9, 1912.

WILLIAM H. CUMBERLAND received his B.A. from the University of Dubuque and his M.A. and Ph.D. from the University of Iowa. He is the author of *The History of Buena Vista College*, (1966, 1991), and *Wallace M. Short, Iowa Rebel* (1983), as well as articles in the *Palimpsest, Annals of Iowa, Books at Iowa*, and *Midwest Review*. For many years he taught at Buena Vista College in Iowa, retiring as emeritus professor of history.

THOMAS RILEY MARSHALL (1854–1925)

Vice President, 1913–1921

(President Woodrow Wilson)

THOMAS RILEY MARSHALL
(Library of Congress)

By Peter T. Harstad

Lawyer, politician, governor of Indiana from 1909 to 1913, one of six two-term vice presidents, popular speaker and raconteur, Thomas Marshall is best known for a quip that became part of American political culture: "What this country needs is a really good five-cent cigar."

A smoker whose personality contrasted sharply with that of President Wilson's, Marshall very likely uttered these words while presiding over the U.S. Senate during the Sixty-third Congress. However, the statement cannot be found in the *Congressional Record* or any other authoritative source close to the event. Marshall's principal biographer, Charles M. Thomas, concluded that the remark was an aside heard by a Senate clerk and others during a long speech by Senator Joseph L. Bristow of Kansas about the country's needs. In his 1970 doctoral dissertation, John E. Brown presented this and other explanations of Marshall's famous utterance.

Marshall deserves to be remembered for more than his humor, which is amply documented in his *Recollections* and elsewhere. Before he arrived on the national scene, Marshall was an effective lawyer and progressive governor of Indiana who sought to adjust the machinery of state government to the twentieth century. The 1912 election that brought Wilson and Marshall to Washington proved to be the national high-water mark for progressivism. Marshall played a role in the progressive agenda of Wilson's first term; then, when war engulfed Europe, he presided over debates in the Senate about American entry into World War I and, subsequently, over bitter debates about the country's participation in the League of Nations.

President Wilson's stroke tested Marshall, who had ambitions beyond the vice presidency. A lesser man might have thrown the country into constitutional turmoil. Instead, Marshall used the vice presidency to stabilize the executive branch and to calm the nation. Operating without precedent during a president's incapacitation, Marshall conducted affairs of state with dignity. A wise and kindly man, he deserves the designation *statesman*.

Born in North Manchester, Indiana (thirty miles west of Fort Wayne), on March 14, 1854, Marshall was a third-generation Hoosier whose paternal grandfather, Riley Marshall, came from Virginia in 1817. Whether the latter "belonged to the first families, the second families, was just well spoken of, or was downright white trash," the vice president could not determine. He thought he might be the only Marshall "who does not trace his origin . . . to the great chief justice." The family had owned slaves in the Old Dominion and had manumitted them, but a great-uncle managed to take some of the blacks to Missouri before they knew they were free. On the eve of the Civil War, that relative owned a plantation and 300 slaves. At this point in his recollections Mar-

shall inserted: "God does not pay at the end of every week, but He pays."

Hard-working people, the Indiana Marshalls made the most of their opportunities. Daniel, Thomas's father, became a country doctor. The vice president's maternal ancestors, Pennsylvanians who came to Indiana via Ohio, were Presbyterians. "That does not necessarily make a good man," he quipped, "but it makes a religious one." In the Indiana setting, it also tended to make a political man.

Thomas and an older sister who did not survive infancy were the only children born to Daniel and Martha Patterson Marshall. Because of vast swamps, malaria was the bane of northeast Indiana in the 1850s. Marshall spun a yarn in which heredity, environment, and malaria explained why he became a Democrat: A man of "domineering character and predatory wealth" lived in town. When summer came and malaria seized the townspeople, that man took sick with third-day ague. "He was an aristocrat. The rest of us shook every other day. We were democrats."

In the Marshall household, each day began with a Presbyterian prayer "that began in Indiana and ended in China." Thereafter "we had a teaspoonful of quinine and then we had breakfast." Thomas admired and respected his parents, both of whom valued learning. One chapter of his *Recollections* is a tribute to the country doctor, "adviser, counselor, friend" personified by his father, a staunch Democrat and minor officeholder. The loving son asserted: "I could be elected to any office" if I could rehabilitate the old family physician.

Thomas believed that he received his sunny disposition from his mother, with whom he lived, except when attending college, until he was forty. During Thomas's early years, Martha Marshall was sickly. Coupled with Dr. Marshall's understanding of medical geography, this explains several family moves. When Thomas was two, the family went west by covered wagon to the prairies near Urbana, Illinois, to try the open-air treatment for Martha's tuberculosis. In the fall of 1858, Dr. Marshall, a Stephen A. Douglas Democrat, took his son to a political debate at Freeport. A suggestive memory led Thomas to believe that he "sat on Lincoln's lap while Douglas was talking, and on Douglas' lap while Lincoln was talking." Although the youthful Marshall liked "the tall man," it pleased the aged raconteur to think that "something of the love of Lincoln and of Douglas for the Union, the Constitution and the rights of the common man flowed into my childish veins."

Again for health reasons, the Marshalls moved to Kansas but stayed only long enough to conclude that it was a dark and bloody ground. Next, the family went to LaGrange, Missouri, across the Mississippi from Quincy, Illinois, where Martha's health was restored. Late in October 1860, Dr. Marshall, a unionist, got into a street altercation with a pro-slavery guerrilla leader. Relatives convinced the doctor that his life was in danger unless he left Missouri immediately. Thomas and his parents saw the sun go down from the stern of the evening boat for Quincy.

Back in Indiana by November, the month Abraham Lincoln was elected president of the United States, the family took up residence at Pierceton, between Warsaw and North Manchester. Here Thomas went to public school for six years. He attended seventh and eighth grades in Warsaw, where an uncle, Woodson Marshall, practiced law, and spent the 1868–69 academic year in high school at Fort Wayne. A fellow student remembered Thomas as "very bright." Sectionalism, Civil War, and the legacy that followed colored Thomas's world. Even as vice president he saw his role as soother and pacificator but not always as compromiser.

After but one year of high school, Thomas went to Wabash College, operated by the Presbyterian church in Crawfordsville, Indiana. The Marshalls were active in that denomination, and Martha hoped that her son would become a Presbyterian minister. Thomas thrived at Wabash College and his personality developed, but not in the direction of the ministry. He studied classical Greek and Latin, modern French and German, mathematics, a cluster of critical thinking courses, science, religion, military drill, and the Constitution of the United States. On a nine-point scale, his lowest college grade was 8.5; in fourteen of his thirty-seven classes he received the highest possible grade.

Fraternities, literary societies, political activities, and the *Geyser*, a student newspaper, offered diversion from the curriculum of the all-male college. A Phi Gamma Delta fraternity member, Marshall actively participated in campus life. Fellow students had confidence in him, particularly when trouble threatened, as it did during Marshall's senior year. Thomas wrote an article that defamed the character of a female lecturer and visitor to Crawfordsville and published it in the *Geyser*. She hired Lew Wallace, Civil War general and Crawfordsville novelist, as her attorney and filed a $20,000 libel suit against Marshall and the *Geyser* staff. Marshall went to Indianapolis and engaged the services of another Civil War general, Benjamin Harrison, destined also to become president of the United States. Harrison extricated the boys from their predicament, charged nothing, and then gave them a stern lecture on ethics. "It was a great lesson to me," Marshall recorded fifty-two years later, "and I have never again been sued for either slander or libel." Through this episode and by visiting courthouses and witnessing trials, the bright young student met leading members of the Indiana bar.

At Wabash College, Marshall learned to reason quickly and keenly and to speak and write well—valuable skills that he would soon put to use. Thomas's Greek professor tried to persuade him to take up that occupation, but by his senior year he had made up his mind to become a lawyer. Elected to Phi Beta Kappa, he graduated with honors in June 1873.

Rather than attend law school (which his family could have paid for had he chosen to do so), Thomas, on the advice of members of the bar, decided to work and study law in the Warsaw law office of his uncle, Woodson Marshall. Why he soon left is not clear, but the chronology of his departure coincided with his parents' move to Columbia City, midway between Warsaw and Fort Wayne.

Before 1873 was out, Marshall was preparing himself for the bar in the offices of Hooper and Olds in Columbia City. Walter Olds took to the bench, opened offices in Fort Wayne, and eventually became a judge of the Indiana Supreme Court. Therefore, accounts asserting that Marshall studied for the bar under a Fort Wayne judge do not conflict with the facts. Marshall was admitted to practice before the Whitley County Circuit Court at age twenty-one.

The Wabash and Erie Canal and several railroads had opened north central Indiana to development well before Marshall came to Columbia City. In his day, the wetlands were being ditched, tiled, and drained. A girl of the nearby Limberlost swamp, writer Gene Stratton-Porter, viewed draining from a nature lover's perspective; farmers regarded it as physical labor. Marshall came to see the "gum-boot era" of Whitley County development from a lawyer's perspective. Draining projects required legal arrangements, hydraulic engineering, capital, and loans. The aftermath of the Panic of 1873 brought mortgage foreclosures, collection cases, and litigation involving farmers, bankers, and merchants. Life was becoming complicated even in the countryside. Frustrated men attempted to solve their problems with their fists. It was a dull Saturday if Marshall did not get a half-dozen assault-and-battery cases. As a young lawyer, he eked out an existence trying them before the justice of the peace.

In time, Marshall's practice diversified and became profitable, but he never specialized in any particular aspect of the law. He liked the county-seat town of 3,000 inhabitants. According to his biographer, "ditch diggers, local bankers, town sots, ministers of the gospel, small town lawyers, and later, diplomats and kings" accepted him as a friend. Here was a man who understood them and their problems. Marshall's matchless humor relieved tense situations and made him good company. By the close of the 1870s, he and his partner, William F. McNagny, were involved with nearly half the cases before the local circuit court. During the 1880s, the influence of Marshall & McNagny spread throughout the Twelfth Congressional District of northeast Indiana. Although Marshall also had other partners for shorter durations, his affiliation with McNagny lasted from 1877 until 1909.

In his *Recollections,* Marshall discussed some of his cases as well as insights he received into the twistings and turnings of human nature while practicing law in Indiana. With tongue in cheek, he claimed that he could tell whether a witness was telling the truth by watching his Adam's apple.

In a 1913 speech to George Washington Law School students in Washington, D.C., Marshall offered his "legal ten commandments," which a reporter paraphrased as follows:

Don't put a fee before a just cause.

Don't worship money to the extent of being willing to write a dishonest contract in order to get a large fee.

Be a peacemaker; that is the lawyer's business.

Don't chase ambulances.

Honor your profession as your own sacred honor; therefore, do not seek or confound litigation.

Don't accept contingent fees.

Use your influence against the system of allowing attorneys' fees in advance of divorce cases . . .; when that has been abolished half the divorce cases will be stopped.

Use your influence to compel a person charged with crime to testify in the cause; the innocent man cannot be harmed thereby.

Take the part of the known criminal, but only to see that justice is tempered with mercy.

Don't inquire as to your client's pocketbook before fixing your fee.

Knowledge of the law and of men could be valuable in politics. Marshall and McNagny, both Democrats, worked for the well-being of their party. As their legal reputations spread, so too did their influence in Democratic circles. In a day when political activity doubled as entertainment, Marshall was in demand as a quick-witted speaker and Democratic torchbearer. In 1892, McNagny ran to represent the Twelfth District in the Fifty-third Congress (1893–95); he won, but failed in his reelection attempt. William Jennings Bryan and "free silver" were not popular in Indiana in 1896, but Marshall hewed to the party line—one of the few Democratic state central committee members to do so.

As Marshall approached forty, he appeared to be successful. He had a good law practice and held the respect of many Hoosiers. On Sundays he attended both morning and evening services at the Presbyterian church. He had taught Sunday school, served on the school board, organized the county fair two years in succession, and gave generously to charities. A Masonic Lodge member, he climbed the grades of the Scottish Rite through the thirty-third degree by 1898. His oratory, at its best in banquet halls and temple dedications, brought resounding applause and more speaking engagements.

But Marshall's genial exterior and gregarious personality masked heartaches; moreover, he drank too much.

During his early years in Columbia City, Marshall had asked Catherine Hooper, daughter of a partner in the the law firm of Hooper and Olds, to marry him. She consented but died soon after buying her trousseau. For the next two decades, Marshall kept the company of several women but did not fall in love with any of them. He lived with his mother. Friends reached the conclusion that he was a confirmed bachelor. While trying a case in Angola few months after his mother's death, Marshall met Lois I. Kimsey, a vivacious twenty-three-year-old deputy county clerk, and married her on October 2, 1895. Marshall adored her and dedicated his *Recollections* to two women "uninjured in the fall of Eden"—his mother and his wife.

Lois Kimsey Marshall helped her husband gain the upper hand over his alcoholism. This did not come easily. By his own account, he never cared for a "drink" of whiskey; he "wanted a barrel." By 1897, according to his biographer, Marshall began to appear in morning court sessions "with after effects of intoxication which made it impossible for him to conduct his business." Marshall's drinking threatened his marriage until in 1898 he took the cure. He continued to struggle with alcoholism but, thereafter, no one saw him drink alcohol in public. "I do not drink," he replied when tempted at political gatherings. When Marshall was governor and then vice president, he and his wife did not serve liquor in their home.

It is unlikely that Marshall would have been successful in Indiana and national politics without a loving wife's encouragement and without Thomas Taggart's influence. As mayor of Indianapolis (1895–1901) and a wheel horse in the Democratic Party on the state and national levels, Taggart had an eye for political talent. Marshall had served with Taggart on the Democratic state central committee beginning in 1896. When the party faithful talked with Marshall about doing his duty and running for Congress in 1906, he declined on grounds that he "might be elected" and then hinted that the only elective office that interested him was the governorship. Republicans had held that office for a decade, but a friend, Louis Ludlow, began to tout Marshall as the Democratic candidate for governor a full year before the 1908 gubernatorial election.

The liquor issue then divided Indiana Republicans and Democrats alike. At the Democratic state convention in March 1908, Taggart's candidate, Samuel M. Ralston, could not muster enough votes in four ballots to carry the convention. To prevent the nomination from going to a temperance candidate, Taggart maneuvered enough votes to Marshall so that he won the nomination on the fifth ballot. Several factions then rallied to Marshall's call for party unity.

Marshall's Wabash College and Masonic connections raised interest beyond the Democratic Party. So too did his speaking style and adept handling of the liquor issue when he began to campaign. To assure his independence, Marshall paid his own campaign expenses. Neither a "dry" nor controlled by the brewers, he favored local option. He also supported such progressive planks in his party's platform as direct election of U.S. senators, primary election laws, tariff reform, and control of trusts. Republican opponent Congressman James E. Watson bogged down when the incumbent governor called a special session of the legislature in September to consider the liquor issue. The Republican majority passed a county option law, whereupon Marshall pilloried the opposition for taking the decision away from the people in the fall election.

Marshall campaigned hard in 1908, using his homespun approach to good effect. Neither formidable in appearance nor particularly handsome, he was friendly and approachable. Well trimmed gray locks covered his large head and a bushy mustache obscured his mouth, into which he frequently stuffed a cigar. Observant reporters noted that he was well groomed, that he wore a Phi Beta Kappa key, and that a dash of whimsy flavored his otherwise dignified appearance. Marshall delivered his points deliberately, "as if addressing a jury," reported the *Indianapolis News* of June 3, 1908; "the whole people seemed to be in a jury box before him."

People liked the man, his progressive message, and the way he delivered it. In the November election, Marshall won a four-year term as governor with a plurality of nearly 15,000 votes. More Hoosiers voted for him in 1908 than for Bryan, the perennial Democratic candidate for president. Marshall also came within 150 votes of outpolling the Republican candidate for president, William Howard Taft. Gubernatorial victories then being rare for Democrats, Marshall's success commanded national attention. Two years later, another progressive Democrat, Woodrow Wilson, would be elected governor of New Jersey.

In office, Marshall distanced himself from the machinery of his party and refused to take orders from party boss Thomas Taggart. As his four-year term unfolded, Marshall proved to be a sound administrator who wielded the powers of his office decisively, including the veto and the use of the militia during labor disputes. He understood the citizens he governed as evidenced by his words and deeds.

The 1910 election, midway in Marshall's term, brought strong Democratic majorities to both houses of the legislature. This enabled the governor and his party to replace the Republicans' county option law governing the sale of intoxicants with their own township option law in 1911. The time had also arrived for action on a progressive agenda related to child labor, correctional institutions, drugs, education, elections, hygiene, railroad safety, trusts, voter registration, and workman's compensation. Governor Marshall signed reform legislation into law in these and other categories. Upon analyzing the details, later generations may conclude that their accomplishments were minimal; for the times, they were significant.

Marshall recognized the limits of what society should attempt through legislation. His theory was that reform should not work downward upon the citizenry but outward from the individual and, when appropriate, be capped off by legislation. The legislature "cannot baptize the state," he insisted.

Because of his interest in penal reform Marshall became known as the Pardoning Governor. One day, he was jostled in a crowd and a man said, "Pardon me," whereupon Marshall replied, "Certainly, what crime have you committed?"

During his tenure as governor, Marshall reached the conclusion that to meet the needs of the twentieth century, Indiana government needed to be overhauled. Amending the 1851 state constitution was exceedingly difficult; therefore, in 1911 Marshall proposed a new and more easily amendable one. Although its principal author was actually Jacob Piatt Dunn, Jr., an Indianapolis lawyer and historian, the document came to be known as the Tom Marshall Constitution. Sections embodying much of the reform thought of the day about state government (including the initiative, referendum, and recall) passed both houses with ease. Curiously, liberalized voting rights were not part of the package.

The question arose: Did the legislature have the power to draft a new constitution and to submit it to the people? Negative answers came back from the circuit court of Marion County and also, by a margin of one vote, from the Indiana supreme court. This rankled Marshall, a stickler on the doctrine of the separation of powers, who thought that the court had overstepped its authority. The U.S. Supreme Court eventually ruled that it had no jurisdiction; therefore the decision of the Indiana supreme court held.

Master politician that he was, Marshall could not steer around the impasse. He closed out his statehouse career as a "liberal with the brakes on."

While he was yet governor, and even before the fate of the Tom Marshall Constitution was sealed, another chapter of Marshall's life was beginning to unfold: He sought the Democratic nomination for president in 1912. Months before the convention, he drummed up speaking engagements for himself in various parts of the country. He had no illusions about his reputation on the national scene but reasoned that he might have a chance at the nomination if the major candidates deadlocked. That prospect was not farfetched because the Democratic nominee then needed the votes of two-thirds of the delegates. Thomas Taggart allegedly led the Indiana delegation to Baltimore in June 1912 with the goal of securing the vice-presidential nomination for Indiana and its popular governor, although Marshall and Taggart were not political cronies (nor were Woodrow Wilson and "Boss" James Smith, Jr., of New Jersey).

The fifth man to be nominated at Baltimore, Marshall received only one vote from beyond Indiana in the initial balloting. On the tenth ballot, Champ Clark of Missouri received a majority of the delegates' votes but could not muster enough to clinch the nomination. The convention deadlocked. On the twenty-eighth ballot, Indiana switched all but one of its votes to Wilson. Marshall's biographer offered the explanation that Taggart used the occasion to gain favor for a vice-presidential slot for Marshall, and further, that Taggart also used his influence with delegations from Illinois and other states to push Wilson over the top and to shore up support for a Wilson-Marshall ticket. On the forty-sixth ballot, Wilson received the necessary two-thirds majority. The vice-presidential nomination for Marshall then came easily. It made political sense to counterbalance a liberal easterner of southern birth with a popular midwestern liberal "with the brakes on." Marshall was not a confidant of Wilson, but Wilson acquiesced in the selection of his running mate.

During a vigorous campaign, Wilson and Marshall traveled the country separately, focusing on the tariff and the trusts. As he had done in his 1908 gubernatorial campaign, Marshall paid his own expenses. He began his campaign in the Northeast in late August, worked his way to the West Coast, and then came back to Indiana. Marshall reserved his strongest rhetoric for lambasting Theodore Roosevelt, the Progressive candidate. In the thick of the campaign, he attended a Scottish Rite banquet along with William Howard Taft, the Republican candidate for president. The Democratic ticket won overwhelmingly in the electoral college.

While the Marshalls were preparing to leave Indiana for Washington, D.C., the Phi Gamma Delta fraternity held a national meeting in Indianapolis. It was on this occasion that Marshall, now a superb after-dinner speaker, told the story of the man who had two sons, one of whom went to sea and drowned and the other of whom entered politics and became vice president. "The poor father died of a broken heart—he never heard of either one afterward."

Marshall began his vice presidency auspiciously on March 4, 1913. A special honor guard consisting of the Black Horse Troop of cadets from his home state's Culver Military Academy escorted Marshall to the inauguration ceremony (and did so again four years later). In his inaugural speech, termed "novel and naive" by *The New York Times,* Marshall referred to the "forced silence" he was about to enter as the presiding officer of the Senate. The realities of the vice presidency began to dawn on Marshall when he found his office, a single room near the Senate chamber. He described it as "a monkey cage, except that the visitors do not offer me any peanuts."

Washington society received the Marshalls graciously. Thomas attributed this to his nimble tongue, which could pay a compliment and "tell a story out of the book of my life, which had not been read by the people of that city." He might have added that his wife added gaiety to private parties and dignity to functions of state. The Marshalls did not have sufficient wealth to entertain lavishly and needed the income from the vice president's speaking engagements to afford even their modest lifestyle. In demand throughout the country, Marshall entertained his audiences and also stumped for the president's program. He spoke of Wilson as a man of ideas who had the courage to express them, the desire to get things done, and "the nerve to insist on their being done."

While Marshall was learning the rules of the tradition-bound Senate, progressivism flowered. With the passage of the Underwood Tariff Act in October 1913, Wilson and Marshall fulfilled their tariff-reform campaign promises. In Marshall's opinion, banking issues generated "the most illuminating and exhaustive discussion of a public question ever held in the Senate." The Federal Reserve Act, also passed in 1913, gave flexibility to the money supply and overhauled the nation's banking system. The Clayton Antitrust Act of 1914 delivered on more campaign promises.

Marshall presided over the Senate while that body debated and passed landmark measures. His friendliness and evenhandedness won him the respect of senators of all political persuasions. As one who had been present at the Lincoln-Douglas debates and whose family had witnessed intense sectionalism, it gave Marshall great satisfaction one day to observe

Senator John Hollis Bankhead of Alabama, a former Confederate soldier, locked arm in arm with Senator Knute Nelson of Minnesota, a former Yankee soldier.

The vice president enjoyed his front-row seat on the great American drama. However, he soon ascertained that he was "of no importance to the administration beyond the duty of being loyal to it and ready, at any time, to act as a sort of pinch hitter; that is, when everybody else on the team had failed, I was to be given a chance." He therefore decided to accept the situation,

> to take it in a good-natured way; to be friendly and well disposed to political friend and . . . foe alike; to be loyal to my chief and at the same time not to be offensive to my associates; and to . . . deal justly with those over whom I was merely nominally presiding.

During the eight years that Marshall spent presiding over the Senate, he did not cast a tie-breaking vote on any legislation of paramount importance.

Every two years, Marshall traveled the country on behalf of Democratic candidates for the House and Senate. As was the case in his Indiana days, he proved to be a loyal and useful party member. In 1916, the Democrats renominated Wilson and Marshall. The Republicans nominated Charles Evans Hughes for president and Charles W. Fairbanks as his running mate. This was awkward for the two vice-presidential candidates because they were fellow Hoosiers, fraternity brothers, and friends. The Democrats ran on their reform record, but by election day the war in Europe overshadowed domestic issues.

Both Marshall and Wilson failed to carry their home states. When it was clear that they had won by a narrow margin nationally, Marshall, quoting Shakespeare, telegraphed Wilson:

> 'TIS NOT SO DEEP AS A WELL
> NOR SO WIDE AS A CHURCHDOOR;
> BUT 'TIS ENOUGH 'TWILL SERVE.

The two men exchanged pleasantries, but no deep relationship developed that could be counted upon to sustain them through a serious crisis. The 1916 victory made Marshall the first vice president since John C. Calhoun to be reelected.

Marshall's *Recollections* provides commentary on events leading to the American declaration of war on April 6, 1917, the war itself, and its aftermath. Nothing what transpired caused Marshall to revise the conclusions he had reached earlier about the vice presidency.

Himself no early or rabid enthusiast for American entry into the war, Marshall refused to be swept along by wartime hysteria. An incident involving Wisconsin Senator Robert M. La Follette motivated the vice president to revise a senate procedure. As did other midwestern progressives, La Follette drew fire for opposing U.S. entry. When a Senate committee temporized about how it should respond to petitions from citizens calling for La Follette's expulsion from the Senate, Marshall halted the Senate's tradition of acting upon petitions from individual citizens and held to this policy for the rest of his term.

The war changed Marshall's duties: In addition to presiding over the Senate and making political speeches, he also traveled the country in support of the Liberty Loan campaigns. According to his biographer, the war transformed "the merry companionable 'Tom' Marshall" into "a serious, serviceable and earnest Vice-President."

When Wilson went to Paris after the armistice, Marshall presided over cabinet meetings—the first vice president to do so. But in accordance with his scruples over the separation of powers, he informed cabinet members that he was "acting in an unofficial and informal way . . . out of deference to your desires and those of the President." He explained that it would be embarrassing "to be in a confidential relationship to both the legislative and the executive branches."

Wilson returned to the United States in February 1919 to discuss both early drafts of the peace treaty and the League of Nations with the senators. With Marshall presiding, an acrimonious debate broke out in the Senate during the waning days of the third session of the Sixty-fifth Congress. The senators filibustered all night. Nerves became frayed and some said things in anger. When Marshall banged down the gavel on March 4, 1919, to close the session, he declared the Senate adjourned "Sine Deo" (without God).

Characteristically, Marshall's humor belittled no one; this time it did have a bite.

The major challenge of Marshall's vice presidency struck in late September 1919, intensified a week later, and continued until the end of his term. On September 25, President Wilson took sick on his return to Washington, D.C., from a national speaking tour presenting his case for the League of Nations to the people. His physician, Dr. Cary T. Grayson, informed the press that the president had "suffered a complete nervous breakdown" (in fact, it was a stroke) and would rest in the White House. Marshall began to fill in for the president on ceremonial occasions, but for several days he knew no more than the public about the situation's seriousness. On October 2, for example, he welcomed the king and queen of the Belgians and their son to the United States on the president's behalf.

That day the president suffered a second stroke, a cerebral thrombosis that left him a physical and mental invalid. Marshall received a briefing on the gravity of the situation a few days later in a bizarre manner. J. Fred Essary, the *Baltimore Sun*'s respected Washington correspondent, made his way quietly to the vice president's office and explained that the massive stroke of October 2 left the president deathly ill. The stunned vice president did not speak or even look up. The reporter waited for a response from Marshall but received none and left. Years later when Essary and Marshall met in Indiana, Marshall apologized for the incident: "I did not even have the courtesy to thank you for coming over and telling me. It was the first great shock of my life."

Wilson's advisers had method in their manner of informing Marshall. They did so unofficially through a nongovernmental source so that the vice president would have no grounds for invoking Article II of the Constitution and assuming the presidency due to the president's "Inability to discharge the Powers and Duties of the said Office."

In his 1992 book *Ill Advised: Presidential Health and Public Trust,* historian Robert H. Ferrell stated flatly: "The president should have resigned immediately." Instead, Wilson, his physician, his wife, and his secretary, Joseph P. Tumulty, disguised his illness. The vice president repeatedly tried to visit the stricken president but was not allowed to see him until his last day in office, March 4, 1921.

Volumes have been written about Mrs. Wilson's "petticoat government," as Senator Albert Fall called it. Edith Boiling Wilson termed it "her stewardship," which probably went so far as to guide the president's hand as he signed necessary papers to sustain him in the presidency. Even in full health, Wilson had not regarded Marshall highly (although he had headed off a move to drop Marshall from the ballot in 1916). Wilson's advisers had less regard for Marshall than did their chief. Colonel Edward M. House, for example, told a reporter that an "unfriendly fairy godmother" had presented Marshall with a keen sense of humor. "Nothing is more fatal in politics." He acknowledged that Marshall made friends, "but they looked upon him as a jester."

Tumulty and Secretary of State Robert Lansing both left accounts describing a conference they had with Dr. Grayson on October 3, 1919. The threesome discussed the possibility of having Marshall "assume the executive authority temporarily in the absence of precedents as to what constituted disability under the Constitution." Heated discussion followed, with the upshot that Tumulty and Grayson concurred that neither man would certify the president's disability. Tumulty then notified Lansing that "if anybody outside of the White House circle attempted to certify to the President's disability, that Grayson and I would stand together and repudiate it."

Not privy to such discussions and barred from seeing the president, Marshall realized that his inquiries into the president's health might be interpreted as self-serving or worse. In the deluge of advice that came to him, people of many political persuasions urged Marshall to seize the presidency; he consistently declined to do so. Marshall's secretary, Mark Thistlethwaite, asked him if he would assume the presidency if Congress decided that Wilson was unable to serve. "No," Marshall replied. "It would not be legal until the President signed it, or until it had a two-thirds vote. . . ." The only conditions under which Marshall would have taken over, according to his biographer, would have been for Congress to have passed such a resolution and for Mrs. Wilson and Dr. Grayson to have approved it in writing. "I am not going to seize the place and then have Wilson—recovered—come around and say 'get off, you usurper.'"

There the issue rested for the remainder of Marshall's term. "These were not pleasant months for me," Marshall recorded in his *Recollections.* He remained reluctant to ask about the president's health "for fear some censorious soul would accuse me of a longing for his place. I never have wanted his [Wilson's] shoes," he wrote. No evidence contradicts the genuineness of this assertion.

An ambitious man could have made much of the situation; an unscrupulous one could have thrown the nation into turmoil. Aware of this, Marshall on one occasion confided to his wife: "I could throw this country into civil war, but I won't." Historian John D. Hicks concluded that had Marshall countenanced the idea, "it is probable that he might have been declared president." Marshall rose above personal ambition. His idols were two Democrats, Stephen A. Douglas and Samuel J. Tilden (who showed restraint in the disputed presidential election of 1876). He wrote:

They are the two men in all American history who when the peace and good order of their country were at stake cast aside every hope of personal preferment for the sake of the Republic.

As vice president, Marshall did what he could from September 1919 to March 4, 1921, to keep the executive branch of the government functioning. (Ratified in 1967, Amendment Twenty-five of the U.S. Constitution addresses the issue of the incapacitation of the president and the transfer of powers to the vice president.) Marshall hosted foreign dignitaries with republican dignity. While presiding over the Senate, he remained loyal to the president's objective of supporting the League of Nations. Had he been president, it is likely that he would have been more flexible in dealing with the Senate. His considered opinion was that more than executive flexibility would have been required to get two-thirds of the senators to approve Article Ten of the League covenant, which provided for collective action against aggressors.

Marshall was not proud of his nation's rejection of the League of Nations. He wrote in his *Recollections* that it reminded him

> of a man going to the relief of his neighbor who was being assaulted by a burglar. After he had assisted in throwing the burglar out of the house, although his neighbor was wounded and in sore stress, he picks up his hat, says good night and goes home.

Following the Republican national convention of June 1920, Marshall greeted his possible successor, Calvin Coolidge, with a message of commiseration. His telegram read: "Please accept my sincere sympathy." Only for fleeting moments following the vice presidency did Marshall entertain thoughts of continuing his political career. He moved back to Indianapolis and used his time to travel, speak, and write. In 1925, he offered to the public *Recollections of Thomas R. Marshall, Vice-President and Hoosier Philosopher—A Hoosier Salad* "in the hope," as

he explained in the front matter, "that the Tired Business Man, the Unsuccessful Golfer and the Lonely Husband whose wife is out reforming the world may find therein a half hour's surcease from sorrow." He also served as a trustee of his alma mater, Wabash College. In 1922, President Harding appointed Marshall to the U.S. Coal Commission.

Marshall died on June 1, 1925, of a heart attack while on a visit to Washington, D.C. The body was returned to Indianapolis and is buried in Crown Hill Cemetery. The Marshalls had no children.

John D. Hicks's decades-old assertion that Marshall "was perhaps the most popular vice president the country ever had" still holds.

References

Thomas R. Marshall, *Recollections of Thomas R. Marshall, Vice-President and Hoosier Philosopher—A Hoosier Salad* (Indianapolis, Ind.: The Bobbs-Merrill Co., 1925); Charles M. Thomas, *Thomas Riley Marshall: Hoosier Statesman* (Oxford, Ohio: The Mississippi Valley Press, 1939); John Eugene Brown, "Woodrow Wilson's Vice President: Thomas R. Marshall and the Wilson Administration" (Ph.D. dissertation, Ball; State University, 1970); David Bennett, *He Almost Changed the World: The Life and Times of Thomas Riley Marshall* (Bloomington, Ind.: Author House, 2007).

PETER T. HARSTAD, now retired and living in Lakeville, Minnesota, received his Ph.D. in history from the University of Wisconsin, Madison in 1963. He spent most of his career in three "I" states: as professor of history at Idaho State University, 1963–72; as director of the State Historical Society of Iowa, 1972–81; and as executive director of the Indiana Historical Society, 1984–2001. He continues to publish on a variety of subjects, most of them related to the history of the Midwest.

CALVIN COOLIDGE (1872–1933)

Vice President, 1921–1923

(President Warren G. Harding)

CALVIN COOLIDGE
(Library of Congress)

By Paul L. Silver

Calvin Coolidge has provoked a range of views. He is often stereotyped as "Silent Cal" and a thoroughly unaggressive administrator, but has also been described as sound and wise, particularly in his handling of the Boston police strike, and as thoughtful and well informed. Both biographer Claude Fuess and Thomas Silver (in a more recent study of the treatment of Coolidge by historians) have argued that their subject was unfairly maligned by politicians and academicians. Indeed Fuess, in his 1940 biography, *Calvin Coolidge: The Man from Vermont,* concludes his introduction with the statement that its subject "was not only a useful public servant but a great and good man."

Coolidge, one of two Vermont-born presidents, both of whom reached that high office through the vice presidency, was born, appropriately, on July 4, 1872, in Plymouth, Vermont. Most of the technological marvels with which we are familial—the telephone, radio, movies, television, computers, and such—were long in the future, and Coolidge's native state was more remote from the centers of culture and power than it is a century and more later. Interstate highways and E-mail tie Vermont to the rest of New England and the country today; in the 1870s Vermont was more detached, and Plymouth was a small community that was rather remote from population centers even within the state. Though he spent most of his adult life outside the state of his birth, Coolidge never lost his devotion to and admiration for it, and he declared his feelings on several occasions, notably September 21, 1928, at Bennington, where he said frankly: "Vermont is a state I love."

In the crossroads town of Plymouth, Calvin's father, John Coolidge, storekeeper and landowner, was also active in local politics and a sometime member of the state legislature. Calvin's education, both at the local ungraded school at Black River Academy and, briefly, at St. Johnsbury Academy, covered a variety of subjects including English grammar, Latin, Greek, French, mathematics, history, and rhetoric. He performed capably with an interest in history and biography, though Fuess in his 1940 biography characterized young Coolidge as "an ordinary boy, who seemed likely to end his days on the farm or in the village store."

Coolidge's life had its share of tragedy as well as chores, education, and entertainment. His mother, Victoria, died when Calvin was twelve years old, and his sister Abigail, of whom he was very fond and who was three years younger than he, died of appendicitis in 1890 leaving a lonely brother and father. The void in the father's life was filled after six years as a widower by Carrie Brown with whom Calvin was close for the remainder of her life.

In fall 1891, the young Vermonter did what no member of the family and few in southern Vermont had done: he went off to college. Amherst College was in the 1890s a small liberal arts institution that introduced young Coolidge to the wider world both of learning and of people beyond Vermont. His shyness and reserve made his absorption into the community slower than for others, though he made friends, participated in fraternity activities, and achieved some prominence as a speaker, delivering an oration as part of his commencement exercises. Coolidge biographer Donald McCoy summarized this part of his subject's life and looked ahead when he wrote that the graduates

marched out into life and among them marched Calvin Coolidge, who though not last among them in college was far from being first. As so often happens, some of the top members of the class were to disappear into the jungles of life and a number of the obscure were to become worthies in their communities, businesses, and professions. Calvin Coolidge, marching to his own tune, was to surpass them all.

The young graduate's next stop was Northampton, Massachusetts, in which he spent a good part of the rest of his life, both before and after his presidency. He had already decided to study law, but during the summer after graduation, in 1895, he discarded the idea of attending law school because of the cost and opted instead for reading law with an established lawyer, clerking in that lawyer's firm and being admitted to the bar by examination. (This is still an option in Vermont, though not in many other states.) At the end of two years of clerking and reading law, he was presented by one of the lawyers in the firm in which he worked, examined by a committee of lawyers and judges, and admitted to the bar forthwith, opening his law office in Northampton in February 1898.

At virtually the same time, Coolidge began his rise up the political ladder. Unlike Herbert Hoover, who ran for only one political office—president of the United States—winning once and losing once, the young lawyer started at the bottom as a campaign worker in the effort of Henry Field, a partner in the firm in which Coolidge had clerked, to become mayor of

Northampton. He was also chosen to be on the Republican city committee and a delegate to a local convention and in December 1898 was elected to the Northampton city council, the first of many elective offices he held. He used this relatively insignificant position to learn the mechanics and people of the political process. He then won election by the city council to the city solicitor's post, served two terms, and was defeated for a third. This was one of his few defeats; another was for a position on his chosen city's school committee.

Prior to his next political move, Coolidge met Grace Goodhue, also a Vermonter, who after graduating in 1902 from the University of Vermont, had accepted a teaching position in Northampton. Though they seemed almost opposite in personality as well as in diversity of interests, Grace and Calvin found each other congenial and in the summer of 1905 decided to be married; the ceremony took place in Burlington in October.

Following a short honeymoon, the couple returned to Northampton where he resumed his law practice and political career. The latter next moved to the state level, Coolidge having won a seat in the Massachusetts house of representatives. Though he is often seen as a staunch conservative, the young legislator's record was reasonably progressive. In his two terms as representative, he supported direct election of U.S. senators, women's suffrage, a six-day workweek, and fewer hours of work for women and children.

After two terms as a representative, the young attorney had a brief period out of office but in 1909 was the Republican candidate for mayor of Northampton, an office he also held for two terms, "beginning," as Donald McCoy notes, "his continuous service in public office until he left the White House twenty years later." As mayor he worked to better the fire and police departments, increase teachers' pay, and improve the city streets, and he did it all efficiently and honestly.

A state senate seat from Hampshire County was Coolidge's next political office. The young politician's return to Boston coincided with the turmoil in the Republican Party marked at the national level by the split between President William Howard Taft and former President Theodore Roosevelt and in Massachusetts by the textile strike in Lowell. At a critical point in this latter contentious dispute, a legislative committee was appointed with Coolidge at its head. Because of his previous record, he was acceptable to both labor and management, and while the settlement reached did not entirely please the strikers, in general Coolidge was perceived as having acted in a fair manner. He served a total of three terms—three years—as state senator; in the final year he was chosen as president of the senate. In the latter position he had considerable power, including the naming of committees and the assignment of bills to those committees. Once again, both as senator and senate president, Coolidge had retained the support of conservatives and moderates and favored measures of interest to the progressives. He backed both women's suffrage and a minimum wage for women as well as a state income tax and primary elections, and he renewed his support for direct election of U.S. senators. Further, as senate president Coolidge was perceived as fair, honest, and efficient with a concern for stability and economy.

Coolidge's upward climb continued with his election in 1915 as lieutenant governor; here, too, he served three one-year terms. In this position, though he did not preside over the senate, he was chair of the governor's council, which had the job of advising the governor on matters as wide ranging as finances, appointments, and pardons. At Governor Samuel McCall's behest, Coolidge was assigned the task of speaking frequently across the state, thus improving his chances for higher office by making him and his ideas and his aura of soundness and stability widely known.

Among those whose attention Coolidge attracted was Frank Stearns, a wealthy Boston merchant who was ultimately to be a major backer of the future president. With Stearns's financial and promotional help, Coolidge became the Republican gubernatorial candidate and entered a campaign made more difficult by a split in the Republican organization between then Governor McCall and U.S. senator John Weeks. Indeed Coolidge at one point thought he might lose the election, and though he won, he did so by the relatively small margin of 16,000 votes.

The new governor began the first of his two one-year terms with an inaugural address characterized by Claude Fuess as "one of his most liberal pronouncements." In it the governor urged the legislature to work diligently and under the law for all citizens:

> Let there be a purpose in all your legislation to recognize the right of man to be well born, well nurtured, well educated, well employed, and well paid. This is no gospel of ease and selfishness, or class distinction, but a gospel of effort and service, of universal application.

In his tenure as governor, Coolidge dealt with the problems and dislocations of the months immediately following World War I. Professor McCoy's assessment of the governor's performance—"an effective, responsible, and conscientious executive"—seems fair. His actions and statements during perhaps the single most difficult event of his governorship, the Boston police strike, more than any other action thrust him into national prominence. Historians disagree about the specific events and most particularly Coolidge's role in them. Some such as McCoy accuse him of being hesitant and uncertain, while others such as Fuess and Silver praise his firmness, determination, and consistency, particularly in his support of Police Commissioner Edward Curtis.

The Boston police strike occurred in the late summer of 1919, a year in which various disputes had occurred as labor went after gains it had refrained from seeking during World War I. The most notable dispute was the threatened Seattle general strike early in the year, though Massachusetts had had its share of strikes, including a work stoppage by telephone workers and a street railway workers' strike in Boston. Coolidge entered that dispute, helping to achieve an agreement under which the workers went back to work while matters in dispute were arbitrated; eventually the workers achieved significant improvement in their wages.

Two primary issues dominated the police strike—the wages, hours, and working conditions of the police, and the effort to form a union and affiliate with the American Federation of Labor. The governor was fully aware of the long hours, the low wages, and the dirty police stations, and said so. However, he consistently backed Police Commissioner Curtis, who refused to allow the Boston police officers to join a union and found guilty those who disobeyed his orders and received a charter from the A.F. of L. Curtis delayed implementing punishment in hopes that these leaders would cease their association with the A.F. of L. Further, just prior to the strike, these men were suspended instead of being dismissed. Silver and McCoy disagree on how vigorous, forthright, and involved the governor was in all of this, but it seems reasonably clear that Coolidge consistently supported Police Commissioner Curtis and, while sympathizing with the policemen, would not condone the strike.

When policemen walked off the job and disorder and violence resulted, Mayor Andrew Peters removed Commissioner Curtis, who was shortly reinstated by Coolidge. Peters had called out the State Guard within Boston; Coolidge called out most of the rest, and order was restored. A.F. of L. Head Samuel Gompers sent telegrams to the governor in which Gompers asserted that the police commissioner had denied the right of policemen to affiliate. The governor replied in his own telegram that became the single most-famous statement in the whole controversy. In it he declared: "The right of the police of Boston to affiliate has always been questioned, never granted, is now prohibited." He added that it was wrong to leave the city unprotected, declaring: "There is no right to strike against the public safety by anybody, anywhere, any time." Coolidge's actions heartened the people of Boston. His telegram, and particularly the above sentence, were quoted across the country, and together his actions and statements helped to propel the governor onto the national scene and into the vice presidency.

In 1920, Governor Coolidge entertained ambitions to be the Republican Party's nominee for president. He had support within Massachusetts and some outside of it, but many Massachusetts delegation members to the Republican national convention were pledged to Leonard Wood, and its most prominent member, Senator Henry Cabot Lodge, would not support Coolidge, in part because of the governor's association with the Murray Crane faction in Massachusetts politics and because, in the opinion of Claude Fuess, of differences in style and background as well as the senator's determination to retain what Fuess calls Lodge's "supremacy in Massachusetts politics." The convention, deadlocked between Wood and Governor Frank G. Lowden of Illinois, was firmly in the control of what Coolidge in his autobiography referred to as "a coterie of United States Senators." These leaders succeeded in nominating for president Senator Warren G. Harding of Ohio, but they were blocked in their efforts to have Wisconsin Senator Irvine L. Lenroot chosen by the delegates as the vice-presidential nominee. Oregon delegation member Wallace McCamant placed the Massachusetts governor's name in nomination, and it was seconded by North Dakota, and though several others were also named, the convention running away from the senatorial group's control quickly chose Coolidge, the nomination being made unanimous.

In the meantime, back in Boston, the governor, perhaps disappointed at not making a better showing in the effort to gain the top place on the ticket, left his Boston residence for a walk and returned from it for a long talk with his wife Grace. When the results from the convention were telephoned to Coolidge, he told his wife: "Nominated for Vice President!" She at first thought he might be kidding, but when it was clear that he was not, she said: "You are not going to accept it, are you?" to which he replied: "I suppose shall have to." Coolidge then prepared a short statement in which he declared the nomination "unsought" and accepted "as an honor and a duty." He added:

> It will be especially pleasing to be associated with my old friend Senator Warren G. Harding, our candidate for President. The Republican Party has adopted a sound platform, chosen a wise leader and is united. It deserves the confidence of the American people. That confidence I shall endeavor to secure.

Coolidge's role in the campaign was not large and usually not outside of New England. He made a speech in Philadelphia in October and in the same month, on orders from the Republican national committee, made an eight-day swing through the South with other party leaders. Coolidge protested the assignment as keeping him too long away from his responsibilities in Massachusetts and added that "my abilities do not lie in that direction," but he carried out the assignment. Following a speech and parade in New York City, he returned to his home state and concluded his campaign with speeches in Boston.

The new vice president's role in the Harding administration promised, at least at the beginning of the campaign, to be significant, certainly larger than was usually the case. On June 30, 1920, Harding and Coolidge had breakfast at the presidential candidate's Washington, D.C., residence. At the press conference that followed, Harding said:

> I think the vice president should be more than a mere substitute in waiting. In reestablishing coordination between the Executive Office and the Senate, the vice president can and ought to play a big part, and I have been telling Governor Coolidge how much I wish him to be not only a participant in the campaign, but how much I wish him to be a helpful part of a Republican administration. The country

needs the counsel and the becoming participation in government of such men as Governor Coolidge.

The Harding-Coolidge ticket easily defeated the Democrats, headed by James M. Cox. The Republicans campaigned on a "return to normalcy" theme that had great national appeal after the war. Harding and Coolidge took 61 percent of the popular vote.

After being sworn in 1921, Coolidge took over his prescribed duty of presiding over the Senate and attended cabinet meetings though according to both Claude Fuess and Donald McCoy, rarely involved himself in the discussions that took place. Coolidge presided over the Senate in a competent and, after one or two troublesome situations, cautious manner. In his autobiography, he declared that "presiding over the Senate was fascinating to me" but in the next paragraph said, wryly, that "the Senate had but one fixed rule, subject to exception of course, which was to the effect that the Senate would do anything it wanted to do whenever it wanted to do it." He thereafter relied on the secretary to the Senate for information on questions of parliamentary procedure.

The vice president also participated in various ceremonial events, and made numerous speeches, either as representative of the Harding administration or to boost his personal income. He later laconically summarized this aspect of his vice-presidential career: "During these two years I spoke some and lectured some. This took me about the country in travels that reached from Maine to California, from the Twin Cities to Charleston. I was getting acquainted." This was not an insignificant benefit to him because, as he himself noted, he had no experience at the federal level and needed to learn the ways of Washington.

He participated in the capital's social side, often accepting invitations to luncheons and dinner—surprisingly perhaps, given his shyness and well-known aversion to idle chatter. Once, when asked about this, he replied "Got to eat somewhere!" This and other stories merely strengthened his reputation for taciturnity punctuated by an occasional dry jest.

During his vice-presidential years Coolidge, though not a major force in either the Washington political arena or social scene, remained a power in Massachusetts politics. Donald McCoy attributes this in part to what came to be called "Coolidge luck," by which he, though not always the strongest candidate, had moved up the ladder from one elective office to another in Massachusetts and then on to the vice presidency. In fact, many expected that this same good fortune would move him into the presidency. People in Northampton reportedly said: "I wouldn't give two cents for Warren Harding's life."

Coolidge's strength in his home state was also based on his political faction's need for a well-known figure to head the group after the death of its longtime leader, Murray Crane, as well as on the strength of that faction, holding as it did in addition to the vice presidency the speakership of the U.S. House of Representatives and the Massachusetts governorship. In addition, the vice president was perceived as a primary reason why Massachusetts Republicans had done well in the elections of 1920.

However, in Washington Coolidge, though supportive of the president, was not close to him or his cronies, having little in common with people like Charles Forbes and Harry Daugherty, of whose activities and character he must have become aware. Fuess noted that: "It could not have been agreeable for Calvin Coolidge, with his innate Puritanical virtue, to watch the deterioration of the Harding administration." While the president was cordial to his vice president, in private he referred to him as "that little fellow from Massachusetts." Claude Fuess asserted, nonetheless, that "Harding had great confidence in Coolidge, consulted him frequently, and was influenced by him to a marked degree." Donald McCoy disagrees, saying rather gently that he found no direct evidence to back up Fuess's assertion, and believes that "The relationship between the Chief Executive and the Vice President, though friendly, was not close." Robert K. Murray, in *The Politics of Normalcy,* is more blunt: Fuess, he says, in arguing that Harding had a high opinion of Coolidge and often sought his views "was wrong on both counts." Mrs. Harding was much less friendly to the vice president than was her husband. In response to an offer of an impressive house as the vice president's residence, Mrs. Harding purportedly said: "Not a bit of it, not a bit of it. I am going to have that bill defeated. Do you think I am going to have those Coolidges living in a house like that? An hotel apartment is plenty good enough for them." A bill to have Congress accept the offered house and appropriate money to maintain it was not passed, though it is unclear whether Mrs. Harding was actually involved.

Perhaps more significant, Coolidge had few close friends and was not aided in making more by those, like Lodge, whom he had known before his arrival in Washington. Indeed, Senator Henry F. Ashurst of Arizona noted in his diary in early 1923 that Senate Republicans were seeking another vice-presidential nominee for the coming election.

In any case, President Harding was increasingly distressed by what he learned of the indiscretions and illegalities of his subordinates. When he left Washington for a trip to Alaska and the West Coast, he was not well. Coolidge had seen Harding at the end of the congressional session in March 1923, then spent much of the time between then and midsummer in Northampton, and in early July drove to Vermont to spend several weeks in Plymouth. It was here that the news of President Harding's death reached him early on the morning of August 3, 1923. Thus ended Coolidge's service as vice president, years which he later termed "a period of most important preparation."

The notification of the vice president and his swearing in as president, the oath being administered by his father, a notary, make a charming and well-known story. The absence of a telephone at the Coolidge home, the rural setting, his father's role in the proceedings all captured the public's attention and that of his-

torians since. It is interesting to note that while this was the first instance of a father swearing in his son as president, there was some question as to whether John Coolidge, a state official and not a federal one, had the authority to do this. To cover this possibility, the oath was administered a second time by a judge of the Supreme Court of the District of Columbia.

Later on the day of his initial swearing-in, the new president traveled to Washington to begin to establish himself as the head of his own administration. He first issued a proclamation of a period of mourning for Harding, then met with various government leaders, urged all cabinet members to retain their posts, and chose a personal secretary. His choice was C. Bascom Slemp, a Virginia congressman and highly knowledgeable individual whose appointment was taken to mean Coolidge's intention to seek nomination and election in 1924.

The new president's concern for Mrs. Harding was striking: He took care of some details personally, told her that she could stay in the White House as long as she wished, and delayed his own family's move into the executive mansion almost four days beyond her departure. "It was," said Professor McCoy, "a magnificent performance for the taciturn Yankee, and for a man who knew how little Mrs. Harding had thought of him."

Coolidge might have found his life as vice president a bit boring, leaving him with time on his hands. As president, he now had more than enough to keep him fully occupied. An increasingly pressing matter—a series of matters, really—involved Harding administration scandals that were becoming public. The president was under significant pressure both to keep and to dismiss Attorney General Harry M. Daugherty. Coolidge eventually did ask for Daugherty's resignation in March 1924, after the attorney general refused to open Justice Department files to a Senate investigation. Professor McCoy asserts that the president "had kept his head and his self respect: he had not acted until he had unquestionable reason to do so." He had indicated earlier, said McCoy, that he was not going to condemn a man on the basis of adverse public opinion or loose-knit circumstantial evidence, a virtue perhaps better understood after the McCarthyite scares of the 1950s than it was in the 1920s.

Though occasionally a target of the Teapot Dome investigations, Coolidge was not seriously linked to this scandal, and his cautious and judicious actions combined with several praiseworthy appointments, notably of Harlan Fiske Stone as attorney general, helped to bring the president through this crisis in as good shape as was likely.

Coolidge's relations with Congress in 1923 and 1924 were rather contentious, involving the Immigration Act, which the president signed though he criticized the provisions excluding Japan from any immigration quota, and a veterans' bonus bill on which he was opposed by major Republican leaders in Congress and which he nevertheless vetoed. The veto was being overridden. Also in this period the McNary-Haugen bill, an effort to raise farm prices by buying up surplus production of several major commodities at prewar prices and selling abroad for whatever could be gained, failed to pass the Congress; it would subsequently be passed and be vetoed by Coolidge. On most major issues, the president had been defeated and abused by the Congress, though the public still had great confidence in him.

The campaign of 1924 began, in the opinion of Robert K. Murray, with the congressional election of 1922. For Coolidge it began with his accession to the presidency. In his autobiography, the former president wrote, somewhat disingenuously, about his role:

Many people at once began to speak about nominating me to lead my party in the next campaign. I did not take any position in relation to their efforts. Unless the nomination came to me in a natural way rather than as the result of any artificial campaign, I did not feel it would be of any value.

While the campaign was not personally directed by the president and while, as he noted in his autobiography, he made no "purely political speeches" during the campaign, he did make remarks at ceremonial occasions and did not in any way discourage efforts to gain for him the Republican nomination at the party's 1924 convention. He certainly indicated what he liked or disliked about the plans others made for his nomination. National Committeeman (subsequently chair of that committee) William M. Butler took charge, ensuring a united Massachusetts delegation, and then controlled equally firmly the following campaign.

The Republicans were aided in 1924 by the deep divisions within the Democratic Party, the inept campaign conducted by Democratic nominee John W. Davis, and the lack of public interest in anything the Progressives and Robert M. La Toilette had to offer. The scandals, particularly the Teapot Dome oil scandal, touched the Democrats as well as the Republicans and certainly did not damage Coolidge in any significant way. To the degree that the Democrats attacked the Republicans about the scandals, some have argued, the Republicans believed it necessary to support the president more firmly. John W. Davis's summary, in a later oral history interview, is on the mark: "I went about the country telling people I was going to be elected, and I knew I hadn't any more chance than a snowball in hell. . . . Not only was the Democratic party ripped apart, but it was impossible to hang the responsibility for the Harding era ills on Coolidge." Coolidge had run on this Harding record and program, and the public supported that program and the stability that the president offered.

In his full term as president, Coolidge continued his support for Andrew Mellon's tax policies and the secretary of the treasury's program for debt reduction; remained consistent in his opposition to the McNary-Haugen bill; continued his effective combination of action and inaction in regard to the scandals of the Harding administration; and dealt with numerous other matters, including U.S. relations with

Latin American countries. The tax policies have long been criticized as evidence of Secretary Mellon's effort to shift the tax burden from the rich to the middle class and the poor and in general to reduce government revenues and improve the condition of business. It is clear that Calvin Coolidge favored the business community and admired many of its leaders, but Thomas B. Silver, in his work *Coolidge and the Historians,* comes down strongly in support of Coolidge administration tax policies and excoriates John D. Hicks and Arthur M. Schlesinger, Jr., for distortion, inaccuracy, bias, and overlooking sources and documents that would not support their case.

Though the president had favored American participation in the World Court, he did not push the Congress on this matter, nor did he achieve American membership. He also did not back efforts to have the United States join the League of Nations. Among the legacies of World War I were the war debts owned the United States by various nations. It is not clear that Coolidge ever said "they hired the money, didn't they," but he opposed the cancellation of those obligations, though he did agree to a reduction in the interest rates on these debts.

In summer 1927, Coolidge vacationed in South Dakota and there handed to news reporters a brief announcement that said: "I do not choose to run for President in nineteen twenty-eight." Historians and others have debated ever since exactly why Coolidge made the announcement and what he really meant by it. Claude Fuess declared that this statement was the result of "a deliberate and carefully planned decision." Coolidge, Fuess added, "never allowed his emotions to dominate his reason, and he knew precisely what he was doing when he prepared the statement which precipitated so much controversy." McCoy, after noting that contemporaries of the president, including Herbert Hoover, his successor, reached differing conclusions, asserts that "there was and still is no absolute proof of what Coolidge had in mind." In his autobiography, the former president wrote that "I had never wished to run in 1928

and had determined to make a public announcement at a sufficiently early date so that the party would have ample time to choose someone else. An appropriate occasion for that announcement seemed to be the fourth anniversary of my taking office." Certainly the president believed he had been clear and, as usual, concise. He offered no comment when he personally handed the announcement to the reporters.

The effect of the announcement was to encourage others to be more active in their campaigns. The eventual Republican nominee in 1928, Herbert Hoover, spoke to Coolidge on two occasions in that year in an effort to elicit further comment. Interested in entering the Ohio primary, Hoover asked the president if he, Coolidge, would be in that primary and was told that he would not. To Hoover's question about his own entry, the president answered, "Why not?" Two months later Hoover believed he had the backing of approximately 400 delegates of the 1,000 who would attend the convention. In another meeting with Coolidge, the candidate said that he would be happy to try to swing these delegates to the president, who replied: "If you have four hundred delegates, you better keep them." Hoover was apparently convinced that the president did not want to be renominated and pursued his own ultimately successful effort to become his party's candidate.

Whether or not Coolidge was pleased with Hoover's actions has been a subject of some comment. On the one hand, he is reported to have said: "That man [Hoover] has offered me unsolicited advice for six years, all of it bad!" and referred to Hoover as the "wonder boy." On the other hand, as McCoy notes, Hoover had remained in Coolidge's cabinet and was supported by the president in the 1928 election campaign.

On March 4, 1929, Coolidge's public career of more than twenty years ended, and he returned to Northampton, where he remained interested in politics. He wrote articles for popular magazines, published his autobiography in 1929, and in 1930 contracted with McClure Syndicate for a daily column to be headed

"Thinking Things Over with Calvin Coolidge." Increasingly, in 1932, the former president said he felt "worn out." On January 5, 1933, after working at his office with his secretary on some correspondence, he went home and was shortly thereafter found dead of coronary thrombosis.

Many have attempted to evaluate the life and career of Calvin Coolidge. An examination of some of the literature on this public servant casts up some of the following attributes. Coolidge was decent, honest, and politically ambitious in the best sense of the word, with a circumscribed view of the world. He revered stability and largely accepted society and government as he found them. Even Claude Fuess, a staunch defender of the former president, declared that "Coolidge during his career displayed very little constructive imagination" and in his speeches no "evidence of broad vision stretching into the shadowy future." Coolidge had a successful public career in part because he was honest, decent, and hardworking, and in part because he appealed to a public that did not want politicians to demonstrate broad vision and imagination.

Editor's Note to the Fourth Edition: In what is a distinct change of interpretation of the presidency of Calvin Coolidge, Robert E. Gilbert in 2003 published *The Tormented President: Calvin Coolidge, Death, and Clinical Depression* (Westport, Conn.: Praeger), in which he maintains that Coolidge's sometime odd behavior and famed taciturn manner were not merely expressions of his New England cultural heritage and personal idiosyncrasies but that, following the death of sixteen-year-old Calvin, Jr., in 1924, the president sank into a deep, clinical depression that conditioned his actions and public demeanor from then on.

REFERENCES

Calvin Coolidge, *The Autobiography of Calvin Coolidge* (New York: Cosmopolitan Book Corporation, 1929); Robert H. Ferrell, *The Presidency of Calvin Coolidge* (Lawrence: University of Kansas Press, 1998); Claude M. Fuess, *Calvin Coolidge: The Man from Vermont* (Boston: Little, Brown, 1940); Claude M. Fuess, *Calvin Coolidge: Twenty Years After* (Worcester, Mass.: American Antiquarian Society, 1954); Donald R. McCoy, *Calvin Coolidge: The Quiet President* (New York: The Macmillan Company, 1967); Robert K. Murray, *The Politics of Normalcy: Governmental Theory and Practice in the. Harding-Coolidge Era* (New York: W.W. Norton and Company, Inc., 1973); Robert K. Murray, *The Harding Era: Warren G. Harding and His Administration* (Minneapolis: The University of Minnesota Press, 1969); David Greenberg, *Calvin Coolidge* (New York: Times Books, 2007); Thomas B. Silver, *Coolidge and the Historians* (Durham, N.C.: Carolina Academic Press for the Claremont Institute, 1982); William Allen White, *A Puritan in Babylon: The Story of Calvin Coolidge* (New York: The Macmillan Company, 1938); manuscript collections at the Library of Congress, Forbes Library in Northampton, Massachusetts, Amherst College, and Holy Cross College.

PAUL S. SILVER is professor of history at Johnson State College, Johnson, Vermont. He received his B.A. from Oberlin College and his M.A. and Ph.D. from the University of Pennsylvania. He has been at Johnson State College since 1971; previously he taught at Pennsylvania Military College (now Widener University) and the University of Akron. He has particular interests in the Progressive Movement and the New Deal. Also a clarinetist, Professor Silver has been a member of the Vermont Philharmonic Orchestra and was for sixteen years a member of Cadenza, a woodwind quintet. He has been a member of numerous pit orchestras accompanying musical theater productions.

CHARLES GATES DAWES (1865–1951)

Vice President, 1925–1929

(President Calvin Coolidge)

CHARLES GATES DAWES
(Library of Congress)

By Robert A. Waller

The inauguration of the vice president immediately preceding that of the president is usually a ritualistic, routine affair worth only a passing note in newspaper accounts describing the beginning of a new administration. Not so the festivities surrounding the inauguration of the thirtieth vice president, Charles Gates ("Hell and Maria") Dawes, on March 4, 1925. As a successful Chicago businessman, former comptroller of the currency, and former purchasing agent for the American Expeditionary Forces during World War I, Dawes used the occasion for the lengthy diatribe against the Senate's antiquated rules, especially the filibuster, which interfered with effective and efficient dispatch of the people's business. The Dawes proposals for the reform of the Senate captured national headlines that overshadowed the inaugural address of President Calvin Coolidge as he began his second term in the White House. This incident foretold the political chasm between Capitol Hill and 1600 Pennsylvania Avenue in the mid-1920s. What circumstances and experiences caused this set of conditions to prevail during the next four years?

Charles Gates Dawes was born on August 27, 1865, in Marietta, Washington County, Ohio, the oldest son of Rufus Republic Dawes (a lumber merchant, Civil War general, and Republican member of Congress, 1881–83) and Mary Berman (Gates) Dawes. After receiving his basic education at Marietta Academy, he attended Marietta College and earned a Bachelor of Arts degree in civil engineering in 1884 with auxiliary interests in music, especially flute and piano. At the age of nineteen, he studied law at the Cincinnati Law School, earning the LL.B. in 1886. Following admission to the Ohio bar that same year, Dawes continued to work for the Marietta, Columbus and Northern Ohio Railway Company as a civil engineer. Eventually he became chief engineer for construction.

On the invitation of James W. Dawes (his father's cousin and former governor of Nebraska), Dawes moved to Lincoln in April 1887. Admitted to the bar there, he began his legal practice with the firm of Dawes, Coffroth and Cunningham, His law office was two floors above that of William Jennings Bryan. The two exchanged political barbs occasionally but became lifelong friends with ideas firmly planted in opposing party platforms. Bryan's brother Charles (later Nebraska governor and 1924 Democratic vice-presidential candidate) was also a member of this frontier community. Another of Dawes's Lincoln acquaintances was a young second lieutenant instructor in military affairs at the University of Nebraska named John J. Pershing. In addition to the legal practice, Dawes became vice president of the Lincoln Packing Company and a director of the American Exchange National Bank, forerunners of his commercial interests.

On January 24, 1889, Dawes married Caro D. Blymyer (1865–1957), a Cincinnati girl whom he had met while a law school student.

They had two children, Rufus Fearing and Carolyn, and adopted two, Dena McCutcheon and Virginia. Rufus, a Princeton student, drowned in a Lake Geneva boating accident on September 5, 1912. Among the many philanthropies associated with the future vice president was the Rufus Fearing Dawes Hotel for Destitute Men, with facilities in Chicago and in Boston. In memory of his mother, Dawes also established the Mary Dawes Hotel for Women in Chicago, which provided bed, bath, and breakfast in clean, inexpensive quarters for the impoverished. Another Dawes philanthropy was the Chicago Grand Opera Company.

While his Lincoln law practice proved lucrative, Dawes's successes in the administrative reorganization of faltering companies led him to move to the Chicago area in January 1895. Though he lived in Evanston, Chicago became his operations base, and subsequent careers would take him to Washington (four times), France, and Great Britain. Dawes's early business interests included real estate ventures and the accumulation of a public utilities empire centered on the North Shore Gas Company in 1900. Ultimately, Metropolitan Gas and Electric Company became a holding company that owned seven companies with twenty-eight plants in ten states.

In a state known for its factionalism within the two major political parties, Dawes's Republicanism brought a fresh perspective. Through his congressman father, Charles Dawes had met Mark Hanna and William McKinley. Although only twenty-nine and an Illinois resident for only two years, Dawes volunteered to rally Illinois Republican support on behalf of McKinley's presidential nomination in 1896. He delivered the four delegates-at-large to McKinley.

President McKinley rewarded Dawes with appointment as comptroller of the currency, a position in which he served from 1898 to 1901. Dawes had published an eighty-three-page tract on *The Banking System of the United States* in 1894 in which he supported the gold standard and argued for better public comprehension of the need for "proper understanding of the monetary problems of the day." From this perspective Dawes proposed banking structure reforms that would obviate the conditions that had caused the depression of the 1890s. He also collected $25 million due to the federal government from various national banks that had failed.

In October 1901, Dawes resigned from the comptroller's position to campaign for election to the U.S. Senate from Illinois. State legislatures selected upper house members to Congress until 1913. Dawes believed that he could be nominated and then elected with the McKinley administration's help, with assistance from federal officeholders, and with the personal friendship of Hanna and McKinley, but the assassination of McKinley changed the political equation. Theodore Roosevelt was not friendly with Hanna; Dawes's hopes for a senatorial role faded.

Rebuffed by the party kingmakers, Dawes withdrew from the race and poured his considerable energies and talents into business and banking affairs. From 1902 until 1921 he served as president of the Central Trust Company of Illinois (the Dawes Bank). Then he served as chairman of the board until he went to Washington as vice president in 1925.

In 1915, Dawes published *Essays and Speeches,* a 400-page collection of his observations on the nation's economy, trust policy, the Federal Reserve System, political reform, and public philanthropy. His conservative views were kept in the public eye and his business ventures prospered.

Then World War I intervened. Despite his age (fifty-two), he volunteered for the army artillery. Ultimately his enlistment was accepted, and he was commissioned a major in the Seventeenth Engineer Corps (Railway) on June 11. Promoted to lieutenant colonel on July 16, Dawes was in one of the advance units of the American Expeditionary Forces sent directly to France. Commanding General John J. Pershing plucked Dawes from the ranks on

September 27, 1917, to coordinate all purchases for the U.S. Army overseas. Commissioned a colonel on January 16, 1918, and a brigadier general on October 15, 1918, Dawes carefully regulated purchases to avoid inflated prices and duplicate buying. Following the war he published a two-volume *Journal of the Great War* (1921) which logged his wartime experiences as chief of supply procurement for the A.E.F. under Pershing.

When the Allied and Associated Nations' forces were unified under Marshal Ferdinand Foch, Dawes became the U.S. member of the Military Board of Allied Supply, continuing to work his business magic in this inter-nation environment. For these services he received the Distinguished Service Medal awarded by his own government and several military recognitions as well from the Belgian, British, French, and Italian governments. At the war's end, Dawes became a member of the Allied Liquidation Commission. While most doughboys headed home, he remained behind in an administrative capacity to dispose of the accumulated war materials and supplies. The task completed to his satisfaction, Dawes resigned from the Army on August 31, 1919. He held a brigadier general position in the Officer's Reserve Corps from 1921 to 1926.

Dawes returned to the United States to resume direct responsibility for his far-flung business interests. Politically he was a supporter of Woodrow Wilson's campaign to ratify the Versailles Treaty and to participate in the League of Nations. Understandably, Dawes was drawn into the inevitable postwar investigation of military spending. By taking a closer look at how the Democrats had conducted the war, Republican congressmen hoped to expose graft and corruption. Dawes went before the committee, not as a guilty-looking Democrat or profiteer but as a justifiably outraged, hand-waving, shouting ex-general who happened also to be a Republican. His seven hours of testimony in 1921 did much to take the wind out of the investigation.

His congressional inquisitors asked him many questions concerning the price the United States had paid for mules from Spain. Dawes roared this response, as stated in the *New York Times* of February 3 and 4, 1921:

Sure we paid. We didn't dicker. Why, man alive, we had to win the war. We would have paid horse prices for sheep if sheep could have pulled artillery to the front. Oh, it's all right now to say we bought too much vinegar and too many cold chisels, but we saved the civilization of the world. Damn it all, the business of an army is to win the war, not to quibble around with a lot of cheap buying. Hell and Maria, we weren't trying to keep a set of books, we were trying to win the war!

Long after this committee is dead and gone and forgotten the achievements of the American army will stand as an everlasting blaze of glory. You have tried to make a mountain out of a molehill. The people are tired of war talk and fault finding. The army was American, neither Republican [n]or Democratic.

From that day forward, he was known as "Hell and Maria" Dawes. In point of fact, he had said "Helen Maria" (an expletive he was fond of using in polite company), but he spoke so rapidly that the stenographers did not catch the distinction.

After this episode, Dawes's prominence catapulted him into consideration for the Republican presidential nomination in 1920. The men in the famous smoke-filled room turned instead to Ohio's Senator Warren G. Harding. Dawes declined an offer to become Harding's secretary of the treasury but instead accepted appointment for one year as first director of the Bureau of the Budget, with promises of unfaltering presidential support. Harding finally achieved in the Budget and Accounting Act of 1921 what Theodore Roosevelt, William Howard Taft, and Woodrow Wilson had sought in their efforts to rationalize the fiscal operations of the federal government. As Dawes recorded in his published notes, *The First Year*

of the Budget of the United States (1923), the purpose of the Bureau was ". . . to inaugurate a system of coordinating business control over the various departments and independent establishments of government which, for one hundred and thirty-two years, have been almost completely decentralized." From the start it was clear that the bureau would deal with no question of policy "except that of economy and efficiency." It was to be "impersonal, impartial and non-political." With characteristic energy and zeal from Room 372½ in the Treasury building, Dawes threw himself into the task of organizing a new unit of presidential administration. Drawing upon his Washington acquaintances from the turn of the century and his military compatriots, he quickly assembled the staff and established the principles under which the bureau would operate. At this time, he acquired the habit of smoking the underslung pipe that became his trademark thereafter.

True to his word, Dawes resigned in July 1922 after launching an agency that was to continue virtually unchanged until the Reorganization Act of 1939. Although he hoped to return to his Chicago business pursuits full-time, he instead at Coolidge's request became chairman of a League committee of experts that was addressing the unsettled question of war reparations. What came to be known as the Dawes Plan (announced on April 9, 1924) suggested methods of balancing the German budget and stabilizing that nation's currency. Undoubtedly this is the work for which Dawes is most noted. It gained him the Nobel Prize for Peace in 1925.

This international prominence enhanced Dawes's credentials for the Republican vice-presidential nomination in 1924. As with most incumbent presidents, the Coolidge nomination was virtually assured. "Silent Cal" left the choice of a running mate to the Republican convention. The initial choice was Illinois former Governor Frank O. Lowden (whom Dawes supported), an ardent spokesperson for the plight of the mid-western farmer. Since the party platform on this issue was unsatisfactory to the Prairie State's ex-governor, he declined by telegraph.

The party chieftains consulted about an alternative candidate while the convention recessed. Among the remaining contenders were Senator Charles Curtis of Kansas (the floor whip); Secretary of Commerce Herbert C. Hoover; and Dawes, whose chairmanship of the Reparations Commission made him newsworthy and noteworthy. Dawes, selected on the third ballot (682½ votes to Hoover's 334½), recorded in *Notes as Vice President* (1935) that he gained the honor ". . . notwithstanding the efforts of the Chairman of the Republican National Committee who . . . endeavored to unite his followers for Hoover." It is significant that Dawes was not blessed by President Coolidge. Distant, if not actually hostile, relations between the Republican standard-bearers could be forecast.

In spite of possible tensions, the Republican nominees conferred in Washington on July 1 with Party Chairman William M. Butler. A campaign strategy was agreed upon with the president, partially due to inclination and partly due to Calvin, Jr.'s tragic death, staying close to the White House or to Vermont. Dawes assumed the bulk of the speech making and traveling. The content of the vice president's acceptance speech was established, and the law-and-order theme became the campaign's leitmotiv. Dawes reported traveling 15,000 miles and making 108 speeches on behalf of the Grand Old Party.

Interestingly, Dawes virtually ignored Democratic candidates John W. Davis and Charles W. Bryan, his acquaintance from Lincoln days. His focus instead was on the third-party candidacies of Robert M. La Follette and Burton K. Wheeler. Especially repugnant to Dawes was a Progressive Party platform plank urging an Constitutional amendment to give Congress the power to override judicial review of legislation. Dawes prophesied to his audiences: "The bill of inalienable rights, the general recognition of which is the foundation of civilization, would be, under the La Follette proposition, at the mercy of Congress." While reporters covering his campaign tired of the repetitious theme, Dawes retorted: "There is one issue in this campaign, and only one. That is whether you stand on the rock of common sense with Calvin Coolidge, or in the sinking sands of Socialism."

Another of the themes in Dawes's campaign swings was opposition to the Ku Klux Klan, a topic that Chairman Butler encouraged him to avoid. He spoke out vigorously, sometimes to the discomfort of local dignitaries seated behind him on the platform, who would have preferred to ignore the subject. Typical are these remarks made at Augusta, Maine, on August 24, 1924:

> Appeals to racial, religious, or class prejudice by minority organizations are opposed to the welfare of all peaceful and civilized communities. Our Constitution stands for religious tolerance and freedom.
>
> I have told you why I am opposed to the Klan. Take what I say into your hearts and consciences and think it over calmly. However it may be with the mind, there is no acrimony in conscience.

Such a stand was not popular in some circles at that time, but it indicated Dawes's independence and spirit of fairness.

"Keeping Cool with Coolidge" was the order of the day. Neither the Democrats nor the Progressives were able to lay the Harding scandals at the doors of Coolidge or Dawes. The voters affirmed their support for prosperity on November 5, 1924, by providing a Republican landslide: a popular plurality of 7 million votes and an electoral college majority of 382 votes to 136 for Davis-Bryan. La Follette and Wheeler garnered 4.5 million popular votes, but only 13 electoral votes from La Follette's home state of Wisconsin.

Normally the period between election and inauguration is one of speculation as the press and the public contemplate the new administration's direction. In those days the vice president's role did not loom large in the considerations, but Vice President-elect Dawes made his wishes known. President Harding had established the practice of asking Vice President Coolidge to attend cabinet meetings. President-by-accident Coolidge had admitted that such exposure was helpful when he was unexpectedly thrust into the Oval Office. The Constitution itself makes no provision for a cabinet, let alone a role for the vice president in attending.

When faced with the prospect of being invited to attend cabinet meetings, Dawes rebelled in a very public and embarrassing manner. In his *Diary* Dawes wrote: "After my election, not knowing how Coolidge felt about it, I wrote him stating my views on the subject." He further explained:

> Long before my election and before I had any thought that I would ever have an individual interest in the question, I said the plan . . . was unwise. The Cabinet and those who sit with it always should do so at the discretion and inclination of the President. Our Constitution so intended it. The relationship is confidential, and the selection of a confidant belongs to him who would be injured by the abuse of confidence, however unintentional. No precedent should be established which creates a different and arbitrary method of selection.
>
> Should I sit . . . the precedent might prove injurious to the country. With it fixed, some future President might face the embarrassing alternative of inviting one whom he regarded as unsuitable into his private conferences or affronting him in the public eye by denying him what had been generally considered his right.
>
> My friendship and high respect for President Coolidge are such that it would be personally a pleasure to sit . . . but I will not do so because, in my judgment, it involves a wrong principle.

Unexplainedly, Dawes did not write personally and privately to his superior to forestall an expected but nonexistent invitation. Rather, he made his views known through a press interview on February 5, 1925, as reported in the *New York Times* even before the letter reached the president. The editorial pandemonium that resulted reflected no credit on the vice president but increased the strain between the chief executive and his supposed right hand. Coolidge followed his custom of silence, so the controversy was one-sided, though prolonged.

Beyond Dawes's public expression of constitutional qualms about the role of the vice president vis-à-vis the cabinet, his publications offer no insight about the further rationale behind his position. Reporters speculated about the hidden agenda. Among the best of these is the analysis presented by Arthur Sears Herring in the *Chicago Tribune* (November 27, 1924), which listed these considerations: (1) as a potential presidential candidate in 1928 Dawes did not wish to be too closely associated with Coolidge's policies should there be a need to criticize them in the future; (2) given Dawes's reputation for pungent and spontaneous expressions of views, Coolidge had no desire to upset the tranquility of his meetings with an irascible competitor; (3) philosophical differences of opinion on such issues as agricultural subsidies and veterans' bonuses made Dawes unpopular in the Coolidge inner circle; and (4) practical experience had suggested to Coolidge that friction would be reduced if executive and legislative spheres remained separate. Whatever the real reason in the matter, the gratuitous manner in which the issue had been aired served to strain relations between Dawes and Coolidge. Rarely has such an unwarranted slight been made to a president by a vice president.

President Coolidge's comments in his *Autobiography* (1929) suggest that Dawes was not invited to sit with the cabinet because he was perceived to be both indiscreet and insubordinate. In spite of Dawes's strict constructionist approach and Coolidge's personality assessment, the practice of the vice president sitting with the cabinet was resumed by the Herbert Hoover–Charles Curtis team and by every succeeding presidential administration.

This tactic to enhance the role of the vice president was only interrupted, not derailed, by Dawes's very indiscreet argument for the status quo.

The next clash between the federal government's two principals occurred on inauguration day, March 4, 1925. Coolidge anticipated the day as the culmination of a thirty-year career in public life and savored the opportunity to create an agenda and atmosphere for his own administration. Dawes, on the other hand, saw the occasion of the "other" inauguration as an opportunity to bring his businesslike approach to conducting the affairs of the U.S. Senate over which he was to preside. Unfortunately, a blustery inaugural address from the new vice president overshadowed Coolidge's day in the sun.

Never having held elective office or presided over a deliberative legislative body, the new Senate presiding officer endeavored to establish his leadership style. As reported in the March 4, 1925, *Congressional Record* he noted:

> What I say upon entering this office should relate to its administration and the conditions under which it is administered. Unlike the vast majority of deliberative and legislative bodies, the Senate does not elect its presiding officer. He is designated for his duties by the Constitution of the United States.

So far, so good.

Dawes continued that he was elected by the people of the United States. Thus he viewed his trust to be opposed on behalf of the people to the implementation of Senate Rule XXII, the one concerning a filibuster. He continued:

> That rule which, at times enables Senators to consume in oratory those last precious minutes of a session needed for momentous decisions, places in the hands of one or a minority of Senators a greater power than the veto power exercised under the Constitution by the President of the United States.

For nearly twenty minutes, he vigorously and pungently attacked the rules conducive to filibustering. He concluded with the declaration that: "Reform in the present rules is demanded, not only by American public opinion, but, I venture to say, in the individual consciences of a majority of the members of the Senate itself." As presiding officer, Dawes considered it his duty to call attention to defective methods in the conduct of Senate business.

Reporters noted an "icy silence" in the Senate chamber when Dawes finished his tirade. If the senators did not appreciate the tongue-lashing about their archaic rules, the nation's reporters applauded the good copy "Hell and Maria" Dawes provided them. Dawes proceeded to add insult to injury. The customary practice following the remarks had been for the vice president to call the thirty-two newly elected senators in groups of four to the Senate well for an individual inauguration ceremony to facilitate public relations opportunities and to sign the roll as duly sworn members of the new Congress. Tiring of this tedious practice after the second group of four, the vice president called all the remaining senators to the well for administration of the oath en masse. In his haste to conclude the proceedings, Dawes neglected to have the roll inscribed. He endeavored to inject some much needed efficiency into the operations of the government, but he succeeded in offending Senate sensibilities.

During the ensuing four years, Dawes returned frequently to this efficiency theme in speeches and articles. While he viewed his attack on the cloture system with a sense of achievement, neither the Senate nor the public moved to make or demand changes. His valedictory comments on March 4, 1929, gave him one last opportunity to chide his colleagues when he administered the oath of office to his successor, Charles Curtis. Dawes again urged the easing of the cloture rules. His brief remarks ended with a cryptic, good-natured phrase, "I take nothing back." Scarcely two minutes later, the new vice president assured his former colleagues that he was "not one of the makers of the law nor is he consulted about the rules governing your actions." The Dawes tilt at the windmill of Senate procedures had come to naught, for the rule remains virtually unchanged.

However, the Dawes remarks had other consequences. Senators and Capitol reporters could think and talk of nothing else but Dawes's campaign to streamline the operations of the nation's oldest deliberative body. President Coolidge's own inauguration ceremony and his carefully crafted address were quickly overlooked and easily forgotten. The focus this inauguration day in news headlines and coverage was this version of the "Dawes Plan" for revamping the U.S. Senate. Another source of irritation between the president and the vice president was identified. Although Coolidge professed in his *Autobiography* never to have been perplexed by the Senate rules, at the time the president clearly thought the timing of the issue was inauspicious.

Excitement over the Dawes's declaration of war on the Senate rules continued as the president sent over a batch of administrative appointments for approval. When Coolidge named Attorney General Harlan Fiske Stone to the Supreme Court, he nominated Charles B. Warren of Michigan as his successor. Democrats and insurgent Republicans united to oppose the confirmation on the ground that Warren was too closely tied to the Sugar Trust, which would make him an unsuitable candidate to enforce the nation's laws against combinations in restraint of trade. The debate was long and fierce, occupying the first several days on the calendar of the new Congress.

As presiding officer of the Senate, the vice president breaks tie votes. On the average a vice president exercises this privilege twice in a term. On March 10, the debate on the Warren appointment continued. Dawes was notified that at least six more senators wished to be heard on the issue that day. After checking with both floor leaders, Curtis and Joseph T. Robinson, who assured him that no vote would be taken later that day, Dawes went to the new

Willard Hotel, then the home of vice presidents, and took an after-lunch nap.

In the Senate, however, the action quickened. Curtis, now believing that the savage assaults on Warren were having an impact, decided to press for an immediate vote. As the roll call progressed, it became apparent that the result would be close. E. Ross Bartley, the vice president's secretary, telephoned to request that Dawes return to the Senate in case there should be a tie. When the result was a 40 to 40 deadlock, the Republicans tried several parliamentary maneuvers to delay, but their efforts proved unavailing. The death blow was given when Lee S. Overman of North Carolina, the lone Democrat who had voted for confirmation, announced a change in his vote. By the time Dawes arrived in the chamber, there was no tie to break. The vote now stood at 39 for confirmation and 41 against. For the first time since Andrew Johnson's presidency, the Senate had rejected a cabinet appointment.

Privately, Coolidge held Dawes accountable, but publicly he said nothing. In a rare show of temper and tenacity, Coolidge resubmitted the nomination six days later. This time Warren was rejected, 39 for and 46 against. Dawes never had the opportunity to make amends for his absence; indeed, it may have been less than coincidence that Dawes was asleep at the switch. At the 1924 Republican convention, the one vote in the Michigan delegation against Dawes and for Hoover was cast by delegate Charles B. Warren. It is probably a curious happenstance but reporters wondered if there were substance in the speculation.

As can be imagined, Dawes suffered considerable ridicule and embarrassment over his failure to be present to support the administration's nominee. Having been lectured on decorum, duties, and responsibilities, the senators now reciprocated. Most clever of all was the needling presented by Senator George W. Norris of Nebraska in the March 12, 1925, *Congressional Record*. Recalling that Dawes was the great-great grandson of William Dawes, the forgotten patriot who rode with Paul Revere on that famous night in '75, Norris offered this parody based on "Sheridan's Ride":

Hurrah, hurrah for Dawes!
Hurrah, hurrah for this highminded man!
And when his statue is placed on high,
Under the dome of the Capitol sky,
The great Senatorial temple of fame,
There with the glorious general's name,
Be it said, in letters both bold and bright:
'O, Hell and Maria, he has lost us the
fight!'

The *New Republic* on March 25, 1925, was far more severe in its criticism. After describing the wild taxi ride up Pennsylvania Avenue, the editor concluded that: "It is extremely doubtful whether he will again be able to get himself taken seriously in political circles." Some wag added the indignity of hanging a sign on the Willard: "Dawes slept here!" Within five months the vice president had thrice placed himself beyond the pale when cooperation with the new administration was expected. It is little wonder that Dawes's four years as vice president are devoid of significant legislative or policy impact. Unlike his success as an administrator of great affairs, Dawes seemed ill suited to the legislative halls.

Where the Dawes name figures prominently in the years 1925–29, it frequently appears in opposition to administration stands. For example, Dawes favored the soldiers' bonus legislation, which Coolidge found it necessary to veto as an unprincipled raid on the federal treasury. The greatest source of irritation over policy arose over the plight of American farmers and the role of the federal government in providing relief. The Republican Party platform of 1924 had recognized that a farm problem existed and promised to study the issue to achieve a solution. Coolidge elected to ignore Dawes's recommendations for select committee membership to explore the issue.

The farm bloc, meanwhile, rallied around the McNary-Haugen legislation as offering the best hope for relief from depressed prices due to surpluses. Without publicly proclaiming his assent to this particular legislation, Dawes gained a reputation for providing an office headquarters for proponents of parity prices and surplus disposal abroad. In February 1927 Dawes's parliamentary intervention enabled the McNary-Haugen bill to come to a vote; it passed the Senate and met the inevitable veto from the White House. Coolidge did not appreciate the fact that he was forced to take a negative action on this political hot potato. He faulted the senators and Dawes for having passed the buck when the proffered legislation could have remained dormant in Congress. Dawes's usual conservatism on policy matters with budgetary implications was dampened when it came to matters affecting farmers and veterans. Expressing support for these two groups could prove beneficial if he had aspirations in 1928 to retain the vice presidency or to run for the presidency.

The presidential political picture for 1928 became both clearer and clouded when Coolidge announced on the fourth anniversary of his succession to the presidency that he did not "choose" to run in 1928. Political pundits were unclear whether he meant it or wished to be drafted for another term. In an interview long after the fact, Dawes told Chicago historian William T. Hutchinson that "a man close to Coolidge" had reported that the president "ardently desired" the nomination and was "sore as a pup" when the Republican convention bypassed him. Acting on this assumption, Dawes made little effort to seek the presidency himself, although he doubtless would have been willing to serve if nominated.

In the 1928 Republican convention, Dawes received four votes (one from Illinois, one from Ohio, and two from Missouri) for president. He figured more prominently in the vice-presidential selection because he was the incumbent. The inner circle at the convention agreed that Dawes should have a chance to "qualify" for the renomination. The principal sticking point was his attitude toward the resolution of the farm problem. With Hooverites dominating the convention, the GOP platform refused to endorse McNary-Haugenism. Instead, there was a general palliative that appropriate but alternative relief measures would be sought. When questioned by the kingmakers on the issue, Dawes agreed that Coolidge's vetoes had probably shelved the opportunity to pass the McNary-Haugen principles for the next four years. When asked to make a public declaration to that effect, Dawes's hackles rose and he refused to abandon this farm relief measure. Thus, his name was eliminated from the eligibles. The convention then turned to Hoover's rival, Charles Curtis, who had been most active in the stop-Hoover movement.

After a term as presiding officer of the Senate, Dawes came to respect the institution in spite of its perceived flaws. As a valedictory summary of the role he had played, he wrote the following:

The office is what the man in it makes it—which applies to all public offices. The fact that the Vice President in the Senate Chamber cannot enter into debate is considered a disadvantage, yet for that reason he is removed from the temptation to indulge in the pitiable quest of that double objective so characteristic of many Senate speeches—the placating of general public opinion and of an opposing local constituency at the same time. For his prestige as a presiding officer, it is to his advantage that he neither votes nor speaks in the Senate Chamber. Outside . . . his position as Vice President gives him a hearing by the general public as wide as the accorded any Senator, other things being equal. If he lacks initiative, courage, or ideas, he of course will be submerged; but that is true also of a Senator or any other parliamentary member.

Whatever may be said to the contrary, as anyone discovers who occupies the office, the people hold it in great respect. While I shall serve eight months more . . . and make future mistakes, I see the prospect of closing my public career at least without discredit. The occupancy of a public office, unless decorated with public respect, is a curse to anyone.

There were no future "mistakes," so the self assessment showed a credible record.

Charles Gates Dawes's public service was not yet ended. Toward the close of his vice presidential term, he had accepted an invitation from President Horacio Vásquez of the Dominican Republic to serve as chairman of an economic commission that would study and revise that new republic's finances. This he did within a month with the aid of a team of U.S. experts. Even before this task was concluded, President Hoover appointed Dawes as ambassador to Great Britain in April 1929. In the Court of St. James, he became involved in the preliminary discussions leading to the London Conference on Naval Limitation in 1930. After resigning this diplomatic post in 1932, Dawes became deeply involved in assuring the financial success of the Chicago World's Fair, known as the Century of Progress.

The Hoover administration was not yet through with his services. As an anti-Depression measure, the Congress had established the Reconstruction Finance Corporation in February 1932. The RFC aimed to provide loans to the states for relief and to provide direct governmental loans to collapsing businesses. Hoover convinced Dawes to accept the presidency of this precursor of the New Deal. He resigned on June 6, 1932, to return to Chicago to protect his banking interests, now known as Central Republic Bank and Trust Company, from a series of consolidations, including getting a controversial $90 million RFC loan for his endangered bank, a loan repaid in full by 1944.

During the 1930s and 1940s, Dawes busied himself with several publications recounting his experiences, including *Notes as Vice President* (1935), *A Journal of Reparations* (1939), *A Journal as Ambassador to Great Britain* (1939), and *A Journal of the McKinley Years* (1951). He served as Chairman of the Board for Chicago's City National Bank and Trust Company from 1932 until his death in Evanston on April 23, 1951, at the age of eighty-five. He was buried in Chicago's Rosehill Cemetery. With a certain irony, the year 1951 experienced a revival of his 1911 musical composition "Melody in A Major"; Now with lyrics and a new title, "It's All in the Game," the song became one of the most popular of that year.

Among historians and political scientists, the ranking and rating of presidents is a professional avocation, but similar attention has not been accorded vice presidents unless elevated to the Oval Office. The typical rating system ranges from great, near great, above average, and below average, to failure. Based on the evidence, a rating of "above average" seems appropriate when restricting the judgment to the vice-presidential years when Dawes exhibited a forceful, independent, and efficient spirit as the Senate's presiding officer. If his total career as author, banker, servant of four presidents, winner of a Nobel Peace Prize, and administrator par excellence were included, then the evaluation becomes "near great." In the pantheon of vice presidents since 1789, Charles Gates Dawes stands among the luminaries.

REFERENCES

Carl William Ackerman, *Dawes—the Doer!* (New York: ERA Publications, 1924); Paul Roscoe Leach, *That Man Dawes* (Chicago: The Reilly and Lee Co., 1930); John Erwin Pixton, "The Early Career of Charles G. Dawes [to 1905]" (Ph.D. diss, University of Chicago, 1952); Richard Garrett Sherman, "Charles G. Dawes: An Entrepreneurial Biography, 1865–1951" (Ph.D. diss, State University of Iowa, 1960); and Bascom N. Timmons, *Portrait of an American: Charles G. Dawes* (New York: Henry Holt and Co., 1953).

Books by Dawes: *The Banking System of the United States and Its Relation to the Money and Business of the Country* (Chicago: Rand, McNally and Co., 1894); *The First Year of the Budget of the United States* (New York: Harper and Bros., 1923); *Essays and Speeches* (Boston: Houghton Mifflin Co., 1915); *A Journal as Ambassador to Great Britain* (New York: Macmillan Co., 1939); *A Journal of the Great War,* 2 vols. (Boston: Houghton Mifflin Co., 1921); *A Journal of the McKinley Years* (Chicago: Lakeside Press, 1950); *A Journal of Reparations* (London: Macmillan, 1939); *How Long Prosperity?* (Chicago: A.N. Marquis, 1937); *Notes as Vice President, 1928–1929* (Boston: Little, Brown and Co., 1935); Charles G. Dawes Papers at Northwestern University Library include 20,000 letters by Dawes, 10,000 letters to him, and journals from 1887 to 1907.

ROBERT A. WALLER is an emeritus professor of history with service at the University of Illinois–Urbana and at Clemson University in South Carolina. Since retiring, he has published two articles on the activities of the Civilian Conservation Corps in South Carolina and is completing research on a third. Additionally, he teaches classes on twentieth-century political history for the The Villages "College," the educational arm of his Florida retirement community.

CHARLES CURTIS (1860–1936)

Vice President, 1929–1933

(President Herbert Hoover)

CHARLES CURTIS
(Library of Congress)

By William E. Unrau

Charles Curtis was born in North Topeka, Kansas, on January 25, 1860, the son of Orren Arms Curtis, a Union soldier, and Ellen Gonville Pappan, a quarter-blood member of the Kansa (now Kaw) Indian tribe. As the only person of Indian blood and legal membership in an Indian tribe to be elevated to the second-highest office in the land, Curtis has been the focus of considerable interest as well as disagreement regarding the precise character of his genealogy. On occasion the popular press in the twentieth-century described him as one-quarter Kaw or as one-eighth Kaw and one-eighth Osage. The official Kaw tribal census taken in 1929, the year he assumed the vice presidency, listed Curtis as one-eighth Kaw, but in 1940 another tribal census changed it to one-quarter Kaw. In the interim, and over objections Curtis himself voiced soon after he relinquished the vice presidency, one scholar expressed certainty that Curtis was a half blood.

The available documents confirm that on the maternal side Curtis was a blood descendant of Kansa Chief White Plume, who married a daughter of the distinguished Osage Chief Pawhuska sometime prior to 1825. Unlike the majority of his tribe, White Plume came under the influence of Catholic missionaries from St. Louis and insisted that the marriage of one of his nieces to Louis Gonville, a French fur trader from Canada, be conducted by a Catholic priest in what White Plume considered a legitimate manner. The Kansa half-blood daughter of this union, Julie, was raised a Catholic and eventually married Louis Pappan, another French trader from the St. Louis area. Pappan entered the ferry business near the Kansa reservation and the future site of North Topeka, where his wife gave birth to Ellen (sometimes Helen), who was educated in a Catholic convent in St. Louis. In 1859, Ellen married Orren Arms Curtis, native of Indiana, and on January 25, 1860, the future vice president was born to them on Kaw Allotment Four, a tract of land in North Topeka granted to Ellen's mother by the Kansa Treaty of 1825. Charles Curtis was thus an eighth-blood Kaw with, perhaps, a modest Osage heritage, and by Indian Office standards of the day, a legal member of the Kaw tribe.

Ellen Pappan Curtis saw to it that her infant son received a Catholic baptism in the St. Mary's Immaculate Conception Church on the Potawatomi reservation nearby. She also taught young Charles the French language and apparently was determined to raise him apart from the Kaw tribe, then located on a reservation some sixty miles west of North Topeka. Her untimely death in 1863 altered the situation dramatically. A few months after Ellen's death Orren Curtis married but soon divorced Rachel Hatch. Perhaps deeming it necessary to remove himself from the setting of his recent bereavement and domestic difficulties, he secured an officer's appointment in the Fifteenth Kansas Cavalry for service against the Confederacy in

Missouri and Arkansas. Thus at age three Charles and his older sister Permelia were placed in their maternal grandmother, Permelia Hubbard Curtis's care; with her husband William and their family, who had followed Orren from Indiana to Kansas Territory in 1860. While her husband engaged in Indian land speculation in the North Topeka vicinity, Permelia ruled her family (including her young Indian grandson) with stern dedication. As Charles Curtis's sister recalled years later, membership in the Republican Party and the Methodist Church were seen by the grandmother as prerequisites to the good life on earth as well as to eternal salvation. In 1866, however, young Charles was abruptly placed in the care of Julie Gonville Pappan, his maternal grandmother, on the Kaw reservation at Council Grove.

Why Charles was sent to live with his Indian grandmother is difficult to determine. The Civil War was over and the Council Grove reservation was dominated by full-bloods alien to their mixed-blood relatives in eastern Kansas. Certainly there were few Republicans and even fewer Methodists among the Kaw traditionalists. The most plausible explanation is that in 1866 there were rumors of an impending Kaw removal treaty, one that once and for all might settle their tribal land affairs in Kansas. With the possibility of a generous financial settlement, it was desirable for Charles and his sister to be reservation residents, thus guaranteeing their legal tribal membership and qualifying them for annuity disbursements. Or it simply may have been a case of the two grandmothers wishing to share in the expense and responsibilities of raising the young mixed bloods. Whatever the case, Charles Curtis lived with his Indian grandmother until the Southern Cheyenne raid on the Kaw reservation in spring 1868.

On June 3, 1868, some 100 mounted Southern Cheyenne from the High Plains to the west appeared at Council Grove and heaped insults on the Kaws with whom they had been bickering for several years. A few shots were fired and shouts and insults from both sides continued for about four hours, but no one was injured. In fact there was no serious military danger because federal troops from nearby Fort Riley were prepared to intervene in case threats on either side turned to violence. The Cheyennes did steal some food and livestock from nearby non-Indian farms, but they later agreed to pay for the modest amount of plunder taken. Young Curtis was unaware of these details but in later years never wearied of challenging those who suggested that he had fled the reservation for fear of personal Injury. To the contrary, he claimed that tribal leaders gave him the responsibility of traveling alone and on foot to North Topeka to alert Kansas authorities and the mixed bloods of the Cheyenne attack. The records indicate that Kansas Governor Samuel Crawford was informed of the attack by Joseph James, Kaw half-blood interpreter, under orders of Kaw Agent E.S. Stover. James, a distant relative of Curtis, apparently took the young mixed-blood with him on his mission to Topeka and to the less perilous home of William and Permelia Curtis. Certainly these events contributed to Curtis's developing aversion for traditionalist reservation life—an aversion that intensified in the face of his father's enlistment in the Nineteenth Kansas Cavalry later that year for military action against the tribe that had "attacked" his Kaw relatives at Council Grove.

Excluding some hesitation before he decided, in 1874, to stay in Topeka rather than join his tribe on a new reservation in future Oklahoma, Curtis's interest and involvement with his tribe or with Indian affairs in general were minimal until he entered national politics two decades later. Yet, his name remained on the Kaw annuity roll until 1878, when it was officially deleted by the Indian Office for his having failed to reside with his people in Indian Territory. Even so, he continued to retain the status of a legal Kaw for the reason that his maternal grandmother was so designated by the Kansa Treaty of 1825.

Curtis attended common school in North Topeka and worked on weekends as a hack driver and fruit salesman in the railyards near his grandfather's hotel. During the summer months, he also rode as a jockey at county fairs in Kansas and at racetracks in Indian Territory and Texas. In 1876, he entered Topeka High School and in 1879 began to read law under Topeka attorney Aderial H. Case. Soon he was handling some of Case's minor court appearances and in 1881, at age twenty-one, the future vice president was certified by the Kansas bar. Criminal law became his specialty and the Republican Party his political preference, as it was of most Topekans of that time. On November 27, 1884, Curtis married Anna E. Baird of Topeka, to which union were born two daughters and one son: Permelia, Harry, and Leona, in that order.

Following his election as Shawnee County Attorney in 1884, Curtis's rigid enforcement of the recently passed (1880) Kansas prohibition amendment brought the young politician to Republican leaders' attention in the Jayhawk state. Illicit saloon keepers in Topeka had supported Curtis's election in 1884 on the belief that as an Indian he surely was also against prohibition and thus would go easy on them; in fact, he virtually ended the illegal flow of alcohol in Topeka and in 1886 was easily reelected to the Shawnee County prosecutor's office. In the meantime he had organized a home-talent theatrical company to stage several well-attended renditions of the famous antidrinking play *Ten Nights in a Barroom,* which spoke well of his political savvy and ambition in a state where the Republican Party was reaping great dividends on the volatile prohibition issue. Years later, he recalled how important his Grandmother Curtis's counsel was at this point in his political career.

In the 1892 election that saw Kansas cast its vote for the Populist James B. Weaver and elect a Populist legislature and governor, Curtis made headline news by being elected to Congress oh the Republican ticket, representing Kansas's old Fourth District. It was a dramatic victory for the conservative Curtis and a testimony to his remarkable talent for working what

William Allen White termed the human side of politics. White, who knew Curtis well, recalled that issues never interested or bothered the Indian. Indeed, said White, in all his life he had never encountered a politician who could better soothe a hostile audience with a smile, a handshake, piercing dark eyes, and seemingly endless small talk at strictly the human level of communication. Curtis always carried a book containing the names of his constituents, which he carefully memorized prior to a political appearance so that he could address audience members by first name and know something about their jobs, marriages, children, relatives, local gossip, and the like. According to one report from the nation's capital after he became a congressman, Curtis received 1,400 letters from folks back in Kansas in one 24-hour period and that with the help of a battalion of secretaries answered every one within the day, often including some personal note taken from his constituent book. One national reporter was persuaded that the famous Curtis handshake and smile could convince a stone image of sincere intent and that few politicians could match his palavering and small talk on the campaign stump or his ability to deflect serious questions regarding the pressing political issues of the day.

There was another side to the Curtis popularity, what some observers attributed to a land of natural wisdom consequent to an indiscriminate fusion of Indian blood and white, at a time when the government's policy of forced assimilation and tribal dissolution was beginning to prompt public concerns regarding the decline—indeed, the demise—of the continent's first North Americans. In Congress, the hardworking mixed blood from Kansas exploited the "Vanishing American" belief with dramatic fineness. As a member of committees dealing with tribal annuities, Indian Territory legislation, development and exploitation of public lands vis-à-vis tribal claims dating back to the beginning of the republic, and, after 1903, as chairman of the powerful House Committee on Indian Affairs, Curtis assumed a dominant role in the present and future status of the American Indians.

He vigorously supported the distribution and allotment of tribal lands on grounds that individual land ownership would promote assimilation and provide Indian families with the means to engage in the competition that in his mind was the very cornerstone of the democratic process. He sponsored the Curtis Act of 1898, which abolished tribal courts and established the legal machinery for dissolution of the once-powerful Five Civilized Tribes in Indian Territory, and more than any other person in Congress, Curtis laid the foundation for Oklahoma statehood. He championed the legal rights of full-bloods and mixed bloods alike and especially orphaned Indian children, while at the same time earning lucrative fees as an attorney representing energy companies that were swindling tribal governments of their natural resources in oil, timber, gas, and coal. He also assumed a leadership role in the legal destruction of his own tribe while gaining valuable allotments for himself and his children in the Kaw Allotment Bill of 1902.

With his shabby hat, ruffled trousers, and generally unkempt look, "Charley" (as both his supporters and critics often called him) preferred to work behind the scenes. For him, formal debate on the House floor was a waste of time and, more important, confusing to the public who neither knew nor could understand the inner workings of politics. Getting things done with a slap on the back and the sealing of a deal "without a fuss" in committee were the more efficient (and productive) tactics of democracy in action. As a fixer, concluded one Washington reporter shortly after the Kaw allotment business had been completed and Oklahoma statehood was a sure thing, Curtis clearly was one of the best in the business.

The fact is that Curtis was a conservative Republican regular who during the Populist and Progressive Eras was able by sheer power of personalized politics to ignore important economic and social issues. He furthered his political career by appearing to be a concerned protector of high tariffs and hard money against the threat of foreign competition, and he evoked the enduring nature of the capitalistic dream. He stood as living proof that an Indian could succeed at the highest levels of government, and when all else failed, he was not above waving the "bloody shirt" to remind his constituents that Lincoln, the Republican Party, and Jayhawk soldiers like his father had saved the Union from Democratic slave mongers in his beloved home state of Kansas.

Curtis remained in the U.S. House until 1907, when he was selected to fill the unexpired term of Kansas Senator Joseph R. Burton. He was returned to the Senate in 1914, where he served continuously until he became vice president in 1929. With his abiding interest in party organization and parliamentary detail, it surprised no one that he was selected to head the Senate Rules Committee or that he eagerly accepted the onerous responsibilities of party whip. At least at the onset of "normalcy" following World War I, keen political observers were not surprised that Curtis—vocal opponent of the League of Nations and avid supporter of high tariffs, restrictive immigration, and reduced federal spending—joined Henry Cabot Lodge, Frank Brandegee, and George Harvey in the smoke-filled room at the Republican convention in Chicago in 1920 to cast his lot for the darkhorse nomination of Warren G. Harding. With Senator Lodge's death one week after Coolidge's election in 1924, Curtis reached the apex of his political career by being selected Senate majority leader.

President Coolidge soon realized that congressional determination to act independently of the executive branch was a fact of political life and that Curtis's legislative support was indispensable to the executive strategy. So it was, again and again, that the so-called "silent" president relied on Curtis's support of the conservative agenda, which at bottom line was economy in government, disengagement at the international level, and support of private enterprise unobstructed by government interference—regardless of the economic implications for industrial workers or, for that matter, Curtis's own agrarian constituents, who were beginning to suffer severe economic depression several years prior to the stock crash of 1929.

No better example may be cited than Curtis's legislative support of the McNary-Haugen Farm Bill of 1927, a federal assistance program for the agrarian sector, and then his hearty upholding of Coolidge's veto of that same legislation soon thereafter. Thus when Coolidge announced in October 1927 that he would not seek another term, it came as no surprise that the mixed-blood Indian from Kansas had set his sights on the White House. He was confident that the Republicans owed him a presidential nomination for his hard work and party regularity, and that an anticipated deadlock between front-runners Herbert C. Hoover of California and Frank Lowden of Illinois might result in a draw in the 1928 Republican Convention in Kansas City—ironically, only a few miles from where Curtis's Indian grandmother more than half a century earlier had advised him to take the white man's way.

The convention's selection of Hoover was a severe blow to Curtis's personal ego and political ambition. Even though he stated publicly that to nominate Hoover would place a heavy burden upon the Republican Party, Curtis agreed to second place on the ticket after Hoover was selected on the first ballot. Curtis won easily on the vice-presidential ballot with 1,025 votes—215 more than Hoover had received for the presidency—thus indicating firm recognition of his tireless and dedicated service to his party. Subsequently, on the campaign stump, however Curtis was no great asset to the Republican ticket. As in the past, he relied on platitudinous and repetitious speeches and handshaking rather than on addressing the complex economic and social issues of the times. Some dismissed him as an anachronistic Harding crony. Others made derogatory remarks regarding his heritage, and on one important whistlestop appearance in the Midwest (where his support was strongest), Curtis clumsily played into the hands of an angry farm heckler by angrily charging him with being too dumb to understand the nation's mounting economic crisis.

Even so, his close political supporters in Washington viewed him as a statesman of great accomplishment. Just prior to his taking the oath of office, Curtis was showered with praise by his good friend and colleague, Senator Reed Smoot of Utah. Smoot dwelt at length on Curtis's long and dedicated career in both houses of Congress, applauded Curtis for his industry and self-reliance, and emphasized how the Indian from Kansas had reached his zenith without benefit of money or powerful influences. Continued Smoot, as reported in the *Congressional Record*:

> Senator, now Vice President Curtis, began life amid primitive and humble surroundings. In his veins runs the blood of a Puritan Englishman, a French-Canadian, and an Indian maiden. That remarkable fusion brought forth the real American, whose career demonstrates the boundless possibilities in the land we love. . . . We will feel more tolerant, more considerate, and more wise, as we look into his kindly eyes. We will profit by the example you have set for us.

As vice president, Curtis busied himself wielding the gavel over the Senate. He moved from a modest residential section in Washington to a ten-room suite in the Mayflower Hotel and hosted hundreds of official dinner parties. President Hoover invited him to attend cabinet meetings, but Curtis's advice was seldom sought—perhaps, as one observer noted, because he had little to offer. He sought to influence farm policy but with little success. He supported prohibition and protective tariffs, criticized the Federal Reserve System on grounds that its actions were too speculative and that it drained too much money from the country to the city, supported Hoover's dispersal of the Bonus Marchers, and in general called on the entire nation to support courts, the country, and the Constitution. The Depression, insisted Curtis repeatedly, was simply a natural occurrence that inevitably would run it course and give way to even greater prosperity.

During the presidential campaign of 1932, Curtis continued to deliver dull and plodding speeches that insisted that the Depression was nearly over and that prosperity was just around the corner if only the Hoover–Curtis team were retained in office. In fact, Curtis's campaign efforts had a negative effect on voters and played havoc with Hoover's attempt to win a second term.

When early election returns indicated a Democratic victory in 1932, Curtis stubbornly predicted that the Republicans would prevail in the end, and according to most accounts, he was genuinely shocked with the Hoover-Curtis defeat. Even his home state of Kansas cast its support for Franklin D. Roosevelt, which may explain Curtis's decision to remain in Washington after the election to resume his law practice while maintaining a nominal association with his old law firm in Topeka. On February 8, 1936, the former vice president died of a heart attack in the Washington home of his half-sister, Dolly Gann (his wife Anna had preceded him in death in 1924). Final interment was in a Topeka cemetery, not far from where he was born three-quarters of a century earlier.

REFERENCES

William E. Unrau, "Charles Curtis: Politics of Allotment," in *Indian Lives: Essays on Nineteenth and Twentieth Century Native American Leaders*, L.G. Moses and Raymond Wilson, eds. (Albuquerque: University of New Mexico Press, 1985); William E. Unrau, *Mixed Bloods and Tribal Dissolution: Charles Curtis and the Quest for Indian Identity* (Lawrence: University Press of Kansas, 1989); William E. Unrau, "The Mixed-Blood Connection: Charles Curtis and Kaw Detribalization," in *Kansas and the West: Bicentennial Essays in Honor of Nyle H. Miller*, Forrest R. Blackburn, ed. (Topeka: Kansas State Historical Society, 1976); Don C. Seitz, *From Kaw Tepee to Capitol: The Life Story of Charles Curtis, Indian,*

Who Has Risen to High Estate (New York: Frederick A. Stokes, 1928); Marvin Ewy, "Charles Curtis of Kansas: Vice President of the United States, 1929–1933," *Emporia State Research Studies,* 10 (December 1961) 1–58; Dolly Gann, *Dolly Gann's Book* (Garden City, N.Y.: Doubleday, Doran, 1933).

WILLIAM E. UNRAU is Distinguished Professor Emeritus at Wichita State University, where he specialized in the history of Indian/white relations and the American West. His books include *White Man's Wicked Water: The Alcohol Trade and Prohibition in Indian County, 1802–1892* (University Press of Kansas, 1996) and *The Rise and Fall of Indian Country, 1825–1855* (University Press of Kansas, 2007).

JOHN NANCE GARNER (1868–1967)

Vice President, 1933–1941

(President Franklin D. Roosevelt)

JOHN NANCE GARNER
(Library of Congress)

By J. Kent Calder

Best remembered for his acerbic quips about the worthlessness of the office, John Nance Garner of Texas was one of this country's most powerful vice presidents. He served fifteen terms in the House of Representatives before his inauguration on March 4, 1933, and during his last term in the House he was elected Speaker. No vice president has ever brought to the office as much legislative experience and influence, and only one other man, Schyler Colfax, has ever served as both vice president and Speaker of the House of Representatives. As President Franklin D. Roosevelt's liaison with Congress, Garner played a major role in pushing through the legislation that initiated the New Deal. Early in his second tern, however, Garner split with the president, and their resulting feud led to Garner's unprecedented presidential challenge in 1940 and one of the great stories of American political history.

Born in a log cabin in Red River County in East Texas on November 22, 1868, two weeks after the election of President Ulysses S. Grant and Vice President Colfax, Garner was the fourth in line with his name. His father, John Nance Garner III, had come to Texas from Tennessee at the age of six with his widowed mother, Rebecca Walpole Garner, a descendant of Sir Robert Walpole of England. The Walpoles of Tennessee were affluent and cultured, as were the Garner and Nance families, into which Rebecca married. After the Walpoles lost their fortune in the panic of 1837, they followed the trail to Texas that fellow Tennesseans such as Sam Houston and Davy Crockett had blazed. Rebecca's good management and hard work, along with that of her two Sons and three daughters, enabled the family to survive, but the children did not receive the education that had been customary for their ancestors.

Nevertheless, John Nance Garner III inherited qualities that helped to make him a successful cotton grower, even in Reconstruction Texas. He was honest, companionable, thrifty, and determined to succeed. By the time Texas came back into the Union in 1870, he had begun to build the impressive and comfortable colonial home that his son, the future vice president, grew up in. It was the place where neighbors gathered to discuss politics and agriculture, share a drink from the ever-present whiskey barrel, and play poker. These occasions shaped the attitudes and interests of the future politician.

Garner long remembered the resentment in Texas, and especially in his own house, that surrounded the prospect of Grant seeking a third term in 1876. Texas Democrats who hailed from Tennessee were well aware of the efforts of their revered Andrew Jackson to push a constitutional amendment through Congress that would have limited a president to one term of four or six years. Garner also retained vivid memories of the premature celebration of Samuel J. Tilden's election to the presidency, as well as the disappointment with which those around him greeted the electoral commission's desig-

nation of Rutherford B. Hayes as president. The most significant event of the campaign year for Garner, however, occurred when he attended with his father a political rally at Coon Soup Hollow and heard the declamations of two candidates for constable. The youngster came away from this event with a desire to become an orator.

Garner attended local schools and did well as a student, though one teacher described him as "not physically capable of prolonged application." At a boarding school in nearby Bogata, he acquired a love of literature from a stern teacher with an excellent library. When he was fifteen, he decided to further his education by going to school in adjoining Lamar County, where a relative, J.R. Walpole, was a teacher. According to biographer Bascom N. Timmons, Garner told his mother: "I don't wish to ask father for assistance. I don't believe I will have to." He supported himself by playing shortstop on semiprofessional baseball teams and by working at odd jobs. His ideas on fiscal responsibility were fully formed at an early age. Even as a student he continually added to his bank account. "My father told me that if I had a dime and owed no one I was solvent," he later recounted.

At the age of eighteen, Garner enrolled at Vanderbilt University in Nashville, Tennessee. Although he considered attending the newly established University of Texas, he succumbed to the ancestral pull of Tennessee. He stayed only one semester. While he might have overcome his educational inadequacies with hard work, physical ailments brought his college career to an abrupt halt. Developing problems with his eyes and lungs, Garner consulted a doctor. "He told me I wouldn't live many years," the vice president remembered; "I decided under these circumstances the money I'd saved was worth more than an education, so I took it and went home."

Returning to Texas, Garner studied law in Clarksville and continued to supplement his income by playing baseball. He was admitted to the bar in 1890 at the age of twenty-one and set up his own practice, which did not prosper. In 1892, he ran unsuccessfully for city attorney and soon afterward was diagnosed with tuberculosis. Seeking a drier climate, he found an opening with the law firm of Clark and Fuller in the south-central Texas town of Uvalde. Years later Garner recalled that his father advised him upon leaving to "Tell the truth and be a gentleman."

The young lawyer's first impressions of Uvalde were not positive. "Hell's bells," Timmons records Garner as saying to himself when he arrived, "I'd rather be dead in Clarksville than alive here." Nevertheless, he immediately opened a bank account with the $150 he had brought with him and finalized arrangements to join the law firm henceforth known as Clark, Fuller & Garner. Appointed to fill a vacancy as county judge, the junior partner rode the circuit in the nine surrounding counties, bringing in substantial revenue for the firm, regaining his health, and developing useful contacts that would later serve his political ambitions. When Garner ran for the regular term, Mariette (Ettie) Rheiner organized the opposition to his candidacy because of his reputation for drinking and playing poker. He married her on November 25, 1895. The couple's only child, Tully, named after Garner's law partner, was born on September 26, 1896, breaking the line of John Nance Garners.

Defeated for reelection in 1896, the aspiring politician set his sights on a seat in the Texas house of representatives, which he acquired in 1898. He served on the Appropriations Committee, where he opposed pork-barrel legislation and established a reputation for championing economy in government and mediating disputes. Although he sought regulation of large corporations, including insurance companies and railroads, he also understood the need for economic development. Reelected in 1900, Garner chaired the redistricting committee that created a new federal congressional district, the Fifteenth, which contained twenty-two counties, including his own. He had been frank with his colleagues about his intentions to be elected to the new

seat, and in 1903 his straightforwardness paid off when he became the Fifteenth's Democratic representative in the Fifty-eighth Congress.

Thirty-four years old at the time of his election, Garner entered the House on a sound financial footing and with well-developed political ideas. His law practice, ranch, and bank holdings provided assets of nearly $50,000, and his political focus from the beginning was on fiscal issues. He considered an income tax the most equitable means of raising revenue, and he was a strong supporter of good economic management in government. "It is just as necessary to watch the expenditure of the people's money after it is collected as it is to devise means for taxing people to produce revenue," he proclaimed during his first campaign; "I, therefore, oppose centralization of government at Washington." As a southerner, a westerner, and a Democrat, Garner also strongly opposed a protective tariff.

Though he was a talented debater, the young legislator maintained a low profile in the Republican House, which Speaker Joseph G. Cannon had just begun to dominate. Instead of making speeches, Garner became an ardent student of legislation and people. "For the first few years," he said, "I just answered roll calls, looked after chores for my constituents, studied, played poker and got acquainted." When Cannon assigned the freshman congressman to the Committee on Railways and Canals, however, Garner immediately introduced legislation calling for a survey for a coastal canal to connect his district along the Gulf of Mexico to the Mississippi and Ohio rivers, much to the astonishment of the committee's chairman. According to the *Galveston News* one purpose of Garner's bill was "just to find out if such a committee really existed." "Mr. Garner is always admirable in the beginning of a game to find out exactly how it is played." The Garner bill eventually became a law, and many years later the 1,100-mile-long Gulf Intracoastal Waterway became a reality.

Just as honesty, industry, and amiability enabled his father to prosper under the trying conditions of post-Civil War Texas, Congressman Garner became extremely popular as a minority member of the House of Representatives by exercising similar traits. Known as Cactus Jack to constituents and colleagues for his unsuccessful proposal to make cactus the state flower, he made friends with both Democrats and Republicans. Shortly after Garner entered the House, the *Houston Post* reported that he "had not been in the Capital two weeks before he was acquainted with more members of the House and the Senate and with public men generally than many members who have been here for years."

He met Joe Cannon during a poker game at the exclusive Boar's Head poker club. Biographer Timmons's account of the meeting has Garner ending the contest and winning a large pot by beating the Speaker's three aces with four fours. "Will that be enough, Mr. Speaker?" queried the freshman. "Sir," Cannon answered, "any man who can do that honestly—honestly mind you—has my profound admiration." By all accounts, the meeting was expensive for Cannon, but the two were thereafter fast friends. Garner, nevertheless, remained a committed Democrat and in 1910 played a leading role in the successful revolt against the Speaker's authoritarian leadership. As a result, the Texan established himself as an expert in parliamentary maneuvering and one of the party's most promising leaders.

In 1905, Cannon moved Garner to the Foreign Affairs Committee, where he served for the next eight years. After his first state dinner, the second-term congressman pulled no punches in providing his impressions: "As near as I have been able to figure out the chief functions of the Committee on Foreign Affairs is [*sic*] to attend as many dinners and banquets and do as little work as possible." Despite such opinions, or perhaps because of them, Garner eventually became the committee's ranking Democrat. While on the committee, he met junior Republican member Nicholas Longworth of Cincinnati, Ohio, establishing the foundation for what would become an extraordinary friendship.

Talented and ambitious, Garner advanced steadily in the House. He became party whip in 1909 and, after Woodrow Wilson's election to the presidency and the brief return of Democratic dominance to the legislature, a member of the Ways and Means Committee in 1913. Although Garner was not as influential in the new administration's first term as he had been with the two previous Republican presidents, he played an important role in financial legislation. He also made it clear that he would continue to advocate economy for Democrats just as he had for Republicans. He fought for a graduated income tax against those who favored a flat-rate tax and succeeded when his plan was enacted as a part of the Underwood Tariff Act of 1913. He supported as well currency and banking reform efforts that led to the institution of the Federal Reserve System.

Cactus Jack's status within the Wilson administration rose during World War I, however, as the president's relations with Speaker Champ Clark and Ways and Means Chairman Claude Kitchen soured. Having lost the Democratic majority in the House in the 1916 election, Wilson made Garner his liaison in that body. If the country was going to war, it would have to raise revenue, and Garner became the president's point man and the acknowledged expert on tax and tariff issues. Yet, even as he endeavored to raise the necessary sums to support the war, he never lost sight of his fundamental belief in fiscal responsibility. Garner told Wilson:

> This war is going to cost us from $10,000,000,000 to $20,000,000,000 a year. Congress has never had any experience in raising such sums. The problem now is to get it to thinking in such astronomical terms. After the war the problem will be to get it out of the habit of thinking in such terms.

The Republican landslide of 1920 left only 132 Democrats in the House. Having no relish to serve again in the minority, Garner made retirement plans. The Ku Klux Klan, however, changed his mind. When Garner discovered that Texas congressmen had joined the organization, he publicly condemned it. The Klan, then, burned a cross near Garner's home and announced plans to facilitate his retirement. As usual Garner did not campaign, but he did win the election.

During the ensuing years of Republican ascendancy, Garner pursued his established policy of making friends rather than speeches. Only a handful of Democrats with more seniority had survived the 1920 election in the House, clearing the Texan's way for accelerated advancement within the party. In 1923, he became the ranking minority member of the Ways and Means Committee and chairman of the House Democratic Committee on Committees. Six years later he attained the post of minority leader, and at the same time his friend and political adversary Nicholas Longworth became Speaker.

These years marked the beginning of a Washington institution presided over by Garner and Longworth in which the two party leaders dispensed political wisdom and influenced legislation in a nonpartisan atmosphere made cordial by whiskey. Not yet liberated from Prohibition by the Twenty-first Amendment, the two legislators resorted to euphemism when describing the practice of sharing a drink with colleagues. They were "striking a blow for liberty," and meetings became known as the "Board of Education."

During one of the first meetings of the board, Garner informed his counterpart that passage of the Smoot–Hawley tariff bill, then being considered, would allow the Democrats to regain a majority in the House and lead to Longworth's defeat as Speaker. "Put a ring around that date, December 7, 1931," he warned, "if you have a calendar that far ahead." Smoot—Hawley was enacted on June 17, 1930, and Garner's prophecy was fulfilled. He became the thirty-ninth Speaker of the House of Representatives on the very date he had foretold. He did not succeed Longworth, though, for his friend and rival had died the previous April.

As Speaker, Garner presided over a slim Democratic majority of three. Keeping that majority intact and available for votes on a daily basis was a task that demanded the full measure of the new Speaker's legislative experience and skill. In the midst of a deteriorating economic crisis, Garner decided that he could best serve the country by supporting the relief program of President Herbert Hoover's Republican administration rather than by thwarting it. "I'll be criticized for following Hoover and not offering a program of our own and I'll be accused of sabotaging Hoover," he told Timmons; "I'm not going to let it bother me. I've got skin as thick as cowhide."

The speed with which proposed legislation, such as the creation of the Reconstruction Finance Corporation, a moratorium on European debts, and strengthening of the Federal Reserve system, passed through the House of Representatives in the early part of the session astonished the White House. By February 1932, however, when the president praised Democrats for their nonpartisanship, a number of prominent party members had begun to revolt. Representative Fiorello H. La Guardia of New York, who controlled as many as fifteen votes and generally supported the Speaker, was quoted as saying: "This isn't a session of Congress. This is a kissing bee."

When Garner pushed for a federal sales tax in order to counter the rapidly growing budget deficit, he was defeated. In one of his rare speeches before the House on March 29, a few days before the vote, he outlined his fundamental beliefs regarding the importance of maintaining the financial integrity of the country. "The paramount duty of the House of Representatives," he stated, "is to levy sufficient taxes of some kind, of some nature, that will sustain the credit of this country in the eyes of the world, as well as our own people." Although the Speaker regained lost political ground with this "camp meeting" speech, his mishandling of sales tax legislation, according to some commentators, weakened his candidacy as his party's presidential nominee and boosted that of Franklin D. Roosevelt.

Backed by publisher William Randolph Hearst, Garner was a serious presidential contender in the spring of 1932. Although the Speaker did not campaign actively, he controlled the crucial votes of California and Texas by the time the Democrats convened in Chicago. When it became apparent by the convention's third ballot that Cactus Jack had no chance for the nomination, he released his delegates to Roosevelt. Indebted to Garner and to the state of Texas, Roosevelt offered the Speaker the vice-presidential nomination, which Garner reluctantly accepted. "Hell, I'll do anything to see the Democrats win one more national election," he told his friend and colleague Sam Rayburn. On November 8, 1932, as the regionally and ideologically balanced Roosevelt-Garner ticket carried 42 of the 48 states, the new vice president also regained his seat in the House. Though in theory he had a choice in the matter of which office to accept, in actuality he had none. He resigned from Congress on March 4, 1933, and began his eight-year tenure as vice president.

Upon assuming the office, he described for the press the nature of its power, or its lack thereof: "The Vice-President has no . . . offices to bestow or favors to extend. He can only make power for himself sometimes by his personality and ability. Only if by his association with men they come to have friendship for him and faith in and respect for his judgment can he be influential." Understanding well the limitations of the office, perhaps no holder was ever in such a good position to maximize its potential. Though the role was new, it was still familiar, and few could equal the capacity of John Nance Garner for making friends or for commanding the respect of his peers. The Board of Education moved to the Senate side of the Congress along with Garner, and 20 percent of the body he now presided over contained men who had served with him in the House.

Astutely, Roosevelt assigned Garner to serve as his liaison with Congress and requested that as such the vice president also attend cabinet meetings. Concerned about potential resentment in the Senate, Garner accepted the offer under the conditions that he would not make public statements or recommendations for public office or national policy unless asked to do so. Not only did the vice president utilize his vast legislative knowledge to push administration measures through the Senate, but he exercised as well considerable clout in the House. He maintained excellent relations with both Senate Majority Leader Joseph T. Robinson and House Speaker William B. Bankhead. Moreover, his numerous friends in the House included the powerful Texas delegation, which supplied no fewer than eight regular committee chairmanships at any time during the New Deal years. As historian Lionel V. Patenaude explains: "Little New Deal legislation could go through Congress without passing through one of these committees."

Garner served the president especially well during the One Hundred Days, a special legislative session from March 9 to June 16, 1932, that inaugurated the New Deal and extended executive power beyond that of any previous peacetime president. He believed the emergency measures were necessary to combat the deepening economic crisis and that they had saved the country. By early 1934, however, along with many conservative businessmen and politicians, he thought that the crisis was over and that government spending should be curtailed. In October, Garner asked the president to "cut down as far as possible, the cost of government," and Roosevelt indicated that he would do so.

Feeling pressure from both ends of the political spectrum, Roosevelt hesitated for a few months before deciding to follow the advice of other key advisers in co-opting the initiatives of the Left by introducing new programs of reform. Though the vice president disagreed with the liberal measures of the Second Hundred Days, referring to a number of them such as the Wagner National Labor Relations Act, the Social Security Act, and the Revenue Act as "plain damn foolishness," he nevertheless worked diligently and effectively during 1935 to secure their passage. At this point his party loyalty overcame his distaste for what he believed the New Deal had become. Yet, he found it increasingly difficult to tolerate the new capitalized phrase, especially as administration officials began referring to themselves as "New Dealers" rather than Democrats.

Despite his misgivings, the landslide Democratic victory of 1936 was immensely satisfying to the vice president. Remembering the overwhelming Republican victories of the 1920s, when some thought that the Democratic Party had outlived its usefulness, Garner took great pleasure in the vast majorities his party now realized in both the Senate and the House and also in the number of governorships and state legislatures that Democrats controlled. The new federal government's duty as he saw it was to "amend, amend, amend." "We have passed a lot of experimental legislation," he stated, "and any experimental legislation has to be amended in the light of the experience with it. . . . We are not putting out a fire now." The lopsided victory only served to fuel the president's arrogance, however, and as the administration moved further to the Left, the differences between the president and the vice president grew. Their inevitable split came not long after the historic 1936 election.

The first significant fissure appeared because of disagreements between Roosevelt and Garner on how to handle the sit-down strikes that closed the automotive industry at the end of 1936. New Deal initiatives that protected the right of workers to organize and bargain collectively had provided new impetus to a moribund labor movement, and by 1936 the Committee for Industrial Organization, led by John L. Lewis, had begun major organization drives in the automobile and steel industries. Late in the year, automobile workers in Detroit adopted the sit-down strike, in which they refused to leave the shop until they were granted collective bargaining. Though Roosevelt disagreed with the method, he refused to denounce the strikers, whose right to unionize the Wagner Act protected. Garner, on the other hand,

saw sit-down strikes as illegal: "They permitted men to take over other people's property," he recalled protesting in a cabinet meeting. "In Texas we would call that stealing," he said. In January 1937, the president and the vice president exchanged heated words over the sit-down strikes, and thereafter Garner worked behind the scenes to oppose his boss.

The ever widening rift became irreparable during the fight over the president's Court Reform Plan. Thwarted by a Supreme Court that had by 1936 ruled against New Deal laws in seven of nine major cases, Roosevelt sought to rectify the problem by naming as many as fifty new federal judges, including six Supreme Court justices, and by limiting the power of judges who had served ten or more years or reached the age of seventy. Though Congress had the power to determine the size of the Court, the president had not consulted that body before introducing the bill, which its elder statesmen, as well as the vice president, considered an affront. Garner eventually worked out a compromise that added no new judges, but his vacation to Uvalde in the midst of the struggle publicized the split not only between Garner and Roosevelt but also between the liberals and the conservatives within the party.

Roosevelt's unsuccessful efforts in 1938 to purge from Congress the senators and representatives who had opposed him by campaigning against them in their district primaries exacerbated the divisions within the administration. By 1938, Garner was the second most powerful man in Washington and the leader of conservative opposition to the New Deal, that voted against nearly all of the president's congressional initiatives. In that year the Texas state Democratic convention endorsed Garner as a candidate for president in 1940, as did the Texas legislature in March 1939. Opinion polls showed him to be the leading candidate if Roosevelt did not run, and in June a Garner-for-President campaign committee formed.

The concept of a third term for any president was anathema to Garner: "I would be against a third term on principal even if I approved every act of Roosevelt's two terms," he told Bascom Timmons; "I would oppose my own brother for a third term." If Roosevelt was ever undecided about whether or not to run, his path became clearer as Garner gained momentum. He was certainly not going to allow a successor to undo all that he had accomplished. Believing that Roosevelt's third-term campaign was inevitable, Garner declared his candidacy for the presidency in December 1939, three months after Great Britain and France declared war on Germany. It was the first time since the development of the party system that a sitting president and a vice president competed for their party's nomination.

Crushed in the primaries by the presidential machine, Cactus Jack Garner ended his campaign at the Chicago convention in July 1940 when Roosevelt received the Democratic nomination with Henry A. Wallace as his running mate. Roosevelt defeated Republican nominee Wendell L. Willkie in the fall election by a comfortable margin as Garner retired from public life to his home in Uvalde. He lived there quietly until his death on November 7, 1967, a couple of weeks before his ninety-ninth birthday. In 1965, when asked by a Washington journalist for suggestions on running the government, he admonished: "Stop the spending!"

Garner's vice-presidential legacy is mixed. While he played a major role in implementing Roosevelt's programs during the first term, he might also be held accountable for preventing completion of the New Deal. His entire career, however, serves as a testament to the importance of legislative power. As vice president, he resisted the transfer of power from the legislative to the executive branch that occurred dur-ing his tenure. A colorful character who always provided good copy for the journalists, Garner is perhaps most often recalled for his widely misquoted statement that the office of vice president was not "worth a pitcher of warm spit." (He actually said "piss.") After his first term, he said: "The job is delightful. I like it. But it is almost entirely unimportant." Although he had little regard for the office, some historians, such as Lionel V. Patenaude, have called him "the most powerful Vice President in the history of the United States."

REFERENCES

Bascom N. Timmons, *Garner of Texas: A Personal History* (New York: Harper and Brothers Publishers, 1948); Patrick L. Cox, "John Nance Garner," in *Profiles in Power, Twentieth-Century Texans in Washington, D.C.* (Austin, Tex.: University of Texas Press, 2005); Lionel V. Patenaude, *Texas, Politics and the New Deal* (New York: Garland Publishing, Inc., 1983); Michael J. Romano, "The Emergence of John Nance Garner as a Figure in American National Politics, 1924–1941" (Ph.D. diss., St. John's University, 1974); Robert A. Caro, *The Years of Lyndon Johnson: The Path to Power* (New York: Random House, 1982).

J. KENT CALDER is executive director of the Texas State Historical Association, located on the campus of the University of North Texas in Denton. He is a graduate of the University of Texas at Arlington and Butler University in Indianapolis, Indiana. He edited the Indiana Historical Society's magazine, *Traces,* from 1989 to 1998.

HENRY AGARD WALLACE (1888–1965)

Vice President, 1941–1945

(President Franklin Delano Roosevelt)

HENRY AGARD WALLACE
(Library of Congress)

By Mark L. Kleinman

Henry Wallace is usually remembered for the events that followed his tenure as vice president, particularly for his resounding defeat as a third-party candidate for the presidency on the Communist-tainted Progressive Party ticket in 1948. Yet during the three decades prior to his political demise in 1948, Wallace had a highly successful public career of which his term as vice president during U.S. participation in World War II was something of a culmination. As vice president, he set modern historical precedent by playing a real administrative role in government. He also gained worldwide notoriety during his vice presidential years as a champion of international political and economic democracy, calling for what he termed the "Century of the Common Man." Through the 1910s, 1920s, and early 1930s, the decades before he became vice president, Wallace was a highly successful agricultural scientist as well as an

315

influential farm editor and Midwestern agrarian spokesman. He was also a central participant in Franklin D. Roosevelt's New Deal as secretary of agriculture, overseeing what are considered some of the most successful programs of the New Deal years.

Despite Wallace's very real successes, from the time he began his political career in 1933 he was often attacked as an impractical, starry-eyed idealist. These attacks were augmented during the 1948 presidential campaign by widespread assertions that Wallace was a dupe of the Communist Party and later by the general cultural climate of the early cold war years and the McCarthy era. Such characterizations also gained impetus from persistent rumors of Wallace's actual interests in different forms of spiritualism. Wallace's reputation, both contemporary and historical, was probably damaged as well by an awkward, somewhat distant personality. Indeed, by nature he was not a politician at all; he was rather a reformer and, to a great degree, a visionary.

Wallace was born on a farm outside the village of Orient, Iowa, south of Des Moines, the third in an agrarian leadership "dynasty" of three Henry Wallaces. His grandfather, "Uncle Henry," from whom Henry A. gained much of his spiritualistic bent, went to Iowa from Pennsylvania in the 1860s as a progressive minister in the United Presbyterian Church, but he later left the ministry for reasons of health and took up farming and farm journalism. With his sons, Uncle Henry took over a small farm journal in 1895 and transformed it, as *Wallace's Farmer,* into one of the leading farm newspapers in the nation. In 1921, his eldest son, Henry C. Wallace, took up the portfolio of secretary of agriculture in the Harding administration, and Henry C.'s son Henry A. Wallace—trained in the agricultural sciences at Iowa, State College and already an international pioneer in corn hybridization—took over the editorship of *Wallace's Farmer.* In 1914, Henry A. had married Ilo Browne of Indianola, Iowa. They had three children and were married for more than fifty-years.

It was in his editorials in *Wallace's Farmer* that Wallace worked out the framework and much of the detail of the extensive critique of modern American culture that lay behind his social, political, and international affairs commentary of the 1930s and 1940s. In thousands of editorial columns and articles written between 1921 and 1933, Wallace presented social criticism analogous in many ways to that of various commentators of the era, liberal and conservative. The centerpiece of Wallace's perspective, framed by his spiritualism and his science, was a quintessential American communal philosophy. He developed a commentary grounded in midwestern American agrarian values. Above all, he invoked the ethic of "cooperation," a touchstone of nineteenth-century agrarian politics in the United States. Around the notion of cooperation, Wallace fashioned an analog to the European constructions of socialism and communism, a vision of a different and, in his view, better American civilization based on ideals that he saw embodied in an increasingly threatened rural culture.

Wallace's profound curiosity about the spiritual world led him, during the 1920s, to explore Hinduism, Bahaism, astrology, and Native American religion. He focused the most, however, on the "wisdom religion" of Theosophy, a belief system eminently suited to his philosophical intertwining of science and spiritualism. Wallace's attraction to the movement led to his involvement in something of a network of spiritualists by the early 1930s.

The best known and most controversial of Wallace's spiritual associations was that with Russian emigré artist, poet, essayist and Theosophist Nicholas Roerich. In the 1920s and 1930s, Roerich promoted an international treaty providing for the protection of the art treasures of all nations during wartime. The so-called Roerich Pact became a reality in 1935 with Wallace, a champion of the pact and a member of Franklin Roosevelt's cabinet, as the signatory for the United States. At about the same time, Wallace, as secretary of agriculture, commissioned Roerich to lead a Department of Agriculture expedition to Asia in search of drought resistant grasses that might be of some benefit to the drought-ravaged American Midwest. The expedition ultimately collapsed in an embarrassing international relations controversy that arose out of some dubious political activities that Roerich undertook while in China. Wallace contributed to the controversy by first defending Roerich unquestioningly against various accusations of misconduct and then completely disengaging from him when it became apparent that the accusations were accurate.

Wallace first entered government as Franklin Roosevelt's secretary of agriculture at the commencement of the New Deal in 1933. He moved quickly to address the desperate circumstances into which American farmers had slipped during the previous twelve years. Shortly after taking office, he called a national agricultural conference to determine what sort of emergency legislation to create. Wallace backed what was known as the Voluntary Domestic Allotment Plan (VDAP), a strategy he had advocated in various forms since the late 1920s. The VDAP called for controlling agricultural production by limiting the acreage of certain crops under cultivation in a given year. The aim of the legislation that contained the VDAP, the Agricultural Adjustment Act (AAA) of 1933, was to restore "reasonable parity" between the prices of farm products and manufactured goods. Farmers would voluntarily agree to produce less of various commodities and would receive in return compensatory payments funded by a special tax on companies that processed agricultural commodities. This would not only raise farm income in the short term but, by decreasing the overall supply of the specific commodities, raise agricultural prices over the long term as well. Wallace and his advisers intended to establish an agricultural system that would guarantee farmers a fair enough return on their production so as to enable them to function for the foreseeable future as consumers in the larger U.S. economy.

The program was wide ranging and controversial, and certain aspects of its controversy redounded negatively upon Wallace himself. This was particularly true regarding aspects of the AAA that in 1933–34 required large portions of the American cotton crop to be plowed under and thousands of baby pigs to be slaughtered in order to drive up cotton and pork prices. The destruction of the piglets was particularly controversial at a time when some 25 percent of American workers were without work and millions more were unable to provide themselves and their families with basic necessities. Although the administration made real attempts to distribute the surplus piglets and crops when appropriate, perceptions of the policy proved easily manipulable by Roosevelt's and Wallace's political opponents. Indeed, exaggerated allusions to the episode were used against Wallace from time to time for the rest of his public career.

In fact, the policy of crop destruction was utilized only during the first year of the AAA and in the case of wheat was not necessary at all. The wheat allotment program worked from the start, greatly helped along by a drought that radically decreased the size of the American wheat crop, augmenting the effects of the AAA's policy. The results in wheat foreshadowed the overall relative success that the entire act attained. By 1936, farm income in the United States increased by some 50 percent, while farm debt plummeted by several billion dollars. In this sense, agricultural policies under Wallace's supervision arguably can be characterized as the New Deal's most effective.

Also controversial was the AAA's impact on tenant farmers, particularly in the cotton agriculture of the South. Because the program decreased the need for farm labor, many tenant farmers were pushed off their land by owners who opted to put the tenants' acreage out of production. The AAA tried to moderate the effects, but at the local level affairs were generally dominated by landlords. The situation led to a battle within the AAA between liberal reformers and more-traditional agrarians. In the end Wallace was put in an untenable position, one over which he was deeply torn: he sympathized with the reformers but acceded to the political practicality of the agrarians (including the need to maintain Democratic support for the administration in the South). His ultimate and infamous "purge" of the liberals from the AAA in 1935 was the only way Wallace believed he could preserve support for the overall reform program.

Despite being declared unconstitutional by the Supreme Court in 1936—a fate shared with many other components of the early New Deal—the AAA survived the New Deal era essentially intact. This was in great part due to the fact that Wallace and his advisers were prepared for just this eventuality, having watched New Deal industrial policy succumb altogether to a negative Supreme Court decision the year before. Within months, virtually all of the AAA's components were re-created in constitutionally acceptable forms and in some cases have remained in place to the present day.

Wallace's ascension to the vice presidency was also characterized by controversy. Roosevelt, running for an unprecedented third term, chose Wallace to run with him in 1940 both for the latter's demonstrated administrative abilities and as a counterbalance to the concessions Roosevelt had made to conservatives in the Democratic Party during his first two terms. At the Democratic convention that summer, Roosevelt was insistent, explicitly threatening to decline the presidential nomination if the Democrats rejected Wallace as his running mate. In this context, the convention experience was humiliating for Wallace. Delegates who resented Roosevelt's dictatorial behavior, as well as those who were specifically opposed to Wallace, focused their anger on Wallace who was shocked by the crowd's vehemence. Ilo Wallace was driven to tears by the antagonism aimed at her husband. Wallace eventually won the nomination in a close vote over House Speaker William Bankhead of Alabama, but was unable to deliver his acceptance speech to the convention due to the delegates' hostility. He gave it the following month instead at a campaign kickoff in Des Moines, Iowa.

Wallace took on something like an enforcer's role in the campaign of 1940, frequently attacking the Republicans in the realm of foreign affairs. Most pointedly, he tried to taint them with the stain of Nazism, arguing that FDR's efforts in global affairs were impeded internationally by Hitler and domestically by partisan opponents. He developed an image of a protofascism nascent in the United States arising out of isolationism and monopolistic corporate capitalism, both of which he associated with the Republican Party. Wallace's quite vicious attacks drew a great deal of criticism not only from the Republicans but also from less partisan sources, including the moderate press. His rhetorical strategy was attacked for being unjust and even irresponsible in its exaggeration. Indeed, it is clear that Wallace did go too far in some of the aspersions he cast on the Republicans in 1940, but he did so out of his real belief that the United States had to move quickly to prepare for an inevitable war and that any group that hindered that preparation was, in effect, "appeasing" the fascists. In the wake of the Munich crisis of 1938 and the advent of the ideologically powerful "Munich analog," Wallace's view was not in any sense an extraordinary one for a liberal in the United States to hold by 1940.

Wallace undertook his first vice-presidential task prior to actually taking office. A few weeks after the election Roosevelt appointed the vice president-elect to head a U.S. delegation to the December 1 inauguration of Manuel Ávila Camacho as president of Mexico. It was an assignment that gave Wallace an opportunity to work to bring about the realization of his long-time hope for hemispheric cooperation, a goal he had advocated since entering government. Wallace was an excellent choice for the mission. As his interest in Latin America had blossomed over the years, he had become an ardent student of Latin American culture as well as of the Spanish language. By the time he left for Mexico, he was fully conversational in

Spanish, which greatly impressed the Mexicans. His penchant for visiting with the common people as well as his ability to communicate in their native tongue drew enthusiastic responses wherever he traveled.

While in Mexico, Wallace conducted an extensive correspondence with Washington in which he advocated an amicable settlement of several issues of contention between the United States and Mexico, most connected to the reformist policies of the outgoing president, Lázaro Cárdenas. It was Cárdenas's administration that had expropriated foreign—including U.S.—oil companies' holdings in Mexico in 1938, causing an international dispute that had seriously threatened the viability of Roosevelt's Good Neighbor Policy throughout Latin America. Wallace contended that the new Mexican regime was likely to be amenable to reaching some sort of final settlement of the oil issue. Doing so would in turn open the door to further Mexican—U.S. cooperation, and Wallace hoped that such cooperation would take a course close to his own heart. He believed that the United States could greatly help the Mexicans by, among other things, setting up an agricultural experiment station in Mexico. As a farm leader and now former secretary of agriculture, he knew how helpful such stations had been to U.S. farmers over the years. Wallace felt that if the United States established such an agency in Mexico, it might have a similarly beneficial impact on Mexican agriculture and so ultimately improve the lives of thousands of impoverished Mexicans.

After the inauguration, Wallace had little difficulty taking up the formal tasks of the vice president. He proved himself fully capable of presiding over the Senate, both in terms of mastering procedure and acquainting himself with its members. By nature Wallace had little interest in the convoluted political machinations of the senators. He did, however, attempt to raise their health consciousness by getting rid of his predecessor's infamous liquor cabinet (Wallace was for the most part a teetotaler) and presenting himself as a physical fitness role

model through his constant participation in sports ranging from boxing to tenths. He also maintained the wide range of intellectual interests that he had pursued since his youth. His office was known for its extensive and varied collection of reading material. In addition, as vice president, Wallace continued to nurture U.S. cooperation with Latin America by keeping up his Spanish language studies, supporting a national radio program that popularized Latin American culture in the United States, and advocating various educational and cultural exchange programs between the United States and the other nations of the Western Hemisphere.

In July 1941, Wallace was given a task that established a new administrative aspect for the office of vice president. Roosevelt appointed him to head the Economic Defense Board (EDB), made up of eight members of the cabinet. The agency was renamed the Board of Economic Warfare (BEW) after Pearl Harbor, and Wallace remained as its wartime director.

The BEW's primary responsibility was locating and obtaining items of strategic importance to the United States from all over the globe. In supervising these operations, Wallace came into direct and highly visible bureaucratic conflict with Secretary of Commerce Jesse Jones, a conservative Texas Democrat who was also director of the Reconstruction Finance Corporation (RFC) as well as, ultimately, federal loan disbursement in general. The main circumstance behind the controversy was that the RFC was the BEW's "banker," which meant that disagreements over procurement, whether philosophical or in regard to specific goals, were likely to lead to classic bureaucratic battles. For Wallace, there were two interconnected concerns that together formed the crux of the conflict: efficient matériel procurement and the assumption that procurement policies had to be socially just, not only for humanitarian reasons but also to attain optimum efficiency. The problem was that Wallace and his subordinates at the BEW believed that the simple fact of being at war meant that peacetime assumptions regarding the flow of goods were to be disregarded. The exigencies of war demanded innovation and particularly might mean foregoing what would normally be considered sober business practices. For Wallace's BEW the profit motive was not a driving strategic principle, but for millionaire businessman Jones and his like-minded team, following sound business practices was of paramount importance.

The intertwining of Wallace's concern for procurement efficiency with his liberal humanitarianism was evident in his regard for the well-being of the workers in other nations who were producing the supplies the BEW sought to procure, especially in Wallace's much-beloved Latin America. To Wallace the working conditions and health of those he had come to term collectively the common man were bound to the question of efficiency. Healthy workers would produce more and do so more efficiently, benefiting the United States both during and after the war. What was humane actually made the best business sense.

By spring 1943, the conflict between Wallace and Jones ranged over various procurement issues. It had also become acrimonious and public, the latter quality being one that Roosevelt ultimately would not tolerate. Jones had used a Senate Banking and Currency Committee hearing the year before to attack the BEW's rubber procurement policy. Wallace and his assistant, Milo Perkins, given an opportunity to respond, implied that Jones and the RFC through their obstructionism had failed to protect the nation's strategic interests in numerous instances. The whole exchange appeared in newspapers across the country. In June 1943, the BEW was attacked in an inflammatory manner on the Senate floor by Jones's allies. This, along with similar, concurrent attacks in the House, led Wallace and Perkins to issue a lengthy press release detailing the impediments created by Jones and the RFC in the creation of adequate stockpiles of a whole list of strategic materials. The statement included the assertion that by obstructing BEW efforts at obtaining supplies of quinine for U.S. troops in the Pacific

theater, the RFC had actually caused the deaths of U.S. servicemen. Jones responded with public outrage, insisting that Wallace in effect had called him a traitor.

Roosevelt intervened at first indirectly, having Wallace and Jones meet under mediation to attempt a reconciliation. They agreed to a public statement, but Jones decided after the fact to issue a statement of his own that once more attacked in vehement language Wallace's criticism of the RFC. Then on July 5 he issued his own press release in response to Wallace's and Perkin's of the previous month. The obvious failure of reconciliation over the next week impelled Roosevelt to direct action. On July 15 he abolished the BEW altogether by executive order, thus ending the conflict. While the RFC did lose some of its authority over foreign contracts, the president's action clearly was a defeat for Wallace, and the episode contributed to the mounting desire of conservative Democrats to force him from the vice-presidency the following year. At the time, however, Wallace accepted his defeat with equanimity,

Wallace's poise in the face of public defeat may have derived in part from the fact that by the time of the BEW's liquidation in summer 1943 he had firmly established himself not only as the United States's leading progressive liberal, but also as the nation's great champion of cooperative internationalism. He had done so in May 1942 when he gave what was the best-known and perhaps most important speech of his career. Formally titled "The Price of Free World Victory," the speech, widely published and republished over subsequent weeks and months, became known by its most poignant phrase, the "Century of the Common Man." It was an address that not only articulated Wallace's liberal internationalism as it had evolved through the 1920s and 1930s, but also laid out his vision for postwar global affairs as well. He attacked U.S. tariff policy as he had in the 1920s for the manner in which it had contributed to international economic upheaval, and he spoke to the historical and moral contexts of the war, characterizing it dramatically as a "fight to the death between the free world and the slave world." Wallace once more attacked fascism abroad and industrial monopoly at home as the great threats to both international and domestic democracy. He declared that modern technological knowledge could overcome inequities in the world and create the "shared abundance" he had long championed. At the same time, he was demanding, as director of the BEW, foreign procurement contracts that protected the health and well-being of the workers of other nations, Wallace asserted in "Century of the Common Man" that modern technological know-how made such a demand wholly reasonable. Wallace insisted that by 1942 modern technology was capable of ensuring "that everybody in the world has the privilege of drinking a quart of milk a day." The statement was not an offer to use national wealth without restraint to support the world's poor, as it was often and sometimes deliberately misconstrued. Rather, Wallace was arguing that the knowledge existed to enable the citizens of all nations to attain the means to apply themselves with the necessities of life. His use of the dietary metaphor arose from his belief that children who ate well would learn well—well enough to master the technology that would industrialize their nations, enabling those nations to participate in the cooperative postwar global prosperity that Wallace envisioned. With such hopes in mind, Wallace declared that this war against fascism could be viewed as one more, perhaps culminating step in a "Great Revolution of the people" that began with the American Revolution and continued with the French, Latin American, German, and Russian revolutions.

By 1944, Wallace was an extremely popular political figure in the United States. A July Gallup poll showed that 65 percent of Democratic voters favored his renomination as vice president. He was viewed by many Americans as the torchbearer of progressive liberal domestic reform and the great champion of cooperation in international affairs. Because of such perceptions, as well as the battles he fought with Jesse

Jones while at the helm of the BEW, conservative Democrats were determined by summer 1944 to force him from the vice presidency, particularly in view of widespread doubt that Roosevelt's health would allow the president to complete a fourth term. Roosevelt's own feelings on retaining Wallace as vice president remained ambiguous throughout the spring and early summer, but by the time of the Democratic convention in mid-July, his actions worked against Wallace's renomination.

Earlier in the year, Wallace had proposed to Roosevelt that he make a vice-presidential tour of Soviet Asia and China. Wallace expected both to become areas of important social, economic, and political development in the postwar era. Roosevelt readily agreed, perhaps seeing the trip as a way to remove the vice president from the domestic political scene. Thus from late May through early July, Wallace traveled in Asia while preconvention political machinations in the United States heated up. He visited mines, farms, and factories in Russia and made speeches that he hoped would establish the foundation for what he termed "world security on the basis of broader understanding." In Siberia, Wallace was received warmly and with great respect, in part because of his clearly exceptional agricultural knowledge. But he was also welcomed enthusiastically because he had taken the time, characteristically, during the months preceding the trip to study enough of the Russian language to enable himself to deliver a speech in his hosts' native tongue. Upon his return to the United States, Wallace recounted the great respect he felt for Soviet accomplishments in Siberia, in notable comparison to the serious doubts and even disdain he felt for the corruption he witnessed under Chiang Kai-shek's regime in China. He was only vaguely aware that much of what he was shown by the Russians—model factories and mining towns peopled by enthusiastic workers—was a false front put up by the Soviets to guarantee his positive report to the U.S. president and people.

By the time Wallace returned home, his hold on the vice presidency was quite tenuous.

Despite the strong support he had among rank-and-file Democrats, southern democratic leaders and party bosses wanted him out. In conversation, the president himself was vaguely contradictory, telling Wallace that if he, Roosevelt, were a delegate to the convention, "he would vote for Henry Wallace" but that there were many in the party who felt otherwise. By the time of the convention, Roosevelt's perhaps false ambivalence led him to desert Wallace effectively by indicating that he would be willing to share the ticket with either Supreme Court Justice William O. Douglas or Senator Harry S. Truman of Missouri, both of whom were viewed by party conservatives as acceptably moderate alternatives.

Roosevelt was formally renominated on the evening of July 20, and Wallace made a dramatic speech from the platform seconding the president's nomination. In bold terms, he asserted a powerfully progressive position, including a call for racial equality in education, economics, and politics. He spoke with a candor that probably cost him whatever chance remained for the renomination. The speech was followed by a huge demonstration on Wallace's behalf. Some historians have argued that had the party bosses not succeeded in having the convention adjourned at that moment, Wallace might have been nominated the same evening. In fact, much of the demonstration was made by Wallace supporters in the galleries who were not actual delegates. In any case, the convention was adjourned and the next day Wallace was beaten in the balloting by Truman.

After his reelection that November, Roosevelt nominated Wallace for secretary of commerce, and Wallace's confirmation by the Senate became yet another acrimonious battle over his liberalism. He finally won confirmation, hut not before his Senate opponents stripped the position of its traditional control of important federal lending agencies. Nevertheless, Wallace was heading the Department of Commerce when Roosevelt died in April 1945 and Harry S. Truman became president.

Truman kept Wallace in the cabinet, at first believing that he needed Wallace to retain the support of the left wing of the Democratic Party, which continued to view Truman with great skepticism. But by summer 1946, Wallace was increasingly in disagreement with Truman over the course of U.S. foreign policy, particularly over U.S. relations with the Soviet Union, the nation's World War II ally. In a letter he wrote to the president in July, Wallace predicted not only the arms race to come but the sort of international paranoia and tension that would result from such a race. He laid the blame for tensions at the feet of both nations but suggested that the United States could ease them by slowing down the tremendous expansion of its military establishment that was taking place especially in atomic weapons and delivery systems.

In September, Wallace reiterated many of the same points in a speech he gave at a progressive political rally at Madison Square Garden in New York. The speech engendered great controversy, both within the administration and the national press. The positions that Wallace advocated seemed to oppose strongly those being established by Secretary of State James Byrnes, who was in Paris at the time, attending a meeting of foreign ministers. It was ultimately at Byrnes's irate insistence that Truman demanded Wallace's resignation from the cabinet.

After leaving public office Wallace became the editor of the *New Republic* magazine. Through his editorials, he continued to oppose the Truman administration's hard line toward the Russians as well as what he viewed as the increasingly conservative course of U.S. politics. By late December 1947, motivated by such issues, he decided to run for the presidency against Truman on the ticket of the resurrected Progressive Party. For Wallace, the campaign of 1948 was a culmination of the various controversies that had followed him throughout his public career. To those of his critics who viewed him as too far to the Left, his association with communists in the Progressive Party seemed to prove their greatest fears, and his path-breaking insistence on integrated rallies while campaigning in the South enraged conservative Southern Democrats even while it foreshadowed aspects of the Civil Rights movement of the 1950s and 1960s.

Wallace's relationship with Nicholas Roerich, particularly its spiritual aspects, became an issue during the campaign of 1948 as well. Their association was brought to light by conservative columnist Westbrook Pegler, who smeared Wallace by publishing and critically interpreting several letters Wallace had written during the 1930s to Roerich and Roerich's secretary on both political and spiritual issues. Pegler harped on aspects of the correspondence in such a way as to make it seem that Wallace had been under the mystical sway of Roerich, with Roerich pejoratively characterized as Wallace's guru. Wallace's failure to squarely address the Roerich connection as well as the larger issue of his spiritualistic inclinations contributed to the further degradation of his reputation in the midst of the disastrous campaign.

Throughout the campaign, Wallace was portrayed in the mainstream press as a foolish dupe of the Communists. Truman and the anticommunist liberals who eventually came to support him went so far at times as to imply Wallace's disloyalty. The election itself was anticlimactic: The Progressives were crushed in the presidential election, with Wallace receiving only 1.1 million votes, less than 2.5 percent of all those cast.

The debacle of the 1948 election was the effective end of Wallace's public career. Although he did speak out on various issues occasionally over the next decade and a half, he in fact retired to a farm he had purchased in upstate New York, returning to his earliest passion, experimental agricultural genetics. He spent his later years developing various strains of garden flowers, hybrid corn, chickens, and strawberries. In 1964, he was diagnosed with amyotrophic lateral sclerosis (Lou Gehrig's disease) and after a year battling the illness he succumbed to it, dying on November 18, 1965, at the age of 77.

REFERENCES

Norman D. Markowitz, *The Rise and Fall of the People's Century: Henry A. Wallace and American Liberalism 1941–1948* (New York: The Free Press, 1973); Edward L. and Frederick H. Schapsmeier, *Henry A. Wallace of Iowa: The Agrarian Years, 1910–1940* (Ames: The Iowa State University Press, 1968) and *Prophet in Politics: Henry A. Wallace and the War Years, 1940–1965* (Ames: The Iowa State University Press, 1970); *The Price of Vision: The Diary of Henry A. Wallace, 1942–1946*, John M. Blum, ed. (Boston: Houghton Mifflin, 1973); Torbjorn Sirevag, *The Eclipse of the New Deal and the Fall of Vice-President Wallace, 1944* (New York: Garland Publishing, 1985); Graham White and John Maze, *Henry A. Wallace: His Search for a New World Order* (Chapel Hill: The University of North Carolina Press, 1995); John C. Culver and John Hyde, *American Dreamer: The Life and Times of Henry A. Wallace* (New York: Norton, 2000).

MARK L. KLEINMAN now lives and works in Sacramento, California, where he helps manage the Preserving Wild California program and serves as a professional consultant on environmental issues. Before leaving academia, he was an associate professor of U.S. history at the University of Wisconsin, Oshkosh. He received his Ph.D. in history in 1991 from the University of California, Los Angeles. He is the author of *A World of Hope, a World of Fear: Henry A. Wallace, Reinhold Niebuhr and American Liberalism* (Ohio University Press, 2000).

HARRY S. TRUMAN (1884–1972)

Vice President, January 20–April 12, 1945

(President Franklin D. Roosevelt)

HARRY S. TRUMAN
(Library of Congress)

By Robert H. Ferrell

Harry S. Truman was appallingly ill-prepared for the grand questions of military strategy and foreign policy that would take most of his time as president, and for that lack of preparedness the blame has to rest on his predecessor, Franklin Delano Roosevelt, who told him virtually nothing before or after his inauguration as vice president. As Lieutenant Commander William M. Rigdon of the White House Map Room, the president's secret operations center in the White House, put it: "I was custodian of the President's secret war files, but not once had I been instructed to show any document to the Vice President. He simply had not been worked into the Roosevelt administration." The vice president saw the president only a few times, mostly with other people; he met privately with the president twice.

Beyond question, Truman was well informed on domestic politics and on those issues might be considered one of the best-informed vice presidents in all of American history. He had been in the Senate for ten years and knew the membership of the upper house and many members of the lower house. He knew the principal officers of the administration, for beginning in 1941 he had been chairman of a special Senate committee to investigate the war effort. The committee was very active, making reports that involved conversation with, and reception of documents from, the highest government officials as well as the principal officers of corporations with war orders. He sometimes excoriated administration officials in his reports, which the committee always issued unanimously.

But when it came to military strategy and foreign policy, he knew no more than what the average intelligent reader of the nation's newspapers would have learned. That, alas, was not much, for censorship kept many details, and most serious disagreements among the Allies, out of the newspapers.

Truman was sixty years old when he became vice president—older than the usual holder of the nation's second-highest elective office. He had not gotten into politics early in his life. After graduation from high school in 1901 he spent three years working in Kansas City banks, 1903–06, and for the next eleven years, until 1917, he was a farmer on a big 600 acre farm near Grandview, Missouri, a few miles south of Kansas City. After two years in the U.S. Army in World War I, he and a regimental friend, Edward Jacobson, conducted a Kansas City haberdashery for three years until it failed in the economic recession after the war.

Beginning in 1923, the banker-farmer-soldier-haberdasher took a two-year term as "county judge," county commissioner, of Jackson County, the county of Kansas City in 1923–24, and then after losing an election because of a division among the local Democrats, Truman came back as "presiding judge" for two four-year terms (1927–34) presiding over a three-man court. In this task, Truman's political instincts developed markedly because much of his duties consisted of ensuring that the county possessed good roads. At this time, automobiles were rapidly increasing and road construction was one of the large county tasks throughout the United States. By the time Truman ended his two terms as his county's principal executive officer, Jackson County had one of the best road systems in the nation, comparable with Wayne County (Detroit) and Westchester County, next to New York City. He accomplished this in an honest way, without graft, despite the presence in Kansas City of Boss Thomas J. Pendergast, whose fiefdom was included in Judge Truman's bailiwick. Truman managed good relations with Boss Tom by not challenging—as indeed he could not have even if he had wanted—Pendergast within the city and simultaneously keeping the county honest.

In the senatorial election of 1934, Truman was backed by Pendergast, as was necessary for anyone running for office from western Missouri, against the rival faction of the Democratic Party in St. Louis, and Truman won the primary in a three-way race. His first term in the Senate was difficult, as he was a newcomer, but gradually it became apparent to the Senate's leadership that he was a work horse, not a show horse, and after shepherding through the upper house the Civil Aeronautics Act of 1938, he became coauthor with Senator Burton K. Wheeler of Montana of the Truman-Wheeler Transportation Act of 1940, a combination of rules governing water and rail transport in the country, a major administrative achievement.

Truman's tightest race, moreso than the presidential election of 1948, was his bid for senate reelection in 1940, against the destroyers of the Pendergast machine, Federal Attorney Maurice Milligan and Governor Floyd C. Stark (a nurseryman of "Stark Delicious" apples fame). Stark had Roosevelt's secret support, and Truman squeaked through the primary because of 8,000 machine votes in St. Louis, votes from what were described as delivery wards, which came to him because of a trade of Kansas City and other votes in an intraparty contest for the governorship. Truman's plurality in the state was less than 8,000.

In his second Senate term, he quickly turned to the special committee, which consumed his time until he was nominated for the vice presidency.

The nomination in summer 1944 was a piece of derring-do by the Democratic Party bosses. It was not so much an effort to choose Truman as to remove the sitting vice president, Henry A. Wallace, whom the party leaders distrusted and—the word is not too strong—despised. Wallace was an amateur in politics, and had never run for office until 1940, when Roosevelt put him on the national ticket. He did not enjoy politics and politicians, and said openly that he was interested in issues, not people—a prime error for any would-be successful candidate. Roosevelt began to tire of Wallace when the vice president tangled with Secretary of Commerce Jesse H. Jones in 1943, even though Jones was no favorite of the president, who privately described the crusty Texan as Jesus H. Jones. The contention between the vice president and secretary became public, and to the surprise of observers, for it was not the president's usual way with squabbling subordinates, he pronounced a plague on both their houses. Roosevelt continued to say publicly and privately that he admired Wallace and that he was the obvious vice-presidential candidate. A cabal consisting of party treasurer Edwin W. Pauley, party secretary George B. Allen, the president's appointments secretary Major General Edwin M. Watson, together with national chairman Robert E. Hannegan and preceding chairman and then Postmaster General Frank C. Walker, thereupon determined to destroy Wallace. General Watson kept Wallace admirers out of the president's office and brought in Wallace antagonists. Gradually, the group brought the president around to their point of view.

The party leaders had made their calculation carefully, and it was uncomplicated in the extreme. The reason for ridding the ticket of Wallace was in part distrust and dislike, but also a belief that Roosevelt could not survive a fourth term and whoever was vice president would become president. After Roosevelt's return from the Teheran Conference late in 1943, his health had visibly worsened. He seemed to suffer from bronchitis. The party leaders did not know what ailed him, though there was talk of cancer, but it was obvious, they believed, that the president needed a healthy vice president and a trustworthy party man, such as Truman.

Roosevelt indeed was wearing out. On March 27, 1944, well before Truman's nomination at the Democratic national convention in Chicago on July 21, the president underwent a physical examination at Bethesda Naval Hospital and was seen by the staff cardiologist, Howard G. Bruenn, who was appalled by the president's condition. Bruenn knew the minute he helped lift the president out of the wheelchair onto the hospital table for the examination that Roosevelt was in trouble, for the president was short of breath. From that moment on, the diagnosis was of the worst: Bruenn found him in heart failure. The results of the examination were not made public, nor told to the president—who never asked Bruenn about his condition nor inquired whether Bruenn, who thereafter saw him almost daily and virtually became his personal physician, was a cardiologist (although the president did know that, as he indirectly mentioned to Secretary of the Treasury Henry Morgenthau, Jr., the night before he died).

One might ask why the leaders allowed Roosevelt to run. The truth was that the president 'wanted to run, and he was so powerful a figure within the party that no one dared try to convince him otherwise. Moreover, the party needed him. That year the Republicans nominated an attractive candidate, Governor Thomas E. Dewey of New York, and only "the champ," the party's strongest vote getter since Andrew Jackson, could win against Dewey.

At the convention Truman was duly nominated but not without a fight by Wallace, who defied the president. Through intermediaries Roosevelt had advised him not to run. There was a strong bid by a White House insider, the ambitious James F. Byrnes, who scented not the vice presidency but the presidency as did Wallace. Byrnes was a former member of the House and the Senate, associate justice of the Supreme Court, and Roosevelt's "assistant president," to use the president's phrase, beginning in 1942 The president told both Wallace and Byrnes in advance of the convention that he was backing them, but after maneuvering them out he passed the nomination to Truman. The nominee had claimed that he did not want the nomination, which is the usual claim in American politics, but it is difficult to believe that Truman, who was ambitious, did not want the nomination that he knew meant the presidency. Moreover, to have been forward in seeking the post would not have endeared him to Roosevelt, who disliked Byrnes for that reason. The nominee also had labored under a singular awkwardness, namely, that his wife, Bess, for reasoning that defies imagination, did not want to live in the White House as she knew the nomination would mean, in view of Roosevelt's ill health.

Truman had not seen Roosevelt since March and met with him on August 18 for luncheon outside the White House on the south lawn, where the two Democratic candidates posed for photographers, and then after Roosevelt sent them, away the president told Truman about the atomic bomb, albeit in general terms, for the president's daughter, Anna Boettiger, soon joined them. The vice-presidential nominee was alarmed by Roosevelt's physical condition. Afterward he spoke with his senatorial assistant, Harry H. Vaughan, and said: "I had no idea he was in such a feeble condition. In pouring cream in his tea, he got more cream in the saucer than he did in the cup." He told Vaughan that the trouble did not seem mental, but that physically the president was going to pieces.

On September 7, the vice-presidential nominee and a World War I friend, Edward D. (Eddie) McKim, attended a White House reception, where McKim studied the president for an hour and a half. Afterward when he and Truman left the mansion, he stopped Truman and said: "Hey bud, turn around and take a look. You're going to be living in that house before long." Truman's response was: "Eddie, I'm afraid I am."

The resultant campaign did not focus on the vice-presidential candidate but upon Roosevelt, even though the president did not campaign much, if only because he was physically unable. Truman's speeches received little attention. The candidate afterward told a reporter friend that he drew crowds of two or three dozen, all over the country.

At a huge rally in Madison Square Garden, Truman had an unnerving experience, but it was about the only one—other than an accusation that he once had been a member of the Ku Klux Klan (which was not the case). He and Vice President Wallace were scheduled to enter the auditorium together. Truman had to wait until the very last moment before Wallace arrived because Wallace had decided to walk to the rally and it took more time than he anticipated. Truman was not certain about this explanation and was inclined to believe that this former rival for the nomination was stalling so he could make a separate entrance and receive applause from the pro-Wallace crowds. Nevertheless, they walked in together, arm in arm. After the two men entered that important evening, there were no more problems. A Truman confederate was in charge of broadcasting the meeting over the radio, and when each man was introduced separately, he saw to it that the "gain" was up for Truman and down for Wallace so that the radio audience, much more important than the Garden audience, would receive the proper impression.

After taking the oath from Vice President Wallace in an abbreviated ceremony held behind the White House because of wartime conditions and the need for ceremonial modesty, Truman remained the same unassuming individual he had been before. He continued in the same Connecticut Avenue apartment he had been living in since 1941, a five-story Moorish-style brick building dating to the 1920s. There, Trumans lived with their daughter Margaret (a junior and history major at George Washington University), and Mrs. Truman's mother, in two bedrooms with a single bath, a living room, a dining room, and a kitchen. The vice president received secret service protection, albeit with a single agent on duty.

The family enjoyed much the same life as before, except that the hectic duties of the investigating committee, together with heavy mail from Missouri constituents and the need to attend votes if not debates on the Senate floor, now were matters of the past.

The vice presidency appears to have been a time of relaxation for Truman. Bess Truman certainly enjoyed herself, and it was perhaps memory of that last, unfettered time that caused her toward the end of her husband's presidency to show some willingness to continue living in Washington where, after Truman's retirement from the White House, he might possibly remain as junior senator from Missouri in the way that John Quincy Adams a century and more before had gone to the House of Representatives. There was a pleasant round of parties in which the vice president and his lady substituted for the busy (or so said the newspaper accounts) chief executive.

Otherwise the family members did what pleased them. In a letter to her husband's cousin, Ethel Noland, Bess conveyed a charming scene of domestic contentment. "Marg," she wrote, "has gone to a picture show and Harry to a poker party. Mother is practically asleep in her chair—so it's very peaceful." The date of this idyllic scene was the day before President Roosevelt left Washington for Warm Springs, for a much-needed rest.

During this period, the vice president liked to show Missouri visitors and friends what he described as his "gold-plated" office ("pretty good for a country boy"), the special suite in the Capitol that went with his recent elevation. He kept his old Senate office, which made him feel more at home, especially the back room, with its wall covered with photographs and cartoons of his Senate years—the room he referred to as "the doghouse," in which he used to confer with important visitors.

He was sensitive to his new duties, and to a reporter for the *New York Times* he gave an interview that in its frankness showed what lay in store for reporters who for years had endured Roosevelt's general evasions of awkward questions. "What are you going to do with your spare time?" the reporter asked. "Study history," was the response. But then Truman got down to something more interesting. He said he would not follow the vice-presidential example of Charles G. Dawes during President Coolidge's second term. (Dawes had spent his time telling the Senate not to waste time, had gone to sleep at a crucial moment during a confirmation, and spent the rest of the time telling everyone how to shape up.) Nor would he follow that of his predecessor. He warmed to the latter example. He said,

> Well, while Garner was Vice President there was hardly a day when at least half the members of the Senate did nor see him in his office or talk to him somewhere around the Capitol. In the past four years I doubt if there are half a dozen Senators all told who have been in the Vice President's office. You can draw your own conclusions.

One of the first tasks Truman undertook as vice president was to fly out to Kansas City when Boss Tom Pendergast died on January 26, 1945. Pendergast was an ex-convict, having gone to Leavenworth in 1939, where he spent a year and a day for income tax evasion (he had forgotten to tell the internal revenue bureau about a huge bribe he had taken from fourteen fire insurance companies in exchange for obtaining for them a favorable settlement of $11 million in impounded premiums). Without hesitation Truman attended the funeral, going out in an army bomber; he could have found something to keep him away but refused.

"He was always my friend," he told reporters unabashedly, "and I have always been his."

Vice President Truman saw Roosevelt only a few times—Roosevelt either was abroad at the Yalta Conference or at Warm Springs. On such occasions Truman was inconspicuous. One of Roosevelt's secretaries, Roberta Barrows, remarked years later when Truman had become famous, that: "Three or four times, he claims he came, but I can't remember the visits at all." He went to the White House for the president's meetings with the Big Four, the leaders in the House and Senate, but there were only a few meetings. The cabinet meetings did not count for anything. Truman told his biographer, Jonathan Daniels, that "Roosevelt never discussed anything important at his Cabinet meetings. Cabinet members, if they had anything to discuss, tried to see him privately after the meetings." He saw the president by appointment privately only on March 8 and March 19.

During the vice presidency, Truman had to perform one difficult task, which was to ensure the confirmation of former Vice President Wallace as secretary of commerce. This was no simple assignment, and Truman later told Daniels that when Roosevelt told him he was going to give Wallace the commerce department, his initial response was "Jesus Christ!"

The Wallace confirmation was nothing if not complicated. Wallace's preference for commerce was understandable. The president had felt sorry for his former running mate and faithful vice president for four years, and told Wallace, with more generosity than perhaps he should have displayed, that he, Wallace, could have any cabinet department save the department of state and the military departments. Without hesitation, Wallace asked for commerce, the department then presided over by his mortal enemy, Byron Jones.

FDR may not have felt too badly about the choice, for he was angry with Jones, who in the arrangements for the recent national convention in Chicago had seemed to be behind a division in the Texas delegation between pro-Roosevelt and anti-Roosevelt forces—Jones's nephew was a member of the anti-Roosevelt faction. The president proposed that Jones become an ambassador, an assignment Jones first indignantly rejected. He then left the cabinet in a huff.

However, for the president and thereby for Truman, who had to preside over the arrangement, the confirmation of Wallace at once turned into a bitter fight. Jones's partisans, who were many, especially in the South and among conservatives generally, raised up the possibility that Wallace would be unable to handle the Reconstruction Finance Corporation, the lending agency that was a part of Jones's bailiwick. Soon senators were whispering that with Wallace ranning the RFC, federal money would go out for every fad and scheme in creation, perhaps for giving each Hottentot a quart of milk. The latter accusation had been invented by the president of the National Association of Manufacturers, but it hurt Wallace's reputation. President Roosevelt, during discussions with the then vice president over renomination, had mentioned the canard.

The Wallace confirmation hearings and debate on the Senate floor turned into a great argument, which in its purposes probably was twofold. One was genuine concern that Wallace could not handle federal money. The other was, one strongly suspects, an indirect revolt against the president. During the war, Roosevelt represented the government to his fellow citizens and also to the nations of the world, and now that the war was coming to an end, the time had come to embarrass the president, to cut him down to size. Wallace's confirmation could be the occasion.

In the event, Truman was forced to break a tie—contrived or real must be a question—in favor of Wallace.

It is interesting that during Truman's short vice presidency he cast another deciding vote, two days before Roosevelt's death, that broke a Senate deadlock over whether recipients of lend-lease could use such funds for postwar reconstruction. Without Truman's intervention, all nonmilitary lend-lease shipments would have ceased upon the end of the war. One of Truman's early embarrassments in the presidency would be cessation of lend-lease to the Soviet Union, announced shortly after the end of the war in Europe, an order that he signed without reading it or thinking about it and which he was forced to change after furious protests from Moscow. Earlier he had broken the Senate tie on this issue, in favor of nonmilitary shipments.

During the vice presidency, Truman sought as best he could not to think of what lay ahead, although he knew full well. In a television series years later, entitled *Decision: The Conflicts of Harry S. Truman,* he said that: "It would have been very foolish not to realize that President Roosevelt was a very sick man. It became perfectly obvious to me that due to [his] health I would eventually inherit the presidency." When he saw FDR on March 19, "His eyes were sunken, his magnificent smile was missing from his careworn face. He seemed a spent man."

But as the weeks passed, the future seemed to extend itself and spring was in die air in the capital. One of Truman's ardent supporters (in part because of belief that Truman had to replace Wallace because of the president's ill health), the New Orleans builder of flat-bottomed landing craft, Andrew J. Higgins, had sent Truman his congratulations in November 1944 and ended on the note of "keep your good health." On April 4, 1945, Truman wrote Higgins: "I am just a figurehead now and don't have any hand in what takes place." Two days later he went from Washington to Buffalo and was accompanied by a single secret service agent.

What he did not know was that after the president came home from the Yalta Conference and made the speech to Congress sitting down in the well of the House chamber—the speech that seemed distressingly anecdotal, in which he mentioned his infirmity because of poliomyelitis—the president's immediate assistants were so concerned for Roosevelt's health that there was talk of a veritable regency. Anna Roosevelt took Jonathan Daniels aside—the

later Truman biographer was then a White House aide—and expressed her fears, not of the president's death but of his increasing incapacity. She hinted at a regency in which she and her husband John would hold what would be dynastic positions.

As he remembered, "I was to be a sort of front." Daniels was shocked. He did not think it would work. Important people such as Congress of Industrial Organizations leader Philip Murray would not be willing to come to the White House to speak with a regent; they would insist on seeing the president. Daniels was so taken aback by the very idea that when he made an oral history for the Harry S. Truman Library, he enjoined his interlocutor not to release this portion of his history until he, himself, was ready to release it—even though by that time eighteen years had elapsed since President Roosevelt had died.

An interesting aspect of Anna Roosevelt's tentative proposal of a regency was that it did not even consider a role for the vice president. It was an evidence of how low in esteem Truman was held in the Roosevelt White House.

The afternoon of April 12, 1945, seemed at first like every other afternoon in the Senate, for discussion concerned water power and irrigation. Senator William Langer of North Dakota was holding forth on that subject, with the vice president in the chair. Leverett Saltonstall of Massachusetts was almost the only other senator on the floor, and a page approached him with a pink slip in Truman's handwriting: "Governor, will you take this seat for a while? I want to see a soldier boy from home in my office." Saltonstall nodded and went down to sit on the dais. Truman said he would be gone no more than half an hour. Someone had placed an apple on his desk, and Saltonstall asked what he would do if he, the senator, ate the apple. The vice president said he would have to fine the senator. About an hour and a half later he returned, recessed the Senate, and walked over to the other side of the capitol for a drink with the Speaker of the House, Sam Rayburn, and some friends.

Then lightning struck in the form of a telephone message from Stephen T. Early from the White House. In a tight voice, he asked the vice president to come to the front entrance of the White House and go directly up to the family quarters on the second floor. There Mrs. Roosevelt rose to meet Truman, put her arm around his shoulder, and said gently: "The President is dead."

He asked Mrs. Roosevelt if there was anything he could do for her.

She asked the new president if there was anything they could do for him.

Truman's subsequent presidency of almost eight years, until January 20, 1953, was marked by partisanship, some of it caused by the fact that Truman himself was a partisan, accustomed to fight rather than negotiate. The times also were out of joint, as too many things were happening too quickly, and public opinion—and for that matter congressional opinion—could not always keep up.

The initial problem was to end the wars in Europe and Asia. The European war petered out after the suicide of Adolf Hitler, but ending the Japanese war seemed to require what Secretary of War Henry L. Stimson described as a shock. This was effected by nuclear bombs dropped on Hiroshima and Nagasaki.

Thereafter came reconversion, accompanied by labor strife and inflation. In 1945 and again in 1949 President Truman asked for expansion of the New Deal measures of his predecessor and with only a few exceptions, such as amendment of the Social Security Act, discovered that the country had turned conservative in domestic measures, unwilling to support further change until the 1960s and the presidential administration of Lyndon B. Johnson. Perhaps Truman's most notable domestic action was to stand up for the rights of black Americans in a way that his predecessor had not done and that looked forward to the Supreme Court decision of *Brown v. Board of Education of Topeka* (1954). During Truman's administration the armed forces were desegregated.

Perhaps his most notable domestic failure was to institute an internal security check on federal employees that not merely turned up almost no Communists but gave an excuse for extremists to abuse Americans' civil liberties under claim that they, the extremists, were protecting internal security.

In foreign policy, the Missouri president made a large contribution and in the Truman Doctrine (1947), Marshall Plan (1948), and North Atlantic Treaty (1949) turned the country away from the policy of isolation. Isolation had been championed by Presidents George Washington and Thomas Jefferson, embodied in the Monroe Doctrine, and confirmed in U.S. withdrawal from the political affairs of Europe after World War I. President Roosevelt told Premier Joseph Stalin at Yalta that U.S. troops would not remain in Europe. It was Truman who turned policy to what for the next half century would be a marked participation in the affairs of Europe and the world. This change was evident in his swift intervention in the Korean War in 1950.

After the presidency, Truman went back to the rambling Victorian house in Independence, from which he could see the skyscrapers of Kansas City ten miles to the west, and was active in writing his memoirs and raising money to build the Harry S. Truman Library on a knoll in a park a few blocks from his house. In his spare time, he made speeches around the country in support of Democratic candidates and causes. In 1964, his physical energy flagged. He was confined ever more to his house, where he died in 1972.

Underestimated during his presidency (in 1951 a Gallup popularity poll gave him a rating of 23 out of 100, one point below the rating of President Richard M. Nixon on the eve of his resignation), Truman's striking qualities came again to public attention in the early 1970s, at the time of the nation's defeat in the Vietnam War and President Nixon's increasing troubles and resignation. "Trumania" made its appearance; Truman's memory took on evidences of a cult, and popular enthusiasm for the Man of

Independence has continued to the present day. Scholarly appreciations have been less enthusiastic, although it is of interest that three biographies in 1992–95, one of which received the Pulitzer Prize and was a massive best-seller, all announced his greatness.

REFERENCES

Robert H. Ferrell, *Choosing Truman: The Democratic Convention of 1944* (Columbia: University of Missouri Press, 1994); R. H. Ferrell, *Harry S. Truman: A Life* (Columbia: University of Missouri Press, 1994); Alonzo Hamby, *Man of the People: The Life of Harry Truman* (New York: Oxford University Press 1995); Merle Miller, *Plain Speaking: An Oral Biography of Harry S. Truman* (New York: Berkley Publishing, 1974); David McCullough, *Truman* (New York: Simon and Schuster, 1992); Robert Dallek, *Harry S. Truman* (New York: Times Books, 2008); Roberta Barrows, Jonathan Daniels, Edward D. McKim, and Harry H. Vaughan oral histories, Harry S. Truman Library, Independence, Mo.

ROBERT H. FERRELL is professor emeritus of history at Indiana University in Bloomington. He is the author of books on U.S. foreign policy and author or editor of many books on President Truman.

ALBEN W. BARKLEY (1877–1956)

Vice President, 1949–1953

(President Harry S. Truman)

ALBEN W. BARKLEY
(Library of Congress)

By James K. Libbey

Barkley was a progressive politician and a partisan Democrat who became one of the "working" vice presidents in American history. It was during his term that the Heraldic Branch of the United States Army designed a special seal and flag for the Office of the Vice President.

Willie Alben Barkley was born near the village of Lowes, Kentucky, on November 24, 1877. His parents, John Wilson and Electra Eliza Barkley, immersed the child in the sanctity of family designations by christening him not only with the name of John's father, Alben, but also for good measure with "Willie" to honor uncles on both sides of the family. The first name, however, was favored by neither father nor mother who grew into the habit of calling their firstborn by his middle name, especially after Grandfather Alben died in 1880. Moreover, their son came to dislike his christened name and later changed it to Alben William Barkley.

Whether Willie or Alben, the son's name was not as important to the child as the nearly primitive environment and subsistence existence that surrounded his early years. Barkley was born in a log cabin. Sometimes half-jokingly and yet half-seriously, he would ponder the rustic birthright that had been a stepping stone into the White House for several of America's illustrious presidents. Such rustic circumstances, though, were not due to the family's existence on the wild frontier. John Barkley was an impoverished tenant farmer who specialized in raising dark tobacco, the sugary leaf used for chewing instead of smoking.

Without benefit of modern impediments to nature's course, the harsh but loving life shared by John and his wife produced like clockwork a succession of seven siblings for Alben. While children and their labor can be a blessing for a farm owner, the biennial appearance of a new mouth to feed spelled financial disaster for the tenant farmer. Almost frenetically, the Barkleys moved from one rented farm to another at least six times between 1877 and 1891 in John's efforts to provide for his family. Thus Alben was raised in an impecunious household whose members bordered daily on achieving the in-distinction of being described as indigent.

Alben probably did not realize that he was poor until a family shopping trip to Mayfield when he was twelve revealed that store clerks wore Sunday suits during the week. He had, though, little time to contemplate his humble surroundings. From an early age he had to accept his share of work. As the Barkley family grew larger and Alben grew older, he began to assist his father on the farm, to help his mother with household chores, and to watch over his younger brothers and sisters. The interludes between sessions in country schools were filled with chopping wood, splitting rails, digging out stumps, setting tobacco, plowing fields, and dozens of other backbreaking tasks. All this work at an early age helped build a strong young man with a physical constitution that gave Alben enough durability to enjoy a long life in robust health.

At least twice in their early years together, the Barkleys had to draw deep from the wellspring of neighbors' good graces when their home was destroyed or damaged, first by fire and then by tornado. Spontaneously, friends gathered clothes and furniture and lent their labor to help the beleaguered family rebuild their home. As a result, the Barkleys never locked their smokehouse door; and if neighbors wanted to borrow tools, utensils, or food, they always received a welcome greeting. Certainly, this general lesson in reciprocity, so fundamental to the covenant of humanity in rural America and so basic to human relations, was driven home to the oldest Barkley child.

A primeval equality emerged from this hard rural life, reinforced in part by the old English custom of calling out each year all males regardless of race and fortune to improve county roads. These positive values were strengthened in Alben Barkley by a happy but strict upbringing by religious parents. His father held the position of elder in the Presbyterian church of Lowes, and his mother refused to light the stove on Sundays unless the pastor joined them for dinner. Liquor and playing cards never entered the home, and without radio, television, CD players, and other electronic gadgets that often promiscuously fill the modern mind, conversation absorbed the Barkleys' evening hours, and Alben Barkley became an apt student of the art.

In 1891, John Barkley made a decision of great importance to Alben's future. 'With the help of friends and neighbors, the family packed three wagons, tied their Jersey cow to one, and moved twenty-five miles southwest from Lowes to Clinton, the Hickman County seat. The nearby Mississippi River and the town's two colleges combined to provide Alben with a cultural atmosphere far in excess of anything he had experienced in Lowes. The move little helped the family fortunes, for John, expert in tobacco, found meager success in raising corn.

Despite John's failure to improve the family's status through farming, Alben was able to fulfill his youthful desire for a college education. Shortly after the family had settled into the new home, Alben enrolled in Marvin College.

Alben never graduated from high school, but then, to describe Marvin as a "college" in modern terms would be as impossible as equating Alben's country education with the rigid K–12 grades so familiar to us today. Marvin, a Methodist school no longer in existence, accepted adolescents and trained them for adulthood. A single building housed most of its activities, and years later Alben could remember the names and count the numbers of his class of 1897 on a single hand. In this personal atmosphere, Alben's fine mind, which had been stimulated mainly by the raw frontier-like life of Lowes, grew with the knowledge and civilizing influences of tradition and the humanities. He would also become a lifelong Methodist,

He could attend Marvin only because of the kind patronage of President J.C. Speight, who provided the youth with a job as janitor. Five years later Barkley graduated, earning a Bachelor of Arts degree and a medal for oratory. Because Marvin functioned as a preparatory institute, his BA represented something between a high school diploma and a college degree. Regardless, his study of classical rhetoric and debates over current issues sharpened his interest in law and politics, an interest heightened by the success of his mentor, Speight, in winning a seat to the Kentucky State Senate in 1896.

Understandably, then, Barkley wanted to continue his education. He borrowed money, moved to Atlanta, Georgia, and enrolled as a sophomore in Emory College (now a university), a Methodist school closely connected with Marvin. Barkley spent the 1897–98 academic year in Georgia studying the classics and making speeches as a member of Emory's Few Debating Society His poverty, though, forced him to return to Clinton and to accept a teaching position in the intermediate department of Marvin College. It was an unwise decision: the college struggled to pay its faculty and Barkley floundered as a teacher. In the midst of a disastrous term, his father abandoned the hazards of a farm for the security of a paycheck by moving his family to Paducah and accepting employment at a cordage mill. Forced to rent a room and buy his meals and uncertain about his college pay and teaching abilities, Barkley resigned from Marvin in December 1898 and joined his parents in Paducah, the city that later became synonymous with his name.

Barkley abandoned his dream of earning a law degree. Instead, he took the self-study route available at the time. He prevailed upon Charles K. Wheeler, Democratic representative for Kentucky's First Congressional District, to give him access to the attorney's library. In the summer of 1899, barristers William S. Bishop and John K. Hendrick hired Barkley as their law clerk. After two years of reading and working in the law, he passed the bar exam and opened his own office in 1901. Moreover, he received an appointment from Hendrick's friend, Judge L.D. Husbands, to serve as court reporter for the circuit court. The steady income subsidized Barkley's law practice and enabled him to pay off his college debts. Sensitive to his shortcomings in formal education, Barkley also saved money to attend, in 1902, a two-month law course at the University of Virginia. He listened to fifty lectures by leading experts and gained confidence in the law. As important, he used his leisure time to tour the campus and read about its architect, Thomas Jefferson. These readings left an indelible mark on his character. Then and thereafter he tended to measure people and politics against the Jeffersonian ideal of the common man.

Meanwhile, Barkley entered Paducah's social milieu with an enthusiasm that bordered on frenzy. One explanation for his behavior is that he had to overcome his outsider status by building those contacts that other lawyers, native to Paducah, acquired as their birthright. He joined the Broadway Methodist Episcopal Church, attended dances and socials, and sought membership in every local organization in sight. Each club not only acquired an energetic member but also a talented speaker. His rich baritone voice could be heard mellifluously preaching a lay sermon on Sunday from behind a Methodist pulpit or gleefully telling an anecdote on Monday before a sportsmen's group. Besides making a name for himself, Barkley's activities brought another benefit. He met and courted Dorothy Brower of Paducah and Tiptonville, Tennessee. Married on June 23, 1903, in Tiptonville, their shared lives produced three children: David Murrell (1906), Marian Frances (1909), and Laura Louise (1911).

A year after his marriage, Barkley chose to enter the Democratic primary for county attorney. Simple ambition accounts for his decision; nevertheless, the campaign he waged is interesting because he demonstrated a style and pattern that served him well in most elections between then and 1954. First, he announced his candidacy in December 1904, well in advance of the March primary. Similar to most later contests, the primary rather than the general election was the key to gaining office in the heavily Democratic region. Second, Barkley's campaign hinged on his performance and often on his resources. Generally, the organization and leadership of his campaigns emerged solely at the time and place of his physical presence. Third, and for the humble post of county attorney, he overwhelmed the voters with personal appearances. Indeed, the energy and drive he displayed became his hallmark. Fourth, Barkley's gregarious nature fused with another quality he long possessed: a supreme ability to make speeches and engage opponents in debates. Finally, he won the 1905 election because of his rural background and his kinship with farmers, who showered him with their votes.

Barkley prosecuted approximately 300 individuals who transgressed the law and saved taxpayers thousands of dollars by challenging padded contracts and inflated claims against the county government. His diligent work and speaking abilities earned him a statewide reputation. In 1907, the Democratic State Central Committee invited him to serve on the Speak-

ers' Bureau, and the State Association of County Attorneys elected him to the post of president. Barkley's rising star contrasted sharply with the sour image of the scandal-ridden Democratic courthouse clique. Not surprisingly, the local Democratic Club looked to Barkley to save the party by tapping him as the Democratic nominee for county judge. The 1909 election turned out to be the most vicious campaign in Barkley's career. His victory, in an unusual year when Republicans captured a majority of seats on the fiscal court, marked Barkley as a formidable political force.

Judge Barkley repaid his most loyal constituents—farmers—by nearly bankrupting McCracken County in order to widen and gravel each county road. Road building, in fact, became the prime feature of his administration. But he also inaugurated a number of progressive measures, such as appointing a purchasing agent and auditing county books, that served as benchmarks of integrity for later officeholders. In the midst of a vigorous term, Barkley told the press late in 1911 that he planned to be a candidate for First District representative to the U.S. Congress. The abrupt move can only be understood by the fact that Barkley had decided early in public life to make Congress a milestone if not a capstone to his political career. Ollie James precipitated the judge's plans when the incumbent congressman revealed his intention to seek a seat in the U.S. Senate. Once again, the Democratic primary proved crucial, as Barkley faced three strong contenders, including his former employer, Hendrick.

Barkley quickly plucked for himself two issues most dear to the hearts of farmers: lowering the tariff and lowering the boom on railroads through stricter regulation by the Interstate Commerce Commission. Moreover, he advocated federal support for highway construction. His opponents chided the judge for his liberal views and maligned him with die socialist tag. Midway through the 1912 campaign, however, Democrats at the Baltimore national convention selected Woodrow Wilson as the party's presidential nominee and adopted a progressive platform that bolstered Barkley's position. Adroitly, he converted the socialist label into party regularity. With the support of First District farmers, Barkley garnered nearly half the votes in the four-way primary and easily won the general election. He would be reelected six times to the U.S. House of Representatives and serve on the important Interstate and Foreign Commerce Committee.

Barkley's early years in Congress further shaped the political views he would hold in his maturity. He admired President Wilson and found that they shared a number of similarities, including a regional heritage and a strong belief in party. By the same token, Wilson went out of his way to cultivate the favor of Barkley and other lawmakers elected for the first time under the Wilson ticket. It was easy, then, for Barkley to enlist in Wilson's New Freedom program, which tried to restore economic competition by sweeping away special privileges. He strongly supported, among many others, the Clayton Antitrust Act of 1914, but once Barkley accepted the idea that federal power should be used to break up monopoly, he pragmatically moved beyond the New Freedom to seek governmental solutions to a variety of social problems. Thus by 1916 he spoke in favor of legislation restricting the use of child labor in interstate commerce and coauthored a bill to ban the sale of liquor in the District of Columbia.

The Shepard-Barkley Act laid the foundation for future prohibition measures. While the experiment in abstinence eventually turned sour and had to be abandoned, the issue put Barkley in the national limelight and in the forefront of the Progressive movement. Colleagues in Congress, from Maine to Missouri, asked him to spark their campaigns with his wit. Because his own reelection was generally assured after the primary, he could afford to spend most electoral seasons from 1916 to 1922 giving hundreds of talks for fellow Democrats and gaining credit as a party stalwart. Coupled with his solid base of support in western Kentucky, Barkley's brush with national prominence subtly colored his own ambition.

On November 11, 1922, he declared his candidacy for the 1923 gubernatorial race in Kentucky.

The single four-year term provided in the state constitution tends to make the governorship either a launching pad for higher office or a rewarding honor to a lengthy political career. Because Barkley had no thought of retiring, most commentators argue that the 1923 canvass merely set the stage for his quest for a seat in the U.S. Senate. Regardless, he conducted a spirited campaign and exhibited such stamina that journalists labeled him the Iron Man. Understandably, Iron Man Barkley advocated the immediate completion of Kentucky's highway network as well as substantial improvements for public education, but he also attacked coal-mining and horse-racing interests by suggesting higher taxes on coal and a ban on pari-mutuel betting. While he narrowly lost the primary, his behavior during and after the campaign gained the plaudits of most Commonwealth Democrats and strengthened his hand for the future. When Barkley announced for the Senate in 1926, no Democrat opposed him in the primary, and even the coal and racing lobbies quietly supported his bid, if only to prevent the reformer from running for governor in 1927.

Barkley unseated Republican incumbent Richard P. Ernst in the general election and, after fourteen years in the House, moved to the Senate in 1927. Assigned to the Library, Finance, and Banking and Currency committees and later to the Interstate Commerce Committee, he possessed a status far beyond his official position as a newly elected junior senator. As early as 1928, Democrats seriously considered Barkley for the second spot on the presidential ticket, and by 1932 he was selected temporary chairman and keynote speaker for the Democratic national convention. The intervening years witnessed the onslaught of the Great Depression. Barkley's background, experience, and progressive lineage enabled him to assume a major role as a national spokesman and political leader during the dramatic and eventful years of the several administrations of President Franklin D. Roosevelt.

The Wilsonian liberal became an apostle of the New Deal, a term more synonymous with Barkley than with any other figure of the 1930s except Roosevelt himself Barkley assisted Senate Majority Leader Joseph T. Robinson in debating measures, effecting compromises, and securing votes for a host of New Deal bills. So identified did Barkley become with FDR's program that he often served as its defender on national radio. Moreover, Roosevelt picked this loyal lieutenant for the unique role of delivering the second consecutive keynote address before the party's convention of 1936, and, when Robinson died in July 1937, FDR urged Democratic senators to elect Barkley as Robinson's successor. The new Senate majority leader faced an early and major defeat in managing FDR's court-packing plan. Nevertheless, his accomplishments far outweighed his failures, and Barkley impressed his contemporaries by his mastery of legislative detail and his skill in the art of persuasion.

These skills received their greatest test during World War II. FDR's focus on foreign affairs left to Barkley extraordinary powers over domestic issues. The senator generally cooperated with the president, but he also felt compelled to preserve those internal interests of the nation's people that Roosevelt neglected because of external events. Barkley, then, slipped uneasily between roles as the administration's cheerleader and watchdog. He attacked, for example, the War Production Board for its habit of assigning military contracts to large rather than small businesses, and in February 1944 when FDR turned down as too little a tax bill, Barkley engineered a stinging rebuke to presidential power by successfully leading the fight to override FDR's veto. Barkley resigned his majority leader post, but his Democratic colleagues immediately reelected him. The whole affair established a precedent for autonomy not found among earlier congressional leaders.

The episode may have also profoundly affected contemporary events, for it kept Bark-ley from becoming president when FDR died on April 12, 1945. In [944, Roosevelt changed vice presidents, picking Harry S. Truman to be his running mate. Political analysts admit that the February incident cost Barkley the chance of having his name, rather than Truman's, in the second spot on the Democratic ticket. Regardless, the seemingly indestructible Barkley endured after FDR's death as the statesman of American politics and as "Mr. Democrat" for his party. Although Barkley suffered the loss of his wife Dorothy to heart disease in 1947, he achieved new heights of popularity in the postwar years. He received awards for distinguished congressional service, ranked ahead of President Truman as the most requested of the Democratic Speakers' Bureau, and vied with war hero General Dwight D. Eisenhower as the most "fascinating American," according to *Look* magazine.

Small wonder that in 1948, when Democrats seemed to be on the ropes and awaiting the knockout punch, Truman asked the popular Kentuckian to serve again as keynote speaker for the party's convention. Barkley's rousing defense of New Deal liberalism so stirred the delegates that Truman felt compelled to name the senator as his running mate. It was a decision the president would not regret. In fact, the pair proved to be a dynamic team. While Truman mercilessly assaulted the nation by train, Barkley audaciously captured the attention of the electorate by his novel use of the airplane. He flew 150,000 miles and delivered 250 speeches, providing an awesome display of vocal and physical powers. When the November tally was complete, Truman and Barkley had fashioned a major upset.

On January 20, 1949, Barkley stopped being a senator when fellow Kentuckian and Supreme Court Associate Justice Stanley F. Reed administered the oath of office that converted Barkley into the nation's thirty-fifth vice president. He was proud of the honor bestowed on him by his party's nomination and the people's votes, though he never made a fuss over the additional distinction that he was also the oldest man to enter into these duties. However, coping with obscurity, not age, had been the prerequisite of office before Barkley walked onto the stage. In fact, one of Barkley's more famous but unoriginal anecdotes—removed from his repertoire after he became vice president—told to a friend shortly before the 1948 convention stated: "There once was a farmer who had two sons. Both boys showed great promise early in life. But the elder son went to sea and the younger son was elected Vice President and neither has been heard from since."

Barkley and many of his contemporaries had good reason to stop joking about the vice presidency after he took the oath of office. Not only did the Kentuckian bring stature to the position, but the course of the president's life reminded the voters that Truman was the third vice president to move up to the White House in the first forty-five years of the twentieth century. Over the years, the vice president had become more than just the Senate's presiding officer and tiebreaker and the president's replacement in time of tragedy. The office permitted its occupant to appoint a few Senate committees, sign congressional resolutions, select five candidates each for the Naval Academy and West Point, and represent the government on the Smithsonian Institution's Board of Regents.

Truman wanted Barkley's legislative experience made available to the entire executive branch of government and so insisted on Barkley's presence for each cabinet-level meeting. Also, 'when a congressional bill created the National Security Council, that important policy-making body included the vice president. Finally, Barkley's national fame and speaking abilities prompted the administration to use the vice president as its principal spokesman. One reporter calculated that in the first eight months of 1949, Barkley traveled across the country to deliver forty major addresses in support of the president's positions. This constant visibility in the national limelight turned Barkley's joke about the vice presidency on its ear.

Recognizing that Barkley brought extraordinary qualities to his post, President Truman ordered the Heraldic Branch of the U.S. Army to design a special seal and flag for the Office of the Vice President. These prestigious symbols, however, were not nearly so endearing as the tide Barkley and his family gave to the office. One evening in the spring of 1949 he spent a quiet time with daughter Marian and grandson Stephen Truitt. The conversation turned to the awkward address, *Mr. Vice President,* that people used when they met Barkley. Ten-year-old Stephen thought *Gramps* should insert two *e*'s between the initials *V.P.* to form *Veep*. At his next news conference the proud grandfather told this story and the reporters picked up and began to employ the title *Veep* when they wrote articles about the vice president. Unlike the symbols of office created by the Heraldic Branch, Barkley did not pass this label on to his successors. The Veep became a special sign for Barkley alone and one that would be used with affection than and thereafter.

As if Barkley had not broken enough new ground to alter permanently the importance and style of the vice presidency, he added another first. On July 8, 1949, he attended a party given by the Clark Cliffords on board the White House yacht *Margy.* One of the guests, Jane Rucker Hadley, caught the attentions and later the affections of the Veep. Mrs. Hadley—vivacious, attractive, and charming—was the middle-aged widow of a St. Louis attorney and secretary for the Wabash Railroad. She had come to Washington for a brief vacation with her close friends, the Cliffords. The moonlit night and the strains of "Some Enchanted Evening" struck a romantic chord in die hearts of Jane and the Veep. Although Jane returned to St. Louis, Barkley's affinity for planes allowed him to woo her in a cross-country romance that every American faithfully followed in the daily press. This whirlwind courtship ended on November 18, 1949, when Alben and Jane shared marriage vows in a simple ceremony before close friends and relatives. Thus Barkley was the first vice president to wed while he held that office.

Not all the accomplishments and activities Barkley undertook as vice president acquired the sympathetic interest of the nation. In his traditional and constitutional function as the Senate's presiding officer, the Veep more than once engaged in controversies that mirrored beliefs and principles he had long held and also shared with the administration. The most publicly disputed act Barkley performed occurred in March 1949. He ruled on a motion to end a ten-day filibuster conducted by southern senators who opposed a civil rights bill then being considered. Technically the motion, not the legislation, caused a bitter debate, and both sides had quoted Barkley extensively to buttress their views. The Veep's decision on the motion placed him squarely on the side of those legislators who strove to implement civil rights, but before he presented his emotion-packed ruling he led off with an anecdot& "The Chair" Barkley said "feels somewhat like the man who was being ridden out of town on a rail. Someone asked him how he liked it. He said if it weren't for the honor of the thing, he would just as soon walk."

Barkley's peers marked his ruling as scurrilous or statesmanlike depending on their position, but few senators could sustain any genuine hatred for a man who so deftly encapsulated a potentially distasteful ruling in a syrup of digestible humor. Fortunately for the Veep's emotional stability, most of his chores in the Senate could be quietly performed or tactfully and wittily fulfilled without arousing the rancor that occurred over the civil rights motion. Congress responded to Barkley's masterful charm by awarding him a special gold medallion for his service, and on March 1, 1951, the thirty-eighth anniversary of his first year in Congress, President Truman made a surprise visit to the Senate chamber to honor the Veep. Truman carried a special gavel for the Senate's president, a gavel fashioned from the ancient timbers of the renovated White House.

Despite his unique role, executive knowledge, and high visibility, Barkley's age (seventy-four) prevented his dark-horse candidacy for president from reaching the finish line during the 1952 convention. January 1953 found Barkley unemployed and without political office for the first time in nearly a half-century. After a brief stint with his own national television show "Meet the Veep," Barkley and his bride retired to their Angles estate in Paducah, where he wrote his memoirs with the assistance of journalist Sidney Shalett. Retirement, however, did not suit Barkley, and, perhaps to redress the "too old" label that had ended his 1952 candidacy for president, he entered the 1954 Senate race, defeating Republican incumbent John Sherman Cooper by 80,000 votes. Barkley relished his return to Congress as a freshman legislator, though his colleagues honored him with an appointment to the prestigious Senate Foreign Relations Committee. He also remained a popular, much sought after speaker. Thus on April 30, 1956, he traveled to Lexington, Virginia, to give a keynote speech before a mock convention conducted by students at Washington and Lee University. At the conclusion of his address, he suffered a fatal heart attack, dying as he had lived, in the public arena. He was buried in Paducah.

REFERENCES

James K. Libbey, *Dear Alben: Mr. Barkley of Kentucky* (Lexington: University Press of Kentucky, 1979); Alben W. Barkley Papers, King Library, University of Kentucky, Lexington; Alben W. Barkley, *That Reminds Me* (Garden City, N.Y.: Doubleday, 1954); Jane R. Barkley, *I Married the Veep* (New York: Vanguard, 1958); Polly Ann Davis, "Alben W. Barkley: Senate Majority Leader and Vice President" (Ph.D. diss., University of Kentucky, 1963); Gerald S. Grinde, "The Early Political Career of Alben W. Barkley, 1877–1937" (Ph.D. diss., University of Illinois, 1976); Charles A. Leistner, "The Political Campaign Speaking of Alben W. Barkley" (Ph.D. diss., University of Missouri, 1958); William Ray Mofield, "The Speaking Role of Alben Barkley in the Campaign of 1948" (Ph.D. diss., Southern Illinois University, 1964); William O. Reichert, "The Political and Social Thought of Alben W. Barkley" (M.A. thesis, University of Kentucky, 1950); Jack R. Yakey, "Prelude to Defeat: Alben Barkley's Quest for the 1952 Democratic Presidential Nomination" (M.A. thesis, Central Missouri State University, 1973).

JAMES K. LIBBEY is a former administrator at Eastern Kentucky University in Richmond, Kentucky, and was professor of social sciences at Embry-Riddle Aeronautical University. He is the author of more than a hundred historical publications, including a book and seven articles on Alben W. Barkley.

RICHARD MILHOUS NIXON (1913–1994)

Vice President, 1953–1961

(President Dwight Eisenhower)

RICHARD M. NIXON
*(By permission of the Richard Nixon
Library & Birthplace)*

By Joan Hoff

Richard Milhous Nixon, born in Yorba Linda California, on January 9, 1913, became the thirty-seventh president of the United States in 1969. On August 9, 1974, as a result of the Watergate affair, he resigned during his second term, becoming the only president in the country's history to leave office in this manner. Before this unprecedented event, however, he had served eight relatively uneventful years as vice president under Dwight D. Eisenhower.

The Irish ancestors of both his mother and his father dated back to the colonial period, and each grew up in the Midwest before migrating to California. Although Frank Nixon became a Quaker upon marrying Hannah Milhous in 1908, Nixon commented in his *Memoirs* (1978) that the type of Quakerism his family practiced-first in Yorba Linda and then in Whittier—resembled the Protestant churches in the area rather than the stricter version the Milhous family had known in Butlerville, Indiana. Nixon's novelist cousin Jessamyn West was more explicit in a 1976 interview with Fawn Brodie, saying: "[There was] no difference between preachers in the Yorba Linda Quaker church and hard shell Baptists. . . . [They were] very evangelical. . . . and rambunctious, singing, crying, going up [to the] front [of the church]." West hastened to add, however, that the Nixons did not personally participate in this unorthodox Quaker display of emotions, although she herself had once become a "born-again."

Because his father was neither a particularly good nor a lucky businessman, Nixon grew up as many boys of his generation did, poor but by no means impoverished. Although he was imbued with a 1920s ethos that combined hard work with the dream of unlimited opportunity, his father was only a marginally successful grocer. As a result, Nixon grew up realizing how difficult it was to make a living and acutely sensitive about preserving his own good name financially. (This is one of the reasons he defended himself in his 1952 "Checkers" speech so emotionally against charges of setting up a slush fund and why he went to great lengths at the height of Watergate to point out repeatedly that he and his aides had not profited financially from the affair.) "The problems you have during the time you are growing up as a member of a working family," Nixon later told an early biographer, "are the ones that stay with you all of your life."

A good student because he applied himself, Nixon excelled scholastically at both Whither High School and College. His special talent turned out not to be football but debating, although he doggedly tried to make "first string" on his high school and college football teams. Interestingly, these interests helped him develop skills he later used as a politician: perseverance and rhetorical attack. They also reinforced his combative, aggressive personality and came to be both respected and resented in the course of his long political career.

After earning a scholarship to Duke Law School in 1934, Nixon worked even harder in law school, graduating third in his class. However, he did not obtain the hoped-for offer from a prestigious law firm upon graduation, so be returned to Whittier, where he practiced law from 1937 until 1942. Perhaps his meeting, courtship, and marriage to Thelma Catherine (Pat) Ryan between 1938 and 1940 constituted the most memorable episodes in Nixon's life prior to his entering politics in 1946.

World War II found the newlyweds in Washington, D.C., where Nixon worked in the tire-rationing section of the Office of Price Administration (OPA). Quickly disillusioned with the red tape of government bureaucracy, Nixon obtained a commission and served in the South Pacific between 1942 and 1946, rising to the rank of lieutenant commander. There was nothing particularly distinguished about either his civilian or military career during these years, and those 'who knew him best did not perceive any overt political ambition.

Like most American politicians since 1945, Nixon's views on government and domestic, as well as foreign, policies appear more influenced by his adult experiences beginning first with the Great Depression and then with World War II than with any unresolved childhood psychological crises or ideological influences that he may have experienced as a young man while going to school or establishing himself as a lawyer.

In contrast to his rather nondescript background, Nixon's political career prior to assuming the presidency proved as controversial as it was meteoric. Elected to the Eightieth Congress in 1946 at the age of thirty-three, he served two terms and then ran successfully in 1950 for the California seat in the U.S. Senate. By 1952, he was elected vice president of the United States at thirty-nine and only narrowly missed being elected president in 1960 when forty-seven. Eight years later, Nixon won the presidency in an almost equally close contest.

Nixon's twenty-three years as a politician before becoming president were peppered with controversy beginning in 1946 when he defeated the five-term liberal Democratic

Congressman Jerry Voorhis, and later in 1950 when he defeated the equally liberal Democrat Helen Gahagan Douglas for a Senate seat. In both campaigns, Nixon charged his opponents with having left-wing political views. In retrospect, however, the latest biographies of Nixon either strongly imply or actually conclude that because of the increasing postwar conservatism, he probably would have defeated Voorhis and Douglas without any Red-baiting.

Before becoming a Senator in 1950, as a freshman House of Representatives member of the House Committee on Un-American Activities (HUAC), Nixon initiated the successful attempt to end the diplomatic and governmental career of Alger Hiss by exposing his connections with the Communist Party in the 1930s. Nixon achieved national prominence during the course of this investigation of the relationship between self-confessed member of a communist spy ring Whittaker Chambers and Hiss who was convicted of perjury on January 21, 1950, after Nixon had been elected to the Senate.

Later studies of the Hiss case concluded that he was guilty of perjury as charged, and documents released from Russian archives in the 1990s indicated that Hiss, indeed, bad passed documents to the USSR. At the time, liberals never forgave Nixon for stumbling onto the "pumpkin papers" (five rolls of microfilm that contained photographs of secret State Department documents hidden in Chambers's pumpkin patch) and then using them to promote his own career in the early years of the cold war.

Advisers to Dwight Eisenhower recommended that Nixon become the general's running mate in 1952, in part because of his well-publicized anticommunist activities. But, as Herbert Brownell later said, Nixon was also chosen because "he was young, geographically right [being from California], had experience both in the House and the Senate with a good voting record and was an excellent speaker." Moreover, he was a team player, had expert knowledge of domestic politics, and among Republicans had become a popular critic of Truman and Democrats. Nixon viewed his own role on the ticket as that of peacemaker between the Eisenhower and Robert Taft factions in the Republican Party that had developed before the convention when the two men vied with each other for the presidential nomination.

Within two months after accepting the nomination, however, Nixon faced a charge published on September 18 that he had created a private slush fund of slightly more than $18,000 from rich southern Californians. Nixon acknowledged the existence of such a fund, saying that he was actually saving the taxpayers money by using private donations to pay for political expenses in excess of the amounts allowable by law to a senator. After the *Washington Post* and New York *Herald Tribune* called for his resignation from the ticket and when a few of Eisenhower's advisers began to wonder if he should, Nixon decided to go on nationwide television on September 23, 1952, to defend himself.

In this broadcast, he presented embarrassingly detailed information about his family's finances, including the fact that his wife Pat did not own a fur coat like so many Democratic politicians' wives but only "a respectable Republican cloth coat." This speech is probably best remembered, however, because of his maudlin declaration that his children would keep a dog named Checkers, even though the cocker spaniel had been a political gift.

The mere hint at financial wrongdoing threatened Nixon's sense of working-class integrity, and so he felt impelled to defend the fund with an emotional and very personal financial narrative. His performance in this broadcast also demonstrated his by then famous ability to attack opponents by innuendo. In this instance, he drew upon statements he had already made on the West Coast about his wife's cloth coat compared to the mink ones worn by wealthy Democrats, the fact that Democratic vice presidential candidate John Sparkman had placed his wife on the federal payroll, and that Adali Stevenson also had such a fund. For good measure and in typically overkill fashion, he also implied that he was being unfairly charged because of his role in the Hiss case and reiterated the Republican campaign slogan of corruption, communism, and Korea.

This speech has been so satirized and condemned by Nixon haters from 1952 down to the present that it is often forgotten that it marked Nixon's debut as a successful television personality. Denounced for its emotionalism, its illogical assertions, and its implicit attacks on Democrats, much of what Nixon said he had already previewed during the campaign on live audiences with good results. Its success among Republicans at large sealed its fate among his opponents as the worst political speech in history. Some have even maintained that the memory of it contributed to his defeat in 1960 and that dislike for Nixon among left-of-center intellectuals stemmed as much from the "Checkers" talk as from his early campaigns against Voorhis and Douglas, and his role in the Hiss case.

One thing is sure: when seen today in its uncut version, it still makes for powerful television and shows Nixon at his debating best— looking directly into the camera and delivering an effective, engaging, and emotional speech. Not until John Kennedy made similar use of television in 1960 did Democratic liberals think such performances could be respectable. Today personal testimonials by politicians about their private lives have become so commonplace that few question their authenticity or effectiveness. Nixon successfully defended himself in this famous Checkers speech, forcing Eisenhower to keep him on the Republican ticket as vice president.

Except for the anticommunist hysteria known as McCarthyism, the 1950s were relatively quiet domestic years for the country, as well as for Nixon politically, despite the fact that he later placed five of his *Six Crises* (1962) in that decade. Of these, probably only one was—the 1952 charge about a slush fund. Fol-

lowing the guilty verdict in the Hiss case, Nixon did not take much advantage of McCarthyism (a term meaning charging people indiscriminately and without substantiation of being communists) in the first half of the 1950s.

Despite his early Red-baiting campaigns in California and the Hiss affair, it became clear that Nixon simply did not make the single-minded pursuit of domestic communists *the* major goal of his public life. He was too much of a political pragmatist and centrist to place all his eggs in one basket.

Although he found Joseph McCarthy "personally likable," he recognized that his extremism was "leading him and others to destruction." Instead, he "kept some distance between himself and McCarthy" as McCarthyism emerged in the early 1950s and Eisenhower used Nixon "to put . . . out brushfires started by McCarthy" because as vice president he had credibility on both sides of the issue. Despite numerous private meetings with McCarthy at the president's request, in which he attempted to modify or redirect the subcommittee's activities, by 1954 Nixon could not tolerate the direct attacks on the administration of the Senate's Permanent Investigations Subcommittee (known as the McCarthy Committee) hearings of alleged spying at the army base at Fort Monmouth, Wisconsin. As president of the Senate, Nixon appointed the select committee that ultimately voted to censure McCarthy on December 2, 1954.

During his first term as vice president, Nixon concentrated on becoming an expert on international affairs, making many trips abroad and becoming acquainted with leading heads of state. The first, in 1953, lasted sixty-nine days, during which Nixon visited nations in Asia and the Middle East. He later said in his memoirs that the trip had been highly educational and convinced him that "foreign policy was a field in which [he] had great interest and at least some ability."

While Nixon was vice president, the Eisenhower administration faced several serious foreign policy crises. The first occurred in spring 1954 when the French were defeated and overrun at their military outpost in Vietnam called Dien Bien Phu. Despite the fact that the United States had heavily financed the French occupation of Vietnam since World War II, Eisenhower decided—against the advice of Nixon, Secretary of State John Foster Dulles, and Admiral Arthur Radford of the Joint Chiefs of Staff—not to bomb or commit U.S. troops there once the French withdrew. Thus, Nixon's first attempt to influence foreign policy as vice president failed. Although the United States did not sign the 1954 Geneva Accords dividing Vietnam into North and South, it promised not to oppose the settlement by force. Nonetheless, in the same year the United States took the lead in setting up the Southeast Asia Treaty Organization (SEATO), pledged to the defense of South Vietnam. In 1956, the Eisenhower administration refused to honor nationwide elections in Vietnam because it was clear that the South under Ngo Dinh Diem would lose. In July, Nixon made a thirteen-day trip to the Far East, visiting South Vietnam on the second anniversary of Diem as president, thus giving him the approval of the administration.

In October, during the 1956 presidential campaign, two foreign policy crises occurred almost simultaneously: the popular rebellions in Poland and the Hungary and the Israeli invasion of Egypt over control of the Suez Canal. Nixon quickly made headlines by calling Nikita Khrushchev the Butcher of Budapest. The United States did nothing to aid the uprisings after rhetorically encouraging such actions in Eastern Europe. In his memoirs, Nixon said that he thought Eisenhower and Dulles were wrong in pressuring Britain, France, and Israel (with the concurrence of the USSR) into withdrawing their forces from the Suez because it meant that "from this time forward the United States should by necessity be forced to 'go it alone' in the foreign policy leadership of the free world." Thus, as vice president, he once again failed to affect foreign policy under the Eisenhower administration.

Part of the problem was, as Nixon himself said in a July 1958 interview in *Saturday Evening Post,* as vice president under Eisenhower he was more willing to take risks than the president: "I am not necessarily a respecter of the *status quo* in foreign affairs. I am a *chance taker* in foreign affairs. I would take chances for peace." However, he approved of allowing the CIA to help overthrow the national government of Iran in 1953, of sending marines into Lebanon in 1958, and of organizing indigenous military units to invade both Guatemala and Cuba.

The election year of 1956 proved difficult for Nixon not only because of foreign policy crises not resolved to his satisfaction, but also because his place on the ticket as vice president was once again challenged. This time it was by Harold Stassen, who in the summer of 1956 was at the height of his prominence as Eisenhower's "Secretary of Peace" and cabinet-level adviser because of his conduct of Geneva "Open Skies" disarmament talks with the Soviets. In July, Stassen apparently told the president that a private poll showed that Nixon would lose the Republicans more votes (4 to 6 percent of the electorate) than other possible running mates, such as Governor Christian Herter of Massachusetts.

At the beginning of the year Eisenhower had announced he would run again but refused to announce his choice for vice president. In fact he offered Nixon a cabinet post, excepting State and Justice, saying that he needed administrative experience if he wanted to run for president in 1960. When Nixon responded that he would be happy to serve again, Eisenhower did not respond negatively. Stassen announced in July that he would support Herter for vice president. Nixon immediately obtained the endorsement of 180 of 203 Republican members of the House, and Eisenhower responded by offering Herter a State Department job if he did not vie for the vice presidential nomination. Herter then offered to renominate Nixon at the forthcoming Republican convention. Not until the convention in August did Stassen finally capitulate and agree to second Nixon's renomination.

It is still not clear who prompted Stassen to initiate a "dump Nixon" campaign. Columnist Drew Pearson said that it was Milton Eisenhower, the president's brother, but he specifically denied this charge in a private letter to Nixon. There is circumstantial evidence indicating that Dulles may have encouraged Stassen to discredit himself and therefore remove him from his cabinet position because Stassen had more direct access to the president than had the secretary of state. In 1957, Stassen was transferred to the State Department and immediately resigned to run unsuccessfully for governor of Pennsylvania.

In addition to the 1952 Checkers speech, two other media events at the end of the decade enhanced Nixon's political fortunes and popularity with the general public: the stoning of his car in Caracas in 1958 and his 1959 "kitchen" encounter with Soviet leader Nikita Khrushchev in Moscow, during which the two men jabbed their fingers at one another and argued the merits of their two very different systems of government and economies. In a word, Nixon was a television success in the 1950s before he became a television failure in the 1960s following two major political defeats. None of these three events, however, added up to a common pattern of constant controversy or crises, as much as they represented sporadic and potentially negative incidents that Nixon turned into politically profitable media opportunities during the valuable, but often discouraging, learning process he underwent during his two terms as vice president.

His major publicity faux pas occurred in 1958 when the State Department leaked to *The New York Times* information about 5,000 letters, 80 percent of which opposed the administration's policy of defending Quemoy and Matsu, two small offshore islands held by the Chinese Nationalists that the Chinese Communists shelled periodically. Nixon overreacted, threatening government employees who "sabotaged" foreign policy through leaks. Accused of

"fascist tendencies" by the press, the vice president sent out a defensive form letter and later said that he was only defending Dulles's Far East policies against a small group in the State Department. At the same time, he launched a full-scale attack on the previous foreign policy of Harry Truman and Dean Acheson as having promoted appeasement and war rather than peace. Eisenhower forced Nixon to say that he did not "question the sincerity or patriotism of those who criticize our policies."

Always outside President Eisenhower's private group of advisers, especially those on the National Security Council who advised the president on foreign policy, and occasionally humiliated by Ike in public, Nixon bided his time and mended his own political fences by courting both moderate and conservative Republicans and creating a "centrist" image of himself among supporters within his own party. This ensured his presidential nomination in 1960. Eisenhower gave him few formal responsibilities during the 1950s; yet, in eight years Nixon permanently upgraded the office of vice president and gave it a much more meaningful and institutionalized role. In part he accomplished this through several well-publicized trips abroad on behalf of the president in the 1950s. (Nixon nostalgically repeated the 1953 trip to Asia and the Middle East as ex-president in 1985.)

The vice presidency also assumed greater importance because Eisenhower suffered a heart attack in 1955, a bout with ileitis in 1956, and a stroke in 1957. Throughout all these illnesses, Nixon handled himself with considerable tact and self-effacement while presiding over nineteen cabinet sessions and twenty-six meetings of the National Security Council. Following his stroke, President Eisenhower worked out a plan with Nixon, Secretary of State Dulles, and Attorney General William Rogers to create the office of acting president in the event he became incapacitated from illness. This formal agreement substituted under Presidents Eisenhower and Kennedy for a constitutional amendment (not ratified until 1967) that granted the vice president full authority to govern when the president could not discharge the powers and duties of his office.

Nixon was so well positioned to run for the presidency in 1960 that despite the trouncing the Republicans experienced in the 1958 midterm elections and potential challenges from the governors of New York and California—Nelson Rockefeller and Ronald Reagan—he won the Republican nomination for president. Once again, he received only lukewarm support from Eisenhower because their relationship had always been an ambiguous one. The president had always approved of Nixon's aggressiveness and partisanship but questioned his maturity. It did not help when Eisenhower was asked at a press conference in August about Nixon's role in the decision-making process and replied: "If you give me a week, I might think of one. I don't remember."

Instead of taking an active public role in Nixon's campaign, Eisenhower held back. Nixon later said in his memoirs that this was because Eisenhower did not want to "overshadow my own appearances," while the president remembered that Nixon did not want him in the campaign until the very end. (Moreover, he ignored Eisenhower's advice not to debate Kennedy, because Nixon was still bedazzled by his victory over Khrushchev in their "debate" the year before.) Whichever interpretation of Eisenhower's lack of participation in the campaign is true, it proved a costly mistake as Kennedy successfully zeroed in on a mythical missile gap and other failures of the Republican administration to be tough enough on communism.

Nixon's unsuccessful campaign against John F. Kennedy for the presidency was fraught with ironies and political lessons he never forgot—not the least of which was that he had to answer the charge that he was soft on communism in Castro's Cuba without being able to reveal that the administration had a plan to invade the island. He also was left holding the bag after Eisenhower lied about the mission of a U-2 spy plane shot down by the Russians. Once

again Nixon had to defend an administration that looked inept in dealing with communism abroad when he had not been privy to many of the foreign policy decisions he defended.

To make matters worse, the press repeatedly described Kennedy as a "youthful frontrunner" representing a new generation, when in fact both men came from approximately the same age cohort, Nixon being only four years older than his forty-three-year-old Democratic opponent. In the course of the campaign, Kennedy was successfully packaged to appear what, in fact, he turned out not to be: a devoted father and family man in good health, an intellectual, a bona fide war hero, and a liberal Democrat. The fact that Nixon's congressional and vice-presidential records on social issues, especially civil rights and foreign policy, were more liberal than Kennedy's were lost in this media blitz, as were JFK's womanizing, chronic back ailments and Addison's disease, mediocre cultural and intellectual interests, his cold warriorism, his conservative fiscal views, and his cautious, at best, attitudes about social reform. Nixon also learned the hard way that television would play a most significant role in the 1960 election—the closest one in U.S. history since Grover Cleveland defeated James G. Blame in 1884. Nixon's successful television tactics of the 1950s proved outmoded in one-on-one debates with Kennedy. Almost overnight, the man who had been touted as a "handsome" young returning veteran in 1946 became "ugly" after he "lost" four nationally televised debates with Kennedy in September and October—losses based not on substantive points made but on style and image. Nothing new was said or revealed in any of the debates, and those who listened to them thought Nixon carried the day, but those who watched them on television rallied to Kennedy.

Nixon's speaking style had long been described as "effective" but not "eloquent." It stemmed from his high school and college days, when he had employed standard debating techniques such as thorough preparation, immediate feedback to improve the next time around, and the use of surprise attacks whenever possible rather than defensive tactics. These debating techniques stood him in good stead until the rules of political debate changed dramatically with television, as Nixon found out so painfully in the 1960 debates with John Kennedy. Forced then to adapt to a situation where scoring points did not matter as much as image, Nixon adapted his debating skills after 1960 to the age of television more successfully than is usually thought.

Even more frustrating to Nixon during the 1960s presidential campaign was his inability to capitalize on his civil rights record among African American voters. As vice president, Nixon had been a stronger supporter of civil rights in the 1950s than either Eisenhower, Kennedy, or Johnson. When he presided over the Senate, his rulings consistently favored those who opposed the use of filibusters to block civil rights legislation, and he chaired the Committee on Government Contracts that oversaw enforcement of nondiscrimination provisions of government contracts, recommending in his final report the establishment of "a positive policy of nondiscrimination" by employers that he later supported as president. In the fall of 1957, during the integration crisis at Little Rock Central High, Nixon strongly defended the administration's use of troops against attacks from southern newspaper editors and congressmen, even though he was never able to persuade Eisenhower to meet directly with African American leaders. He later said that he supported civil rights for blacks and equal rights for women not because it would "help" members of either group but because "it was fair" and good for the nation because it prevented "wasted talent."

Nixon always denied that he was a conservative on civil rights at any time during his career, citing his support as vice president for the 1957 Civil Rights Act and Equal Right Amendment every time it was introduced in Congress. Although he adopted a white-oriented southern strategy for the Republican Party in the late 1960s, earlier in the 1960 presidential campaign Nixon had expected to be able to increase black support for the Republican Party beyond Eisenhower's 39 percent in 1956 because of his previous civil rights record and Martin Luther King, Jr.'s, personal promise to register African Americans for the Republican Party in the South. He also had the support in 1960 of such prominent African American athletes as Jackie Robinson.

After the Democrats nominated Kennedy, whose Catholicism brought an unexpected number of white southern Protestants over to the Republican Party, Nixon appealed more carefully to both blacks and whites in the South than he had originally intended. As it turned out, Kennedy's highly publicized intervention when Martin Luther King, Jr., was arrested in October won over a crucial number of black voters, including Robinson. Before this incident King (and Robinson) had openly praised Nixon above all other presidential candidates for caring about the race issue. Despite Kennedy's "grandstanding" on King's arrest and subsequent jailing, Nixon still captured 32 percent of the black vote in 1960, but in such a close election that was not enough. Later, as a very public private citizen in the 1960s, Nixon, unlike George Bush, supported the Civil Rights Acts of 1964 and 1966—not southern segregationist planks in Republican state platforms. Nixon also consistently opposed the poll tax and supported antilynching legislation. Far from being a bland supporter of civil rights, Nixon's record was better than any of the political opponents he ran against for the Senate, vice president, and president (with the exception of Hubert Humphrey).

To his credit, Nixon did not challenge the election he lost to John F. Kennedy by only 113,000 popular votes (less than one-half vote per precinct nationwide), although there was every indication that the Democrats did not legally win in either Illinois or Texas, whose combined electoral college tally tipped the election in their favor, 303 to 219. Moreover, there were confused returns from Alabama and such close votes in Missouri, New Mexico, Nevada, and Hawaii that a shift of less than 12,000 votes would have given Nixon a majority in the electoral college. Such luminaries of the Republican Party as Bryce Harlow, Herbert Klein, Len Hall, Thruston Morton, and even Eisenhower all urged Nixon to challenge the results because of the many reported cases of fraud, but he steadfastly refused. "Our country can't afford the agony of a constitutional crisis," Nixon remarked in an unconsciously prescient moment to a reporter who had unearthed a number of voting irregularities in Illinois and Texas, "and I damn well will not be a party to creating one just to become President or anything else." Nonetheless, after 1960, Nixon resolved never again to take any preelection lead for granted—not in 1968 or even in 1972. All future campaigns became "no holds barred" contests.

During his years as Eisenhower's vice president, Nixon campaigned widely for Republican candidates and in the process obtained the unenviable reputation of being the party hatchet man, especially because of his attacks on Adlai Stevenson, twice the Democratic presidential candidate in the 1950s. As a result, elements within the press, many academics, and liberals in general found it easier to criticize the conservatism of the Eisenhower administrations by concentrating on the personality and campaign tactics of his vice president rather than by attacking a popular president. What they overlooked in his performance then (and later after he became president) was his consistent support for liberal educational reform, civil rights, and for moderate, as well as conservative, Republican candidates on the campaign trail, thereby building up a broad base of support among Republicans that belied the one dimensional view his critics projected of him.

Richard Nixon's apprenticeship under Eisenhower left him with strong negative impressions about cabinet government in general, and the National Security Council in particular—impressions he would act on later when he became president in 1969. He is considered one of the most successful vice presidents, if for no other reason than his institutionalization of that office, so that future occupants could play a more significant role in policy formulation that he had been able to in the 1950s.

By 1968, Richard Milhous Nixon was once again positioned to win his party's nomination for the United States presidency. This time, unlike in 1960, he faced a Democratic Party hopelessly divided over the Indochinese war and haplessly led by Hubert Humphrey in the wake of LBJ's unexpected refusal to run again, Robert Kennedy's assassination, and a strong third-party bid by George C. Wallace. During the 1968 campaign, Nixon's more-liberal opponent Hubert Humphrey appeared to be defending past U.S. efforts to win the Vietnam War more than was Nixon, his Republican opponent whom many considered to be an original cold warrior. Had President Johnson halted the bombing of North Vietnam and renewed the Paris peace talks before the end of October, Humphrey might have been able to squeeze by Nixon, for the election results proved to be almost as close as they had been in 1960, with Nixon winning by 500,000 popular votes and receiving 301 electoral votes compared to 191 for Humphrey and 46 for Wallace In 1972, Nixon won by a landslide with 520 electoral votes to 17 for George McGovern and a margin of almost 18 million popular votes.

Had Nixon left office after his first term, his administration would have been remembered as one of the most successful since the World War II, largely because of his often overlooked domestic achievements and his highly publicized, but rather ephemeral, foreign policy. Unfortunately, he precipitated the constitutional crisis known as Watergate and was forced, in August 1974, to resign from office or face a Senate impeachment trial.

In the areas of civil rights, it was Nixon, not Eisenhower, Kennedy, or Johnson, who actually desegregated southern schools rather than simply talk about it. His administration also enforced such affirmative actions programs as the Philadelphia "set-asides," one in the construction industry, and increased funding that so the

Equal Economic Opportunity Commission could effectively implement the 1964 Civil Rights Act, making his civil rights record with respect to women and Native Americans one of the best. With respect to the environment, Nixon both led and accepted from Congress the first concrete federal legislation on this issue. His administration was also impressive in retrospect for its reorganization of the executive branch of government that most of his successors in office simply emulated or tinkered with but did not basically change, including his restructuring of the National Security Council. Nixon failed to achieve welfare and health care reform, but his bold attempts in both areas (opposed by liberals and conservatives alike at the time) remain the most comprehensive suggestions made by any president after FDR and before Bill Clinton and the One Hundred Fourth Congress.

Of all his innovative foreign policy endeavors, only one—the opening of China—survived. Détente with the Soviet Union became a dirty word in the Ford administration and was not pursued by Presidents Ford, Carter, or Reagan until Gorbachev appeared on the scene. Nixon formulated no coherent Middle East foreign policy before the 1973 October war and then it consisted largely of Kissinger's shuttling around telling both the Arabs and Israelis what they wanted to hear. This proved more show than substance. Nor did Nixon develop a third-world policy except to use certain countries as pawns in the geopolitical battle with the USSR. In fact, his policy toward Africa favored the white minority regimes in that part of the world.

But it was the Watergate scandal that will forever cast a shadow on Nixon's presidency because it involved the highest officials of government. The cover-up by the president and his top aides of the original break-in and bugging at Democratic national committee headquarters located in Washington, D.C.'s Watergate complex on June 17, 1972, and related corrupt or criminal political activities ultimately resulted in the indictment, conviction, and sentencing of twenty men. These included the top White House aides to Nixon (John Ehrlichman and H.R. Halde-man), the president's counsel (John W. Dean III), the president's special assistant (Charles Colson), one former cabinet member (Attorney General John Mitchell, Jr.), and others who worked for the Committee for the Reelection of the President (CRP, but usually derogatorily referred to as CREEP) and/or the White House Special Investigative Unit known more commonly as the Plumbers, whose members engaged in break-ins before Watergate occurred.

Most of these men functioned as Republican election officials or presidential advisers in whom public trust had been placed. A few Plumbers such as E. Howard Hunt, James McCord, and G. Gordon Liddy—all former CIA or FBI agents—were specifically employed by the White House with private funds to carry out political espionage; they in turn hired the four Cubans arrested in the Watergate complex. All served time for their participation in the original crime of burglary and bugging of the Democratic Party national offices. Despite multiple investigations and books, many factual questions remain unanswered about both the Watergate incident itself and its still-disputed historical significance. Yet, most scholars and journalists, and quite a few prolific ex-felons, continue to skew Nixon's legacy as president by attributing too much of Nixon's foreign policy to Kissinger; by almost entirely ignoring his constructive domestic achievements; and by refusing to recognize the downhill course in American politics that Watergate exacerbated, but neither originated nor ended. The system worked during Watergate in that it held Nixon and his aides accountable, but it has not held any other major politician or policy maker constitutionally accountable since.

REFERENCES

Stephen B. Ambrose, *Nixon,* 3 vols. (New York: Simon and Schuster, 1987, 1989, 1991); Fawn M. Brodie, *Richard Nixon: The Shaping of His Character* (New York: W.W. Norton, 1981); Belinda Kornitzer, *The Real Nixon: An Intimate Biography* (New York: Rand McNally, 1960); Earl Mazo and Stephen Hess,

Nixon: A Political Portrait (New York: Harper & Row, 1968); Joan Hoff, *Nixon Reconsidered* (New York: Basic Books, 1994); Roger Morris, *Richard Milhous Nixon: The Rise of an American Politician* (New York: Holt, 1990); *Richard M. Nixon: Memoirs,* 3 vols. (New York: Grosset & Dunlap, 1978); *Richard M. Nixon, Six Crises* (New York: Doubleday, 1962); Herbert S. Parmet, *Richard Nixon and His America* (Boston: Little, Brown, 1990); Tom Wicker, *One of Us: Richard Nixon and the American Dream* (New York: Random House, 1991); Carry Wills, *Nixon Agonistes: The Crisis of the Self-Made Man* (Boston: Houghton Mifflin, 1970); Rick Perlstein, *Nixonland: The Rise of a President and the Fracturing of America* (New York: Scribner, 2009); Conrad Black, *Richard Nixon: A Life in Full* (Public Affairs, 2008); *Frost Nixon: The Original Watergate Interviews* (DVD) (Los Angeles: Liberation Entertainment, 2008).

JOAN HOFF is the distinguished professor of history at Montana State University, Bozeman. She is the former director of the Contemporary History Institute at Ohio University and the former director of the Center for the Study of the Presidency in New York City. A specialist on contemporary U.S. foreign policy and politics and women's legal status, she is the author of *American Business and Foreign Policy, 1920–1933* (1973); *Ideology and Economics: United States Relations with the Soviet Union, 1918–1933* (1971); *Herbert Hoover: Forgotten Progressive* (1975); *Law, Gender and Injustice: A Legal History of U.S. Women* (1991); *Nixon Reconsidered* (1994); and *The Cooper's Wife Is Missing: The Trials of Bridget Cleary* (2001). She published *Faustian Foreign Policy from Woodrow Wilson to George W. Bush* in 2008.

LYNDON BAINES JOHNSON (1908–1973)

Vice President, 1961–1963

(President John F. Kennedy)

LYNDON BAINES JOHNSON
(Library of Congress)

By G. L. Seligmann

For some—Adams, Jefferson, Van Buren, Nixon, and Bush—the vice presidency was but one rung in ascending the political ladder. For others—Tyler, Fillmore, Andrew Johnson, Arthur, Teddy Roosevelt, Coolidge, Truman, and Ford—it was the route to an office they probably would not have otherwise held. For many—Aaron Burr, George clinton, Levi P. Morton, and Alben Barkley, among others—it marked the peak of their political careers. For a few—John Nance Garner comes to mind—it was a decline in their political power. But for none did the office of vice president represent such a low point of their political career, sandwiched between the considerable power of a Senate majority leader and the awesome power of the presidency as it did for Lyndon Baines-Johnson.

Johnson was born in 1908 in the hill country of Texas, the eldest of Sam and Rebekah Johnson's four children. Sam was a teacher, farmer, and sometime member of the Texas state legislature, but he went broke early in the agricultural depression of the 1920s and moved his family to Johnson City, named after Lyndon's grandfather. Johnson graduated from high school in 1924 and spent a year as a laborer in California, followed by a return to Johnson City and a series of menial jobs. At age eighteen, Johnson borrowed a small stake and enrolled in Southwest Texas State Teachers College in San Marco. He struggled to pay his way through school and dropped out for a year to teach Hispanic children in the small town of Cotulla—an experience that had great influence on his later views of what society owed the poor and the disadvantaged.

After teaching in Houston briefly following graduation from college, Johnson embarked on his first job in politics, moving to Washington as secretary to Texas millionaire Representative Richard Kleberg. The young aide became an ardent New Dealer, absorbing and championing the programs of FDR. While serving at his Washington post, Johnson met, wooed, and married a Texan, Claudia Alta Taylor (known to all as Lady Bird). The couple eventually had two daughters, Lynda Bird and Luci Baines.

In 1935, Johnson became Texas state director of the New Deal National Youth Administration, but he was elected U.S. Representative in 1937 and returned to Washington, where his good personal connections and immense legislative skills moved him rapidly ahead. He briefly served on active military duty during the first months of World War II but returned to Congress at the president's request.

LBJ's most important electoral race came in the Texas state Democratic primary for the U.S. Senate in 1948. Whoever won the Democratic nomination was assured of winning the Senate seat. LBJ ran a vigorous and energetic campaign, using a helicopter to jump from appearance to appearance, but the voting came down to a margin of a mere 87 votes out of more than 988,000 cast. Johnson's victory was almost certainly due to fraudulent vote count-

ing and a stuffed ballot box in a key precinct. Despite challenges, the thin margin held, and LBJ went to the Senate, where his rise was meteoric. He became Senate minority leader and was reelected to his Senate seat by a huge margin in 1954 as part of a national Democratic victory, following which he assumed the office of Senate majority leader. He rapidly became one of the more powerful Senate leaders in modern times, able to manipulate people and processes masterfully.

Why then, in 1960, did Johnson accept nomination as Kennedy's running mate, which was a major retreat from his very powerful position as Senate majority leader? What motivated this quintessential political power seeker to agree to serve, over the opposition of very powerful elements within the Democratic Party, in an office succinctly characterized by a former vice president and a fellow hill-country Texan as "not worth a bucket of warm spit"? Then, too, why did presidential nominee John F. Kennedy offer the number-two spot to LBJ over the opposition of influential groups, while simultaneously removing LBJ from his position of power—a position that could be very useful to a Democratic president? These are not simply rhetorical questions, although no definitive answer can be given to either. Moreover, it is in the probable answers to these questions that one can find the clues to explaining and understanding the LBJ vice presidency.

From JFK's perspective, the offer. can be readily understood. A powerful Senate majority leader would be of little value to a defeated Democratic candidate. LBJ's presence on the ticket would be valuable in the region where a New England Catholic would be most vulnerable—the South. The powerful elements on the Democratic left that feared, disliked, and mistrusted LBJ did not fear, dislike, or mistrust JFK, indeed, he and his close circle had strong ties to these groups, and the nominee knew full well that when all was said and done these groups would support the Democratic candidate. There was, moreover, in addition to this calculated political analysis another reason for adding Johnson to the ticket. Senator Kennedy believed that in the case of his incapacity or death, Johnson was qualified by virtue of knowledge, temperament, and ability to fill the office of the president. To be sure, rumors circulated at the time and since, often by members of JFK's outer circles, that the offer was made in the expectation that it would be refused. No evidence, however, other than the rumors themselves exists to validate this contention.

Given the reasons for making the offer, the question then becomes: Why was it accepted? The answers to this question both complement and go beyond JFK's reasons for making the offer. Johnson agreed with the arguments that he would strengthen the Democratic ticket where it was the weakest—the South and the West. But LBJ's reasons were not altogether altruistic. In 1968 he would be sixty years old, and he wanted to be president of the United States. The office of the vice president, if used well, could aid in that goal. LBJ knew well the nature, strength, and depth of the liberal Democrats' opposition to him. He believed that he could use the eight years as vice president to demonstrate to these groups that he was not the enemy they thought him to be. As a senator from Texas, even with the prestige of being Senate majority leader, he could not be too far ahead of his Texas constituents. He knew well the first two rules of politics: (I) Represent your constituency, and (2) do not break (1) until you are strong enough at home to withstand the challenge. Having won the 1948 primary vote by eighty-seven illegal votes, LBJ was in no position to challenge the conservative tastes of the Texas electorate. His 3–1 victory in 1954 had made it possible to begin to move away from distinctive conservative voting patterns toward the center of the national Democratic Party. As vice president, he would no longer be tied to a purely Texas voting base.

In the late 1950s, essentially four groups made up the liberal wing of the Democratic Party—big city bosses, labor, intellectuals, and civil rights groups—and, to be sure, the groups overlapped on occasion. Of these four groups, only the bosses supported Johnson.

Labor leaders, refusing to recognize the political realities of an eighty-seven vote victory in an antilabor state, opposed him for voting for both the Taft-Hartley and Landrum-Griffin bills. In this they were encouraged by the almost impotent liberal wing of the Texas Democrats. This union opposition Johnson understood, and although he considered it wrongheaded, he felt it could be finessed over the next eight years.

The gap between LBJ and the intellectual community was one of both substance and style. These professional nonpoliticians were never comfortable with what their idol, JFK, called "the nature and the necessity for compromise and balance." Johnson's J.C. Penney—polyester style clashed with their tweedy Brooks Brothers look. They talked about things and, in only talking, avoided the hard-and-fast realities of practical politics. He did things and thus was forced to confront realities headlong. But LBJ knew he needed them, so he wooed them, and for this reason, plus the fact that he was the choice of JFK, they accepted him in the short run.

The opposition of civil rights leaders was a more difficult thing. They did not trust LBJ, and although he had gotten the best civil rights bills possible through the Congress in 1957 and 1960, they doubted his conversion. In this lack of trust they, like their labor allies, failed to take Texas political realities into account. In addition, they did not consider LBJ's racially liberal political antecedents. His father, Sam Ealy Johnson, when in the Texas legislature, had voted for a resolution opposing the Ku Klux Klan and had, indeed, called the Klan "un-American." Furthermore, LBJ's early experience teaching Mexican American children in South Texas, an experience which later led him to note "somehow you never forget what poverty and hatred can do when you see its scars in the face of a child," had taught him much. To the civil rights community, LBJ had joined the successful southern filibuster in 1949 against the Fair Employment Practices Commission, and in this opposition they had chosen not to hear some of what the new senator was saying:

Perhaps no prejudice is so contagious or so unreasoning as the unreasoning prejudice against men because of their birth, the color of their skin, or their ancestral background. Racial prejudice is dangerous because it is a disease of the majority endangering minority groups. . . . For those who would keep any group in our nation in bondage, I have no sympathy or tolerance. Some may feel moved to deny this group or that the homes, the education, the employment which every American has the right to expect, but I am not one of those.

Perhaps it is natural that words so out of place in a filibuster against a civil rights measure might be missed.

In 1957, LBJ had maneuvered a civil rights bill through the Senate at the cost of eliminating a section concerning contempt trials from the final bill. The part of the original bill had provided for nonjury contempt trials for those who violated the bill's provisions. This tide quickly became the focus of the southern and conservative opposition to the measure. In a successful effort to pass this early civil rights measure, New Mexico Democrat Clinton P. Anderson, a liberal senator of impeccable credentials, moved to remove the embattled title. In this maneuver Anderson was joined by such liberals as Hubert H. Humphrey, Jacob Javits, and JFK, but the fury of the civil rights leaders fell on Johnson. That the offending section was in violation of our legal traditions made no difference to these civil rights leaders. They believed the only way to secure civil rights convictions in the South was to bypass jury trials, and this weapon had been stripped from them. It would be difficult indeed to win this group's support, but to become president in 1968 LBJ had to have it, and the office of vice president would give him eight years to change their opinions.

These then were the reasons JFK wanted LBJ on the ballot and the reasons LBJ accepted second-place billing to a younger, less experienced man. He brought strength to the ticket and he wanted the position. When Robert F. Kennedy informed his brother and others that Johnson is "willing to fight for it," he did not mean, as Arthur M. Schlesinger, Jr. and others have argued, that LBJ would fight the nominee for the vice president slot, but rather that LBJ would join JFK to fight for the nomination. Indeed, such close friends of JFK as Joseph Alsop and Philip Graham had consistently predicted a JFK-LBJ ticket.

With the ticket completed, the campaign commenced. As expected, Johnson campaigned extensively but not exclusively in the South, and his campaigning was most effective. As was expected, Kennedy's Catholicism was a major issue in the South, often masking southern opposition to other issues. Afraid to confront the electorate in open support of their party's nominee, many Deep South politicians used the candidate's religion as their out. Against this hypocrisy, LBJ used an indirect but not very subtle approach:

I know you boys know how strong your people feel about this Catholic thing. Both Senator Kennedy and I think you should vote your conscience on this matter. Course we do want to win pretty badly and I am going to feel real bad if we don't. Now I don't know how them Irish Catholics take losing but I would be real surprised if they like it. But that's just something him and me are gonna have to live with. Course now I'm still gonna be majority leader and Senator Kennedy is going to be much more of a leader then he is now and that'll help some. And of course both of us have good memories. But now on this religion thing you just go ahead and go with your conscience and your people.

Given this sort of treatment, many southern politicos were able to rise above their religious prejudices.

The election was a squeaker, but Texas, helped by JFK's defense of his religious beliefs before a group of Houston Baptist ministers and a backlash of sympathy caused by the hostile if not threatening treatment Senator and Mrs. Johnson received from a group of Republican conservatives in Dallas, as well as several other southern states helped put the Kennedy–Johnson ticket over the top. The JFK-LBJ gamble had paid off.

The administration began as have all recent administrations with the president and vice president in complete accord as to how to involve the vice president more completely and at a higher level than previous vice presidents. As Johnson put it: "If there is one the President can turn to, I want it to be me." But additionally Johnson thought he could continue his rigid control of the Democratic majority in the Senate. The method to be used was for LBJ instead of newly elected Majority Leader Mike Mansfield of Montana to preside over the meetings of the Democratic Caucus. When this idea was presented to the Democratic senators, it was accepted by a 46 to 17 vote after some complicated political and parliamentary maneuvers. Although the vote was almost 3–1 in Johnson's favor and the opposition almost all liberals, it was a large enough bloc to convince Johnson the idea was a mistake. He never again attended a Senate Democratic Caucus meeting.

True to his word, JFK assigned several meaningful tasks to his vice president. LBJ, in addition to his general political duties in the United States, was often sent abroad to represent the president and the country, a job for which he soon demonstrated considerable proficiency. Domestically he was placed in charge of the Space Council and the Presidential Committee on Equal Employment Opportunity, two positions of importance both to the new administration and to Johnson's political future.

To Kennedy, the race to control space was one the country had been publicly losing since *Sputnik* and central to his concept of how to deal with the Soviet Union. Consequently the Space Council, which set and coordinated our national space effort, was of great importance. Therefore, although the Space Council had been underutilized during the Eisenhower years, JFK and LBJ revitalized its activities. Johnson, who had long pushed U.S. efforts in this area, threw his full energies into the project. These efforts, while neither dramatic nor well studied, of course, resulted in placing a man on the moon during the Nixon administration. In addition to the Space Council's support of the moon landing program, it also played a leading role in developing COMSAT (Communication Satellite).

Perhaps the major reason this important activity has been so ignored lies in the fact that it was so noncontroversial. It was an area that found those oftimes opponents. Johnson and Robert Kennedy, in full agreement. It was also an area where the president appreciated the advice he was getting from the vice president. President Kennedy did not welcome the general and political advice that was LBJ's forte because of his ego and self-perceived personal strengths. However, the vice president's expertise in the area of space issues, dating back to LBJ's long-standing congressional interest, was such that he could give JFK the kind of technical advice the president wanted.

Yet another area where Johnson was given a number of assignments and achieved considerable success was that of representing the United States abroad. His first trip abroad, to Senegal, set the pattern. After performing his official duties celebrating Senegalese Independence Day, he and Lady Bird were off and running. Awakening at 4:30 A.M., the Johnsons traveled by car to the small fishing and peanut-growing village of Kayar, some miles distant from Dakar, the capital. There they met the people, shook hands, and kissed babies. When asked by the village chief why he was there, Johnson replied:

I came to Dakar for Independence Day festivities because of President Kennedy's deep interest in Africa, but I came to Kayar because I was a farm boy too in Texas. It's a long way from Texas to Kayar, but we both produce peanuts and both want the same thing: a higher standard of living for the people.

Later, during a visit to Lebanon, Johnson discussed dump trucks with a Beirut road crew. When he asked what the truck held and was told five yards, he noted that his first job was filling a one-yard capacity truck with a shovel. He then noted to a nearby Lebanese official: "You're going to realize great benefits from work like this. In my country, one of the most important developments was getting the farmers out of the mud. In my own state of Texas now, no farmer has to drive more than a mile to get to a paved road." To the Ivy League—educated State Department personnel and the intelligentsia who understood JFK and joked about Johnson, this was "Uncle Cornpone" at his worst. His hosts, however, loved it. In Teheran on a state visit Johnson shook an estimated 300 hands in 5 minutes. It was as though, one reporter noted, "he was running for Shah."

It was this gregariousness that resulted in Johnson's invitation to the illiterate Pakistani cameleer, Basher Ahmed, to visit the United States. An offhand invitation, "You all come to Washington and see us some day" was given to Ahmed, who took it seriously. When news of this hit the anti-American elements of the Pakistani press, it was passed on to Washington. LBJ then arranged through the People-To-People program for the Pakistani to come to the United States. The vice president and the camel driver toured the United States, where Ahmed's natural dignity and the vice president's presence turned a casual remark into a major news story. When Basher Ahmed's return trip was routed through Mecca so that he could make his pilgrimage, the diplomatic triumph was complete.

However, Johnson's major overseas triumph was his trip to Berlin, undertaken as one U.S. response to the construction of the Berlin Wall. There were three purposes to the trip: to make clear U.S. neutrality in the political struggle between Konrad Adenauer and Willi Brandt; to inform the German people and their leaders of the U.S. position on Berlin; and to attempt to moderate the West German political leaders' near hysteria. The first goal was achieved by Johnson's meeting with Chancellor Adenauer in Bonn and later his appearance in Berlin with the city's mayor, Willi Brandt. U.S. support of a Western-controlled Berlin was highlighted by the return of retired General Lucius Clay, the commander of the city during the Berlin blockade, and by the dispatch overland of a token force of some 1,500 additional combat troops. Support for the city was further made clear in the vice president's speech to the Berliners. "I have come to Berlin by direction of President Kennedy. . . . To the survival and to the creative future of this city we Americans have pledged, in effect what our ancestors pledged in forming the United States . . . 'Our Lives, Our Fortunes, and Our Sacred Honor. . . .'" More formal perhaps, less dramatic possibly than JFK's *Ich bin em Berliner*" but no less effective under the circumstances.

The same could be said of his trip earlier in 1961 to Southeast Asia. Here also, the purpose of the trip was to signal U.S. support of an ally, South Vietnam's President Diem. As with all of his overseas trips, Johnson's scope of maneuver was carefully defined. In his reassurances and his commitments, he could not go beyond the president's guidelines. On this trip, in addition to bolstering the South Vietnamese government's resolve, he was to urge other U.S. allies in Southeast Asia to support one another and to hold firm. While believing that Diem was too aloof to be a truly successful leader, LBJ's report to the president noted that Diem was the best choice in that troubled country. The significance of this report in determining future U.S. policy and involvement in the affairs of South Vietnam is impossible to determine.

Although his overseas trips were extremely successful, they did not result in Johnson's being seen as an indispensable part of the leadership team. Indeed the repetitious, clichélike quality of the president's remarks—"strengthened the forces of freedom," "well represented," "an in-valuable service"—tended to give the impression that these missions were pro-forma endeavors. Despite this, these trips did demonstrate Johnson's ability to negotiate with foreign leaders and to communicate with the people.

Although helpful in his long-term quest for the presidency, these activities were at best peripheral. Johnson was widely viewed as a conservative on domestic and, particularly, racial matters and this was an impression he had to change. His best hope of reshaping his image lay in chairing the President's Committee on Equal Employment. Here he could demonstrate to the civil rights community, to the intellectuals, and to the liberal union leadership that his commitment to racial equality was heartfelt and real.

Prior to 1961, the government's involvement in the area of equal employment opportunities had been ineffective. To be sure, Nixon, a strong supporter of these goals, had tried but had lacked both a public mandate and the determined support of President Eisenhower, and he had consequently fallen short of his hoped-for goal. Perhaps Johnson could do better. Again there was no public mandate for this activity, but JFK had at least talked about it in his campaign and he had certainly gotten, and needed, the African American vote. In fact, not only had JFK endorsed the concept of equal employment, but he also had noted that the situation could be changed by a presidential "stroke of a pen." Given the possibilities and the potential, Johnson had good reason to view the situation with optimism.

This optimism was reinforced by the president's willingness to accept Johnson's suggestion that longtime friend and confidante Abe Fortas draw up a new executive order creating the President's Committee on Equal Employment. Under the terms of Fortas's directives, all government contractors would have to agree not to practice racial discrimination. The way

the pledge was worded was designed to put the burden of proof on the contractors to prove that they didn't discriminate, not on an appellant to prove they did.

The first test of the new policy came when the Lockheed Corporation's Marietta, Georgia, plant received a billion-dollar government contract. Despite the fact that the company only employed blacks in menial jobs and that restrooms, eating facilities, water fountains, and so forth were segregated, the company submitted the necessary certificates of nonsegregation only to have them rejected by the committee. Despite intense political pressure brought by Johnson's former political mentor Richard Russell and others, the committee held firm and the company integrated its facilities. It was a major victory for the policies and demonstrated that local racial patterns would yield to economic pressure.

However, even before this victory, prominent committee members were complaining that LBJ's political style was playing havoc with the committee's proceedings. In addition to these complaints, there was also dissatisfaction with the president's choice of the committee's executive and associate executive director. For director, JFK had chosen one of his earliest southern supporters and a former college roommate of his dead brother Joseph, Robert Troutman, an Atlanta businessman. Troutman had seriously and courageously supported the goals of the committee, but he also advocated a "go slow" approach that several committee members opposed; the associate director, John Feild, was just the opposite—he supported compulsion where Troutman argued voluntary compliance. The result was conflict and confusion. Because both men were presidential appointees, the matter had to be resolved by Kennedy, but LBJ was caught in the middle. He agreed with Troutman's approach, but he didn't approve of Troutman. Johnson's suggestion was to reorganize the staff structure, creating a single head of staff who would work closely with the vice president. Eventually, JFK accepted this idea and Troutman and Feild were replaced by

Hobart Taylor, Jr., an African American personally selected by LBJ. From then on things went better; still, by 1962 not much had been achieved.

Frustrated by this lack of progress, the president asked Robert Kennedy to look into the matter. The attorney general, who had long suspected Johnson's sincerity on ending segregation, compiled data on black employment by the federal government. The record was not encouraging. Appearing at one of the committee's meetings, Kennedy dropped this information into their laps with the very strong implication that the president expected results—and soon. The attack was unexpected and devastating. Although LBJ was not mentioned by name, it was clear that RFK was implying that the White House lacked faith in LBJ's ability and/or desire to improve the employment situation.

To make things worse, the charge was not a particularly valid one. Within the administration and in his public speeches, LBJ had done much to keep the issue of civil rights in the forefront. In an eloquent 1963 speech delivered at Gettysburg as a part of the Civil War centennial, Johnson had begun his remarks by noting that "One hundred years ago the slave was freed. One hundred years later the Negro remains in bondage to the color of his skin." He went on to note that the dead at Gettysburg were neither answered nor honored when our reply to the Negro is "patience." His conclusion noted that: "Until justice is blind to color, until all education is unaware of race, until opportunity is unconcerned with the color of men's skins, emancipation will be a proclamation, but emancipation will not be a fact."

Shortly after this speech Johnson, in a lengthy and recorded telephone conversation, gave Theodore Sorenson, JFK's principal speech-writer, a lecture on how the president should push his civil rights legislation. At one point in this remarkable conversation, LBJ advised Sorenson to have the president speak on the matter in the Deep South. LBJ went on to say that the president should ask his audience how they thought he could order a black soldier to risk death for his country when that soldier couldn't eat in a restaurant in the city where he was speaking. The audience might disagree with the president, the vice president noted, but they would respect him. Sadly, JFK never gave this speech.

By this time, it was clear that although LBJ had enemies in the administration he still had the president's support. Johnson had walked the narrow path between appearing to be unimportant and suggesting that he was more important than the President. Yet, the rumors and the attacks continued: Johnson had been out of the loop during the crisis over a potentially crippling strike in the steel industry; he had not been a major player in the Cuban missile crisis; he was "Uncle Cornpone" with the funny accent and the inferior education; he wore boots, not deck shoes; he was the square dancer at what was later to be called Camelot.

Despite Johnson's best efforts, he was still distrusted by liberals, and in Texas that distrust approached loathing. Being unable to defeat either LBJ or his lieutenant, John Connally, the best hope of Texas liberals was to work with Johnson's other enemies to remove him from the national ticket. That was easier said than done, but still they tried. They hoped to unite behind Senator Ralph Yarborough and seize control of the state party while sending a message to Washington that LBJ was more of a hindrance than a help in securing the state's twenty-five electoral. Johnson's response was to attempt the defeat of Yarborough. Both strategies cast a cloud over the chances of JFK carrying the state in the 1964 election.

Thus it was that the president and the vice president and their wives came to Texas in November 1963 to make peace within the Texas Democratic Party. Kennedy would support Connally for governor and Ralph Yarborough for the Senate. The nature of Texas politics had made it impossible for LBJ to gain the Democratic nomination in his own right. The nature of Texas politics would thrust him into the presidency.

By midafternoon of November 22, Kennedy was dead, and LBJ had been sworn in as the thirty-sixth president of the United States. Johnson did a masterful job of rallying the country during his first months in office and used his great legislative skills to pass programs that had been stalled under Kennedy, notably a landmark civil rights act and a tax cut. In addition, LBJ pushed through Congress a series of programs aimed at attacking poverty in the United States.

By the 1964 presidential election, LBJ had solidified his position as national leader and was able to portray skillfully his conservative Republican opponent, Arizona Senator Barry Goldwater, as a dangerous right-wing warmonger. Johnson and his running mate, Hubert Humphrey, smashed the Republican ticket, winning 61 percent of the popular vote and taking 44 states in one of the greatest landslides in history.

LBJ used this mandate to push through Congress a monumental package of social legislation, which he referred to as the Great Society. Large-scale government programs in health, education, environmental protection, and minority rights that were put in place set the U.S. domestic agenda for the following thirty years. At LBJ's behest, Congress passed more than 200 bills that created more than 500 programs.

Unfortunately for Johnson, his domestic successes were not mirrored in the foreign policy area. He had inherited an intractable problem in Southeast Asia in the form of U.S. involvement in the ongoing war between South and North Vietnam. Often against his better judgment, Johnson slowly allowed the war to escalate until it included tens of thousands of U.S. troops on the ground and a massive bombing campaign against Communist North Vietnam. By 1966, the war was the consuming issue in the United States, with large-scale protests and political divisions becoming standard fare. LBJ strove mightily to solve the problem and to open negotiations with the communists but was essentially frustrated at every turn.

When domestic violence broke out in the form of riots in the black ghettos of several U.S. cities, Johnson's hold on the country slackened even more, and in March 1968 he stunned the nation by announcing that he would not run for a second full term as president. His lame-duck efforts to bring the war to a close failed, and he retired to his ranch near Johnson City.

Lyndon Baines Johnson died of heart failure in January 1973, only one day before his successor announced an end to the war.

REFERENCES

Leonard Baker, *The Johnson Eclipse: A President's Vice-President* (New York: The Macmillan Company, 1966); Paul L Conkin, *Big Daddy From the Pedernales Lyndon Baines Johnson* (Boston: Twayne Publishers, 1986); Rowland Evans and Robert Novak, *Lyndon B. Johnson: The Exercise of Power* (New York: New American Library, 1966); Doris Kearns, *Lyndon Johnson and the American Dream* (New York: Signet Books, 1976); Merle Miller, *Lyndon: An Oral Biography* (New York: Putnam, 1988); Arthur M. Schlesinger Jr., *A Thousand Days: John F. Kennedy in the White House* (Boston: Houghton Mifflin and Co., 1965); Thomas S. Langston, *Lyndon Baines Johnson* (Washington: C Q Press, 2002); The Miller Center et al., *The Presidential Recordings: Lyndon B. Johnson (The Kennedy Assassination and the Transfer of Power, November 1963–January 1964)* 3 vols. and DVD (New York: W. W. Norton, 2005); Randall B. Woods, *LBJ: Architect of American Ambition* (New York: Free Press, 2006); John L. Bullion, *Lyndon B. Johnson and the Transformation of American Politics* (New York: Pearson Longman, 2008); Robert D. Johnson, *All the Way with LBJ: The 1964 Presidential Election* (New York: Cambridge University Press, 2009).

G. L. SELIGMANN received a B.A. and an M.A. in history from New Mexico A&M (now New Mexico State University) in 1957 and 1958 and a Ph.D. in history from the University of Arizona in 1967. His special research interest is

New Mexico politics in the late nineteenth and early twentieth centuries. In 1964, he directed the Johnson-Humphrey campaign for the Third Congressional District of Louisiana, thus triggering an ongoing fascination with LBJ. He has given several papers on the general topic of LBJ and his biographers and published "LBJ versus His Biographers: A Review Essay" in *Social Science Quarterly*. He is on the faculty of the University of North Texas and is past president of H-Net Humanities and Social Sciences Online.

HUBERT H. HUMPHREY, JR. (1911–1978)

Vice President, 1965–1969

(President Lyndon Baines Johnson)

HUBERT H. HUMPHREY, JR.
(Library of Congress)

By Karen M. Hult

For observers of U.S. politics from the late 1940s into the 1970s, the name Hubert Humphrey likely triggers a torrent of memories. Among such images may be his 1948 speech pleading with the Democratic Party "to get out of the shadow of states' rights and walk forthrightly into the bright sunshine of human rights," the ebullient "Happy Warrior" on the presidential campaign trail, his incongruous reference to the "politics of joy" in the midst of televised coverage of violent demonstrations during the 1968 Democratic convention, or a haggard U.S. senator advising a president while himself dying of cancer.

Humphrey's vice presidency was scarcely the high point of a long and distinguished career of public service. As vice president, Humphrey struggled to balance loyalty to a domineering and often ungrateful Lyndon Johnson, his own sense of responsibility to the nation, and his searing ambition to be president himself. Despite sporadic involvement in foreign policy and more regular participation in domestic policy and politics, Humphrey's talents and energies were largely checked—and his weaknesses magnified—by a suspicious president and a polarizing polity. Little wonder then that Hubert Humphrey compared being vice president to ". . . being naked in the middle of a blizzard with no one to even offer you a match to keep you warm."

Humphrey was a quintessentially public man. Not only did he spend most of his adult life in elective office, but he also was deeply committed to preserving and enhancing democratic governance. Throughout, too, Humphrey evidently craved recognition and affection and strove untiringly (if futilely) to become president.

Hubert Horatio Humphrey, Jr., though a second son, was named after his father; the junior Humphrey also had an elder and a younger sister. Humphrey was born in Wallace, South Dakota, but he spent most of his childhood in nearby Doland, where the family moved when he was four. In both Humphrey's telling and that of others, the roots of his love of politics and of many of his policy commitments can be traced to these early years. Humphrey's father, a pharmacist and small-drugstore owner, was an especially important influence. The young boy's rhetorical skills and political values were nurtured by a father who regularly read his children Woodrow Wilson's Fourteen Points and William Jennings Bryan's Cross of Gold speech and who conducted ongoing political debates at the drugstore soda fountain. Although the senior Humphrey was one of only a handful of Democrats in South Dakota, he was well respected, later serving as mayor and state legislator.

Like most members of his generation, Humphrey was deeply affected by the Great Depression. Economic troubles began early in South Dakota as its agricultural economy faltered and banks closed even before the devastating dust storms began. Humphrey's parents lost their house in 1927 and eventually moved to Huron, South Dakota, where his father opened another pharmacy in 1931. Hubert Humphrey, Jr., recalled being impressed by his parents' capacity to survive such setbacks without becoming bitter. Although he watched as his father extended credit and accepted barter for goods, he also became a staunch supporter of Franklin Delano Roosevelt and the New Deal.

The Depression also interfered with the young Humphrey's college plans. Initially, he and his older brother Ralph attended the University of Minnesota during alternate years. However, both returned home in March 1931 to help their father with the new drugstore. The following winter, Hubert completed a six-month course at Capitol College of Pharmacy in Denver, apparently resigned to life as a small-town pharmacist.

Humphrey married Muriel Buck in September 1936, but, he remembered, "[t]he depression, the dust storms, and the demands of family on a newlywed couple were finally too much." Using Muriel Buck Humphrey's savings, the two moved back to Minneapolis in September 1937, where Hubert resumed college; Muriel, who did not return to school, worked as a bookkeeper. In Minneapolis, the trademark Humphrey energy and speaking talents quickly surfaced. Humphrey completed his degree in political science in June 1939, graduating *magna cum laude*; he also was elected to Phi Beta Kappa and won a Big Ten debating championship.

Humphrey's next stop was Louisiana State University, which awarded him a graduate fellowship to study political science. At least by his own account, the year Humphrey spent at LSU taught him painful lessons about the discrimination blacks suffered in the United States and exposed him to southern politics (an experience he would draw on later in the Senate).

After finishing a master's degree (with a thesis on the political philosophy of the New Deal), Humphrey returned to the University of

Minnesota to begin doctoral work. Needing more money than a teaching assistantship provided to support a growing family (his first child was born in 1939, with three others to follow), however, he started working in summer 1940 in a series of Works Progress Administration (WPA) positions. Humphrey trained adult-education teachers in Duluth, directed the Workers' Education Program for the Twin Cities, and served as state director of workers' services. By 1942, Humphrey was charged with liquidating WPA programs in the state, and in 1943 he was named assistant director of the Minnesota War Manpower Commission. Despite persistent efforts to join the armed services, though, Humphrey initially failed physicals and then received deferments as a "critical" domestic worker.

Humphrey's childhood fascination with politics persisted. Meanwhile, his university connections put him in contact with several political activists, and his WPA positions had introduced him to local labor leaders. It did not take much encouragement to convince Humphrey to challenge the incumbent mayor of Minneapolis in 1943. Although he ultimately lost to the sitting mayor, Humphrey was able to reach a runoff, drawing support from the local AFL and the Jewish and black communities.

Although Humphrey next accepted a teaching job at Macalester College in St. Paul, he later readily admitted: "[T]eaching . . . was a pale second choice. . . . I was permanently hooked on politics." Meanwhile, the future vice president plunged into numerous political activities. Working with local labor groups had catalyzed his opposition to the communist left that had infiltrated Minnesota unions. Humphrey worked with Philip Murray (the president of the national CIO) to rid the Minnesota chapter of communists. More important for later national political endeavors, Humphrey also became one of the founders of Americans for Democratic Action, which sought to articulate an ideology that was both strongly anticommunist and liberal. In addition, concerned about the inability of liberal candidates to win statewide elections, Humphrey enlisted the help of the national Democratic Party (itself worried about the narrow Roosevelt victory in Minnesota in 1940) to achieve the "fusion" of the Minnesota Democratic Party with the Farmer-Labor Party. With the merger accomplished, in 1944 Humphrey ran FDR's campaign in the state and attended his first national convention as a delegate.

Humphrey succeeded at moving into politics full time when he was elected mayor of Minneapolis in 1945. The new mayor moved quickly to "clean up" the city, notorious for its police corruption, gambling, and prostitution. He also worked to reduce racism and anti-Semitism among police officers and is credited with creating the nation's first municipal Fair Employment Practices Commission.

Although Humphrey was easily reelected in 1947, the sirens of national politics beckoned. As he later wrote: "The Cold War and international events seemed more compelling than veterans' housing and liquor licenses."

In 1948, the mayor exploded into national consciousness, igniting a firestorm of controversy. At the Democratic convention, he spoke advocating passage of a strong civil rights plank to the party's platform, an action that most in the party hierarchy opposed and a majority of the platform committee refused to take. To the surprise of many (including Humphrey himself), the plank was approved, triggering Strom Thurmond and thirty-five other southern delegates to walk out. Although mobilization by key big city bosses (led by Ed Flynn from the Bronx) mostly accounted for the plank's success, Humphrey's speech is likely the most remembered and most effective speech he ever delivered. (Surprising to critics of Humphrey's longwindedness may be that the speech was a mere ten minutes long.)

The year 1948 also marked Humphrey's first election to the U.S. Senate, where he would serve until 1964 and again from 1970 to 1978. He was the first Democrat to be elected to the Senate from Minnesota since it became a state in 1858.

At the outset, Humphrey faced considerable opposition and mistrust. He recounted: "My actions at the Democratic convention had elicited bitterness and antagonism far beyond what I expected. . . . [I was] treated like an evil force that had seeped into sanctified halls." The new senator made matters worse by violating hoary institutional norms. For example, he was silent for a mere six weeks; then, the urge to speak that would generate criticism throughout his career took over. "His cocky attitude caused [a Republican senator] to whisper to a colleague during a Humphrey speech that the brash Minnesotan reminded him of some tomatoes he once planted 'too early in the spring and the frost got them.'"

Humphrey's biggest mistake during this early period was giving a floor speech that criticized the Joint Committee on Reduction of Nonessential Federal Expenditures, chaired by the powerful Harry Byrd from Virginia. Worse yet, the novice senator attacked the committee when Byrd was away attending to his ill mother. Despite Humphrey's apology, the next day Byrd delivered a scathing lecture on the floor of the Senate on the institution's norms; more than twenty-five senators followed to deliver their own attacks.

As humiliating as this well-reported experience was to Humphrey, it showed his resilience and willingness to learn from his mistakes. Earning the respect of his colleagues took time and hard work, features that would mark the rest of Humphrey's tenure. In the Senate, Humphrey's breakthrough came when he and Paul Douglas from Illinois offered a series of amendments to 1950 tax legislation. Although virtually all of the proposed changes lost, the two senators were well prepared. The acknowledged experts on the Finance Committee congratulated the pair on the constructive and responsible nature of a week-long debate.

After this rocky start, Humphrey embarked on an extraordinarily productive Senate career. In his first two terms, the Minnesota senator sponsored 1,044 bills and joint resolutions. Moreover, among these proposals were several

pathbreaking initiatives. Humphrey, for example, was one of the architects of P.L.–480 (which evolved into Food for Peace), authored the 1958 National Defense Education Act, and was instrumental in the creation of the Arms Control and Disarmament Agency and the ratification of the 1963 Limited Nuclear Test Ban Treaty.

Not all of Humphrey's proposals, of course, immediately became law. For example, the first bill Humphrey introduced in 1949 was to establish a program providing health care to the elderly through the Social Security system, a direct ancestor of Medicare, enacted in 1965. Meanwhile, throughout his Senate service, Humphrey took special interest in legislation in the areas of civil rights, public education, labor, and the Peace Corps. Long interested in foreign affairs (and acutely aware that presidential candidates are expected to have some foreign policy credentials), Humphrey pushed for the creation of a Senate subcommittee on nuclear disarmament in 1955 (which he chaired) and also served for a time as the Congressional Delegate to the United Nations.

Once Kennedy was elected president, Humphrey was chosen by the Senate Democrats as majority whip under Mike Mansfield, a position that made him the chief enforcer of party loyalty in the Senate. Far more energetic and adept at legislative maneuvering than the majority leader, Humphrey was an effective advocate for JFK's legislative program. After Kennedy's assassination, Humphrey joined Johnson in pushing hard to get the remaining Kennedy agenda through Congress. Most observers (including the new president) credit Humphrey with being instrumental in securing Senate passage of major legislation like the 1964 omnibus tax bill and the Civil Rights Act of 1964.

At the same time, Humphrey could not boast an unblemished record of accomplishment in the Senate. For example, perhaps reflecting Humphrey's own strong anticommunism, he did not distinguish himself by opposing Senator Joseph McCarthy, even though he was a member of McCarthy's Government

Operations Committee. Indeed, some of Humphrey's language was written into the Communist Control Act of 1954, which sought to outlaw the Communist Party altogether.

More generally, at least one former legislative assistant has questioned the depth and quality of the Minnesota senator's deliberativeness:

[Humphrey was] a whirling dervish who absorb[ed] things fantastically quick, but the idea of Humphrey reading a book or sitting down long enough to seriously think about the implications of what he was doing is hard to imagine. He was so active that I don't think he had time to think about the big things.

The U.S. Senate, of course, also was where Humphrey and Lyndon Johnson developed the difficult and complex relationship that would so bedevil the former's vice presidency. Each man always claimed to have deep, genuine affection for the other; moreover, their relationship produced mutual benefits. For example, Humphrey credited LBJ (along with his LSU debate partner Russell Long) with establishing his credibility among southern senators. For his part, Johnson saw Humphrey as his link with the liberal-intellectual wing of the Democratic Party, which had long suspected the Texan. After JFK was assassinated, Humphrey worked to convince many Kennedy advisers to stay on in the White House and contributed the memorable phrase, "Let us continue" to LBJ's first speech as president.

One also can interpret LBJ's actions in a less benign light. According to historian Paul Conkin, Johnson "used and wooed" Humphrey when they were senators, making the latter "a bit of a protege. He befriended him and to some extent bought his loyalty." As minority leader, for instance, LBJ got Humphrey on the coveted Foreign Relations Committee in January 1953. Thus, "Lyndon recognized his worth, flattered his ego, and inhibited Humphrey from agitating domestic issues that divided Senate Democrats" because the Minnesota senator had to give up assignments on the Agriculture and the Labor and Public Welfare committees. More fundamentally, Conkin argues, LBJ had

. . . considerable disdain for men like Humphrey. Behind his exuberance and talkativeness . . . , Humphrey was an intellectual with a few scholarly credentials. This side of him, and his identification with the Senate's northern liberals, created elements of jealousy and resentment on Johnson's part.

Despite his clear love of the Senate, Humphrey, like many of his colleagues there, nursed presidential ambitions. For this, he offered few apologies: "I thought lack of ambition was sinful and that a politician without it was ready for retirement." In 1956, Humphrey became one of the first candidates ever to campaign openly for the Democratic vice-presidential nomination. He believed that Adlai Stevenson had promised to name him as his running mate, and Humphrey was stunned when Stevenson opened the nomination to convention vote. Utterly unprepared, Humphrey ran fifth on the first ballot and then shifted his support to Senate colleague Estes Kefauver, who won the nomination on the second ballot.

Again, Humphrey rebounded from a humiliating experience and shifted his attention to the presidency, becoming the first formal candidate in 1960. He entered only two primaries—Wisconsin and West Virginia—and was decisively defeated by John Kennedy in both. The Humphrey camp attributed Kennedy's Wisconsin victory to a heavy Catholic "crossover" vote, but the Minnesota senator's disastrous loss in West Virginia produced more lasting scars. In West Virginia, he was hamstrung by the issue of Kennedy's Catholicism, which had surfaced in Wisconsin: Humphrey could scarcely discuss it without appearing to be a religious bigot. At least as important, the Kennedy campaign had insurmountable funding and organizational advantages. Humphrey was most bitter, however, about Franklin Delano Roosevelt, Jr.'s, attack on his World War II service record, which Humphrey believed

Robert Kennedy instigated (though whether this was the case is considerably less clear). Humphrey withdrew after garnering only 39.2 percent of the vote in West Virginia to JFK's 60.8 percent. The West Virginia contest produced lasting coolness between Humphrey and the Kennedys and apparently led the Minnesota senator to reject out of hand tentative offers from the Kennedy camp to become the vice-presidential nominee. Ever the good soldier, though, Humphrey did help quell a liberal revolt against LBJ at the 1960 Democratic convention.

Humphrey's ambition to attain higher office soon resurfaced, accelerated by events. Relatively soon after JFK's assassination, Humphrey began "an intensive effort to woo labor leaders I knew, journalists and commentators who wrote and rewrote the vice-presidential story, and leaders of the business community, an area where I was very weak." Despite strong support from party, civil rights, and labor leaders, he found himself competing for the nomination with his fellow senator from Minnesota, Eugene McCarthy. Characteristically, Johnson toyed with Humphrey, adding conditions for the nomination and refusing to make an iron-clad commitment until well after the convention had started. Humphrey remembered campaigning hard, delighting in the first plane solely under his campaign's command, the redoubtable "Happy Warrior."

Serving as vice president likely was the most agonizing period of Hubert Humphrey's public life. Still, Humphrey maintained his frenetic pace. He made twelve foreign trips as vice president, visiting thirty-one countries—a record unequaled until the vice presidency of Humphrey's Minnesota protégé, Walter Mondale. Like his immediate predecessors, Humphrey was a member of the cabinet and the National Security Council. He also for a time coordinated the federal government's civil rights programs as chair of the President's Council on Equal Opportunity. In addition, the vice president chaired, among others, advisory councils to the Office of Economic Opportunity and the Peace Corps, the President's Council on Youth Opportunity, the National Aeronautics and Space Council, and the President's Council on Recreation and Natural Beauty. Much like Johnson before him, Humphrey worked with Congress to help pass the administration's programs, including the flurry of Great Society initiatives in the mid-1960s. The vice president sought as well, with ever mounting difficulty, to be LBJ's link to liberals, blacks, and Democratic party leaders.

In early 1965, LBJ moved local government liaison from the White House (where it had been lodged since the Eisenhower years) to the vice-president's office. Mayors generally were pleased with the new arrangements, praising Humphrey's staffing, his personal interest in the nation's cities, and his office's ability to resolve snarls involving federal grants quickly. For his part, Humphrey's aides claimed that he spent more of his time on this than on any of his other assigned tasks.

Like many vice presidents, however, Humphrey soon faced challenges from senior White House staffers, who were concerned about protecting both the president's interests and their own political and policy turfs. Humphrey clashed most frequently with Johnson aide Joseph Califano who directed an ever-expanding domestic policy operation within the White House Office. Rather quickly, the Equal Opportunity Council that Humphrey chaired was abolished and the vice president lost his civil rights responsibilities to Califano.

Even more galling perhaps were the ongoing indignities to which the president subjected Humphrey. Despite their apparent closeness as senators and his own unhappy experiences as vice president, LBJ sometimes treated his vice president—as he did many others—with cruelty and contempt. Conkin contends that LBJ, the master manipulator, "had a hook in [Humphrey]—Humphrey's presidential ambitions—and on occasions he twisted it." At a time when Humphrey was delivering as many as twenty-five prepared major speeches a month, he was forced to get direct presidential approval to use a White House plane or boat, and his speeches needed to be approved by senior White House aides. Humphrey's only visit to Camp David was at Jimmy Carter's invitation in 1977.

Vietnam, however, presented by far the worst problems for Humphrey. The new vice president's growing doubts about U.S. involvement in Vietnam almost immediately got him in trouble with LBJ. Despite his preconvention pledges to Johnson that he would never disagree with the president in a meeting with others present, at a National Security Council session in February 1965 Humphrey expressed concerns about both using retaliatory air strikes to bring North Vietnam to the negotiating table and expanding U.S. presence more generally. Humphrey followed up with a memo elaborating on his arguments, once more violating a rule of the leak-obsessed LBJ. As a result, the vice president was excluded for nearly a year from the inner circle of presidential foreign policy advisers and not invited to Johnson's informal Tuesday lunches, the chief forum for discussing Vietnam. Meanwhile, according to David Halberstam, ". . . every one of the other principals [including the other "dove," George Ball], wanting to keep their own effectiveness and credibility with this tempestuous President . . . became wary of being seen with Humphrey; he had become a cripple and everyone else knew it."

Humphrey's status within the administration rose marginally as he proved to be a capable roving presidential ambassador in early trips to India and France. Finally, in February 1966, the President sent Humphrey (on less than a day's notice) on a grueling two-week trip to nine Asian countries. To underscore his continuing lack of trust, though, LBJ also ordered White House aides to accompany him and report back daily on the vice president's activities. The ostensible purpose of the trip was to spread the "Honolulu Doctrine": the U.S. approach in Southeast Asia would increasingly focus on the pursuit of positive social and economic development goals. Instead, the U.S. party was treated to the kind of positive reporting by the South Vietnamese on the war's progress that George Romney would later call brainwashing. In Humphrey's case, the trip worked as intended, and he came home persuaded of the correctness of U.S. policy (though his doubts would return after a second trip in 1967).

For a time, the vice president became, in the words of his biographer, Johnson's "most articulate and indefatigable advocate of the war." Once again, Humphrey was invited to participate in high-level foreign policy discussions; yet, his hard-charging defense of administration policy also produced serious rifts with old liberal allies, and his general approval ratings in public opinion polls dropped.

As the Johnson years continued, controversy over Vietnam mounted—both within the administration and more generally in the country. This polarizing conflict, along with the vice president's own doubts, his painful separation from former friends and growing vilification on college campuses, and his sense of loyalty to, and ultimate dependence upon, Lyndon Johnson plagued Humphrey even after LBJ withdrew from the presidential race on March 31, 1968. Although Humphrey quickly threw his own hat into the ring, he feared that Johnson would reenter the race (especially after Robert Kennedy was killed in early June) until he actually received the formal Democratic nomination.

The 1968 Democratic convention was, from Humphrey's perspective, disastrous. Not only did Johnson forces retain control over virtually all of the logistics of the convention, but because there was an incumbent president likely to seek reelection, it had been scheduled late in the summer, reducing time for intraparty wounds to heal and for an effective fall campaign plan to be crafted and put in place. Control of the platform committee by Johnson loyalists and the Soviet invasion of Czechoslovakia virtually on the eve of the convention conspired to make compromise on a Vietnam plank impossible. Meanwhile, a national television audience watched violent protests on

Chicago streets as delegates inside the convention hall celebrated.

For much of the fall campaign, Humphrey was hampered by his unwillingness to express his own views on Vietnam. LBJ continued to demand absolute consistency with administration policy on Vietnam from his vice president. Humphrey reluctantly complied until the end of September, evidently driven both by the high value he placed on loyalty and by the concern that any apparent straying from the administration line could disrupt the Paris peace talks. In September, Humphrey trailed Republican nominee Richard Nixon by more than fifteen points and faced extraordinary difficulties raising funds and mobilizing traditional Democratic supporters. While Independent candidate George Wallace was siphoning away blue-collar and southern voters, many liberals deeply opposed Johnson's Vietnam policies. Of the three candidates, Humphrey endured by far the most interference from antiwar activists, who tried to keep him from delivering speeches and engaged in numerous verbal and physical confrontations with the candidate and his entourage.

Finally, Humphrey escaped LBJ's "fatal embrace" in a speech he delivered in Salt Lake City on September 30. Although the speech failed to outline any major departures from current policy, it did signal the vice president's increased willingness to halt U.S. bombing of North Vietnam and to pursue peace more vigorously. Opinion polls narrowed considerably, and many Democratic constituencies returned to spark the last weeks of the campaign. The renewed enthusiasm, however, was not enough. Humphrey lost to Nixon by less than 1 percent of the votes cast nationally.

In such a close election, a variety of factors could have tipped the scales. Not surprisingly, some Humphrey supporters blamed the lack of presidential support for his vice president. LBJ made only one campaign speech for Humphrey until their joint appearance in the Houston Astrodome in early November; nor was the machinery of the federal government used for partisan purposes during the campaign. John-son aide Harry McPherson has observed that Johnson evidently had mixed feelings about the vice president's candidacy:

On the one hand, an old and deep affection for Humphrey; his own lifelong fidelity to the Democratic party; and surely a desire that the Administration's record be vindicated by the election of its Vice President. On the other, apprehension that Humphrey was preparing to repudiate the war policies for which he had once been a zealous advocate; the desire to remain "above politics" in the search for peace; and, surely, resentment that another man now carried the banner that was his by right of achievement . . ."

Others point to characteristic weaknesses in all three of Humphrey's bids for the presidency. First, the candidate himself routinely talked too long, obscuring his message and plunging daily schedules into chaos. (Indeed, Conkin reports: "LBJ once remarked to Lady Bird: 'If only I could breed him to Calvin Coolidge.'") More important, Humphrey's campaign organizations tended to be weak, shot through with staff infighting and sometimes stunning gaps in expertise. His close friend and personal physician Edgar Berman has contended that Humphrey had a staff of "warm hearts and fuzzy heads." Meanwhile, Berman continued, Humphrey was a "terrible" fund-raiser, and his campaigns routinely faced financial problems.

Out of national elective office after the election for the first time twenty years, Humphrey went home to Minnesota. He accepted offers to teach at both Macalester College and the University of Minnesota, became the chairman of the board of the Encyclopedia Britannica Education Foundation, and sat on several other boards of directors. Yet, the former vice president was wounded by the resistance of some students and faculty to his return to college campuses, and he clearly missed being out of the national spotlight.

Humphrey leaped at the chance to run again for elective office when Eugene McCarthy decided not to seek reelection to the U.S. Senate in 1970. Returning to the Senate created its own adjustment problems: not only was Humphrey again a lowly junior senator with no seniority, but the Senate itself had changed. Still, he set out to try to reestablish his credentials among liberals—voting, for example, to cut off financial support for the supersonic transport, which environmentalists opposed.

Humphrey made a final bid for the presidency in 1972. He ran second to Wallace in the Florida primary but trailed both Wallace and McGovern in Wisconsin. Despite familiar funding problems, Humphrey then swept the primaries in Pennsylvania, Ohio, Indiana, and West Virginia. Again, though, financial and organizational weaknesses haunted him. George McGovern won the California primary and became the Democratic nominee.

For reasons that may never be clear, Humphrey at the last minute decided not to run for his party's nomination in 1976, declaring that he did not want to be "humiliated again at this stage" of his life. He was diagnosed as having bladder cancer in August 1976, but his physician insists that he had a clean bill of health in the spring.

In spite of the cancer diagnosis, Humphrey was reelected to the Senate in 1976. He also advised President Carter and served as an advocate for his programs in the Senate. As his illness worsened, Humphrey talked with Nixon and specifically asked that the former president be invited to his Washington funeral service. Hubert Humphrey died in January 1978 and became only the twenty-second person to lie in state in the Capitol Rotunda. Nixon did attend Humphrey's funeral, his first visit to the capital since his resignation.

Hubert Humphrey's public life was marked by significant achievement and considerable disappointment, which reflected both the immense challenges of the times and his own characteristic strengths and weaknesses. His era was marked by periods dominated by oversimplification, dramatic overstatement, and extreme rhetoric. Yet, Humphrey viscerally disliked confrontation and seemed to genuinely believe that

". . . there is not a single problem in this country that is not subject to reason and negotiation and at least some form of conciliation. . . ." The urge to compromise produced clear successes in civil rights and in Senate leadership but less-impressive results in challenging McCarthyism or responding to polarization over Vietnam.

More generally, Humphrey's strengths and weaknesses seem inextricably linked. For example, his almost superhuman energy helped mobilize others to generate social change but on occasion likely drove out thoughtful reflection. The "lesson" that Humphrey drew from his first electoral defeat in 1943—that "loyalty, above all else, seems important"—served him well in building coalitions and attracting lifelong supporters. It also, however, heightened his vulnerability to LBJ's manipulation. The vice president's unwillingness to challenge U.S. policy in Vietnam consistently and openly was a consequence, one magnified and only belatedly overcome by Humphrey's presidential ambitions. Nonetheless, given the complexities and constraints of both the man and his times, Hubert Humphrey was a valuable contributor to the polity he so revered.

REFERENCES

Edgar Berman, M.D., *Hubert: The Triumph and Tragedy of the Humphrey I Knew* (New York: G.P. Putnam's Sons, 1979); Vaughn Davis Bornet, *The Presidency of Lyndon B. Johnson* (Lawrence: University Press of Kansas, 1983); Paul K. Conkin, *Big Daddy from the Pedernales; Lyndon Baines Johnson* (Boston: Twayne Publishers, 1986); Robert Dallek, *Lone Star Rising: Lyndon Johnson and His Times, 1908–1960* (New York: Oxford University Press, 1991); Albert Eisele, *Almost to the Presidency: A Biography of Two American Politicians* (Blue Earth, Minn.: The Piper Company, 1972); Dan B. Fleming, Jr., *Kennedy vs. Humphrey, West Virginia, 1960: The Pivotal Battle for the Democratic Presidential Nomination* (Jefferson, N.C.: McFarland and Company, 1992); Joel Goldstein, *The Modern Vice Presidency: The Transformation of a Political Institution* (Princeton, N.J.: Princeton University Press, 1982); David Halberstam, *The Best and the Brightest*

(Greenwich, Conn.: Fawcett Publications, 1972); Hubert H. Humphrey, *The Education of a Public Man: My Life and Politics,* Norman Sherman, ed. (Minneapolis: University of Minnesota Press, 1991); Harry McPherson, *A Political Education: A Washington Memoir* (Boston: Houghton Mifflin, 1988); David M. Welborn and Jesse Burkhead, *Intergovernmental Relations in the American Administrative State: The Johnson Presidency* (Austin: University of Texas Press, 1989); Jeff Taylor, *Where Did the Party Go?: William Jennings Bryan, Hubert Humphrey, and the Jeffersonian Legacy* (Columbia: University of Missouri Press, 2006).

KAREN M. HULT is professor of political science at Virginia Polytechnic Institute and State University, book review editor of *Presidential Studies Quarterly,* and is currently on the editorial board of *Rhetoric & Public Affairs.* She was previously on the boards of the *American Journal of Political Science* and *Presidential Studies Quarterly.* Her publications include *Empowering the White House: Governance under Nixon, Ford, and Carter* (with Charles Walcott, University Press of Kansas, 2004), *Agency Merger and Bureaucratic Redesign, Governing Public Organizations: Politics, Structure, and Institutional Design* (with Charles Walcott), *Governing the White House: From Hoover through Johnson* (with Charles Walcott), and numerous journal articles. Her primary scholarly interests are the design and dynamics of government organizations.

SPIRO THEODORE AGNEW (1918–1996)

Vice President, 1969–1973

(President Richard M. Nixon)

SPIRO T. AGNEW
(Library of Congress)

By John Robert Greene

On August 8, 1968, at about 1:00 P.M., Richard M. Nixon went down to the ballroom of his Miami Beach hotel to talk to the press for the first time since winning the Republican Party's nomination for the presidency. The room was buzzing with anticipation, as everyone expected that Nixon would use the occasion to announce the name of his running mate. Smart money was riding on either one of Nixon's two defeated rivals for the nomination—New York Governor Nelson Rockefeller and California Governor Ronald Reagan—or on longtime Nixon confidant Robert Finch. When Nixon announced his choice—Governor Spiro T. Agnew of Maryland—the press was stunned. As Nixon walked out of the room without taking any questions, several reporters cried out, "Spiro *Who?*"

The son of a Greek immigrant, Spiro Theodore Agnew attended Johns Hopkins University and Baltimore Law School before his education was interrupted by World War II. He married Elinn Judefind in 1942, during the war (the couple eventually had four children). He served in Europe as a captain in an armored division. He received his law degree from Baltimore in 1947 and began a law practice while seeking a career in politics. A Republican in a heavily Democratic state, it took until 1957 for Agnew to secure his first official post, an appointment to the Baltimore County Zoning Board of Appeals. Five years later, in a surprising upset, he was elected Baltimore County Executive. The Baltimore Democratic Party spent much of Agnew's tenure planning to unseat him in 1966. Recognizing that reelection was probably out of the question, Agnew began to sound out Maryland Republican leaders about a run for governor. He was not given much of a chance, but no other Republican wanted the nomination. Agnew once again won in an upset, thanks to the rabidly segregationist stand of his Democratic opponent and the correspondingly solid support of Agnew by the Baltimore black community.

Agnew's black support helped earn him a label as a moderate, sometimes left-of-center Republican. Part of this reputation was borne out by events, as Agnew put forth a progressive Fair Housing Act and appointed many blacks to statewide positions. However, Agnew's moderate tendencies were not deeply held, as was soon evidenced by his actions following the riots in Baltimore after the April 1968 assassination of Martin Luther King, Jr. Agnew called some 100 of the city's black leaders to his Annapolis office and, rather than offering them sympathy and help, berated them and laid the blame for the riots squarely at their door. Agnew called them "caterwauling, riot-inciting, burn-America-down type of leaders," and saw to it that his harangue was leaked to reporters in detail.

Agnew's response to the black leadership appealed to Pat Buchanan, then working as a speechwriter for Richard Nixon's campaign to win the 1968 presidential nomination. Buchanan reported Agnew's tirade to his boss, who arranged for a dinner with Agnew and Nixon law partner John Mitchell, then serving as Nixon's campaign manager. During the course of the dinner, Nixon asked Agnew if he would place his name in nomination before the convention. Agnew agreed, and Nixon came away from the dinner convinced that the governor would make a good running mate. This was a remarkable stroke of luck for Agnew, who not weeks before had been a supporter of Nelson Rockefeller's presidential candidacy, only to be left behind and embarrassed (literally standing in front of the Maryland press corps, about to make a speech of support) when Rockefeller announced that he wasn't sure that he wanted to run.

Despite Agnew's stroke of good fortune, he was far from Nixon's first choice. Nixon offered the vice-presidential nod first to Robert Finch, who, citing the appearance of cronyism, declined. Nixon then asked House Minority Leader Gerald Ford, who also declined in hopes of becoming the Speaker of the House after a Republican victory that fall. Nixon then turned to Agnew, arguing to those in the party who did not know the governor (it was reported that when Nixon told him of his final choice, Ford laughed out loud) that he was a good speaker who had shown courage during the Baltimore riots.

Yet the choice was a carefully considered one. Agnew—like Nixon in 1952—was largely chosen for his appeal to a constituency that distrusted the head of its ticket: the conservative wing of the Republican Party. It is clear that many early supporters of Alabama Governor George Wallace, not wanting to "waste their vote" on a third-party candidate, finally came home to the Republican Party because of Agnew. Nixon also had an important campaign role for Agnew, one that Nixon had been assigned by the head of *his* ticket in 1952. Dwight Eisenhower, who was anxious to run a campaign that showed him to be "presidential," instructed Nixon to go on the attack, while Ike took the smoother, high road. Sixteen years later, with an equal desire to be perceived as presidential timber but with Vietnam hovering as an issue that threatened to destroy any candidate who mishandled it, Nixon wanted to deflect as much attention from himself as possible. Thus, the low road was consigned to Agnew, and it was a road that he traveled well. During the campaign, Agnew called Maryland reporter, Eugene Oishi, a "fat Jap" (apologizing later, saying that they were old friends); he responded to the criticism that he was not campaigning in many inner cities by snapping that "when you've seen one slum, you've seen them all"; and he accused Democratic candidate Hubert Humphrey of being "squishy-soft on communism." Nixon's choice had proved to be a masterful one. Far from being embarrassed that Agnew was panned by the press, Nixon was pleased that Agnew's press contingent had doubled before October, thus deflecting attention from the issues of the day. More important, in an election that was this close (Nixon won with just 43.4 percent of the popular vote), postelection polls made it clear that, as Nixon had predicted, many conservatives voted for the Republican ticket *because* of Agnew's rhetoric.

However, despite Agnew's political value, Nixon was not about to allow him to have an active role in the formation of administration policy. From the start, Agnew was given low-level assignments, kept out of the limelight, and given only limited access to the president. Agnew himself made the situation worse by exhibiting a decided lack of political tact. As the first man since Calvin Coolidge to step directly to the vice presidency from a state-house, it was logical that he be put in charge of relations with other state executives. The Office of Intergovernmental Relations was thus created as part of the Office of the Vice President in 1969. However, Agnew was far from diplomatic in his dealings with his former colleagues—Rockefeller simply refused to talk with him, sending his messages to Nixon through National Security Adviser Henry Kissinger. As chair of a Space Advisory Committee,

Agnew's dogged support of a costly manned mission to Mars angered the White House. As a statutory member of the National Security Council, he advocated the immediate bombing of the Viet Cong sanctuaries in Cambodia and Laos. This belief mirrored Nixon's own, but Agnew was so strident about his support that Nixon, feeling that he had been overshadowed by an adviser, cut Agnew out of the foreign policy loop for the rest of the administration. The CIA even reported that while on an African trip, Agnew had told leaders that he opposed Nixon's overtures to the People's Republic of China. Agnew did make one solid contribution to the administration's policy: Sharing Nixon's belief of Indian self-determination, Agnew's National Council on Indian Opportunity committee officially proposed the establishment of an Indian Revenue Sharing Program in October 1971, a plan that was supported by the Department of the Interior and eventually adopted. But this was not enough. By 1970, Nixon was openly speculating with his aides about getting rid of Agnew by naming him to the Supreme Court—then he could name John Connally, Nixon's choice as his heir apparent, vice president.

However, as much as he would have liked to have done so, Nixon was not able to rid himself of Agnew. By mid-1970, it was clear that Nixon was losing support of the conservative wing of the Republican Party, largely due to its opposition to détente with China and the Soviet Union. Despite Nixon's problems, Agnew found a home in the right wing, thanks to some of the most inflammatory rhetoric of the modern political period. Unneeded in Washington, Agnew hit the road, using speeches largely crafted by Buchanan. His first target was what he perceived to be a growing permissiveness on the part of the U.S. middle-class toward their children. At the University of Utah in May 1969, he railed against the dress of college students ("I didn't raise my son to be a daughter"). The next month at Ohio State, Agnew charged that any society that feared its young was "effete." Later that fall in

New Orleans, he attacked the "effete corps of impudent snobs" who were teaching in the colleges and universities and poisoning the minds of the nation's young. These liberals soon were labeled with one of the most famous of the Agnewisms, "Radiclibs." But his most famous attack came in November 1969, when Agnew turned on the nation's broadcast media. In a speech at the Midwest Republican Conference held in Des Moines, Agnew savaged a media "whose minds were made up in advance" on Nixon's Vietnam policies. Agnew charged the networks with a conspiracy to slant the news through "a handful of commentators who admit their own set of biases," and encouraged like-minded people to call in and voice their support of his attack. All three networks were flooded with phone calls and telegrams; Agnew had become a celebrity.

By July 1970, several Republican congressional candidates, including Robert Taft of Ohio, publicly stated that they did not want Agnew campaigning for them in the off-year elections that fall, but Nixon wanted Agnew on the campaign trail. Using Agnew as the administration's chief campaign surrogate would allow Nixon to stay in Washington and avoid the political fray. It would also allow the administration to strike out at Republicans who had criticized the administration's policy on Vietnam without involving the president. With Buchanan at his side, the vice president plunged into the first substantive job given him by Nixon since their election. As he had been in 1968, Agnew was both coarse and effective. His attacks on antiwar New York Republican Senator Charles Goodell were so stinging (in a reference to the first person who had undergone a sex-change operation, Agnew called Goodell the "Christine Jorgensen of the Republican Party") that they brought private complaints from Republican Party leaders like Ford. Regardless of Ford's objections, Goodell lost his race, and the White House was ecstatic. Agnew played a large part for the administration in keeping its off-year losses to a minimum that fall.

Agnew's worth to the Nixon administration was clearly as a campaigner who galvanized the far right with his outlandish oratory. Despite his belief that his vice president was not up to the job, Nixon was quick to announce—during a January 2, 1972, televised interview with CBS's Dan Rather—that Agnew would stay on the ticket that fall. During the campaign, Agnew went after Democratic presidential candidate George McGovern, calling him "one of the greatest frauds ever to be considered as a presidential candidate by a major American party." Agnew also followed Democratic vice-presidential contender Sargent Shriver from city to city, answering the speeches of the former director of the Peace Corps with speeches that specialized in claiming that Shriver's position on the ticket was a result of his being an in-law of liberal senator Edward M. Kennedy.

Agnew's invective was less necessary in 1968 than in 1972 (the Republican ticket won with 60.7 percent of the popular vote). It also did not earn for him a place at Nixon's side during the second term. Quite the contrary; because the Constitution disqualified him from seeking a third term, Nixon no longer needed Agnew to rally the conservatives on the campaign trail. Immediately following the campaign, any access he may have had to Nixon virtually disappeared. Agnew was stripped of the Office of Intergovernmental Relations and virtually shut out of White House councils.

Yet, Agnew soon had much greater worries than a lack of access. In Baltimore, U.S. Attorney George Beall had found evidence that real estate developers in and around Baltimore County had been paying kickback money to Agnew since 1962. The payments began as a quid pro quo for lucrative building contracts, but one developer, Lester Matz, fell behind, and at least two installments were delivered to Agnew after he became vice president. Throughout the spring of 1973, Agnew had heard the rumors of an investigation, but the Watergate revelations had spurred the press to new heights of investigative reporting. Agnew dared not interfere with the investigation, lest an enterprising reporter pick up the scent.

Nixon had already heard. On April 14, 1973, during a meeting with Chief of Staff H. R. Haldeman and Domestic Policy Adviser John Ehrlichman, Nixon was first given details of the investigation. This news settled on a White House that had long been bunkering itself against Watergate; Nixon made it clear that there would be no attempt made to cover up Agnew's transgressions. Left without White House support, it was only a matter of time before the press picked up the story. On August 6, the *Wall Street Journal* called Agnew to tell him that it was running a story that reported that there was an investigation underway. That same day, Attorney General Elliot Richardson, who had been kept appraised of the investigation by Beall, met with Nixon and told him that Beall's case against Agnew was airtight.

The next day, August 7, Nixon met with Agnew. The vice president emerged to report that the president supported him in his fight against charges that Agnew labeled "damned lies." But Nixon's support never consisted of anything more than benign neglect. Watergate-implicated White House aides, including Haldeman and Ehrlichman, had been allowed to resign, as Nixon was faced with investigations by both the Congress and a Justice Department Special Prosecutor, both of whom wanted to hear recordings from an Oval Office taping system. As Nixon fought the battle of the tapes—which had every indication, even as early as the summer of 1973, of being a fight that would find its way to the Supreme Court—Nixon clearly wanted to rid himself of Agnew as soon as was politically possible. Before the end of August, he sent Alexander Haig, Haldeman's replacement as chief of staff, to ask the vice president to resign. Agnew refused, holding out until mid-September when both Haig and White House Counsel J. Fred Buzhardt told Agnew that he had no chance. Agnew's lawyer contacted Beall, and the plea bargaining began.

But when the *Washington Post* reported on September 22 that bargaining had begun,

a seething Agnew tried one more offensive. Ordering the plea bargaining to come to a halt, he demanded to be afforded the formal impeachment process before the House of Representatives. This terrified the administration—once the impeachment process had been dusted off and tested, Agnew's case might well serve as a model for Nixon's own. Fortunately for Nixon, Speaker of the House Carl Albert refused to intervene. Agnew then tried one last gambit. Arguing that the Constitution prevented a sitting vice president from being indicted for a crime, his lawyers filed a suit against the Justice Department, enjoining them not to turn over any further evidence to the grand jury. On October 4, the court ruled that while a president was protected from indictment, a vice president was not.

Agnew had no further legal avenues, and his attempt to garner public opinion had failed miserably. The country was Watergate-weary; both the president and the people wanted Agnew gone, and the vice president finally accepted the inevitable. On October 10, Agnew appeared in a federal courtroom in Baltimore to plead nolo contendere (no contest) to a charge of income tax evasion. He received a $10,000 fine and a three-year jail sentence, which was suspended immediately. Later that afternoon, Agnew delivered his resignation to Secretary of State Kissinger. On October 12, Nixon announced that he would nominate Gerald Ford to replace Agnew under the terms of the Twenty-fifth Amendment.

Five days after his resignation, on October 15, Agnew delivered a farewell address to the nation. It was vintage Agnew, as he continued to claim his innocence and to blame the media for his problems. In the national sigh of relief that followed the Ford nomination, Agnew's protests fell largely on deaf ears.

In the more than two decades after he left the vice presidency—a period that saw Agnew retreat into a retirement that did not include either an attempt to return to public office or to the public arena—Agnew continued to maintain his guiltlessness. In his memoirs, *Go*

Quietly . . . or Else (1980), Agnew widened his indictment to include Attorney General Richardson and Nixon himself. In May 1995, the Republican-dominated Congress accorded Agnew an honor which, to that point, he had been the only vice president not to receive: His bust was included with the other vice presidents just outside Statuary Hall on the Senate side of the U.S. Capitol building—in a ceremony that received a great deal of media attention.

Spiro Agnew died on September 18, 1996, at age 77 in a hospital in Berlin, Maryland. He was admitted with a previously undiagnosed case of acute leukemia and died within three hours.

REFERENCES

Spiro Agnew, *Go Quietly . . . or Else* (New York: William Morrow and Co., 1980); Richard M. Cohen and Jules Witcover, *A Heartbeat Away: The Investigation and Resignation of Vice President Spiro T. Agnew* (New York: Viking Press, 1977); John Robert Greene, *The Limits of Power: The Nixon and Ford Administrations* (Bloomington: University of Indiana Press, 1992); Anthony J. Lukas, *Nightmare: The Underside of the Nixon Years* (New York: Viking Press, 1976); Jules Witcover, *White Knight: The Rise of Spiro Agnew* (New York: Random House, 1972); Jules Witcover, *Very Strange Bedfellows: The Short and Unhappy Marriage of Richard Nixon and Spiro Agnew* (New York: Public Affairs, 2007).

JOHN ROBERT GREENE is the Paul J. Schupf Professor of History and Humanities at Cazenovia College, Cazenovia, New York, where he has taught since 1969. In 1993, the faculty voted him the honor of Distinguished Faculty Member. Greene holds both a B.A. and M.A. from St. Bonaventure University and a Ph.D. from Syracuse University. His fifteen books include *The Presidency of George Bush* (1999); *The Limits of Power: The Nixon and Ford Administrations* (1992) and *The Presidency of Gerald R. Ford* (1995). His biography of Betty Ford, *Candor and Courage in the White House*, was published in the fall of 2004. He is also the author of two books in the Presidential Profiles series: *The Nixon and Ford Years* (2006) and *George H. W. Bush* (2006).

GERALD RUDOLPH FORD (1913–2006)

Vice President, 1973–1974

(President Richard M. Nixon)

GERALD R. FORD
(Library of Congress)

By John Robert Greene

On October 10, 1973, pleading no contest to a charge of income tax evasion, Vice President Spiro Agnew resigned. Later that day, President Richard Nixon asked House Minority Leader Gerald R. Ford (a Republican from Michigan) to a private meeting at the White House. Aware that he would be the first president to utilize the Twenty-Fifth Amendment, ratified in 1967 to give the president the opportunity to fill a vice presidential vacancy by "nominat[ing] a vice president who shall take office upon confirmation by a majority vote of both houses of Congress," and equally aware that Watergate had squandered away much of his support on Capitol Hill, Nixon wanted Ford's advice on potential candidates who would be confirmable. After Ford left, Nixon spoke with advisers Bryce Harlow and Melvin Laird and Democratic Speaker of the House Carl Albert. All three men told the president that Gerald

Ford was the only confirmable choice. Nixon instructed Laird to call Ford to sound him out about the nomination.

That evening, Laird called Ford at his home to inquire whether Ford would accept the vice-presidential nomination if offered the position by the president. Despite the protests of his wife, Betty, who said that she wanted him to run for one more term in the House and then retire, Ford agreed. The next day in the Oval Office, Nixon formally asked Ford if he wanted the job, and Ford accepted. Later that evening, Nixon publicly announced his choice of Ford to the nation, and those assembled in the room to hear the announcement went wild with cheering and whistling. Somewhat surprised, Nixon turned to Ford and whispered: "They like you."

Born in 1913 in Omaha, Nebraska, Leslie Lynch King was brought to Grand Rapids by a mother who had been the victim of spousal abuse. Once divorced, Dorothy King married Gerald R. Ford Sr., who gave his name to her only child. Young Jerry—called Junior by his neighborhood friends—was reasonably well insulated from the suffering of the Great Depression by the success of his stepfather's paint and varnish company. As a result, he had a relatively carefree childhood, one that centered around school, Boy Scouting, and football. As a football player, Ford had few peers. He was an All-City and All-State center for South High and won a full-year's tuition ($100) to the University of Michigan. In his senior year of college, Ford was regarded as one of the country's best centers, and in the balloting for the 1935 Collegiate All-Star Game played against the Chicago Bears at Soldier Field, Ford was the number four vote getter of fans around the nation. Had he not chosen to study law at Yale University that fall, Ford might have played for either the Detroit Lions or the Green Bay Packers, both of which offered him a professional football contract.

Ford earned his law degree from Yale University in 1941 and after a brief stint practicing law in Grand Rapids joined the Navy in 1942.

After service in the South Pacific he returned to Grand Rapids, and in 1948 married Elizabeth Bloomer, a union that produced three sons and a daughter. In the same year, Ford was elected to the first of twelve consecutive terms in the House of Representatives. Throughout his years in Congress, Ford developed an expertise in the area of defense appropriations, as well as a reputation as a member whose political word could be trusted. It was this reputation for evenhandedness that was Ford's biggest asset as he rose up the leadership ladder.

In January 1963, he was elected head of the House Republican Conference, and in December of that year, President Lyndon Johnson tapped Ford to serve on the commission to investigate the assassination of John F. Kennedy. Thanks in part to the national recognition earned from his participation on the Warren Commission, Ford was chosen House minority leader in January 1965. He served in this position under both Lyndon Johnson and Richard Nixon until Nixon turned to him to replace Agnew in the fall of 1973.

In his memoirs, Nixon was crystal clear why he chose Gerald Ford for the vice presidency: "There was no question that he [Ford] would be the easiest to get confirmed." Yet, before the nomination could go to the floor of both houses of Congress, it had to clear both the Senate Rules Committee and the House Judiciary Committee. Anti-Nixon feeling ran deep on Capitol Hill, and Ford could expect to face many questions that were Watergate related. The overwhelming majority of the questions probed Ford's personality and his institutional views; his views on policy were virtually ignored. This comes as no great surprise—it was widely assumed, by Democrat and Republican alike, that in Ford, the Congress was confirming the next president.

For the most part, Ford said all the right things during his committee testimony. He argued that he saw himself as "a ready conciliator between the White House and Capitol Hill" (he would say in a later interview with Dom

Bonafede of the *National Journal Reports* that while he felt that he *did* have an obligation to both president and Congress, "the obligation to Congress is one of my own choosing") and described himself as a "moderate on domestic affairs, conservative on fiscal affairs, but a very dyed-in-the-wool internationalist in foreign policy."

Ford testified that no official had the right to disobey a direct order of the Court. He also promised to be more accessible to, and honest with, both the public and the Congress. In response to a question on whether or not he would have the power to prevent or terminate any investigation or prosecution of his predecessor, Ford replied that "I do not think the public would stand for it. I think—and whether he has the technical authority or not, I cannot give you a categorical answer." On the few questions of policy, however, he indicated a solid agreement with the policies of the Nixon administration. He continued his long-standing loyalty to Nixon when he made it clear that he felt that Nixon was "completely innocent" of any wrongdoing in Watergate.

The hearings were far from a cakewalk, however. There were several serious accusations raised against Ford. He was questioned about contributions totaling some $11,500 in 1970 from several business groups and a union, the Marine Engineers Beneficial Association, which had a rather unsavory reputation. Ford stated "categorically" that no funds collected on his behalf in 1970 "were for my personal benefit," and testified that he had endorsed all the checks over to the Kent County Republican Committee. He was also grilled on his role as Nixon's chief defender on the floor of the Congress, his civil rights record, and claims that as minority leader he had used his influence to slow down the initial phases of the investigation into financial improprieties during the 1972 election, an investigation that later implicated the Nixon White House.

The oddest charges were made by an ex-lobbyist acquaintance of Ford's. Robert N. Winter-Berger, former public relations man and lobbyist, had claimed in a 1972 book, *The Washington Payoff,* that in 1966 he had paid a friend $1,000 and "a number of favor" to be introduced to Ford. Winter-Berger viewed this "a good investment," one that Ford "knew about . . . and it did not faze him." Winter-Berger's book went on to document the number of times that he had visited Ford's office and a vacation that he had arranged for the Minority Leader "at the home of some friends of mine in Kentucky." He further charged that Ford had routinely granted favors for Winter-Berger associates in return for campaign contributions; one enumerated was that Winter-Berger had arranged for $125,000 to be contributed to the Republicans by Francis Kellogg, a State Department official, in return for consideration for his being named assistant to the secretary of state, a position that carried the rank of ambassador. In a second book, *The Gerald Ford Letters,* written after Ford had been confirmed as vice president, Winter-Berger claimed that he had rewritten speeches for Ford, consulted with Ford on the congressman's wardrobe, and had been instrumental in pushing Ford to get an extension on the visa of a New York psychiatrist who was facing deportation to his native Holland. Winter-Berger also claimed that he had "loaned" Gerald Ford about $15,000 and that he had introduced Ford to a New York psychiatrist who had treated Ford for nervous exhaustion.

Ford's memoirs reflect how he felt at the time:

> All these allegations, of course, were lies. . . .
> I had met Winter-Berger—I didn't dispute that—but it didn't take me long to determine that I didn't want anything to do with him. I had told my staff that and they made sure that he was kept out of my way.

Ford countered by offering to take a lie-detector test, but it was unnecessary; Winter-Berger's story immediately began to self-destruct. The *Ann Arbor News* reported that Winter-Berger's newest claims directly contradicted an April 17,

1972, interview with one of their reporters, during which Winter-Berger was quoted as contending that "Jerry Ford never personally received a cent from me." The House Rules Committee decided to call Winter-Berger in on November 7 to testify during a closed session. During that testimony, one committee member confronted Winter-Berger with a copy of his tax returns, which showed that he only had a gross income of about $28,306 over the three-year period of the loan. Reeling, Winter-Berger tried to change his story. After hearing his contradictory testimony, the committee did not try to hide its scorn.

The votes to confirm Ford's nomination were overwhelmingly positive. The Senate Rules Committee supported him, 9–0. Nine days later, the House Judiciary Committee voted 24–8. In the full House, the vote was 387–35; in the Senate, it was 92–3. All of the nay votes were cast by Democrats. Nixon wanted to have the swearing-in at the White House; however, a Nixon aide told Robert Hartmann, then Ford's Chief of Staff, that he was afraid that Nixon would be booed when he walked down the center aisle with Ford. Adamant, Ford insisted upon the Capitol, and Nixon finally agreed. Ford's December 6, 1973, swearing-in was a simple ceremony, followed by a short speech from the new vice president during which he cautioned the nation not to over-inflate their expectations of his abilities, quipping that "I am a Ford, not a Lincoln."

As soon as he was confirmed, Ford solicited the advice of many of his Capitol Hill colleagues as he searched for a job description. Some of the most prescient advice, in a letter now deposited in the Gerald R. Ford Library, came from a former vice president, Minnesota Senator Hubert Humphrey, who characterized the office as "awkward . . . at best. The man who occupies it will have many responsibilities and no authority with the one exception [of the tie-breaking power in the Senate]." Humphrey recognized that the vice president was expected to serve as the "alter-ego of the president," but cautioned Ford that "it is important for a vice

president to remember that he is not the president, and, therefore, can only speak for the government when he is authorized to do so." Nixon's staffers had the same idea. Bruce Kehrli, staff secretary to Alexander Haig and then Nixon's chief of staff, grandly announced in a meeting with Robert Hartmann that "what we want to do is to make the Vice President as much as possible a part of the White House staff." Hartmann remembered in his memoirs that "as I shook [Kehrli's] damp hand, it occurred to me that this was really intended to be a compliment."

Ford would later tell a reporter that "I feel that I am an active, participating vice-president." That was certainly the case. Either by statute or by tradition, the vice president was a member of the cabinet, vice chairman of the Domestic Council, and a member of the National Security Council. Nixon also appointed Ford as the chairman of both the Committee on the Right of Privacy and of his Energy Action Group. However, Ford shed two assignments that had been routinely turned over to the vice president—that of White House liaison for Indian Affairs and the role of administration representative with the governors and mayors.

Yet, it was in his role as Nixon's lightning rod that Ford played his most public role as vice president. During his confirmation hearings, Senator Mark Hatfield asked Ford if he thought that Nixon could still save his presidency. Ford's reply: "I think so. It's going to take a lot of help from a lot of people. And I intend to devote myself to that." True to his word, Ford was constantly on the road, defending the president to any audience who would listen. During his eight months in office, more than 500 groups in forty states heard the vice president speak to them. He also gave more than fifty press conferences, and more than eighty interviews. Ford consistently gave an uncompromising defense of Nixon, and it was almost his undoing. On January 15, 1974, before the American Farm Bureau Federation in Atlantic City, Ford identified the president's antagonists as "a few extreme partisans," whose "aim is total victory for themselves and the total defeat not only of President Nixon but of the policies for which he stands." The next day, both Nixon and Ford's staff acknowledged that the speech had been drafted by the White House speechwriters. Sharp press criticism followed, and rather than be castigated any further as a Nixon shill, Ford hired two speechwriters of his own. The Farm Bureau speech was a turning point for Ford. From that point on, he was less effusive in his defense of Nixon. For example, when on May 1, 1974, the White House made public only a highly sanitized version of the Watergate tapes, Ford quipped that he was a "little disappointed."

The mutually exclusive requirements of political loyalty (he was, after all, vice president, and Nixon had been one of his oldest friends in Congress) and good political common sense (Nixon was clearly doomed) played havoc with Ford. In his memoirs, Ford lamented:

By the nature of the office I held, I was in an impossible situation. I couldn't abandon Nixon, because that would make it appear that I was trying to position myself to become president. Nor could I get too close to him, because if I did, I'd risk being sucked into the whirlpool myself.

The closest he came to admitting it in public was in a June 8, 1974, speech at Logan, Utah: "why do I uphold the president one day and the next day side with Congress, which is deliberating his impeachment? . . . [I will] remain my own man, fix my own course and speak my own conscience. . . ." Yet his time for political agony was almost over. Events sped through the consciousness of the United States in summer 1974 with a blinding speed. On July 22, the Supreme Court ordered that the White House release all the subpoenaed tapes.

Ford spent the first days of August preparing for the inevitable. On August 1, he met with Haig, who floated the idea of a deal—Nixon's resignation for the promise of a presidential pardon by Ford for any and all offenses that Nixon may have committed during Watergate—Ford turned Haig down in the presence of two aides. On Friday, August 2, Ford met with the Senate leadership to discuss plans for the now probable Senate trial of Nixon, and it was agreed that Ford should not even attend but should be waiting in the wings to take the oath of office when Nixon was convicted. On August 5, the day that the tapes were finally released, Ford announced that

I have come to the conclusion that the public interest is no longer served by repetition of my previously expressed belief that on the basis of all the evidence known to me and to the American people, the president is not guilty of an impeachable offense.

In a cabinet meeting the next day—the final cabinet meeting of the Nixon administration—Ford told the president that "had I known and had it been disclosed to me what has been disclosed in reference to the Watergate affair in the last twenty-four hours, I would not have made a number of the statements that I have made, either as Minority Leader or as Vice President of the United States." In his memoirs, Ford was blunter: "No longer was there the slightest doubt in my mind as to the outcome of the struggle. Nixon was finished."

Equally convinced that the end was near, Haig asked for another meeting with Ford. On the morning of August 7, Ford remembered that Haig was formal: "Mr. Vice-President, I think it's time for you to prepare to assume the office of President." He was right. The next morning, Nixon summoned Ford to the White House. Nixon told his vice president that "I have made the decision to resign. It's in the best interest of the country." He paused, and then quietly said, "Jerry, I know you'll do a good job." Following Nixon's speech to the nation that evening, Ford came out onto the steps of his home in Alexandria, Virginia, and spoke to reporters, saying that "this is one of the most difficult and very saddest incidents I've ever witnessed." He praised Nixon for making "one of the greatest personal sacrifices for the country and one of the finest personal decisions on behalf of all of us as Americans by his decision to resign."

The next day, at about 12:00 P.M., the East Room of the White House was filled with staffers who, less than an hour before, had been teary eyed as they attended Nixon's farewell to them. Chief Justice Warren Burger, just off an Air Force jet that had whisked him back from a conference in the Netherlands, walked in alone, wearing a full black judicial robe. When Ford entered with his wife Betty at his side, he was met with an almost cathartic standing ovation. As the oath of office was administered, Ford's voice never wavered. His first speech as president was clearly his best speech as president. In words that would, for many, become both the symbol of the administration and the standard by which it would be judged, Ford attempted to bring an end to Watergate:

> I believe that truth is the glue that holds government together, not only our government but civilization itself. That bond, though strained, is unbroken at home and abroad. . . . In all my private and public acts as your president, I expect to follow my instincts of openness and candor with full confidence that honesty is always the best policy in the end. . . . My fellow Americans, our long national nightmare is over. Our constitution works. Our great republic is a government of laws and not of men. Here, the people rule. . . .

As he closed, Ford came close to tears when he asked the country to pray for Richard Nixon and his family so that "our former President, who brought peace to millions, find it for himself. . . ."

Ford's presidency was a difficult one. Not having the luxury of a three-month transition period as president-elect, he had little time to plan, and he and his advisers faced many dilemmas: The economy, beset both by inflationary pressures and rapid unemployment, grew worse by the day. The nation growled at his pardon of Richard Nixon, a proclamation that came so early in his administration that, despite Ford's protests to the contrary, the majority of people believed he had made a deal with Nixon. Although he was not responsible for U.S. failure in Vietnam, it was on Ford's watch that the North Vietnamese began their final offensive against the South—the most vivid image held by many people of the Ford years was that of helicopters evacuating thousands from the U.S. embassy in Saigon. There were moments of national pride—most notably the rescuing of the crew of the *Mayaquez,* a tanker ship that had been detained by the Cambodian government, and the national celebration of the bicentennial anniversary of the signing of the Declaration of Independence on July 4, 1976.

However, as the nation headed toward the presidential election of 1976, Ford found himself faced with a challenge from within his own party: Conservatives, led by California governor Ronald Reagan, assailed Ford as a weaker clone of Nixon, and Reagan came breathlessly close to upsetting Ford for the Republican nomination. Weakened by the Reagan challenge, the Ford campaign did not withstand the fall challenge by Jimmy Carter, and the former governor of Georgia won the White House back for the Democrats for the first time since 1968. Ford retired to private life, dividing his time between homes in California and Colorado.

As the years passed after Ford's defeat in the 1976 presidential election, the public and the news media began to forget the negatives of his presidential term, and Ford gradually achieved the status of elder statesman, both for the nation and his party. He played a lot of golf, but he also was titular head of several important government commissions and held both ceremonial and consultative posts for government and nonprofits.

On the whole, Ford was circumspect on public and party issues, but from a speech in 2001 onward he was forthright in supporting equal rights for gay and lesbians, a stance that set him at odds with the conservative wing of the GOP, which had turned that issue into a political hot button from 2000 onward. Ford also voiced criticism of the Bush-Cheney decision to invade Iraq using the excuse of weapons of mass destruction, which proved not to exist, but did so only in a clandestine interview with author and journalist Bob Woodward. Ford insisted that the interview remain unpublished until after his death.

As it turned out, Ford had a long life after the presidency—the longest of any former chief executive—and when he died at age 93 of heart disease on December 26, 2006, at his home in California, he was the oldest living former president, surpassing Ronald Reagan by only a few days.

As a former president, Gerald Ford was given the fullest and most elaborate national funeral honors. His body was flown to Washington, D.C., aboard the plane that usually served as Air Force One, and he lay in state at the Capitol on the same catafalque that had held Abraham Lincoln's body. Following a funeral service at the National Cathedral, his casket was flown to Michigan, where he was buried at the Gerald Ford Presidential Museum in Grand Rapids.

REFERENCES

John Robert Greene, *The Presidency of Gerald R. Ford* (Lawrence: The University Press of Kansas, 1995); James Cannon, *Time and Chance: Gerald Ford's Appointment with Destiny* (New York: HarperCollins, 1994); Gerald R. Ford, *A Time to Heal: The Autobiography of Gerald R. Ford* (New York: Harper and Row, 1979); Lester Sobel, ed. *Presidential Succession: Ford, Rockefeller, and the Amendment* (New York: Facts On File, 1975); Douglas Brinkley, *Gerald R. Ford* (New York: Times Books, 2007); Thomas M. DeFrank and Gerald R. Ford, *Write It When I'm Gone: Remarkable Off-the-Record Conversations with Gerald R. Ford* (New York: G. P. Putnam's Sons, 2007).

See the entry for Spiro Agnew for a biographical note on John Robert Greene

NELSON A. ROCKEFELLER (1908–1979)

Vice President, 1974–1977

(President Gerald Ford)

NELSON A. ROCKEFELLER
(Library of Congress)

By Leroy O. Dorsey

Nelson Aldrich Rockefeller represented a larger-than-life figure in American history who achieved nearly every prize he desired except the one he most sought: the presidency. As an heir to one of the largest family fortunes in America, Rockefeller funded many philanthropic projects. As a special counsel to six presidents, he helped to shape U.S. foreign and domestic policy. As four-time governor of New York State, he promoted major social and political reforms. During these decades of public philanthropy and political service, Rockefeller pursued the office of the presidency. Ironically, after three unsuccessful attempts to become president as well as his legendary disdain to be second in anything, Rockefeller accepted President Gerald Ford's offer to become the forty-first vice president of the United States.

Rockefeller's term as vice president held many trials and triumphs. Despite his political savvy and ability to manage people, Rockefeller faced numerous challenges. He encountered a highly controversial and lengthy confirmation process for the vice presidency. He experienced the emotionally draining conflicts fostered among competing interests in the Ford White House, and endured the overwhelming demands placed on him as both vice president and staff assistant to the president. Having survived these challenges, Rockefeller succeeded in making the vice presidency more substantively involved in the policy processes of the contemporary presidency. Given the fact that he neither sought nor wanted the vice presidency, he took an office that is often considered virtually useless and propelled it into a position that initiated and developed policy proposals that had far-reaching consequences for the country. Furthermore, he lent a sense of energy to a presidential administration that might well have languished in the aftermath of Watergate if not for him.

Born in Bar Harbor, Maine, in 1908, Rockefeller was a third-generation heir to the name and fortune of the Rockefellers. In fact, both sides of his family had attained prestige and wealth. Maternal grandfather Nelson Aldrich became a self-made millionaire and was a respected majority leader in the U.S. Senate for seventeen years. Paternal grandfather, John D. Rockefeller had formed the Standard Oil Corporation and by 1908 had seized control of nearly every aspect of oil production in the United States; as a result of this, John D. had become what President Theodore Roosevelt labeled a "malefactor of great wealth."

Rockefeller lived with his parents and five siblings in several of their family homes, including a town house in New York City and a country estate at Pocantico Hills, Westchester. Despite the magnificence of these homes—complete with art treasures, family infirmaries, and private playgrounds—Rockefeller's father instilled in him many of the traditional values that his father had taught him, frugality and

altruism being primary among them. When Rockefeller received his allowance of thirty cents a week at age eight, his father allowed him to spend only ten cents on himself with the remainder to be split equally between savings and charity, and like his grandfather, Rockefeller became adept at making money. As a young boy he raised rabbits to be sold to the Rockefeller Institute, raised vegetables that he sold to the family kitchen, and performed household chores for money. Both his mother and his father wanted their son to respect the physical and financial benefits of hard work.

Rockefeller found his formal education, especially in the early years, to be difficult due to left-handedness and dyslexia. In the early 1900s, many people considered left-handedness an aberration. To counter this "abnormality" in his son, Rockefeller's father would inflict a mild pain by snapping an elastic band on his son's right hand when Nelson used his left hand. Although he became right handed in most activities, this conversion process probably intensified his learning disability: Rockefeller transposed numbers and juxtaposed letters in words. These problems nearly caused him to fail the ninth grade and placed him in his high school class's bottom third. While his grades prevented him from attending Princeton University like his older brother, he remained undaunted. Working tirelessly and with unflinching perseverance, and confident to the point of cockiness in his own abilities, Rockefeller improved his grades enough to allow him to enter Dartmouth College in 1926.

Rockefeller's college years helped to crystallize his beliefs and character. First, his experience with fraternities, which he considered snobbish, made him more aware of the need to promote democratic institutions and to consider the welfare of people not as privileged as himself. Second, college became an arena for Rockefeller to face tough competition and to experience both defeat and victory. In a foreshadowing of later events, he lost the class presidency and became instead the class vice president. His first political upset, however, did not prevent him from achieving success as a scholar. Rockefeller's senior thesis, a forty-five-page essay on Standard Oil, earned him an A and the respect of his teachers, fellow students, and family; in addition, it gave him greater insight into the power and the consequent responsibility of the Rockefellers. In 1930, he earned membership in Phi Beta Kappa and graduated *cum laude*.

Less than a month after graduation, Rockefeller married Mary Todhunter Clark whom he had courted during his school vacations. Nicknamed Tod, she also had come from a distinguished family: her family's estate in Philadelphia had been granted to them by their ancestor, King George III, and her maternal grandfather had served as president of the Pennsylvania Railroad. During their thirty-one-year marriage, Tod gave birth to five children. With a keen intelligence and wit, and the requisite social graces, she appeared to be the perfect mate (albeit temporarily).

After an around-the-world honeymoon lasting nine months, which included appointments with business associates and foreign leaders at every stop, Rockefeller and his wife returned to New York City in 1931. Despite the Depression, he had his choice of business opportunities. He quickly became bored with a minor post at Standard Oil and so went to work with his uncle at Chase Bank. During the morning, Rockefeller learned the banking business and in the afternoon devoted his energy to a company he started, Special Work, Inc; its mission involved finding tenants for the new Rockefeller Center, then the world's largest office complex. Rockefeller excelled at leasing space and at public relations for the Center. He frequently made the news with special ceremonies and speeches that paid tribute to the opulent structure. He proved so successful in the promotion of Rockefeller Center that his father named him its executive vice president in 1937 and its president in 1938. One year later Rockefeller became more involved with his second love: art. Having acquired a genuine appreciation for fine art from his mother, he eagerly accepted the position of president of the Museum of Modern Art.

It, was, however, a small investment that Rockefeller made in the Creole Petroleum Company (CPC) in 1935, a Venezuelan subsidiary of Standard Oil, that altered the course of his life. After becoming a member of the CPC board of directors, he recruited a group of oil and economic experts to accompany him on a fact-finding mission to Latin America. He discovered that the U.S. executives of the Venezuelan CPC chose not to learn the native tongue, managed the company autocratically, and even separated themselves from the workers with barbed wire fences. Thanks to Rockefeller's report to the CPC board of directors on his return to the United States, the company instituted major reforms to serve better the interests of the host country. Rockefeller also took note of the growing anti-U.S. sentiment being created by companies like the CPC and the cultivation of that negative sentiment by German, Japanese, Italian, and Soviet agents. If these were left unchecked, he believed, Latin America would fall prey to the Axis powers and lead ultimately to the ruin of the Rockefeller interests and those of the United States.

Rockefeller's fervent interest in Latin America brought him to the attention of President Franklin Roosevelt. Roosevelt wanted him to head a program that would strengthen Latin American ties to the United States. After clearing it with his family, Rockefeller headed the Office of the Coordinator for Inter-American Affairs (CIAA) in 1940, earning a salary of one dollar a year. Working long hours every day as well as emerging relatively unscathed from bureaucratic in-fighting, Rockefeller made this small office one of the most popular agencies to work for during World War II, earning for himself a notoriety evidenced by his picture on the cover of *Life* magazine in 1942. Thanks to him, Latin American commodities were purchased at higher than market prices by the United States and other allied countries, which, in turn, caused critical shortages for the Axis powers; U.S. companies in Latin America were forced to terminate their anti-U.S. agents or be blacklisted by the State Department; and the CIAA's information campaign involving newspapers, radio, and movies met and turned back the tide of Nazi propaganda in Latin America. Roosevelt, impressed and pleased with Rockefeller's accomplishments, appointed him assistant secretary of state for American republic affairs in 1944. As assistant secretary he lobbied successfully to have the fascist-ruled Argentina admitted to the United Nations and reinforced the Monroe Doctrine by maneuvering the United Nations into agreeing that aggression against one American region was equivalent to aggression against all of the Americas.

Despite his accomplishments, Rockefeller's appointment as assistant secretary came to an end eight months after the death of Roosevelt. President Truman felt no strong loyalty to Rockefeller, and when Truman's newly appointed secretary of state wanted to chose his own assistant, the president gladly accepted Rockefeller's resignation in 1945.

Returning to New York, Rockefeller again took control of Rockefeller Center. Unsatisfied and eager once again to command global attention, he launched the American International Association (AIA) in 1946, a nonprofit and philanthropic organization designed to aid in the modernization of Brazil's and Venezuela's health, education, and agricultural infrastructure. Over time, the AIA helped to build roads and reduce infant mortality. In conjunction with the AIA, Rockefeller also started the International Basic Economy Corporation (IBEC) in 1947, a private, commercial organization whose mission was to introduce Latin America to such U.S. enterprises as supermarkets and mass distribution. As a result of the IBEC, hundreds of U.S. businesses invested in Latin America.

Rockefeller's private ventures regarding cultural and technological progress in Latin America again gained him entry into the White House. In 1949, President Truman announced his Point Four program to introduce scientific advances into underdeveloped areas. With some

prodding by Rockefeller, Truman invited him in 1950 to chair the International Advisory Board (IAB) to enact that program. The board's recommendation to consolidate all overseas economic functions currently distributed among twenty-three agencies into a single office, the Office of Overseas Economic Administration, antagonized Special Assistant to the President Averell Harriman. Harriman wanted an organization that stressed military rather than economic assistance in Latin America. When Truman approved the Harriman agency, Rockefeller resigned from the IAB in 1951.

When the Republican Party regained the White House a year later with the election of Dwight Eisenhower, Rockefeller again seized the opportunity to return to Washington. He enjoyed much success in the Eisenhower administration. As chair of an advisory committee to study the reorganization of the federal government, Rockefeller helped establish the Department of Health, Education, and Welfare and in 1953 became its first undersecretary. His position, which involved improving health and educational facilities, soon gave way to yet another coveted position in 1953: special assistant to the president concerning foreign affairs. In this role, Rockefeller developed programs that would increase understanding and cooperation among countries; the media popularly termed his work psychological warfare. Rockefeller persuaded Eisenhower to adopt a plan proposed to him by his consultant, Harvard professor of government Henry Kissinger. Called Open Skies, the Rockefeller-Kissinger plan not only proposed that the United States and the Soviet Union allow inspectors from each country to examine military establishments as a necessary step to nuclear disarmament, but it also proposed that both countries allow aerial inspections of their territories to reduce the risk of surprise attacks. Rockefeller again waited for recognition of his service by being appointed to a cabinet post and was again disappointed.

Frustrated, Rockefeller resigned and left Washington in 1955. From his experiences in the Eisenhower White House, he recognized the limitations of being in someone else's power and now sought the power that derives from being popularly elected. With the announcement of his candidacy for governor in 1958, Rockefeller staged an aggressive and expensive media campaign that highlighted his dedication to work diligently for the public welfare. This, coupled with his inherent charm, won him the governorship of New York for the first of four times.

During his fifteen years as New York governor, Rockefeller achieved an impressive record of accomplishments. To tackle the urban problems of the state, he created the Urban Development Corporation to clear slum areas and aid in the construction of low-income housing. His antidrug program, initially opposed from almost all quarters due to the harsh penalties Rockefeller called for, was eventually instituted with only minor changes. Regarding education, he expanded the New York State university system to the point that it was the largest system of higher education anywhere in the world at that time. He successfully pushed for legislation that outlawed racial discrimination in housing and the lending practices of financial institutions. His youth centers served to provide training and jobs for troubled young adults. He also promoted construction on a grand scale. To make Albany worthy of being the capital of New York, Rockefeller initiated the South Mall project; by its completion, the Empire State Plaza had been constructed and constituted an eighteen-acre complex of government buildings, a. cultural center, and a shopping mall. To attract industry and business, Rockefeller oversaw the building of the twin 110-story towers of the World Trade Center. Other benefits New Yorkers received because of Governor Rockefeller included a State Council on the Arts that promoted cultural development in the performing arts, establishment of the first mandatory police training course, and the development of open land as recreational areas.

Rockefeller's terms as governor were not without their moments of controversy. Perhaps the most dramatic involved the Attica prison riot in September 1971 and Rockefeller's response to it. For five days, inmates seized control of the prison, taking thirty-nine guards hostage. Despite repeated pleading by the prison commissioner and others on the scene, Rockefeller refused to come to Attica personally. He did, however, order the state police to retake the prison. In the assault, thirty-nine inmates and hostages were killed, constituting the highest loss of life in U.S. penal history. The McKay Commission, authorized to study the riot and its aftermath, criticized both the amount of force used in retaking the prison and Rockefeller's failure to appear on the scene and take charge personally.

His triumphs and trials as governor, however, did not slow his drive for achieving his most sought after goal: the presidency.

Buoyed by his landslide victory for the governorship in 1958, Rockefeller turned his attention to winning the White House in 1960. He recruited a large personal staff, which he divided between speech writing, research, image management, and logistics. After two months of cultivating support and generating headlines, Rockefeller decided that he could not stop Richard Nixon from winning the primaries, given the latter's position as vice president to the immensely popular President Eisenhower. Rockefeller withdrew from the race but he was not silent. In 1959, he issued a statement that essentially condemned the Republican Party for its failure in leadership. This plus the revelation of Rockefeller's plan to coerce Nixon into accepting several Rockefeller-platform elements caused Rockefeller to be viewed as a party spoiler.

Despite this 1960 election image, Rockefeller found himself a leading contender for his party's nomination in the 1964 election. After Nixon's defeat in 1960 and his subsequent defeat in a California race for governor, Rockefeller became the favorite, given the new and untested faces in the GOP, but his front-runner status failed to last because of several questionable decisions. Support began to erode when he reneged on a campaign promise not to raise taxes as governor of New York. His support continued downward when he attacked the Republican Party's conservative right in an attempt to associate himself with the civil rights issue. Finally, he angered the morally concerned citizenry when in 1962 he divorced his wife after three decades and fourteen months later married a woman nineteen years his junior. Margaretta Fitler Murphy, nicknamed Happy, was a thirty-six-year-old divorcée who appeared to have given up her own four children to indulge her romance with Rockefeller. When the votes were counted, Rockefeller had lost the chance for the presidency again.

Rockefeller's third try at the presidency in 1968 also proved abortive. As that presidential election neared, Rockefeller assured his supporters in February 1967 that he would run again; however, he stunned them weeks later when he formally declared that be would not seek the nomination. The events of late March and early April worked to lead Rockefeller back into the race: President Johnson refused to seek another term and Dr. Martin Luther King, Jr., was assassinated, with the ghettos in many major cities erupting in turmoil as a result. In yet another reversal, Rockefeller believed it was his duty to resume running, but his on-again-off-again campaign, coupled with his increasing alienation of Republican delegates by attempting to capture the poor and black constituencies after Robert Kennedy's assassination in June 1968, placed him behind Nixon in the primaries again.

Rockefeller's governorship and bids for the presidency did not prevent him from continuing his service to the presidency. Having a strong friendship and mutual respect with Lyndon Johnson, Rockefeller frequently brought the president's attention to civil rights, water pollution, and education. From 1965 to 1970, Rockefeller served as a Johnson appointee to the Advisory Commission on Intergovernmental Relations, allowing him to bring together mayors and other country officials in order to pressure Washington into overhauling the federal grant system and to focus national atten-

tion on such issues as welfare reform. Even his enmity toward Nixon did not prevent Rockefeller from aiding his chief rival, nor did it stop Nixon from utilizing Rockefeller's talent. Nixon and Rockefeller met frequently to discuss domestic legislation. When Nixon asked Rockefeller to undertake a special mission to develop a successful U.S. policy toward Latin America, Rockefeller accepted. After a seven-month trip through Latin America, considered by some to be ill conceived, Rockefeller presented Nixon with a critically acclaimed "Report on the Americas" that proposed the refinancing of Latin America's foreign debt and that called for a more-tolerant attitude toward the military regimes in that region of the world.

It was perhaps fitting that Rockefeller served in the Nixon White House when his rival faced his greatest crisis. In 1972, the police arrested five men during a break-in at Democratic National Committee offices in Washington's Watergate Hotel and office complex. Later that year, and despite repeated denials from the president, suspicions rose that Nixon himself had personal knowledge of that event before the fact. With the release of the White House tapes contradicting Nixon's assertion that he knew nothing about Watergate, and facing impeachment, Nixon became the first person to resign the presidency on August 9, 1974.

With Vice President Gerald Ford's ascension to the presidency, Rockefeller immediately became the subject of speculation regarding Ford's choice for his vacated office. However, the New York governor was not the president's first choice; these were Wisconsin Representative Melvin Laird with whom Ford had had a long congressional relationship and Republican National Committee Chairman George Bush, With Bush the target of reports that linked him to a secret "slush fund" in the Nixon White House and Laird's refusal of the appointment, Ford turned to Rockefeller. In spite of Rockefeller's reluctance to be the vice president and his current work with the Commission on Critical Choices for Americans (an organization that he created in 1973 to brought together the best minds of the time to address the problems facing the country), he believed it his duty to work with the untried president to alleviate the economic and social problems facing the nation.

The first test of that duty came in fall 1974 with the vice-presidential confirmation process. The country eagerly awaited the hearings that would reveal the specifics regarding Rockefeller wealth and power. No one at the time knew that the process would go on for four grueling months, taking their toll on Rockefeller's wife Happy as she underwent a radical mastectomy and on Rockefeller himself as he defended his finances, explained his personal transgressions, and awaited to begin work in the White House.

The length of the confirmation process stemmed from the need for Congress to satisfy its concern that there would be no conflict of interest given Rockefeller's vast holdings in major corporations—corporations that worked almost daily with the executive branch. If he succeeded the president, Congress reasoned, the Rockefeller fortune merged with the power of the presidency could be economically unsettling.

On the first day of hearings before the Senate Rules and Administration Committee in September, Rockefeller attempted to lay to rest what he considered the erroneous belief concerning his family's fortune and their economic power. According to him, he personally owned less than 1 percent and his family combined owned less than 3 percent in any oil company. To help lessen the supposed conflict of interest issue, Rockefeller offered to place all his securities in one blind trust while vice president, keeping only his real estate and art in his name. Although less than what many people anticipated, Rockefeller estimated his total worth at $178 million.

For three days, Rockefeller's confirmation went smoothly; then the trouble began. During October, two potentially damaging revelations came to light. The FBI disclosed that Rockefeller had funded a disparaging book about his opponent, former Supreme Court Justice Arthur Goldberg, during his 1970 reelection bid for governor. This seemingly "dirty trick" raised the specter of Watergate in the public's mind. Rockefeller explained that he did not know what the book was going to say; he just referred the backers of the project to his brother Laurence for financing. Rockefeller admitted that he had made a hasty error and he apologized to his former opponent. The Senate concluded that Rockefeller was only guilty of poor judgment. The second revelation involved large financial gifts and loans Rockefeller had given to New York State officials while he was governor. On this point, Rockefeller made no apologies. To him, his gifts reflected no more than the respect and admiration he felt for many of those officials. In addition, Rockefeller maintained that these gifts could not be bribes because the recipients were already working for him. The Senate committee disliked Rockefeller's practice but found no evidence of any wrongdoing. With the Senate's vote of 90 to 7 to confirm, and the House's vote of 287 to 128 in favor, Rockefeller officially became vice president on December 19, 1974.

The vice president has traditionally undertaken certain tasks, and Rockefeller's vice presidency was no different. As a vice president, Rockefeller presided over the Senate. He learned there that, unlike in the New York State legislature, the Senate would not meekly bow before him. In a representative episode, Rockefeller, attempting to facilitate a decision in the Senate, refused to recognize two senators who wanted to speak before the roll call for votes was continued. A senator informed Rockefeller that he had the authority to ignore members of the Senate but that it was discourteous of him to exercise that authority. Two months passed before Rockefeller apologized for his breach of Senate etiquette. Rockefeller also toured foreign countries on goodwill missions and traveled throughout the United States promoting the administration. For example, regarding his tour of U.S. cities, Rockefeller made a series of speeches during the bicentennial year that acquainted Americans with the administration's concerns about the energy crisis, national health, and religion.

Other traditional vice-presidential duties included membership on several national commissions. As chairperson of the Commission on CIA Activities within the United States, Rockefeller investigated whether any of the CIA's activities were illegal and beyond the scope of its charter. The National Commission on Productivity and Work Quality sought to increase the productivity and morale of the American worker. The Commission on the Organization of Government for the Conduct of Foreign Policy worked to clarify the relationship between the legislative and executive branches regarding foreign policy making. Finally, as chairperson of the President's Panel on Federal Compensation, Rockefeller developed recommendations that would make compensation practices fair to both the employees and the public.

For Rockefeller, however, commission work took too much time away from cultivating a central role in the Ford White House and in developing program policies. Contrary to vice-presidential tradition, Rockefeller wanted a substantive policy role, so he preferred his assignments as vice chairman of the Domestic Council, as the panel chairman responsible for achieving the nation's energy independence, and as the chairman of an advisory group whose task was to establish a White House Science Advisory Unit.

The Domestic Council had been created to evaluate domestic programs, to integrate them for maximum efficiency, and to determine how they could be funded. Under John Erlichman's direction during the Nixon administration, the Domestic Council became such a powerful entity that it dominated the domestic cabinet secretaries and involved itself in departmental program activities. With the Watergate scandal and Erlichman's resignation, the council found its power severely limited. In addition, the newly created Economic Policy Board (EPB) and the Energy Resources Council (ERC) overlapped responsibilities with the Domestic Council, creating the potential for further weakening of the council's power.

From this weakened position, Rockefeller hoped to establish the Domestic Council to a prominent position regarding domestic matters. He first proposed to become the council's executive director, but this met with strong opposition. Not only did President Ford's legal advisers publicly conclude that it was legally impossible for Rockefeller to hold the vice-chair and executive director's position simultaneously, but White House Coordinator Donald Rumsfeld privately informed Rockefeller that he and he alone would be responsible for the paper flow to and from the president. Unable to maneuver himself into the coveted position, Rockefeller proposed that two of his associates, James Cannon and Richard Dunham, assume the roles of executive directive and deputy directory, respectively. His new proposal similarly agitated the White House staff. Rumsfeld countered by proposing his own nominee for the executive directorship and lobbied his choice to President Ford. Angered by Rumsfeld's actions, Rockefeller sent a memo to the president stating that he would withdraw from the Domestic Council if his proposal was not met. To prevent a major division in his administration, Ford backed Rockefeller.

With his associates in place, Rockefeller worked next to regain the Domestic Council's position over the EPB and the ERC. To that end, the vice president called for and got those offices to agree to become part of the council's task force to establish long-range goals for the administration regarding social programs and subordinate their power to Rockefeller's unit.

Rockefeller, however, failed to achieve control over the Domestic Council, as it had been created to serve the president's needs, not the vice president's. As a result, Cannon, Rockefeller's associate, made it clear that as executive director he worked for and gave his loyalty to Ford. Furthermore, when Ford offered Deputy Director Dunham the opportunity to chair the Federal Power Commission, he accepted.

Rockefeller had lost the means to control the council and so largely withdrew from it.

Rockefeller's involvement with the Domestic Council did not mark the end of his attempt to influence domestic policy programs. He believed that he could still direct those policies with the authority he derived from the vice-president's office. Rockefeller began by establishing a group to review the nation's social programs and by getting that group recognized by the Domestic Council; this latter action ensured the legitimacy of the review group as more than a Rockefeller operation. With this authorization, Rockefeller's group developed detailed proposals concerning economic growth, resource development, and human welfare and for improving the national infrastructure. These proposals, Rockefeller hoped, would become the basis for Ford's 1976 State of the Union message. A few months before that message, however, Ford announced a budget cut that would all but destroy any chance of the review group's proposals from being accepted. Daunted but not defeated, Rockefeller instructed the group to revise its proposals to meet the new budget limitations. The vice president then sent a memo to the president that outlined the group's revised recommendations. Sensing the futility of having his proposals accepted, Rockefeller officially withdrew from the Domestic Council in December 1975. Just as Rockefeller had guessed, less than one month later, Ford's State of the Union address contained not one of his recommendations.

Another controversial episode in Rockefeller's quest to direct domestic policy involved his proposal to create a federal energy development corporation to aid in making the nation energy independent. In early 1975, Ford warned the nation that it was too dependent on importing foreign oil to meet its rising energy demands. The process by which the nation could achieve energy independence intrigued Rockefeller, and he set his staff to the task of determining how that could be done. After months of investigation, Rockefeller presented to Ford his proposal for the creation of the Energy Resources Finances Corporation (ERFCO). According to the vice president, ERFCO would act as a federally sponsored corporation to stimulate the private sector to generate investment needed to help the administration achieve its goals regarding energy independence. Those goals included oil-imports reduction and energy-technology and resources development to make the United States a leading supplier of the world's energy needs. Opponents of Rockefeller and ERFCO informed the president that the corporation would not solve the energy problem and that its broad power would be disruptive to the investment community; their doubts caused Ford to hesitate in authorizing ERFCO but not to deny it outright. Thus, Rockefeller began to work with the Federal Energy Administration to revise ERFCO and to generate support for it on Capitol Hill.

In August 1975, Rockefeller submitted a revised proposal for ERFCO, now called the Energy Independence Authority (EIA), for a smaller version of the initial federally sponsored corporation. Ford accepted this proposal and publicly declared the EIA as the means to make the nation energy independent. To promote the EIA, Rockefeller became one of only three vice presidents to appear in the Senate to give congressional testimony in its behalf. However, his EIA would not be realized: just as the Democratic majority in Congress had stalled other of Ford's energy programs, the EIA suffered the same fate.

Another assignment Ford gave to Rockefeller late in 1974 concerned whether the White House needed to revive its science advisers' board and, if so, in what form. Rockefeller began by tapping his Commission on Critical Choices for Americans for the members of his advisory group. In February 1975, the vice president submitted to Ford recommendations that included the chief executive's need to have an independent source of scientific judgment available to him and the establishment by congressional action of an Office of Technology and Science (OTS). Ford supported the creation of an OTS but balked at the scale suggested by

Rockefeller, for example, a support staff of seventeen professionals; Ford wanted five. After several discussions with his advisers, Ford submitted a proposal to Congress that was virtually identical to Rockefeller's: instead of seventeen professionals, Ford agreed to fifteen, and the name was changed to the Office of Science and Technology Policy (OSTP).

With the proposal moving through Congress, albeit slowly, Rockefeller next tackled the areas on which the OSTP would focus. Rockefeller recommended to Ford that he be allowed to bring together a contingent from the scientific community that would advise the OSTP on anticipated advances in technology and on technology policy and their affect on economic growth; Ford approved the recommendation. In early May 1976, Ford signed the National Science and Technology Policy, Organization, and Priorities Act into law, which created the OSTP within the executive office, establishing its director as a presidential adviser on matters of science and technology who also sat on the Domestic Council. Essentially, Rockefeller took an assignment that called only for recommendations regarding the reestablishment of the White House's science advisory unit and expanded that unit's scope and influence.

Rockefeller's dual positions as a White House staff assistant and as the vice president gave him the ability to push beyond the limits usually associated with each individual role. In the former position, he prepared and developed various proposals that were adopted as administration initiatives; with his latter position, he generated support for those initiatives in Congress and in the private sector. This benefit from the duality of roles also came with several costs. First, the number of assignments given to and personally undertaken by Rockefeller strained his ability to give adequate attention to any of them, and despite the vice president's ability to surround himself with the most capable people, he found himself extended as never before. Second, Rockefeller's domestic policy development and the zeal he showed in attempting to push past any opposition threatened

senior White House staff so much that Rockefeller's ideas were resisted in varying degrees regardless of their merit. Third, Rockefeller's understanding with Ford that the president wanted an active vice president proved illusory. Rockefeller learned that Ford was unwilling to redefine the vice-presidential role in domestic policy development until Rockefeller threatened to withdraw from an active role on the Domestic Council.

What successes Rockefeller won during his twenty-five months as vice president came at perhaps the greatest cost. His constant clashes and frequent frustrations with key personnel in the Ford White House won him virtually no friends and no allies, so when the Ford camp looked to the 1976 election, it decided that the president would be better off without Rockefeller. Ford approached Rockefeller and explained that he was not asking Rockefeller to withdraw from the Republican ticket but that if he did some problems might be eliminated. On November 3, 1975, ever vigilant to do his duty for the nation, Rockefeller agreed. Despite his dismissal from the ticket, the vice president continued to do his job dutifully. When asked to nominate Senator Robert Dole for the vice presidency, Rockefeller complied and introduced Dole to New York State voters. But Rockefeller's acquiescence was short lived: at State University Rockefeller, being taunted by some students, responded by "giving them the finger"—a moment captured by a newspaper photographer that could have symbolized his long-suppressed frustration with his vice presidency.

Once again a private citizen in January 1977, Rockefeller withdrew from active involvement with politics and busied himself with various private enterprises over the next two years. He created The Nelson Rockefeller Collection, Inc., to market reproductions of his artwork, started a second company to publish books regarding his artwork, and remade his property at King Ranch in Texas into a jungle by stocking it with exotic African animals. Furthermore, Rockefeller assisted the soon-to-be deposed Shah of Iran in finding a home in the United States.

In his own mind, Rockefeller believed that he was a failure because he never reached his most-sought-after goal—the presidency—but his advocates as well as his critics would have to disagree. He almost single-handedly rehabilitated his family's reputation by promoting numerous philanthropic causes in the Rockefeller name, aided several chief executives in developing U.S. foreign and domestic agendas that still influence the country today, governed the most politically and socially complex state in the country and did so successfully, and left a legacy that few people could ever hope to repeat.

Nelson Rockefeller died of a heart attack on January 26, 1979, while in the much-publicized private company of a young female "research assistant."

REFERENCES

Stewart Alsop, *Nixon & Rockefeller: A Double Portrait* (Garden City, N.Y.: Doubleday & Company, Inc., 1960); Elizabeth A. Cobbs, *The Rich Neighbor Policy: Rockefeller and Kaiser in Brazil* (New Haven, Conn.: Yale University Press, 1992); Robert H. Connery and Gerald Benjamin, *Rockefeller of New York: Executive Power in the Statehouse* (Ithaca, N.Y.: Cornell University Press, 1979); Frank Gervasi, *The Real Rockefeller: The Story of the Rise, Decline and Resurgence of the Presidential Aspirations of Nelson Rockefeller* (New York: Atheneum, 1964); Michael Kramer and Sam Roberts, *"I Never Wanted To Be Vice-President of Anything!": An Investigative Biography of Nelson Rockefeller* (New York: Basic Books, Inc., 1976); Joseph E. Persico, *The Imperial Rockefeller: A Biography of Nelson A. Rockefeller* (New York: Simon and Schuster, 1982); Nelson A. Rockefeller, *The Future of Federalism* (Cambridge, Mass.: Harvard University Press, 1962); Nelson A. Rockefeller, *The Future of Freedom: Vice President Nelson A. Rockefeller Speaks out on Issues Confronting Americans in Bicentennial 1976* (Washington, D.C.: U.S. Government Printing Office, 1976); Nelson A. Rockefeller, "Overview," *Critical Choices for Americans: Reports on Energy, Food & Raw Materials—Vital Resources,* Volume 1 (Lexington, Ky.: D.C. Heath and Company, 1977); Nelson A. Rockefeller, *The Rockefeller Report on the Americas: The Unofficial Report of a United States Presidential Mission for the Western Hemisphere* (Chicago, Ill.: Quadrangle Books, 1969); Michael Turner, *The Vice President as Policy Maker: Rockefeller in the Ford White House* (Westport, Conn.: Greenwood Press, 1982); James E. Underwood and William J. Daniels, *Governor Rockefeller in New York: The Apex of Pragmatic Liberalism in the United States* (Westport, Conn.: Greenwood Press, 1982).

LEROY G. DORSEY holds a Ph.D. from Indiana University and is an associate professor of communications at Texas A&M University in College Station, Texas. He is the author of *We Are All Americans, Pure and Simple: Theodore Roosevelt and the Myth of Americanism* (University of Alabama Press, 2007) and edited *The Presidency and Rhetorical Leadership* (2002), published by Texas A&M University Press. Other research has been published in *The Quarterly Journal of Speech, Presidential Studies Quarterly,* and *Rhetoric & Public Affairs.* Dorsey specializes in and teaches courses in presidential rhetoric, American oratory, and myth and popular culture.

WALTER F. MONDALE (B. 1928)

Vice President, 1977–1981

(President Jimmy Carter)

WALTER F. MONDALE
(Library of Congress)

By Frank Kessler

Those who study the institution of the vice presidency and its rising stature will no doubt point to Walter F. Mondale as a man who, more than any of his predecessors, remade the much-maligned graveyard of the executive branch into an office to be sought after. Unlike some of his predecessors in this one-time dead letter office, Mondale did not fit the stereotype of a ticket balancer. Perhaps his varied career in politics gave him the vision to see more in the office that has provided many a one-liner for starving stand-up comics. He decided to try to make something of a position that had been characterized as a "fifth wheel of the vehicle of government" and an afterthought of the Constitutional convention.

Mondale became a close, trusted adviser to President Jimmy Carter, and it is evident that Carter valued Mondale's intellect and breadth of experience with the Democratic Party constituent groups and Washington political scene. He knew his place in the administration and that was not merely cowering in the wings. Mondale saw himself as "in the loop" as he noted in a *National Journal* interview:

I'm automatically included in things, invited to things. That was not the case in the beginning . . . but now we've got institutional experience. The next Vice President is going to say, "Well, I should be in the White House (too.)" I may have more influence now than I ever had in the Senate. I'm able to be heard on any matter I want to be heard on.

Mondale was able to make statements like this because of his lifelong ties with labor, minority groups, and traditional Democratic Party leaders. These ties offered potential reservoirs of support and savvy under the party umbrella for Jimmy Carter, whose limited experience as Georgia governor left him lacking the necessary network to govern effectively. During the campaign and throughout the four years of the Carter administration, Mondale served as a special liaison with unions and party honchos, especially in the urban Northeast where Gaiter's poll numbers were so deficient.

Given the disrepute surrounding the vice president's office, one might wonder why Mondale sought it. First of all, he had nothing to lose by running because he could return to his seat in the Senate, but, more than that, it fit his pursuit of politics as a career. In the forward to his book on the power of the presidency, *Accountability of Power* (1975), Mondale writes about the early Nixon years: "The sense of helpfulness and humanity that underlay the Great Society was already gone, having been destroyed by the [Vietnam] war." He also complained that this new attitude was due to "a new national strategy to create suspicion, division, and a sense of selfishness in the American people." This point speaks volumes on Mondale's acceptance of the positive role of government and led him to the view that public

servants should aspire to bring out the noble in their constituents rather than pandering to their basest, most selfish instincts.

Mondale's family heritage and political lineage provide much of the explanation for his political career.

He was born in 1928 to Theodore Mondale, son of a Norwegian immigrant, and his second wife, Claribel. His father became a Lutheran minister but left the church because of its insistence on predestination and denial of free will and lack of social concern. The elder Mondale later joined the Methodists. Young Walter Frederick (known as Fritz) was raised with the Social Gospel at home and in church. The painful slow death from encephalitis of Reverend Mondale's first wife, Jessie, along with his inability to pay for care after going bankrupt in the Depression no doubt reinforced the message of social justice that he imparted to his family. Possibly because of his father's move from Lutheranism to Methodism and his older brother's decision to become a Unitarian minister, Mondale developed an openness to other religious views and traditions. As one of his biographers, Finlay Lewis, wrote: "While religion pervaded almost every aspect of family life, it was a happy and optimistic faith. . . ."

Mondale demonstrated leadership in high school and seems to have decided on a political career during those formative years. When the time came just after World War II for him to attend college, he chose Macalester College in St. Paul, Minnesota. The school, even though undergoing a change of direction from its Presbyterian roots, was still hardly a political hotbed. While Mondale was a freshman, though, he became involved with Students for Democratic Action (SDA), affiliated with the Americans for Democratic Action (ADA), and campaigned for the reelection of Minneapolis reform mayor Hubert H. Humphrey, a onetime Macalester professor whose enthusiasm, boundless energy, optimistic spirit, and deep compassion for the poor and minorities were most attractive to Fritz. Humphrey eventually became his mentor and provided an introduction for young Mondale to eventual Minnesota governor Orville Freeman, among other state party leaders, and national Democratic leaders whose company Humphrey frequented. Humphrey's election as mayor of Minneapolis in fact had been a testament to the success of his and the ADA's efforts to unite the old Farmer–Labor Party with its labor union ties to the state Democratic Party, a coalition that came to be known as the Democratic Farmer–Labor Party (DFL).

As one might expect from a person with career aspirations, Mondale was involved in political and international organizations and debate clubs at college. His years at Macalester were volatile ones for the Minnesota Democratic Party and college liberals in general because communist influences threatened the party, the campus ADA, and the Farmer-Labor coalition. Mondale was honing his world view in the fight against McCarthy-era paranoia about communism. Communism and activism against it divided liberals from the late 1940s forward.

While in college, at the age of twenty, Mondale offered his services to help manage what would be the successful Humphrey race for the U.S. Senate. The candidate's positions were a perfect fit for Mondale because both were New Dealers and both had a deep sense of commitment to ameliorating social injustice (no doubt deepened by Mondale's days working the farm harvest fields shoulder to shoulder with migrant workers). In addition, both felt at home with the major constituent interest groups of the party, especially labor, and both were committed to an active role for the federal government in dealing with social problems. He took on a Republican stronghold, organized it with no funds from the state organization, and helped ring up solid majorities for both Humphrey and President Truman there.

After Humphrey's election, Mondale dropped out of college (a sabbatical of sorts) to take a job in Washington, D.C., to help pay his mounting debts from attending Macalester, which was an expensive private school. He worked as secretary for the SDA but became disenchanted with its paucity of resources both in staff and finances. His biographers would note that this was a period of frustration and self-doubt for Mondale. A certain need to please his father seemed to pressure him toward success in politics; in addition, his small-town upbringing encouraged insecurities about the big city life that was required in national politics. All this led to self-doubt and personal reflection and compensation via bouts of extraordinary and unremittingly hard work.

Within two years, Mondale returned from Washington, D.C., to finish college at the less-expensive University of Minnesota. There he became involved in trying to take the stodgy, more conservative state Democratic Party to the Left, where it could meet the more liberal Farmer–Labor party. He worked to recruit new young progressive candidates to run for office. In the process, he was building his contacts for a race of his own at some later date.

Upon completion of a political science degree from the university, Mondale considered his options and concluded that the armed services would provide the means for him to finish his education through the GI Bill. He enlisted in the army but proved too "radical" for some of his senior officers, and after being rejected for training in the Counter Intelligence Corps because of "loyalty" reasons, Mondale served his commitment uneventfully. On his discharge, he returned to attend the University of Minnesota law school before embarking on a legal career. To him, law was the perfect way to both make a living and permit him to dabble in politics. He commented once to a biographer that he felt that a person needed something other than politics to fall back on—if something offended one's conscience too deeply in politics, one could just walk away.

At his core, Mondale was a populist who distrusted people born into wealth and privilege. He viewed himself as the quintessential champion of the common man against the greed of corporate barons bent on profit regardless of the impact on the human condition. He was also raised in a state that valued a civil service of policy development and reform instead of the patronage systems commonly associated with party organizations in the majority of the states.

After graduation from law school, Mondale and his wife, Joan Adams, settled in Minneapolis. His first job was with a firm known for the political careers of its members. For the next few years, he spent his time helping others be elected. Then, in 1960, Mondale was appointed by Governor Orville Freeman, whose state campaign Mondale had managed, to fill out the unexpired term of the flamboyant Minnesota Attorney General Miles Lord, who had resigned.

Ever the party stalwart and unwilling to divide the Democratic Farmer-Labor Party, Mondale decided not to run in 1962 for the governorship against then Lieutenant Governor Karl Rolvaag, though others had urged him to do so after his impressive win in his race to retain the job of attorney general in 1960. Some would suggest this decision demonstrated that Mondale was unwilling to take a gamble, but he had given his word to support Rolvaag two years earlier and, he told others, he felt unprepared to make the leap to the governor's mansion.

As luck would have it, had he taken the governor's job, he might not have been called upon by Hubert Humphrey to mediate successfully a critical impasse that developed at the Atlantic City Democratic national convention in 1964. Mondale's skills as a conciliator were showcased as the party grappled with the mostly black Mississippi Freedom Democratic Party's challenge, which sought to have the freedom slate of delegates rather than the regular Democrats seated as the rightful convention delegates from the state.

Mondale's next step up the political ladder could be more accurately characterized as a prodigious leap. With the selection of Hubert Humphrey in 1964 to share the national ticket with Lyndon Johnson, Humphrey's U.S. Senate seat fell vacant. The line of suitors was long

indeed and contained some state party heavyweights, including Governor Rolvaag himself; former governor and U.S. Secretary of Agriculture Orville Freeman; Walter Heller, John Kennedy's chair of the Council of Economic Advisers; Carl Rowan; and even Miles Lord, whom Mondale had replaced as Minnesota attorney general.

In a 1962 speech, Mondale had placed himself clearly on the liberal side of most public policy issues because he believed that the United States had enough determination to remove the remaining vestiges of poverty and racism in society by using current institutions. He put it this way: "We in America have now all the wealth, the sociological and political know-how to root out poverty and its causes." He viewed it to be primarily government's responsibility to see that every citizen had an equal chance to succeed. His liberal credo had a conservative side as well because he tended to view job training and education as possible solutions to the problems of race and poverty. With Humphrey's backing and Rolvaag's gratitude that Mondale had not challenged him for the governorship, Mondale garnered the coveted appointment as senator. Once again he was in the right place at the right time; still, he had put himself in the right place via loyalty and determination and successful efforts on other people's behalf.

The new young senator arrived in the nation's capital during one of the most intense periods in American history. Goldwater conservatives seemed to be in retreat, and the heady days of the Great Society saw the liberal Democrats living up to promises the party had made since 1948 in education, health care, and civil rights for black Americans.

Mondale, the Senate neophyte, quickly learned that the flowcharts of the legislative process and Senate rules were not as crucial as understanding the political culture of the place. He learned from his predecessor that having a hide like an armadillo was a definite political asset in the clubby atmosphere of the U.S. Senate. Because he had only two years left in Humphrey's term before he would have to stand for election in his own right, Mondale was forced to moderate his potential impact on the Senate. More than most of his colleagues who had six years to work with when they came in, Mondale had to pick his battles carefully, set his priorities, and calibrate his legislative votes with an eye toward the way they would-sell back home. His biographers note that working in his Senate office in those days was akin to having Attila the Hun for a boss. In fairness to him, though, he pushed himself every bit as hard.

During his Senate years, Mondale tended to view Vietnam War as something that the president and the executive branch were more capable of dealing with than the Congress. Mondale believed that expert advisers to the president were honest and correct in their assessment of the winability of the conflict. His real areas of interest and expertise were more domestic than foreign. When the day for his reelection came, Mondale retained the loyalties of Minnesota's New Deal Democrats and won with almost 54 percent of the vote. He would later admit that he had not been as critical of the war as he should have been. With Humphrey in the vice presidency, Mondale evidently felt constrained from criticizing the administration on foreign policy, an area that had not been his own personal strong suit. Mondale would later concede that he had miscalculated on supporting the war and that it was the greatest mistake of his career.

On his return to Washington for a full Senate term of his own, Mondale was unwilling to back down from the Great Society and civil rights programs despite the fact that public opinion seemed to hold that too much effort and treasure was going into those areas and not enough into crime prevention and success in Vietnam. He pressed for a fair housing bill, education, job training programs, and housing supplements and rent subsidies. His position was the opposite of the views that Nixon would galvanize as those of the "silent majority" in 1968.

Other pro–civil-rights leaders feared white backlash from Mondale's proposed "open hous-ing" initiatives. Still Mondale, instead of seeking compromise as one might have predicted from him, pressed forward on principle. The concern at that time centered around whether the old FDR coalition could be melded with the new antiwar types. The November elections could demonstrate whether the coalition, which had held sway since the 1930s, was so badly frayed that the very fabric of the party itself seemed to be beyond repair. The coalition of minorities, labor, and big city machines could still nominate candidates but could no longer automatically elect them. The movement of antiwar Democrats, with its outreach to youth, suburbanites, and the academic community, helped create the historic riot-tainted Chicago Democratic national convention that helped to seal Humphrey's fate despite the incredible comeback that Mondale as one of Humphrey's campaign managers had helped to engineer. In almost a prophetic comment about his own situation later, Mondale tried to defend Humphrey from student hecklers by noting that no one is ever at his best in the vice presidency: "No man has ever done well there. You must judge Humphrey on his entire record, not just his years in the vice presidency." No doubt Humphrey's defeat chastened his protégé about the efficacy of governmental efforts when executive bureaucracies can lead the nation astray, as happened over Vietnam.

In the aftermath of Humphrey's defeat and his own return to the Senate, Mondale began to reexamine previous standard liberal solutions to social problems publicly, much in the way he had moved away from support for the Vietnam conflict. He felt the frustration of the United States being the richest nation on earth and yet having so many children in poverty. He lectured his fellow liberals, complaining that it was time for them to face the fact that their approaches had been too Washington centered, insensitive to public concern, overlooking of recipients' needs. His solution was to propose for the children of the poor alternative federally funded programs in the nutrition, health, and educational services.

Nevertheless, as he traveled the nation giving speeches for House and Senate candidates in the off-year elections, Mondale intoned more traditional party mantras. In his partial term as senator, he focused most of his time on domestic concerns, and little of his energy was spent on foreign policy, with the exception of trade matters that affected the agricultural constituencies in his state. Within a year or so of the beginning of his second term and with his opposition to the Vietnam War becoming more recognized, he began to examine foreign policy, as several of his biographers assert, to position himself to run for president someday soon.

Any success in his aspirations to a chair in the Oval Office depended on his ability to mount a credible coalition behind him. Mondale was unprepared for the reality of the New Deal coalition's fragmentation. It was as if he expected the demographics of Minnesota's Democrats would be the same across the nation. As he traveled the nation in support of Democratic House candidates, he preached an orthodox New Deal gospel to a flock that had lost a number of its sheep. Some erstwhile middle-class Democrats made up what Nixon deftly categorized as the silent majority and began to do what Mondale had never imagined—join the party of the "rich and the powerful." As they departed their urban neighborhoods, fleeing taxes, political corruption, blight, and crime, they became the new Republicans of the inner suburbs. Issues like those and new ones like integration, busing, school choice, school prayer, and (after *Roe v. Wade*) abortion became the new hot-button issues. Southern Democrats and suburban Catholics were especially vulnerable to breaking away. Richard Nixon's call to the "forgotten American," with its emphasis on patriotism, law enforcement, and a call for a return to "traditional values" resonated well with many of the one-time Democrats. Unlike other senators, who such as Gary Hart of Colorado had incorporated these shifts into their campaign rhetoric, Mondale was a latecomer to this reality, though he had become increasingly skeptical whether the liberal creed would work in practice by the 1970s.

Earlier in his Senate career, Mondale had recognized a need to find a middle ground in policy areas while not abandoning his lifelong principles. He called for the creation, for example, of a Senate Select Committee on equal educational opportunity to see if the problems in education for minorities could be catalogued and thoroughly examined and if a middle ground between liberals and disenchanted conservative Democrats could be found. His move to the political center might well have been partly in response to the decision of Hubert Humphrey to do so to win Eugene McCarthy's old Senate seat in 1970 and his warnings to the DFL that such changes were necessary. This recognition that a more centrist message was more salable did not daunt Mondale's concern for poor children. His child care initiatives had broad party support in 1971, but his $2 billion program for dealing with children whose parents had to work was stymied by Nixon's veto pen. Interestingly enough, the vote for override in the Senate was only seven votes short of the needed two-thirds. It did not do much for Mondale's attempt to be seen as more moderate to lead a coalition made up of labor, civil rights groups, the women's liberation forces, big city mayors, and advocates of zero population growth.

Unfortunately for his children's initiative, Mondale's own polls in his races for the Senate in 1972 were showing a white backlash, and as a result, his campaign for the Senate tried to downplay his past role in advancing liberal agendas. He kept his political distance as far as possible from his neighboring senator from South Dakota, George McGovern, whose capture of the Democratic Party nomination in 1972 left the party's national wing in a shambles. Mondale's campaign-manager experience left him with the discernment to realize that the coalition that McGovern cobbled together by ingenious crafting of the party rules could not get him into the White House.

As noted earlier, Mondale the principled champion of the people could also be Mondale the cautious, as the situation dictated. He was not eager to play the ant trying to move the rubber-tree plant; high hopes gave way to foundational pragmatism. One of his biographers, Steven Gillon, notes that on a number of occasions Mondale was known to say that he didn't like "to waste his time slaying windmills," a phrase he must not have cleared with his speechwriters. From this point on, he was not noted for tilting at dragons either. He seemed to sense intuitively that some melding of these new and the old traditional Democrats would be required for a successful pursuit of the Oval Office. For these reasons, he told McGovern that he would not want to be considered as vice-presidential candidate on the ticket. Why should he sacrifice a Senate seat so he could win in 1972 to rearrange deckchairs on the *Titanic*? He expected that other opportunities for national office would come along when he would not have to gamble to consider them. Of course, we know that his instincts were quite correct. Unfortunately for Mondale, his pragmatism made him the target of sarcasm, especially from the political Left. One DFL wag reportedly commented, when Mondale had an emergency appendectomy in 1974: "I hope the surgeon inserted some guts before sewing him up."

Mondale's success in getting early childhood education programs through the Senate made him the darling of national media and added him to the list of names put forward by the "great mentioners" in the national press corps who could anoint presidential candidates as possibles or curse them to political oblivion by merely providing no ink or airtime. Mondale's longtime Senate office chief of staff Dick Moe and compatriots Mike Berman and Jim Johnson were his political brain trust, drafting the plan for Mondale's self-positioning to be the Democratic nominee in 1976. Like a fair damsel holding suitors at arm's length, Mondale would tell the press he was thinking of running, he was 99 percent sure he would, that probably he would run but not give a definitive yes.

As Moe, Berman, Johnson, and the Mondale family prepared to clear the decks so they could give their undivided attention to the campaign, Mondale became increasingly unsure whether he had the desire, stamina, and masochism to make the race. Six months of cat and mouse with the press corps and giving speeches across the nation did not appreciably improve his standing in the Gallup and Harris polls in November. Reminiscent of his decision not to seek the governor's race earlier, Mondale seemed to be wimping out. Hindsight is always 20/20, but it would have been interesting to see if, after Ted Kennedy dropped out and Senator Henry "Scoop" Jackson and Governor George Wallace's support began to falter, Mondale could have knocked an unknown governor from Georgia named Jimmy Carter out of the race.

In a *Minnesota Tribune* interview, Mondale indicated that his heart was not in the effort. He explained his stunning decision not to run by saying:

> In order to be a serious presidential candidate, I was going to have to ask others to commit themselves—to pledge parts of their lives to the campaign. Being uncertain myself as to whether I really wanted to seek the office, I just didn't feel I could ask others to make the commitment. I did not have the overwhelming desire to be president which is essential for the kind of campaign that it required. I don't think anyone should be president who is not willing to go through fire.

In looking back on his decision, Mondale told a friend that it was the indignity of it all in campaigning that soured him on the process. Every place he went, he was someone new to the voters there. He was constantly having to sell himself. He was never the fascinating speaker that the age of instant communications required.

As the election of 1976 approached, Jimmy Carter surprised virtually everyone except himself as he represented the Democratic Party in the quadrennial contest with the Republicans for the Oval Office. Unlike his predecessors, he spent quite a bit of time thinking about who ought to be his vice president and who would bring the most to the ticket and the job itself. During a November 1991 meeting of the Miller Center for Public Policy's Commission on the Selection for Vice President, Center Director Kenneth Thompson recorded Carter's recollections on the matter. According to Thompson's synopsis, Carter first assessed the people running against him. As Georgia governor, he had the 1972 candidates down to the capital to visit with him. He had aspirations to run for president or vice president himself. It had been reported that Carter's close aide Hamilton Jordan and his friend Dr. Peter Bourne had approached the McGovern camp, offering the governor as a vice-presidential candidate.

In summer 1976, after the Carter nomination was all but assured and weeks before he won on the first ballot at the New York Democratic national convention, he began to talk to Jordan and old friends like Charles Kirbo about how to select a running mate. He reported fifteen years later to those gathered at the Miller Center Forum that he put together a list of thirty candidates in a leather-bound book, along with a list of names of his choices for high cabinet positions. He had Kirbo interview some of the vice-presidential possibilities and later winnowed the list down to ten or so. He invited Senators Jackson of Washington, Church of Idaho, Muskie of Maine, and Mondale and two others to visit with him at Plains.

Carter realized that he needed someone with major Washington experience, a quality clearly lacking in his personal entourage. He finally chose between Muskie and Mondale. To Carter, the issue beyond experience was compatibility or chemistry between him and his choice, rather than the standard philosophical or geographic balance factors commonly used by his predecessor candidates for president. Mondale had impressed him by doing his homework on the issues, and ultimately, the phone call and invitation to join the ticket went out to him. When Carter was asked about the vice presidency during the 1976 campaign, he expressed an unprecedented view of the vice president's role, evidently with a Mondale-type in mind. He indicated that he was:

> certainly determined to make the Vice Presidency a substantive position. . . . I hope to have the kind of Vice President, if I am elected, who would share with me all the purposes of the administration in an easy and unrestrained way. . . . I think the country loses when a competent Vice President is deprived of any opportunity to serve in a forceful way.

During the campaign, Mondale participated in a first: He and Republican counterpart Bob Dole traded jabs in the first televised vice-presidential debate, organized by the League of Women Voters. When the joust was finished, Dole had scored debating points, but Mondale had shown himself to be not only a worthy candidate for vice president, but also a person of intelligence and finesse capable of being president on his own should the worst occur.

Mondale served as an important bridge to the liberal constituencies among which he had labored for his entire political career. Those same labor, minority, and other activist liberal groups were concerned about Carter's lack of specificity on issues and tendency to sound like a Republican in Democrat's clothing, with his calls for budgetary austerity, cutting bureaucracy, and civic virtue. It was Mondale's ties to the groups that Carter had seemingly run against in primaries that helped the ticket get out the vote necessary to win by one of the smallest margins in American history on election day. The big-city political organizations and labor unions delivered the needed turnout for the narrow victory. Mondale put on the final push in Illinois, New Jersey, Ohio, Pennsylvania, New York, and Wisconsin that combined to total 147 of the necessary 270 electoral votes to win. Pundits would note later that the Democrats in 1976 had resurrected the old New Deal coalition, with Carter bringing back the South and Mondale cementing the other traditional groups. By 1980, it would be clear that 1976 might have been an apparition of the ghost of victories past, but the body of the old coalition did not rise.

Given the rough road Mondale knew both Nelson Rockefeller and Hubert Humphrey had to travel as vice presidents and the psychological abuse to which they had been subjected by the presidents or their staff, he made sure that he and Carter were on the same wave length about the office very early in the game. In fact, Moe (in an interview on the Mondale staff as a part of the Carter Presidency Project oral histories, January 15 and 16, 1982 under auspices of the University of Virginia's Miller Center), reported that both Carter and Mondale felt that the vice presidency had been wasted in the past. They determined that if Mondale would be on the ticket, the two of them would talk over his role right after the election. Moe noted that Hamilton Jordan met with Moe and Mike Berman with the suggestion that the two staffs be fused. This experience of working together in the campaign would make the transition to governing in an integrated staffing mode much easier. Carter asked Mondale after the election to draft a memo of what he thought his role ought to be.

Mondale, after talking with Rockefeller and Humphrey and their staffs, concluded that it was a mistake for vice presidents to have institutional responsibilities because these impinged on other people's turf and created other problems. Also, responsibilities for specific programs and issues would keep the vice president from being useful as an adviser on more crucial issues. For Mondale's perception of the office to work, he told Carter he would need three things: unimpeded access to the president, access to all the information to which the president had access, and no make-work duties. In an interview after he had assumed the office, Mondale noted that "in the past Vice Presidents often took on minor functions in order to make it appear their role was significant, when if they were President they wouldn't touch them at all."

Few would argue that Mondale was anything but a respected adviser who had both the experience and stature to handle almost anything for the president. Both the vice president and his staffers were permitted to see virtually every paper that went through the Oval Office. He and his staff interacted regularly with the president, his staff, and key cabinet-level personnel. These interactions included a weekly lunch with the president; attending with the president weekly congressional leadership sessions; twice-weekly intelligence briefings with the White House chief of staff, the National Security assistant, and the CIA director; and participating in Friday foreign-policy breakfasts with Carter, National Security Assistant Brzezinski, Jordan, and the secretary of state (first Muskie, then Vance).

The integration of the two staffs was virtually unprecedented and permitted Mondale access to decision making even when he was not in the country. Carter had suggested that they share a common staff, but Mondale had sense enough to know he would want the independence of having his own people. At one point Carter had said publicly that he wanted Mondale to be his staff chief; as if to make the point that the staffs would be integrated, Mondale suggested and Carter agreed that Moe be both chief of staff to the vice president and senior adviser to the president. There was no precedent for such a move. Carter also told the White House staff: "If you get a request from Fritz, treat it as from me." On another occasion Carter, according to Moe, told the staff: "If I hear anybody critical of Fritz, you're out of here." Carter did not always follow Mondale's advice or that of the staff, but he always sought it out and listened.

It was Mondale who supervised a combined staff effort to set the early agenda of the incoming administration. The report suggested, on December 28, 1976, to the assembled cabinet-staff level personnel and the president fourteen key agenda points for the administration in the first hundred days, and it proposed the image the president would want to project. Carter acknowledged to the assembled administration personnel: "Fritz has done a good job." That good job would be rewarded with the ultimate indication of clout, an office in the West Wing near the Oval Office. Mondale was the first vice president to even have an office in the White House, a precedent that has been followed ever since.

Mondale is credited with being able to influence the president to select several key cabinet and major staff personnel including Health, Education, and Welfare Secretary Joseph Califano. Mondale also lobbied successfully to get people loyal to him in key administration positions: David Aaron, Mondale's chief foreign policy adviser in the Senate, became deputy national security adviser in the new administration. Close Mondale staffer Bert Camp became presidential deputy for domestic policy. So closely were the staffs intermingled that Hamilton Jordan, early in the administration, said: "I consider that I work for Mondale. He is my second boss, the way Carter is my first boss." Unlike his predecessors Humphrey and Rockefeller, Mondale was given no special project types of things to administer. Carter was especially concerned that Mondale be able to assume the presidency prepared in foreign affairs.

As vice president, Mondale took it upon himself to try to improve administration relations with the civil rights community, organized labor, and traditional liberal party leaders, whose support he would need to govern effectively. He encouraged Carter to accept a little pork barrel (eighteen water-control projects) to retain congressional support for his other initiatives. His recommendations and those of Domestic Policy Adviser Stu Eisenstadt convinced Carter to stand for affirmative action as a principle when confronted with the *Baake* case, which claimed reverse discrimination against white students seeking admission to medical school. Attorney General Griffin Bell had planned to argue the case entirely differently until the president intervened.

While Mondale had a good batting average early in the administration in being able to con-

vince Carter to follow his suggestions, he was not an insider. The vice president found that, though he always had access, he was not assured that the president would either turn to him for advice or agree with his assessments of situations. Carter was more of an economic conservative than his more liberal vice president. Mondale fought for a higher minimum wage and lost; he advocated a $50 tax rebate and lost again to Carter's commitment to balance the budget before the end of the term; and he had no better luck advocating increased farm price supports.

During fall 1977, Carter commented on Mondale's role in the administration, saying: "Fritz doesn't waste his influence. He does excellent background study. And his staff is superb. He also uses my staff, some of whom are his former staff members, very effectively." Further, Carter noted, "And it's really kind of a rare thing for me not to go along with his position because Fritz tries to put himself in the role of a president and not just present a fairly radical argument one way or the other in an irresponsible way."

Unfortunately for Mondale's traditional liberal views on the economy and public policy, continuing inflation encouraged Carter to follow his more conservative instincts and constrict the growth of new programs. Moe would later comment that he "spent a lot of time trying to keep domestic initiatives adequately funded and to prevent the marginal cuts that would do nothing for the economy but would create a firestorm of resentment and opposition."

The Carter regulars from Georgia and his media guru, Gerald Rofshoon, all urged belt tightening. Rafshoon once commented: "We were giving them ninety percent of their agenda and all they talked about was the ten percent they were not getting." Cutting back on spending and slowing the economy presented the danger of some unintended consequences such as unemployment. The Carter austerity package without massive cuts in defense opened the door for a Ted Kennedy challenge at the 1980 convention. Mondale's political instincts had proven correct. Once again, he found himself placed in the mediator's role that had characterized his career going back to college days. His liberal colleagues in the Senate, representing interest groups from the left of the party spectrum, were expecting that Mondale would successfully do their bidding when pressure for cuts came; instead they concluded that he caved in to pressure to please the president.

Liberals were also frustrated with Carter foreign policy in the Middle East because it tilted too much toward solutions that addressed Arab concerns without sufficiently bringing U. S. Jewish leaders into policy formulation. Language in a joint U.S.-Soviet declaration on solutions in the Middle East called for efforts to "ensure the legitimate rights of the Palestinian people." The language was highly incendiary to the U.S. Jewish community, which had tended to vote strongly Democratic in key electoral college states. Mondale was expected to put out the fire without being able to change the policy.

Mondale also expressed serious misgivings about the president's request that all staff and cabinet people tender their resignations in late July to prepare for a second-half of the term review. Even though the vice president thought the firings were a bad idea and expressed that to key presidential staffers, he was unable to halt the process and was out of town on a vice-presidential road show when the ax fell on so many "non-loyal" appointees. Unfortunately for Mondale, as the president and his staff became more knowledgeable about Washington, they felt the need to bypass the very constituencies Mondale was supposed to be a bridge to for the administration. Though he had advanced the role of the vice presidency far beyond anything his predecessors had been able to do, he realized, as he told a *National Journal* interviewer: "Jimmy Carter is the President; I know that." Though Mondale was required to pick up the campaigning slack left by Carter's decision not to campaign while Americans were being held hostage in Iran, it would not be his last presidential campaign.

From his selection to be Carter's running mate, Mondale wrote a new chapter in the history of the vice presidency. Carter's selection process, his suggestion that he felt that the office had been wasted, the merger of campaign staff, and the close ties between presidential and vice-presidential staff after the inauguration represented a new direction for the number-two office. In addition, Mondale's ability to write his own job description, see everything the president saw, have an office in the West Wing, and avoid make-work commission roles positioned the vice president to be an adviser to the president instead of a "Secretary of Catchall Affairs," as Nixon had characterized his duties in the Eisenhower years. Mondale would advise subsequent vice presidents how to get the most out of the office and in enhancing the role of the office to better serve the person who selected him as running mate. Mondale's proximity to power illustrates an important point about power and influence: Just being there doesn't always mean you will have influence.

Even as the campaign of 1980 was winding down, Mondale seemed to be looking ahead in a speech at the Woodrow Wilson Center at Princeton. In speaking to true-believing liberals, Mondale with sobering candor said, "Progressives need to adjust the liberal values of social justice and compassion to a new age of limited resources."

After the dust settled from the drubbing that Carter and Mondale took at the hands of Reagan and Bush, one might have expected Mondale's comment that he needed time to study and rethink the party message instead of making a bid for the Senate, as Hubert Humphrey had done. In fact, his attendance at numerous issue seminars across the country and trips overseas lent credence to his comments. At the same time, though, he was considering a run for the presidency in his own right. He made sure that he had representatives on the Democratic Party commission that wrote the party rules on convention delegation selection and seating criteria, and he reinvigorated his contacts with the old party constituencies.

Though he tried to project the image of a new progressive, he was still perceived in poll after poll as being an old-line liberal Democrat. It was that perception that encouraged Senator Gary Hart of Colorado to toss his hat into the ring and give Mondale the fight of his life in the party primaries.

Mondale's campaign seemed to be an uphill climb. His choice of Geraldine Ferraro as his running mate was indeed precedent shattering. Though he criticized PACs and their influence, he was embarrassed to have to respond to press and Hart complaints that Mondale had, in fact, created several PACs to funnel money into the campaign. Hart embarrassed him across the nation with the taunt: "Give the money back, Walter." Both Jimmy Carter and Ronald Reagan had won on their first general election by projecting the "outsider" image. Obviously Mondale, with all his Senate experience, was destined to be seen as just another tainted insider, He did not help his new-Democrat image when he announced in his convention acceptance speech: "If you elect me, I'll raise your taxes; so will Mr. Reagan; he won't tell you, I just did."

Some would attribute his eventual loss in 1984 to his positions on issues, while others saw Reagan as an incumbent president whose messages resonated well with larger segments of the increasingly conservative national constituency. As Mondale and his campaign staff realized, if the Democrats were to reclaim the White House in 1984, they would have to bring the middle class voters into the coalition of labor, citizen lobby groups, feminists, civil rights supporters, and old traditional urban Democrat machines. That promised to be no easy proposition. Some would fault Mondale's campaign style as the root of his problems: His message was not focused enough to some; he never learned how to use the media the way Reagan had, others would complain. His strength was within the traditional Democratic coalition put together around FDR, but that strength proved also to be a weakness because it labeled him as a traditional liberal at a time when a conservative middle class was turning elections.

Mondale's loss in 1984 then, in the main, was more due to an inability to articulate a new message for the Democratic Party, which had worn out its welcome to many of its past constituents who left the city ethnic neighborhoods for the suburbs. Six months after his defeat, he held a press conference in St. Paul to indicate that he did not intend to run for another term in the Senate. He withdrew from elective and appointed public life, but President Bill Clinton plucked him from the private sector in 1992 to serve as U.S. ambassador to Japan.

Mondale made one more brief appearance on the campaign trail in 2002, after Minnesota's popular liberal Democratic U.S. senator Paul Wellstone was killed in a plane crash 11 days before the November election. Mondale stepped forward at the urging of state party leaders and Wellstone's family to fill the late senator's place on the ballot against Republican former mayor of St. Paul Norm Coleman. Mondale, by then 74 years old, lost to Coleman, 49 percent to 47 percent, and he retired from electoral politics for the second time.

While it could be argued that his race for president will ensure his place in the history books, Mondale deserves recognition for the way his incumbency affected the ability of the vice presidents of the United States to advise the president and prepare the junior partner of the presidential ticket should the unthinkable happen. History may also record him, as well, as the last of a New Deal breed capable of getting the Democratic nomination for president. His message of compassion and civil rights in an age of middle-class consumerism and personal self-fulfillment became the ultimate hard sell.

REFERENCES

Steve M. Gillon, *The Democrats' Dilemma: Walter F. Mondale and the Liberal Legacy* (New York: Columbia University Press 1992); Finley Lewis, *Mondale: Portrait of An American Politician* (New York: Harper and Row, 1980); Kenneth Thompson, ed., *The Selec-*

tion of Vice Presidents (Charlottesville, Va.: Commission to Study Vice Presidential Selection, The Miller Center, University of Virginia, 1990–92); Interview with Richard Moe (including Michael Berman), Miller Center Interviews, Carter Presidency Project, v. XII, January 15–16, 1982, Jimmy Carter Library, Atlanta, Georgia. The author wishes to thank both the Miller Center at the University of Virginia and its director Kenneth Thompson and Martin J. Elzy, assistant director of the Jimmy Carter Library, for their help in making the oral history interviews available.

FRANK KESSLER is a political scientist with a Ph.D. from the University of Notre Dame. He has been recipient of NEH and NSF research grants, is author of *Dilemmas of Presidential Leadership: Of Caretakers and Kings* (Prentice Hall, 1983), and has been on the National Steering Committee of the Presidency Research Group and Board of Editors for *Presidential Studies Quarterly*. Recently, he presented a paper on the Bush Millennium Challenge Accounts at the Third World Development Conference. He formerly taught political science at Missouri Western College in St. Joseph, Missouri, and in the graduate American studies and political science programs at the University of Missouri–Kansas City. He is now at Benedictine College in Atchison, Kansas.

GEORGE HERBERT WALKER BUSH (B. 1924)

Vice President, 1981–1989

(President Ronald Reagan)

GEORGE H. W. BUSH
(Courtesy of Bush Presidential Materials Project)

By L. Edward Purcell

After George Bush returned to his Detroit hotel room on the evening of August 16, 1980, and changed into casual clothes, he settled in to wait for delegates to the Republican Party convention, to which he had just delivered a speech, to nominate Ronald Reagan as the party's candidate and for Reagan to then name Gerald Ford as his running mate. Before that could happen, however, the Secret Service phoned to say several agents had taken over a room two floors below in Bush's hotel. Bush understood what the call meant: he was likely to become vice president of the United States.

For Bush, the vice presidency was the penultimate stop on his way to the White House. It would fill out a sterling résumé that had only two more slots left open at the top, and it would position Bush to run for the White House.

As he wrote: "everybody belittles the office of the Vice President, not many people turn it down."

Born in Milton, Massachusetts, in June 1924, Bush was the second son of a wealthy New England family. His father, Prescott Bush, was a tall, handsome, well-to-do member of the northeastern social and economic elite, a gifted amateur golfer and singer and eventually a U.S. Senator from Connecticut (the family moved to Greenwich not long after George's birth). The elder Bush worked in his father-in-law's investment banking firm of Brown Brothers, Harriman. Bush's mother, Dorothy Walker, was less public than her husband but just as much a part of the genteel establishment. The family summered at Kennebunkport, Maine, where George's namesake grandfather owned the beachfront "Walker's Point," and where George acquired his love of boating, fishing, swimming, and tennis.

Bush was precocious and began his education at Greenwich Country Day School a year earlier than the norm. At age twelve, he was sent to Phillips Academy at Andover, Massachusetts, where by all accounts he developed into an extremely likeable young man, gifted in athletics and more than respectable in the classroom. His graduation from Andover was delayed by a serious illness, but during his senior year he was class president, captain of the baseball team, a member of the soccer and basketball varsity squads, and editor of the school newspaper.

Although he was speaking of a slightly later period of Bush's life, former Rhode Island Senator John F. Chafee once described George as

. . . one of those fellows who was sort of a golden boy: Everything he did he did well. . . . My first impression was that he was—and I don't mean this in a derogatory way—in the inner set, the movers and shakers, the establishment.

Bush finished prep school six months after the Japanese bombed Pearl Harbor, and against the wishes of his parents and the advice of his mentors, he spurned college and enlisted in the Navy, applying immediately for a commission and aviator's training. The Navy waived its usual requirement that demanded two years of college from pilots and allowed Bush to become—at eighteen years of age—die country's youngest flight trainee. Within a year, Bush earned his wings as a torpedo bomber pilot and headed toward the war in the Pacific.

He was assigned to a squadron aboard the carrier *San Jacinto* (known to its crew as the "San Jack"), flying a three-man TBM torpedo bomber. In June 1944, during an attack on Japanese bases on the Mariana Islands, Bush and his crew were forced to take off from the deck of their carrier into heavy fire. They were hit and the aircraft went down, but all survived the ditching and were rescued. In September, they were not so lucky. Bush and his crew were flying a combat mission against a Japanese radio station on the island of Chichi Jima (part of the same group as Iwo Jima) when the plane took a severe antiaircraft hit during a strafing run. After completing his attack, Bush turned his crippled plane toward the open sea. As the aircraft went down, Bush and his crew bailed out. The two crewmen were never seen again. Bush escaped alive but discovered that his life raft was slowly drifting toward the Japanese base and certain capture, perhaps death. Rather miraculously, the American submarine USS *Finback* appeared from the depths and rescued the downed pilot. After a month aboard the sub, Bush was put ashore at Pearl Harbor and, after a brief return to the *San Jacinto,* he was shipped home to the United States. For his heroism, he received the Distinguished Flying Cross. Bush was thus one of the five twentieth-century American presidents who were combat veterans when they became commander in chief.

Shortly after arriving home, Bush married Barbara Pierce, the daughter of a New York publisher. He had met her before the war when she was a student at Ashley Hall girls' school, and she dropped out of Vassar to marry Bush. The newlyweds moved to Norfolk, Virginia, where Bush was assigned as a flight instructor until the war's end. Eventually, the union produced four sons and two daughters, one of whom died tragically from childhood leukemia.

After his discharge from the Navy in 1945, Bush returned to Connecticut and enrolled at Yale, his father's alma mater. He was one of the thousands of veterans who descended on American campuses in the years immediately after the war. Many of whom, like Bush, were married and mature and eager to pick up lives interrupted by duty during the conflict.

Bush was again in a hurry, and he was admitted to an accelerated degree program at Yale. Despite the pressures of extra courses and the distractions of marriage and a family (his eldest son, George W. Bush who in 2000 was elected president was born in 1947), Bush managed to participate in extracurricular life at the Ivy-League school. He was captain of the excellent school baseball team, playing in the finals of the national collegiate world series twice, and he played varsity soccer. He also was a member of a social fraternity and elected to Yale's famed secret society, the Skull and Bones. He graduated as a Phi Beta Kappa economics major in the spring of 1948.

At this stage, Bush took a surprising decision about a career. With his many family connections in the eastern business world, he could have chosen among many gilt-edged job offers. Instead, he arranged for an entry-level position with a Texas oil company and moved his fledgling family to Odessa, in the heart of the oil patch, a major disjuncture from his previous country-club life in Connecticut. The Bushes at first lived modestly in a shotgun-style house while George learned the oil business from the ground up. After a short tour as a salesman in California, Bush settled in Midland, Texas. In 1951, he and a friend, John Overbey, formed an oil development company with financial backing from George's uncle. Two years later, the duo merged their interests with the Liedtke brothers, William and Hugh, to form Zapata Petroleum.

Bush was a hard-working businessman in an industry having one of its periodic boom spells, and the company prospered. In 1959, Bush's interest in offshore drilling rigs prompted him to move to Houston and become head of a split-off business, Zapata Offshore, which rented equipment to producers. The new firm was a profitable enterprise that eventually employed more than 200 workers.

The success of his oil-rig business coincided with Bush's growing interest in politics. As a Republican in heavily Democratic Texas, Bush was not well placed for a quick rise, and he at first devoted himself to hard work at the grassroots level. Most of his interests revolved around the Harris County Republican Party (which encompassed conservative districts in Houston), and he was selected as county chairman in 1963. The following year, Bush decided to try for elective office and mounted a campaign for the U.S. Senate. He won the GOP primary, but when pitted against popular Democrat Ralph Yarborough, Bush was no match, despite heavyweight campaign help from Senator Barry Goldwater and Vice President Richard Nixon.

Realizing the futility of running statewide in Texas as a Republican, Bush refocused his ambitions and in 1966 entered the race for the newly reapportioned seat in the U.S. House of Representatives from the prosperous Seventh District of Houston. At the same time, Bush decided to get out of the oil business, and he sold his interest in Zapata Offshore for around $1.1 million—a modest fortune by Texas standards but nonetheless a tribute to his business energy and acumen. Henceforth, Bush would devote himself to politics and officeholding as he began to build a spectacular record of public service. The first step was taking the House seat by winning more than 57 percent of the district's vote.

When he moved his family to Washington, D.C., early in 1967, Bush began a twenty-five year period of nearly uninterrupted officeholding. Except for a few years in the late 1970s, his next quarter-century revolved around national government and politics. The Bush ties to Texas were strong, but because the family moved so frequently, the most stable residence was probably the compound at Kennebunkport, Maine, where the Bushes vacationed often during the years of public life. (Eventually the Bushes were able to buy Walker's Point from George's family and take over the main house.)

During Bush's first term in the House, he was favored by the party leadership and got a superior appointment for a freshman representative to the House Ways and Means Committee. He was a strong supporter of American participation in the war in Vietnam, and although he voted for the Fair Housing Act in 1968, he was no more than lukewarm in supporting other causes backed by black Americans.

In all of this, as well as the rest of his political career, Bush confirmed his own nature and reflected what would become his public image: he was a good party man of deep loyalty. He could count on moving to the top through good connections and he could handle any job assigned to him, but he was unmotivated by any deep conviction or fire in the belly.

Bush won a second House term in 1968, and emboldened by the national Nixon–Agnew Republican victory—he had been briefly considered as Nixon's running mate before the election—he decided to once again try for the Texas Senate seat held by Ralph Yarborough. Bush's conclusion that Yarborough was vulnerable proved correct when the latter was beaten in the Democratic primary by Lloyd Bentsen. The contest between Bentsen and Bush proved a lively affair, with President Nixon throwing all his support behind the congressman from Houston. Nixon also privately promised Bush an appointment to a high post if he lost. In the end, Bentsen won the Senate seat by nearly six percentage points, a result attributed to Bush's failure to attract even token support among black Texas voters.

True to his word, President Nixon rewarded Bush by appointing him to the post of U.S. ambassador to the United Nations. Bush enjoyed his duties in New York but discovered that he was being used by the administration—headed on foreign policy matters by Secretary of State Henry Kissinger—as a diplomatic decoy. Bush vigorously pursued the longtime American policy of defending Taiwan as the official representative of China to the UN, while behind the scenes, Kissinger and Nixon prepared to recognize the mainland Communist Chinese, which they eventually did, leading to the expulsion of Taiwan from the world body.

Despite the seeming embarrassment of his term at the UN, Bush was still in political favor, and in 1972, Nixon appointed him to head the GOP as chairman of the Republican National Committee. The most important event during Bush's watch as head of the party was the infamous break-in at the Watergate by operatives of Nixon's reelection committee. Bush was not involved, but he was placed in the uncomfortable position of having to defend Nixon throughout the subsequent investigation and scandal. Bush's loyalty was tested, but he remained steadfastly a supporter of the president to the bitter end, crisscrossing the country to make speech after speech in defense of Nixon. Not until the day before Nixon's resignation did Bush formally withdraw his support and acknowledge the president's guilt.

When Gerald Ford became president on Nixon's departure, Bush hoped to be named vice president. With Nelson Rockefeller's selection instead, Bush was placated by the offer of his choice of ambassadorships to either Great Britain or France—the two posts generally considered to be the plums of the foreign service. Instead of accepting either, Bush surprised Ford and asked to be named to the relatively less important post of head of the U.S. mission to Communist China. He and Barbara moved to Beijing in 1974, and although they were tireless travelers and consumers of tourist culture, George himself had little to do. Kissinger handled almost all important communications with the Chinese government and usually consulted Bush only as an afterthought.

In December 1975, Bush was offered an escape to a job with real responsibility when

Ford asked him to take over as head of the besieged Central Intelligence Agency. The CIA had come under heavy attack for lying to Congress and for concealing bungled attempts to assassinate several world leaders, including Fidel Castro. Bush had few if any qualifications for the job except for his well-known charm, loyalty, and capacity for hard work. After he became director in January 1976, however, Bush was successful in improving agency operations and did a good deal to improve internal morale and to resuscitate the CIA's reputation, especially on Capitol Hill. With Jimmy Carter's election victory in November, however, Bush's days at the CIA were numbered. When the Democrats swept into office, he was replaced and moved back to Houston, out of a government job for the first time in a decade.

Bush joined the executive committee of Houston's First International Bank and gained several lucrative seats on corporate boards, but his main occupation from 1977 to 1979 was campaigning on behalf of Republican candidates and laying plans for his own political future. Bush's goal, of course, was the White House.

In May 1979, he announced his intention to run for the G.O.P. presidential nomination in 1980. Although he was well known nationally in some party circles from his days as Republican Party chairman, Bush's name was not much of a public commodity. He had held only one elective office—his seat in the U.S. House—and despite his tours in diplomatic posts and at the CIA, the general population knew very little about him. Even in his home territory, he was something of a cipher. His introduction to a 1978 Dallas Republican Men's Club luncheon meeting as a "prospective Republican nominee for president" was met with disbelieving silence.

Nonetheless, Bush mounted a spirited campaign for the nomination. He assembled a group of consultants and a staff and set up a campaign headquarters in Alexandria, Virginia, just across the Potomac from Washington, D.C. His chief advisers were his old friends James A. Baker III,

a former undersecretary of commerce under Gerald Ford, and Robert Mosbacher. Bush also used the family compound at Kennebunkport as a meeting center to plan strategy.

The Republican front-runner for the nomination was former movie star and California governor, Ronald Reagan. Behind Reagan came a cluster of hopefuls including Bush, Robert Dole, John Connally, Howard Baker, Phil Crane, and John Anderson, but none of them had the public recognition or momentum of Reagan. Bush's main task was to separate himself from the pack and become Reagan's chief competitor. He took a step toward this by coming in first in a Maine straw poll of Republicans (Reagan was not on the ballot), but the high point of Bush's campaign for the nomination came in late January 1980 when he actually beat out Reagan and the others in the Iowa party caucuses. He basked in the fame of his Iowa "victory," appearing on the cover of *Newsweek,* but a strong showing by Reagan in the New Hampshire primary all but finished the campaign. By May, even though Bush had won primaries in Massachusetts, Connecticut, Pennsylvania, and Michigan, it was clear that Reagan, with a thirty-point lead in the polls, would be the choice of the party, and the best Bush could hope for was to get the call as vice president.

Bush went to the Republican convention in Detroit prepared to accept the vice presidency, but as he later commented, he "knew you don't campaign for the vice presidency, because it's a calling. And the caller is whoever happens to be the presidential nominee." Reagan's first choice for his vice president was former president Gerald Ford, whom Reagan's pollsters told him would be the strongest addition to the GOP ticket. Plans to nominate Ford were well advanced when Ford shot himself in the foot during a TV interview with Walter Cronkite. Ford outlined his idea of what in his mind was to be nearly a copresidency, with Reagan handling domestic matters and Ford in charge of foreign affairs. The Reagan camp was outraged and turned immediately to Bush, despite lingering resentment of some of Bush's anti-Reagan primary campaign tactics (especially a crack Bush made about Reagan's "voo-doo economics").

When the call from Reagan finally came to his hotel room that night in Detroit, George Bush was happy to accept the second spot on the ticket. He did not know Reagan well personally—historically, few vice presidents seem to have had much acquaintance with their running mates—but Bush believed they were close enough in political philosophy to make the combination work. "The bottom line," he wrote, "both politically and economically, was that Reagan and I agreed that solving the country's economic problems would require not only tax cuts but massive cuts in government spending, along with a wholesale reduction in federal red tape and overregulation."

The election itself was not much of a contest. Jimmy Carter appeared to a majority of American voters to have lost his grasp on government and policy, and the Reagan-Bush ticket swept into office with a plurality of almost 9.5 million popular votes and a margin of 489 to 49 in the electoral college. In January, Bush moved back to Washington, D.C., and into the vice presidential residence on the grounds of the Naval Observatory, although his vice-presidential schedule allowed for frequent visits to Kennebunkport.

Bush's two terms as vice president saw him take on the sort of tasks that have come to characterize the office in the late twentieth century: heading task forces to cut government paperwork and to combat drugs and attending state funerals around the globe (he once quipped "You die; I fly"), but his tenure was also marked by very dramatic episodes.

During his first year in office, Bush was circumspect and intentionally low key. He knew that several of the president's longtime California supporters mistrusted him and that the ultraconservatives in the party thought him unsound even though he consistently refused to take a stand or comment on ideology. He quietly set out to establish a personal relationship with Reagan in the hope that it would solidify his political position. As Bush later commented that ". . even when Presidents and Vice Presidents see eye to eye on the issues, their long-term political relationship can only be as strong as their personal relationships." The tactic worked, and within a few weeks Reagan had warmed to Bush. The two shared a private lunch weekly, where the president relaxed, talked about issues, and auditioned new jokes. As have other recent vice presidents, Bush had an office in the West Whig of the White House and had access to all documents and classified communications of the president, allowing him to maintain a high state of preparedness to step forward if need be.

The need arrived suddenly on March 3, 1981, when Reagan, White House press secretary Jim Brady, a Secret Service agent, and a policeman were shot down on the street outside the Capital Hilton by a would-be assassin. Reagan was seriously wounded and rushed to George Washington Hospital with a bullet lodged in his chest. Brady had taken an even more grievous wound to the head and barely survived.

At the time of the attack, George Bush was in Fort Worth, Texas, dedicating a historic site. He was airborne in Air Force Two when a rather cryptic message came through the communications net from Secretary of State Alexander Haig that the president had been shot. A certain amount of chaos reigned at the White House in the hours immediately after the attack on Reagan—Haig made an unfortunate appearance before the press, for example, in which he claimed to be in charge, an assertion that displayed an incredible ignorance of the constitutional line of succession—and not much clear information made its way from Washington to Bush's plane. Most of what he learned about the situation came from commercial television broadcasts monitored on Air Force Two on a tiny black-and-white set.

When the plane landed at Andrews Air Force Base, south of Washington, Bush was pressured to take a Marine helicopter directly to the White House in order to avoid the delay of rush-hour traffic, but he firmly declined and insisted on being flown to the Naval Observatory and then traveling by limousine. For Bush this was an important symbolic action. He wanted to be certain that Americans and foreign friends and foes knew that the government in Washington would continue to function in steady hands, but he wanted to avoid all appearance of impudence or impropriety. He told his advisers: ". . . only the president lands on the South Lawn."

At 7:00 P.M., Bush called a meeting of the cabinet and then spoke to a press conference where he reassured the nation and the world that the United States government was still functioning.

As his friendly biographer Fitzhugh Green has noted, Bush showed a nice touch in his willingness to assume authority as needed, without giving an unseemly appearance of a thirst for power. On the other hand, some former Reagan aides have criticized Bush for being too passive during his term as vice president. The truth is that Bush was very cautious in almost every situation to avoid an aggressive or self-seeking stance, but he was more than willing to speak out or take on responsibility if asked, and President Reagan came to rely on him in important situations. When Secretary of State Haig and National Security Advisor Richard Allen got into an exceedingly acrimonious power fight, for example, Reagan resolved the problem by appointing Bush as head of the White House crisis management team, which gave the vice president a limited but crucial position of power within the administration.

Bush was always very clear about his understanding of the vice president's role. He was firm in stating his view that a vice president must be circumspect at all times, and intense loyalty is the highest of vice-presidential virtues. In his autobiography, Bush listed his five rules of the vice presidency:

1. There is only *one* president.
2. No political opportunism.
3. No news leaks.
4. All Interviews must be on the record.
5. The vice president owes the president his best judgment.

In the 1984 election, the Reagan-Bush team ran against former Vice President Walter Mondale and his running mate, Geraldine Ferraro. The result was a monumental landslide for the incumbent Republican team. The weather in Washington turned nasty for the Reagan-Bush second inauguration and the ceremony was moved inside to the Capitol Rotunda, but otherwise the slide into a second term was almost uneventful.

By mid-1985, however, events again turned dramatic. During a routine physical, doctors discovered that Reagan had suspicious-looking polyps attached to his intestines. A biopsy showed the growths to be cancerous, and the president was scheduled for surgery. The question then arose whether to evoke the provisions of the Twenty-fifth Amendment to the Constitution, which called for the president to turn over powers temporarily to the vice president in case of physical incapacity. Reagan would be under anesthetic for the surgery and for awhile, at least, unable to function. Reagan's advisers decided to hedge the situation slightly, and at 11:30 A.M. on July 13, Reagan signed a letter (just before going under anesthetic) temporarily transferring the power of the presidency to Bush. When the president regained consciousness six hours later, he signed a second letter to reclaim his office. Although the episode may have been little more than a footnote to history, it demonstrated a vastly different approach to the question of a president's fitness for office than had been the case many times before, most notably the two-and-a-half years of Woodrow Wilson's complete debility.

Perhaps the only controversial aspect of Bush's vice presidency revolved around what came to be known as the Iran-contra affair. Members of the Reagan team, notably U.S. Marine Colonel Oliver North, put into play a scheme to sell missiles to Iran and send the proceeds to finance right-wing guerrillas in Nicaragua, who were trying to overthrow the elected government of the left-wing Sandinistas. When the illegal maneuvers became a public scandal and led to congressional hearings and criminal convictions, some Democrats and members of the news media wanted to explore Bush's knowledge of the affair and possible involvement. He had been, after all, head of the CIA and of task forces dealing with terrorism and drugs and therefore might be expected to have had a hand in the administration's clandestine activities. Although his role has never been explained to his critics' complete satisfaction, Bush denied involvement in the Iran-contra exchange, although he did admit to learning of North's activities. Subsequent official inquiries little focused on Bush.

As the end of Reagan's second term approached, Bush stepped forward and claimed the GOP nomination for president, despite a challenge from Robert Dole, who shook Bush with an early victory in the Iowa caucuses. The Democrats nominated Massachusetts Governor Michael Dukakis, who chose Bush's old Texas political nemesis Lloyd Bentsen as his vice-presidential running mate. Coming out of the Democratic convention in late July, the Democratic candidates had a seventeen-point lead in the polls.

Bush selected Dan Quayle, a relatively obscure senator from Indiana, to fill out the Republican ticket and set forth on a masterfully crafted campaign to defeat the Democrats. By focusing on what his pollsters and strategists said were Dukakis's perceived weaknesses, especially a supposed softness on crime, and emphasizing brisk, positive media sound bites, Bush closed the gap. He was especially effective in calling attention to "a kinder, gentler America," and telling Americans to "Read my lips. No new taxes." When combined with a brutal attack on Dukakis's record on crime—most famously involving an ad about furloughed black Massachusetts rapist and killer Willie Horton—the positive strategy worked. Bush and Quayle won the election by claiming nearly 54 percent of the popular vote and taking forty of the fifty states. Bush thus became the first sitting vice president to be elected directly to the presidency since Martin Van Buren took over from Andy Jackson in 1836.

Bush's term as president proved to be eventful, to say the least. Within the first year, communist control of Eastern Europe collapsed with shocking suddenness. The Berlin Wall came down. Communist regimes fell everywhere, and the Russian empire itself disintegrated. Bush's administration managed to negotiate this new situation and reached arms-reduction agreements that heralded the end of the cold war, a situation that would have seemed unthinkable only a few years earlier.

Bush also led the nation into a full-scale war—the first since Vietnam—after the army of Iraqi dictator Saddam Hussein invaded Kuwait in 1990 and threatened Saudi Arabia. With the West's oil supplies on the line, Bush skillfully built a United Nations coalition, including several Mideastern Arab nations, that demanded Hussein's withdrawal. In early 1991, the coalition, comprised mostly of American forces, carried out a massive air war followed by a devastating ground attack that crushed the Iraqi army in Kuwait, although the coalition stopped short of occupying Baghdad and ousting Hussein. Bush's popularity soared as he justly claimed credit for what most Americans saw as a chest-puffing victory that laid to rest the ghostly legacy of failure in Vietnam. It was somewhat shocking, therefore, that by 1992 Bush's standing with the voters had been pummeled and that the relatively obscure Democratic governor of Arkansas, Bill Clinton, was able to chase Bush out of office after only one term.

The cause was almost certainly a sharp downturn in the economy and Bush's need to renege on his loud campaign promise not to raise taxes. Even though the economy was well along toward recovery, Bush ran a lackluster campaign until close to the end, and he was unable to catch Clinton.

Following his defeat. Bush moved back to Houston, where he and his wife built a new house in a posh section of town and settled into a comfortable retirement. Bush was active on the speechmaking circuit and reportedly commanded up to $100,000 a speech. He worked on a book with former foreign policy advisor Brent Scowcroft, and in 1993, he visited Kuwait at the invitation of the nation's ruler and narrowly avoided an assassination attempt by the Iraqis. In general, George Bush kept a low public profile after 1992, spending much time with his family (including thirteen grandchildren), both in Houston and Kennebunkport even after the election of his eldest son, George W., as president in 2000. He teamed up in a seemingly unlikely but extremely successful alliance with former president Bill Clinton to cochair an international fund-raising effort to aid victims of the 2004 Indian Ocean tsunami and Hurricane Katrina.

Perhaps the most public notice came from his skydiving exploits, first on his 80th birthday and again at the age of 83 to mark the opening of his presidential library on the campus of Texas A & M at College Station. On the latter occasion, he dove in tandem with a member of the U.S. Army's Golden Knights. Afterward, Bush commented, "Just because you're 83 is no reason to sit around and drool."

REFERENCES

George Bush (with Brent Scowcroft), *A World Transformed* (New York: Scribner's, 1999); George Bush (with Victor Gold), *Looking Forward: An Autobiography* (New York: Doubleday, 1987); Michael Duffy and Dan Goodgame, *Marching in Place: The Status Quo Presidency of George Bush* (New York: Simon and Schuster, 1992); Fitzhugh Green, *George Bush: An Intimate Portrait* (New York: Hippocrene Books, 1989); John Robert Greene, *The Presidency of George Bush* (Lawrence, Kans.: University Press of Kansas, 1999); Haynes Johnson, *Sleepwalking through History: America in the Reagan Years* (New York: W.W. Norton, 1991); Pamela Kilian, *Barbara Bush: A Biography* (New York: St. Martin's Press, 1992); Nicolas King, *George Bush: A Biography* (New York: Dodd, Mead, 1980); Jane Mayer and Doyle McManus, *Landslide: The Unmaking of the President, 1984–1988* (Boston: Houghton Mifflin, 1988); Edwin Meese, *With Reagan: The Inside Story* (Lanham, Md.: Regnery Gateway, 1992); Peggy Noonan, *What I Saw at the Revolution: A Political Life in the Reagan Era* (New York: Random House, 1990); Ronald Reagan, *An American Life* (New York: Simon and Schuster, 1990); Larry Speakes, *Speaking Out: The Reagan Presidency from Inside the White House* (New York: Scribner's, 1988); David Stockton, *The Triumph of Politics: How the Reagan Revolution Failed* (New York: Harper & Row, 1986); Tom Wicker, *George Herbert Walker Bush: A Penguin Life* (New York: Penguin, 2004).

See the entry for George Clinton for a biographical note on L. EDWARD PURCELL.

J. DANFORTH QUAYLE (B. 1947)

Vice President, 1989–1993

(President George H. W. Bush)

J. DANFORTH QUAYLE
*(Courtesy of the Dan Quayle Center/United States Vice
Presidential Museum, Huntington, Indiana)*

By Shirley Anne Warshaw

The Republicans dominated the White House throughout the 1980s, first with the Reagan–Bush administration and then the Bush–Quayle administration. Elected in 1988, George Herbert Walker Bush and J. Danforth Quayle continued the Reagan legacy of fiscal conservatism, slimming the federal bureaucracy, and deficit reduction, in addition to a continued defense buildup. By the 1992 election cycle, however, the tide of public opinion had turned against the Republican agenda and moved toward the domestic and economic stimulus themes of the Democrats. The Democratic ticket of Bill Clinton and Al Gore defeated the one-term Republican Bush/Quayle team and turned the reins of government over to the Democrats for the first time in twelve years.

419

When George Bush chose the relatively obscure junior senator from Indiana as his vice-presidential running mate in 1988, he had taken a calculated risk that Dan Quayle could galvanize the conservative right wing of the Republican Party for an electoral victory. Quayle and Bush hardly knew each other, but Quayle had forged a reputation as a strong supporter of family values, the prolife movement, and conservative principles. Quayle solidified for the Bush–Quayle ticket the conservative vote that had supported Ronald Reagan for the past two elections. Bush, himself a moderate, needed to balance the ticket in order to maintain conservative support.

The November 8, 1988, election proved Bush's risk of Dan Quayle to be well taken, for the voters handily turned away Democrat Massachusetts Governor Michael S. Dukakis and his running mate, senior Texas Senator Lloyd Bentsen. Bush controlled the election, carrying 40 states with 48.9 million votes, 53 percent of the total, and an impressive 426 electoral votes. Dukakis carried only 10 states, with 41.8 million votes or 46 percent of the total, and 111 electoral votes.

The emergence of Dan Quayle as a national political figure was part of a concerted effort on his part to move into the national scene. As Bush became the clear front-runner for the Republican nomination in 1988, Quayle embarked on a campaign to capture the vice-presidential nomination. As early as 1986, just after being reelected to the Senate, he had begun to explore ways to become a contender for the nomination. He gave high profile speeches on the Senate floor throughout spring 1988, became an active participant in the weekly lunches of Senate Republicans that George Bush regularly attended, and frequently stopped in Bush's office in the Senate.

Quayle's most deliberate move toward gaining the vice-presidential nomination was lobbying to give the keynote address at the 1988 Republican convention. Quayle commented that "I lobbied a little bit, very discreetly. . . . I thought I'd be . . . good." In late spring, Quayle began actively to garner the support of the Republican Party's conservative wing through his opposition to the INF (Intermediate Nuclear Forces) Treaty being debated on the Senate floor. He later became a major opponent of the 1988 defense budget, arguing that the Democrats had cut the budget beyond acceptable limits. When the defense bill was passed by the Democratic-controlled Senate, Quayle became the leading advocate of a presidential veto and frequently met with Vice President Bush. Bush eventually supported the Quayle position and convinced President Reagan to veto the bill.

The decision to consider Dan Quayle for the 1988 Republican ticket came on July 25, 1988, as the Democratic convention was ending. Bush phoned Quayle at his McLean, Virginia, home and told him he was one of several people under consideration as the vice-presidential nominee. By August 16, when the New Orleans Republican convention was in full operation, Quayle emerged as the successful candidate. Quayle's addition to the ticket provided Bush with not only political and geographic balance but also the increasingly important generational balance. Dan Quayle represented the politically active postwar generation. At the relatively young age of forty-one, Quayle had become one of the nation's youngest vice-presidential nominees, representing burgeoning baby boomers. Only Richard Nixon, who was elected in 1952 at age thirty-nine with Dwight D. Eisenhower, had been younger when elected to the nation's second highest office.

J. Danforth Quayle entered the world as part of a prominent Indianapolis publishing family. Born to James and Corinne Quayle on February 4, 1947, in Huntington, Indiana, Dan Quayle grew up in a small midwestern town where his father was a second-tier manager of a newspaper owned by his father-in-law, Eugene Pulliam. When he was eight years old, the Quayle family moved to Arizona, where Jim Quayle joined another newspaper. Finally, in 1963, when Quayle was sixteen years old, the family returned to Huntington when his father bought the *Huntington Herald-Press* from Pulliam.

Quayle's childhood was one of strong family ties and conservative values. His father, a John Birch Society member, had been a powerful influence on the development of Quayle's conservative value system. Life was comfortable for the Quayles and included such luxuries as a country-club membership and, as one family friend recalled, "plenty of time to play golf." It was also a childhood full of politics, with both his parents serving on precinct committees and heavily involved in Republican politics. In 1968, Quayle signed on as a volunteer at the Republican national convention and became a driver for the Nixon staff, all of which was encouraged by his parents.

Quayle's strong family ties were a key reason for his decision to attend DePauw University in Greencastle, Indiana, where both his parents and his grandfather had gone. After graduating there in 1969, he entered the Indiana National Guard to meet his military obligation before he could be drafted. A year later, Quayle entered the Indiana University–Indianapolis Law School with the class of 1973. His interest in politics was fueled during his tenure at law school; he held jobs in both the attorney general's and the governor's offices.

While in law school Quayle met another law student, Marilyn Tucker, whom he married in 1972. After graduation, they returned to Huntington, Indiana, where Quayle took over the family newspaper as associate publisher of the *Huntington Herald-Press,* which was owned by his grandfather and run by his father. In addition, he opened a law firm, known as Quayle and Quayle, with his wife.

The political career of Dan Quayle began as soon as he left law school, with his decision to buy a house in Huntington because of its location. Quayle wanted to run for the state legislature and sought a house in a district from which he thought he could be elected. However, he subsequently chose to bypass the state legislature and make a run for the U.S. House

of Representatives in 1976. Marilyn Quayle served as his campaign strategist and became the liaison with Republican state leaders, meeting with county party leaders and organizing local political events. She was widely credited with managing the campaign and ensuring its political and financial success.

Quayle's 1976 campaign for the House focused on the issues of welfare reform, increased defense spending, and criticism of the New York City bailout. Rather than run on the president's coattails, Quayle chose to distance himself from Gerald Ford, whose popularity had fallen after his pardon of Richard Nixon. Quayle ousted Democrat J. Edward Roush, who had represented the Fourth Congressional District for 16 years, winning the election by a margin of 19,000 votes, 55 percent to 45 percent, despite trailing Roush by 16 points during the summer before the election.

Quayle's congressional victory was a combination of clever attacks on a tax-and-spend liberal Congress, of which Roush was a prominent member, and actively seeking support from the Christian right. A Fort Wayne newspaper noted that "Congressman-elect Quayle called for a limited government, an end to deficit spending, and a stop to the federal bureaucracy's cancerous growth." In January 1977, at the tender age of twenty-nine, Quayle was sworn into the U.S. Congress and focused his energies on what he called "excessive government spending."

Quayle's voting House record reflected the conservative values that he had espoused during the campaign and was scored by the conservative Americans for Constitutional Action as one of the highest in the Congress, averaging in the mid-ninetieth percentile. The liberal Americans for Democratic Action scored his voting record as unacceptable, averaging in the fifteenth percentile. After two House terms, Quayle took a major political risk by challenging the Democratic incumbent, Birch Bayh, for the U.S. Senate. When the leading Republican contender to challenge Bayh, Governor Otis Bowen, announced that he would not run for the Senate seat, Quayle announced that he would. On May 14, 1979, Quayle entered the race.

Quayle's decision to challenge Bayh, an eighteen-year Senate veteran, was based on his belief that the public was ready for a new generation of leadership committed to reducing federal expenditure. During seven televised debates during the 1980 campaign, Quayle repeatedly hammered away at the liberal voting record that Bayh had maintained.

Quayle's attacks were in step with the conservative trend of the 1980 election: Republican presidential candidate Ronald Reagan was similarly attacking President Jimmy Carter's administration. Quayle tried to draw parallels between Democrats Bayh and Carter, including their support for a gasoline tax. Quayle adeptly used the media in his drive for the Senate; for example, he held a press conference using a local McDonald's as the backdrop for presenting a chart that listed the onerous federal regulations that governed making a hamburger. Indiana supported Quayle, as it did Ronald Reagan, with 54 percent of the vote to Bayh's 46 percent. Four years after being elected to the House, Quayle had been elected to the Senate. In January 1981 when the Ninety-seventh Congress convened, Indiana had two Republican Senators, Richard Lugar and J. Danforth Quayle.

The Reagan Revolution ushered Quayle into the Senate along with the first Republican majority since Dwight Eisenhower, and the new majority was committed to cutting taxes, reducing federal regulation, and increasing national defense. The Republicans' goal was to restructure the federal government's role in policy making by both ending numerous programs and devolving other programs to the state level. The Reagan Republicans were also committed to a major buildup in national defense, including military hardware and manpower.

Quayle's 1980 campaign had been a natural fit with the conservative Republican trend of the Reagan Revolution. Quayle campaigned as an advocate of prayer in public schools and tuition tax credits for private schools. He opposed abortion and supported voluntarism to replace government services.

His committee assignments were generally a solid mix with his electoral base and his ambition toward higher office. His appointment to the Labor and Human Resources Committee provided input into social legislation, his appointment to the Budget Committee allowed constant overview of budget cutting, and his appointment to the Armed Services Committee ensured national attention.

During his first year in office, it was the Armed Services Committee that dominated Quayle's attention as it held hearings on the proposed sale of AWACS surveillance airplanes by the Reagan administration to Saudi Arabia. The debate became heated, as Israel brought pressure on the Senate to abandon the sale. Relatively early in the debate, Quayle tried to broker a satisfactory deal between the opponents of the AWACS sale and those in favor of it. A deal was forged and the Senate voted to support Reagan's plan of sale, giving Quayle instant credibility as a knowledgeable, active player who was willing to deal in high-stakes issues.

Although the Armed Services Committee had served Quayle well in his bid to move past freshman status and gain credibility among his colleagues, he decided to focus his attention on the Labor and Human Resources Committee, where he would immediately gain control of a subcommittee. Committee Chair Orrin Hatch, a Republican from Utah, assigned Quayle the Subcommittee on Employment chairmanship, which controlled the $8 billion Comprehensive Employment and Training Act (CETA), which would expire on September 30, 1982. The focus of the subcommittee would be to determine whether to extend CETA and, if extended, at what level.

Quayle was extremely sensitive to the issues of unemployment and job training. Indiana, which had a large auto manufacturing base, suffered from nearly an 18 percent unemployment rate among autoworkers. During his 1980 campaign against Birch Bayh, Quayle had said that "300,000 people were without jobs and that Birch Bayh was to blame." Now Quayle moved aggressively to seek ways to spur the economy and to protect the unemployed. He immediately pored over the CETA program, trying to understand its assets and liabilities. The Reagan administration had recommended significant program cuts and restructuring of the remaining programs primarily into block grants.

After a detailed review, Quayle recommended continuing the program, essentially in its previous form but with a trimmed down budget, and not moving toward block grants. The White House was not eager to support his proposal but viewed it as acceptable and moved on with its own legislative agenda. As he had in the Armed Services Committee AWACS issue, Quayle had mastered the details of the CETA issue and gained bipartisan respect for his ability to move swiftly to resolution. One of Quayle's strengths during his early tenure on the Labor and Human Resources Committee was his ability to build such bipartisan support both on the subcommittee and within the full committee. With a nominal 9–7 Republican majority, which included the liberal-leaning Connecticut Republican Lowell Weicker, success depended upon such bipartisan support.

As Quayle moved to become a leading player in labor and employment issues, he needed the aid of longtime labor supporter Democrat Edward Kennedy of Massachusetts. By early 1983, Quayle had forged an alliance with Kennedy, Labor and Human Resources Committee's senior member, to replace the CETA bill and to introduce a replacement Senate bill, S2036, focusing on job training for the unemployed. Headlines read that the unlikely alliance of conservative Dan Quayle and liberal Ted Kennedy would work together for the "Quayle–Kennedy Training for Jobs Bill."

The Reagan administration opposed the bill primarily because of its costs but additionally because of general opposition to any bill supported by Kennedy. Reagan's economic cab-inet council, chaired by Treasury Secretary Donald Regan, opposed the jobs training bill, so Quayle found himself being opposed by the White House and supported by Kennedy, a position he was uncomfortable maintaining. Surprisingly, Quayle chose to remain loyal to S2036 and to continue his alliance with Kennedy in the Senate.

Quayle successfully convinced Orrin Hatch, chair of the full committee, to lend his support to the bill on the grounds that the Republicans had to provide leadership in economic issues. Hatch, who was running for reelection, finally moved into the Quayle camp and began to lobby the White House. The intense lobbying by Hatch and Quayle proved successful, and on September 21, 1983, Reagan endorsed the Job Training Partnership Act to replace the CETA program. The Senate quickly approved the bill, 97–0, followed by a House vote of 339–12 in favor of the bill. It became Public Law 97–300, largely due to Quayle.

Quayle's leadership had resulted in one of the few pieces of significant legislation passed by the divided Ninety-seventh Congress. He noted of the Ninety-seventh Congress that "we've passed the two budgets, the two tax bills, and the voting rights bill. Add the job training bill and that's just about it for this Congress."

The jobs training bill proved to be central not only to the Ninety-seventh Congress's legislative record but also to Quayle's legislative accomplishments. When he campaigned for reelection in 1986, he focused his campaign on his success in providing a key piece of economic legislation. He often cited "the 163,000 people in Indiana who have been trained" as a result of the act.

Quayle's opponent in the 1986 senatorial race was Valparaiso University Professor Jill Long. Being essentially unknown, she was able to raise only $100,000, compared to the $2 million raised by Quayle. The election result was predictable, with Quayle garnering 61 percent of the vote, the largest percentage margin any Indiana Senator had ever received in a general election. As Quayle's campaign manager noted, the jobs bill "was the whole campaign."

By 1988, Dan Quayle was beginning to look toward what he called "career advancement." He aggressively pursued the second seat on the Republican presidential ticket. Six months before the Republican convention, Quayle began to leak his interest in the job, noting his solid conservative credentials, his success at building bipartisan coalitions, and his support within his own generation. When the call came from George Bush on the night of August 16, 1988, it was the result of a highly orchestrated effort by Dan Quayle, his wife Marilyn, and the Quayle Senate staff.

Although Bush had called Quayle in July to test his interest in the job, no one on the Bush campaign had contacted Quayle since then, and no one had alerted Quayle that he would be the final choice. Bush had not had a single substantive conversation with Quayle about the campaign's goals and objectives. When Quayle was finally contacted during the convention, he was as surprised as the nation.

Quayle's first public appearance as the vice-presidential nominee at the Republican convention, however, was less than ideal. He entered the convention hall out of breath, having walked several blocks from his hotel. He was hot, tired, and overly eager to please. Once next to Bush, he continually grabbed Bush's arms and said, "Let's go get them." The media disparagingly described Quayle not as a major asset to the ticket but as a cheerleader for the presidential nominee.

Quayle's performance during the first days after the convention continued to support the image of the ticket's minor player. Quayle floundered through questions about his personal wealth (appraised in 1988 at $859,700 by Price Waterhouse), average academic achievements, country-club background, and service in the National Guard. The question of military service was repeatedly raised as the press sought to learn why Quayle had chosen the National Guard rather than an active-duty assignment that might have led to a tour in Vietnam.

In spite of his initial high profile, Quayle stayed out of the limelight throughout most of the 1988 campaign. Bush dominated the national media and generally moved Quayle into state political and fund-raising activities. Quayle's most visible campaign moments came in October during the nationally televised vice-presidential debate with Democratic nominee Lloyd Bentsen. Both Bush and Quayle had agreed to debate their individual opponents through the nonpartisan Commission on Presidential Debates. When Quayle and Bentsen were on the stage together, Quayle tried to draw attention to their age and generational difference. Just when this tactic might have been successful, Quayle went the extra step and tried to draw a parallel between himself and the youthful John F. Kennedy during the 1960 presidential debates. Bentsen retorted that he had known John F. Kennedy and that Quayle "was no John Kennedy." This was the lasting impression of the debate, one in which Bentsen had gained the upper hand.

Although Bentsen won the vice-presidential debate, presidential candidate Michael Dukakis did not gain the same advantage in his debates with Bush. The electorate saw Bush as the more experienced statesman and leader and by the November election had turned its support to the Bush–Quayle team in spite of a 17 percent lead by Dukakis–Bentsen during the summer. In large measure, the election had turned on a negative campaign, particularly the charge made by Bush that Dukakis's liberal approach to crime as governor of Massachusetts had allowed a convicted murderer, Willie Horton, to be furloughed. Horton was later convicted of committing rape and torture while on furlough. Bush and Quayle capitalized on public intolerance of crime and eventually garnered 53 percent of the popular vote and 426 electoral votes.

Once in office, Bush did not seek to bring Quayle into the inner circle. In an effort to gain status among administration members, Quayle sought avenues for gaining attention. One of the more obvious tactics was to try to meet with international leaders, which would bring national media attention and ensure frequent briefings with Bush. This idea, however, was quickly derailed by Secretary of State James Baker, who saw diplomatic initiatives as the State Department's sole province. Quayle, who had only a limited personal relationship with the new president, would always be outmaneuvered in policy issues by Baker, who enjoyed a thirty-five year friendship with Bush.

With both domestic and foreign policy involvement moved out of the scope of routine responsibilities, Quayle returned to his roots in Congress and within the Republican Party. He regularly met with members of the Senate Republican leadership in his Senate office, provided for his Constitutional role as the president of the Senate, to discuss bills in progress. He served both to relay presidential positions on major bills and to lobby on their behalf. During the 1990 battle over the budget, Quayle became a key member of Bush's congressional liaison staff as he worked to build conservative support for the budget bill. In spite of a campaign promise not to raise taxes in the famous "Read my lips" statement, the Bush administration supported tax increases as a means to curb the mounting deficit crisis The White House assigned Quayle to meet with members of Congress to build support and sooth the tensions that were mounting over a sense of betrayal. Although Quayle did not support the budget bill (which he called "the most serious test of loyalty I'd experience during the administration"), he lobbied on behalf of the tax increase.

In addition to his role as congressional liaison, Quayle took up the mantle of political liaison for the White House, meeting with key Republican leaders and raising millions of dollars for the National Republican Committee and for state and local Republican candidates.

Throughout his term of office, Quayle contributed to two major policy areas: federal regulation and space research. As chair of the National Space Council, Quayle worked to protect NASA's programs and to continue support for the Freedom space station.

In the more high-profile Council on Competitiveness, Quayle and his staff reviewed every new federal law and oversaw the departmental production of the regulations to implement the law. Their task was to minimize the number of regulations imposed on either private business or state and local government as means of reducing the cost of doing business. The business community had repeatedly complained in recent years that the federal government had imposed too many regulatory mandates to allow a competitive environment.

Among the many regulatory issues that the Council on Competitiveness addressed were those raised by the Environmental Protection Agency (EPA). Under William Reilly's leadership, the EPA moved to support aggressively the reauthorization of the Clean Air Act in 1991 and often battled with both White House Chief of Staff John Sununu and Quayle's Competitiveness Council on clean-air standards to be incorporated into the new bill. Quayle fought with Reilly over the biodiversity treaty signed in Rio de Janeiro, Brazil, and over wetlands legislation. The public saw both the EPA and Quayle as overly zealous, seeking to address environmental problems in less-than-satisfactory ways.

The Persian Gulf War in 1991 was the single area that provided cohesiveness among the senior White House staff and the vice president. As a National Security Council member, Quayle was regularly briefed on Iraq's movements and about U.S. troop buildup. In less-structured discussions among senior White House staff, Quayle was consistently included. He was, however, generally a passive member of the group as Sununu dominated the questioning of national security advisor Brent Scowcroft and Joint Chiefs of Staff Chairman Colin Powell.

By 1992, Dan Quayle had not worked his way into the Bush inner circle, a circle generally dominated by Sununu and, after Sununu's ouster, Samuel Skinner. Quayle had to be content traveling the nation on behalf of Republican candidates (a task he hoped would pay off when he moved into a presidential campaign as the ticket's lead member) and managing the Competitiveness Council.

Although sitting presidents rarely have vigorous opposition during the second-term reelection campaign, in 1992 the Democrats attacked what they perceived to be a relatively weak Republican administration. Democratic presidential nominee Bill Clinton and his running mate, Senator Al Gore, charged the Bush–Quayle administration for its failure to manage the domestic economy. The Bush–Quayle campaign focused on its Persian Gulf War success but never gained broad-based public support. Clinton won the election with 43 percent of the popular vote. Ross Perot, millionaire industrialist from Texas, similarly challenged Bush and gained 19 percent of the popular vote.

George Bush and Dan Quayle gracefully acknowledged their defeat in the 1992 election and offered their support to the fledgling Clinton–Gore administration. Both Bush and Quayle opened their offices during the transition to provide advice and information to the new tenants of 1600 Pennsylvania Avenue.

After the Clinton administration's January 20, 1993, inauguration, Quayle returned to his native Indiana and joined the conservative Hudson Institute, a think tank near Indianapolis. There, he focused on issues of competitiveness in the marketplace, continuing his efforts from the Competitiveness Council.

Although Quayle was widely viewed as a major contender for the 1996 Republican presidential nomination, he pulled his name out of contention during the fall of 1995. He had suffered several health problems during 1995, including a hospitalization for a blood clot in the leg, and appeared to have difficulty raising the necessary funds for a national election. His formal withdrawal from the race, however, was based on his decision to remain close to his wife and three teenage children, Tucker, Benjamin, and Corinne. Citing his deep commitment to his family, Quayle explained that his children

came first in his life. He left the door open to a continuing political career, noting that he was still a young man with many years remaining to pursue politics. However, in the years since, Quayle has kept a low profile and appears to have left the national political scene for good. He now lives in Scottsdale, Arizona, and is chairman of an international division of Cerberus Capital Management.

The legacy of Dan Quayle is one of consistency: throughout his political career Quayle remained loyal to his personal values of family and church and to his conservative political values of a reduced role for government. His political future, however, remains in question; the U.S. public will not easily forget the vice president who erroneously "corrected" the spelling of an elementary school child. The child had spelled "potato" on the blackboard at his school, but Dan Quayle made him change it to "potatoe." Although accuracy in spelling is not a criteria for attaining national office, most Americans prefer their candidates to be able to spell "potato" correctly.

REFERENCES

David S. Broder and Bob Woodward, *The Man Who Would Be President* (New York: Simon and Schuster, 1992); Richard F. Fenno, Jr., *The Making of a Senator: Dan Quayle* (Washington, D.C.: Congressional Quarterly Press, 1989); Dan Quayle, *Standing Firm* (New York: HarperCollins, 1994).

SHIRLEY ANNE WARSHAW is professor of political science at Gettysburg College, specializing in presidential decision making. Her most recent book is *The Co-Presidency of Bush and Cheney* (Stanford Politics and Policy, 2009), and she is also the author of *Keys to Power: Managing the Presidency* (second edition, Longman, 2004) and *The Clinton Years* (Facts On File, 2004). She is a frequent commentator on National Public Radio and other media outlets on elections and the presidency.

ALBERT ARNOLD GORE, JR. (B. 1948)

Vice President, 1993–2001

(President Bill Clinton)

ALBERT A. GORE, JR.
(Office of the Vice President)

By Scott W. Rager

During his tenure in the vice presidency, Al Gore, Jr., played a more substantial role in decision and policy making than many of his recent predecessors. Highly regarded for his energy and competence, Gore, with President Bill Clinton's encouragement, redefined the office, expanding both its power and influence. He served as one of Clinton's main advisers on foreign policy and became strongly identified with several key administration domestic issues, including the reorganization of government, the environment, and communications technology.

Born on March 31, 1948, in Carthage, Tennessee, Al Gore was the second child of Albert and Pauline LaFon Gore. His parents and older sister, Nancy, were dynamic individuals who set high standards of personal achievement for Gore to emulate.

Albert Gore, Sr., a former educator and lawyer, was a protégé of Franklin Roosevelt's secretary of state, Cordell Hull. First elected to Tennessee's Fourth Congressional District in 1938, he served seven terms in the U.S. House of Representatives (1939–1953) and three terms in the Senate (1953–1971). Pauline LaFon Gore was the second woman ever to graduate from Vanderbilt University Law School and practiced law for a year prior to her marriage on April 17, 1937. Nancy Gore, ten years older than her brother, was also a graduate of Vanderbilt University and became one of the founding members of President John F. Kennedy's Peace Corps.

Al Gore, Jr., was raised in two entirely different environments. One was the family cattle farm in rural Carthage, Tennessee; the other was Washington, D.C. Until the age of nine, he lived and attended school in Carthage. After moving to the capital, Gore's formal education continued at St. Albans School for Boys, a prestigious Washington prep school where he excelled in both academic and athletic pursuits. Equally valuable, however, was the informal tutelage he received in American politics and government while living in Washington.

Upon graduation from St. Albans in 1965, Gore, who had won a National Merit Scholarship, was admitted to Harvard, where he majored in political science and became active in student government. His senior thesis, written under the direction of Dr. Richard Neustadt, was titled: "The Impact of Television on the Conduct of the Presidency, 1947–1969" and dealt with the effect of presidential debates on elections. Gore appeared headed for a career in politics. His parents, particularly his father, had encouraged him in that direction, but upon graduating in 1969, Gore made a decision that sidelined all his career plans for several years; he enlisted in the army.

This decision, one of the most difficult of his life, had nothing to do with approval or support for the Vietnam War—like many of his Harvard classmates, Gore had been a war protester. Obtaining exemption from the draft would have presented no particular problem for him, but he sensed the severe ramifications avoidance of military service might have for Al Gore, Sr., who had already been severely criticized for his own antiwar stance. Despite the fact that he later campaigned in uniform for his father, Gore was unable to prevent the senator's defeat in 1970. Still, military service, which included a tour of duty as an army journalist in Vietnam, would later prove invaluable for his own political career.

Upon completing Army enlistment in May 1971 Gore returned to Tennessee to find a career. Deeply disillusioned by the war, he abandoned the idea of entering politics and was left without a clear idea of what he intended to do. Shortly after enlisting, Gore had married the former Mary Elizabeth "Tipper" Aitcheson in May 1970. Reunited with his wife, Gore settled in Nashville, where he became a reporter for the *Tennessean*. That fall he also entered Vanderbilt School of Divinity, hoping to resolve some spiritual questions raised by his war experiences.

While covering the local and state political beat for the *Tennessean,* Gore found his interest in political activity rekindled and realized that his own abilities qualified him to be involved in government. In preparation for a political career, Gore transferred to Vanderbilt Law School in 1974 but never completed the degree because an opportunity came for him to run for the House of Representatives. The Fourth District congressional seat held by Joseph L. Ervin for thirty-two years was being vacated, and Gore could not pass up the chance to represent his home district. Despite his youth and lack of experience, he easily defeated an independent with 96 percent of the vote, winning the seat his father had once held.

At twenty-eight, Gore was the youngest man ever elected to Congress from the Fourth District. During his four terms in the House, he earned a reputation for responsibility, competency, and hard work. So genuine was his desire to keep in touch with the electorate, he held more than 1,600 town meetings. His agenda in Congress included nuclear arms control, health, communications, and environmental issues. With respect to the latter, as member of the Energy and Commerce Oversight Subcommittee, Gore led the investigation on illegal hazardous-waste dumping and helped bring about the creation of the Superfund in 1980, which provided $1.6 billion for toxic waste cleanup. Recognition for his dedication and diligence as a legislator came from several quarters, most notably from the *Washington Monthly,* which named him among the six most effective members of Congress, and from the Jaycees, who chose him as one of the "Ten Most Outstanding Young Men in America."

In 1983, Senator Howard Baker, the Republican majority leader from Tennessee, announced that he would not seek reelection for another term. Again, following in his father's footsteps, Gore ran for the Senate. In the fall 1984 election, despite a Republican landslide in other races, he handily defeated his Republican opponent, Victor H. Ashe, winning 61 percent of the vote. Although the victory was a triumph, with it had come sadness; during the campaign Gore's sister, Nancy, to whom he was very close, died of cancer.

In the Senate, Gore maintained the agenda he had set for himself in the House. Still dedicated to nuclear arms control, as a member of the Armed Services Committee he was able to play an instrumental role in working out a Democratic agreement with the Reagan administration to limit the deployment of MX missiles. Gore also proposed a $1.2 million trimming of Reagan's $3.7 million budget for development of the Strategic Defense Initiative but failed to generate enough support for his compromise measure with either the liberal or conservative camps.

As a member of the Commerce, Science, and Transportation Committee, Gore sponsored the National High Performance Computer Technology Act, which set into motion the creation of a national super computer network.

Continuing his advocacy for improved health care, Gore worked for the creation of a computerized network to match organ donors with patients needing transplants. Another of his causes involved placing stronger warnings on cigarettes and warnings on alcoholic beverages.

Gore further enhanced his reputation as one of Congress's leading experts on the environment. Fact-finding trips to gather information on the state of the environment took him to both the North and South poles and to Brazil. In June 1992, he led the Senate delegation to the Earth Day Summit. His best-selling book, *Earth in the Balance: Ecology and the Human Spirit,* published in 1992, expressed his thoughts on the environment and laid out a comprehensive plan for global action.

The high-profile and excellent legislative record achieved by Gore while in Congress provided him with an impressive base from which to launch a bid for the Democratic presidential nomination in 1988. The competition was stiff: Senator Gary Hart of Colorado, Senator Joe Biden of Delaware, Governor Michael Dukakis of Massachusetts, Representative Dick Gephardt of Missouri, and Reverend Jesse Jackson of Illinois. Gore initially focused on the environment as the chief issue of his campaign, but that tactic failed to attract as much public attention as he had hoped. His performance in the New Hampshire primary was lackluster. Determined campaigning and a refocus of his agenda helped Gore to rebound to win five of fourteen Super Tuesday states in March, but disappointing results in the crucial New York primary finally convinced him to suspend his efforts. The Democratic nomination ultimately went to Michael Dukakis, who lost the election to George Bush, Ronald Reagan's vice president.

By no means did his failure to win the Democratic Presidential nomination in 1988 diminish Gore's desire to seek the office again. He very likely would have pursued it in 1992 if a life-changing event had not intervened. In

April 1989, Gore's six-year-old son Albert was struck and nearly killed by a car. The boy sustained massive internal and external injuries that required extensive surgery at Johns Hopkins Hospital in Baltimore and took months to heal. His son's recuperation eventually was complete, but the experience caused Gore to do serious soul searching, and the entire family went through therapy to overcome the trauma. This experience was the most important factor in Gore's decision not to run for president during the 1992 cycle.

That Gore might instead consider being a candidate for the vice presidency in 1992 seemed at best a remote possibility; based upon his past remarks, he considered the second position a political dead end. But this assessment obviously changed. When Warren Christopher, head of Arkansas Governor Bill Clinton's vice-presidential search team, contacted Gore about his availability as a potential candidate, he consented to have his name added to a list which, in its final form, included forty individuals. At the end of June, Gore met privately with Clinton. Subsequent to that meeting the Tennessee senator secured a place on the vice-presidential shortlist that had five others: Congressman Lee Hamilton and Senators Harris Wofford, Bob Kerry, Jay Rockefeller, and Bob Graham.

The decision to choose Gore was not difficult for Clinton, who recognized a man of exceptional drive, ability, and intellect. Also important was the fact that on a personal and political level Gore suited Clinton almost perfectly. The two shared many similarities. In addition to being from the same region, they were both Southern Baptists, both baby boomers in their forties (Gore is nineteen months younger than Clinton), and both graduates of prestigious universities. More significant, both Clinton and Gore were so-called New Democrats, a group whose core philosophy was based in making government more efficient and responsible. It did not seem to worry Clinton that Gore might be perceived as being too much like him, which could give rise to an argument that the ticket lacked diversity, particularly in

respect to region. He was more concerned that the South and border states went solidly for him, and Gore's participation made that outcome more probable.

The ticket was also strengthened by Gore in a critical area where Clinton was thought to be weak: personal character. The Gores' marriage, unlike the Clintons', was one of the most solid in Washington. Furthermore, Al and Tipper, the parents of one son and three daughters, were strong proponents of "family values." Their reputation was further bolstered by Tipper Gore's crusade for labeling rock music to inform parents about obscene lyrics.

Finally, Gore's acknowledged expertise on environmental matters and foreign affairs made a Clinton presidency more attractive to several key groups within the electorate. His outstanding record as an environmental advocate meant Gore could potentially win the support of affluent suburbanites and West Coast voters. Equally important, he was also an expert and a moderate on foreign policy issues. During the Gulf crisis, Gore was among only ten Democrats who voted to authorize President Bush to use U.S. forces to drive Iraqi strongman Saddam Hussein's forces from Kuwait. This and the fact that he had served in the army during the Vietnam War (unlike Bill Clinton who had avoided military service) would provide reassurance to both veterans' groups and Reagan Democrats who might otherwise be wary of a Clinton-led administration.

Before he was officially offered the vice-presidential slot, Gore had consulted with his family, and together they had agreed that he should accept if asked to join Clinton on the ticket. Gore realized that if all went well, he would stand a very good chance of becoming the Democrats' next nominee for the presidency. When Clinton called with the offer on July 20, Gore was ready with his answer.

Clinton's choice was widely applauded at the Democratic convention and served to win the support of some of his former critics. Only Jesse Jackson expressed concern with the selection, remarking: "It takes two wings to fly but here you have two of the same wing." The selection seemed to strike a responsive chord with the public as well. A *Newsweek* poll showed that 44 percent of those surveyed expressed a greater willingness to vote for Clinton after Gore was added to the ticket, compared with 21 percent who indicated they were less willing and 27 percent who indicated no change in their position.

The main issue of the Clinton–Gore program was the need for change and fresh ideas, particularly regarding a solution to revive the country's then sagging economy, but from the beginning of the campaign it was clear that the Democratic strategy would also involve making an issue of the vice presidency and the two individuals seeking that position. At their first news conference, Clinton focused on this issue, saying that in choosing Gore he had "tried to take political considerations out" of the selection process "and ask (instead) who would be the best person." He stressed that Gore would be a vice president immediately prepared to assume the presidency if anything happened to him. A poll subsequently taken by *Time* magazine indicated that the public did perceive Gore as more qualified than Dan Quayle to become president by a margin of 61 percent to 21 percent.

A televised debate between Gore and Quayle at Georgia Tech in Atlanta on the evening of October 13, 1992, served to further enhance Gore's position. Also participating in the debate was Admiral James Stockdale, the running mate of Ross Perot, whose on-again-off-again campaign was once more on. While Quayle did a much better job than many had expected, polls taken afterward showed that Gore fared best when people were asked who had won. Fifty percent of the respondents chose him over Quayle, who received 27 percent, and Stockdale, who received 7 percent.

Energetic and enthusiastic during the often grueling three-and-a-half-month race, veteran campaigner Gore was a true asset to the team and regularly demonstrated the improvements he had made in relating to an audience; less in evidence was the Al Gore who had once been described as somewhat "wooden," "obsequious," and "boring." Together, he and Bill Clinton displayed a dynamism often missing from the campaign of their Republican opponents.

Bush, particularly, seemed to lack his old fire and fighting zeal. Perhaps due to overconfidence, the incumbent president had begun his campaign too late. In October, he and Quayle were still running ten points behind Clinton and Gore in the polls, and a desperate Bush resorted to calling his opponents names. Hoping to cast aspersions on the Democratic team's grasp of geopolitics, the president said that his dog Millie knew more about foreign affairs than those "two bozos." Bush also attempted to make a jest out of Gore's dedication to environmental matters by calling him "Ozone Man." Such tactics, however, only succeeded in calling attention to the failing Bush–Quayle campaign and swayed little support toward the Republicans.

The November 4 election went much as had been expected; Clinton–Gore won 43 percent of the vote. Bush–Quayle took 38 percent and Perot-Stockdale trailed far behind with 19 percent.

President-elect Clinton fully appreciated the important part Al Gore had played in winning the election and publicly expressed his desire to have him take a more substantial role in governing than had many of his predecessors in the vice presidency. Before the January 20 inaugural, Gore assisted in picking the subcabinet and the White House staff and from the first days of the new administration was integral to the decision-making process. He became a general adviser to the president and counseled Clinton on nearly all major issues.

Gore's input on foreign policy was particularly sought after by the president. The former Senate Armed Services Committee member's advice tended to be that of a moderate hawk. After the June 1993 assassination attempt made on the life of George Bush during a visit to the Middle East, Gore was in the vanguard of those advisers urging Clinton to order a retaliatory military strike against Saddam Hussein. Gore also initially argued that aggressive force should be used to solve the crisis in Bosnia-Hercegovina but relented when President Clinton was unable to rally support among the allies. By midterm, the president had increased his reliance on Gore, who was devoting 25 percent of his working hours to foreign policy. Diplomatic trips to Russia helped Gore to develop a relationship with his counterpart, Prime Minister Victor Chernomyrdin, and led to the creation of the Gore–Chernomyrdin Commission, formed by Presidents Clinton and Boris Yeltsin to encourage greater economic cooperation between the United States and Russia. Gore's carefully cultivated relationship with Chernomyrdin became a back channel for communications between Washington and Moscow. The vice president further eased tension in Eastern Europe through his secret negotiations with Ukranian President Leonid Kravchuk, which resulted in the surrender of the Ukraine's nuclear weapons stockpile.

During fall 1993, the vice president also played a vital role in winning support for the North American Free Trade Agreement (NAFTA), which allowed free trade with Mexico. Opponents of the controversial policy maintained that U.S. companies would be likely to move their factories to Mexico to take advantage of the cheap labor. The anti-NAFTA rhetoric of Ross Perot was particularly poisonous. Heading the administration's damage control operation was Al Gore, who challenged Perot to a televised debate. The forum was CNN's *Larry King Live*. On November 9, 1993, Gore and Perot debated the pros and cons of NAFTA and took phone-in questions from the audience. The outcome of the debate was a clear win for Gore. The NAFTA agreement subsequently passed, and Gore was sent to Mexico to discuss implementation of the plan with President Carlos Salinas de Gortari.

Gore played a no-less-significant role in the planning and implementing of the Clinton administration's domestic policy. His highest-profile activity involved heading the National Performance Review, which was initially charged with conducting an examination of every department in the federal government and then formulating recommendations for "reinventing government." This process, according to Gore, would involve "not just cutting wasteful spending, but also improving our services and making our government work better." "We want," he concluded, "major reforms and major innovations." Typically thorough, Gore hired expert consultants; sought advice from federal, state, and local government officials; and held town meetings with employees from each cabinet department. Within six months, by early September 1993, the report was ready. Contained in it were 800 recommendations expected to save $108 billion in five years and to eliminate a quarter-of-a-million federal jobs within fifteen years. The plan was announced without much fanfare but resonated with the public in a way that the White House never anticipated it would. When national health care reform, the administration's greatest effort, stalled in Congress, Gore's efficiency project was given a higher priority and was destined to become a major issue in the second half of Clinton's term.

Acting as the administration's chief spokesman for the environment and for technological advancement rounded out Vice President Gore's duties. In pursuit of the latter, he played a major role in planning and promoting a new telecommunications strategy for development of the national information superhighway. The proposal, dubbed the National Information Infrastructure, called for connecting libraries, schools, and other public institutions to computer networks and increasing the federal support for research into online technologies.

Without question, Gore established himself as a Clinton administration key player, becoming "a vice-president who counts," according to a *U.S. News and World Report* article of July 1993. Unfortunately, the mediocre overall record of the administration's first two years tended to obscure Gore's successes. Little progress had been made with health care and welfare reform, and by midterm President

Clinton was plagued with personal problems. Polls indicated low public approval for the president, an outcome in part linked to ongoing investigations into financial arrangements made while he was governor of Arkansas. Dissatisfaction with the administration was registered in the 1994 elections, when the Republican party took over control of Congress for the first time in forty years. Vice President Gore's reputation and personal integrity remained unblemished through all of the Clinton administration's first-term trials, however.

His long-term political future seemed to be in serious doubt in 1994 when the president's chances for reelection appeared to be slight, but in a remarkable political comeback, Bill Clinton fought off the defeats of midterm and along with Gore took a commanding lead in the election polls by mid-1996. The Republicans, who had appeared to be completely in command when they took control of Congress, fumbled the presidential race badly. Senate Majority Leader Robert Dole, a candidate for the vice presidency twenty years before, won the GOP nomination but failed to ignite any sparks among the electorate. He was one of the oldest presidential candidates ever and showed what seemed to be campaign weariness from the beginning. His selection of the energetic Jack Kemp did little to combat the effective public team of Clinton and Gore.

Having maintained a double-digit lead in the polls right up until election-day, Clinton and Gore won easily with 49 percent of the vote to 41 percent for the Republicans and 8 percent for H. Ross Perot.

Editor's Addendum to the Third Edition:
The come-from-behind victory put Al Gore into position to become the Democratic Party candidate for president in the 2000 election, if he could avoid political pitfalls during his second term. However, this proved to be difficult, as a series of remarkable events overtook Gore and the Clinton presidency in the four years following the 1996 victory, only to be capped by one of the most closely contested and hotly disputed elections in the nation's electoral history.

Gore was scarcely into his second term when his theretofore squeaky-clean image began to tarnish. He had been unusually active in raising campaign funds for the election (Republicans in Washington referred to Gore as the "Solicitor in Chief"), and it appeared that he had overstepped or trod close to the bounds of legality in two cases. In 1995, both he and President Clinton had made political fund-raising calls from their official offices in the West Wing of the White House, which was in violation of federal laws governing fund-raising by elected officials. The following year, Gore had attended a questionable fund-raising event at a Buddhist temple in California, where thinly disguised campaign contributions slipped through the legal cracks.

In March 1997, the Justice Department began an investigation of Gore's fund-raising activities. He was forced to respond publicly, and he fumbled badly in explaining his presence at the Buddhist temple, where it was determined illegal activity had taken place although there was no direct link to the vice president. Worse, when Gore appeared in a televised press conference to defend the fund-raising calls made from his White House office, he insisted that he had been under "no controlling legal authority," a phrase that the Republicans immediately pounced on with withering ridicule.

Compounding his political difficulties, when Gore traveled to China later the same month, he appeared in public with Chinese premier Li Peng, widely believed in the West to have ordered the crackdown and massacre in Tiananmen Square in 1989. Gore was shown on American television clinking champagne glasses in what appeared to be a jolly toast.

These highly public missteps might have been, to an impartial observer, counterbalanced by Gore's solid record of accomplishments as vice president, but his activities on behalf of the environment, deficit reduction, the regulation of tobacco as a dangerous drug, and support for "v" chip technology to shield children from harmful television shows lacked glamour in the political arena and seldom reached the same level of public consciousness as his gaffes. Unfortunately for Gore, his boldness and forcefulness as a behind-the-scenes adviser in the second Clinton administration were seldom matched in his public appearances, where he appeared to remain stiff and wooden.

Gore continued to work with Viktor Chernomyrdin, even though the latter was ousted as Russian prime minister. In 1999, the vice president was crucial in working out an agreement with Chernomyrdin, who was Russia's envoy to Yugoslavian dictator Slobodan Milosevic, a tactic to persuade the Yugoslavs to withdraw from Kosovo. Chernomyrdin and Gore met in Washington at Gore's official residence to hammer out the proposal that Milosevic finally accepted.

Most of Gore's efforts were overshadowed, however, by the national political crisis precipitated by the revelation that President Clinton had probably lied under oath about his relationship with a young White House intern named Monica Lewinsky. The allegations stemmed from a deposition Clinton gave in January 1998 in regard to a suit for sexual harassment brought against him by state employee Paula Jones when he had been governor of Arkansas. Special Prosecutor Kenneth Starr, who for years had been investigating an allegedly crooked land deal in Arkansas involving President and Mrs. Clinton without success in pinning anything on the First Couple, discovered that the president and Lewinsky had probably carried out a series of sexual liaisons in the White House, and the prosecutor maneuvered Clinton into what appeared to be perjury. Clinton, who had taken the bait during his testimony—he denied ever being alone with Lewinsky—exacerbated his problems by apparently trying to cover up the mess and buy off Lewinsky with a cushy job.

Gore felt shock and betrayal over the Lewinsky scandal. He had been brought onto the Clinton ticket originally to balance the president's reputation as a womanizer, and now the vice president was faced with the need to back a president whose personal behavior was completely at odds with Gore's beliefs and lifelong example of marital fidelity. Moreover, as the year wore on, Gore came under more and more pressure. By fall, when Starr released a report with graphic details of the president's sexual exploits, Gore was forced to take a public stand of support for Clinton, despite his personal feelings. When Clinton was finally impeached by the U.S. House of Representatives in December, Gore appeared on the White House lawn with Clinton and loyally declared him to be "one of our greatest presidents."

Clinton was acquitted of the articles of impeachment after a trial in the U.S. Senate in 1999, but the cloud of the affair hung over the remaining months of the Clinton-Gore administration and created a big problem for Gore as he began to outline his plans for a run at the presidency. Clinton was a powerful campaigner and fund-raiser who, in the normal course of things, could have been relied on to boost Gore's candidacy, but after the impeachment scandal, Clinton was perceived as a political liability with much of the electorate. Although Gore had shown unwavering public loyalty as Clinton's vice president, he decided to keep Clinton at arm's length during the 2000 presidential campaign.

Gore's chief rival for the Democratic nomination was Bill Bradley, the former U.S. senator from New Jersey and a star college and professional basketball player. Bradley had high visibility, especially among those who remembered his days on the court, but he was uninspiring as a speaker and campaigner, and if anything even stiffer in public than Gore. Nonetheless, polls in fall of 1999 showed Bradley tied with Gore in New Hampshire, the site of the first presidential primary. Gore eventually moved ahead of Bradley, however, and not only won the highly publicized Iowa party caucuses in January 2000 but also took the prize in New Hampshire and by March chased Bradley out of the running. *Newsweek* commented that Gore had been "lucky to face a Democrat even less personable than himself."

Gore originally set up his campaign headquarters in Washington, D.C., but when it became apparent that his organization was top heavy with expensive consultants and was apparently bogged down in the political culture of the capital, Gore moved his headquarters to Nashville, Tennessee. He had named former U.S. official Tony Coelho as chief campaign manager but changed other staffers frequently during the early months of the campaign. At one point, in order to change his image, Gore dumped his trademark blue suits and began to appear in earth-toned knit shirts, and he tried to incorporate personal anecdotes into his speeches.

In May, President Clinton, who was mostly relegated to giving advice to his wife, Hillary Rodham Clinton, who was running for the U. S. Senate from New York, burst forth into the presidential campaign when he was quoted in the *New York Times* as criticizing Gore's strategy and organization. When this blow was coupled with polls that showed him badly trailing George W. Bush, son of the former president and presumptive G.O.P. nominee for president, Gore was motivated to shake up his campaign again. He fired Coelho and hired William Dailey, a former cabinet member and son of the famous Chicago mayor, as his new campaign manager, and almost the entire campaign was re-staffed and refocused during the slow summer weeks before the national conventions. The new strategy was to concentrate on Gore's experience and accomplishments before he became vice president and to sharpen the message about the nation's prosperity during Gore's time in the administration.

In early August, Gore took a bold step by naming Joseph Lieberman, a moderate Democratic senator from Connecticut, as his running mate. Lieberman was an Orthodox Jew—the first of his religion to be nominated to such a high post—and had been one of the most vocal Democrats in condemning President Clinton during the Lewinsky affair. Not only was Lieberman an animated speaker who gave renewed life to the campaign, but his selection helped Gore distance himself even further from the president. Gore neglected to inform Clinton of his choice before leaking the news to the press.

At the Democratic National Convention in Los Angeles, later in August, Gore made perhaps his biggest impact of the campaign. As he arrived on the speakers' platform to give his acceptance speech, he spontaneously embraced Tipper and gave her a prolonged, lusty kiss, which received cheers from the crowd and favorable media comment for weeks after. Overall, Gore came out of the convention with a much bigger bounce in the polls than expected—they showed him ahead of Bush by as much as ten points, which proved to be his high point.

During the weeks following the conventions, the rival candidates seemed to take turns fumbling. Bush in particular had trouble when speaking informally, and he often mangled the English language in ways that the television commentators and late-night comedians found irresistible. Gore was at the opposite end of the scale, still appearing stiff and unbending (a physical pose he adopted in part to deal with chronic back trouble) and criticizing and shaking up his campaign staff with frequent changes in advisers.

Gore also did surprisingly poorly during the three presidential debates in early October, by which time the polls showed the race to be a dead heat. He had long been a skilled debater—he had demolished Ross Perot on live television—and his staff hoped Gore could show up Bush as an inarticulate intellectual lightweight. During the first debate in Boston, however, Bush did well in his presentation, and Gore hurt his own performance by too audibly sighing and shaking his head while Bush was speaking. Gore also made two slim exaggerations about his record, which the Bush camp jumped on immediately. Since Gore had previously been caught making exaggerated claims, most famously that he "invented" the Internet, the new problems hurt.

Gore fared better during the second debate a few days later, although he may have overcompensated for his previous podium manner by retreating into his accustomed stiffness. The debate was overshadowed by affairs in the Mideast, where renewed violence between Palestinians and Israelis claimed the headlines and the evening news. The third debate, conducted in town meeting style, was inconclusive according to media pundits, but the poll numbers narrowed between Gore and Bush even further.

It became clear during the final weeks of the campaign that the race was too close to call ahead of time. The undecided voters would be the key: whichever way they leaned on Election Day would probably decide the winner. Although the polls showed Bush with a slight lead, it was within the pollsters' margin of error. At this stage, the fringe candidacy of Ralph Nader, a long-time consumer advocate and government gadfly who carried the banner of the Green Party, took on new significance, since most analysts—including those on Gore's staff—felt he would take votes from Gore. Both of the major candidates began to carefully calculate their chances in the large states with big numbers of electoral votes, since it appeared the final numbers would be close.

A few of his staff and consultants urged Gore to bring Clinton from under wraps and unleash his proven ability to mobilize black voters, a group that appeared to be crucial to victory, but in the end the vice president decided to keep Clinton away from the spotlight. Gore pushed himself mercilessly during the final days of the campaign, hopscotching from place to place and putting in incredibly long hours in an effort to swing the key states.

When Election Day finally arrived, everyone expected a close contest, but no one anticipated the prolonged drama that ensued.

As the returns began to come in on November 7 and were tabulated by the television networks, the closeness of the election became clear to all. What was unclear was who the winner was. The nation had grown accustomed to relying on television commentators to project winners in specific states, based on exit interviews at polling places and early returns, but this election completely confounded this process. All the networks fumbled and they began to waffle, awarding key states to either Gore or Bush and then taking them away. As the night wore on, the confusion become greater and greater.

By the last hours of Election Day, it appeared that the contest would be settled for whoever got the twenty-five electoral votes of Florida, where margins of victory seemed to be razor thin. Gore followed the returns from his headquarters in Nashville, and when the networks and his own staff decided at around 2:00 A.M. that Florida would go to Bush, Gore called his opponent and offered his concession. He then started in a motorcade toward Nashville's War Memorial Park to make his concession speech to a crowd of supporters who had been waiting through the rainy, cold night.

As the cars drove through the streets toward the memorial, however, Bill Dailey began to receive new reports from Florida that Bush's margin in the swing state—where the Republican candidate's brother, Jeb, was governor—was narrowing to the vanishing point. Dailey frantically called Gore on his cell phone and told him to stay away from the platform. When Gore and the campaign staff finally arrived at the park and conferred, Gore decided he should wait out the decision in Florida, and he then called Bush and rescinded his concession in a tense phone conversation.

As dawn broke the following day, one of the most dramatic stories in United States election history began to unfold, and the election process was "clouded by uncertainty" over who had won the electoral votes of Florida and would therefore become the next president.

It appeared that Bush had won by fewer than 300 votes out of a total of nearly 6 million cast in the state. However, there were reports of irregularities or at least confusion over thousands of votes in key counties, and thousands of overseas absentee ballots were still to arrive and be counted. Moreover, Florida state law called for recounts if an election was close, so the process of recounting the hand-punched ballots would be crucial.

In a rare occurrence, the margin of victory in a presidential election appeared to be smaller than the margin of error in the electoral process. Literally a handful of votes would make the difference, and the actual physical process of voting was too crude to accurately handle this margin.

Both Gore and Bush sent small armies of lawyers and advisers to Florida. Gore selected former secretary of state Warren Christopher to head his team. Christopher faced off against James Baker, himself a former cabinet officer and long-time political operative.

At first, machine recounts of disputed ballots narrowed Bush's lead even further but did not reverse the outcome. However, it was discovered that 19,000 ballots in Palm Beach County alone had been disqualified. The Gore campaign began immediately to demand hand recounts there and in other key counties, which were traditionally Democratic. To complicate matters further, although the elected state officers in Florida were Republicans, including Katherine Harris, the secretary of state, and the state legislature was controlled by the G.O.P., the local canvassing boards, which were charged under state law to conduct the manual recounts, were controlled by Democrats.

As the hand recounts began, in full view of the television cameras, the public came to know every permutation of the term *chad*, referring to the tiny rectangle of paper that was punched out by voters as a way to indicate their preferences. Since Florida recount law allowed recount canvassers to determine the intent of the voter, many chads that were partially punched (said to be "pregnant," "dimpled," or "hanging") were counted as votes after agonizing scrutiny by the canvassers.

It was soon evident that although Bush's lead was likely to increase when all the absentee ballots were in, the hand recounts in Democratic counties could well reverse the victory and give the state to Gore. As a result, Bush's campaign brought suit in federal court to stop the hand recounts. Gore's team countered with its own suits (joined by many individual Florida voters who brought suits of their own). Within days of the election, it appeared that the courts would play a significant role in deciding the election.

Two deadlines further complicated matters. Under a federal law, which had been passed in response to the contested 1876 election, if Florida's electoral votes were certified and submitted to Congress before December 12, then they could not be contested. The final deadline was December 18, when the electors around the country were due to cast their votes and actually elect a president.

Florida secretary of state Katherine Harris, who had close ties to the Bush camp, stepped forward a week after Election Day and announced that she was preparing to certify the state's election for Bush, based on his initial 300-vote lead. However, she was immediately placed under a court order restraining her from making arbitrary decisions about the official vote count. Two days later, the Florida Supreme Court, most of whose members were Democratic appointees, ruled that the hand counts should continue at all possible speed toward the deadline of December 12, but the court provided no guidelines for how to count partially punched ballots.

More potential constitutional and legal complexities were raised when the leaders of the Republican state legislature announced plans to convene and select its own slate of electors, without regard to the balloting, which appeared on the face of it to be constitutionally possible.

After more give and take, and the entry of an appeal to the United States Supreme Court by the Bush campaign to vacate the Florida Supreme Court's rulings, Katherine Harris certified the Bush victory on November 26, giving a total margin of 537 votes. Four days later, the Florida legislature called a special session. At this stage there were more than forty-five lawsuits in the Florida courts concerning the election. On December 8, the state supreme court ordered a massive hand recount of 45,000 votes, which when begun started to whittle down Bush's tally, rapidly approaching a reversal of the election totals. The recount was halted, however, by the U.S. Supreme Court, which agreed to hear arguments and make a final ruling.

On December 12, the justices of the United States Supreme Court voted five to four to overturn the rulings of the Florida Supreme Court, and, since there was no time for the recount procedure to be redefined and begun again, the Court's ruling effectively awarded the election in Florida, and therefore the presidency, to Bush, marking the only time the Supreme Court decided a national presidential election.

Gore, forced to accept defeat by the Court, finally conceded the election to George W. Bush and adopted a gracious and dignified demeanor. He was the overall winner of the national popular vote by more than half a million votes, but he fell four electoral votes short of the required majority. Gore thus became the fourth presidential candidate in U.S. history to win more votes than his opponent but still lose the election. He had roughly 49 percent of the vote to Bush's 48.

Gore had the unenviable duty of presiding over a joint session of Congress that tallied the electoral votes. He received 266 to Bush's 271. An elector from the District of Columbia withheld her vote as a protest against the district's lack of congressional representation.

On inauguration day, a month later, Gore left office and became a private citizen for the first time in nearly twenty-five years. He busied himself initially with visiting professorships at Columbia University, Middle Tennessee State, Fisk University, and the University of California at Los Angeles. With a wry, bittersweet humor, he introduced himself to classes with: "Hi, I'm Al Gore. I used to be the next President of the United States." Gore also moved into the world of business by becoming an adviser to Google, the rapidly growing internet search engine company, and vice chairman of a West Coast financial firm. He broadened his business interests in 2003 by joining the board of directors of Apple Computer.

During the two years after his defeat, Gore stayed in the political background, especially after the terrorist attacks of September 11, 2001, seemed to call for a period of solidarity with the administration. Nonetheless, supporters began to urge him to consider running again in 2004, and following Republican victories in the 2002 mid-term elections, which gave them control of both houses of Congress, Gore appeared to move toward reemergence as a political figure. He gave speeches that were critical of the Bush-Cheney administration's movement toward war in Iraq and of the administration's economic record. In December 2002, however, he announced definitively that he would not run for the nomination, wanting, he said, to focus the upcoming campaign on issues and not on a rematch between him and Bush. Gore nonetheless continued to speak publicly and forcefully against the Bush administration, especially after the war in Iraq started to look like a mistake to the president's opponents and a scandal arose over the abuse of Iraqi prisoners in Abu Ghraib prison in Baghdad.

In spring 2004, Gore tapped the money left over from his 2000 campaign and a special fund set up to pay for the 2000 recount in Florida. He donated more than $6 million to various Democratic Party organizations, thereby helping to fund their attempts to defeat Bush and Cheney. When the Democratic ticket lost to the Republicans in the November election, Gore turned again to the world of private enterprise, helping to form an international investment firm and promoting a cable news network he cofounded.

Those who predicted that Gore would sooner or later decide to again enter electoral politics were disappointed, and few could have predicted his rather amazing career path between 2004 and the triumph in 2008 of the Democrats' unlikely presidential candidate Barack Obama and the return of the Democratic Party to power.

During that four-year interval, Gore not only amassed a considerable financial fortune, but, perhaps more remarkably, when he addressed the Democratic National Convention in Denver in August 2008, he did so as a man who had starred in an Oscar-winning movie and won the Nobel Peace Prize. Unlike so many other former vice presidents, Al Gore had not faded from public view.

Not only did the global investment firm he chaired, Generation Investment Management, prosper at the same time it supported environment-friendly investing, but Gore made a large income from other activities, such as sitting on the board of Apple and serving as a senior adviser to Google, which became during this period one of the largest and highest-earning companies in the world. His stock holdings in these companies alone would have made him a rich man. He also became a partner in what proved to be a successful venture capital company. By 2008, the financial news cable TV network Bloomberg News reported that Gore was able to invest $35 million in an environmentally informed hedge fund.

Perhaps more remarkably, Gore became the star of the entertainment world when his relatively dry illustrated lecture on the impending dangers of global warming was turned into a surprisingly sprightly documentary film called *An Inconvenient Truth.* Gore had long been derided by his political enemies as a empty-headed tree hugger due to his interest in preserving and protecting the environment. Conservative Republicans in particular had attacked him heavily for what they saw as unrealistic ideas that would harm American prosperity. However, after Gore left office and suffered defeat to George Bush at the hands of the Supreme Court, the weight of the scientific evidence finally began to shift public opinion about the danger of global warming. Gore's lecture, fully illustrated with convincing images and graphics, formed the core of the movie, with a little tweaking from Hollywood professionals.

When the documentary won an Oscar for best documentary feature (and amassed very large box office receipts for a documentary) in 2006, Gore shared the stage amid the glitter of the Oscar night presentation when the film's director was handed the coveted statue, and the former vice president made a short speech, following in the footsteps of Hollywood's brightest stars.

He then published a book based on the film, *An Inconvenient Truth: The Planetary Emergency of Global Warming and What We Can Do About It,* which became a best seller. Gore also won a Grammy for his recorded reading of the book. Almost incidentally, Gore won an Emmy for the work of his cable TV network, Current TV.

These honors paled, however, in 2007, when he was awarded the Nobel Peace Prize for his efforts to save the planet. He shared the award with the UN's Intergovernmental Panel on Climate Change (IPCC). The prize citation described Gore, according to the *New York Times,* as "probably the single individual who has done most to create greater worldwide understanding of the measures that need to be adopted." In late November, Gore responded to an invitation from President Bush to meet in the White House to receive the president's congratulations in person—a meeting that must have been heavy with irony.

As the 2008 presidential election came closer, Gore's name was often put forward as someone who could unite the Democratic Party and who could ride his recent fame to a successful campaign, especially since, according to poll results, the public had begun to turn against the Bush-Cheney administration's insistence on the rightness of the wars in Iraq and Afghanistan. A majority had come to see the administration as incompetent and driven by an inappropriate reliance on ideological criteria. The contentious primary battles between Senator (and former First Lady) Hillary Clinton and Senator Barack Obama also seemed to play into the possibility that Gore could step forward at a key moment and claim the Democrats' nomination.

Gore, himself, however, consistently denied he was interested in running again for president, and he reaffirmed his desire to continue his efforts on the issues of global warming and planetary danger. He stood apart from the long preconvention campaigning and did not endorse a candidate until June, when Obama had finally nailed down the nomination.

After the Democratic sweep of the November elections, there was considerable speculation that Obama would offer Gore a spot in his cabinet, but Gore confined his role to that of an adviser.

REFERENCES

Albert Gore, *The Path to Survival* (New York: Rodale Press, 2009); ———, *Our Choice* (New York: Simon & Schuster, 2009); ———, *Our Purpose: The Nobel Prize Lecture, 2007* (New York: Rodale Press, 2008); ———, *The Assault on Reason* (New York: Penguin Press, 2007); ———, *An Inconvenient Truth: The Planetary Emergency of Global Warming and What We Can Do About It* (New York: Rodale Press, 2006); ———, *Earth in the Balance* (New York: Rodale Press, 1992, new release, 2006); Bruce A. Ackerman, *Bush v. Gore: The Question of Legitimacy* (New Haven, Conn.: Yale University Press, 2002); *Biography of Vice President Al Gore,* Press Office, Vice President of the United States; Donna Brazile, *Cooking with Grease: Stirring the Pots in American Politics* (New York: Simon & Schuster, 2004); Douglas Brinkley, *36 Days: The Complete Chronicle of the 2000 Presidential Election Crisis* (New York: Times Books, 2001); Vincent Bugliosi and Gary Spence, *Betrayal of America: How the Supreme Court Undermined the Constitution and Chose Our President* (New York: Thunder's Mouth Press/Nation Books, 2001); Betty Buford, *Al Gore: United States Vice President* (Hillside, N.J.: Enslow Publishers, Inc., 1994); James McGregor Burns, Georgia Jones Sorenson, et al., *Dead Center: Clinton-Gore Leadership and the Perils of Moderation* (New York: Scribner's, 1999); Alex Cockburn, *Al Gore: A User's Manual* (New York: Verso, 2000); *Deadlock: The Inside Story of America's Closest Election* (New York: Public Affairs, 2001); Alan Dershowitz, *Supreme Injustice: How the High Court Hijacked Election 2000* (New York: Oxford University Press, 2001); E.J. Dionne and William Kristol, *Bush v. Gore: The Court Cases and the Commentary* (New York: Thunder's Mouth Press/Nation Books, 2001); E. D. Dover, *The Disputed Presidential Election of 2000: A History and Reference Guide* (Westport, Conn.: Greenwood Press, 2003); R. M. Dworkin, *A Badly Flawed Election: Debating Bush v. Gore, the Supreme Court, and American Democracy* (New York: New Press, 2002); Tipper Gore, *Picture This: A Visual Diary* (New York: Broadway Books, 1996); Abner Greene, *Understanding the 2000 Election: A Guide to the Legal Battles That Decided the Presidency* (New York: New York University Press, 2001); Hank Hillen, *Al Gore, Jr.: His Life and Career* (New York: Carol Publishing Group, 1992); David Maraniss and Ellen Nakashima, *The Prince of Tennessee: The Rise of Al Gore* (New York: Simon & Schuster, 2000); Richard Posner, *Breaking the Deadlock: The 2000 Election, the Constitution, and the Courts* (Princeton, N.J.: Princeton University Press, 2001); Larry Sabato, *Overtime!: The Election 2000 Thriller* (New York: Longmans, 2002); Robert Simon, *Divided We Stand: How Al Gore Beat George Bush and Lost the Presidency* (New York: Crown Publishers, 2001); Cass R. Sunsten, *The Vote: Bush, Gore, and the Supreme Court* (Chicago: University of Chicago Press, 2001); Jeffrey Toobin, *Too Close to Call: The Thirty-Six Day Battle to Decide the 2000 Election* (New York: Random House, 2001); Bill Turque, *Inventing Al Gore: A Biography* (Boston: Houghton Mifflin, 2000); Bob Zelnick, *Gore: A Political Life* (Washington, D.C.: Regnery Publishing Company, 1999); Peter J. Boyer, "The Political Scene: Gore's Dilemma," *The New Yorker,* November 28, 1994, 101–110; David Remnick, "The Wilderness Campaign: Al Gore Lives on a Street in Nashville," *The New Yorker,* September 13, 2004, 57–71; Walter Shapiro, "Gore: A Hard-Won Sense of Ease," *Time,* July 20, 1992, 28–29; Kenneth T. Walsh, "A Vice President Who Counts," *U.S. News and World Report,* July 19, 1993, 29–33.

SCOTT W. RAGER is a historian of U.S. politics and of congressional development who received his Ph.D. from the University of Illinois in 1991. His main research focus has been on Joseph Gurney Cannon, Speaker of the House from 1903–1911. He is a contributor to the book, *Masters of the House: Congressional Leadership Over Two Centuries* (Westview Press, 1998). Rager is a faculty member in the department of history at Heartland Community College in Normal, Illinois.

RICHARD BRUCE CHENEY (1941–   )

Vice President, 2001–2009

(President George W. Bush)

RICHARD B. CHENEY
(AFP/CORBIS)

By L. Edward Purcell

Richard Cheney came to the vice presidency as part of a ticket that won office with half a million fewer votes than its opposition and only by virtue of a split decision of the United States Supreme Court that awarded Cheney and his running mate, George W. Bush, one of the most disputed elections in American history. Nonetheless, Cheney was then widely perceived, even by his enemies, as a man with a sterling résumé and qualifications whose term as vice president might well be significant.

When cataclysmic events overtook the Bush-Cheney administration, beginning with the terrorist attacks of September 11, 2001, and continuing through the preemptive invasions of Afghanistan and Iraq (and prolonged and costly anti-insurgency wars), Cheney became without question the most active vice president in the history of the office. By all accounts, he was the chief architect of many of the Bush administration's policies, including foreign policy and the invasion of Iraq, and he became a strident advocate and spokesman for the Republican Party's ultraconservative, no-holds-barred politics.

Cheney had a long career in government and high office in Washington, D.C., before his selection as Bush's running mate, and he moved to his new position directly from a Fortune 500 oil services company that he had taken to new heights of prosperity, yet he came from quite ordinary, if not to say humble, origins and was almost the antithesis of Bush, who had been born into a political family that was financially well off.

The forty-sixth vice president was born in Lincoln, Nebraska, the eldest of three children. His parents were native Nebraskans. His father was a soil conservation agent for the U.S. Department of Agriculture. The family lived on a pleasant dead-end street that provided Cheney with a childhood playground.

When Cheney was twelve or thirteen (accounts vary), the family moved to the oil-boom town of Casper, Wyoming. There he entered high school, where he excelled in football, becoming captain of the team despite his short stature and light build, and met his future wife, Lynne Vincent, who was a baton twirler and homecoming queen. Cheney traced his lifelong love of the outdoors to his adolescence spent hunting and fishing in Wyoming.

Even as a boy, Cheney impressed people with his seriousness and purposefulness. He was capable of boyish pranks but was regarded by his classmates as someone destined for high achievement. One companion later said: "He was decent and everything, not serious but earnest, just straight as a die, just true."

In fall 1959, after graduating from high school in Casper, Cheney traveled to the East Coast to take up a scholarship he had won to Yale University. Unfortunately, he was unhappy at the Ivy League school and soon flunked out. He commented later in life that "I had a lack of direction, but I had a good time."

Cheney returned to Casper and worked for a while as a lineman for the local utility company, but his romantic relationship with Lynne spurred him to return to school. She was herself an exceptional student, and Cheney concluded that she would never be happy married to him if he neglected his education. He attended Casper Community College for one semester and then enrolled at the University of Wyoming, where he settled down to serious work. He and Lynne were married in August 1964, and he received his bachelor's degree at the end of the following school year. He stayed at the university for another year, earning a master's degree.

In 1966, the couple moved to Madison, Wisconsin, and entered graduate school, Dick in a Ph.D. program in political science and Lynne in British literature.

Cheney—a future secretary of defense—avoided service in the Vietnam War through a series of student deferments, although he was reclassified in mid-1964 into the top category and was probably close to being drafted when Lynne gave birth to the couple's first child, Elizabeth, in 1966. As a father, Cheney received an additional deferment that lasted until he reached the age of twenty-six and passed out of the draft pool. When quizzed in later life about his deferments, Cheney maintained that he would have served if called up.

In 1968, Cheney interrupted his Ph.D. program—his dissertation on various models of roll-call voting remained unfinished (Lynne got her degree, however)—and moved to Washington, D.C., for a one-year internship sponsored by the American Political Science Association. He never resumed academic pursuits but instead began a government career that had a steep upward spiral.

While an intern, Cheney wrote a memo that caught the attention of Donald Rumsfeld, a U.S. representative from Illinois. Cheney was soon on Rumsfeld's staff and moved along with his mentor when Rumsfeld became director of the Office of Economic Opportunity under President Richard Nixon. Within a year, Cheney was a staff assistant in the White House and eventually was appointed as assistant director of the Cost of Living Council.

Despite its rapid rise, Cheney's career was short-circuited for a time by the Watergate scandal and the collapse of the Nixon administration. In 1973, Cheney took a job with a Washington, D.C., investment firm, where he forged the beginnings of his personal fortune and waited out the end of the Watergate drama. After Nixon's resignation, Cheney returned to government service as staff assistant and head of the transition team for Gerald Ford, the new president. In late 1975, Cheney became Ford's chief of staff (replacing Rumsfeld, who moved on to become secretary of defense), one of the youngest people ever to hold that position.

When Ford lost to Democrat Jimmie Carter in the election of 1976, Cheney, who had been at the center of Ford's campaign and received some of the blame for the Republican candidate's narrow defeat, returned to Wyoming. The thinly populated state had only a single U.S. representative, so the political opportunities of the position for someone of Cheney's precocious record were limited; however, the Democrat who held the office decided to retire, and Cheney entered the race.

During the primary campaign, Cheney suffered the first of three heart attacks, a serious event for someone only thirty-seven years old. The attack proved to be relatively mild, but Cheney was forced to the sidelines to recuperate for nearly six weeks, although with the help of a California ad agency, he cleverly turned the episode into a campaign positive by stressing the philosophical maturity he had gained during his brush with mortality. Despite charges that he was a carpetbagger, having been absent from the state for so long, Cheney easily defeated his Republican primary opponent and won the general election in a landslide, claiming the first of what proved to be five terms in the U.S. House.

Cheney's record in Congress was a model of consistency. He predictably voted on the conservative side of almost every issue, opposing abortion rights for women and voting against welfare, for example. He won a very high rating from the American Conservative Union and one of the lowest possible scores from the liberal Americans for Democratic Action, although he eventually joined the moderates on environmental policy when parts of Wyoming were threatened by development under Reagan's secretary of interior James Watt.

Shortly after arriving in the House, Cheney resumed his rise to higher office when he became Republican minority whip. By all accounts he handed his duties with an effective combination of firmness and low-key charm that contrasted sharply with some of the G. O.P.'s subsequent whips, such as Newt Gingrich. Cheney kept the party's troops in line, but he made few enemies and many admirers, although he was reported to be extremely tough in private when facing down the opposition.

While in Congress, Cheney suffered two more heart attacks, in 1984 and again in 1988. After the third attack, he underwent quadruple bypass surgery and appeared to enjoy a full recovery, although as the years went on, the repairs grafted to the arteries of his heart could be assumed to start to wear out.

Meanwhile, Lynne Cheney forged an enviable Washington career of her own, being appointed by President Reagan in 1986 to become chairperson of the National Endowment for the Humanities, a post she served in until the end of the first Bush administration in 1993. She and Dick also collaborated on a study of congressional leaders, published as *Kings of the Hill: How Nine Powerful Men Changed the Course of American History* (a book that was reissued in paperback in 2000 shortly before Dick was nominated for the vice presidency).

In 1989, Cheney returned to the administrative side of government when President George Bush nominated him as secretary of defense. Cheney was Bush's second choice, after the Senate turned down Senator John Tower, a notoriously heavy drinker, but the selection proved to be sound. Cheney, although not a veteran of military service himself, immediately took hold of the job, studying assiduously and bringing to office his capacity for hard work and skillful management. With his background in Congress, Cheney proved to be an effective spokesperson for the administration's proposals to expand military spending for expensive programs such as the B-2 Stealth bomber. He also oversaw the planning and execution of the American incursion into Panama to oust dictator Manuel Noriega.

Cheney's grandest moments, however, came in 1990 and 1991, when the United States and its allies carried on the biggest military operation since the Vietnam War. When Iraqi dictator Saddam Hussein invaded oil-rich neighbor Kuwait in August 1990, he threatened the oil supply of the West and appeared poised to roll on down the Arabian Peninsula into Saudi Arabia—the United States's closest ally in the region. President Bush immediately declared that the United States would resist the incursions, and while the president set about forging an alliance against Iraq and galvanizing support in the United Nations, Secretary Cheney began to mobilize American ground, air, and naval forces to descend on the region. Four days after Hussein's move across the border of Kuwait, Cheney flew to Saudi Arabia and met with King Fahd, persuading the Saudis to accept the presence of tens of thousands of American troops on Saudi soil and to fight alongside the Western allies against a fellow Arab state. When this came to pass, it inadvertently set in motion an intense hatred of America by a rich young Saudi named Osama bin Laden, who eventually became the country's nemesis.

Over the following months, Cheney and his handpicked head of the Joint Chiefs of Staff, General Colin Powell, organized and helped plan a campaign to reclaim Kuwait and defeat Saddam Hussein, even though the Iraqis had what appeared on paper to be a large and powerful army and a significant air force. The American plan was to build up a large force in the Gulf region as rapidly as possible and then launch a massive air attack on Iraq, followed by a ground assault across the desert.

The air assault began in January 1991, news of which was dramatically brought to the American public by live reports from Baghdad by CNN correspondents who described the first-night bombing runs by American warplanes. Over the following days, the war plans engineered in part by Cheney appeared to be moving toward a huge success, despite Iraqi missile attacks on Israel (Cheney helped quell Israel's desire for direct retaliation). A sanitized version of the war played out each night on U.S. television. When the ground assault was launched in February, the allied forces rapidly overran Iraqi positions and swept around the main Iraqi force in a giant flanking maneuver. Tens of thousands of Iraqi soldiers were killed on the "Highway of Death" while trying to escape from Kuwait.

Cheney's role in what was called Operation Desert Storm brought him into the limelight and raised his public stock extremely high, along with Colin Powell and General Norman Schwarzkopf, the crusty theater commander. Despite some nagging criticism that the ground attack was called off too soon before ousting Hussein from power, the Gulf War marked a high point of popularity for the Bush administration in general.

The fall from power was, therefore, all the more difficult when President George Bush was defeated in the national election of 1992 by the Democratic team of Bill Clinton and Al Gore.

Cheney was suddenly out of office. He remained in Washington for a time, working as a senior fellow at the American Enterprise Institute, a conservative think-tank, along with Lynne. In 1995, the couple moved to Dallas, Texas, and Dick became chief executive of Halliburton Company, which provides engineering and construction services to oil-industry clients worldwide. Halliburton prospered under Cheney's leadership, expanding its share of the market (it acquired one of its main rivals along the way) and increasing annual revenues. Cheney's salary and stock options made him a very wealthy man over the course of the five years he was head of Halliburton. He also served on the corporate boards of such large companies as Union Pacific, Electronic Data Services, and Proctor and Gamble.

Despite his sojourn in private life, Cheney kept open his many channels of influence among his old colleagues and associates in Washington and from the first Bush administration. As Bush's son George W. Bush, who was governor of Texas and also a former oil industry executive, began to assemble advisers for a run at the Republican nomination for president in 2000, Cheney was drawn into the campaign. After George W. Bush defeated his main Republican opponent, Senator John McCain of Arizona, in the spring primaries, he asked Dick Cheney to head the search for a vice presidential candidate.

After two months of looking for potential running mates for Bush, Cheney finally decided to consider the post for himself, despite his pledge to the Halliburton board that he would not be a candidate.

In mid-July, Cheney signaled that he would be Bush's choice by changing his voter registration back to Wyoming, where he had not lived for decades but where he still owned a vacation home. The Twelfth Amendment to the U.S. Constitution bars a state's electors from voting for both presidential and vice presidential candidates from their state, so in order to not risk losing the thirty-two electoral votes from Texas, Cheney and Bush had to appear to be from different states.

A few days later, Bush announced Cheney's selection for the G.O.P. ticket.

The choice was greeted by the nearly universal opinion that Cheney would bring a wealth of high-level experience and seriousness to the ticket—elements that Bush seemed to lack—but that he was too stolid and boring to enliven the campaign. It was clear that Bush had decided to forgo a running mate who would be a vigorous campaigner in favor of someone whom he could rely on for advice and who could be trusted to carry out even the heftiest assignments. It was widely commented that Cheney would supply "gravitas" to the G.O.P.

ticket. Cheney's connection to George W. Bush's father's administration was another plus, since in a real sense the younger Bush was hoping to redeem the loss his father suffered at the hands of the Democrats in 1992.

Questions were raised almost immediately about Cheney's history of heart problems, but the Bush-Cheney campaign got famed Texas heart surgeon Denton Cooley to testify to Cheney's good health, based on a call by Cooley to Cheney's doctor.

Cheney proved to be—as predicted—a very low-key campaigner for the most part. He appeared less than completely comfortable at times when giving speeches, but he was direct and effective in meeting people and discussing issues. His opposite number, Connecticut Senator Joe Lieberman, chosen as Al Gore's running mate, was an ebullient figure to whom the news media gave much favorable attention, contrasting the rather somber Cheney to the lively Lieberman.

However, when the two vice presidential candidates met for a televised debate in October, Cheney's strong points and depth of background and character were prominently displayed. The debate was a friendly, unstructured, sit-down encounter between Lieberman and Cheney, and they covered a great deal of substance and displayed considerable knowledge. Both candidates demonstrated intelligence and wit. Several pundits expressed the opinion after the debate that the two vice presidential candidates were more impressive than the figures at the head of their respective tickets.

Cheney suffered a few distressing moments during the campaign, when the news media brought up unpleasantries such as his arrest in the 1960s for drunken driving (a particularly sensitive issue since George W. Bush openly admitted to a serious drinking problem during his younger days), the fact that he had failed to vote during most of the previous two decades, and his earlier admission that he passed a series of bad checks through the notorious Capitol bank when he was a congressman. He was also attacked for the $13 million retirement package he stood to receive from Halliburton and his contrastingly puny charitable contributions during his years in private life. On the whole, however, the media gave Cheney almost a free pass on personal issues.

During the confused and contentious period following the election (see the entry on Al Gore for a detailed narrative of the election dispute), Cheney initially stayed out of public view. Bush assigned him the major task of overseeing a potential transition of power, and Cheney spent most of his time organizing for what he hoped would eventually become the Bush-Cheney administration. His efforts to deal with the monumental tasks of transition were made difficult, of course, by the decreasing amount of time available between a conclusion to the election and the inauguration.

On the morning before Thanksgiving, Cheney awoke early with chest pains. Lynne rushed him to a Washington, D.C., hospital, where the first tests were negative, but follow-ups showed he had experienced a slight heart attack. His doctors performed an angioplasty and inserted a stent (a small device designed to reinforce arteries) to ease the flow of blood to Cheney's heart.

At first, Bush, who may simply have been ill-informed at that early stage, denied that Cheney had a heart attack, but within hours, the campaign issued a full statement.

Luckily, Cheney recovered rapidly from the episode, and within a few days of leaving the hospital appeared to be back to business, although vowing to follow his doctor's advice.

As the election dispute over Florida's crucial electoral votes wound to a conclusion before the U.S. Supreme Court, Cheney's value to the Bush administration—already thought by some to be virtually on the level of a prime minister, owing to Bush's inexperience—grew even greater when an extremely close election recount in Oregon's senatorial race resulted in an even split among Republicans and Democrats in the U.S. Senate. The only constitutional duty of any vice president, that of presiding over the Senate, which during most of U.S. history has been purely ceremonial, suddenly became crucial to the Republican Party's control. In the event of a fifty-fifty tie on any issue, Cheney would cast the deciding vote.

As he assumed office on January 20, 2001, alongside President George W. Bush, having already been instrumental in the transition and in bringing Colin Powell and Donald Rumsfeld into the new cabinet, Cheney was poised to become one of the nation's most important vice presidents ever.

Cheney's unusually powerful status was due to several factors. First of all was his high-level legislative and administrative experience, which had placed him at the center of many of the major political and historical events of the Nixon, Ford, Reagan, and George H. W. Bush administrations. But many vice presidents before him had also been experienced and successful politicians, only to fade from power almost immediately after taking office. Cheney, however, differed significantly from most of his immediate predecessors in his lack of personal presidential ambition—all vice presidents going back to Nixon had tried to use their office as a springboard for a run at the presidency—but after a brief flirtation with presidential ambition in 1993, Cheney had given up, and by 2000, he clearly presented no political threat to George W. Bush or any other potential Republican hopeful.

Cheney also had a long relationship with the new president prior to his selection as a running mate, and he had not been added to the ticket merely to provide balance or to pull in a swing state—Bush joked tongue in cheek that he had selected Cheney for Wyoming's three electoral votes. Their relationship was much stronger and deeper than most vice presidents and presidents had enjoyed in the past, and Bush was willing, perhaps eager, to give Cheney a large measure of responsibility and actual power. It seemed clear that Cheney, in the words of Richard Moe (formerly a chief aide to Vice President Walter Mondale), had been selected as the vice presidential candidate, not to help win the election, but rather to "help govern," which is exactly what he proceeded to do.

Within weeks it was obvious that Cheney would not be shunted off to harmless or relatively insignificant projects, as was the norm for vice presidents, but that he would be at the heart of policy making in the new administration. Cheney imposed himself vigorously during the transition and early days of the Bush administration by placing many of his friends and long-time associates, almost all of whom shared his aggressive neoconservative viewpoints, in key administration spots. In addition to pushing for the appointment of Donald Rumsfeld, his former boss and patron, as secretary of defense, Cheney swung high-level appointments for Paul Wolfowitz in the Pentagon, Elliott Abrams as head of the Middle East Office on the National Security Council, and several others.

Whereas previous vice presidents had to be content with a weekly lunch and the occasional private meeting with their presidents, Cheney met frequently with Bush, and they made it routine to confer privately before each cabinet meeting. Before many weeks had gone by, observers noted that Cheney appeared to be able to step into almost any aspect of the administration and virtually take over, often brushing aside cabinet members or other administration officials. Previous vice presidents had hoped to influence policy; Cheney actually seized power at the behest of Bush, who appeared to be content to let his more experienced second in command flex his muscles.

Although President George W. Bush was a wealthy man, mostly as the result of riding the advice and help of his rich friends, Cheney was much wealthier due to his years with Halliburton. When he took the vice-presidential nomination, Cheney separated officially from the giant company, but his retirement package and the sale of part of his stock (the rest was put in a blind trust) gave him a very large net worth, which he later estimated as up to $80 million. He also continued to receive deferred annual income from Halliburton. In 2001, his first year in office, Cheney earned $196,600 as vice president and received an additional $205,298 in deferred income from Halliburton. The Halliburton payments dropped to around $150,000 a year thereafter, but they continued to represent a strong financial and personal tie between the company and Cheney, a fact that would raise eyebrows during 2003 and 2004 when Halliburton received billion dollar no-bid contracts from the government.

Early in the new administration, Cheney's continued ill health reappeared as a point of concern. His heart problems resurfaced shortly after his inauguration, and he was hospitalized after complaining of chest pains. His doctors again operated and reopened one of the stents that that had been placed in his coronary arteries the previous fall. Two months later, surgeons implanted a combination pacemaker and defibrillator in Cheney's chest in order to correct irregular heart beats and protect against future attacks. This treatment seemed to work, and the vice president on the whole experienced little further difficulty during his first term, although he had a brief episode of shortness of breath during the fall 2004 election campaign.

Rather ironically, given his own medical history, Cheney became the first vice president to take responsibility for the government under Section 3 of the Twenty-fifth Amendment to the Constitution, which calls for the vice president to take over if the president is medically incapacitated. On June 29, 2001, George W. Bush underwent a colonoscopy, and before going under the anesthetic, he signed a letter temporarily transferring presidential power to Cheney. Twenty minutes later, Bush woke up, but Cheney did not return authority to the president for nearly two more hours while Bush recovered from the effects of the procedure (which showed no problems with the presidential colon).

At his inauguration, Cheney had anticipated that his role as president of the Senate, his only formal constitutional function, would offer a chance to make major contributions to achieving the administration's and the Republican Party's agendas, since the 50-50 split after the fall 2000 election gave him the deciding vote in case of ties; however, when moderate Vermont Republican senator Jim Jeffords was outraged by his treatment during the Bush administration's push for a tax cut and subsequently quit the party and threw his vote to the Democrats (although claiming to be an Independent), Cheney's position in the Senate became irrelevant. He was unusually active, however, in lobbying for the administration in the U.S. House of Representatives, where he had previously served as an elected member, and he set up an office in the House building, the first such vice-presidential office there in memory.

In May 2001, George W. Bush gave Cheney the task of formulating a new national energy policy in order to meet what appeared to be a growing crisis. Cheney convened a task force composed apparently in large part of oil and nuclear energy industry businesspeople and lobbyists, many of whom Cheney worked with as CEO of Halliburton, which was a major player in the energy industry. Not surprisingly, the National Energy Policy Development Group, as it was called, came up with a plan to exploit new potential gas and oil fields at almost any costs, including bending long-standing environmental protection rules, and with almost no attention to energy conservation measures.

When eventually challenged by law suits from environmental and consumer advocate groups and the watchdog Government Accounting Office, Cheney refused to divulge who had taken part in the task force or anything about how it had arrived at its conclusions, citing executive privilege. The case dragged on for three years and became a point of increasing contention, especially after energy giant Enron Corporation went spectacularly bankrupt and its executives, including Ken Lay, who had advised Cheney and contributed heavily to the Cheney-Bush campaign in 2000, were convicted of massive fraud and corruption. Cheney and the administration fought vigorously to withhold information, and in December 2003, the case was sent to the U.S. Supreme Court.

Even more controversy erupted when it was revealed that a month after the Court accepted the case, Associate Justice Antonin Scalia went on a private hunting trip with Cheney. Scalia declined to recuse himself from the case, and in June 2004—in the midst of a presidential campaign year—the high court confirmed Cheney's right to silence and sent the case back to the lower courts.

Although Cheney's vice-presidential role during his first months in office had been much larger than usual in American history, it paled in comparison to his position after the events of September 11, 2001.

Cheney was in the White House that morning when four hijacked commercial airliners were converted to suicide weapons by Islamic fundamentalists, members of al-Qaeda, an international organization under the command of wealthy Saudi Arabian Osama bin Laden. Two of the airliners struck the twin towers of the World Trade Center in New York City, causing their fiery collapse and the deaths of more than 2,700 office workers, bystanders, and police and firemen who had rushed to try to rescue victims. A third hijacked plane crashed into the Pentagon in Washington, killing 252 and damaging the building, which had served as headquarters of the U.S. military since World War II.

President Bush was in Sarasota, Florida, at the time of the attack, visiting a grade school classroom, and he was unable to rapidly respond to the news of the emergency. Cheney, on the other hand, rushed to a bunker under the White House, along with National Security Advisor Condoleezza Rice and several top aides and officials, and assumed command. He conferred with the president by phone, but Cheney seized the initiative and ordered military aircraft to shoot down any other airliners if they appeared to offer a threat. The fourth hijacked airliner was, in fact, headed for Washington, D.C., and may have been targeting the White House or the U.S. Capitol building, but heroic passengers on board rushed the cockpit and caused the plane to crash into a field in Pennsylvania, killing all the passengers and hijackers aboard. Cheney's orders came too late and were never properly transmitted to the pilots.

Bush was persuaded by the Secret Service, backed by Cheney's advice, to stay away from the capital, which might be the target of more attacks. The president boarded *Air Force One* and flew first to an air base in Louisiana and then to Offut Air Force Base in Omaha, Nebraska, the home of the Strategic Air Command and one of the most secure locations in the country. Bush conferred by phone with Cheney and members of the cabinet and the National Security Council, and before the end of the day, he returned to Washington.

In the weeks following the attack, Cheney's role in the government took on even more importance. His deep knowledge and experience, including his stint as secretary of defense during the Gulf War, were called on as the Bush administration searched for a response to the terrorism and what Bush declared to be a state of war with al-Qaeda and its sponsors. However, in order to protect the line of succession, Cheney moved from Washington to what was described as "an undisclosed, secure location," and he essentially disappeared from public view for several weeks.

Osama bin Laden and al-Qaeda had been harbored for several years in Afghanistan, a war-torn nation where a fanatical Islamic faction, called the Taliban, had taken power in the political and military turmoil that followed the withdrawal of the Soviet Union. Bush and his advisers decided to attack al-Qaeda and its training camps directly, so in October 2001, the United States launched a full-scale attack on the Taliban. Aided by Great Britain and with the cooperation of the military dictatorship in neighboring Pakistan, United States air power struck at al-Qaeda and the Afghan rulers. The United States also recruited thousands of anti-Taliban fighters known as the Northern Alliance, made up mostly of militias lead by domestic opponents of the Taliban, to carry out most of the ground fighting, thus holding the numbers of American soldiers and marines in the country to a minimum, a doctrine proposed by Cheney's former mentor and current secretary of defense, Donald Rumsfeld. Cheney himself remained in the background, usually away from Washington, but he appeared to have supported Rumsfeld's plan.

By December, massive displays of air power had crushed the Taliban and—along with the help of the Northern Alliance fighters—had expelled the radical Muslim leaders from most of the country. However, a lack of American ground troops and a reluctance of Afghan proxies to press home a difficult search in a remote mountain area of the country allowed Osama bin Laden to escape across the border into a part of Pakistan were there was effectively no government control or military presence. An American-backed government was installed in Kabul, the Afghan capital, but the object of the war had escaped capture or death.

In January 2002, President Bush delivered an aggressive State of the Union Address. In this and later speeches, the president outlined a series of policies and ideas that were to a large measure backed by and even advocated by Vice President Cheney. Along with Rumsfeld, Rice, Wolfowitz, and other neoconservatives, Cheney urged a new international course for the United States, one that would veer away from decades of previous policy.

The neoconservatives shared a belief in the overriding importance of U.S. military power and the need to focus national attention on matters of security before thinking of global economic or environmental issues. They also saw the United States's military preeminence after the collapse of the Soviet empire as a positive, and they further believed the United States should be aggressive in asserting itself on the international stage. Many of these ideas had been succinctly stated in 1992 in a policy paper called the "Defense Planning Guidance Paper," drafted by Paul Wolfowitz under the direction of then secretary of defense Dick Cheney. At the heart of the new policies was the belief that the traditional U.S. reliance on containment, deterrence, and multiparty solutions to world problems should be replaced by self-determined and self-interested action on the international stage, including the use of preemptive warfare if necessary, regardless of world opinion or support. Cheney became the chief spokesperson and most vocal advocate of these neoconservative views.

It became obvious early in 2002 that the Bush-Cheney administration was determined to turn its gaze from Afghanistan to Iraq, where longtime dictator Saddam Hussein continued to viciously oppress his own people and to taunt the United States and its allies who had defeated Iraq in the Persian Gulf War in 1991 but had stopped short of displacing Hussein. The neoconservatives in the government now fixed on the supposed "weapons of mass destruction" they claimed Hussein had secretly developed or was in the process of developing. These imagined weapons included both biological agents and nuclear devices, along with the long-range rockets to deliver them. To add weight to their condemnation of Hussein, Cheney and the president claimed that U.S. intelligence agencies had uncovered direct ties between al-Qaeda and the Iraqi regime. As it turned out, Iraq had no weapons of mass destruction and there were no ties between Hussein and al-Qaeda, but Cheney continued to make these assertions in speeches years after they were proved false. Central Intelligence Agency head George Tenet told the press he had personally corrected Cheney several times, but the vice president persisted in his mistaken beliefs, or at least he persisted in asserting their truth in his public speeches.

The mid-term elections of November 2002 gave the Republicans control of the U.S. Senate and strengthened its majority in the House of Representatives, which emboldened the administration to push ahead with its aggressive stance against Iraq. With the coming of the new year, it was apparent that almost nothing could prevent a war. In March 2003, Bush with the approval of Congress launched a preemptive, all-out war on Iraq with air attacks and ground assaults aimed at Baghdad. The goals of the war, according to the administration, were to find and render harmless the suspected weapons of mass destruction officials believed Hussein harbored, to sever the supposed ties to al-Qaeda, to effect "regime change" (in other words dethrone Saddam Hussein), and to turn Iraq into a model Arab Middle Eastern democracy.

Joined by British troops and token contingents from several other countries, notably Poland and Spain, the American-led forces swept rapidly toward the Iraqi capital, and by the first week of April, they seized Baghdad and chased Hussein into hiding. After only 43 days of combat, President Bush declared an end to major fighting. Unfortunately, things began to go badly almost immediately. The neo-conservative doctrine had called for a minimum of troops, so there was insufficient armed manpower on the scene to prevent mass looting and civil chaos in the wake of the U.S. military victory. The predictions that Americans would be greeted as saviors proved also to have been a miscalculation, one espoused with particular fervor by Cheney based on his relationship with expatriate Iraqi power seekers, and the degenerating situation was made worse by the administration's decision to disband the Iraqi army and governmental bureaucracy, thereby creating a large body of unemployed dissidents who fed on the religious and ethnic divisions that ran deeply through Iraqi society. Despite frantic searching, no weapons of mass destruction were found anywhere in the country. Over the ensuing months, Iraqi insurgents mounted increasingly effective and large-scale attacks on U.S. forces and on Iraqis who cooperated with the United States and the interim Iraqi government the administration set up. American and Iraqi casualties due to roadside attacks, ambushes, and suicide bombers increased steadily, despite the capture of Saddam Hussein and most of his principal henchmen by the end of the year.

Cheney continued his public role as chief cheerleader for the administration's Iraqi War policies, and behind the scenes, he continued to guide much of the decision making, often backstopping Secretary of Defense Rumsfeld and frustrating the efforts of more moderate Secretary of State Colin Powell. Cheney himself became the focus of attention when reports began to surface that Halliburton, his old employer, had received gigantic no-bid war contracts and had then overcharged the government by millions of dollars. The news media and members of Congress discovered that the company, which by the second year of the war had accumulated $11 billion in contracts, had not only gouged the government but had performed poorly in many areas. Cheney, who was still receiving deferred salary from Halliburton, came in for media criticism, especially when Halliburton also drew Securities and Exchange Commission scrutiny for alleged fraudulent accounting during Cheney's time as CEO, but remarkably, the criticism seemed to slide off his back.

In January 2004, Cheney made one of his infrequent trips abroad—a chief duty of most previous vice presidents had been to travel often to funerals and second-level international conferences, but Cheney's unique position in the Bush administration and the wars in Afghanistan and Iraq had kept him at home—and he addressed an audience of political, business, and religious leaders at a world economic conference in Davos, Switzerland. In his speech and follow-up comments and conversations, Cheney appeared to soften somewhat the Bush administration's hard-line, independent stance. Accompanied by Lynne, he then flew to Italy where he met both the prime minister and the pope, and he visited U.S. troops stationed there. He also uncharacteristically went out of way to speak to and court the news media, making what appeared to be a conscious effort to rebuild America's public image in Europe.

While the vice president was in Europe, the 2004 presidential election began to heat up with the first party caucuses in Iowa, where Massachusetts senator John Kerry defeated the field of Democratic hopefuls, including first-term South Carolina senator John Edwards, who Kerry eventually selected as his running mate after further Kerry victories in the March "Super Tuesday" primaries. There was little doubt that Bush would retain Cheney as his vice president, although a few media pundits speculated that Cheney's gruff image might pull down the Republican ticket.

The major campaign issues were clear: the war against terrorism; the war in Iraq; the economy; and what were termed as "moral values." Cheney's well-publicized role as chief administration adviser and Bush's counselor cast him as an aggressive supporter of the war efforts, although his campaign effectiveness on the economy was questionable. On the whole, his image as an elder statesman and his reputation as a no-holds-barred, behind-the-scenes manipulator served the Republican ticket well. Cheney's opposite number, Senator John Edwards, had an abundance of boyish good looks and a winning public personality, but when it came to power issues, such as terrorism and the war in Iraq, he seemed a lightweight in comparison to Cheney.

Nonetheless, Cheney and Bush had to fight against a rising tide of bad news from Iraq during the campaign. In May, photos were circulated showing sexual and physical abuse of Iraqi prisoners by U.S. troops acting as guards. Not only were the images and accounts shocking, but matters were made worse by the fact that Abu Ghraib prison, the site of the abuses, had been the most notorious of Saddam Hussein's torture facilities. And, as the summer of the campaign wore on, the ferocity of the insurgency rose as a drumbeat of attacks caused more and more casualties. At the same time, terrorists (many of them now genuinely tied to al-Qaeda) began to routinely kidnap westerners and then videotape their beheadings for public broadcast on Arab television networks. The severe religious and social fault lines of Iraqi society also complicated attempts by the United States to move Iraq toward democratic elections, with the long-suppressed Shiite Muslim majority clamoring for power and many minority Sunni Muslims, who had enjoyed control under Hussein, supporting the insurgency.

On the campaign issue of moral values, Cheney would have seemed logically to be on firm ground due to his assertive conservatism, but he found himself in a pinch. The major issue in the public mind was gay marriage, which had surfaced prominently when a Massachusetts court approved same-sex marriage and officials there began to issue marriage licenses to gay couples. The mayor of San Francisco also seized on the issue and married hundreds of gay couples on the steps of city hall. President Bush's response—pushed hard early in the campaign by his right-wing fundamentalist supporters—was to propose a constitutional amendment to ban same-sex marriage in the United States. Eleven states put similar amendments on their ballots for the November election.

The problem for Cheney was that one of his daughters, Mary, was openly lesbian. Thus, he and Lynne were placed in a difficult position when the issue of homosexuality, cloaked in the topic of gay marriage, came to the front in 2004. Four years earlier, in his vice-presidential debate with Joe Lieberman, Cheney had defended the right of individuals "to enter into any kind of relationship they want to enter into," and said it was "really no one else's business." Now, in 2004, with Bush and the Republican conservatives pushing for a formal amendment to the U.S. Constitution, Cheney was forced at first to backpedal and appeared to support the president, although the vice president verbally skirted the issue whenever possible.

As the campaign pressure increased, however, Cheney was confronted with Mary's lesbianism and the issue of same-sex marriage more and more frequently. In August, after Lynne had said in public that the issue should be left up to the states, a clear step away from the party line, Cheney finally shifted his position in a speech at a campaign rally, saying that "freedom means freedom for everyone" when asked directly about his stance. He qualified his position somewhat by adding that the president made policy, not the vice president. The final eruption of the gay marriage–lesbian daughter issue came late in the campaign, when, during his third debate with Bush, Democratic candidate Kerry illustrated a point by specifically citing Mary Cheney's lesbianism, a comment that drew sharp retorts from both Cheney parents.

The gay marriage amendment notwithstanding, Bush and Cheney put on an aggressive campaign against their opponents. At every opportunity, they pounded home their superiority when it came to fighting terrorism, defending the country, and pursuing the war in Iraq. Despite revelations of intelligence failures brought to light during the campaign by a nonpartisan commission on the September 11 attacks—a commission Bush and Cheney had tried without success to stonewall—and circumstantial evidence that Cheney may have attempted to influence prewar intelligence reports on Saddam Hussein (he was still making the old spurious charges about Hussein's links to al-Qaeda well into the fall campaign), the polls showed most voters trusted the Bush-Cheney team more on these issues than they did the Democrats.

Cheney and Edwards met in October for a single face-to-face debate, which for the most part was amicable and revealed both men to be knowledgeable and confident. The most contentious moment came when Cheney tried to paint Edwards as a senatorial slacker, saying that as the presiding president of the Senate, he had never met the South Carolina senator until the evening of the debate. Edwards left this unchallenged, but within hours, news media and internet web sites produced evidence that the two had met several times, including a Washington breakfast where they had been photographed together. Cheney also miscited a web site and sent viewers by mistake to a site critical of the administration. Neither of these two gaffes did much to damage Cheney's standing, however.

When it came to the final voting in November, despite polls showing a close race, the Bush-Cheney ticket won easily, taking 51 percent of the national popular vote. Turnout was high by recent election standards with almost

120 million voters making their selections. The final results in Iowa and New Mexico were not known for several days due to the closeness of the vote in those states, but—unlike the prolonged agony of the 2000 election—the practical outcome was known by the next morning. In the end, Bush-Cheney won 286 electoral votes to 252 for Kerry-Edwards (when the electoral college voted officially in December, one Minnesota elector voted for Edwards for both president and vice president, so Kerry's final total was 251). Moreover, the Republicans gained seats in both houses of Congress, raising for the administration the prospect of pushing through almost any legislative initiatives. Tellingly, constitutional amendments against same-sex marriage passed in all eleven states where they were on the ballot, and voters reported to pollsters that moral values had been a decisive set of issues.

However, the reelection of the Bush-Cheney ticket proved to be the high point of the vice president's two terms in office. Within two years, the Republicans lost control of Congress, and the public began to turn against the administration's failing policies in the Middle East. Moreover, although Cheney was not directly involved, the Bush administration's shortcomings were prominently and tragically displayed when Hurricane Katrina hit New Orleans and the Gulf Coast in August 2005. The Bush-Cheney practice of appointing political cronies to key government jobs as a way to entrench conservative Republican power backfired when the Federal Emergency Management Agency (FEMA), which had proven highly effective under the previous Democratic administration in dealing with natural disasters, failed miserably to meet the challenge of one of the worst storms to hit the United States. Public approval of both Bush and Cheney began to decline and was on a downhill slide for the rest of Cheney's time in office.

In general, Cheney dug in and resisted efforts by the news media or anyone else to call him to account for his behind-the-scenes activities as vice president. He mounted a campaign to insist that his official vice presidential papers should not be subject to acquisition by the National Archives Administration (as required by law) nor should congressional investigations have access to his office documents. He claimed executive privilege allowed him to exercise his natural inclinations toward secrecy—as had been demonstrated earlier in his refusal to make public the members of his energy advisory board—and that he and the president were above the law in this matter. He even went so far as to seem to claim that the vice presidency was a fourth branch of government, neither executive or legislative, and therefore not subject to the restrictions of either.

As public opinion began to turn sharply against the administration's prolonged war in Iraq, Cheney's immoveable position that the war had been necessary to protect Americans against the potential threat posed by Saddam Hussein and Hussein's supposed link to al-Qaeda became more and more marginalized. Two significant developments demonstrated Cheney's increasingly aggressive tactics to try to shore up his long-proclaimed contentions that Hussein had been actively conspiring with al-Qaeda and trying to acquire an atom bomb.

The first was not to be revealed clearly until after Cheney left office. In 2004, Cheney told the *Rocky Mountain News* in an interview that went unnoticed at the time that significant intelligence had been obtained from captured al-Qaeda leaders by means of what came to be known as "enhanced" interrogation techniques—in other words, torture. In 2009, after Barack Obama and the Democrats took office, there were lurid and troubling revelations that Cheney himself had approved torture of prisoners by the CIA. In fact, a former CIA official revealed that Cheney had specifically directed the agency to use torture to find a connection between al-Qaeda and Hussein. By the time Cheney left office, public opinion had clearly condemned the practice of torture as a violation of a long-held national policy and of the basic values of the nation. Nevertheless, Cheney insisted in 2009 in television interviews and public speeches to conservative groups that the practice of water boarding, in which prisoners were repeatedly subjected to simulated drowning, and other harsh measures were not torture, and even if they were they were necessary to acquire important information from the prisoners. He also, in early 2009, attacked the new Democratic administration for, in his view, endangering American lives by forgoing torture of terrorist prisoners and announcing the closing of the extralegal detention camp at Guantánamo Bay, Cuba.

The second development was a repercussion of Cheney's attempts to find evidence that Saddam Hussein was preparing to build weapons of mass destruction. No physical evidence of Cheney's allegations—which had been key to the Bush administration's justification for launching the invasion of Iraq—had ever been found after the United States took control of the country and defeated Hussein. Nevertheless, Cheney continued to insist that even if no evidence existed, the Iraqi dictator had *intended* to assemble such weapons.

This fixation eventually involved Cheney in a complex set of events that involved former Bush administration ambassador Joseph Wilson, Wilson's wife, Valerie Plame, and Cheney's chief of staff, Lewis "Scooter" Libby.

Wilson had been sent to Niger by the White House to investigate rumors that Hussein had been trying to buy African yellowcake uranium, which would have indicated he was moving toward developing nuclear weapons. However, Wilson found no such evidence and reported that to the White House, where his conclusions were unwelcome. Despite the lack of intelligence, President Bush made the assertion in his State of the Union address that Hussein was building an atom bomb. Wilson subsequently refuted in public the president's claims, an action that infuriated Cheney and others high in the administration.

The affair might have ended there, but Cheney and his cronies decided to hit back at Wilson. An unnamed high official leaked a story to a conservative columnist Robert Novak, who published a story in the *Washington Post* that revealed that Wilson's wife, Valerie Plame, was a covert CIA agent—in other words, the administration outed one of its own undercover operatives, ruining her career in the intelligence agency. The public outcry and anger among congressional Democrats resulted in a series of hearings, investigations, and an eventual trial of Scooter Libby, who was Cheney's chief of staff and most trusted aide. Neither Libby nor anyone else was convicted of the federal crime of revealing the name of a secret agent, but Libby was convicted in 2007 of related charges—obstruction of justice and perjury—and was sentenced to 30 months in prison and a fine of $250,000. President Bush commuted the prison term, but he did not give Libby the pardon Cheney wanted, and so his former chief of staff was stuck paying the fine and was unable to resume his legal career because he was now a convicted felon.

As Cheney's positive public image began to erode, a careless moment during one of his favorite pursuits, hunting, damaged him even further. On a quail hunt in Texas in February 2006, Cheney mistakenly fired his shotgun at his host, seventy-eight-year-old Harry Whittington, hitting the lawyer in the face and neck. Whittington also took some errant birdshot to the chest, and he had a mild heart attack as the result. Although there were rumors that the hunting party had been drinking beer before the accident, Cheney was cleared by the local sheriff. He could not escape the wrath of television commentators, however, especially the ridicule of the influential television commentator, Jon Stewart, who continued for months after the event to deride Cheney as someone "who shot an old man in the face."

In November 2006, the Republicans lost control of the House of Representatives, greasing the slide toward their eventual defeat in the presidential race in 2008. The loss of the conservatives' congressional power base (GOP conservative leader Tom Delay resigned after being indicted) only seemed to reinforce Cheney's determination to stand by his actions and previous policies, and his rare public pronounce-ments continued to hew to the conservative playbook, even down to hinting five years after having been proven wrong that Saddam Hussein had been a serious threat to the United States due to his ties to al-Qaeda.

Cheney himself was the target of an assassination attempt by al-Qaeda in February 2007 while visiting an American base in Afghanistan, a nation where the extremist Taliban had regrouped and was beginning to reclaim parts of the country they had lost in 2002. An al-Qaeda suicide bomber ignited his bomb near the front gates of the base while Cheney was actually on the far side of the compound. He was barely aware that there had been an explosion.

For the second time in his term as vice president, Cheney became the actual acting president while Bush was sedated for a colonoscopy. The handover of authority lasted only a few hours in July 2007, however, and Bush resumed office as soon as he was out of the recovery phase. It was later reported that Bush had by this stage of his presidency begun to lose faith in Cheney and no longer relied on the vice president's advice, although Bush did little or nothing to rein in Cheney's unconstitutional, self-assumed powers.

By mid-2008, it had become obvious that the GOP was in serious danger not only of failure to regain control of Congress, but of losing the White House also. When the U.S. economy began a nearly unprecedented collapse, which eventually turned into a colossal meltdown of the financial system and a severe corresponding downturn in both the national and global economies, the voting public's lingering support for the Republicans thumped. The Bush-Cheney record did almost nothing to shore up support for Senator John McCain, the GOP presidential nominee, and the young, charismatic Democratic nominee Barack Obama took a lead in the polls. Obama's election as the first black, or more properly mixed-race, president sent a thrill throughout much of the world and was taken in general to be a refuta-tion of Cheney and Bush. Dick Cheney was perhaps the most powerful vice president in U.S. history.

REFERENCES

Shirley Anne Warshaw, *The Co-Presidency of Bush and Cheney* (Palo Alto: Stanford University Press, 2009); Barton Gellman, *Angler: The Cheney Vice Presidency* (New York: Penguin Press, 2008); Robert Sam Anson, *The Opportunist Dick Cheney's Path to Power* (New York: Simon & Schuster, 2007); Charlie Savage, *Takeover: The Return of the Imperial Presidency and the Subversion of American Democracy* (New York: Little, Brown, 2007); Murray Waas and Jeff Lomonaco, *The United States v. I. Lewis Libby* (New York: Union Square Press, 2007); Stephen F. Hayes, *The Untold Story of America's Most Powerful and Controversial Vice President* (New York: HarperCollins, 2007); Lou Dubose and Jake Bernstein, *Vice: Dick Cheney and the Hijacking of the American Presidency* (New York: Random House, 2006); John Nichols, *Dick: The Man Who Is President* (New York: New Press, 2004). Beginning in 2000, almost daily coverage of Cheney could be found on the pages and web sites of many newspapers, including most notably the *New York Times* (URL: http://www.nytimes.com) and the *Washington Post* (URL: http://www.washingtonpost.com), and the syndicated print stories and web sites of news organizations such as the Associated Press (URL:http://dailynews.yahoo.com) and Knight-Ridder Washington Bureau (URL: http://www.krwashington.com). Also useful were reports of broadcast news on the web sites of CNN (URL: http://www.cnn.com), CBS News (URL: http://www.cbsnews.com), and MSNBC (URL: http://www.msnbc.com). Unfortunately, most of the daily web site journalism and comment was fleeting and was replaced as the sites were updated. Two television interviews by Cheney with Tim Russert on "Meet the Press" can be viewed online: "Meet the Press," March 16, 2003, URL: http://www.mtholyoke.edu/acad/intrel/bush/cheneymeetthepress.html. Downloaded December 10, 2004; and "Meet the Press," September 10, 2004, URL: http://www.msnbc.msn.com/id/3080244. Downloaded December 10, 2004. Other online transcripts include an interview with Neil Cavuto, June 25, 2004, URL:

http://www.foxnews.com/story/0,2933,123794,00.html. Downloaded August 25, 2004; and a panel discussion on PBS, "The Cheney Factor," March 12, 2001, URL: http://www.pbs.org/newshour/bb/white_house/jan-june01/cheney_3-12.html. Downloaded August 25, 2004. One of the best profiles is Nicholas Lemann, "The Quiet Man: Dick Cheney's Discreet Rise to Unprecedented Power," in the May 7, 2001, edition of *The New Yorker,* which may be read online URL: http://new-yorker.com/archive/content/?040906fr_archives06. Downloaded December 12, 2004. The transcript of a radio broadcast interview by Amy Goodman with Spencer Ackerman entitled "The Radical Mind of Dick Cheney," is at URL: http://www.democracynow.org/article.pl?sid=03/11/26. Downloaded on August 2, 2004. See also portions of James Mann, *Rise of the Vulcans: The History of Bush's War Cabinet* (New York: Viking, 2004) and Bob Woodward, *Plan of Attack* (New York: Simon & Schuster, 2004) for events of 2003 and 2004.

See the entry for GEORGE CLINTON for a biographical note on L. EDWARD PURCELL.

JOSEPH ROBINETTE BIDEN, JR. (1942–)

Vice President, 2009–

(President Barack Obama)

JOSEPH R. BIDEN, JR.
(United States Congress)

By Laurie McNown

Joseph Robinette Biden, Jr., was elected to the office of the vice president after representing the state of Delaware in the United States Senate for 36 years. Few who have occupied the vice presidency could claim to bring to the job such a depth of knowledge of Washington and its institutions as did Biden. During his years in the Senate, he had played key roles in important Supreme Court nominations, had been in the forefront of congressional foreign policy decisions, and had conducted two unsuccessful bids for the presidency.

Joe Biden's roots are in Scranton, Pennsylvania, where he was born on November 20, 1942. For financial reasons, his family moved to Delaware, where he grew up and has lived the rest of his life until moving into the official vice president's residence in Washington after his election. As a child, Biden spoke with a stutter, which he cured by memorizing and reciting long literary passages. During his education in high school at the Archmere Academy and at the University of Delaware, Biden's focus was more on sports and friends than on academics.

During his junior year at the university, he met Neilia Hunter, a student at Syracuse University. After graduating from the University of Delaware in 1965 with degrees in political science and history, he started law school in Syracuse to be close to Neilia, and they were married in 1966.

Biden demonstrated little zeal for the intricacies of law school and by his own account became an "arrogant and sloppy" law student. After failing a course due to plagiarizing a source and then retaking it, he eventually graduated near the bottom of his class in 1968. After graduation, Biden went to work in the public defender's office, but he left to start his own firm. He soon became involved with the Delaware Democratic Party and won a seat on the New Castle County Council.

In 1972, no Delaware Democrat wanted to run against the well-known and well-financed Republican incumbent. In a campaign with few resources except the energy and dedication of his family, Biden upset the sitting senator by a slim margin. At the time of his election, Biden was 29 but he would turn 30 before he was to be sworn in in January.

A few weeks after the election, Biden was setting up his new office in Washington while his wife and three young children shopped for a Christmas tree in Delaware. A truck hit her station wagon, and she was killed along with Biden's infant daughter and their sons were seriously injured. During the initial shock in the aftermath of the tragedy, Biden decided to not take his Senate seat, but he was persuaded to change his mind by friends and leaders in the party. He was sworn into office in the hospital where his sons were recovering.

In 1977, Biden married Jill Jacobs. In addition to the two sons, Beau and Hunter, from his first marriage, the family grew to include a daughter, Ashley. Jill Biden has worked as an educator in high school and community colleges teaching English and writing, and in 2007, she earned a doctorate degree from the University of Delaware. The Bidens' two sons both earned law degrees. His oldest son, Beau, was elected as Delaware's attorney general in 2006. Beau's Army National Guard unit was deployed to Iraq the day after his father participated in the vice presidential debate during the campaign. Ashley Biden works as a social worker.

Biden became a well-known national figure in 1987 in two separate and well-publicized roles. First, in his continuing role as chair of the Senate Judiciary Committee, he presided over one of the most contentious Supreme Court confirmation battles in Senate history. And, as he led the hearings, he attempted to keep his bid for the Democratic nomination for president alive.

In late June 1987, Associate Justice Lewis Powell announced his retirement from the Supreme Court. Powell had been appointed by President Nixon and during his 17 years on the Court had developed the reputation as a moderate and independent voice, casting the decisive vote on many important decisions. While the replacement of this centrist justice was seen by some as an opportunity to shift the Court to a comfortable conservative majority, it was viewed as a threat by others who desired more balance on the Court. As such, Powell's retirement received even more attention than most vacancies.

On July 1, 1987, President Reagan nominated Robert Bork to fill Justice Powell's seat. Bork's qualifications for Supreme Court justice were beyond question. He had been a professor of law at Yale University, served as Solicitor General in the Nixon and Ford administrations as well as acting Attorney General, and had been a judge on the important U.S. Court of Appeals for the District of Columbia circuit.

Shortly after Reagan's nomination of Judge Bork, Senator Biden issued a statement in which he declared that he would resist efforts by the administration to "impose an ideological agenda upon our jurisprudence." He indicated that a confirmation of Bork would alter the balance of the Court. Biden's concerns were echoed by others on the committee, especially Senator Ted Kennedy, as well as women's and civil rights groups who spoke out against the nomination.

The concern of those who opposed Bork's nomination rested on opposition to the legal theory he had helped to develop and had advocated during his distinguished career. Bork was a leading proponent of originalism, a theory that advocates that the interpretation of the Constitution should be consistent with the intent of those who wrote and ratified it. An opposing theory of the Constitution is sometimes described as the living constitution and posits that the meaning of the Constitution is constantly evolving within the context of society. It was on this fundamental question of constitutional interpretation that Biden opposed the Bork nomination. In a statement that he released before the confirmation hearings, Biden promised that he would "examine with special care any nominee who is predisposed to undo long-established protections that have become part of the social fabric that binds us as a nation." The case perceived to be most vulnerable to reinterpretation from the originalist perspective was the famous case that protected the right of women to abortions, *Roe v. Wade* (1973), which had been decided on generalized rights of privacy inferred from other constitutional rights. A judge using originalism as a standard would likely vote to overturn this case, as there is no explicit right to privacy in the Constitution. Furthermore, using this doctrine, the matter of abortion rights would remain as a state issue.

As chair of the committee, Biden promised a "full and thorough and fair" review of Judge Bork. Biden also promised the candidate that the committee would allow any and all witnesses that Bork put forth to testify. Yet, Biden also assured opponents of the nomination that he would lead the fight against confirmation.

The five days of questioning Judge Bork captured the attention of the American public in an unprecedented and spirited discussion of constitutional philosophy. Bork's supporters charged that many on the panel and press simplified Bork's theories and unfairly politicized his positions. Bork's keen intellect was evident, and his demeanor was that of a law professor giving a seminar. But, Biden, the politician, was keenly aware that the American public was watching and forming opinions on the jurist. As he wrote in his autobiography, "Ninety-nine out of a hundred law professors and constitutional scholars must be fascinated by this colloquy . . . And ninety-nine out of a hundred average citizens must have been thinking *Bork can't come up with a good reason to stop the government from intruding in my bedroom?*"

Senator Biden, as chair of the Judiciary Committee, had explicitly pursued a strategy of defeating the nominee on the grounds that his judicial philosophy was out of the mainstream of contemporary thought. Biden reasoned that if the president used ideology as qualification for appointment, the Senate should use that attribute in assessing its confirmation vote.

Judge Bork's confirmation was reported negatively out of the Judiciary Committee. Bork did not withdraw his nomination, but the full Senate failed to confirm him on a vote of 58-42 with several members crossing party lines. This vote represents an important moment in the history of the modern Senate when the ideology of the nominee, as well as qualifications and character, was used as a criterion for the approval of a nomination to the Supreme Court.

It was while presiding over the confirmation hearings of Robert Bork that the presidential bid of Joe Biden disintegrated. Biden had announced his candidacy in June of 1987, and after front-runner Gary Hart dropped out of the race, he was considered a strong candidate in a field of Democratic candidates that was not particularly well known to the public or politically strong. Biden's competition included Michael Dukakis, Richard Gephardt, Al Gore, and Jesse Jackson. The press often referred to this group as "the Seven Dwarfs."

At a debate at the Iowa State Fair in August 1987, Biden closed his remarks with a point he had used as part of his standard stump speech. He posed the question: "Why is it that Joe Biden is the first in his family ever to go to a university?" And the answer was not that other Bidens had been not been bright. The problem was that government was not active in helping citizens realize their potential.

Biden had used this speech many times before the closing of the debate in Iowa and had credited Neil Kinnock, a British Labour leader whose words and ideas he was using. Biden has always maintained that his omission of attribution was inadvertent and cited his other speeches that did recognize the source. However, the Dukakis campaign circulated a video with a split screen of the Biden speech compared to the Kinnock speech to the press. The *New York Times* ran a front-page story on the speech and soon the story was national news. It was revealed that Biden had given speeches in which there were similarities to ones that had been given by other politicians such as Hubert Humphrey and Robert F. Kennedy. And reporters discovered that Biden had failed a class during his first year of law school for not properly citing a source. Biden claimed that he did not understand the need for multiple citations rather than the one footnote for nearly five pages of material that he had used. In another revelation years later, he claimed to have graduated in the top half of his law school class when he had actually graduated seventy-sixth of eighty-five students. Taken together, these incidents allowed the press to paint a portrait of the candidate as either dishonest in his portrayal of himself and his accomplishments or careless in his reporting of his accomplishments.

Less than two weeks after the *New York Times* article detailing the similarities in Biden and Kinnock's speeches, the Biden campaign for the presidency was finished. Proclaiming that his candidacy had been overwhelmed by "the exaggerated shadow" of his past mistakes, he withdrew from the Democratic nomination race. The *New York Times* noted that "Mr.

Biden chose to swallow most of his private anger and place the burden for the end of his candidacy on himself." He also stressed the importance of choosing between his campaign and his responsibilities as chair of the Judiciary Committee in the Bork hearings. Bork's nomination was defeated one month later.

During the campaign and the Bork hearings, Senator Biden suffered from frequent and often excruciating headaches, and the pain was initially diagnosed as a pinched nerve in his neck. But, after he collapsed in February 1988 in a hotel room in Rochester, an aneurysm just below the base of the left side of his brain was discovered. After being given last rites in a hospital in Delaware, he was transferred to Walter Reed Medical Center where he underwent eight hours of surgery. Later, as a complication from his recovery, he underwent a second surgery for a blood clot in his lung. And, then, in May, he had yet another operation for a second aneurism in an artery on the right side of his brain.

Biden's collapse and first operation had come just as Michael Dukakis was winning the Iowa primary that he had hoped to compete in himself. By the time Biden returned to the Senate, seven months after his collapse in Rochester, Dukakis was the presidential nominee of the Democratic Party. Just days before his return, Dukakis rehired John Sasso, his former campaign manager, who had been forced out of his campaign after it was revealed that he was responsible for the leaked tape of the comparisons between the Biden and Kinnock speeches. At the time of his return to the Dukakis campaign, Sasso released a statement to the press saying: "What I did back in September [1987] was an error in judgment and I am sorry it hurt Senator Biden and his family. . . . On other occasions, he certainly had quoted and given attribution to Neil Kinnock and I do not believe in any way he intended to mislead the American people." This vindication was clearly important to Biden as he reports it in his autobiography.

The recounting of Joe Biden's life has often been framed by the three crises of his wife's death, his aborted presidential bid, and his aneurysms. In 2007, he told the *New York Times* that he had gained different insights from each of these events. "The accident taught him, he said, 'to always let the people you love know you love them, and never let something go unsaid.' The aneurysm taught him that 'it's a hell of a lot easier being on the operating table than in the waiting room.' As for the 1987 race, Mr. Biden said he learned that he could pull himself back up after the crippling experience of having his character questioned, 'particularly when it's your own fault.'"

After the very intense years of 1987 and 1988, Senator Biden returned to his duties on two important committees, the Senate Judiciary Committee and the Senate Foreign Relations Committee. He served as chair of the Judiciary Committee from 1987 to 1995 and as chair of the Foreign Relations Committee starting in 2001, holding that position while the Democrats had the majority in the chamber. It was in his role as chair of the Judiciary Committee that Biden found himself in the center of another-high profile nomination battle in 1991.

Thurgood Marshall, the first African American to serve on the Supreme Court, announced his retirement in late June 1991. Marshall, by any measure, had been an important figure in legal history. In 1954, he had argued the landmark *Brown v. the Board of Education* before the Supreme Court. In 1967, saying that it was "the right thing to do, the right time to do it, the right man and the right place," President Lyndon Johnson named him to that court. And in his twenty-four years on the Court Marshall had provided an unwavering voice in support of civil rights, the constitutional protection of individual rights, the rights of criminal suspects, and programs such as affirmative action. In his time on the bench, the Court had become more conservative, reflecting appointments by Nixon, Ford, Reagan, and the first president Bush. At the time of his retirement, Marshall was the most liberal justice on the Court as evidenced by the fact that in his final term he dissented in twenty-five

of 112 cases. As such, he was seen to fill two important roles on the court, one related to race and one related to ideology.

President George H. W. Bush nominated Clarence Thomas to fill the vacancy created by Marshall's resignation. In choosing Thomas, the Bush appointment would maintain the racial makeup of the Court but would shift the ideological balance. Thomas was one of the few African-Americans conservative jurists who could be considered qualified for the appointment. He had served as Chairman of the Equal Employment Opportunity Commission and had been appointed to the U.S. Court of Appeals for the District of Columbia Circuit by President Bush only fifteen months before the nomination to the Supreme Court. Thomas was viewed as being a reliable conservative voice. Although his judicial philosophy was not well articulated, legal observers noted similarities to Bork's originalist thought.

The Thomas confirmation became a flashpoint for both liberal and conservative groups. Liberal groups such as the National Organization of Women, the NAACP, and the Urban League opposed the nomination on the basis of concerns over issues such as abortion and affirmative action. Conservative groups vowed that they would fight to prevent another "borking" of a nominee. And Joe Biden was at the center of conflict.

Soon after the hearing began, rumors began to circulate concerning charges of sexual harassment against Thomas leveled by a former colleague at the Equal Employment Opportunity Commission, Anita Hill, who was a professor of law at the University of Oklahoma. According to the legal writer Jeffrey Rosen, who was an intern on the Judiciary Committee at the time, Biden's strategy in the hearings was to focus on issues such as property rights and federal power. He initially wanted to handle the charges of sexual harassment confidentially. After the press began to report on the charges, he allowed Ms. Hill to testify but he did not allow three additional witnesses who could corroborate the allegations of Thomas's interest in pornography.

The Judiciary Committee sent the nomination to the full Senate without a recommendation either way. Thomas was confirmed by the Senate in a narrow vote of 52 to 48.

Biden's middle road seemed to please few. At the time, Thomas called his confirmation hearings a "high-tech lynching." His view of the proceedings had not moderated in his 2007 memoir, sixteen years after the hearings. On the other hand, Biden received heavy criticism from women's groups and liberal legal organizations for not allowing a full examination of the harassment charges. Unlike the Bork hearings, which he gave extensive coverage to, Biden does not explore this dramatic and contentious incident.

One of the most fundamental differences between the philosophies of Bork and Thomas on one hand and Biden on the other concerned the role of the federal government. As adherents of originalism, the nominees believed in a limited role for the national government and state responsibility for most government actions that affected individual citizens. Biden points to his preparation for the Bork hearings as having the effect of crystallizing his own philosophy of the role of government. "Bork and his adherents thought [that government] should get out of the way and let society and the markets operate as they pleased. I thought government was obligated to be active in helping its citizens. I thought government should serve people."

Biden's philosophy of an activist government is apparent in what he calls "the single most significant legislation I've crafted during my thirty-five-year tenure in the Senate." The Violence Against Women Act (VAWA) was passed by Congress in 1994 and signed into law by President Clinton. Extensions of this act were passed in 2000 and 2005 (and it is up for renewal in 2010). Senator Biden had begun working on this issue in 1990, and the majority staff of the Senate Judiciary Committee issued a report in 1993, in which he stated, in part: "I have become convinced that violence against women reflects as much a failure of our Nation's collective moral imagination as it does the failure of our Nation's laws and regulations . . . These findings reveal a justice system that fails by any standard to meet its goals—apprehending, convicting, and incarcerating violent criminals . . ."

Working with a coalition of women's organizations and progressive groups, Biden and the Judiciary Committee crafted a bill that included an approach that utilized federal, state, and local programs, supported by grants for prevention and victim services. In addition, it provided for increased investigation and prosecution of violent crimes against women. More than $1.6 billion of funding for six years was authorized for these programs in the original VAWA.

It is difficult to measure the effectiveness of preventative measures, but there is general agreement that the act has been instrumental in decreasing violence against women. It has also spurred changes in many state laws. For example, all states have changed laws that treated date or spousal rape as a lesser crime than stranger rape. The act has been criticized for focusing on the criminal justice system rather than a more holistic approach to violence.

It is interesting to note that one aspect of this act allowed victims of domestic abuse to sue for damages in federal court. This is precisely the type of expansion of federal authority that Bork opposed and considered unconstitutional under the originalist philosophy. The VAWA had sought authority to provide this remedy partially under the commerce clause.

In overturning this provision, Chief Justice Rehnquist's opinion had echoes of Bork: "We accordingly reject the argument that Congress may regulate noneconomic, violent criminal conduct based solely on that conduct's aggregate effect on interstate commerce. The Constitution requires a distinction between what is truly national and what is truly local. In recognizing this fact we preserve one of the few principles that has been consistent since the Clause was adopted." And, Associate Justice Clarence Thomas wrote in an extremely brief concurring opinion: "I write separately only to express my view that the very notion of a 'substantial effects' test under the Commerce Clause is inconsistent with the original understanding of Congress' powers and with this Court's early Commerce Clause cases. By continuing to apply this rootless and malleable standard, however circumscribed, the Court has encouraged the Federal Government to persist in its view that the Commerce Clause has virtually no limits. Until this Court replaces its existing Commerce Clause jurisprudence with a standard more consistent with the original understanding, we will continue to see Congress appropriating state police powers under the guise of regulating commerce."

Senator Biden served on the Senate Foreign Relations Committee from January 1975 until he left the Senate to become vice president. He became ranking minority member of this important committee in 1997 and chair (when the Democrats had the majority in the Senate) after 2001. Although he served concurrently on the Judiciary Committee, his primary focus shifted to foreign affairs.

In his role as the chair of the committee, it has often been difficult to make simple categorizations relating to Biden's positions on foreign affairs. While he often supported using military force to achieve U.S. foreign policy objectives, he also emphasized more diplomatic engagement with adversaries. Liberals often criticized him for his somewhat aggressive views relating to use of force in Iraq while conservatives expressed unease with his calls for diplomatic engagement and his criticism of executive claims to war powers.

Some observers pointed to inconsistencies in Biden's approach to foreign affairs. For example, in 1991, Biden voted against authorizing the use of force in Iraq for the first Gulf War. In this case, the UN Security Council Resolution had authorized members of the United Nations in to use "all necessary means to uphold and implement" a previous resolution, which demanded that Iraq withdraw its forces from Kuwait. As such, an argument could be made

that the international community backed intervention. However, Biden voted in favor of authorizing the 2003 invasion of Iraq, which had not been approved by the Security Council. Many in the international community, therefore, viewed this as an illegitimate act of aggression on the part of the United States. Biden later became a critic of President Bush's handling of the war and said that he regretted his vote to authorize force.

In his years dealing with American foreign policy, Biden regularly advocated American military intervention in various venues. For example, in the early 1990s, he was an early and strong voice for American involvement and the lifting of an arms embargo to stop the ethnic cleansing of Muslims in Bosnia in the wake of the breakup of Yugoslavia. In advocating these policies he was opposed by President George H. W. Bush and later President Clinton. This policy did, however, become the basis of a NATO peacekeeping effort.

It is often noted that few politicians have the years of experience and knowledge of varied places and situations in the world that Senator Biden possesses. In recounting a visit by Biden to Romania in 1999, the former U.S. ambassador to that country gave his impression of the senator at the time. The ambassador wrote in the *Wall Street Journal* that he was impressed by the questions Biden asked about the current state of Romanian politics and policies. The ambassador noted: "Because Mr. Biden has known all the major Romanian leaders since before the dictator Nicolae Ceausescu was ousted in 1989, the questions were Ph.D. level, not Romania 101."

In 2006, Senator Biden wrote in a *New York Times* opinion piece that Bosnia had been preserved a decade earlier by dividing it into ethnic federations. He proposed adapting this idea to Iraq by creating three relatively autonomous regions for the Kurds, the Shiites, and the Sunni, with a central government in Baghdad responsible for foreign affairs and oil revenues. In September 2007, the Senate passed a nonbinding measure supporting the plan that expressed only the will of the Senate. The White House rejected the plan.

The partition plan played a central role in Senator Biden's short-lived run for the Democratic nomination for the 2008 presidential race. Biden entered the race in January 2007, running on his experience in the Senate and his expertise on foreign policy matters. His campaign got off to a rocky start when the press focused not on his impressive resume but on one of his famous verbal gaffes instead. Biden had characterized fellow candidate Barack Obama as "the first mainstream African-American who is articulate and bright and clean and a nice-looking guy." And, while Biden conceded that he had been quoted correctly, he stated that his words had been taken out of context or misunderstood. He later said that "fresh" would have been a better word than "clean" but many saw the remark as either offensive, insensitive, or at best as evidence that Biden's worst enemy on the campaign trail was his own voice. However, his voice did provide for one of the most memorable one-liners of the campaign. During a debate with the Democratic candidates in October 2007, he said of Republican hopeful Rudy Guiliani, "There's only three things he mentions in a sentence: a noun, and a verb and 9/11."

Senator Biden's bid for the Democratic nomination never gathered much momentum. The national mood for change and the very high-profile and well-financed campaigns of two fellow senators, Hillary Clinton and Barack Obama, dominated the Democratic political scene. Biden dropped out of the race after finishing a disappointing fifth in the Democratic caucuses in Iowa. He won less than 1 percent of the delegates and had raised less than $12 million.

After Biden's withdrawal from the race, there was speculation that he might be chosen for the position of secretary of state. On *Meet the Press* in June, he was asked if he wanted the job of the vice president. Biden replied that, clearly, he did not want to be asked, but if the presumptive nominee were to ask, he would, of course, say yes.

In August, shortly before the Democratic Convention was to convene in Denver, Obama sent a text message to his supporters announcing his choice of Joe Biden for vice president. The choice of Biden, who had decades in Washington politics, came with both positives and negatives for the Obama campaign. Biden's foreign policy experience was seen as the major credential that he brought to the ticket. But the cost of that experience was, that in picking an insider, Obama's message of change was somewhat undercut. The *New York Times* assessed Biden as ". . . known to much of the public as a gabby, gaffe-prone, backslapping Irish boy from Scranton, Pa., [but] in private councils and in the corridors of the Senate he is known as an ambitious, astute, calculating politician always looking at the next step." When chosen for the second slot on the ticket, Biden was sixty-five years old and had been in the Senate for thirty-five years. (Obama was forty-seven and had been in the Senate for less than four years.)

During the very secretive selection process, it had been assumed that Biden was one of the finalists along with Senator Evan Bayh of Indiana and Governor Tim Kaine of Virginia. Some Democrats advocated the choice of Hillary Clinton in order to help facilitate the healing of the party and bring the defeated candidate's supporters more fully into the Obama camp. Some Clinton supporters were vocal about their disapproval of the choice.

Vice presidential candidates are usually chosen either for what they can bring to the campaign or what they might bring to an administration. Although Biden was clearly able to prevail in his elections to the Senate from Delaware, he had not been successful on the national electoral stage. His home state's three electoral votes were certainly not reason enough to choose him. As a Roman Catholic he could be seen to represent a key voting bloc, but his moderated stance on abortion was a problem for many in this group. And, with his well-known tendency to produce gaffes, it was fair to say that Senator Biden's selection to be the vice presidential nominee was due to qualities he could offer after the election.

In the general election campaign, the press focused primarily on the two nominees, Obama and Senator John McCain and on the Republican vice presidential nominee, Sarah Palin. The one major event for Biden during the debate was his televised debate with Palin. In this debate, it was important for Palin to appear knowledgeable and articulate and for Biden to avoid any major gaffes. It was also key that Biden not appear to be condescending toward his inexperienced opponent. Both succeeded in their missions, with Palin exceeding expectations and Biden giving one of the best debate performances of his career. Most commentators and public opinion polls indicated that Biden won the debate. This vice presidential debate was watched by 73 million people—more than watched any of the presidential debates.

Afterward, the election speculation focused on what type of vice president Biden would be and what his role in the White House would involve. Interest in this subject was sharper than usual given the unusual role that Vice President Dick Cheney played in the Bush White House and was fueled by a remark that Biden made during the campaign when he said that Cheney was probably "the most dangerous" vice president in American history. Biden also stated that Cheney was "dead wrong" in his views about unfettered presidential powers during wartime and that he intended to "restore the balance" in power between the presidency and the vice presidency.

In December, after the election Cheney defended his stance on vice presidential powers and mocked Biden's pledge to be less expansive in his interpretation of the powers of the office. Cheney said: "If he wants to diminish the office of the vice president, that's obviously his call . . . President-elect Obama will decide what he wants in a vice president and, apparently, from the way they're talking about it, he does not expect him to have as consequential a role as I have had during my time."

Reports indicated that Biden did not want to be a shadow secretary of state and the choice of Hillary Clinton for this role seemed to preclude such a role. Indications were that Biden was seeking a position of general adviser with input on all important decisions. His knowledge of the institution and people in Congress could prove to be useful, but the Senate has a long tradition of being a closed institution and not welcoming interference from outsiders, even if those people came from the Senate. Ultimately, a vice president's job is defined by the president and the relationship that develops between the two.

References

Joseph Biden, *Promises to Keep* (New York: Random House, 2007); John M. Broder, "A Father's Tough Life Inspiration for Biden," *New York Times* (10/23/08). Available online. URL: http://www.nytimes.com/2008/10/24/us/politics/24biden.html?scp=1&sq=biden%20father%20tough%20&st=cse. Accessed September 14, 2009.

LAURI MCNOWN teaches at the University of Colorado. She also works extensively in the professional development of civic educators, such as secondary school teachers. She has lectured on American government in Indonesia, Namibia, Egypt, Libya, and Croatia, and she has lived and taught in Kathmandu, Beijing, Hanoi, and Sydney, as well as the university's Semester at Sea.

APPENDICES

CHRONOLOGY OF EVENTS

1774

September–October

The First Continental Congress, with representatives from all the American colonies except Georgia, meets in Philadelphia to discuss grievances with Great Britain.

1775

April

American militiamen at Lexington and Concord in Massachusetts clash with British regulars, setting off six years of warfare.

May

The Second Continental Congress convenes in Philadelphia and takes responsibility for fighting the war and serving loosely as a central government for what become the thirteen states. The body becomes the Confederation Congress in 1781 with the adoption of the Articles of Confederation and remains in existence until superseded by the fist U.S. Congress in 1789.

1776

July

Congress adopts the Declaration of Independence.

1781

March

The Articles of Confederation, first proposed in 1775, finally go into effect, thereby establishing a new form of government for the United States.

October

Commander in chief George Washington forces the surrender of the British army commanded by Lord Cornwallis at Yorktown, Virginia, bringing to an end most of the actual fighting, although the treaty-making process drags on for two more years.

1783

April

Congress ratifies the treaty of peace with Great Britain; the treaty is not signed officially until September, ending the Revolutionary War.

1785

May

Congress passes the Land Ordinance that specifies how public land is to be sold to the public. The law calls for a survey of land into rectilinear townships and sections, which are then to be sold in 640-acre lots at $1 an acre. Specific size and price of lots are changed frequently in future decades, but the principles and procedures of selling public land follow this precedent.

1786

September

Armed malcontents, led by former Revolutionary War officer Daniel Shays, confront state militia near Springfield, Massachusetts, setting off widespread fears of civil insurrection and a crisis of confidence in the government of the Confederation. Shays's Rebellion, as it is known, is eventually put down by federal troops in February of the following year.

1787

May–September
Delegates from the states (Rhode Island is missing) assemble in Philadelphia to consider revising the form of national government. The result is the Constitution of the United States. The new plan calls for a national executive consisting of a president and a vice president to be chosen by electors from the states. The candidate receiving the highest number of electoral votes will be president and the second highest will be vice president. The duties of the vice president are to succeed to the presidency on the death, resignation, or removal of the president and to preside as president of the Senate, one of the two bodies of the new U.S. Congress.

July
The Confederation Congress gives final approval to the Northwest Ordinance, one of its greatest accomplishments. The law sets forth the steps and requirements for admitting new states to the Union from the Old Northwest Territory (the modern states of Ohio, Indiana, and Illinois) and provides a blueprint for further political expansion.

October
The proposed Constitution is submitted to the state legislatures for ratification. Nine of the thirteen states must approve if the plan is to go into effect, and apolitical struggle ensues in several key states during the following months.

1788

June–July
The Constitution is officially ratified with the approval of New Hampshire in June, but success of the new government is not assured until the Virginia and New York legislatures concur a month later.

1789

February
Electors chosen by the states (in a variety of ways) cast their votes for president and vice president.

April
The new U.S. Senate meets in New York City (the temporary capital) and counts the electoral votes: George Washington is elected as the first president with 69 votes; John Adams is vice president with 34. Adams arrives in New York before Washington and takes his oath of office on April 21. Washington is inaugurated on April 30. He chooses Thomas Jefferson of Virginia as his first secretary of state; Alexander Hamilton of New York is secretary of the Treasury.

1790

June
A site for the new national capital is chosen in northern Virginia on the Potomac River; meanwhile, the government will convene in Philadelphia, to which it moves in December.

1791

December
The first ten amendments to the Constitution, known as the Bill of Rights, are ratified and go into effect. Several states insisted that such a list of rights be added before they agreed to ratify the new form government.

1792

February
Congress passes the first of several Succession Acts, which specify who will ascend to the presidency if both the president and vice president die, resign, or are removed from office. Neither

this law, which puts the president pro tem of the Senate and the Speaker of the House in line, nor subsequent laws alter the vice president's first right of succession.

October

The cornerstone of the White House is laid in Washington, D.C.

November

The second national election for president and vice president is held. When the votes are counted a month later, Washington again wins with 132 votes, with Adams repeating as vice president with 77.

1793

April

"Citizen" Edmond Genêt arrives as the minister from the revolutionary government of France. His presence galvanizes the developing political parties in the United States, with the Jefferson Madison Democratic Republicans enthused about the French Revolution and the Hamilton-Adams Federalists distrustful and anxious. Genet's silly behavior and offenses toward Washington over the summer months discredit him and his cause. He is recalled in August but seeks political asylum in the United States, eventually marrying future vice president George Clinton's daughter.

1794

August–November

Farmers in western Pennsylvania stage violent protests against the federal tax on whiskey. Washington counters the so-called Whiskey Rebellion with a show of force, and the protesters back down.

November

John Jay, chief justice of the Supreme Court, concludes a treaty with Great Britain that attempts to settle American and British claims arising from the Revolution, as well as several other issues such as the closing of British posts in the Old Northwest. The treaty becomes a controversial political issue when its provisions are made public several months later. It is narrowly ratified by Congress in June of the following year but continues to divide the country.

1796

February

France is outraged at the provisions of the Jay Treaty between the United States and Great Britain and brings relations with the United States almost to the point of war. During the following months, there will be armed conflict at sea between ships of the two countries.

May

A new Land Act establishes a system by which public land can be bought on credit at auction. The minimum price set is high enough to eliminate many potential small buyers.

September

Washington issues his Farewell Address, signaling his withdrawal from public life.

December

John Adams, a Federalist and the sitting vice president, wins the national election for president with seventy-one electoral votes. His rival, Thomas Jefferson, comes in second with sixty-eight votes and thereby becomes vice president, although of the opposing party from the new president. Several others receive electoral votes, including Federalist Thomas Pinckney, who is only nine votes behind Jefferson.

1797

March

Adams and Jefferson are inaugurated. The Constitution calls for this long interval between election and taking office, which has potential for causing problems if and when the office of president changes hands from one party to the next. The original framers of the Constitution did not foresee the formation of parties and have made no allowance for them or the conflict they imply.

October

Three U.S. diplomats, Charles C. Pinckney, Elbridge Gerry, and John Marshall, arrive in Paris on a mission to patch up differences with the French and conclude a peace treaty. Instead, French foreign minister Talleyrand attempts to extort nearly a quarter-million-dollar bribe before opening negotiations. The incident becomes known as the XYZ Affair, after the pseudonyms of the three French agents sent by Talleyrand with the demand for money. Pinckney and Marshall return to the United States, but Gerry is forced to stay. Americans are outraged when the affair is reported.

1798

May

The United States and France enter a period of active but undeclared war known as the Quasi War. President Adams has overseen a build up of American naval forces and is authorized by Congress to raise a new army and to have U.S. warships capture French naval vessels if they attempt to stop U.S. shipping.

June–July

The Federalists use the Quasi War as an excuse to pass a series of Alien and Sedition Acts, aimed at stifling government critics from the opposing Democratic-Republican Party. Several politicians and journalists are arrested and jailed under the repressive laws, but in the end, the measures backfire and turn voters against the Federalists.

1799

December

George Washington dies at Mt. Vernon and is mourned by the entire nation.

1800

April–May

Candidates for president and vice president are chosen by congressional party caucuses. Incumbent John Adams will run again as the the Federalist candidate with Charles C. Pickney as his running mate. The Democratic Republicans nominate Thomas Jefferson for president and Aaron Burr for vice president.

May

President Adams recognizes that some of his cabinet members are secretly working against him in conjunction with Alexander Hamilton. He dismisses several disloyal officers but loses the broad support of his Federalist Party, in part because he works toward peace with France.

November

The government leaves Philadelphia for the new capital of Washington City on the Potomac, where John and Abigail move into the president's residence, later known as the White House.

1801

February

The presidential electoral ballots, cast the previous December, are finally counted, resulting in a potential political catastrophe. Thomas Jefferson and Aaron Burr have tied with 73 votes each. It was intended that some Democratic–Republican electors refrain from voting for Burr, thereby making him vice president, but there has been a slip-up. To Jefferson's consternation, Burr sees a chance to achieve his ambition to become president, and he refuses to concede to Jefferson. The contested election is thrown into the House of Representatives, which is controlled by Jefferson's Federalist enemies. After a prolonged deadlock, some Federalists decide that Jefferson is the lesser evil and swing enough votes to make him president. The affair reveals a major defect in the electoral system.

1801

March

Jefferson and Burr are inaugurated in Washington City, the new national capital.

1802

February

Congress appropriates funds to arm U.S. vessels in the Mediterranean Sea against the pirate nation of Tripoli. The United States has paid tribute to pirate kingdoms along the Barbary coast of North Africa for several years, but the Pasha of Tripoli has declared war. The conflicts with the pirate states will continue off and on for many years—the current war with Tripoli drags on until 1805—and the problems are not settled until 1815 when U.S. naval hero Stephen Decatur defeats Algiers, Tunis, and Tripoli and secures American rights.

1803

May

American envoys in Paris agree to a treaty with France that will transfer a huge area west of the Mississippi River to the United States. The French offer to sell the land has come as a surprise, but President Jefferson seizes the opportunity. In exchange for about $15 million, the United States acquires a region between the river and the Rocky Mountains that eventually will be carved into thirteen states. The Louisiana Purchase is the largest and most significant single act of expansion in American history. The Senate approves the purchase in October.

August

An expedition put afoot by Jefferson and led by Meriweather Lewis and William Clark sets off to explore a route across the newly acquired Louisiana Purchase to the Pacific Ocean.

December

Congress passes the Twelfth Amendment, which alters the flawed presidential electoral process. The new amendment calls for presidential and vice-presidential candidates to run as a paired ticket, with separate electoral votes for each office. No longer will the vice president be elected by the second-highest number of votes for president, thereby eliminating the possibility of a repeat of the Aaron Burr–Thomas Jefferson conflict that arose after the election of 1800. Final ratification of the change will come from the states in the fall of 1804.

1804

February

Democratic–Republican members of Congress meet in a caucus to nominate candidates. They pick Jefferson to run for a second term and replace Burr with veteran New York governor George Clinton.

July

Vice President Aaron Burr has lost a bid for the governorship of New York State, and he blames the opposition of former Secretary of the Treasury Alexander Hamilton, who is the leader of the Federalist Party. Burr challenges Hamilton to a duel. When the two meet at Weehawken, New Jersey, the Vice President shoots his opponent dead and is forced to flee arrest warrants in New York and New Jersey. Later in the year, he resumes his place in Washington as president of the Senate, despite the warrants.

December

The Democratic–Republican ticket of Jefferson and Clinton smashes the Federalist candidates, Charles Cotesworth Pinckney and Rufus King, taking the presidency and vice presidency by a margin of 162 electoral votes to 14.

1805

March

Jefferson is inaugurated for a second term; Clinton for his first.

1806

January

When Secretary of State James Madison reports to Congress on the British practice of impressment—stopping U.S. merchant ships and forcibly recruiting sailors—he draws attention to what has been and will continue to be a long-term source of conflict between the two nations. The struggle over impressment and the right of free passage at sea will continue for several years and eventually become a major reason for the war of 1812.

1807

February

Former Vice President Aaron Burr is arrested in Alabama and charged with a conspiracy to attack Spanish territory in the West in order to form an independent nation. His murky motives seem nefarious, and he is eventually indicted in Virginia on a federal charge of treason. He is acquitted in September at a trial presided over by U.S. Chief Justice John Marshall, and he escapes prosecution on the old charges of murdering Hamilton by sailing to Europe.

December

At the request of President Jefferson, Congress passes the Embargo Act, which makes it illegal for Americans to trade with foreign nations or to sail ships to foreign ports. Jefferson hopes thereby to avoid further conflict over freedom of the seas and impressment and at the same time to stimulate regional U.S. manufacturing. The result, however, is an economic disaster for the United States. Mercantile states of the Northeast are particularly hard hit.

1808

January

The African slave trade is finally banned by law. The Constitution had contained a provision that stalled ending the trade until this year. Slavery itself, of course, remains legal in all the southern states; most northern states eliminated it during or soon after the Revolution.

December

A complex political situation develops over the question of who will succeed Jefferson as president. The Democratic–Republican congressional caucus has nominated James Madison (with Jefferson's blessing) for president and renominated Vice President George Clinton. However, a separate faction opposes the southern leadership of the party, and it nominates Clinton for president, making him simultaneously the running mate of Madison and one of his chief opponents. The Federalists again put up Charles Cotesworth Pinckney and Rufus King. Madison easily wins the presidency, although Clinton gets a few electoral votes for the top office. By a margin of 113 to 47, Clinton is elected as vice president for a second term, once again beating King.

1810–1811

In a series of confusing events, the British and French pass conflicting and devious regulations about trade and seizures of American ships. The United States responds with aggressive stances against first one and then the other.

Deceived by the French, the U.S. government finally focuses on a policy of nonintercourse with the British, which brings on increased conflict and confrontation.

1811

November
A new generation of politicians, known as War Hawks, takes over control of Congress and begins to press for war against Great Britain. John C. Calhoun of South Carolina and Henry Clay of Kentucky are leaders of the war faction.

1812

April
Vice President George Clinton dies in Washington, D.C.

May
Democratic–Republican congressmen from the southern states caucus and renominate Madison for president and choose John Langdon for vice president, but Langdon refuses and the vice-presidential nomination then goes to Elbridge Gerry. Dissident, antiwar Democratic-Republicans in the North nominate DeWitt Clinton for president with the backing of the waning Federalists. The Federalists put up Jared Ingersoll for vice president.

June
The United States declares war on Great Britain. Ironically, the British government rescinds its aggressive policy on the high seas, which is the pretext for the American declaration of war, before Congress acts, but the news fails to reach the United States in time. Western and southern states enthusiastically support the war, but almost all of New England is bitterly opposed. The country has a difficult time recruiting an army (many state militia units refuse to fight outside their state boundaries) and leadership is

for the French most part dismal. Even though the British are distracted by their prolonged war against Napoleon, they nonetheless succeed in almost all the land campaigns against the Americans. Only at sea do U.S. forces enjoy repeated victories, including the destruction of a British frigate in August by the USS *Constitution* ("Old Ironsides").

December
Madison wins a second term as president by defeating DeWitt Clinton. Gerry wins the vice presidency, actually garnering more electoral votes than Madison due to the split in the Democratic–Republican Party over the war.

1813

April
After a series of defeats, the U.S. land forces finally have some success and momentarily capture the city of York in Canada (now Toronto). They burn the government buildings and then retreat.

September
British victories during the summer are to a degree negated by Commodore Oliver Hazard Perry's naval victory on Lake Erie. He sends the message: "We have met the enemy and they are ours." Three weeks later, General William Henry Harrison defeats the British and their Indian allies at the Battle of the Thames.

1814

August
With resources freed by the temporary defeat of Napoleon, the British launch a reinvigorated campaign to win the war in America. They invade Maryland and defeat the American army at Bladesburg. President Madison and the U.S. government flee Washington as the British advance. Temporarily taking control of the city, the British burn the Capitol and White House,

although neither are destroyed. The British withdraw after a few days, and Madison returns to Washington.

September
The British attack Baltimore from the sea, but are beaten back after bombarding Fort McHenry with rockets and artillery, inspiring "The Star Spangled Banner."

November
Vice President Elbridge Gerry dies in Washington, D.C., becoming the second consecutive vice president to die in office.

December
American and British peace commissioners in Europe sign a treaty ending the war, but news of the peace travels slowly.

1815

January
Unaware that the war is officially over, a British army attacks American forces outside New Orleans. The Americans inflict a terrible defeat on the British, killing or wounding more than 2,000, while suffering only eight dead themselves. U.S. general Andrew Jackson emerges as the nation's greatest military hero, even though the battle was pointless.

1816

March
After considerable debate, Congress charters the second Bank of the United States as a quasi-public, quasi-private financial institution to help regulate the national currency and to some degree allow control of aspects of the economy. It is a controversial creation, seen by some in American society as a satanic device used by the rich class to keep the common man down. Others see the bank as necessary for financial order, although it usually favors the property-holding portions of society. The bank will frequently be at the center of political controversy over the next twenty years.

March
The Democratic-Republicans nominate Secretary of State James Monroe for president through the congressional caucus system. Daniel Tompkins of New York, a strong wartime governor, is selected as his running mate. The Federalists, their days in American politics nearly at an end, nominate old reliable Rufus King for president and John Howard for vice president.

December
Monroe and Tompkins win with 183 electoral votes.

1819

January
The nation is hit with a severe economic crash (known in the nineteenth century as a panic) when Congress passes a law restricting credit. Many in the West and South have gone into debt to buy land, and the panic hits them hard. By year's end, many Americans have lost everything. This is only the first in what proves to be a recurring series of financial panics.

1820

February–March
As the United States expands westward, the central divisive question of slavery pushes itself forward onto the national agenda. The slave South wants to take slavery into the new territories; the North wants the new regions to be free. At stake is the essence of what the United States will become and adherents on each side will find it increasingly difficult to compromise. In 1820, however, when the admission of Maine into the Union as a free state is at issue, opponents manage to work out a trade-off by admitting Missouri as a slave state, thus maintaining

the national political balance for the time being. The law also bans slavery north of latitude 36 degrees 30 minutes (the Missouri border).

December
Monroe and Tompkins run for reelection virtually unopposed because the Federalists opposition has collapsed and no new party has formed to take its place. Monroe wins with 231 electoral votes to just 1 for Massachusetts's John Quincy Adams (son of former president John Adams).

1822

May
Denmark Vesey, a free black man, plots an uprising of black slaves in South Carolina, but the plan is foiled before it gets off the ground. Vesey and thirty-four others are executed. Revelation of the plan frightens white slaveholders who begin to build an even more repressive legal system to lock blacks into slavery. More uprisings, many involving considerable bloodshed, continue over the next four decades, and southern white response is increasingly harsh and preemptory.

July
War hero Andrew Jackson is nominated for the presidency in 1824 by his home state legislature in Tennessee. The old system of nomination by caucus has collapsed with the demise of the party system. Several months later, the Kentucky legislature nominates Henry Clay.

1824

February
The absence of well-organized political parties results in a chaotic presidential nomination process. Andrew Jackson and Henry Clay have been nominated two years previous. In February, a small minority of the Democratic-Republicans in Congress hold a rump caucus and nominate Secretary of the Treasury William Crawford. The next day, John Quincy Adams is nominated

by a political meeting in Boston. John C. Calhoun also has presidential ambitions, but he stands aside and agrees to accept the vice presidency no matter who is elected president.

December
As might have been predicted with the nation so split among candidates, the election turns sour. Jackson has a clear plurality in the popular vote, but he has only ninety-nine electoral votes, not enough to reach the constitutionally required majority. Adams has eighty-four; Crawford forty-one; and Clay thirty-seven. Calhoun, however, receives 182 electoral votes for vice president and is elected, albeit without a president. The contest must go to the House of Representatives for resolution.

1825

February
The House votes for president, and John Quincy Adams wins even though he was significantly outpolled by Jackson in the popular vote. When Henry Clay is named as Adams's secretary of state, the Jackson faction howls that there was a "corrupt bargain" to deprive Jackson of the prize. New parties are formed in the wake of the dispute: Jackson's followers become the precursors of modern-day Democrats, and Clay's adherents join with other political factions to form first the National Republicans and then the Whig Party.

March
John Quincy Adams and John C. Calhoun are inaugurated. Adams and his father are the only father-son combination to win the presidency.

1826

July 4
John Adams and Thomas Jefferson die within hours of each other on the fiftieth anniversary of the Declaration of Independence.

1828

May

An unusually high tariff (import tax) is passed by Congress. The tariff, along with the national bank and the federal land sales office, is one of the principal factors in the national economy (there is no central financial system and no income tax at this time), so a high tariff is a matter for great political controversy. This 1828 "Tariff of Abominations" and its successors will spark trouble for years to come.

December

John C. Calhoun, although he is the incumbent vice president under President John Quincy Adams, is elected for a second term as the running mate of Andrew Jackson. Adams and his running mate, Richard Rush, are soundly defeated. Adams will later return to Washington as a long-serving representative from Massachusetts.

1829

March

Andrew Jackson's inauguration is capped by a boisterous reception at the White House, symbolizing the transition of the American political system from the more sedate era of the Early Republic to a period dominated by the political power of the "common man."

1830

September

Henry Clay receives an early nomination for the presidency from a convention of a faction of the National Republicans.

1831

April

What is known as the Peggy Eaton Affair comes to a head in Washington with the resignation of all but one of Jackson's cabinet members. Secretary of War John Eaton's wife, Peggy, had been deemed to be low in social standing and deficient in morals (she was a former barmaid) by the wives of most of the other cabinet members, and they refused to receive her socially. Jackson was outraged, in part because of the experience of his own late wife, Rachel, who had suffered public scorn because of revelations of a defective divorce from her first husband. Only Martin Van Buren among Jackson's cabinet supports the president and Mrs. Eaton. What may seem a trifling matter becomes a serious political split between Jackson and his cabinet. Jackson is an extremely pugnacious man who thrives on confrontation and conflict, and he pushes the feud to the end. Vice President Calhoun's sharp differences with the president come to the surface during this episode.

1831

August

Vice President John C. Calhoun is nominated for president in next year's election by a public meeting in New York City.

September

The Anti-Mason Party, a third-party splinter group founded on the basis of a widespread belief in a conspiracy by the Masons, holds a convention and drafts the first party platform. The Anti-Masons eventually merge with other factions to help form the Whig Party.

1832

May

The Democratic Party, which has evolved from the original Democratic-Republicans of Thomas Jefferson and James Madison, holds its first convention. The delegates nominate Andrew Jackson as their presidential candidate and Martin Van Buren of New York for vice president. The convention method of nomination will dominate until the late twentieth century.

July

President Jackson vetoes a bill to recharter the National Bank, which he sees as a corrupt enemy of the people. This sets off a fierce political debate, but the Senate fails to override the veto. The bank is dead and with it all mechanisms to control the currency and the national economy. Jackson further demolishes the national economy the following year when he withdraws federal deposits from the national bank and distributes them to "pet" (favorite) private banks around the country.

November

South Carolina precipitates a national crisis by passing a law that nullifies the high import tariffs of 1828 and 1832, which have hurt the agricultural South. The state prepares troops and declares it will leave the Union if opposed by the federal government. Vice President Calhoun is the intellectual force behind the nullification movement.

December

Jackson and Van Buren win easily over Clay and John Sergeant. A few days later, Vice President Calhoun resigns to take up a seat as senator from South Carolina. The nullification controversy heats up with warnings from Jackson that no state can secede.

1833

January–February

After both sides bluster and rattle sabers, the controversy over nullification and the national tariff is settled with a compromise that lowers the tariff and saves face all around.

December

The growing antislavery and abolitionist movements gain momentum with the organization of the American Anti-Slavery Society in Phila-

delphia. During the next thirty years, the abolitionist forces, centered in the northern states, come to exert increasing social, cultural, and political pressure on the slaveholding South. The activities of the abolitionists will do much to bring about the Civil War.

1834

April

A growing coalition of political interests is christened the Whig Party (named after a faction of the British Parliament) by Henry Clay, one of its leaders. The party is made up of anti-Jackson factions of the old National Republican and the Democratic parties. They are joined by pro-states' rights supporters of nullification and slavery and by the Anti-Masons. Until its demise in the political convulsions of the 1850s, the Whig Party is a major factor in U.S. political life, managing to elect two presidents (both of whom die in office) and many members of Congress.

1835

January

The Whig Party has adopted a strategy of disruption that encourage states and regions to nominate several people for the presidency, hoping to throw the election into the House of Representatives. Daniel Webster is nominated in January by a meeting in Massachusetts and later by other northeastern states. The month before, Hugh L. White of Tennessee has been nominated by a small congressional caucus and then by several southern state legislatures. John L. McLean is nominated by the legislature in Ohio, but declines. William Henry Harrison, a war hero from Ohio, is nominated by several state legislatures. The vice-presidential situation is also clouded and complex. There are two major Whig nominations: Frances Granger and John Tyler. Philip Barbour is nominated in Georgia but declines. The electoral possibilities seem endless.

May

The national Democratic convention nominates Vice President Martin Van Buren for president and Kentuckian Richard Johnson for vice president.

October

A group of dissident Democrats, known as Loco Focos, meets in New York City and adopts an anti-Jackson platform, further confusing the national political scene.

1836

March–April

Open warfare breaks out in the Mexican province of Texas, which is largely populated by slaveholding former U.S. citizens. A Mexican army under President Santa Anna captures and kills garrisons at the Alamo and Goliad and seems poised to defeat the ragtag Texas army. However, on April 21, Texas commander Sam Houston surprises the Mexicans at San Jacinto and achieves complete victory, capturing Santa Anna and killing hundreds of Mexican soldiers. Texans and many in the United States assume that the United States will recognize and eventually absorb the new independent Republic of Texas, but the matter proves over the coming decade to be controversial and divisive, in large part because of the issue of slavery.

December

The Whig strategy is foiled when Martin Van Buren wins 170 electoral votes, 97 more than his closest Whig rival and enough to make president. He is the last sitting vice president to succeed to the White House until George Bush does it 152 years later. Van Buren's running mate, Richard Johnson, is not so lucky. Enough electoral votes are siphoned off by the Whig vice-presidential candidates so that Johnson just fails to get the required majority. For the first and only time, selection of the vice president goes to the House of Representatives.

1837

February

The House of Representatives votes 33–16 to make Richard Johnson vice president.

May

Another financial panic hits the country, probably as the result of Jackson's policies, especially his move late in his last term to tighten credit by requiring payment for land sales in hard currency. Van Buren is blamed, however.

1839

November

Abolitionists form the Liberty Party and nominate James B. Birney for president and Thomas Earle for vice president.

December

The Whig Party nominates William Henry Harrison, a military hero of the War of 1812, for president and John Tyler, a Virginia slaveholder, for vice president.

1840

May

Meeting in convention, the Democrats renominate Martin Van Buren for president, but there is enough opposition to Richard Johnson to stifle a formal renomination by the convention, which votes to leave the vice-presidential candidacy up to the states. No serious rivals to Johnson emerge, however, after James K. Polk drops out.

December

The Whig ticket of Harrison and Tyler sweeps to victory, and the Whigs capture a majority in Congress. The new party should be able to control national policies for several years to come.

1841

April

Only a month after taking office, President Harrison dies of pneumonia, making John Tyler the first vice president to succeed to the presidency. For a while, Tyler's status is unclear—some in Washington want to declare him merely acting president—but he demands and receives full status as the chief executive. To the dismay of the Whigs, Tyler proves to have little in common with the rest of the party, and he usually backs measures supported by the Democrats. Within a short while, Tyler lacks all support of his own party.

1844

May

The Whigs hold a national convention and nominate Henry Clay for president and Theodore Frelinghuysen for vice president. Clay has waffled on the major issue of annexing Texas, so the party ignores the question when drafting a platform.

The Democrats have a fierce convention struggle. Van Buren cannot gain enough votes for the nomination, despite an early lead, and a relative longshot, James K. Polk, eventually wins. His running mate is George M. Dallas of Pennsylvania. The Democratic platform stresses annexing Texas at all costs and takes an aggressive stance toward Great Britain on the question of the Oregon border.

Dissident Democrats simultaneously nominate incumbent President John Tyler, who was originally elected to the vice presidency as a Whig, but he withdraws from the campaign three months later.

December

Polk and Dallas win the election. Clay's strength has been drained to some degree in the North by the strong showing of James G. Birney the anti-slavery Liberty Party candidate.

1845

February–December

Through a series of complicated legal and political maneuvers, Texas becomes a state. President James K. Polk has pushed hard for annexation, which becomes a reality after some constitutional legerdemain by Congress and a vote for annexation by a convention in Texas. Annexation is certain to mean war with Mexico.

1846

May

Provocations on each side lead to a violent clash along the Mexican border. At President Polk's urging, Congress declares war on Mexico and authorizes the raising of an army. The war is bitterly opposed by many in the northern and western free states but strongly supported by southerners. U.S. troops invade Mexico almost immediately, opening what will be a bloody contest.

June

Wishing to concentrate on matters with Mexico, Polk agrees to a treaty with Great Britain over the Oregon border question. Americans in California declare a revolt against Mexico and proclaim the Republic of California, although they agree to transfer power to a U.S. military officer a few weeks later.

August

When passing an appropriation to pay for land anticipated to come to the United States from Mexico after the war, Congress considers but eventually rejects the Wilmot Proviso that would assure that all territories acquired must exclude slavery. U.S. forces take Los Angeles in California and Santa Fe in New Mexico, consolidating control over the former Mexican provinces, although they must put down a revolt later in summer by Mexican residents in Southern California.

September

The U.S. army of invasion under General Zachary Taylor takes Monterrey. By the end of the year, he holds a large area in northern Mexico.

1847

February

General Taylor wins a major victory at Buena Vista against large odds.

March

General Winfield Scott takes Veracruz after an amphibious assault.

April

General Scott wins at Cerro Gordo and two other smaller battles.

August

Initial peace negotiations between the United States and Mexico fail.

September

The antiimmigrant American Party (called the Know Nothings) organizes and nominates General Zachary Taylor for president and Henry Dearborn of Massachusetts for vice president.

September

After a fierce battle at Chapultepec, General Scott captures Mexico City, effectively bringing the war to a close.

1848

March

By the Treaty of Guadalupe Hidalgo, the United States acquires a vast region in the West and Southwest from Mexico, including most of the modern-day states of New Mexico, Arizona, California, Utah, and Nevada.

May

The Democratic convention nominates Lewis Cass of Michigan for president (Polk declines to run for a second term) and William 0. Butler of Kentucky for vice president.

June

The Whigs nominate war hero Zachary Taylor, with New York's Millard Fillmore as his running mate. The fragmentation of national politics that comes to characterize the next dozen years is prefigured this year by nominations from several splinter groups, none of which are yet serious contenders, however.

July

The first national convention supporting women's rights meets at Seneca Falls, New York. Although not successful at the national level for several generations to come, the women's suffrage movement exerts a powerful influence on American life and politics from this time on.

August

Antislavery supporters form the Free Soil Party and nominate former President Martin Van Buren for president and Charles Francis Adams of Massachusetts for vice president.

December

Whig candidates Zachary Taylor and Millard Fillmore win the election when the Free Soilers drain support for the Democratic ticket.

1849

February

News of the discovery of gold in the northern California hills ignites a huge rush of fortune seekers. Tens of thousands of "Forty-Niners" set out by sea and overland for the goldfields. While some miners strike it rich, most fail and eventually leave broke.

1850

January–September

Henry Clay leads a fight for a political compromise that will defuse the issue of extending slavery into the new territories taken from Mexico. After prolonged negotiations, debate, and maneuvering, Congress finally passes a series of measures that are known as the Compromise of 1850 and include admitting California as a free state, organizing the territories of New Mexico and Utah, allowing Texas to remain a slave state, abolishing slavery in the District of Columbia, and putting in place a strong new Fugitive Slave Act.

July

President Zachary Taylor dies in office and Millard Fillmore becomes president.

1851

February

Reflecting resistance to the Fugitive Slave law in northern states, citizens of Boston rescue an escaped slave from jail. In several other places, antislave mobs frustrate U.S. marshals and southern slave hunters.

1852

March

Harriet Beecher Stowe publishes *Uncle Tom's Cabin*, which becomes immensely popular and helps to galvanize northern public opinion against slavery.

June

The Democratic national convention nominates Franklin Pierce of New Hampshire for president and William Rufus King of Alabama for vice president. The party backs the Compromise of 1850.

August

The Free Soil Party nominates John P. Hale of New Hampshire for president and George Julian of Indiana for vice president. The party platform condemns the Compromise of 1850.

November

The Democratic state wins in a landslide, 254 electoral votes for Pierce to Winfield Scott's 42. The Free Soil candidates fare poorly in the popular vote.

1853

March

Franklin Pierce is inaugurated in Washington, D.C. Vice President William King is inaugurated (by special dispensation of Congress) in Cuba, where he has gone to seek better health.

April

Vice President King dies at his home in Alabama, never having taken up his duties.

December

The United States signs a treaty with Mexico for the purchase of a small parcel of land along the southern Arizona and New Mexican borders, which becomes known as the Gadsden Purchase.

1854

January

Hope for a peaceful solution to the question of slavery in the West evaporates when Illinois Senator Stephen Douglas introduces the Kansas-Nebraska Act, which would organize these two territories as a preliminary to statehood and would allow territorial residents to vote on whether to be slave or free (a concept known as "popular sovereignty"). Because both territories would be above the 36 degrees 30 minute limit on slavery established by the Missouri Compromise in 1820, the act is destined to reopen the political conflict between free and slave states, North and South.

February
Antislave opponents of the Kansas-Nebraska bill form the Republican Party at a meeting in Wisconsin. The new party grows rapidly and brings under its banner a variety of antislavery factions, including the Free Soilers, northern Democrats, and antislavery Whigs.

1855–1858

Factions in Kansas Territory fight over adopting a constitution and applying for statehood as a free or a slave state. The conflicts are complex and increasingly violent. The region will come to be known as Bleeding Kansas and is seen as the cockpit of the great struggle for the soul of the nation. By the end of 1856, there is open warfare in Kansas with armed attacks by proslavery forces on the antislavery capital at Lawrence and murderous retaliation by antislavery advocates such as John Brown.

Both sides draft their own constitutions and ask for statehood. The situation is so volatile that neither side wins. Kansas remains a territory until after the outbreak of the Civil War.

1856

February
The Know-Nothing Party nominates former president Millard Fillmore.

June
The Democrats meet in a stormy convention and nominate James Buchanan of Pennsylvania for president. Buchanan has been out of the country, and his views on slavery have not been widely reported. John C. Breckinridge is selected as the vice presidential candidate. The

party hopes to avoid a split over slavery and the Kansas-Nebraska question.

Later in the month, the new Republican Party meets in its first national convention and nominates John C. Frémont of California and William L. Dayton of New Jersey.

December
Buchanan and Breckinridge win the national election in a race that is divided clearly along slave versus free lines. The Democrats have managed to eke out enough votes for an electoral college win, but the regional split seems likely to grow worse and spell trouble for the older party, especially in face of growing Republican strength. The Whig Party, strong enough to elect two presidents during the 1840s, is virtually dead.

1857

March
The Missouri Compromise is rendered unconstitutional by the decision of the U.S. Supreme Court in the *Dred Scott* case, in which a black slave had sued for his freedom after his owner had taken him into free territory in Illinois. The effect is to say that the federal government has no power to bar slavery from northern or western states and territories. The ruling also declares slaves ineligible to be citizens.

August
Businesses start to fail with the onset of another of the nation's periodic financial panics.

1859

October
Fanatical Kansas abolitionist John Brown and a small group of followers attempt to seize the federal arsenal at Harper's Ferry, Virginia, hoping to set off a massive slave insurrection. Brown is captured by federal troops (led by Virginia

colonel Robert E. Lee) and hanged for treason in early December. The incident becomes a focal point for conflict over slavery.

1860

April
The final split of the nation is presaged by presidential politics. The Democratic Party holds a convention but is unable to select a candidate after southern delegates walk out.

May
Fragmentation continues with the formation of the Constitution Party and the nomination of John Bell of Tennessee and Edward Everett of Massachusetts.

The most significant political development comes in Chicago, where the Republican Party nominates Illinois lawyer and former Congressman Abraham Lincoln, with Hannibal Hamlin of Maine as his running mate. The southern slave states, especially the so-called fire-eaters such as South Carolina, have made it clear they will not remain in the Union if Lincoln is elected.

June
A second Democratic convention nominates Stephen Douglas for president, but only because all but his supporters have left the party. Southern Democrats meet separately and nominate their own candidate, Vice President John C. Breckinridge with Joseph Lane of Oregon as his running mate. The election will turn solely on the issue of slavery and which section shall dominate the federal government. The Democrats are badly divided along sectional lines and the way is clear for a Republican victory, although in general probably only a minority of voters support the party.

November
Lincoln and Hamlin win with a majority of electoral college votes but a minority in the popular vote.

December
A convention in South Carolina votes to secede from the Union. Despite some attempts to find a new compromise, it is clear that with Lincoln in the White House, the nation will break apart.

1861

January
More Southern slave states vote for secession. Eventually eleven states—all in the slave South—will withdraw from the Union to form the Confederacy.

March
At his inauguration, Lincoln calls for unity, but the Confederacy has already come into being with Jefferson Davis of Mississippi as its president.

April
Warfare begins as Confederate artillery batteries in Charleston, South Carolina, fire on federal troops at Fort Sumter in the harbor. President Lincoln calls for volunteers to put down the rebellion of the Confederate states.

July
The first great battle of the Civil War is fought near Manassas Virginia, not far from Washington. The larger Union army is routed by the better-led and tougher Confederate troops, although the Southerners fail to follow up their victory with a march on the national capital. The first years of the war reflect the basic confrontation established early in the conflict: the Union will have huge numbers of well-equipped and well-trained soldiers but few good generals, including the blustering but timid commander George McClellan; the Confederacy will have limited resources in manpower (slaves are not allowed to fight) and matériel but discover a corps of superb generals, headed by Robert E. Lee, which allows them to win battle after battle and stave off overall defeat for years.

1862

Although eventually winning major victories in the West, the Union forces in the East have little success and retreat ignominiously from a failed attempt to invade Virginia from the coastline. Lee assumes command of the Army of Northern Virginia and decides on an invasion of Maryland, after defeating a Union Army in a second battle at Manassas. In September, Lee's troops meet McClellan's at the Battle of Antietam. The result is a stalemate after the bloodiest single day of combat in American history. Lee is forced to retreat, but McClellan fails to follow up.

1863

With the important but mostly symbolic declaration of the Emancipation Proclamation in January, Lincoln isolates the Confederacy from potential British support and explicitly makes slavery one of the major issues of the war. More costly battles continue, both in the West and the East. The war approaches a kind of climax in midyear. Union forces under General Ulysses S. Grant take Vicksburg, Mississippi, and gain control of the great river. Lee attempts another invasion of the north and meets a huge Union army near Gettysburg, Pennsylvania, where a horrendous three-day battle ends with the Confederate Army broken on federal defensive positions. Lee is forced to retreat south, but again the Union generals fail to pursue and allow him to regroup. There is no longer any possibility that the South can win the war in the field, but Lee can prolong the bloody conflict for many months.

1864

The Union forces begin a costly but inevitable advance across the South from Tennessee, moving toward Atlanta, which falls in September.

Grant is given overall command by Lincoln and begins to move toward the Confederate capital at Richmond, Virginia. The eastern theater turns into a horrible meatgrinder, with battle after battle resulting in huge casualty lists. After reaching the outskirts of Richmond, the Union army sets up a trench-warfare siege. At the end of the year, Union general William T. Sherman leads his army from Atlanta on a destructive march to the seacoast cities of Savannah and Charleston.

June
The Republican Party (calling itself the National Union Party) renominates Abraham Lincoln for president but discards Vice President Hamlin in favor of Tennessee's Andrew Johnson, a former Democrat.

August
The Democrats nominate General George McClellan for president and George Pendleton of Ohio for vice president.

November
Lincoln and Johnson win a narrow popular victory over the Democrats, with the soldier vote the likely crucial factor.

1865

March
Lincoln delivers a conciliatory speech at his second inauguration in Washington. He expresses the desire to bind the nation's wounds "with malice toward none and charity for all."

April
Union troops occupy Richmond. Lee surrenders his army to Grant at Appomattox Court House, Virginia. The war is essentially over. President Lincoln is shot in the head by prosouthern sympathizer John Wilkes Booth while attending a play in Washington. He dies the next day, and Andrew Johnson becomes president.

December

The thirteenth Amendment, abolishing slavery and involuntary servitude, is ratified.

1865–1876

The death of President Lincoln marks the beginning of a long struggle to reconstruct the nation, a struggle that centers on the issues of how to extend political, social, and economic rights to black former slaves and how to reincorporate the states of the Confederacy into the Union. The struggle is sharp, played out against a background of corrupt and incompetent leadership and in the end reaches no satisfactory conclusions. President Andrew Johnson begins immediately to implement his vision of accepting the southern states back into national life, but he is thwarted by powerful anti-southern figures in Congress. He is impeached and nearly convicted. The strident reconstructionists pass several constitutional amendments and laws that extend citizenship and voting and economic rights to former slaves, and they punish the former Confederate states with military occupation and withheld sovereignty. Eventually, however, the power of the reconstructionists wanes, and more cynical men take charge. By 1876, Reconstruction is dead and the South has managed to resubjugate the region's black population and to regain its political potency.

1866

April

Congress passes a civil rights bill over President Johnson's veto. The law grants citizenship and full civil rights to former slaves.

1867

March

Congress passes, over the president's veto, a reconstruction act that sets up military governments in the southern states and requires ratification of the proposed fourteenth Amendment, which protects blacks' rights and punishes former Confederates, before a state can be readmitted to the Union. Congress also passes the Tenure in Office Act that weakens the president and will be used against Johnson.

In the same month, Secretary of State William Seward concludes a treaty with Russia for the purchase of Alaska for $7.2 million.

1868

February

Congress impeaches President Andrew Johnson on the formal grounds that he has violated the Tenure in Office Act by his attempts to fire his secretary of war. In fact, the struggle is over reconstruction policies and political control of the nation.

March

Johnson is tried on impeachment charges in the Senate and is effectively acquitted by one vote in a highly dramatic scene.

May

The Republicans nominate war hero Ulysses S. Grant for president with Schuyler Colfax of Indiana as his running mate.

July

The Democrats nominate New York's Horatio Seymour and Francis P. Blair of Missouri.

Later in the month, the Fourteenth Amendment is formally ratified.

November

Republicans Grant and Colfax win by a large margin in the electoral college, although the popular vote is relatively close and turns on the votes of former slaves.

1869

May
Crews working from different directions meet in Utah and complete the first transcontinental rail line.

1870

March
The Fifteenth Amendment to the Constitution is ratified. It says a citizen's right to vote may not be abridged by the states on account of race, color, or previous servitude. However, the exclusion of women voters continues.

1872

May
A group of splinter Liberal Republicans nominate Horace Greeley of New York and Gratz Brown of Missouri as a rival ticket to President Grant. Two months later, the Democrats also nominate the Greeley–Brown ticket.

June
The regular Republican convention renominates Grant for president but discards Vice President Schuyler Colfax, who has been touched by the many scandals of the Grant administration, in favor of Henry Wilson of Massachusetts.

September
The worst of the Grant-era scandals becomes public when it is revealed that several influential members of congress have set up a phony construction company, called the Crédit Mobilier, in order to grab millions of dollars of public money from railroad-building contracts.

November
Despite the scandals, Grant and Wilson are elected by 286 electoral votes to 66.

1873

September
A new financial panic hits the country with massive numbers of business failures. The New York Stock Exchange closes its doors temporarily.

1876

June
The Republicans nominate Rutherford B. Hayes of Ohio for president and William Wheeler of New York as his running mate.

Flamboyant General George Armstrong Custer and 260 men and officers of his 7th Cavalry are killed in a battle with a large number of Sioux and Cheyenne warriors at the Little Big Horn River. Public reaction prompts a massive campaign against the remaining free Indians of the West.

The Democrats nominate Samuel Tilden of New York for president and Thomas Hendricks of Indiana for vice president.

November
Disputed and possibly fraudulent voting in some of the former Confederate states clouds the election. Tilden has won majority of the popular vote, but contested returns throw the election into the House of Representatives.

1877

January
The House selects a special commission to settle the disputed presidential election. Originally, the commission was to have been divided evenly between Democrats and Republicans with the deciding vote held by an independent, but the balance is upset when the independent is appointed to a Senate seat and the Republicans gain control. A deal is finally struck between Republicans and white southern Dem-

ocrats: Hayes and Wheeler are put in office in return for final withdrawal of federal troops from the South and a free hand for whites to subjugate blacks.

1877

July
A series of nationwide strikes opens what becomes a prolonged struggle between labor and business owners.

1878

February
The Greenback Party, which favors paper money and free silver, joins with members of the Labor Party. The coalition will elect more than a dozen members to Congress.

Congress passes the Bland-Allison Act that calls for limited silver coinage.

1880

June
The Republicans nominate James A. Garfield of Ohio for president, defeating a movement to nominate Grant for a third term. New Yorker Chester A. Arthur is Garfield's running mate. The party has split into factions called Stalwarts (supporters of Grant) and Half-Breeds (led by James G. Blaine). Garfield is the Half-Breed candidate and Arthur is a Stalwart.

The Greenback-Labor Party nominates James B. Weaver and B.J. Chambers.

The Democrats nominate Pennsylvania Civil War general Winfield Scott Hancock and Indiana's William H. English.

November
Republicans Garfield and Arthur win 214 electoral votes to 155.

1881

July
President James A. Garfield is shot at a train station in Washington, D.C. The assailant is a deranged office seeker inflamed by the political rhetoric of the Stalwart and the Half-Breed conflicts.

September
Garfield dies after painful suffering, and Chester A. Arthur becomes president.

1883

January
Congress passes the landmark Pendleton civil service reform act. Somewhat surprisingly, President Arthur, who has been thought of as the exemplar of the political spoils system, supports the reform movement.

1884

June
The mainline Republicans again nominate James G. Blaine for president, pairing him this time with John Logan of Illinois.

The dissident Liberal Republicans vote to support the Democratic candidate, who has not yet been selected. These splinter Republicans, known as Mugwumps (supposedly an Indian term for "big chief"), despise Blaine.

July
The Democratic Party nominates New York Governor Grover Cleveland and Indiana's Thomas Hendricks. The Republican Mugwumps give their support.

November
Cleveland and Hendricks narrowly defeat the Republicans after a nasty campaign marked by scurrilous personal attacks.

1885

November

Vice President Thomas Hendricks, who has been in poor health for months, dies in Indianapolis.

1886

January

Congress passes a Presidential Succession Act that defines the succession of cabinet members to the presidency if both executives and heads of Congress die or are disabled.

May

A labor meeting in Chicago's Haymarket Square is disrupted by a bomb that kills several police. Spurred by widespread fear of political terrorism, authorities arrest, convict, and hang several accused anarchists.

1887

February

A new law governs contested electrons states will now determine the validity of their own vote totals. Congress will become involved only in extreme cases.

In the same month, the Interstate Commerce Act becomes law. It has far-reaching effects in allowing the federal government to regulate business in the public interest.

1888

June

The Democratic national convention renominates President Grover Cleveland and names Allen Thurmand of Ohio as his running mate.

The Republicans nominate Benjamin Harrison of Indiana and Levi P. Morton of New York.

November

In another of the weird presidential elections that plague the second half of the nineteenth century, Harrison and Morton are elected, although Cleveland and Thurmand receive 5,000 more popular votes nationwide. The Republicans have won in key electoral states and win easily in the electoral college, 233 to 168.

1890

July

The Sherman Antitrust Act is passed and signed. It is intended to limit the size and power of big corporations but is frequently used against labor unions in coming years. Later in the month, Congress passes the Sherman Silver Purchase Act, increasing the coinage of silver.

1891

May

The Populist Party is founded, basing its strength on western and southern farmers and laborers. The party uses inflammatory rhetoric to urge a variety of "radical" measures such as government ownership of the railroads and the eight-hour day.

1892

June

Amid increased national agitation between labor and business, the Republicans again nominate President Benjamin Harrison. Vice President Levi P. Morton is replaced on the ticket by New York's Whitlaw Reid.

The Democrats nominate former President Grover Cleveland with Illinois's Adlai Stevenson as his running mate.

July

The Populists nominate old war horse James B. Weaver for president and James Field of Virginia for vice president.

November

Cleveland and Stevenson win the election. Cleveland becomes the only president to serve two nonconsecutive terms.

1893

February–June

A financial crisis grows rapidly after the failure of a major railroad. The nation's gold reserves have been drained due to the silver purchase policy, and the economy collapses in the worst panic of the century. The dislocations are long lasting, even after revocation of the Sherman Silver Purchase Act.

July

President Grover Cleveland has secret surgery for cancer of the mouth aboard a yacht off Long Island, New York. Vice President Stevenson is not informed of Cleveland's illness or operation, although the hugely corpulent president goes under a dangerous general anesthetic. The president recovers and resumes his duties.

1894

April

Hundreds of protestors, known as Coxey's Army after leader Jacob Coxey, march on Washington, D.C., to agitate against unemployment caused by the financial depression.

May

Workers for the Pullman rail-car company in Illinois go out on strike. The confrontation with ownership develops into a violent struggle involving the federal and state governments and the U.S. Army. Several people are killed and much properties damaged before the strike is called off.

1896

May

The U.S. Supreme Court upholds the "separate but equal" doctrine that allows public facilities and schools to be segregated on racial lines.

June

The Republican national convention nominates William McKinley of Ohio for president and Garret Hobart of New Jersey for vice president.

July

There is no clear choice for the presidential nomination at the Democratic convention until Williams Jennings Bryan captures the delegates with his "cross of gold" speech in which he extols the free coinage of silver. His running mate is Arthur Sewell of Maine.

September

Breakaway Democrats who favor the gold standard instead of free silver meet in a separate convention and nominate John Palmer of Illinois and Simon Buckner of Kentucky.

November

McKinley and Hobart win easily.

1897

June

The United States signs a treaty that annexes the territory of the Hawaiian Islands (although the official act is delayed for nearly a year). The islands have been in the grip of powerful U.S. planters for some time.

1898

February

After the U.S. battleship *Maine* blows up in Havana harbor, agitation increases for a war with Spain over Cuba.

April

After months of posturing, Spain and the United States declare war on each other. The struggle during the coming weeks will be one sided, although the U.S. Army is ill prepared and suffers badly from poor organization and disease during its invasion of Cuba. The Navy, on the other hand, performs well against a weak Spanish fleet in the Philippines. The United States wins before the summer is out, creating an instant overseas empire.

May

The U.S. Asiatic Fleet under Admiral George Dewey destroys the Spanish fleet at the battle of Manila Bay.

June

U.S. Marines land at Guantanamo Bay, Cuba, followed by a large army invasion force near Santiago.

July

U.S. troops suffer heavy casualties in taking strategic hills surrounding Santiago. Theodore Roosevelt achieves lasting heroic fame for leading a prominent assault near San Juan Hill. Later in the month, the Spanish capitulate, and the United States formally accepts surrender in August. The peace allows Cuban independence and passes control of Puerto Rico, the Philippines, and Guam to the United States.

1899

November

Vice President Hobart dies in Paterson, New Jersey.

1900

June

The Republicans renominate McKinley for president with war hero and former New York Governor Theodore Roosevelt for vice president.

July

The Democratic convention again selects William Jennings Bryan as the party's standard bearer. Former vice president Adlai Stevenson joins him on the ticket.

November

McKinley wins a second term with Roosevelt as his vice president.

1901

September

President McKinley is shot by an anarchist while visiting an exhibition in Buffalo, New York. He dies thirteen days later, and Theodore Roosevelt is sworn in as president.

1904

June

The Republican Party nominates President Theodore Roosevelt to head the election ticket, although his vocal opposition to monopolies and large business combinations has created some dissension among party's leaders. Charles Fairbanks of Indiana, a conservative, is chosen as vice-presidential candidate.

July

The Democrats nominate Alton B. Parker of Illinois and Henry G. West of West Virginia.

November

Republicans Roosevelt and Fairbanks win with a plurality of a quarter-million popular votes. Roosevelt sees the victory as confirmation of his policies and, during his second term, pushes for more restrictions on big business, including a flurry of new laws and court decisions.

1906

November
President Theodore Roosevelt travels to the Isthmus of Panama to view progress on the great canal project he has strongly supported. The canal is completed seven years later.

1907

October
A major financial panic hits the country. Complete collapse of the economy is avoided, but a year-long depression follows.

1908

June
Roosevelt is seen as having already served two terms, so the Republicans nominate William Howard Taft of Ohio as his successor. John Sherman of New York is his vice-presidential running mate.

July
The Democrats again nominate reliable William Jennings Bryan with John W. Kern of Indiana for vice president.

November
Taft and Sherman win with a large margin of more than 1.2 million votes. Taft will expand on Roosevelt's anti-big business and trust-breaking policies but without Roosevelt's flair for publicity.

1912

January
Reformers organize the Progressive Party to rally opponents of big business from both of the traditional parties. Former president Theodore Roosevelt, anxious for power once again, becomes a prominent member.

June
The mainline Republicans reject Roosevelt and renominate President Taft and Vice President Sherman. Roosevelt thereupon bolts and later in the summer forms his own third party, the Bull Moose Party, based on the Progressive Party. Hiram Johnson of California is chosen as TR's running mate.

July
The Democrats stage an exhausting convention fight in which warhorse William Jennings Bryan finally gives way to New Jersey's reform governor, Woodrow Wilson. Thomas Marshall of Indiana is nominated for vice president.

October
Vice President Sherman dies and is replaced on the Republican ticket by New York's Nicolas Butler. During the same month, ex-president Roosevelt is shot and wounded by a would-be assassin in Milwaukee. He miraculously survives the attack.

November
Wilson and Marshall win by a large margin, surpassing the combined total of Roosevelt and Taft. The electoral vote is 435 for Wilson, 88 for Roosevelt, and 8 for Taft.

1913

February
The Sixteenth Amendment, which imposes an income tax, is ratified.

May
The Seventeenth Amendment passes, providing for the popular election of senators (who have been chosen by state legislatures until now).

1914

August
A general war breaks out in Europe with all the great powers in opposing alliances—the

Central Powers against the Allies. Vicious fighting during the first weeks of the war establish a stalemated line of battle that stretches north to south across Western Europe. The United States led by President Wilson, declares neutrality.

October

Congress passes the Clayton Antitrust Act which proves to be a milestone in economic and business legislation. One effect of the law is to free labor unions from persecution under antitrust restrictions.

1915

May

Germany attempts to counter Great Britain's naval blockade of the Continent by using a deadly new sea weapon, the modern submarine. The British passenger ship *Lusitania* is sunk without warning, taking more than a 100 Americans to their deaths. The United States is outraged and moves closer to favoring war against the Central Powers.

1916

March

Mexican bandit Pancho Villa raids into New Mexico. President Wilson sends an expeditionary force under General John Pershing to chase Villa. The force crosses into Mexico but has no success. The invasion nearly sets off a war between the two countries.

June

The Progressives hold a convention and offer the nomination to Roosevelt, who declines. They then nominate a ticket of Charles Evans Hughes and John Parker.

The Republican convention also nominates Hughes, but selects Charles Fairbanks as the vice-presidential candidate. Many Progressives

come back into the Republican fold after the joint nomination for president.

President Woodrow Wilson and Vice President Thomas Marshall are renominated by the Democrats. The party slogan claims that Wilson "kept us out of war."

November

Wilson and Marshall win again.

1917

January

Germany resumes unrestricted submarine warfare, which has been on hold, and announces it will sink neutral civilian ships without warning. Four days later, Wilson breaks diplomatic relations with Germany.

April

President Woodrow Wilson asks Congress to declare war on Germany. This marks the first-time the United States has entered into a conflict in Europe and will alter temporarily the historic isolationist stance of the nation. Although the United States is completely unprepared to fight on a large scale, within months the country will mobilize and train an army and begin to gear up industrial production to help the Allies. By any absolute measure, the U.S. contribution to the Allied effort in Europe is modest, but it comes at a crucial time when all the long-term combatants are depleted and exhausted; it will help to decide the contest.

June

The first contingent of U.S. troops under Commander John J. Pershing lands in France. By year's end, there will be close to 200,000 American soldiers in France; by war's end two million.

1918

January

President Wilson announces his program of Fourteen Points that he insists be the basis for any peace after the war. To his European allies, the declaration seems irrelevant and naive.

June
U.S. Marines and soldiers win a battle at Belleau Wood, but at a horrendous cost in casualties.

September
The Americans win a significant victory at St. Mihiel.

November
The Central Powers give up the struggle and conclude an armistice with the victorious Allies, bring the "war to end all wars" to a conclusion. Making a lasting peace will prove impossible.

1919

January
The peace conference to set terms for postwar Europe meets in Paris. Wilson will attend with high hopes of implementing his Fourteen Points, but diplomats from France and Great Britain will brush him aside and impose harsh terms on the defeated Central Powers, especially Germany. Wilson will be rebuffed as a hopeless idealist.

In the same month, the ill-considered Eighteenth Amendment to the Constitution reaches ratification, outlawing the manufacture and sale of liquor in the United States.

June
The Treaty of Versailles concludes the war. The treaty includes a League of Nations, one of President Wilson's pet ideas, but the U.S. Senate will refuse to ratify the agreement in a fit of isolationist reaction to the war and to the loss of more than 130,000 American lives in Europe.

September
President Wilson suffers a stroke after touring the country in an unsuccessful attempt to drum up support for the League of Nations. He is incapacitated, but his wife and advisers refuse to let the nation know of his true condition, even keeping Vice President Thomas Marshall in the dark. Wilson never really recovers, and the nation is left without a true chief executive until the next inauguration. Mrs. Wilson and a few advisers run the country in Wilson's name.

1920

January
As a part of the continuing reaction against the war, the nation enters a paranoid phase of public fear and oppression, known as the Big Red Scare. Using the Bolshevik revolution in Russia as an excuse, the U.S. Attorney General arrests and persecutes hundreds of innocent people on suspicion of subversive activities.

June
The Republican Party nominates Warren G. Harding of Ohio for president and Calvin Coolidge of Massachusetts for vice president.

July
The Democrats nominate James M. Cox of Ohio and Franklin Delano Roosevelt (a cousin of TR) for vice president.

August
The Nineteenth Amendment gives women the vote, a victory achieved only after decades of struggle.

November
Harding and Coolidge win with a margin of more than 7 million votes.

1923

August
President Warren Harding dies of pneumonia in a San Francisco hotel room on his way back from a visit to Alaska. Vice President Calvin

Coolidge is sworn in as president by his father, a rural Vermont justice of the peace.

October
The Teapot Dome oil scandal breaks into the news. Government officials, including the secretary of interior and cronies of former President Harding, are guilty of selling strategic oil reserves for profit.

1924

May
Congress passes the first comprehensive legal restrictions on immigration. Although the full force of the law will not go into effect until 1929, the act marks a major change in U.S. policy and shuts down the massive movement of people from Europe to the United States.

June
The Republicans nominate President Coolidge to run for a term on his own with Charles Dawes of Illinois as his running mate.

July
The Democrats nominate John Davis of West Virginia and Charles Bryan of Nebraska as the party's national ticket. The fading Progressives have previously nominated Robert La Follette and Burton K. Wheeler.

November
Coolidge and Dawes win by a large margin: 382 electoral votes to 136 for Davis and Bryan and 13 for the Progressives.

1928

June
Interpreting Coolidge's statement that he does not choose to run as declining nomination, the Republicans select Herbert Hoover of California to head their ticket. Charles Curtis of Kansas is nominated for the vice presidency.

The Democrats nominate New York Governor Al Smith as the first serious Roman Catholic candidate for president. His running mate is Joseph T. Robinson of Arkansas.

November
The Republicans win the election easily with 21.3 million votes to the Democrats' 15 million.

1929

October
The New York stock market collapses in a single day, and the price of shares goes into a free-fall decline that will eventually wipe out billions of dollars of paper wealth. The crash heralds the beginning of the Great Depression, which will last a decade and not be reversed until the outbreak of war in Europe stimulates the U.S. economy.

1932

January
The Reconstruction Finance Corporation is created to use federal funds to prop up banks, financial institutions, and other key parts of the economy. Most see this as too little and too late on the part of the Hoover administration.

May–July
A so-called Bonus Army of World War I veterans descends on Washington, D.C., to demand full payment of their war bonuses. After camping out in the capital, they are ruthless dispersed by the Army.

June
The Republicans renominate Hoover and Curtis.

The Democrats nominate Franklin Delano Roosevelt of New York and John Nance Garner of Texas.

November

The Democrats sweep into office with a Roosevelt–Garner landslide. They take 472 electoral votes to the Republican' 59.

1933

February

The Twentieth Amendment, known as the lame-duck amendment, is ratified, changing the inauguration date for the president and vice president from March to January. This will eliminate the traditional long waiting period between election and taking office

Later in the month, Franklin Delano Roosevelt, who is waiting out the time until his inauguration under the old arrangement, is shot at while riding in an open car in Miami, Florida, by a would-be assassin. The president-elect escapes harm, but Chicago mayor Anton Cermak, who is with FDR, is fatally wounded.

March–June

President Franklin Delano Roosevelt launches his New Deal, a comprehensive program of executive action and legislation, aimed at economic recovery and relief. He closes the nation's banks temporarily in order to stop a panic, reorganizes the federal government, creates a Civilian Conservation Corps to employ young workers, takes the country off the gold standard, promotes the Federal Emergency Relief Act and the Agricultural Adjustment Act as instruments of direct relief, sets up federal regulation of the stock market, creates a federal employment service, and gains passage of the National Industrial Recovery Act that in turn spawns the National Recovery Administration and the Public Works Administration. These and other agencies, such as the Resettlement Administration and the Works Progress Administration, form the basis for the New Deal and, although often modified and added to, the fundamental policies and programs influence American life for decades to come.

December

The states ratify the twenty-first Amendment, which repeals the Nineteenth Amendment and ends Prohibition.

1935

May

The U.S. Supreme Court strikes down the National Industrial Recovery Act, bringing FDR's New Deal into question and beginning a struggle between the Court and the president.

July

Congress passes the National Labor Relations Act, which allows unions to organize freely.

August

President Roosevelt signs the Social Security Act, probably the most far reaching of all New Deal programs, which provides unemployment insurance, disability benefits, and pensions to almost all workers. During the same month, he also signs an act that establishes federal taxes on inheritances and gifts.

1936

January

The Supreme Court rules that the Agricultural Adjustment Act, a key part of the New Deal for farmers, is unconstitutional.

June

The Republican Party nominates Alf Landon of Kansas for president and Frank Knox of Illinois for vice president.
The Democrats renominate FDR and Vice President John Nance Garner.

November

FDR and Garner score a huge landslide over the Republicans. The Democratic incumbents win 523 electoral votes to 8 for Landon and

Knox. The margin of the popular vote is more than 11 million.

1937

January
President Franklin Delano Roosevelt and Vice President John Nance Garner become the first to be inaugurated in January following a previous November election.

February
FDR announces a plan to "pack" the Supreme Court by creating places for up to six new judges. He ultimately fails to get the legislation passed.

1938

February
The Agricultural Adjustment Act is revived in a new form.

1939

September
Germany invades Poland, setting off war in Europe. The United States has remained neutral under law as the belligerents have jostled toward the outbreak of war, but FDR openly favors the British.

1940

March–June
German military forces roll over all opposition and occupy much of France and northern Europe. Only Great Britain, which has evacuated its small army across the English Channel, remains as a viable opponent to Hitler, and FDR moves to strengthen ties with the British, but stops well short of armed support.

June
The Republican national convention selects relative unknown Wendell Wilkie of Indiana as presidential nominee with Charles McNary of Oregon as his running mate.

July
FDR breaks the tradition set by George Washington and is nominated for a third term. He discards John Nance Garner in favor of Henry Wallace of Iowa as his vice presidential choice.

September
The United States begins the Lend Lease program to supply the British with what is essentially the gift of fifty destroyers. The country edges further and further from neutrality. At the end of the month, FDR announces an embargo of steel to all belligerents except Britain. The real target of the embargo is Japan, which is also hit with a U.S. embargo on oil.

November
FDR and Wallace win a relatively narrow victory in the popular vote, with a margin of less than 2 million votes, although the electoral college vote is 449–82. FDR becomes America's only three-term president.

1941

January
Speaking at his third inaugural, President Roosevelt announces his "Four Freedoms": freedom of speech, freedom of worship, freedom from want, and freedom from fear.

December
The Americans are stunned on December 7 by a devastating sneak air attack by the Japanese Imperial Fleet on U.S. military bases at Pearl Harbor, Hawaii. The next day, President Roosevelt asks Congress for a declaration of war against Japan. A few days later, the United States also declares war on Germany and Italy.

America's neutrality is ended, and a titanic international struggle begins. The war will be fought on two major fronts, Europe and the Pacific, with significant conflicts in the China–Burma–India theater. It will consume unimaginable amounts of energy and matériel and result in millions of casualties worldwide. At the beginning, the nation is ill prepared for war and things go badly, especially in the Pacific. Eventually, America's natural resources, industrial capacity, and manpower are mobilized and expanded on a huge scale, and these factors ultimately tip the military balance in favor of the United States and its allies. The Italians and Germans are defeated after bloody invasions of Europe by the Allies, and Japan is forced to surrender by the explosion of atoms bombs over two Japanese cities, By the end of the war in 1945, the United States will have become the dominant world power, armed with nuclear weapons, and ready to assume a role in international affairs that would have been impossible to imagine only a few years previous.

1942

February
The U.S. Navy in the Pacific attempts to regroup after the Philippines, Wake Island, Guam, and a host of lesser-known islands fall to the Japanese, but a major defeat in the Java Sea further weakens U.S. forces. On the home front, President Roosevelt organizes wartime government control and administration of key parts of the economy and authorizes a program to intern Japanese Americans.

April
The United States forces a stalemate in the naval battle of the Coral Sea and stalls further Japanese advances on Australia.

May
In a huge battle near Midway Island, the U.S. carrier fleet defeats a large Japanese naval force and turns back an invasion plan.

August
U.S. ground forces land on Guadalcanal Island and begin a prolonged, costly campaign against the Japanese who hold the island. Both sides pour resources into the series of land, air, and sea battles, which the Americans eventually win.

During the same month, U.S. bombers flying from England make their first air strikes on German bases in France. A large buildup of air forces in England is underway as well as planning for the assembly of a cross-Channel invasion.

November
American and Allied forces under General Dwight Eisenhower land in North Africa and seize former French territories in Morocco and Algiers.

In Eastern Europe, German forces are turned back at Stalingrad, but the campaign into Russia has resulted in extreme casualty rates among both armed forces and civilians.

1943

January
After more than a year of war, the home front looks vastly different than during peacetime. The federal government controls prices, wages, and production in almost all industrial and manufacturing segments of the economy. Scarce or strategically important goods are rationed. The Selective Service System (the draft) and patriotic enthusiasm have pulled hundreds of thousands of young men and women into the armed forces, and they are replaced in the domestic workforce mostly by women who have never worked outside the home before. Almost every family in the America is affected by wartime separation and disruption.

President Roosevelt travels to North Africa for a conference with the leaders of the Allies at Casablanca. They set policy for the continuation of the war, including an agreement to demand unconditional surrender from the Germans.

May

After a long teeter-totter struggle, the Germans withdraw from North Africa and leave the Allies victorious there.

July

The Allies invade the island of Sicily as a preamble to invasion of Italy. Later in the same month, Benito Mussolini, the Italian fascist dictator, gives up power.

September

The Allies invade Italy, and the new Italian government effectively ceases to resist. The Germans, however, move into the breach and will eventually stop the Allied advance up the Italian peninsula.

November–December

President Roosevelt meets other Allied leaders in a series of conferences in Cairo, Egypt, and Teheran, Iran. They agree to demand unconditional surrender from Japan and on the timing of the war in Europe. The president later announces that U.S. General Dwight Eisenhower will become the Supreme Allied Commander for the anticipated invasion of Europe.

1944

January–February

U.S. forces capture Japanese bases in the Marshall Islands in the Pacific, beginning a long and exceedingly costly campaign of "island-hopping" aimed at taking all of Japan's strategic bases and eventually attacking the Japanese home islands.

January–March

Allied attempts to advance through central Italy are stopped by the Germans, and a stalemate develops. Massive daylight air raids are launched against German cities from bases in England, but very little strategic damage results despite horrendous casualty rates among air crews. U.S., British, and Canadian forces continue an unparalleled build-up of power in England in preparation of the planned invasion of Europe.

June

On D-Day, June 6, the Allies invade France at beaches in Normandy. Air superiority allows the landings to succeed, despite high casualty rates. When the invasion forces join and begin to move inland, the end of the war in Europe can be glimpsed even though many months of death and destruction remain. Hitler and the German nation are also pressed from the East by the advancing Russian Red Army.

In the Pacific later in the month, the Japanese are decisively defeated at the naval battle of the Philippines, and U.S. forces continue a costly advance toward the Japanese islands.

The Republicans nominate New York Governor Thomas Dewey as their candidate for the presidency with governor John Bricker of Ohio for vice president.

July

The Democratic Party convenes and renominates President Roosevelt for a fourth term. Few can imagine pursuing the war without him in the White House, although in reality he is very ill. Vice President Wallace is removed from the ticket in favor of Missouri Senator Harry S. Truman.

August

Guam falls to a U.S. invasion in the Pacific, and the Allied advance in Europe continues to push the Germans back. Late in the month, the Allies enter Paris, which the Germans have abandoned intact.

October

U.S. forces land in the Philippine Islands, led by General Douglas McArthur, who had vowed to return when forced to flee the Japanese in 1942. A decisive naval victory in Leyte Gulf destroys a major portion of the remaining Japanese fleet, and the Japanese turn to suicide kamikaze air attacks on U.S. ships.

November
Roosevelt and Truman win with a 3.5 million popular-vote edge. The president will enter a fourth term with his third vice president.

December
A desperate German attack in Belgium momentarily halts Allied advances with the Battle of the Bulge.

1945

February
At a conference at Yalta in the Crimea, President Roosevelt and other Allied leaders plan for the postwar international organization that eventually becomes the United Nations.

March
In the Pacific, Americans capture Iwo Jima and move on to attack Okinawa as the last step before invasion of Japan itself. In Europe, Allied troops cross the Rhine into Germany as the Russians close in from the East.

April
President Franklin Delano Roosevelt dies of a massive stroke while at his resort home in Warm Springs, Georgia. Vice President Harry S. Truman, relatively unknown to the public and a sharp contrast to FDR in style and personality, assumes the office of the president at a crucial time in U.S. and world history. He pledges to continue FDR's wartime policies.

May
Germany surrenders, bringing the war in Europe to an end. The Allies divide Berlin and occupied Germany into four sectors.

July
After a massive secret research and development program, U.S. scientists explode the world's first atom bomb at a base in New Mexico. President Truman is informed of the successful test while at a conference with Allied leaders at Potsdam, Germany.

August
On August 6, an American B-29 bomber drops an atom bomb on the Japanese city of Hiroshima, resulting in extraordinary casualties and destruction. The United States immediately calls on Japan to surrender, but the demand is rejected. President Truman has ordered the bomb dropped in hope of forestalling a bloody invasion of the Japanese home islands. He orders another bombing, and the city of Nagasaki is hit with an atom bomb on August 9. Five days later, the Japanese government agrees to end the war.

September
Japan formally surrenders. The war is over.

1946

January
America begins a series of social and economic postwar adjustments. Several industries are hit by major strikes, for example, as unions try to upgrade wages and working conditions held in check during the war. As hundreds of thousands of veterans are demobilized and return to the civilian world, national leaders fear economic dislocation, but the fears prove wrong. Using the benefits granted under the so-called G.I. Bill of Rights, veterans enroll in college in record numbers and many buy houses, propelling an economic expansion.

March
British Prime Minister Winston Churchill, during a speech in the United States, draws attention to the "Iron Curtain" that has descended across Eastern Europe where the Soviet Union has established political and military control. Churchill's analysis points to a growing international conflict between the communist East and

the democratic West. As the world's first atomic power and in the aftermath of the devastating war that impoverished Britain and France, the United States is forced to assume leadership of what its politicians call the "free world."

1947

March
President Truman announces the Truman Doctrine that will provide American aid to anti-communist regimes. At the same time, he institutes a loyalty program to guard against Communists in the federal government.

June
Secretary of State George Marshall, formerly the commanding general of U.S. forces, announces a massive program of aid to rebuild the nations of Western Europe. The policy becomes known as the Marshall Plan and is the nation's first large-scale involvement in peacetime European affairs. During the same month, Congress passes the Taft-Hartley Act over President Truman's veto. The act outlaws closed union shops.

July
Amendments to the Presidential Succession Act of 1886 places the Speaker of the House as next in line for the presidency after the vice president.

1948

March–April
Strikes in the coal and rail industries hamper the economy, but the forecast postwar depression fails to materialize.

June
The Republicans again nominate Thomas Dewey for president with Governor of California Earl Warren as his running mate. The party hopes to regain the presidency for the first time since 1932.

A few days after the convention makes its choice, the Soviets create a European crisis by blocking access to the occupied German capital of Berlin. The United States responds with a massive airlift of supplies, food, and fuel. This marks the first major confrontation between the United States and the Soviet Union and begins the so-called cold war, a forty-year period of mutual antagonism and aggression. Because the Soviets now have the secrets of the atom bomb (gained through spies in the United States), mutual global destruction is a growing possibility, but the cold war always stops just short of warfare.

July
The Democrats meet in a convention full of conflict and put a civil rights plank into their platform. They nominate President Truman for a full term with Alben Barkley of Kentucky as his running mate. Democratic delegates from the southern states walk out in protest of the civil rights plank, and later in the month, they convene their own convention as the States' Rights Party—known as the Dixiecrats—and nominate Senator Strom Thurmond of South Carolina for the presidency and Fielding Wright as his running mate. Dissatisfied leftwing Democrats form a fourth party, resurrecting the name Progressive, and nominate former vice president Henry Wallace. The Democrats seem to be fragmented and at the mercy of the strong Republican ticket.

At the end of the month, President Truman signs an executive order that ends segregation in the armed forces and the federal government.

August
A growing anticommunist trend gains momentum when journalist Whittaker Chambers accuses state department official Alger Hiss of being a Soviet spy.

November
Against all odds and in the face of polling reports to the contrary, Truman and Barkley

win the election. Truman's attacks on Congress during a train-tour campaign have had their effect. He and Barkley poll more than 24 million popular votes to slightly less than 22 million for the Republican ticket. The Dixiecrats and the Progressives between them get 1.3 million.

1949

January
President Truman calls his package of domestic proposals the Fair Deal. They include expansion of social security, a hike in the minimum wage, a national health insurance system, more federal aid to education, civil rights legislation, and government-sponsored housing. Little is actually passed during his administration, but the proposals extend the domestic ideas of FDR's New Deal.

April
The United States signs the first treaties that eventually form the North Atlantic Treaty Organization (NATO), a key factor in the cold war military stalemate.

1950

February
Senator Joseph McCarthy begins a loud campaign against communists in government with unsubstantiated charges of communists in the State Department. Before the movement known as McCarthyism is finished and McCarthy himself discredited four years later, a wave of communal hysteria will turn the nation on its head. McCarthyism will destroy the lives of hundreds of innocent victims while leaving real spies and subversives little affected.

June
The communist government of North Korea launches an invasion of the Republic of South Korea. The United States immediately sends troops and planes to help defend the South and secures a UN resolution authorizing armed intervention by a United Nations force. The resulting conflict is a vicious, costly war (although labeled only as a "police action") that will eventually involve massive combat between the United States and Communist China and end in a stand-off at the original borders.

November
Puerto Rican nationalists try to kill President Truman in an attack on Blair House, where the president and his family are living during renovations to the White House. A guard and one of the would-be assassins are killed, but the president is safe.

1951

February
The Twenty-second Amendment is ratified, limiting presidents to two elected terms.

April
Soviet spies Ethel and Julius Rosenberg are sentenced to death in a controversial case that polarizes much of the nation. During the same month, President Truman removes General Douglas McArthur from command in Korea. McArthur has defeated the North Koreans but baited the Chinese into entering the war and now refuses to heed Truman as commander in chief. The removal further disrupts national unity, as many conservatives, support McArthur as a symbol of anti-Communism. The dismissed general is asked by Congress to address a joint session, an extraordinary occurrence.

1952

March
President Truman publicly declines to run for renomination, although he is still eligible under Twenty-second Amendment.

June

The Supreme Court overrules President Truman's recent takeover of the steel industry, setting off a massive strike in a crucial industry. Later in the month, Congress passes an immigration restriction law over the president's veto. The new act sets national origin quotas.

At their convention, the Republicans nominate World War II commander Dwight "Ike" Eisenhower for president with Californian Richard Nixon as running mate.

July

The Democrats nominate Adlai Stevenson of Illinois and Alabama's John Sparkman.

November

The Republican ticket wins easily with 442 electoral votes to 89 for the Democrats. Eisenhower becomes the first Republican president in twenty years. Less than two weeks after the balloting, the United States successfully tests the first hydrogen bomb in the Pacific.

December

Fulfilling a campaign pledge, President-elect Eisenhower travels to Korea to visit the troops and assess the United States position there. The fighting has diminished, but the truce talks are at stalemate.

1953

July

The belligerents sign an armistice in Korea but cannot agree on an official end to the war. Both sides will continue indefinitely to face each other across an uneasy border. The United States will permanently station 40,000 troops in South Korea.

1954

April

The Senate begins hearings on the U.S. Army, which has been accused by Senator Joseph McCarthy. During the course of the televised hearings, McCarthy will be completely discredited and his hold on the nation will be finally broken.

May

The U.S. Supreme Court in the *Brown v. Board of Education* decision declares separate-but-equal segregation unconstitutional and sets the stage for a long struggle to end legal racial discrimination in the United States.

1955

September

President Eisenhower suffers a heart attack while in Denver. The seriousness of his condition is shielded from the general public, but he eventually recovers after a three-week hospital stay.

December

Rosa Parks refuses to give up her seat on a bus to a white man and sets in motion a long campaign by black citizens in the South to challenge and vanquish public segregation laws. The decade-long series of activities comes to be known as the Civil Rights movement and brings leaders such as Martin Luther King, Jr., to national prominence. In general, the movement uses nonviolent means, such as boycotts, demonstrations, and "freedom" marches, to protest discrimination in housing, transportation, education, and voting rights.

1956

June

President Eisenhower again falls ill, this time with a bout of ileitis. He undergoes surgery and recovers normally.

August

Despite his two episodes of ill health, President Eisenhower is renominated by the Republican

Party, as is Vice President Nixon. The Democrats again nominate Adlai Stevenson, but put Estes Kefauver of Tennessee up as his running mate.

November

Eisenhower and Nixon win again, outpolling their opponents by a landslide margin of almost 10 million votes.

1957

September

The state National Guard is called out by the governor in Little Rock, Arkansas, to prevent black students from integrating the high school. Violence escalates until President Eisenhower sends in U.S. Army troops to enforce the law and escort black students to class.

October

Americans are shocked when the Soviet Union successfully launches the space satellite *Sputnik*. Efforts to respond with a U.S. launch fail when the U.S. rockets explode on their pads. The humiliation stimulates massive spending on a space-and-rocket defense program and on heightened educational efforts in science and mathematics.

1960

March–July

John F. Kennedy, a wealthy young senator from Massachusetts, uses the state primary system to gain enough delegate votes to win the Democratic nomination. His bold tactics spell the end of the party convention system as the mechanism to nominate presidential candidates.

May

Soviet missiles shoot down a U.S. U-2 spy plane over Russia and capture the CIA pilot. The incident precipitates a crisis in cold war relations but leads to nothing more than threats.

July

The Democratic convention names Lyndon Johnson of Texas as Kennedy's running mate. The Republicans nominate Vice President Nixon and Henry Cabot Lodge of Massachusetts.

September

Nixon and Kennedy stage the first televised presidential campaign debate. Kennedy, the more telegenic candidate, is thought to have "won."

November

Kennedy and Johnson win by a very thin margin of not much more than 100,000 votes. Widespread rumors of voting fraud in Illinois and Texas do not change the outcome.

1961

March

The Twenty-third Amendment to the Constitution is ratified, giving voters in the District of Columbia the vote.

April

An armed force of Cuban refugees from Florida attempts to invade Cuba, hoping to oust Communist dictator Fidel Castro. The Central Intelligence Agency has trained and armed the invaders, but the Cuban military crushes the landings at the Bay of Pigs.

May

Alan Shepard, Jr., becomes the first American in space when he rides a rocket-propelled capsule in a looping, suborbital flight to the edge of the Earth's atmosphere.

1962

October

The Soviets precipitate the worst cold war crisis by attempting to install missiles in Cuba. U.S. intelligence detects the building of sites and the shipment of missiles, and President Kennedy orders a naval blockade of Cuba and aggressively warns the Soviets to withdraw the weapons. After a tense confrontation, the Soviets back down.

1963

April–May

Black civil rights activists stage large-scale demonstrations and marches in Birmingham, Alabama. Leader Dr. Martin Luther King, Jr., is jailed. Violence continues while U.S. Attorney General Robert Kennedy (the president's brother) tries to intervene.

June

Alabama Governor George Wallace attempts to keep black students out of the state university but finally is forced to allow two to enroll.

August

Dr. Martin Luther King, Jr., addresses a large civil rights rally on the Mall in Washington, D. C. He tells the crowd that "I have a dream. . . ." This becomes one of the central events of the civil rights campaign.

November

President John F. Kennedy is assassinated by a sniper while traveling in a motorcade in Dallas, Texas. The nation is stunned by his death and the subsequent events, which are widely seen on television. Vice President Lyndon Johnson is sworn in aboard a plane bound for Washington, D.C. The alleged assassin, Lee Harvey Oswald, is killed publicly by a bystander while in police custody, giving rise to decades of speculation about conspiracy.

1964

March

President Johnson begins an ambitious domestic program with his war on poverty. His over-

all program of welfare spending, civil rights legislation, and education improvements will try to implement his vision of what he calls the Great Society.

July

The president signs a civil rights act that ends legal discrimination.

The Republicans nominate Arizona Senator Barry Goldwater for the presidency. William Miller of New York is his running mate.

August

U.S. destroyers off the coast of Communist North Vietnam in the Gulf of Tonkin are reportedly attacked by North Vietnamese boats. They retaliate and U.S. planes bomb the mainland. Congress subsequently passes resolutions authorizing further armed attacks by U.S. forces.

This sequence ushers in the beginning of serious American involvement in what proves to be the most disastrous foreign war in U.S. history. President Lyndon Johnson is persuaded by his advisers that the United States has vital interests in stopping a takeover of South Vietnam by the nationalist communist regime of Ho Chi Minh in the north, which is allied with southern Vietcong rebel guerrilla fighters and supplied by the Soviet Union. The United States props up a series of weak governments in the south and begins a massive infusion of troops, planes, and ships by which it is hoped the technologically unsophisticated Communists can be defeated. The hope proves false, however, and no amount of manpower, technology, or bombing can ultimately dissuade or defeat the Vietcong and the North Vietnamese. During Johnson's administration, the United States pours more and more into Vietnam, reaching a high point of more than a half-million troops by 1968. The home front, however, proves a complete disaster as conflict over the war erupts everywhere in American society, particularly on college and university campuses. While many Americans support the war effort, millions do not, and protests, draft evasion, and desertion take on major political and social power. Johnson is chased from office by the dissension and replaced by Richard Nixon, who tries to wind down America's direct involvement on the ground and negotiate a peace. The war stretches on and on, however, and no peace is reached until 1973. The regime in the south collapses and the United States has to face the trauma of a defeat in war and in spirit.

August

The Democrats nominate incumbent President Johnson and name Minnesota's Hubert Humphrey as the vice-presidential candidate.

November

Johnson and Humphrey win by a huge margin of nearly 16 million popular votes, taking 44 states to 6 for the Republicans.

1965

February

The conflict in Vietnam begins to escalate as Vietcong guerrillas attack a U.S. base and the president orders bombing in retaliation.
Radical black leader Malcom X is assassinated in New York City by members of the Black Muslim organization, of which he was previously a principal leader.

March

State troopers in Selma, Alabama, attack civil rights marchers. President Johnson eventually nationalizes the state National Guard and sends federal troops to protect the demonstrators.

July

President Johnson signs an act creating Medicare, a national health insurance program for the elderly and disabled.

August

Large-scale race riots erupt in the Watts section of Los Angeles. These are the first in a series of destructive riots in urban black ghettos over the following three years.

October

An immigration reform bill becomes law. It abolishes the quota system and opens the way for renewal of larger-scale immigration and for the first time allows significant immigration from Asia.

1966

January

President Johnson orders bombing of North Vietnam, which had been suspended since December, to resume.

March

Protestors in several cities stage large demonstrations against the war in Vietnam.

June

The U.S. Supreme Court rules in the *Miranda* decision that accused criminals must be informed of their rights.
     U.S. planes begin to bomb the North Vietnamese capital of Hanoi.

July

One of decade's the most violent and destructive race riots takes place in Detroit. Damage is in the hundreds of millions of dollars, and thousands of inner-city residents are left homeless by fire. President Johnson sends in Army troops to help restore order.

1967

October–December

Massive antiwar demonstrations in Washington, D.C., and many other cities, including New York, result in large-scale arrests of demonstrators.

1968

January

The Vietcong and North Vietnamese unleash a series of attacks on the eve of the Tet New Year.

The attacks destroy the American perception that the war is going well. Antiwar student riots renew in the United States.

March

Anti-war Democratic presidential candidate Eugene McCarthy wins a primary in New Hampshire and shakes the Democratic Party. Attorney General Robert Kennedy announces his candidacy in the wake of evidence of President Johnson's unpopularity. Former Vice President Richard Nixon has previously announced his run for the Republican nomination. President Lyndon Johnson surprises the nation with a declaration that he will not seek the nomination for another term.

April

Civil rights leader Martin Luther King, Jr., is assassinated in Memphis, Tennessee. Rioting and protests result.

Students seize administration buildings at Columbia University to protest the war.

June

Robert Kennedy is assassinated in Los Angeles, where he is campaigning for the presidential nomination.

August

The Republican convention nominates Richard Nixon and he names Maryland Governor Spiro Agnew as his running mate.

The Democratic party convention in Chicago nominates Vice President Hubert Humphrey and Maine Senator Edmund Muskie, but the convention and the city are totally disrupted by brutal street battles between police and antiwar demonstrators.

November

Nixon and Agnew win a tight race with a margin of slightly more than 800,000 million votes out of nearly 80 million cast. Third-party segregationist candidate George Wallace pulls almost 9.5 million votes.

1969

June

President Nixon announces a new policy of Vietnamization that is planned to place the burden of ground fighting on the South Vietnamese regime and will mean gradual withdrawal of U.S. troops.

July

U.S. astronauts Neil Armstrong and Buzz Aldrin set foot on the moon, marking one of humankind's greatest technological achievements. A second lunar landing follows in November.

1970

May

Ohio national guardsmen fire on student demonstrators at Kent State University, killing four and wounding nine. A few days later, two students are killed at Jackson State College in Mississippi in a similar incident.

1971

April

The twenty-sixth Amendment is adopted, granting the right to vote to eighteen-year olds.

1972

January

President Nixon announces a peace proposal for Vietnam.

February

Nixon visits Communist China and announces resumption of partial diplomatic and economic relations.

March

The North Vietnamese reject the U.S. peace proposals and stage a massive attack into South Vietnam. President Nixon orders the mining of major North Vietnamese ports and the resumption of bombing.

May

The president visits the Soviet Union and signs an agreement to freeze nuclear weapons.

June

Operatives of the Committee to Reelect the President break in to Democratic National Party headquarters at the Watergate building in Washington, D.C. They are caught in the act, and the subsequent investigation snowballs until eventually the president and almost all of his key aides and associates are implicated in a series of illegal actions. The break-in becomes part of the greatest political scandal in American history. Nixon will resign the presidency in the face of imminent impeachment, and many of his coconspirators will serve prison time.

July

The Democratic convention nominates South Dakota's George McGovern, who wins on the strength of primary victories and manipulation of delegate rules. He chooses Missouri Senator Thomas Eagleton as his running mate.

August

Eagleton is forced to withdraw from the Democratic ticket when it is revealed that he has suffered psychiatric disorders and has been treated with electroshock therapy. He is replace by Sargeant Shriver.

The Republican Party renominates President Richard Nixon and Vice President Spiro Agnew.

November

Nixon and Agnew are reelected for a second term with one of the most emphatic victories in American political history. They win more than 60 percent of the popular vote. McGovern and Shriver win electoral votes only from Massachusetts.

December

After peace talks breaks down, President Nixon orders new bombing of North Vietnam. Most of the ground fighting is now in the hands of the South Vietnamese.

1973

January

In *Roe v. Wade,* the U.S. Supreme Court rules that state laws against voluntary abortion are unconstitutional. The decision legalizes abortion and touches off a long, rancorous, sometimes violent debate over the next two decades.

A peace agreement is signed in Paris that will end the war in Vietnam. The United States is to withdraw all of its troops. The agreement tacitly acknowledges the victory of the Vietcong and the North Vietnamese.

June–July

Testimony before the Senate committee investigating the Watergate break-in implicates high White House and reelection committee officials, including the president himself. The break-in was authorized at the highest levels as were attempts to cover up. A White House aide reveals that all conversations are routinely recorded by order of the president.

October

Vice President Spiro Agnew is forced to resign his office after pleading "no contest" (a legal admission of guilt) to charges of corruption and bribe taking while governor of Maryland. Some of the illegal payments were made to Agnew after he took office as vice president. President Richard Nixon, himself under intense investigation for political wrongdoing, appoints Michigan Representative Gerald Ford as vice president, using the Twenty-fifth Amendment for the first time. Previous vacancies in the vice presidency have remained unfilled.

A few days later, Nixon precipitates another crisis in what is known as the Saturday Night Massacre. He orders his attorney general to fire a special prosecutor who has been seeking the secret White House tapes. When the attorney general refuses and resigns along with his assistant attorney general, the solicitor general finally agrees to fire the special prosecutor. This sequence is greeted with a storm of outrage.

During the same month, an economic crisis threatens as the result of an oil embargo by Arab oil-producing nations. The nation reacts with a burst of interest in energy saving during the year-long embargo. Long lines at the gas pumps and other signs of distress mask the fact that actual, shortages are negligible.

December
After intense hearings prompted by the possibility of a presidential impeachment, Gerald Ford is sworn in as vice president.

1974

March
High-ranking members of the president's staff are indicted on criminal charges connected with Watergate. President Nixon is named as an "unindicted co-conspirator."

July
After a favorable Supreme Court ruling, the House Judiciary Committee finally gets tapes of White House conversations about Watergate from the president. The committee then approves articles of impeachment that charge the president with criminal misconduct in obstructing justice and violating his oath of office in connection with the Watergate cover-up.

August
Richard Nixon resigns as president in order to avoid impeachment and trial. Vice President

Gerald Ford is immediately sworn in as the new president. Before the end of the month, Ford nominates New York's Nelson Rockefeller as vice president.

September
President Ford gives former President Nixon a full pardon. Later in the month, he grants amnesty to Vietnam War draft evaders and deserters.

December
Nelson Rockefeller takes the oath of office as vice president. His confirmation has been delayed by long and critical investigative hearings.

1975

January
The North Vietnamese move to take Saigon, and the final U.S. evacuees flee the country.

September
President Gerald Ford narrowly escapes an assassination attempt in San Francisco when a woman shoots at him with a handgun from a crowd. Her arm is jostled by a bystander as she fires.

1976

May
President Gerald Ford wins Republican presidential nomination primaries in several key states. Georgia governor Jimmy Carter takes similar victories in crucial state Democratic Party primaries. The party conventions no longer have a meaningful role in selecting party candidates as the focus has shifted almost entirely to state caucuses and primaries, which can be influenced by media campaigns.

July
Jimmy Carter officially receives the Democratic nomination and selects Minnesota's Walter Mondale as his running mate.

August

President Gerald Ford is nominated by the Republican convention and chooses Kansas Senator Robert Dole for the vice presidential nomination.

November

Carter and Mondale beat Ford and Dole in a relatively close race. The Democrats take 297 electoral votes to the Republicans' 241.

1978

June

The Supreme Court rules in the *Bakke* case that affirmative action racial quotas are illegal, although affirmative action guidelines that favor racial or ethnic minorities are not in themselves against the Constitution.

1979

January

The United States ends diplomatic relations with the government of Taiwan and resumes full normal relations with Communist China.

November

Following a takeover in Iran by radical Muslims and the ouster of the U.S.-backed Shah, students in Tehran seize the U.S. embassy and take sixty-six hostage when the Shah is allowed into the United States for medical treatment. The resulting prolonged crisis cannot be solved by U.S. diplomacy, and an attempt at a military rescue mission fails miserably. President Carter's popularity suffers as a result.

1980

July

California's former Governor Ronald Reagan takes the Republican nomination for the presidency and selects George Bush as his running mate.

August

The Democrats renominate incumbents Carter and Mondale.

November

Reagan and Bush score a smashing victory. They win 489 electoral votes to the Democrats' 49.

1981

March

President Reagan is shot down by a would-be assassin on the street in front of a Washington, D.C., hotel. Vice President Bush flies back from a visit to Texas and temporarily takes control of the U.S. government. Reagan recovers from his wounds after surgery and resumes the powers of his office.

1982

August

Hundreds of U.S. Marines are sent to Beirut, Lebanon, to as part of a multinational peacekeeping force.

1983

April

The U.S. embassy in Beirut is destroyed by a terrorist car bomb. Seventeen U.S. embassy personnel and sixty-three people in total are killed.

October

Islamic terrorists strike again in Beirut, blowing up the Marine headquarters with a suicide truck bomb. Two hundred forty-one Marines are killed in the attack.

Two days later, the United States invades the tiny Caribbean island nation of Grenada, responding to a Cuban communist take over of the the island's government.

1984

April–May
President Ronald Reagan makes a five-day visit to mainland China.

July
The Democrats nominate former vice president Walter Mondale as their presidential candidate. He selects New York's Geraldine Ferraro as his running mate, the first woman to be so nominated by a major party. The Democratic ticket's chances seem slight in view of President Reagan's overwhelming popularity.

August
The Republicans again name Reagan and Bush as their candidates.

November
Reagan and Bush win in a huge landslide with nearly a 16.9-million-vote plurality. They take 49 of the 50 states (Mondale and Ferraro win only in Minnesota) and claim 525 electoral votes to the Democrats' 13.

1985

June
President Reagan has surgery for cancer of the colon. While he is under anaesthetic and during the first hours of recovery, Vice President George Bush takes over the powers of chief executive.

1986

January
The space shuttle *Challenger* explodes and crashes shortly after takeoff, killing the entire crew. It is the worst disaster of the entire U.S. space program.

April
The United States hits Libya with an air attack in retaliation for Libya's sponsorship of terrorism.

August
Congress approves a request from the president for financial aid to the anticommunist contra rebels in Nicaragua. The White House policy is to unseat the communist government in the Central American nation.

October
A major tax code revision becomes law, lowering taxes for many U.S. taxpayers. At the same time, a record national deficit of $220.7 billion is announced. This comes despite the passage five years earlier of a law mandating deficit reduction.

November
The first details of the so-called Iran–contra affair become public. The president's National Security Advisor and his assistant have engineered a complicated deal that involved secretly selling arms to Iran and diverting the proceeds to the anticommunist rebel army in Nicaragua. The president claims ignorance of the entire affair. Congress investigates, as does a special prosecutor. The scandal eventually causes a major shake-up in the administration and criminal indictments of former White House officials, but the president himself evades widespread blame.

1987

October
The stock market crashes spectacularly in the greatest single-day loss in history. The Dow-Jones market average falls more than 500 points. Although the fall is vastly worse than the 1929 crash, the long-term effects are slight

and no major economic dislocation results. By December, the market rebounds and finishes up overall for the year.

1988

May
The U.S. Senate approves a major arms-reduction treaty with the Soviet Union, calling for elimination of many land-based missiles.

July
The Democrats nominate the winner of the primaries, Massachusetts governor Michael Dukakis for the presidency with Texan Lloyd Bentsen as his running mate.

August
The Republicans nominate Vice President George Bush, who has easily defeated his rivals in the primaries. He selects a senator from Indiana, Dan Quayle, as the vice-presidential candidate.

November
The Republican ticket wins easily, taking 426 electoral votes to 112 for the Democrats. The popular vote margin is close to 7 million votes.

1989

August
As the result of a free election, Tadeusz Mazowiecki, an official of the Polish labor union, Solidarity, is named as the nation's first non-communist prime minister since World War II. This is the beginning of a series of astonishing events that culminate in the transformation of eastern Europe. One by one during 1989 and 1990, communist bloc nations throw out their communist governments and install freely elected officials. The decades-old restrictions on travel, commerce, and political life disappear as the Iron Curtain lifts. The most important symbolic event is the destruction of the Berlin Wall

in November 1989, followed within a year by the reunification of East and West Germany. By 1991, even the Soviet Union is dissolved and replaced by rampantly nationalistic new countries. In Russia, Boris Yeltsin takes office as an elected democratic president. All of this has a huge impact on U.S. foreign and domestic policy: the cold war is over and the United States is the only remaining world superpower.

August
Congress approves a $166-billion bailout for the failed savings-and-loan industry. More and more tax money is required before the end of the hugely expensive affair.

December
U.S. forces invade Panama and seek to arrest Panamanian dictator Manuel Noriega, who has bellicosely threatened U.S. interests and is accused of drug trafficking. Twenty-three U.S. soldiers are killed in the invasion, but Noriega is eventually taken into custody in January.

1990

August
Iraqi strongman Saddam Hussein invades Kuwait and threatens the Western world's oil supply. President George Bush pushes resolutions through the United Nations and organizes a coalition against Iraqi. The coalition builds a huge military force—mostly from the United States—in the Persian Gulf region, basing the ground troops in Saudi Arabia. It is clear by the end of the year that a massive attack is imminent. The United States alone has more than 500,000 military personnel in the region by December.

1991

January
A series of air attacks on Iraq employ long-range cruise missiles, stealth bombers, and

high-tech "smart" bombs to devastate Iraqi defenses and offensive capability. The Iraqis retaliate with "Scud" missile attacks on Israel but do not dissuade the coalition. After flying more than 40,000 air sorties, the U.S.-led coalition launches a ground attack than crushes the Iraqis in a battle of 100-hours duration. The defeated Iraqis set fire to the Kuwaiti oil fields, and the coalition in an ill advised move stops short of taking Baghdad and deposing Hussein. The Persian Gulf War has preserved U.S. access to relatively cheap oil but has failed to dislodge a persistently irritating Mideast foe and achieves little lasting benefit.

October
Despite President Bush's extremely high standing in the popularity polls after the Gulf War, the economy begins to erode, and Arkansas Governor Bill Clinton announces he will make a run for the Democratic nomination in the 1992 primaries. Clinton's main opponents for the nomination will be Jerry Brown and Paul Tsongas.

President's Bush's appointment of judge Clarence Thomas to the Supreme Court proves to be controversial when the jurist is accused of sexual harassment. Televised hearings eventually result in his confirmation.

December
Conservative Republican Pat Buchanan announces a primary challenge to President George Bush for the presidential nomination. The Soviet Union officially disbands after more than 70 years of existence.

1992

March–April
President Bush and Bill Clinton win respective primaries and take the leads in the races for their party nominations. Texas millionaire H. Ross Perot announces he will run for president as an independent. Polls show Bush has a lead over Clinton, with Perot surprisingly strong.

In Los Angeles, destructive riots break out after several L.A. policemen are acquitted by an all-white jury of beating black motorist Rodney King at the scene of a traffic arrest the previous March. The beating was videotaped by an onlooker, and the police have been seen repeatedly on television viciously assaulting King. The riots continue over several days and result in the deaths of fifty-two victims and cause at least $1 billion damage. Federal troops and state National Guard are called into quell the violence.

May
The Twenty-seventh Amendment to the Constitution is finally ratified when Michigan becomes the thirty-eighth state to approve. The amendment, which says that sitting Congress may not raise its own salaries, was proposed and first put to the ratification process in 1789 by James Madison. The measure has been pending for more than 200 years.

June
More primary victories clinch the Democratic nomination for Bill Clinton.

July
Clinton is officially nominated at the Democratic national convention, and he chooses Tennessee Senator Al Gore as his running mate. Perot surprises the nation and his supporters by dropping out of the race. Clinton begins an attack on President Bush that centers on the poor state of the economy—economic indicators continue to decline and unemployment remains high.

August
President Bush and Vice President Quayle are renominated by the Republican convention.

September
Perot declares he will reenter the race. The three candidates stage a televised debate, as do the vice-presidential candidates.

November

Clinton and Gore are elected with 43 percent of the popular vote, taking thirty-two states and 370 electoral votes. Bush and Quayle win only eighteen states and 168 electoral votes. Perot finishes strongly with almost 19 percent of the popular vote but no electoral votes.

December

The United States sends troops to Somalia as part of a UN peacekeeping force, hoping to stifle civil war and ameliorate a war-induced famine among the civilian population. President Bush visits the troops late in the month.

1993

February

Islamic terrorists bomb the World Trade Center in New York City. Six people die, and more casualties are avoided by sheer luck when the terrorists misposition their explosive-laden truck. This is the first major attack by foreign terrorists on U.S. soil. The FBI arrests the plotters and later in the year averts further attacks in the New York area by more arrests.

April

An FBI assault on the stronghold of the Branch Davidian religious cult outside Waco, Texas, results in the death of seventy-two of the cult members, including several children. The incident becomes a rallying point for violent anti-government militias.

November

Congress narrowly ratifies the North American Free Trade Agreement, which will open trade borders with Canada and Mexico.

December

Fifteen U.S. troops are killed in a clash with warlords in Somalia. The United States decides to withdraw.

1994

September

The United States sends peacekeeping troops to Haiti to help a restore a U.S.-backed president after engineering the ruling junta's withdrawal.

1995

April

A massive truck bomb destroys a federal office building in Oklahoma City, killing 168 men, women, and children. Two radical antigovernment domestic militia terrorists are arrested and accused of the attack shortly after the blast.

December

The United States sends troops into Bosnia as part of a United Nations force that will try to enforce a truce between the Bosian Serbs, the Muslims, and the Croatians, who have been at war since the breakup of Yugoslavia.

1996

January

Senate leader Robert Dole begins a primary campaign for the Republican nomination. He will beat back a minor challenge from ultraconservative Pat Buchanan in the coming months and take the nomination easily. President Clinton has seemed vulnerable, but a rapidly improving economy strengthens the president's position.

August

Robert Dole is nominated by the Republicans, and he chooses New York's Jack Kemp as his vice-presidential running mate. They are well behind the Democratic incumbents Bill Clinton and Al Gore in the polls. Ross Perot is also again in the race, but trailing his popularity of four years previous.

November

President Clinton and Vice President Gore easily defeat Dole and Kemp, taking 49 percent of the popular vote and claiming 373 electoral votes. The Republicans have 41 percent of the popular vote and 113 in the electoral college. Perot has dropped to 8 percent of the popular vote.

1997

January

Bill Clinton and Al Gore are sworn in as president and vice president for second terms. Having beaten the odds to win the national election, they now embark on campaigns to advance their domestic agenda while facing a U.S. House and Senate still controlled by Republicans. Gore, who appears to be the heir apparent to Clinton as a presidential candidate, hopes to spearhead domestic issues that will keep him favorably in the public eye.

June

The jobless rate hits 4.8 percent, the lowest figure in more than twenty years, signaling the robust health of the American economy. Over the next three years, the stock market indexes and all other measures of economic activity reach extraordinary heights, pushed most publicly by the rapid formation and growth of new Internet-based businesses (known as "dot coms" because their names include the Internet designation ".com" at the end). Almost all sectors of American society seem to share in the record-breaking prosperity, which gives a strong boost to the approval ratings of President Clinton.

December

U.S. Attorney General Janet Reno, who has been held over in office despite widespread criticism of her actions during the first Clinton-Gore term, absolves both Clinton and Gore of legal responsibility for making what appear to have been illegal campaign fund-raising calls

from their official White House offices. She rules out charges and further investigation.

1998

January

President Clinton is called to testify privately in a sexual harassment case brought against him by former Arkansas state employee Paula Jones, who during the 1992 campaign had accused the president of making improper sexual advances toward her when he was Arkansas governor. Clinton later turns down an offer by Jones's attorneys to settle the case because he is reluctant to make an embarrassing public apology. During his deposition, Clinton denies a sexual relationship with a young White House intern named Monica Lewinsky.

June

President Clinton makes an official visit to China, a nation he has attempted to woo into closer ties with the United States. Clinton's domestic opponents accuse him of ignoring the well-documented human rights abuses of the Chinese government in order to advance economic trade and easier diplomatic relations.

July

Special Counsel Kenneth Starr, who has taken over the long-running investigation into fraudulent land deals in Arkansas in which both President Clinton and First Lady Hillary Rodham Clinton appear to have been involved, although no evidence of impropriety by either has surfaced, subpoenas President Clinton to testify to the Whitewater grand jury.

August

Monica Lewinsky testifies to the grand jury, alleging she took part in a series of sexual encounters with President Clinton in the White House while she was an intern there. Public revelations of her testimony set off a national uproar, and Starr—supported by the president's political enemies—pushes forward his case against the president for perjury under oath during his grand jury testimony and obstruction of justice, based on the president's alleged attempts to cover up his relationship with Lewinsky and to suppress her testimony.

Terrorists blow up U.S. embassies in Kenya and Tanzania, killing and injuring dozens of people. The attack is suspected to be the result of a plot by Muslim terrorist mastermind Osama bin Laden, an immensely rich Saudi who hates the United States and is said to train terrorists from a base in Afghanistan.

After first publicly denying during a national telecast that he had sexual relations with Monica Lewinsky, President Clinton is forced to admit his involvement.

September

Special Counsel Kenneth Starr's report to the U.S. Congress on President Clinton's false grand jury testimony and his relationship with Lewinsky is released to the public. It describes in explicit detail a series of sexual acts between Clinton and the intern, which the Republican members of Congress conclude make Clinton guilty of perjury since he denied the relationship under oath.

December

The U.S. House of Representatives brings articles of impeachment against President Bill Clinton, marking only the second time in U.S. history that a president has been impeached. The vote, which is mostly along political party lines, claims Clinton committed perjury before the Whitewater grand jury and attempted to obstruct justice during the investigation.

1999

January

The trial of President Clinton on articles of impeachment opens in the U.S. Senate, which the Republicans control. Chief Justice of the U.S. Supreme Court William Rehnquist presides. If convicted, Clinton will become the first U.S. president to be officially ousted from office.

February

After considerable debate, oratory, and legal wrangling, the Senate votes fifty-five to forty-five to acquit the president. Ten Republicans have joined the Senate Democrats.

April

Three teenage high school students arm themselves with a small arsenal and attack their classmates and teachers at Columbine High School in Colorado. They kill thirteen and then commit suicide. The carnage and the televised aftermath shock the nation, but it is only one of a series of school shootings by teenagers during the 1990s.

March

NATO launches a series of air attacks, carried out mostly by the U.S. Air Force, against Yugoslavia after the Serb-dominated nation begins what observers fear is a war of extermination against Muslims in the province of Kosovo. The air strikes continue for seventy-eight days and visit serious destruction on Belgrade and other cities before the Yugoslavian president, Slobodan Milosevic, relents and agrees to pull out of Kosovo.

June

A NATO peacekeeping force enters Kosovo on the heels of a Yugoslavian pullout.

September

Widespread and highly publicized fears about the so-called Y2K problem, which holds that computers will shut down or malfunction on January 1, 2001, reach a loud pitch that will continue until the end of the year, when all the anxieties prove to be groundless.

November

The Coast Guard rescues a six-year-old Cuban boy, Elián Gonzáles, from the waters off Florida where he is found floating in an inner tube, the survivor of an ill-fated attempt by refugees to flee Communist Cuba. His mother has drowned in the escape attempt, so he is turned over to anti-Castro relatives in Miami, even though his father is still in Cuba and claims custody of the boy.

2000

January
The presidential campaign hits high gear with the Iowa party caucuses, which supply the news media with the first slight but concrete signs of the electorate's preferences. Vice President Al Gore defeats his only serious Democratic opponent, former U.S. senator and basketball star Bill Bradley. On the Republican side, Texas governor George W. Bush (the son of former president George Bush, who was defeated by the Clinton/Gore ticket eight years previous) defeats Arizona senator and Vietnam P.O.W. hero John McCain.

February
In the New Hampshire primary election, the first actual voting for the candidates, Gore again defeats Bradley, but Senator McCain soundly whips Governor Bush, confounding most pundits and predictions.

In the subsequent primary in South Carolina, where Bush ducks comment on the hot topic of whether to remove the Confederate flag from the state capitol, the Texas governor beats McCain, but McCain returns the favor and beats Bush in the Michigan primary.

March
Despite his strong early showing, McCain concedes defeat after Bush takes more primaries. He was unable to match Bush's massive campaign chest. Bill Bradley also concedes his party's nomination to Al Gore, who will attempt to become only the second vice president since Martin Van Buren to succeed to the presidency by election (Bush's father was the other).

April
Federal agents raid the home of Elián González's relatives in Miami and forcibly remove the boy from his uncle's custody. The relatives have refused to return the boy to his father despite a court order. The move enrages the Cuban exile community in Florida.

June
A federal judge orders the breakup of computer software giant Microsoft. Although the decision is suspended pending a drawn-out appeal process, the uncertainty caused by the judgment underscores a decline in the stock market, particularly the high-flying technology stocks and "dot coms" that have driven the U.S. economy to extreme highs. By year's end, many of the most publicized dot coms go out of business, and the nation appears to slip into a recession or near recession after years of expansion and prosperity.

July
The Middle East peace talks between Israel and the Palestinians break down. President Clinton has been the chief sponsor of the talks, which were held at his presidential retreat at Camp David, Maryland.

Texas Governor George W. Bush announces former Secretary of Defense Richard B. Cheney as his choice as a vice-presidential running mate. Cheney is seen as an undynamic but highly experienced and respected choice, a good counterbalance to the slightly lightweight reputation of the presidential candidate.

August
The Republican National Convention nominates Bush and Cheney as the G.O.P. ticket. Vice President Al Gore selects Senator Joseph Lieberman as his running mate, making Lieberman the first Jewish candidate for the office of vice president. The Democratic Convention nominates the pair, who lead their Republican opponents in the national polls.

September

The six-year-long investigation of the Whitewater Arkansas real estate affair—which touched off the impeachment of President Clinton—comes to an end with an announcement that no charges will be brought against the president or First Lady Hillary Rodham Clinton, who is running for a U.S. Senate seat from the state of New York.

October

Fighting breaks out on the West Bank and in the Gaza Strip, bringing the Mideast peace process to an end and dashing hopes for an American-brokered peace.

The U.S.S. *Cole* is attacked by suicide terrorist bombers while in port for refueling in Yemen. Seventeen U.S. sailors are killed and thirty seven wounded.

The presidential candidates meet in their first campaign debate in Boston. They cover foreign policy, tax cuts, and Medicare. Green Party candidate Ralph Nader is not only barred from participating but also turned away at the door when he tries to attend the debate.

Two days later, the vice-presidential candidates meet for their only debate. The affair is low-key and extremely cordial, showing off the two men to considerable advantage.

Bush and Gore debate for the second time and forgo the contentiousness that characterized their first meeting. Bush later calls the debate a "love fest."

The final debate between the presidential candidates takes place in St. Louis and is organized in the style of a town hall meeting, as Bush and Gore respond to questions from the audience. Overall, Bush does much better than expected against Gore, who entered the campaign with a strong reputation as a formal debater.

November

National polls show the campaign to be extremely close and getting closer as November 7 approaches. The actual election proves to be the most confused and disputed in more than a century, with neither candidate able to claim a victory at day's end. The national news media's exit polling techniques break down entirely, and the television commentators swing back and forth during their reporting, first awarding the victory to one candidate and then the other. At one point, Vice President Gore believes he has lost the race, and he calls Governor Bush to concede. However, on his way to make his concession speech, Gore learns that the key state of Florida, whose twenty-five electoral votes will provide the margin of victory in the Electoral College, is still very much in doubt, so the vice president calls Bush and rescinds the concession.

The Republicans hold their control of the U.S. House of Representatives, but the Senate appears to be split fifty-fifty, pending a contested race in Oregon, making the final selection of a vice president crucial to control of the national legislature, since the new vice president will most likely have the deciding vote in the Senate if the even split holds up (as it does). Hillary Rodham Clinton takes the U.S. Senate seat for New York, making her the first wife of a U.S. president ever to hold elected office.

Following election night, a long, drawn-out series of events surrounding the counting of the popular votes in Florida, where Bush has a very slim margin—only a few hundred votes out of nearly 6 million cast—grips the nation for weeks. No one can say for certain who has won the key Florida electoral votes, not even George W. Bush's brother, Jeb, who is governor of the state, but lawyers, political-party operatives, state officeholders, and judges wrangle over the validity of punchcard ballots, hand recounts in key counties, and disqualified absentee ballots. Recounts are on and off again as the two campaigns turn to the courts. The state's Republican secretary of state, Katherine Harris, certifies Bush as the winner, but her action is challenged. The Republican-controlled state legislature appears ready to select its own slate of electors. During the weeks of confusion, vice-presidential candidate Dick Cheney suffers a mild heart attack but appears to recover quickly.

December
Although Vice President Al Gore and Senator Joe Lieberman appear to be closing the gap on Bush and Cheney in the recount of Florida votes, their hopes for victory in the Electoral College are dashed when a Bush appeal is upheld by the U.S. Supreme Court in a five-to-four decision that rules the recounts must stop and Bush will therefore win the state's electoral votes. Gore finally concedes defeat. Bush wins the Electoral College vote, 271 to 266 (one Gore elector from the District of Columbia withholds her ballot), even though Gore and Lieberman have won the overall popular vote by more than half a million votes. Only three other times has the winner of the popular vote lost the presidency in the Electoral College, and never with such a huge popular plurality.

2001

January
George W. Bush and Richard B. Cheney are inaugurated. Cheney has overseen the Bush administration transition and played a major role in selecting the Bush cabinet, and his will be the deciding vote in the evenly divided U.S. Senate.

May
Republican Vermont senator James Jeffords drops his party affiliation and declares himself to be an Independent, which breaks the 50-50 deadlock in the Senate and allows the Democrats to take control of the upper legislative house, depriving Vice President Dick Cheney of his role as tiebreaker.

June
President George W. Bush signs legislation cutting taxes at a historically high level. The cut is expected to cost $1.35 trillion over ten years.

The measure, which fulfills a major Bush-Cheney campaign pledge, includes cash tax rebates for almost all American taxpayers, repeal of the estate tax, and reduction of taxes on high incomes.

September
On the morning of September 11, Muslim suicide terrorists, acting under the orders of Osama bin Laden, a radical Saudi Arabian advocate of violence against the United States, hijack airliners and fly two of them into the twin towers of the World Trade Center in New York City. The massive impacts, explosions, and fires result in the collapse and destruction of the two huge buildings and the deaths of over 2,700 victims, including office workers, service personnel, bystanders, and firefighters and police who rush to the scene. Remarkably, thousands of people are able to escape before the buildings collapse. Shortly after the attack in New York, a third hijacked plane crashes into U.S. military headquarters at the Pentagon in Washington, D.C., killing 252 and damaging part of the building. A fourth hijacked airliner, thought to be targeting the White House or the U.S. Capitol Building, goes down in Pennsylvania after some of the 44 passengers heroically rush the hijackers flying the plane. The attacks are the first against U.S. territory since the Japanese bombing of Pearl Harbor 60 years before.

On the morning the terrorists strike, President Bush is in Sarasota, Florida, visiting a grade school. Vice President Dick Cheney assumes emergency command from a White House bunker, but his orders to shoot down the hijacked planes come too late. In the chaos and confusion following the attack, Bush flies first to an airfield in Louisiana and then heavily secured Offut Air Force Base in Nebraska, where he confers by videophone with Cheney and the National Security Council, before returning to Washington. Commercial air traffic is suspended temporarily, all planes in the air are asked to land, and the U.S. military is on high alert as rescue workers begin to search the ruins of the Twin Towers for survivors. New York City, considered by many to be the center of U.S. and world commerce, is paralyzed.

Vice President Cheney withdraws to a secret location in order to assure continuity of government in case the president is killed in further attacks on Washington. It is soon confirmed that Osama bin Laden and al-Qaeda, his terrorist organization, are responsible for the attacks, and Bush declares a virtual war on terrorism and vows to hunt down the terrorists no matter where they are, including in their training camps and headquarters in Afghanistan, a war-torn nation controlled by a radical fundamentalist Muslim militia known as the Taliban.

October

The United States, aided by Great Britain and with the cooperation of the government of Pakistan, launches an air campaign against the Taliban and suspected terrorists in Afghanistan. Cooperative anti-Taliban militias known as the Northern Alliance are designated as the primary ground forces in what develops as an all-out attack on the fundamentalist rulers of the nation and al-Qaeda. The air war destroys the terrorists' bases and sends them on the run. Taliban resistance is fierce in some areas of the country, but the campaign against them seems to head toward an inevitable military victory for the United States and its Afghan allies. Osama bin Laden, however, eludes capture or death and flees to a rugged mountainous region near the border to a remote and ungoverned area of Pakistan.

On the home front, an unknown perpetrator mails letters laden with deadly anthrax spores to members of the U.S. Congress and newspapers and television news networks in New York City. Two postal workers die after contracting the disease and many more are made sick by the infection in Washington, New York, and New Jersey, where contaminated mail had been handled.

December

The Taliban surrender their control of Afghanistan to U.S.-backed forces. A push, lasting into the following spring, to find and kill bin Laden fails, and he apparently escapes into Pakistan, where he survives in isolated safety and continues to direct al-Qaeda terrorist activities worldwide.

2002

January

President Bush delivers a defiant and aggressive State of the Union speech, honoring the victims and heroes of September 11, and he identifies the threat to the United States from what he terms "the axis of evil": Iraq, Iran, and North Korea.

February

Energy giant Enron Corporation goes bankrupt in one of the largest financial disasters in United States history, taking down thousands of employees with it and shaking key parts of the national economy. A subsequent criminal investigation reveals a story of financial corruption and manipulation by the highest corporate officers.

March

Fighting continues along the Afghan-Pakistani border, where remnants of the Taliban and al-Qaeda have dug in. The operations are characterized by heavy air and bombing assaults by U.S. planes, but the bulk of the ground action is assigned to allied Afghan fighters.

Elsewhere, renewed suicide bombings carried out against Israeli civilians prompt the Israeli government to attack Palestinian camps. The mounting bloodshed undermines any attempt to start up a peace process again

The U.S. Senate passes a major campaign finance reform law, which places limits on "soft" contributions to political parties or candidates.

May

President Bush concludes a tour of Europe by signing a nuclear arms reduction agreement with Russian president Vladimir Putin. The pact calls for both countries to reduce their nuclear stockpiles by two-thirds over the next ten years.

June

In the wake of the attacks of the previous fall, President Bush proposes a large-scale reorganization of parts of the executive branch of government in order to deal with the threat of terrorism. He wants Congress to approve a new cabinet-level Department of Homeland Security into which would be folded more than 22 existing agencies, including the Coast Guard, the Customs Service, the Secret Service, the Federal Emergency Management Agency, and the Naturalization and Immigration Service. The president had established an Office of Homeland Security soon after the September 11 attacks, but it lacked sufficient authority and status.

October

President Bush, urged on by Vice President Dick Cheney, Secretary of Defense Donald Rumsfeld, and other hawkish "neoconservatives" in the administration, seeks congressional approval for a preemptive military strike against Saddam Hussein of Iraq. In a televised speech, Bush claims that Iraq has direct ties to al-Qaeda and is preparing biological and chemical weapons of mass destruction along with missile systems capable of attacking the United States. He bases his contentions on what prove to be erroneous reports from the Central Intelligence Agency and, as it will turn out, there are no Iraqi ties to al-Qaeda or weapons of mass destruction, but he wins authority nonetheless and begins war plans.

November

The Republicans score major gains in off-year congressional elections, winning control of the House of Representatives and taking back a majority in the U.S. Senate. President Bush's strong popularity—his approval rating stands at 60 percent—is credited with sparking the victory for his party supporters. He had campaigned widely and vigorously for Republicans and will now be in a position to win congressional approval for both his pro-business domestic reforms and his aggressive foreign policy. His proposed Homeland Security Department clears Congress later in the month.

2003

January

President Bush devotes much of his State of the Union address to the threat posed to the country by Saddam Hussein and Iraq. He again accuses Hussein of developing weapons of mass destruction, warns foreign states who may harbor terrorists, and he alerts U.S. military forces to the possibility of war.

February

Disaster strikes the nation's space program when the Space Shuttle *Columbia* breaks up while attempting reentry. All seven crew members are killed when the shuttle's heat shield fails and the craft disintegrates, scattering debris in a wide swath across Texas and Louisiana.

March

After a prolonged buildup, the United States launches a preemptive war against Iraq, beginning with an intensive air bombardment, followed by a ground invasion. U.S. forces are joined by British troops and token contingents from several more countries, which comprise what President Bush calls the "coalition of the willing." Vice President Cheney plays a key role in planning the effort to unseat Iraqi strongman Saddam Hussein. The invasion force, pushing off from staging bases in Kuwait, moves quickly through Iraqi resistance, although there is fierce fighting in southern parts of the country.

April

By the first week of April, U.S. forces have reached the Iraqi capital of Baghdad and seized the airport and other key spots. They also control the highways leading in and out of the city. Within a few more days, the U.S. penetrates to the center of Baghdad and occupies Saddam Hussein's presidential palaces. The Iraqi leader and his government flee into hiding. The coalition consolidates its military grip on the country, but large-scale looting breaks out in the absence of police or security forces. The military situation is under control, but there is civil and social chaos as the old regime collapses.

May

President Bush declares an end to major fighting in Iraq after a 43-day military campaign. One by one, major figures in the Hussein regime are captured or surrender, but Hussein himself remains at large. The search for the weapons of mass destruction that the Bush administration had posited as the excuse for the invasion of Iraq turns up no evidence of actual weapons or of significant research and development facilities. In the months to come, it becomes clear that Hussein had—as he claimed —no weapons and had long ago abandoned his attempts to produce them. Iraqi insurgents begin attacks on U.S. forces, but the resistance is at a relatively low level.

On the domestic front, Congress passes and President Bush signs a $350 billion tax cut, the third largest in U.S. history.

July

U.S. forces surround and kill Saddam Hussein's two sons in the northern Iraqi town of Mosul. Officials hope this will quell the rising tide of attacks on Americans, most of them carried out with improvised bombs or with weapons that fell into the insurgents' hands in the chaos following the U.S. invasion. Despite this optimism, anti-American attacks increase. In the southern city of Najaf, a Shiite Muslim cleric stirs up anti-American furor among the fighters of his private militia.

A joint congressional committee issues a report on intelligence failures that led up to the September 11, 2001, attacks. The report faults the CIA and FBI for missing faint but clear signs of an impending attack, and it recommends an overhaul of U.S. intelligence agencies and the creation of a new intelligence czar.

August

A massive electrical power failure strikes much of the Northeast, the Midwest, and parts of Canada. What begins as a relatively minor incident mushrooms into a major problem as the blackout cascades along the power grid, and 50 million people lose electricity.

In Iraq, insurgents blow up United Nations headquarters in Baghdad, killing the top U.N. official. The attack signals increased resistance by anti-American insurgents, who begin also to target international aid groups and the fledging American-trained Iraqi police and security forces. Late in the month, another bomb in Najaf kills 80 people, including a leading Shiite cleric and leader.

September

President Bush asks Congress for an $87 billion appropriation to fund the war and reconstruction in Iraq, citing the former Iraqi regime's supposed central role in international terrorism. Despite assurances by U.S. administration officials, insurgent attacks in Iraq appear to be rising. Rejection by key European nations of U.N. resolutions proposed by the United States signals increasing diplomatic isolation.

October

Violence in Iraq continues to grow. Congress approves the president's appropriation request.

November

The Supreme Judicial Court of Massachusetts strikes down a governmental ban on gay marriage, eventually setting off a well-publicized wave of gay unions in Massachusetts and other states, which becomes an important political issue for the upcoming presidential campaign.

December

Under tight secrecy and security, President Bush makes a surprise visit to troops in Iraq, where violence against foreigners and Iraqis working with the United States continues to increase. Shiites, who are in the majority in the country, call for elections.

On December 13, former Iraqi dictator Saddam Hussein is captured when he is discovered hiding in a hole in the ground. His bearded and disheveled image is broadcast widely, and the U.S. administration hopes his capture will dampen the insurgency. He is taken to a security facility and held for interrogation and eventual trial.

2004

January

The presidential campaign gets underway with party caucuses in Iowa, where Democratic Massachusetts senator John Kerry scores a surprise victory, and previous Democratic frontrunner Howard Dean self-destructs. In his annual State of the Union address, President Bush defends his administration's policies and actions, stressing his successful fight against terrorism and defending the war in Iraq. However, violence in Iraq persists.

February

President Bush submits a $2.4 trillion budget to Congress, projecting a $521 billion deficit, not including the costs of the wars in Afghanistan and Iraq. In a statement later in the month, he proposes an amendment to the U.S. Constitution that would ban gay marriage.

March

Senator Kerry clinches the Democratic Party nomination for president by wins in nine out of ten "Super Tuesday" primaries. His chief rival, South Carolina senator John Edwards, withdraws, but Kerry eventually chooses the first-term senator, a lawyer, as his vice-presidential running mate.

On March 11, several bombs explode on commuter trains in Madrid, Spain, killing 190 and wounding 1,400 people. The attack, the work of al-Qaeda and the worst modern terrorist attack ever in western Europe, comes only days before a national election. The pro-American ruling Conservative Party's fumbling—it tries to blame Basque separatists—results in a victory for the opposition Socialist Workers Party. The new anti-American prime minister withdraws Spain from the coalition and evacuates Spanish troops from Iraq.

April

Heavy fighting intensifies on several fronts in Iraq. The dissident Shiite cleric, Moqtada al-Sadr, incites his large armed militia to revolt against the American occupation, and Sunni insurgents continue direct attacks. U.S. Marines begin a large-scale assault on the Sunni stronghold in the city of Fallujah but are ordered to withdraw before reaching a conclusion with the enemy. Secretary of State Colin Powell reveals his previous assertions about weapons of mass destruction in Iraq were wrong.

May

Investigative American journalists reveal that U.S. troops guarding prisoners at the Abu Ghraib prison in Baghdad, infamous as a center for torture under dictator Saddam Hussein, have been abusing Iraqi prisoners. Photos show naked prisoners humiliated, forced to simulate homosexual acts, and physically abused by U.S. troops, including one female soldier. The widely distributed pictures further fuel anti-American sentiment among many Muslims. Individual U.S. soldiers are eventually prosecuted for criminal behavior at the prison.

A videotape is released on the internet showing the beheading of a kidnapped American by masked Iraqi insurgents. More kidnappings and graphic beheadings of Americans and other foreigners follow throughout the summer.

June

In a hastily arranged ceremony, the American administrator of the U.S.-led Provisional Authority in Iraq hands over sovereignty to a temporary Iraqi government and departs the country. Roughly 150,000 U.S. troops remain, however, as violent resistance from insurgents continues to grow.

The bipartisan commission named to study the September 11, 2001, terrorist attacks makes its formal report, which, based on wide-ranging research and interviews, concludes that U.S. government leaders had failed to understand or fully appreciate the threat of terrorism. The commission especially notes the failure of U.S. intelligence agencies and recommends the creation of a national intelligence director to oversee all civilian and military intelligence.

John Kerry and John Edwards are formally nominated as presidential and vice-presidential candidates by the Democratic Party national convention held in Boston.

August

A major hurricane hits Florida and the Southeast, the first of a record four hurricanes over the following weeks. More than a hundred people are killed by the storms and 2,500 homes destroyed. Estimated insured damages top $22 billion. The presidential campaign sees both tickets running hard in key states.

September

President George W. Bush and Vice President Dick Cheney are renominated by the Republican Party national convention held in New York City. The campaign builds intensity, with both sides attacking strongly. The Bush-Cheney ticket defends its record against terrorism and derides the Democrats' abilities to carry on what it sees as a global war. Kerry and Edwards are slow to hit their campaign stride but cite a weak and struggling national economy and massive loss of jobs under the Republican administration.

October

Vice President Dick Cheney and Democratic challenger John Edwards meet in a face-to-face televised debate in Cleveland, following the first of three debates between the presidential candidates. Cheney declares the administration's policies in Afghanistan and Iraq to have been correct, and he levels sharp attacks on his opponents, especially Kerry. He accuses Edwards of absenteeism in the Senate, claiming (falsely as it turns out) that as presiding officer of the Senate he had never met Edwards. National polls show a close race, with the Republicans holding a slight advantage.

In Iraq, insurgents continue to escalate their war of terror and violence as the U.S. and the interim Iraqi government remain committed to holding national elections in January 2005. Much of the strength of the insurgency is in Sunni sections of the country. The Sunnis have long held power in Iraq but will likely lose in democratic elections to the large Shiite majority.

November

President Bush and Vice President Cheney are reelected with 51 percent of the popular vote, 59 million to 55.4 million for Kerry-Edwards. Unlike the 2000 election, the decisive results are clear on election night, even though winners in Iowa and New Mexico remain unclear for several days. The Republicans make gains in Congress and will keep control of both the House of Representatives and the Senate. Voter turnout is high, close to 120 million. Polling of voters shows concern for "moral values" to have been one of the keys to the outcome (ballot initiatives to ban gay marriage pass in all 11 states where they are on the ballot), and voters express confidence in Bush and Cheney to continue the war on terrorism.

Immediately after the election at home, U.S. forces in Iraq launch a campaign against the insurgent stronghold of Fallujah, which results in fierce house-to-house fighting and high casualties. Despite U.S. successes, the insurgency appears to continue to grow.

December

Bowing to political pressure, Congress passes and President Bush signs a law to reorganize the nation's intelligence agencies under a new national director. The law is a watered down version of the recommendations made by the commission that reported on the September 11, 2001, attacks.

Insurgent attacks on fledgling Iraqi police and security forces continue, and a suicide bomber penetrates a U.S. Army camp near the city of Mosul and blows himself up in a crowded mess hall, killing 22 and wounding many more.

2005

January

President George W. Bush and Vice President Dick Cheney are inaugurated for a second term.

On the last day of the month, Iraqis vote in a democratic election. The majority Shiites win, with the ethnic Kurds second. Sunni Muslims on the whole boycott the election. Iraqis elect an Iraqi transitional government to draft a permanent constitution. Although some violence and a widespread Sunni boycott occur, most of the eligible minority Kurd and Shitte populations participate, giving the new government the hoped-for democratic legitimacy.

February

The Web site YouTube is launched, revolutionizing how individuals use the Internet to both view and post user-generated content, such as movie and TV clips, music videos, and other visual media. When coupled with cell phones that can record short pieces of video, YouTube soon adds a powerful and widespread ability to publicize the activities of politicians and begins to limit the chances of hiding mistakes in public speaking and conversation.

April

Pope John Paul II dies, and German cardinal Joseph Alois Ratzinger is elected as the 265th pope, taking the name Benedict XVI. He is theologically conservative, and both his teachings and writings defend traditional Catholic doctrine and values.

May

The infamous Watergate inside source, Deep Throat, reveals himself to be W. Mark Felt, a former top FBI official, who admits that he was the anonymous source during the 1972 investigations by *Washington Post* reporters Woodward and Bernstein that eventually drove President Richard Nixon from office.

In Iraq, hopes for a quick end to the insurgency and a withdrawal of U.S. troops are ruined as suicide bombers tear through Iraq, often targeting concentrations of mainly Shiite civilians. Over 700 Iraqi civilians and 79 U.S. soldiers are killed.

June

In a 5 to 4 four decision, the U.S. Supreme Court decrees that the Connecticut city of New London had the right to exercise a state eminent domain law to require several homeowners to cede their property for commercial use that will generate tax revenue for the city. This court case is widely derided and causes much consternation among some property owners.

July

Justice Sandra Day O'Connor announces her retirement from the U.S. Supreme Court, creating the first opening in eleven years. President Bush chooses his White House counsel Harriet E. Miers as O'Connor's replacement, but objections from both the political right and left force the inexperienced and apparently unprepared Miers to withdraw on October 27 after below-par interviews and cross-examination by members of Congress. President Bush then nominates Samuel A. Alito Jr, who is confirmed to the bench of the Supreme Court on January 31, 2006.

August

Hurricane Katrina, a massive category 5 storm, causes severe damage along the Gulf coast from

Texas to central Florida, with the greatest concentration of damage in New Orleans, where levee failures flood large portions of the city and drive residents into makeshift refuges. Hundreds seek shelter in the city's domed football arena, where conditions deteriorate rapidly with little food and no water or sanitation. There is also almost no medical help, and crime—sometimes violent—becomes common in the arena. Conditions elsewhere in the city are not much better. Hundreds of victims are rescued by boat or helicopter after being stranded on rooftops of their flooded homes, and hundreds more barely survive after finding high ground on portions of an interstate highway.

The city appears to be almost destroyed by the aftermath of the storm, and thousands of homes and buildings all along the Gulf Coast in Mississippi and Alabama have also been destroyed or crucially damaged. The toll of human life and property is staggering, yet the Federal Emergency Management Agency (FEMA), to whom the survivors look for aid, seems paralyzed and fails to respond competently to the situation. Despite President Bush's televised promise to aid Katrina's victims, it soon becomes clear that the current administration has failed spectacularly, and public confidence in Bush begins a decline. Hurricane Katrina is the largest natural disaster in U.S. history.

September

The California state legislature becomes the first in the nation to approve same-sex marriages. The Religious Freedom and Civil Marriage Protection Act passed by a vote of 41 to 35.

Chief Justice William H. Rehnquist dies after a long battle with thyroid cancer. President George W. Bush's nominee for the position, John G. Roberts, Jr., meets with some opposition, but he performs smoothly in Judiciary Committee hearings, and the full Senate confirms him by a 78 to 22 vote. Roberts is subsequently sworn in as chief justice.

House Majority Leader Tom Delay, a leading architect of GOP strength in Congress, is indicted on campaign finance charges and eventually is forced to leave office. His departure signs a further decline in public support for the Republican administration and party.

October

Iraqis go to the polls and ratify their new constitution.

Vice President Cheney and his closest staffer have become deeply involved in yet another Bush administration scandal. Lewis "Scooter" Libby, Cheney's chief of staff, is indicted on charges of perjury and obstruction of justice. In 2003, an unnamed high official leaked the name of a covert CIA operative to a *Washington Post* journalist, and the agent was compromised. The CIA operative in question, Valerie Plame, is the wife of former U.S. ambassador Joseph Wilson, who had angered members of the Bush administration by refuting President Bush's claim (made in his State of the Union address) that Iraq had attempted to buy uranium in Niger. After a long investigation, Libby has been identified as the source of the leak and is indicted on federal charges. He resigns the next day as Cheney's right-hand man. Libby is subsequently convicted in March 2007 and sentenced to 30 months in prison and a fine of $250,000. Four months later, President Bush commutes the prison sentence, but Libby must pay the fine and is still classified as a convicted felon.

December

The Iraqi people elect a national assembly, with participation from Sunni, Kurd, and Shiite groups.

2006

January

The Iraq War deteriorates into a complex and savage struggle that resembles a civil war, with Iraqis by the thousands killed in fierce sectarian reprisal attacks. The U.S. military death toll nears 3,000. President Bush balks at embracing many of the key suggestions of a bipartisan study group. Iraqi authorities struggle to assert control and avoid fracture, but a protest against a summit between President Bush and Iraqi Prime Minister Nouri al-Maliki starts a three-week boycott of the new parliament that effectively stalls governmental operations.

Simultaneously, the Taliban launch a violent resurgence in Afghanistan, operating from safe haven bases across the Pakistani border.

North Korea begins underground nuclear testing that threatens regional peace and stability for China, Japan, and South Korea. This action creates global anxiety about the proliferation of nuclear weapons that could be sold to terrorist groups on the black market.

February
The al-Askari Mosque, one of the holiest sites for Shiite Muslims, is bombed in the Iraqi city of Samarra. The bombing is believed to have been the work of al-Qaeda in Iraq, and it sets off a convulsion of sectarian violence that continues for months. Death squads roam the cities and countryside, leaving scores of dead and often mutilated bodies in the streets each morning. The country appears to be slipping into a sectarian civil war, with the United States playing the role of a helpless bystander.

May
The new national government of Iraq takes office, following approval by the members of the Iraqi National Assembly. This government succeeds the Iraqi transitional government, which had continued in office after the American invasion in a caretaker capacity until the formation of this permanent government.

November
The Iraqi interim government brings Saddam Hussein to trial. He is eventually found guilty of committing crimes against humanity on charges related to the executions of 148 Iraqi Shiites suspected of planning an assassination attempt against him. He is sentenced to death by hanging and executed in December.

The Democrats claim a large victory in the November 7 off-year election. They recapture control of the House of Representatives, which they had lost in the middle of Bill Clinton's second term, with a large majority. They also gain a narrow edge in the Senate and capture statehouses nationwide, thus sending a powerful message of a desire for change throughout the nation. California Democrat Nancy Pelosi becomes the first female speaker of the House. Combined with the distressing state of affairs in Iraqi, the Democratic takeover in Congress marks the beginning of a steep downhill slide in the Bush-Cheney political fortunes and the Bush administration's ability to govern effectively.

One day after the election, Donald Rumsfeld resigns as defense secretary. Although his brusque style initially won some admiring reviews, Rumsfeld has come to be viewed as underestimating Iraq's challenges while alienating the military and members of Congress. By mid-December, President Bush nominates a new secretary of defense, former CIA director Robert Gates, who easily gains bipartisan congressional confirmation and is sworn in early the following month.

December
The official report of the bipartisan Iraq Study Group Report, set up to gauge the overall success of the American effort, is released. The study concludes that the situation in Iraq is rapidly deteriorating as U.S. forces seem to be caught in a hopeless mission. The report recommends increasing diplomatic relationships with Iran and Syria while intensifying efforts to train Iraqi troops.

2007

January
President Bush announces a surge in Iraq with the deployment of more than 20,000 additional troops to provide security to Baghdad and Al Anbar Province. The major element of the strategy is a change in focus for the U.S. military

that will, the administration hopes, then provide the time and conditions conducive to reconciliation among political and ethnic factions.

Former first lady and now senator Hillary Rodham Clinton of New York announces her campaign for the Democratic nomination for the presidential election of 2008.

February
In a possible assassination attempt on Vice President Cheney, a suicide bomber kills 23 people and wounds 20 more outside the Bagram Air Base in Afghanistan during the vice president's visit. Qari Yousef Ahmadi, a Taliban spokesman, claims Osama bin Laden supervised the attack. Cheney is on the far side of the base when the suicide bomber ignites his explosives and is nowhere near the explosion. He reports to the news media that he merely heard a distant loud bang.

April
New Century Financial files for bankruptcy, the first in a slew of mortgage company failures that slowly begin to overtake the financial industry. Defaults on subprime mortgages (mortgages granted to borrowers who meet only the bare minimum lending requirements and who often have misrepresented themselves on mortgage applications) had been rising slowly for a few years and were up over 90 percent from the year before. Banks worldwide with money in mortgage-backed securities begin to realize many of their investments are worthless, and the major stock market indexes see their values drop, prompting central banks in the United States and Europe to inject extra cash into their financial systems. As the global economy teeters, columnists blamed companies' predatory lending practices, which offered cash to people who could not afford loans and who failed to understand the terms of their loans.

A tragedy unfolds on the campus of Virginia Tech university. A disturbed student Cho Seung-Hui shoots thirty-seven students and five professors in the deadliest shootings on a U.S. college campus.

May
Iraqi parliamentary lawmakers sign onto a legislative petition calling on the U.S. to set a timetable for withdrawal from the region.

July
Vice President Cheney once again serves as acting president, this time for only about two and a half hours while President Bush undergoes a colonoscopy that requires sedation. The president resumes his powers and duties the same day.

September
Planned troop reductions in Iraq begin, with President Bush backing a limited withdrawal of soldiers in order to bring U.S. troop numbers back to their level before the surge at the beginning of the year.

October
Wildfires spread across southern California, destroying at least 1,500 houses and over half a million acres of land from Santa Barbara County to the U.S.-Mexico border. Major contributing factors were drought, hot weather, and the strong Santa Ana winds, with gusts reaching 85 mph.

2008

January
Senator Barack Obama of Illinois wins a major victory in the contest for the Democratic nomination for president, when he takes the Iowa caucus, with Senator John Edwards placing second, and Senator Hillary Rodham Clinton coming in third. Since Obama is the son of a white American mother and a black Kenyan father, the win in predominately white and conservative Iowa gives Obama's campaign a huge boost, which he subsequently uses to argue that he is a viable candidate. He becomes the first serious black candidate for the presidency. After a poor showing in Iowa, Delaware senator Joe

Biden drops out of the presidential campaign. Obama gains ground in national polling over the next week, with all polls predicting a victory for him in the New Hampshire primary. However, Clinton scores a surprise win, narrowly defeating Obama in New Hampshire and restoring some luster to her campaign.

The primary campaign fractures during the next few days, when remarks by Bill Clinton and Hillary Clinton are perceived as labeling Obama as a limited, racially oriented candidate and otherwise denying the post-racial significance and accomplishments of his campaign. Despite attempts by both Hillary Clinton and Obama to downplay the issue, Democratic voting becomes more polarized as a result, with Clinton losing much of her support among African Americans. She loses by a two-to-one margin to Obama in the South Carolina primary, setting up, with Edwards dropping out, an intense two-person contest for the 22 state primaries on February 5—Super Tuesday.

February
In the Super Tuesday primaries, Clinton and Obama almost evenly split the overall popular vote, but Obama wins more pledged convention delegates for his share of the popular vote because he better exploits the Democratic proportional allocation rules. Clinton, over the coming three months, wins some of the remaining primary contests, but not enough to overcome Obama's growing lead.

After more than half a century of rule, Fidel Castro, ruler of Cuba, relinquishes power to his younger brother Raul, who many hope will be a moderate reformer.

The resurgence of the Taliban in Afghanistan grows and gathers momentum. The Islamic extremists begin to regain control of Afgan territory, and the U.S. and NATO forces are too thin to offer effective resistance. The Afgan government in Kabul proves ineffective in resisting the Taliban.

Global inflation reaches historic levels, and domestic inflation hits a ten to twenty year high for many nations.

June
Following the final primaries, Obama gains enough delegates to become the presumptive Democratic nominee. Clinton reluctantly ends her campaign, which she has pursued to the bitter end, and endorses Obama.

July
The U.S. economy increasingly shows signs of serious trouble. The housing market is distressed in many regions and begins to collapse nationwide. It slowly dawns on Americans that something is drastically wrong with the fundamental structure of the market economy. Wheeling and dealing financial companies and banks have used the vehicle of subprime and questionable loans to fuel a spectacular period of huge profits, but now the underlying housing values begin to decline rapidly, bringing into question the value of many historic, big-name banks and financial institutions that have invested heavily in the convoluted housing market and financial products derived from it.

To add to domestic economic troubles, global economic issues produce hyper-volatile energy markets. The price of crude oil soars as high as $150 a barrel before crashing to $33 in December. The average price for a gallon of regular gas peaks at $4.11, then plunges below $1.70

August
Russia attacks neighboring South Ossetia, a breakaway province of the NATO–aspirant former Soviet republic of Georgia, sending the message that Moscow will tolerate no interference from an expanding NATO or challenges by Georgia's nationalist president Mikheil Saakashvili. Europeans eventually broker a peace agreement after Russian forces crush Georgian resistance and occupy a large part of territory claimed by Georgia. The peace is largely on Moscow's terms.

Barack Obama is officially nominated at the Democratic National Convention, and he chooses Delaware senator Joe Biden as his running mate. The nomination of a black candidate is an historic first, and polls show he has a significant lead over the Republican presumptive candidate, Arizona senator John McCain, who has routed his opponents in the Republican primaries.

September
The Republicans nominate Senator John McCain, and he selects Governor Sarah Palin of Alaska as his running mate, the first woman to be nominated by the Republican Party. McCain's selection is apparently intended to appeal to the female vote and to attract diehard Hillary Clinton supporters who have balked at the Obama nomination. Palin proves to be a feisty, hardcore conservative campaigner, but she begins almost immediately to reveal her thin knowledge of international and domestic affairs. Her gaffes in interviews and public appearances continue to pile up, causing many independent voters to swing to the Obama-Biden ticket, which takes what proves to be an unbeatable lead in the national polls.

Lehman Brothers, a venerable investment banking company, declares bankruptcy, revealing that much of its supposed value has been based on "toxic" mortgage-backed securities. An appeal to the Bush administration to save the company is rejected. Insurance company AIG soon follows Lehman Brothers to the brink of insolvency but is saved by the U.S. Treasury with a massive bailout, having been deemed too big to allow to fail—administration officials fear a complete collapse of the national financial system if AIG goes bankrupt. The stock market experiences huge losses, home prices fall even further, and a surge of foreclosure and financial failures follows. It becomes the worst economic crisis since the Great Depression of the 1930s. The Bush administration devises a plan to bail out the largest banks and financial companies that will cost the federal government hundreds of billions of dollars. (Eventually, over $1 trillion is spent by Bush and his successor in various rescue and stimulus packages.) The unemployment rate also begins to climb, and it becomes

clear that the Big Three U.S. automakers, who have been giant factors in the domestic economy for decades, are now in serious economic peril or virtually bankrupt. Ford Motor Company appears to be in the best condition of the three, but Chrysler and General Motors can continue to operate only through massive government handouts. Many ordinary Americans now see their retirement savings severely depleted or destroyed and their savings and investments tattered. The financial pain is deep and severe, although the largest banks survive due to the massive infusions of federal bailout money.

November
Proving the pre-election polls to be accurate, Democratic senator Barack Obama and Senator Joe Biden defeat Senator John McCain and Governor Palin, with 365 electoral votes and 52.9 percent of the popular vote. The Republicans claim 173 electoral votes and 45.7 percent of the popular vote. Barack Obama becomes the first black or mixed-race president after a campaign of ingenuity and inventiveness that marked a generational shift in American politics through innovative campaign tactics and the use of the Internet to raise huge sums of money. His election is celebrated across the nation and the world as a political and social landmark.

December
The Iraqi government approves the U.S.-Iraq Status of Forces Agreement. It establishes that U.S. combat forces will withdraw from Iraqi cities by June 2009, and that all U.S. forces will be completely out of Iraq by the end of 2011.

2009

January
Barack Obama is inaugurated as the forty-fourth president and Joe Biden as the forty-seventh vice president before a huge crowd numbering over 2 million on the great national green that stretches from the west side of the Capitol to the Lincoln Memorial.

VICE PRESIDENTS OF THE UNITED STATES

(In Alphabetical Order with Years of Service)

Adams, John (1789–1797)

Agnew, Spiro Theodore (1969–1973)

Arthur, Chester Alan (1881)

Barkley, Alben W. (1949–1953)

Biden, Joseph (2009–   )

Breckinridge, John Cabell (1857–1861)

Burr, Aaron (1801–1805)

Bush, George Herbert Walker (1981–1989)

Calhoun, John Caldwell (1825–1832)

Cheney, Richard Bruce (2001–2009)

Clinton, George (1805–1812)

Colfax, Schuyler (1869–1873)

Coolidge, Calvin (1921–1923)

Curtis, Charles (1929–1933)

Dallas, George Mifflin (1845–1849)

Dawes, Charles Gates (1925–1929)

Fairbanks, Charles Warren (1905–1909)

Fillmore, Millard (1849–1850)

Ford, Gerald Rudolph (1973–1974)

Garner, John Nance (1933–1941)

Gerry, Elbridge (1813–1814)

Gore, Albert Arnold, Jr. (1993–2001)

Hamlin, Hannibal (1861–1865)

Hendricks, Thomas Andrews (1885)

Hobart, Garret Augustus (1897–1899)

Humphrey, Hubert H., Jr. (1965–1969)

Jefferson, Thomas (1797–1801)

Johnson, Andrew (1865)

Johnson, Lyndon Baines (1961–1963)

Johnson, Richard Mentor (1837–1841)

King, William Rufus de Vane (1853)

Marshall, Thomas Riley (1913–1921)

Mondale, Walter F. (1977–1981)

Morton, Levi Parsons (1889–1893)

Nixon, Richard Milhous (1953–1961)

Quayle, J. Danforth (1989–1993)

Rockefeller, Nelson A. (1974–1977)

Roosevelt, Theodore (1901)

Sherman, James Schoolcraft (1909–1912)

Stevenson, Adlai Ewing (1893–1897)

Tompkins, Daniel D. (1817–1825)

Truman, Harry S. (1945)

Tyler, John (1841)

Van Buren, Martin (1833–1837)

Wallace, Henry Agard (1941–1945)

Wheeler, William A. (1877–1881)

Wilson, Henry (1873–1875)

Vice Presidents of the United States

(Listed by State)

("b" indicates state of birth; "c" location of career)

Alabama
King, William Rufus de Vane (c)

California
Nixon, Richard Milhous

Delaware
Biden, Joseph (c)

Indiana
Colfax, Schuyler
Hendricks, Thomas Andrews (c)
Fairbanks, Charles Warren
Marshall, Thomas Riley
Quayle, J. Danforth

Illinois
Stevenson, Adlai Ewing (c)
Dawes, Charles Gates (c)

Iowa
Wallace, Henry Agard

Kansas
Curtis, Charles

Kentucky
Johnson, Richard Mentor
Breckinridge, John Cabell
Stevenson, Adlai Ewing (b)
Barkley, Alben W.

Maine
Hamlin, Hannibal
Rockefeller, Nelson A. (b)

Massachusetts
Adams, John
Gerry, Elbridge
Wilson, Henry
Bush, George Herbert Walker (b)

Michigan
Ford, Gerald Rudolph

Missouri
Truman, Harry S.

Nebraska
Cheney, Richard Bruce (b)
Dawes, Charles Gates (c)
Ford, Gerald Rudolph (b)

New York
Burr, Aaron (c)
Clinton, George
Tompkins, Daniel D.
Van Buren, Martin
Fillmore, Millard
Wheeler, William A.
Arthur, Chester Alan (c)
Morton, Levi Parsons (c)
Roosevelt, Theodore
Sherman, James Schoolcraft
Rockefeller, Nelson A. (c)

New Jersey
Hobart, Garret Augustus
Burr, Aaron (b)

North Carolina
King, William Rufus de Vane

Ohio
Hendricks, Thomas Andrews (b)
Fairbanks, Charles Warren
Dawes, Charles Gates (b)

Pennsylvania
Biden, Joseph (b)
Dallas, George Mifflin

South Carolina
Calhoun, John Caldwell

South Dakota
Humphrey, Hubert H., Jr. (b)

Tennessee
Johnson, Andrew
Gore, Albert Arnold, Jr.

Texas
Garner, John Nance
Johnson, Lyndon Baines
Bush, George Herbert Walker (c)

Vermont
Arthur, Chester Alan (b)
Morton, Levi Parsons (b)
Coolidge, Calvin

Virginia
Jefferson, Thomas
Tyler, John

Wyoming
Cheney, Richard Bruce (c)

UNSUCCESSFUL
VICE-PRESIDENTIAL CANDIDATES
By Year of Contest

1792	George Clinton (Antifederalist)	1896	Arthur Sewell (Democrat)
1796	Thomas Pinckney (Federalist)	1900	Adlai Stevenson (Democrat)
	Aaron Burr (Democratic-Republican)	1904	Henry G. Davis (Democrat)
1800	Charles C. Pinckney (Federalist)	1908	John W. Kern (Democrat)
1804	Rufus King (Federalist)	1912	Nicolas Butler (Republican)
1808	Rufus King		Hiram W. Johnson (Progressive)
1812	Jared Ingersoll (Federalist)	1916	Charles W. Fairbanks (Republican)
1816	John Howard (Federalist)	1920	Franklin D. Roosevelt (Democrat)
1820	no opponent	1924	Charles W. Bryan (Democrat)
1824	Nathan Sanford (no party)		Burton K. Wheeler (Progressive)
	Nathaniel Macon (no party)	1928	Joseph T. Robinson (Democrat)
1828	Richard Rush (National Republican)	1932	Charles Curtis (Republican)
1832	John Sergeant (National Republican)	1936	Frank Knox (Republican)
1836	Francis Granger (Whig)	1940	Charles McNary (Republican)
	John Tyler (Whig)	1944	John Bricker (Republican)
1840	Richard M. Johnson (Democrat)	1948	Earl Warren (Republican)
1844	Theodore Frelinghuysen (Whig)		Felding Wright (States' Rights)
1848	William O. Butler (Democrat)	1952	John Sparkman (Democrat)
	Charles Francis Adams (Free Soil)	1956	Estes Kefauver (Democrat)
1852	William A. Graham (Whig)	1960	Henry Cabot Lodge (Republican)
1856	William L. Dayton (Republican)	1964	William Miller (Republican)
1860	Edward Everett (Constitutional Union)	1968	Edmund Muskie (Democrat)
	Hershell V. Johnson (Democrat)	1972	Sergeant Shriver (Democrat)
	Joseph Lane (National Democrat)	1976	Robert Dole (Republican)
1864	George Pendleton (Democrat)	1980	Walter F. Mondale (Democrat)
1868	Francis P. Blair (Democrat)	1984	Geraldine Ferraro (Democrat)
1872	B. Gratz Brown (Liberal Republican and Democrat)	1988	Lloyd Bentsen (Democrat)
		1992	J. Danforth Quayle (Republican)
1876	Thomas Hendricks (Democrat)		James Stockdale (Independent)
1880	William English (Democrat)	1996	Jack Kemp (Republican)
1884	John A. Logan (Republican)	2000	Joseph Lieberman (Democrat)
1888	Allen G. Thurman (Democrat)	2004	John Edwards (Democrat)
1892	Whitlaw Reid (Republican)	2008	Sarah Palin (Republican)

GENERAL REFERENCES

Abbott, Philip. *Accidental Presidents: Death, Assassination, Resignation, and Democratic Succession.* New York: Palgrave Macmillan, 2008.

Alotta, Robert I. *#2: A Look at the Vice Presidency.* New York: Julian Messner, 1981.

American Political Leaders, 1789–2000. Washington, D.C.: Congressional Quarterly Press, 2000.

Barzman, Sol. *Madmen and Geniuses: The Vice Presidents of the United States.* Chicago: Follett Publishing Co., 1974.

Baumgartner, Jody C. *The American Vice Presidency Reconsidered.* Westport, Conn.: Praeger Publishers, 2006.

Byrne, Gary C., and Paul Marx. *The Great American Convention: A Political History of Presidential Elections.* Palo Alto, Calif.: Pacific Books, 1976.

Center for the Study of the Presidency. Special Issue on the Modern Vice Presidency. *Presidential Studies Quarterly* 38, no. 3 (July 2008).

Cleere, Gail S. *The House on Observatory Hill: Home of the Vice Presidents of the United States.* Washington, D.C.: Department of the Navy, 1989; reprinted, Diane Publishing Co., 1993.

Congress, Biographical Directory of the U.S. http://bioguide.congress.gov/biosearch.asp.

Curtis, Richard, and Maggie Wells. *Not Exactly a Crime: Our Vice Presidents from Adams to Agnew.* New York: Dial Press, 1972.

Daily, William O., Edward A. Hinck, and Shelly S. Hinck. *Politeness in Presidential Debates: Shaping Political Fare in Campaign Debates from 1960 to 2004.* Lanham, Md.: Rowman & Littlefield Publishers, 2008.

Dell, Christopher. *Vice Presidents of the United States, 1789–1978: Brief Biographical Notes.* Washington, D.C.: Library of Congress, Congressional Records Service, 1978.

Diller, Daniel C., and Stephen L. Robertson. *The Presidents, First Ladies, and Vice Presidents, 1789–1997.* Washington, D.C.: Congressional Quarterly Press, 1998.

Di Salle, Michael V., and Lawrence G. Blockman. *Second Choice.* New York: Hawthorne Books, 1966.

Dorman, Michael. *The Second Man.* New York: Delacorte Press, 1968.

Dunlap, Leslie W. *Our Vice Presidents and Second Ladies.* Metuchen, N.J.: Scarecrow, 1988.

Durbin, Thomas M., and Michael V. Seitzinger. *Nomination and Election of the President and Vice President of the United States.* Washington, D.C.: Government Printing Office, 1992.

Genovese, Michael A. *Encyclopedia of the American Presidency.* New York: Facts On File, Inc., 2004.

Goldstein, Joel K. *The Modern Vice Presidency: The Transformation of a Political Institution.* Princeton, N.J.: Princeton University Press, 1982.

Harwood, Michael. *In the Shadow of the Presidents.* New York: J. B. Lippincott, 1966.

Hatch, Louis C., and Earl L. Shoup. *A History of the Vice Presidency of the United States.* Westport, Conn.: Greenwood Press, 1970.

Hatfield, Mark O., and Wendy Wolff. *Vice-Presidents of the United States, 1789–1993.* Washington, D.C.: Government Printing Office, 1997.

Healy, Diana Dixon. *America's Vice Presidents.* New York: Atheneum, 1989.

Hoopes, Roy. *The Changing Vice-Presidency.* New York: Crowell, 1981.

Justice, Keith L. *Presidents, Vice Presidents, Cabinet Members, Supreme Court Justices, 1789–2003.* Jefferson, N.C.: McFarland & Co., 2003.

Kane, Joseph N., Janet Podell, and Steven Anzovin. *Facts about the Presidents: A Compilation of Biographical and Historic Information.* 7th ed. New York: H. W. Wilson, 2001.

Kelter, Bill. *Veeps.* Marietta, Ga.: Top Shelf, 2008.

Kengor, Paul. *Wreath Layer or Policy Player: The Vice President's Role in Foreign Policy.* Lanham, Md.: Lexington Books, 2000.

Kinkade, Vance R. *Heirs Apparent: Solving the Vice Presidential Dilemma.* Westport, Conn.: Praeger, 2000.

Laird, Archibald. *The Near Great—Chronicle of the Vice Presidents: A Collection of Photographs and Inscriptions and a Record of Historic Events.* North Quincy, Mass.: Christopher Publishing House, 1980.

Lanman, Charles. *Biographical Annals of the Civil Government of the U.S. during Its First Century.* Washington, D.C.: 1876; reprinted, Gale Publishing, 1976.

Lechelt, Jack. *The Vice Presidency in Foreign Policy: From Mondale to Cheney.* El Paso, Tex.: LFB Scholarly Publications, 2009.

Levin, Peter. *Seven by Chance: The Accidental Presidents.* New York: Farrar, Straus, & Co., 1948.

Levy, Leonard W., and Lewis Fisher, eds. *The Encyclopedia of the American Presidency.* New York: Simon & Schuster, 1994.

Light, Paul C. *Vice Presidential Power: Advice and Influence in the White House.* Baltimore, Md.: Johns Hopkins University Press, 1984.

Lott, Jeremy. *The Warm Bucket Brigade: The Story of the American Vice Presidency.* Nashville, Tenn.: Thomas Nelson, 2007.

Natoli, Marie D. *American Prince, American Pauper: The Contemporary Vice Presidency in Perspective.* Westport, Conn.: Greenwood Press, 1985.

Nelson, Michael, ed. *Guide to the Presidency,* 3rd ed., 2 vols. Washington, D.C.: Congressional Quarterly Press, 2003.

———. *A Heartbeat Away.* New York: Priority Press Publications, 1988.

Office of the Vice President of the United States, 1789–1978. Washington, D.C.: Office of the Vice President, Government Printing Office, 1971.

Patterson, Bradley H. *To Serve the President: Continuity and Innovation in the White House Staff.* Washington, D.C.: Brookings Institution Press, 2008.

Relyea, Harold, and Charles V. Arja. *The Vice Presidency of the United States: Evolution of the Modern Office.* New York: Nova Science Publishers, 2002.

Schindler, Allan P. *Unchosen Presidents: The Vice-Presidency and Other Frustrations of Presidential Succession.* Berkeley, Calif.: University of California Press, 1976.

Schlesinger, Arthur M., Jr., and Fred L. Israel, eds. *History of the American Presidential Elections, 1789–1968.* 4 vols. New York: Chelsea House, 1971.

Schlup, Leonard, and Thomas Sutton (eds.). *The American Vice Presidency in the Last Half of the Nineteenth Century: A Documentary History.* Lewiston, Me.: Edwin Mellen Press, 2007.

Shade, William G., and Ballard C. Campbell, eds. *American Presidential Campaigns and Elections.* 3 vols. Armonk, N.Y.: Sharpe Reference, 2003.

Sobel, Robert, and David B. Sicilia, eds. *The United States Executive Branch: A Biographical Dictionary of the Heads of State and Cabinet Officials.* Westport, Conn.: Greenwood Press, 2003.

Southwick, Leslie, *Presidential Also Rans and Running Mates, 1788–1996.* Jefferson, N.C.: MacFarland & Co., 1998.

Tally, Steve. *Bland Ambition: From Adams to Quayle—The Cranks, Criminals, Tax Cheats, and Golfers Who Made It to the Vice Presidency.* San Diego, Calif.: Harcourt Brace Jovanovich, 1992.

Treese, Joel D. and Dorothy J. Countryman, eds. *Biographical Directory of the U. S. Congress, 1774–1996.* Alexandria, Va.: Congressional Quarterly Books, 1996.

Tompkins, Dorothy. *Selection of the Vice President.* Berkeley, Calif.: Institute of Governmental Studies, University of California, 1974.

United States Senate. *The Vice Presidential Bust Collection.* Washington: Senate Commission on Art, 2004.

Vexler, Robert I. *The Vice-Presidents and Cabinet Members: Biographies Arranged Chronologically by Administration.* Dobbs Ferry, N.Y.: Oceana Publications, 1975.

Walch, Timothy, ed. *At the President's Side: The Vice Presidency in the Twentieth Century.* Columbia, Mo.: University of Missouri Press, 1997.

Waldrup, Carole Chandler. *The Vice Presidents: Biographies of the 45 Men Who Have Held the Second Highest Office in the Land.* Jefferson, N.C.: MacFarland & Co., 1996.

Warshaw, Shirley Anne. *The Co-Presidency of Bush and Cheney.* Palo Alto: Stanford University Press, 2009.

Waugh, Edgar W. *Second Consuls: The Vice Presidency; Our Greatest Political Problem.* Indianapolis, Ind.: Bobbs-Merrill, 1956.

Williams, Irving G. *The Rise of the Vice Presidency.* Washington, D.C.: Public Affairs Press, 1956.

Witcover, Jules. *Crapshoot: Rolling the Dice on the Vice-Presidency.* New York: Crown, 1992.

Young, Donald. *American Roulette: The History and Dilemma of the Vice Presidency.* New York: Holt, Rinehart and Winston, 1965.

Young, Klyde, and Lamar Middleton. *Heirs Apparent: The Vice Presidents of the United States.* Freeport, N.Y.: Books for Libraries Press, 1969.

GENERAL WEB SITES:

www.angelfire.com/az/theredbadge/vps.html
www.christers.net/veeps
www.VicePresidents.com

Index

Photos and illustrations are indicated by *italic* locators. Locators for main entries are set in **boldface;** locators for material in the chronologies are followed by *c;* locators for material in the appendixes are followed by *a.*

election of 1824 62, 64–66,
109–110
election of 1828 68
historical significance 73–74
and Jackson 68–70
and Johnson (R.) 88–89
"Onslow-Patrick Henry"
correspondence 66–67
personal qualities 64
resignation from vice presidency
71
as secretary of state 73, 105
as secretary of war 64
in South Carolina politics 71–72
on state's rights 70–71, 72
tariff crisis 71–72
theory of concurrent majority
73
on uses of political power 67–
68
and Van Buren 78, 79–80, 83–
84
vice presidency 68–71
in War of 1812 64
Calhoun, Patrick 64
Califano, Joseph 368, 406
California statehood 124–125, 151
Callender, James 23
Cameron, J. Donald 193
Cameron, Simon 152
Camp, Bert 406
Cannon, James 393
Cannon, Joseph 256, 262, 309,
310
Carr, Peter 23
Carr, Samuel 23
Carrow, Edith Kermit 244
Carter, Jimmy 510–511c
election of 1976 384, 403–405,
443
election of 1980 407, 415
and Mondale 397–398, 404–
407
Cass, Lewis 111, 116, 118, 133
Central Intelligence Agency 346,
393, 413–414, 450, 453–454
Chambers, Whittaker 344
Chandler, William E. 197
Chapman, Reuben 133
Chase, Salmon P. 162
Chase, Samuel 31
Cheetham, James 30
Cheney, Elizabeth 442
Cheney, Lynn Vincent 442, 443,
446, 451–452
Cheney, Mary 452
Cheney, Richard Bruce v, vi, 441,
441–456, 518–531c
Bush's (G. W.) relationship with
446

in Congress 443
early life 441–442
education 442
election of 2000 446–447, 448
election of 2004 451–453
energy policy 448
and gay marriage 452
health 443, 445–446, 447
secretary of defense 444
vice presidency 446–455
Chernomyrdin, Victor 432, 434
China 321, 347, 351, 375, 413,
433
Chinn, Julia 91
Christian, Letitia 106
Christopher, Warren 430, 437
Cincinnati, Society of 48
civil rights
antebellum Indiana 200
Arthur administration 197
Carter administration 406
after Civil War 177–178, 202
election of 1892 221, 222
election of 1960 349, 355–356
election of 1964 400
equal employment opportunity
359, 368
Ford's politics 384–385
gay and lesbian rights 384–385,
452, 453
Hendricks's politics 202
Humphrey's political efforts
365, 366
Johnson's (L.) record 355–356,
359–360
Mondale's politics 400, 401,
406
Nixon's legislative
accomplishments 349, 350–
351
Truman administration 331
Wallace's (H. A.) politics 322–
323
civil service reform
in Arthur administration 196
in Cleveland administration
205–206, 244–245
election of 1880 193
election of 1884 205
in Gore term 432
in Hayes administration 184
and Wilson (H.) 179
Civil War 152–154
Arthur in 192
beginning of 143–144, 176,
182, 201
conscription 176
Copperheads in Congress 201
early North-South disagreements
70–72, 73, 97, 99

efforts to prevent 107
Hamlin's activities 152–154
Hendricks's politics 201–202
Reconstruction 160–161, 169,
177–179
Roosevelt family in 242
status of African Americans after
177
Clark, Champ 274, 310
Clark, Mary Todhunter 388
Clarke, Evelyn 166
Clay, Cassius M. 152
Clay, Henry
and Burr 32
and Clinton (G.) 44
death of 140–141
election of 1824 64–66
election of 1840 122
election of 1844 110, 111, 112
election of 1848 123
on slavery 124, 151
tariff of 1833 72
and Tompkins 62
and Tyler 99, 100–101, 102
and Van Buren 80, 82–83, 85
Clay, Lucius 358
Cleary, Joseph 121
Cleveland, Grover 489–491c
election of 1884 205, 220
election of 1888 214
election of 1892 220–222
election of 1896 234
and Hendricks 205–206
illness and operation of 1892
223
presidency 223–224, 233
and Stevenson 220–221, 224
Clifford, Clark 339
Clinton, Catherine 36
Clinton, Cornelia 36, 41, 44
Clinton, DeWitt
and Clinton (G.) 35, 40
election of 1812 53, 57–58, 77
in New York politics 41
and Tompkins 56–57, 58, 59,
60–61, 62
and Van Buren 77, 78
Clinton, George vi, 34, **34–44**,
474–475c
Burr and 27, 29, 42
death of 44
early life 35
election of 1788 5
election of 1804 31
election of 1808 43–44, 57
Genêt affair 41
as governor of New York 37–
40, 41–42
historical significance 35
in national politics 41–42

E

F

early life and education 259–260

election of 1908 263, 265–266

family background 259–260

historical significance 263–264, 267

illness and death 266–267

in New York politics 260

Payne-Aldrich Tariff Bill 264

personal qualities 259, 261, 263–264

political beliefs 263–265

scandal rumors 265–266

vice presidency 259, 263–266

Sherman, John 187, 192–193

Sherman, William T. 161, 162

Sherman Antitrust Act 248–249

Shriver, Sargent 376

Skelton, Martha Wales 17

slavery

ban on trade 22, 43

Breckinridge's views 139

Colfax's beliefs 167

Compromise of 1850 125, 126, 127, 133, 167

constitutional ban 168

Dallas's views 117

election of 1848 116, 123–124

election of 1852 134

election of 1860 142–143

Fillmore vice presidency/presidency 119–120, 124–125, 127

Hamlin's views 148, 149, 150–151

Hendricks's politics 200, 201

issues in election of 1844 112

Jefferson and 16, 17, 23

Johnson (R.)'s personal life and 91

Kansas-Nebraska Bill 151

Missouri Crisis and Compromise 60, 96, 97–98

New York legislation 59

popular sovereignty proposal 116, 141

in Taylor administration 124–125

and Texas annexation 104–105

and westward expansion 119–120, 124–125

in Wilson's politics 174–175, 176–177

Slemp, C. Bascom 285

Smallpox War 47

Smith, Abigail 2

Smith, William, the younger 35

Smith, William Henry 254, 255

Smoot, Reed 305

Snyder, Simon 59

social services

educational system 86–87, 93, 178

Great Society reforms 361

Mondale's policies 401–402

Progressive Party platform of 1912 250

Quayle's labor legislation 422–423

Tompkins's policy 57

Sorenson, Theodore 360

Southeast Asia Treaty Organization 346

Soviet Union. *See also* Russia

in Afghanistan 449

collapse of 417, 449

Nixon administration 346, 347, 351, 375

Wallace in 321

space race 357

Spain 450

Spanish-American War 228, 238, 245–246

Sparkman, John 344–345

Spencer, Ambrose 77

Stalwarts 190, 193, 194–195, 196, 210, 212

Stamp Act 2, 46

Stanbery, Henry 162

Stanton, Edwin 160, 162, 163, 169

Stark, Lloyd C. 325–326

Starr, Kenneth 434

Stassen, Harold 346–347

Stearns, Frank 281–282

Stevens, Thaddeus 159, 162, 168

Stevenson, Adlai Ewing *218,* **218–230,** *490–491c*

and Cleveland 220–221, 224

in Congress 219–220

early life 219

election of 1860 219

election of 1884 220

election of 1890 220

election of 1892 220–222

election of 1896 225–227

election of 1900 228–229, 247

historical significance 229

and Hobart 236

in Illinois politics 219

isolationist policies 229

later life 229

personal qualities 218–219

political beliefs 219

postal appointment 220

vice presidency 223–226

Stevenson, Adlai Ewing, II 345, 367

Stevenson, Andrew 78–79

Stewart, John 454

Stimson, Henry L. 331

Stockdale, James 431

Stone, Harlan Fiske 296

Strategic Air Command 449

Street, Anna Livingston Read 210

Stuart, David 8

Summary View of the Rights of British America 17

Sumner, Charles 175, 177, 179

Sununu, John 425

Supreme Court

Bork confirmation hearings 458–459

Bush v. Gore 438, 441, 446

on Commerce Clause 462–463

Enron controversy 448

executive employment of justices 28

Thomas confirmation hearings 461–462

Swartwout, Samuel 79

Sylvester, Francis 76

T

Taft, Robert 376

Taft, William Howard 250, 256, 263, 265, 493c

Taggart, Thomas 272–273, 274

Taliban 448–449

Talleyrand-Périgord, Charles-Maurice de 12–13

Tammany Hall 29, 41, 57, 60, 205

Taney, Roger B. 82

Tappen, Cornelia 36

Tawney, James A. 262

tax policy

Adams's (J.) views 8

Bush administration 425

Cleveland administration 223–224

Coolidge administration 286–287

federal v. state authority 38, 48

tariff of 1842 114–115

tariffs of 1820s/1830s 70–72, 80–81, 97

Wilson administration 310

Taylor, Claudia Alta 354

Taylor, Hobart, Jr. 359–360

Taylor, John 28

Taylor, John W. 77

Taylor, Zachary 116, 120, 123, 125, 482–483c

Tazewell, Henry 20

Teapot Dome 286

Tecumseh 88

Tenet, George 450

Tennessee statehood 28

Wallace, George C. 350, 370, 374, 403
Wallace, Henry Agard v, vi, *315*, **315–323**, 498–500*c*
  early life and education 316
  election of 1940 314, 318
  election of 1944 321–322, 326, 327
  election of 1948 322–323
  historical significance 315–316
  internationalist perspective 320–321
  and Jesse Jones 319–320, 326
  later life 323
  philosophical and spiritual beliefs 316
  and Roerich 316–317, 323
  Roosevelt's relationship with 321–322, 326
  as secretary of agriculture 317–318
  as secretary of commerce 322, 329
  vice presidency 318–322
Wallace, Henry C. 316
Wallace, Ilo 316
Wallace, Lew 270
War of 1812 23, 52–53, 58, 64, 88
Warren, Charles B. 296
Warren Commission 380
Washington, George
  Adams's relationship with 6, 7–8
  and Clinton (G.) 36–37, 40–41
  Conway Cabal against 48
  election of 3–4
  near-fatal illness of 9
  presidency 18
  reelection 10
  retirement 28
  on vice presidency 4–5
water boarding 454
Watergate affair 351, 376–377, 383–384, 391, 413
Watson, Edwin M. 326
Watt, James 443
weapons of mass destruction 385, 450, 454
Webster, Daniel 61, 82, 104, 125, 126
Weed, Thurlow 121, 122–123, 124, 192
Welles, Gideon 152

West, Jessamyn 343
westward expansion
  election of 1848 123–124
  Fillmore vice presidency/presidency 119–120
  Jefferson's policy 18, 22
  Johnson (R.) family in 87, 88–89
  Polk administration 115–116
  postal services 167
  slavery issues 119–120, 124–125
  Tyler administration 104–105
Wheeler, Burton K. 293, 325
Wheeler, Charles K. 335
Wheeler, Mary 182
Wheeler, William A. *181*, **181–189**, 488–489*c*
  in Congress 183
  early life and education 181–182
  election of 1856 182
  election of 1876 183–186
  election of 1880 187
  and Hamlin 153
  later years 188
  in New York politics 182–183
  personal qualities 183, 189
  vice presidency 184–187, 188
Whig Party 100, 101, 102–103, 105, 175
Whiskey Rebellion 19
White, Hugh Lawson 82, 100
Whittington, Harry 454
Wicker, Lowell 423
Wilkie, Wendell L. 314
Wilkins, William 109, 110–111
Wilkinson, James 32
Willis, Benjamin A. 210
Wilmot, David 114
Wilmot Proviso 116, 150, 166
Wilson, Harriet Malvina 174
Wilson, Henry *173*, **173–180**, 488*c*
  antislavery politics 174–175, 176–177
  civil rights activities 177–178
  in Civil War 176–177
  in Congress 175, 177–179
  death of 180
  early life 173
  election of 1872 171, 179
  historical significance 180

  in Massachusetts politics 174
  personal qualities 174
  political affiliations 175
  Reconstruction politics 177–179
  vice presidency 179
Wilson, Joseph 454
Wilson, Woodrow 493–495*c*
  and Barkley 337
  election of 1912 251, 266, 274
  election of 1916 251, 257, 275–276
  and Garner 310
  Marshall's relationship with 275–276, 277
  presidency 275–276
  stroke 276
Winter-Berger, Robert N. 381–382
Witherspoon, John 139
Wofford, Harris 430
Wolcott, Oliver 11, 13
Wolfowitz, Paul 447, 449
women, violence against 462–463
Wood, John 30
Wood, Leonard 245, 283
Woodbury, Levi 111
Woodford, Stewart L. 184
Woodward, Bob 385
World Trade Center 448
World War I 251, 276, 291, 310
World War II 331, 338, 343, 411
Wright, Silas 81, 111
Wyth, George 16–17

X

XYZ affair 12–13, 51–52

Y

Yale University 412, 442
Yancey, William Lowndes 133
Yarborough, Ralph 360, 412, 413
Yates, Robert 27
Yeltsin, Boris 432

Z

Zuczek, Richard v

every Tailhook Convention since 1986 without any intervention by navy officials, civilian women's groups rallied to Coughlin's cause. The fallout resulted in new SEXUAL HARASSMENT policies and training for personnel, along with the slogan "Not in Our Navy."

Further Reading

Boo, Katherine. "Universal Soldier: What Paula Coughlin Can Teach American Women." *Washington Monthly* 24 September 1992, 37–40.

Frost-Knappman, Elizabeth, and Kathryn Cullen-Dupont. *Women's Rights on Trial*. Detroit: Gale Publishing, 1997.

Take Our Daughters to Work Day / Take Our Daughters and Sons to Work Day

First held in 1993 in New York City, Take Our Daughters to Work Day is dedicated to exposing young women to the diversity of career options available to them. The goal of the program is to "focus attention on the needs and concerns of girls and to help them stay focused on their future during adolescence," according to Ms. Foundation, the creator of Take Our Daughters to Work Day. The foundation encourages parents to take girls ages 8–12 to work with them on the fourth Thursday in April. Each year is organized around a theme selected by organizers, and the Ms. Foundation provides educational resources. In 2003, the Ms. Foundation changed the nature of the project to include boys as well as girls, and the day is now called, "Take our Daughters and Sons to Work Day." Additional information can be found at www.daughtersandsonstowork.org

Tarbell, Ida (Ida Minerva Tarbell) (1857–1944) *author, journalist*   Born on November 5, 1857, in western Pennsylvania, Ida Tarbell was one of the first female graduates of Allegheny College (1880). After a brief period of work as a teacher and an extended stay in France, she started writing for *McClure's Magazine*. She wrote

Ida M. Tarbell, 1922 (LIBRARY OF CONGRESS)

biographical articles on Napoleon and Madame Roland and ultimately many pieces on Abraham Lincoln; however, she was most famous at *McClure's* for her 16-part study of the Standard Oil Company and John D. Rockefeller's rise in business, later published as a book entitled *The History of the Standard Oil Company* (1904). This exposé led to a public outcry and, ultimately, the Supreme Court–mandated breakup of the Standard Oil Trust.

In 1906, Tarbell helped found the *American Magazine* with other leading journalists from *McClure's*. Her first major assignment for this magazine was a history of the tariff, and the success of her research is shown by President Woodrow Wilson's invitation to Tarbell to serve on the U.S. Tariff Commission (the first woman to be asked); she declined in order to focus on her writing. She also wrote two book-length series of articles published as *The Business of Being a Woman* (1914) and *The Ways of Woman*

(1915). These works argued against the claims of suffragists that women were innately different from men and that women could not pursue both a career and a family life, and she believed that women should recognize that wife and mother were the most appropriate roles to play. In 1939, Tarbell published her autobiography *All in a Day's Work: An Autobiography*. She died on January 6, 1944, at the age of 86.

Further Reading

Brady, Kathleen. *Ida Tarbell: Portrait of a Muckraker.* Pittsburgh: University of Pittsburgh Press, 1989.
Fitzpatrick, Ellen. *Muckraking: Three Landmark Articles.* Boston: Bedford/St. Martins, 1994.
Kochersberger, Robert, ed. *More than a Muckraker: Ida Tarbell's Lifetime in Journalism.* Knoxville: University of Tennessee Press, 1994.

—Claire Curtis

Tauscher, Ellen (1951–) *congressperson* Ellen Tauscher was born on November 15, 1951, in Newark, New Jersey. She attended Seton Hall University, earning a bachelor's degree in early childhood education in 1974. Prior to entering public service, she was an investment banker and member of the New York Stock Exchange. After moving to California in 1989, she founded the first national research service to help parents verify the background of CHILD CARE workers.

Tauscher was active as a Democratic fundraiser before seeking election herself in 1996. She won reelection in 1998 and 2000 against vigorous Republican opposition, even though the 10th district is heavily Republican. Redistricting after the 2000 census left the district more Democratic, and she has not faced serious opposition since, winning reelection in 2006. Tauscher is vice chair of the Democratic Leadership Council and is also a member of the Blue Dog Coalition. In the 109th Congress, she served on the House Committee on Armed Services and the Committee on Transportation and Infrastructure. She is the vice chair of the Democratic Congressional Campaign Committee (DCCC).

Further Reading

Barone, Michael. *The Almanac of American Politics.* Washington, D.C.: National Journal Group, 2006.
"Tauscher, Ellen O'Kane." In *Biographical Directory of the United States Congress, 1774–present.* Available online. URL: http://bioguide.congress.gov/scripts/biodisplay.pl?index=T000057. Accessed on January 8, 2007.
"Representative Ellen O. Tauscher (CA)." In *Project Vote Smart.* Available online. URL: http://votesmart.org/bio.php?can_id=BC029008. Accessed on January 8, 2007.

—Angela Kouters

Taylor, Margaret (Margaret Mackall Smith Taylor) (1788–1852) *first lady* Margaret Mackall Smith was born on September 21, 1788, to Walter and Ann Mackall Smith, wealthy planters in Calvert County, Maryland. When she was 21, she traveled to Kentucky to visit a married sister, and there she met army lieutenant Zachary Taylor. They were married the following year, on June 21, 1810, in a log house.

The Taylors moved from one army post to the next, often enduring long periods of separation. In relatively primitive conditions, Margaret gave birth to five daughters and one son. In 1820, two of her daughters died from bilious fever in Bayou Sara, Louisiana. Margaret herself suffered an illness serious enough that Zachary Taylor received a dispatch informing him of his wife's impending death. After her recovery, the older children were sent east to be educated. Despite this nomadic life, their surviving daughters married army men, and their son, Richard, became a lieutenant general in the Confederate army. (Daughter Sarah Knox Taylor married Lieutenant Jefferson Davis but died soon afterward from malarial fever.)

In 1840, Zachary Taylor was assigned to Baton Rouge, and Margaret refurbished a Spanish cottage on the Mississippi. For nearly five years, she lived a stable life with her husband, daughter Mary Elizabeth (Betty), and son Richard. In 1845, General Taylor was dispatched to Mexico, returning with a nickname ("Old Rough and Ready") and a national reputation as a war hero. Margaret was sure that they could now retire to the settled life she had dreamed of, but the Whig Party had already begun drafting Zachary Taylor as a presidential candidate. His election in 1848 was viewed by Margaret as a "plot to deprive her of his company and shorten his life."

Upon Zachary's election, the Taylors moved to the White House, but Margaret (now 60 years old) rejected the role of first lady. The public knew little about her, but since her husband was a national hero, his opponents tried to attack him by discrediting her, describing her, for instance, as an "old crone with a corn cob pipe." Since she rarely appeared in public, there was little direct evidence to the contrary. Upon arriving in Washington, she designated her daughter Betty as the official White House hostess and decorated the family quarters on the second story to resemble their Louisiana home, entertaining family and friends in the residence.

On July 4, 1850, Zachary Taylor attended an event outdoors and returned overheated. He fell ill and died five days later, on July 9, from "cholera morbus." Margaret was devastated and quickly moved out of the White House. Her desire to bury her husband according to her own wishes rather than the norms of the day gave rise to rumors that she had poisoned him. She refused to have his body embalmed and took him back to Louisiana for burial. Rumors of her involvement in his death persisted for nearly 140 years until Taylor's body was exhumed. Margaret Taylor lived for the remainder of her life with her daughter Betty and her family in East Pascagoula, Mississippi. She died on August 14, 1852.

Further Reading
Bauer, Jack. *Zachary Taylor: Soldier, Planter, Statesman of the Old Southwest*. Newton, Conn.: American Political Biography, 1993.

National First Ladies Library. *Biographies: First Ladies of the United States*. Available online. URL: http://www.firstladies.org/biographies. Accessed on January 4, 2007.
Schneider, Dorothy, and Carl J. Schneider. "Margaret Mackall Smith Taylor" *First Ladies: A Biographical Dictionary*. New York: Checkmark Books, 2001, 79–82.

Taylor v. Louisiana (368 U.S. 57) (1975)

Billy Jean Taylor was arrested in St. Tammany Parish, Louisiana, and charged with aggravated kidnapping, armed robbery, and rape. Taylor challenged the list of available jurors on the basis that women had been systematically excluded thereby denying him his constitutional right to a fair trial by "a jury of a representative segment of the community." In Louisiana, women were not called for jury service unless they specifically registered with the clerk of court for jury duty. The court rejected Taylor's motion, and he was convicted and sentenced to death. When the Louisiana Supreme Court sided with the lower court, Taylor appealed to the U.S. Supreme Court. Taylor's attorney provided statistics on the small number of women registering for jury service and the very small number of women actually appearing on jury lists. There were no women among the 175 available jurors for Taylor's criminal trial. The state claimed that Taylor, as a male, lacked the standing to challenge the exclusion of women from jury service.

Although Louisiana repealed the provision Taylor was challenging before the U.S. Supreme Court issued its ruling, the Court ruled that Taylor's Sixth and Fourteenth Amendment rights had indeed been violated by the state's gender-based system of jury selection. Taylor's conviction was reversed. Justice Byron R. White wrote: "The requirement of a jury's being chosen from a fair cross section of the community is fundamental to the American system of justice." The Court concluded that this requirement was violated by systematically excluding women from the pool. This ruling overturned *HOYT V. FLORIDA* (1961) and serves as another example of the Court's incremental dismantling of the barriers to full citizenship for women.

Further Reading

Lindgren, J. Ralph, Nadine Taub, Beth Ann Wolfson, and Carla M. Palumbo. *The Law of Sex Discrimination,* 3rd ed. Belmont, Calif.: Thomson Wadsworth, 2005.

temperance movement The temperance movement introduced women to political activism. The movement emerged in the early 19th century as a male-dominated reform. Women were generally only welcome at temperance gatherings if they agreed to listen and not to speak. A frustrated AMELIA BLOOMER decided to give women a greater voice in temperance and became the first woman publisher when she founded *The Lily* in 1849. ELIZABETH CADY STANTON and SUSAN B. ANTHONY were also angered by the refusal of temperance men to welcome women as equals. In 1852, Anthony and Stanton founded the Women's New York State Temperance Society, which addressed temperance but also ventured into the controversial realm of women's rights by advocating the right to vote and to divorce drunken husbands.

After the Civil War, women flooded into the temperance movement to protect the home and family. In the early 1870s, a Women's Temperance Crusade spread through New York and Ohio, with participant Annie Wittenmyer subsequently founding the WOMAN'S CHRISTIAN TEMPERANCE UNION (WCTU) in 1874. Wittenmyer wanted to focus exclusively on temperance, but younger members wanted to embrace a broad program of reform. In 1879, FRANCES WILLARD gained control of the WCTU and linked the organization to a range of political issues, including women's SUFFRAGE. The organization was predominantly white, with African-American women continuing their 19th-century focus on racial matters.

Prohibition in 1919 initially appeared as a triumph for women's activism. The celebration was short-lived as women increasingly came to object to government intrusion in private life. The Women's Organization for National Prohibition Reform helped achieve repeal of the Eighteenth Amendment in 1933. The collapse of Prohibition brought the temperance movement to an end.

Further Reading

Blocker, Jack S., Jr. *"Give to the Winds Thy Fears": The Women's Temperance Crusade, 1873–1874.* Westport, Conn.: Greenwood Press, 1995.

Bordin, Ruth. *Woman and Temperance: The Quest for Power and Liberty, 1873–1900.* New Brunswick, N.J.: Rutgers University Press, 1990.

Neumann, Caryn E. "The End of Gender Solidarity: The History of the Women's Organization for National Prohibition Reform in the United States, 1929–1933." *Journal of Women's History* 9 (1997): 31–51.

—Caryn E. Neumann

Temple, Shirley See BLACK, SHIRLEY TEMPLE.

Terrell, Mary Church (1863–1954) *writer, civil rights activist* Mary Church was born in Memphis, Tennessee, on September 23, 1863, to parents who were both former slaves; her father became a successful businessman. After attending public schools in Ohio, Mary graduated from OBERLIN COLLEGE in 1884, having studied in Europe for two of her college years. While at Oberlin, she edited the school magazine, reaching out through its readership to comment on many political issues of the day. After her graduation, Church taught at a variety of schools and universities in Ohio and in Washington D.C., and was a member of the NATIONAL AMERICAN WOMAN SUFFRAGE ASSOCIATION (NAWSA). Upon her marriage to Robert Terrell in October 1891, she had to give up teaching (as most teaching posts were limited to unmarried women), and she devoted more time and energy to SUFFRAGE and civil rights.

Mary Church Terrell first attended a NAWSA meeting in 1898. She spoke up to express her hope that the association would "include in the resolution the injustices of various kinds of which colored people are the victims" (as quoted in her autobiography). SUSAN B. ANTHONY supported Terrell's initiatives, and the two maintained a correspondence and friendship through their activist work. Terrell advocated within NAWSA that the fight for suffrage not be limited to suffrage for white women. She appealed (unsuccessfully) to President Benjamin Harrison in 1892 to publicly condemn lynching, and in that same year she founded the COLORED WOMAN'S LEAGUE of Washington. The league, whose members were mostly teachers, worked to provide free kindergartens, training for kindergarten teachers, adult education classes, and day care. Terrell wrote in an article: "There is every reason for all who have the interests of the race at heart to associate themselves with the League, so that there might be a vast chain of organizations extending the length and breadth of the land devising ways and means to advance our cause."

In 1895, Terrell was appointed to the District of Columbia Board of Education, the first woman of color appointed to such a position in the United States. While active on the school board, she advocated for teachers of color, most of whom were women. She worked to promote schools for black students in Washington during a time of segregation, and she saw firsthand the harm inherent in the system of "separate but equal." She founded and became the first president of the NATIONAL ASSOCIATION OF COLORED WOMEN (NACW) in 1896 because many of the national women's organizations would not allow women of color to join as members. The NACW focused on anti-lynching effects, Jim Crow laws, SUFFRAGE, and other issues of daily importance to women of color, including kindergartens, retirement homes and homes for young women coming to the city to work.

In 1904, Terrell was the only black woman invited to speak at the Berlin International Congress of Women; she delivered her address in English, German, and French. In 1909, with MARY WHITE OVINGTON and others, she helped form the National Association for the Advancement of Colored People (NAACP), and 10 years later, she was elected vice president of the Washington chapter of the NAACP.

During Terrell's suffrage work, she picketed the White House with members of the CONGRESSIONAL UNION FOR WOMAN SUFFRAGE (joining ALICE PAUL and LUCY BURNS) during World War I, although women of color were often asked not to march, for fear their presence would anger southern politicians. She noted with pride in her autobiography the recognition she received from the NATIONAL WOMAN'S PARTY for that period of picketing while also noting that her absence from the picket line when arrests were made ensured her ability to keep working for suffrage and civil rights. Had she been arrested, her race would have been used against her and she would not have been able to work so prominently in her later activism.

After the Nineteenth Amendment was passed, Terrell became active in the Republican Party. In the 1930s, she traveled throughout the East Coast campaigning for Republican candidates. She also traveled to Europe and in 1937 spoke before the International Assembly of the World Fellowships of Faith in London. In her international travels, Terrell was acknowledged as an intellectual and her work abroad often reinvigorated her for her tasks back in the United States. In 1940, she published her autobiography, *A Colored Woman in a White World.* She testified before Congress numerous times in the early 1940s for passage of anti-lynching laws, and in her last years she continued to fight segregation in Washington, D.C. She was active in the fight for the EQUAL RIGHTS AMENDMENT, and she was involved in direct action campaigns for civil rights, picketing segregated restaurants and stores in Washington, D.C., into her 90s. Mary Church Terrell died on July 24, 1954, a few months after the Supreme Court made its historic decision in *Brown v. Board of Education,* beginning a process of desegregation of the schools.

See also ANTI-LYNCHING MOVEMENT.

Further Reading

Carlton-LaNey, Iris. *African American Leadership: An Empowerment Tradition in Social Welfare History.* Washington, D.C.: NASW Press, 2001.

Jones, Beverly Washington. *Quest for Equality: The Life and Writings of Mary Eliza Church Terrell, 1863–1954.* New York: Carlson Publishers, 1990.

Terrell, Mary Church. *A Colored Woman in a White Woman's World.* New York: G.K. Hall, 1996.

—Claire Curtis

third-wave feminism Third-wave FEMINISM emerged in the late 1990s, the product of young activists primarily between the ages of 15 and 30. In part a reaction to the claims that "feminism is dead," third-wave feminists are activists working to engage young women on a wide range of issues to advance the status of women.

Liberal feminists, primarily intent on breaking down barriers to full inclusion in traditionally male-dominated areas, including work, education, law, and politics, largely shaped the second wave of feminism in the 1960s and 1970s. Liberal feminists were most interested in getting women in the door—but before the work of dismantling the "sticky floor" and the "glass ceiling," the movement lost steam. Third wave feminists are the first generation of girls and women to grow up with feminism and the goal of gender equality as a given. They are interested in challenging the very definitions of gender and sexuality and in expanding the scope of feminism beyond Western ideals to include the global concerns of all people. Third-wave feminism is characterized by an interest in "intersectionality," defined as the ways in which cross-cutting identities of sex, race, class, and sexuality shape human interests and behavior.

One more controversial component of third-wave feminism is the ascendance of "girlie culture" or "lipstick feminism." Advocates claim that being female is just as valuable as being male, and being female includes enjoying female sexuality and femininity. Examples of this form of female self-empowerment include movies such as *Buffy the Vampire Slayer,* activist groups such as Riot Grrrl, and books such as Elizabeth Wurtzel's *Bitch: In Praise of Difficult Women* (1999). This focus, more than any other, has produced the so-called rift between second-wave and third-wave feminists. Second wavers decry girlie culture as an egocentric focus on the personal and cultural rather than a political strategy for change. The divide has a generational component to it as well, since third-wave feminists tend to be in their teens, 20s, and 30s, while second wavers are primarily over 40.

There are a number of third-wave feminist organizations, including the Third Wave Foundation (www.thirdwavefoundation.org), headquartered in New York City.

Further Reading

Baumgardner, Jennifer, and Amy Richards. *Manifesta: Young Women, Feminism, and the Future.* New York: Farrar, Straus and Giroux, 2000.

Gillis, Stacy, Gillian Howie, and Rebecca Munford, eds. *Third Wave Feminism: A Critical Exploration.* New York: Palgrave, 2004.

Henry, Astrid. *Not My Mother's Sister: Generational Conflict and Third Wave Feminism.* Bloomington: Indiana University Press, 2004.

Thomas, Helen (1920–) *journalist* Born on August 4, 1920, in Winchester, Kentucky, and raised in Detroit, Michigan, Helen Thomas is known for her probing political journalism. She was one of nine children born to Lebanese parents who did not write or read English. In 1942, Thomas earned a journalism degree from Wayne State University and began work for the *Washington Daily News* as a "copy girl." The following year, she became a United Press International (UPI) wire service reporter, writing on women's topics for the radio wire service. She subsequently wrote UPI's "Names in the News" column, and in the late 1950s, she covered reports on federal agencies. She was president of the Women's National Press Club from 1959 to 1960.

In 1960, Thomas began covering the White House and U.S. presidents for UPI as White House Bureau Chief; she held the assignment until she resigned in 2000. Thomas now serves as a White House correspondent and writes for King Features Syndicate.

Often referred to as "the Dean" or "the First Lady" of the White House Press Corps, Thomas has travelled extensively with the presidents she has covered. In 1972, she was the only print journalist to travel with President Richard M. Nixon on his historic trip to China. During the Watergate scandal that ultimately led to Nixon's resignation, Thomas was the recipient of several late-night phone calls from MARTHA MITCHELL, the wife of Attorney General John Mitchell. Of Nixon's fall from power, she said, "There was no way he could save himself. It was like a Greek tragedy."

Thomas was the first woman officer of the National Press Club after it opened its doors to women members, the first woman member and president of the White House Correspondents Association, and the first woman member of the Gridiron Club. In 1998, she received the International Women's Media Foundation Lifetime Achievement Award and was honored by President Bill Clinton as the first recipient of the Helen Thomas Lifetime Achievement Award.

Thomas developed a reputation for the often tough and direct questions she posed to sitting presidents. In 2003, President George W. Bush took issue with Thomas's critiques, moved her seat assignment to the back of the room, and ended the long-standing tradition of allowing Thomas to close the press conference with "Thank you, Mr. President." About her career in journalism, Thomas said, "We in the press have a special role since there is no other institution in our society . . . that can hold the President accountable. I do believe that our democracy can endure and prevail only if the American people are informed."

Further Reading
Thomas, Helen. *Front Row at the White House: My Life and Times.* New York: Scribner, 2000.

Thomas, Martha Carey (1857–1935) *educator, suffragist, president of Bryn Mawr College* Born in Baltimore, Maryland, on January 2, 1857, Carey Thomas (who preferred to be known by her middle name) was raised by Quaker parents who believed in secondary education of girls. Her mother and aunt were involved in the WOMAN'S CHRISTIAN TEMPERANCE UNION. Thomas herself pursued both college and graduate degrees over the initial objections of her father. In 1877, she graduated from Cornell and was accepted at Johns Hopkins University, but she was denied the opportunity to attend lectures. She went on to receive a Ph.D. from the University of Zurich (after being denied a degree, because she was a woman, at the University of Leipzig). When she returned to the United States in 1884, she was hired as a dean of the college and professor of English at the newly founded Bryn Mawr College for women. She eventually became the president of Bryn Mawr in 1894, a job that she held until 1922. With longtime companion Mary Garrett, she founded the Bryn Mawr School for Girls in Baltimore in 1885 and worked to get women admitted to the Johns Hopkins Medical School by raising $500,000 to help the financially unstable institution.

Thomas also worked for women's SUFFRAGE, serving as president of the National College Women's Equal Suffrage League, and was a member of the NATIONAL AMERICAN WOMAN SUFFRAGE ASSOCIATION. In addressing the North American Woman Suffrage Association in Buffalo in 1908, she said "The man's world must become a man's and a woman's world. Why are we afraid?" Thomas worked to ensure that the women who attended Bryn Mawr were given the tools to compete in the world (Bryn Mawr differed from other women's colleges by offering a required curriculum and few electives).

After the passage of the Nineteenth Amendment, Carey Thomas supported the NATIONAL WOMAN'S PARTY efforts to pass an EQUAL RIGHTS AMENDMENT.

Further Reading

Helen Horowitz. *Power and Passion of M. Carey Thomas,* Chicago: University of Illinois Press, 1999.

—Claire Curtis

Thornburgh v. American College of Obstetricians and Gynecologists (476 U.S. 747)

(1986) The issue in this case was whether a Pennsylvania state law that required physicians to inform women contemplating an ABORTION of the detrimental physical and psychological effects was constitutional. The U.S. Supreme Court struck down most of the provisions of the Pennsylvania statute and reiterated the Court's earlier statements that the states are not free, under the guise of protecting maternal health or potential life, to intimidate women into continuing pregnancies. The Court found that the Pennsylvania statute "wholly subordinate[d] constitutional privacy interests and concerns with maternal health [to the state's] effort to deter a woman from making a decision that, with her physician, is hers to make." The Court ruled that the mandatory informed consent provisions impermissibly intruded on the discretion of the physician and counselor to ensure effective counseling and unduly interfered with a woman's right to make abortion decisions. The Court also struck down the provision requiring physicians to use the method of abortion that would preserve the life of the fetus unless it presented a significantly lesser medical risk to the life or health of the mother. Finally, the Court struck down the statute's reporting requirements as an invasion of privacy of any woman who chose abortion because of the possibility that her decision and identity would become known. The Court also struck down the requirement that a second physician be present to take care of aborted viable fetuses because it had no exception for medical emergencies in the event the woman's life was at risk. The Court declined to address whether the provisions for parental/judicial consent unduly burdened minors' rights.

Tillmon, Johnnie (1926–1995) *welfare movement activist* Johnnie Tillmon was known for her grassroots activism within the national WELFARE RIGHTS MOVEMENT. As a poor, black, single mother of six, Tillmon became one of the welfare movement's most vociferous and articulate advocates.

Born on April 10, 1926, the daughter of a sharecropper in Scott, Arkansas, Tillmon headed to California in 1959 hoping for a better life. There, after a series of illnesses, she was forced to leave her job as a laundress. Out of work and with six mouths to feed, Tillmon ended up on the welfare line. Her direct experiences with the welfare system served as the catalyst for Tillmon's activism. After experiencing harassment at the hands of welfare agents in the form of midnight raids seeking to determine whether an able-bodied man resided in her house and if there were signs of additional sources of support, and learning from others of similar experiences, Tillmon formed Aid to Needy Children (ANC) Mothers Anonymous in 1963.

ANC–Mothers Anonymous became one of the first local welfare rights organizations in the United States. The organization acted as a support system and resource tool for poor women seeking "an adequate welfare income, job-training to transition out of welfare, and day care." Recognizing the important connection between welfare policy implementation and decision-making by politicians, Tillmon actively encouraged poor women to register to vote, participate in political campaigns, and protest and demonstrate against unjust policies.

In her famous *Ms.* MAGAZINE interview in 1972, "Welfare Is a Woman's Issue," Tillmon described the American welfare system as "the most prejudiced institution in the country." She equated it with a super-sexist marriage in which "you trade in a man for *the man*." Tillmon perceived the welfare system as one that is even more dominating and controlling than the opposite sex. She lamented that in order for poor women to receive aid, welfare agents could exercise authority over their sexuality and bodies. Tillmon's ANC group could be considered the parallel to the women's liberation movement in the sense that it marked the beginning of the poor women's liberation movement. Tillmon strongly believed that welfare was a woman's issue for all women to address collectively. Unlike the mainstream women's movement, which tended to focus on women's liberation without analyzing how issues of class and race intersected with women's rights, Tillmon attempted to redefine the debate.

Soon after its founding, ANC–Mothers Anonymous became affiliated with the National Welfare Rights Organization (NWRO). As head of the NWRO from 1972 until it folded in 1975, Tillmon was responsible for redirecting the welfare debate in the United States. She called on welfare activists to rethink welfare and poverty as primarily an issue that affects women. She believed that all women regardless of race and class had a responsibility to fight the oppressive welfare system. This is reflected in her 1972 *Ms.* magazine interview, wherein she notes, "For me, Women's liberation is simple. No woman in this country can feel dignified; no woman can be liberated, until all women get off their knees." In other words, for Tillmon, injustices suffered by welfare recipients were a threat to justice for all women involved in the liberation movement. Tillmon died on November 23, 1995, in Los Angeles, CA.

See also WELFARE POLICY.

Further Reading

Kelly, Kori. "Conflict and Strategy in the National Welfare Rights Movement." *Berkeley McNair Research Journal,* volume 8, winter 2000. Accessed at www-mcnair.berkeley.edu/2000jan.html.
Steffan, Nancy. "Welfare Is a Women's Issue." *Ms. Magazine* (Spring 1972): 111–116.

—Hollis France

Title IX of the Education Amendments of 1972   In 1970, President Richard Nixon's Task Force on Women's Rights and Responsibilities called discrimination in education "one of the most damaging injustices women suffer." Title IX, also known as the Education Amendments of 1972, banned sex discrimination at all levels of formal education. The language of this legislation mirrors other equal-protection legislation: "No person in the United States shall, on the basis of sex, be excluded from participation in, be denied the benefits of, or be subjected to discrimination under any education program or activity receiving federal financial assistance."

Cosponsored by Congresswoman Edith Green and Senator Birch Bayh, the bill met little opposition from within Congress or from lobbyists when it was introduced. In fact, Green specifically asked women's organizations *not* to testify on behalf of the legislation, fearing the publicity would attract opponents and endanger the bill's chances for passage. While it was designed to eliminate the crippling barriers in all sorts of educational programs, institutions, and curriculum, the law is now almost exclusively described in relation to increasing women's access to sports programs—even in accounts of the women's movement or women's history. The legislation specified that no federal funds could go to educational institutions that were already receiving federal dollars and practiced sex discrimination in any of its programs, including admissions, athletics, financial aid, counseling, facilities, and employment. Today Title IX extends to issues of SEXUAL HARASSMENT, pregnancy, parental status, and marital status.

As a result of Title IX regulations, schools dropped admissions quotas that limited the number of women enrolled in some professional programs (e.g., engineering, medicine, and law) and were required to evaluate men and women under the same set of admission standards. Congress did not, however, end SINGLE-SEX EDUCATION. Private, single-sex institutions were not required to change the character of their mission or their admissions process. The legislation merely prohibited public coeducational institutions from becoming single-sex in composition and required that once men and women were admitted, they had to be treated equally and have equal access to all aspects of the educational experience. This meant that girls could not be "advised" to pursue a traditional course of study, such as home economics, nor could boys be relegated to vocational courses like shop. Title IX, moreover, required gender-neutral counseling, meaning that special efforts to redirect girls into nontraditional courses in higher mathematics, sciences, or vocational training were not permitted. Segregation by sex was still allowed in sex-education classes or in ability-grouped physical education classes, and school-affiliated organizations could maintain their traditional sex segregation if they were purely social rather than academic or professional in character. This meant that social fraternities and sororities on college campuses could remain single-sex.

Title IX has been very successful in opening the doors to education. More women than ever before are enrolled in colleges and universities. In 1979, the number of women surpassed the number of men enrolled in college for the first time, and the upward trend has continued ever since. Most demographers expect that increase to continue, even as the proportion of male enrollees continues to decline. They also predict that between 1995 and 2007, the total number of both full- and part-time women students enrolled in college may increase by 19 percent to 9.2 million, compared with a 12 percent increase for men, to 6.9 million. By 2007, 5.4 million women are expected to be enrolled full-time, an increase of more than 30 percent since 1995. The 4.2 million men projected to be full-time students in 2007 represent only a 13 percent increase over the same time period.

The most immediate and vociferous opposition to Title IX came from college and high school athletic directors and coaches. The National Collegiate Athletic Association (NCAA) initially tried to lobby Congress and the Department of Health, Education and Welfare to exclude athletics from Title IX coverage. When total exclusion was unsuccessful, the NCAA argued, again unsuccessfully, that only the programs within an institution that actually received federal dollars should be subject to the equity provisions. Since few athletics programs at either the college or the high school level are direct recipients of federal dollars, this interpretation would mean a de facto Title IX exemption for athletics. The Office of Civil Rights, the primary enforcement agency, rejected the NCAA's efforts, maintaining that if any program took federal money, the entire institution was subject to Title IX compliance. In 1974, the NCAA supported the Tower Amendment, which would have exempted men's intercollegiate football and basketball (the revenue-generating sports). A House-Senate conference committee rejected the amendment, leaving the NCAA to challenge the constitutionality of the gender-equity provision in the courts.

Although initially unsuccessful, a 1984 Supreme Court case, GROVE CITY COLLEGE V. BELL, temporarily gave Title IX opponents what they sought. The U.S. Supreme Court ruled that only those programs receiving federal funds must comply with the statute. Congress acted (over President Ronald Reagan's veto) in 1988 to reinstate the original intent of Title IX by passing the Civil Rights Restoration Act. Four years later, in COHEN V. BROWN UNIVERSITY, a federal court ruled that Brown University had violated Title IX's provisions when it cut two women's teams and two men's teams. Although the university cut the same number of varsity teams for men and women, several women on the gymnastics team filed suit, claiming that the effect of Brown's action violated Title IX. Cutting the two women's programs had saved the university more than $62,000, while eliminating the two men's programs saved only $16,000. In other words, female athletes were disproportionately affected by the cuts.

The regulations under Title IX provide three ways an institution can show that it is offering equitable opportunities for women athletes. First, a school can show that the percentage of its female athletes is substantially proportionate to the percentage of women in its student body. Second, if there is no evidence of proportionality, schools are required to show that they are actively engaged in a meaningful process that will provide equity for women. In 2003, for example, the University of Maryland promoted its cheerleading squad and women's water polo to varsity status to create more scholarships and playing opportunities for female athletes on campus. By moving into compliance, the University of Maryland was able to return some scholarships to eight underfunded men's programs. Third, a school is in compliance if it is meeting the actual level of athletic interest among women. It is this third provision that has energized opponents to Title IX. In Brown University's case, the institution argued that while 51 percent of its student body was female, only 38 percent of its intercollegiate athletes were women, suggesting that it was more than meeting the "interest test" required for compliance. It is difficult, however, to ignore the circularity of the interest argument. Girls and women are interested in sports when they have the opportunity to play sports.

Title IX's impact on women's interest and participation in sports was almost immediate and has been overwhelmingly successful. For example, in 1961, nine states actually prohibited interscholastic sports for females, presumably because of the stereotype that females were too delicate for physical activity and not suited for competitive sports. In 1971, only 7.5 percent of the nearly 4 million high school athletes were female. By 1997, the 25th anniversary of Title IX, girls made up more than 40 percent of the 6 million-plus high school athletes. However, in 2001, girls at the high school level received 1.1 million fewer opportunities to play sports than their male counterparts. Prior to Title IX, women made up 15 percent of college athletes, but received 2 percent of the total athletic budget. While more than 53 percent of the under-

graduates at Division I schools today are female, they receive only 41 percent of the opportunities to play sports, and women's programs accounted for only 36 percent of overall university athletic budgets, 32 percent of recruiting funds, and 28 percent of coaches' salaries. In 2000–01, the average college in Division I spent more than $3 million on women's sports and $5.8 million on men's sports. In June 2002, the National Women's Law Center released a list of 30 colleges it said failed to give female athletes a fair share of athletic scholarship dollars. The report estimated the difference between male and female scholarship money at the 30 schools came to nearly $6.5 million for the 2000–01 academic year. Those at the top of the list of 30 included the University of Miami, Kansas State, and Notre Dame.

In June 2002, President George W. Bush appointed a 15-person Commission on Athletic Opportunity to examine Title IX on eight specific questions. The very first question asked whether Title IX standards for assessing equal opportunity in athletics were working to promote opportunities for men and women, suggesting that the impetus for forming the commission in the first place was to determine whether implementation of Title IX was "unfair" to men. The commission held town meetings throughout the country to gather information before submitting a report to the secretary of education. Several of the proposals threatened to dismantle Title IX protections and current interpretations of compliance requirements, spurring women's groups and education activists around the country into action. Two female commission members, Donna de Varona (a two-time Olympic gold medal swimmer and chairperson of the U.S. Olympic Committee's government relations committee) and Julie Foudy (former member of the USA women's soccer team and president of the Women's Sports Foundation) issued a minority report taking exception to many claims made by the full committee report and emphasizing the discrimination women and girls still face in education an athletics. On July

11, 2003, the Bush administration announced that there would be no changes to the mechanisms currently in place to measure compliance, and in fact, none of the recommendations from the Commission on Opportunity in Athletics have been adopted.

Title IX has proven to be a very powerful tool in opening education to girls and women. As noted above, efforts to weaken provisions requiring gender equity in education have faced serious and sustained opposition.

Further Reading

American Association of University Women. *How Schools Shortchange Girls: A Study of Major Findings on Girls and Education.* Wellesley, Mass.: Wellesley College Center for Research on Women, 1992.

National Coalition of Women and Girls in Education (NCWGE). "Title IX at 30: Report Card on Gender Equity." Washington, D.C.: NCWGE, 2002.

Weistart, John. "Equal Opportunity? Title IX and Intercollegiate Sports." *Brookings Review* 16 (1998): 39–43.

"Women's Rights Groups Win Title IX Victory," Women's Sports Foundation. Available online. URL: www.womenssportsfoundation.org/cgi-bin/iowa/issues/media/article.html.

Title VII of the Civil Rights Act of 1964

Title VII makes it illegal to restrict jobs to one sex or the other based purely on sex or stereotypical assumptions about gender-linked abilities, but gender segregation is still pervasive throughout the labor force. Three-quarters of all women who work do so in just 20 occupations, each of which is nearly 80 percent female.

The EQUAL EMPLOYMENT OPPORTUNITY COMMISSION (EEOC), now responsible for administering all of the nation's equal protection provisions, was created under the CIVIL RIGHTS ACT OF 1964 and charged from the start with developing guidelines for Title VII's implementation. It was clear that the EEOC was not going to be very ambitious in writing guidelines on sex discrimination, and women's organizations such as the NATIONAL ORGANIZATION FOR WOMEN

(NOW, founded in 1966) rallied to pressure the commission to act more diligently.

The specific provisions in Title VII most relevant to sex discrimination are found in section 703(a): "It shall be an unlawful employment practice for an employer (1) to fail or refuse to hire or to discharge any individual, or otherwise to discriminate against any individual with respect to his compensation, terms, conditions, or privileges of employment, because of such individual's race, color, religion, sex, or national origin; or (2) to limit, segregate, or classify his employees or applicants for employment in any way which would deprive or tend to deprive any individual of employment opportunities or otherwise adversely affect his status as an employee, because of such individual's race, color, religion, sex, or national origin."

An important exception to Title VII's coverage arises from what is called a BONA FIDE OCCUPATIONAL QUALIFICATION (BFOQ): "Notwithstanding any other provision of this subchapter (1) it shall not be an unlawful employment practice for an employer to hire and employ employees . . . on the basis of his religion, sex, or national origin in those certain instances where religion, sex, or national origin is a bona fide occupational qualification reasonably necessary to the normal operation of that particular business enterprise." Many of the challenges to Title VII coverage in employment have been brought under BFOQ exceptions.

Like many policies passed by Congress, the basic provisions and language of Title VII have been subject to interpretation by the Supreme Court. Two of the statute's critical phrases have provided the basis for such cases. Title VII prohibits discrimination practices "because of sex." Congress did not specify exactly what it intended in choosing this particular language, so the courts decided what each means through a succession of cases. In 1912, Justice Oliver Wendell Holmes best articulated for the Court the basic principle of the equal-protection clause that allows some sex-based laws to stand, even now in the face of Title VII's prohibition of sex discrimination: "The Fourteenth Amendment does not interfere [with state legislation] by erecting fictitious equality where there is real difference" (*Quonguing v. Kirkendall*, 233 U.S. 59, 63). Unlike race, which the Court views as an immutable characteristic that bears no relationship to job performance, sex is assumed to create real and meaningful differences in a man's or a woman's ability to get and hold some jobs. However, the determination of the relevance of sex differences to employment cannot be based on assumptions of women as a group or any stereotypical characteristics as a group and must be based in fact.

See also GENDER STEREOTYPES.

Further Reading

Hesse-Biber, Sharlene, and Gregg Lee Carter. *Working Women in America: Split Dreams* New York: Oxford University Press, 2000.

Matthaei, Julie A. *An Economic History of Women in America: Women's Work, the Sexual Division of Labor, and the Development of Capitalism.* New York: Schocken Books, 1982.

Valian, Virgina. *Why So Slow? The Advancement of Women* Cambridge, Mass.: MIT Press, 1998.

Totenberg, Nina (1944–) *radio journalist*

Nina Totenberg was born on January 14, 1944, and attended Boston University. Before joining National Public Radiio (NPR) in 1975, she served as Washington editor of *New Times Magazine* and, prior to that, worked as a legal affairs correspondent for the *National Observer*. In 1979, she married Colorado senator Floyd Haskell, who died in 1998. She married physician H. David Reines in 2006.

In her role as legal affairs correspondent for NPR, Nina Totenberg has provided the nation with extensive coverage of the Supreme Court and interviewed every political mover and shaker in the country, many justices more than once. In the process, she has earned a reputation as a tenacious and well-respected journalist. Her reports air regularly on NPR's newsmagazine *All Things Considered* and on *Morning Edition* and *Weekend Edition*. It was Totenberg, honored eight times by the American Bar Association for continued excellence in legal reporting, who broke the story about University of Oklahoma law professor ANITA HILL's allegations of SEXUAL HARASSMENT by future justice Clarence Thomas when she worked for him at the EQUAL EMPLOYMENT OPPORTUNITY COMMISSION. Totenberg's investigative journalism also rocked Capitol Hill with her disclosure of Supreme Court nominee Douglas Ginsburg's use of marijuana, a fact that ultimately led to his withdrawal from consideration.

Totenberg made broadcast history in 1998 by being the first radio journalist to receive the Sol Taishoff Award for Excellence in Broadcasting from the National Press Foundation. In spring 2004, she was the only broadcast journalist granted advance access to the papers of Supreme Court justice Harry Blackmun five years after his death. Blackmun had been the author of the landmark ROE V. WADE abortion rights opinion. A prolific writer, Totenberg is a frequent contributor to national newspapers and magazines.

Further Reading

Totenberg, Nina. *The Complete Transcripts of the Clarence Thomas-Anita Hill Hearings: October 11, 12, 13, 1991.* Chicago: Academy Chicago Pub, 1994.

—Thea Lapham

Triangle Shirtwaist Company fire

On the night of March 25, 1911, 146 workers, mostly immigrant women and young girls, died in the Triangle Shirtwaist Company. A lower Manhattan sweatshop, the Triangle Shirtwaist factory typified working conditions for many women in the early 20th century, with long hours, extremely low wages, and lack of even basic safety precautions. When the fire erupted in the Asch Building on the afternoon of March 5, 1911, nearly 500 employees were in the building. The doors on the ninth floor were locked, the fire escape did not reach the ground, and firefighters' ladders were not long enough to reach the upper floors. Some women chose to jump to their deaths rather than perish in the fire.

The incident led to immediate calls for improved working conditions throughout the city of New York and the nation. The INTERNATIONAL LADIES' GARMENT WORKERS' UNION (ILGWU) organized relief efforts for the families of the victims, including payments to survivors and placement of orphans. The ILGWU also demanded reforms. A year later, a strike in Lawrence, Massachusetts, sent 20,000 textile workers to the streets, and appeal for women's SUFFRAGE increased based on the need to enact legislation to protect women workers.

Max Blanck and Isaac Harris, the owners of the Triangle Shirtwaist Factory, were charged with knowingly locking the doors to the ninth-floor exit. Despite testimony from dozens of witnesses who testified that workers had to exit the main gate and have their pocketbooks inspected after every shift, the men were found not guilty. They later paid $75 per life lost in a civil suit. Nonetheless, some reforms were enacted after the Triangle Shirtwaist fire. While earlier strikes, including the "Uprising of 20,000" in 1911, resulted in improved conditions at individual factories, the aftermath of the Triangle Shirtwaist Company fire involved legislation on both the state and national levels. The Factory Commission of 1911, headed by Samuel Gompers, president of the American Federation of Labor, recommended legislation that required exit doors open outward and prohibited locked exit doors. The legislation was passed and eventually became the foundation of the Occupational Safety and Health Administration (OSHA). New York City created the Bureau of Fire Prevention to establish regulations, and many other cities followed suit.

Further Reading

McClymer, John F. *The Triangle Strike and Fire.* Fort Worth: Harcourt Brace College Publishers, 1998.

—Angela O'Neil

Truman, Bess (Elizabeth Virginia Wallace Truman) (1885–1982) *first lady*

Elizabeth Virginia (Bess) Wallace was born in Independence, Missouri, on February 13, 1885, to David Willock and Margaret Gates Wallace. While her mother's family was wealthy, her father's employment was spotty, and Bess was keenly aware of the tensions created by her mother's expectations and her father's failure to provide. As a child, Bess was athletic, personable, and exuded self-confidence. She was an excellent student, but her life was irrevocably changed when her father committed suicide in 1903. In shame, Margaret Gates moved the family to the Gates family mansion in Independence.

Although Bess's grandparents provided the financial support for her to finish high school at the prestigious Barstow School in Kansas City, she did not accompany her classmates as they entered college. Rather, she returned to Independence to care for her mother and brothers. There she became reacquainted with Harry Truman, a childhood friend, now running the family farm in Grandview, Missouri. Within three years, the couple were engaged, but they did not marry until Harry returned from World War I (June 28, 1919). Following their honeymoon, the couple established their home in the Gates family mansion. Bess helped Harry, who had entered the haberdashery business, and continued to care for her mother. The business failed, and Harry entered politics, being elected judge for the Eastern District of Jackson County in 1922. In 1924, their only child, Mary Margaret, was born.

Bess greeted Harry's decision to seek a U.S. Senate seat in 1934 with ambivalence, but she agreed to stand beside him as he announced his candidacy and campaigned with him on a limited basis. His victory meant a move to Washington, D.C.—a move she viewed with hesitancy. Once in residence, however, she found that she liked the small-town feel of Washington, although she returned to Independence regularly each summer to care for her mother and oldest brother, who remained in the Gates homestead. In Washington, Bess learned the formalities of making and receiving calls. She spent time with cabinet wives as well as Secretary of Labor FRANCES PERKINS and First Lady ELEANOR ROOSEVELT. Bess followed the legislative process closely and frequently handled correspondence in Harry's congressional office. By 1940, she was more comfortable with her political life and greeted the prospect of reelection more positively by campaigning with Harry, greeting voters at their home, and working behind the scenes. In July 1941, Harry put Bess on the payroll in his congressional office, which she ran while he toured investigating defense expenditures following Pearl Harbor.

In 1944, Harry Truman was offered the vice presidency. Bess knew well the state of Franklin Roosevelt's health and doubted that he would survive a fourth term, thereby leaving Harry to inherit the presidency in the midst of a war. She feared for the safety of her daughter Margaret and loathed the prospect of the public spotlight on her family, most especially the disclosure of her father's suicide. Harry ultimately agreed to join the ticket, but Bess did not campaign as actively on his behalf as she had in his last Senate campaign. She spent most of the summer in Independence, and when he was elected, she declined to speak on political issues. On April 12, 1945, when President Roosevelt died, she paid a condolence call on Eleanor Roosevelt and stood by her husband as he was sworn into office. Upon inspecting the White House, she found it in terrible disrepair. She undertook extensive refurbishment before moving her family into the living quarters and quickly assembled a staff, but declined to follow in Eleanor Roosevelt's footsteps of political involvement.

As first lady, Bess did not give speeches, hold press conferences, or respond to press queries for the record. She held teas for women reporters but refused to be quoted, opting instead to reply in one-word written responses or a "no comment." Fleeing what she termed "the great White jail," she frequently returned to Independence,

leaving the president alone in Washington. During the close of World War II, she curtailed formal entertaining at the White House. However, throughout the country's "return to normalcy," she surprised even her supporters in her ability to restore elegance to formal entertaining. By 1948, she had suspended all but the most important state reception, fearing that the dilapidated condition of the White House posed a threat to the personal safety of her guests.

Bess and Margaret Truman campaigned with Harry in 1948, accompanying him on his famous whistle-stop tour across the country. Bess waved from the back of the train platform but rarely made any public statements. Harry's reelection assured, the family moved into Blair House after structural engineers discovered problems so severe that they considered demolishing the White House and starting over. The Trumans insisted that as much of the original structure as

Elizabeth Virginia Wallace Truman, ca. 1950 (LIBRARY OF CONGRESS)

possible be saved, and Bess was forced to move many of the large social gatherings to locations around Washington; the 1949 inaugural ball, for example, was held in the National Gallery of Art. She entertained only as much as she felt she must, preferring to spend her time in the company of her immediate family. Blair House presented security problems, and she worried even more after a Puerto Rican nationalist tried to shoot his way into the residence, killing one guard and wounding another.

Because of the Twenty-Second Amendment, Harry Truman was unable to seek a third term in 1952, and the election of Dwight D. Eisenhower meant that the three Trumans could return to a quiet life in Independence. In retirement, Harry supported the family financially by completing his memoirs and selling the family farm to developers. (Former presidents did not receive a federal pension at that time.) The couple traveled widely, oversaw the construction of the Truman Library, celebrated Margaret's marriage to *New York Times* editor Clifton Daniel in 1956, and welcomed their first grandchild in 1957. When John F. Kennedy was assassinated in 1963, federal secret service protection was granted to all former presidents and their families. Bess accepted it but refused to allow agents on her property.

Harry Truman died in 1972 and, at Bess's request, was memorialized at a small funeral in Independence rather than in Washington. After his death, she continued to follow politics and even allowed herself to be named honorary chair of Missouri senator Tom Eagleton's reelection campaign in 1974 and Congressman Jim Symington's campaign for the Senate in 1976. She worked with former members of the Truman administration on the creation of the Truman Scholarship program, designed to bring more young people into government service. Bess Truman died on October 18, 1982, at the age of 97, making her the longest-lived first lady in U.S. history. She is buried next to her husband in the courtyard of the Truman Library in Independence, Missouri.

Further Reading

Cottrell, Debbie Mauldin. "Elizabeth Virginia (Bess) Wallace Truman." In *American First Ladies: Their Lives and Their Legacy,* 2nd ed., edited by Lewis L. Gould, 303–310. New York: Routledge, 2001.

National First Ladies Library. *Biographies: First Ladies of the United States.* Available online. URL: http://www.firstladies.org/biographies. Accessed on January 4, 2007.

Schneider, Dorothy, and Carl J. Schneider. "Elizabeth (Bess) Virginia Wallace Truman" *First Ladies: A Biographical Dictionary,* 250–260. New York: Checkmark Books, 2001.

Truth, Sojourner (Isabella Hardenbergh)

(ca. 1797–1883) *abolitionist, women's rights activist, temperance advocate*   Sojourner Truth was born into slavery as Isabella Hardenbergh—her surname reflecting that of her first owner, Johannes Hardenbergh—in about 1797. The Hardenbergh farm, located in Hurley County, New York, was near the Hudson River and in sight of the Catskill Mountains. When Isabella was born, her parents, James and Elizabeth, had already seen several children sold away; Isabella knew only one of 10 siblings, a brother named Peter. She was sold to the Neely family at the age of nine for $100. Isabella had grown up speaking Dutch and spoke no English, and when she could not understand the Neelys' commands, they beat her. Within about a year, she was sold to the Schriver family.

In 1810, John Dumont purchased Isabella for $175. She worked both in the fields for Dumont and in the house for his wife. Although she suffered cruel treatment at the hands of both masters, it was Mrs. Dumont that she later described as "cruel and harsh" in her autobiographical narrative. Some scholars have speculated that Isabella may have suffered from sexual abuse by Mrs. Dumont.

Around 1815, Isabella met a slave named Robert who was owned by another master. Although the two wanted to marry, Robert's owner refused permission for the union since any children born to the couple would belong to Dumont. After Robert was caught with Isabella, he was savagely beaten and never returned. Isabella subsequently gave birth to a daughter she named Diana. In 1817, apparently at Dumont's insistence, she married an older slave named Thomas, with whom she had four more children: Peter, James, Elizabeth, and Sophia. James died while still an infant.

On July 4, 1827, the emancipation of every slave in New York was ordered. However, John Dumont refused to let Isabella go, even though they had reached an agreement that she would be freed one year in advance of New York's emancipation date "if she would do well and be faithful." Dumont reneged on the promise after Isabella suffered a disfiguring hand accident, arguing that her injury had reduced her productivity. Isabella therefore walked away from slavery on her own terms. After working the fall harvest, including spinning 100 pounds of wool yarn, she escaped with only her infant daughter Sophia. Dumont pursued her but agreed to accept $20 for the balance of the year prior to emancipation from Isaac and Maria Van Wagenen. Like the Dumonts, the Van Wagenens were prominent members of the Dutch Reformed Church, but unlike the Dumonts, they opposed slavery and invited Isabella to call them by their given names. During the year she stayed with them, she worked for the return of her five-year-old son Peter, who had first been leased and then sold to a slaveholder in Alabama. A group of Quakers helped Isabella pursue Peter's return through the courts. He was eventually returned but had been badly abused.

Isabella found her voice as a preacher and began attending a local Methodist church. In 1829, she left Ulster County and traveled, ultimately settling for a time in New York City. On June 1, 1843, she changed her name to Sojourner Truth to reflect her new life as a travelling teller of truth. She began a life of evangelism and spiritualism, in spite of the fact that she could neither read nor write. In 1844, she joined the

Sojourner Truth, 1864 (LIBRARY OF CONGRESS)

Northampton Association of Education and Industry, a 500-acre farm cooperative in Massachusetts. The community had been founded by abolitionists and had over 200 members who voiced strong support for religious tolerance and women's rights. It was here that Sojourner Truth met such well-known abolitionists as William Lloyd Garrison and Frederick Douglass. When the cooperative folded, she continued to live with one of the association's founders, George Benson and dictated her memoirs to Olive Gilbert, another member of the cooperative. *The Narrative of Sojourner Truth: A Northern Slave* was published by William Lloyd Garrison in 1850. Truth sold the book for income as she traveled and gave antislavery speeches based on her personal experiences as a slave. When George Benson left Northampton, Sojourner Truth bought his house and lived there when she was not giving speeches. In 1851, she gave her most famous speech to the Ohio Women's Rights Convention in Akron, Ohio. The speech is now titled "Ain't I a Woman?" in reference to her repeated refrain (see Appendix of this volume for the entire text).

Truth's involvement in the spiritualism movement influenced her travels, and she often settled with Quaker groups or within other utopian communities. In 1857, she sold her Northampton home and purchased a house in Harmonia, Michigan. When the Civil War broke out, Truth spoke for the Union cause and worked with other freed slaves for the National Freedman's Relief Association in Washington, D.C. A painting depicts her meeting with Abraham Lincoln. In 1863, HARRIET BEECHER STOWE's article "Sojourner Truth, the Libyan Sibyl" was published in the *Atlantic Monthly*. Although Truth took issue with some of the facts and with Stowe's characterization of her as an "African," the work brought new prominence to Sojourner Truth's story in ways that her own *Narrative* never did. Stowe's article and, later, William Story's statue of the same title transformed Sojourner Truth the woman into Sojourner Truth the symbol.

When the war ended, Truth continued her work to assist newly freed slaves. In the 1870s, she campaigned (unsuccessfully) for the federal government to provide land in the West to freedmen and their families. Although she continued to preach about women's rights and temperance, the plight of the "Exodusters" (freed slaves migrating north and west) became the primary focus of her speeches at churches throughout the upper Midwest. In the early 1880s, Truth returned to Battle Creek, Michigan, where her daughters Diana and Elizabeth lived with their children. She died on November 26, 1883, and she is buried at Oak Hill Cemetery.

In 1997, Battle Creek celebrated the 200th anniversary of Truth's birth by commissioning a statue of her by artist Tina Allen. In 1998, the Sojourner Truth Institute of Battle Creek was established as an affiliate of the Battle Creek Community Foundation "to expand the historical and biographical knowledge of her life's work and carry on her mission by teaching, demonstrating and promoting projects that accentuate the ideals and principles for which she stood." The institute, in conjunction with the Heritage Battle Creek Research Center, houses one of the most extensive collections of Sojourner Truth artifacts and records in the United States.

Further Reading
Gilbert, Olive. *Narrative of Sojourner Truth,* edited by Margaret Washington. New York: Vintage Books, 1993.
Mabee, Carlton. *Sojourner Truth: Slave, Prophet, Legend.* New York: New York University Press, 1993.
Newhouse, Susan Mabee. *Sojourner Truth: Slave, Prophet, Legend.* New York: New York University Press, 1995.
Painter, Nell Irvin. *Sojourner Truth: A Life, A Symbol.* New York: W.W. Norton and Company, 1996.

—Thea Lapham

Tubman, Harriet (Araminta Ross Tubman)

(ca. 1820–1913) *abolitionist, suffragist, underground railroad conductor* Born to slaves in Bucktown, Maryland about 1820, Harriet Tubman was often referred to as the "Black Moses" of the Underground Railroad. The designation honored her tireless commitment to helping slaves navigate their way to freedom and safety via a series of "safe houses" along a northern route. She is celebrated throughout history as one of the most successful "conductors" on the Underground Railroad.

Originally named Araminta, Harriet later took her mother's name. When she was 25, she married John Tubman, a free African American. In 1849, she fled from her Maryland slave owner and found freedom in Philadelphia, but she could not free herself from the memory of friends and family left behind. It was her love and compassion that compelled Harriet Tubman to risk her life over and over again to rescue those who could not rescue themselves.

During the Civil War, Tubman's stealth and self-sacrifice continued. Blessed with an uncanny sense of direction and an ability to recognize landmarks, the illiterate emancipator helped to free countless slaves. She communicated her message of freedom—including which routes to travel and what time to flee—using biblical quotes and the lyrics of spirituals. Throughout her long years of service as a scout, nurse, and spy for the U.S. government, Tubman was never caught, and she never lost a single one of her approximately 300 "passengers" along the Underground Railroad.

After the Civil War, Tubman became increasingly involved in women's issues and frequently attended meetings in Seneca Falls, New York,

the birthplace of the women's SUFFRAGE movement. In 1896, she helped to found the NATIONAL ASSOCIATION OF COLORED WOMEN. She died on March 10, 1913, in Auburn, New York.

Further Reading

Humez, Jean McMahon. *Harriet Tubman: The Life and the Life Stories.* Madison: University of Wisconsin Press, 2004.

Larson, Kate Clifford. *Bound for the Promised Land: Harriet Tubman, Portrait of an American Hero.* New York: Ballantine Books, 2003.

—Thea Lapham

Tyler, Julia Gardiner (1820–1889) *first lady*
The second wife of President John Tyler, Julia Gardiner was born into wealth and influence on May 4, 1820, on Gardiner's Island, New York. She was the third of four children of lawyer David Gardiner and heiress Juliana McLachlan Gardiner. The family was acutely aware of the advantages of marital alliances, social exclusivity, and money. Julia was schooled in an elite private academy for girls and trained in the female subjects of the times: music, French literature, ancient history, and composition. When she was 19, she went on a year-long European tour designed to meet appropriate suitors. On a visit to Washington in early 1842, the family was invited to a reception at the White House, where Julia was first introduced to President John Tyler. Priscilla Cooper Tyler, the president's daughter-in-law, presided as official hostess as First Lady LETITIA TYLER was confined to a wheelchair in a second-floor bedroom.

President Tyler invited the Gardiner family to the White House often, and the families grew close. By 1843, although still in mourning for his first wife, who had died in September 1842, he decided that he wanted to marry Julia. She rejected his first proposal, but a second one articulated in front of Julia's sister was conveyed to her parents. They were pleased with the development and used it as an opportunity to get a political appointment for her brother

Harriet Tubman (LIBRARY OF CONGRESS)

before agreeing to the marriage. On June 26, 1844, John Tyler and Julia Gardiner were secretly married in New York City. He revealed the marriage to his children and to the country only after it had taken place. John Tyler's oldest children (three who were older than Julia) were shocked by their father's secret marriage so soon after their mother's death. Although all but one would ultimately reconcile; the eight months remaining of John Tyler's term were often tense.

At 24 years old, Julia was the youngest first lady in history, and she sought advice from DOLLEY MADISON. Like her mentor, she loved to entertain and brought many of the flourishes and customs of European courts to the White House—for instance, beginning the tradition of "Hail to the Chief" being played when the president entered at official state functions. Julia created her own "court," made up of four close female relatives, to serve as her "ladies in waiting." She also created positive press attention by secretly employing her own press secretary to "sound Julia's praises far and near in Washington." She used the few perks of the office to her personal advantage and extended them to her entire family as well, such that the entire Gardiner clan enjoyed the franking privilege to send mail without cost.

Though born a New Yorker, Julia quickly moved to adopt her husband's southern political views as her own. She wrote to her brother, "I have turned my back upon New York and aim to become a thorough Virginian." Indeed, as first lady she urged her husband to accomplish the annexation of Texas in 1845, even though previous attempts had failed in the Senate. In an effort to help, she lobbied senators at her balls, hoping flirtation would turn their votes. When President Tyler signed the legislation three days before leaving office, he gave her the gold pen he used to sign it. At her last ball before leaving the White House, she entertained 3,000 people, including several foreign ministers.

After leaving the White House, the Tylers moved to Sherwood Forest, a plantation on the James River near Richmond, Virginia. Together they had seven children between 1846 and 1860. Julia's Gardiner money and John's land-holdings meant that the family lived in style, but it also meant that they supported a large number of dependents including children, relatives, and slaves. Over time, their commitments exceeded her money and the plantation's yield, and they were forced to turn to her family for money. Although John Tyler had hoped to avoid a national split over slavery, after the 1859 attack at Harpers Ferry led by John Brown and futile attempts at keeping the peace as Virginia's special commissioner, he returned to Sherwood Forest in 1861 advocating secession. Julia openly supported the Confederate cause, even urging her 13-year-old son to enlist in the Junior Guard.

In January 1862, John Tyler was in Richmond for the Confederate House of Representatives meeting when Julia had a dream that he was dangerously ill. Although she found him well when she arrived, he lapsed into sickness just days later and died on January 18, 1862. Julia was left to raise their seven children, the oldest 15 and the youngest just two.

The war years found Julia at odds with the rest of the Gardiner family, particularly her brother David. When she tried to move her children to her mother's house in New York to escape the fighting, she found David's family already in residence. She ordered him to leave, he refused, and ultimately she ferried her children back to Sherwood Forest. Out of respect for her former position, the Union army maintained a sentry around her plantation, and when she traveled north with her children, she did so on a Union-issued pass and with federal protection. Even so, she continued her work in support of the Confederacy by distributing pamphlets, collecting relief supplies, and campaigning for General George McClellan to replace Abraham Lincoln as president.

Upon her mother's death, Julia entered a legal battle with her brother David over the Gardiner estate. This was the first of several lawsuits she was involved in at war's end, many in an attempt to regain property seized by Union troops during the war. In 1872, she moved back to Washington, but the depression of 1873 required her to sell off all her property with the exception of Sherwood Forest, which remains in the hands of her descendants. She lobbied to receive a federal pension as a president's widow and an additional monthly sum as a widow of a veteran of the War of 1812. She was successful on both counts. On July 10, 1889, at the age of 69, she died of a cerebral stroke. She is buried next to John Tyler in Richmond, Virginia.

Further Reading

Mayo, Edith P. "Julia Tyler." In *The Smithsonian Book of First Ladies: Their Lives, Times, and Issues,* pp. 58–63. New York: Henry Holt and Company, 1996.

National First Ladies Library. *Biographies: First Ladies of the United States.* Available online. URL: http://www.firstladies.org/biographies. Accessed on January 4, 2007.

Schneider, Dorothy, and Carl J. Schneider. "Julia Gardiner Tyler" *First Ladies: A Biographical Dictionary,* pp. 62–69. New York: Checkmark Books, 2001.

Seagar, Robert. *And Tyler Too: A Biography of John and Julia Gardiner Tyler.* New York: McGraw-Hill, 1963.

Tyler, Letitia (Letitia Christian Tyler) (1790–1842) *first lady*   Very little is known of Letitia Christian Tyler as none of her letters have survived. The daughter of a wealthy and politically prominent family, she was born at Cedar Grove Plantation, just outside Richmond, Virginia, on November 12, 1790. On March 29, 1813, she married John Tyler at Cedar Grove. The Tylers used an inheritance from her parents to build a large home on land owned by John. Beginning in 1815, Letitia bore the first of nine children (seven survived infancy). Much of Letitia's life during this period was focused on tending her children and the plantation's slaves.

In 1825, John Tyler was elected governor of Virginia, and two years later, he was elected to the U.S. Senate. After resigning in 1836, he moved the family to Williamsburg. In 1839, Letitia Tyler suffered a stroke that left her partially paralyzed and bedridden. When Tyler was elected as William Henry Harrison's vice president in the election of 1840, he had planned to remain in Williamsburg. However, when Harrison died a month after taking office, President Tyler left for Washington. Letitia moved to Washington and was installed in a second-floor bedroom where she received guests and visiting dignitaries. Her daughter-in-law, Priscilla Cooper Tyler, served as official hostess for President Tyler. In 1842, Letitia suffered a second stroke, and she died on September 10. Her husband would later marry JULIA GARDINER TYLER in 1844.

Further Reading

National First Ladies Library. *Biographies: First Ladies of the United States.* Available online. URL: http://www.firstladies.org/biographies. Accessed on January 4, 2007.

Schneider, Dorothy, and Carl J. Schneider. "Letitia Christian Tyler." *First Ladies: A Biographical Dictionary.* New York: Checkmark Books, 2001, 56–61.

U

UAW v. Johnson Controls, Inc. (499 U.S. 187) (1991) In 1987, displaced female employees alleged that Johnson Controls, Inc.'s fetal-protection plan constituted gender discrimination in violation of TITLE VII OF THE CIVIL RIGHTS ACT OF 1964, as amended by the PREGNANCY DISCRIMINATION ACT of 1978. The company, a battery manufacturer, prohibited fertile women from holding jobs that required exposure to lead out of concern for the unborn children. No similar exclusion was applied to men. The trial court ruled for the employer, finding that the women had failed to prove essential elements of their claim. The Seventh Court of Appeals concurred, finding that airborne lead within the battery plants represented a significant fetal health hazard. The court described previous appellate decisions allowing such policies under the business necessity defense and agreed that this theory should apply here as well.

In a unanimous decision, the U.S. Supreme Court reversed the Seventh Circuit Court Decision, finding policies that represent such overt gender discrimination to be unlawful under traditional TITLE VII analysis *unless* the plan meets a narrow BONA FIDE OCCUPATIONAL QUALIFICATION (BFOQ) defense. In this case, the policy requiring infertility did not satisfy the BFOQ. A majority of the court found that Johnson Controls' plan could not be maintained, since that defense could not be stretched to encompass the company's concerns for fetal safety.

Further Reading

The OYEZ Project. "*Automobile Workers v. Johnson Controls, Inc.,* 499 U.S. 187 (1991)." Available online. URL: http://www.oyez.org/cases/case?case=1990–1999/1990/1990_89_1215. Accessed on January 11, 2007.

United Daughters of the Confederacy (UDC)

Initially established as the National Association of the Daughters of the Confederacy on September 10, 1894, the organization was rechristened a year later as the United Daughters of the Confederacy (UDC). It was subsequently incorporated under the laws of the District of Columbia on July 18, 1919.

Only the name changed, however. The group's objectives, established during the 1894 organizational meeting in Nashville, Tennessee, remained the same: the promotion of history, education, benevolence, honor, and patriotism. Since then, time has done nothing to erase the

UDC's dedication toward those initial objectives. The UDC collects and preserves rare books, documents, diaries, letters, personal records, and other papers of historical importance relating to the period between 1861 and 1865. The collection is stored at the UDC Memorial Building in Richmond, Virginia. The building is also home to the Caroline Meriwether Goodlett Library and the Helen Walpole Brewer Library.

A fund established in 1910 to help Confederate women in need continues to assist those descended from Confederate veterans. A 32.5-foot bronze monument featuring 32 life-sized figures still stands in the Confederate section of Arlington National Cemetery in Arlington, Virginia. Members of the UDC worked to raise funds for the monument, which was unveiled on June 4, 1914. The UDC does not just limit its benevolence to the people, places, and ideology of the Confederate era, however. During World War I, the organization's 100,000 members purchased $24,843,368 worth of war bonds and savings stamps, donated $841,676 to the Red Cross and other relief work, and made several other large donations. The UDC made similar donations during World War II and the Korean War, continuing on through the Vietnam conflict and Operation Desert Shield/Desert Storm.

Further Reading

Cox, Karen L. *Dixie's Daughters: The United Daughters of the Confederacy and the Preservation of Confederate Culture.* Gainesville: University Press of Florida, 2003.

—Thea Lapham

United Nations Decade for Women (1976–1985)

Following the International Women's Year conference held in Mexico City in 1975, the United Nations adopted a resolution proclaiming the period between 1976 and 1985 as the United Nations Decade for Women: Equality, Development and Peace. The focus was designed to encourage member states to examine their progress relative to benchmarks established in the World Plan of Action adopted at the first International Women's Year Conference. In 1985, women from around the world gathered in Nairobi, Kenya, to review the achievements of the United Nations Decade for Women and to create a 10-year action plan for the advancement of women. The Nairobi conference consisted of two important processes: an official process, which brought together delegations from the United Nations member countries; and a nongovernment (NGO) process, which brought together representatives of women's organizations from around the world to a parallel NGO Forum.

The Nairobi conference of 1985 represented the largest gathering of women in the history of the United Nations and produced a benchmark document: "Forward Looking Strategies for the Advancement of Women to the Year 2000." As part of the strategy developed at Nairobi, it was determined that within 10 years, a UN conference would be convened to report on the implementation of the Forward Looking Strategies. This conference was held in Beijing on September 4–15, 1995, and had four objectives: to review and appraise the advancement of women since 1985, to mobilize women and men at both the policy-making and grassroots levels, to adopt a "Platform for Action," and to determine the priorities to be followed in 1996–2001 for implementation of the strategies within the UN system.

Ten years later, in 2005, at the 49th session of the UN Commission on the Status of Women, governments met to review their successes and failures in achieving the goals of Beijing. The Beijing+10 review provided an opportunity for NGO representatives from around the world, who monitor and contribute to the governmental discussions, to share their experiences in pushing for implementation of the Beijing strategies in their home countries.

See also INTERNATIONAL WOMEN'S DAY.

Further Reading

United Nations Inter-Agency Network on Women and Gender Equality. Available online. URL: www.un.org/womenwatch. Accessed on June 30, 2006.

United States v. Susan B. Anthony (24 F.Cas. 829) (1873)

"Miss Susan B. Anthony . . . upon the 5th day of November, 1872, . . . voted. . . . At that time she was a woman," said the U.S. district attorney in presenting the indictment against SUSAN B. ANTHONY. On November 1, 1872, Susan B. Anthony registered to vote in Rochester, New York, and four days later she voted in the election. She was arrested and charged with "knowingly casting an illegal vote in a federal election." In casting a vote, Anthony was pursuing a strategy to advance women's suffrage by arguing that the right to vote falls under the provisions of the Fourteenth Amendment. As citizens, women were entitled to the "privileges and immunities" of citizenship, including the privilege of voting. When Anthony was declared incompetent to testify on her own behalf because of her sex, her attorney, Henry R. Seldon, testified the language of the Fourteenth Amendment gave women the right of SUFFRAGE, and that he had counseled Anthony to exercise her right to vote. When the defense rested its case, Judge Ward Hunt read a statement to the all-male jury and directed them to find Anthony guilty. He denied Seldon's request to poll the jury and denied a request for a new trial. Before sentencing Anthony, Hunt asked, "Has the prisoner anything to say why sentence should not be pronounced?" but then denied Anthony the chance to deliver her statement. Anthony's sentence was a fine of $100 as well as court costs. Anthony replied, "May it please your honor, I will never pay a dollar of your unjust penalty. . . . Resistance to tyranny is obedience to God." Anthony did not pay the fine, nor did she ever cast a legal vote. Anthony's trial experience, and the Supreme Court's narrow interpretation of a Fourteenth Amendment claim in a case brought by VIRGINIA MINOR in *MINOR V. HAPPERSETT*, convinced her that women were not going to win the vote through the courts and that suffragists should dedicate their efforts to state referenda and a federal amendment. Anthony traveled extensively around the country promoting state women suffrage initiatives and legislation. The Nineteenth Amendment to the U.S. Constitution granting women suffrage, also known as the Susan B. Anthony Amendment, was ratified in 1920, 14 years after her death.

See also MINOR V. HAPPERSETT (1875).

Further Reading

Lindner, Douglas O. "The Trial of Susan B. Anthony, 1873. In *Famous American Trials*. Available online. URL: http://tinyurl.con/4s6nb. Accessed on June 30, 2006.

United States v. Virginia et al. (518 U.S. 515) (1996)

The Virginia Military Institute (VMI) boasted a long and proud tradition as Virginia's only exclusively male public undergraduate higher learning institution. The U.S. solicitor general brought suit against the state of Virginia and VMI, alleging that the school's male-only admissions policy violated the Fourteenth Amendment's equal protection clause. On appeal from the District Court ruling favoring VMI, the Fourth Circuit Court reversed the lower court's decision, finding VMI's admissions policy to be unconstitutional. In response, Virginia proposed to create the Virginia Women's Institute for Leadership (VWIL) as a parallel program for women at Mary Baldwin College. On appeal from the District Court's affirmation of the plan, the Fourth Circuit Court ruled that despite the difference in prestige between the VMI and VWIL, the two programs would offer "substantively comparable" educational benefits. The U.S. solicitor general appealed to the Supreme Court.

In a 7-1 decision, the Court held that VMI's male-only admissions policy was unconstitutional. Because it failed to show "exceedingly persuasive justification" for VMI's gender-biased admissions policy, Virginia had violated the Fourteenth Amendment's equal-protection clause. The state failed to support its claim that single-sex education contributes to educational diversity because it did not show that VMI's male-only admissions policy was created or maintained in order to further educational diversity. Furthermore, Virginia's VWIL could not ever offer women the same benefits as VMI offered men. The VWIL would not provide women with the same rigorous military training, faculty, courses, facilities, financial opportunities, or alumni reputation and connections that VMI afforded its male cadets. Finally, the Fourth Circuit's "substantive comparability" between VMI and VWIL was used in error; rather, "all gender-based classifications today" must be evaluated with "heightened scrutiny."

This case is as close as the Supreme Court has ever come to employing a standard of skepticism similar to the "strict scrutiny" applied to cases where distinctions are made on the basis of race. In essence, when evaluated with "heightened scrutiny," Virginia's plan to create the VWIL could not provide women with the same opportunities as VMI provided its men, and so it failed to meet the requirements of the equal-protection clause.

Justice RUTH BADER GINSBERG wrote the majority opinion for the Court, a forceful statement in support of full gender equality. Justice Clarence Thomas did not participate. Although The Citadel in South Carolina had been involved in years of litigation to fight gender integration, the college moved immediately to admit women on the basis of this decision.

Further Reading

The OYEZ Project. "*United States v. Virginia,* 518 U.S. 515 (1996)." Available online. URL: http://www. oyez.org/cases/case?case=1990–1999/1995/1995_ 94_1941. Accessed on January 12, 2007.

V

Velázquez, Nydia Margarita (1953–   ) *congressperson* Nydia Margarita Velázquez was born on March 28, 1953, in Yabucoa, Puerto Rico; she is one of nine children. Velázquez started school early, skipped several grades, and became the first person in her family to receive a college degree. At the age of 16, she entered the University of Puerto Rico in Rio Piedras, and she graduated magna cum laude in 1974 with a degree in political science. After earning a master's degree from New York University in 1976, Velázquez taught at the University of Puerto Rico, Humacao (1976–81) and then taught Puerto Rican studies (1981–83) at City University of New York's Hunter College. In 1983, she was appointed special assistant to Democratic congressman Edolphus Towns (Brooklyn). One year later, she became the first Latina appointed to serve on the New York City Council.

In 1992, Velázquez became the first Puerto Rican woman elected to the U.S. House of Representatives, and she has been reelected ever since. In February 1998, she was named ranking democratic member of the House Small Business Committee. In 2001, she called for a repeal of the 1996 welfare law, arguing that there should be no time limits on welfare and that benefits should be available to legal immigrants. Velázquez serves on the House Committee on Financial Services as well as the Small Business Committee.

Further Reading

Barone, Michael. *The Almanac of American Politics*. Washington, D.C.: National Journal Group, 2006.

"Representative Nydia M. Velázquez." In *Project Vote Smart*. Available online. URL: http://votesmart. org/biophp?can_id=H2631103. Accessed on January 8, 2007.

"Velázquez, Nydia Margarita." In *Biographical Directory of the United States Congress, 1774–present*. Available online. URL: http://bioguide.congress.gov/ scripts/biodisplay.pl?index=V000081. Accessed on January 8, 2007.

—Angela Kouters

Villard, Fanny (Helen Frances Garrison Villard) (1844–1928) *suffragist, peace advocate* Born Helen Frances Garrison on December 16, 1844, Fanny Garrison was the only daughter of abolitionist William Lloyd Garrison. Fanny taught piano until marrying Henry

Villard, a war correspondent for the *New York Tribune,* on January 3, 1866. Together they had four children. Though he continued to work as a journalist, Henry Villard speculated in railroad financing and was so successful that he became president of Northern Pacific Railway in 1881. This in turn enabled him to acquire the *New York Evening Post.* Henry and Fanny Villard also owned the *Nation,* edited by her brother, Wendell Phillips Garrison. Henry Villard died in 1900.

Fanny Villard joined the SUFFRAGE movement in 1906 and was active in a number of interracial and humanitarian causes. She and her son Oswald were founding members of the National Association for the Advancement of Colored People (NAACP). An uncompromising pacifist, she led a 1914 Peace Parade of 1,200 women down New York's 5th Avenue to protest World War I and helped to organize the WOMEN'S PEACE PARTY (WPP). After the war, she helped to establish the Women's International League for Peace and Freedom (WILPF). She was also a relentless worker to improve social conditions, managing the New York Diet Kitchen Association for almost 50 years. Fanny Villard died on July 5, 1928, at the age of 83.

Further Reading

Venet, Wendy Hamand. *Neither Ballots nor Bullets: Women Abolitionists and the Civil War.* Charlottesville: University Press of Virginia, 1991.

Vindication of the Rights of Woman, A (Mary Wollstonecraft) (1792)

Liberal political philosophy provides the basis for the fundamental claims to equality for liberal feminists in the United States and elsewhere. Liberalism stresses the importance of rational thought, autonomous action, and choice on the part of each person. Reason is what most clearly distinguishes humans from other forms of animal life. Individual autonomy empowers an individual to make choices in her or his own best interest, thereby elevating individual rights above the common good. Liberal theorists believe that the political and legal systems can be used to promote a liberal agenda for all people. However, early liberal theorists such as Thomas Hobbes, John Locke, and Jean-Jacques Rousseau excluded women from claims to full citizenship. All three believed that natural and biological differences between men and women precluded women from full participation in the social contract—in public life at large and politics specifically. English feminist Mary Wollstonecraft (1759–97) challenged that basic assumption, arguing instead that any weakness exhibited by women did not result from her biological sex but rather from her lack of education and isolated social position.

In her book *A Vindication of the Rights of Woman,* published in 1792, Wollstonecraft notes that custom has decreed woman to be weak, and she claims that this weakness has been brought about through the teachings of society.

Mary Wollstonecraft (LIBRARY OF CONGRESS)

Wollstonecraft declares that humanity is based on the acquisition of reason and virtue and that this acquisition is open to both men and women. Thus, woman is not weaker, but society has made her so in order to enhance men's own feelings of superiority. In this sense, men and women both lose virtue and reason in a system of enforced superiority. Wollstonecraft argues for the necessity of education for both males and females in coeducational facilities: "To render mankind more virtuous, and happier of course, both sexes must act from the same principle; but how can that be expected when only one is allowed to see the reasonableness of it? To render also the social compact truly equitable, and in order to spread those enlightening principles, which alone can ameliorate the fate of man, women must be allowed to found their virtue on knowledge, which is scarcely possible unless they be educated by the same pursuits as men."

Wollstonecraft objected particularly to the argument made concerning women by Rousseau, whose *Emile*—which outlines the ideal upbringing and education for a free man—takes up the subject of women in the final chapter with his portrayal of Sophie, the woman who is to be Emile's ideal spouse. However, where Emile is raised to defy convention and pursue both reason and virtue, Sophie is made to accord herself with the dictates of custom, thus denying both her capacity for reason (which Rousseau denied that she had) and her ability to reach true virtue (which Rousseau deemed would be found in her conformity). Wollstonecraft, who agreed with many of Rousseau's claims about the necessity for humans to use reason and achieve freedom in obedience to the dictates of reason, disagreed with Rousseau's designation of the female sex as somehow unable to achieve this freedom. Thus, she advocates the liberal feminist position that men and women are both capable of achieving humanity's highest ends, writing: "Let woman share the rights, and she will emulate the virtues of man." According to Wollstonecraft, men and women have the same capacities, even though they may end up playing differing roles in the family and in society. *A Vindication of the Rights of Woman* proved inspirational to many 19th-century American feminists and laid the foundation for much of the era's reaction against the SEPARATE SPHERES IDEOLOGY.

See also FEMINISM.

Further Reading

Wollstonecraft, Mary. *Vindication of the Rights of Women,* by Mary Wollstonecraft. New York: Penguin Classics, 1985.

—Claire Curtis

Violence Against Women Act (VAWA)
(1994)   The Omnibus Crime Bill of 1994 was signed into law by President Bill Clinton on September 13, 1994. While the bill encompasses legislation that affects both men and women alike, it is of critical importance for its inclusion of two key initiatives—the Violence against Women Act (VAWA) and the Assault Weapons Ban. Women legislators played instrumental roles in ensuring that VAWA and the Assault Weapons Ban made their way into the final crime bill.

VAWA ensured that women who were the victims of gender-motivated crimes would be protected under federal law. Specifically, Title III of VAWA defines gender-motivated crimes as "bias" or "hate" crimes that deprive victims of civil rights. Prior to the passage of VAWA, punishment for acts of violence against women was subject to the whims of each individual state.

While Senator Joseph Biden (D-DE) was responsible for introducing and shepherding VAWA through the legislative process, congresswomen from the Senate and House were also instrumental in ensuring VAWA's passage. PATRICIA SCHROEDER (D-CO), LOUISE SLAUGHTER (D-NY), and Connie Morella (R-MD), along with Charles Schumer (D-NY) were VAWA's chief sponsors in the House. Collectively and individually, female members of the Senate and House were able to work across party lines to ensure that brutality against women such as DOMESTIC

VIOLENCE and other gender-motivated crimes would be addressed by the federal government through increased funding for education, law enforcement, and punishment.

The Crime Bill of 1994 also contained the Assault Weapons Ban. This outlawed the production of semiautomatic assault weapons and ammunition clips holding more than 10 rounds except for military or police use. Its principal architect was Senator DIANNE FEINSTEIN (D-CA). The ban's successful passage in the House and Senate demonstrates the power of women working collectively to achieve important yet controversial pieces of legislation. When all was said and done, 91 percent of Democratic congresswomen voted in favor of the ban, compared to only 66 percent of their male colleagues from the same party. Fifty-eight percent of Republican congresswomen favored the ban, while only 19 percent of Republican congressmen voiced their support.

Further Reading

Dodson, Debra L., et al. *Voices, Views and Votes: The Impact of Women in the 103rd Congress.* New Brunswick, N.J.: Center for American Women and Politics, Rutgers University, 1995.

—Krista Jenkins

Voluntary Parenthood League (VPL) MARY WARE DENNETT was the driving force behind the creation of the Voluntary Parenthood League (VPL). With Jessie Ashley and Clara Gruening Stillman, she founded the National Birth Control League in 1915 after renouncing the militant tactics of rival birth control advocate MARGARET SANGER. Based in Albany, New York, the first order of business was to draft a statement calling for New York legislatures to change laws regarding birth control information. By 1918, Dennett had become executive secretary of the organization and renamed it the Voluntary Parenthood League. As in 1915, the priority of the VPL was to eliminate the laws that kept birth control information from being dissemi-

nated. However, the League's political efforts were never realized, and all legislation submitted to Congress died in committee.

The VPL also worked to educate the general public about sex. Although the organization concentrated its efforts on lobbying the U.S. Congress for an "open bill" that would decriminalize any public discussion of contraception under the COMSTOCK ACT of 1873, it also addressed other feminist and constitutional concerns. When the VPL voted in 1925 to support Sanger's position on opposing restrictions on the distribution of birth control information by doctors, Dennett resigned as its director. By 1927 the league had disbanded, yet its contribution to the birth control debate was significant. Like Sanger's rival AMERICAN BIRTH CONTROL LEAGUE, the VPL used birth control as a free-speech issue, a springboard for sex education and a tool for expressing its importance in American society.

Further Reading

Chen, Constance. *The Sex Side of Life: Mary Ware Dennett's Pioneering Battle for Birth Control and Sex Education.* New York: W.W. Norton, 1996.
Gordon, Linda. *The Moral Property of Women: A History of Birth Control Politics in America.* Chicago: University of Illinois Press, 2002.
Papers of Mary Ware Dennett and the Voluntary Parenthood League. Schlesinger Library, Radcliffe Institute, Harvard University Women's Studies Manuscript Collection, microfilm.

—Patricia Walsh Coates

***Vorchheimer v. School District of Philadelphia* (430 U.S. 703)** (1977) This case involved a female high school student's request to attend all-male Central High School in Philadelphia. Although Girl's High School also offered a college preparatory curriculum, Susan Lynn Vorchheimer argued that Central High's science classes were superior to those offered at Girl's High. Her application for admission was denied because of her sex. The District Court ruled that the separate school policy was unconstitutional. The Court of Appeals for the Third Circuit reversed that decision, ruling that "under some circumstances sex differences may be legally justified." The appellate ruling determined that the sexes were equally affected by the city's policy of maintaining single-sex academic high schools. Because the city presented evidence that there were educational advantages to be gained from SINGLE-SEX EDUCATION, the court held that the policy was substantially related to the city's educational objectives and therefore constitutional. In 1977, the U.S. Supreme Court voted to affirm the lower court's decision.

Further Reading

The OYEZ Project. "*Vorchheimer v. School District Of Philadelphia,* 430 U.S. 703 (1977)." Available online. URL: http://www.oyez.org/cases/case?case=1970–1979/1976/1976_76_37. Accessed on January 12, 2007.

W

wage gap   The wage gap is defined as the ratio of female wages to male wages. Regardless of occupation, level of experience, skills, or education, the wage gap remains. According to the U.S. Census Bureau's statistics for 2006, women earned just 77 cents for each dollar earned by a male. While TITLE IX OF THE EDUCATION AMENDMENTS OF 1972 and TITLE VII OF THE CIVIL RIGHTS ACT OF 1964 opened doors to education and employment in well-paying professions previously limited to men, the EQUAL PAY ACT (1963), the first among the major federal equality initiatives, has not been effective in eliminating the wage gap. There is no dispute over the existence of a gender wage gap. There is substantial disagreement, however, over the cause of the wage gap. Is it the result of gender discrimination? Or is the wage gap the result of other factors that are correlated with gender, such as educational attainment, occupational choice, prior work experience, or tenure on the job? How much, if any, of the wage gap can be attributed to choices that women make in planning for a job or career?

Those who argue that the wage gap is not the result of discrimination point to occupational segregation that leaves some job categories disproportionately filled with women or men. For example, the Bureau of Labor Statistics (2003) reported that women made up 98 percent of the nation's kindergarten teachers, 96 percent of its secretaries and administrative assistants, and 90 percent of its nurses. Likewise, men made up 99 percent of the nation's auto mechanics, 97 percent of its construction workers, and 96 percent of its firefighters. This would not matter if the pay scales for occupations requiring about the same level of education and training were equivalent; however, they are not. In 2004, the median income for kindergarten teachers was $20,980, but the median income for auto mechanics was $28,810, according to the Bureau of Labor Statistics. Public school kindergarten teachers must hold a bachelor's degree, have completed an approved teacher education program, and be licensed. Formal automotive technician training is the best preparation for this increasingly technical job, but it is not always required for employment. Those who argue that the wage gap is not the result of discrimination often point to the "crowding" hypothesis. Women voluntarily select low-wage occupations and, in doing so, produce a large labor supply, thereby depressing wages. It is difficult to tell how freely women and men choose their occupations because years of formal and informal gender norm socialization has at the very least shaped their choices. Diana Furchtgott-Roth, a member of George W. Bush's Council of Economic Advisers, testified before the Equal Employment Opportunity Commission that "The average wage gap is not proof of widespread discrimination, but of women making choices about their educational and professional careers in a society where the law has granted them equality of opportunity to do so."

Although women make up a greater proportion of full-time enrollments in colleges and universities today (58 percent in 2007), that has not always been the case. The aggregate education attainment is still higher for men than for women. Therefore, some argue that the pay differential will diminish as women's education catches up over time. However, a recent study by the AMERICAN ASSOCIATION OF UNIVERSITY WOMEN (AAUW) found that just one year out of college, women working full time already earn less than their male counterparts, even when they work in the same field. The report, titled *Behind the Pay Gap,* found that women earn only 80 percent of what men earn, and within a decade, that proportion drops to 69 percent. As the study notes, looking at earnings one year out of college is about as level a playing field as you can possibly find because men and women have few care-giving obligations and similar workforce experience. "The persistence of the pay gap among young, college-educated, full-time workers suggests that educational achievement alone will not close the pay gap. We need to make workplaces more family friendly, reduce sex segregation in education and in the workplace, and combat discrimination that continues to hold women back in the workplace," said Catherine Hill, AAUW director of research.

Another prevalent explanation for the wage gap is women's exit from the paid labor force for childbearing, leaving them with fewer "continuous years" of work when compared with men. This was certainly true until the 1980s, although today most women (64 percent in 2007, according to the Bureau of Labor Statistics) with young children remain in the workforce. For women and men with similar education, continuous years in the workforce, age, and occupation, the wage gap is much smaller (though it still exists). The difference appears to stem from women's "choice" to have children. Comparing men and women with the same experience and education in 1991, women without children averaged 95 percent of men's wages while women with children made just 75 percent of men's wages. The presence of children accounted for women's, but not men's, lower wages, according to two other studies. This, according to wage gap detractors, is due to a woman's choice to spend time with her children, accept more flexible, lower-paying jobs to do so, or to aspire to less demanding occupations in anticipation of having children. And, what about women's wages when they return to the work force after caring for their children? The Center for Work-Life Policy, a research organization founded by Sylvia Ann Hewlett of Columbia University, found that women lose an average of 18 percent of their earning power when they temporarily leave the workforce. Women in business sectors lose 28 percent. Although there are contrary trends at work (see OPT-OUT REVOLUTION), experts expect that the wage differential will decline over time owing to declining fertility rates over the last decade and more continuous labor force participation by young female workers.

Those who believe that the gender wage gap is the result of labor market discrimination often argue that "equal pay for equal work" ignores the persistence of patriarchy and the powerful role that gender plays in shaping people's lives. Instead, they advocate a comparable worth pay structure. Under this system, jobs would be rated according to a series of criteria, such as educational requirements, manual dexterity requirements, job stress, risk of injuries, etc. Jobs that have similar ratings would then be assigned the same rate of pay. So, for example, a secretary (a job largely held by women) and a truck driver (a job largely held by men) might be assigned similar ratings because both involve long periods of sitting, similar levels of training, and repetitive tasks. When the Equal Pay Act of 1963 was debated in Congress, women's rights advocates pushed for a comparable worth strategy, but business interests argued that determining the comparability of jobs would increase the level of government in private business.

The Fair Pay Act (currently sponsored by Senator Tom Harkin of Iowa and Delegate ELEANOR HOLMS NORTON of the District of Columbia) and the Paycheck Fairness Act (currently sponsored by Senator HILLARY RODHAM CLINTON of New York and Representative ROSA DELAURO of Connecticut) are both designed to remediate the wage gap. The Fair Pay Act would amend the FAIR LABOR STANDARDS ACT of 1938 and would prohibit discrimination in pay based on sex, race, or national origin and require employers to pay equal wages for work at "equivalent" jobs. For enforcement purposes, the Fair Pay Act allows class-action lawsuits to be filed and provides for compensatory and punitive damages. The Paycheck Fairness Act is designed to strengthen the Equal Pay Act of 1963 by improving remedy provisions, making it easier to bring class-action Equal Pay Act claims; requiring employers to submit pay data identified by sex, race, and national origin to the EQUAL EMPLOYMENT OPPORTUNITY COMMISSION (EEOC); prohibiting employers from punishing employees who share salary information with coworkers; and closing the "affirmative defense" loophole so that employers can only defend a pay differential when it is caused by something other than sex and is related to job performance. Both of these bills have been introduced in multiple sessions of congress, but neither bill has reached the floor of the Senate or House for a vote. Both bills are before the 110th Congress.

This new legislation may be even more important in fighting wage discrimination given the U.S. Supreme Court's 5-4 ruling in LEDBETTER V. GOODYEAR TIRE AND RUBBER CO. on May 29, 2007. Lilly Ledbetter, the lone female supervisor at a tire plant in Gadsden, Alabama, filed suit alleging that her pay was substantially less than that of the male supervisors employed in the same plant due to illegal sex discrimination and, therefore, constituted a violation of Title VII of the Civil Rights Act of 1964. The Court held that the effects of past discrimination do not restart the clock for filing claims with the EEOC and that Ledbetter's suit was not timely because she could not demonstrate specific acts of discrimination within the proscribed time period. Justice Ruth Bader Ginsburg dissented, arguing that pay disputes often arise in small increments, making women hesitant to file a claim in federal court. Only when the disparities become overwhelmingly evident are women likely to proceed with a legal action. This ruling will make it more difficult to bring wage discrimination cases under Title VII.

The persistence of the wage gap even in the face of federal legislation mandating equal pay demonstrates the limits of the law to address forms of sex discrimination arising from women's traditional social roles in the private sphere. In addition to policy changes, there are other forms of direct action to challenge the wage gap. One example is the WAGE [Women Are Getting Even] Project, directed by Evelyn Murphy, former lieutenant governor of Massachusetts and author of the book *Getting Even: Why Women Don't Get Paid Like Men and What to Do About It* (New York: Simon and Schuster, 2005). WAGE provides research on the wage gap, teaches women how to determine if their wages are depressed relative to others in their field, and arms them with effective strategies for negotiating a wage increase. Most important, the WAGE Web site serves as a method of communication for employees to share wage information and thereby increase their own bargaining power.

The wage gap is a reality for women in the United States. Although there may be disagreement over its cause, there is no disputing the fact that women earn less than men.

See also GENDER STEREOTYPES.

Further Reading

Day, Judy Goldberg, and Catherine Hill. *Behind the Pay Gap.* Washington, D.C.: American Association of University Women Educational Foundation, 2007.

Furchtgott-Roth, Diana, and Christine Solba. *Women's Figures: An Illustrated Guide to the Economic Progress of Women in America.* Washington, D.C.: AEI Press and the Independent Women's Forum, 1999.

Mezey, Susan Gluck. 2003. *Elusive Equality: Women's Rights, Public Policy, and the Law.* Boulder, Colo.: Lynne Rienner, 2003.

National Committee on Pay Equity. Available online. URL: www.pay-equity.org.

Walker, Mary Edwards (1832–1919) *physician, feminist, Congressional Medal of Honor winner* Mary Edwards Walker was born on November 26, 1832, in Oswego, New York, to a family involved in abolition and other reform movements. Her father, Alvah Walker, believed in the education of girls, and Mary graduated from Syracuse Medical College in 1855. She became an early enthusiast for women's rights and was particularly passionate about the issue of dress reform. She eagerly adopted AMELIA BLOOMER's "Turkish pantaloons" and would later wear a man's evening suit to lecture on women's rights. In 1856, Mary Walker married another physician, Albert Miller, wearing trousers and a man's coat; she kept her own name throughout her life. Walker and Miller established a medical practice together in Rome, New York, but few were ready to be seen by a woman doctor, and the practice struggled. The marriage failed after 13 years.

When the Civil War started, Walker traveled to Washington, D.C., to enlist with the Union army. Denied a commission because of her sex, she volunteered as an army surgeon. In 1863, she was appointed assistant surgeon of the army and was transferred to the 52nd Ohio Infantry. In 1864, she was captured by Confederate soldiers, arrested as a spy, and imprisoned

Mary Edwards Walker, ca. 1911 (LIBRARY OF CONGRESS)

for four months in Richmond, Virginia. Her release came along with four other surgeons in a trade for 17 Confederate doctors. She returned to the 52nd Ohio Infantry until the war ended. Upon returning home to New York, she received a pension, but in a value smaller than most war widows.

On November 11, 1865, President Andrew Johnson signed a bill to present Dr. Mary Edwards Walker with the Congressional Medal of Honor for Meritorious Service, in order to recognize her contributions to the war effort without having to award her an army commission. She was the only woman to have this honor. In 1917, Congress declared that such an award could only be given for "actual combat" with enemy soldiers, and Walker's medal (along with 910 others) was revoked. Walker refused to return her medal and wore it every day until she died. President Jimmy Carter posthumously restored the medal in 1977.

Following the war, Walker became a writer and lecturer on such issues as women's rights, health care, and temperance. She was also an advocate for dress reform and often wore men's clothing to protest restrictive women's clothes—a practice that resulted in arrest several times. On the issue of SUFFRAGE, she argued that a woman's right to vote was already contained within the Constitution and that requiring a constitutional amendment (and thus arguing for such an amendment) was redundant. She wrote her "Crowing Constitutional Argument" in 1907. Dr. Mary Edwards Walker died on February 21, 1919, just three months before Congress passed the Nineteenth Amendment.

Further Reading

Leonard, Elizabeth D. *Yankee Women: Gender Battles in the Civil War.* New York: W.W. Norton, 1995.

—Claire Curtis

Warren, Mercy Otis (1728–1814) *poet, playwright, historian, Revolutionary War patriot*   Mercy Otis was born September 14, 1728 in Barnstable, Massachusetts, the third of 13 children. Growing up in the midst of a lively Patriot family, she spent her childhood and teen years receiving a good general education as well as becoming politically conscious of the growing political conditions surrounding her as the American colonies headed toward revolution. In 1754, she married James Warren and moved to Plymouth, Massachusetts. Her father's house served as a meeting place for revolutionaries, and as an adult, Warren felt it was her duty to participate in the Patriot cause. Her first play, *The Adulateur,* was published in 1772 and served as the first of many propaganda pieces that she produced in support of the American Revolution. During the War, Mercy Warren hosted political meetings in her Plymouth home. She developed her close friendship with John and ABIGAIL ADAMS during this period and continued to correspond with the couple throughout her life.

After the war, Warren continued to write and publish poetry, and in 1805, her *History of the Rise, Progress, and Termination of the American Revolution,* was published. This three-volume work offered a unique insider's perspective to the war and also set the groundwork for future female authors. Warren's entire life revolved around writings and commentary about the political situation of the United States during the Revolutionry War and Early Republic periods, and she also worked for educational reforms for women. Mercy Otis Warren died in her Plymouth home on October 19, 1814.

Further Readings

Bohrer, Melissa Lukeman. *Glory, Passion, and Principals: The Story of Eight Remarkable Women at the Core of the American Revolution.* New York: Anita Books, 2003.

Richards, Jeffery H. *Mercy Otis Warren.* New York: Twaine Publishing, 1995.

Zagarri, Rosemarie. *A Woman's Dilemma: Mercy Otis Warren and the American Revolution.* Wheeling, Ill.: Harlan Davidson, 1995.

—Sharon Romero

Washerwomen's Strike of 1881   Organized by African-American laundresses in Atlanta, Georgia, in the summer of 1881, the Washerwomen's Strike illustrates the difficulties minority women faced when they attempted to form labor organizations.

Before the advent of new technology in the late 19th century, laundry was such an arduous task that even families with limited means hired washerwomen. These women either worked inside the employer's home or took the laundry away and returned with it later. African-American women in both North and South, their job options limited by discrimination, frequently worked as laundresses and in other service occupations. Workers in the era increasingly turned to organizing in pursuit of better wages, but since laundry work was considered an unskilled job, it fell outside the purview of the dominant, craft-oriented labor organizations. Moreover, an African-American washerwoman faced both gender and racial discrimination.

Few unions considered either group suitable candidates for organization.

With the assistance and encouragement of local churches, a group of African-American laundresses organized into the Washerwomen's Association of Atlanta. They then struck for a wage increase of $1 per 12 pounds of wash. Leaders relied on door-to-door mobilization in Atlanta's tightly knit African-American community to attract support. At its peak, the strike drew 3,000 participants, including women in other domestic-service jobs. Atlanta's white community retaliated with a variety of measures. One city councilman threatened that Atlanta would require every laundress in the city to pay a $25 licensing fee; the measure, however, was not adopted. Local authorities arrested and sometimes fined several strike leaders. Under the weight of these actions, the movement lost momentum and ultimately dissolved without the washerwomen winning any increase in wages.

Further Reading

Hunter, Tera W. "Domination and Resistance: The Politics of Wage Household Labor in New South Atlanta." *Labor History* 34 (1993): 205–220.

Jones, Jacqueline. *Labor of Love, Labor of Sorrow: Black Women, Work, and the Family from Slavery to the Present.* New York: Vintage Books, 1985.

Rabinowitz, Howard N. *Race Relations in the Urban South, 1865–1890.* New York: Oxford University Press, 1978.

—Eileen V. Wallis

Washington, Martha (Martha Dandridge Custis Washington) (1731–1802) *first lady*

Martha Dandridge was born on June 2, 1731, in New Kent County, Virginia, to John and Frances Jones Dandridge. Her father was a planter on a modest 500-acre plantation known as Chestnut Grove. The Dandridges were members of the gentry class, meaning that Martha received a "lady's education" emphasizing music, the arts, dress, fine sewing, dancing, demeanor and household management. She was sufficiently educated in reading, writing, and mathematics for her to run a household and correspond with her mother once she moved away and established a household of her own. Mores of the times held that educating women any further might make her seem "undesirably bookish" to suitors.

In 1748, when Martha was 17 years old, 39-year old Daniel Parke Custis, son of the wealthy although eccentric John Custis, began to court her. John Custis finally acquiesced to the marriage a year later, and the wedding took place in 1750. The couple moved to Daniel Custis's plantation, called White House, and children soon followed: Daniel Parke (b. 1751), Frances Parke (b. 1753), John Parke (b. 1754), and Martha Parke (b. 1756). Between 1754 and 1757, two children (Daniel and Frances), Martha's father, and her husband all died. At the age of 26, Martha was a wealthy widow of two young

Martha Washington (Library of Congress)

children and responsible for a large estate. Little in her background prepared her to oversee more than 17,000 acres and several hundred slaves. She rose to the challenge, however, and assumed responsibility for farming, buying supplies, maintaining the property, paying debts, tending to the needs of the plantation's workforce, and fighting off a decades-old lawsuit that threatened the solvency of the enterprise. She did not hesitate to call on male friends and relatives for guidance. Her wealth and her competence immediately attracted suitors, including George Washington. They met in spring 1758 and were married on January 6, 1759. His new wife's property now his, George began renovations to his home, Mount Vernon, in anticipation of moving his family there. Until then, Martha and her two children moved to Williamsburg, where George Washington was a representative in the national assembly.

By 1767, the family was settled at Mount Vernon. George treated Martha's children as his own, and they called him "Pappa." Martha and George never had children of their own. Martha Washington was a loving but overprotective mother, rarely letting her children out of her sight. Despite criticizing her own mother's overindulgence in childrearing, she doted on her son John (known as "Jacky"). Her youngest child, Martha "Patsy" Custis, was in delicate health and suffered from epileptic seizures. At the time, there was no medical treatment for seizures, and Patsy died as a result of her disease in June 1773. Jacky grew up self-indulgent and indolent, making little effort in his studies. Although nominally enrolled in King's College, he announced his engagement to Nelly Calvert, a member of a prominent Maryland family. Upon Patsy's death, he returned to Mount Vernon, and he and Nelly were married in February 1774. Meanwhile, the Washingtons welcomed family, friends, and acquaintances to Mount Vernon on a regular basis. In fact, the house was enlarged on several occasions to make room for the frequently long stays of family members and to give Martha and George more privacy.

In May 1775, Washington accepted command of the Continental Army and agreed to move the troops to Boston. Upon leaving for Boston, he wrote to Martha, "I retain an unalterable affection for you, which neither time or distance can change." That fall, George invited Martha to join him at the army's winter encampment outside Boston. For Martha, the journey represented the first time she had traveled north of Alexandria, Virginia, and the first time she observed firsthand the celebrity associated with her husband's public role. At his Harvard headquarters, she set about improving the morale of officers, enlisted men, and their families. The Continental Congress did not provide sufficient funds to supply the army with food or clothing, meaning that officer's wives often traveled along with them to cook, mend, and tend to the needs of the troops. Martha Washington formed a sewing and knitting circle to mend for bachelor soldiers and provide bandages for the hospital.

When the Americans took over Boston, the Washingtons moved to New York in the summer of 1776. When the Declaration of Independence was signed on July 4, 1776, Martha added the threat of execution for treason to her list of worries for her husband. In October 1776, the Americans were defeated in New York and Martha moved back to Mount Vernon, where she could attend to the affairs of the plantation rather than accompany George to Philadelphia. Even so, Martha continued to join her husband and his troops in his winter headquarters for the eight long years of the war, regardless of the conditions or the risk of capture or harm. She offered moral support to her husband and material support to the troops in the form of clothing, food, and medical care. During the winter of 1779–80, the British were so close that soldiers guarded the windows of the Washingtons' bedroom each night as they slept. In the spring and summer, Martha returned to Mount Vernon, often accompanied by family members. When Jacky contracted "camp fever" during a visit with his father in Yorktown, efforts to nurse him back to health were in vain. He died in 1781, leaving behind a widow and four young children. The Washingtons offered to adopt the two youngest. Although no formal papers were ever executed, Eleanor Parke Custis (b. 1779) and George Washington Custis (b. 1781) lived with Martha as her children for the rest of their lives.

By 1783, the war was over, and George Washington joined Martha once again at Mount Vernon. The Washingtons believed that they would be free to resume their private lives and recede from national attention. Their home at Mount Vernon attracted a steady stream of visitors, leading George to establish regular visiting hours. Politics once again disrupted domestic life as the fragile government created under the Articles of Confederation nearly collapsed, overwhelmed by economic depression and political infighting. In 1787, General Washington attended the Constitutional Convention in Philadelphia, where he was made presiding officer. Once the new Constitution was signed, he returned to Mount Vernon, only to be informed of his election to the presidency in April 1789. Although Martha was sorely disappointed that public duty would again eclipse their plans for retirement, she resigned herself to the new challenge and joined him in New York (then the site of the capitol) two months after his inauguration.

Both Washingtons faced the task of defining the executive in the newly formed government. As both head of state and head of government, the U.S. president and his wife were challenged to set precedents appropriate to democratic principles while improving the image and reputation of the young United States in the eyes of the world. It seemed to both that some degree of formality and dignity should set them apart from the rest of the nation's citizens, and yet the title Martha selected for herself (Mrs. Washington) aptly illustrates the conscious attempt to avoid aristocratic airs. The Washingtons were mobbed by visitors, forcing them once again to set up a formal visiting schedule. President Washington held meetings for men only on Tuesday

afternoons, and Martha held Friday evening "drawing room" receptions, which the president attended as a guest. She did not like the new limitations on her freedom of movement and the social obligations imposed by her emerging role as first lady. In 1790, she wrote to her niece back at Mount Vernon: "I live a very dull life hear and know nothing that passes in the town—I never go to any publik place, indeed I think I am more like a state prisoner than anything else, there is certain bounds set for me which I must not depart from—and as I can not doe as I like I am obstinate and stay home a great deal." However, Martha was a gracious national hostess, and her social ease softened the president's stiff ceremonious edge.

In 1790, Congress decided to move the nation's capital to a site near Georgetown, but in the meantime government would move to Philadelphia. Martha was glad to return to a busier social scene and to be closer to Mount Vernon. She looked forward to the end of Washington's term and balked at the notion of a second term. In a rare expression of her own opinion, she protested against talk of another four years in office. Ultimately, as she had done on so many previous occasions, she apologized and said nothing further when, in 1793, George was unanimously reelected. The second term was far more difficult than the first. International tensions, the ongoing French Revolution, and increasingly shrill criticism of Washington's leadership made bridging the political divisions in the nation difficult. Thomas Jefferson, Henry Knox, and Alexander Hamilton all resigned their cabinet positions in the second term and returned to private life. Finally, in 1797, George Washington stood beside John Adams as he took the oath of office as the nation's second president. George and Martha Washington were now free to return to Mount Vernon to pursue the private life they had planned for so long. It was to be short-lived.

Their return to Virginia brought with it familiar patterns in resettling. The plantation had suffered from years of neglect. George devoted his attention to overseeing building repairs and bringing the land back into shape. His popularity meant that throngs of visitors descended on the household. Ultimately they invited George's nephew, Lawrence Lewis, to join the family as secretary and deputy host. Lewis married Nelly on February 22, 1799. In late November 1799, George was supervising plantation activities when he came down with a severe cold and respiratory infection. He died on December 14 with Martha by his side.

George had assigned Martha lifetime use of his property, although at this point in her life, she assigned the management to her grand-daughter Nelly and her husband, Lawrence Lewis. She moved out of the bedroom she and George had shared into a small garret room where she stayed mostly to herself after his death. Almost three years later, Martha Washington died on May 22, 1802, of a prolonged fever and was buried beside her husband in the tomb he had designed.

Martha Washington's role as a real partner in establishing the expectations and public role of the American executive cannot be over-stated. She was acutely aware of the importance of the precedent she and George Washington were setting as the nation's first president and first lady. She did not have an elevated image of herself or of the office, but instead under-stood the delicate balance between humility and maintaining the prestige of the presidency. Many of the constraints on her personal aspirations are still imposed on first ladies today. In many respects, George and Martha Washington embodied the culture of "civic virtue" that came to characterize elite Americans in the late 17th century—duty to the public first and to oneself second. Martha Washington's devotion to her husband, her family, and the nation's hard-won independence made her the foremost woman of her times.

Further Reading
Brady, Patricia. "Martha Washington and the Creation of the Role of First Lady." In *The Presidential Companion: Readings on the First* Ladies, edited by Robert P. Watson and Anthony J. Eksterowicz. Columbia: University of South Carolina Press, 2003.

Schneider, Dorothy, and Carl J. Schneider. "Martha Dandridge Custis Washington." *First Ladies: A Biographical Dictionary.* pp. 1–10. New York: Checkmark Books, 2001.

Wasserman Schultz, Debbie (1966–) *congressperson* Debbie Wasserman Schultz was born on September 27, 1966, in Queens, New York. A mother of three, she is married to Steve Schultz and currently lives in Weston, Florida. Prior to her election to Congress, Wasserman Schultz was a program administrator and an instructor at a Florida college as well as a state legislative aide to Peter Deutsch. In 1993, she was elected to the Florida House; then 26, she was the youngest female legislator in the state's history. In 2000, she was elected to the Florida Senate. During her tenure in the Florida legislature, Wasserman Schultz was considered one of its most liberal members. She pursued gender-equity legislation and a bill to guarantee that equal numbers of men and women were appointed to state boards. She also undertook a campaign to make language in official state documents more "gender neutral."

Wasserman Schultz won her first campaign for the U.S. House of Representatives in 2004, winning 70 percent of the vote. During the campaign, her opponent charged that she would not have enough time to adequately serve the district because she had three young children at home. Wasserman Schultz was appointed to the Democratic Steering and Policy Committee and is a member of House Speaker NANCY PELOSI's "30-Something Working Group," an organization for House Democrats under 40 years of age. The group concentrates on issues affectng young people, including Social Security. Wasserman Schultz also has joined the bipartisan Congressional Cuba Democracy Caucus.

Further Reading

Barone, Michael. *The Almanac of American Politics.* Washington, D.C.: National Journal Group, 2006.

"Representative Debbie Wasserman Schultz (FL)." In *Project Vote Smart.* Available online. URL: http://votesmart.org/bio.php?can_id=CS026460. Accessed on January 8, 2007.

"Wasserman Schultz, Debbie." In *Biographical Directory of the United States Congress, 1774–present.* Available online. URL: http://bioguide.congress.gov/scripts/biodisplay.pl?index=W000797. Accessed on January 8, 2007.

—Angela Kouters

Further Reading

Barone, Michael. *The Almanac of American Politics.* Washington, D.C.: National Journal Group, 2006.

"Representative Maxine Waters (CA)." In *Project Vote Smart.* Available online. URL: http://votesmart.org/bio.php?can_id=H0451103. Accessed on January 8, 2007.

"Waters, Maxine." In *Biographical Directory of the United States Congress, 1774–present.* Available online. URL: http://bioguide.congress.gov/scripts/biodisplay.pl?index=W000187. Accessed on January 8, 2007.

—Angela Kouters

Waters, Maxine (1938–) *congressperson* Born on August 15, 1938, in St. Louis, Missouri, Maxine Waters earned a bachelor's degree from California State University, Los Angeles, in 1974. She worked as a teacher and a volunteer coordinator in the Head Start program prior to entering public service. In 1976, Waters was elected to the California State Assembly, where she served from 1977 to 1990. Upon the retirement of incumbent congressman Augustus F. Hawkins in 1990, Waters sought election as a Democrat to the U.S. House of Representatives for California's 29th congressional district. She won and has been reelected ever since.

Maxine Waters is a fairly controversial member of the House. As a first-term representative, she gained fame by walking into the Oval Office and telling President George H. W. Bush that his "time is up." Waters cochaired the 1992 presidential campaign of Bill Clinton. Following the presidential election in 2000, she tried to object to the electoral votes being counted and certified, arguing that rampant voter fraud made the result illegitimate. In addition to her service on the House Committee on Banking and Committee on the Judiciary, Waters has served as chair of the Congressional Black Caucus. She is also a member of the Congressional Progressive Caucus. Her husband, Sidney Williams, is a former U.S. ambassador to the Bahamas.

Watson, Diane (Diane Edith Watson) (1933–) *congressperson* Born in Los Angeles, California, on November 12, 1933, Diane Watson earned a bachelor's degree in education from the University of California, Los Angeles (1955), a master's degree in school psychology from California State University, Los Angeles (1958), and a doctorate in educational administration from Claremont Graduate School (1987). She has worked as a psychologist, as a faculty member at California State University, and as a health occupation specialist with the Bureau of Industrial Education of the California Department of Education. She was elected to the Los Angeles Unified District School Board in 1975 and to the California State Senate in 1978. She served as the U.S. ambassador to Micronesia before entering the House of Representatives as a Democrat following the 2000 election. In the House, Watson serves on the Committee on Government Reform and the Committee on International Relations. She is also a member of the Congressional Progressive Caucus. In 1993, she sponsored the California Birth Defects Monitoring Program Act, which led to research into the causes of birth defects. Watson was reelected in 2006.

Further Reading

Barone, Michael. *The Almanac of American Politics.* Washington, D.C.: National Journal Group, 2006.

"Representative Diane E. Watson (CA)." In *Project Vote Smart*. Available online. URL: http://votesmart.org/bio.php?can_id=BS021500. Accessed on January 8, 2007.

"Watson, Diane Edith." In *Biographical Directory of the United States Congress, 1774–present*. Available online. URL: http://bioguide.congress.gov/scripts/biodisplay.pl?index=W000794. Accessed on January 8, 2007.

—Angela Kouters

Webster v. Reproductive Health Services (492 U.S. 490) (1989)

In 1986, the state of Missouri enacted legislation that placed a number of restrictions on ABORTIONS. The statute's preamble indicated that "the life of each human being begins at conception," and the law codified the following restrictions: public employees and public facilities were not to be used in performing or assisting abortions unnecessary to save the mother's life, encouragement and counseling to have abortions was prohibited, and physicians were to perform viability tests on women in their 20th (or more) week of pregnancy. Lower courts struck down the restrictions.

In a controversial and highly divisive decision, the U.S. Supreme Court held that none of the challenged provisions of the Missouri legislation were unconstitutional. First, the Court held that the preamble had not been applied in any concrete manner for the purposes of restricting abortions and thus did not present a constitutional question. Second, the Court held that the due-process clause did not require states to enter into the business of abortion and did not create an affirmative right to governmental aid in the pursuit of constitutional rights. Third, the Court found that no case or controversy existed in relation to the counseling provisions of the law. Finally, the Court upheld the viability testing requirements, arguing that the state's interest in protecting potential life could be applied before the point of viability. The Court made very clear that it was not revisiting the central holding in *ROE V. WADE*. Justice SANDRA DAY O'CONNOR refused to join four others in overturning *Roe;* however, *Webster* demonstrated how vulnerable the right to abortion articulated in *Roe* had become. The decision was 4-1-4, with O'Connor squarely in the middle and forever identified as the abortion swing vote.

Further Reading

The OYEZ Project. "*Webster v. Reproductive Health Services,* 492 U.S. 490 (1989)." Available online. URL: http://www.oyez.org/cases/case?case=1980–1989/1988/1988_88_605. Accessed on January 12, 2007.

Weddington, Sarah (Sarah Ragle Weddington)

(1947–) *lawyer, reproductive rights activist* A nationally known attorney and spokesperson on a variety of public issues, Sarah Ragle Weddington was born on February 5, 1945, graduated from the University of Texas School of Law in 1967. In 1972, she was elected to the Texas State House of Representatives, where she served three terms.

In 1973, the 26-year-old attorney successfully argued the case of *ROE V. WADE* before the United States Supreme Court. She received no compensation and had to pay the C.O.D. charge on the telegram letting her know she had won the highly controversial ABORTION rights case. The landmark ruling, which gives women, not the government, the right to decide if abortion is right or wrong for them remains under continued threat of partial or full repeal.

Between 1978 and 1981, Weddington worked as an assistant to President Jimmy Carter in Washington, D.C. From her office in the west wing of the White House, she directed the administration's work on women's issues and organized a series of information sessions for top state leaders. She also worked extensively with the recruitment and retention of minority women for governmental positions. Later, she became the director of the Texas Office of State-Federal Relations in Washington, D.C. In 1980, Weddington received the

Planned Parenthood Federation of America's Margaret Sanger Award, the organization's highest honor. In 1993, the National Council of Jewish Women presented her with its prestigious "Woman of Distinction Award."

An adjunct associate professor at the University of Texas, Weddington is a frequent speaker on the global lecture circuit. Topics include legal cases, leadership, health, and women's issues. She is a founding member of the Foundation for Women's Resources and remains active in the organization.

Further Reading

Hull, N.E.H., and Peter Hoffer. *Roe v Wade: The Abortion Right Controversy in American History.* Landmark Law Cases and American Society. Lawrence: University Press of Kansas, 2001.

Weddington, Sarah. *A Question of Choice.* East Rutherford, N.J.: Penguin USA, 1993.

—Thea Lapham

Weeks v. Southern Bell Telephone and Telegraph (408 F.2d 228 [5th Cir.])

(1969)   Several cases have been brought before the courts on the basis of the BONA FIDE OCCUPATIONAL QUALIFICATION (BFOQ) exception to TITLE VII OF THE CIVIL RIGHTS ACT OF 1964. One of the earliest, *Weeks v. Southern Bell Telephone and Telegraph* (1969), challenged a rule that prevented women, but not men, from holding positions that required lifting more than 30 pounds. Lower courts ruled that the company had based its decision to limit women's employment on stereotypes rather than on real abilities of its employees or applicants. Similarly, in *ROSENFELD V. SOUTHERN PACIFIC COMPANY* (1971), the Ninth Circuit Court of Appeals ruled against Southern Pacific's policy of excluding women from certain jobs that were deemed "unsuitable" for women because (1) they involved irregular hours and lifting weights of up to 25 pounds, and (2) state laws limited working conditions for women under a variety of protective statutes. The court ruled that nei-

ther reason constituted a BFOQ exception to Title VII because both relied on GENDER STEREOTYPES of women's abilities rather than on a finding of fact.

See also *BRADWELL V. ILLINOIS.*

Weinberger v. Wiesenfeld (420 US 636)

(1975)   In this case, a widowed father challenged the Social Security survivor's benefit rules that allowed mothers, but not fathers, to stay home, raise their underage children, and collect benefits after their spouse had died. After the death of his wife, Stephen Wiesenfeld applied for Social Security CHILD CARE benefits so that he could stay home with his infant son. His claim was rejected. The interpretation of the law at the time held that a widow with children was entitled to benefits (called "mother's insurance benefits") based on her late husband's Social Security taxes. A widower was ineligible for the same benefits unless he could prove that he had been economically dependent on his wife prior to her death. Attorney RUTH BADER GINSBURG, working for the American Civil Liberties Union's Women's Rights Project, argued the case before the U.S. Supreme Court.

Wiesenfeld was one of a series of cases Ginsburg and other Women's Rights Project attorneys selected in order to challenge the traditional GENDER STEREOTYPES on which laws that discriminated by sex were often based. In her brief, Ginsburg argued that the strict assignment of sex roles in the statute did not reflect the reality of millions of Americans. What was intended to protect and benefit women was in reality part of a larger web of laws that denied both men and women the equal protection of the laws. Ginsburg wrote: "When Paula Wiesenfeld died, her social insurance provided less protection to her family than the social insurance of a wage-earning man. . . . The payout to her survivors was subject to a deep discount."

The U.S. Supreme Court ruled unanimously that this provision of the Social Security laws violated "the right to equal protection secured by the Due Process Clause of the Fifth Amendment" and was therefore unconstitutional. In a sign that the Court was ready to dismiss some long-held social stereotypes about men and women, six of the justices accepted Ginsburg's argument that the distinction between widows and widowers was founded on an "archaic and overbroad generalization not tolerated under the Constitution, namely that male workers' earnings are vital to their families' support, while female workers' earnings do not significantly contribute to their families' support." *Wiesenfeld* was the first of a series of cases challenging the constitutionality of Social Security measures that amounted to "double-edged" discrimination.

See also SOCIAL SECURITY AND WOMEN.

Further Reading
The OYEZ Project. "*Weinberger v. Wiesenfeld,* 420 U.S. 636 (1975)." Available online. URL: http://www. oyez.org/cases/case?case=1970–1979/1974/1974_ 73_1892. Accessed on January 12, 2007.

welfare policy In the early days of the United States, relief for the poor was largely the responsibility of town governments, although family was the primary support for the needy. The modern "welfare system" did not emerge until the 1930s and the onset of the Great Depression. With the private support structures previously provided by families in shambles, people in need turned to the government. The sheer number of people without employment, housing, or bare subsistence overwhelmed local government resources. GRACE ABBOTT, head of the federal Children's Bureau, reported that by spring 1933, 20 percent of the nation's schoolchildren showed evidence of poor nutrition, housing, and medical care. An estimated 200,000 boys left home to wander the streets and beg because of the poor economic condition of their families.

The emphasis during the first two years of President Franklin Roosevelt's "New Deal" was to provide work relief for the millions of unemployed Americans. Federal money flowed to the states to pay for public works projects, which employed the jobless. Some federal aid also directly assisted needy victims of the depression. The states, however, remained mainly responsible for taking care of the "unemployables" (widows, poor children, the elderly poor, and the disabled). Yet states as well as private charities were unable to keep up the support of these people at a time when tax collections and personal giving were declining steeply. On August 18, 1935, Roosevelt signed the Social Security Act. It set up a federal retirement program for persons over 65, which was financed by a payroll tax paid jointly by employers and their workers. In addition to old-age pensions and unemployment insurance, the Social Security Act established a national welfare system. The federal government guaranteed one-third of the total amount spent by states for assistance to needy and dependent children under age 16 (but not their mothers). Additional federal welfare aid was provided to destitute elderly people, the blind, and disabled children. Although financed partly by federal tax money, the states could still set their own eligibility requirements and benefit levels. This aspect of the law demanded by southern states allowed them to limit benefits available to the African-American population. Thus, the U.S. federal welfare system was, from its inception, shaped by assumptions about race and gender.

In 1936, when the federal AID TO FAMILIES WITH DEPENDENT CHILDREN (AFDC) program began, it provided cash aid to about 500,000 children and their parents. By 1969, the number had grown to nearly 7 million. President Lyndon B. Johnson's "War on Poverty" added noncash benefits to AFDC recipients and others, including food stamps (1964), Medicaid (1965), and, nearly a decade later, the Supplemental Security Income (SSI) program (1974). By the 1990s, AFDC supported an estimated 15 percent of the nation's children. Worries grew that a federal system of subsidies created dependence rather than assistance toward self-sufficiency and full employment. The FAMILY SUPPORT ACT OF 1988 was one of the first attempts to require work as a condition of benefits and to impose limits on the length of eligibility. In 1996, President Bill Clinton signed the PERSONAL RESPONSIBILITY AND WORK OPPORTUNITY RECONCILIATION ACT (PRWORA). Temporary Assistance for Needy Families (TANF) replaced AFDC as the primary vehicle to deliver federal welfare support. PRWORA ended welfare as an entitlement and replaced that ethos with strict limits on eligibility, introduced stiffer work requirements, and allowed states to impose lifetime benefit caps and other restrictions. Education, job training, and CHILD CARE support is administered by the states through a system of bloc grants.

See also WELFARE RIGHTS MOVEMENT.

Further Reading

Abramovitz, Mimi. *Regulating the Lives of Women: Social Welfare Policy from Colonial Times to the Present.* Boston: South End Press, 1988.

Gordon, Linda. *Pitied but Not Entitled: Single Mothers and the History of Welfare.* New York: Free Press, 1994.

Nadasen, Premilla. *Welfare Warriors: The Welfare Rights Movement in the United States.* New York: Routledge, 2005.

welfare rights movement   The welfare rights movement grew out of the belief that welfare unduly stigmatized women along race, class, and gender lines. The largest single organization dedicated to promoting welfare rights from 1966 to 1975 was the National Welfare Rights Organization (NWRO), founded by Congress of Racial Equality (CORE) activist and university chemistry professor George Wiley. Under the NWRO's mantle, tens of thousands of welfare recipients demanded more income and justice for their families. At its peak in 1969, NWRO membership was estimated at 22,000 families nationwide, mostly black, with local chapters in nearly every state and major city. The NWRO galvanized its members to bring about tangible improvements in the welfare system and, in the process, changed the attitudes of thousands of women who joined the organization. Its "minimum standards" campaign, linking the level of benefits with the actual cost of living, resulted in a substantial increase in the size of the income transfer in states like New York. Members also demanded changes in the way they were treated by personnel in welfare offices. While under Wiley's leadership, the movement was broadly focused on poor people rather than predominantly on poor women and on providing guaranteed income to the poor regardless of race, ethnicity, or gender. The transition in leadership from Wiley to JONNIE TILLMON in 1972 was preceded by a period of organizational turmoil, as many in the membership demanded more decision-making power and visibility for "recipients" (largely female and black) and less for the organization's middle-class leadership (largely male and white). However, as the transition unfolded and Wiley ultimately resigned his post as executive director, little was done to train the next cohort in the skills necessary to maintain an organization let alone a movement. The social and political climate was changing as well. Lyndon B. Johnson's Democratic administration (with its focus on the Great Society anti-poverty initiatives) had given way to Richard M. Nixon's Republican administration. Nixon publicly vowed to dismantle many of the Great Society programs. In 1969, he proposed the Family Assistance Plan (FAP) with dramatic reductions in state welfare budgets and a guaranteed family income that would place a family of four well below the federal poverty line. NWRO countered by challenging legislators to "Live on a Welfare Budget" for a week and to publicly detail their experiences.

Nixon's FAP proposal exposed another schism in the organization over who should be eligible for guaranteed income. The male-dominated staff of NWRO gave preference to "intact families" (those with a father and a mother present), but this ignored the reality that the majority of recipients and organization members were women in female-headed households. They argued that the primary focus should be on providing more jobs and training programs for women as well as child care assistance so that they could work and parent. By 1972, the organization's members demanded that black women be placed in key positions so that their needs would be more centrally reflected in the movement's priorities.

When elected executive director in 1972, Johnnie Tillmon recast the NWRO's emphasis on poverty and welfare as specifically women's issues. In an interview with Ms. MAGAZINE that same year, she said, "For me, Women's Liberation is simple. No woman in this country can feel dignified; no woman can be liberated, until all women get off their knees. That's what NWRO is all about—women standing together, on their feet." In her own essay, "Welfare Is a Woman's Issue," appearing in the spring 1972 issue of Ms., she challenged women to recognize welfare as matter of survival, as something that could happen to anyone but most especially to women. She characterized welfare as the most "prejudiced institution in the country, even more than marriage" likening AFDC to a "super-sexist marriage" where "the man" (meaning government) runs everything. Although initially greeted as a savior by the membership, Tillmon was never able to overcome the substantial financial deficit she inherited, and the National Welfare Rights Organization was dissolved in 1975.

Further Reading

Davis, Martha. *Brutal Need: Lawyers and the Welfare Rights Movement, 1960–1973.* New Haven, Conn.: Yale University Press, 1993.

Kotz, Mary and Nick Kotz. *A passion for equality: George Wiley and the Movement.* New York: Norton, 1977.

Piven, Frances Fox. "Welfare Movement Rises." *Nation* 8 May 2000. Available online. URL: www.the-nation.com/20000508/piven.

West, Guida. The National Welfare Rights Movement. New York: Prague Publishers, 1981.

Wells-Barnett, Ida B. (Ida Bell Wells-Barnett) (1862–1931) *anti-lynching activist, journalist, suffragist, African-American rights leader*

Ida Bell Wells-Barnett led a remarkable life and had a career that consistently challenged discrimination based on race, class, and gender. She was born on July 16, 1862, in Holly Springs, Mississippi, to slaves Jim Wells and Elizabeth ("Lizzie Bell") Warrenton, who believed strongly in education and sent Ida to school after the family was freed at the conclusion of the Civil War. Following the war, Jim Wells became involved with the Freedman's Aid Society and was a founder of Shaw University (now Rust College) in Holly Springs. Ida, the oldest of eight children, assumed full responsibility for her siblings at age 16 when her parents died of yellow fever in 1878. She received her education at Rust College and taught school in Mississippi. In 1881, she moved to Memphis, Tennessee to teach at a country school. She also continued her education at Fisk University in Nashville during summer sessions. In 1883, Wells bought a share of the *Memphis Free Speech*. In order to support herself, she traveled the South selling subscriptions to the newspaper.

In 1884, in one of her first political acts, Ida Wells was physically removed from a train operated by the Chesapeake and Ohio Railroad Company after refusing to sit in the Jim Crow car when she had paid full fare. She sued the railroad and was awarded $500 in damages by the local circuit court, but the railroad appealed to the Tennessee Supreme Court, and the verdict was overturned. While in Memphis, Wells began her journalism career, writing first about her experiences with the lawsuit and later about the dismal affects of poverty on black public school education. Under the pen name Iola, her articles appeared in local and national newspapers. Her editorials arguing that poor facilities and untrained teachers contributed to the poor education black children received led to her firing as a teacher.

In March 1892, three black men in Memphis were lynched. Lynching was not uncommon, but it was usually covered by the charge that black men were killed because they had raped white women. Wells knew that rape was not the impetus for this lynching and wrote about what really happened: Thomas Moss, Calvin McDowell, and Henry Seward were owners of a successful grocery store, and the owners of a competing white grocery store wanted to eliminate the competition. They broke into the store, and one white male was shot. More than 100 black men (including Moss, McDowell and Seward) were arrested. A lynch mob broke into the jail and dragged the store owners out of town, murdering all three. Ida Wells wrote: "There is nothing we can do about the lynching now, as we are out-numbered and without arms. . . . There is therefore only one thing left to do; save our money and leave a town which will neither protect our lives and property, nor give us a fair trial in the courts, but takes us out and murders us in cold blood when accused by white persons." As a result of Wells's article, many blacks left Memphis, and those that stayed organized a boycott of white-owned businesses.

Wells wrote numerous articles exposing lynching as a "racist device for eliminating financially independent Black Americans" and as purposeful acts intended to scare the entire black population and suppress any advancement. *Southern Horrors: Lynch Law in All Its Phases,* published in 1892, was a compilation of her research notes and articles written during her investigation. In one article, she wrote that it was possible for white women to be attracted to black men, and in fact it was white women who were responsible for encouraging relationships with black men. The offices of the *Free Speech* were burned, and Wells left town for New York under a cloud of death threats. She wrote about her experiences for the *New York Age.*

In 1893, Wells moved to Chicago, where she continued to investigate and write about the causes and consequences of lynching in America. In 1895, she published *A Red Record: Tabulated Statistics and Alleged Causes of Lynching in the United States: 1892, 1893, and 1894,* based on her findings. She began giving lectures on the horrors of lynching and calling upon political leaders to sponsor legislation to outlaw racial lynching. Wells also took her cause abroad and found widespread support in England and Scotland. In 1895, she married Ferdinand Lee Barnett, an attorney and founder of the *Chicago Conservator* (the first black newspaper in Chicago). He sold his shares in the newspaper to Wells and over time she bought out the other owners, becoming the sole owner of the publication by the age of 33. With her husband's support, Ida successfully combined marriage with raising four children and continuing her reform activities.

Ida Wells-Barnett was a founder of the National Afro-American Council and one of only two African-American women to sign the call transforming the organization into the National Association for the Advancement of Colored People (NAACP) in 1909. She championed African American voting rights and founded the ALPHA SUFFRAGE CLUB, the first female SUFFRAGE club in Illinois. She received much publicity in 1913 when she refused to march in the segregated rear section of the NATIONAL AMERICAN WOMAN SUFFRAGE ASSOCIATION parade in Washington, D.C. Her involvement with women's suffrage increased her interest in politics. In 1924, she ran for the presidency of the NATIONAL ASSOCIATION OF COLORED WOMEN but lost to MARY MCLEOD BETHUNE. In 1930, she campaigned for the Illinois State Senate but lost the election. On March 25, 1931, she died of kidney disease at her home in Chicago.

In 1974, Wells-Barnett's former home in Chicago was placed on the National Register of Historic Places. In 1990, the U.S. Postal Service issued a stamp to honor her life. Never satisfied with what had been written about her, she published an autobiography during her lifetime: *Crusade for Justice: The Autobiography of Ida B. Wells* (1928) and maintained a diary that was published in 1995 as *The Memphis Diary of Ida B. Wells: An Intimate Portrait of the Activist as a Young Woman*. The Ida B. Wells-Barnett Papers can be found at the University of Chicago in Chicago, Illinois.

See also ANTI-LYNCHING MOVEMENT.

Further Reading

De Costa-Willis, Miriam, eds. *The Memphis Diary of Ida B. Wells: An Intimate Portrait of the Activist as a Young Woman*. Boston: Beacon Press, 1995.

McMurry, Linda O. *To Keep the Waters Troubled: The Life of Ida B. Wells*. Oxford: Oxford University Press, 2000.

Royster, Jacqueline. *Southern Horrors and Other Writings: The Anti-Lynching Campaign of Ida B. Wells, 1892–1900*. New York: Bedford/St. Martins, 1996.

Schechter, Patricia A. *Ida B. Wells Barnett and American Reform, 1880–1930*. Chapel Hill: University of North Carolina Press, 2001.

Wells, Ida B. *Crusade for Justice: The Autobiography of Ida B. Wells,* edited by Alfreda Duster. Chicago: University of Chicago Press, 1991.

—Delia C. Gillis

White House Project   Founded in 1998, the White House Project is a national nonpartisan organization dedicated to promoting women's leadership with the goal of electing more women to public office, and especially to electing a woman president of the United States. In support of this goal, the White House Project sponsors a number of training programs and provides information on training programs and internships sponsored by other organizations. Programs and training workshops are organized around three themes: pipeline, perception, and platform. Much of the organization's most visible work is designed to fill the pipeline with highly qualified female candidates for public office at all levels of government. However, consistent with research on candidate emergence, the White House Project has devoted considerable attention to encouraging young women's interest in politics.

In a study conducted in spring 2000 for the White House Project Education Fund, researchers interviewed young women and men to learn more about the pipeline of the future. The study found that young people, particularly women, are extraordinarily dedicated to their communities and to solving problems within those communities. Although they hold negative attitudes about politics and politicians in general, more than four in 10 young adults would consider running for office themselves. Young women are more inclined to get involved in politics if they believe they will be able to accomplish their goals and address issues they care about through political involvement. Those who have held leadership positions in their school or community and who have been encouraged to seek office are far more likely than other women to express a desire to seek political office. Encouragement has twice the power of any other factor in predicting whether a young woman will consider running for office. Therefore, the organization argues, young women can be cultivated to seek elective office.

One way of beginning that cultivation early is by providing role models. Research by the White House Project Education Fund suggests that providing girls with role models, mentors, and opportunities to practice politics before they reach adulthood makes a positive difference in women's interest and political ambition. One initiative in this regard that draws ridicule from some quarters and praise from others is the "Barbie for President" doll, first released in April 2000 and re-released in August 2004 by Mattel in conjunction with the White House Project and Girls, Inc.

The 2004 Barbie for President doll is a part of a new White House Project initiative, "Go Vote. Go Run. Go Lead. Go Girl." Marie Wilson, founder and president of the White House Project, characterizes the Barbie as "a case of invading the culture rather than fighting it, and using the tools of the culture to teach valuable lessons about democracy." The White House Project's "Girl Power" Web page provides girls with a number of activities related to women in politics and leadership. In partnership with the Girl Scouts, girls between the ages of 5 and 11 can work on projects leading to a White House Project leadership patch, known as the "Ms. President" badge.

Projects organized around the theme of perception include "SheSource," an online resource database of women experts in every field. She-Source fosters a more representative public dialogue on important issues by increasing the number of female "experts" called upon by the media. Likewise, the White House Project has developed promotional programs to support women in film and television.

Projects organized around the platform theme are designed to produce messages that women can deliver with authority in an effort to shape the national agenda. For example, the White House Project is engaged in an attempt to reshape the national security debate in a way that allows women to speak with authority in an arena largely dominated by men.

The organization maintains an informative Web site with links to training programs and internships across the country as well as links to research reports and data on women in politics at http://www.thewhitehouseproject.org/.

See also PIPELINE THESIS.

Whitman, Christine Todd (1946–) *governor of New Jersey* Christine Todd Whitman served as New Jersey's first female governor from 1993 to 2000. Born in New York City on September 26, 1946, she descended from a political family with strong ties to the Republican Party. Her husband, John R. Whitman, also has ties to the GOP—his grandfather was once governor of New York. Whitman began her political career on the Somerset County Board of Chosen Freeholders, but it was her 1990 campaign against incumbent New Jersey senator Bill Bradley that put her on the national political scene. She lost to Bradley but received an impressive 48 percent of the vote by making then-Governor James Florio's tax increases the cornerstone of her campaign.

In 1993, Whitman, a Republican, ran for governor against Florio and won by just 26,000 votes. She suffered through several scandals during the campaign, but it was after her election when she had to deal with the most serious issue. Her campaign manager reported that people working for her had paid election workers in Democratic neighborhoods to stay home; African-American ministers had also been bribed to suppress turnout among their parishioners. No support for these allegations was discovered, however.

As governor, Whitman faced serious challenges. The state budget deficit was nearly $1 billion when she took office in 1994, yet she asked the legislature to enact a 5 percent tax cut. She went on record as saying that she hoped these cuts would not force municipalities to raise taxes to cover missing state aid, but also said that she would not be responsible if this did happen. She was active in promoting reforms in education and in improving the state's environmental record. For example, the number of days New Jersey violated the federal one-hour air quality standard for ground level ozone dropped from 45 in 1988 to 4 in 2000. In 1999, Governor Whitman vetoed a bill that outlawed partial birth abortion. Although her veto was overridden by the legislature, the law was ultimately determined to be unconstitutional. As New Jersey's first female governor, she appointed New Jersey's first African American State Supreme Court Justice, its first female State Supreme Court Chief Justice and its first female Attorney General. Whitman was the first governor ever chosen to give the Republican response to President Clinton's State of the Union address in 1995. Her performance started people talking about the possibilities of her candidacy for vice president in 1996. Robert Dole, the Republican candidate, ultimately chose Jack Kemp as his running mate. She co-chaired the 1996 Republican Convention with George W. Bush.

In 2001, Whitman left the governorship to accept President George W. Bush's offer of a cabinet position as the administrator of the Environmental Protection Agency (EPA). Her tenure at the EPA was difficult. She was not viewed as "conservative enough" by many in the Bush administration, while she was perceived as not "green enough" by environmentalists. She was also viewed as "out of step" with the administration at times. The president had promised during the 2000 campaign to curb carbon dioxide emissions from power plants, which contribute to global warming. Just days after Whitman announced actions publicly to make good on his promise, the president rejected the Kyoto treaty on global warming. A week before her June 27, 2003, departure from the agency, the EPA prepared to release a major report on the state of the environment, commissioned by Whitman in 2001. Prior to the report's release, the national media reported that the White House had edited out major sections on global warming, including data on climate change and a section on the likely human contribution to global warming. In February 2006, a federal judge found that Whitman had misled the public about the safety of the air quality near the site of the World Trade Center collapse following the terrorist attacks on September 11, 2001. This finding came as a part of a lawsuit filed by rescue workers and on behalf of schoolchildren who say they were exposed to contamination and that the site has never been properly cleaned. Whitman denied these allegations.

In early 2005, she released a book entitled *It's My Party, Too: Taking Back the Republican Party . . . And Bringing the Country Together Again,* a critique of what she views as the divisive campaign and governing styles of the George W. Bush administration and the party's current leadership. Upon the release of her book, Whitman formed a political action committee called It's My Party Too–PAC that has since joined forces with the Republican Leadership Council, cochaired by Whitman, John Danforth (former Senator from Missouri), and Michael Steele (lieutenant governor of Maryland). The council advocates "for the historic Republican principles of liberty, individual responsibility, and personal freedom," according to its Web site (www.republican-leadership.com).

Further Reading

Aron, Michael. *Governor's Race: A TV Reporter's Chronicle of the 1993 Florio/Whitman Campaign.* Piscataway, N.J.: Rutgers University Press, 1994.
Beard, Patricia. *Growing Up Republican: Conversations with Christine Todd Whitman.* New York: HarperCollins, 1996.
McClure, Sandy. *Christie Whitman for the People: A Political Biography.* Amherst, N.Y.: Prometheus Books, 1996.

Whitner v. South Carolina (328 S.C. 1, 492 S.E.2d 777) (1997)

This is a 1997 South Carolina State Supreme Court decision holding that pregnant women who risk harm to their viable fetuses may be prosecuted under the state child-abuse laws. It is specifically targeted at women who use illegal drugs during pregnancy.

In this case, the South Carolina Supreme Court upheld the use of the state's child-abuse and endangerment statute to prosecute cocaine-addicted pregnant women for child abuse. Although the word *child* in the statute is defined as a "person under the age of eighteen," the court held that a viable fetus met the definition and therefore warranted protection by the state. Generally, these policies are promoted as deterrents to adverse behavior among pregnant women; however, there is little evidence that arrest and prosecution deters drug or alcohol addiction in any form. More likely, these policies discourage other pregnant women from seeking prenatal care out of fear of criminal prosecution.

The *Whitner* decision poses significant questions for all pregnant women. The state supreme court decreed that *anything* a pregnant woman does after viability that causes "potential harm" to the fetus is child abuse. "Anything" may include a list of activities that healthy pregnant women now take for granted—athletics, strenuous exercise, conditions of employment, diet or travel.

Further Reading

Woliver, Laura R. *The Political Geographies of Pregnancy*. Urbana: University of Illinois Press, 2002.

—J. Celeste Lay

widow's tradition (widow's mandate)   One of the paths to Congress for women well into the 20th century was an appointment, or a victory in a special election, to complete the unexpired term of their deceased husbands. Between 1916 and 1940, 54 percent of all women members succeeded their husbands. Of the 224 women ever to serve in Congress, 46 (roughly 21 percent) have entered Congress following the deaths of their husbands. Four women serving in the 109th Congress succeeded their husbands.

The "widow's tradition" or the "widow's mandate" has strong support from the voting public. A Rutgers University study found that when widows stand as candidates in special elections, they win 84 percent of the time. There are a number of reasons for this tradition, including what some scholars call "sentimental nepotism" or a form of "sentimental tribute." Feminists do not view the practice with much favor because it puts women in the role of "stand in" rather than service as an independent representative. In fact, proponents of the practice often say that a wife is most likely to mirror the deceased member's goals, legislative agendas, and voting habits, suggesting that she has been his confidant in the past and assuming that she does not possess an independent political perspective of her own. As more women are elected to the House and Senate in their own right, the practice may decline. Alternatively, as women gain a larger share of the seats in Congress, we may witness a "widower's tradition" emerge.

Further Reading

Gertzog, Irwin N. *Congressional Women: Their Recruitment, Integration and Behavior,* 2nd ed. Westport, Conn.: Praeger, 1995.

Center for American Women and Politics, Eagleton Institute of Politics, Rutgers. "Women Who Succeeded their Husbands: Fact Sheet." (2005) Available online. URL: http://www.cawp.rutgers.edu/Facts/Officeholders/widows.pdf. Accessed on June 30, 2006.

Willard, Emma (Emma Hart Willard) (1787–1870) *women's rights advocate, educator*   Emma Willard was an American educator and pioneer in woman's education. Born Emma Hart on February 23, 1787, in Berlin, Connecticut, she attended and later taught in the local academy there. In 1807, she took charge of the Female Academy at Middlebury, Vermont. Two years later, she married Dr. John Willard. In 1814, she opened a school in her home (Middlebury Female Seminary), where she taught subjects not then available to women. Since she herself was denied admission to Middlebury College on account of her sex, she borrowed her nephew's books to teach herself higher mathematics, Greek, astronomy, botany, geology, biology, chemistry, and geography, among other subjects.

In 1818, after Emma Willard addressed the New York legislature with an appeal for support of her plan for improving female education, Governor George Clinton invited her to move to New York. She did so and opened a school at Waterford, but promised financial support was not forthcoming, and the school closed in 1821. In September that same year, however, Troy Female Seminary was founded under Willard's leadership. The Troy Female Seminary later became famous as the Emma Willard School for its offering of collegiate education to women and new opportunity to women teachers.

Willard formulated her ideas about women's education in a draft she called "A Plan for Improving Female Education." She strongly supported the establishment of public schools and educated hundreds of teachers in her schools for girls. She wrote a number of textbooks, a journal of her trip abroad in 1830, and a volume of poems, including "Rocked in the Cradle of the Deep." In 1838, Willard retired from active management of the Troy Female Seminary, which was later renamed in her honor. She devoted the remainder of her life to the improvement of common schools and to the cause of woman's education. She died in Troy, New York, on April 15, 1870, at the age of 83. The Emma Willard School remains today in Troy, New York, with an enrollment of 314 girls from the United States and 22 foreign countries.

Further Reading

Lutz, Alma. *Emma Willard, Daughter of Democracy.* Boston: Houghton Mifflin, 1929.
———. *Emma Willard, Pioneer Educator of American Women.* Boston: Beacon Press, 1964.

—Cynthia Melendy

Willard, Frances (Frances Elizabeth Caroline Willard)

(1839–1898) *educator, temperance reformer, suffragist* Born in Churchville, New York, on September 28, 1839, Frances Willard was raised in Wisconsin from the age of seven. At 18, she moved to Evanston, Illinois, where she graduated from the Northwestern Female College in 1859. She taught school after graduation, and after extended travels in Europe she became president of the Evanston College for Ladies, which became affiliated with Northwestern in 1873. Willard resigned from her position as dean of women in 1874 when she was elected secretary of a new Chicago temperance organization. She traveled to Cleveland for a temperance convention and was elected secretary of the WOMAN'S CHRISTIAN TEMPERANCE UNION (WCTU); she was elected president of the WCTU in 1879 and remained president for the rest of her life.

As president of the WCTU, Willard focused on numerous domestic social justice issues, including women's SUFFRAGE, women's health, equal pay for equal work, education, and PROS-

TITUTION. Internationally, she worked to abolish narcotics trafficking. Under Willard's leadership, the WCTU organized into a system of local chapters that affiliated with state chapters that were in turn guided by the national chapter. Willard could thus focus the attention of the organization on particular reforms, especially temperance. Under Willard, the WCTU played a leadership role in the suffrage movement (in part because its membership base was so large), first putting it on their national platform in 1882. Prior to this, Willard had advocated the more moderate "home protection" rule, asking that women be granted the vote on the issue of alcohol alone. She argued that advocating temperance without simultaneously advocating a woman's right to vote on the matter of temperance (and other issues primarily relevant to women and children) would fail. Citing what she called the "Do Everything" policy, Willard argued: "Let us not be disconcerted, but stand bravely by that blessed trinity of movements, Prohibition, Woman's Liberation, and Labour's Uplift" (from her 1893 address before the World WCTU Convention).

In 1888, Willard, with SUSAN B. ANTHONY, founded simultaneously the National Council of Women and the International Council of Women, which advocated peace, health, and education; the councils urged, but did not demand, suffrage in order to attract the attention of more moderate nations. The National Council of Women acted as a central organization for the variety of smaller organizations advocating for women's rights. Bringing together multiple organizations in twice-yearly conferences, the council provided a way to focus the activities of the numerous women-led organizations throughout the country.

In 1891, Willard helped form the World WCTU and was subsequently elected its president. The following year, she moved to England, where she became increasingly interested in socialist politics as the key to bringing about progressive change. She was not, however, able to convince socialists of the value of temperance nor members of the TEMPERANCE MOVEMENT of the value of socialism. After her death on February 17, 1898, the WCTU shifted its attention back to a more particular focus on temperance and the prohibition of alcohol.

Further Reading

Giele, Janet Zollinger. *Two Paths to Equality.* New York: MacMillan Library Reference, 1995.

Mattingly, Carol. *Well Tempered Women: Nineteenth Century Temperance Rhetoric.* Carbondale: Southern Illinois University Press, 2000.

Willard, Frances E. *Writing Out My Heart: Selections from the Journal of Frances E. Willard,* edited by Carolyn D. Gifford. Urbana: University of Illinois Press, 1995.

—Claire Curtis

Wilson, Edith (Edith Bolling Galt Wilson)

(1872–1961) *first lady*   Edith Bolling was born in Whytheville, Virginia, on October 15, 1872, the fourth of 11 children. Her father, William Bolling, was a descendant of southern farmers forced off their land during the Civil War. He turned to law and served as a judge during his daughter's childhood. Edith grew up in a multigenerational household, caring for her grandparents. Unlike most of her immediate predecessors in the White House, she had little formal education. She was home-schooled by her grandmother but attended Martha Washington College for one year when she was 15 and later spent a year at Powell Girl's School in Richmond. She cared very little about studies and showed no intellectual curiosity in public issues or women's rights, nor in arts or literature.

While visiting her married sister in Washington, Edith met Norman Galt, a cousin to her brother-in-law. At 28, Norman was nine years her senior but wealthy thanks his family's jewelry business. The couple married on April 30, 1896. Upon the death of his relatives, Norman became the sole owner of the jewelry store, and the couple lived an ostentatious lifestyle. In 1903, Edith gave birth to a son who died three days later. She was never again pregnant, but she was dedicated to her extended family and cared for a number of ailing relatives and her own mother until their deaths. In 1908, Norman died, leaving her heir to the jewelry store. She hired a manager and kept the store, although she later sold it to the employees.

A close friend, Alice Gertrude Gordon, wife of Dr. Cary Grayson, played a critical role in introducing Edith Bolling Galt to President Woodrow Wilson. Dr. Grayson had served as White House physician to two former presidents and now cared for ELLEN WILSON. Upon the first lady's death in August 1914, Wilson's three daughters and his closest allies realized that he would not survive long himself without a wife and intimate companion. Although not even a year had passed since Ellen's death, Edith met Wilson in March 1915, and he began courting her soon thereafter. Wilson proposed for the first time on May 3, 1915. Edith declined, but she later accepted after he convinced her that continued refusals might jeopardize his ability to lead the nation. With war raging in Europe, she accepted, and they were married at her home on December 18, 1915.

After a brief honeymoon, Edith settled into the White House. She did little to change the building, and the war in Europe curtailed any expectations that she entertain. Instead, she concentrated on Woodrow Wilson, becoming his closest confidant and an eager student of public affairs, both foreign and domestic, in order to better serve his needs. She provided him with distractions, accompanying him to the theater and on drives around the city. She opposed the suffragists picketing the White House; their anti-Wilson slogans infuriated her, and she referred to them as "disgusting." She cared nothing for the SUFFRAGE cause, since she herself cared nothing for public issues apart from her support of the president's agenda. When the Democrats nominated Woodrow Wilson for a second term, Edith campaigned with and for her husband. He won the election by a narrow margin.

In Wilson's second term, Edith took an even more active role in his official business. When the United States entered World War I on April 6, 1917, she devoted herself to ensuring his health and well-being. She began to limit his advisers' access to him, particularly those she thought were disloyal or pursued agendas contrary to Wilson's own. The first lady participated in the war effort by volunteering with the Red Cross and selling Liberty Bonds, and she urged other Washington wives to economize, setting an example in her own plain dress. She allowed a flock of sheep to graze on the White House lawn to save in mowing expenses, and donated the wool to charitable causes.

After the armistice on November 11, 1918, Edith accompanied the president to Europe for the peace conference. The Treaty of Versailles was signed on June 28, 1919, and the Wilsons returned to Washington to seek its ratification as well as support for the League of Nations. Once home, they encountered fierce opposition in the Senate, led by Henry Cabot Lodge. On April 3, 1919, Woodrow Wilson suffered the first of several strokes. Weakened but not disabled, he refused to abandon the campaign for the League of Nations and decided to take his case directly to the American people, setting off on a cross-country speaking tour by train. The effort exhausted him, left him with severe headaches, and likely resulted in another stroke that impaired his ability to speak. The Wilsons returned to Washington without completing the tour.

Once back in the White House, Edith conspired with Woodrow's doctors to conceal the president's condition from Congress and the public. She limited visitors and guests and took over most of the business of state, although she denied ever doing so and claimed that the president made every decision she communicated. Another stroke left him partially paralyzed and his thinking impaired. Still she refused to acknowledge his limitations, but for all practical purposes, government from the White House stopped. There were no provisions at the time

Edith Bolling Galt Wilson, ca. 1918 (Library of Congress)

for succession due to disability rather than death. She and Wilson's closest advisers did not think Vice President Thomas Marshall a worthy successor, and Wilson refused to resign.

Accusations of "petticoat government" did not deter Edith from carrying on Woodrow's attempts to win approval for the League of Nations. Wilson refused any compromise on it, and after being rebuked by her husband for urging him to make concessions, Edith refused to mention modifications with him again. She blamed the eventual demise of the League of Nations (and later, World War II) on Henry Cabot Lodge, calling him a "a snake in the open."

Once the president's health improved somewhat, Wilson took Edith's advice on making changes to his cabinet. He dismissed his secretary of state, Robert Lansing, for holding cabinet meetings in his absence. Edith Wilson had long disliked Lansing, and scholars attribute his resignation to her insistence. Apparently the Wilsons briefly flirted with thoughts of a third term in office, but this was untenable by anyone's calculations, and Warren Harding was elected president in 1920. Edith Wilson took the Harding slogan of a return to normalcy as a personal insult. She did very little to ease their transition into the White House, and Woodrow Wilson was himself too weak even to attend the swearing-in ceremony.

After leaving the White House in 1921, the Wilsons moved to a house on S Street where the former president received visitors and accepted honors until he died on February 3, 1924. Edith Wilson lived on in Washington but paid little attention to politics or public causes. In 1939, she published *My Memoir,* widely held as a sentimental treatment of her life with Wilson rather than an accurate account of history. She carefully controlled access to Wilson's letters and papers, forbidding them to be seen by former White House officials she did not like. Historians now believe she played a much larger role in governing during Wilson's long disability than she ever admitted to and, in the process, made it more difficult for other presidential wives to take an active role in the public affairs of state. Edith's insistence that Woodrow's illness be kept from government officials and from the public went largely unchallenged by cabinet members and the vice president. Ratification of the Twenty-fifth Amendment in 1967, providing a means for temporarily relieving a president of official duties because of disability or incompetence, makes a repeat of this scenario unlikely today.

Edith Wilson died of heart failure on December 28, 1961. At 89, she was the third longest-lived first lady after BESS TRUMAN and LADY BIRD JOHNSON.

Further Reading

McCallops, James S. *Edith Bolling Galt Wilson: The Unintended President.* New York: Nova History Publications, 2003.

National First Ladies Library. *Biographies: First Ladies of the United States.* Available online. URL: http:// www.firstladies.org/biographies. Accessed on January 4, 2007.

Schneider, Dorothy, and Carl J. Schneider. "Edith Bolling Gault Wilson." *First Ladies: A Biographical Dictionary,* pp. 190–200. New York: Checkmark Books, 2001.

Wilson, Ellen (Ellen Louise Axon Wilson)

(1860–1914) *first lady*   Ellen Louise Axon was born in Savannah, Georgia, on May 15, 1860. Her father, Samuel Edward Axon, was an ordained Presbyterian minister, and her mother, Margaret Jane Hoyt Axon, was the daughter of a Presbyterian minister. Ellen was the oldest of four children born to the couple. Her father served as a chaplain to the Georgia Infantry during the Civil War, leading to an extended absence from home. In 1866, the family moved to Rome, Georgia, and Samuel Axon took over the pastoral duties at the First Presbyterian Church. Margaret Axon died giving birth to Ellen's only sister in 1881. Ellen was 21 years of age and took over household duties and the care of her two brothers (the baby was sent to her mother's sister to raise). Although Ellen had demonstrated real talent as an artist, her family responsibilities and finances limited her ability to paint and formally study art. Her father suffered from mental illness and deteriorated steadily after her mother's death.

In April 1883, Ellen met Woodrow Wilson, an attorney visiting from Atlanta. Wilson proposed marriage in September, and Ellen accepted. Before the couple could be married, Ellen's father died, most likely a suicide. Ellen tried to break off the engagement, but Woodrow refused to hear of it, and they were married on June 24, 1885. The couple moved to Pennsylvania, where Woodrow accepted a faculty position at Bryn Mawr College. While playing the role of faculty wife, Ellen also enrolled in classes herself. She studied German, history, political economy and political philosophy so that she could help her husband with his monographs. In addition, she maintained her own reading list, centering on literature and political philosophy. She also gave birth to three daughters between 1886 and 1889. In autumn 1890, Woodrow accepted a position at Princeton University, and they moved to New Jersey. Ellen home-schooled her three daughters and served as a surrogate parent to her brothers, now both enrolled in universities. In 1902, Woodrow Wilson was elected president of Princeton.

The Wilsons moved into the presidential mansion, and Ellen grudgingly took on the responsibilities for entertaining. She stated that although it was simply a part of daily life and not worth complaining about, entertaining obligations often bored her. Woodrow's position afforded several opportunities for her to travel to Europe, and she used these trips to further her study in art and architecture. Ellen's broad intellectual interests and liberal education made her a popular and effective hostess for the university. She also served as a constant support to her husband, who suffered from bouts of insecurity, depression, and stomach illness.

In 1905, Ellen's youngest brother and his entire family died in a drowning accident. The loss was devastating for both Ellen and Woodrow. She withdrew from her family and turned to philosophy for answers. He reportedly turned to the company of Mary Peck. Ellen referred to this relationship as the "most painful part" of their marriage. She also returned to her art during this period, moving to the Lyme Summer School of Art in Lyme, Connecticut, to study with a professional instructor.

In autumn 1910, Woodrow resigned from Princeton, accepted the Democratic nomination to run for governor of New Jersey, and was elected. As the governor's wife, little was expected from Ellen by way of formal entertaining. However, she continued to entertain in their Princeton home and toured the state with Woodrow, taking on a far more public role than she had in the past. She devoted more time to charities and emerged as a trusted campaign advisor. In 1912, Woodrow Wilson accepted the Democratic nomination for president. Ellen

developed a good rapport with the press while campaigning with her husband. She was known for speaking frankly, but also for her discretion. Although Ellen was persuaded by her daughters to support SUFFRAGE for women, Woodrow's longstanding patriarchal attitudes caused her to remain publicly silent on the issue. The campaign took its toll on Ellen's physical stamina, worrying her daughters and her husband.

Woodrow was elected, and just before moving to Washington, Ellen held her first one-woman show at the Arts and Crafts Guild in Pennsylvania. Hanging 50 landscapes, she sold 23 of them. Wilson cancelled the traditional inaugural ball as an unnecessary expense, and the family spent its first night in the White House dining alone. Over the next few months, however, Ellen entertained with vigor. She held receptions, teas, musicales, and dinners and played host to numerous overnight guests. She hired Woodrow's cousin, Helen Bones, as her social secretary and was also assisted by her daughters. She, like other first ladies, refurbished the White House and planned to expand the family quarters by adding five additional bedrooms. She helped Woodrow with his speeches and offered private advice on appointments. More often than not, he listened to Ellen's advice, recognizing her insight into human nature and personalities.

The public side of First Lady Ellen Wilson grew dramatically. She involved herself in a number of reform efforts targeted at improving living conditions for the poor and most specifically blacks living in alleys surrounding the Capitol. Mrs. Wilson personally toured the worst areas and accepted an honorary chair of the Women's Department of the District of Columbia's National Civic Federation's housing committee. Women's engagement in politics and progressive causes was at its peak at this point, and many looked to Ellen Wilson for inspiration. She offered her full support for legislation to improve slum living conditions but remained silent on the question of women's suffrage.

In 1913, the first lady was diagnosed with Bright's disease, an ailment that debilitates the kidneys and was untreatable at the time. Ellen did not want to burden anyone with her illness and therefore kept the diagnosis to herself. She retreated with her daughters to the mountains of New Hampshire for the summer, but actively planned her daughter Jessie's White House wedding and kept up her correspondence. After the fall wedding, she plunged back into her philanthropic work. During this time, she also worked with the White House gardener to establish a rose garden on the grounds. This area has since become synonymous with formal political ceremonies.

In March 1914, Ellen fell while in her bedroom and was slow to recover. She planned and attended daughter Eleanor's May 1914 wedding, but declined rapidly after the wedding. Woodrow Wilson remained unaware of the seriousness of his wife's condition until August that year. On August 6, 1914, Ellen Wilson died in the White House. Before she died, she asked her doctor, "If I go away, promise me that you will take good care of my husband." Soon after her death, Congress passed the Alley Dwelling Bill to demolish slums and build new housing using federal money. It was legislation Ellen had worked for.

Although Ellen Wilson's tenure as first lady was short, she was the first to take on public causes of her choice and to promote her own political-social reform agenda. Although her first dedication was to her husband's well-being and his career, she was not eclipsed by him in the same way that most of her predecessors had been.

Further Reading

Sallee, Shelley. "Ellen Louise Axson Wilson." In *American First Ladies: Their Lives and Their Legacy,* 2nd ed., edited by Lewis L. Gould, pp. 227–236. New York: Routledge, 2001.

National First Ladies Library. *Biographies: First Ladies of the United States.* Available online. URL: http://www.firstladies.org/biographies. Accessed on January 4, 2007.

Schneider, Dorothy, and Carl J. Schneider. "Ellen Louise Axson Wilson" *First Ladies: A Biographical*

Dictionary, pp. 182–189. New York: Checkmark Books, 2001.

Wilson, Heather (1960–) *congressperson*

Heather Wilson was born on December 30, 1960, in Keene, New Hampshire. She joined the air force at the age of 17, graduating from the U.S. Air Force Academy in 1982. Wilson was a Rhodes Scholar and continued her education at Oxford University, earning a Ph.D. in international relations in 1985. Wilson became director for European defense policy and arms control on the National Security Council in 1989. She founded Keystone International, Inc., in 1991 to promote business development in the United States and Russia. She is the former secretary of the New Mexico Children, Youth, and Family Department.

In 1998, Wilson was elected to the U.S. House of Representatives as a Republican in a special election to replace the late Steven Schiff. She represents New Mexico and is the first female veteran to be elected to Congress. In the House, she serves on the Committee on Energy, the Committee on Commerce, and the House Select Committee on Intelligence. In February 2006, Wilson uncharacteristically went against President George W. Bush by calling for a full congressional inquiry into the National Security Agency's warrantless surveillance of U.S. citizens. She won reelection in 2006 by a margin of 875 votes.

Further Reading

Barone, Michael. *The Almanac of American Politics.* Washington, D.C.: National Journal Group, 2006.

"Representative Heather A. Wilson (NM)." In *Project Vote Smart.* Available online. URL: http://votesmart.org/bio.php?can_id=CNM54181. Accessed on January 8, 2007.

"Wilson, Heather." In *Biographical Directory of the United States Congress, 1774–present.* Available online. URL: http://bioguide.congress.gov/scripts/

biodisplay.pl?index=W000789. Accessed on January 8, 2007.

—Angela Kouters

Winnemucca, Sarah (Thocmetony, Sarah Winnemucca Hopkins) (ca. 1844–1891)

author, Native American activist Sarah Winnemucca, Northern Paiute leader and activist, was born around 1844 in what is now western Nevada. Her Paiute name was Thocmetony ("Shell Flower"). Her grandfather, Chief Truckee, and father, Chief Winnemucca, both provided tribal leadership during a time of white encroachment onto Indian lands. By the time she was 14, Sarah Winnemucca spoke three Indian dialects, English, and Spanish, and had spent some time being educated in an American convent school. In 1871, she went to work for the Bureau of Indian Affairs as an interpreter, and in 1878 she fought in the Bannock War. She married three times, the last time to Lt. L. H. Hopkins, with whom she ran a school for Indian children in Nevada.

In 1860, during the Pyramid Lake War, Winnemucca became acting chief of her Paiute nation. She recognized that the federal government had taken much of their reservation rights, making many of her people homeless. Determined to help, in 1880 Winnemucca traveled to Washington, D.C., to present her people's case. The federal government promised reforms that never came. Although she never again fully trusted the government, throughout the 1880s she continued to deliver public speeches on her people, American Indian rights, and the need for reform across the United States. Winnemucca found allies in Elizabeth Peabody and Mary Peabody Mann, reformers who helped her raise money. In 1883 she became the first American Indian woman to publish a personal and tribal history with her *Life among the Piutes: Their Wrongs and Claims.*

Sarah Winnemucca died of tuberculosis at Henry's Lake, Nevada, on October 17, 1891. She continues to have a lasting influence as an example of political leadership and as a voice for American Indian rights.

Further Reading

Canfield, Gae Whitney. *Sarah Winnemucca of the Northern Paiutes.* Norman: University of Oklahoma Press, 1983.

Hopkins, Sarah Winnemucca. *Life among the Piutes: Their Wrongs and Claims.* Bishop, Calif.: Chalfant Press, 1969.

Zanjani, Sally. *Sarah Winnemucca.* Lincoln: University of Nebraska Press, 2001.

—Eileen V. Wallis

Winning Plan

CARRIE CHAPMAN CATT organized the "Winning Plan" as the focus for the NATIONAL AMERICAN WOMAN SUFFRAGE ASSOCIATION (NAWSA) based on the principle that each state that granted women the vote could then be pressed to support the effort on the federal level. In 1916, at a NAWSA convention in Atlantic City, New Jersey, she unveiled her Winning Plan. It involved campaigning simultaneously for SUFFRAGE on both state and federal levels and compromising for partial suffrage in resistant states. She ended her speech with these words: "Do not stand in the way of the next step in human progress. No one living who reads the signs of the times but realizes that woman suffrage must come. We are working for the ballot as a matter of justice and as a step for human betterment."

Catt's emphasis on the importance of state, in addition to congressional, action arose from her belief that passage of a suffrage amendment through Congress, let alone its ratification, would never be attained without increasing the number of "suffrage states," which could compel their congressmen and senators as well as their legislatures to support the amendment. This effort pioneered grassroots democracy since suffragists began tracking the votes of the politicians and realized once states had some form of suffrage, support for the federal amendment became de facto.

Further Reading

Catt, Carrie Chapman, and Nettie Rogers Shuler. *Woman Suffrage and Politics: The Inner Story of the Suffrage Movement.* New York: C. Scribner's Sons, 1923.

Evans, Sara M. *Born for Liberty.* New York: The Free Press, 1989.

—Paula Casey

WISH List (Women in the Senate and the House) An organization modeled on EMILY's LIST on the Democratic side, WISH (Women in the Senate and House) List supports Republican pro-choice women for public office. Founded by Glenda Greenwald in 1992, WISH List is a donor network of "members" who agree to support candidates on the list. The organization vets the candidates and carefully selects women they determine can win and then offers the candidate training and forwards "bundles" of checks written by the list's members. In the 2002–03 cycle, WISH List endorsed nearly 200 candidates and saw a majority of them win office. WISH List remains the country's largest fund-raising network for pro-choice Republican women. The organization maintains a Web site at www.thewishlist.org.

Wollstonecraft, Mary See *Vindication of the Rights of Woman, A.*

Woman's Christian Temperance Union (WCTU) The Woman's Christian Temperance Union (WCTU), founded in 1874 in Cleveland, Ohio, considers itself the "oldest continuing non-sectarian women's organization in the world." Most early members were white, middle-class women, although men could be "honorary members," without voting privileges. Initially focused on the harmful influences of alcohol on society, the WCTU rapidly expanded its concern to other issues affecting family life and Christian moral values and adopted a position of moral suasion in the "social purity" campaigns of the Progressive era. The union's righteous stance gave women a powerful legitimacy for venturing out of their homes and into the political sphere. Recognizing their potential political strength, they organized at local, state, national, and international levels. FRANCES WILLARD, president of the WCTU from 1879 to 1898, urged women to learn public speaking and to "be involved in every social issue needing a woman's perspective. . ."

The WCTU's approach became twofold: (1) advocating government intervention to legislate censorship of harmful influences, and (2) production of their own alternatives, including promoting the WCTU's agenda with literature, radio shows, movies, and children's programs.

From its beginning, the WCTU has pressed for reforms: kindergartens, foster homes for abused children, physical education for women, woman SUFFRAGE, shelters and reformatories for women, and matrons for jails housing women prisoners. WCTU members fought to raise the age of consent for women, improve working conditions, promote child labor laws, increase minimum wages, and eradicate white slavery. They still distribute temperance and other literature published by their own Signal Press and publish a quarterly journal, the *Union Signal.* The WCTU was among the first organizations to keep a professional lobbyist in Washington, D.C., and in 1945 became a charter member of the United Nations Non-Governmental Organizations.

Current issues reflect the original purpose of protecting families and society, as the WCTU continues work to halt alcoholism and tobacco and drug abuse, fight fetal alcohol syndrome, eliminate pornography, and demand alcohol-free sports on television. The WCTU also supports the "sanctity of life" stance against ABORTION and opposes embryonic stem-cell research. Resolved to protect "traditional" family values, they support the current move to amend the U.S. Constitution to define marriage as a "sacred union between one man and one woman." The organization maintains a Web site at www.wctu.org.

Further Reading
Parker, Alison M. *Purifying America: Women, Cultural Reform, and Pro-Censorship Activism, 1873–1933.* Chicago: University of Illinois Press, 1997.
Willard, Frances. *Woman and Temperance.* New York: Arno, 1972.

—Billie Ford

Woman Suffrage Party The Woman Suffrage Party was organized by women in New York in 1909 in order to campaign for a state woman SUFFRAGE amendment. The party organized parades and public speeches as well as a specific response strategy to attacks by anti-suffragists. More than 800 women attended the first party convention, held at Carnegie Hall in New York City. Membership expanded to nearly 500,000 by 1917, when New York finally granted women the right to vote. Many in the suffrage movement viewed this victory as a good omen for final passage of the federal SUSAN B. ANTHONY Amendment. Ultimately that, too, was ratified as the Nineteenth Amendment in 1920.

Women Accepted for Voluntary Emergency Service (WAVES) Women Accepted for Voluntary Emergency Service (WAVES) was established as the Women's Reserve of the U.S. Navy in 1942. During World War II, more than 100,000 female volunteers served with the navy overseas and at home. In 1944, President Franklin Roosevelt racially integrated the WAVES, and membership rose even higher. Members of the organization served in a number of capacities, including (but not limited to) air traffic controllers, pilot instructors, aircraft mechanics, and clerical workers. This organization, unlike many of the other auxiliary-type organizations that formed during the 1940s, lasted until 1978, when women were fully integrated into the regular armed forces.

Women of All Red Nations (WARN) In 1974, more than 300 women from 30 Native American tribal communities attended the inaugural conference of Women of All Red Nations (WARN) in Rapid City, South Dakota. The founders of this first pan-tribal women's organization included Madonna Thunder Hawk (Lakota), Lorilei DeCora (Ho Chunk), and Janet McCloud (Tulalip). A number of WARN members had been involved with the American Indian Movement (AIM) and had participated in the 1973 occupation of Wounded Knee. Native American women founded WARN in part because the federal government's persecution of AIM after the 1973 occupation had created the need for new leadership. Their experiences working within AIM, which mirrored those of African-American and white women of the civil rights movement, also compelled these activists to address issues specific to Native American women, especially the forced sterilization of Native American women at Indian Health Service hospitals, DOMESTIC VIOLENCE, substance abuse, and other threats to American Indian women's health.

While championing Native American sovereignty generally, WARN activists have argued that that sovereignty depends upon the protection of Native Americans' "personal sovereignty." American Indian women have played an important role in the environmental justice movement. In highlighting the high rates of birth defects, miscarriages, and deaths associated with nuclear mining and storage on Indian land, WARN linked women's health and the survival of Native peoples to preserving environmental health. WARN has also fought to restore and secure treaty rights, campaigned to eliminate derogatory Indian mascots in sports, sought more accurate historical accounts of Native peoples, and protested the commercialization of Indian culture. The organization serves as an important voice for Native America on critical issues of education, health, cultural identity, and the environment.

—Paul C. Rosier

Women's Action Alliance   See STEINEM, GLORIA.

Women's Airforce Service Pilots (WASP)

During World War II, after rejecting several proposals to use qualified women pilots for flying duties, army commanders agreed to the formation of two groups designed to assist in meeting the need for pilots to ferry aircraft. The Women's Auxiliary Ferrying Squadron (WAFS) and the Women's Flying Training Detachment were both activated in September 1942. Both were designed to employ women as civilians in military tasks. WAFS was intended to use qualified females to ferry aircraft for the Air Corps Ferrying Command (later the Air Transport Service), and the second was to include an intensive training program to qualify women to replace men in a number of flying duties. In 1943, the two programs were merged into one organization, Women's Airforce Service Pilots (WASP), headed by Jacqueline Cochran.

The WASP pilot training program had 1,074 graduates who ferried aircraft, including bombers and fighters; towed targets for gunnery; and served as instrument instructors in the Eastern Flying Training Command. By late 1944, the WASP organization was disbanded. WASP members remained civil service employees who did not receive the pay and benefits given to male pilots. In 1977, President Jimmy Carter signed legislation providing procedures for former WASPs to be granted veteran status, although with limited benefits. It was not until 1979 that the first WASPs were given discharge certificates, and it was 1984 before they were awarded World War II Victory Medals.

Women's Army Corps (WAC)

More than 150,000 American women served in the Women's Army Corps (WAC) during World War II. First founded in 1942 as the Women's Army Auxiliary Corps (WAAC), it was integrated into the regular army in 1943 and became known as the Women's Army Corps. Representative Edith Nourse Rogers (R-MA) proposed legislation to create the organization. There was considerable opposition to the bill when it was introduced. With women in the armed services, one representative asked, "Who will then do the cooking, the washing, the mending, the humble homey tasks to which every woman has devoted herself; who will nurture the children?" After a long and acrimonious debate, which filled 98 columns in the *Congres-*

Poster created by the Recruiting Publicity Bureau of the United States Army, 1943 (LIBRARY OF CONGRESS)

sional Record, the bill finally passed the House, 249-86. The Senate approved the bill by a vote of 38-27 in May. When President Franklin D. Roosevelt signed the bill into law the next day, he set a recruitment goal of 25,000 for the first year. WAAC recruiting topped that goal by November, at which point Secretary of War Henry L. Stimson authorized WAAC enrollment at 150,000, the original ceiling set by Congress. Major OVETA CULP HOBBY served as the WAC's first director.

Members of the WAC were the first women (other than nurses) to serve within the ranks of the United States Army. Both the army and the American public initially had difficulty accepting the concept of women in uniform. However, political and military leaders, faced with fighting a two-front war, realized that women could supply the additional resources desperately needed in the military and industrial sectors. Given the opportunity to make a major contribution to the national war effort, women seized it. Healthy, unmarried women of "excellent character" without dependents who could pass an intelligence test could join the WAC. The large number of women who served demonstrates their desire to both be of service to their country and expand their own individual opportunities beyond domesticity. The WAC remained a separate unit of the U.S. Army until 1978, when male and female forces were integrated.

Further Reading

Bellafaire, Judith A. *The Women's Army Corps: A Commemoration of World War II Service.* Carlisle, Pa.: Center for Military History, 1993.

Cott, Nancy F. *No Small Courage: A History of Women in the United States.* New York: Oxford University Press, 2000.

Women's Bureau

Established by Congress in 1920, the Women's Bureau continues to act under the aegis of the Department of Labor, with a mandate to represent the needs of wage-earning women in the public-policy process in the United States. The bureau counts among its successes the inclusion of women's work under the FAIR LABOR STANDARDS ACT of 1938, the EQUAL PAY ACT of 1963, and legislation for family and medical leave and protection against discrimination in hiring. The bureau has played an important role in linking grassroots women's groups to government from the early post-SUFFRAGE era to the present, and it has undertaken valuable research, analysis, and reporting on women in the labor market.

Initially established in July 1918 as a temporary agency called Women in Industry Service, the bureau achieved a permanent place within the federal bureaucracy after lobbying by women's groups. Mary Anderson, a founder of the National Women's Trade Union League, was appointed director from 1920 to 1945, and under her leadership the bureau continued the earlier efforts of Progressive era reformers in the area of women and work. Further, the bureau was one of a number of groups that opposed the EQUAL RIGHTS AMENDMENT (ERA) for fear that it would jeopardize earlier legislation that had been passed to protect women workers.

During the administration of John F. Kennedy (1961–63) and the appointment of ESTHER PETERSON, a former lobbyist for the American Federation of Labor and the Congress of Industrial Organizations (AFL-CIO), the bureau played a primary role in the PRESIDENT'S COMMISSION ON THE STATUS OF WOMEN. The bureau later reversed its longstanding position on the ERA with the appointment in 1969 of Elizabeth Koontz, a champion of minority rights.

Further Reading

Freeman, Jo. *The Politics of Women's Liberation.* New York: David McKay, 1976.

Laughlin, Kathleen. *Women's Work and Public Policy: A History of the Women's Bureau, U.S. Department of Labor, 1945–1970.* Boston: Northeastern University Press, 2000.

Sealander, Judith. *As Minority Becomes Majority: Federal Reaction to the Phenomenon of Women in the Work Force, 1920–1963.* Westport, Conn.: Greenwood Press, 1983.

—Leanne Dustan

Women's Campaign Fund (WCF)

The Women's Campaign Fund (WCF) is the oldest national nonpartisan political action committee (PAC) dedicated to electing pro-choice women. Founded shortly after the Supreme Court decision in ROE V. WADE in 1974, the WCF strives to preserve access to reproductive choice by helping to elect progressive women to political office. The WCF's goal is to increase the number of progressive women, regardless of party, serving in political office. To this end, they raise funds but also provide strategic consulting, fund-raising, networking, field campaigning and get-out-the-vote assistance. Since its founding, the fund has contributed to over 2000 campaigns. Recent successful WCF-supported candidacies include Senators HILLARY RODHAM CLINTON, MARY LANDRIEU, and OLYMPIA SNOWE; and Representatives JUDY BIGGERT, STEPHANIE HERSETH, and NITA LOWEY, as well as Speaker of the House NANCY PELOSI. The Women's Campaign Fund was reorganized and renamed The Women's Campaign Forum in 2006. The organization maintains a Web site at: www. wcfonline.org.

Women's Educational Equity Act (WEEA)

(1974)   TITLE IX OF THE EDUCATION AMENDMENTS OF 1972 requires gender-neutral treatment of men and women in education. The results have been more opportunities for women and fewer overt barriers to college admission and career choices. However, without proactive counseling and intervention strategies designed to increase the numbers of girls in nontraditional courses of study, the opportunities created by Title IX are likely to go unrealized. In 1974, Congress passed the Women's Educational Equity Act (WEEA), which authorized funds to promote bias-free textbooks and curriculum, support research on gender equity, and revamp teacher-training programs. The effort was significantly underfunded by Congress and ignored by Republican administrations through Ronald Reagan and George H. W. Bush. It was not until the AMERICAN ASSOCIATION OF UNIVERSITY WOMEN (AAUW) published its 1992 report "How Schools Shortchange Girls" that a credible effort to support WEEA materialized. Fiscal year 1996 had no appropriation for WEEA; however, between 1997 and 1999, funding remained constant at $3 million a year. As part of the original legislation, a national Equity Resource Center was established. It remains active as a clearinghouse for teacher training, developing equity curriculum materials, and conducting research related to gender equity in education.

In September 2004, Congress passed the Maloney/Woolsey/Sanchez amendment, which provided $3 million to fund the WEEA in 2005. The Heritage Foundation, a conservative Washington-based think tank, lobbied to end program funding, arguing that WEEA was outdated: "On nearly every indicator of academic success girls outperform boys. The GENDER GAP in reading and writing achievement, Advanced Placement participation, honors course participation, high school and college graduation rates, and other indicators favor girls. Boys, however, are more likely to be in Special Education, to repeat a grade, to be suspended, or to be involved with crime, drugs, and alcohol." In 2001, the Heritage Foundation issued a report titled *Wasting Dollars: The Women's Educational Equity Act,* in which it argued that "focusing on non-existent problems like gender inequity diverts funds and attention from the real—and critical—problems in America's educational system." The National Coalition for Women and Girls in Education, however, lobbied hard for the amendment and funding. WEEA is the only remaining program solely focused on advancing gender equity, and it is one of the smallest programs in the Department of Education. Equity advocates remain concerned about the way in which funds have been allocated. Previously, over one-third of the appropriation was used to fund the WEEA Equity Resource Center, but the Department of Education has redirected those dollars to fund a study of SINGLE-SEX EDUCATION.

Further Reading

American Association of University Women. *How Schools Shortchange Girls: A Study of Major Findings on Girls and Education.* Wellesley, Mass.: Wellesley College Center for Research on Women, 1992.

Kafer, Krista. "Girl Power: Why Girls Don't Need the Women's Educational Equity Act." The Heritage Foundation, Web Memo #536, September 8, 2004. Available online. URL: http://www.heritage.org/Research/Education/win563.cfm. Accessed on January 24, 2007.

Women's Equity Action League (WEAL)

The Women's Equity Action League (WEAL) was founded in Cleveland, Ohio, in 1968. The league had a network of state affiliates, but the national organization remained small (no more than 2000). WEAL sought to attract more conservative women who disliked the more radical or confrontational politics of the NATIONAL ORGANIZATION FOR WOMEN (NOW). Instead of focusing on "controversial" issues such as reproductive rights, equity in divorce, and rape laws, WEAL members devoted their efforts to winning economic advancement for women and eliminating sexism in educational institutions. They had notable success in establishing equity in estate taxation, eliminating gender-specific job listings, and removing sex-based bias in vocational education training programs. WEAL is perhaps best known, however, for its initiatives to reduce sexism in American colleges and universities. Its members filed hundreds of lawsuits against schools that received federal operating aid, successfully arguing that any recipient of federal contracts had to conform to already existing affirmative action guidelines contained in the federal Civil Rights Act of 1965. Although small in membership, its members included many influential people in politics, academia, and business. WEAL members strongly endorsed the EQUAL RIGHTS AMENDMENT. WEAL membership dwindled at the state and national level in the mid-1970s as members moved on to other feminist organizations such as the NATIONAL WOMEN'S POLITICAL CAUCUS.

Women's Era Club   See NEW ERA CLUB.

Women's National Loyal League   See NATIONAL WOMAN'S LOYAL LEAGUE.

Women's Peace Party

The Women's Peace Party was organized in 1915 by Crystal Eastman, JANE ADDAMS, and CARRIE CHAPMAN CATT in response to the outbreak of World War I. More than 3,000 people attended the first meeting held in the Willard Hotel in Washington, D.C. Frustrated by what they perceived as ineffectual action by male-dominated peace groups, members of the Women's Peace Party argued that women were more ably suited to lobby to preserve life since women are the "custodians of life." They claimed a moral imperative to oppose war. Following the war, the organization merged with the Women's International League for Peace and Freedom (WILPF).

Women's Policy, Inc.   See CONGRESSIONAL CAUCUS FOR WOMEN'S ISSUES / WOMEN'S POLICY, INC.

Women's Political Union (Equality League of Self-Supporting Women)

The Women's Political Union was an offspring of the British Women's Social and Political Union founded by Emmeline Pankhurst and her two daughters, Christabel and Sylvia Pankhurst. In the United States, the Women's Political Union was founded by HARRIOT STANTON BLATCH (daughter of ELIZABETH CADY STANTON), a participant in the British SUFFRAGE campaign. Blatch had been to England, where she had observed the methods used by suffragists there to get their message across. She returned to the United States in 1902 determined to engage in some of the same tactics. In 1907, she organized women into the Equality League of Self-Supporting Women, later named the Women's Political Union. This organization is credited with holding the first suffrage parade in 1910. They later merged with ALICE PAUL'S CONGRESSIONAL UNION FOR WOMAN SUFFRAGE in 1915.

Woodhull, Victoria (Victoria California Claflin Woodhull) (1838–1927) *suffragist, publisher, first woman presidential candidate* Controversial women's rights activist Victoria Woodhull was born Victoria California Claflin on September 28, 1838. The uneducated daughter of a petty criminal, she followed an unconventional path to prominence. Woodhull was married three times—the first time to Dr. Canning Woodhull when she was just 15—and divorced twice. As a young woman, she supported her family by engaging in clairvoyant healing along with her sister, Tennessee Claflin. It was in this role that the two gained the trust and financial backing of wealthy businessman Cornelius Vanderbilt. With his support, they opened the first female brokerage house on Wall Street in 1870. Soon thereafter, Woodhull and Claflin began publishing the controversial newspaper *Woodhull and Claflin's Weekly,* which became a source of radical ideas. It was the first newspaper to publish Karl Marx's *The Communist Manifesto* in English.

Woodhull, an advocate of sexual equality (or "free love" as it was known to its detractors), became the first woman to address a congressional committee when she presented a memorial (speech by a citizen) on behalf of woman's SUFFRAGE in January 1871. She and her friends formed the Equal Rights Party, and in 1872 Woodhull became its nominee for president, hoping to get former slave and abolitionist Frederick Douglass as her running mate. Although Douglass declined to run with Woodhull, the party wanted to unite advocates of suffrage for women with civil rights activists. In 1872, Woodhull published the details of an affair between prominent reform preacher Henry Ward Beecher and the wife of a colleague in the *Weekly,* in part to reveal the double standard applied to the sexes. Woodhull and her sister were arrested under the COMSTOCK ACT, which prohibited sending obscene materials through the mail. Although both were acquitted, the scandal ended Woodhull's political career. She spent her last years in England and died on June 9, 1927.

Further Reading

Gabriel, Mary. *Notorious Victoria: the Life of Victoria Woodhull, Uncensored.* Chapel Hill: Algonquin Books of Chapel Hill, 1998.
Underhill, Lois Beachy. *The Woman Who Ran for President: The Many Lives of Victoria Woodhull.* Bridgehampton, N.Y.: Bridgehampton Works Publishing, 1995.

—Laura Prieto

Woodward, Charlotte (Charlotte Woodward Pierce) (1829–1921) *suffragist* Charlotte Woodward was born in 1829 into a Quaker family. She began making her living at 15 as a teacher but later sewed gloves as piecework in Waterloo, New York. Excited to hear of the upcoming SENECA FALLS CONVENTION for women's rights, she made the trip there with several other young women from the rural environs of Syracuse. She participated in both days of the convention, July 19–20, 1848. At its conclusion, she signed the DECLARATION OF SENTIMENTS AND RESOLUTIONS, which included radical demands for equal rights and SUFFRAGE for women. In doing so, Woodward joined only 100 of the roughly 300 women and men who attended the convention. She later married and lived most of the rest of her life in Philadelphia. Like all but a handful of the Seneca Falls convention attendees, Woodward never became a suffrage leader, but she remained dedicated to the cause throughout her life. When the suffrage movement split over the issue of black male suffrage after the Civil War, she joined the AMERICAN

WOMAN SUFFRAGE ASSOCIATION. She was also a member of the Association for the Advancement of Women.

The only woman to sign the Declaration of Sentiments (1848) still living when the United States passed the Nineteenth Amendment in 1920, Charlotte Woodward (who apparently never voted) symbolically links the generations of activists who struggled to extend the vote to women. She exemplifies the unsung, grass-roots members of the movement whose long years of dedication made success possible. In 1921, shortly before her death at 92, she sent a trowel to the NATIONAL WOMAN'S PARTY to be used in laying a cornerstone of their new headquarters in Washington, D.C. The inscription read: "In Memory of the Seneca Falls Convention in 1848: presented by its sole survivor, Mrs. Charlotte L. Pierce, in thanksgiving for progress made by women and in honor of the National Woman's Party, which will carry on the struggle so bravely begun."

Further Reading

Gurko, Miriam. *The Ladies of Seneca Falls: The Birth of the Woman's Rights Movement.* New York: Schocken Books, 1974.

Wellman, Judith. *The Road to Seneca Falls: Elizabeth Cady Stanton and the First Women's Rights Convention.* Urbana: University of Illinois Press, 2004.

—Laura R. Prieto

Woolsey, Lynn (Lynn C. Woolsey) (1937–)

congressperson   Lynn Woolsey was born on November 3, 1937, in Seattle, Washington. She was educated at the University of Washington and the University of San Francisco, earning a degree in human resources and organizational behavior in 1980. She was a human resources manager a teacher at the College of Marin and the Dominican University of San Rafael before entering public service as a member of the Petaluma, California, City Council (1985–92). She served as vice mayor of Petaluma in 1989 and again in 1992.

In the 1992 primary to succeed Congresswoman BARBARA BOXER, who successfully ran for the Senate, Woolsey defeated a crowded field easily and went on to win the general election. Woolsey is a progressive democrat who has established a liberal voting record in the House and has worked to gain more funding for poor women and children and to improve the child support collection system. She believes in universal health care and is an advocate of ABORTION rights. Woolsey is one of two women in the House who have received welfare. In the 109th Congress, she served on the Committee on Education and the Workforce and the Committee on Science.

Lynn Woolsey is a critic of the 2003 invasion of Iraq and has introduced a number of resolutions on troop withdrawal. In 2006, she gave war protester Cindy Sheehan a guest pass for the State of the Union address. Sheehan was removed from the gallery for wearing a shirt with a political message. Woolsey was reelected in 2006.

Further Reading

Barone, Michael. *The Almanac of American Politics.* Washington, D.C.: National Journal Group, 2006.

"Representative Lynn C. Woolsey (CA)." In *Project Vote Smart.* Available online. URL: http://votesmart. org/bio.php?can_idíH0226103. Accessed on January 8, 2007.

"Woolsey, Lynn C." In *Biographical Directory of the United States Congress, 1774–present.* Available online. URL: http://bioguide.congress.gov/scripts/ biodisplay.pl?index=W000738. Accessed on January 8, 2007.

—Angela Kouters

Wright, Frances (Fanny Wright) (1795–1852)

lecturer, writer, feminist, utopian   Born in Dundee, Scotland, on September 6, 1795, Frances Wright, known as Fanny, was a pioneer in many areas: the first woman to speak publicly from a podium in the United States, the first woman to advocate woman's inherent equality to men, the first to question the utility of religion and to denounce the power of the clergy. She was an early advocate of free public education and a pioneering antislavery activist and antiracist advocate, as well as a social reformer.

The daughter of a wealthy family, Wright became smitten with the United States after a trip there as a teenager. Upon her return to England, she published *Views of Society and Manners in America* (1821). She went back to America with the marquis de Lafayette in 1824 and officially became an American citizen in 1825. Influenced by the socialist Robert Dale Owen, the wealthy heiress purchased land in west Tennessee for a model communal plantation that she called Nashoba and where she planned to educate her slaves for freedom. Her ill-planned, underfunded, and understaffed experiment failed, however, in part due to her support for miscegenation. Traveling as far west as St. Louis, Wright lectured throughout the East and Midwest on the need for education for women and the need to free people's minds from the shackles of religion. In 1829, she settled in New York, where, with Owen, she published the *Free Enquirer,* a socialist newspaper advocating universal SUFFRAGE, the abolition of slavery, and BIRTH CONTROL, among other controversial topics. She also published her book *Course of Popular Lectures.*

In 1831, Wright was devastated by the death of her sister. That same year, she married Phiquepal D'Arusmont, moved to France, and had a daughter. Her marriage was an unhappy one. As was the custom of the day, upon marriage, all of Wright's wealth became her husband's to disperse as he saw fit. She returned to the United States in 1835, and in 1844, she purchased a house in Cincinnati and sued D'Arusmont to regain her American properties. She divorced him, lost custody of her daughter, and continued writing and lecturing, though she was no longer as radical as before. Although her daughter, Sylvia, became a Christian and saw her mother's newspaper *Free Enquirer* as "infidel trash," she nonetheless raised a marble monument to Wright, whom she never understood, after her death on December 13, 1852. Wright's letters and lectures were collected and reprinted in *Life Letters and Lectures* (1972).

Further Reading

James, Edward T., Janet Wilson James, and Paul S. Boyer, eds. *Notable American Women 1607–1950: A Biographical Dictionary,* vol. 1. Cambridge, Mass.: Belknap Press, 1971.

Morris, Celia. *Fanny Wright: Rebel in America.* Urbana: University of Illinois Press, 1992.

—Paula Casey

Y

Yard, Molly (Mary Alexander Yard) (1912–2005) *feminist, women's rights activist* Mary Alexander Yard, known as Molly, was born on July 6, 1912, Chengdu, the capital of Szechwan Province in China. Her father was a Methodist missionary, and the family lived in China until Molly was 13 years old. Because she was the third of three daughters, upon her birth, Chinese friends gave her father an ornate brass bowl as a consolation gift, to show their sympathy for yet another girl child. Yard later said that living in a country where women were so discriminated against made her a feminist almost from birth.

As a student at Swarthmore College in the early 1930s, Yard began her life of social activism by protesting fraternities and sororities because of the exclusion of a Jewish student in her own sorority, Kappa Alpha Theta. Although she was trained as a social worker, she found her inability to change the social condition frustrating and soon turned to activism in the trade union movement. She graduated in 1933 with a degree in political science. Yard became active in the American Student Union, serving first as the national organization secretary and eventually as chair. In this capacity, she met and later worked with ELEANOR ROOSEVELT. In 1938, Yard married Sylvester Garrett, but she kept her own name. When the couple tried to open a joint bank account, they were told they could only do so if Ms. Yard was Mr. Garrett's mistress rather than his spouse. Together the couple had three children, two sons and a daughter. Sylvester Garrett, a noted labor arbitrator, died in 1996.

Molly Yard became active in Democratic Party politics in California when she worked on behalf of HELEN GAHAGAN DOUGLAS in her campaign for the U.S. Senate against Richard M. Nixon. After the family moved to Pittsburgh, Yard worked in presidential campaign politics on behalf of John F. Kennedy in 1960 and George McGovern in 1972, as well as numerous state and congressional campaigns. Yard herself only ran for office once but was unsuccessful in her bid to win a seat in the Pennsylvania state legislature in 1964. She was also a founder of the Americans for Democratic Action, an independent liberal lobbying organization.

Yard's civil rights commitments were broad and deep, but her work on behalf of women's rights was extensive. She first became active in the NATIONAL ORGANIZATION FOR WOMEN (NOW) in 1974 while still in Pennsylvania. By 1978, however, she had gone to work on the national staff as part of the campaign to ratify the EQUAL RIGHTS AMENDMENT (ERA). She worked as a lobbyist in the effort until the ERA's demise in 1982. During this time, she became a leader within NOW and one of the organization's primary legal and political strategists and a prolific fundraiser. She served as a senior staff member for the NOW Political Action Committee from 1978 to 1984. Between 1985 and 1987, she served as NOW's political director and dedicated her energies to defeating anti-abortion legislation in several states.

In 1987, at the age of 75, Molly Yard won election as president of NOW, serving until she suffered a stroke in 1991. During her tenure, membership swelled by 110,000 and the organization collaborated with other progressives to defeat the Supreme Court nomination of Judge Robert Bork. NOW's agenda during her presidency included ABORTION rights, promoting gay and lesbian rights, and electing more women to public office. She was doggedly committed to protecting the gains for women and girls won under TITLE IX OF THE EDUCATION AMENDMENTS OF 1972 and against threats to weaken its provisions and negative interpretations by the federal courts.

Following her stroke, Yard continued to work for the Feminist Majority. She gave her last public speech at the Feminist Expo, sponsored by the Feminist Majority, in 2000. Molly Yard received the Feminist Majority Foundation's lifetime achievement award for "tireless work for women's rights, for women and girls in sports, for the Equal Rights Amendment for Women, for civil rights for all Americans, for her championing of the trade union movement, and her devotion to world peace and non-violence." She died in her sleep at age 93 at a nursing home in Pittsburgh, Pennsylvania, on September 20, 2005. Although Molly Yard was a tireless advocate for social change and women's rights, very little has been written about her life, and no official biography is known.

Further Reading

Fox, Margalit. "Molly Yard, Advocate for Liberal Causes, Dies at 93," *New York Times,* 22 September 2005. Available online. URL: www.nytines.com/2005/09/22/national/22yard.html.

Year of the Woman (1992) "The Year of the Woman" is a phrase commonly used to describe the 1992 congressional elections. Historic numbers of women ran for and won seats in the United States House of Representatives and Senate. Specifically, 11 women ran for Senate seats (10 Democrats and 1 Republican) and 106 women were major-party candidates for House and delegate seats (70 Democrats and 36 Republicans). Out of these, five women were elected to the Senate, including two from the state of California (DIANNE FEINSTEIN and BARBARA BOXER, both Democrats); and CAROL MOSELEY BRAUN, an Illinois Democrat, became was the first African-American woman and the first woman of color to be elected to the U.S. Senate. Twenty-four women were elected to the U.S. House of Representatives. Among them were NYDIA VELÁSQUEZ, a New York Democrat who became the first Puerto Rican woman to serve in Congress.

Women were successful in the 1992 congressional elections in large part due to events that took place on the national stage highlighting such problems as SEXUAL HARASSMENT and sex discrimination. The ANITA HILL–Clarence Thomas controversy politicized thousands of women who had never before donated money to a candidate or thought about seeking office themselves. Carol Mosely Braun challenged incumbent Illinois senator Alan Dixon in the Democratic primary, beat him, and went on to win not only his U.S. Senate seat but a place on the Senate Judiciary Committee. The NATIONAL WOMEN'S POLITICAL CAUCUS effectively channeled women's dismay over an all-male, all-white Senate Judiciary Committee by asking, "What if . . . " in a fund-raising letter intended to raise money in support of female Senate candidates such as Braun.

The need for more women in public office was never more visible than in 1992. Women candidates promised that women's interests and experiences would be more fairly represented in policy-making, and voters responded.

Further Reading

Carroll, Susan J. and Ronnee Schreiber. "Media Coverage of Women in the 103rd Congress." In *Women, Media and Politics,* edited by Pippa Norris. New York: Oxford University Press, 1997, pp. 131–148.

Handlin, Amy. *Whatever Happened to the Year of the Woman? Why Women Still Aren't Making it to the Top of Politics.* New York: Arden Press, 1998.

—Krista Jenkins

Z

Zbaraz v. Hartigan (484 U.S. 171) (1987)
This case concerned the Illinois Parental Notice of Abortion Act of 1983. The act required a minor to notify her parents, or seek a court order instead, and wait 24 hours before having an ABORTION. The Illinois federal district court found both provisions of the act unconstitutional. On appeal, the Seventh Circuit Court agreed that the waiting period was unconstitutional, citing several other cases; however, the court took note that the U.S. Supreme Court had never ruled on a waiting period for minors only. The court upheld the parental notification provision but delayed enforcement until the confidentiality of the minors seeking court orders could be assured. In 1987, the U.S. Supreme Court voted to uphold the appellate court's decisions (4-4).

APPENDICES

TABLES AND STATISTICAL PORTRAITS

1. FIRSTS FOR WOMEN IN U.S. POLITICS

2. WOMEN IN THE U.S. CONGRESS, 1917–2009

3. WOMEN OF COLOR IN THE U.S. CONGRESS, 1965–2007

4. WOMEN IN THE U.S. HOUSE OF REPRESENTATIVES, 1917–2007

5. WOMEN IN THE U.S. SENATE, 1922–2007

6. WOMEN IN STATEWIDE ELECTIVE OFFICE, 1969–2007

7. PERCENTAGE OF WOMEN IN STATE LEGISLATURES, 1971–2007

8. WOMEN APPOINTED TO CABINET POSITIONS, 1933–2007

9. WOMEN'S REPRESENTATION IN NATIONAL LEGISLATURES
AROUND THE WORLD

10. FIRST LADIES OF THE UNITED STATES OF AMERICA

1. Firsts for Women in U.S. Politics

1872   Victoria Woodhull, a stockbroker, publisher, and protégé of Cornelius Vanderbilt, runs for president of the United States on the Equal Rights Party ticket.

1884   Belva Lockwood, the first woman admitted to practice law before the U.S. Supreme Court, runs for president on the Equal Rights Party Ticket; she did so again in 1888.

1887   Susanna Salter is elected mayor of Argonia, Kansas, the first woman mayor in the country.

1894   Three women are elected to the Colorado House of Representatives, the first women elected to any state legislature. They were Clara Cressingham, Carrie C. Holly, and Frances Klock.

1896   Martha Hughes Cannon is elected to the Utah State Senate, becoming the first woman state senator.

1900   Frances Warren of Wyoming becomes the first woman delegate to a Republican National Convention. In the same year, Elizabeth Cohen of Utah is chosen as an alternate to the Democratic National Convention. When another delegate falls ill, Cohen becomes the first woman delegate to a Democratic National Convention.

1917   Jeannette Rankin, a Republican from Montana, enters the U.S. House of Representatives, the first woman ever elected to Congress. She serves from 1917 to 1919 and again from 1941 to 1942; a pacifist, she is the only lawmaker to vote against U.S. entry into both world wars.

1920   After 72 years of struggle, the Nineteenth Amendment to the Constitution is ratified, giving women the right to vote.

1920   The League of Women Voters (initially the National League of Women Voters) is founded by members of the National American Woman Suffrage Association as a means of encouraging informed participation by the new female electorate.

1922   Rebecca Latimer Felton, a Georgia Democrat, becomes the first woman to serve in the U.S. Senate. She is appointed to fill a vacant seat temporarily; she serves for only two days before giving up her seat to the man who had been elected to it.

1924   Bertha K. Landes, Republican city council president at the time, becomes acting mayor of Seattle, the first woman to lead a major American city. Two years later, she is elected mayor in her own right in a campaign run by women. She lost in her bid for a second full term.

1924   Lena Springs of South Carolina chairs the credentials committee at the Democratic National Convention and receives several votes for the vice presidential nomination.

1925   Nellie Tayloe Ross, a Wyoming Democrat, becomes the nation's first woman governor, elected to replace her deceased husband. She serves for two years. Later, she becomes vice chair of the Democratic National Committee and director of the U.S. Mint. At the 1928 Democratic National Convention, she received 31 votes on the first ballot for vice president.

1925   Representative Mae Ella Nolan (R-CA) becomes the first woman chair a congressional committee when, during the 68th Congress, she chairs the Committee on Expenditures in the Post Office Department.

1931   Hattie Wyatt Caraway (D-AR), is appointed to the U.S. Senate to succeed her late husband, the first of many women to reach the Senate in this way. She subsequently becomes the first woman ever elected to the Senate, where she served two full terms. She is the first woman to chair a Senate committee—the Committee on Enrolled Bills, a minor post.

1933   When she is appointed by President Franklin D. Roosevelt as secretary of labor, Frances Perkins becomes the first woman ever to serve in a presidential cabinet. She serves until 1945.

1933   Ruth Bryan Owen, a former congresswoman, becomes the first woman to hold a major diplomatic post when she is appointed by President Roosevelt as minister to Denmark. She holds this post until 1936, when her marriage to a Dane and resulting dual citizenship make her ineligible to serve.

1933   Minnie Davenport Craig (R-ND) becomes the first woman to hold the position of Speaker of the House in a state legislature.

1945   Representative Chase G. Woodhouse (D-CT) is the first woman to hold the position of secretary in the House Democratic Caucus.

1952   Two women, India Edwards and Judge Sarah Hughes, are proposed as Democratic vice-presidential candidates. Both withdraw their names before the balloting so the choice of presidential nominee Adlai Stevenson, Senator Estes Kefauver, could be nominated by acclamation.

1955   Consuelo Bailey, a Vermont Republican, becomes the first woman ever elected lieutenant governor of a state. In that role, she served as president of the state Senate. She had previously served as Speaker of the state House of Representatives, thus becoming the only woman in the country ever to preside over both chambers of a state legislature.

1964   Senator Margaret Chase Smith, a Maine Republican, is nominated for the presidency by Vermont senator George Aiken at the Republican national convention. Smith had campaigned briefly for the post, limiting herself to periods when the Senate was not in session. Elected to the House of Representatives in 1940 (to replace her dying husband) and the Senate in 1948, Smith had already made history by becoming the first woman to serve in both houses of Congress.

1965   Patsy Takemoto Mink, a Democrat from Hawaii, becomes the first woman of color

and the first woman of Asian–Pacific Islander descent in the House of Representatives. She served until 1977 and was reelected in 1990, serving until her death on September 28, 2002.

1966   The National Organization for Women is established to combat discrimination against women in every sphere. Its aim is to "bring women into full participation in the mainstream of American society now."

1968   Shirley Chisholm, a New York Democrat, becomes the first black woman to serve in Congress. She remains in the House of Representatives until 1982.

1971   The Center for the American Woman and Politics is founded at the Eagleton Institute of Politics at Rutgers, the State University of New Jersey.

1971   The National Women's Political Caucus (NWPC) is formed at a Washington, D.C., meeting of more than 300 feminists. Its aims are to increase women's access to political power in the major parties and to encourage and support women committed to women's rights who seek elective and appointive office.

1972   Congresswoman Shirley Chisholm runs for president in the Democratic primaries. At the party's national convention, she garnered 151.25 delegate votes before Senator George McGovern clinched the nomination. At the same convention, Frances (Sissy) Farenthold, a former Texas state legislator who twice ran for governor of that state, finished second in the balloting for the vice-presidential nomination, receiving more than 400 votes.

1972   Jean Westwood chairs the Democratic National Committee. The first woman to hold that position, she serves until just after the election, when she was replaced by Robert Strauss.

1974   The Women's Campaign Fund is formed for the purpose of "electing qualified progressive women of both parties to public office at every level." It is the first national political action committee with the specific goal of funding women's campaigns.

1977 Patricia Roberts Harris is appointed by President Jimmy Carter to serve as Secretary of Housing and Urban Development during 1977–79. From 1979 to 1981, she served as secretary of Health and Human Services. She was the first black woman to serve in a presidential cabinet and the first woman to hold two different cabinet positions.

1978 Nancy Landon Kassebaum, a Kansas Republican, is elected to the United States Senate. Prior to her election, all of the women who served in the Senate had succeeded their husbands in Congress or had first been appointed to fill out unexpired terms.

1980 For the first time, a national party's nominating convention delegates included equal numbers of men and women. At its convention in New York, the Democratic Party also added to its charter a requirement that future conventions have equal numbers of female and male delegates.

1981 Sandra Day O'Connor, a former Republican state legislator from Arizona who had served on a state appeals court, is appointed by President Ronald Reagan as the first woman ever to sit on the U.S. Supreme Court.

1984 Congresswoman Lynn Morley Martin (R-IL) is elected to the first of two terms as vice chair of the Republican Conference in the House, the first time a woman has held an elected position in the congressional party's hierarchy.

1984 Third-term congresswoman Geraldine A. Ferraro (D-NY), secretary of the House Democratic Caucus, becomes the first woman ever to run on a major party's national ticket when she was selected by Walter F. Mondale as his vice-presidential running mate.

1985 Madeline Kunin, a Democrat, is elected governor of Vermont. She becomes the first woman to serve three terms as governor (1985–91).

1987 Kay Orr, a Republican from Nebraska, is the first Republican woman elected governor of a state, as well as the first woman to defeat another woman in a gubernatorial race (former Lincoln mayor Helen Boosalis).

1987 Jan Faiks, a Republican from Alaska, becomes the first woman to hold the position of president of a state senate (1987–88).

1989 Ileana Ros-Lehtinen, a Florida Republican, becomes the first Hispanic woman and first Cuban American to be elected to Congress. She is elected in August 1989 in a special election and continues to serve.

1990 Joan Finney, a Kansas Democrat, becomes the first woman to defeat an incumbent governor. She served as governor from 1991 to 1995.

1991 Representative Barbara Kennelly (D-CT) becomes the first woman to hold the position of House Democratic chief deputy whip.

1992 Nydia Velázquez, a New York Democrat, is elected in 1992, becoming the first Puerto Rican woman to serve in Congress. She continues to serve.

1992 Carol Moseley Braun, an Illinois Democrat, becomes the first African-American woman and the first women of color to be elected to the U.S. Senate. She is also the first African-American woman to win a major-party Senate nomination. She served until 1999.

1993 Janet Reno becomes the first woman to serve as U.S. attorney general (1993–2001).

1993 Representative Nancy Lee Johnson (R-CT) becomes the first woman to hold the position of secretary in the House Republican Conference.

1993 Representative Rosa DeLauro (D-CT) becomes the first woman to hold the position of secretary to the House Democratic Conference. She later serves as assistant to the House democratic leader in the 107th Congress.

1994 Christine Todd Whitman is elected as the first female governor of New Jersey, serving two terms (1994–2004).

1995 Senator Barbara Mikulski (D-MD) becomes the first woman to hold the position of secretary to the Senate Democratic Conference.

1995 Senator Nancy Landon Kassebaum (R-KS) becomes the first woman to chair a major Senate committee, the Committee on Labor and Human Resources.

1997 Madeleine K. Albright becomes the first woman to serve as U.S. secretary of state (1997 to 2001). Although she becomes the highest-ranking woman in the U.S. government, as a naturalized citizen, she would not have been eligible to become president. She had previously served as U.S. ambassador to the United Nations (1993 to 1997).

1997 Aida Alvarez becomes the first Hispanic woman, as well as the first person of Puerto Rican heritage, to hold a cabinet-level position when she is appointed administrator of the U.S. Small Business Administration.

1998 Tammy Baldwin, a Democrat from Wisconsin, becomes the first openly gay or lesbian person elected to Congress as a nonincumbent. She is also Wisconsin's first woman elected to Congress.

2001 Hillary Rodham Clinton becomes the first woman elected to the U.S. Senate from New York, the only first lady ever elected to public office.

2001 Condoleezza Rice becomes the first woman to hold the post of National Security Advisor.

2001 Elaine Chao becomes the first Asian-American woman to serve in a presidential cabinet when she is appointed secretary of labor.

2001 Gale Norton becomes the first woman to serve as secretary of the interior.

2001 Ann Veneman is appointed to be the first female secretary of agriculture. She had previously been the first woman to serve as secretary of the California Department of Food and Agriculture.

2001 Christine Todd Whitman of New Jersey becomes the first female former governor to serve in a presidential cabinet-level position when she is appointed administrator of the Environmental Protection Agency.

2001 Senator Kay Bailey Hutchison (R-TX) becomes the first woman to hold the position of vice chair of the Senate Republican Conference.

2001 Senator Patty Murray (D-WA) becomes the first woman to serve as chair of the Democratic Senatorial Campaign Committee.

2001 Representative Nancy Pelosi (D-CA) is elected by her colleagues as House Democratic whip, becoming the highest-ranking woman in the history of the U.S. Congress.

2001 Representative Nita Lowey (D-NY) becomes the first woman to chair the Democratic Congressional Campaign Committee.

2002 Representative Nancy Pelosi (D-CA) becomes the first woman to head her party in Congress when she is elected by her colleagues as House democratic leader.

2002 With the election of Linda Sánchez (D-CA), for the first time two sisters serve together in the House of Representatives.

2003 Arizona becomes the first state where a woman governor succeeded another woman governor. Jane Dee Hull (R) is succeeded by Janet Napolitano (D).

2005 Washington becomes the first state to have both a woman governor—Christine Gregoire (D)—and two women serving in the U.S. Senate—Patty Murray (D) and Maria Cantwell (D).

2007 Representative Nancy Pelosi (D-CA) becomes the first woman to serve as Speaker of the House of Representatives.

Source: Center for American Women and Politics, Eagleton Institute of Politics, Rutgers, the State University of New Jersey, 2007.

2. Women in the U.S. Congress 1917–2009

Congress	Women in Senate	Women in House	Total # of Women
65th 1917–1919	0	1	1
66th 1919–1921	0	0	0
67th 1921–1923	1	3	4
68th 1923–1925	0	1	1
69th 1925–1927	0	3	3
70th 1927–1929	0	5	5
71st 1929–1931	0	9	9
72nd 1931–1933	1	7	8
73rd 1933–1935	1	7	8
74th 1935–1937	2	6	8
75th 1937–1939	2	6	8
76th 1939–1941	1	8	9
77th 1941–1943	1	9	10
78th 1943–1945	1	8	9
79th 1945–1947	0	11	11
80th 1947–1949	1	7	8
81st 1949–1951	1	9	10
82nd 1951–1953	1	10	11
83rd 1953–1955	2	11	13
84th 1955–1957	1	16	17
85th 1957–1959	1	15	16
86th 1959–1961	2	17	19
87th 1961–1963	2	18	20
88th 1963–1965	2	12	14
89th 1965–1967	2	11	13
90th 1967–1969	1	11	12
91st 1969–1971	1	10	11
92nd 1971–1973	2	13	15
93rd 1973–1975	0	16	16
94th 1975–1977	0	19	19
95th 1977–1979	2	18	20
96th 1979–1981	1	16	17
97th 1981–1983	2	21	23
98th 1983–1985	2	22	24
99th 1985–1987	2	23	25
100th 1987–1989	2	23	25
101st 1989–1991	2	29	31
102nd 1991–1993	4	28	32
103rd 1993–1995	7	47	54
104th 1995–1997	9	48	57

(continues)

Congress	Women in Senate	Women in House	Total # of Women
105th 1997–1999	9	54	63
106th 1999–2001	9	56	65
107th 2001–2003	13	59	72
108th 2003–2005	14	60	74
109th 2005–2007	14	65	79
110th 2007–2009	16	71	87

Source: Center for American Women and Politics, Eagleton Institute of Politics, Rutgers, State University of New Jersey, 2007. Available online. URL: http://www.cawp.rutgers.edu/Facts/Officeholders/cong.pdf.

3. Women of Color in the U.S. Congress 1965–2009

Congress	Women in Senate	Women in House	Total # of Women
89th 1965–1967	0	1	1
90th 1967–1969	0	1	1
91th 1969–1971	0	2	2
92th 1971–1973	0	2	2
93th 1973–1975	0	5	5
94th 1975–1977	0	5	5
95th 1977–1979	0	4	4
96th 1979–1981	0	2	2
97th 1981–1983	0	2	2
98th 1983–1985	0	2	2
99th 1985–1987	0	1	1
100th 1987–1989	0	2	2
101st 1989–1991	0	4	4
102nd 1991–1993	0	6	6
103rd 1993–1995	1	12	13
104th 1995–1997	1	14	15
105th 1997–1999	1	17	18
106th 1999–2001	0	19	19
107th 2001–2003	0	21	21
108th 2003–2005	0	20	20
109th 2005–2007	0	21	21
110th 2007–2009	0	21	21

Source: Center for American Women and Politics, Eagleton Institute of Politics, Rutgers, State University of New Jersey, 2007. Available online. www.rci.rutgers.edu/~cawp/Facts/Officeholders/color.pdf.

4. WOMEN IN THE U.S. HOUSE OF REPRESENTATIVES 1917–2007

NAME	DATES	METHOD ACQUIRED
Jeannette Rankin (R-MT)	1917–1919; 1941–1943	Elected
Alice Mary Roberton (R-OK)	1921–1923	Elected
Winnifred Sprague Mason Huck (R-IL)	1922–1923	Elected
Mae Ella Nolan (R-CA)	1923–1925	Widow's tradition
Florence Prag Kahn (R-CA)	1925–1937	Widow's tradition
Mary Teresa Norton (D-NJ)	1925–1951	Elected
Edith Nourse Rogers (R-MA)	1925–1960	Widow's tradition
Katherine Gudger Langley (R-KY)	1927–1937	Elected
Pearl Peden Oldfield (D-AR)	1929–1931	Widow's tradition
Ruth Hanna McCormick (R-IL)	1929–1931	Elected
Ruth Bryan Owen (D-FL)	1929–1933	Elected
Ruth Sears Baker Pratt (R-NY)	1929–1933	Elected
Effiegene Locke Wingo (D-AR)	1930–1933	Widow's tradition
Willa McCord Blake Eslick (D-TN)	1932–1933	Widow's tradition
Virginia Ellis Jenckes (D-IN)	1933–1939	Elected
Kathryn Ellen O'Loughlin (D-KS)	1933–1935	Elected
Isabella Selmes Greenway (D-AZ)	1933–1937	Elected
Marian Williams Clarke (R-NY)	1933–1935	Widow's tradition
Caroline Love Goodwin O'Day (D-NY)	1935–1943	Elected
Nan Wood Honeyman (D-OR)	1937–1939	Elected
Elizabeth Hawley Gasque (D-SC)	1938–1939	Widow's tradition
Jessie Sumner (R-IL)	1939–1947	Elected
Clara Gooding McMillan (D-SC)	1939–1941	Elected
Frances Payne Bolton (R-OH)	1940–1969	Widow's tradition
Margaret Chase Smith (R-ME)	1940–1969	Widow's tradition
Florence Reville Gibbs (D-GA)	1940–1941	Widow's tradition
Katharine Edgar Byron (D-MD)	1941–1943	Widow's tradition
Veronica Grace Boland (D-PA)	1942–1943	Widow's tradition
Clare Boothe Luce (R-CT)	1943–1947	Elected
Winifred Claire Stanley (R-NY)	1943–1945	Elected
Willa Lybrand Fulmer (D-SC)	1944–1945	Widow's tradition
Emily Taft Douglas (D-IL)	1945–1947	Elected
Helen Gahagan Douglas (D-CA)	1945–1951	Elected
Chase Goin Woodhouse (D-CT)	1945–1947 1949–1951	Elected
Helen Douglas Mankin (D-GA)	1946–1947	Elected
Eliza Jane Pratt (D-NC)	1946–1947	Elected
Georgia Lee Lusk (D-NM)	1947–1949	Elected
Katharine Price Collier St. George (R-NY)	1947–1965	Elected
Reva Zilpha Beck Bosone (D-UT)	1949–1953	Elected

(continues)

NAME	DATES	METHOD ACQUIRED
Cecil Murray Harden (R-IN)	1949–1959	Elected
Edna Flannery Kelly (D-NY)	1949–1969	Elected
Marguerite Stitt Church (R-IL)	1951–1963	Elected
Ruth Thompson (R-MI)	1951–1957	Elected
Maude Elizabeth Kee (D-WV)	1951–1965	Widow's tradition
Vera Daerr Buchanan (D-PA)	1951–1955	Widow's tradition
Gracis Bowers Pfost (D-ID)	1953–1963	Elected
Leonor Kretzer Sullivan (D-MO)	1953–1977	Widow's tradition
Mary Elizabeth Pruett Farrington (R-HI)	1954–1957	Widow's tradition
Iris Faircloth Blitch (D-GA)	1955–1963	Elected
Edith Starrett Green (D-OR)	1955–1974	Elected
Martha Wright Griffiths (D-MI)	1955–1974	Elected
Coya Cjesdal Knutson (D-MN)	1955–1959	Elected
Kathryn Elizabeth Granahan (D-PA)	1956–1963	Widow's tradition
Florence Price Dwyer (R-NJ)	1957–1973	Elected
Catherine Dean May (R-WA)	1959–1971	Elected
Edna Oakes Simpson (R-IL)	1959–1961	Widow's tradition
Jessica McCullough Weis (R-NY)	1959–1963	Elected
Julia Butler Hansen (D-WA)	1960–1974	Elected
Catherine Dorris Norrell (D-AR)	1961–1963	Widow's tradition
Louise Goff Reece (R-TN)	1961–1963	Widow's tradition
Corinne Boyd Riley (D-SC)	1962–1963	Widow's tradition
Charlotts Thompson Reid (R-IL)	1963–1971	Elected
Irene Bailey Baker (R-TN)	1964–1965	Widow's tradition
Patsy Takemoto Mink (D-HI)	1965–1977 1990–2002	Elected
Lera Millard Thomas (D-TX)	1966–1967	Widow's tradition
Margaret M. Heckler (R-MA)	1967–1983	Elected
Shirley Anita Chisholm (D-NY)	1969–1983	Elected
Bella Savitzky Abzug (D-NY)	1971–1977	Elected
Ella Tambussi Grasso (D-CT)	1971–1975	Elected
Louise Day Hicks (D-MA)	1971–1973	Elected
Elizabeth Andrews (D-AL)	1972–1973	Widow's tradition
Yvonne Brathwaite Burke (D-CA)	1973–1979	Elected
Marjorie Sewell Holt (R-MD)	1973–1987	Elected
Elizabeth Holtzman (D-NY)	1973–1981	Elected
Barbara Charline Jordan (D-TX)	1973–1979	Elected
Patricia Scott Schroeder (D-CO)	1973–1997	Elected
Corinne Claiborne (Lindy) Boggs (D-LA)	1973–1991	Widow's tradition
Cardiss Collins (D-IL)	1973–1997	Widow's tradition
Millicent Hammond Fenwick (R-NJ)	1975–1983	Elected
Martha Elizabeth Keys (D-KS)	1975–1979	Elected
Marilyn Laird Lloyd (D-TN)	1975–1995	Elected
Helen Stevenson Meyner (D-NJ)	1975–1979	Elected
Vorgonoa Dodd Smith (R-NE)	1975–1991	Elected

NAME	DATES	METHOD ACQUIRED
Gladys Noon Spellman (D-MD)	1975–1981	Elected
Shirley Neil Pettis (R-CA)	1975–1979	Widow's tradition
Barbara Ann Mikulski (D-MD)	1977–1987	Elected
Mary Rose OaKar (D-OH)	1977–1993	Elected
Beverly Barton Butcher Byron (D-MD)	1979–1993	Widow's tradition
Geraldine Ann Ferraro (D-NY)	1979–1985	Elected
Olympia Jean Snowe (R-ME)	1979–1995	Elected
Bobbi Fiedler (R-CA)	1981–1975	Elected
Lynn Morley Martin (R-NJ)	1981–1991	Elected
Margaret Scafati Roukema (R-NJ)	1981–2003	Elected
Claudine Schneider (R-RI)	1981–1991	Elected
Barbara Bailey Kennelly (D-CT)	1982–1999	Elected
Jean Spencer Ashbrook (R-OH)	1982–1983	Widow's tradition
Katie Beatrice Hall (D-IN)	1982–1985	Elected
Barbara Boxer (D-CA)	1983–1993	Elected
Nancy Lee Johnson (R-CT)	1983–2007	Elected
Marcia Carolyn Kaptur (D-OH)	1983–	Elected
Barbara Farrell Vucanovich (R-NV)	1983–1997	Elected
Sala Burton (D-CA)	1983–1987	Widow's tradition
Helen Delich Bentley (R-MD)	1985–1995	Elected
Jan Meyers (R-KS)	1985–1997	Elected
Catherine S. Long (D-LA)	1985–1987	Widow's tradition
Constance A. Morella (R-MD)	1987–2003	Elected
Elizabeth J. Patterson (D-SC)	1987–1993	Elected
Patricia Fukuda Saiki (R-HI)	1987–1991	Elected
Louise McIntosh Slaughter (D-NY)	1987–	Elected
Nancy Pelosi (D-CA)	1987–	Elected
Nita M. Lowey (D-NY)	1989–	Elected
Jolene Unsoeld (D-WA)	1989–1995	Elected
Jill Long (D-IN)	1989–1995	Elected
Ileana Ros-Lehtinen (R-FL	1989–	Elected
Susan Molinari (R-NY)	1990–1997	Elected
Barbara-Rose Collins (D-MI)	1991–1997	Elected
Rosa L. DeLauro (D-CT)	1991–	Elected
Joan Kelly Horn (D-MO)	1991–1993	Elected
Eleanor Holmes Norton (D-DC)	1991–	Elected
Maxine Waters (D-CA)	1991–	Elected
Eva Clayton (D-NC)	1992–2003	Elected
Corrine Brown (D-FL)	1993–	Elected
Leslie Byrne (D-VA)	1993–1995	Elected
Maria Cantwell (D-WA)	1993–1995	Elected
Pat Danner (D-MO)	1993–2001	Elected
Jennifer Dunn (R-WA)	1993–2005	Elected
Karan English (D-AZ)	1993–2005	Elected

(continues)

NAME	DATES	METHOD ACQUIRED
Anna G. Eshoo (D-CA)	1993–	Elected
Tillie Fowler (R-FL)	1993–2001	Elected
Elizabeth Furse (D-OR)	1993–1999	Elected
Jane Harman (D-CA)	1993–1999	
	2001–	Elected
Eddie Bernice Johnson (D-TX)	1993–	Elected
Blanche Lambert Lincoln (D-AR)	1993–1997	Elected
Carolyn B. Maloney (D-NY)	1993–	Elected
Marjorie Margolies-Mezvinsky (D-PA)	1993–2003	Elected
Cynthia McKinney (D-GA)	1993–2003	
	2005–2007	Elected
Carrie P. Meek (D-FL)	1993–2003	Elected
Deborah Pryce (R-OH)	1993–	Elected
Lucille Roybal-Allard (D-CA)	1993–	Elected
Lynn Schenk (D-CA)	1993–1995	Elected
Karen Shepherd (D-UT)	1993–1995	Elected
Karen Thurman (D-FL)	1993–2003	Elected
Nydia M. Velazquez (D-NY)	1993–	Elected
Lynn Woolsey (D-CA)	1993–	Elected
Helen Chenoweth-Hage (R-ID)	1995–1997	Elected
Barbara Cubin (R-WY)	1995–	Elected
Enid Greene (Waldholtz) (R-UT)	1995–1997	Elected
Shelia Jackson-Lee (D-TX)	1995–	Elected
Sue Kelly (R-NY)	1995–2007	Elected
Zoe Lofgren (D-CA)	1995–	Elected
Karen McCarthy (D-MO)	1995–2005	Elected
Sue Myrick (R-NC)	1995–	Elected
Lynn Rivers (D-MI)	1995–2003	Elected
Andrea Seastrand (R-CA)	1995–1997	Elected
Linda Smith (R-WA)	1995–1999	Elected
Juanita Millender-McDonald (D-CA)	1996–2007	Elected
JoAnn Emerson (R-MO)	1996–	Widow's tradition
Julia Carson (D-IN)	1997–	Elected
Donna MC Christensen (D-VI)	1997–	Elected
Diana DeGette (D-CO)	1997–	Elected
Kay Granger (R-TX)	1997–	Elected
Darlene Hooley (D-OR)	1997–	Elected
Carolyn Cheeks Kilpatrick (D-MI)	1997–	Elected
Carolyn McCarthy (D-NY)	1997–	Elected
Anne Northup (R-KY)	1997–2006	Elected
Loretta Sanchez (D-CA)	1997–	Elected
Debbie Stabenow (D-MI)	1997–2001	Elected
Ellen Tauscher (D-CA)	1997–	Elected
Lois Capps (D-CA)	1998–	Widow's tradition
Mary Bono (R-CA)	1998–	Widow's tradition

NAME	DATES	METHOD ACQUIRED
Barbara Lee (D-CA)	1998–	Elected
Heather Wilson (R-NM)	1998,–	Elected
Tammy Baldwin (D-WI)	1999–	Elected
Shelley Berkley (D-NV)	1999–	Elected
Judith Borg Biggert (R-IL)	1999–	Elected
Stephanie Tubbs Jones (D-OH)	1999–	Elected
Grace Napolitano (D-CA)	1999–	Elected
Janice Schakowsky (D-IL)	1999–	Elected
Shelly Capito (R-WV)	2001–	Elected
Jo Ann Davis (R-VA)	2001–	Elected
Susan Davis (R-CA)	2001–	Elected
Melissa Hart (D-PA)	2001–2007	Elected
Betty McCollum (D-MN)	2001–	Elected
Hilda Solis (D-CA)	2001–	Elected
Diane E. Watson (D-CA)	2001–	Elected
Marsha Blackburn (R-TN)	2003–	Elected
Madeleine Bordallo (D-GU)	2003–	Elected
Virginia Brown-Waite (R-FL)	2003	Elected
Katherine Harris (R-FL)	2003–2007	Elected
Denise Majette (D-GA)	2003–2005	Elected
Candice Miller (R-MI)	2003–	Elected
Marilyn Musgrave (R-CO)	2003–	Elected
Linda T. Sanchez (D-CA)	2003–	Elected
Stephanie Herseth (D-SD)	2004–	Elected
Melissa Bean (D-IL)	2005–	Elected
Thelma Drake (R-VA)	2005–	Elected
Virginia Foxx (R-NC)	2005–	Elected
Kathy McMorris (R-WA)	2005–	Elected
Gwen Moore (D-WI)	2005–	Elected
Allyson Schwartz (D-PA)	2005–	Elected
Debbie Wasserman-Schultz (D-FL)	2005–	Elected
Doris O. Matsui (D-CA)	2005–	Widow's tradition
Jean Schmidt (R-OH)	2005–	Elected
Michele Bachmann (R-MN)	2007–	Elected
Nancy Boyda (D-KS)	2007–	Elected
Kathy Castor (D-FL)	2007–	Elected
Yvette Clarke (D-NY)	2007–	Elected
Mary Fallin (R-OK)	2007–	Elected
Gabrielle Giffords (D-AZ)	2007–	Elected
Kirsten Gillibrand (D-NY)	2007–	Elected
Mazie Hirono (D-HI)	2007–	Elected
Carol She-Porter (D-NH)	2007–	Elected
Betty Sutton (D-OH)	2007–	Elected

Source: U.S. House of Representatives. "Women in Congress: Chronological List of Members."
Congresswomen's Biographies. Available online. URL: http://bioguide.congress.gov/congresswomen/chrono.asp.

5. WOMEN IN THE U.S. SENATE 1922–2007

NAME	DATES	METHOD ACQUIRED
Rebecca Latimer Felton (D-GA)	1922 (24 hours)	Appointed
Hattie Wyatt Caraway (D-AR)	1931–1945	Appointed then elected, widow's tradition
Rose McConnell Long (D-LA)	1936–1937	Appointed then elected widow's tradition
Dixie Bibb Graves (D-AL)	1937–1938	Appointed by Gov. Bibb Graves (husband)
Gladys Pyle (R-SD)	1938–1939	Elected
Vera Cahalan Bushfield (R- SD)	1948	Appointed, widow's tradition
Margaret Chase Smith (R-ME)	1949–1973	Elected (previously elected to U.S. House, widow's tradition)
Eva Kelley Bowring (R-NE)	1954	Appointed
Hazel Hempel Abel (R-NE)	1954	Elected
Maurine Brown Neuberger (D-OR)	1960–1967	Elected, widow's tradition
Elaine S. Edwards (D-LA)	1972	Appointed by Gov. Edwin Edwards (husband)
Muriel Humphrey (D-MN)	1978	Appointed, widow's tradition
Maryon Allen (D-AL)	1978	Appointed, widow's tradition
Nancy Landon Kassebaum (R-KS)	1978–1997	Elected
Paula Hawkins (R-FL)	1981–1987	Elected
Barbara Mikulski (D-MD)	1987–present	Elected
Jocelyn Burdick (D-ND)	1992	Appointed, widow's tradition
Dianne Feinstein (D-CA)	1993–present	Elected
Barbara Boxer (D-CA)	1993–present	Elected
Carol Moseley-Braun (D-IL)	1993–1999	Elected
Patty Murray (D-WA)	1993–present	Elected
Kay Bailey Hutchinson (R-TX)	1993–present	Elected
Olympia Jean Snowe (R-ME)	1995–present	Elected
Sheila Frahm (R-KS)	1996	Appointed
Mary Landrieu (D-LA)	1997–present	Elected
Susan Collins (R-ME)	1997–present	Elected
Blanche Lincoln (D-AR)	1999–present	Elected
Hillary Rodham Clinton (D-NY)	2001–present	Elected
Deborah Stabenow (D-MI)	2001–present	Elected
Maria E. Cantwell (D-WA)	2001–present	Elected
Jean Carnahan (D-MO)	2001–2002	Appointed, widow's tradition
Lisa Murkowski (R-AK)	2002–present	Appointed by Gov. Frank Murkowski (father)
Elizabeth Dole (R-NC)	2003–present	Elected
Claire McCaskill (D-MO)	2007–present	Elected
Amy Klobuchar (D-MN)	2007–present	Elected

Source: United States Senate. "Women in the Senate." Available online. URL: http://www.senate.gov/artandhistory/history/common/briefing/women_senators.htm.

6. WOMEN IN STATEWIDE ELECTIVE EXECUTIVE OFFICE 1969–2007

YEAR	TOTAL WOMEN	TOTAL POSITIONS	PERCENT WOMEN
2007	76	315	24.1
2005	79	315	25.1
2004	81	315	25.4
2003	81	316	25.6
2001	89	323	27.6
2000	92	323	28.5
1999	89	323	27.6
1998	82	323	25.4
1997	82	324	25.4
1996	80	324	25.6
1995	84	324	25.9
1994	73	324	22.5
1993	72	324	22.2
1992	60	324	18.5
1991	59	324	18.2
1990	47	323	14.6
1989	46	322	14.3
1988	41	322	12.7
1987	45	323	13.9
1986	45	323	13.9
1985	43	323	13.3
1984	38	323	11.8
1983	34	324	10.5
1982	34	324	10.5
1981	34	324	10.5
1980	34	N/A	N/A
1979	35	327	10.7
1978	32	N/A	N/A
1977	33	333	9.9
1976	32	N/A	N/A
1975	33	337	9.8
1974	26	N/A	N/A
1973	26	342	7.6
1972	24	N/A	N/A
1971	24	343	7.0
1970	24	N/A	N/A
1969	23	346	6.6

Source: Center for American Women and Politics, Eagleton Institute of Politics, Rutgers, State University of New Jersey, 2007. Available online. URL: www.rci.rutgers.edu/~cawp/Facts/Officeholders/stwidehist.pdf.

7. Percentage of Women in State Legislatures 1971–2007

Year	Women Legislators	% Total of Legislators
2007	1734	23.5
2005	1663	22.5
2003	1654	22.4
2002	1662	22.7
2001	1666	22.4
2000	1670	22.5
1999	1664	22.4
1998	1617	21.8
1997	1605	21.6
1996	1539	20.7
1995	1532	20.6
1993	1524	20.5
1991	1368	18.3
1989	1270	17.0
1987	1170	15.7
1985	1103	14.8
1983	991	13.3
1981	908	12.1
1979	770	10.3
1977	688	9.1
1975	604	8.0
1973	424	5.6
1971	344	4.5

Source: Center for American Women and Politics, Eagleton Institute of Politics, Rutgers, State University of New Jersey, 2007. Available online. URL: http://www.cawp.rutgers.edu/Facts/Officeholders/stleg.pdf.

8. Women Appointed to Cabinet Positions 1933–2007

Appointee	Position	Appointed By	Dates
Frances Perkins	Secretary of Labor	F. D. Roosevelt	1933–1945
Oveta Culp Hobby	Secretary of Health, Education and Welfare	Eisenhower	1953–1955
Carla Anderson Hills	Secretary of Housing and Urban Development	Ford	1975–1977
Juanita A. Kreps	Secretary of Commerce	Carter	1977–1979
Patricia R. Harris	Secretary of Housing and Urban Development	Carter	1977–1979
Patricia R. Harris	Secretary of Health and Human Services	Carter	1979–1981
Shirley M. Hufstedler	Secretary of Education	Reagan	1981–1985

APPOINTEE	POSITION	APPOINTED BY	DATES
Jeane J. Kirkpatrick	United Nations Ambassadori*	Reagan	1981–1985
Margaret M. Heckler	Secretary of Health and Human Services	Reagan	1983–1985
Elizabeth H. Dole	Secretary of Transportation	Reagan	1983–1987
Anne McLaughlin	Secretary of Labor	Reagan	1987–1989
Elizabeth H. Dole	Secretary of Labor	G. H. W. Bush	1989–1991
Carla Anderson Hills	Special Trade Representative*	G. H. W. Bush	1989–1993
Lynn Morley Martin	Secretary of Labor	G. H. W. Bush	1991–1993
Barbara H. Franklin	Secretary of Commerce	G. H. W. Bush	1992–1993
Madeleine K. Albright	United Nations Ambassador*	Clinton	1993–1997
Hazel R. O'Leary	Secretary of Energy	Clinton	1993–1997
Carol M. Browner	Administrator, Environmental Protection Agency*	Clinton	1993–2001
Janet Reno	Attorney General	Clinton	1993–2001
Donna E. Shalala	Secretary of Health and Human Services	Clinton	1993–2001
Alice M. Rivlin	Director, Office of Management and Budget*	Clinton	1994–1996
Laura D'Andrea Tyson	Chair, National Economic Council*	Clinton	1995–1997
Janet L. Yellen	Chair, Council of Economic Advisors*	Clinton	1997–1999
Madeleine K. Albright	Secretary of State	Clinton	1997–2001
Aida Alvarez	Administrator, Small Business Administration*	Clinton	1997–2001
Charlene Barshefsky	U.S. Trade Represerative*	Clinton	1997–2001
Alexis Herman	Secretary of Labor	Clinton	1997–2001
Janice R. Lachance	Director, Office of Personnel Management*	Clinton	1997–2001
Christine Todd Whitman	Administrator, Environmental Protection Agency*	G. W. Bush	2001–2003
Elaine Chao	Secretary of Labor	G. W. Bush	2001–present
Gale Norton	Secretary of Interior	G. W. Bush	2001–present
Condoleezza Rice	National Security Advisor	G. W. Bush	2001–2005
Ann Veneman	Secretary of Agriculture	G. W. Bush	2001–2005
Margaret Spellings	Secretary of Education	G. W. Bush	2005–present
Condoleezza Rice	Secretary of State	G. W. Bush	2005–present

* Position considered cabinet-level during this administration.

Source: Center for American Women and Politics, Eagleton Institute of Politics, Rutgers, State University of New Jersey, 2003. Available online. URL: http://www.cawp.rutgers.edu/Facts/Officeholders/fedcab.pdf.

9. WOMEN'S REPRESENTATION IN NATIONAL LEGISLATURES AROUND THE WORLD

FIFTEEN COUNTRIES RANKING HIGHEST FOR WOMEN'S REPRESENTATION
NATIONAL PARLIAMENT—LOWER HOUSE—2006

COUNTRY	PROPORTION OF WOMEN MEMBERS
Rwanda	48.8% (rank 1)
Sweden	47.3% (rank 2)
Costa Rica	38.6% (rank 3)
Finland	38.0% (rank 4)
Denmark	36.9% (rank 5)
Netherlands	36.7% (rank 6)
Cuba	36.0% (rank 7)
Spain	36.0% (rank 8)
Argentina	35.0% (rank 9)
Mozambique	34.85 (rank 10)
Belgium	34.7% (rank 11)
Iceland	33.3% (rank 12)
South Africa	32.8% (rank 13)
Austria	32.2% (rank 14)
New Zealand	32.2% (rank 14)
Germany	31.6% (rank 15)
United States	16.2% (rank 66)

Source: Inter-Parliamentary Union. "Women in Parliaments: World Classification," as of November 30, 2006. Available online. URL: www.ipu.org/wmn-e/world.htm.

10. FIRST LADIES OF THE UNITED STATES OF AMERICA

FIRST LADY	PRESIDENT	DATES
Martha Dandridge Custis Washington	George Washington	1789–1797
Abigail Smith Adams	John Adams	1797–1801
Dolley Payne Todd Madison	James Madison	1809–1817
Elizabeth Kortright Monroe	James Monroe	1817–1825
Louisa Catherine Johnson Adams	John Quincy Adams	1825–1829
Anna Tuthill Symmes Harrison	William Henry Harrison	1841
Letitia Christian Tyler	John Tyler	1841–1842 (died)
Julia Gardiner Tyler	John Tyler	1844–1845
Sarah Childress Polk	James K. Polk	1845–1849
Margaret Mackall Smith Taylor	Zachary Taylor	1849–1850
Abigail Powers Fillmore	Millard Fillmore	1850–1853

First Lady	President	Dates
Jane Means Appleton Pierce	Franklin Pierce	1953–1857
Mary Ann Todd Lincoln	Abraham Lincoln	1861–1865
Eliza McCardle Johnson	Andrew Johnson	1865–1869
Julia Dent Grant	Ulysses S. Grant	1869–1877
Lucy Ware Webb Hayes	Rutherford B. Hayes	1877–1881
Lucretia Rudolph Garfield	James A. Garfield	1881
Frances Clara Folsom Cleveland	Grover Cleveland	1885–1889
Caroline Lavinia Scott Harrison	Benjamin Harrison	1889–1893
Frances Folsom Cleveland	Grover Cleveland	1893–1897
Ida Saxton McKinley	William McKinley	1897–1901
Edith Kermit Carow Roosevelt	Theodore Roosevelt	1901–1909
Helen Herron Taft	William H. Taft	1909–1913
Ellen Louise Axson Wilson	Woodrow Wilson	1913–1914 (died)
Edith Bolling Galt Wilson	Woodrow Wilson	1915–1921
Florence Mabel Kling Harding	Warren G. Harding	1921–1923
Grace Anna Goodhue Coolidge	Calvin Coolidge	1923–1929
Lou Henry Hoover	Herbert Hoover	1929–1933
Eleanor Roosevelt	Franklin D. Roosevelt	1933–1945
Bess Wallace Truman	Harry S. Truman	1945–1953
Mamie Geneva Doud Eisenhower	Dwight D. Eisenhower	1953–1961
Jacqueline Lee Bouvier Kennedy	John F. Kennedy	1961–1963
Lady Bird Johnson	Lyndon B. Johnson	1963–1969
Pat Nixon	Richard M. Nixon	1969–1974
Betty Ford	Gerald R. Ford	1974–1977
Rosalynn Carter	Jimmy Carter	1977–1981
Nancy Reagan	Ronald Reagan	1981–1989
Barbara Pierce Bush	George H. W. Bush	1989–1993
Hillary Rodham Clinton	Bill Clinton	1993–2001
Laura Welch Bush	George W. Bush	2001–2009

Source: American Memory, Library of Congress. "Time Line of Presidents and First Ladies." Available online. URL: http://memory.loc.gov/ammem/odmdhtml/pptime.html.

NOTE: Five women married to future presidents did not live long enough to be first lady. They are: Martha Wayles Skelton Jefferson, Rachel Donelson Robards Jackson, Hanna Hoes Van Buren, Ellen Lewis Herndon Arthur, Alice Hathaway Lee Roosevelt. These women, as well as the many women who served as White House hostesses, are not included in this volume.

PRIMARY DOCUMENTS

SIGNIFICANT SPEECHES DELIVERED BY WOMEN AND SELECTED PRIMARY DOCUMENTS FROM THE WOMEN'S RIGHTS MOVEMENT

1. Address to the first Women's Rights Convention, Elizabeth Cady Stanton (1848)

2. Declaration of Sentiments and Resolutions, Elizabeth Cady Stanton (1848)

3. "Ain't I a Woman?" Sojourner Truth (1851)

4. Address to the Woman's National Loyal League, Angelina Grimké Weld (1863)

5. Speech after Being Convicted of Voting in the 1872 Presidential Election, Susan B. Anthony (1873)

6. "What it Means to be Colored in the Capital of the United States," Mary Church Terrell (1906)

7. "The Fundamental Principle of a Republic," Anna Howard Shaw (1915)

8. "The Crisis," Carrie Chapman Catt (1916)

9. Address to the United States Congress, Carrie Chapman Catt (1917)

10. U.S. Constitution: Nineteenth Amendment, Women's Suffrage Rights (1920)

11. "A Moral Necessity for Birth Control," Margaret Sanger (1921)

12. Declaration of Conscience, Margaret Chase Smith (1950)

13. The National Organization for Women's 1966 Statement of Purpose

14. "Equal Rights for Women," Shirley Chisholm (1969)

15. Text of the Proposed Equal Rights Amendment

16. Opening Statement to the House Judiciary Committee Proceedings on the Impeachment of Richard Nixon, Barbara Jordan (1974)

17. Democratic Convention Keynote Address: "Who Then Will Speak for the Common Good?" Barbara Jordan (1976)

18. Address Accepting the Nomination for Vice President, Geraldine Ferraro (1984)

19. Keynote Address to the 1988 Democratic National Convention, Ann Richards (1988)

20. Commencement Address at Wellesley College, Barbara Pierce Bush (1990)

21. "Women's Rights are Human Rights," Hillary Rodham Clinton (1995)

1. ADDRESS TO THE FIRST WOMEN'S RIGHTS CONVENTION

ELIZABETH CADY STANTON, JULY 19, 1848, SENECA FALLS, NEW YORK

We have met here today to discuss our rights and wrongs, civil and political, and not, as some have supposed, to go into the detail of social life alone. We do not propose to petition the legislature to make our husbands just, generous, and courteous, to seat every man at the head of a cradle, and to clothe every woman in male attire. None of these points, however important they may be considered by leading men, will be touched in his convention. As to their costume, the gentlemen need feel no fear of our imitating that, or we think it in violation of every principle of taste, beauty, and dignity; notwithstanding all the contempt cast upon our loose, flowing garments, we still admire the graceful folds, and consider our costume far more artistic than theirs. Many of the nobler sex seem to agree with us in this opinion, for the bishops, priests, judges, barristers, and lord mayors of the first nation on the globe, and the Pope of Rome, with his cardinals, too, all wear the loose flowing robes, thus tacity acknowledging that the male attire is neither dignified nor imposing. No, we shall not molest you in your philosophical experiments with stocks, pants, high-heeled boots, and Russian belts. Yours be the glory to discover, by personal experience, how long the kneepan can resist the terrible strapping down which you impose, in how short time the well-developed muscles of the throat can be reduced to mere threads by the constant pressure of the stock, how high the heel of a boot must be to make a short man tall, and how tight the Russian belt may be drawn and yet have wind enough left to sustain life.

But we are assembled to protest against a form of government existing without the consent of the governed—to declare our right to be free as man is free, to be represented in the government which we are taxed to support, to have such disgraceful laws as give man the power to chastise and imprison his wife, to take the wages which she earns, the property which she inherits, and, in case of separation, the children of her love; laws which make her the mere dependent on his bounty. It is to protest against such unjust laws as these that we are assembled today, and to have them, if possible, forever erased from our statute books, deeming them a shame and a disgrace to a Christian republic in the nineteenth century. We have met to uplift woman's fallen divinity upon an even pedestal with man's. And, strange as it may seem to many, we now demand our right to vote according to the declaration of the government under which we live. This right no one pretends to deny. We need not prove ourselves equal to Daniel Webster to enjoy this privilege, for the ignorant Irishman in the ditch has all the civil rights he has. We need not prove our muscular power equal to this same Irishman to enjoy this privilege, for the most tiny, weak, ill-shaped stripling of twenty-one has all the civil rights of the Irishman. We have no objection to discuss the question of equality, for we feel that the weight of argument lies wholly with us, but we wish the question of equality kept distinct from the question of rights, for the proof of the one does not determine the truth of the other. All white men in this country have the same rights, however they may differ in mind, body, or estate.

The right is ours. The question now is: how shall we get possession of what rightfully belongs to us? We should not feel so sorely grieved if no man who had not attained the full stature of a Webster, Clay, Van Buren, or Gerrit Smith could claim the right of the elective franchise. But to have drunkards, idiots, horse-racing, rum-selling rowdies, ignorant foreigners, and silly boys fully recognized, while we ourselves are thrust out from all the rights that belong to citizens, it is too grossly insulting to the dignity of woman to be longer quietly submitted to. The right is ours. Have it, we must. Use it, we will. The pens, the tongues, the fortunes, the indomitable wills of many women are already pledged to secure this right. The great truth that no just government can be formed without the consent of the governed we shall echo and re-echo in the ears of the unjust judge, until by continual coming we shall weary him. There seems now to be a kind of moral stagnation in our midst. Philanthropists have done their utmost to rouse the nation to a sense of its sins. War, slavery, drunkenness, licentiousness, gluttony, have been dragged naked before the people, and all their abominations and deformities fully brought to light, yet with idiotic laugh we hug those monsters to our breasts and rush on to destruction. Our churches are multiplying on all sides, our missionary societies, Sunday schools, and prayer meetings and innumerable charitable and reform organizations are all in operation, but still the tide of vice is swelling, and threatens the destruction of everything, and the battlements of righteousness are weak against the raging elements of sin and death. Verily, the world waits the coming of some new element, some purifying power, some spirit of mercy and love. The voice of woman has been silenced in the state, the church, and the home, but man cannot fulfill his destiny alone, he cannot redeem his race unaided. There are deep and tender chords of sympathy and love in the hearts of the downfallen and oppressed that woman can touch more skillfully than man.

The world has never yet seen a truly great and virtuous nation, because in the degradation of woman the very fountains of life are poisoned at their source. It is vain to look for silver and gold from mines of copper and lead. It is the wise mother that has the wise son. So long as your women are slaves you may throw your colleges and churches to the winds. You can't have scholars and saints so long as your mothers are ground to powder between the upper and nether millstone of tyranny and lust. How seldom, now, is a father's pride gratified, his fond hopes realized, in the budding genius of his son! The wife is degraded, made the mere creature of caprice, and the foolish son is heaviness to his heart. Truly are the sins of the fathers visited upon the children to the third and fourth generation. God, in His wisdom, has so linked the whole human family together that

any violence done at one end of the chain is felt throughout its length, and here, too, is the law of restoration, as in woman all have fallen, so in her elevation shall the race be recreated.

"Voices" were the visitors and advisers of Joan of Arc. Do not "voices" come to us daily from the haunts of poverty, sorrow, degradation, and despair, already too long unheeded. Now is the time for the women of this country, if they would save our free institutions, to defend the right, to buckle on the armor that can best resist the keenest weapons of the enemy—contempt and ridicule. The same religious enthusiasm that nerved Joan of Arc to her work nerves us to ours. In every generation God calls some men and women for the utterance of truth, a heroic action, and our work today is the fulfilling of what has long since been foretold by the Prophet—Joel 2:28: "And it shall come to pass afterward, that I will pour out my spirit upon all flesh; and your sons and your daughters shall prophesy." We do not expect our path will be strewn with the flowers of popular applause, but over the thorns of bigotry and prejudice will be our way, and on our banners will beat the dark storm clouds of opposition from those who have entrenched themselves behind the stormy bulwarks of custom and authority, and who have fortified their position by every means, holy and unholy. But we will steadfastly abide the result. Unmoved we will bear it aloft. Undauntedly we will unfurl it to the gale, for we know that the storm cannot rend from it a shred, that the electric flash will but more clearly how to us the glorious words inscribed upon it, "Equality of Rights."

Source: Accessed at the National Park Service. URL: http://www.nps.gov/wori/address.htm.

2. DECLARATION OF SENTIMENTS AND RESOLUTIONS

ELIZABETH CADY STANTON
SENECA FALLS CONVENTION, 1848

When in the course of human events, it becomes necessary for one portion of the family of man to assume among the people of the earth a position different from that which they have hitherto occupied, but one to which the laws of nature and of nature's God entitle them, a decent respect to the opinions of mankind requires that they should declare the causes that impel them to such a course.

We hold these truths to be self-evident: that all men and women are created equal; that they are endowed by their Creator with certain inalienable rights; that among these are life, liberty, and the pursuit of happiness; that to secure these rights governments are instituted, deriving their just powers from the consent of the governed. Whenever any form of government becomes destructive of these ends, it is the right of those who suffer from it to refuse allegiance to it, and to insist upon the institution of a new government, laying its foundation on such principles, and organizing its powers in such form, as to them shall seem most likely to effect their safety and happiness. Prudence indeed, will dictate that governments long established should not be changed for light and transient causes; and accordingly all experience hath shown that mankind are more disposed to suffer, while evils are sufferable, than to right themselves by abolishing the forms to which they were accustomed. But when a long train of abuses and usurpations, pursuing invariably the same object evinces a design to reduce them under absolute despotism, it is their duty to throw off such government, and to provide new guards for their future security. Such has been the patient sufferance of the women under this government, and such is now the necessity which constrains them to demand the equal station to which they are entitled.

The history of mankind is a history of repeated injuries and usurpations on the part of man toward woman, having in direct object the establishment of an absolute tyranny over her. To prove this, let facts be submitted to a candid world.

He has never permitted her to exercise her inalienable right to the elective franchise.

He has compelled her to submit to laws, in the formation of which she had no voice.

He has withheld from her rights which are given to the most ignorant and degraded men—both natives and foreigners.

Having deprived her of this first right of a citizen, the elective franchise, thereby leaving her without representation in the halls of legislation, he has oppressed her on all sides.

He has made her, if married, in the eye of the law, civilly dead.

He has taken from her all right in property, even to the wages she earns.

He has made her, morally, an irresponsible being, as she can commit many crimes with impunity, provided they be done in the presence of her husband. In the covenant of marriage, she is compelled to promise obedience to her husband, he becoming, to all intents and purposes, her master—the law giving him power to deprive her of her liberty, and to administer chastisement.

He has so framed the laws of divorce, as to what shall be the proper causes, and in case of separation, to whom the guardianship of the children shall be given, as to wholly regardless of the happiness of women—the law in all cases, going upon a false supposition of the supremacy of man, and giving all power into his hands.

After depriving her of all rights as a married woman, if single, and the owner of property, he has taxed her to support a government which recognizes her only when her property can be made profitable to it.

He has monopolized nearly all of the profitable employments, and from those she is permitted to follow, she receives but a scanty remuneration. He closes against her all the avenues to wealth and distinction which he considers most honorable to himself. As a teacher of theology, medicine, or law, she is not known.

He has denied her the facilities for obtaining a thorough education, all colleges being closed against her.

He allows her in Church, as well as State, but a subordinate position, claiming Apostolic authority for her exclusion from the ministry, and, with some exceptions, from any public participation in the affairs of the Church.

He has created a false public sentiment by giving to the world a different code of morals for men and women, but which moral delinquencies which exclude women from society, are not only tolerated, but deemed of little account in man.

He has usurped the prerogative of Jehovah himself, claiming it as his right to assign for her a sphere of action, when that belongs to her conscience and to her God.

He has endeavored, in every way that he could, to destroy her confidence in her own powers, to lessen her self-respect, and to make her willing to lead a dependent and abject life.

Now, in view of this entire disfranchisement of one-half the people of this country, their social and religious degradation—in view of the unjust laws above mentioned, and because women do feel themselves aggrieved, oppressed, and fraudulently deprived of their most sacred rights, we insist that they have immediate admission to all the rights and privileges which belong to them as citizens of the United States.

In entering upon the great work before us, we anticipate no small amount of misconception, misrepresentation, and ridicule; but we shall use every instrumentality within our power to effect our object. We shall employ agents, circulate tracts, petition the State and National legislatures, and endeavor to enlist the pulpit and the press in our behalf. We hope this Convention will be followed by a series of Conventions embracing every part of the country.

Source: Elizabeth Cady Stanton, Susan B. Anthony, and Matilda Joslyn Gage, eds., *History of Women's Suffrage,* vol. 1. Rochester, NY: Charles Mann, 1881.

3. "Ain't I a Woman?"

Sojourner Truth
Women's Convention in Akron, Ohio, May 29, 1851.

Well, children, where there is so much racket there must be something out of kilter. I think that 'twixt the Negroes of the South and the women at the North, all talking about rights, the white men will be in a fix pretty soon. But what's all this here talking about?

That man over there says women need to be helped into carriages, and lifted over ditches, and to have the best place everywhere. Nobody ever helps me into carriages, or over mud-puddles, or gives me any best place! And ain't I a woman? Look at me! Look at my arm! I have ploughed, and planted, and gathered into barns, and no man could head me! And ain't I a woman? I could work as much and eat as much as a man—when I could get it—and bear the lash as well! And ain't I a woman? I have borne thirteen children, and seen them most all sold off to slavery, and when I cried out with my mother's grief, none but Jesus heard me! And ain't I a woman?

Then they talk about this thing in the head; what's this they call it? ["Intellect," whispered someone near.] That's it, honey. What's that got to do with women's rights or Negroes rights? If my cup won't hold but a pint, and yours holds a quart, wouldn't you be mean not to let me have my little half-measure full?

Then that little man in black there, he says women can't have as much rights as men, because Christ wasn't a woman! Where did your Christ come from? Where did your Christ come from? From God and a woman! Man had nothing to do with Him. . . .

If the first woman God ever made was strong enough to turn the world upside down all alone, these women together ought to be able to turn it back, and get it right side up again! And now they are asking to do it, the men better let them.

Obliged to you for hearing me, and now old Sojourner ain't got nothing more to say.

Source: Accessed at Historic Speeches, sojust. net. Available online. URL: http://www.sojust.net/ speeches/truth_a_woman.html.

4. Address to the National Woman's Loyal League

Angelina Grimké Weld, May 14, 1863

I came here with no desire and no intention to speak; but my heart is full, my country is bleeding, my people are perishing around me. But I feel as a South Carolinian, I am bound to tell the North, go on! go on! Never falter, never abandon the principles which you have adopted. I could but say thus when it was proclaimed in the Northern States that the Union was all that we sought. No, my friends, such a Union as we had then, God be praised that it has perished. Oh, never for one moment consent that such a Union should be reestablished in our land. There was a time when I looked upon the Fathers of the Revolution with the deepest sorrow and the keenest reproach. I said to their shadows in another world, "Why did you leave this accursed system of slavery for us to suffer and die under? why did you not, with a stroke of the pen, determine—when you acquired your own independence—that the principles which you adopted in the Declaration of Independence should be a shield of protection to every man, whether he be slave or whether he be free?" But, my friends, the experience of sixty years has shown me that the fruit grows slowly. I look back and see that great Sower of the world, as he traveled the streets of Jerusalem and dropped the precious seed, "Do unto others as ye would that others should do unto you." I look at all the contests of different nations, and see that, whether it were the Patricians of Rome, England, France, or any part of Europe, every battle fought gained something to freedom. Our fathers, driven out by the oppression of England, came to this country and planted that little seed of liberty upon the soil of New England. When our Revolution took place, that seed was only in the process of sprouting. You must recollect that our Declaration of Independence was the very first National evidence of the great doctrine of brotherhood and equality. I verily believe that those who were the true lovers of liberty did all they could at that time. In their debates in the Convention they denounced slavery—they protested against the hypocrisy and inconsistency of a nation declaring such glorious truths, and then trampling them underfoot by enslaving the poor and oppressed, because he had a skin not colored like their own; as though a man's skin should make any difference in the recognition of his rights, any more than the color of his hair or his eyes. This little blade sprouted as it were from the precious seeds that were planted by Jesus of Nazareth. But, my friends, if it took eighteen hundred years to bring forth the little blade which was seen in our Declaration, are we not unreasonable to suppose that more could have been done than has been done, looking at the imperfection of human nature, looking at the selfishness of man, looking at his desire for wealth and his greed for glory?

Had the South yielded at that time to the freemen of the North, we should have had a free Government; but it was impossible to overcome the long and strong prejudices of the South in favor of slavery. I know what the South is. I lived there the best part of my life. I never could talk against slavery without making my friends angry—never. When they thought the day was far off, and there was no danger of emancipation, they were willing to admit it was an evil; but when God in His providence raised up in this country an Anti-slavery Society, protesting against the oppressions of the colored man, they began to feel that truth which is more powerful than arms—that truth which is the only banner under which we can successfully fight. They were comparatively quiet till they found, in the election of Mr. Lincoln, the scepter had actually departed from them. His election took place on the ground that slavery was not to be extended—that it must not pass into the Territories. This was what alarmed them. They saw that if the National Government should take one such step, it never would stop there; that this principle had never before been acknowledged by those who had any power in the nation.

God be praised. Abolitionists never sought place or power. All they asked was freedom; all they wanted was that the white man should take his foot off the negro's neck. The South determined to resist the election of Mr. Lincoln. They determined if Fremont was elected, they would rebel. And this rebellion is like their own Republic, as they call it; it is founded upon slavery. As I asked one of my friends one day, "What are you rebelling for? The North never made any laws for you that they have not cheerfully obeyed themselves. What is the trouble between us?" Slavery, slavery is the trouble. Slavery is a "divine institution." My friends, it is a fact that the South has incorporated slavery into her religion; that is the most fearful thing in this rebellion. They are fighting, verily believing that they are doing God service. Most of them have never seen the North. They understand very little of the working of our institutions; but their politicians are stung to the quick by the prosperity of the North. They see that the institution which they have established can not make them wealthy, can not make them happy, can not make them respected in the world at large, and their motto is, "Rule or ruin."

Before I close, I would like, however strange it may seem, to utter a protest against what Mrs. Stanton said of colonizing the aristocrats in Liberia. I can not consent to such a thing. Do you know that Liberia has never let a slave tread her soil?—that when, from the interior of the country, the slaves came there to seek shelter, and their heathen master pursued them, she never surrendered one? She stands firmly on the platform of freedom to all. I am deeply interested in this colony of Liberia. I do not want it to be cursed with the aristocracy of the South, or any other aristocracy, and far less with the Copperheadism of the North. If these Southern aristocrats are to be colonized, Mrs. President, don't you think England is the best place for them? England is the country which has sympathized most deeply with them. She has allowed vessels to be built to prey upon our commerce; she has sent them arms and ammunition, and everything she could send through the West India Islands. Shall we send men to Liberia, who are ready to tread the black men under their feet? No. God bless Liberia for what she has done, and what she is destined to do.

I am very glad to say here, that last summer I had the pleasure of entertaining several times, in our house, a Liberian who was well educated in England. He had graduated at Oxford College, and had a high position there. His health broke down, and he went to Liberia. "When I went to Liberia," said he, "I had a first-rate education, and I supposed, of course, I would be a very superior man there; but I soon found that, though I knew a great deal more Greek and Latin and mathematics than most of the men there, I was a child to them in the science of government and history. "Why," said he, "you have no idea of the progress of Liberia. The men who go there are freemen—citizens; the burdens of society are upon them; and they feel that they must begin to educate themselves, and they are self-educated men. The President of Liberia, Mr. Benson, was a slave about seven years ago on a plantation in this country. He went to Liberia. He was a man of uncommon talents. He educated himself to the duties which he found himself called upon to perform as a citizen. And when Mr. Benson visited England a year ago, he had a perfect ovation. The white ladies and gentlemen of England, those who were really anti-slavery in their feelings—who love liberty—followed him wherever he went. They opened their houses, they had their soirees, and they welcomed him by every kind of demonstration of their good wishes for Liberia."

Now, Mrs. President, the great object that I had in view in rising, was to give you a representative from South Carolina. I mourn exceedingly that she has taken the position she has. I once had a brother who, had he been there, would have stood by judge Pettigrew in his protest against the action of the South. He, many years ago, during the time of nullification in 1832, was in the Senate of South Carolina, and delivered an able address, in which he discussed these very points, and showed that the South had no right of secession; that, in becoming an integral part of the United States, they had themselves voluntarily surrendered that right. And he remarked, "If you persist in this contest, you will be like a girdled tree, which must perish and die. You can not stand."

Source: Accessed at Historic Speeches, sojust. net. Available online. URL: http://www.sojust.net/ speeches/grimké_weld_wlnl.html.

5. Speech after Being Convicted of Voting in the 1872 Presidential Election

Susan B. Anthony
Philadelphia, Pennsylvania (1872)

Friends and fellow citizens: I stand before you tonight under indictment for the alleged crime of having voted at the last presidential election, without having a lawful right to vote. It shall be my work this evening to prove to you that in thus voting, I not only committed no crime,

but, instead, simply exercised my citizen's rights, guaranteed to me and all United States citizens by the National Constitution, beyond the power of any state to deny.

The preamble of the Federal Constitution says:

"We, the people of the United States, in order to form a more perfect union, establish justice, insure domestic tranquility, provide for the common defense, promote the general welfare, and secure the blessings of liberty to ourselves and our posterity, do ordain and establish this Constitution for the United States of America."

It was we, the people; not we, the white male citizens; nor yet we, the male citizens; but we, the whole people, who formed the Union. And we formed it, not to give the blessings of liberty, but to secure them; not to the half of ourselves and the half of our posterity, but to the whole people—women as well as men. And it is a downright mockery to talk to women of their enjoyment of the blessings of liberty while they are denied the use of the only means of securing them provided by this democratic-republican government—the ballot.

For any state to make sex a qualification that must ever result in the disfranchisement of one entire half of the people, is to pass a bill of attainder, or, an ex post facto law, and is therefore a violation of the supreme law of the land. By it the blessings of liberty are forever withheld from women and their female posterity.

To them this government has no just powers derived from the consent of the governed.

To them this government is not a democracy. It is not a republic. It is an odious aristocracy; a hateful oligarchy of sex; the most hateful aristocracy ever established on the face of the globe; an oligarchy of wealth, where the rich govern the poor. An oligarchy of learning, where the educated govern the ignorant, or even an oligarchy of race, where the Saxon rules the African, might be endured; but this oligarchy of sex, which makes father, brothers, husband, sons, the oligarchs over the mother and sisters, the wife and daughters, of every household—which ordains all men sovereigns, all women subjects, carries dissension, discord, and rebellion into every home of the nation. Webster, Worcester, and Bouvier all define a citizen to be a person in the United States, entitled to vote and hold office.

The only question left to be settled now is: Are women persons? And I hardly believe any of our opponents will have the hardihood to say they are not. Being persons, then, women are citizens; and no state has a right to make any law, or to enforce any old law, that shall abridge their privileges or immunities. Hence, every discrimination against women in the constitutions and laws of the several states is today null and void, precisely as is every one against Negroes.

Source: "On A Woman's Right to Vote." Accessed at Historic Speeches, Sojust.net. Available online. URL: http://www.sojust.net/speeches/susananthony.html.

6. "WHAT IT MEANS TO BE COLORED IN THE CAPITAL OF THE UNITED STATES"

MARY CHURCH TERRELL, OCTOBER 10, 1906, UNITED WOMEN'S CLUB, WASHINGTON, D.C.

Washington, D.C., has been called "The Colored Man's Paradise." Whether this sobriquet was given to the national capital in bitter irony by a member of the handicapped race, as he reviewed some of his own persecutions and rebuffs, or whether it was given immediately after the war by an ex-slave holder who for the first time in his life saw colored people walking about like freemen, minus the overseer and his whip, history saith not. It is certain that it would be difficult to find a worse misnomer for Washington than "The Colored Man's Paradise" if so prosaic a consideration as veracity is to determine the appropriateness of a name.

For fifteen years I have resided in Washington, and while it was far from being a paradise for colored people, when I first touched these shores, it has been doing its level best ever since to make conditions for us intolerable. As a colored woman I might enter Washington any night, a stranger in a strange land, and walk miles without finding a place to lay my head. Unless I happened to know colored people who live here or ran across a chance acquaintance who could recommend a colored boarding house to me, I should be obliged to spend the entire night wandering about. Indians, Chinamen [sic], Filipinos, Japanese and representatives of any other dark race can find hotel accommodations, if they can pay for them. The colored man alone is thrust out of the hotels of the national capital like a leper.

As a colored woman I may walk from the Capitol to the White House, ravenously hungry and abundantly supplied with money with which to purchase a meal, without finding a single restaurant in which I would be permitted to take a morsel of food, if it was patronized by white people, unless I were willing to sit behind a screen. As a colored woman I cannot visit the tomb of the Father of this country, which owes its very existence to the love of freedom in the human heart and which stands for equal opportunity to all, without being forced to sit in the Jim Crow section of an electric car which starts from the very heart of the city—midway between the Capitol and the White House. If I refuse thus to be humiliated, I am cast into jail and forced to pay a fine for violating the Virginia laws. Every hour in the day Jim Crow cars filled with colored people, many of whom are intelligent and well to do, enter and leave the national capital.

As a colored woman I may enter more than one white church in Washington without receiving that welcome which as a human being I have a right to expect in the sanctuary of God. Sometimes the color blindness of the usher takes on that peculiar form which prevents a dark face from making any impression whatsoever upon his retina, so that it is impossible for him to see colored people at all. If he is not so afflicted, after keeping a colored man or woman waiting a long time, he will ungraciously show these dusky Christians who have had the temerity to thrust themselves into a temple where only the fair of face are expected to worship God to a seat in the rear, which is named in honor of a certain personage, well known in this country, and commonly called Jim Crow. Unless I am willing to engage in a few menial occupations, in which the pay for my services would be very poor, there is no way for me to earn an honest living, if I am not a trained nurse or a dressmaker or can secure a position as teacher in the public schools, which is exceedingly difficult to do. It matters not what my intellectual attainments may be or how great is the need of the services of a competent person, if I try to enter many of the numerous vocations in which my white sisters are allowed to engage, the door is shut in my face.

From one Washington theater I am excluded altogether. In the remainder certain seats are set aside for colored people, and it is almost impossible to secure others. I once telephoned to the ticket seller just before a matinee and asked if a neat appearing colored nurse would be allowed to sit in the parquet with her little white charge, and the answer rushed quickly and positively thru [sic] the receiver—NO. When I remonstrated a bit and told him that in some of the theaters colored nurses were allowed to sit with the white children for whom they cared, the ticket seller told me that in Washington it was very poor policy to employ colored nurses, for they were excluded from many places where white girls would be allowed to take children for pleasure.

If I possess artistic talent, there is not a single art school of repute which will admit me. A few years ago a colored woman who possessed great talent submitted some drawings to the Corcoran Art School, of Washington, which were accepted by the committee of awards, who sent her a ticket entitling her to a course in this school. But when the committee discovered that the young woman was colored, they declined to admit her, and told her that if they had suspected that her drawings had been made by a colored woman, they would not have examined them at all. The efforts of Frederick Douglass and a lawyer of great repute who took a keen interest in the affair were unavailing. In order to cultivate her talent this young woman was forced to leave her comfortable home in Washington and incur the expense of going to New York. Having entered the Woman's Art School of Cooper Union, she graduated with honor, and then went to Paris to continue her studies, where she achieved signal success and was complimented by some of the greatest living artists in France.

With the exception of the Catholic University, there is not a single white college in the national capital to which colored people are admitted, no matter how great their ability, how lofty their ambition, how unexceptionable their character or how great their thirst for knowledge may be. A few years ago the Columbian Law School admitted colored students, but in deference to the Southern white students the authorities have decided to exclude them altogether.

Some time ago a young woman who had already attracted some attention in the literary world by her volume of short stories answered an advertisement which appeared in a Washington newspaper, which called for the services of a skilled stenographer and expert typewriter. It is unnecessary to state the reasons why a young woman whose literary ability was so great as that possessed by the one referred to should decide to earn money in this way. The applicants were requested to send specimens of their work and answer certain questions concerning their experience and their speed before they called in person. In reply to her application the young colored woman, who, by the way, is very fair and attractive indeed, received a letter from the firm stating that her references and experience were the most satisfactory that had been sent and requesting her to call. When she presented herself there was some doubt in the mind of the man to whom she was directed concerning her racial pedigree, so he asked her point blank whether she was colored or white. When she confessed the truth the merchant expressed great sorrow and deep regret that he could not avail himself of the services of so competent a person, but frankly admitted that employing a colored woman in his establishment in any except a menial position was simply out of the question.

Another young friend had an experience which, for some reasons, was still more disheartening and bitter than the one just mentioned. In order to secure lucrative employment she left Washington and went to New York. There she worked her way up in one of the largest dry goods stores till she was placed as saleswoman in the cloak department. Tired of being separated from her family, she decided to return to Washington, feeling sure that, with her experience and her fine recommendation from the New York firm, she could easily secure employment. Nor was she overconfident, for the proprietor of one of the largest dry goods stores in her native city was glad to secure the services of a young woman who brought such hearty credentials from New York. She had not been in this store very long, however, before she called upon me one day and asked me to intercede with the proprietor in her behalf, saying that she had been discharged that afternoon because it had been discovered that she was colored. When I called upon my young friend's employer he made no effort to avoid the issue, as I feared he would. He did not say he had discharged the young saleswoman because she had not given satisfaction, as he might easily have done. On the contrary, he admitted without the slightest hesitation that the young woman he had just discharged was one of the best clerks he had ever had. In the cloak department where she had been assigned, she had been a brilliant success, he said. "But I

cannot keep Miss Smith in my employ," he concluded. "Are you not master of your own store?" I ventured to inquire. The proprietor of this store was a Jew, and I felt that it was particularly cruel, unnatural and cold-blooded for the representative of one oppressed and persecuted race to deal so harshly and unjustly with a member of another. I had intended to make this point when I decided to intercede for my young friend, but when I thought how a reference to the persecution of his own race would wound his feelings, the words froze on my lips. "When I first heard your friend was colored," he explained, "I did not believe it and said so to the clerks who made the statement. Finally, the girls who had been most pronounced in their opposition to working in a store with a colored girl came to me in a body and threatened to strike. 'Strike away,' said I, 'your places will be easily filled.' Then they started on another tack. Delegation after delegation began to file down to my office, some of the women my very best customers, to protest against my employing a colored girl. Moreover, they threatened to boycott my store if I did not discharge her at once. Then it became a question of bread and butter and I yielded to the inevitable—that's all. Now," said he, concluding, "if I lived in a great, cosmopolitan city like New York, I should do as I pleased, and refuse to discharge a girl simply because she was colored." But I thought of a similar incident that happened in New York. I remembered that a colored woman, as fair as a lily and as beautiful as a Madonna, who was the head saleswoman in a large department store in New York, had been discharged, after she had held this position for years, when the proprietor accidentally discovered that a fatal drop of African blood was percolating somewhere thru [sic] her veins.

Not only can colored women secure no employment in the Washington stores, department and otherwise, except as menials, and such positions, of course, are few, but even as customers they are not infrequently treated with discourtesy both by the clerks and the proprietor himself. Following the trend of the times, the senior partner of the largest and best department store in Washington, who originally hailed from Boston, once the home of William Lloyd Garrison, Wendell Phillips, and Charles Sumner, if my memory serves me right, decided to open a restaurant in his store. Tired and hungry after her morning's shopping a colored school teacher, whose relation to her African progenitors is so remote as scarcely to be discernible to the naked eye, took a seat at one of the tables in the restaurant of this Boston [sic] store. After sitting unnoticed a long time the colored teacher asked a waiter who passed her by if she would not take her order. She was quickly informed that colored people could not be served in that restaurant and was obliged to leave in confusion and shame, much to the amusement of the waiters and the guests who had noticed the incident. Shortly after that a teacher in Howard University, one of the best schools for colored youth in the country, was similarly insulted in the restaurant of the same store.

In one of the Washington theaters from which colored people are excluded altogether, members of the race have been viciously assaulted several times, for the proprietor well knows that colored people have no redress for such discriminations against them in the District courts. Not long ago a colored clerk in one of the departments who looks more like his paternal ancestors who fought for the lost cause than his grandmothers who were the victims of the peculiar institution, bought a ticket for the parquet of this theater in which colored people are nowhere welcome, for himself and mother, whose complexion is a bit swarthy. The usher refused to allow the young man to take the seats for which his tickets called and tried to snatch from him the coupons. A scuffle ensued and both mother and son were ejected by force. A suit was brought against the proprietor and the damages awarded the injured man and his mother amounted to the munificent sum of one cent. One of the teachers in the Colored High School received similar treatment in the same theater.

Not long ago one of my little daughter's bosom friends figured in one of the most pathetic instances of which I have ever heard. A gentleman who is very fond of children promised to take six little girls in his neighborhood to a matinee. It happened that he himself and five of his little friends were so fair that they easily passed muster, as they stood in judgment before the ticket seller and the ticket taker. Three of the little girls were sisters, two of whom were very fair and the other a bit brown. Just as this little girl, who happened to be last in the procession, went by the ticket taker, that argus eyed sophisticated gentleman detected something which caused a deep, dark frown to mantle his brow and he did not allow her to pass. "I guess you have made a mistake," he called to the host of this theater party. "Those little girls," pointing to the fair ones, "may be admitted, but this one," designating the brown one, "can't." But the colored man was quite equal to the emergency. Fairly frothing at the mouth with anger, he asked the ticket taker what he meant, what he was trying to insinuate about that particular little girl. "Do you mean to tell me," he shouted in rage, "that I must go clear to the Philippine Islands to bring this child to the United States and then I can't take her to the theater in the National Capital?" The little ruse succeeded brilliantly, as he knew it would. "Beg your pardon," said the ticket taker, "don't know what I was thinking about. Of course she can go in." "What was the matter with me this afternoon mother?" asked the little brown girl innocently, when she mentioned the affair at home. "Why did the man at the theater let my two sisters and the other girls in and try to keep me out?" In relating this incident, the child's mother told me her little girl's question, which showed such blissful ignorance of the depressing, cruel conditions which confronted her, completely unnerved her for a time.

Altho [sic] white and colored teachers are under the same Board of Education and the system for the children of both races is said to be uniform, prejudice against the colored teachers in the public schools is manifested in a variety of ways. From 1870 to 1900 there was a colored superintendent at the head of the colored schools. During all that time the directors of the cooking, sewing, physical culture, manual training, music and art departments were colored people. Six years ago a change was inaugurated. The colored superintendent was legislated out of office and the directorships, without a single exception, were taken from colored teachers and given to the whites. There was no complaint about the work done by the colored directors, no more than is heard about every officer in every school. The directors of the art and physical culture departments were particularly fine. Now, no matter how competent or superior the colored teachers in our public schools may be, they know that they can never rise to the height of a directorship, can never hope to be more than an assistant and receive the meager salary therefore, unless the present regime is radically changed.

Not long ago one of the most distinguished kindergartners in the country came to deliver a course of lectures in Washington. The colored teachers were eager to attend, but they could not buy the coveted privilege for love or money. When they appealed to the director of kindergartens, they were told that the expert kindergartner had come to Washington under the auspices of private individuals, so that she could not possibly have them admitted. Realizing what a loss colored teachers had sustained in being deprived of the information and inspiration which these lectures afforded, one of the white teachers volunteered to repeat them as best she could for the benefit of her colored co-laborers for half the price she herself had paid, and the proposition was eagerly accepted by some.

Strenuous efforts are being made to run Jim Crow streetcars in the national capital. "Resolved, that a Jim Crow law should be adopted and enforced in the District of Columbia," was the subject of a discussion engaged in last January by the Columbian Debating Society of the George Washington University in our national capital, and the decision was rendered in favor of the affirmative. Representative Heflin, of Alabama, who introduced a bill providing for Jim Crow street cars in the District of Columbia last winter, has just received a letter from the president of the East Brookland Citizens' Association "indorsing [sic] the movement for separate street cars and sincerely hoping that you will be successful in getting this enacted into a law as soon as possible." Brookland is a suburb of Washington.

The colored laborer's path to a decent livelihood is by no means smooth. Into some of the trades unions here he is admitted, while from others he is excluded altogether. By the union men this is denied, altho [sic] I am personally acquainted with skilled workmen who tell me they are not admitted into the unions because they are colored. But even when they are allowed to join the unions they frequently derive little benefit, owing to certain tricks of the trade. When the word passes round that help is needed and colored laborers apply, they are often told by the union officials that they have secured all the men they needed, because the places are reserved for white men, until they have been provided with jobs, and colored men must remain idle, unless the supply of white men is too small.

I am personally acquainted with one of the most skilful laborers in the hardware business in Washington. For thirty years he has been working for the same firm. He told me he could not join the union, and that his employer had been almost forced to discharge him, because the union men threatened to boycott his store if he did not. If another man could have been found at the time to take his place he would have lost his job, he said. When no other human being can bring a refractory chimney or stove to its senses, this colored man is called upon as the court of last appeal. If he fails to subdue it, it is pronounced a hopeless case at once. And yet this expert workman receives much less for his services than do white men who cannot compare with him in skill.

And so I might go on citing instance after instance to show the variety of ways in which our people are sacrificed on the altar of prejudice in the Capital of the United States and how almost insurmountable are the obstacles which block his [sic] path to success. Early in life many a colored youth is so appalled by the helplessness and the hopelessness of his situation in this country that, in a sort of stoical despair he resigns himself to his fate. "What is the good of our trying to acquire an education? We can't all be preachers, teachers, doctors and lawyers. Besides those professions, there is almost nothing for colored people to do but engage in the most menial occupations, and we do not need an education for that." More than once such remarks, uttered by young men and women in our public schools who possess brilliant intellects, have wrung my heart.

It is impossible for any white person in the United States, now matter how sympathetic and broad, to realize what life would mean to him if his incentive to effort were suddenly snatched away. To the lack of incentive to effort, which is the awful shadow under which we live, may be traced the wreck and ruin of scores of colored youth. And surely nowhere in the world do oppression and persecution based solely on the color of the skin appear more hateful and hideous than in the capital of the United States, because the chasm between the principles upon which this Government was founded, in which it still professes to believe, and those which are daily practiced under the protection of the flag, yawns so wide and deep.

Source: Accessed at American Rhetoric.com. Available online. URL: http://www.american.rhetoric.com/speeches/marychurchterellcolored.htm.

7. "THE FUNDAMENTAL PRINCIPLE OF A REPUBLIC"

ANNA HOWARD SHAW, JUNE 21, 1915, OGDENBURG, NEW YORK

When I came into your hall tonight, I thought of the last time I was in your city. Twenty- one years ago I came here with Susan B. Anthony, and we came for exactly the same purpose as that for which we are here tonight. Boys have been born since that time and have become voters, and the women are still trying to persuade American men to believe in the fundamental principles of democracy, and I never quite feel as if it was a fair field to argue this question with men, because in doing it you have to assume that a man who professes to believe in a Republican form of government does not believe in a Republican form of government, for the only thing that woman's enfranchisement means at all is that a government which claims to be a Republic should be a Republic, and not an aristocracy. The difficulty with discussing this question with those who oppose us is that they make any number of arguments but none of them have anything to do with Woman's Suffrage; they always have something to do with something else, therefore the arguments which we have to make rarely ever have anything to do with the subject, because we have to answer our opponents who always escape the subject as far as possible in order to have any sort of reason in connection with what they say.

Now one of two things is true: either a Republic is a desirable form of government, or else it is not. If it is, then we should have it, if it is not then we ought not to pretend that we have it. We ought at least be true to our ideals, and the men of New York have for the first time in their lives, the rare opportunity on the second day of next November, of making the state truly a part of the Republic. It is the greatest opportunity which has ever come to the men of the state. They have never had so serious a problem to solve before, they will never have a more serious problem to solve in any future of our nation's life, and the thing that disturbs me more than anything else in connection with it is that so few people realize what a profound problem they have to solve on November 2. It is not merely a trifling matter; it is not a little thing that does not concern the state, it is the most vital problem we could have, and any man who goes to the polls on the second day of next November without thoroughly informing himself in regard to this subject is unworthy to be a citizen of this state, and unfit to cast a ballot.

If woman's suffrage is wrong, it is a great wrong; if it is right, it is a profound and fundamental principle, and we all know, if we know what a Republic is, that it is the fundamental principle upon which a Republic must rise. Let us see where we are as a people; how we act here and what we think we are. The difficulty with the men of this country is that they are so consistent in their inconsistency that they are not aware of having been inconsistent; because their consistency has been so continuous and their inconsistency so consecutive that it has never been broken, from the beginning of our Nation's life to the present time. If we trace our history back we will find that from the very dawn of our existence as a people, men have been imbued with a spirit and a vision more lofty than they have been able to live; they have been led by visions of the sublimest truth, both in regard to religion and in regard to government that ever inspired the souls of men from the time the Puritans left the old world to come to this country, led by the Divine ideal which is the sublimest and the supremest ideal in religious freedom which men have ever known, the theory that a man has a right to worship God according to the dictates of his own conscience, without the intervention of any other man or any other group of men. And it was this theory, this vision of the right of the human soul which led men first to the shores of this country.

Now, nobody can deny that they are sincere, honest, and earnest men. No one can deny that the Puritans were men of profound conviction, and yet these men who gave up everything in behalf of an ideal, hardly established their communities in this new country before they began to practice exactly the same sort of persecutions on other men which had been practiced upon them. They settled in their communities on the New England shores and when they formed their compacts by which they governed their local societies, they permitted no man to have a voice in the affairs unless he was a member of the church, and not a member of any church, but a member of the particular church which dominated the particular community in which he happened to be. In Massachusetts they drove the Baptists down to Rhode Island; in Connecticut they drove the Presbyterians over to New Jersey; they burned the Quakers in Massachusetts and ducked the witches, and no colony, either Catholic or Protestant allowed a Jew to have a voice. And so a man must worship God according to the conscience of the particular community in which he was located, and yet they called that religious freedom, they were not able to live the ideal of religious liberty, and from that time to this the men of this government have been following along the same line of inconsistency, while they too have been following a vision of equal grandeur and power.

Never in the history of the world did it dawn upon the human mind as it dawned upon your ancestors, what it would mean for men to be free. They got the vision of a government in which the people would be the supreme power, and so inspired by this vision men wrote such documents as were went from the Massachusetts legislature, from the New York legislature and from the Pennsylvania group over to the Parliament of Great Britain, which rang with the profoundest measures of freedom and justice. They did not equivocate in a single word when they wrote the Declaration of Independence; no one can dream that these men had not got the sublimest ideal of democracy which had ever dawned upon the souls of men. But as soon as the war was over and our government was formed, instead of asking the question, who shall be the governing force in this great new Republic, when they brought those thirteen little territories together, they began to eliminate instead of include the men who should be the great governing forces, and they said, who shall have the voice in this great new Republic, and you would have supposed that such men as fought the Revolutionary War would have been able to answer that every man who has fought, everyone who has given up all he has and all he has been able to accumulate shall be free, it never entered their minds. These excellent ancestors of yours had not been away from the old world long enough to realize that man is of more value than his purse, so they said every man who has an estate in the government shall have a voice; and they said what shall that estate be? And they answered that a man who had property valued at two hundred and fifty dollars will be able to cast a vote, and so they sang "The land of the free and the home of the brave." And they wrote into their Constitution, "All males who pay taxes on $250 shall cast a vote," and they called themselves a Republic, and we call ourselves a Republic, and they were not quite so much of a Republic that we should be called a Republic yet. We might call ourselves angels, but that wouldn't make us angels, you have got to be an angel before you are an angel, and you have got to be a Republic before you are a Republic. Now what did we do? Before the word "male" in the local compacts, they wrote the word "Church-members"; and they wrote in the word "taxpayer." Then there arose a great Democrat, Thomas Jefferson, who looked down into the day when you and I are living and saw that the rapidly accumulated wealth in the hands of a few men would endanger the liberties of the people, and he knew what you and I know, that no power under heaven or among men is known in a Republic by which men can defend their liberties except by the power of the ballot, and so the Democratic party took another step in the evolution of the Republic out of a monarchy and they rubbed out the word "taxpayer" and wrote in the word "white", and then the Democrats thought the millennium had come, and they sang " The land of the free and the home of the brave" as lustily as the Republicans had sung it before them and spoke of the divine right of motherhood with the same thrill in their voices and at the same time they were selling mother's

babies by the pound on the auction block—and mothers apart from their babies. Another arose who said a man is not a good citizen because he is white, he is a good citizen because he is a man, and the Republican party took out that progressive evolutionary eraser and rubbed out the word "white" from before the word "male" and could not think of another word to put in there- they were all in, black and white, rich and poor, wise and otherwise, drunk and sober; not a man left out to be put in, and so the Republicans could not write anything before the word "male", and they had to let the little word, "male" stay alone by itself.

And God said in the beginning, "It is not good for man to stand alone." That is why we are here tonight, and that is all that woman's suffrage means; just to repeat again and again that first declaration of the Divine, "It is not good for man to stand alone," and so the women of this state are asking that the word "male" shall be stricken out of the Constitution altogether and that the Constitution stand as it ought to have stood in the beginning and as it must before this state is any part of a Republic. Every citizen possessing the necessary qualifications shall be entitled to cast one vote at every election, and have that vote counted. We are not asking as our Anti-Suffrage friends think we are, for any of awful things that we hear will happen if we are allowed to vote; we are simply asking that that government which professes to be a Republic shall be a Republic and not pretend to be what it is not.

Now what is a Republic? Take your dictionary, encyclopedia, lexicon or anything else you like and look up the definition and you will find that a Republic is a form of government in which the laws are enacted by representatives elected by the people. Now when did the people of New York ever elect their own representatives? Never in the world. The men of New York have, and I grant you that men are people, admirable people, as far as they go, but they only go half way. There is still another half of the people who have not elected representatives, and you never read a definition of a Republic in which half of the people elect representatives to govern the whole of the people. That is an aristocracy and that is just what we are. We have been many kinds of aristocracies. We have been a hierarchy of church members, than an oligarchy of sex.

There are two old theories, which are dying today. Dying hard, but dying. One of them is dying on the plains of Flanders and the Mountains of Galicia and Austria, and that is the theory of the divine right of kings. The other is dying here in the state of New York and Massachusetts and New Jersey and Pennsylvania and that is the divine right of sex. Neither of them had a foundation in reason, or justice, or common sense.

Now I want to make this proposition, and I believe every man will accept it. Of course he will if he is intelligent. Whenever a Republic prescribes the qualifications as applying equally to all the citizens of the Republic, when the Republic says in order to vote, a citizen must be twenty-one years of age, it applies to all alike, there is no discrimination against any race or sex. When the government says that a citizen must be a native-born citizen or a naturalized citizen that applies to all; we are either born or naturalized, somehow or other we are here. Whenever the government says that a citizen, in order to vote, must be a resident of a community a certain length of time, and of the state a certain length of time and of the nation a certain length of time, that applies to all equally. There is no discrimination. We might go further and we might say that in order to vote the citizen must be able to read his ballot. We have not gone that far yet. We have been very careful of male ignorance in these United States. I was much interested, as perhaps many of you, in reading the Congressional Record this last winter over the debate over the immigration bill, and when that illiteracy clause was introduced into the immigration bill, what fear there was in the souls of men for fear we would do injustice

to some of the people who might want to come to our shores, and I was much interested in the language in which the President vetoed the bill, when he declared that by inserting the clause we would keep out of our shores a large body of very excellent people. I could not help wondering then how it happens that male ignorance is so much less ignorant than female ignorance. When I hear people say that if women were permitted to vote a large body of ignorant people would vote, and therefore because an ignorant woman would vote, no intelligent women should be allowed to vote, I wonder why we have made it so easy for male ignorance and so hard for female ignorance.

When I was a girl, years ago, I lived in the back woods and there the number of votes cast at each election depended entirely upon the size of the ballot box. We had what was known as the old-tissue ballots and the man who got the most tissue in was the man elected. Now the best part of our community was very much disturbed by this method, and they did not know what to do in order to get a ballot both safe and secret; but they heard that over in Australia, where the women voted, they had a ballot which was both safe and secret, so we went over there and we got the Australian ballot and we brought it here. But when we got it over we found it was not adapted to this country, because in Australia they have to be able to read their ballot. Now the question was how could we adapt it to our conditions? Someone discovered that if you should put a symbol at the head of each column, like a rooster, or an eagle, or a hand holding a hammer, that if a man has intelligence to know the difference between a rooster and an eagle he will know which political party to vote for, and when the ballot was adapted it was a very beautiful ballot, it looked like a page from Life.

Now almost any American could vote that ballot, or if she had not that intelligence to know the difference between an eagle and a rooster, we could take the eagle out and put in the hen. Now when we take so much pains to adapt the ballot to the male intelligence of the United States, we should be very humble when we talk about female ignorance. Now if we should take a vote and the men had to read their ballot in order to vote it, more women could vote than men. But when the government says not only that you must be twenty-one years of age, a resident of the community and native born or naturalized, those are qualifications, but when it says that an elector must be a male, that is not a qualification for citizenship; that is an insurmountable barrier between one half of the people and the other half of the citizens and their rights as citizens. No such nation can call itself a Republic. It is only an aristocracy. That barrier must be removed before the government can become a Republic, and that is exactly what we are asking right now, that the last step in the evolutionary process be taken on November 2d. and that this great state of New York shall become in fact as it is in theory, a part of a government of the people, by the people, and for the people.

Men know the inconsistencies themselves; they realize it in one way while they do not realize it in another, because you never heard a man make a political speech when he did not speak of this country as a whole as though the thing existed which does not exist and that is that the people were equally free, because you hear them declare over and over again on the Fourth of July "under God the people rule." They know it is not true, but they say it with a great hurrah, and they repeat over and over again that clause from the Declaration of Independence. "Governments derive their just powers from the consent of the governed," and they see how they can prevent half of us from giving our consent to anything, and then they give it to us on the Fourth of July in two languages, so if it is not true in one it will be in the other, "vox populi, vox Dei." "The voice of the people is the voice of God," and the orator forgets that in the people's voice there is a soprano as well as a bass. If the voice of the people is the voice of God, how are we ever going to know what God's voice is when we are content to listen to a bass solo? Now if it is true that the voice of the people is the voice of God, we will never know what the Deity's voice in government is until the bass and soprano are mingled together, the result of which will be the divine harmony. Take any of the magnificent appeals for freedom, which men make, and rob them of their universal application and you take the very life and soul out of them.

Where is the difficulty? Just in one thing and one thing only, that men are so sentimental. We used to believe that women were the sentimental sex, but they can not hold a tallow candle compared with the arc light of the men. Men are so sentimental in their attitude about women that they cannot reason about them. Now men are usually very fair to each other. I think the average man recognizes that he has no more right to anything at the hands of the government than has every other man. He has no right at all to anything to which every other man has not an equal right with himself. He says why have I a right to certain things in the government; why have I a right to life and liberty; why have I a right to this or this? Does he say because I am a man? Not at all, because I am human, and being human I have a right to everything which belongs to humanity, and every right which any other human being has, I have. And then he says of his neighbor, and my neighbor he also is human, therefore every right which belongs to me as a human being, belongs to him as a human being, and I have no right to anything under the government to which he is not equally entitled. And then up comes a woman, and then they say now she's a woman; she is not quite human, but she is my wife, or my sister, or my daughter, or an aunt, or my cousin. She is not quite human; she is only related to a human, and being related to a human a human will take care of her. So we have had that caretaking human being to look after us and they have not recognized that women too are equally human with men. Now if men could forget for a minute I believe the anti-suffragists say that we want men to forget that we are related to them, they don't know me if for a minute they could forget our relationship and remember that we are equally human with themselves, then they would say yes, and this human being, not because she is a woman, but because she is human is entitled to every privilege and every right under the government which I, as a human being am entitled to. The only reason men do not see as fairly in regard to women as they do in regard to each other is because they have looked upon us from an altogether different plane than what they have looked at men; that is because women have been the homemakers while men have been the so-called protectors, in the period of the world's civilization when people needed to be protected. I know that they say that men protect us now and when we ask them what they are protecting us from the only answer they can give is from themselves. I do not think that men need any very great credit for protecting us from themselves. They are not protecting us from any special thing from which we could not protect ourselves except themselves. Now this old time idea of protection was all right when the world needed this protection, but today the protection in civilization comes from within and not from without.

What are the arguments, which our good Anti-friends give us? We know that lately they have stopped to argue and call suffragists all sorts of creatures. If there is anything we believe that we do not believe, we have not heard about them, so the cry goes out of this; the cry of the infant's mind; the cry of a little child. The anti-suffragists' cries are all the cries of little children who are afraid of the unborn and are forever crying, "The goblins will catch you if you don't watch out." So that anything that has not been should not be and all that is right, when as a matter of fact if the world believed that we would be in a statical condition and never move, except back like a crab. And so the cry goes on.

When suffragists are feminists, and when I ask what that is no one is able to tell me. I would give anything to know what a feminist is. They say, would you like to be a feminist? If I could find out I would, you either have to be masculine or feminine and I prefer feminine. Then they cry that we are socialists, and anarchists. Just how a human can be both at the same time, I really do not know. If I know what socialism means it means absolute government and anarchism means no government at all. So we are feminists, socialists, anarchists, and Mormons or spinsters. Now that is about the list. I have not heard the last speech. Now as a matter of fact, as a unit we are nothing, as individuals we are like all other individuals.

We have our theories, our beliefs, but as suffragists we have but one belief, but one principle, but one theory and that is the right of a human being to have a voice in the government, under which he or she lives, on that we agree, if on nothing else. Whether we agree or not on religion or politics we are concerned. A clergyman asked me the other day, "By the way, what church does your official board belong to?" I said I don't know. He said, "Don't you know what religion your official board believes?" I said, "Really it never occurred to me, but I will look them up and see, they are not elected to my board because they believe in any particular church. We had no concern either as to what we believe as religionists or as to what we believe as women in regard to theories of government, except that one fundamental theory in the right of democracy. We do not believe in this fad or the other, but whenever any question is to be settled in any community, then the people of that community shall settle that question, the women people equally with the men people. That is all there is to it, and yet when it comes to arguing our case they bring up all sorts of arguments, and the beauty of it is they always answer all their own arguments. They never make an argument, but they answer it. When I was asked to answer one of their debates I said, " What is the use? Divide up their literature and let them destroy themselves."

I was followed up last year by a young, married woman from New Jersey. She left her husband home for three months to tell the women that their place was at home, and that they could not leave home long enough to go to the ballot box, and she brought all her arguments out in pairs and backed them up by statistics. The anti-suffragists can gather more statistics than any other person I ever saw, and there is nothing so sweet and calm as when they say, " You cannot deny this, because here are the figures, and figures never lie." Well they don't but some liars figure.

When they start out they always begin the same. She started by proving that it was no use to give the women the ballot because if they did have it they would not use it, and she had statistics to prove it. If we would not use it then I really can not see the harm of giving it to us, we would not hurt anybody with it and what an easy way for you men to get rid of us. No more suffrage meetings, never any nagging you again, no one could blame you for anything that went wrong with the town, if it did not run right, all you would have to say is, you have the power, why don't you go ahead and clean up.

Then the young lady, unfortunately for her first argument, proved by statistics, of which she had many, the awful results which happened where women did have the ballot; what awful laws have been brought about by women's vote; the conditions that prevail in the homes and how deeply women get interested in politics, because women are hysterical, and we can not think of anything else, we just forget our families, cease to care for our children, cease to love our husbands and just go to the polls and vote and keep on voting for ten hours a day 365 days in the year, never let up, if we ever get to the polls once you will never get us home, so that the women will not vote at all, and they will not do anything but vote. Now these are two very strong anti-suffrage arguments and they can prove them by figures. Then they will tell you that if women are permitted to vote it will be a great expense and no use because wives will vote just as their husbands do; even if we have no husbands, that would not effect the result because we would vote just as our husbands would vote if we had one. How I wish the anti-suffragists could make the men believe that; if they could make men believe that the women would vote just as they wanted them to do you think we would ever have to make another speech or hold another meeting, we would have to vote whether we wanted to or not.

And then the very one who will tell you that women will vote just as their husbands do will tell you in five minutes that they will not vote as their husbands will and then the discord in the homes, and the divorce. Why, they have discovered that in Colorado there are more divorces than there were before women began to vote, but they have forgotten to tell you that there are four times as many people in Colorado today as there were when women began to vote, and that may have some effect, particularly as these people went from the East. Then they will tell you all the trouble that happens in the home. A gentleman told me that in California and when he was talking I had a wonderful thing pass through my mind, because he said that he and his wife had lived together for twenty years and never had a difference in opinion in the whole twenty years and he was afraid if women began to vote that his wife would vote differently from him and then that beautiful harmony which they had had for twenty years would be broken, and all the time he was talking I could not help wondering which was the idiot because I knew that no intelligent human beings could live together for twenty years and not have a differences of opinion. All the time he was talking I looked at that splendid type of manhood and thought, how would a man feel being tagged up by a little woman for twenty years saying, "Me too, me too." I would not want to live in a house with a human being for twenty years who agreed with everything I said. The stagnation of a frog pond would be hilarious compared to that. What a reflection is that on men. If we should say that about men we would never hear the last of it. Now it may be that the kind of men being that the anti-suffragists live with is that kind, but they are not the kind we live with and we could not do it. Great big overgrown babies! Cannot be disputed without having a row! While we do not believe that men are saints, by any means, we do believe that the average American man is a fairly good sort of fellow.

In fact my theory of the whole matter is exactly opposite, because instead of believing that men and women will quarrel, I think just the opposite thing will happen. I think just about six weeks before election a sort of honeymoon will start and it will continue until they will think they are again hanging over the gate, all in order to get each other's votes. When men want each other's votes they do not go up and knock them down; they are very solicitous of each other, if they are thirsty or need a smoke or—well we don't worry about home. The husband and wife who are quarreling after the vote are quarreling now. Then the other belief that the women would not vote if they had a vote and would not do anything else; and would vote just as their husbands vote, and would not vote like their husbands; that women have so many burdens that they cannot bear another burden, and that women are the leisure class.

I remember having Reverend Dr. Abbott speak before the anti-suffrage meeting in Brooklyn and he stated that if women were permitted to vote we would not have so much time for charity and philanthropy, and I would like to say, "Thank God, there will not be so much need of charity and philanthropy." The end and aim of the suffrage is not to furnish an opportunity for excellent old ladies to be charitable. There are two words that we ought to be able to get along without, and they are charity and philanthropy. They are not needed in a Republic. If we put in the word "opportunity" instead, that is what Republics stand for. Our doctrine is not to extend the length of our bread lines or the size of our soup kitchens, what we need is for men to have the opportunity to buy their own bread and eat their own soup. We women have used up our lives and strength in fool charities, and we have made more paupers than we have ever helped by the folly of our charities and philanthropies; the unorganized methods by which we deal with the conditions of society, and instead of giving people charity we must learn to give them an opportunity to develop and make themselves capable of earning the bread; no human being has the right to live without toil; toil of some kind, and that old theory that we used to hear "The world owes a man a living" never was true and never will be true. This world does not owe anybody a living, what it does owe to every human being is the opportunity to earn a living. We have a right to the opportunity and then the right to the living thereafter. We want it. No woman, any more than a man, has the right to live an idle life in this world, we must learn to give back something for the space occupied and we must do our duty wherever duty calls, and the woman herself must decide where her duty calls, just as a man does.

Now they tell us we should not vote because we have not the time, we are so burdened that we should not have any more burdens. Then, if that is so, I think we ought to allow the women to vote instead of the men, since we pay a man anywhere from a third to a half more than we do women it would be better to use up the cheap time of the women instead of the dear time of the men. And talking about time you would think it took about a week to vote.

A dear, good friend of mine in Omaha said, "Now Miss Shaw," and she held up her child in her arms, "is not this my job." I said it certainly is, and then she said, "How can I go to the polls and vote and neglect my baby?" I said, "Has your husband a job?" and she said, "Why you know he has." I did know it; he was a banker and a very busy one. I said, "Yet your husband said he was going to leave and go down to the polls and vote," and she said, "Oh yes, he is so very interested in elections." Then I said, "What an advantage you have over your husband, he has to leave his job and you can take your job with you and you do not need to neglect your job." Is it not strange that the only time a woman might neglect her baby is on election day, and then the dear old Antis hold up their hands and say, "You have neglected your baby." A woman can belong to a whist club and go once a week and play whist, she cannot take her baby to the whist club, and she has to keep whist herself without trying to keep a baby whist. She can go to the theatre, to church or a picnic and no one is worrying about the baby, but to vote and everyone cries out about the neglect. You would think on Election Day that a woman grabbed up her baby and started out and just dropped it somewhere and paid no attention to it. It used to be asked when we had the question box, "Who will take care of the babies?" I did not know what person could be got to take care of all the babies, so I thought I would go out West and find out. I went to Denver and I found that they took care of their babies just the same on election day as they did on every other day; they took their baby along with them, when they went to put a letter in a box they took their baby along and when they went to put their ballot in the box they took their baby along. If the mother had to stand in line and the baby got restless she would joggle the go-cart and when she went in to vote a neighbor would joggle the go-cart and if there was no neighbor there was the candidate and he would joggle the cart. That is one day in the year when you can get a hundred people to take care of any number of babies. I have never worried about the babies on Election Day since that time.

Then the people will tell you that women are so burdened with their duties that they can not vote, and they will tell you that women are the leisure class and the men are worked to death: but the funniest argument of the lady who followed me about in the West: Out there they were great in the temperance question, and she declared that we were not prohibition, or she declared that we were. Now in North Dakota which is one of the first prohibition states, and they are dry because they want to be dry. In that state she wanted to prove to them that if women were allowed to vote they would vote North Dakota wet and she had her figures; that women had not voted San Francisco dry, or Portland dry, or Chicago dry. Of course we had not voted on the question in Chicago, but that did not matter. Then we went to Montana, which is wet. They have it wet there because they want it wet, so that any argument that she could bring to bear upon them to prove that we would make North Dakota wet and keep it wet would have given us the state, but that would not work, so she brought out the figures out of her pocket to prove to the men of Montana that if women were allowed to vote in Montana they would vote Montana dry. She proved that in two years in Illinois they had voted ninety-six towns dry, and that at that rate we would soon get over Montana and have it dry. Then I went to Nebraska and as soon as I reached there a reporter came and asked me the question, " How are the women going to vote on the prohibition question?" I said, " I really don't know. I know how we will vote in North Dakota, we will vote wet in North Dakota; in Montana we will vote dry, but how we will vote in Nebraska, I don't know, but I will let you know just as soon as the lady from New Jersey comes."

We will either vote as our husbands vote or we will not vote as our husbands vote. We either have time to vote or we don't have time to vote. We will either not vote at all or we will vote all the time. It reminds me of the story of the old Irish woman who had twin boys and they were so much alike that the neighbors could not tell them apart, so one of the neighbors said, " Now Mrs. Mahoney, you have two of the finest twin boys I ever saw in all my life, but how do you know them apart." "Oh," she says, "That's easy enough, any one could tell them apart. When I want to know which is which I just put my finger in Patsey's mouth and if he bites it is Mikey."

Now what does it matter whether the women will vote as their husbands do or will not vote; whether they have time or have not; or whether they will vote for prohibition or not. What has that to do with the fundamental question of democracy, no one has yet discovered. But they cannot argue on that; they cannot argue on the fundamental basis of our existence so that they have to get off on all of these side tricks to get anything approaching an argument. So they tell you that democracy is a form of government. It is not. It was before governments were; it will prevail when governments cease to be; it is more than a form of government; it is a great spiritual force emanating from the heart of the Infinite, transforming human character until some day, some day in the distant future, man by the power of the spirit of democracy, will be able to look back into the face of the Infinite and answer, as man can not answer today, "One is our Father, even God, and all we people are the children of one family." And when democracy has taken possession of human lives no man will ask from him to grant to his neighbor, whether that neighbor be a man or woman; no man will then be willing to allow another man to rise to power on his shoulders, nor will he be willing to rise to power on the shoulders of another prostrate human being. But that has not yet taken possession of us, but some day we will be free, and we are getting nearer and nearer to it all the time; and never in the history of our country had the men and women of this nation a better right to approach it than they have today; never in the history of the nation did it stand out so splendidly as it stands today, and never ought we men and women to be more grateful for anything than that there presides in the White House today a man of peace.

As so our good friends go on with one thing after another and they say if women should vote they will have to sit on the jury and they ask whether we will like to see a woman sitting on a jury. I have seen some juries that ought to be sat on and I have seen some women that would be glad to sit on anything. When a woman stands up all day behind a counter, or when she stands all day doing a washing she is glad enough to sit; and when she stands for seventy-five cents she would like to sit for two dollars a day. But don't you think we need some women on juries in this country? You read your paper and you read that one day last week or the week before or the week before a little girl went out to school and never came back; another little girl was sent on an errand and never came back; another little girl was left in charge of a little sister and her mother went out to work and when she returned the little girl was not there, and you read it over and over again, and the horror of it strikes you. You read that in these United States five thousand young girls go out and never come back, don't you think that the men and women the vampires of our country who fatten and grow rich on the ignorance and innocence of children would rather face Satan himself than a jury of mothers. I would like to see some juries of mothers. I lived in the slums of Boston for three years and I know the need of juries of mothers.

Then they tell us that if women were permitted to vote that they would take office, and you would suppose that we just took office in this country. There is a difference of getting an office in this country and in Europe. In England, a man stands for Parliament and in this country he runs for Congress, and so long as it is a question of running for office I don't think women have much chance, especially with our present hobbles. There are some women who want to hold office and I may as well own up. I am one of them. I have been wanting to hold office for more than thirty-five years. Thirty-five years ago I lived in the slums of Boston and ever since then I have wanted to hold office. I have applied to the major to be made an officer; I wanted to be the greatest office holder in the world, I wanted the position of the man I think is to be the most envied, as far as the ability to do good is concerned, and that is a policeman. I have always wanted to be a policeman and I have applied to be appointed policeman and the very first question that was asked me was, "Could you knock a man down and take him to jail?" That is some people's idea of the highest service that a policeman can render a community. Knock somebody down and take him to jail! My idea is not so much to arrest criminals, as it is to prevent crime. That is what is needed in the police force of every community. When I lived for three years in the back alleys of Boston. I saw there that it was needed to prevent crime and from that day? This I believe there is no great public gathering of any sort whatever where we do not need women on the police force; we need them at every moving picture show, every dance house, every restaurant, every hotel, and every great store with a great bargain counter and every park and every resort where the vampires who fatten on the crimes and vices of men and women gather. We need women on the police force and we will have them there some day.

If women vote, will they go to war? They are great on having us fight. They tell you that the government rests on force, but there are a great many kinds of force in this world, and never in the history of man were the words of the Scriptures proved to the extent that they are today, that the men of the nation that lives by the sword shall die by the sword. When I was speaking in North Dakota from an automobile with a great crowd and a great number of men gathered around a man who had been sitting in front of a store whittling a stick called out to another man and asked if women get the vote will they go over to Germany and fight the Germans? I said, "Why no, why should we go over to Germany and fight Germans?" "If Germans come over here would you fight?" I said, "Why should we women fight men, but if Germany should send an army of women over here, then we would show you what we would do. We would go down and meet them and say, "Come on, let's go up to the opera house and talk this matter over." It might grow wearisome but it would not be death.

Would it not be better if the heads of the governments in Europe had talked things over? What might have happened to the world if a dozen men had gotten together in Europe and settled the awful controversy, which is today discriminating the nations of Europe? We women got together there last year, over in Rome, the delegates from twenty-eight different nations of women, and for two weeks we discussed problems which had like interests to us all. They were all kinds of Protestants, both kinds of Catholics, Roman, and Greek, three were Jews and Mohamedans, but we were not there to discuss our different religious beliefs, but we were there to discuss the things that were of vital importance to us all, and at the end of the two weeks, after the discussions were over we passed a great number of resolutions. We discussed white slavery, the immigration laws, we discussed the spread of contagious and infectious diseases; we discussed various forms of education, and various forms of juvenile criminals, every question which every nation has to meet, and at the end of two weeks we passed many resolutions, but two of them were passed unanimously. One was presented by myself as Chairman on the Committee on Suffrage and on that resolution we called upon all civilizations of the world to give to women equal rights with men and there was not a dissenting vote.

The other resolution was on peace. We believed then and many of us believe today, notwithstanding all the discussion that is going on, we believe and we will continue to believe that preparedness for war is an incentive to war, and the only hope of permanent peace is the systematic and scientific disarmament of all the nations of the world, and we passed a resolution and passed it unanimously to that effect. A few days afterward I attended a large reception given by the American ambassador, and there was an Italian diplomat there and he spoke rather superciliously and said, "You women think you have been having a very remarkable convention, and I understand that a resolution on peace was offered by the Germans, the French women seconded it, and the British presiding presented it and it was carried unanimously." We none of us dreamed what was taking place at that time, but he knew and we learned it before we arrived home, that awful, awful thing that was about to sweep over the nations of the world. The American ambassador replied to the Italian diplomat and said, "Yes, Prince, it was a remarkable convention, and it is a remarkable thing that the only people who can get together internationally and discuss their various problems without acrimony and without a sword at their side are the women of the world, but we men, even when we go to the Hague to discuss peace, we go with a sword dangling at our side." It is remarkable that even at this age men can not discuss international problems and discuss them in peace.

When I turned away from that place up in North Dakota that man in the crowd called out again, just as we were leaving, and said, "Well what does a woman know about war anyway?" I had read my paper that morning and I knew what the awful headline was, and I saw a gentleman standing in the crowd with a paper in his pocket, and I said, "Will that gentleman hold the paper up." And he held it up, and the headline read, "250,000 Men Killed Since the War Began". I said, "You ask me what a woman knows about war? No woman can read that line and comprehend the awful horror; no woman knows the significance of 250,000 dead men, but you tell me that one man lay dead and I might be able to tell you something of its awful meaning to one woman. I would know that years before a woman whose heart beat in unison with her love and her desire for motherhood walked day by day with her face to an open grave, with courage, which no man has ever surpassed, and if she did not fill that grave, if she lived, and if there was laid in her arms a tiny little bit of helpless humanity, I would know that there went out from her soul such a cry of thankfulness as none save a mother could know. And then I would know, what men have not yet learned that women are human; that they have human hopes and human passions,

aspirations and desires as men have, and I would know that that mother had laid aside all those hopes and aspirations for herself, laid them aside for her boy, and if after years had passed by she forgot her nights of sleeplessness and her days of fatiguing toil in her care of her growing boy, and when at last he became a man and she stood looking up into his eyes and beheld him, bone of her bone and flesh of her flesh, for out of her woman's life she had carved twenty beautiful years that went into the making of a man; and there he stands, the most wonderful thing in all the world; for in all the Universe of God there is nothing more sublimely wonderful than a strong limbed, clean hearted, keen brained, aggressive young man, standing as he does on the border line of life, ready to reach out and grapple with its problems. O, how wonderful he is, and he is hers. She gave her life for him, and in an hour this country calls him out and in an hour he lies dead; that wonderful, wonderful thing lies dead; and sitting by his side, that mother looking into the dark years to come knows that when her son died her life's hope died with him, and in the face of that wretched motherhood, what man dare ask what a woman knows of war. And that is not all. Read your papers, you can not read it because it is not printable; you cannot tell it because it is not speakable, you cannot even think it because it is not thinkable, the horrible crimes perpetrated against women by the blood drunken men of the war.

You read your paper again and the second headlines read, "It Costs Twenty Millions of Dollars a Day," for what? To buy the material to slaughter the splendid results of civilization of the centuries. Men whom it has taken centuries to build up and make into great scientific forces of brain, the flower of the manhood of the great nations of Europe, and we spend twenty millions of dollars a day to blot out all the results of civilization of hundreds and hundreds of years. And what do we do? We lay a mortgage on every unborn child for a hundred and more years to come. Mortgage his brain, his brawn, and every pulse of his heart in order to pay the debt, to buy the material to slaughter the men of our country. And that is not all, the greatest crime of war is the crime against the unborn. Read what they are doing. They are calling out every man, every young man, and every virile man from seventeen to forty-five or fifty years old; they are calling them out. All the splendid scientific force and energy of the splendid virile manhood are being called out to be food for the cannon, and they are leaving behind the degenerate, defective imbecile, the unfit, the criminals, the diseased to be the fathers of children yet to be born. The crime of crimes of the war is the crime against the unborn children, and in the face of the fact that women are driven out of the home shall men ask if women shall fight if they are permitted to vote.

No, we women do not want the ballot in order that we may fight, but we do want the ballot in order that we may help men to keep from fighting, whether it is in the home or in the state, just as the home is not without the man, so the state is not without the woman, and you can no more build up homes without men than you can build up the state without women. We are needed everywhere where human problems are to be solved. Men and women must go through this world together from the cradle to the grave; it is God's way and the fundamental principle of a Republican form of government.

Source: Accessed at Historic Speeches, sojust. net. Available online. URL: http://www.sojust.net/speeches/anna_shaw_republic.html.

8. "THE CRISIS"

CARRIE CHAPMAN CATT, SEPTEMBER 7, 1916, ATLANTIC CITY, NEW JERSEY

I have taken for my subject, "The Crisis," because I believe that a crisis has come in our movement which, if recognized and the opportunity seized with vigor, enthusiasm and will, means the final victory of our great cause in the very near future. I am aware that some suffragists do not share this belief; they see no signs nor symptoms today which were not present yesterday; no manifestations in the year 1916 which differ significantly from those in the year 1910. To them, the movement has been a steady, normal growth from the beginning and must so continue until the end. I can only defend my claim with the plea that it is better to imagine a crisis where none exists than to fail to recognize one when it comes; for a crisis is a culmination of events which calls for new considerations and new decisions. A failure to answer the call may mean an opportunity lost, a possible victory postponed.

The object of the life of an organized movement is to secure its aim. Necessarily, it must obey the law of evolution and pass through the stages of agitation and education and finally through the stage of realization. As one has put it: "A new idea floats in the air over the heads of the people and for a long, indefinite period evades their understanding but, by and by, when through familiarity, human vision grows clearer, it is caught out of the clouds and crystalized into law." Such a period comes to every movement and is its crisis. In my judgment, that crucial moment, bidding us to renewed consecration and redoubled activity has come to our cause. I believe our victory hangs within our grasp, inviting us to pluck it out of the clouds and establish it among the good things of the world.

If this be true, the time is past when we should say: "Men and women of America, look upon that wonderful idea up there; see, one day it will come down." Instead, the time has come to shout aloud in every city, village and hamlet, and in tones so clear and jubilant that they will reverberate from every mountain peak and echo from shore to shore: "The woman's Hour has struck." Suppose suffragists as a whole do not believe a crisis has come and do not extend their hands to grasp the victory, what will happen? Why, we shall all continue to work and our cause will continue to hang, waiting for those who possess a clearer vision and more daring enterprise.

On the other hand, suppose we reach out with united earnestness and determination to grasp our victory while it still hangs a bit too high? Has any harm been done? None!

Therefore, fellow suffragists, I invite your attention to the signs which point to a crisis and your consideration of plans for turning the crisis into victory.

FIRST: We are passing through a world crisis. All thinkers of every land tell us so; and that nothing after the great war will be as it was before. Those who profess to know, claim that 100 millions of dollars are being spent on the war every day and that 2 years of war have cost 50 billions of dollars or 10 times more than the total expense of the American Civil War. Our own country has sent 35 millions of dollars abroad for relief expenses.

Were there no other effects to come from the world's war, the transfer of such unthinkably vast sums of money from the usual avenues to those wholly abnormal would give so severe a jolt to organized society that it would vibrate around the world and bring untold changes in its wake.

But three and a half millions of lives have been lost. The number becomes the more impressive when it is remembered that the entire population of the American Colonies was little more than three and one-half millions. These losses have been the lives of men within the age of economic production. They have been taken abruptly from the normal business of the world and every human activity from that of the humblest, unskilled labor to art, science and literature has been weakened by their loss. Millions of other men will go to their homes, blind, crippled and incapacitated to do the work they once performed. The stability of human institutions has never before suffered so tremendous a shock. Great men are trying to think out the consequences but one and all proclaim that no imagination can find color or form bold enough to paint the picture of the world after the war. Brit-

ish and Russian, German and Austrian, French and Italian agree that it will lead to social and political revolution throughout the entire world. Whatever comes, they further agree that the war presages a total change in the status of women.

A simple-minded man in West Virginia, when addressed upon the subject of woman suffrage in that State, replied, "We've been so used to keepin' our women down, 'twould seem queer not to." He expressed what greater men feel but do not say. Had the wife of that man spoken in the same clear-thinking fashion, she would have said, "We women have been so used to being kept down that it would seem strange to get up. Nature intended women for door-mats." Had she so expressed herself, these two would have put the entire anti-suffrage argument in a nut-shell.

In Europe, from the Polar Circle to the Aegean Sea, women have risen as though to answer that argument. Everywhere they have taken the places made vacant by men and in so doing, they have grown in self-respect and in the esteem of their respective nations. In every land, the people have reverted to the primitive division of labor and while the men have gone to war, women have cultivated the fields in order that the army and nation may be fed. No army can succeed and no nation can endure without food; those who supply it are a war power and a peace power.

Women by the thousands have knocked at the doors of munition factories and, in the name of patriotism, have begged for the right to serve their country there. Their services were accepted with hesitation but the experiment once made, won reluctant but universal praise. An official statement recently issued in Great Britain announced that 660,000 women were engaged in making munitions in that country alone. In a recent convention of munition workers, composed of men and women, a resolution was unanimously passed informing the government that they would forego vacations and holidays until the authorities announced that their munition supplies were sufficient for the needs of the war and Great Britain pronounced the act the highest patriotism. Lord Derby addressed such a meeting and said, "When the history of the war is written, I wonder to whom the greatest credit will be given; to the men who went to fight or to the women who are working in a way that many people hardly believed that it was possible for them to work." Lord Sydenham added his tribute. Said he, "It might fairly be claimed that women have helped to save thousands of lives and to change the entire aspect of the war. Wherever intelligence, care and close attention have been needed, women have distinguished themselves." A writer in the London *Times* of July 18, 1916, said: "But, for women, the armies could not have held the field for a month; the national call to arms could not have been made or sustained; the country would have perished of inanition and disorganization. If, indeed, it be true that the people have been one, it is because the genius of women has been lavishly applied to the task of reinforcing and complementing the genius of men. The qualities of steady industry, adaptability, good judgement and concentration of mind which men do not readily associate with women have been conspicuous features."

On fields of battle, in regular and improvised hospitals, women have given tender and skilled care to the wounded and are credited with the restoration of life to many, heroism and self-sacrifice have been frankly acknowledged by all the governments; but their endurance, their skill, the practicality of their service, seem for the first time, to have been recognized by governments as "war power." So, thinking in war terms, great men have suddenly discovered that women are "war assets." Indeed, Europe is realizing, as it never did before, that women are holding together the civilization for which men are fighting. A great search-light has been thrown upon the business of nation-building and it has been demonstrated in every European land that it is a partnership with equal, but different responsibilities resting upon the two partners.

It is not, however, in direct war work alone that the latent possibilities of women have been made manifest. In all the belligerent lands, women have found their way to high posts of administration where no women would have been trusted two years ago and the testimony is overwhelming that they have filled their posts with entire satisfaction to the authorities. They have dared to stand in pulpits (once too sacred to be touched by the unholy feet of a woman) and there, without protest, have appealed to the Father of All in behalf of their stricken lands. They have come out of the kitchen where there was too little to cook and have found a way to live by driving cabs, motors and streetcars. Many a woman has turned her hungry children over to a neighbor and has gone forth to find food for both mothers and both families of children and has found it in strange places and occupations. Many a drawing-room has been closed and the maid who swept and dusted it is now cleaning streets that the health of the city may be conserved. Many a woman who never before slept in a bed of her own making, or ate food not prepared by paid labor, is now sole mistress of parlor and kitchen.

In all the warring countries, women are postmen, porters, railway conductors, ticket, switch and signal men. Conspicuous advertisements invite women to attend agricultural, milking and motor-car schools. They are employed as police in Great Britain and women detectives have recently been taken on the government staff. In Berlin, there are over 3,000 women streetcar conductors and 3,500 women are employed on the general railways. In every city and country, women are doing work for which they would have been considered incompetent two years ago.

The war will soon end and the armies will return to their native lands. To many a family, the men will never come back. The husband who returns to many a wife, will eat no bread the rest of his life save of her earning.

What then, will happen after the war? Will the widows left with families to support cheerfully leave their well-paid posts for those commanding lower wages? Not without protest! Will the wives who now must support crippled husbands give up their skilled work and take up the occupations which were open to them before the war? Will they resignedly say: "The woman who has a healthy husband who can earn for her, has a right to tea and raisin cake, but the woman who earns for herself and a husband who has given his all to his country, must be content with butterless bread?" Not without protest! On the contrary, the economic axiom, denied and evaded for centuries, will be blazoned on every factory, counting house and shop: "Equal pay for equal work"; and common justice will slowly, but surely enforce that law. The European woman has risen. She may not realize it yet, but the woman "door-mat" in every land has unconsciously become a "door-jamb"! She will have become accustomed to her new dignity by the time the men come home. She will wonder how she ever could have been content lying across the threshold now that she discovers the upright jamb gives so much broader and more normal a vision of things. The men returning may find the new order a bit queer but everything else will be strangely unfamiliar too, and they will soon grow accustomed to all the changes together. The "jamb" will never descend into a "door-mat" again.

The male and female anti-suffragists of all lands will puff and blow at the economic change which will come to the women of Europe. They will declare it to be contrary to Nature and to God's plan and that somebody ought to do something about it. Suffragists will accept the change as the inevitable outcome of an unprecedented world's cataclysm over which no human agency had any control and will trust in God to adjust the altered circumstances to the eternal evolution of human society. They will remember that in the long run, all things work together for good, for progress and for human weal.

The economic change is bound to bring political liberty. From every land, there comes the expressed belief that the war will be followed by a mighty, oncoming wave of democracy for it is now well known that the conflict has been one of governments, of kings and Czars, Kaisers and Emperors; not of peoples. The nations involved have nearly all declared that they are fighting to make an end of wars. New and higher ideals of governments and of the rights of the people under them, have grown enormously during the past two years. Another tide of political liberty, similar to that of 1848, but of a thousandfold greater momentum, is rising from battlefield and hospital, from camp and munitions factory, from home and church which, great men of many lands, tell us, is destined to sweep over the world. On the continent, the women say, "It is certain that the vote will come to men and women after the war, perhaps not immediately but soon. In Great Britain, which was the storm centre of the suffrage movement for some years before the war, hundreds of bitter, active opponents have confessed their conversion on account of the war services of women. Already, three great provinces of Canada, Manitoba, Alberta, and Saskatchawan [sic], have given universal suffrage to their women in sheer generous appreciation of their war work. Even Mr. Asquith, world renouned [sic] for his immovable opposition to the Parliamentary suffrage for British women, has given evidence of a change of view. Some months ago, he announced his amazement at the utterly unexpected skill, strength and resource developed by the women and his gratitude for their loyalty and devotion. Later, in reply to Mrs. Henry Fawcett, who asked if woman suffrage would be included in a proposed election bill, he said that when the war should end, such a measure would be considered without prejudice carried over from events prior to the war. A public statement issued by Mr. Asquith in August, was couched in such terms as to be interpreted by many as a pledge to include women in the next election bill.

In Great Britain, a sordid appeal which may prove the last straw to break the opposition to woman suffrage, has been added to the enthusiastic appreciation of woman's patriotism and practical service and to the sudden comprehension that motherhood is a national asset which must be protected at any price. A new voters' list is contemplated. A parliamentary election should be held in September but the voters are scattered far and wide. The whole nation is agitated over the questions involved in making a new register. At the same time, there is a constant anxiety over war funds, as is prudent in a nation spending 50 millions of dollars per day. It has been proposed that a large poll tax be assessed upon the voters of the new lists, whereupon a secondary proposal of great force has been offered and that is, that twice as much money would find its way into the public coffers were women added to the voters' list. What nation, with compliments fresh spoken concerning women's patriotism and efficiency, could resist such an appeal?

So it happens that above the roar of cannon, the scream of shrapnel and the whirr of aeroplanes, one who listens may hear the cracking of the fetters which have long bound the European woman to outworn conventions. It has been a frightful price to pay but the fact remains that a womanhood, well started on the way to final emancipation, is destined to step forth from the war. It will be a bewildered, troubled and grief-stricken womanhood with knotty problems of life to solve, but it will be freer to deal with them than women have ever been before.

"The Woman's Hour has struck." It has struck for the women of Europe and for those of all the world. The significance of the changed status of European women has not been lost upon the men and women of our land; our own people are not so unlearned in history, nor so lacking in National pride that they will allow the Republic to lag long behind the Empire, presided over by the descendant of George the Third. If they possess the patriotism and the sense of nationality which should be the inheritance of an American, they will not wait until the war is ended but will boldly lead in the inevitable march of democracy, our own American specialty. Sisters, let me repeat, the Woman's Hour has struck!

SECOND: As the most adamantine rock gives way under the constant dripping of water, so the opposition to woman suffrage in our own country has slowly disintegrated before the increasing strength of our movement. Turn backward the pages of our history! Behold, brave Abbie Kelley rotten-egged because she, a woman, essayed to speak in public. Behold the Polish Ernestine Rose startled that women of free America drew aside their skirts when she proposed that they should control their own property. Recall the saintly Lucretia Mott and the legal-minded Elizabeth Cady Stanton, turned out of the [W]orld's Temperance convention in London and conspiring together to free their sex from the world's stupid oppressions. Remember the gentle, sweet-voiced Lucy Stone, egged because she publicly claimed that women had brains capable of education. Think upon Dr. Elizabeth Blackwell, snubbed and boycotted by other women because she proposed to study medicine. Behold Dr. Antoinette Brown Blackwell, standing in sweet serenity before an Assembly of howling clergymen, angry that she, a woman dared to attend a Temperance Convention as a delegate. Revere the intrepid Susan B. Anthony mobbed from Buffalo to Albany because she demanded fair play for women. These are they who builded with others the foundation of political liberty for American women. Those who came after only laid the stones in place. Yet, what a wearisome task even that has been! Think of the wonderful woman who has wandered from village to village, from city to city, for a generation compelling men and women to listen and to reflect by her matchless eloquence. Where in all the world's history has any movement among men produced so invincible an advocate as our own Dr. Anna Howard Shaw? Those whom she has led to the light are Legion. Think, too, of the consecration, the self-denial, the never-failing constancy of that other noble soul set in a frail but unflinching body—the heroine we know as Alice Stone Blackwell! A woman who never forgets, who detects the slightest flaw in the weapons of her adversary, who knows the most vulnerable spot in his armor, presides over the Woman's Journal and, like a lamp in a lighthouse, the rays of her intelligence, farsightedness and clear-thinking have enlightened the world concerning our cause. The names of hundreds of other brave souls spring to memory when we pause to review the long struggle.

The hands of many suffrage master-masons have long been stilled; the names of many who laid the stones have been forgotten. That does not matter. The main thing is that the edifice of woman's liberty nears completion. It is strong, indestructible. All honor to the thousands who have helped in the building.

The four Corner-stones of the foundations were laid long years ago. We read upon the first: "We demand for women education, for not a high school or college is open to her"; upon the second, "We demand for women religious liberty for in few churches is she permitted to pray or speak"; upon the third, "We demand for women the right to own property and an opportunity to earn an honest living. Only six, poorly-paid occupations are open to her, and if she is married, the wages she earns are not hers"; upon the fourth, "We demand political freedom and its symbol, the vote."

The stones in the foundation have long been overgrown with the moss and mould of time, and some there are who never knew they were laid. Of late, four cap-stones at the top have been set to match those in the base, and we read upon the first: "The number of women who are graduated from high schools, colleges and universities is legion"; upon the second, "The Christian Endeavor, that mighty, undenominational church militant, asks the vote for the women and the Methodist Episcopal Church, and many another, joins that appeal"; upon the third, "Billions of dollars worth of property are earned [and] owned by women; more than 8 millions of women are wage-earners. Every occupation is open to them"; upon the fourth: "Women vote in 12 States; they share in the determination of 91 electoral votes."

After the cap-stones and cornice comes the roof. Across the empty spaces, the rooftree has been flung and fastened well in place. It is not made of stone but of two planks—planks in the platform of the two majority parties, and these are well supported by planks in the platforms of all minority parties.

And we who are the builders of 1916, do we see a crisis? Standing upon these planks which are stretched across the top-most peak of this edifice of woman's liberty, what shall we do? Over our heads, up there in the clouds, but tantalizing [sic] near, hangs the roof of our edifice—the vote. What is our duty? Shall we spend time in admiring the capstones and cornice? Shall we lament the tragedies which accompanied the laying of the cornerstones? or, shall we, like the builders of old, chant, "Ho! all hands, all hands, heave to! All hands, heave to!" and while we chant, grasp the overhanging roof and with a long pull, a strong pull and a pull together, fix it in place forevermore?

Is the crisis real or imaginary? If it be real, it calls for action, bold, immediate and decisive.

Let us then take measure of our strength. Our cause has won the endorsement of all political parties. Every candidate for the presidency is a suffragist. It has won the endorsement of most churches; it has won the hearty approval of all great organizations of women. It was won the support of all reform movements; it has won the progressives of every variety. The majority of the press in most States is with us. Great men in every political party, church and movement are with us. The names of the greatest men and women of art, science, literature and philosophy, reform, religion and politics are on our lists.

We have not won the reactionaries of any party, church or society, and we never will. From the beginning of things, there have been Antis. The Antis drove Moses out of Egypt; they crucified Christ who said, "Love thy neighbor as thyself" [Matt. 19:19, 22:39]; they have persecuted Jews in all parts of the world; they poisoned Socrates, the great philosopher; they cruelly persecuted Copernicus and Galileo, the first great scientists; they burned Giordano Bruno at the stake because he believed the world was round; they burned Savonarola who warred upon church corruption; they burned Eufame McIlyane [sic] because she used an anaesthetic; they burned Joan d'Arc for a heretic; they have sent great men and women to Siberia to eat their hearts out in isolation; they burned in effigy William Lloyd Garrison; they egged Abbie Kelley and Lucy Stone and mobbed Susan B. Anthony. Yet, in proportion to the enlightenment of their respective ages, these Antis were persons of intelligence and honest purpose. They were merely deaf to the call of Progress and were enraged because the world insisted upon moving on. Antis male and female there still are and will be to the end of time. Give to them a prayer of forgiveness for they know not what they do; and prepare for the forward march.

We have not won the ignorant and illiterate and we never can. They are too undeveloped mentally to understand that the institutions of today are not those of yesterday nor will be those of tomorrow.

We have not won the forces of evil and we never will. Evil has ever been timorous and suspicious of all change. It is an instinctive act of self-preservation which makes it fear and consequently oppose votes for women. As the Hon. Champ Clark said the other day: "Some good and intelligent people are opposed to woman suffrage; but all the ignorant and evil-minded are against it."

These three forces are the enemies of our cause.

Before the vote is won, there must and will be a gigantic final conflict between the forces of progress, righteousness and democracy and the forces of ignorance, evil and reaction. That struggle may be postponed, but it cannot be evaded or avoided. There is no question as to which side will be the victor.

Shall we play the coward, then, and leave the hard knocks for our daughters, or shall we throw ourselves into the fray, bare our own shoulders to the blows, and thus bequeath to them a politically liberated womanhood? We have taken note of our gains and of our resources and they are all we could wish. Before the final struggle, we must take cognizance of our weaknesses. Are we prepared to grasp the victory? Alas, no! our movement is like a great Niagara with a vast volume of water tumbling over its ledge but turning no wheel. Our organized machinery is set for the propagandistic stage and not for the seizure of victory. Our supporters are spreading the argument for our cause; they feel no sense of responsibility for the realization of our hopes. Our movement lacks cohesion, organization, unity and consequent momentum.

Behind us, in front of us, everywhere about us are suffragists—millions of them, but inactive and silent. They have been "agitated and educated" and are with us in belief. There are thousands of women who have at one time or another been members of our organization but they have dropped out because, to them the movement seemed negative and pointless. Many have taken up other work whose results were more immediate. Philanthropy, charity, work for corrective laws of various kinds, temperance, relief for working women and numberless similar public services have called them. Others have turned to the pleasanter avenues of clubwork, art or literature.

There are thousands of other women who have never learned of the earlier struggles of our movement. They found doors of opportunity open to them on every side. They found well-paid posts awaiting the qualified woman and they have availed themselves of all these blessings; almost without exception they believe in the vote but they feel neither gratitude to those who opened the doors through which they have entered to economic liberty nor any sense of obligation to open other doors for those who come after.

There are still others who, timorously looking over their shoulders to see if any listeners be near, will tell us they hope we will win and win soon but they are too frightened of Mother Grundy to help. There are others too occupied with the small things of life to help. They say they could find time to vote but not to work for the vote. There are men, too, millions of them, waiting to be called. These men and women are our reserves. They are largely unorganized and untrained soldiers with little responsibility toward our movement. Yet these reserves must be mobilized. The final struggle needs their numbers and the momentum those numbers will bring. Were never another convert made, there are suffragists enough in this country, if combined, to make so irresistible a driving force that victory might be seized at once.

How can it be done? By a simple change of mental attitude. If we are to seize the victory, that change must take place in this hall, here and now!

The old belief, which has sustained suffragists in many an hour of discouragement, "woman suffrage is bound to come," must give way to the new, "The Woman's Hour has struck." The long drawn out struggle, the cruel hostility which, for years was arrayed against our cause, have accustomed suffragists to the idea of indefinite postponement but eventual victory. The slogan of a movements sets its pace. The old one counseled patience; it said, there is plenty of time; it pardoned sloth and half-hearted effort. It set the pace of an educational campaign. The "Woman's Hour has struck" sets the pace of a crusade which will have its way. It says: "Awake, arise, my sisters, let your hearts be filled with joy—the time of victory is here. Onward March."

If you believe with me that a crisis has come to our movement—if you believe that the time for final action is now, if you catch the rosy tints of the coming day, what does it mean to you? Does it not give you a thrill of exaltation; does the blood not course more quickly through your veins; does it not bring a new sense of freedom, of joy and of determination? Is it not true that you who wanted a little time ago to lay down the work because you were weary with long service, now, under the compelling influence of a changed mental attitude, are ready to go on until the vote is won. The change is one of spirit! Aye, and the spiritual effect upon you will come to others. Let me borrow an expression from Hon. John Finlay: What our great movement needs now is a "mobilization of spirit"—the jubilant, glad spirit of victory. Then let us sound a bugle call here and now to the women of the Nation: "The Woman's Hour has struck." Let the bugle sound from the suffrage headquarters of every State at the inauguration of a State campaign. Let the call go forth again and, again and yet again. Let it be repeated in every article written, in every speech made, in every conversation held. Let the bugle blow again and yet again. The Political emancipation of our sex call[s] you, women of, America, arise! Are you content that others shall pay the price of your liberty? Women in schools and counting house, in shops and on the farm, women in the home with babes at their breasts and women engaged in public careers will hear. The veins of American women are not filled with milk and water. They are neither cowards nor slackers. They will come. They only await the bugle call to learn that the final battle is on.

Source: Accessed at Historic Speeches, sojust. net. Available online. URL: http://www.sojust.net/ speeches/catt_the_crisis.html.

9. Address to the United States Congress

CARRIE CHAPMAN CATT, NOVEMBER 4, 1917

Woman suffrage is inevitable. Suffragists knew it before November 4, 1917; opponents afterward. Three distinct causes made it inevitable.

First, the history of our country. Ours is a nation born of revolution, of rebellion against a system of government so securely entrenched in the customs and traditions of human society that in 1776 it seemed impregnable. From the beginning of things, nations had been ruled by kings and for kings, while the people served and paid the cost. The American Revolutionists boldly proclaimed the heresies: "Taxation without representation is tyranny." "Governments derive their just powers from the consent of the governed." The colonists won, and the nation which was established as a result of their victory has held unfailingly that these two fundamental principles of democratic government are not only the spiritual source of our national existence but have been our chief historic pride and at all times the sheet anchor of our liberties.

Eighty years after the Revolution, Abraham Lincoln welded those two maxims into a new one: "Ours is a government of the people, by the people, and for the people." Fifty years more passed and the president of the United States, Woodrow Wilson, in a mighty crisis of the nation, proclaimed to the world: "We are fighting for the things which we have always carried nearest to our hearts: for democracy, for the right of those who submit to authority to have a voice in their own government."

All the way between these immortal aphorisms political leaders have declared unabated faith in their truth. Not one American has arisen to question their logic in the 141 years of our national existence. However stupidly our country may have evaded the logical application at times, it has never swerved from its devotion to the theory of democracy as expressed by those two axioms. . . .

With such a history behind it, how can our nation escape the logic it has never failed to follow, when its last unenfranchised class calls for the vote? Behold our Uncle Sam floating the banner with one hand, "Taxation without representation is tyranny," and with the other seizing the billions of dollars paid in taxes by women to whom he refuses "representation." Behold him again, welcoming the boys of twenty-one and the newly made immigrant citizen to "a voice in their own government" while he denies that fundamental right of democracy to thousands of women public school teachers from whom many of these men learn all they know of citizenship and patriotism, to women college presidents, to women who preach in our pulpits, interpret law in our courts, preside over our hospitals, write books and magazines, and serve in every uplifting moral and social enterprise. Is there a single man who can justify such inequality of treatment, such outrageous discrimination? Not one. . . .

Second, the suffrage for women already established in the United States makes women suffrage for the nation inevitable. When Elihu Root, as president of the American Society of International Law, at the eleventh annual meeting in Washington, April 26, 1917, said, "The world cannot be half democratic and half autocratic. It must be all democratic or all Prussian. There can be no compromise," he voiced a general truth. Precisely the same intuition has already taught the blindest and most hostile foe of woman suffrage that our nation cannot long continue a condition under which government in half its territory rests upon the consent of half of the people and in the other half upon the consent of all the people; a condition which grants representation to the taxed in half of its territory and denies it in the other half a condition which permits women in some states to share in the election of the president, senators, and representatives and denies them that privilege in others. It is too obvious to require demonstration that woman suffrage, now covering half our territory, will eventually be ordained in all the nation. No one will deny it. The only question left is when and how will it be completely established.

Third, the leadership of the United States in world democracy compels the enfranchisement of its own women. The maxims of the Declaration were once called "fundamental principles of government." They are now called "American principles" or even "Americanisms." They have become the slogans of every movement toward political liberty the world around, of every effort to widen the suffrage for men or women in any land. Not a people, race, or class striving for freedom is there anywhere in the world that has not made our axioms the chief weapon of the struggle. More, all men and women the world around, with farsighted vision into the verities of things, know that the world tragedy of our day is not now being waged over the assassination of an archduke, nor commercial competition, nor national ambitions, nor the freedom of the seas. It is a death grapple between the forces which deny and those which uphold the truths of the Declaration of Independence. . . .

Do you realize that in no other country in the world with democratic tendencies is suffrage so completely denied as in a considerable number of our own states? There are thirteen black states where no suffrage for women exists, and fourteen others where suffrage for women is more limited than in many foreign countries.

Do you realize that when you ask women to take their cause to state referendum you compel them to do this: that you drive women of education, refinement, achievement, to beg men who cannot read for their political freedom?

Do you realize that such anomalies as a college president asking her janitor to give her a vote are overstraining the patience and driving women to desperation?

Do you realize that women in increasing numbers indignantly resent the long delay in their enfranchisement?

Your party platforms have pledged women suffrage. Then why not be honest, frank friends of our cause, adopt it in reality as your own, make it a party program, and "fight with us"? As a party measure—a measure of all parties—why not put the amendment through Congress and the legislatures? We shall all be better friends, we shall have a happier nation, we women will be free to support loyally the party of our choice, and we shall be far prouder of our history.

"There is one thing mightier than kings and armies"—aye, than Congresses and political parties—"the power of an idea when its time has come to move." The time for woman suffrage has come. The woman's hour has struck. If parties prefer to postpone action longer and thus do battle with this idea, they challenge the inevitable. The idea will not perish; the party which opposes it may. Every delay, every trick, every political dishonesty from now on will antagonize the women of the land more and more, and when the party or parties which have so delayed woman suffrage finally let it come, their sincerity will be doubted and their appeal to the new voters will be met with suspicion. This is the psychology of the situation. Can you afford the risk? Think it over.

We know you will meet opposition. There are a few "women haters" left, a few "old males of the tribe," as Vance Thompson calls them, whose duty they believe it to be to keep women in the places they have carefully picked out for them. Treitschke, made world famous by war literature, said some years ago, "Germany, which knows all about Germany and France, knows far better what is good for Alsace-Lorraine than that miserable people can possibly know." A few American Treitschkes we have who know better than women what is good for them. There are women, too, with "slave souls" and "clinging vines" for backbones. There are female dolls and male dandies. But the world does not wait for such as these, nor does liberty pause to heed the plaint of men and women with a grouch. She does not wait for those who have a special interest to serve, nor a selfish reason for depriving other people of freedom. Holding her torch aloft, liberty is pointing the way onward and upward and saying to America, "Come."

To you and the supporters of our cause in Senate and House, and the number is large, the suffragists of the nation express their grateful thanks. This address is not meant for you. We are more truly appreciative of all you have done than any words can express. We ask you to make a last, hard fight for the amendment during the present session. Since last we asked a vote on this amendment, your position has been fortified by the addition to suffrage territory of Great Britain, Canada, and New York.

Some of you have been too indifferent to give more than casual attention to this question. It is worthy of your immediate consideration. A question big enough to engage the attention of our allies in wartime is too big a question for you to neglect.

Some of you have grown old in party service. Are you willing that those who take your places by and by shall blame you for having failed to keep pace with the world and thus having lost for them a party advantage? Is there any real gain for you, for your party, for your nation by delay? Do you want to drive the progressive men and women out of your party?

Some of you hold to the doctrine of states' rights as applying to woman suffrage. Adherence to that theory will keep the United States far behind all other democratic nations upon this question. A theory which prevents a nation from keeping up with the trend of world progress cannot be justified.

Gentlemen, we hereby petition you, our only designated representatives, to redress our grievances by the immediate passage of the Federal Suffrage Amendment and to use your influence to secure its ratification in your own state, in order that the women of our nation may be endowed with political freedom before the next presidential election, and that our nation may resume its world leadership in democracy.

Woman suffrage is coming—you know it. Will you, Honorable Senators and Members of the House of Representatives, help or hinder it?

Source: Accessed at Historic Speeches, sojust. net. Available online. URL: http://www.sojust.net/speeches/catt_congress.html.

10. U.S. CONSTITUTION: NINETEENTH AMENDMENT

WOMEN'S SUFFRAGE RIGHTS, 1920

Section 1. The right of the citizens of the United States to vote shall not be denied or abridged by the United States or by any State on account of sex.

Section 2. Congress shall have power to enforce this article by appropriate legislation.

Source: Accessed at Legal Information Institute, Cornell Law School. Available online. URL: http://www.law.cornell.edu/constitution/constitution.amendmentxix.html.

11. "A MORAL NECESSITY FOR BIRTH CONTROL"

MARGARET SANGER ON BEHALF OF THE AMERICAN BIRTH CONTROL LEAGUE, NOVEMBER 18, 1921, NEW YORK CITY

The meeting tonight is a postponement of one which was to have taken place at the Town Hall last Sunday evening. It was to be a culmination of a three day conference, two of which were held at the Hotel Plaza, in discussing the Birth Control subject in its various and manifold aspects.

The one issue upon which there seems to be most uncertainty and disagreement exists in the moral side of the subject of Birth Control. It seemed only natural for us to call together scientists, educators, members of the medical profession and the theologians of all denominations to ask their opinion upon this uncertain and important phase of the controversy. Letters were sent to the most eminent men and women in the world. We asked in this letter, the following questions:

1. Is over-population a menace to the peace of the world?
2. Would the legal dissemination of scientific Birth Control information through the medium of clinics by the medical profession be the most logical method of checking the problem of over-population?
3. Would knowledge of Birth Control change the moral attitude of men and women toward the marriage bond or lower the moral standards of the youth of the country?
4. Do you believe that knowledge which enables parents to limit the families will make for human happiness, and raise the moral, social and intellectual standards of population?

We sent such a letter not only to those who, we thought, might agree with us, but we sent it also to our known opponents. Most of these people answered. Every one who answered did so with sincerity and courtesy, with the exception of one group whose reply to this important question as demonstrated at the Town Hall last Sunday evening was a disgrace to liberty-loving people, and to all traditions we hold dear in the United States. I believed that the discussion of the moral issue was one which did not solely belong to theologians and to scientists, but belonged to the people. And because I believed that the people of this country may and can discuss this subject with dignity and with intelligence I desired to bring them together, and to discuss it in the open.

When one speaks of moral, one refers to human conduct. This implies action of many kinds, which in turn depends upon the mind and the brain. So that in speaking of morals one must remember that there is a direct connection between morality and brain development. Conduct is said to be action in pursuit of ends, and if this is so, then we must hold the irresponsibility and recklessness in our action is immoral, while responsibility and forethought put into action for the benefit of the individual and the race becomes in the highest sense the finest kind of morality.

We know that every advance that woman has made in the last half century has been made with opposition, all of which has been based upon the grounds of immorality. When women fought for higher education, it was said that this would cause her to become immoral and she would lose her place in the sanctity of the home. When women asked for the franchise it was said that this would lower her standard of morals, that it was not fit that she should meet with and mix with the members of the opposite sex, but we notice that there was no objection to her meeting with the same members of the opposite sex when she went to church.

The church has ever opposed the progress of woman on the ground that her freedom would lead to immorality. We ask the church to have more confidence in women. We ask the opponents of this movement to reverse the methods of the church, which aims to keep women moral by keeping them in fear and in ignorance, and to inculcate into them a higher and truer morality based upon knowledge. And ours is the morality of knowledge. If we cannot trust woman with the knowledge of her own body, then I claim that two thousand years of Christian teaching has proved to be a failure.

We stand on the principle that Birth Control should be available to every adult man and woman. We believe that every adult man and woman should be taught the responsibility and the right use of knowledge. We claim that woman should have the right over her own body and to say if she shall or if she shall not be a mother, as she sees fit. We further claim that the first right of a child is to be desired. While the second right is that it should be conceived in love, and the third, that it should have a heritage of sound health.

Upon these principles the Birth Control movement in America stands. When it comes to discussing the methods of Birth Control, that is far more difficult. There are laws in this country which forbid the imparting of practical information to the mothers of the land. We claim that every mother in this country, either sick or well, has the right to the best, the safest, the most scientific information. This information should be disseminated directly to the mothers through clinics by members of the medical profession, registered nurses and registered midwives.

Our first step is to have the backing of the medical profession so that our laws may be changed, so that motherhood may be the function of dignity and choice, rather than one of ignorance and chance. Conscious control of offspring is now becoming the ideal and the custom in all civilized countries. Those who oppose it claim that however desirable it may be on economic or social grounds, it may be abused and the morals of the youth of the country may be lowered. Such people should be reminded that there are two points to be considered. First, that such control is the inevitable advance in civilization. Every civilization involves an increasing forethought for others, even for those yet unborn. The reckless abandonment of the impulse of the moment and the careless regard for the consequences, is not morality. The selfish gratification of temporary desire at the expense of suffering to lives that will come may seem very beautiful to some, but it is not our conception of civilization, or is it our concept of morality.

In the second place, it is not only inevitable, but it is right to control the size of the family

for by this control and adjustment we can raise the level and the standards of the human race. While Nature's way of reducing her numbers is controlled by disease, famine and war, primitive man has achieved the same results by infanticide, exposure of infants, the abandonment of children, and by abortion. But such ways of controlling population is no longer possible for us. We have attained high standards of life, and along the lines of science must we conduct such control. We must begin farther back and control the beginnings of life. We must control conception. This is a better method, it is a more civilized method, for it involves not only greater forethought for others, but finally a higher sanction for the value of life itself.

Society is divided into three groups. Those intelligent and wealthy members of the upper classes who have obtained knowledge of Birth Control and exercise it in regulating the size of their families. They have already benefited by this knowledge, and are today considered the most respectable and moral members of the community. They have only children when they desire, and all society points to them as types that should perpetuate their kind.

The second group is equally intelligent and responsible. They desire to control the size of their families, but are unable to obtain knowledge or to put such available knowledge into practice.

The third are those irresponsible and reckless ones having little regard for the consequence of their acts, or whose religious scruples prevent their exercising control over their numbers. Many of this group are diseased, feeble-minded, and are of the pauper element dependent entirely upon the normal and fit members of society for their support. There is no doubt in the minds of all thinking people that the procreation of this group should be stopped. For if they are not able to support and care for themselves, they should certainly not be allowed to bring offspring into this world for others to look after. We do not believe that filling the earth with misery, poverty and disease is moral. And it is our desire and intention to carry on our crusade until the perpetuation of such conditions has ceased.

We desire to stop at its source the disease, poverty and feeble-mindedness and insanity which exist today, for these lower the standards of civilization and make for race deterioration. We know that the masses of people are growing wiser and are using their own minds to decide their individual conduct. The more people of this kind we have, the less immorality shall exist. For the more responsible people grow, the higher do they and shall they attain real morality.

Source: Accessed at American Rhetoric.com. Available online. URL: http://www.americanrhetoric.com/speeches/margaretsangermoralityofbirthcontrol.htm.

12. DECLARATION OF CONSCIENCE

MARGARET CHASE SMITH, JUNE 1, 1950, WASHINGTON, D.C.

Mr. President:

I would like to speak briefly and simply about a serious national condition. It is a national feeling of fear and frustration that could result in national suicide and the end of everything that we Americans hold dear. It is a condition that comes from the lack of effective leadership in either the Legislative Branch or the Executive Branch of our Government.

That leadership is so lacking that serious and responsible proposals are being made that national advisory commissions be appointed to provide such critically needed leadership.

I speak as briefly as possible because too much harm has already been done with irresponsible words of bitterness and selfish political oppor-

tunism. I speak as briefly as possible because the issue is too great to be obscured by eloquence. I speak simply and briefly in the hope that my words will be taken to heart.

I speak as a Republican. I speak as a woman. I speak as a United States Senator. I speak as an American.

The United States Senate has long enjoyed worldwide respect as the greatest deliberative body in the world. But recently that deliberative character has too often been debased to the level of a forum of hate and character assassination sheltered by the shield of congressional immunity.

It is ironical that we Senators can in debate in the Senate directly or indirectly, by any form of words, impute to any American who is not a Senator any conduct or motive unworthy or unbecoming an American—and without that non-Senator American having any legal redress against us—yet if we say the same thing in the Senate about our colleagues we can be stopped on the grounds of being out of order.

It is strange that we can verbally attack anyone else without restraint and with full protection and yet we hold ourselves above the same type of criticism here on the Senate Floor. Surely the United States Senate is big enough to take self-criticism and self-appraisal. Surely we should be able to take the same kind of character attacks that we "dish out" to outsiders.

I think that it is high time for the United States Senate and its members to do some soul-searching—for us to weigh our consciences—on the manner in which we are performing our duty to the people of America—on the manner in which we are using or abusing our individual powers and privileges.

I think that it is high time that we remembered that we have sworn to uphold and defend the Constitution. I think that it is high time that we remembered that the Constitution, as amended, speaks not only of the freedom of speech but also of trial by jury instead of trial by accusation.

Whether it be a criminal prosecution in court or a character prosecution in the Senate, there is little practical distinction when the life of a person has been ruined.

Those of us who shout the loudest about Americanism in making character assassinations are all too frequently those who, by our own words and acts, ignore some of the basic principles of Americanism:

> The right to criticize;
> The right to hold unpopular beliefs;
> The right to protest;
> The right of independent thought.

The exercise of these rights should not cost one single American citizen his reputation or his right to a livelihood nor should he be in danger of losing his reputation or livelihood merely because he happens to know someone who holds unpopular beliefs. Who of us doesn't? Otherwise none of us could call our souls our own. Otherwise thought control would have set in.

The American people are sick and tired of being afraid to speak their minds lest they be politically smeared as "Communists" or "Fascists" by their opponents. Freedom of speech is not what it used to be in America. It has been so abused by some that it is not exercised by others.

The American people are sick and tired of seeing innocent people smeared and guilty people whitewashed. But there have been enough proved cases, such as the Amerasia case, the Hiss case, the Coplon case, the Gold case, to cause the nationwide distrust and strong suspicion that there may be something to the unproved, sensational accusations.

As a Republican, I say to my colleagues on this side of the aisle that the Republican Party faces a challenge today that is not unlike the challenge that it faced back in Lincoln's day. The Republican Party so successfully met that challenge that it emerged from the Civil War as the champion of a united nation—in addition to being a Party that unrelentingly fought loose spending and loose programs.

Today our country is being psychologically divided by the confusion and the suspicions that are bred in the United States Senate to spread like cancerous tentacles of "know nothing, suspect everything" attitudes. Today we have a Democratic Administration that has developed a mania for loose spending and loose programs. History is repeating itself—and the Republican Party again has the opportunity to emerge as the champion of unity and prudence.

The record of the present Democratic Administration has provided us with sufficient campaign issues without the necessity of resorting to political smears. America is rapidly losing its position as leader of the world simply because the Democratic Administration has pitifully failed to provide effective leadership.

The Democratic Administration has completely confused the American people by its daily contradictory grave warnings and optimistic assurances—that show the people that our Democratic Administration has no idea of where it is going.

The Democratic Administration has greatly lost the confidence of the American people by its complacency to the threat of communism here at home and the leak of vital secrets to Russia though key officials of the Democratic Administration. There are enough proved cases to make this point without diluting our criticism with unproved charges.

Surely these are sufficient reasons to make it clear to the American people that it is time for a change and that a Republican victory is necessary to the security of this country. Surely it is clear that this nation will continue to suffer as long as it is governed by the present ineffective Democratic Administration.

Yet to displace it with a Republican regime embracing a philosophy that lacks political integrity or intellectual honesty would prove equally disastrous to this nation. The nation sorely needs a Republican victory. But I don't want to see the Republican Party ride to political victory on the Four Horsemen of Calumny—Fear, Ignorance, Bigotry, and Smear.

I doubt if the Republican Party could—simply because I don't believe the American people will uphold any political party that puts political exploitation above national interest. Surely we Republicans aren't that desperate for victory.

I don't want to see the Republican Party win that way. While it might be a fleeting victory for the Republican Party, it would be a more lasting defeat for the American people. Surely it would ultimately be suicide for the Republican Party and the two-party system that has protected our American liberties from the dictatorship of a one party system.

As members of the Minority Party, we do not have the primary authority to formulate the policy of our Government. But we do have the responsibility of rendering constructive criticism, of clarifying issues, of allaying fears by acting as responsible citizens.

As a woman, I wonder how the mothers, wives, sisters, and daughters feel about the way in which members of their families have been politically mangled in the Senate debate—and I use the word "debate" advisedly.

As a United States Senator, I am not proud of the way in which the Senate has been made a publicity platform for irresponsible sensationalism. I am not proud of the reckless abandon in which unproved charges have been hurled from this side of the aisle. I am not proud of the obviously staged, undignified countercharges that have been attempted in retaliation from the other side of the aisle.

I don't like the way the Senate has been made a rendezvous for vilification, for selfish political gain at the sacrifice of individual reputations and national unity. I am not proud of the way we smear outsiders from the Floor of the Senate and hide behind the cloak of congressional immunity and still place ourselves beyond criticism on the Floor of the Senate.

As an American, I am shocked at the way Republicans and Democrats alike are playing directly into the Communist design of "confuse, divide, and conquer." As an American, I don't want a Democratic Administration "whitewash" or "cover-up" any more than a want a Republican smear or witch hunt.

As an American, I condemn a Republican "Fascist" just as much I condemn a Democratic "Communist." I condemn a Democrat "Fascist" just as much as I condemn a Republican "Communist." They are equally dangerous to you and me and to our country. As an American, I want to see our nation recapture the strength and unity it once had when we fought the enemy instead of ourselves.

It is with these thoughts that I have drafted what I call a "Declaration of Conscience." I am gratified that Senator Tobey, Senator Aiken, Senator Morse, Senator Ives, Senator Thye, and Senator Hendrickson have concurred in that declaration and have authorized me to announce their concurrence.

Source: Accessed at Gift of Speech: Women's Speeches from Around the World, Sweetbriar College. Available online. URL: http://gos.sbc.edu/s/chasesmith.html.

13. THE NATIONAL ORGANIZATION FOR WOMEN'S 1966 STATEMENT OF PURPOSE

NOTE: This is a historic document, which was adopted at NOW's first National Conference in Washington, D.C., on October 29, 1966. The words are those of the 1960s, and do not reflect current language or NOW's current priorities.

We, men and women who hereby constitute ourselves as the National Organization for Women, believe that the time has come for a new movement toward true equality for all women in America, and toward a fully equal partnership of the sexes, as part of the world-wide revolution of human rights now taking place within and beyond our national borders.

The purpose of NOW is to take action to bring women into full participation in the mainstream of American society now, exercising all the privileges and responsibilities thereof in truly equal partnership with men.

We believe the time has come to move beyond the abstract argument, discussion and symposia over the status and special nature of women which has raged in America in recent years; the time has come to confront, with concrete action, the conditions that now prevent women from enjoying the equality of opportunity and freedom of choice which is their right, as individual Americans, and as human beings.

NOW is dedicated to the proposition that women, first and foremost, are human beings, who, like all other people in our society, must have the chance to develop their fullest human potential. We believe that women can achieve such equality only by accepting to the full the challenges and responsibilities they share with all other people in our society, as part of the decision-making mainstream of American political, economic and social life.

We organize to initiate or support action, nationally, or in any part of this nation, by individuals or organizations, to break through the silken curtain of prejudice and discrimination against women in government, industry, the professions, the churches, the political parties, the judiciary, the labor unions, in education, science, medicine, law, religion and every other field of importance in American society.

Enormous changes taking place in our society make it both possible and urgently necessary to advance the unfinished revolution of women toward true equality, now. With a life span lengthened to nearly 75 years it is no longer either necessary or possible for women to devote the greater part of their lives to child-rearing; yet childbearing and rearing, which continues to be a most important part of most women's lives, still is used to justify barring women from equal professional and economic participation and advance.

Today's technology has reduced most of the productive chores which women once performed in the home and in mass-production industries based upon routine unskilled labor. This same technology has virtually eliminated the quality of muscular strength as a criterion for filling most jobs, while intensifying American industry's need for creative intelligence. In view of this new industrial revolution created by automation in the mid-twentieth century, women can and must participate in old and new fields of society in full equality—or become permanent outsiders.

Despite all the talk about the status of American women in recent years, the actual position of women in the United States has declined, and is declining, to an alarming degree throughout the 1950's and 60's. Although 46.4% of all American women between the ages of 18 and 65 now work outside the home, the overwhelming majority—75%—are in routine clerical, sales, or factory jobs, or they are household workers, cleaning women, hospital attendants. About two-thirds of Negro women workers are in the lowest paid service occupations. Working women are becoming increasingly—not less—concentrated on the bottom of the job ladder. As a consequence full-time women workers today earn on the average only 60% of what men earn, and that wage gap has been increasing over the past twenty-five years in every major industry group. In 1964, of all women with a yearly income, 89% earned under $5,000 a year; half of all full-time year round women workers earned less than $3,690; only 1.4% of full-time year round women workers had an annual income of $10,000 or more.

Further, with higher education increasingly essential in today's society, too few women are entering and finishing college or going on to graduate or professional school. Today, women earn only one in three of the B.A.'s and M.A.'s granted, and one in ten of the Ph.D.'s.

In all the professions considered of importance to society, and in the executive ranks of industry and government, women are losing ground. Where they are present it is only a token handful. Women comprise less than 1% of federal judges; less than 4% of all lawyers; 7% of doctors. Yet women represent 51% of the U.S. population. And, increasingly, men are replacing women in the top positions in secondary and elementary schools, in social work, and in libraries—once thought to be women's fields.

Official pronouncements of the advance in the status of women hide not only the reality of this dangerous decline, but the fact that nothing is being done to stop it. The excellent reports of the President's Commission on the Status of Women and of the State Commissions have not been fully implemented. Such Commissions have power only to advise. They have no power to enforce their recommendation; nor have they the freedom to organize American women and men to press for action on them. The reports of these commissions have, however, created a basis upon which it is now possible to build. Discrimination in employment on the basis of sex is now prohibited by federal law, in Title VII of the Civil Rights Act of 1964. But although nearly one-third of the cases brought before the Equal Employment Opportunity Commission during the first year dealt with sex discrimination and the proportion is increasing dramatically, the Commission has not made clear its intention to enforce the law with the same seriousness on behalf of women as of other victims of discrimination. Many of these cases were Negro women, who are the victims of double discrimination of race and sex. Until now, too few women's organizations and official spokesmen have been willing to speak out against these dangers facing women. Too many women have been restrained by the fear of being called "feminist." There is no civil rights movement to speak for women, as there has been for Negroes and other victims of discrimination. The National Organization for Women must therefore begin to speak.

WE BELIEVE that the power of American law, and the protection guaranteed by the U.S. Constitution to the civil rights of all individuals, must be effectively applied and enforced to isolate and remove patterns of sex discrimination, to ensure equality of opportunity in employment and education, and equality of civil and political rights and responsibilities on behalf of women, as well as for Negroes and other deprived groups. We realize that women's problems are linked to many broader questions of social justice; their solution will require concerted action by many groups. Therefore, convinced that human rights for all are indivisible, we expect to give active support to the common cause of equal rights for all those who suffer discrimination and deprivation, and we call upon other organizations committed to such goals to support our efforts toward equality for women.

WE DO NOT ACCEPT the token appointment of a few women to high-level positions in government and industry as a substitute for serious continuing effort to recruit and advance women according to their individual abilities. To this end, we urge American government and industry to mobilize the same resources of ingenuity and command with which they have solved problems of far greater difficulty than those now impeding the progress of women.

WE BELIEVE that this nation has a capacity at least as great as other nations, to innovate new social institutions which will enable women to enjoy the true equality of opportunity and responsibility in society, without conflict with their responsibilities as mothers and homemakers. In such innovations, America does not lead the Western world, but lags by decades behind many European countries. We do not accept the traditional assumption that a woman has to choose between marriage and motherhood, on the one hand, and serious participation in industry or the professions on the other. We question the present expectation that all normal women will retire from job or profession for 10 or 15 years, to devote their full time to raising children, only to reenter the job market at a relatively minor level. This, in itself, is a deterrent to the aspirations of women, to their acceptance into management or professional training courses, and to the very possibility of equality of opportunity or real choice, for all but a few women. Above all, we reject the assumption that these problems are the unique responsibility of each individual woman, rather than a basic social dilemma which society must solve. True equality of opportunity and freedom of choice for women requires such practical, and possible innovations as a nationwide network of child-care centers, which will make it unnecessary for women to retire completely from society until their children are grown, and national programs to provide retraining for women who have chosen to care for their children full-time.

WE BELIEVE that it is as essential for every girl to be educated to her full potential of human ability as it is for every boy—with the knowledge that such education is the key to effective participation in today's economy and that, for a girl as for a boy, education can only be serious where there is expectation that it will be used in society. We believe that American educators are capable of devising means of imparting such expectations to girl students. Moreover, we consider the decline in the proportion of women receiving higher and professional education to be evidence of discrimination. This discrimination may take the form of quotas against the admission of women to colleges, and professional schools; lack of encouragement by parents, counselors and educators; denial of loans or fellowships; or the traditional or arbitrary procedures in graduate and professional training geared in terms of men, which inadvertently discriminate against women. We believe that the same serious attention must be given to high school dropouts who are girls as to boys.

WE REJECT the current assumptions that a man must carry the sole burden of supporting himself, his wife, and family, and that a woman is automatically entitled to lifelong support by a man upon her marriage, or that marriage, home and family are primarily woman's world and responsibility—hers, to dominate—his to support. We believe that a true partnership between the sexes demands a different concept of marriage, an equitable sharing of the responsibilities of home and children and of the economic burdens of their support. We believe that proper recognition should be given to the economic and social value of homemaking and child-care. To these ends, we will seek to open a reexamination of laws and mores governing marriage and divorce, for we believe that the current state of "half-equity" between the sexes discriminates against both men and women, and is the cause of much unnecessary hostility between the sexes.

WE BELIEVE that women must now exercise their political rights and responsibilities as American citizens. They must refuse to be segregated on the basis of sex into separate-and-not-equal ladies' auxiliaries in the political parties, and they must demand representation according to their numbers in the regularly constituted party committees—at local, state, and national levels—and in the informal power structure, participating fully in the selection of candidates and political decision-making, and running for office themselves.

IN THE INTERESTS OF THE HUMAN DIGNITY OF WOMEN, we will protest, and endeavor to change, the false image of women now prevalent in the mass media, and in the texts, ceremonies, laws, and practices of our major social institutions. Such images perpetuate contempt for women by society and by women for themselves. We are similarly opposed to all policies and practices—in church, state, college, factory, or office—which, in the guise of protectiveness, not only deny opportunities but also foster in women self-denigration, dependence, and evasion of responsibility, undermine their confidence in their own abilities and foster contempt for women.

NOW WILL HOLD ITSELF INDEPENDENT OF ANY POLITICAL PARTY in order to mobilize the political power of all women and men intent on our goals. We will strive to ensure that no party, candidate, president, senator, governor, congressman, or any public official who betrays or ignores the principle of full equality between the sexes is elected or appointed to office. If it is necessary to mobilize the votes of men and women who believe in our cause, in order to win for women the final right to be fully free and equal human beings, we so commit ourselves.

WE BELIEVE THAT women will do most to create a new image of women by acting now, and by speaking out in behalf of their own equality, freedom, and human dignity—not in pleas for special privilege, nor in enmity toward men, who are also victims of the current, half-equality between the sexes—but in an active, self-respecting partnership with men. By so doing, women will develop confidence in their own ability to determine actively, in partnership with men, the conditions of their life, their choices, their future and their society.

This Statement of Purpose was co-authored by Betty Friedan, author of The Feminine Mystique, *and Dr. Pauli Murray, an African-American Episcopal minister.*

Source: National Organization for Women, Washington, D.C. Available online. URL: www.now.org/history/purpos66.html.

14. "EQUAL RIGHTS FOR WOMEN"

SHIRLEY CHISHOLM (D-NY)
ADDRESS TO THE UNITED STATES HOUSE OF REPRESENTATIVES, MAY 21, 1969, WASHINGTON, D.C.

Mr. Speaker, when a young woman graduates from college and starts looking for a job, she is likely to have a frustrating and even demeaning experience ahead of her. If she walks into an office for an interview, the first question she will be asked is, "Do you type?"

There is a calculated system of prejudice that lies unspoken behind that question. Why is it acceptable for women to be secretaries, librarians, and teachers, but totally unacceptable for them to be managers, administrators, doctors, lawyers, and Members of Congress?

The unspoken assumption is that women are different. They do not have executive ability, orderly minds, stability, leadership skills, and they are too emotional. It has been observed before, that society for a long time, discriminated against another minority, the blacks, on the same basis—that they were different and inferior. The happy little homemaker and the contented "old darkey" on the plantation were both produced by prejudice.

As a black person, I am no stranger to race prejudice. But the truth is that in the political world I have been far oftener discriminated against because I am a woman than because I am black.

Prejudice against blacks is becoming unacceptable although it will take years to eliminate it. But it is doomed because, slowly, white America is beginning to admit that it exists. Prejudice against women is still acceptable. There is very little understanding yet of the immorality involved in double pay scales and the classification of most of the better jobs as "for men only."

More than half of the population of the United States is female. But women occupy only 2 percent of the managerial positions. They have not even reached the level of tokenism yet no women sit on the AFL-CIO council or Supreme Court There have been only two women who have held Cabinet rank, and at present there are none. Only two women now hold ambassadorial rank in the diplomatic corps. In Congress, we are down to one Senator and 10 Representatives.

Considering that there are about 3½ million more women in the United States than men, this situation is outrageous.

It is true that part of the problem has been that women have not been aggressive in demanding their rights. This was also true of the black population for many years. They submitted to oppression and even cooperated with it. Women have done the same thing. But now there is an awareness of this situation particularly among the younger segment of the population.

As in the field of equal rights for blacks, Spanish-Americans, the Indians, and other groups, laws will not change such deep-seated problems overnight. But they can be used to provide protection for those who are most abused, and to begin the process of evolutionary change by compelling the insensitive majority to reexamine its unconscious attitudes.

It is for this reason that I wish to introduce today a proposal that has been before every Congress for the last 40 years and that sooner or later must become part of the basic law of the land—the equal rights amendment.

Let me note and try to refute two of the commonest arguments that are offered against this amendment. One is that women are already protected under the law and do not need legislation. Existing laws are not adequate to secure equal rights for women. Sufficient proof of this is the concentration of women in lower paying, menial, unrewarding jobs and their incredible scarcity in the upper level jobs. If women are already equal, why is it such an event whenever one happens to be elected to Congress?

It is obvious that discrimination exists. Women do not have the opportunities that men do. And women that do not conform to the system, who try to break with the accepted patterns, are stigmatized as "odd" and "unfeminine." The fact is that a woman who aspires to be chairman of the board, or a Member of the House, does so for exactly the same reasons as any man. Basically, these are that she thinks she can do the job and she wants to try.

A second argument often heard against the equal rights amendment is that is would eliminate legislation that many States and the Federal Government have enacted giving special protection to women and that it would throw the marriage and divorce laws into chaos.

As for the marriage laws, they are due for a sweeping reform, and an excellent beginning would be to wipe the existing ones off the books. Regarding special protection for working women, I cannot understand why it should be needed. Women need no protection that men do not need. What we need are laws to protect working people, to guarantee them fair pay, safe working conditions, protection against sickness and layoffs, and provision for dignified, comfortable retirement. Men and women need these things equally. That one sex needs protection more than the other is a male supremacist myth as ridiculous and unworthy of respect as the white supremacist myths that society is trying to cure itself of at this time.

Source: Accessed at Historic Speeches, sojust. net. Available online. URL: http://www.sojust.net/speeches/shirley_chisholm_women.html.

15. TEXT OF THE PROPOSED EQUAL RIGHTS AMENDMENT

(AS PROPOSED TO THE STATE LEGISLATURES IN 1972)

Section 1. Equality of rights under the law shall not be denied or abridged by the United States or by any state on account of sex.

Section 2. The Congress shall have the power to enforce, by appropriate legislation, the provisions of this article.

Section 3. This amendment shall take effect two years after the date of ratification.

Source: Accessed at http://www. equalrightsamendment.org/overview/htm.

16. OPENING STATEMENT TO THE HOUSE JUDICIARY COMMITTEE PROCEEDINGS ON THE IMPEACHMENT OF RICHARD NIXON

CONGRESSWOMAN BARBARA JORDAN, JULY 25, 1974, WASHINGTON, D.C.

Mr. Chairman, I join my colleague Mr. Rangel in thanking you for giving the junior members of this committee the glorious opportunity of sharing the pain of this inquiry. Mr. Chairman, you are a strong man, and it has not been easy but we have tried as best we can to give you as much assistance as possible.

Earlier today we heard the beginning of the Preamble to the Constitution of the United States, "We, the people." It is a very eloquent beginning.

But when that document was completed, on the seventeenth of September in 1787, I was not included in that "We, the people." I felt somehow for many years that George Washington and Alexander Hamilton just left me out by mistake. But through the process of amendment, interpretation, and court decision I have finally been included in "We, the people."

Today I am an inquisitor. I believe hyperbole would not be fictional and would not overstate the solemnness that I feel right now. My faith in the Constitution is whole, it is complete, it is total. I am not going to sit here and be an idle spectator to the diminution, the subversion, the destruction of the Constitution.

"Who can so properly be the inquisitors for the nation as the representatives of the nation themselves?" (Federalist, no. 65) The subject of its jurisdiction are those offenses which proceed from the misconduct of public men." That is what we are talking about. In other words, the jurisdiction comes from the abuse of violation of some public trust. It is wrong, I suggest, it is a misreading of the Constitution for any member here to assert that for a member to vote for an article of impeachment means that that member must be convinced that the president should be removed from office. The Constitution doesn't say that. The powers relating to impeachment are an essential check in the hands of this body, the legislature, against and upon the encroachment of the executive. In establishing the division between the two branches of the legislature, the House and the Senate, assigning to the one the right to accuse and to the other the right to judge, the framers of this Constitution were very astute. They did not make the accusers and the judges the same person.

We know the nature of impeachment. We have been talking about it awhile now. "It is chiefly designed for the president and his high ministers" to somehow be called into account. It is designed to "bridle" the executive if he engages in excesses. "It is designed as a method of national inquest into the public men." (Hamilton, Federalist, no. 65) The framers confined in the Congress the power if need be, to remove the president in order to strike a delicate balance between a president swollen with power and grown tyrannical, and preservation of the independence of the executive. The nature of impeachment is a narrowly channeled exception to the separation-of-powers maxim; the federal convention of 1787 said that. It limited impeachment to high crimes and misdemeanors and discounted and opposed the term "maladministration." "It is to be used only for great misdemeanors," so it was said in the North Carolina ratification convention. And in the Virginia ratification convention: "We do not trust our liberty to a particular branch. We need one branch to check the others."

The North Carolina ratification convention: "No one need be afraid that officers who commit oppression will pass with immunity."

"Prosecutions of impeachments will seldom fail to agitate the passions of the whole community," said Hamilton in the Federalist Papers, no. 65. "And to divide it into parties more or less friendly or inimical to the accused." I do not mean political parties in that sense.

The drawing of political lines goes to the motivation behind impeachment; but impeachment must proceed within the confines of the constitutional term "high crimes and misdemeanors."

Of the impeachment process, it was Woodrow Wilson who said that "nothing short of the grossest offenses against the plain law of the land will suffice to give them speed and effectiveness. Indignation so great as to overgrow party interest may secure a conviction; but nothing else can."

Common sense would be revolted if we engaged upon this process for insurance, campaign finance reform, housing, environmental protection, energy sufficiency, mass transportation. Pettiness cannot be allowed to stand in the face of such overwhelming problems. So today we are not being petty. We are trying to be big because the task we have before us is a big one.

This morning, in a discussion of the evidence, we were told that the evidence which purports to support the allegations of misuse of the CIA by the president is thin. We are told that that evidence is insufficient. What that recital of the evidence this morning did not include is what the president did know on June 23, 1972. The president did know that it was Republican money, that it was money from the Committee for the Re-Election of the President, which was found in the possession of one of the burglars arrested on June 17.

What the president did know on June 23 was the prior activities of E. Howard Hunt, which included his participation in the break-in of Daniel Ellsberg's psychiatrist, which included Howard Hunt's participation in the Dita Beard ITT affair, which included Howard Hunt's fabrication of cables designed to discredit the Kennedy administration.

We were further cautioned today that perhaps these proceedings ought to be delayed because certainly there would be new evidence forthcoming from the president. The committee subpoena is outstanding, and if the president wants to supply that material, the committee sits here.

The fact is that yesterday, the American people waited with great anxiety for eight hours, not knowing whether their president would obey an order of the Supreme Court of the United States.

At this point I would like to juxtapose a few of the impeachment criteria with some of the president's actions.

Impeachment criteria: James Madison, from the Virginia ratification convention. "If the president be connected in any suspicious manner with any person and there be grounds to believe that he will shelter him, he may be impeached."

We have heard time and time again that the evidence reflects payment to the defendants of money. The president had knowledge that these funds were being paid and that these were funds collected for the 1972 presidential campaign.

We know that the president met with Mr. Henry Petersen twenty-seven times to discuss matters related to Watergate and immediately thereafter met with the very persons who were implicated in the information Mr. Petersen was receiving and transmitting to the president. The words are "if the president be connected in any suspicious manner with any person and there be grounds to believe that he will shelter that person, he may be impeached."

Justice Story: "Impeachment is intended for occasional and extraordinary cases where a superior power acting for the whole people is put into operation to protect their rights and rescue their liberties from violations."

We know about the Huston plan. We know about the break-in of the psychiatrist's office. We know that there was absolute complete direction in August 1971 when the president instructed Ehrlichman to "do whatever is necessary." This instruction led to a surreptitious entry into Dr. Fielding's office.

"Protect their rights." "Rescue their liberties from violation." The South Carolina ratification convention impeachment criteria: those are impeachable "who behave amiss or betray their public trust."

Beginning shortly after the Watergate break-in and continuing to the present time, the president has engaged in a series of public statements and actions designed to thwart the lawful investigation by government prosecutors. Moreover, the president has made public announcements and assertions bearing on the Watergate case which the evidence will show he knew to be false.

These assertions, false assertions, impeachable, those who misbehave. Those who "behave amiss or betray their public trust." James Madison again at the Constitutional Convention: "A president is impeachable if he attempts to subvert the Constitution."

The Constitution charges the president with the task of taking care that the laws be faithfully executed, and yet the president has counseled his aides to commit perjury, willfully disregarded the secrecy of grand jury proceedings, concealed surreptitious entry, attempted to compromise a federal judge while publicly displaying his cooperation with the processes of criminal justice.

"A president is impeachable if he attempts to subvert the Constitution."

If the impeachment provision in the Constitution of the United States will not reach the offenses charged here, then perhaps that eighteenth century Constitution should be abandoned to a twentieth-century paper shredder. Has the president committed offenses and planned and directed and acquiesced in a course of conduct which the Constitution will not tolerate? That is the question. We know that. We know the question. We should now forthwith proceed to answer the question. It is reason, and not passion, which must guide our deliberations, guide our debate, and guide our decision."

Source: Accessed at Gifts of Speech: Women's Speeches from Around the World, Sweetbriar College. Available online. URL: http://gos.sbc.edu/j/jordan3.html.

17. Democratic Convention Keynote Address: "Who Then Will Speak for the Common Good?"

Barbara Jordan, July 12, 1976, New York City

One hundred and forty-four years ago, members of the Democratic Party first met in convention to select a Presidential candidate. Since that time, Democrats have continued to convene once every four years and draft a party platform and nominate a Presidential candidate. And our meeting this week is a continuation of that tradition.

But there is something different about tonight. There is something special about tonight. What is different? What is special? I, Barbara Jordan, am a keynote speaker.

A lot of years passed since 1832, and during that time it would have been most unusual for any national political party to ask that a Barbara Jordan deliver a keynote address . . . but tonight here I am. And I feel that notwithstanding the past that my presence here is one additional bit of evidence that the American Dream need not forever be deferred. Now that I have this grand distinction what in the world am I supposed to say? I could easily spend this time praising the accomplishments of this party and attacking the Republicans but I don't choose to do that.

I could list the many problems which Americans have. I could list the problems which cause people to feel cynical, angry, frustrated: problems which include lack of integrity in government; the feeling that the individual no longer counts; the reality of material and spiritual poverty; the feeling that the grand American experiment is failing or has failed. I could recite these problems and then I could sit down and offer no solutions. But I don't choose to do that either.

The citizens of America expect more. They deserve and they want more than a recital of problems.

We are a people in a quandary about the present. We are a people in search of our future. We are a people in search of a national community.

We are a people trying not only to solve the problems of the present: unemployment, inflation . . . but we are attempting on a larger scale to fulfill the promise of America. We are attempting to fulfill our national purpose; to create and sustain a society in which all of us are equal.

Throughout out history, when people have looked for new ways to solve their problems, and to uphold the principles of this nation, many times they have turned to political parties. They have often turned to the Democratic Party.

What is it, what is it about the Democratic Party that makes it the instrument that people use when they search for ways to shape their future? Well I believe the answer to that question lies in our concept of governing. Our concept of governing is derived from our view of people. It is a concept deeply rooted in a set of beliefs firmly etched in the national conscience, of all of us.

Now what are these beliefs?

First, we believe in equality for all and privileges for none. This is a belief that each American regardless of background has equal standing in the public forum, all of us. Because we believe this idea so firmly, we are inclusive rather than an exclusive party.

Let everybody come.

I think it no accident that most of those emigrating to America in the 19th century identified with the Democratic Party. We are a heterogeneous party made up of Americans of diverse backgrounds.

We believe that the people are the source of all governmental power; that the authority of the people is to be extended, not restricted. This can be accomplished only by providing each citizen with every opportunity to participate in the management of the government.

They must have that.

We believe that the government which represents the authority of all the people, not just one interest group, but all the people, has an obligation to actively underscore, actively seek to remove those obstacles which would block individual achievement . . . obstacles emanating from race, sex, economic condition. The government must seek to remove them.

We are a party of innovation. We do not reject our traditions, but we are willing to adapt to changing circumstances, when change we must. We are willing to suffer the discomfort of change in order to achieve a better future.

We have a positive vision of the future founded on the belief that the gap between the promise and reality of America can one day be finally closed. We believe that. This my friends, is the bedrock of our concept of governing. This is a part of the reason why Americans have turned to the Democratic Party. These are the foundations upon which a national community can be built.

Let's all understand that these guiding principles cannot be discarded for short-term political gains. They represent what this country is all about. They are indigenous to the American idea. And these are principles which are not negotiable.

In other times, I could stand here and give this kind of exposition on the beliefs of the Democratic Party and that would be enough. But today that is not enough. People want more. That is not sufficient reason for the majority of the people of this country to vote Democratic. We have made mistakes. In our haste to do all things for all people, we did not foresee the full consequences of our actions. And when the people raised their voices, we didn't hear. But our deafness was only a temporary condition, and not an irreversible condition.

Even as I stand here and admit that we have made mistakes I still believe that as the people of America sit in judgment on each party, they will recognize that our mistakes were mistakes of the heart. They'll recognize that.

And now we must look to the future. Let us heed the voice of the people and recognize their common sense. If we do not, we not only blaspheme our political heritage, we ignore the common ties that bind all Americans.

Many fear the future, Many are distrustful of their leaders, and believe that their voices are never heard. Many seek only to satisfy their private work wants. To satisfy private interests.

But this is the great danger America faces. That we will cease to be one nation and become instead a collection of interest groups: city against suburb, region against region, individual against individual. Each seeking to satisfy private wants.

If that happens, who then will speak for America?

Who then will speak for the common good? This is the question which must be answered in 1976.

Are we to be one people bound together by common spirit sharing in a common endeavor or will we become a divided nation?

For all of its uncertainty, we cannot flee the future. We must not become the new puritans and reject our society. We must address and master the future together. It can be done if we restore the belief that we share a sense of national community, that we share a common national endeavor. It can be done.

There is no executive order; there is no law that can require the American people to form a national community. This we must do as individuals and if we do it as individuals, there is no President of the United States who can veto that decision.

As a first step, we must restore our belief in ourselves. We are a generous people so why can't we be generous with each other? We need to take to heart the words spoken by Thomas Jefferson:

Let us restore to social intercourse the harmony and that affection without which liberty and even life are but dreary things.

A nation is formed by the willingness of each of us to share in the responsibility for upholding the common good.

A government is invigorated when each of us is willing to participate in shaping the future of this nation.

In this election year we must define the common good and begin again to shape a common good and begin again to shape a common future. Let each person do his or her part. If one citizen is unwilling to participate, all of us are going to suffer. For the American idea, though it is shared by all of us, is realized in each one of us.

And now, what are those of us who are elected public officials supposed to do? We call ourselves public servants but I'll tell you this: we as public servants must set an example for the rest of the nation. It is hypocritical for the public official to admonish and exhort the people to uphold the common good. More is required of public officials than slogans and handshakes and press releases. More is required. We must hold ourselves strictly accountable. We must provide the people with a vision of the future.

If we promise as public officials, we must deliver. If we as public officials propose, we must produce. If we say to the American people it is time for you to be sacrificial; sacrifice. If the public official says that, we (public officials) must be the first to give. We must be. And again, if we make mistakes, we must be willing to admit them. We have to do that. What we have to do is strike a balance between the idea, the belief, that government ought to do nothing. Strike a balance.

Let there be no illusions about the difficulty of forming this kind of a national community. It's tough, difficult, not easy. But a spirit of harmony will survive in America only if each of us remembers that we share a common destiny.

I have confidence that we can form this kind of national community.

I have confidence that the Democratic Party can lead the way. I have confidence. We cannot improve on the system of government handed down to us by the founders of the Republic, there is no way to improve upon that. But what we can do is to find new ways to implement that system and realize our destiny.

Now, I began this speech by commenting to you on the uniqueness of a Barbara Jordan making the keynote address. Well I am going to close my speech by quoting a Republican President and I ask you that as you listen to these words of Abraham Lincoln, relate them to the concept of national community in which every last one of us participates:

As I would not be a slave, so I would not be a master. This expresses my idea of Democracy. Whatever differs from this, to the extent of the difference, is no Democracy.

Source: Accessed at Historic Speeches, sojust. net. Available online. URL: http://www.sojust.net/ speeches/barbara_jordan_1976dnc.html.

18. ADDRESS ACCEPTING THE NOMINATION FOR VICE PRESIDENT

GERALDINE FERRARO, JULY 19, 1984, SAN FRANCISCO, CALIFORNIA

Ladies and gentlemen of the convention:

My name is Geraldine Ferraro. I stand before you to proclaim tonight: America is the land where dreams can come true for all of us. As I stand before the American people and think of the honor this great convention has bestowed upon me, I recall the words of Dr. Martin Luther

King Jr., who made America stronger by making America more free. He said, "Occasionally in life there are moments which cannot be completely explained by words. Their meaning can only be articulated by the inaudible language of the heart." Tonight is such a moment for me.

My heart is filled with pride. My fellow citizens, I proudly accept your nomination for Vice President of the United States.

And I am proud to run with a man who will be one of the great presidents of this century, Walter F. Mondale. Tonight, the daughter of a woman whose highest goal was a future for her children talks to our nation's oldest party about a future for us all. Tonight, the daughter of working Americans tells all Americans that the future is within our reach, if we're willing to reach for it. Tonight, the daughter of an immigrant from Italy has been chosen to run for [Vice] President in the new land my father came to love.

Our faith that we can shape a better future is what the American dream is all about. The promise of our country is that the rules are fair. If you work hard and play by the rules, you can earn your share of America's blessings. Those are the beliefs I learned from my parents. And those are the values I taught my students as a teacher in the public schools of New York City.

At night, I went to law school. I became an assistant district attorney, and I put my share of criminals behind bars. I believe if you obey the law, you should be protected. But if you break the law, you must pay for your crime.

When I first ran for Congress, all the political experts said a Democrat could not win my home district in Queens. I put my faith in the people and the values that we shared. Together, we proved the political experts wrong. In this campaign, Fritz Mondale and I have put our faith in the people. And we are going to prove the experts wrong again. We are going to win. We are going to win because Americans across this country believe in the same basic dream.

Last week, I visited Elmore, Minnesota, the small town where Fritz Mondale was raised. And soon Fritz and Joan will visit our family in Queens. Nine hundred people live in Elmore. In Queens, there are 2,000 people on one block. You would think we would be different, but we're not. Children walk to school in Elmore past grain elevators; in Queens, they pass by subway stops. But, no matter where they live, their future depends on education, and their parents are willing to do their part to make those schools as good as they can be. In Elmore, there are family farms; in Queens, small businesses. But the men and women who run them all take pride in supporting their families through hard work and initiative. On the 4th of July in Elmore, they hang flags out on Main Street; in Queens, they fly them over Grand Avenue. But all of us love our country, and stand ready to defend the freedom that it represents.

Americans want to live by the same set of rules. But under this administration, the rules are rigged against too many of our people. It isn't right that every year the share of taxes paid by individual citizens is going up, while the share paid by large corporations is getting smaller and smaller. The rules say: Everyone in our society should contribute their fair share. It isn't right that this year Ronald Reagan will hand the American people a bill for interest on the national debt larger than the entire cost of the federal government under John F. Kennedy. Our parents left us a growing economy. The rules say: We must not leave our kids a mountain of debt.

It isn't right that a woman should get paid 59 cents on the dollar for the same work as a man.

If you play by the rules, you deserve a fair day's pay for a fair day's work. It isn't right that, if trends continue, by the year 2000 nearly all of the poor people in America will be women and children. The rules of a decent society say: When you distribute sacrifice in times of austerity, you don't put women and children first. It isn't right that young people today fear they won't get the Social Security they paid for, and that older Americans fear that they will lose what they have already earned. Social Security is a contract between the last generation and the next, and the rules say: You don't break contracts.

We are going to keep faith with older Americans. We hammered out a fair compromise in the Congress to save Social Security. Every group sacrificed to keep the system sound. It is time Ronald Reagan stopped scaring our senior citizens.

It isn't right that young couples question whether to bring children into a world of 50,000 nuclear warheads. That isn't the vision for which Americans have struggled for more than two centuries. And our future doesn't have to be that way. Change is in the air, just as surely as when John Kennedy beckoned America to a new frontier; when Sally Ride rocketed into space; and when Reverend Jesse Jackson ran for the office of President of the United States.

By choosing a woman to run for our nation's second highest office, you send a powerful signal to all Americans: There are no doors we cannot unlock. We will place no limits on achievement. If we can do this, we can do anything.

Tonight, we reclaim our dream. We are going to make the rules of American life work fairly for all Americans again. To an Administration that would have us debate all over again whether the Voting Rights Act should be renewed and whether segregated schools should be tax exempt, we say, Mr. President: Those debates are over. On the issue of civil rights, voting rights, and affirmative action for minorities, we must not go backwards. We must—and we will—move forward to open the doors of opportunity.

To those who understand that our country cannot prosper unless we draw on the talents of all

Americans, we say: We will pass the Equal Rights Amendment.

The issue is not what America can do for women, but what women can do for America.

To the Americans who will lead our country into the 21st century, we say: We will not have a Supreme Court that turns the clock back to the 19th century.

To those concerned about the strength of American and family values, as I am, I say: We are going to restore those values—love, caring, partnership—by including, and not excluding, those whose beliefs differ from our own. Because our own faith is strong, we will fight to preserve the freedom of faith for others.

To those working Americans who fear that banks, utilities, and large special interests have a lock on the White House, we say: Join us; let's elect a people's president; and let's have government by and for the American people again.

To an Administration that would savage student loans and education at the dawn of a new technological age, we say: You fit the classic definition of a cynic; you know the price of everything, but the value of nothing.

To our students and their parents, we say: We will insist on the highest standards of excellence, because the jobs of the future require skilled minds. To young Americans who may be called to our country's service, we say: We know your generation will proudly answer our country's call, as each generation before you.

This past year, we remembered the bravery and sacrifice of Americans at Normandy. And we finally paid tribute—as we should have done years ago—to that unknown soldier who represents all the brave young Americans who died in Vietnam. Let no one doubt, we will defend America's security and the cause of freedom around the world. But we want a president who tells us what America's fighting for, not just what we are fighting against.

We want a president who will defend human rights, not just where it is convenient, but wherever freedom is at risk—from Chile to Afghanistan, from Poland to South Africa. To those who have watched this administration's confusion in the Middle East, as it has tilted first toward one and then another of Israel's long-time enemies and wonder: "Will America stand by her friends and sister democracy?" We say: America knows who her friends are in the Middle East and around the world. America will stand with Israel always.

Finally, we want a President who will keep America strong, but use that strength to keep America and the world at peace. A nuclear freeze is not a slogan: It is a tool for survival in the nuclear age. If we leave our children nothing else, let us leave them this Earth as we found it: whole and green and full of life.

I know in my heart that Walter Mondale will be that president.

A wise man once said, "Every one of us is given the gift of life, and what a strange gift it is. If it is preserved jealously and selfishly, it impoverishes and saddens. But if it is spent for others, it enriches and beautifies." My fellow Americans: We can debate policies and programs, but in the end what separates the two parties in this election campaign is whether we use the gift of life for others or only ourselves.

Tonight, my husband, John, and our three children are in this hall with me. To my daughters, Donna and Laura, and my son, John Junior, I say: My mother did not break faith with me, and I will not break faith with you.

To all the children of America, I say: The generation before ours kept faith with us, and like

them, we will pass on to you a stronger, more just America.

Thank you.

Source: Accessed at Gifts of Speech: Women's Speeches from Around the World, Sweetbriar College. Available online. URL: http://gos.sbc.edu/f/ferraro.html.

19. KEYNOTE ADDRESS TO THE 1988 DEMOCRATIC NATIONAL CONVENTION

GOVERNOR ANN RICHARDS OF TEXAS, JULY 19, 1988, ATLANTA, GEORGIA

Thank you. Thank you. Thank you, very much.

Good evening, ladies and gentlemen. Buenas noches, mis amigos.

I'm delighted to be here with you this evening, because after listening to George Bush all these years, I figured you needed to know what a real Texas accent sounds like.

Twelve years ago Barbara Jordan, another Texas woman, Barbara made the keynote address to this convention, and two women in a hundred and sixty years is about par for the course.

But if you give us a chance, we can perform. After all, Ginger Rogers did everything that Fred Astaire did. She just did it backwards and in high heels.

I want to announce to this Nation that in a little more than 100 days, the Reagan-Meese-Deaver-Nofziger-Poindexter-North-Weinberger-Watt-Gorsuch-Lavelle-Stockman-Haig-Bork-Noriega-George Bush [era] will be over!

You know, tonight I feel a little like I did when I played basketball in the 8th grade. I thought I looked real cute in my uniform. And then I heard a boy yell from the bleachers, "Make that basket,

Birdlegs." And my greatest fear is that same guy is somewhere out there in the audience tonight, and he's going to cut me down to size, because where I grew up there really wasn't much tolerance for self-importance, people who put on airs. I was born during the Depression in a little community just outside Waco, and I grew up listening to Franklin Roosevelt on the radio. Well, it was back then that I came to understand the small truths and the hardships that bind neighbors together. Those were real people with real problems and they had real dreams about getting out of the Depression. I can remember summer nights when we'd put down what we called the Baptist pallet, and we listened to the grown-ups talk. I can still hear the sound of the dominoes clicking on the marble slab my daddy had found for a tabletop. I can still hear the laughter of the men telling jokes you weren't supposed to hear—talkin' about how big that old buck deer was, laughin' about mama puttin' Clorox in the well when the frog fell in.

They talked about war and Washington and what this country needed. They talked straight talk. And it came from people who were living their lives as best they could. And that's what we're gonna do tonight. We're gonna tell how the cow ate the cabbage. I got a letter last week from a young mother in Lorena, Texas, and I wanna read part of it to you. She writes,

"Our worries go from pay day to pay day, just like millions of others. And we have two fairly decent incomes, but I worry how I'm going to pay the rising car insurance and food. I pray my kids don't have a growth spurt from August to December, so I don't have to buy new jeans. We buy clothes at the budget stores and we have them fray and fade and stretch in the first wash. We ponder and try to figure out how we're gonna pay for college and braces and tennis shoes. We don't take vacations and we don't go out to eat. Please don't think me ungrateful. We have jobs and a nice place to live, and we're healthy. We're the people you see every day in the grocery stores, and we obey the laws. We pay our taxes.

We fly our flags on holidays and we plod along trying to make it better for ourselves and our children and our parents. We aren't vocal any more. I think maybe we're too tired. I believe that people like us are forgotten in America."

Well of course you believe you're forgotten, because you have been.

This Republican Administration treats us as if we were pieces of a puzzle that can't fit together. They've tried to put us into compartments and separate us from each other. Their political theory is "divide and conquer." They've suggested time and time again that what is of interest to one group of Americans is not of interest to any one else. We've been isolated. We've been lumped into that sad phraseology called "special interests." They've told farmers that they were selfish, that they would drive up food prices if they asked the government to intervene on behalf of the family farm, and we watched farms go on the auction block while we bought food from foreign countries.

Well, that's wrong!

They told working mothers it's all their fault—their families are falling apart because they had to go to work to keep their kids in jeans and tennis shoes and college. And they're wrong!! They told American labor they were trying to ruin free enterprise by asking for 60 days' notice of plant closings, and that's wrong. And they told the auto industry and the steel industry and the timber industry and the oil industry, companies being threatened by foreign products flooding this country, that you're "protectionist" if you think the government should enforce our trade laws. And that is wrong. When they belittle us for demanding clean air and clean water for trying to save the oceans and the ozone layer, that's wrong.

No wonder we feel isolated and confused. We want answers and their answer is that "something is wrong with you." Well nothing's wrong with you. Nothing's wrong with you that you can't fix in November!

We've been told—We've been told that the interests of the South and the Southwest are not the same interests as the North and the Northeast. They pit one group against the other. They've divided this country and in our isolation we think government isn't gonna help us, and we're alone in our feelings. We feel forgotten. Well, the fact is that we are not an isolated piece of their puzzle. We are one nation. We are the United States of America.

Now we Democrats believe that America is still the county of fair play, that we can come out of a small town or a poor neighborhood and have the same chance as anyone else; and it doesn't matter whether we are black or Hispanic or disabled or a women [sic]. We believe that America is a country where small business owners must succeed, because they are the bedrock, backbone of our economy.

We believe that our kids deserve good daycare and public schools. We believe our kids deserve public schools where students can learn and teachers can teach. And we wanna believe that our parents will have a good retirement and that we will too. We Democrats believe that social security is a pact that cannot be broken.

We wanna believe that we can live out our lives without the terrible fear that an illness is going to bankrupt us and our children. We Democrats believe that America can overcome any problem, including the dreaded disease called AIDS. We believe that America is still a country where there is more to life than just a constant struggle for money. And we believe that America must have leaders who show us that our struggles amount to something and contribute to something larger—leaders who want us to be all that we can be.

We want leaders like Jesse Jackson. Jesse Jackson is a leader and a teacher who can open our hearts and open our minds and stir our very souls. And he has taught us that we are as good as our capacity for caring, caring about the drug problem, caring about crime, caring about education, and caring about each other.

Now, in contrast, the greatest nation of the free world has had a leader for eight straight years that has pretended that he can not hear our questions over the noise of the helicopters. And we know he doesn't wanna answer. But we have a lot of questions. And when we get our questions asked, or there is a leak, or an investigation the only answer we get is, "I don't know," or "I forgot."

But you wouldn't accept that answer from your children. I wouldn't. Don't tell me "you don't know" or "you forgot." We're not going to have the America that we want until we elect leaders who are gonna tell the truth; not most days but every day; leaders who don't forget what they don't want to remember. And for eight straight years George Bush hasn't displayed the slightest interest in anything we care about. And now that he's after a job that he can't get appointed to, he's like Columbus discovering America. He's found child care. He's found education. Poor George. He can't help it. He was born with a silver foot in his mouth.

Well, no wonder. No wonder we can't figure it out. Because the leadership of this nation is telling us one thing on TV and doing something entirely different. They tell us that they're fighting a war against terrorists. And then we find out that the White House is selling arms to the Ayatollah. They tell us that they're fighting a war on drugs and then people come on TV and testify that the CIA and the DEA and the FBI knew they were flying drugs into America all along. And they're negotiating with a dictator who is shoveling cocaine into this country like crazy. I guess that's their Central American strategy.

Now they tell us that employment rates are great, and that they're for equal opportunity. But we know it takes two paychecks to make ends meet today, when it used to take one. And the opportunity they're so proud of is low-wage, dead-end jobs. And there is no major city in America where you cannot see homeless men sitting in parking lots holding signs that say, "I will work for food."

Now my friends, we really are at a crucial point in American history. Under this Administration we have devoted our resources into making this country a military colossus. But we've let our economic lines of defense fall into disrepair. The debt of this nation is greater than it has ever been in our history. We fought a world war on less debt than the Republicans have built up in the last eight years. You know, it's kind of like that brother-in-law who drives a flashy new car, but he's always borrowing money from you to make the payments.

Well, but let's take what they are most proudest of—that is their stand of defense. We Democrats are committed to a strong America, and, quite frankly, when our leaders say to us, "We need a new weapons system," our inclination is to say, "Well, they must be right." But when we pay billions for planes that won't fly, billions for tanks that won't fire, and billions for systems that won't work, "that old dog won't hunt." And you don't have to be from Waco to know that when the Pentagon makes crooks rich and doesn't make America strong, that it's a bum deal.

Now I'm going to tell you, I'm really glad that our young people missed the Depression and missed the great Big War. But I do regret that they missed the leaders that I knew, leaders who told us when things were tough, and that we'd have to sacrifice, and that these difficulties might last for a while. They didn't tell us things were hard for us because we were different, or isolated, or special interests. They brought us together and they gave us a sense of national purpose. They gave us Social Security and they told us they

were setting up a system where we could pay our own money in, and when the time came for our retirement we could take the money out. People in the rural areas were told that we deserved to have electric lights, and they were gonna harness the energy that was necessary to give us electricity so my grandmama didn't have to carry that old coal oil lamp around. And they told us that they were gonna guarantee when we put our money in the bank, that the money was going to be there, and it was going to be insured. They did not lie to us.

And I think one of the saving graces of Democrats is that we are candid. We talk straight talk. We tell people what we think. And that tradition and those values live today in Michael Dukakis from Massachusetts.

Michael Dukakis knows that this country is on the edge of a great new era, that we're not afraid of change, that we're for thoughtful, truthful, strong leadership. Behind his calm there's an impatience to unify this country and to get on with the future. His instincts are deeply American. They're tough and they're generous. And personally, I have to tell you that I have never met a man who had a more remarkable sense about what is really important in life.

And then there's my friend and my teacher for many years, Senator Lloyd Bentsen. And I couldn't be prouder, both as a Texan and as a Democrat, because Lloyd Bentsen understands America. From the barrio to the boardroom, he knows how to bring us together, by regions, by economics, and by example. And he's already beaten George Bush once.

So, when it comes right down to it, this election is a contest between those who are satisfied with what they have and those who know we can do better. That's what this election is really all about. It's about the American dream—those who want to keep it for the few and those who know it must be nurtured and passed along.

I'm a grandmother now. And I have one nearly perfect granddaughter named Lily. And when I hold that grandbaby, I feel the continuity of life that unites us, that binds generation to generation, that ties us with each other. And sometimes I spread that Baptist pallet out on the floor, and Lily and I roll a ball back and forth. And I think of all the families like mine, like the one in Lorena, Texas, like the ones that nurture children all across America. And as I look at Lily, I know that it is within families that we learn both the need to respect individual human dignity and to work together for our common good. Within our families, within our nation, it is the same.

And as I sit there, I wonder if she'll ever grasp the changes I've seen in my life—if she'll ever believe that there was a time when blacks could not drink from public water fountains, when Hispanic children were punished for speaking Spanish in the public schools, and women couldn't vote.

I think of all the political fights I've fought, and all the compromises I've had to accept as part payment. And I think of all the small victories that have added up to national triumphs and all the things that would never have happened and all the people who would've been left behind if we had not reasoned and fought and won those battles together. And I will tell Lily that those triumphs were Democratic Party triumphs.

I want so much to tell Lily how far we've come, you and I. And as the ball rolls back and forth, I want to tell her how very lucky she is that for all our difference, we are still the greatest nation on this good earth. And our strength lies in the men and women who go to work every day, who struggle to balance their family and their jobs, and who should never, ever be forgotten.

I just hope that like her grandparents and her great-grandparents before that Lily goes on to raise her kids with the promise that echoes in homes all across America: that we can do better, and that's what this election is all about.

Thank you very much.

Source: Accessed at Gifts of Speech: Women's Speeches from Around the World, Sweetbriar College. Available online. URL: http://gos.sbc.edu/r/richards.html.

20. COMMENCEMENT ADDRESS AT WELLESLEY COLLEGE

BARBARA PIERCE BUSH, JUNE 1, 1990, WELLESLEY, MASSACHUSETTS

Thank you very, very much, President Keohane. Mrs. Gorbachev, Trustees, faculty, parents, and I should say, Julia Porter, class president, and certainly my new best friend, Christine Bicknell—and, of course, the Class of 1990. I am really thrilled to be here today, and very excited, as I know all of you must be, that Mrs. Gorbachev could join us. These are exciting times. They're exciting in Washington, and I have really looked forward to coming to Wellesley. I thought it was going to be fun. I never dreamt it would be this much fun. So, thank you for that.

More than ten years ago, when I was invited here to talk about our experiences in the People's Republic of China, I was struck by both the natural beauty of your campus and the spirit of this place.

Wellesley, you see, is not just a place but an idea—an experiment in excellence in which diversity is not just tolerated, but is embraced. The essence of this spirit was captured in a moving speech about tolerance given last year by a student body president of one of your sister colleges. She related the story by Robert Fulghum about a young pastor, finding himself in charge of some very energetic children, hits upon the game called "Giants, Wizards, and Dwarfs." "You have to decide now," the pastor instructed the children, "which you are—a giant, a wizard, or a dwarf?" At that, a small girl tugging at his pants leg, asked, "But where do the mermaids stand?" And the pastor tells her there are no mermaids. And she says, "Oh yes there are—they are. I am a mermaid."

Now this little girl knew what she was, and she was not about to give up on either her identity, or the game. She intended to take her place wherever mermaids fit into the scheme of things. "Where do the mermaids stand? All of those who are different, those who do not fit the boxes and the pigeonholes?" "Answer that question," wrote Fulghum, "And you can build a school, a nation, or a whole world." As that very wise young woman said, "Diversity, like anything worth having, requires effort—effort to learn about and respect difference, to be compassionate with one another, to cherish our own identity, and to accept unconditionally the same in others.

You should all be very proud that this is the Welles-ley spirit. Now I know your first choice today was Alice Walker—guess how I know!—known for *The Color Purple*. Instead you got me—known for the color of my hair. Alice Walker's book has a special resonance here. At Wellesley, each class is known by a special color. For four years the Class of '90 has worn the color purple. Today you meet on Severance Green to say goodbye to all of that, to begin a new and a very personal journey, to search for your own true colors.

In the world that awaits you, beyond the shores of Waban—Lake Waban, no one can say what your true colors will be. But this I do know: You have a first class education from a first class school. And so you need not, probably cannot, live a "paint-by-numbers" life. Decisions are not irrevocable. Choices do come back. And as you set off from Wellesley, I hope that many of you will consider making three very special choices.

The first is to believe in something larger than yourself, to get involved in some of the big ideas of our time. I chose literacy because I honestly

believe that if more people could read, write, and comprehend, we would be that much closer to solving so many of the problems that plague our nation and our society.

And early on I made another choice, which I hope you'll make as well. Whether you are talk-ing about education, career, or service, you're talking about life—and life really must have joy. It's supposed to be fun.

One of the reasons I made the most important decision of my life, to marry George Bush, is because he made me laugh. It's true, sometimes we've laughed through our tears, but that shared laughter has been one of our strongest bonds. Find the joy in life, because as Ferris Bueller said on his day off, "Life moves pretty fast; and ya don't stop and look around once in a while, ya gonna miss it." (I'm not going to tell George ya clapped more for Ferris than ya clapped for George.)

The third choice that must not be missed is to cherish your human connections: your relation-ships with family and friends. For several years, you've had impressed upon you the importance to your career of dedication and hard work. And, of course, that's true. But as important as your obligations as a doctor, a lawyer, a business leader will be, you are a human being first. And those human connections—with spouses, with children, with friends—are the most important investments you will ever make.

At the end of your life, you will never regret not having passed one more test, winning one more verdict, or not closing one more deal. You will regret time not spent with a husband, a child, a friend, or a parent.

We are in a transitional period right now, fasci-nating and exhilarating times, learning to adjust to changes and the choices we, men and women, are facing. As an example, I remember what a friend said, on hearing her husband complain to his buddies that he had to babysit. Quickly setting him straight, my friend told her husband that when it's your own kids, it's *not* called baby-sitting.

Now maybe we should adjust faster; maybe we should adjust slower. But whatever the era, whatever the times, one thing will never change: fathers and mothers, if you have children, they must come first. You must read to your children, and you must hug your children, and you must love your children. Your success as a family, our success as a society, depends not on what happens in the White House, but on what happens inside your house.

For over fifty years, it was said that the winner of Wellesley's annual hoop race would be the first to get married. Now they say, the winner will be the first to become a C.E.O. Both of those stereotypes show too little tolerance for those who want to know where the mermaids stand. So I want to offer a new legend: the winner of the hoop race will be the first to realize her dream—not society's dreams—her own personal dream.

Who knows? Somewhere out in this audience may even be someone who will one day follow in my footsteps, and preside over the White House as the President's spouse—and I wish him well.

Well, the controversy ends here. But our conversation is only beginning. And a worthwhile conversation it has been. So as you leave Wellesley today, take with you deep thanks for the courtesy and the honor you have shared with Mrs. Gorbachev and with me.

Thank you. God bless you. And may your future be worthy of your dreams.

Source: Accessed at Gifts of Speech. Women's Speeches from Around the World, Sweetbriar College. Available online. URL: http://gos.sbc.edu/b/bush.html.

21. "WOMEN'S RIGHTS ARE HUMAN RIGHTS"

REMARKS TO THE UNITED NATIONS FOURTH WORLD CONFERENCE ON WOMEN PLENARY SESSION
HILLARY RODHAM CLINTON, FIRST LADY OF THE UNITED STATES
SEPTEMBER 5, 1995, BEIJING, CHINA

Mrs. Mongella, Under Secretary Kittani, distinguished delegates and guests:

I would like to thank the Secretary General of the United Nations for inviting me to be part of the United Nations Fourth World Conference on Women. This is truly a celebration—a celebration of the contributions women make in every aspect of life: in the home, on the job, in their communities, as mothers, wives, sisters, daughters, learners, workers, citizens and leaders.

It is also a coming together, much the way women come together every day in every country.

We come together in fields and in factories. In village markets and supermarkets. In living rooms and board rooms.

Whether it is while playing with our children in the park, or washing clothes in a river, or taking a break at the office water cooler, we come together and talk about our aspirations and concerns. And time and again, our talk turns to our children and our families.

However different we may be, there is far more that unites us than divides us. We share a common future. And we are here to find common ground so that we may help bring new dignity and respect to women and girls all over the world—and in so doing, bring new strength and stability to families as well.

By gathering in Beijing, we are focusing world attention on issues that matter most in the lives of women and their families: access to education, health care, jobs and credit, the chance to enjoy basic legal and human rights and participate fully in the political life of their countries.

There are some who question the reason for this conference.

Let them listen to the voices of women in their homes, neighborhoods, and workplaces. There are some who wonder whether the lives of women and girls matter to economic and political progress around the globe.

Let them look at the women gathered here and at Huairou—the homemakers, nurses, teachers, lawyers, policymakers, and women who run their own businesses. It is conferences like this that compel governments and people everywhere to listen, look and face the world's most pressing problems.

Wasn't it after the women's conference in Nairobi ten years ago that the world focused for the first time on the crisis of domestic violence?

Earlier today, I participated in a World Health Organization forum, where government officials, NGOs, and individual citizens are working on ways to address the health problems of women and girls.

Tomorrow, I will attend a gathering of the United Nations Development Fund for Women. There, the discussion will focus on local—and highly successful—programs that give hard-working women access to credit so they can improve their own lives and the lives of their families.

What we are learning around the world is that if women are healthy and educated, their families will flourish. If women are free from violence, their families will flourish. If women have a chance to work and earn as full and equal partners in society, their families will flourish.

And when families flourish, communities and nations will flourish.

That is why every woman, every man, every child, every family, and every nation on our planet has a stake in the discussion that takes place here.

Over the past 25 years, I have worked persistently on issues relating to women, children and families. Over the past two-and-a-half years, I have had the opportunity to learn more about the challenges facing women in my own country and around the world.

I have met new mothers in Jojakarta, Indonesia, who come together regularly in their village to discuss nutrition, family planning, and baby care.

I have met working parents in Denmark who talk about the comfort they feel in knowing that their children can be cared for in creative, safe, and nurturing after-school centers. I have met women in South Africa who helped lead the struggle to end apartheid and are now helping build a new democracy.

I have met with the leading women of the Western Hemisphere who are working every day to promote literacy and better health care for the children of their countries. I have met women in India and Bangladesh who are taking out small loans to buy milk cows, rickshaws, thread and other materials to create a livelihood for themselves and their families.

I have met doctors and nurses in Belarus and Ukraine who are trying to keep children alive in the aftermath of Chernobyl.

The great challenge of this Conference is to give voice to women everywhere whose experiences go unnoticed, whose words go unheard.

Women comprise more than half the world's population. Women are 70% percent of the world's poor, and two-thirds of those who are not taught to read and write.

Women are the primary caretakers for most of the world's children and elderly. Yet much of the work we do is not valued—not by economists, not by historians, not by popular culture, not by government leaders.

At this very moment, as we sit here, women around the world are giving birth, raising children, cooking meals, washing clothes, cleaning houses, planting crops, working on assembly lines, running companies, and running countries.

Women also are dying from diseases that should have been prevented or treated; they are watching their children succumb to malnutrition caused by poverty and economic deprivation; they are being denied the right to go to school by their own fathers and brothers; they are being forced into prostitution, and they are being barred from the bank lending office and banned from the ballot box.

Those of us who have the opportunity to be here have the responsibility to speak for those who could not.

As an American, I want to speak up for women in my own country—women who are raising children on the minimum wage, women who can't afford health care or child care, women whose lives are threatened by violence, including violence in their own homes. I want to speak up for mothers who are fighting for good schools, safe neighborhoods, clean air and clean airwaves; for older women, some of them widows, who have raised their families and now find that their skills and life experiences are not valued in the workplace; for women who are working all night as nurses, hotel clerks, and fast food cooks so that they can be at home during the day with their kids; and for women everywhere who simply don't have time to do everything they are called upon to do each day.

Speaking to you today, I speak for them, just as each of us speaks for women around the world

who are denied the chance to go to school, or see a doctor, or own property, or have a say about the direction of their lives, simply because they are women. The truth is that most women around the world work both inside and outside the home, usually by necessity.

We need to understand that there is no formula for how women should lead their lives. That is why we must respect the choices that each woman makes for herself and her family. Every woman deserves the chance to realize her God-given potential. We also must recognize that women will never gain full dignity until their human rights are respected and protected.

Our goals for this Conference, to strengthen families and societies by empowering women to take greater control over their own destinies, cannot be fully achieved unless all governments—here and around the world—accept their responsibility to protect and promote internationally recognized human rights.

The international community has long acknowledged—and recently affirmed at Vienna—that both women and men are entitled to a range of protections and personal freedoms, from the right of personal security to the right to determine freely the number and spacing of the children they bear.

No one should be forced to remain silent for fear of religious or political persecution, arrest, abuse or torture.

Tragically, women are most often the ones whose human rights are violated. Even in the late 20th century, the rape of women continues to be used as an instrument of armed conflict. Women and children make up a large majority of the world's refugees. When women are excluded from the political process, they become even more vulnerable to abuse.

I believe that, on the eve of a new millennium, it is time to break our silence. It is time for us to say here in Beijing, and the world to hear, that it is no longer acceptable to discuss women's rights as separate from human rights.

These abuses have continued because, for too long, the history of women has been a history of silence. Even today, there are those who are trying to silence our words. The voices of this conference and of the women at Huairou must be heard loud and clear: It is a violation of human rights when babies are denied food, or drowned, or suffocated, or their spines broken, simply because they are born girls.

It is a violation of human rights when women and girls are sold into the slavery of prostitution.

It is a violation of human rights when women are doused with gasoline, set on fire and burned to death because their marriage dowries are deemed too small.

It is a violation of human rights when individual women are raped in their own communities and when thousands of women are subjected to rape as a tactic or prize of war.

It is a violation of human rights when a leading cause of death worldwide among women ages 14 to 44 is the violence they are subjected to in their own homes.

It is a violation of human rights when young girls are brutalized by the painful and degrading practice of genital mutilation.

It is a violation of human rights when women are denied the right to plan their own families, and that includes being forced to have abortions or being sterilized against their will.

If there is one message that echoes forth from this conference, it is that human rights are women's rights—and women's rights are human rights. Let us not forget that among those rights are the right to speak freely—and the right to be heard.

Women must enjoy the right to participate fully in the social and political lives of their countries if we want freedom and democracy to thrive and endure.

It is indefensible that many women in nongovernmental organizations who wished to participate in this conference have not been able to attend—or have been prohibited from fully taking part.

Let me be clear. Freedom means the right of people to assemble, organize, and debate openly. It means respecting the views of those who may disagree with the views of their governments. It means not taking citizens away from their loved ones and jailing them, mistreating them, or denying them their freedom or dignity because of the peaceful expression of their ideas and opinions.

In my country, we recently celebrated the 75th anniversary of women's suffrage. It took 150 years after the signing of our Declaration of Independence for women to win the right to vote.

It took 72 years of organized struggle on the part of many courageous women and men. It was one of America's most divisive philosophical wars. But it was also a bloodless war. Suffrage was achieved without a shot being fired.

We have also been reminded, in V-J Day observances last weekend, of the good that comes when men and women join together to combat the forces of tyranny and build a better world.

We have seen peace prevail in most places for a half century. We have avoided another world war.

But we have not solved older, deeply-rooted problems that continue to diminish the potential of half the world's population.

Now it is time to act on behalf of women everywhere. If we take bold steps to better the lives of women, we will be taking bold steps to better the lives of children and families too.

Families rely on mothers and wives for emotional support and care; families rely on women for labor in the home; and increasingly, families rely on women for income needed to raise healthy children and care for other relatives.

As long as discrimination and inequities remain so commonplace around the world—as long as girls and women are valued less, fed less, fed last, overworked, underpaid, not schooled and subjected to violence in and out of their homes—the potential of the human family to create a peaceful, prosperous world will not be realized.

Let this Conference be our—and the world's—call to action.

And let us heed the call so that we can create a world in which every woman is treated with respect and dignity, every boy and girl is loved and cared for equally, and every family has the hope of a strong and stable future.

Thank you very much.

God's blessings on you, your work and all who will benefit from it.

Source: Accessed at Historic Speeches, sojust.net. URL: http://www.sojust.net/speeches/hillaryclinton_women.html.

BIBLIOGRAPHY

Abramovitz, Mimi. *Regulating the Lives of Women: Social Welfare Policy from Colonial Times to the Present.* Boston: South End Press, 1996.

Abzug, Bella, and Mim Kelber. *Gender Gap: Bella Abzug's Guide to Political Power for American Women.* Boston: Houghton Mifflin, 1984.

Ackman, Dan "Wal-Mart and Sex Discrimination by the Numbers." *Forbes* 23 June, 2004.

Addams, Jane. *Twenty Years at Hull-House: with Autobiographical Notes.* Edited by Victoria Bissell Brown. Boston: Bedford/St. Martin's, 1999.

Albright, Madeleine, and Bill Woodward. *Madame Secretary: A Memoir Madeleine Albright.* New York: Miramax Books, 2003.

Alpern, Kenneth D. ed. *The Ethics of Reproductive Technology.* New York and Oxford: Oxford University Press, 1992.

American Association of University Women. *How Schools Shortchange Girls: A Study of Major Findings on Girls and Education.* Wellesley, Mass.: Wellesley College Center for Research on Women, 1992.

Anderson, Christopher. *Citizen Jane: The Turbulent Life of Jane Fonda.* New York: Henry Holt, 1990.

Anderson, Marian. *My Lord, What a Morning.* New York: Viking Press, 1956.

Anderson, Peggy. *The Daughters: An Unconventional Look at America's Fan Club—the D.A.R.* New York: St. Martin's Press, 1974.

Anderson, William, and David Wade. *The World of Louisa May Alcott.* New York: HarperPerennial, 1995.

Aron, Michael. *Governor's Race: A TV Reporter's Chronicle of the 1993 Florio/Whitman Campaign.* Piscataway, N.J.: Rutgers University Press, 1994.

Austin, Sara, and Thomas R. Kearns. *Law in Everyday Life.* Ann Arbor: University of Michigan Press, 1993.

Baer, Judith A. *The Chains of Protection: The Judicial Response to Women's Labor Legislation.* Westport, Conn.: Greenwood Press, 1978.

Baird, Robert, and Stuart Rosenbaum. *The Ethics of Abortion: Pro-Life v. Pro-Choice.* New York: Prometheus Books, 2001.

Barbuto, Domenica M., ed. *The American Settlement Movement: A Bibliography.* Bibliographies and Indexes in American History, no. 42. Westport, Conn.: Greenwood Press, 1999.

Barton, William. *The Life of Clara Barton, Founder of the American Red Cross.* New York: AMS Press, 1969.

Basow, Susan. *Gender Stereotypes: Traditions and Alternatives.* Monterey, Calif.: Brooks/Cole Publishing, 1986.

Baumgardner, Jennifer, and Amy Richards. *Manifesta: Young Women, Feminism, and the Future.* New York: Farrar, Straus and Giroux, 2000.

Bayer, Linda. *Ruth Bader Ginsburg.* Philadelphia: Chelsea House Publishers, 2000.

Becker, Susan. *The Origins of the Equal Rights Amendment: American Feminism Between the Wars.* Westport, Conn.: Greenwood, 1982.

Beckman, Linda J., and S. Marie Harvey, eds. *The New Civil War: The Psychology, Culture, and Politics of Abortion.* Washington, D.C.: American Psychological Association, 1998.

Beisel, Nicola. *Imperiled Innocents: Anthony Comstock and Family Reproduction in Victorian America.* Princeton, N.J.: Princeton University Press, 1997.

Benjamin, Anne Myra Goodman. *A History of the Anti-suffrage Movement in the United States from 1895 to 1920: Women Against Equality.* Lewiston, N.Y.: Edwin Mellen Press, 1991.

Berry, Mary Frances. *The Politics of Parenthood: Childcare, Women's Rights, and the Myth of the Good Mother.* New York: Penguin Books, 1993.

———. *Why ERA Failed: Politics, Women's Rights and the Amending Process of the Constitution.* Bloomington: Indiana University Press, 1986.

Bigelow, Carlisle Barbara. *Contemporary Black Biography: Profiles from the International Black Community,* vol. 2. Detroit: Gale Research Inc., 1992.

Black, Shirley Temple. *Child Star: An Autobiography.* New York: McGraw-Hill, 1988.

Blackwell, Alice Stone. *Lucy Stone: Pioneer of Women's Rights.* Charlottesville: University Press of Virginia, 2001.

Blackwell, Elizabeth. *Pioneer Work in Opening the Medical Profession to Women.* New York: Prometheus Books, 2005.

Blair, Karen J. *The Clubwoman as Feminist: True Womanhood Redefined, 1868–1914.* New York: Holmes and Meier Publishers, 1980.

Blanchard, Dallas A. *The Anti-Abortion Movement and the Rise of the Religious Right: From Polite to Fiery Protest.* New York: Twayne Publishers, 1994.

Block-Fried, Adrienne. *Amy Beach: Passionate Victorian.* Oxford: Oxford University Press, 1998.

Bloomer, Dexter C. *Life and Writings of Ameilia Bloomer.* 1895. Reprint, New York: Schocken Books, 1975.

Blum, Linda M. *Between Feminism and Labor: The Significance of the Comparable Worth Movement.* Berkeley: University of California Press, 1991.

Bohrer, Melissa Lukeman. *Glory, Passion, and Principals: The Story of Eight Remarkable Women at the Core of the American Revolution.* New York: Anita Books, 2003.

Boo, Katherine. "Universal Soldier: What Paula Coughlin Can Teach American Women." *Washington Monthly.* 24 September 1992, 37–40.

Bordin, Ruth. *Alice Freeman Palmer: The Evolution of a New Woman.* Ann Arbor: University of Michigan Press, 1993.

———. *Woman and Temperance: The Quest for Power and Liberty, 1873–1900.* New Brunswick, N.J.: Rutgers University Press, 1990.

Boston Women's Health Collective. *Our Bodies Ourselves: A New Edition for a New Era.* New York: Simon and Schuster, 2005.

Boydston, Jeanne, Mary Keeley, and Anne Margolis. *The Limits of Sisterhood: The Beecher Sisters on Women's Rights and Woman's Sphere.* Chapel Hill: University of North Carolina Press, 1988.

Braden, Maria. *Women Politicians and the Media.* Lexington: University of Kentucky Press, 1996.

Bradley, Patricia. *Mass Media and the Shaping of American Feminism.* Jackson: University Press of Mississippi, 2003.

Brady, David W., and Kent L. Tedin. "Ladies in Pink: Religion and Political Ideology in the Anti-ERA Movement." *Social Science Quarterly* 54 (1976): 564–575.

Brady, Kathleen. *Ida Tarbell: Portrait of a Muckraker.* Pittsburgh: University of Pittsburgh Press, 1989.

Breslin, Rosemary, and Joshua Hammer. *Gerry!: A Woman Making History.* New York: Pinnacle Books, 1984.

Brown, Cynthia Stokes, ed. *Ready from Within: Septima Clark and the Civil Rights Movement.* Navarro, Calif.: Wild Trees Press, 1986.

Brown, Ruth Murray. *For a "Christian America": The History of the Religious Right.* New York: Prometheus Books, 2002.

Browne, Stephen H. *Angelina Grimké: Rhetoric, Identity and the Radical Imagination.* East Lansing: Michigan State University Press, 2000.

Bryan, Mary Lynn McCree, and Allen Freeman Davis, eds. *100 Years at Hull-House.* Bloomington: Indiana University Press, 1990.

Byrne, Jane. *My Chicago.* Chicago: Northwestern University Press, 2004.

Bysiewicz, Susan. *Ella: A Biography of Ella Grasso.* Old Saybrook, Conn.: Peregrine Press, 1984.

Camhi, Jane Jerome. *Women against Women: American Anti-Suffragism 1880–1920.* New York: Carlson Publishers, 1994.

Campbell, Amy Leigh. *Raising the Bar: Ruth Bader Ginsburg and the ACLU Women's Rights Project.* Philadelphia: Xlibris Corporation, 2004.

Canfield, Gae Whitney. *Sarah Winnemucca of the Northern Paiutes.* Norman: University of Oklahoma Press, 1983.

Carlton-LaNey, Iris. *African American Leadership: An Empowerment Tradition in Social Welfare History.* Washington, D.C.: NASW Press, 2001.

Carroll, Susan J. *Women and American Politics: New Questions, New Directions.* Oxford: Oxford University Press, 2003.

Carson, Clayborne, and Darlene Clark Hine, eds. *Black Women in America: A Historical Encyclopedia.* New York: Carlson Publishing Inc., 1993.

Casper, Gerhard. *Landmark Abortion Cases: Planned Parenthood v. Casey.* Bethesda, Md.: University Publications of America, 1993.

Catt, Carrie Chapman, and Nettie Rogers Shuler. *Woman Suffrage and Politics: The Inner Story of the Suffrage Movement.* New York: C. Scribner's Sons, 1923.

Celeste, Marie. *Intimate Friendships of Elizabeth Ann Bayley Seton: First Native-Born American Saint, 1774–1821.* Lanham, Md.: University Press of America, 2000.

Chen, Constance M. *The Sex Side of Life: Mary Ware Dennett's Pioneering Battle for Birth Control and Sex Education.* New York: W.W. Norton & Co., 1996.

Chesler, Ellen. *Woman of Valor: Margaret Sanger and the Birth Control Movement in America.* New York: Simon & Schuster, 1992.

Chesler, Phyllis. *Sacred Bond: The Legacy of Baby M.* New York: Times Books, 1988.

Chisholm, Shirley. *Unbought and Unbossed: An Autobiography.* New York: Houghton Mifflin Co., 1970.

Chodorow, Nancy. *The Reproduction of Mothering: Psychoanalysis and the Sociology of Gender.* Berkeley: University of California Press, 1978.

Clark, Septima. *Echo in My Soul.* New York: E.P. Dutton, 1962.

Clifford, Deborah. *Mine Eyes Have Seen the Glory: A Biography of Julia Ward Howe.* Boston: Little, Brown, 1979.

Cobble, Dorothy Sue. *The Other Women's Movement: Workplace Justice and Social Rights in Modern America.* Princeton, N.J.: Princeton University Press, 2004.

Collins, Patricia Hill. *Black Feminist Thought: Knowledge, Consciousness, and Politics of Empowerment.* Boston: Unwin Hyman, 1990.

Commager, Henry Steele, ed. *Documents of American History to 1898,* vol. 1. New York: Prentice Hall, 1993.

Conn, Peter. *Pearl S. Buck: A Cultural Biography.* London: Cambridge University Press, 1998.

Conover, Pamela Johnston, and Virginia Gray. *Feminism and the New Right: Conflict over the American Family.* New York: Praeger, 1983.

Conrad, Susan Phinney. *Perish the Thought: Intellectual Women in Romantic America, 1830–1860.* New York: Oxford University Press, 1976.

Cook, Blanche Wiesen. *Eleanor Roosevelt: Volume One, 1884–1933.* New York: Viking, 1992.

Cook, Rebecca, ed. *Human Rights of Women: National and International Perspectives.* Philadelphia: University of Pennsylvania Press, 1994.

Corbett, Katharine T. *In Her Place: A Guide to St. Louis Women's History.* St. Louis: Missouri Historical Society Press, 1999.

Corn, David. "The Death of Mary McGrory." *Nation* 23 April 2004.

Costain, Lela B. *Two Sisters for Social Justice: A Biography of Grace and Edith Abbott.* Urbana: University of Illinois Press, 1983.

Cott, Nancy. "Feminist Politics in the 1920s: The National Woman's Party." *The Journal of American History* 71 (1984): 43–68.

———. *The Grounding of Modern Feminism.* New Haven, Conn.: Yale University Press, 1987.

———. *No Small Courage: A History of Women in the United States.* New York: Oxford Press, 2000.

Cox, Karen L. *Dixie's Daughters: The United Daughters of the Confederacy and the Preservation of Confederate Culture.* Gainesville: University Press of Florida, 2003.

Crawford, Susan Hoy. *Beyond Dolls and Guns: 101 Ways to Help Children Avoid Gender Bias.* Portsmouth, N.H.: Heinemann Press, 1995.

Cromwell, Otelia. *Lucretia Mott.* Cambridge, Mass.: Harvard University Press, 1958.

Cuddy, Lois A., and Claire M. Roche. *Evolution and Eugenics in American Literature and Culture, 1880–1940.* Lewisburg, Pa.: Bucknell University Press, 2003.

Daly, Mary. *Gyn/Ecology: The Metaethics of Radical Feminism.* Boston: Beacon Press, 1978.

Datnow, Amanda, and Lea Hubbard, eds. *Gender in Policy and Practice: Perspectives on Single Sex and Co-Educational Schooling.* New York: Routledge, 2002.

Davis, Allen F. *American Heroine: The Life and Legend of Jane Addams.* London: Oxford University Press, 1973.

Davis, Angela. *The Angela Y. Davis Reader.* Malden, Mass.: Blackwell, 1998.

———. *Blues Legacies and Black Feminism: Gertrude "Ma" Rainey, Bessie Smith, and Billie Holiday.* New York: Pantheon Books, 1998.

———, and Chela Sandoval. *Methodology of the Oppressed.* Minneapolis: University of Minnesota Press, 2000.

———, and Joy James. *Resisting State Violence: Radicalism, Gender, and Race in U.S. Culture.* Malden, Mass.: Blackwell, 1996.

———. *Violence against Women and the Ongoing Challenge to Racism.* Latham, N.Y.: Kitchen Table Women of Color Press, 1992.

———. *Women, Race, and Class.* New York: Vintage Books, 1983.

De Hart, Jane Sherron. "Gender on the Right: Meaning Behind the Existential Scream." *Gender & History* 3 (1991): 246–267.

———, and Donald G. Mathews. *Sex, Gender, and the Politics of the ERA: A State and the Nation.* New York: Oxford University Press, 1990.

DeLeon, David. *Leaders from the 1960s: A Biographical Sourcebook of American Activism.* Westport, Conn.: Greenwood Press, 1994.

D'Emilio, John. *Sexual Politics, Sexual Communities: The Making of a Homosexual Minority in the United States, 1940–1970.* Chicago: University of Chicago Press, 1983.

Dennett, Mary Ware. *Birth Control Laws: Shall We Keep Them, Change Them, Or Abolish Them.* New York: Da Capo Press, 1926.

Dole, Elizabeth, and Bob Dole. *Unlimited Partners: Our American Story.* New York: Simon & Schuster, 1996.

Douglas, Helen Gahagan. *A Full Life: Helen Gahagan Douglas.* Garden City, N.Y.: Doubleday, 1982.

Doyle, Paul A. *Pearl S. Buck.* Twayne's United States Authors Series. New York: Twayne Publishers, 1980.

Drachman, Virginia G. *Sisters in Law: Women Lawyers in Modern American History.* Cambridge, Mass.: Harvard University Press, 1998.

Dubeck, Paula J., and Dana Dunn. *Workplace/Women's Place: An Anthology.* Los Angeles: Roxbury Publishing Company, 2006.

DuBois, Ellen Carol *Elizabeth Cady Stanton–Susan B. Anthony Reader: Correspondence, Writings, Speeches.* Boston: Northeastern University Press, 1992.

———. *Feminism and Suffrage: The Emergence of an Independent Women's Movement in America, 1848–1869.* Ithaca, N.Y.: Cornell University Press, 1978.

———. *Harriot Stanton Blatch and the Winning of Woman Suffrage.* New Haven, Conn.: Yale University Press, 1997.

Dulles, Eleanor Lansing. *Chances of a Lifetime: A Memoir.* Englewood Cliffs, N.J.: Prentice-Hall, 1980.

Duniway, Abigail Scott. *Path Breaking: An Autobiographical History of the Equal Suffrage Movement in Pacific Coast States.* New York: Schocken Books, 1971.

Dunn, Lynne Kathleen. "Joining the Boys' Club: The Diplomatic Career of Eleanor Lansing Dulles." In *Women and American Foreign Policy: Critics, Lobbyists and Insiders,* edited by Edward Crapol. Westport, Conn.: Greenwood Press, 1987.

Echols, Alice. *Daring to be Bad: Radical Feminism in America, 1967–1975.* Minneapolis: University of Minnesota Press, 1989.

Ehrenreich, Barbara. *Nickel and Dimed: On (Not) Getting by in America.* New York: Owl Books, 2002.

———. "A Uterus is No Substitute for a Conscience: What Abu Ghraib Taught Me." *ZNet* 21 May 2004. Available online. URL: http://www.zmag.org/content/showarticle.cfm?ItemJD=5571. Accessed on January 4, 2007.

Elders, M. Joycelyn. *Joycelyn Elders: From Sharecroppers' Daughter to Surgeon General of the United States of America.* New York: William Morrow, 1996.

Elshtain, Jean Bethke. *Jane Addams and the Dream of American Democracy: A Life.* New York: Basic Books, 2002.

Epstein, Barbara Leslie. *The Politics of Domesticity: Women, Evangelism, and Temperance in Nineteenth Century America.* Middletown, Conn.: Wesleyan University Press, 1981.

Evans, Sara. *Born for Liberty: A History of Women in America.* New York: Free Press, 1997.

Ewen, Elizabeth. *Immigrant Women in the Land of Dollars: Life and Culture of the Lower East Side, 1890–1925.* New York: Monthly Review Press, 1985.

Falk, Candace. *Love, Anarchy and Emma Goldman.* New Brunswick, N.J.: Rutgers University Press, 1990.

Faludi, Susan. *Backlash: The Undeclared War Against American Women.* New York: Crown, 1991.

———. *Stiffed: The Betrayal of the American Man.* New York: W. Morrow, 1999.

Farrell, Amy Erdman. *Yours in Sisterhood: Ms. Magazine and the Promise of Popular Feminism (Gender and American Culture).* Chapel Hill: University of North Carolina Press, 1998.

Feldt, Gloria, and Laura Fraser. *The War on Choice: The Right-Wing Attack on Women's Rights and How to Fight Back.* New York: Bantam Books, 2004.

Felsenthal, Carol. *The Biography of Phyllis Schlafly: The Sweetheart of the Silent Majority.* Garden City, N.Y.: Doubleday & Company, Inc., 1981.

Fenwick, Millicent. *Speaking Up.* New York: Harper and Row, 1982.

Ferraro, Geraldine. *Ferraro, My Story.* New York: Bantam Books, 1985.

Firestone, Shulamith. *The Dialectic of Sex.* New York: Bantam Books, 1970.

Fitzpatrick, Ellen. *Endless Crusade: Women Social Scientists and Progressive Reform.* New York: Oxford University Press, 1990.

———. *Muckraking: Three Landmark Articles.* Boston: Bedford/St. Martins, 1994.

Foerstel, Karen. *Biographical Dictionary of Congressional Women.* Westport, Conn.: Greenwood Press, 1999.

Fonda, Jane. *My Life So Far.* New York: Random House, 2005.

Ford, Linda. "Alice Paul and the Politics of Nonviolent Protest." In *Votes for Women: The Struggle for Suffrage Revisited,* edited by Jean H. Baker. New York: Oxford University Press, 2002.

Ford, Linda G. *Iron Jawed Angels: The Suffrage Militancy of the National Woman's Party, 1912–1920.* Lanham, Md.: University Press of America, 1991.

Ford, Lynne E. *Women and Politics: The Pursuit of Equality,* 2nd ed. Boston: Houghton Mifflin, 2006.

Forest, James H. *Love Is the Measure: A Biography of Dorothy Day.* Maryknoll, N.Y.: Orbis Press, 1994.

Forster, Margaret. *Significant Sisters: The Grassroots of American Feminism 1839–1939.* New York: Alfred Knopf, 1985.

Fowler, Robert Booth. *Carrie Catt: Feminist Politician.* Boston: Northeastern University Press, 1986.

Fox, James. *The Five Sisters: The Langhornes of Virginia.* New York: Simon and Schuster, 2000.

Freeman, Jo. *At Berkeley in the Sixties: Education of an Activist, 1961–1965.* Indiana: Indiana University Press, 2004.

———. *A Room at a Time: How Women Entered Party Politics.* Lanham, Md.: Rowland and Littlefield Publishers, 2000.

———. *Women: A Feminist Perspective.* Mountain View, Calif.: Mayfield Publishing Co., 1995.

Friedan, Betty. *Life So Far.* New York: Simon & Schuster, 2000.

Friedman, Jane M. *America's First Woman Lawyer: The Biography of Myra Bradwell.* Buffalo, N.Y.: Prometheus Books, 1993.

Friedman, Leon. *The Supreme Court Confronts Abortion: The Briefs, Argument, and Decision in Planned Parenthood v. Casey.* New York: Farrar, Straus, and Giroux, 1993.

Frost-Knappman, Elizabeth, and Kathryn Cullen-DuPont. *Women's Rights on Trial: 101 Historic Trials from Anne Hutchinson to the Virginia Military Institute Cadets.* Detroit: Gale Publishing, 1997.

Fuller, Paul E. *Laura Clay and the Woman's Rights Movement.* Lexington: The University Press of Kentucky, 1975.

Furchtgott-Roth, Diana, and Christine Solba. *Women's Figures: An Illustrated Guide to the Economic Progress of Women in America.* Washington, D.C.: AEI Press and the Independent Women's Forum, 1999.

Furlow, John W., Jr. "Cornelia Bryce Pinchot: Feminism in the Post-Suffrage Era." *Pennsylvania History* 43 (1976): 329–346.

Gabriel, Mary. *Notorious Victoria: the Life of Victoria Woodhull Uncensored.* Chapel Hill, N.C.: Algonquin Books of Chapel Hill, 1998.

Gelles, Edith B. *Portia: The World of Abigail Adams.* New York: Routledge, 2002.

Giddings, Paula. *When and Where I Enter.* New York: William Morrow & Company, 1984.

Giele, Janet Zollinger. *Two Paths to Equality.* New York: MacMillan Library Reference, 1995.

Gilbert, Olive. *Narrative of Sojourner Truth,* edited by Margaret Washington. New York: Vintage Books, 1993.

Gilbreth, Lillian. *As I Remember: An Autobiography of Lillian Moller Gilbreth.* Norcross, Ga.: Engineering and Management Press, 1998.

Gilchrist, Beth Bradford. *The Life of Mary Lyon.* Boston: Houghton Mifflin, 1910.

Giles, Kevin S. *Flight of the Dove: The Story of Jeanette Rankin.* Beaverton, Oreg.: Touchstone Press, 1980.

Gill, Gillian. *Mary Baker Eddy.* Reading: Perseus Books, 1998.

Gilligan, Carol. *In a Different Voice.* Cambridge, Mass.: Harvard University Press, 1982.

Gillis, Stacy, Gillian Howie, and Rebecca Munford, eds. *Third Wave Feminism: A Critical Exploration.* New York: Palgrave, 2004.

Gilman, Charlotte Perkins. *The Living of Charlotte Perkins Gilman: An Autobiography.* Madison: University of Wisconsin Press, 1991.

Glass, Jennifer L., and Sarah Beth Estes. "The Family Responsive Workplace." *Annual Review of Sociology* 23 (1997): 298–314.

Goldman, Emma. *Living My Life.* New York: AMS Press, 1970.

———, and Alix Kates Shulman, eds. *Red Emma Speaks: An Emma Goldman Reader.* New York: Schocken Books, 1982.

Goldstein, Leslie. *Contemporary Cases in Women's Rights.* Madison: University of Wisconsin Press, 1994.

Gollaher, David. *Voices for the Mad: The Life of Dorothea Dix.* New York: Free Press, 1995.

González, Deena. "La Tules of Image and Reality: Euro-American Attitudes and Legend Formation on a Spanish-Mexican Frontier." In *Building with Our Hands: Directions in Chicana Scholarship,* edited by Beatrmz M. Pesquera and Adela de la Torre. Berkeley: University of California Press, 1993.

———. *Refusing the Favor: The Spanish-Mexican Women of Santa Fe, 1820–1880.* New York: Oxford University Press, 1999.

Goodwin, Doris Kearns. *No Ordinary Time: Franklin and Eleanor Roosevelt: The Home Front in World War II.* New York: Simon & Schuster, 1994.

Gordon, Linda. *The Moral Property of Women: A History of Birth Control Politics in America.* Urbana: University of Illinois Press, 2002.

———. *Pitied but Not Entitled: Single Mothers and the History of Welfare.* New York: Free Press, 1994.

———. *Woman's Body, Woman's Right: A Social History of Birth Control in America.* New York: Grossman Publishers, 1976.

Gordon, Vivian V. *Black Women, Feminism, and Black Liberation: Which Way?* Chicago: Third World Press, 1985.

Gorn, Elliott J. *Mother Jones: The Most Dangerous Woman in America.* New York: Hill and Wang, 2001.

Gorney, Cynthia. *Articles of Faith: A Frontline History of the Abortion Wars.* New York: Simon and Schuster, 2000.

Gould, Lewis L., ed. *American First Ladies: Their Lives and Their Legacy,* 2nd ed. New York: Routledge, 2001.

Graf, Mercedes. "Women Physicians in the Spanish-American War." *Army History* 28 (2000): 5–15.

Grant, Joanne. *Ella Baker: Freedom Bound.* New York: Wiley, 1988.

Grant, Mary Hetherington. *Private Woman, Public Person: An Account of the Life of Julia Ward Howe from 1819–1868.* Brooklyn: Carlson Publishing, 1994.

Green, Elna C. *Southern Strategies: Southern Women and the Woman Suffrage Question.* Chapel Hill: University of North Carolina Press, 1997.

Gregory, Ramond. *Unwelcome and Unlawful: Sexual Harassment in the American Workplace.* Ithaca, N.Y.: Cornell University Press, 2004.

Griffith, Elisabeth. *In Her Own Right: The Life of Elizabeth Cady Stanton.* Oxford: Oxford University Press, 1985.

Grumet, Robert Steven. *Northeastern Indian Lives, 1632–1816.* Amherst: University of Massachusetts Press, 1996.

Guerrila Girls. *Bitches, Bimbos and Ballbreakers: The Guerrilla Girls' Illustrated Guide to Female Stereotypes.* New York: Penguin Books, 2003.

———. *The Guerrilla Girls Bedside Companion to the History of Western Art.* New York: Penguin Books, 1998.

Guinier, Lani. *Lift Every Voice: Turning a Civil Rights Setback into a New Vision of Social Justice.* New York: Simon and Schuster, 1998.

———. *Tyranny of the Majority.* New York: The Free Press, 1994.

Gurko, Miriam. *The Ladies of Seneca Falls: The Birth of the Woman's Rights Movement.* New York: Schocken Books, 1974.

Guy-Sheftall, Beverly, ed. *Words of Fire: An Anthology of African-American Feminist Thought.* New York: The New Press, 1995.

Guzzo, Louis. *Is It True What They Say About Dixy?: A Biography of Dixy Lee Ray.* Mercer Island, Wash.: Writing Works, 1980.

Halberstam, Malvina, and Elizabeth F. Defeis. *Women's Legal Rights: International Covenants and Alternative to ERA?* Dobbs Ferry, N.Y.: Transnational Publishers Inc., 1987.

Hall, Jacquelyn Dowd. *Revolt Against Chivalry: Jessie Daniel Ames and the Women's Campaign against Lynching.* New York: Columbia University Press, 1979.

Handlin, Amy. *Whatever Happened to the Year of the Woman? Why Women Still Aren't Making It to the Top of Politics.* New York: Arden Press, 1998.

Hanson, Joyce A. *Mary McLeod Bethune and Black Women's Political Activism.* Columbia: University of Missouri Press, 2003.

Hardisty, Jean. *Mobilizing Resentment: Conservative Resurgence from the John Birch Society to the Promise Keepers.* Boston: Beacon Press, 1999.

Hare, Lloyd C. M. *The Greatest American Woman, Lucretia Mott.* New York: Negro Universities Press, 1937.

Harrison, Cynthia. *On Account of Sex: The Politics of Women's Issues, 1945–1968.* Berkeley: University of California Press, 1988.

Harrison, Pat. *Jeane Kirkpatrick.* New York: Chelsea House, 1991.

Hartmann, Susan M. *From Margin to Mainstream: American Women and Politics since 1960.* New York: Alfred Knopf, 1989.

Height, Dorothy. *Open Wide the Freedom Gates: A Memoir.* New York: Public Affairs Press, 2003.

Heilbrun, Carolyn. *The Education of a Woman: The Life of Gloria Steinem.* New York: Bantam Doubleday Dell, 1995.

Hennessee, Judith. *Betty Friedan: Her Life.* New York: Random House, 1999.

Henry, Astrid. *Not my Mother's Sister: Generational Conflict and Third Wave Feminism.* Bloomington: Indiana University Press, 2004.

Hill, Anita Faye, and Emma Coleman Jordan, eds. *Race, Gender, and Power in America: The Legacy of the Hill-Thomas Hearings.* New York: Oxford University Press, 1995.

Hill, Mary A. *Charlotte Perkins Gilman: The Making of a Radical Feminist, 1860–1896.* Philadelphia: Temple University Press, 1980.

Hine, Darlene Clark. *Black Women in America: A Historical Encyclopedia.* New York: Carlson Publishing, 1993.

———. *Encyclopedia of Black Women in America: The Early Years 1617–1899.* New York: Facts on File, Inc., 1997.

———. *Encyclopedia of Black Women in America: Law and Government.* New York: Facts on File, Inc., 1997.

———. *Encyclopedia of Black Women in America: Social Activism.* New York: Facts on File, Inc., 1997.

Hodes, Martha, ed. *Sex, Love, Race: Crossing Boundaries in North American History.* New York: New York University Press, 1999.

Hoff, Joan. *Law, Gender, and Injustice: A Legal History of the United States,* New York: New York University Press, 1991.

Holm Jeanne. *Women in the Military: An Unfinished Revolution,* New York: Random House, 1992.

Holt, Rackham. *Mary McLeod Bethune: A Biography.* New York: Doubleday, 1964.

Holzer, Henry Mark, and Erika Holzer. *"Aid and Comfort:" Jane Fonda in North Vietnam.* Jefferson, N.C.: McFarland, 2002.

hooks, bell. *Ain't I a Woman? Black Women and Feminism.* Boston: South End, 1981.

Hopkins, Sarah Winnemucca. *Life Among the Piutes: Their Wrongs and Claims.* Bishop, Calif.: Chalfant Press, 1969.

Horowitz, Daniel. *Betty Friedan and the Making of the Feminine Mystique: The American Left, the Cold War, and Modern Feminism.* Amherst: University of Massachusetts Press, 1998.

Horowitz, Helen Lefkowitz. *Alma Mater: Design and Experience in the Women's Colleges from Their Nineteenth-Century Beginnings to the 1930s.* New York: Knopf, 1984.

———. *Power and Passion of M. Carey Thomas.* Chicago: University of Illinois Press, 1999.

Horton, Joey Dean. *"Girl Lawyer Makes Good: The Story of Annette Abbott Adams."* Women's Legal History Biography Project. Stanford University, 1997.

Howe, Julia Ward, and Carrie Chapman Catt. *Reminiscences, 1819–1899.* Boston: Houghton Mifflin, 1899.

Howe, Louise Kapp. *Pink Collar Workers: Inside the World of Women's Work.* New York: G P Putnam's Sons, 1977.

Humez, Jean McMahon. *Harriet Tubman: The Life and the Life Stories.* Madison: University of Wisconsin Press, 2004.

Hyde, Janet Shibley, and Marilyn J. Essex, eds. *Parental Leave and Child Care: Setting a Research and Policy Agenda*. Philadelphia: Temple University Press, 1991.

Hyman, Paula E., and Deborah Dash Moore, eds. *Jewish Women in America: A Historical Encyclopedia*. New York: Routledge Press, 1997.

Inglehart, Ronald, and Pippa Norris. *Rising Tide: Gender Equality and Cultural Change Around the World*. Cambridge: Cambridge University Press, 2003.

Ireland, Patricia. *What Women Want*. New York: Dutton Books, 1996.

Irwin, Inez Haynes. *The Story of the Woman's Party*. New York: Kraus Reprint Co., 1971.

Jacoby, Robin Miller. *The British and American Women's Trade Union Leagues, 1890–1925: A Case Study of Feminism and Class*. New York: Carlson Publishers, 1994.

Jagger, Allison M. *Feminist Politics and Human Nature*. Totowa, N.J.: Roman and Allanheld, 1983.

Jasper, Margaret C. *Employment Discrimination Under Title VII*. New York: Oceana Publications, 1999.

Jeffrey, Julie Roy. *The Great Silent Army of Abolitionism: Ordinary Women in the Anti-Slavery Movement*. Chapel Hill: University of North Carolina Press, 1998.

Jelen, Ted G., ed. *Perspectives on the Politics of Abortion*. Westport, Conn.: Praeger, 1995.

Johnston, Johanna. *Harriet and the Runaway Book: The Story of Harriet Beecher Stowe and Uncle Tom's Cabin*. New York: Harper and Row, 1977.

Jones, Beverly Washington. *Quest for Equality: The Life and Writings of Mary Eliza Church Terrell, 1863–1954*. New York: Carlson Publishers, 1990.

Jones, Jacqueline. *Labor of Love, Labor of Sorrow: Black Women, Work, and the Family from Slavery to the Present*. New York: Vintage Books, 1985.

Jones, Mother. *The Autobiography of Mother Jones*. Chicago: C.H. Kerr, 1976.

Jordan, Barbara, and Shelby Hearon. *Barbara Jordan-A Self-Portrait*. New York: Doubleday & Co., 1979.

Josephson, Hannah. *Jeanette Rankin, First Lady in Congress*. Indianapolis: Bobbs-Merrill, 1974.

Kaitin, Katherine Karr. "Congressional Responses to Families in the Workplace: The Family and Medical Leave Act of 1987–1988." In *More Than Kissing Babies? Current Child and Family Policy in the United States,* edited by Francine H. Jacobs and Margery W. Davies. Westport, Conn.: Auburn House, 1993.

Karcher, Carolyn. *The First Woman in the Republic: A Cultural Biography of Lydia Maria Child*. Durham, N.C.: Duke University Press, 1994.

Keller, Rosemary. *Patriotism and the Female Sex: Abigail Adams and the American Revolution*. New York: Carlson Publishers, 1994.

Kelly, Rita Mae. *The Gendered Economy: Work, Careers, and Success*. Newbury Park, Calif.: Sage Publications, 1991.

Ken, Andrea. *Lucy Stone: Speaking out for Equality*. New Brunswick, N.J.: Rutgers University Press, 1992.

Kendall, Phebe Mitchell, ed. *Maria Mitchell: Life, Letters, and Journals*. Boston: Lee and Shepard, 1986.

Kenny, Maurice. *Tekonwatoni, Molly Brant, 1735–1795: Poems of War*. Fredonia, N.Y.: White Pine Press, 1992.

Kerber, Linda K., and Jane Sherron De Hart. *Women's America: Refocusing the Past*. New York: Oxford University Press, 2004.

Kessler, Donna J. *The Making of Sacagawea: A Euro-American Legend*. Tuscaloosa: University of Alabama Press, 1996.

Kessler-Harris, Alice. *Out to Work: A History of Wage-Earning Women in the United States*. New York: Oxford University Press, 1982.

Kincade, Diane, ed. *Silent Hattie Speaks: The Personal Journal of Senator Hattie Caraway*. Westport, Conn.: Greenwood Press, 1979.

King, Coretta Scott. *My Life with Martin Luther King, Jr.* New York: Henry Holt, 1969.

Kinnard, Cynthia D. *Antifeminism in American Thought: An Annotated Bibliography*. Boston: G.K. Hall, 1986.

Klatch, Rebecca. *Women of the New Right*. Philadelphia: Temple University Press, 1987.

Knee, Stuart E. *Christian Science in the Age of Mary Baker Eddy*. Westport, Conn.: Greenwood Press, 1994.

Kochersberger, Robert, ed. *More than a Muckraker: Ida Tarbell's Lifetime in Journalism*. Knoxville: University of Tennessee Press, 1994.

Kornfeld, Eve. *Creating an American Culture, 1775–1800*. Boston: Bedford/St. Martins, 2001.

Kraditor, Aileen. *The Ideas of the Woman Suffrage Movement: 1890–1920*. New York: Norton, 1981.

Kroeger, Brooke. *Nellie Bly: Daredevil, Reporter, Feminist*. New York: Three Rivers Press, 1995.

Lancaster, Jane. *Making Time: Lillian Moller Gilbreth, A Life beyond Cheaper by the Dozen.* Boston: Northeastern University Press, 2004.

Lane, Ann J. *To Herland and Beyond: The Life and Works of Charlotte Perkins Gilman.* Charlottesville: University Press of Virginia, 1997.

La Plante, Eve. *American Jezebel: The Uncommon Life of Anne Hutchinson, The Woman Who Defied the Puritans.* New York: HarperCollins, 2004.

Larson, Kate Clifford. *Bound for the Promised Land: Harriet Tubman, Portrait of an American Hero.* New York: Ballantine Books, 2003.

Larson, Lia. *Skirting Tradition: Women in Politics Speak to the Next Generation.* Hollis, N.H.: Hollis Publishing Company, 2004.

Laughlin, Kathleen A. *Women's Work and Public Policy: A History of the Women's Bureau, U.S. Department of Labor, 1945—1970.* Boston: Northeastern University Press, 2000.

Lawless, Jennifer L., and Richard J. Fox. *It Takes a Candidate: Why Women Don't Run for Office.* New York: Cambridge University Press, 2005.

Leach, William. *True Love and Perfect Union: The Feminist Reform of Sex and Society.* New York: Basic Books Inc., 1980.

Lear, Linda. *Rachel Carson: Witness for Nature.* New York: Owl Books, 1998.

Lease, Mary Elizabeth. *The Problem of Civilization Solved.* Chicago, Laird & Lee, 1895.

Leher, Susan. *Origins of Protective Labor Legislation for Women, 1905–1925.* SUNY Series on Women and Work. Albany: State University of New York Press, 1987.

LeMonchek, Linda, and James P. Sterba. *Sexual Harassment: Issues and Answers.* Oxford: Oxford University Press, 2001.

Leonard, Elizabeth D. *Yankee Women: Gender Battles in the Civil War.* New York: W.W. Norton and Company, 1995.

Lerner, Gerda. *The Creation of Patriarchy.* Oxford: Oxford University Press, 1987.

———. *Grimké Sisters from South Carolina: Pioneers for Women's Rights and Abolition.* Oxford: Oxford University Press, 1998.

Levine, Susan. *Degrees of Equality: The American Association of University Women and the Challenge of Twentieth Century Feminism.* Philadelphia: Temple University Press, 1995.

Lindenmeyer, Kriste. *"A Right to Childhood": The U.S. Children's Bureau and Child Welfare, 1912–46.* Urbana: University of Illinois Press, 1997.

Lindgren, J. Ralph, Nadine Taub, Beth Anne Wolfson, and Carla M. Palumbo. *The Law of Sex Discrimination,* 3rd ed. Belmont, Calif.: Wadsworth, 2005.

Lissak, Rivka Shpak. *Pluralism and Progressives: Hull house and the new immigrants, 1890–1919.* Chicago: University of Chicago Press, 1989.

Lowy, Joan A. *Pat Schroeder: A Woman of the House.* Albuquerque: University of New Mexico Press, 2003.

Lubiano, Wahneema, ed. *The House that Race Built.* New York: Vintage Books, 1998.

Luker, Ralph E., ed. *Black and White Sat Down Together: Reminiscences of an NAACP Founder.* New York: Feminist Press, 1995.

Lumsden, Linda J., and William J. Jackson. *Inez: The Life and Times of Inez Milholland.* Bloomington: Indiana University Press, 2004.

Lunardini, Christine. *From Equal Suffrage to Equal Rights: Alice Paul and the National Women's Party, 1910–1928.* New York: New York University Press, 1986.

———. *What Every American Should Know About Women's History: 200 Events that Shaped our Destiny.* Holbrook, Mass.: Adams Media Corporation, 1997.

Mabee, Carlton. *Sojourner Truth: Slave, Prophet, Legend.* New York: New York University Press, 1993.

MacKinnon, Catherine A. *Sexual Harassment of Working Women: A Case of Sex Discrimination.* New Haven, Conn.: Yale University Press, 1979.

MacKinnon, Catherine A., and Andrea Dworkin. *Pornography and Civil Rights: A New Day for Women's Equality.* Minneapolis: Organizing Against Pornography, 1988.

———, eds. *In Harm's Way: The Pornography Civil Rights Hearings.* Cambridge, Mass.: Harvard University Press, 1997.

MacKinnon, Janice R., and Stephen R. MacKinnon. *Agnes Smedley: The Life and Times of an American Radical.* Berkeley: University of California Press, 1988.

Mankiller, Wilma P., with Michael Wallis. *Mankiller: A Chief and Her People.* New York: St. Martin's Press, 1993.

Mansbridge, Jane J. *Why We Lost the ERA*. Chicago: University of Chicago Press, 1986.

Marshall, Susan E. *Splintered Sisterhood: Gender and Class in the Campaign against Woman Suffrage*. Madison: University of Wisconsin Press, 1991.

Marshall-White, Eleanor. *Women, Catalysts for Change: Interpretive Biographies of Shirley St. Hill Chisholm, Sandra Day O'Connor, and Nancy Landon Kassebaum*. New York: Vantage Press, 1991.

Martin, George Whitney. *Madam Secretary, Frances Perkins*. Boston: Houghton Mifflin, 1976.

Mattingly, Carol. *Well Tempered Women: Nineteenth Century Temperance Rhetoric*. Carbondale: Southern Illinois University Press, 2000.

McCarthy, Kathleen. *Women, Philanthropy and Civil Society*. Indianapolis: Indiana University Press, 1991.

McGovern, James R. "Anna Howard Shaw: New Approaches to Feminism." *Journal of Social History* 3 (1969): 135–153.

McGuire, John Thomas. "Making the Democratic Party a Partner: Eleanor Roosevelt, the WJLC, and the Women's Division of the New York State Democratic Party, 1921–1927." *Hudson Valley Regional Review* 18 (2001): 29–47.

Martin, Del, and Phyllis Lyon. *Lesbian/Women*. San Francisco: Bantam, 1972.

Masson, Margaret W. *Margaret Brent, c. 1601–c.1671, Lawyer, Landholder, Entrepreneur*. Centreville, Md.: Tidewater Press, 1977.

Mayo, Edith P., ed. *The Smithsonian Book of the First Ladies: Their Lives, Times, and Issues*. New York: Henry Holt and Company, 1996.

McArthur, Judith N. *Creating the New Woman: The Rise of Southern Women's Progressive Culture in Texas, 1893–1918*. Urbana: University of Illinois Press, 1998.

———, and Harold L. Smith. *Minnie Fisher Cunningham: A Suffragist's Life in Politics*. New York: Oxford University Press, 2003.

McCann, Carole. *Birth Control Politics in the United States, 1916–1945*. New York: Cornell University Press, 1994.

McClymer, John F. *The Triangle Strike and Fire*. Fort Worth: Harcourt Brace College Publishers, 1998.

McFadden, Grace Jordan. "Septima P. Clark and the Struggle for Human Rights." In *Women in the Civil Rights Movement: Trailblazers and Torchbearers, 1941–1965*, edited by Vicki L. Crawford, Jacquelin Anne Rouse, and Barbara Woods, 85–97. Bloomington: Indiana University Press, 1990.

McHenry, Elizabeth. *Forgotten Readers: Recovering the Lost History of African-American Literary Societies*. Durham, N.C.: Duke University Press, 2004.

McNall, Scott G. *The Road to Rebellion: Class Formation and Kansas Populism, 1865–1900*. Chicago: University of Chicago Press, 1988.

Mead, Margaret. *Coming of Age in Samoa*. New York: Perennial Classics, 2001.

Meijer, Molly, ed. *Inventing a Voice: The Rhetoric of American First Ladies of the Twentieth Century*. Lanham: Rowman & Littlefield, 2004.

Melich, Tanya. *The Republican War against Women: An Insider's Report From Behind the Scenes*. New York: Bantam Books, 1998.

Merrill, Arlene Deahl, ed. *Growing Up in Boston's Gilded Age: The Journal of Alice Stone Blackwell, 1872–1874*. New Haven, Conn.: Yale University Press, 1990.

Meyerowitz, Joanne. "Beyond the Feminine Mystique: A Reassessment of Postwar Mass Culture, 1946–1958." In *Not June Cleaver: Women and Gender in Postwar America, 1845–1960*, edited by Joanne Meyerowitz. Philadelphia: Temple University Press, 1994.

Mezey, Susan Gluck. *Elusive Equality: Women's Rights, Public Policy, and the Law*. Boulder, Colo.: Lynne Rienner, 2003.

Michel, Sonya. *Children's Interests/Mothers' Rights: The Shaping of America's Child Care Policy*. New Haven, Conn.: Yale University Press, 1999.

Miller, William D. *Dorothy Day: A Biography*. New York: Harper and Row, 1982.

Millett, Kate. *A.D.: A Memoir*. New York: Norton, 1995.

———. *Going to Iran*. New York: Coward, McCann & Geoghegan, 1982.

———. *The Loony Bin Trip*. Champaign: University of Illinois Press, 1990.

———. *The Politics of Cruelty*. New York: Norton, 1994.

———. *The Prostitution Papers*. New York: Avon, 1973.

———. *Sita*. New York: Simon & Schuster, 1992.

Morello, Karen. *The Invisible Bar: The Woman Lawyer in America 1638 to Present*. New York: Random House, 1986.

Morgan, Robin. *Sisterhood is Global.* Garden City, N.Y.: Anchor, 1984.

Morris, Celia. *Fanny Wright: Rebel in America.* Urbana: University of Illinois Press, 1992.

————. *Storming the Statehouse: Running for Governor with Ann Richards and Diane Feinstein.* New York: Scribner, 1992.

Morris, Sylvia. *Rage for Fame: The Ascent of Clare Booth Luce.* New York: Random House, 1997.

Moskowitz, Ellen H., and Bruce Jennings, eds. *Coerced Contraception? Moral and Policy Challenges of Long-Acting Birth Control.* Washington, D.C.: Georgetown University Press, 1996.

Moynihan, Ruth Barnes. *Rebel For Rights: Abigail Scott Duniway.* New Haven, Conn.: Yale University Press, 1983.

Muncy, Robyn. *Creating a Female Dominion in American Reform, 1890–1935.* New York: Oxford University Press, 1991.

Myers, John L., ed. *The Arizona Governors: 1912–1990.* Phoenix: Heritage Publishers, 1989.

Nalle, Ouida Ferguson. *The Fergusons of Texas, or "Two Governors for the Price of One": A Biography of James Edward Ferguson and His Wife.* San Antonio: Naylor Press, 1946.

Nelson, W. Dale. *Interpreters with Lewis and Clark: The Story of Sacagawea and Toussaint Charbonneau.* Denton: University of North Texas Press, 2003.

Nestor, Agnes. *Woman's Labor Leader: An Autobiography of Agnes Nestor.* Washington, D.C.: Zenger Publishing, 1975.

Neumann, Caryn E. "The End of Gender Solidarity: The History of the Women's Organization for National Prohibition Reform in the United States, 1929–1933." *Journal of Women's History* 9 (1997): 31–51.

Newhouse, Susan Mabee. *Sojourner Truth: Slave, Prophet, Legend.* New York: New York University Press, 1995.

Norgren, Jill. "Before It Was Merely Difficult: Belva Lockwood's Life in Law and Politics." *Journal of Supreme Court History* 23 (1999): 16–42.

Oates, Stephen B. *A Woman of Valor: Clara Barton and the Civil War.* New York: Maxwell MacMillan International, 1994.

O'Connor, Sandra Day. *The Majesty of the Law: Reflections of a Supreme Court Justice.* New York: Random House, 2004.

Okin, Susan Moller. *Women in Western Political Thought.* Princeton, N.J.: Princeton University Press, 1979.

O'Neill, William L. *Everyone Was Brave: The Rise and Fall of Feminism in America.* Chicago: Quadrangle, 1969.

Orenstein, Peggy. *School Girls: Young Women, Self-Esteem, and the Confidence Gap.* New York: Anchor Books, 1995.

Palmer, Beverly Wilson, ed. *Selected Letters of Lucretia Mott.* Urbana: University of Illinois Press, 2002.

Parker, Alison M. *Purifying America: Women, Cultural Reform, and Pro-Censorship Activism, 1873–1933.* Chicago: University of Illinois Press, 1997.

Parker, Gail Thain. *Mind Cures in New England: From the Civil War to World War I.* Hanover, N.H.: University Press of New England, 1973.

Parks, Rosa, with Gregory J. Reed. *Quiet Strength: The Faith, The Hope, and the Heart of a Woman Who Changed a Nation.* Grand Rapids, Mich.: Zondervan, 1995.

Pasachoff, Naomi. *Frances Perkins: Champion of the New Deal.* New York: Oxford University Press, 1991.

Paulissen, May Nelson, and Carl McQueary. *Miriam: The Southern Belle Who Became the First Woman Governor of Texas.* Austin: Eakin Press, 1995.

Peel, Robert. *Mary Baker Eddy: The Years of Authority.* New York: Holt Rinehart and Winston, 1977.

Peterson, Esther, with Winifred Conkling. *Restless: The Memoirs of Labor and Consumer Activist Esther Peterson.* Washington, D.C.: Caring Publishing, 1997.

Petrash, Antonia. *More than Petticoats: Remarkable Connecticut Women.* Guilford, Conn.: Twodot, 2004.

Plimpton, Ruth. *Mary Dyer: Biography of a Rebel Quaker.* Wellesley, Mass.: Branden Books, 1994.

Porterfield, Amanda. *Mary Lyon and the Mount Holyoke Missionaries.* New York: Oxford University Press, 1997.

Pryor, Elizabeth Brown. *Calara Barton: Professional Angel.* Philadelphia: University of Pennsylvania Press, 1987.

Purdue, Theda. *Sifters: Native American Women's Lives.* Oxford: Oxford University Press, 2001.

Rabinowitz, Howard N. *Race Relations in the Urban South, 1865–1890.* New York: Oxford University Press, 1978.

Randall, Mercedes M. *Improper Bostonian: The Life of Emily Greene Balch.* New York: Twayne Publishers, 1964.

Ransby, Barbara. *Ella Baker and the Black Freedom Movement: A Radical Democratic Vision.* Chapel Hill: University of North Carolina Press, 2003.

Ray, Dixy Lee. *Environmental Overkill: Whatever Happened to Common Sense?* New York: HarperPerennial, 1994.

———. *The Nation's Energy Future.* Washington D.C.: Atomic Energy Commission, 1973.

———. *Trashing the Planet: How Science Can Help Us Deal with Acid Rain, Depletion of the Ozone, and Nuclear Waste (Among Other Things).* New York: HarperPerennial, 1992.

Rice, Condoleezza, with Philip Zelikow. *Germany Unified and Europe Transformed: A Study in Statecraft.* Boston: Harvard University Press, 1995.

Rice, Edward. *Margaret Mead: A Portrait.* New York: Harper & Row Publishers, 1979.

Richards, Jeffery H. *Mercy Otis Warren.* New York: Twayne Publishing, 1995.

Risen, James, and Judy L. Thomas. *Wrath of Angels: The American Abortion War.* New York: Basic Books, 1998.

Roberts, Cokie. *Founding Mothers: The Women Who Raised Our Nation.* New York: HarperCollins, 2004.

Rogow, Faith. *Gone to Another Meeting: The National Council of Jewish Women, 1893–1993.* Tuscaloosa: University of Alabama Press, 1993.

Rose, Elizabeth R. *A Mother's Job: The History of Day Care, 1890–1960.* New York: Oxford University Press, 1999.

Rosen, Ruth. *The World Split Open: How the Modern Women's Movement Changed America.* New York: Viking, 2000.

Rosenbaum, Jon H., and Peter C. Sederberg, eds. *Vigilante Politics.* Philadelphia: University of Pennsylvania Press, 1976.

Rossiter, Margaret. *Women Scientists in America: Struggles and Strategies to 1940.* Baltimore: Johns Hopkins University Press, 1982.

Rountree, Helen. "Pocahontas—the Hostage Who Became Famous." In *Sifters: Native American Women's Lives,* edited by Theda Perdue. Oxford: Oxford University Press, 2001.

———. *Pocahontas's People: The Powhatan Indians of Virginia through Four Centuries.* Norman: University of Oklahoma Press, 1990.

Rudd, Jill, and Val Gough, eds. *Charlotte Perkins Gilman: An Optimist Reformer.* Iowa City: University of Iowa Press, 1999.

Saetnan, Ann Rudinow, Nelly Oudshoorn, and Marta Kirejvzyk. *Bodies of Technology: Women's Involvement With Reproductive Medicine.* Columbus: Ohio State University, 2000.

Safire, William, ed. *Lend Me Your Ears: Great Speeches in History.* New York: W.W. Norton, 1997.

Salmon, Marylyn. *Women and the Law of Property in Early America.* Chapel Hill: University of North Carolina Press, 1986.

Sanger, Alexander. *Beyond Choice: Reproductive Freedom in the 21st Century.* New York: PublicAffairs, 2004.

Sanger, Margaret. *Margaret Sanger: An Autobiography.* New York: Cooper Square Press, 1999.

Sarachild, Kathie, ed. *Feminist Revolution.* New York: Random House, 1978.

Sarnecky, Mary. *A History of the United States Army Nurse Corps.* Philadelphia: University of Pennsylvania Press, 1999.

Sax, Leonard. *Why Gender Matters: What Parents and Teachers Need to Know about the Emerging Science of Sex Differences.* New York: Doubleday Press, 2005.

Schapiro, Amy. *Millicent Fenwick: Her Way.* New Brunswick, N.J.: Rutgers University Press, 2003.

Schlaifer, Charles, and Lucy Freeman. *Heart's Work: Civil War Heroine and Champion of the Mentally Ill, Dorothea Lynde Dix.* Gettysburg, Pa.: Stan Clark Military Books, 1991.

Schloesser, Pauline. *Fair Sex: White Women and Racial Patriarchy in the Early American Republic.* New York: New York University Press, 1992.

Schmidt, Patricia L. *Margaret Chase Smith: Beyond Convention.* Orono: The University of Maine Press, 1996.

Schneider, Dorothy, and Carl J. Schneider. *First Ladies: A Biographical Directory.* New York: Checkmark Books, 2001.

Schott, Linda. *Reconstructing Women's Thoughts: The Women's International League for Peace and Freedom Before World War II.* Stanford, Calif.: Stanford University Press, 1997.

Schroeder, Patricia S. *24 Years of House Work . . . and the Place is Still a Mess: My Life in Politics.* Kansas City: Andrews MacMeel Publishing, 1998.

Scott, Anne Firor. *Natural Allies: Women's Associations in U.S. History.* Urbana: University of Illinois Press, 1992.

Seccombe, Karen. *"So You Think I Drive a Cadillac?": Welfare Recipients' Perspectives on the System and Reform.* Boston: Allyn and Bacon, 1998.

Shammas, Carol. "Reassessing Married Women's Property Acts." *Journal of Women's History* 6 (1994): 9–30.

Shar, Christopher. *The Bad and the Beautiful: Gender Stereotypes in Newspaper Coverage of Domestic Violence.* Shippensburg, Pa.: Shippensburg Press, 1996.

Shaw, Anna Howard, with Elizabeth Jordan. *The Story of a Pioneer.* New York: Harper & Brothers Publishers, 1915.

Shaw, Sondra C., and Martha Taylor. *Reinventing Fundraising: Realizing the Potential of Women's Fundraising.* San Francisco: Jossey-Bass Publishers, 1995.

Sherman, Janann. *No Place for a Woman: A Life of Senator Margaret Chase Smith.* New Brunswick, N.J.: Rutgers University Press, 2000.

Sherr, Lynn. *Failure Is Impossible: Susan B. Anthony in Her Own Words.* New York: Times Books, 1995.

———. *The Trial of Susan B. Anthony.* New York: Prometheus Books, 2003.

Shibley, Janey Hyde, and Marilyn J. Essex, eds. *Parental Leave and Child Care: Setting a Research and Policy Agenda.* Philadelphia: Temple University Press, 1991.

Shipler, David K. *The Working Poor: Invisible in America.* New York: Knopf, 2004.

Siegel, Beatrice. *The Year They Walked: Rosa Parks and the Montgomery Bus Boycott.* New York: Four Winds Press, 1992.

Sklar, Kathryn K. *Florence Kelley and the Nation's Work: The Rise of Woman's Political Culture.* New Haven: Yale University Press, 1997.

———, ed. *Notes of Sixty Years: The Autobiography of Florence Kelley.* Chicago: Charles H. Kerr Publishing Co., 1986.

Slaughter, Thomas P. *Exploring Lewis and Clark: Reflections on Men and Wilderness.* New York: Alfred A. Knopf, 2003.

Smedley, Agnes. *China Fights Back: An American Woman with the Eighth Route Army.* London: V. Gollancz, 1938.

Smith, Barbara. *Home Girls: A Black Feminist Anthology.* New York: Kitchen Table Women of Color Press, 1983.

Smith, J. Clay, Jr., ed. *Rebels in Law: Voices in History of Black Women Lawyers.* Ann Arbor: University of Michigan, 1998.

Smitherman, Geneva, ed. *African American Women Speak Out on Anita Hill-Clarence Thomas.* Detroit: Wayne State University Press, 1995.

Solomon, Barbara Miller. *In the Company of Educated Women: A History of Women and Higher Education in America.* New Haven, Conn.: Yale University Press, 1986.

Solomon, Martha. "The Positive Woman's Journey: A Mythical Analysis of the Rhetoric of Stop-ERA." *Quarterly Journal of Speech* 65 (1979): 262–274.

Sommers, Christine Hoff. *The War against Boys: How Misguided Feminism Is Harming Our Young Men.* New York: Simon and Schuster, 2001.

Stanton, Elizabeth Cady, Susan B. Anthony, and Matilda Gage. *History of Woman Suffrage: 1848–1861,* vol. I. Salem, N.H.: Ayer Publishing, 1985.

———, eds. *History of Woman Suffrage,* vol. 2. New York: Fowler & Wells, 1882.

Steinem, Gloria. *Moving Beyond Words: Age, Rage, Money, Power, Sex, Muscles: Breaking the Boundaries of Gender.* New York: Simon and Schuster, 1994.

———. *Outrageous Acts and Everyday Rebellions.* New York: Holt Rhinehart, 1983.

Stevens, Doris. *Jailed for Freedom: American Women Win the Vote.* 1920. Reprint, Troutdale, Oreg.: New Sage Press, 1995.

Stiller, Richard. *Queen of Populists: The Story of Mary Elizabeth Lease.* New York: Crowell, 1970.

Stirling, Nora. *Pearl Buck: A Woman in Conflict.* Piscataway, N.J.: New Century Publishers, 1983.

Stoltzfus, Emilie. *Citizen, Mother, Worker: Debating Public Responsibility for Child Care after the Second World War.* Chapel Hill: University of North Carolina Press, 2003.

Strane, Susan. *A Whole Souled Woman: Prudence Crandall and the Education of Black Women.* New York: W.W. Norton, 1990.

Stuhler, Barbara. *For the Public Record: A documentary history of the League of Women Voters.* Westport, Conn.: Greenwood Press, 2000.

Swain, Martha H. "Caroline O'Day." In *American National Biography,* vol. 16, edited by John A.

Garraty and Mark C. Carnes. New York: Oxford University Press, 1999.

Taylor, Clare. *Women of the Anti-Slavery Movement: The Weston Sisters.* New York: St. Martins, 1995.

Thom, Mary. *Inside Ms.: 25 Years of the Magazine and the Feminist Movement.* New York: Owl Publishing, 1998.

Thomas, Helen. *Front Row at the White House: My Life and Times.* New York: Scribner, 2000.

Thorn, William, Phillip Runkel, and Susan Moutin, eds. *Dorothy Day and the Catholic Worker Movement: Centenary Essays.* Milwaukee: Marquette University Press, 2001.

Tolleson-Rinehart, Sue, and Jeanie R. Stanley. *Claytie and the Lady: Ann Richards, Gender, and Politics in Texas.* Austin: University of Texas Press, 1994.

Toner, Robin. "Mary McGrory, 85, Longtime Columnist, Dies." *New York Times,* 23 April 2004.

Tong, Rosemarie Putnam. *Feminist Thought: A More Comprehensive Introduction.* Boulder, Colo.: Westview Press, 1998.

Totenberg, Nina. *The Complete Transcripts of the Clarence Thomas-Anita Hill Hearings: October 11, 12, 13, 1991.* Chicago: Academy Chicago Publisher, 1994.

Trattner, Walter I. *From Poor Law to Wefare State.* New York: Free Press, 1998.

Tribe, Lawrence. *Abortion: A Clash of Absolutes.* New York: W.W. Norton, 1992.

Tuve, Jeanette. *First Lady of the Law: Florence Ellinwood Allen.* Lanham, Md.: University Press of America, 1984.

Underhill, Lois Beachy. *The Woman Who Ran for President: The Many Lives of Victoria Woodhull.* Bridgehampton, N.Y.: Bridgehampton Works Publishing, 1995.

United Nations Department of Economic and Social Affairs. *The Convention on the Political Rights of Women: History and Commentary.* New York: United Nations, 1955.

Van Voris, Jacqueline. *Carrie Chapman Catt: A Public Life.* New York: Feminist Press at the City University of New York, 1987.

Wagner, Sally Roesch. *Matilda Joslyn Gage: She Who Holds the Sky.* Aberdeen, S.Dak.: Sky Carrier Press, 1998.

———. *The Untold Story of the Iroquois Influence on Early Feminists.* Aberdeen, S.Dak.: Sky Carrier Press, 1996.

———. *A Time of Protest: Suffragists Challenge the Republic 1870–1877.* Aberdeen, S.D.: Sky Carrier Press, 1996.

Ward, Geoffrey. *Not For Ourselves Alone: The Story of Elizabeth Cady Stanton and Susan B. Anthony.* New York: Knopf, 2001.

Ware, Susan. *Beyond Suffrage: Women in the New Deal.* Cambridge, Mass.: Harvard University Press, 1981.

Warshaw, Robin. *I Never Called It Rape.* New York: HarperPerennial, 1994.

Watson, Robert P., and Anthony J. Eksterowicz. *The Presidential Companion: Readings on the First Ladies.* Columbia: University of South Carolina Press, 2003.

Waugh, Joan. *Unsentimental Reformer: The Life of Josephine Shaw Lowell.* Cambridge, Mass.: Harvard University Press, 1997.

Weddington, Sarah. *A Question of Choice.* New York: Penguin Books, 1993.

Wedin, Carolyn. *Inheritors of the Spirit: Mary White Ovington and the Founding of the NAACP.* Hoboken, N.J.: John Wiley and Sons, 1997.

Weinstein, Cindy, ed. *The Cambridge Companion to Harriet Beecher Stowe.* Cambridge: Cambridge University Press, 2004.

Weistart, John. "Equal Opportunity? Title IX and Intercollegiate Sports." *Brookings Review* 16 (1998): 39–43.

Wellman, Judith. *The Road to Seneca Falls: Elizabeth Cady Stanton and the First Women's Rights Convention.* Urbana: University of Illinois Press, 2004.

Wertheimer, Molly Meijer, ed. *Inventing a Voice: The Rhetoric of American First Ladies of the Twentieth Century.* Lanham, Md.: Rowman & Littlefield Publishers, Inc., 2004.

———, ed. *Leading Ladies of the White House: Communication Strategies of Notable Twentieth Century First Ladies.* Lanham, Md.: Rowman & Littlefield Publishers, 2005.

Wheeler, Marjorie Spruill. *One Woman, One Vote: Rediscovering the Woman Suffrage Movement.* Troutdale, Oreg.: New Sage Press, 1995.

Whelan, Imelda. *Modern Feminist Thought: From the Second Wave to "Post Feminism."* New York: New York University Press, 1995.

White, Deborah Gray. *Too Heavy A Load: Black Women in Defense of Themselves, 1894–1994.* New York: W.W. Norton & Co., 1999.

Wiehe, Vernon, and Ann Richards, eds. *Intimate Betrayal: Understanding and Responding to the Trauma of Acquaintance Rape.* Thousand Oaks, Calif.: Sage Publishers, 1995.

Willard, Frances E. Carolyn D. Gifford, ed. *Writing Out My Heart: Selections from the Journal of Frances E. Willard.* Urbana: University of Illinois Press, 1995.

Wilson, Marie. *Closing the Leadership Gap: Why Women Can and Must Help Run the World.* New York: Viking Press, 2004.

Wisensale, Steven K. *Family Leave Policy: The Political Economy of Work and Family in America.* Armonk, N.Y.: M.E. Sharpe, 2001.

Withey, Lynne. *Dearest Friend: The Life of Abigail Adams.* New York: Touchstone, 2002.

Woodward, Grace Steele. *Pocahontas.* Norman: University of Oklahoma Press, 1969.

Wright, Helen. *Sweeper in the Sky: The Life of Maria Mitchell, First Woman Astronomer in America.* New York: Macmillan, 1949.

Yee, Shirley J. *Black Women Abolitionists: A Study in Activism 1828–60.* Knoxville: University of Tennessee Press, 1992.

Yellin, Carol Lynn, and Janann Sherman. *The Perfect 36: Tennessee Delivers Woman Suffrage,* edited by Ilene Jones-Cornwell. Memphis, Tenn.: Iris Press, 1998.

Zagarri, Rosemarie. *A Woman's Dilemma: Mercy Otis Warren and the American Revolution.* Wheeling, Ill.: Harlan Davidson, 1995.

Zoelle, Diana G. *Globalizing Concern for Women's Human Rights: The Failure of the American Model.* New York: St. Martin's Press, 2000.

INDEX

Boldface page numbers denote extensive treatment of a topic. *Italic* page numbers refer to illustrations. Page numbers followed by *t* indicate tables.